New Zealand

Paul Harding
Carolyn Bain
Neal Bedford

LONELY PLANET PUBLICATIONS
Melbourne • Oakland • London • Paris

NEW ZEALAND

BAY OF ISLANDS
Stunning coastal scenery – clear blue waters punctuated by unspoiled coves and islands

ROTORUA
Rich and accessible Maori culture in a landscape of gushing geysers and bubbling mud pools

NAPIER
One of the world's best examples of an Art Deco city

WAIPOUA KAURI FOREST
A sanctuary for the largest remnant of NZ's once-extensive kauri forests

AUCKLAND
A vibrant, cosmopolitan city – the capital of the South Pacific

WAITOMO CAVES
Magical underground limestone landscapes, complete with glowworms and rivers

LAKE TAUPO
A beautiful lake in a magnificent setting – a fishing paradise offering lots of adventure activities

TONGARIRO NATIONAL PARK
Tramp or ski in the volcanic landscape of this World Heritage area.

SOUTH PACIFIC OCEAN

TASMAN SEA

East Cape
Cape Runaway
Hicks Bay
Ruatoria
Tokomaru Bay
Tolaga Bay
Poverty Bay
Gisborne
Mahia Peninsula
Waroa
Hawke Bay
Cape Kidnappers
Napier
Waipawa
Waipukurau
Hastings
Cape Turnagain
Dannevirke
Woodville
Taihape
Palmerston North
Levin
Kaiti

Whakaari (White Island)
Bay of Plenty
Whakatane
Opotiki
Mayor Island
Mt Maunganui
Tauranga
Rotorua
Lake Rotorua
Lake Taupo
Taupo
Turangi
Mt Tongariro
Mt Ngauruhoe
Mt Ruapehu
National Park
Ohakune
Raetihi
Taumarunui
Wanganui
Hawera
Stratford
Mt Taranaki/Egmont
New Plymouth
Cape Egmont
Opunake
North Taranaki Bight
South Taranaki Bight

Coromandel Peninsula
Cape Colville
Thames
Huntly
Hamilton
Ngaruawahia
Cambridge
Te Kuiti
Kawhia
Raglan
Waitomo Caves
Waikato
Great Barrier Island
Little Barrier Island
Hauraki Gulf
Wellsford
Helensville
AUCKLAND
Kaipara Harbour
Dargaville
Whangarei
Hen & Chicken Islands
Poor Knights Islands
Cape Brett
Russell
Paihia
Kerikeri
Kaikohe
Opononi
Kaikohe
Hokianga Harbour
Bay of Islands
Karikari Peninsula
Great Exhibition Bay
North Cape
Kaitaia
Ninety Mile Beach
Cape Reinga

Marlborough Sounds
Farewell Spit
Golden Bay
Cape Farewell
Collingwood

Area	270,534 sq km
Population	3.9 million
Population Density	14 per sq km
Capital	Wellington
Official Languages	English & Maori

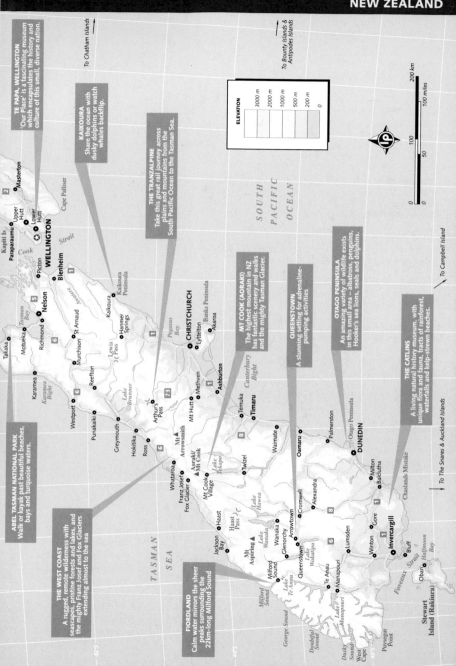

NEW ZEALAND

TE PAPA, WELLINGTON
'Our Place' is a fascinating museum which encapsulates the history and culture of this small, diverse nation.

KAIKOURA
Share the ocean with dusky dolphins or watch whales backflip.

THE TRANZALPINE
Take this great rail journey across plains and mountains from the South Pacific Ocean to the Tasman Sea.

ABEL TASMAN NATIONAL PARK
Walk or kayak past beautiful beaches, bays and turquoise waters.

THE WEST COAST
A rugged, remote wilderness with seascapes, pristine forests and lakes, and the mighty Franz Josef and Fox Glaciers extending almost to the sea.

FIORDLAND
Calm water mirrors the sheer peaks surrounding the 22km-long Milford Sound.

MT COOK (AORAKI)
The highest mountain in NZ has fantastic scenery and walks and the mighty Tasman Glacier.

QUEENSTOWN
A stunning setting for adrenaline-pumping activities

OTAGO PENINSULA
An amazing variety of wildlife exists in this small area – albatross, penguins, Hooker's sea lions, seals and dolphins.

THE CATLINS
A living natural history museum with unique flora and fauna, tracts of rainforest, waterfalls and kelp-strewn beaches.

To Chatham Islands

To Bounty Islands & Antipodes Islands

To Campbell Island

To The Snares & Auckland Islands

ELEVATION
3000 m
2000 m
1000 m
500 m
200 m
0

200 km
100 miles
100
50
0

SOUTH PACIFIC OCEAN

TASMAN SEA

Masterton
Kapiti Is
Paraparaumu
Upper Hutt
Lower Hutt
WELLINGTON
Cape Palliser
Cook Strait
Picton
Blenheim
Takaka
Motueka
Nelson
Richmond
Karamea
St Arnaud
Murchison
Reefton
Westport
Punakaiki
Greymouth
Hokitika
Ross
Lewis Pass
Hanmer Springs
Kaikoura
Kaikoura Peninsula
Lake Brunner
Arthur's Pass
CHRISTCHURCH
Lyttelton
Banks Peninsula
Akaroa
Pegasus Bay
Methven
Mt Hutt
Ashburton
Temuka
Timaru
Waimate
Oamaru
Palmerston
Canterbury Bight
Whataroa
Franz Josef
Fox Glacier
Mt Arrowsmith
Aoraki/Mt Cook
Mt Cook Village
Lake Tekapo
Twizel
Lake Hawea
Lake Wanaka
Haast
Jackson Bay
Haast Pass
Mt Aspiring
Wanaka
Cromwell
Alexandra
Arrowtown
Glenorchy
Queenstown
Lake Wakatipu
Milford Sound
Te Anau
Lake Te Anau
Lake Manapouri
Manapouri
Lumsden
Gore
Winton
Mataura
Invercargill
Bluff
Milton
Balclutha
Dunedin
Otago Peninsula
Chaslands Mistake
George Sound
Doubtful Sound
Dusky Sound
West Cape
Puysegur Point
Foveaux Strait
Stewart Island (Rakiura)
Oban
Halfmoon Bay
Tasman Bay

New Zealand
11th edition – September 2002
First published – December 1977

Published by
Lonely Planet Publications Pty Ltd ABN 36 005 607 983
90 Maribyrnong St, Footscray, Victoria 3011, Australia

Lonely Planet offices
Australia Locked Bag 1, Footscray, Victoria 3011
USA 150 Linden St, Oakland, CA 94607
UK 10a Spring Place, London NW5 3BH
France 1 rue du Dahomey, 75011 Paris

Photographs
Many of the images in this guide are available for licensing from
Lonely Planet Images.
w www.lonelyplanetimages.com

Front cover photograph
A tour bus waits for sheep to clear the road with Aoraki/Mt Cook in
the background (David Wall)

North Island title page photograph
Champagne Pool, Waiotapu Thermal Reserve, Waiotapu
(Simon Bracken)

South Island title page photograph
View of Mt Cook from Hooker Valley (Deanna Swaney)

Watching Wildlife title page photograph
Cabbage tree (David Wall)

Watching Wildlife title page photograph (inset)
Close-up of a Tuatara (David Wall)

Maori Culture & Arts title page photograph
Historic Maori carvings in Otago Museum (Deanna Swaney)

ISBN 1 74059 196 8

text & maps © Lonely Planet Publications Pty Ltd 2002
photos © photographers as indicated 2002

Printed by SNP SPrint (M) Sdn Bhd
Printed in Malaysia

All rights reserved. No part of this publication may be reproduced,
stored in a retrieval system or transmitted in any form by any means,
electronic, mechanical, photocopying, recording or otherwise, except
brief extracts for the purpose of review, without the written permission
of the publisher.

Lonely Planet, the Lonely Planet logo, Lonely Planet Images, CitySync
and eKno are trade marks of Lonely Planet Publications Pty Ltd. Other
trade marks are the property of their respective owners.

**Although the authors
and Lonely Planet try
to make the informa-
tion as accurate as
possible, we accept
no responsibility for
any loss, injury or
inconvenience sus-
tained by anyone
using this book.**

Contents – Text

AUCKLAND REGION 121

NORTHLAND 173

COROMANDEL REGION 223

WAIKATO & THE KING COUNTRY 245

TARANAKI 275

THE WEST COAST 495

CANTERBURY 530

OTAGO 582

SOUTHLAND 639

OUTER ISLANDS 670

LANGUAGE 684

Contents – Maps

WELLINGTON

MARLBOROUGH & NELSON

THE WEST COAST

CANTERBURY

OTAGO

SOUTHLAND

OUTER ISLANDS

MAP LEGEND   back page

MAP INDEX

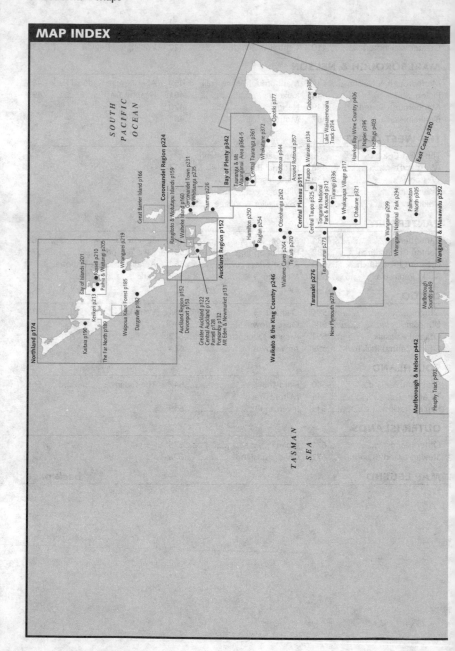

SOUTH
PACIFIC
OCEAN

TASMAN
SEA

Northland p174
Kaitaia p190
The Far North p189
Kerikeri p213
Bay of Islands p201
Russell p210
Paihia & Waitangi p205
Whangarei p219
Waipoua Kauri Forest p185
Dargaville p182

Great Barrier Island p166

Coromandel Region p224
Rangitoto & Motutapu Islands p159
Waiheke Island p160
Coromandel Town p231
Whitianga p235
Thames p226

Auckland Region p152
Devonport p153
Greater Auckland p122
Central Auckland p124
Parnell p128
Ponsonby p132
Mt Eden & Newmarket p131

Auckland Region p152

Waikato & the King Country p246
Hamilton p250
Raglan p254
Otorohanga p262
Waitomo Caves p264
Te Kuiti p270

Bay of Plenty p342
Tauranga & Mt
Maunganui Area p364-5
Central Tauranga p361
Whakatane p372
Opotiki p377
Gisborne p385

Rotorua p344
Around Rotorua p357

Lake Waikaremoana
Track p354
Hawkes Bay Wine Country p406
Napier p396
Hastings p403

East Coast p380

Central Plateau p311
Central Taupo p325
Taupo & Wairakei p334
Tongariro National
Park & Around p312
Turangi p336
Whakapapa Village p317
Ohakune p321

Taranaki p276
Taumarunui p273
New Plymouth p278

Wanganui & Manawatu p292
Wanganui p299
Whanganui National Park p294
Palmerston
North p305

Marlborough & Nelson p442
Marlborough
Sounds p449
Heaphy Track p493

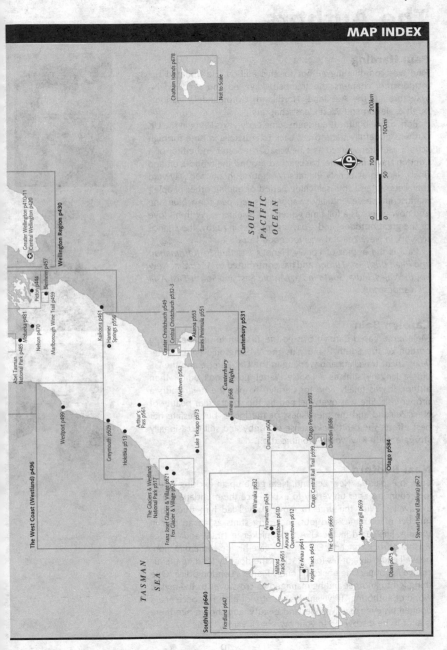

The Authors

Paul Harding

Paul was coordinating author for this edition. He updated the introductory chapters and tramped, kayaked and skydived his way through the Auckland, Northland, Coromandel, Marlborough & Nelson and West Coast chapters.

Born in Melbourne, Paul spent some early years living in the UK but was gratefully transported back to Australia in time for high school. He later worked as a newspaper reporter and editor of a London travel magazine, backpacked around the world a bit and finally landed at Lonely Planet's Melbourne home for wayward travellers. After a soul-searching period of editing other people's manuscripts, he eventually swapped his red pen for a blue one and now works as a full time writer and researcher. With his love of the great outdoors and a passing interest in rugby, the chance to work in New Zealand was too good to refuse.

Paul is the author of Lonely Planet's *Istanbul to Kathmandu* and *Read this First: Europe* and has contributed to *Australia*, *New South Wales*, *India*, *South India*, *Middle East* and *South-East Asia on a shoestring*.

Carolyn Bain

Melbourne-based Carolyn crossed the Tasman to update a large portion of the South Island plus the Wellington Region. After years spent travelling and working in the UK, Europe and the US plus a lengthy stint as a Lonely Planet guidebook editor then author, it was finally time for Carolyn to pay the neighbours a proper visit. She was overwhelmed by the spectacular beauty of New Zealand and the friendliness of the locals, but despite her best efforts she can't make sense of rugby and still occasionally struggles with Kiwi vowel pronunciation.

Neal Bedford

Born in Papakura, New Zealand, Neal gave up an exciting career in accounting after university to experience the mundane life of a traveller. With the urge to move, travel led him through a number of countries and jobs, including stints as an au pair in Vienna, life-guard in the USA, fruit picker in Israel and lettuce washer at rock concerts. Deciding to give his life some direction, he well and truly got his foot stuck in the door by landing the lucrative job of packing books in Lonely Planet's London office. One thing led to another and he managed to cross over to the mystic world of authoring. Travelling his country of birth has once again opened his eyes to its wonder and beauty, and shown him there is a lot to be discovered in your own back yard.

FROM THE AUTHORS
Paul Harding

Thanks, as always, to the people at Lonely Planet who allow me to continue travelling for a living and encourage me along the way. This time thanks to Jane, Corie, Errol, Michael and everyone who eventually worked on the book. Big thanks to co-authors Carolyn and Neal for their hard work, support and those beers in Greymouth and Auckland respectively.

There were many people who made my trip enjoyable and fruitful, either assisting with advice or company. Thanks to Mansel, Margaret, Neil, Nicole and Steve in Auckland for hospitality, advice and brain-storming sessions. Also in Auckland thanks to the travel-industry crew who know how to party – Ali, Rat, Heather, Campbell, Nalisha and others – and to Natalee Hampson at Tourism Auckland. Thanks to Tony for making the time for a reunion in St Arnaud and Nelson. Also thanks to Krista for dinner, Gordon in Hokitika, Alan in Nelson, Barbara Doyle and the crew at Brian Boru Backpackers in Thames, and the captain of the Endeavour Express in Picton.

Staff at various tourist offices and business willingly gave their time along the way, so thanks to all, in particular Fiordland Travel in Queenstown, and visitor centres at Nelson, Kaitaia, Picton (and Marlborough) and Motueka to name a few.

Finally, thanks to anyone who put me in a kayak, pushed me out of a plane or otherwise helped me enjoy this beautiful country.

Carolyn Bain

Firstly, big thank yous to Paul and Neal for being great co-authors and for their assistance on the road and their sympathy as deadlines loomed large. Thanks to Paul for an eventful evening in Greymouth and especially for research assistance in Maruia Springs and Kaikoura. Cheers to Neal for a fun-filled few days in and around Wellington.

My appreciation goes also to a couple of friends whose company on this trip made everything loads more fun: to Sally O'Keefe, for a great couple of weeks spent harassing baby lambs, sampling the local vino and getting the car bogged; and to Jenny Jones for trawling Wellington's cafes with me and for also being crap at flying-by-wire.

Countless Kiwis made my job much easier and more pleasurable and I thank them all for their eagerness to share their local expertise, plus their many acts of kindness. There are too many names to mention here, but special thanks go to the efficient, knowledgeable staff at all the visitors centres, and to Lesley and

Phil Creedy (Invercargill), Lesley Gray (Stewart Island), Iain Leitch (Queenstown), Dion and the team (Mt Cook), John & Helen Chipper (Plimmerton), Jane Tolerton and Marlene & Paul Gasson (Wellington), Hamish Allardice (Wellington), Hamish Johnston & Co (Akaroa) and Graeme Doesler (Kaikoura).

Thanks to all the travellers who used the last edition and wrote to us with comments and recommendations. A special mention must go to Fraser Shearer for his excellent review of Queenstown's nightlife scene. Finally, thanks to Michael Day, Huw Fowles, Corie Waddell, Errol Hunt and the rest of the fine crew at LP Melbourne for getting the final product on the shelves.

Neal Bedford

First of all thanks to LP for giving me this gig (I'm not greasing, I mean it!). Cheers to Paul for all his advice and help throughout the project, and to Carolyn for dragging me to Wellington and forcing me on 'fly by wire', hangover and all.

A huge thank you is directed at all the visitors centres and DOC offices which made my job that much easier and helped stop my stress levels from going through the roof. To all the incredibly friendly locals and enthusiastic travellers I met on the way, thanks for the hints, tips and conversations. To my travelling companions – Jamie Kemp, who should stop chatting up Israelis and Germans, and Paul Bloomfield, who needs to practice on the luge a bit more – *danke* for keeping me off the straight and narrow and for supplying the *Pink Panther* with groovy tunes. A big thumbs up to Alan Ludlam for letting me abuse his hospitality, PlayStation and local knowledge; Judy and Gary Ludlam for coming to the printing rescue; Brad and Debbie for not making me feel too bad for crashing the folks' car and giving me the low-down on Hamilton; Stu (aka Ponch/Nige) and Andy (aka John/Dougal) for Gisborne beaches, Drum & Base and CHiPs; Kirk for Rotorua's highlights; and John and Mel for support, friendship and for finally getting pregnant.

Special thanks to the Brennan Clan and Peter and Anne Hoffmann for putting me up once again. But the most thanks and love goes to Mum and Dad, who kept me fed and supported me throughout.

This Book

Lonely Planet's *New Zealand* guide has been around since 1977, when Tony Wheeler wrote the first edition. Since then subsequent editions have been coordinated by Simon Hayman, Mary Coverton, Tony again, Robin Tinker, Nancy Keller and Jeff Williams.

This 11th edition was coordinated by Paul Harding, who wrote the introductory chapters, Auckland, Coromandel, Marlborough & Nelson, Northland and the West Coast. Neal Bedford wrote Bay of Plenty, Central Plateau, East Coast, Taranaki, Waikato & King Country and Wanganui & Manawatu. Carolyn Bain wrote Canterbury, Otago, Other Islands, Southland and Wellington.

FROM THE PUBLISHER

New Zealand was coordinating inhouse by Michael Day (editing) and Huw Fowles (design and cartography). Michael was helped by Julia Taylor, William Gourlay, George Dunford and Anastasia Safioleas while Huw called on Sally Morgan, Csanad Csutoros, Ray Thomson, Celia Wood, Chris Thomas, Jacqueline Nguyen and Barbara Benson. Errol Hunt and then Victoria Harrison took over layout from Michael when he disappeared to the Middle East.

Elsewhere, Kusnandar did the climate charts, Mick Weldon drew the new illustrations, Jenny Jones designed the cover, Jennifer Mundy (talk2us) kept us right up to date with readers letters and Kerrie Williams (LPI) and Chaman Sidhu tracked down a hundred tricky permissions issues. Errol wrote the 'Watching Wildlife' section and the rugby and Peter Jackson boxed texts and knocked together the index. Authors were commissioned by Corie Waddell and Jane Thompson. Errol and Corie supervised the book inhouse with artwork-checking assistance from Chris Love, Jack Gavran, Jocelyn Harewood, Kieran Grogan, Kim Hutchins and Meredith Mail.

Thanks to *whanau* and friends for fact checking, Ben Wootten for the tour of Weta and to staff of NZ tourist offices who are always willing to go the extra mile.

Kia ora rawa atu and a sad *haere atu* to Greg Alford – thanks for tireless work behind the scenes on this and a million other Asia/Pacific titles.

THANKS
Many thanks to the travellers who used the last edition and wrote to us with helpful hints, advice and interesting anecdotes. Your names appear in the back of this book.

13

Foreword

ABOUT LONELY PLANET GUIDEBOOKS

The story begins with a classic travel adventure: Tony and Maureen Wheeler's 1972 journey across Europe and Asia to Australia. There was no useful information about the overland trail then, so Tony and Maureen published the first Lonely Planet guidebook to meet a growing need.

From a kitchen table, Lonely Planet has grown to become the largest independent travel publisher in the world, with offices in Melbourne (Australia), Oakland (USA), London (UK) and Paris (France).

Today Lonely Planet guidebooks cover the globe. There is an ever-growing list of books and information in a variety of media. Some things haven't changed. The main aim is still to make it possible for adventurous travellers to get out there – to explore and better understand the world.

At Lonely Planet we believe travellers can make a positive contribution to the countries they visit – if they respect their host communities and spend their money wisely. Since 1986 a percentage of the income from each book has been donated to aid projects and human rights campaigns, and, more recently, to wildlife conservation.

Although inclusion in a guidebook usually implies a recommendation we cannot list every good place. Exclusion does not necessarily imply criticism. In fact there are a number of reasons why we might exclude a place – sometimes it is simply inappropriate to encourage an influx of travellers.

UPDATES & READER FEEDBACK

Things change – prices go up, schedules change, good places go bad and bad places go bankrupt. Nothing stays the same. So, if you find things better or worse, recently opened or long-since closed, please tell us and help make the next edition even more accurate and useful.

Lonely Planet thoroughly updates each guidebook as often as possible – usually every two years, although for some destinations the gap can be longer. Between editions, up-to-date information is available in our free, quarterly *Planet Talk* newsletter and monthly email bulletin *Comet*. The *Upgrades* section of our website (W www.lonelyplanet.com) is also regularly updated by Lonely Planet authors, and the site's *Scoop* section covers news and current affairs relevant to travellers. Lastly, the *Thorn Tree* bulletin board and *Postcards* section carry unverified, but fascinating, reports from travellers.

Tell us about it! We genuinely value your feedback. A well-travelled team at Lonely Planet reads and acknowledges every email and letter we receive and ensures that every morsel of information finds its way to the relevant authors, editors and cartographers.

Everyone who writes to us will find their name listed in the next edition of the appropriate guidebook, and will receive the latest issue of *Comet* or *Planet Talk*. The very best contributions will be rewarded with a free guidebook.

We may edit, reproduce and incorporate your comments in Lonely Planet products such as guidebooks, websites and digital products, so let us know if you don't want your comments reproduced or your name acknowledged.

How to contact Lonely Planet:
Online: e talk2us@lonelyplanet.com.au, W www.lonelyplanet.com
Australia: Locked Bag 1, Footscray, Victoria 3011
UK: 10a Spring Place, London NW5 3BH
USA: 150 Linden St, Oakland, CA 94607

Introduction

If you've seen the film *The Lord of the Rings* you'll have caught glimpses of those soaring craggy mountains (the Remarkables), beautiful meadows, rivers and plains. It's only a fraction of what's out there.

New Zealand may be a small, lightly populated country, but it packs an incredible amount into its two lamb chop–shaped islands. New Zealand is like a microcosm of all the world's natural attractions. You can trek on the slopes of active volcanoes; travel through remote, rugged patches of virgin rainforest; walk around thermal geysers and boiling mud, or discover kauri forests with some of the largest and oldest trees on Earth. You can swim with pods of playful dolphins, watch whales, see glaciers descending into rainforests towards the ocean, fish for trout in pristine lakes and streams, and see fur seals and penguins swimming around your boat as you cruise on remote fiords. The adventurous can go white-water rafting, cave rafting, rock and mountain climbing, tandem skydiving, bungy jumping, skiing down long glaciers, and much more. Tramping on some of the world's best-known tracks and winter skiing at dozens of resorts both draw many visitors.

Fresh air, magnificent scenery and outdoor activities are the feature attractions of New Zealand, and visitors who come expecting a pristine, green, well-organised little country are not disappointed.

The two islands are surprisingly different in character. The North Island, with a slightly warmer climate, is best known for the stark volcanic landscapes of Tongariro National Park, Taranaki, Rotorua and the

NEW ZEALAND

Desert Road south from Taupo. But it also has New Zealand's best beaches, remnants of native forest in Northland and Coromandel, and a strong Maori influence. The South Island is greener, softer, slower paced and dominated by the magnificent string of snow-capped Southern Alps and the flooded waterways of Fiordland in the far south.

Though none could seriously be called a metropolis by world standards, New Zealand's major cities each have their own unique character. Auckland is the brash, harbourside business centre, constantly drawing people in from around New Zealand, Asia and the Pacific. As host of the America's Cup, it commands international attention. Wellington, the national capital, is more refined, with a vibrant arts and cafe culture. Christchurch, the main city of the South Island, is like something transplanted from England and has a small university-town feel – the Oxford of the south.

Unlike in its Antipodean neighbour, Australia ('across the ditch', as they say), distances in New Zealand are not great and getting around is easy. Cycling, hitching and driving through the countryside are all popular ways to travel. Finding affordable accommodation is also easy, although it's a good idea to book ahead in the high season. Eating out is becoming an art form – the food (especially the seafood) is fresh and there's plenty of it, and the local wine is excellent and getting better.

Importantly, the Kiwis (the people, not the birds) are by and large a friendly, welcoming lot, keen to share their beautiful country and Maori culture with visitors.

Travellers do have one consistent complaint about New Zealand, though: that they haven't allowed themselves enough time in the country. Look at the map of the world and it doesn't appear to be a big country. However, once you arrive in New Zealand, it soon becomes apparent how much there is to see and do.

If time is no object, we recommend allowing at least six weeks for a visit. Of course, you can still enjoy New Zealand in less time and some travellers make a mad dash through the country and still have a great time.

This book will help to show you all there is to see and do in New Zealand, and assist you in planning your travels. Have a great time. It's a beautiful country.

Facts about New Zealand

HISTORY

It is known from archaeological evidence that there were established communities in New Zealand from around AD 1000 onwards – perhaps much earlier.

Although different tribes have differing legends about the initial settlement of NZ, many oral histories tell of the discovery of NZ by the navigator Kupe in about AD 800. Kupe sailed to Aotearoa from Hawaiki, the ancestral homeland. He visited the North and South Islands then returned from Hokianga to Hawaiki to report his find. Despite the similar names, Hawaiki was not Hawaii; it was probably Ra'iatea (in Maori, Rangiatea), near Tahiti. It was Kupe's wife, Hine-te-aparangi, who named the new land Aotearoa, which means 'Land of the Long White Cloud'.

Other legends tell of the so-called Great Migration in AD 1350, when a fleet of migratory canoes, including *Te Arawa, Aotea* and *Tainui*, left Hawaiki to settle Aotearoa. This 'history', although still widely believed, was a dubious adaptation of Maori legends by early Western historians. While the canoes named almost certainly existed, it is unlikely that they travelled in a fleet.

For the early creation mythology see the special section 'Maori Culture & Arts'.

Early Settlement

Recent evidence indicates that Polynesians, who were to become the Maori, arrived in NZ in a series of migrations over several generations from around AD 1000.

These migrations had been preceded by an eastward seaborne expansion of Austronesians (from the Melanesian/Indonesian chain) some three thousand years earlier. The Lapita people (named after a location in New Caledonia where their distinctive pottery was found) reached Fiji, Tonga and Samoa around 1500 BC. Almost 1000 years later they fanned out further east, reaching as far as Tahiti (Society Islands). Around 1000 years later they were on the move

again, this time to Easter Island, Hawaii, and eventually NZ.

Driven from their homeland by land shortages, war or religious dissent, the settlers on these great canoe voyages found in NZ temperate islands far larger than any islands of the Pacific. Apart from bats, the land was devoid of mammals for hunting, but the sea provided abundant food resources. Of the birdlife, the most spectacular was the huge flightless moa, over 3m tall.

This initially plentiful food supply became one of the staples of early Polynesians, especially on the east of the South Island, where the moa was hunted for its food and feathers. Agriculture was not well developed in this early 'Archaic' period of settlement, perhaps because the climate was so much colder than the Polynesian homeland. There is evidence to suggest that there were three areas of settlement where different resources were utilised. In the warmer north, kumara (sweet potato) cultivation was possible. A central transitional area saw only marginal cultivation. In the far colder south, cultivation wasn't a possibility.

Widespread agricultural societies based on the imported Polynesian crops of kumara, taro and yams came later; this second era of settlement, sometimes known as the 'Classic Maori' period, was only possible with the development of a sophisticated system to protect root crops from frost.

Probably the most devastating effect of the arrival of humans in the untouched environment was the destruction of flora and fauna. Widespread forest fires led to extensive deforestation and large areas of fernland became tussock grassland.

The giant moa was hunted into extinction by about the late 17th century; seal populations were confined to smaller ranges in the south; and introduced rats *(kiore)* and dogs *(kuri)* wreaked havoc on populations of ground-dwelling birds.

With natural resources so depleted it was necessary for the Maori to develop another food supply. Over two centuries (from around 1300 to 1500) the northern tribes became cultivators of fern root and kumara. During this time, under increasing pressure for land and again beginning in the north, the Maori became more warlike and many of the tribes were wiped out by a process of conquest and enslavement. Cannibalism also became prevalent at this time, as did the development of *pa* (forts) for protection against warring tribes.

The Moriori, who inhabited the Chatham Islands, are believed to have settled there from the main NZ islands about 500 years ago. They retained an Archaic culture long after it had vanished from the mainland.

One version of history you may hear is that the Moriori were the first settlers of NZ. Based solely on a study by historian S. Percy Smith (1840–1922), this theory has it that the Moriori (or Maruiwi) were a Melanesian people and were forcibly displaced by the arrival later of the Polynesian Maori. Although discredited since the early 20th century, the theory was taught to NZ school kids until relatively recently and still finds favour among many adults.

European Exploration

In 1642 Dutch explorer Abel Tasman, who had just sailed around Australia from Batavia (modern-day Jakarta, Indonesia), sailed up the west coast of NZ but didn't stay long after his only landing attempt (in Golden Bay) resulted in three members of his crew being killed. He christened the bay 'Murderer's Bay' and the land Niuew Zeeland, after the Netherlands province of Zeeland.

Because Tasman had only sailed up the west coast, there had been speculation that this could be the west coast of the fabled great southern continent. In the logical European cosmology, it was thought that a large southern land must exist to balance the large landmasses in the northern hemisphere.

The Dutch, after this first uncomfortable look, lost interest and NZ was left alone until British navigator and explorer James Cook arrived on the *Endeavour* in 1769. Cook circumnavigated NZ on three voyages, mapping as he went, and many places still bear

Captain Cook claimed NZ for Britain in 1769

the names he gave them. He made friendly contact with the Maori inhabitants on several occasions, with one exception – at Poverty Bay some Maori were killed. Luckily his Polynesian interpreter, Tupaia, was Ra'iatean and spoke a language very similar to NZ Maori. Cook was impressed with their bravery and spirit, and with the potential of this sparsely populated land. After finishing his journey around the coasts of both the North and South Islands and determining that it was not the great southern continent, Cook claimed the entire land for the British Crown and continued on to Australia.

The French explorer Jean-François Marie de Surville was sailing around NZ at the same time as Cook but the two never crossed paths with one another. They came close, off the coast of the North Island, but each was unaware of the other's presence.

New Zealand's first European settlers were itinerant sealers (who soon reduced the seal population to next to nothing) and then whalers (who did the same to the whales). They introduced diseases and prostitution, and created such a demand for preserved heads that Maori chiefs began chopping off their slaves' heads to order (previously they'd only preserved the heads of warriors who had died in battle). Worst of all, Europeans brought firearms. When they exchanged greenstone *mere* (clubs) for muskets, the Maori soon embarked on wholesale slaughter of one another. In what became known as the Musket Wars, Northland's Ngapuhi tribe, led by Hongi Hika, embraced the new technology and sent raiding parties throughout the central North Island as far south as Hawkes Bay on the East Coast and Taranaki in the west.

By 1830 the Maori population was falling dramatically.

European Settlement

Samuel Marsden was the first missionary to bring Christianity to NZ, arriving in 1814, and other missionaries soon followed. The Bible was translated into Maori – the first time the Maori language had been written. By the mid-19th century tribal warfare had abated, cannibalism was fairly well stamped out and the raging impact of European diseases also curbed. But the Maori people now found themselves spiritually assaulted and much of their culture and traditions were irrevocably altered. Their numbers continued to decline.

During the early 19th century European settlers (called Pakeha in Maori) arrived in increasing numbers, some on settlement campaigns organised from Britain. In the 1830s entrepreneurs from Australia raced to carve out holdings in the new land. Growing lawlessness from less-savoury settlers and a deterioration in Maori-Pakeha relations resulted in petitions for British intervention.

The need to establish the rule of law, and increasing French interest in this southern land, finally prompted the British to dispatch James Busby as the British Resident in 1833. It was a low-key effort, illustrated by poor Busby having to pay his own fare from Australia. Once he'd set up shop in Kororareka (now called Russell) in Northland, his efforts to protect the settlers and maintain law and order were hobbled by his lack of supporting forces, arms and authority. He was soon dubbed 'the man of war without guns'.

Treaty of Waitangi

In 1838 the lawlessness problem, unscrupulous 'purchases' of Maori land and the threat of a French colony at Akaroa in the South Island all stirred the British to seek annexation of NZ. Captain William Hobson was sent to replace Busby and persuade the Maori chiefs to relinquish their sovereignty to the British Crown.

The Treaty of Waitangi was drawn up within a few days of Hobson's arrival in NZ. On 5 February 1840, over 400 Maori gathered in front of Busby's residence at Waitangi in the Bay of Islands to hear the treaty read. The Maori chiefs had some objections, so the treaty was amended and they withdrew to debate the issue throughout the night. The following day, with a truly British display of pomp and circumstance, the treaty was signed by Hobson and 45 Maori chiefs, mostly from the Bay of Islands region.

Over the next seven months the treaty was carried throughout NZ by missionaries, traders and officials, eventually being signed by over 500 chiefs. Hobson proclaimed British sovereignty, becoming NZ's first governor and establishing his capital at Kororareka. He moved it to Auckland a year later.

Though the treaty was short and seemed to be simple, it was a controversial document that is still hotly debated in modern-day NZ. Under the terms of the treaty, the chiefs ceded their sovereignty (kawanatanga) to the Queen of England in exchange for the Queen's protection and the granting to Maori people all citizenship rights, privileges and duties enjoyed by citizens of England. The term kawanatanga, however, did not have the same connotation in Maori as 'sovereignty' does in English – the Maori chiefs thus had a different understanding to the British as to what they were signing.

The treaty guaranteed the Maori possession of their land, fisheries and resources (in total, their tino rangatiratanga) and stipulated that they could only sell their land to the Crown. The Queen's agent would then sell the land to settlers in an orderly and fair fashion.

The treaty seemed to promise benefits for both sides, but when settlers arrived and needed land and the Maori didn't want to sell, conflict inevitably resulted. The admirable idea that the government should be a go-between ensuring fairness in all Maori-Pakeha deals fell apart when the government was too tight-fisted to pay the price.

Land Wars

The first visible revolt against the treaty came when Hone Heke chopped down the flagpole at Kororareka which flew the British flag. Despite new poles and more guards, Hone Heke or his followers managed to chop the pole down four times; on the last occasion it was braced with iron to foil further attempts. In 1845, Hone Heke attacked and razed the town of Kororareka. In the skirmishes that followed, the British governor posted a £100 reward for Heke's head, to which the chief responded by offering a matching £100 for the governor's head.

The Northland war was only one in a series of conflicts between the Maori and Europeans. The original benign intent of the Treaty of Waitangi was forgotten as ever-increasing numbers of European settlers arrived. Many land sales were disputed, as chiefs sold land that belonged to the whole tribe or sold land of other tribes, resulting in a new source of tribal conflict.

Meanwhile, the government pressed on with developing the colony. The Constitution Act of 1852 divided the country into six provinces that administered local government and assumed responsibility for land purchases and sales. Alarmed, Maori became increasingly reluctant to sell land. In the Waikato region, a number of tribal chiefs united to elect a Maori 'King' in 1858 and resisted land sales and European settlement in the Waikato and the King Country region until the 20th century (see the Waikato & the King Country chapter).

Tensions between Maori and Europeans escalated into several fully fledged wars with troops from England and Australia aiding the NZ militia. Known collectively as the Land Wars (or Maori Wars), fighting took place in many parts of the country: Northland (1844–46), Taranaki (1860–61 and 1865–69), Waikato/King Country (1863–67) and the East Coast (1868–72). See individual chapters for more historical information.

The most bitterly fought conflicts were in Taranaki. The force of arms enabled imperial troops to vanquish the Taranaki tribes, but later skirmishes erupted in the East Coast region with the rise of Hauhauism, a Maori religious movement which aimed to oust the Europeans. Te Kooti (see the boxed text 'Te Kooti' in the East Coast chapter) also led raiding parties against European settlers in the Taranaki region until he finally retreated to the King Country in 1872.

After the Land Wars the government confiscated huge parcels of Maori land, which, with new legislation allowing private land sales, resulted in the loss of prime Maori land over the rest of the 19th century.

Late 19th Century

While development in the North Island languished because of the conflicts, the South Island prospered, helped by farming and then the discovery of gold. After 1870, the North Island economy began to recover but it remained poorer until last century. In 1876 the colonial government abolished the provincial governments and centralised power in Wellington, the capital since 1865.

European settlement and influence grew and NZ became a productive agricultural country. Sheep farming, the backbone of modern NZ, flourished as refrigerated ships made it possible to sell NZ meat in Europe. NZ became what has been called 'an efficient offshore farm' for England, exporting agricultural products, especially mutton, wool, sheepskin and dairy products, and importing manufactured goods.

Towards the end of the 19th century, NZ went through a phase of sweeping and unprecedented social change. After years of lobbying spearheaded by the remarkable Kate Sheppard, women were given the vote in 1893, 25 years before Britain or the USA and 75 years before Switzerland. An eminent leader at the time, Richard 'King Dick' Seddon and his Liberal Party were responsible for many of the reforms. Their far-sighted social reforms and pioneering legislation included old-age pensions, minimum-wage structures and the introduction of arbitration courts and children's health services.

ALEXANDER TURNBULL LIBRARY, WELLINGTON NZ

Kate Sheppard

Meanwhile the Maori people suffered. NZ grew through immigration (a selective policy), but by 1900 the Maori population had dropped to an estimated 42,000. The Maori were given the vote in 1867, but continued to lose the struggle to hold on to their culture and ancestral lands.

Early 20th Century

New Zealand had become a self-governing British colony in 1856 and a dominion in 1907. By the 1920s it controlled most of its affairs, but it was not a fully independent country until 1947.

Meanwhile NZ fought for the British in the Boer War of 1899–1902 and in WWI. The Kiwi soldiers earned a reputation for skill and bravery – most notably fighting as part of the Australia New Zealand Army Corps (Anzacs) at the famous battle of Gallipoli in 1915 – but also suffered heavy losses, with one in three men aged between 20 and 40 killed or wounded fighting for Britain in WWI. NZ troops also helped the British in WWII, fighting in the European and Middle East arenas. But after 1941,

when war was declared in the Pacific, and NZ was directly threatened, a division was also established in the southwest Pacific.

The post-war years were good to NZ, as the world economy was rebuilt and prices for agricultural products were high. NZ had one of the highest per-capita incomes in the world and a social welfare system envied by many countries.

During the Korean War (1950–53), NZ again sent troops as part of a Commonwealth brigade. Australia, NZ and the USA signed the Anzus defence pact, pledging mutual aid in the event of any attack. In response to the perceived threat of communism, NZ also joined the anticommunist Seato (South-East Asia Treaty Organisation).

During the 1960s and '70s an increased amount of NZ aid was directed to Pacific countries and in 1971 NZ joined the South Pacific Forum, designed for Pacific governments to discuss common problems.

Race Relations

The most important event in the history of NZ race relations was the signing of the Treaty of Waitangi in 1840. Though it signalled the annexation of the country by Britain, its motives – to stop lawlessness and the grab for Maori land – were at least partly humanitarian. In exchange for granting sovereignty over NZ to Britain, the Maori chiefs were promised full exclusive and undisturbed possession of their lands, forests, fisheries and other properties, and the same rights and privileges as British subjects.

As settlement progressed, the terms of the treaty were increasingly ignored. Disputes over land resulted in the Land Wars of the 1860s, which eventually broke the back of Maori resistance. Maori land was appropriated and the treaty, which was never ratified by a NZ parliament, was all but dead.

Despite romantic notions of the Maori people, partly inspired by the 'noble savage' sentiments fashionable in the 19th century, Europeans remained largely separate from Maori society. Though intermarriage was common, for the most part Maori retreated to the more isolated rural areas.

At the turn of the 20th century, when race relations looked at their bleakest, the Maori began to organise and develop leaders skilled in negotiating between Pakeha and Maori communities. The setting aside of Maori seats in parliament gave the Maori a political voice. In the South Island the Ngai Tahu people petitioned parliament over land grievances. The Maori also elected members of parliament specifically to lobby on these issues. The Young Maori Party, composed of Pakeha-educated Maori, pressed for greater education and health services for Maori communities.

Apirana Ngata of the Ngati Porou tribe was an inspiring leader who became Minister of Native Affairs in 1928. He established Maori land development schemes stressing the importance of Maori culture. Ngata was a member of the Young Maori Party with Hone Heke (the nephew of the warrior chief of the same name, of the Ngapuhi tribe), James Carroll (Ngati Kahungunu tribe), Maui Pomare (Tainui) and Peter Buck (also known as Te Rangi Hiroa) of the Ngati Toa tribe. These politicians lobbied the Labour Party persistently and when Labour achieved power in 1935, the government introduced legislation guaranteeing equality in employment, and increased spending on health, housing and education. Though the Maori were conspicuous on the rugby field and keen to sign up to defend the realm in times of war, up until WWII interaction between Pakeha and Maori communities remained minimal.

Despite disparities in education, wealth and power-sharing between Maori and Pakeha, Maori people did enjoy greater acceptance and equality under the law than the indigenous peoples of other European colonised countries. New Zealanders are proud of their record of racial harmony. *Return to Paradise* by James Michener tells of the outraged local reaction when WWII American GIs stationed in NZ tried to treat the Maori like American blacks.

The post-war economic boom saw the greatest change in Maori society, as Maori migrated to the cities, lured by the promise of jobs. Urban Maori mixed with Europeans as never before as the government pursued the policies of assimilation fashionable at the time. But assimilation ensured the dominance of European culture and though Maori culture survived, particularly in rural areas, Maori progressively lost more of their language and traditions.

In the late 1960s a new Maori voice called for a revival in *Maoritanga* (Maori culture). Young activists combined with traditional leaders to provide a new direction, calling for the government to address Maori grievances. The contentious Treaty of Waitangi, always on the Maori agenda, came to the fore as never before, and the concept of 'tino rangatiratanga' became a catch cry for greater self-determination. Increasing radicalism saw Maori take to the streets and engage in land occupations. In the 1970s, historic land disputes involved Raglan golf course and Bastion Point, in Auckland. The rise of black power groups and gangs such as the Mongrel Mob, a prominent Maori biker group, unsettled many in the European community.

The focus on Maori issues spurred the government to give the Maori language greater prominence in schools and the media, to institute the Race Relations Act, banning discrimination, and to introduce the Waitangi Tribunal in 1975 to investigate Maori land claims. Though some claims have resulted in the return of Maori land, other claims have dragged on for many years.

In 1994 the government, in an attempt to extricate itself from the terms of the tribunal, proposed a massive once-and-for-all fiscal envelope of $1 billion to pay out all Maori land claims over the following 10 years. Settlements have already been made. In 1995, there was a notable $170 million reparation to the Tainui for lands confiscated in 1884. In 1997, an agreement between the Crown and the Ngai Tahu was reached.

Perhaps the greatest effect of the Maori revival has been the growing interest in Maoritanga. Maori language, literature, arts and culture are experiencing a renaissance. The establishment of Te Kohanga Reo (language nests) in schools, with sessional or all-day immersion in Maori language and culture, is a definitive step towards the preservation of Maori identity. The Maori population is now overwhelmingly urban and largely integrated into European society, but the loss of traditional culture is being redressed as more and more Maori learn the language and return to *marae* (the traditional ancestral village of a tribe).

Pakeha also have a growing awareness of Maori culture. Certainly the government and intellectuals have embraced the new Maori revival and see an understanding of the Maori culture and at least a basic knowledge of Maori as an advantage. However, there is an undercurrent of unease in the wider community, especially with radical Maori aspirations that call for Maori sovereignty – the establishment of a separate Maori government and judicial system.

The Maori occupation of the Moutoa Gardens in Wanganui in 1995 created great acrimony in the town and other parts of NZ, reflecting unease at the adjustments to the dominant European culture. Though NZ is not the utopia of racial harmony it is sometimes portrayed to be, there is no denying the genuine attempts by the European community to accommodate Maori aspirations. The overall good relations between both communities continues, and NZ's record on race relations remains strong.

Recent History

New Zealand's economy, along with that of much of the rest of the world, nose-dived in the 1970s and '80s. The loss of its traditional European markets for agricultural products, combined with the oil crisis–related price hikes of many of its mineral and manufactured imports, caused a dramatic deterioration in the country's economy. Robert Muldoon's National Party government tried to buy NZ's way out of trouble by running up large foreign debts and investing in wayward industrial development programmes.

In 1984 a Labour government was elected and, in a reversal of political roles, set about a radical restructuring of the economy dubbed 'Rogernomics' after the finance minister, Roger Douglas. As Douglas pressed on with the privatisation of state

MURRAY WEBB / ALEXANDER TURNBULL LIBRARY, WELLINGTON NZ

David Lange

industries and proposals of a flat income tax rate and deregulation of the labour market, Prime Minister David Lange decided enough was enough and sacked him. After the party reinstated Douglas, Lange shocked the nation by resigning in 1989. Labour was in disarray, and the National Party led by Jim Bolger swept to power in 1990.

In 1983 Australia and NZ signed the Closer Economic Relations Trade Agreement, permitting free and unrestricted trade between the two countries. In 1984 NZ took a strong stand on nuclear issues by refusing entry to nuclear-equipped and powered warships. In response, the USA suspended its obligations to NZ within the Anzus defence pact. Although this brave policy has caused many problems for the Kiwis they have continued to stick by it.

NZ also became a leader in the Pacific in its opposition to nuclear testing by the French at Moruroa Atoll in French Polynesia. In 1985 French secret service agents sank the Greenpeace ship *Rainbow Warrior* in Auckland's harbour (see the boxed text 'The *Rainbow Warrior* Trail' in the Northland chapter). In 1995, the French restarted testing in French Polynesia despite worldwide condemnation. NZ was again at the forefront of international protests and dispatched the navy frigate HMNZS *Tui* with a protest flotilla to Moruroa; the NZ ambassador to France was recalled as a mark of NZ's outrage. After a number of controversial detonations the French finally stopped testing.

In the 1996 election, the National Party led by Jim Bolger formed a government in coalition with the minority NZ First Party and its maverick leader, the charismatic Winston Peters. In a bloodless coup the following year, Bolger was ousted and replaced by Jenny Shipley, the country's first woman prime minister.

In late November 1999, Labour won a general election and Helen Clark became NZ's first *elected* woman prime minister. Labour formed a coalition with the left-wing Alliance Party, dependent on the support of the (even more left-wing) Greens. At the time of writing, Kiwis were again preparing to go to the polls, the 'Alliance' Party had disintegrated entirely and Labour was tipped to easily win another term.

Significant events during the 1990s were NZ's 1995 win in the America's Cup yachting race and its subsequent successful defence in 2000 (see the boxed text 'America's Cup 2003' in the Auckland chapter).

GEOGRAPHY

New Zealand stretches 1600km from north to south. It consists of two main islands and some smaller islands, and several far-flung islands hundreds of kilometres away. NZ's territorial jurisdiction extends to Tokelau and the mostly uninhabited islands of the Chathams, Kermadecs, Auckland, Antipodes, Snares, Solander and Bounty, and to the Ross Dependency in Antarctica.

The North Island (115,000 sq km) and the South Island (151,000 sq km) are the two major landmasses. Stewart Island (1700 sq km) lies directly south of the South Island. The country is 10,400km southwest of the USA, 1700km south of Fiji and 2250km east of Australia.

NZ's total land area (270,534 sq km) is greater than that of the UK (244,800 sq km), but almost 36 times smaller than that

of the USA. Its coastline, with many bays, harbours and fiords, is long compared with its landmass.

A notable feature of NZ's geography is the great number of rivers. There's a lot of rainfall in NZ and all that rain has to go somewhere. The Waikato River in the North Island is NZ's longest river (425km). Also in the North Island, the Whanganui River is the country's longest navigable river, which has always made it an important waterway. NZ also has many beautiful lakes; Lake Taupo is the largest, Waikaremoana and Wanaka are two of the most beautiful and Lake Hauroko the deepest (462m).

GEOLOGY

Both the North Island and South Island have some high mountains, formed by two distinct geological processes associated with the westward movement of the Pacific tectonic plate.

The North Island is situated on the southern reaches of the subduction zone, where the oceanic Pacific Plate is sliding underneath the continental Indo-Australian Plate. The resulting volcanic activity has created a number of volcanoes, thermal areas and some equally impressive volcanic depressions.

A rough line of volcanoes, some of which are still active, extends south from the steaming Whakaari (White Island) in the Bay of Plenty past Putauaki (Mt Edgecumbe), Tarawera and the highly active thermal areas in and around Rotorua and Lake Taupo. The latter, NZ's largest lake, was formed by a gigantic volcanic explosion in AD 186 and still has thermal areas bubbling away nearby. South of Lake Taupo are the North Island's spectacularly large volcanoes Tongariro, Ruapehu, Ngauruhoe and the smaller Pihanga. Further southwest is the lone volcanic cone of Mt Taranaki/Egmont.

Other parts of the North Island also have evidence of volcanic activity; in Auckland, for example, there are over 50 volcanic cones, including most of its famous hills (One Tree Hill, Mt Eden etc) that rise up from the plains.

The North Island has some ranges of hills and mountains produced by folding and uplift, notably the Tararua and Ruahine ranges in the southern part of the North Island. In general, though, most of the high places of the North Island were formed by volcanic activity – particularly the high central plateau.

In the South Island the geological process is different. Here the two tectonic plates are smashing into each other, resulting in a process called 'crystal shortening'. This has caused the Southern Alps to rise as a spine, virtually extending along the entire length of the South Island. Thrust faulting, folding and vertical slips all combine to create a rapid uplift of the Southern Alps. Though the Southern Alps receive a lot of rainfall, and hence a lot of erosion, their rate of uplift is enough to keep pace and they are continuing to rise, as much as 10mm a year. Most of the east side of the South Island is a large plain known as the Canterbury Plains. Banks Peninsula, on the east coast, was formed by volcanic activity and joined to the mainland by alluvial deposits washed down from the Southern Alps.

CLIMATE

Lying between 34°S and 47°S, NZ is in the Roaring Forties, so it has a prevailing wind blowing over it from west to east year-round, ranging from gentle, freshening breezes to occasional raging gales in winter. Coming across the Tasman Sea, this breeze is relatively warm and moisture-laden. When the south wind comes up from Antarctica it means cold weather.

Because of their different geological features, the North and South Islands have two distinct rainfall patterns. In the South Island, the Southern Alps act as a barrier for the moisture-laden winds coming across the Tasman Sea, creating a wet climate on the west side of the mountains and a dry climate on the east side. The annual rainfall on the west side is over 7500mm but is only about 330mm on the east.

The South Island's geography also creates a wind pattern in which the prevailing wind, after losing its moisture, blows eastwards

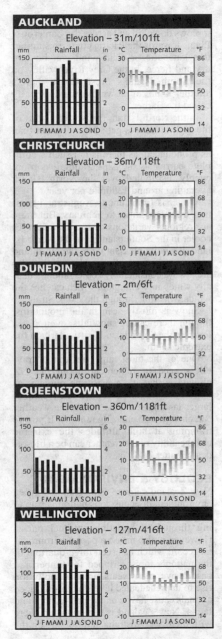

as a dry wind, gathering heat and speed as it blows downhill and across the Canterbury Plains towards the Pacific coast. In summer this katabatic or föhn wind can be hot, dry and fierce. In the Grey River valley on the South Island's West Coast there's another kind of downhill wind, locally called the Barber.

In the North Island, the western sides of the high volcanoes get a lot more rain than the eastern sides but the rain shadow is not as pronounced, as there is not such a complete barrier as the Alps. Rainfall is more evenly distributed over the North Island, averaging around 1300mm per year.

Winter is from June to August and summer from December to February. But there are regional variations: it is a few degrees cooler in the South Island than the North Island. It's quite pleasant up in the Northland region at any time of year. Higher altitudes are always considerably cooler, and it's usually windy in Wellington, which catches the winds whistling through the Cook Strait.

Snow is mostly seen in the mountains, though there can be snowfalls, even at sea level, in the South Island, particularly in the extreme south.

One of the most important things travellers need to remember about the NZ climate is that it's a maritime climate, as opposed to the continental climate typical of larger landmasses. This means the weather can change with amazing rapidity. If you're tramping at high altitudes the extreme changeability of the weather can be a life-or-death matter.

ECOLOGY & ENVIRONMENT

New Zealand's image as a clean and green environmentally conscious nation is true to some extent, certainly while you're tramping through its pristine national parks. However, it also masks a poor environmental record which has seen three-quarters of the nation's forest stripped for timber and pasture over many years, urban air pollution rise to unprecedented levels and introduced animals cause havoc on the native flora and fauna. New Zealand is also right up there with the USA, Australia and Canada on the

ALEXANDER TURNBULL LIBRARY, WELLINGTON NZ

Moa (FW Frohawk, 1906)

list of the worst greenhouse-gas-emitting countries per capita.

Human habitation has been devastating for NZ's unique ground-dwelling birdlife, first with the Maori hunting the giant Moa to extinction, then with European settlers introducing destructive wildlife such as the stoat, chamois and Australian brush-tailed possum (see the special colour section 'Watching Wildlife' for more on the sad story of the decimation of many of NZ's bird species). The possum, of which there are some 70 million roaming the country eating native bush, is a real environmental threat.

The Department of Conservation (Te Papa Atawhai) is working on several 'mainland islands' around the country to eradicate introduced pests and re-establish native flora and fauna. Programmes in Lake Rotoiti in Nelson Lakes National Park and the Trounson Kauri Park are two examples. These follow programmes to clear pests from offshore islands.

Commercial forestry and timber-milling is a big part of NZ's economy. While you'll regularly travel past barren hills stripped of trees and dotted with stumps, the logging industry these days almost entirely uses introduced pine, which grows quickly and can be harvested on a rotational basis. Native timber such as the magnificent kauri is now protected in reserves – though it's a bit late since only 4% of the ancient kauri forests that once covered a million hectares in the country's north remain (see the Northland and Coromandel chapters). Forestry is increasing on the East Cape of the North Island, ostensibly to get at the marijuana plants hiding in there!

The battle to protect those ecologically sensitive areas has been fought and won on various fronts over the years, particularly with the designation of national parks. The creation in 1987 of Paparoa National Park on the South Island's West Coast protected 30,000 hectares of forest after much public pressure was applied. More recently, the Kahurangi National Park was formed, and Stewart Island was declared a national park in 2001.

Hydroelectricity, an environmentally friendly form of energy production, supplies around 70% of NZ's electricity but it hasn't been introduced without controversy. When authorities wanted to raise the levels of Lake Manapouri (Fiordland) in order to maximise output from the West Arm hydro plant, the public outcry resulted in NZ's longest petition (265,000 signatories). The lake was 'saved' and its water level is now monitored by the Guardians of the Lake.

It's hard to believe that New Zealand, with only about 4 million people, should suffer from air pollution, but in urban areas, at least, carbon monoxide (CO) levels regularly exceed WHO standards. Auckland is even reported to have higher levels of CO than London. Over 80% of this pollution comes from vehicle emissions – with limited public transport and growing traffic congestion, there are more than 600,000 slow-moving vehicles getting around Auckland. Vehicle-emission controls in NZ are currently not as strict as many other Western countries but the situation is improving. In 2000 Auckland council adopted a 'Dob in a Smoky Vehicle' campaign to get offending cars off the road. Methane (from agriculture and industry) accounts for about 50% of NZ's greenhouse emissions.

For more information, check out the following environmental organisations: Environment & Conservation Organisations of NZ (W www.converge.org.nz), a network of 70 groups including Greenpeace and Friends of the Earth; Greenpeace (W www.greenpeace.org.nz); New Zealand Conservancy Trust (W www.eartheal.org.nz); NZ Department of Conservation (W www.doc.govt.nz); Greenhouse Policy Coalition (W www.gpcnz.co.nz).

NATIONAL PARKS

In addition to NZ's 14 national parks there are numerous designated forest areas. NZ has 19 forest, three maritime and two marine parks. The excellent pamphlet *Exploring New Zealand's Parks* outlines the national, maritime and forest parks. See the 'New Zealand Parks' map in the Activities chapter.

The Department of Conservation (Te Papa Atawhai), commonly referred to as DOC, looks after parks, tracks, walkways, huts and general tramping facilities. It also administers hundreds of scenic, historic, scientific and nature reserves, and wildlife refuges and sanctuaries. It also has responsibility for the three World Heritage areas – Tongariro National Park, Te Wahipounamu (southwest NZ, incorporating Fiordland, Mt Aspiring, Mt Cook and Westland National Parks) and NZ's subantarctic islands.

The local DOC office is usually the best place for information on nature and outdoor attractions in any area. DOC produces excellent pamphlets on almost any natural attraction. In some towns the visitors centres have the same information and a collection of DOC pamphlets. Also check out W www.doc.govt.nz.

GOVERNMENT & POLITICS

The governmental structure of NZ is modelled on the British parliamentary system, with elections based on universal adult suffrage. The minimum voting age is 18 and candidates are elected by secret ballot. The maximum period between elections is three years but the government of the day can call an early election. Voting is not compulsory, but more than 80% of eligible voters usually turn up.

NZ is a constitutional monarchy. The traditional head of state, the reigning British monarch, is represented in NZ by a resident governor-general, who is appointed for a five-year term. An independent judiciary makes up another tier of government.

The difference between the British Westminster system and the NZ model is that NZ has abolished the upper house and governs solely through the lower house. Known as the House of Representatives, it has 120 seats. The government runs on a party system – the party that wins a majority of seats in an election automatically becomes the government and its leader the prime minister (PM). The main parties are the Labour Party (traditionally a workers' party) and National Party (conservative). The two-party system has traditionally made it difficult for other parties to gain much power.

In 1993, after a referendum, the government introduced the MMP (Mixed Member Proportional) electoral system, a limited form of proportional voting based on the German electoral system. Under MMP, electors have two votes: one vote for a candidate in their electorate and the second for a political party. New Zealand has 62 general electorates and seven Maori electorates (Maori voters can choose to vote in either a general or Maori electorate). The remaining 51 seats are allocated to the parties according to the percentage of party votes received.

After the country's first MMP elections, in 1996, the minority NZ First Party and the National Party formed the country's first coalition government (although Labour achieved the highest number of votes).

The 1999 election saw Labour, headed by Helen Clark, win power after forming a coalition with the leftist Alliance Party. The Greens (seven seats) achieved the balance of power after the allocation of MMP party votes. NZ First lost all but a handful of seats. The far-right ACT Party is also represented.

As we go to press NZ faces another election, which Clark's Labour Party is expected to win handsomely.

ECONOMY

The NZ economy has undergone radical restructuring since 1984, first under Labour and then the National government, moving from a welfare-state, government-involved economy towards a private open-market economy.

By the 1980s NZ had lost its old UK market for agricultural produce, had incurred huge foreign debts; the economy was stagnant and restricted by government controls.

The financial market was then deregulated by floating the NZ dollar and abolishing exchange controls. Restrictions on overseas borrowing and foreign investment were also reduced. Tariffs were lowered, agricultural subsidies abolished and the taxation system was reformed by introducing a goods and services tax (GST), while lowering company and personal income taxes.

The bubble burst in 1987 with the worldwide stock market collapse. New Zealand's speculation boom abruptly ended. Inflation and unemployment topped 10%, growth was nonexistent and the country questioned the restructuring. The main engineer of the economic reforms, Labour's finance minister Roger Douglas, pressed on with a programme of privatisation.

In 1990, the National government continued with the free-market reforms Labour had started, tackling areas a Labour government never could. Welfare programmes were cut (the state-funded health insurance system was abolished), privatisation was increased and, most significantly, the labour market was deregulated.

The reforms have had a major effect on the NZ economy and society. Though still overwhelmingly reliant on agriculture for export income, NZ has made progress in its efforts to diversify its economy. NZ also has a broader world outlook, both in its trade and in general. Since 1960, when Britain bought over half of NZ's exports, NZ has shifted its focus elsewhere, especially to Asia. Australia is now NZ's single-largest trading partner, accounting for over 20% of all trade, but Asia takes 30% of exports, the USA 16.1% and the UK only 9.3%. NZ is also attracting greater investment from Asia, especially Japan and Singapore. The economy is growing at around 3.5%, inflation is under 2.5% and unemployment is around 5.4%.

As the corporate philosophy engulfs NZ, the once-sacrosanct ideals of equality in society have taken a back seat. Income disparity has grown substantially. In the new user-pays NZ, social services have been cut back, or sold off to private enterprise, resulting in higher charges and the axing of some nonprofitable services. In 2001 the government, in what seemd to be a move back to state-owned enterprises, bailed out the ailing national carrier Air New Zealand, and opened a 100% state-owned 'people's bank' called Kiwibank.

Tourism, service industries, manufacturing, small-scale industry and agriculture are important in the NZ economy. In recent figures, the trade, restaurants and hotels sector accounted for the largest proportion of GDP, followed by the financing, insurance, real estate and business services sectors, then manufacturing and then agriculture.

With all the sheep, cattle and farms you see around New Zealand – the country is reckoned to have around 48 million sheep (12.5 per person) and nearly nine million cattle – it's not surprising that agriculture is an important part of the economy. In strictly dollar amounts it accounts for only about 10% of the entire GDP and employs about the same percentage of the country's workforce, but over 50% of all land in the country is devoted to pasture. Agricultural products from sheep, cattle, fish and forestry are NZ's chief exports (50%). Farming is a scientific proposition in NZ, with constant research carried out and the most modern scientific farming methods used.

Principal exports are meat (beef and veal bring in slightly more revenue than lamb and mutton), dairy products, fish, forest products (almost entirely pine and other non-native trees), fruits and vegetables (especially kiwi fruit, apples and pears) and wool. Main imports are machinery and mechanical appliances, electrical machinery and equipment, textiles, motor cars and other goods.

Tourism is also a major source of foreign revenue, although it is estimated as being 0.2% of the world total. Tourist arrivals numbered 1.88 million in 2001.

POPULATION & PEOPLE

Of NZ's population of around 3.88 million people, 74% are NZ European (Pakeha), 13.5% are NZ Maori, 6% are Pacific Island Polynesians and about 6% are Asian.

Many Pacific islands are experiencing a rapid population shift from remote and undeveloped islands to the big cities. Auckland is very much the big city of the South Pacific, with the greatest concentration of Polynesians on earth. It sometimes causes a great deal of argument, discussion and tension, and much of it is not between the recent Pacific immigrants and the Pakeha population, but between the islanders and the Maori, or among the various islander groups themselves.

Asian migration is also increasing. NZ has a sizable Indian community, mostly from Fiji, and has attracted east-Asian migrants, many of them through NZ's recent immigration incentives. Central Auckland has a particularly east-Asian character.

With only about 14 people per sq km, NZ is lightly populated by many countries' standards but is more densely populated than its huge neighbour, Australia (two people per sq km). Over the last 20 years or so the economic situation has led to a mass exodus (often called the 'brain drain') of young New Zealanders to Australia and the

MURRAY WEBB / ALEXANDER TURNBULL LIBRARY, WELLINGTON NZ

Dame Kiri Te Kanawa

UK, although improving economic conditions have helped slow down emigration.

The South Island once had a greater population than the North Island but is now the place to go for elbow room – its population is barely more than that of Auckland. Despite its rural base, NZ is very much an urban country. Altogether, the population of the 15 largest urban areas is nearly 80% of NZ's population.

ARTS

New Zealand has a multifaceted arts scene, with both Maori and Pakeha engaged in all kinds of traditional and modern arts. Although there are distinct Maori arts and European arts, there is rarely a ruling over who can practise particular arts. For example, there are Pakeha who enjoy carving in bone and painting in traditionally Maori styles. Maori songs, some Maori language and *poi* dances are taught in all schools. Likewise, there are many Maori who excel in the traditionally European arts such as theatre and music. Dame Kiri Te Kanawa is one of the world's best-known operatic divas (see the boxed text 'Dame Kiri Te Kanawa' in The East Coast chapter).

Another opera singer of world standing is Dame Malvina Major.

Though the written word was not traditionally a part of Maori culture, NZ is experiencing a movement of dynamic Maori writing in fiction, nonfiction and poetry (see Maori & Pacific Literature later in this section).

For information on Maori Arts see the special section 'Maori Culture & Arts'.

Theatre & Dance

New Zealanders take part in all the traditional European-based art forms including many styles of dance and live theatre. Wellington is particularly well known for its theatre scene, with traditional as well as improvisational and avant-garde theatre companies. At the other major centres – Auckland, Palmerston North, Christchurch and Dunedin – also have active theatre and dance scenes. Smaller towns often actively support a community theatre group.

Music

As with theatre, so with music – the major centres have the liveliest music scenes but even smaller towns can have some interesting music. There's plenty of opportunity for going out in the evening and hearing live music in the larger centres, with a choice of everything from a symphony concert and the ballet to a rock, jazz or blues band. Irish music – both the acoustic ballad minstrel variety and the rousing Irish dance-band style – is very popular in NZ.

Popular Music New Zealand rock music doesn't begin and end in Dunedin, though over the last 10 years you could be forgiven for thinking so. In terms of cutting-edge alternative music, Dunedin is NZ's music capital.

In the 1970s and '80s, Split Enz was NZ's best-known and most successful band. Originally an unusual and eccentric group, their style became more mainstream in the '80s. Like many other NZ bands who achieved success, Split Enz based themselves in Australia and found themselves referred to as a 'great Australian band'. After their break-up in the mid-1980s, band member Neil Finn formed another successful 'Australian' band, Crowded House (at least Crowded House had some Australian members).

It's true to say that in the last 10 years a real homegrown music scene has developed in NZ and more acts are slowly developing international recognition. As one Kiwi music lover said: 'People actually listen to New Zealand music now'.

The best-known recent Kiwi export is the band formerly known as Shihad, who signed to a US record label in 2001, just in time for their name to become a serious liability: it sounds too much like 'jihad'! Look for them now under their new moniker Pacifier.

Other Kiwi bands and singers to look out for include Garageland, Weta, The Feelers, Stella, Tadpole, Paul Ubana Jones, Salmonella Dub (reggae, ska, techno crossover) and Che Fu (hip-hop). NZ is also forging ahead in the techno scene and drum'n'bass outfits like Concord Dawn and Shape Shifter are popular.

Recently, a distinctly Kiwi style has developed, mixing accepted overseas styles with Polynesian influences. This style is exemplified by Chinese-Maori artist Bic Runga, Anika Moa and the Tokelauan group Te Vaka.

The evergreen Dave Dobbyn's popular *Slice of Heaven* is an anthem for the tourist industry, and his many other compositions have distinctly NZ themes.

And what was recently voted NZ's number-one pop song of the past 75 years by music industry bods? An obscure number called *Nature* by the band, Fourmyula.

Visual Arts

The larger centres have museums and art galleries with contemporary and traditional art; smaller towns often have a gallery, which may combine arts and crafts. All the visual arts are represented in NZ, including painting, sculpture, ceramics and a wide variety of handicrafts.

Frances Hodgkins (1869–1947) is NZ's most famous painter, but like author Katherine Mansfield, she achieved her fame overseas and never returned to NZ after 1913.

Her European-influenced oils are hung in galleries worldwide.

New Zealand's most famous portrait painter was Charles Frederick Goldie (1870–1947), whose portraits of Maori with *moko* (tattoos) are so realistic as to be almost photo-like.

The best known of recent NZ painters is modernist Colin McCahon (1919–87), who expressed bold, often controversial themes, and incorporated cryptic messages on his canvases.

Literature

NZ has an active literary scene. For a more detailed study, the *Oxford Companion to New Zealand Literature* (1998) or the *Penguin History of New Zealand Literature* by Patrick Evans, are good places to start.

Probably the most internationally famous NZ writer is Katherine Mansfield (1888–1923), who was born and raised in NZ and later moved to England, where she did most of her writing (see the boxed text 'Katherine Mansfield' in the Wellington Region chapter). See also Books in the Facts for the Visitor chapter.

Frank Sargeson (1903–82) is another distinguished NZ author. Within the country he is probably as well known as Mansfield, especially for his three-volume autobiography, novels and many short stories. Since he lived all his life in NZ, his work did not become as widely known overseas.

For a wide-ranging collection of fiction by NZ women, try *In Deadly Earnest* compiled by Trudie McNaughton.

The author of several fine historical novels about NZ, Maurice Shadbolt has so far published nine novels, four collections of short stories and several nonfiction books. His best-known novel is *The Season of the Jew*, which was chosen by the *New York Times* as one of the best books of 1987. This book follows a band of Maori in the East Coast Land War (see the boxed text 'Te Kooti' in The East Coast chapter).

Novelist, poet and short-story writer Janet Frame is also extremely popular. Her three-volume autobiography (*To the Island, An Angel at my Table* and *Envoy from*

Mirror City) became famous after the film *An Angel at My Table* by acclaimed Kiwi director Jane Campion. *Janet Frame: An Autobiography* is a fascinating insight into her life.

Shonagh Koea is another popular author; her better-known works include *The Woman Who Never Went Home, The Grandiflora Tree, Staying Home and Being Rotten* and *Fifteen Rubies by Candlelight*. Elizabeth Knox, author of award-winning *The Vintner's Luck* (1998) and a string of other acclaimed books including three volumes of autobiographical writing, continues to be a literary success. Her latest offering is *Black Oxen* (2001).

Other favourite authors include Maurice Gee, whose novel *Going West* won the NZ Wattie Book of the Year Award in 1993, Fiona Kidman *(The Book of Secrets)*, Owen Marshall *(Tomorrow We Save the Orphans)*, Philip Temple *(Beak of the Moon)* and Dame Ngaio Marsh, who writes murder mysteries.

Maori & Pacific Literature Witi Ihimaera has edited two books of the series *Te Ao Marama – Contemporary Maori Writing. Volume One: Te Whakahuatanga o te Ao – Reflections of Reality* is an anthology of written and oral Maori literature; *Volume Two: He Whakaatanga o te Ao – The Reality* (1993) has prominent Maori authors examining crucial issues affecting Maori people. Witi Ihimaera, of the Rongowhakaata tribe, is a highly prolific author of novels and short stories. Some of his better-known novels are *The Matriarch, Tangi* and *Pounamu, Pounamu*. His *Bulibasha* is a zany look at the life of Maori sheep-shearing gangs in the East Coast region of the North Island.

Keri Hulme received international acclaim when *The Bone People* won the British Booker McConnell Prize for fiction in 1985. She has published several other novels and books of poetry.

Alan Duff is a controversial author who writes about Maori people in modern New Zealand society. His writing has always generated heated debate. His first novel, *Once Were Warriors*, was made into the film that received international acclaim; his second novel was *One Night Out Stealing*. In 1993 his nonfiction work *Maori: The Crisis and the Challenge* sparked widespread controversy.

NZ has some important Pacific islander authors. Albert Wendt, a Samoan author, who is a professor of English at the University of Auckland, is one of the finest. His novels include *Leaves of the Banyan Tree, Pouliuli, Sons for the Return Home, Ola* and *Black Rainbow;* he has also published two poetry books and two collections of short stories. The excellent *The Shark that Ate the Sun: Ko e Ma go ne Kai e La* by Niuean John Puhiatau Pule is about the Pacific-island experience in NZ.

Children's Literature This is a particularly fertile area of writing, with many NZ writers achieving international success.

David Hill deals with the sensitive subject of children with disabilities in *See Ya, Simon*. Rural life is the setting for Jack Lasenby's *Uncle Trev* and *Harry Wakatipu*. Sports, especially sailing and swimming, are the impetus for some of Tessa Duder's novels (the *Alex* series, *Jellybean* and *Night Race to Kawau*), while William Taylor's novels, aimed at 11- and 12-year-olds, focus on the plight of the underdog.

One of NZ's most successful writers of children's literature is Margaret Mahy. She is author of over 100 titles and winner of the international Carnegie Medal for *The Changeover* and *The Haunting*.

Poetry James K Baxter (1926–72) is possibly the best-known NZ poet. Others include RAK Mason, Allen Curnow, Denis Glover, Hone Tuwhare and the animated Sam Hunt. *Contemporary New Zealand Poetry Nga Kupu Titohu o Aotearoa* edited by Miriama Evans, Harvey McQueen & Ian Wedde is an excellent collection of NZ poetry written both in English and Maori. Wedde and McQueen also edited the comprehensive *Penguin Book of New Zealand Verse*.

Cinema

With actor Russell Crowe (yes, he's a Kiwi) pulling in Academy Awards, and director

As is the case for most Pacific islands, New Zealand's native flora and fauna are for the most part endemic (ie, they're not found anywhere else in the world). Here you'll find the world's largest flightless parrot (kakapo), the only truly alpine parrot (kea), the oldest reptile (tuatara), the smallest bats, some of the oldest trees, and many of the rarest birds, insects and plants in the world.

FAUNA

With no large native land mammals, birds dominate NZ's fauna...

Birds

There is not an enormous variety of endemic birdlife in NZ, but, because the avifauna here evolved in relative peace with very little threat and no large competitors, there are some remarkable, strange specimens about! In such a peaceful, uncompetitive environment, flightless birds such as ground-dwelling kakapo, kiwi and weka not only survived but thrived.

The balance was altered by the arrival of humans – first the Maori, then the Pakeha – as well as the predatory species which both groups introduced. Many species vanished in a blink of the eye relative to NZ's evolutionary history.

Thus, one bird you *won't* spot these days is the famous moa – up to 3.5m tall and weighing in at 200kg of succulent, easily captured flesh. Similarly, the huia, with its remarkably different male and female bills, is extinct. The subantarctic fairy tern is currently the bird closest to extinction; less than 40 remain. Other species in peril are the Chatham Island oystercatcher (around 170), the kakapo (85) and even the famous kiwi itself!

Good bird-spotting books available in NZ include *Which New Zealand Bird?* by Andrew Crowe and *Collins Handguide to the Birds of New Zealand* by Chlöe Talbot Kelly. Websites such as **w** www .nzbirds.com and **w** www.doc.govt.nz have lots of up-to-date information about individual species.

Moa Hotspots
None

Australasian Gannet

This gannet *(takapu)* has three mainland breeding colonies: Farewell Spit (see the Marlborough & Nelson chapter), Muriwai (see Around Auckland in the Auckland chapter) and Cape Kidnappers (see Around Hawkes Bay in the East Coast chapter). Juveniles migrate to Australia and return in four years to breed. These birds dive from great heights, with wings folded back, to catch fish. The yellow head and white body is the most obvious feature of adult birds but immature gannets are speckled brown.

Australasian gannet

Bellbird

The bellbird *(makomako)* is common in both native and exotic forests and is easily identified by its beautiful bell-like call. A member of the honey-eater family, like the tui, it is a fairly unremarkable looking dark-green bird, with a curved honey-eater beak and short tail feathers. Among trees from which it takes nectar are rata, pohutukawa and kowhai. Bellbirds are found all over NZ, except Northland.

Bellbird

Black Stilt

The Mackenzie Country of south Canterbury is the home of the black stilt *(kaki)*, one of the world's rarest wading birds. It is found in swamps and beside braided river beds in South Island river systems. A single population of about 40 adults survives in the wild.

Black stilt

A captive breeding and release programme for the endangered black stilt has been established by the Department of Conservation (DOC) near Twizel in the South Island. Juvenile birds are hand reared and released into the wild at nine months of age.

Sadly, the country's favourite little *kaki*, Mrs Bones, died in January 2002, after personally hatching 68 black stilts. For more information about the black stilt, see Twizel in the Canterbury chapter.

Cormorants & Shags

Gangly, coastal-feeding birds, cormorants and shags are both lovingly referred to as 'shags' in NZ, and distinction is seldom made between the seven species. The black shag *(kawau)*, NZ's largest shag, is common on inland lakes and along sheltered parts of the coastline. It is seen in flocks near shellbanks and sandspits or perched on rocks. The NZ king shag is one of the rarest shags in the world and only found in coastal waters on the southern side of Cook Strait. Pink feet are its distinguishing feature.

Australasian gannet:
Photo by Jason Edwards
Bellbird:
Photo by Sally Dillon
Black stilt:
Photo courtesy of NZ
Department of
Conservation (DOC)
Little shag:
Photo by Jason Edwards

Shag

Pied fantail

Fantail

The acrobatic little fantail *(piwakawaka)* has a reputation as a friendly bird because of its habit of following trampers through the bush. (In fact it's attracted to the insects trampers disturb as they brush past the undergrowth.)

There are two subspecies of fantail, the North Island and South Island; both are common in forests and scrubland, and can even be seen in suburban gardens. Although most fantails are pied (dark brown and white), there are black variants of both species.

Piwakawaka

In Maori tradition, the *piwakawaka* (fantail) is considered a harbinger of doom. It certainly spelled disaster for the mythical Maori hero Maui, whom it betrayed by laughing at an inopportune moment.

Chatham Island Black Robin

By the 1970s the handful of black robins left were confined to little Mangere Island in NZ's Chatham Islands, and by 1980 there were only five black robins left, and only one breeding female (Old Blue). Such a small population would usually spell extinction for a species but, as a last resort, wildlife authorities began a cross-fostering programme using other small bird species.

Chatham Island black robin

The robins must have sensed that the time for their emergence was right. By the end of summer 1985 there were 38 robins. The future of the black robin is no longer bleak and one of the most courageous attempts to save an endangered species has succeeded. There are now around 250 of these birds.

Their more common mainland relatives, the North Island and South Island robins are both greyish in colour, with a whitish breast and that familiar 'little cock robin' bearing.

Kakapo

The kakapo is an example of a bird that evolved in the absence of predators; as far as its ability to survive in the modern, competitive world is concerned, it's a fairly hopeless case. Lovingly described in Douglas Adams' *Last Chance to See* as 'the world's largest, fattest and least-able-to-fly parrot', the kakapo is (perhaps unsurprisingly) severely endangered.

Once a widely dispersed bird, kakapo were confined to Fiordland and Stewart Island by the 1890s and now the only remaining popu-

Kakapo

lations are those that have been shifted to predator-free islands (in the Marlborough Sounds and offshore of Stewart Island). There are only 80 or so kakapo left; few enough that they have been individually named by DOC staff – from Alice to Zephyr (you can read about the individual birds at **w** www.kakaporecovery.org.nz).

The largest parrot in the world (males weigh up to 4kg), the kakapo is flightless, although it can glide a short way downhill (or as Douglas Adams said 'not only has the kakapo forgotten how to fly, but it has also forgotten that it has forgotten how to fly'). The name literally means 'night parrot' in Maori – the kakapo is nocturnal.

You will only be able to observe this bird with the assistance of DOC, and you're probably out of luck. They'll want a pretty good reason before they let you land on any 'kakapo islands' and disturb the birds.

Kea

Kea

The kea is a large parrot decked out in un-parrot-like drab green except for bright red underwings. They inhabit South Island high-country forests and mountains and are amusing, fearless, cheeky and inquisitive birds. There are plenty of opportunities to observe them at the Fox and Franz Josef Glaciers and in Arthur's Pass National Park – particularly at the carparks at the terminal of the glaciers, where they hang around waiting for tourist hand-outs.

The Kea's Diet

High-country carpark signs warn you of the kea's destructive tendencies – they often supplement their traditional diet of bugs and berries with tasty windscreen rubber. In fact, they'll eat almost anything, including, when winters are tough, having a go at sheep's backs!

Kiwi

The best known of all NZ's birds, the kiwi has become the country's most recognised symbol and a nickname for New Zealanders themselves.

It's a small, tubby, flightless bird with defunct vestigial wings, feathers that are more like hair than real feathers and lousy eyesight, but

Kiwi Hotspots

Kiwi are a threatened species, and with the additional difficulty of them being nocturnal, it's only on Stewart Island (see the Outer Islands chapter) that you easily see one in the wild. However, they can be observed in many artificially dark 'kiwi houses':

Kaitaia, Whangarei (Northland)
Auckland Zoo
Otorohanga (King Country)
Rotorua (Bay of Plenty)
Taupo (Central Plateau)
Napier (East Coast)
Mount Bruce in the Wairarapa, Waikanae, Wellington Zoo (Wellington Region)
Hokitika (West Coast)
Christchurch (Canterbury)
Queenstown (Otago)
Stewart Island

Little spotted kiwi

Pied fantail:
Photo courtesy of DOC
Chatham Is black robin:
Photo courtesy of DOC
Kakapo:
Photo courtesy of DOC
Kea:
Photo by Gareth McCormack
Little spotted kiwi:
Photo by Oliver Strewe

strong legs. Most active at night, kiwi are fairly lazy, sleeping for up to 20 hours a day. They spend the rest of the time poking around for worms, sniffed out with the nostrils on the end of their bill.

The female kiwi is larger than the male and much fiercer. She lays an egg weighing up to half a kilogram, huge in relation to her size and about 20% of her body weight. After performing that mighty feat, she leaves the male to hatch it while she guards the burrow. So when the kiwi hatches it associates with its father, completely ignoring its mother.

There are six identified varieties of kiwi: the brown kiwi, of which there are several subspecies (Okarito, Southern Tokoeka and Haast Tokoeka); the little spotted kiwi; and the great spotted kiwi.

Kokako

Of the two kokako species, only the North Island kokako now survives. It is mostly found in Te Urewera National Park; its numbers elsewhere depleted by the destruction of its forest habitat and the introduction of predators. A member of the wattlebird family, like the now-extinct huia, the kokako can be easily recognised by its bluish-grey feathers and blue wattle (the skin hanging from its throat). If you see an orange-wattled kokako bounding and gliding through the forest, let someone know – you may have just rediscovered the vanished South Island kokako!

North Island kokako

Little Blue Penguin

New Zealand's five subspecies of little blue penguin *(korora)* are common in coastal waters from the top of the North Island to Stewart Island.

The smallest species of penguin, *korora* can sometimes be seen coming ashore at night, eg, on beaches along the Otago coast. Its upper parts are blue, underparts white and bill black.

In Australia the *korora* is known as the fairy or little penguin.

Little blue penguin

Morepork

The morepork *(ruru)* is found throughout NZ, with the exception of the east of the South Island. *Ruru* is the country's only endemic owl (it differs from the introduced little owl in that it has a rounded head and larger tail).

The morepork gets its name from its cry of 'quor-quo', which, with a *lot* of imagination, sounds like 'more pork' (in other countries similar

Watching Tip
Many animals must be on constant alert for predators, and will class you as just another one. Engaging a wild animal's attention may disrupt its normal routine and thus reduce its available feeding time. So it is worth respecting an animal's needs and being sensitive to the level of disturbance you are creating.

birds are called mopokes). Its cry at night in the bush is unmistakable (although the novelty wears off after a few hours!). Moreporks would probably eat pork if offered, but usually favour insects such as moths and the large bush weta (see Other Fauna).

New Zealand Falcon
In the high country of the South Island, you'll sometimes see NZ's fearless falcon *(kearea)* hunting for small birds or mice. It can be distinguished from a similar bird of prey – the larger Australasian harrier (which is also common in NZ) – by its very rapid flight (up to 230 km/h!) and longer, straighter tail. *Kearea* are only rarely seen north of central North Island.

Morepork

New Zealand Pigeon
When you first encounter the NZ pigeon *(kereru)* in the forest it is likely that you will be startled by its heavy, thumping wingbeat as it flies from tree to tree. Also called the wood pigeon, it is easily identified by its bright green colouring and white 'apron'.

The bird is widespread in NZ forests and is occasionally seen eating in open fields. A large bird, it is NZ's only endemic species of pigeon. The West Coast, the Catlins, Fiordland and Stewart Island are good places to see them. Their numbers have dropped alarmingly in Northland forests – partly due to illegal hunting.

North Is kokako:
Photo by Jenny & Tony Enderby
Little blue penguin:
Photo by Jason Edwards
Morepork:
Photo by Jason Edwards
NZ pigeon:
Photo by David Wall

NZ pigeon

Parakeets
New Zealand has two species of indigenous parakeet – the yellow-crowned and red-crowned. Both birds are commonly known as *kakariki* (which is also the Maori word for bright green).

The yellow-crowned *kakariki* is seen high in the canopy of forests in the North, South and Stewart Islands, and on many outlying islands. The red-crowned is not likely to be seen on the mainland but rather in lowland forest on offshore islands. Both species lay their eggs from October to January and the males help feed the chicks.

Royal albatross

Pukeko

Pukeko

This attractive (blue and black with a bright-red beak) bird is common throughout the wetter areas of NZ, especially near swamps and lake edges where there are clumps of rushes; often seen on the roadside as you drive past such areas. (Drive carefully; pukeko might be very pretty but they're no brain surgeons – their road sense is negligible.)

The pukeko is a good swimmer, with its extremely large feet, and a good flier too – the feet look extremely comical dangling below it as the bird takes off. Pukeko emit a high-pitched screech when disturbed.

Royal Albatross

New Zealand waters host 14 of the world's 24 species of albatross. *Toroa*, the huge royal albatross, with a wingspan of over 3m, ranges throughout the world but comes to island groups to the south and east of NZ each year to breed. *Toroa* spend three-quarters of their lives at sea and can cover almost 200,000km over the course of a year. New Zealand's one mainland breeding colony is Taiaroa Head on the Otago Peninsula, where they can be observed by visitors (see the Otago chapter).

Takahe

The story of the takahe is one of NZ's most fascinating bird tales. It was first classified by botanists in 1849 but was known to be dying out and was believed extinct by the early 20th century. However, it was found again in the Murchison Mountains, Fiordland, in 1948. Now, there are about 130 birds

Takahe

still in Fiordland, another 60 on predator-free islands, and some in captivity. You can see them at Te Anau (see the Southland chapter) and Mt Bruce (see Wairarapa in the Wellington Region chapter).

Royal albatross:
Photo by Jenny & Tony Enderby
Pukeko:
Photo by Jason Edwards
Takahe:
Photo by David Wall
Weka:
Photo by Paul Kennedy
White heron:
Photo by David Wall

The takahe is a flightless bird with similar colouring to that of the pukeko (blue and dark green with a red beak) but it's darker, bulkier and, of course, much less common. The takahe feeds on tussock shoots, alpine grasses and fern roots. Its habitat is tussock and small patches of beech forest.

Tui

The tui is found throughout NZ's forests. Conspicuous by its white throat feathers (hence its unpoetic alternative name, 'parson bird'), it is most often identified by its voice. The tui is perhaps the most beautiful singing bird in NZ. Parts of its song are an almost liquid call similar to that of the bellbird, but the tui adds clicks, grunts, chuckles and other sounds from its extremely large repertoire of sounds. It also mimics other birds.

Tui are widely distributed and you can see them around much of the country, even in built-up areas – often feeding on flax in suburban backyards. However, forest areas are their preferred habitat. Pelorus Sound, Ulva Island and Oban (Stewart Island) are particularly fertile spotting grounds.

Weka

Weka are found in a wide range of habitats, usually in scrub and on forest margins. There are a few weka on Kapiti Island and in Northland, but they're most common in the South Island.

Another one of NZ's many flightless birds, the weka is most active at dusk, but it can usually be seen scrounging during the day in areas where humans leave rubbish. (Just leave your cooking gear unattended for 10 minutes in any South Island national park to see one!)

White Heron

This heron *(kotuku)* is widely spread throughout the world but seen in relatively small numbers in NZ. It is believed that there are only 200 *kotuku* in the entire country. The sole breeding colony is at Whataroa (see Ross to Okarito in the West Coast chapter) and the best time to see them there is from September to November. After that, they scatter to wetlands and tidal lagoons throughout NZ.

Kotuku

In ancient times, some Maori believed that seeing a white heron *(kotuku)* was a once-in-a-lifetime experience, and it is still considered a sign of good luck to spot one.

The birds are considered the epitome of rare grace and beauty. To call someone a *kotuku* is to pay them the highest of compliments!

Weka

White heron

Whio

Also known as the blue duck (it's actually bluish-grey), this endemic, threatened species of duck is found in fast-flowing rivers of the high country of the North and South Islands, but no further north than East Cape.

Strong swimmers, they feed both on the surface and under water. You can be almost certain that it is a whio if you see a bluish-grey duck surfing and feeding in fast-flowing, turbulent water. (But you're more likely to see one on the NZ$10 note.)

Wrybill

If you fail to recognise this bird with its unique bill (the tip is bent to the right), put the binoculars away and take up stamp collecting – you're obviously no birdwatcher! Wrybills *(ngutuparore)* use that peculiar beak to feed – swinging it sideways through mud to trap marine organisms from the sludge. They migrate within NZ, first nesting in the shingle river beds of Canterbury and Otago then moving north to spend autumn and winter in the warmer estuaries and mud flats of the North Island.

Yellow-eyed Penguin

The yellow-eyed penguin *(hoiho)* is the world's second-rarest species of penguin, its numbers having steadily diminished largely because of the loss of its coastal habitat. *Hoiho* can still be seen, though, along the south-eastern coast of the South Island (see Otago Peninsula in the Otago chapter). As the name implies, a streaked yellow head and eye are its most conspicuous characteristics.

Yellow-eyed penguin

Marine Mammals

Perhaps one of the greatest delights of a trip to NZ, especially the South Island, is a chance to observe the wealth of marine mammals. There are 76 species of whales *(tohora)* and dolphins *(aihe)* on this globe and NZ, as small as it is, is blessed with 35 of these species. Kaikoura, north of Christchurch, is particularly blessed, as nearly half of that number of whales and dolphins have been seen in waters off its shores.

Many species of whales and seals were once hunted in NZ waters – but no longer. The whales, dolphins, seals and sea lions attract not the bludgeon and harpoon but the entranced eyes and cameras of foreign and local observers. The tourist dollars pouring into Kaikoura and elsewhere are worth many times the money made by the previous slaughter for oil and skins.

Whale Hotspots

 Bay of Islands (Northland)
Hauraki Gulf (Auckland)
Kaikoura (Marlborough)

Dusky Dolphin

Dusky dolphins can reach lengths of over 2m, but usually average a bit less. What they lack in size they make up for in spirit. These are the most playful dolphins and those that 'dolphin swimming' participants are most likely to encounter. While in the water, you will see them executing noisy head-first re-entry leaps and somersaults.

Dusky dolphin

Dolphin Hotspots
Bay of Islands (Northland)
Hauraki Gulf (Auckland)
Whitianga (Coromandel Peninsula)
Tauranga & Whakatane (Bay of Plenty)
Picton (Marlborough)
Kaikoura (Marlborough)
Punakaiki (West Coast)
Oamaru (Otago)

They feed on small schooling fish and often round up hundreds of fish in a tight ball, from which members of the pod take turns at feeding. They congregate near the shore from late October to May; after that the pods break up, as winter comes on, and the dolphins move offshore.

Hectors Dolphin

This dolphin is confined to NZ waters. They have a rather dumpy shape, a distinctive rounded fin and reach a length of only 1.4m. Like the dusky dolphin they feed on small schooling fish, but they stay relatively close to shore year-round.

Some years back Greenpeace reported that 230 Hectors, about 30% of the population of the area, had been killed in gill nets around Banks Peninsula over four years; DOC has since declared the area a marine mammal sanctuary.

Sperm Whale

Sperm whales are the largest of the toothed whales – the male often reaches up to 20m in length, while the female is much smaller, with a maximum length of 12m. This is the whale that 'watchers' come to Kaikoura (see the Marlborough & Nelson chapter) to see. Adult males weigh up to 50 tonnes and females just over 20 tonnes; both live for up to 70 years. They dive for long periods (around 45 minutes).

Sperm whale

Yellow-eyed penguin: Photo by David Wall
Dusky dolphins: Photo by Gareth McCormack
Sperm whale: Photo by Neil Irvine

They are hard to locate in the open ocean (just ask Captain Ahab) and the only real giveaway is a blow from their spout or their sonar clicks, detected with hydrophones. Because they each require a huge feeding area, whales are normally seen alone. Sperm whales have a single blowhole, offset on the left side of their head.

Other Fauna

Bats

There are two species of indigenous bat *(pekapeka)* – prosaically named long-tailed and short-tailed – which were NZ's only land mammals before the arrival of humans. Long-tailed bats are similar to the fruit bats or flying foxes of Australia and the Pacific Islands, but the short-tailed bat is endemic to NZ. If you're very, *very* lucky, you may see bats (both species) flitting around forest margins at sunset.

Long-tailed bat

Giant weta

Creepy Crawlies

New Zealand has more than 100 species of **weta**, large invertebrates with a fearsome appearance. The cave weta has long legs and a small body (only 35mm), perfectly adapted for movement on cave walls. In contrast, the bush weta has a large body (50mm) and looks fearsome with a large head and snapping mandibles. It can deliver a painful nip with those scary mandibles, but it's really pretty harmless. The wingless alpine weta, also known as the 'Mt Cook flea', lives in rock crevices above the snowline. The largest weta grow to 100mm in length and can weigh as much as a small bird!

There is only one (slightly) dangerous spider in NZ, the rare **katipo** (see Health in the Facts for the Visitor chapter).

Vermin

All of the deliberately introduced species of mammals have done their fair share of damage, but the most infamous is the **brush-tailed possum**. There are now more than 70 million possums in NZ, eating about 7 million tonnes of vegetation per year and doing terrible damage to particular trees (including rata, totara, kowhai and pohutukawa).

Other introduced pests are rabbits, chamois, thar, deer, pigs (both large, wild Captain Cookers and smaller *kune kune*), goats and stoats. In a classic case of *There Was an Old Woman Who Swallowed a Fly*, stoats were introduced to NZ to eat the (previously introduced) rabbits, but preferred the taste of kiwi.

Brush-tailed possum

Galaxids

New Zealand boasts its own species of 'trout', the giant **kokopu**, one of several galaxid species found in NZ waters. The giant kokopu can be seen at the visitor centre in Haast and at Westland's Water World in Hokitika (see the West Coast chapter).

More important in NZ kitchens, though, is one of the other galaxids, the **inanga**, which is 'whitebait' in its immature stage (and best served with flour, eggs and milk in a whitebait fritter).

A new species of galaxid (*Galaxias gollumoides*), recently discovered in NZ's far south, was named in honour of the slimy Gollum from Tolkien's *Lord of the Rings*.

Reptiles

The **tuatara** is a lizard-like reptile dating back to the age of the dinosaurs (about 220 million years). It is the only surviving member of the order Rhynchocephalia. Active at night, it eats insects, small mammals and birds' eggs, has a rudimentary 'third eye' in the centre of its fore-

Tuatara

head, grows to 60cm in length and may live for 100 years. The tuatara is found on protected offshore islands (eg, The Brothers and Stephens Island in the Marlborough Sounds), which you need special permission to visit. Some specimens are kept in captivity in places such as the Wellington Zoo, Otorohanga Kiwi House, and Southland Museum in Invercargill (where they have been successfully bred).

There are no snakes in NZ.

FLORA

The Maori, Aotearoa's first people, had managed to reduce the land's forest cover down from about 80% to less than 60% in their first eight centuries or so of occupation. But it was after the arrival of large numbers of Europeans, in the 1800s, that the forests really started to suffer. Much of them were soon cleared for timber (eg, the large kauri forests) or to make way for farming.

Despite that, NZ still has some magnificent areas of native forest and bush. About 10% to 15% of its total land area is covered by native flora, much of it in protected parks and reserves (see National Parks in the Facts about New Zealand chapter).

Of the country's 2000 or so flowering plants, about 75% are only found in NZ.

Trees

The progenitors of NZ's two major forest groups, the podocarps and the southern beeches, were found in the ancient supercontinent of Gondwanaland. When the continents drifted apart and the land bridges were eventually lost, over 60 million years ago, NZ's flora evolved in isolation.

For more information about tree species, see the DOC website (**w** www.doc.govt.nz) and these books: *Which Native Tree?* by Andrew Crowe and *New Zealand Trees and Ferns* by Murdoch Riley.

Beeches

New Zealand has several species of beech. The silver beech *(tawhai)* is found in stands in mixed forest on both islands and occurs in subalpine regions. It can grow up to 30m in height and has a silver-grey trunk of up to 2m in diameter. The small rounded leaves have serrated edges,

Long-tailed bat: Photo courtesy of DOC
Giant weta: Photo courtesy of DOC
Brush-tailed possum: Photo by Mitch Reardon
Tuatara: Photo by Oliver Strewe

the small flowers are green and brown, and the fruit is small and woody.

The beautiful mountain beech *(tawhairauriki)* occurs in mountain and subalpine areas from the North Island's Central Plateau to the far south of the South Island. It grows to 22m in favoured sites (but usually to about 15m) and its trunk is about 1m in diameter. Its leaves are dark and pointy, as opposed to the light leaves of the *tawhai*. It has small red flowers and woody fruit and can be seen in splendour in Arthur's Pass National Park and near the Lewis Pass.

Cabbage Tree

The beautiful broad-leafed mountain cabbage tree *(ti kouka)* is found in moist mountain areas where there is plenty of light. It grows to 20m and, when mature, its stems hang downwards. The Pakeha name comes from an old misunderstanding: James Cook's crew ate the leaves of a similar tree, the nikau palm, but *ti kouka* ended up with the name.

Kauri

Kauri trees only grow in Northland and on the Coromandel Peninsula. These large native trees were once ruthlessly cut down for their excellent timber and Northland is covered with evidence of the kauri days (see Trounson Kauri Park and Waipoua Kauri Forest in the Northland chapter). Kauri gum was an important ingredient in varnish and at one time there were many 'gum diggers' who roamed the forests, poking in the ground for hard lumps of kauri gum.

Kauri

> **Kauri Nui**
> A number of individual trees in Northland have special spiritual significance, and bear individual names such as Tane Mahuta (named for the god of the forests) or Te Matua Ngahere (Father of the Forest). Many of these trees are within easy walk of the road through Waipoua Kauri Forest.

Kauri grow to at least 30m tall and are believed to live for up to 2000 years. Their bark is a distinctive blotchy mosaic.

Kowhai

This tree grows to about 11m and has small green leaves and groups of bright yellow flowers – in fact, the Maori word for 'yellow' is *kowhai*. There are three species of this, NZ's national flower, and all are similar in appearance. The tree is found in open areas, near rivers and on the edge of forests. They're popular trees with birds, especially tui, which seek honey from the flowers.

Kowhai

Kauri:
Photo by David Wall
Kowhai:
Photo by David Wall
Nikau:
Photo by David Wall
Pohutukawa:
Photo by David Wall
Flowering rata:
Photo by David Wall

Nikau

The nikau is found throughout lowland areas of the North Island and the north of the South Island, as far south as Banks Peninsula. The best place to see nikau is on the north of the West Coast, from Punakaiki to Karamea; their appearance there could fool you into thinking you are in the tropics. The tree's name, nikau, reveals the tropical roots of the Maori and perhaps also the first settlers' disappointment at finding Aotearoa to be lacking in their number-one foodstuff – *ni kau* is Polynesian for 'no coconuts'.

Nikau

Nikau can grow to 10m in height and in ancient times their fronds were interwoven and used for roofing material by the Maori.

Pohutukawa

This beautiful tree is predominantly found in the north of the North Island, but it has been successfully planted throughout the South Island. Its magnificent crimson flowers appear in December, making it popularly known as the 'Christmas tree'. It can grow up to 20m in height and 2m across at its base, and is usually found close to the sea; good places to see it are along the beaches of the Coromandel Peninsula, Bay of Plenty and East Coast.

Pohutukawa Nui

Individual pohutukawa trees of special significance include the 600-year-old Te Waha o Rerekohu at Te Araroa (see the East Coast chapter).

Even more famous is the 800-year-old pohutukawa, at Cape Reinga, whose roots form the gateway to the Underworld; see Ancestors *(Tipuna)* in the 'Maori Culture & Arts' special section.

Pohutukawa

Flowering rata

Rata

The rata is another tree with beautiful crimson flowers like the pohutukawa, except that its leaves are shiny and pointed at both ends. The northern rata, reaching a height of 25m, grows in the North Island and in Nelson in the South Island. Southern rata predominates in the South Island but is also found in Northland.

What is the nature of the rata? The northern rata starts as a climber on a host tree which it eventually strangles. When this happens the aerial roots disappear and the tree takes on a gnarled appearance.

Rimu

The rimu, or red pine, is the most easily recognised of the podocarps. Rimu are found throughout NZ in areas of mixed forest and grow to a height of more than 50m, with a girth of about 1.5m. The distinctive, narrow, prickly leaves drape down and often have little red cones at the tips of the leafy clusters. The fruit appears as a black nut at the tip of the seed.

Rimu

Rimu was once the most common of the lowland podocarps but its popularity as a building timber has led to its drastic depletion.

Totara

The totara has special significance in NZ, as it was favoured for Maori war canoes because of its soft wood. It can grow to be extremely old, attaining an age of 1000 years or more. The totara has long, pointy leaves, and the male and female cones occur on separate trees. Its red-and-pink stalks attract birds.

Ferns

One of the prominent features of the NZ bush is the proliferation of tree ferns which are intertwined with the undergrowth. There are over 80 species of fern and five species of soft fern. Perhaps the most unusual, appearance-wise, are the **mauku** (hen and chickens fern) and the **raurenga** (kidney fern), and the rarest would be the **para** (horseshoe or king fern). A common sight on NZ hillsides is the bracken fern, growing to 3m or more.

The **mamaku** (black tree fern) is the largest of NZ's ferns, growing to a height of 20m, with the fronds extending to 7m. Mamaku grow throughout the country, and are common in damp forest gullies.

The **ponga** (silver tree fern) is one of NZ's national symbols; it adorns the jumpers of many of NZ's sports representatives and is shown in logos such as NZ wool and NZ tourism. It grows to up to 10m in height and the fronds, which extend up to 4m, are white on the underside and dull green on the upper side.

Ponga

> **Totara Nui**
> One particular totara, named Pouakani, in Pureora Forest Park in the North Island, is said to be more than 1700 years old. Pouakani is an easy walk from the forest park's visitor centre (see the Central Plateau chapter).

Rimu:
Photo by Gareth McCormack
Ponga:
Photo by David Wall

Peter Jackson capturing the movie world's imagination and showcasing the country's beauty with the *Lord of the Rings* trilogy, New Zealand's film industry is finally booming. However, the history of NZ film doesn't really begin until the late 1970s, and from some early stumbling attempts, notable feature films have survived the test of time and launched the careers of NZ directors and actors.

Sleeping Dogs (1977) is an accomplished psychological drama that was at the forefront of the new film industry; it also launched the careers of actor Sam Neill and director Roger Donaldson.

A British–NZ production, *Bad Blood* (1981), is about the gun-toting psychosis of macho NZ, based on the true story of Stan Graham, a nutter oddly afforded hero status in NZ, who went berserk in a rural town during WWII. *Smash Palace* (1981), about a marriage break-up and custody case, was a local success. *Came a Hot Friday* (1984), directed by Ian Mune, is one of NZ's better comedies.

Other films of note are *Utu* (Revenge; 1983), an amateurish but breakthrough Maori film and *The Quiet Earth* (1985), an end-of-the-world sci-fi movie with wit and imagination. *Goodbye Pork Pie* (1980), an exuberant NZ road movie directed by Geoff Murphy, was a box office hit in NZ, as was the later, animated *Footrot Flats* (1986), starring NZ's favourite cartoon character, The Dog.

NZ films moved into art-house cinemas with Vincent Ward's *Vigil* (1984), a brooding film about a girl's coming of age in rain-drenched back country NZ. It proved too ponderously artistic for many Kiwi film-goers but wowed them at Cannes. Ward's follow-up *The Navigator* (1988) is a strange modern/medieval hunt for the Holy Grail.

After Peter Jackson, NZ's best-known director is Jane Campion. Her greatest films explore NZ themes. *An Angel at My Table* (1990), based on Janet Frame's autobiography, shows the fine character development typical of her films. Campion's masterpiece, *The Piano* (1993), about the trials of a mute

woman in NZ's pioneer days, received Cannes and Academy Award success.

During the 1990s the world suddenly noticed NZ's already accomplished movie industry. *Once Were Warriors* (1994), a brutal tale of modern urban Maori life, stunned movie-goers around the world. The sequel *What Becomes of the Broken Hearted?* (1999) had nowhere near as much impact.

Scarfies (1999), a cult flick made on a shoestring budget, relates the misadventures of a group of students, known as 'scarfies' (because they wear university scarfs). More recent films include the dark comedy *Savage Honeymoon* (2000), which laughs at life in Auckland's west; *Stickmen* (2001), a tale of pool and gambling – a sort of Kiwi version of *Lock, Stock and Two Smoking Barrels*; *Rain* (2001), an arty tale of coming of age; and *Snakeskin*, a road movie that screened at the Sundance Film Festival.

See the boxed text 'New Zealand's *Lord of the Rings* – Peter Jackson' for a short summary of Jackson's contribution to NZ's film industry.

SOCIETY & CONDUCT

Maori culture has always been an integral part of NZ and is a strong and growing influence, although NZ culture is essentially European, transplanted by the British to these far-off islands.

European New Zealanders used to hold so strongly to their British traditions that they earned the tag of 'South Seas Poms'. While British culture is still a strong focus for many, a growing diversity of migrants and a wider global outlook has seen a distinct change in NZ society in recent years. Resurgent Maori culture and the new corporate philosophy have also helped to shape a new world view. NZ has always been proud of its traditions, but more than ever the country is exploring its identity.

Though the majority of NZ's population is of English stock, other notable early influences were the Scots and the Dalmatians, the latter coming to dig kauri gum in Northland.

[Continued on page 36]

New Zealand's *Lord of the Rings* – Peter Jackson

Unless you've been living in a hole in the ground for the last five years, you *must* have heard about New Zealand's Peter Jackson and his trilogy of films: *The Lord of the Rings: Fellowship of the Ring* (released in December 2001); *The Two Towers* (2002) and *Return of the King* (2003).

From Exploding Sheep to Middle Earth Peter Jackson was a minor hero to NZ's small film industry long before he scored the *Rings* contract. From his very first film, *Bad Taste*, back in 1987, it was obvious that Jackson was a unique talent (even if some people didn't appreciate the exploding sheep). *Bad Taste* was largely a 'spare weekends' project put together by Jackson and his mates over the period of four years, but it earned Jackson the support of the New Zealand Film Commission, which funded *Meet the Feebles* (1989), a hilarious Muppets-on-acid flick that would have absolutely horrified most NZ taxpayers. Jackson followed *Feebles* with an even sicker splatter movie, *Brain Dead* (1992), an uproarious zombie film; then two more-conservative, but just as creative, films, *Heavenly Creatures* (1994) and *Frighteners* (1996). The success of these two films led to Jackson being awarded the *Lord of the Rings* contract in 1997.

One Movie to Rule Them All... Once the powers in the west (Los Angeles) had given him the nod to film Professor JRR Tolkien's classic, Jackson endeared himself immediately to four million New Zealanders by insisting stubbornly that the films be filmed and produced here in NZ. He also endeared himself to a million Tolkien fans worldwide by insisting just as stubbornly that the film be made in three parts, as intended by the revered professor himself. (The three films were filmed simultaneously over 16 months, with post-production of each film progressing separately after that.)

New Zealand itself had no such reservations; the country embraced the *Rings* films with a passion. Long before *Fellowship* was released, in late 2001, NZ had pretty much declared ownership of Jackson's trilogy. At a time when little else was going right (the economy was a bit down and the country wasn't excelling in the sporting arena), Jackson's films became a vehicle for NZ pride.

Jackson and many others involved in the films had been Tolkien fans since they were knee-high to a Brandybuck; the film-makers' attention to minor, often unnoticable, details was as high as Tolkien's himself, and being faithful to the story was essential. However the screenwriting team did take a few tactical liberties with JRR's story – introducing such controversial modern ideas as complexity of character and (gasp!) strong female roles. In the long run the hard-core cloak-and-20-sided-dice brigade may have been infuriated, but most fans agreed that the end result on film was at least as good as the book. (Personally, I'd say it was better – and I've been known to rattle a 20-sided dice myself.)

MURRAY WEBB / ALEXANDER TURNBULL LIBRARY, WELLINGTON NZ

Jackson – Kiwi director with a magic touch

And fair enough too – the *Rings* films were undeniably a product of NZ. There was all that magnificent local scenery of course, and scruffy, low-key Jackson is the epitome of a Kiwi boy. But many other Kiwis contributed to the films' success: in all, about 2000 NZers had fulltime jobs working on the films, and that's in addition to all the 'extras' (15,000 of them, including a few hundred NZ Army personnel pressed into costume and drafted into battle scenes for *Fellowship*). Finally, there was the crowd of 25,000 recorded roaring like orcs for Jackson's microphones during a NZ vs England cricket match in Wellington – sampled for use in a *Towers* battle scene. Eight NZers were nominated for academy awards for *Fellowship* alone, and Tourism NZ jokingly awarded

New Zealand's *Lord of the Rings* – Peter Jackson

NZ the Oscar for 'Best Supporting Country in a Motion Picture'.

When *Fellowship* was released in late 2001, NZ went positively ballistic: A 6m-tall Moria troll was raised above Wellington's Embassy Cinema, Wellington was renamed Middle Earth for the week, and a Minister for the *Rings* was even named in the NZ government. Jackson himself was made a Companion of the New Zealand Order of Merit for his services in the film industry in January 2002. (Sadly, the NZ government had just recently discontinued awarding knighthoods – so Jackson won't get to be a knight).

Fellowship's effect on NZ's economy was immediate, and huge. At a time when world tourism was suffering, following the September 11 attacks on the USA, *Fellowship* sparked huge worldwide interest in the country of its origin. With a little help from another famous Kiwi – Lucy Lawless *(Xena)* starred in Tourism

Treebeard, from *The Two Towers*

NZ's *Rings* promotional video – the film has helped maintain NZ's important tourism industry. On top of that was the NZ$650 million directly spent on making the films, much of which stayed in NZ.

Tourists in Middle Earth If you're one of those travellers who was inspired to come down under by the scenery of the *Rings* movies, you won't be disappointed. Jackson's decision to film here wasn't mere patriotism. Nowhere else on earth will you find such wildly varied, unspoiled landscapes.

However if you've come seeking scenes of Middle Earth itself, you might be disappointed. Filming occurred at over 150 separate locations, but, despite the fact that a handful of tour companies offer tours to actual film sites, there's not much to see anywhere. NZ's great attraction as Middle Earth, remember, was the *unspoiled* nature of its wilderness, and the Department of Conservation (DOC) wasn't going to let any meddlesome director compromise that – Jackson's agreement with DOC included dismantling all the sets immediately afterwards.

You may recognise some places from the films, however. Eg, Hobbiton (the Matamata region in the Waikato) or Mount Doom (Ngauruhoe, Central Plateau). And if you're in Wellington, Christchurch or Queenstown the information centre should be able to direct you to local *Rings* sites of interest.

If you make it down to Jackson's home town, Wellington, you might as well go see the film(s) a second time (third time, fourth time...) at their spiritual home – the **Embassy Cinema** in Kent Terrace. There are plans in the wind to put all the left-over props from the *Rings* films, presently housed at Weta Studios in Wellington, into a **Lord of the Rings museum** in that fair city. It's unlikely the museum will be up and running during the life of this book (the props are needed in case scenes need refilming) but you could ask at the Wellington visitors centre anyway – the encouragement won't hurt.

If armchair travelling will do, you could get a few old Jackson films out on video to fill rainy nights at backpacker hostels (let's face it – any trip to NZ involves a few rainy nights) looking for Jackson's own performances. He stars as the chainsaw-wielding (beardless) Derek ('I've been born again') and vomit-eating Robert the Alien in *Bad Taste*, and has cameos as the dumb undertaker's assistant in *Brain Dead*, the derelict hobo outside the cinema in *Heavenly Creatures*, an uncoordinated, chain-wearing biker in *Frighteners* and a belching hobbit outside a pub in *Fellowship*.

As director, of course, Jackson has been able to hog all the good roles.

Errol Hunt

[Continued from page 33]

Scottish immigrants arrived in large numbers and their cultural influence is most evident in the far south of the country, where Scottish games are held, the bagpipes still blow and a distinct Scottish brogue can be heard.

The Continuing Saga of a Trans-Tasman Tussle

New Zealanders have long memories, particularly when it comes to the double-dealing of its bigger sibling to the west. Forgive they may, but here are a few things Kiwis are unlikely to forget.

- The Greg and Trevor Chappell underarm scandal of 1981
- Being kicked out of the Anzus treaty by the Americans – just for doing the right thing! – while Australia looked on
- Australia claiming Russell, Split Enz, Fred Hollows, Jane Campion, Phar Lap, pavlova... even Sir Edmund!

ERIC HEATH / ALEXANDER TURNBULL LIBRARY, WELLINGTON NZ

- Australia poaching the 2003 Rugby World Cup
- Sheep jokes
- Being constantly mistaken for Australian by other nationalities
- Possums

If you want to know the history behind these things, simply ask any self-respecting Kiwi. (Then make yourself comfortable!)

More recently, Polynesians have brought their cultures with them from Pacific-island nations. In Auckland you can go to a Samoan rugby match on Saturday afternoon, dance the *tamure* at a Cook Islands nightclub that night and go to a Tongan-language church service on Sunday. Indians and Chinese are NZ's other two major immigrant groups.

Through a common history and culture based on British traditions and a strong geographical link, NZ shares many cultural attributes with, and has long been influenced by, Australia. Many Kiwis have migrated to Australia, or at least travelled to and worked there, but Kiwis are keen to distance themselves from their brasher and patronising cousins across the Tasman. Likening a Kiwi to (or mistaking one for) an Australian rarely goes down well – a bit like comparing Canadians to Americans.

New Zealanders are intensely proud of their country. Aware of their country's small size and relative insignificance on the world stage, national achievements, particularly world-beating sporting achievements, are greeted with great fanfare. NZ also values its independence and is not afraid to take on the world, as it has done in its antinuclear stance, a policy so widely supported that not even conservative governments have been game to reverse it, despite intense international pressure.

New Zealanders value hard work, resourcefulness, honesty, fairness, independence and ruggedness – legacies of their pioneering history. For the visitor, perhaps the most immediately obvious trait of all New Zealanders is their friendliness.

RELIGION

The most common religion in NZ is Christianity. Twenty-four per cent of the population is Anglican (Church of England), 18% is Presbyterian and 15% is Roman Catholic. Other denominations include the Methodist (5%) and Baptist Churches, the Church of Latter-Day Saints (Mormon Church), Jehovah's Witnesses, the Pentecostal Church, Assembly of God and the Seventh-Day Adventist Church.

Other faiths, including Hinduism, Judaism, Islam and the Baha'i faith, are also represented in NZ.

The Ratana and Ringatu faiths, with significant followings, are Maori forms of Christianity. Ringatu was founded by Te Kooti (see the boxed text 'Te Kooti' in The East Coast chapter) after a divine revelation while he was imprisoned on the Chathams. Revitalised by the Tuhoe prophet Rua Kenana in the early 20th century, the church still has a large following in the Bay of Plenty and East Coast, and on the 11th of each month its devotees begin an intensive period of worship which culminates in a communion ritual.

The Ratana Church was founded by Tahupotiki Wiremu Ratana (1870–1939). He performed faith healing and was soon attracting a loyal following of adherents – to them he was Te Mangai, 'The Mouthpiece of God'. Since its founding, the Ratana faith has been an influential force in Maori politics – at one time four Maori seats were held by Ratana members. Ratana Pa near Raetihi, with its twin-towered temple, is the spiritual centre for its 40,000-plus members.

About 20% of Kiwis classify themselves as having no religion.

LANGUAGE

English and Maori are both the official languages of New Zealand. English is spoken by just about everyone in NZ however Maori is the language of everyday conversation in a very small number of rural areas, particularly in Northland or the East Coast. You will often hear Polynesian languages spoken by people in both Auckland and Wellington.

Facts for the Visitor

SUGGESTED ITINERARIES

Many travellers assume that New Zealand, by virtue of its small size relative to Australia, can be covered in a short time – then end up disappointed that they didn't allow enough time. There's a lot to see and do, and even picking a handful of highlights from the North and South islands will require about a month (unless you fly everywhere). Those with special interests, particularly tramping and other outdoor activities, should also see the Activities chapter and factor in extra time. These itineraries assume you have your own transport or are planning a tour and that you want to fit in as much as possible; reliance on public transport will add more time.

One Week – North Island

Spend a day in Auckland, then head up to the Bay of Islands for a cruise and a visit to historic Waitangi. Return to Auckland via the Waipoua Kauri Forest on Northland's west coast and visit the Matakohe Kauri Museum en route. Head down to Rotorua, where you can visit thermal areas and attend a Maori *hangi* and concert evening. From Rotorua, travel west to Waitomo and its magnificent caves, then back to Auckland.

Two Weeks – North Island

Spend a couple of days in Auckland including a cruise out to Rangitoto or Waiheke Island in the Hauraki Gulf. Travel up to the Bay of Islands and continue to the Far North and Cape Reinga, returning to Auckland via the west coast. Head down to the Waitomo Caves (take a detour to the west coast village of Kawhia, rich in Maori history) and across to Rotorua and Taupo, then continue south to the magnificent Tongariro National Park. Try to do the one-day Tongariro Crossing walk here. Continue down the 'Desert Rd' to Wellington, perhaps stopping off along the Kapiti Coast for a 'fly by wire' or seafood lunch. Explore Wellington, including their premier museum, Te Papa,

North Island Highlights

New Zealand has so many superb physical features that you tend to take the country's beauty for granted after a while. Here's our list of not-to-be-missed sights or things to do in NZ (in no particular order), starting with the rugged North Island. Apart from places listed here, see the Activities chapter for the bewildering array of outdoor adventures to be tackled:

- **Northland** – The best of this region includes magnificent west coast kauri forests with gigantic 3000-year-old trees; the stunning Bay of Islands where you can go sailing, swimming and fishing; and Cape Reinga, a place of Maori mythology in the Far North.

- **Rotorua & Taupo** – Rotorua is a centre of thermal activity (boiling mud pools, hissing geysers and eerie lunar landscapes) and abundant Maori culture such as concerts and *hangi*. NZ's largest lake, Taupo, is a haven for activities, and has the stunning volcanic plateau as a backdrop.

- **Tongariro National Park** – This outstanding volcanic landscape, centred on Mt Ruapehu, is a natural highlight of the North Island. As well as fabulous walking, there's winter skiing and unbelievable scenery.

- **Waitomo Caves** – The Waitomo region is riddled with explorable limestone caves full of stalactites, stalagmites and the stellar radiance of glowworms.

- **Auckland & Wellington** – NZ's major cities offer a chance to delve into the country's cosmopolitan culture and to learn the intricacies of NZ's complex racial mix. Visit museums for an insight into NZ culture – Te Papa in Wellington and the Auckland War Memorial Museum shouldn't be missed. These cities also offer the best eating in NZ – check out Auckland's waterfront or Parnell district for international cuisine, and Wellington's hot cafe culture.

then head back up the east coast to Art Deco Napier – indulge yourself at the vineyards in Wairarapa and Hawkes Bay on the way. Return to Auckland via the Bay of Plenty.

One Week – South Island

Spend day one in Christchurch, then travel across to Greymouth on the West Coast, either by the superb road crossing through Arthur's Pass National Park or on the *Tranz-Alpine* train. Travel south to either (or both) Franz Josef or Fox Glacier. From there it's an all-day trip to Queenstown via Haast Pass and Wanaka – perhaps stop in Wanaka and catch a film at Cinema Paradiso. Spend a day or two in Queenstown bungying, jet-boating, cruising the lake and revelling in the nightlife. Head up to beautiful Mt Cook (overnight in the YHA there) then return to Christchurch via Lake Tekapo.

Two Weeks – South Island

Spend a couple of days in Christchurch with side trips to the Port Hills and the French village of Akaroa. Go north to Kaikoura for whale watching or swimming with dolphins, seals and sharks, and indulge in a crayfish meal. Travel up to Nelson via the Marlborough wineries near Blenheim; or alternatively take in the scenic Marlborough Sounds with Picton or Havelock as a base. From Nelson, detour to the Abel Tasman National Park where you can sea kayak and walk, and, if time permits, continue on to Golden Bay (Takaka). Returning to Nelson, head across to the West Coast, perhaps stopping to raft or jetboat in the Buller Gorge. Visit Paparoa National Park, including Punakaiki and its Pancake Rocks, before travelling down the coast to the glaciers and Queenstown. From Queenstown continue south to Te Anau and organise a cruise on Milford or Doubtful Sound. Travel via the Catlins to Dunedin. Explore the Otago Peninsula, with its wonderful wildlife, before returning to Christchurch.

One Month

One month is a reasonable amount of time to see a bit of both islands – combine the two week options for both the South and North

South Island Highlights

If you thought the scenery of the North Island was magnificent, you ain't seen nothing yet! Many travellers rate the greener South Island, with its alpine mountains, fiords and forests, even *more* spectacular. Attractions here include:

- **Kaikoura** – Wedged between mountains and the ocean, whale-watching trips and swimming with dolphins, seals and sharks have made this place famous, and there are myriad other adventure activities.

- **Fox & Franz Josef Glaciers** – Nowhere else do glaciers so close to the equator come this near to sea level and a walk or heli-hike on them is a must. The glaciers are just one highlight on the rugged West Coast. There are also lush native forests, a scenic coastal road and the famous *TranzAlpine* rail link.

- **Mt Cook** – Also known as Aoraki, the highest mountain in the country offers unmatched scenery, good walks and skiing, and mighty glaciers cascading from its flanks.

- **Queenstown** – The home of the bungy jump, and with a fantastic natural setting on the shores of Lake Wakatipu, this is NZ's outdoor activity capital. Queenstown is also a winter sports haven and has the most energetic nightlife in the South Island all year round.

- **Nelson Region** – For sheer diversity of things to see and do, the Nelson region is hard to beat. Walking and kayaking in Abel Tasman National Park, touring wineries, sailing and shopping for arts and crafts are a start.

- **Fiordland** – As wild and remote as it gets. Doubtful Sound and Milford Sound are spectacular fiords, and a cruise on them is a highlight. The region attracts trampers of all nationalities, keen to tackle the world-famous tracks.

- **Otago Peninsula and the Catlins** – The southeastern coastline is a wildlife enthusiast's dream, with an amazing array of fauna – albatross, fairy and yellow-eyed penguins, Hector's dolphins, seals and sea lions. A must!

Islands, and vary as suits, eg, substitute a trip to Napier with an exploration of beautiful Mt Taranaki/Egmont in the north, or Mt Cook for the Catlins and the *TranzAlpine* train journey for Golden Bay in the south. You might decide to sacrifice Northland for a tramp in the Central Plateau.

Two Months

If you really want to experience much of what NZ has to offer then two months is the minimum time required.

In the North Island, you could add the forests and beaches of Coromandel (two to three days), Great Barrier Island (two days), Lake Waikaremoana and Urewera National Park (two to three days), the Bay of Plenty (two days), East Cape and Gisborne (three days), Taranaki (three days) and canoeing on the Whanganui River (three to four days).

Tramping highlights include Lake Waikaremoana, Tongariro Crossing, Tongariro Northern Circuit, Totara Flats in the Tararua Ranges, and Mt Taranaki/ Egmont (see the Activities chapter).

In the South Island, add the beautiful waterways of Marlborough Sounds and the Queen Charlotte Track (three days), Kahurangi National Park and Farewell Spit (three days), Nelson Lakes National Park (two days), Hanmer Springs hot pools (one day), Karamea and Westport (two days), the Haast World Heritage region (two days), Wanaka with Mt Aspiring National Park, skiing and fine walks (four days), Stewart Island (two to seven days), Central Otago cycle trails (two days), Lake Tekapo (two days) and Methven jetboating, skiing and walks (two to three days).

It's easy to spend extra days anywhere – particularly in the main destinations, eg, the Bay of Islands, Rotorua, Auckland, Taupo, Wellington, Kaikoura, Nelson, Queenstown, Dunedin and Christchurch. Chances are the highlight of your trip will be time spent somewhere we haven't even mentioned!

PLANNING
When to Go

New Zealand's busiest tourist season is during the warmer months, from around November to April, with some exceptions – ski resort towns, obviously, will be packed out in winter.

The peak travel time in NZ is the summer school holidays, from late December to late January. During these holidays, transport and every type of accommodation fills up, especially the budget places, so book as far ahead as possible. It may be more pleasant to visit NZ either side of this hectic period. To a lesser extent Easter weekend (March/April), Labour Day weekend (late October) and the mid-year school holidays are also very busy.

November and April are slightly cooler but these months are noticeably quieter and are in many ways the best months to travel.

October and May are quieter still and cheaper months to travel. Though snow falls at higher altitudes, the weather is cool but mild in much of the country. The main tourist industry starts to wind down in May (and slowly cranks up again in October); while most services and activities still operate, a few close.

June to September is the season for winter sports enthusiasts but, away from the busy ski areas, some accommodation, transport services and activities close down. Some of the tramping trails are closed because of snow and ice, as are some of the pass roads. However, NZ is not like some countries where the weather is so miserable that there's no point in going. Winter is cold – freezing in the far south and at higher altitudes – but parts of the North Island, particularly Northland, and the Nelson region of the South Island have mild winters where nights are cold but days can be sunny and pleasant.

What to Bring

Everything you might need is available in New Zealand and the weak NZ dollar makes most things quite cheap, although clothing and luxury items can be relatively expensive by world standards. Come prepared for New Zealand's widely varying and very changeable weather. A T-shirt-and-shorts day at the Bay of Islands can also bring snow and sleet to a high pass in the Southern Alps. In fact, on any of NZ's mountains you can often encounter T-shirt and snow-gear weather on the same day. If you're tramping, proper gear can save your life. Good camping and sports equipment is available in NZ – high-quality gear can be expensive, but equipment can be hired quite cheaply.

Bring waterproof gear and a warm down sleeping bag even if you're not camping or tramping. A sleeping bag will save a lot of money in budget accommodation where linen costs extra.

Maps

Excellent maps are widely available in NZ – everything from street maps and road atlases to detailed topographical maps.

Automobile Association (AA) members (or members of affiliate organisations) can present their cards at any AA office and get many free maps. The AA city, town, regional and highway maps are some of the best available. For car touring off the beaten track, pick up a set of the 1:350,000 district maps. The AA also sells road atlases and large maps of the North and South Islands. The Shell road atlas, Wises' maps and road atlases, and the Minimap series are also excellent and available at AA offices, visitor centres and bookshops.

Land Information New Zealand (LINZ; formerly known as DOSLI) publishes several excellent map series – street, country and holiday maps, maps of national parks and forest parks, detailed topographical maps for trampers, and more. LINZ maps are available at LINZ offices, some bookshops and Department of Conservation (DOC) offices.

TOURIST OFFICES
Local Tourist Offices

Almost every city or town – whether it has any worthwhile attractions or not – seems to have a visitor information centre. Many are united by the Visitor Information Network (VIN), affiliated with the New Zealand Tourism Board (NZTB). These bigger information centres have trained staff, abundant information on local activities and attractions and free brochures and maps. Staff also act as travel agents, booking almost all activities, transport and accommodation. Use the centres: they are an excellent resource for travellers, but bear in mind that most information centres only promote accommodation and tour operators who are paying members of the local tourist association.

Some visitor centres can be understaffed and very busy – it's a good idea to visit close to opening time.

Tourist Offices Abroad

The NZTB has representatives in various countries around the world. The board's head office is at Level 16, 80 The Terrace, Wellington, New Zealand (☎ 04-917 5400, fax 915 3817, ☒ www.purenz.com). Overseas offices include:

Australia (☎ 02-9247 5222, fax 9241 1136)
  Level 8, 35 Pitt St, Sydney, NSW 2000
Germany (☎ 69-971 2110, fax 971 2113)
  Rossmarkt 11, 60311 Frankfurt am Main
UK (☎ 020-7930 1662, fax 7839 8929)
  New Zealand House, Haymarket,
  London SW1Y 4TQ
USA
  California (☎ 310-395 7480, fax 395 5453)
  501 Santa Monica Blvd, Suite 300,
  Santa Monica, CA 90401
  New York (☎ 212-832 8482, fax 832 7602)
  780 3rd Avenue, Suite 1904, New York,
  NY 10017-2024

VISAS & DOCUMENTS
Passport

Almost everyone needs a passport to enter NZ. If you enter on an Australian or NZ passport, or on a passport containing an Australian or NZ residence visa, your passport must be valid on arrival. All others must have passports valid for at least three months beyond the time you intend to stay in NZ.

Visas

Australian citizens or holders of current Australian resident return visas do not need a visa or permit to enter NZ and can stay indefinitely, if they do not have any criminal convictions. Australians do not require a work permit.

Citizens of the UK, and other British passport holders who can show they have permanent UK residency, do not need a visa; they are issued on arrival with a visitor permit to stay for up to six months.

Citizens of the following countries do *not* need a visa and are given a three-month extendable visitor permit upon arrival, provided you can show an onward ticket and sufficient funds ($1000 per month or $400 per month if your accommodation has been prepaid) to support your stay:

Andorra, Argentina, Austria, Bahrain, Belgium, Brazil, Brunei, Canada, Chile, Denmark, Finland, France, Germany, Greece, Hong Kong, Hungary, Iceland, Ireland, Israel, Italy, Japan, Korea (South), Kiribati, Kuwait, Liechtenstein, Luxembourg, Malaysia, Malta, Mexico, Monaco, Nauru, Norway, Netherlands, Oman, Portugal, Qatar, Saudi Arabia, Singapore, Slovenia, South Africa, Spain, Sweden, Switzerland, Tuvalu, UAE, Uruguay, USA, Zimbabwe

Citizens of all other countries require a visa to enter NZ, available from any NZ embassy or consulate (see the list later in this chapter). Visas are normally valid for three months. Check at the immigration website (W www.immigration.govt.nz).

Work & Student Visas It is illegal to work on a visitor permit. If you have an offer of employment, you should apply for a work permit, valid for up to three years, before arriving in NZ. In theory, permission to work is granted only if no NZ job seekers can do the job you have been offered. A work permit can be applied for in NZ after arrival but, if granted, it will only be valid for the remaining time you are entitled to stay as a visitor.

For travellers, the Working Holiday Visa is the best way to supplement your travels. Under this scheme citizens aged 18 to 30 years from the UK, Ireland, Canada, Chile, Denmark, France, Germany, Hong Kong, Italy, Japan, Korea, Malaysia, Netherlands and Sweden can apply for a 12-month visa. It is only issued to those seeking a genuine working holiday, not for permanent work, so you are not supposed to work for one employer for more than three months. You must apply for this visa in (or from) your own country, and must be able to show an onward ticket and evidence of at least NZ$4200 funds. A limited number of visas are issued each year so apply early – for UK citizens it's 8000, for Ireland and Germany it's 1000, Canada 800 and most other countries between 200 and 400. The application fee is the equivalent of NZ$90 to $100 depending on where you apply (refunded if your application is unsuccessful). Since the rules differ slightly for different nationalities, see the Department of Immigration website at W www.immigration.govt.nz/work. Also see the Work section later in this chapter for information on possible jobs. US citizens can consider applying for a work permit through BUNAC.

You can study on a visitor permit if it is one single course not more than three months long. For longer study, you must obtain a student permit.

Visa Extensions Visitor permits can be extended for stays of up to nine months, if you apply for further permits and meet normal requirements. 'Genuine tourists' and a few other categories of people can be granted stays of up to 12 months.

Apply for extensions at any New Zealand Immigration Service office:

Auckland (☎ 09-914 4100, fax 914 4119) 450 Queen Street
Christchurch (☎ 03-365 2520) Carter House, 81 Lichfield St
Dunedin (☎ 03-477 0820) 6th floor, Evan Parry House, 43 Princes St
Hamilton (☎ 07-838 3566) 5th floor, Westpac Building, Victoria St
Wellington (☎ 0508-558855) Level 7, Regional Council Centre, 142–146 Wakefield St

Documents & Copies

No special documents other than your passport are required in NZ.

Bring your driving licence. A full, valid driving licence from your home country is all you need to rent and drive a car in NZ. Members of automobile associations should bring their membership cards – most have reciprocal agreements with New Zealand's AA.

An ISIC card (International Student Identity Card) entitles you to certain discounts, particularly on transport. The international Youth Hostel Association (YHA) card is well worth having even if you don't intend staying in hostels. This card provides a 50% discount on domestic air travel and a 25% discount on major bus lines, plus dozens of discounts on activities. A VIP Backpackers Card offers similar benefits and can be bought in NZ or Australia from VIP hostels.

All important documents (passport data page and visa page, credit cards, travel insurance policy, air/bus/train tickets, driving licence etc) should be photocopied before you leave home. Leave one copy with someone at home and keep another with you, separate from the originals.

Travel Insurance

A good travel insurance policy to cover theft, loss and medical problems is important. Nothing is guaranteed to ruin your holiday plans quicker than an accident or having that brand new camera stolen. The policies handled by STA Travel and other budget travel organisations are usually good value.

Some policies specifically exclude 'dangerous activities' such as scuba diving, parasailing, bungy jumping, motorcycling, skiing and even tramping. Given the emphasis on outdoor activities in New Zealand and the operators' lack of liability, you should be certain you understand what you're covered for in this area.

You may prefer a policy that pays doctors or hospitals direct rather than you having to pay on the spot and claim later. If you have to claim later make sure you keep all documentation. Some policies ask you to call back (reverse charges) to a centre in your home country where an immediate assessment of your problem is made. Check that the policy covers ambulances and emergency medical evacuations by air.

EMBASSIES & CONSULATES
NZ Embassies & Consulates

You can find details of New Zealand embassies and consulates around the world on ☑ www.nzembassy.com.

Australia
High Commission (☎ 02-6270 4211, fax 6273 3194) Commonwealth Ave, Canberra, ACT 2600
Consulate-General (☎ 02-8256 2000, fax 9221 7836) Level 10, 55 Hunter St, Sydney, NSW 2000
Canada (☎ 613-238 5991, fax 238 5707, ☑ www.nzhcottawa.org) Suite 727, Metropolitan House, 99 Bank St, Ottawa, Ont K1P 6G3
France (☎ 01 45 00 43 43, fax 01 45 01 43 44) 7ter, rue Léonard de Vinci, 75116 Paris
Germany (☎ 30-206 210, fax 206 21114) Atrium Friedrichstrasse, Friedrichstrasse 60, 10117, Berlin
Ireland (☎ 01-660 4233, fax 660 4228) 37 Leeson Park, Dublin 6
Netherlands (☎ 70-346 9324, fax 363 2983) Carnegielaan 10, 2517 KH The Hague
UK (☎ 09069 100 100, fax 020-7973 0370) New Zealand House, 80 Haymarket, London SW1Y 4TQ
USA
Embassy (☎ 202-328 4800, fax 667 5227, ☑ www.nzemb.org), 37 Observatory Circle NW, Washington, DC 20008
Consulate-General (☎ 310-207 1605, fax 207 3605) Suite 1150, 12400 Wiltshire Blvd, Los Angeles, CA 90025

Embassies & Consulates in NZ

Most overseas embassies and consulates are in the capital, Wellington (area code ☎ 04). They include:

Australia (☎ 473 6411, ☑ www.australia.org.nz) 72-78 Hobson St
Canada (☎ 473 9577, ☑ www.dfait-maeci .gc.ca/newzealand) 61 Molesworth St
France (☎ 384 2555, ☑ ambafrance-nz.org.nz) 34–42 Manners St
Germany (☎ 473 6063, ☑ www.deutschebotschaftwellington.co.nz) 90–92 Hobson St
Israel (☎ 472 2368, ☑ users.iconz.co.nz/israel/) 13th floor, DB Tower, 111 The Terrace
Japan (☎ 473 1540, ☑ www.japan.org.nz) 18th floor, Majestic Centre, 100 Willis St
Netherlands (☎ 471 6390, ☑ www.netherlands embassy.co.nz) 10th floor, Investment Centre, cnr Featherston and Ballance Sts
UK (☎ 472 6049, ☑ www.brithighcomm.org.nz) 44 Hill St, Thorndon
USA (☎ 472 2068, ☑ usembassy.org.nz) 29 Fitzherbert Terrace, Thorndon

Your Own Embassy

It's important to realise what your own embassy – the embassy of the country of which you are a citizen – can and can't do to help you if you get into trouble.

Generally speaking, it won't be much help in emergencies if the trouble you're in is remotely your own fault. Remember that you are bound by the laws of the country you are in. Your embassy will not be sympathetic if you end up in jail after committing a crime locally, even if such actions are legal in your own country.

In genuine emergencies you might get some assistance, but only if other channels have been exhausted. For example, if you need to get home urgently, a free ticket home is exceedingly unlikely – the embassy would expect you to have insurance. If you have all your money and documents stolen, it might assist with getting a new passport, but a loan for onward travel is out of the question.

CUSTOMS

For the full story on what you can and can't bring into New Zealand, see the NZ customs website at ⓦ www.customs.govt.nz. Customs allowances include 200 cigarettes (or 50 cigars or 250g of tobacco), 4.5L of wine or beer and one 1125mL bottle of spirits or liqueur.

Goods up to a total combined value of NZ$700 are free of duty and GST. Personal effects are not normally counted.

As in most countries the customs people are fussy about drugs, and trained sniffer dogs are occasionally used at NZ airports. Drug paraphernalia, such as bongs and pipes, is also prohibited. Obviously, weapons of any kind are restricted.

Biosecurity is the buzz word for NZ customs. With the country's reliance on the agricultural industry, authorities are very serious about keeping out diseases such as foot and mouth, so quarantine laws are quite strict. Tramping gear such as boots and tents will be checked and may need to be cleaned before being allowed in. The same applies to golf clubs and bicycles. You must declare any plant or animal products (including anything made of wood), and food of any kind. You'll also come in for extra scrutiny if you've come from or via Africa, South-East Asia and South America.

If you're unsure about whether to declare an item or not, then declare it – there are on-the-spot fines of $200 for going through customs without declaring suspect goods.

MONEY
Currency

New Zealand's currency is dollars and cents. There are $5, $10, $20, $50 and $100 notes and 5c, 10c, 20c and 50c, $1 and $2 coins. Unless otherwise noted, all prices quoted in this book are in NZ dollars.

There are no limitations on the import or export of foreign currency. Unused NZ currency can be changed before you leave the country.

Exchange Rates

The currencies of Australia, the UK, USA, European Union and Japan are all easily changed, and at consistently good rates. Most banks will exchange these and several other currencies, but rates may be slightly worse for less frequently changed currencies.

country	unit		NZ$
Australia	A$1	=	$1.30
Canada	C$1	=	$1.40
euro zone	□	=	$2.00
Japan	¥100	=	$1.90
UK	£1	=	$3.20
USA	US$1	=	$2.03

Exchanging Money

Banks are open from 9am to 4.30pm Monday to Friday. Exchange rates may vary a few cents between banks. The main banks include the Bank of New Zealand (BNZ), Westpac Trust, ANZ, BSN Bank and Kiwibank, which is found at post offices.

Travellers cheques are always a safe way to carry money and their exchange rate is slightly better than for cash in NZ. American Express, Visa and Thomas Cook travellers cheques are widely recognised and at most banks there's no service charge for changing them.

Moneychangers *(bureaux de change)* can be found in the major tourist areas and at airports. They have slightly longer weekday hours (9am to 9pm) and are usually open on Saturday and sometimes Sunday. American Express and Thomas Cook offices, found in major cities, have competitive rates and change a wider variety of currencies than most banks. They will change their own travellers cheques commission-free.

ATMs & Credit Cards

Automated Teller Machines (ATMs) at most of the big banks offer access to overseas savings accounts via networks such as Cirrus, Maestro and Plus, but check with your bank before departure. You can get cash advances over the counter at banks or via 24-hour ATMs that display Visa or Master-Card symbols.

Credit cards are a convenient way to carry money if you avoid interest charges by always keeping your account in the black. Visa, MasterCard, Bankcard, JCB, American Express and Diners Club credit cards are the most widely recognised – Visa and MasterCard are accepted practically everywhere. Money can be sent by telegraphic transfer, bank to bank, or – more easily – through a credit card.

Many NZ businesses allow Eftpos (electronic funds transfer at point of sale) purchases, using your ATM or credit card to pay over the counter, but this service usually isn't available to foreign savings accounts (ie, you'll probably have to use your credit card).

For long stays, it may be worth opening a bank account. Westpac and the Bank of New Zealand have many branches around the country and you can request a card for 24-hour ATM access.

Costs

The weak NZ dollar (sometimes disparagingly referred to as the NZ peso) and the consequent high rate of exchange means that NZ can appear quite cheap if you're coming from Europe, the UK, Japan or the US. But like anywhere, while it is possible to travel quite economically in NZ, it's just as easy to spend up big. Costs are generally similar to Australia, although food and luxury items (especially imported goods) tend to be more expensive. Accommodation is reasonable: at backpackers you're looking at paying $17 to $20 per person a night. In motor camps or holiday parks it costs $8 to $10 per person to camp (a little more with power), and you can get a simple cabin from $35 a double. Eating out can cost anywhere from $3 to $5 for simple takeaways, or from $20 to $30 per person for dinner at a medium-priced restaurant.

If you're travelling on a tight budget and camping or staying in backpackers, preparing your own food and getting around on public transport, you could expect to scrape by on as little as $40 a day, provided you don't cover any great distances or try to have too much fun. A more realistic figure, which would allow you to eat out once a day and enjoy a drink or two, would be $60 a day.

If you're staying in cheap guesthouses or motels, eating out once or twice a day, sightseeing and getting around by car, count on at least $80 to $100 per day (per person travelling as a couple), not including the car hire or additional activities.

Some of the many activities that attract people to NZ – such as tramping, swimming, lazing on beaches and bird-watching – cost nothing . However, any organised adventure activities such as jetboating, skydiving, bungy jumping, kayaking etc need to be considered separately – a few days in Queenstown could be enough to blow anybody's budget!

In this book we round most prices up to the nearest 50c – or dollar, with higher prices – with the exception of prices where having the right coinage can be important.

Tipping

Tipping is by no means entrenched in NZ – many Kiwis still regard it as a foreign custom – but it is becoming more widespread, particularly with the growth in fine dining and cafe culture. In cities and major tourist centres (Auckland, Wellington,

Queenstown), tipping in good cafes and restaurants will be expected, or at least appreciated. Tip if you feel the service was good – 5% to 10% of the bill is usually enough.

Taxes

GST (Goods and Services Tax) adds 12.5% to the price of just about everything in NZ. Prices quoted almost invariably include GST, but look out for any small print announcing that the price is GST exclusive.

POST & COMMUNICATIONS
Post

New Zealand post offices are generally called 'post shops' now – most have been removed from the traditional old buildings and set up in modern shop-style premises – and are open from 9am to 5pm Monday to Friday. You can have mail addressed to you care of 'Poste Restante, Main Post Shop' in whichever town you require. Mail is usually held for 30 days. Post shops acting for post restante in the main centres are Wellesley St, Auckland; Bunny St, Wellington; Cathedral Square, Christchurch; and Metro, 283 Princess St, Dunedin.

Within NZ, standard post costs $0.40 for medium letters and postcards, and $0.90 for letters larger than 120mm by 235mm. Fast Post, promising next-day delivery between Auckland, Wellington and Christchurch, and two-day delivery for rural areas, costs $0.80/$1.30 for medium/large letters.

For international mail, use Fast Post; just affix a Fast Post sticker or use a Fast Post envelope and make sure it goes in the Fast Post box. This way it costs $1.50 to send postcards anywhere in the world.

For international airmail letters (maximum weight of 200g) there are only two zones: for Australia & South Pacific the cost is $1.50/2.50/3.50 for medium/large/extra large; to anywhere else in the world it's $2/3/5. Approximate delivery time is three to six days for Australia and the Pacific, six to 12 days for the rest of the world.

For parcels there are five international zones and pricing depends on weight (minimum 100g) and whether you send econ-

---

Getting Mobile

If you want to get hooked up to the mobile phone network in New Zealand, you currently have two choices: NZ Telecom or Vodafone. If you want to bring your own phone and go on a prepaid service using a local SIM card, Vodafone (Ⓦ www.vodafone.co.nz) is the one. Any Vodafone shop (found in most major towns) will set you up with a SIM card and phone number (about $45, including $30 worth of calls), and prepaid cards can be purchased at newsagents and shops practically anywhere. Telecom also has a prepaid system, but you must buy one of its phones to get on the network (there are no SIM cards).

Mobile numbers preceded by ☎ 025 and ☎ 027 (CDMA) are Telecom, numbers preceded by ☎ 021 are Vodafone. Mobile phone coverage is good in towns and most parts of the North Island, but it can be patchy away from the main towns in the South Island.

---

omy (which takes from two to six weeks) or air (three to 12 days). As a guide, a 1/5/10kg parcel sent by airmail costs roughly $12/39/58 to Australia; $26/93/155 to North America and Asia; and $28/102/167 to Europe and the UK. Economy parcel post is about 20% cheaper.

Telephone

NZ Telecom (Ⓦ www.telecom.co.nz) operates the public phone and local call networks. From private residential phones, local calls are free, while rates for long-distance calls through the various suppliers are competitive but constantly changing.

From payphones local calls cost a flat rate of 50c, out-of-area calls start at around 50c per minute, international calls have a minimum charge of $3 and the cost builds up at an alarming rate; toll-free call cards mean you can get around these high charges.

Almost all pay phones in NZ are now card-operated and a few still take coins. Cardphones accept NZ Telecom cards ($5, $10, $20 or $50), available from visitor centres, shops and newsagencies. The larger cities have some credit-card phones.

Long-distance and international calls can be dialled directly from pay phones. For international calls dial ☎ 00, then the country code, area code (drop the initial zero) and number.

To avoid the high charges of making long-distance calls from public phones, use one of the various discount call cards which can be used with any phone. With these prepaid phonecards (to values of $10 to $50), you dial a (toll-free) ☎ 0800 number and then a PIN number printed on the card (hidden by a scratch panel) before direct dialling your overseas calls. The cards, available from shops, newsagents, service stations, backpacker hostels and hotels, include Eziphone, NetTel, Smartel, Kia Ora card and Telecom's YABBA. Calls to the UK, USA and Australia can be as low as $0.15 a minute, or even lower if the card uses a local access number rather than a toll free number.

Lonely Planet's eKno Communication Card is aimed specifically at travellers and provides cheap international calls as well as a range of messaging services including free email. However, for local calls alone you're usually better off with a local phonecard and you should compare eKno rates with local cards if you're going to be making a lot of calls. You can join online at W www.ekno.lonelyplanet.com, or by phone from NZ by dialling ☎ 0800-11 44 84. Once you have joined, to use eKno from NZ, dial ☎ 912 8211 from Auckland or ☎ 0800-11 44 78 elsewhere.

Emergency calls are not charged. Toll-free numbers in NZ are preceded by a ☎ 0800 or ☎ 0508 code. Cardphones may require you to insert a card, even though the call is not charged. The ☎ 0900 code attracts a charge higher than local calls. Mobile phone numbers are preceded by the ☎ 021 or ☎ 025 code and also attract a higher rate.

Country Direct The toll-free Country Direct service enables you to phone directly to an operator in an overseas country for reverse-charge calls, bypassing the NZ operator. The connection fee and call is then charged to the number you dial. Details, including Country Direct numbers, are listed in the front of telephone directories or are available from the NZ international operator. The access number varies, depending on the number of phone companies in the country you call, but is usually ☎ 000 9 (followed by the country code).

Fax

Many hotels, motels and even backpackers have fax machines. Most towns of any size have at least one business offering fax services, and post offices often do too, but faxes are expensive. The charge is about $5, plus the telephone toll charges. Receiving a fax costs around $1 per page.

Email & Internet Access

Email is the No.1 way for travellers to keep in touch, not only with family and friends at home but with each other. Practically every

NZ Area Codes	
Auckland and Northland	☎ 09
Coromandel Peninsula, Bay of Plenty, Waikato and Central Plateau	☎ 07
East Coast, Hawkes Bay, Wanganui, Manawatu and Taranaki	☎ 06
Wellington Region	☎ 04 & 06
South Island	☎ 03

When dialling within a region you still have to use the area code between towns, often for a town just a few kilometres down the road.

All the numbers in this book are listed with their area codes.

Useful Numbers	
Directory assistance in NZ	☎ 018
Emergency (police, ambulance, fire brigade)	☎ 111
International directory service	☎ 0172
New Zealand country code	☎ 64

backpackers hostel has Internet access for guests' use, as do many holiday parks, motels and guesthouses. Libraries generally have public Internet access, but bear in mind that this is provided mainly for research purposes, not for travellers to check their email, and often you'll have to book a time slot.

In any city, reasonable-sized town, or anywhere that travellers congregate, you'll find Internet cafes. The cost ranges from $4 to $10 an hour but is usually around $6 (at a minimum of $2 for 15 minutes).

DIGITAL RESOURCES

The World Wide Web is a rich resource for travellers. You can research your trip, hunt down bargain air fares, book hotels, check on weather conditions or chat with locals and other travellers about the best places to visit (or avoid!).

There's no better place to start your Web search than the Lonely Planet website (W www.lonelyplanet.com), with succint summaries on travelling to most places on earth, postcards from other travellers and the Thorn Tree bulletin board, where you can ask questions before you go or dispense advice when you get back. You can also find travel news, and the subWWWay section links you to the most useful travel resources elsewhere on the Web.

A Web search on NZ will turn up thousands of useful sites and as many useless ones. Many specific sites have been included in the relevant chapters and sections. Good starting points are:

KiwiNewZ An up-to-date site with lots of links, although its primary focus is Queenstown and the Southern Lakes region. W www.KiwiNewZ.com

Noticeboard A good online travel directory. W www.notice-board.com

NZ.Com NZ guidebook, news and resources. W www.nz.com

NZ Government General information on the country, government services and regulations (immigration and census figures). W www.govt.nz

Search Engines Two search engines useful for looking up all things Kiwi. W www.searchnz .co.nz and W www.nzsearch.co.nz

Stuff A news and views site produced by Independent newspapers. W www.stuff.co.nz

Telecom The NZ telephone directory online. W www.whitepages.co.nz

Te Puna The National Library of NZ has a great Web directory. W tepuna.natlib.govt.nz

BOOKS

For details of NZ literature, see Literature under Arts in the Facts about New Zealand chapter.

The biggest national bookstore chain is Whitcoulls – it has a major store on Queen St, Auckland. London Bookshops and Dymocks are also large chains with a wide variety of books, including sections specialising in NZ books. The larger cities have a good selection of other general and specialist bookshops, including Smith's in Christchurch, a browser's heaven, and the Hard to Find Bookstore in Auckland.

Lonely Planet

Tramping in New Zealand describes nearly 50 walks in all parts of NZ. *Cycling New Zealand* gives a comprehensive coverage of all the main routes, and has heaps of tips. The *Auckland* city guide describes the City of Sails and surrounds in detail.

Other Guidebooks

Innumerable specialist travel guides have been written about tramping, skiing, cycling, scuba diving, surfing, fishing, birdwatching and many other activities. See the Activities chapter for details.

The *Mobil New Zealand Travel Guide* by Diana & Jeremy Pope is a good resource for history, background information and interesting stories about the places you visit. It comes in two volumes – *North Island* and *South Island*.

The Reader's Digest *Guide to New Zealand* was written by Maurice Shadbolt, one of the country's pre-eminent authors, who provides wonderful insights into NZ's history, culture and attractions.

History

Although a little outdated, *A History of New Zealand* by Keith Sinclair is a readable and

[Continued on page 65]

Maori Culture & Arts

ALEXANDER TURNBULL LIBRARY, WELLINGTON NZ

Death of Major Von Tempskey at Te-Ngutu-o-te-Manu, New Zealand, 7th September 1868 (Kennett Watkins, 1893)

Wata at Otumatua on the North Shore of Cooks Strait (Charles Heaphy, 1841)

DAVID WALL

Maori cultural performers at the annual Ngaruawahia Regatta, north of Hamilton

TURNBULL LIBRARY, WELLINGTON NZ

Ornamental design on a maori rafter, 1890s.

CULTURE

'Maoridom' is a complex cosmos, and it is only possible to describe an infinitesimal speck of its depth in such a short section. For a description of the coming of the Maori to New Zealand (both popular myth and substantiated theory) see History in the Facts about New Zealand chapter.

Mythology
IN THE BEGINNING...

Top: Thigh pattern. *Waikairo* tattooing on a left thigh. (Horatio Gordon Robley, circa 1864–1930; image courtesy of Alexander Turnbull Library, Wellington NZ)

Bottom Left: *Maui Fishing New Zealand out of the Ocean* (Wilhelm Dittmer, 1907)

Bottom Right: *Hawaiki* (Wilhelm Dittmer, 1907)

In the Beginning there was Te Kore – nothingness, and after nine nothingnesses, came Te Ata – the Dawn. And from the womb of the darkness came Ranginui, the Sky Father, and Papatuanuku, the Earth Mother. The two were united and bore many children.

The six most important children of Ranginui and Papatuanuku were Tawhiri-matea, god of winds and storms; Tangaroa, god of the ocean; Tane-mahuta, god of the forest; Haumia-tike-tike, god of wild food such as fern roots and berries; Rongo-matane, god of peace and cultivated food such as the kumara; and Tu-matauenga, the god of war and humans.

After aeons of living in darkness because their parents were joined together and no light came between them, the children of Ranginui and Papatuanuku could take it no longer; they wanted light. They debated what they should do. Eventually they decided that they should separate their parents so that light could enter the world.

ALEXANDER TURNBULL LIBRARY, WELLINGTON NZ

ALEXANDER TURNBULL LIBRARY, WELLINGTON NZ

They each tried, and failed, to separate Ranginui and Papa-tuanuku. Finally it was Tane-mahuta's turn to try, and he pushed and strained, his shoulders to the ground and his feet to the sky, and finally succeeded in forcing his parents apart. Light flooded into the world.

But all the six gods were male, and for the earth, Papa, to be inhabited Tane had to procreate with a woman. After unsuccessful tries with immortals he created a woman out of soil and gave her the breath of life. The Earth-formed maid Hine-ahuone had a daughter Hine-titama, the Dawn Maid, and Tane procreated with her ensuring the birth of humanity.

AND THEN CAME AOTEAROA...

A long time after the creation of the world – after Tane-mahuta had a daughter, who also became his wife and bore him other daughters, and after many other things had happened – the demigod Maui, who lived in Hawaiki, went out fishing with his five brothers.

They went further and further out to sea. When they were a long way out, Maui took out his magic fish-hook (the jaw of his sorcerer grandmother), tied it to a strong rope, then dropped it over the side of the canoe. Soon he caught an immense fish and, struggling mightily, pulled it up to the surface. He leapt into the water and beat the fish with his greenstone *mere* (club). This fish became the North Island of NZ, called Te Ika a Maui (The Fish of Maui) by the ancient Maori. Wellington Harbour is the fish's mouth, the Taranaki and East Coast areas are its two fins, Lake Taupo is its heart and the Northland peninsula is its tail. Mahia Peninsula in Hawke Bay is Te Matau a Maui (The Fish-hook of Maui) – the hook with which he caught the giant fish. Maui's *mere* created the mountains and valleys when the fish was clubbed.

The South Island was known as Te Waka o Maui (The Canoe of Maui), the one in which he was sitting when he caught the fish. Kaikoura Peninsula was where he braced his foot while hauling up the fish. It was called Te Taumanu o te Waka o Maui (The Thwart of Maui's Canoe).

Stewart Island, south of the South Island, was known as Te Punga a Maui (The Anchor of Maui) – the anchor stone that held the canoe steady as Maui hauled in the giant fish.

Tribal Society

Maori society was (and to a large degree still is) tribal – the Maori refer to themselves in terms of their *iwi* (tribe), often named after an ancestor, such as Ngati Kahungunu (The Descendants of Kahungunu) or Ngapuhi (The Descendants of Puhi).

The largest *iwi* are the Ngapuhi with nearly 100,000 members, Ngati Porou (55,000), Ngati Kahungunu (45,000) and Ngai Tahu, the main South Island *iwi* (30,000). Many different *iwi* are related by their

ALEXANDER TURNBULL LIBRARY, WELLINGTON NZ

descent from one *waka*, or migratory canoe (see History in the Facts about New Zealand chapter). For example, the Waikato and Ngati Maniapoto tribes were historically allied because of their common descent from those who arrived on the *Tainui* canoe.

Often of more relevance than the *iwi* was the *hapu* (the subtribe), and the village structure based around *whanau* (extended family groups). *Whanau* combined to form communal villages centred around the *marae* (the sacred ground in front of the *whare whakairo*, the carved meeting house where the tribe's ancestral spirits live). The *marae* was the focus of Maori culture because it was where the tribe gathered. It was on the *marae* and in the *whare whakairo* that ceremonies were held, and elders and others of authority addressed the community.

Society was hierarchical, with positions of leadership largely hereditary, and almost always male. The tribes were headed by an *ariki*, or supreme chief, while *hapu* were led by a *rangatira*, or local chief. The final say in *whanau* matters rested with the male head of the family, the *kaumatua*. At the bottom of the pecking order were the *taurekareka* (slaves) taken from opposing tribes in battle.

Within each *hapu* there were clear lines of responsibility between chiefs, men, women and slaves as to which daily tasks they would perform. Men prepared the agricultural plots (and chiefs participated

Above: Mita Taupopoki speaking on a *marae* (photographer unknown, circa 1915)

in this also) but women did the planting; men fished in the open sea and dove for shellfish and the women were allowed to bring food out to them; only slaves and women were allowed to cook, weave and make cloaks; and only men were allowed to go to war, build canoes, tattoo or carve. The delineation of responsibility was ruled by complex laws of *tapu* (taboo).

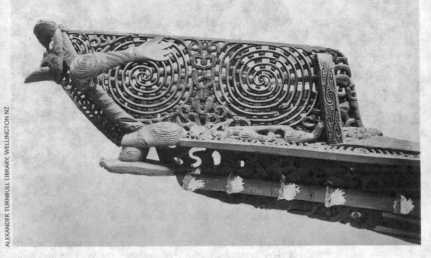

ALEXANDER TURNBULL LIBRARY, WELLINGTON NZ

KEY VALUES

The four essential pillars of Maori society were spirituality, the land, hospitality and ancestors.

Spirituality (Wairua) Maori (Polynesian) religion was complex, with a pantheon of gods representing the sea, sky, war, agriculture etc. Spirituality was expressed in all aspects of the daily lives of the Maori.

The *tohunga* (priests) could communicate with the gods and knew the rituals associated with offerings, but were also responsible for maintaining the history, genealogy, stories and songs of the tribe. The *tohunga* were not just priests but included many different experts: *tohunga ta moko* (expert tattooists), *tohunga whakairo* (master wood-carvers) and *tohunga tarai waka* (shipwrights). The *tohunga* would request that a god come to rest in his god stick *(toko)* during consultation. Symbols such as the god stick did not have the same religious significance as, say, the crucifix in Christianity, but were merely temporary resting places *(taumata atua)* for the gods.

Essential to Maori beliefs and society were the notions of *mauri* (active life force) and *wairua* (soul or spirit) that reside in all things, and *mana* (personal spiritual power or prestige). All things were imbued

Above: Carved prow of a *waka* (photographer unknown, circa 1910).

with *mauri*, but upon death it was the *wairua* which went to the spirit world. If a stone used to signify the *mauri* of a particular river was removed, then it was believed that its inhabitants (fish, eels, birds) would go elsewhere.

Mana, or personal spiritual power, was possessed by chiefs and from them it flowed through to their tribe. Gods had *mana*, and it was inherent in the *karakia* (prayers or chants) that the *tohunga* made to them. The chanting *tohunga* invariably had *mana*. It could be lost – a chief captured in battle would lose his, and that of his tribe. A warrior who killed the *mata ika* or 'first fish' – the first enemy killed – in a battle would attain considerable *mana*.

Tapu applied to forbidden objects, such as sacred ground or a chief's possessions, and also to actions prohibited by the tribe. Its application could be temporary or permanent; canoe builders would be given *tapu* in a ceremony prior to commencing work, and war parties would be given a blood tapu which was removed when they returned to their families. *Noa* was the quality of 'ordinariness', the opposite of *tapu*, and applied to everyday objects, cooked food, women and to captured male slaves.

Land (Whenua) The land will sustain forever if it too is looked after. Geographical features such as *maunga* (mountains) and *awa* (rivers) often delineated tribal boundaries, and were an important genealogical indicator.

Some *maunga* were personified and, even today, each tribe (of the 160 tribal and sub-tribal groups) has one or more sacred *maunga*. Tribal *whakapapa* (genealogies) always refer to the names of mountains, as they were an important part of the social grid (see the boxed text 'Ko Tongariro te Maunga').

Many *maunga* were given European names in an almost deliberate attempt to tame the 'wilderness'. This practice was more prevalent in areas with small Maori populations (such as the colonised towns of the South Island) while places in heartland Maori regions like King Country, Te Urewera and Taupo retained their original names.

Ko Tongariro te Maunga

In this famous quote in 1856 Te Heuheu Iwikau, the hereditary *ariki* (high chief) of the Tuwharetoa tribe established his credentials by identifying himself and his tribe with his mountain and his 'sea':

Ko Tongariro te maunga, ko Taupo te moana, ko Ngati Tuwharetoa te iwi, ko Te Heuheu te tangata

'Tongariro is the mountain, Taupo is the sea, Ngati Tuwharetoa is the tribe, Te Heuheu is the person'

Hospitality (Manaaki) This is an extremely important pillar of Maori society, based on the principle that people are the most important thing in the world.

Ancestors (Tipuna) The proper reverence for ancestors was important to the ancient Maori and, in the absence of a written language, long *whakapapa* (oral genealogies), stretching back hundreds of years to people who arrived by *waka* from Hawaiki, were committed to memory. *Whakapapa* defined ancestral and family ties and determined everyone's place in the tribe. The Maori saw themselves not as individuals but as part of the collective knowledge and experience of all of their ancestors.

Burial practices differed between tribes but the *tangi* (funeral) was similar. The *wairua* of the departed was told to *haere ki te Po* (go to the Underworld). At Te Rerenga-Wairua, Cape Reinga in the far north, the soul slid down the roots of a lone pohutakawa tree (which still stands), took a last look at Aotearoa from the summit of Ohau in the Three Kings Islands, and then rejoined the ancestral spirits in Hawaiki (simultaneously the name for the Underworld and the ancestral homeland).

Below: Four carved posts from the meeting house at the Waiohiki Marae (William Williams, circa 1890s)

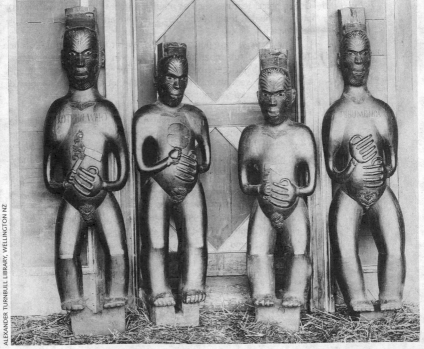

ALEXANDER TURNBULL LIBRARY, WELLINGTON NZ

THE MARAE

Strictly, the 'marae' is the open area in front of the *whare whakairo* (the carved meeting house), but today the term is used to describe the entire complex of buildings as well.

Today, many Maori are re-establishing contact with the *marae* of their tribe. But even the *marae* are subject to the winds of change. Traditional tribal leadership has evolved into today's trust boards, whose power bases are the *marae* in rural areas. The trust boards are under increasing attack from young, urban Maori who see the old leaders as too conservative and exclusive. With elders' adherence to traditional etiquette and Maori language, many urban Maori not brought up on the *marae* feel excluded and want a greater say in tribal affairs and negotiations with the government.

Recent census figures show that three-quarters of all Maori can name their *iwi*, an increase since the previous census. Many Maori are now attempting to trace their *whakapapa*.

Below: Maori women weaving, Te Whai-a-te-Motu meeting house, Mataatua Marae, Ruatahuna (photographer unkown, circa 1910)

Visiting a Marae Probably the best way to gain some understanding of Maoritanga (Maori culture) is by visiting a *marae*. It is a place that is sacred to the Maori and should be treated with great

ALEXANDER TURNBULL LIBRARY, WELLINGTON NZ

respect. The most important of the many customs and conventions of the *marae* are:

- The *marae* is a place of kinship *(whanaungatanga)*, friendship *(manaakitanga)*, love *(aroha)*, spirituality *(wairua)* and the life force *(mauri)*
- Respect for elders *(whakarongo ki nga kaumatua)*
- The *marae* is a place where life and death merge, where the living *(nga hunga ora)* give great honour to the dead *(nga hunga mate)*
- The preservation and use of the Maori language *(te reo Maori)*

A welcoming ritual called *te powhiri ki te manuhiri* is followed every time *manuhiri* (visitors) come onto the *marae*. The manuhiri and the *tangata whenua* (hosts) bring with them the memories of their dead, and both groups pay their respects to one another's deceased. The ceremony removes the *tapu* and permits the *manuhiri* and *tangata whenua* to interact. The practice varies from *marae* to *marae*. Note that shoes must be removed before entering a *whare whakairo*.

Te powhiri ki te manuhiri may proceed as follows: a *karanga* (welcoming call) is made by women of the tangata whenua to the manuhiri. It could also include a *taki* or *wero* (ceremonial challenge). The manuhiri reply to the karanga and proceed on to the *marae*. They pay their respects and sit where indicated, generally to the left (if facing outwards) of the *whare whakairo*.

Mihi (welcoming speeches) are given by the *tangata whenua* from the *taumata tapu* (threshold) in front of the meeting house. Each speech is generally supported by a *waiata* (song), generally led by the women. When the *mihi* is finished the *manuhiri* reply. (It is important to mention the *iwi*, *hapu*, *maunga* and *awa* of respective ancestors.) The *tapu* is deemed to have been lifted from the *manuhiri* when the replies are finished. The *manuhiri* then greet the *tangata whenua* with handshakes and the *hongi* (pressing of noses).

In some places the *hongi*, a sharing of life breath, is a single press, in others it is press, release, press. It is never a rubbing together of noses, a popular misconception.

Before the *manuhiri* leave the *marae* they make *poroporoaki* (farewell speeches), which take the form of thanks and prayer.

The important thing to remember, as a visitor, is that once invited you are extremely welcome on the *marae*, as hospitality is a cornerstone of Maori culture. Once protocol has been satisfied, you have become part of an extended family and your welfare is the primary concern of the *tangata whenua*. They want to see you fed and looked after, almost spoiled, because you are a guest. Such hospitality is fantastic and lucky visitors to New Zealand are increasingly being given the opportunity to enjoy it, often on one of the *marae* tours that are becoming popular.

If you do receive hospitality such as food and lodging, it is customary to offer a *koha*, or donation, to help towards the upkeep of the *marae*. When the roles are reversed and you are the *tangata whenua*, remember that the care of your guests becomes your first concern. See Maori Culture under Books in the Facts for the Visitor chapter for some guides to *marae* protocol.

The term *hui* you often hear refers to a meeting or congregation. It is usually a large group gathering to discuss important issues, or to engage in cultural competitions (for example, action songs).

ALEXANDER TURNBULL LIBRARY, WELLINGTON NZ

WAR *(PAKANGA)*

Perhaps the greatest social change in Maori culture was the progression from a peaceful hunter-gatherer society to a warlike society as land pressures increased. Associated with this was the migration from open *kainga* (unfortified settlements) to *pa tuwatawata* (fortified enclosures), especially in the richer northern region where kumara and fern root thrived.

One of the best ways to promote the *mana* of a tribe was through battle, so the Maori had a highly developed warrior society. War had its own worship, sacrifices, rituals, dances and art forms. Tribes

ALEXANDER TURNBULL LIBRARY, WELLINGTON NZ

Top: Two *wahaika*, the whale-bone form of the *patu* (photographer unknown, circa 1900–70)

Bottom: Six Maori men wearing feather cloaks and carrying spears (J Cowan, circa 1914)

engaged in numerous battles over territory, for *utu* (revenge or payment) or for other reasons, with the losers often becoming slaves or food. Cooking and eating an enemy not only delivered the ultimate insult but also passed on the enemy's life force or power. Usually a *taua muru* (plundering raid) rather than a pitched battle was enough to settle a matter. But reprisal raids were demanded often as a matter of *utu* or restoration of a *hapu's mana*, leading to an almost constant state of warfare.

The defensive villages, or *pa*, to which the Maori retreated when attacked, were built on terraced hill tops with concentric defensive walls and elaborate earth defences. If the outer wall was breached the defenders could retreat to the next fortified inner terrace. Many of these earthworks are still visible, eg, the sculptured Auckland hills. These defensive earthworks were successfully adapted to deal with cannon and musket fire during the Land Wars in the 1840s and 1860s – the world's first example of trench warfare.

Weapons included the wooden long clubs (*taiaha*, *pouwhenua* and *tewhatewha*) and short clubs known as *patu*, including the greenstone *mere*. Although the long clubs resembled spears they were never thrown.

ARTS

Maori arts are dramatic and include various arts that people of European backgrounds might not be familiar with.

SONG *(WAIATA)* & DANCE *(HAKA)*

Traditionally the Maori did not keep a written history; their history was kept in long, specific and stylised songs and chants. As in many parts of the world where oral history has been practised, oratory, song and chant developed to become a magnificent art in Maori culture.

The Maori arts of song (*waiata*) and dance (*haka*, see the boxed text) include some special features, such as the *poi* dance, hand games (*mahi ringaringa*) and other action songs.

The highly expressive action song (*waiata kori*) is perhaps the most beloved tradition, and a highlight of a visit to NZ could be learning some songs with members of a Maori cultural group. Usually the men performed with vigorous actions, whereas the movements of women were graceful and flowing, reflecting some of the artistic forms of Asia.

The poi dance (*haka poi*) is distinctive to the NZ Maori. Originally the poi were made of flax but many types of material are now used. There were long and short poi, with the long poi being the easier of the two dances. The most famous dance is the *waka poi*, with the women sitting in a row as if in a canoe; normally the poi dance is performed standing.

Maori musical instruments included two forms of flute – the *putorino* played with the mouth and the *koauau*, a nose flute; and the

Facing Page: Sir Apirana Ngata (1874–1950) takes the lead in a *haka* at the Waitangi celebrations (B Snowdon, 1940)

Haka

The word *haka* is Maori for any form of dance but it's come to be associated with the war chant (*haka taparahi*) that preceded a battle or challenged suspicious visitors.

Delivered with fierce shouting, flexing arm movements that resemble fists pummelling the side of someone's head, and thunderous stamping to grind whatever is left into the dust, it is indeed a frightening sight.

Each tribe had its own *haka*, but the most famous and widely used comes from Te Rauparaha (1768–1849), chief of the Ngati Toa tribe. He was one of the last great warrior chiefs, carving a course of mayhem from Kapiti, near Wellington, to the South Island, where many southern Maori were slaughtered by his advance. Made famous by the All Blacks national rugby team, Te Rauparaha's *haka* is:

Ka mate, ka mate (It is death, it is death)
Ka ora, ka ora (It is life, it is life)
Tenei te tangata puhuruhuru (Behold the hairy man)
Nana nei i tiki mai
I Whakawhiti te ra (Who caused the sun to shine)
Upane, upane (Abreast, keep abreast)
Upane, ka upane (The rank, hold fast)
Whiti te ra (Into the sunshine)

It is said to have originated when Te Rauparaha was fleeing from his enemies. A local chief hid him in an underground kumara store, where Te Rauparaha waited in the dark, expecting to be found. When the store was opened and the sun shone in, it was not his enemies but the hairy local chief telling him they had gone. Te Rauparaha climbed the ladder to perform this victorious *haka*.

ALEXANDER TURNBULL LIBRARY, WELLINGTON NZ

MAORI CULTURE & ARTS

ALEXANDER TURNBULL LIBRARY, WELLINGTON NZ

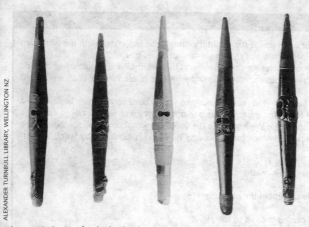

trumpet *(pu)*, of which the best known is the shell version with a wooden mouthpiece. There was no drum to provide a beat, this being provided by rhythmical stamping.

CARVING *(WHAKAIRO)*

Despite remaining a stone age culture (it would have been difficult to get beyond that stage in NZ, since there are few metals apart from gold) the Maori evolved elaborate artistic traditions. The chisels *(whao)* used were of basalt or greenstone, and cord drills were used for making holes.

Woodcarving *(whakairo rakau)* became increasingly refined, peaking in the period immediately before European arrival. Facing the *marae*, ornate *whare whakairo* were built with powerful wooden carvings depicting ancestors, as well as *tukutuku* (wall panelling) and symbolic paintings on rafters and other parts of buildings.

The human figure was the central motif with enlarged head, mouth and eyes. To imitate exactly the human form, a creation of the gods, would be a form of insult. Another prevalent feature, often seen in window lintels and along the barge boards of canoes, is the *manaia,* a 'bird-headed man' identifiable by a human-shaped head with a beak.

Beautifully carved *waka taua* (war canoes) were a source of great *mana* for a tribe and were protected by *tapu*. Built of kauri or totara, they were up to 25m (80 feet) in length and the bow and stern pieces were elaborately fashioned and carved by *tohunga tarai waka*. Being *tapu*, women were not allowed to travel in them.

A variety of household items were also intricately carved such as feather boxes to hold huia feathers *(a waka huia)* and other treasures *(taonga);* the handle of adzes *(toki);* funnels for feeding people that were temporarily too *tapu* to touch cooked food; and digging sticks *(ko)*.

Today you can check out woodcarvings in Rotorua, see artisans at work (such as at Te Whakarewarewa cultural village) and in some cases buy direct from the artists. Carvers produce tremendous forms such as

ALEXANDER TURNBULL LIBRARY, WELLINGTON NZ

Facing page: Maori wind instruments known as *putorino* (date and photographer unknown)

Right: Wooden carved door displaying the coat of arms for the Maori Kings (Te Paki o Matariki) at the Maori meeting house Te Mahinarangi, Turangawaewae Marae, Ngaruawahia (John Houston, 1939)

leaping dolphins, as well as the sometimes highly intricate traditional Maori carvings. Expect to pay a small fortune for high-quality work. Of course, many poor examples are turned out for the tourist trade and that's most likely what you'll find lining souvenir shops in Auckland.

Maori bone carvings are another fine art form undergoing something of a renaissance. Maori artisans have always made bone carvings, but nowadays they feed the tourist industry. *Tiki*, interesting human and animal figures, such as dolphins and sea birds, are carved from bone. Bone fish-hook pendants, carved in traditional Maori and modernised styles, are most common and worn on a thong or a chain around the neck.

ALEXANDER TURNBULL LIBRARY, WELLINGTON NZ

ALEXANDER TURNBULL LIBRARY, WELLINGTON NZ

Head of Maori Chief
Showing full Tatoo (Moko-pu)
Names of Incisions

Upper forehead-*Titi*. The 8 bands below-*Tiwhana*. Curling under
eyebrows over nose-*Rewha*. Curling outer corner of eyes-*Pukaru*.
Ornament over nose-*Kohiti*. Spiral upper nose-*Ngu*. Spiral on
nostrils-*Pongiangia*. Notching down nose-*Whakatara*. From nostrils
to chin-*Rerepehi*. On chin-*Kauwae*. Spiral on cheek-*Kowiri*. Spiral
on jaw-*Koromaha*. Notching near these spirals-*Wera*. From spiral
on cheek to ear-*Paepae*. Under ear-*Putaringa*. On both lips-*Ngutupara.*

Abalone shell, called paua in NZ, is carved into some beautiful ornaments and jewellery, and some tacky ones. It is also used as an inlay
in many Maori carvings. Shells are used as ashtrays in places where
paua is plentiful, but it's illegal to take natural paua shells out of NZ.
Only processed ornaments can be taken with you.

TATTOOS *(MOKO)*
The higher classes were decorated with intricate *moko*, or tattoos –
women only had moko on their chins and lips, while high-ranking men
not only had tattoos over their entire face but also over other parts of
their body (especially their buttocks). The tattoos were created using
bone chisels and a mallet and blue pigment.

CLOTHING *(KAKAHU)*
The Maori made clothing from dog's fur, flax, feathers and other materials. The two principal items of clothing were the kilt and the cloak.

The *maro* (male kilt) was scanty and designed to cover the penis,
whereas the *rapaki* (female kilt) was much larger. At times men often
wore a *whitiki* or *tatua* (belt of dried flax). A woman's flaxen belt was
called a *tu*.

The *piupiu* (skirt) worn in cultural performances is a modern innovation, as is the colourful *pari* (bodice).

The usual *kahu* (cloaks) were made of flax but some were of
dogskin or bird skins sewn together. The most prized of the cloaks,
used for ceremonial purposes, were the *kahu huruhuru* (feather

ALEXANDER TURNBULL LIBRARY, WELLINGTON NZ

cloaks), often using huia or kiwi feathers and fringed with *taniko* (dog's fur). Other feathers used were from the tui, kaka, pukeko, takahe and kereru (wood pigeon).

GREENSTONE *(POUNAMU)*

Greenstone (jade or nephrite, called *pounamu* in Maori) was highly prized by the Maori. The South Island, where pounamu was found, was called Te Wahi Pounamu (The Place of Greenstone) or Te Wai Pounamu (The Water of Greenstone). Since greenstone is found predominantly on the West Coast, expeditions undertaken by the Maori to collect it often took months, following treacherous trans-alpine trails.

Working the stone with their primitive equipment was no easy task either, but they managed to produce some exquisite items.

Pounamu ornaments and *mere* (war clubs) were great treasures. The *heitiki* is one of the most popular greenstone mementos purchased in NZ. Its name literally means 'hanging human form', as Tiki was the first

Facing Page Left: Portrait of an unidentified woman (Samuel Carnell, circa 1870)

Facing Page Right: Head of a fully tattooed Maori man, with cloak and *tiki*. (derived from a drawing by H. G. Robley of Tomika Te Mutu, chief of Ngai-te-Rangi, Tauranga, circa 1860s)

Right: Maori needle, tattooing chisel and birdholding ring, alongside pieces of greenstone. (Samuel Heath Head, circa 1890–1930)

Tama & the Greenstone

The legend of Tama explains why there are differing types of greenstone in the South Island. Tama's three wives (Hine-kawakawa, Hine-kahurangi and Hine-pounamu) were abducted by the taniwha Poutini. At Anita Bay near Milford Sound he found one wife, Hine-pounamu, turned into greenstone, and when he wept his tears gave the stone a flecked appearance, hence the name of *tangiwai* (water of weeping) given to that type of stone. Tama's companion, Tumu-aki, breached *tapu* by putting his burnt fingers in his mouth while cooking some birds, so Tama was not able to find his other wives. Like the first discovered, they were turned into greenstone – *kawakawa* and *kahurangi*. The careless Tumu-aki was turned into a mountain and *tutaekoka*, a fourth form of greenstone, was named to remember the birds they had eaten.

man created and *hei* is 'to hang'. They are tiny, stylised Maori figures, usually depicted with their tongue stuck out in a warlike challenge, worn on a thong or chain around the neck. They've got great *mana* or power, but they also serve as fertility symbols, so beware!

Heitiki were passed on through generations – it was believed that each ancestor who wore it added something to its value. Other popular motifs are the *manaia*, the *taniwha* (monster) and the *marakihau* (sea monster).

The best places to buy greenstone items are Hokitika and Greymouth in the South Island. Collections of both ancient and modern pieces are held at Te Papa Museum in Wellington, and at the Otago (Dunedin), Canterbury (Christchurch) and Auckland Museums. Traditionally, greenstone is bought as a gift for another person, not for yourself.

Left: *Tohunga* using a cord drill to drill a hole in greenstone (James Ingram McDonald, 1921)

Pounamu hei tiki – greenstone

PHOTO © TE PAPA, B.024907, MICHAEL HALL

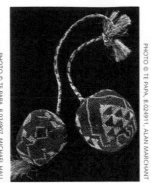

Poi made from lace bark

PHOTO © TE PAPA, B.024911, ALAN MARCHANT

PHOTO © TE PAPA, F.002889/10, MICHAEL HALL

The entrance to the whare whakairo, Whakarewarewa in Rotorua

DAVID WALL

Heru – ornamental comb

DAVID WALL

Ngaruawahia Regatta at Turangawaewae Marae, residence of Maori Queen Dame Te Atairangikaahu

RICHARD I'ANSON

Big Sheep, Hokitika

DAVID WALL

DAVID WALL

Big Kiwi Fruit, Te Puke, Bay of Plenty

DAVID WALL

Big Carrot, Ohakune

PAUL KENNEDY

Big Surfer, Colac Bay, Southland

DAVID WALL

Big Dog Info Centre, Tirau

[Continued from page 48]

entertaining general history, from the Maori account of the creation to the present.

The People and the Land – Te Tangata me Te Whenua: An Illustrated History of New Zealand 1820–1920 by Judith Binney, Judith Bassett & Erik Olssen is also good.

The *New Zealand Historical Atlas: Visualising New Zealand – Ko Papatuanuku e Takoto Nei* is the most exciting NZ publication (1997) for years. Numerous colour spreads cover the prehistory, history and demography of the islands in detail. The text is easy to read and the graphs, diagrams, maps and illustrations highlight interesting aspects of the country's development – Maori migration, the kauri harvest, the sheep-meat industry, sport and leisure, women in paid work, suburban streets etc.

Two Worlds: First Meetings between Maori and Europeans 1642–1772 by Anne Salmond is an account of the first contact between the Maori and the European explorers. It's a fascinating anthropological history telling the story as it was experienced by both sides.

The 19th-century Land Wars between Europeans and Maori are looked at in a new and interesting way in *The New Zealand Wars* by James Belich.

Christopher Pugsley's *Anzac* is a pictorial account of NZ troops' involvement in the ill-fated 1915 Gallipoli campaign during WWI, an important element of the national psyche.

One of the most important and controversial elements of NZ history is the Treaty of Waitangi. Many books have been written about the treaty and the debates surrounding it. One of the best is *The Treaty of Waitangi* (as well as *An Illustrated History of the Treaty of Waitangi*) by Claudia Orange.

Biography

Some fascinating history has been told through biography. *The Dictionary of New Zealand Biography* is a multivolume collection of hundreds of short NZ biographies.

Three biographies about Maori elders are particularly interesting. *Eruera: The Teachings of a Maori Elder* by Eruera Stirling, as told to Anne Salmond, won the Wattie Book of the Year Award, one of NZ's highest literary awards. *Te Puea* by Michael King tells the story of the Maori King Movement's Te Puea Herangi, one of the most influential women in modern Maori history. *Whina*, also by King, tells the story of the Ngapuhi elder Whina Cooper, another important Maori figure, who organised her first public protest at 18 and at age 95 welcomed an international audience to the XIV Commonwealth Games in Auckland in 1990.

The Book of New Zealand Women – Ko Kui Ma Te Kaupapa edited by Charlotte Macdonald, Merimeri Penfold & Bridget Williams is an anthology of over 300 biographical essays of NZ women – a great resource.

Contemporary Autobiography One of NZ's favourite characters, the late Barry Crump was a writer and rugged adventurer, more the Bukowski than the bastard of the bush. He is the author of many popular books, including *A Good Keen Man* (1960), *Hang On a Minute Mate* (1961) and many others published after these, which still sell even after all these years.

Being Pakeha by Michael King is the autobiography of one of NZ's foremost Maori historians, who is a Pakeha.

An Autobiography by the poet Lauris Edmonds (1924–2000) is a frank account of an emergent writer's life. Her poetry, written in a relaxed style, is a delight to read; some of the best is in *Wellington Letter: A Sequence of Poems* (1980).

Mihi Edwards is a contemporary Maori elder who writes readable books telling the story of her life growing up Maori in Pakeha culture and how Maori were punished if they spoke their language in school. Her books include *Mihipeka: Early Years* and *Mihipeka: Time of Turmoil*.

Maori Culture

In recent years NZ has experienced a renaissance of interest in Maori culture, a subject covered by many excellent books. Maori language books are mentioned in the Language chapter at the end of the book.

Te Marae: A Guide to Customs & Protocol by Hiwi & Pat Tauroa is a useful little how-to book for non-Maori visiting a marae for the first time.

Hui: A Study of Maori Ceremonial Gatherings by Anne Salmond is an excellent, more scholarly book about Maori gatherings on the *marae* with insights into Maori culture.

Te Ao Hurihuri: Aspects of Maoritanga edited by Michael King is a great collection of writings on many aspects of Maori culture, written by a number of respected Maori authors.

Tikanga Whakaaro: Key Concepts in Maori Culture by Cleve Barlow is a book in English and Maori in which the author explains 70 terms central to Maori culture.

Maori Customs and Crafts compiled by Alan Armstrong, a small book in the Pocket Guide series, describes and illustrates many different Maori customs and crafts.

A number of good books have been written about the rich legends, myths and stories of the Maori people. An excellent one is the illustrated *Maori Myths and Tribal Legends* retold by Antony Alpers. Another smaller volume is the illustrated *Maori Myth and Legend* by AW Reed.

Traditional Maori Stories, introduced and translated by Margaret Orbell, is a fine book of Maori stories in English and Maori.

Greenstone Trails: The Maori and Pounamu by Barry Brailsford is a fascinating archaeological and historical account of trails used by the Maori when they crossed the Southern Alps to trade the precious stone.

Chatham Islands

Moriori: A People Rediscovered by Michael King tells of the Moriori people of the Chatham Islands and debunks some of the common notions about them. King also wrote *A Land Apart: The Chatham Islands of New Zealand*, with photographs by Robin Morrison, which offers good coverage of the history and stories of these remote islands.

Art & Architecture

There are plenty of high-quality art books on NZ's well-known artists and Maori arts and crafts. The magnificent *Taonga Maori: A Spiritual Journey Expressed through Maori Art* by the Australian Museum (Sydney) has colour photographs and insightful text on some of the best Maori art.

Architecture is not what people usually think of when contemplating NZ, but the book *The New Zealand House* by Michael Fowler (architect) & Robert van de Voort (photographer) is a fascinating presentation. It features an amazing variety of NZ home architecture, with colour photos of everything from grand Victorian palaces to homemade rolling caravan inventions.

Cartoons

No overview of Kiwi publishing could be complete without mention of NZ's favourite comic strip, *Footrot Flats* by Murray Ball. Many books have been published of the adventures of the focal character, The Dog, a mongrel black-and-white sheepdog, and his master Wal, the farmer. It's a delightful look into rural NZ farming life as told from the sheepdog's point of view.

NEWSPAPERS & MAGAZINES

There is no truly national paper although the *New Zealand Herald* (W www.nzherald .co.nz/nznews) in Auckland, the *Dominion* (Wellington) and the *Press* (Christchurch) have wide circulations. Backing up the city newspapers are numerous local dailies.

The closest to a national weekly news magazine is the *Listener* an excellent publication which provides a weekly TV and radio guide, plus articles on the arts, social issues and politics. International publications (eg, *Time* and *Newsweek*) are available in most towns.

Local magazines of merit are *Cuisine*, which features innovative uses of local produce, and *North & South*, which has articles on all aspects of NZ culture.

RADIO & TV

There are four national commercial TV stations (in some areas only a couple can be received) plus Sky, a subscriber television service with news, sports, movie and documentary channels.

Many regional or local commercial radio stations broadcast on the AM and FM bands. Of particular interest are National Radio (837kHz), good for current affairs, Concert FM (96FM) for classical and jazz and Radio Pacific (95.6FM) and Newstalk ZB (97.0FM) for talkback. There are also university stations in the big cities, tribal-based stations, and special interest stations such as Mai FM (88.6FM), a popular Maori youth station.

VIDEO SYSTEMS

Three video systems are used in the world, and each one is completely incompatible with the others. Video recorders in NZ operate on the PAL system, used in Australia and most of Europe.

PHOTOGRAPHY & VIDEO

Photographic and video supplies, equipment and maintenance are all readily available, but prices tend to be higher than in other countries.

Fuji, Kodak and Agfa are the most popular films. Film and processing prices can vary, so it pays to shop around. For prints, one-hour photo developing shops are all over NZ. Slide film is expensive ($15 to $20 for a roll of Kodak Ektachrome 36/100ISO and up to $28 a roll for professional film such as Fuji Provia). Slide processing can be done overnight in Auckland ($15 to $25 a roll) but if it has to be sent away (ie, to Auckland) it takes about a week. Auckland is a good place to stock up on film.

The native bush in NZ is dense and light levels can be very low – more-sensitive (eg, 400 ISO) film will help.

TIME

Being close to the international date line, NZ is one of the first places in the world to start the new day (Pitt Island in the Chatham Islands gets the first sunrise each new year). NZ is 12 hours ahead of GMT (Greenwich Mean Time, also known as UTC) and two hours ahead of Australian Eastern Standard Time.

In summer NZ observes daylight-saving time, where clocks are put forward by one hour on the last Sunday in October; clocks are wound back on the first Sunday of the following March. Ignoring daylight-saving time, when it is noon in NZ it is 10am in Sydney, 8am in Singapore, midnight in London, 8pm the previous day in New York and 5pm the previous day in San Francisco. The Chathams are 45 minutes ahead of the mainland.

ELECTRICITY

Electricity is 230V AC, 50Hz, as in Europe and Australia; Australian-type three-blade plugs are used. Appliances designed for DC supply or different voltages need a transformer. It's not usually possible to operate appliances such as clocks or computers under a different frequency.

WEIGHTS & MEASURES

New Zealand uses the metric system, but you'll still encounter vestiges of the old imperial system. If you go sky diving they'll take you up to 9000 feet rather than 2743m and if you ask someone how much they weigh, the answer may be in kilograms, pounds or stones (a stone is 14 pounds).

HEALTH

There are no vaccination requirements to enter NZ, which is largely a clean, healthy, disease-free country with few health concerns. Medical attention is of a high quality but the state-subsidised health system has long since disappeared. Hospital services are expensive so take out travel insurance with decent medical coverage.

The same health precautions apply as in other developed countries. Of extra note for trampers in NZ is the presence of giardia in some lakes, rivers and streams, but it is rare. There is also a risk of catching amoebic meningitis if you bathe in natural hot thermal pools (see Infectious Diseases under Environmental Hazards).

Predeparture Planning

Health Insurance Make sure that you have adequate health insurance. See Travel Insurance under Visas & Documents earlier in this chapter for details.

Immunisations You don't need any vaccinations to visit NZ. It's always a good idea to keep your tetanus immunisation up to date no matter where you are – boosters are necessary every 10 years.

Other Preparations Make sure you're healthy before you start travelling. If you are going on a long trip make sure your teeth are OK. If you wear glasses take a spare pair and your prescription.

If you require a particular medication take an adequate supply, as it may not be available locally. Take part of the packaging showing the generic name rather than the brand, which will make getting replacements easier. It's a good idea to have a legible prescription or letter from your doctor to show that you legally use the medication to avoid any problems.

Basic Rules

Water Tap water is clean and safe to drink in NZ. Water in lakes, rivers and streams is often OK, but giardia (see Infectious Diseases later) has been found in these sources. DOC can advise on the occurrence of giardia in national parks and forest areas it administers. Water from these sources should be purified before drinking.

The simplest way of purifying water is to boil it. Vigorous boiling should be satisfactory, but at high altitude water boils at a lower temperature and should be boiled for longer in these environments.

Consider purchasing a water filter for a long trip. There are two main kinds of filter. Total filters take out all parasites, bacteria and viruses and make water safe to drink. They are often expensive, but they can be more cost effective (and more environmentally friendly) than buying bottled water. Simple filters take out dirt and larger foreign bodies from the water so that chemical solutions work much more effectively; if water is dirty, chemical solutions may not work at all.

Environmental Hazards

Hypothermia Too much cold can be dangerous, particularly if it leads to hypothermia. Hypothermia is a real and present danger in NZ due to the country's extremely changeable weather. Visitors die from hypothermia every year, mostly because they have gone out walking without adequate preparation. Within the space of a few minutes bright, warm weather can change to freezing winds, rain and hail. Always be prepared for cold, wet or windy conditions even if you're just out walking or hitching; it's especially important if you're tramping out in the bush, away from civilisation.

Hypothermia occurs when the body loses heat faster than it can produce it and the core temperature of the body falls. It is surprisingly easy to progress from very cold to dangerously cold due to a combination of wind, wet clothing, fatigue and hunger, even if the air temperature is above freezing. It is best to dress in layers; silk, wool and some of the new artificial fibres are all good insulating materials. A hat is important, as a lot of heat is lost through the head. A strong, waterproof outer layer (and a 'space' blanket for emergencies) is essential. Carry basic supplies, including food containing simple sugars to generate heat quickly, and fluid to drink.

Symptoms of hypothermia are: exhaustion, numb skin (particularly toes and fingers), shivering, slurred speech, irrational or violent behaviour, lethargy, stumbling, dizzy spells, muscle cramps and violent bursts of energy. Irrationality may take the form of sufferers claiming they are too warm and trying to take off their clothes.

To treat mild hypothermia, first get the person out of the wind and/or rain, remove their clothing if it's wet and replace it with dry, warm clothing. Give them hot liquids – not alcohol – and some high-energy, easily digestible food. Do not rub victims: instead, allow them to slowly warm themselves. This should be enough to treat the early stages of hypothermia. The early recognition and treatment of mild hypothermia is the only way to prevent severe hypothermia, which is a critical condition.

Motion Sickness Eating lightly before and during a trip will reduce the chances of motion sickness. If you are prone to motion sickness try to find a place that minimises movement – near the wing on aircraft, close to midships on boats, near the centre on buses. Fresh air usually helps; reading and cigarette smoke don't. Commercial motion-sickness preparations, which can cause drowsiness, have to be taken before the trip commences. Ginger (available in capsule form) and peppermint (including mint-flavoured sweets) are natural preventatives.

Sunburn You can get sunburnt surprisingly quickly, even through cloud. Use a sunscreen, a hat, and a barrier cream for your nose and lips. Calamine lotion, or a commercial after-sun preparation, is good for mild sunburn. Protect your eyes with good-quality sunglasses, particularly if you will be near water, sand or snow.

Infectious Diseases

Diarrhoea Simple things like a change of water, food or climate can all cause a mild bout of diarrhoea, but a few rushed toilet trips with no other symptoms is not indicative of a major problem.

Dehydration is the main danger with any diarrhoea, particularly in children or the elderly, as it can occur quite quickly. Under all circumstances *fluid replacement* (at least equal to the volume being lost) is the most important thing to remember. Weak black tea with a little sugar, soda water, or soft drinks allowed to go flat and diluted 50% with clean water are all good replacements.

Giardiasis This is caused by a common parasite, Giardia lamblia. Symptoms include stomach cramps, nausea, a bloated stomach, watery, foul-smelling diarrhoea and frequent gas. Giardiasis can appear several weeks after you have been exposed to the parasite. The symptoms may disappear for a few days and then return; this can go on for several weeks.

You should seek medical advice if you think you have giardiasis but if this is not possible, tinidazole or metronidazole are the recommended drugs. Treatment is a 2g single dose of tinidazole or 250mg of metronidazole three times daily for five to 10 days.

Fungal Infections These occur more commonly in hot weather and are usually found on the scalp, between the toes (athlete's foot) or fingers, in the groin and on the body (ringworm). You get ringworm (which is a fungal infection, not a worm) from infected animals or other people. Moisture encourages these infections.

To prevent fungal infections wear loose, comfortable clothes, avoid artificial fibres, wash frequently and dry yourself carefully. If you get an infection, wash the infected area daily with a disinfectant or medicated soap and water, and rinse and dry well. Apply an antifungal cream or powder such as tolnaftate. Try to expose the infected area to air or sunlight as much as possible and wash all towels and underwear in hot water, change them often and let them dry in the sun.

HIV & AIDS Infection with the human immunodeficiency virus (HIV) may lead to acquired immune deficiency syndrome (AIDS), which is a fatal disease. Any exposure to blood, blood products or body fluids may put the individual at risk. The disease is often transmitted through sexual contact or dirty needles – vaccinations, acupuncture, tattooing and body piercing can be potentially as dangerous as intravenous drug use.

Amoebic Meningitis This very serious disease can be a danger if you bathe in natural hot thermal pools. Fortunately, it's no danger if you know how to protect yourself from it.

The amoeba that causes the disease can enter your body through the orifices of your head, usually the nose but occasionally the ears as well. Once it gets inside the nose it bores through the tissues and lodges in the brain. It's easy not to catch the disease – just keep your head out of water!

Symptoms of amoebic meningitis may have a slow onset – it could be several days or even several weeks before the first symptoms are noticed. Symptoms may at first be similar to the flu, later progressing to severe headaches, stiffness of the neck, hypersensitivity to light and then even coma. It can be treated with intravenous anti-amoebic drugs.

Cuts, Bites & Stings

Mosquitoes & Sandflies Mosquitoes appear after dusk. In some parts of the country – notably the West Coast of the South Island and especially in summer – they can come in huge clouds. Avoid bites by covering bare skin and using an insect repellent. Insect screens on windows and mosquito nets on beds offer good protection, as does burning a mosquito coil or using a pyrethrum-based insect spray.

Another six-legged New Zealander that can drive you wild is the tiny black sandfly. Sandfly bites can be even more irritating than mosquito bites; since the insects live on the ground, sandfly bites are mainly on the feet and ankles. Wearing shoes, thick socks and plenty of insect repellent is practically a necessity where sandflies are present.

The most effective insect repellent, DEET (N, N-diethyl-m-toluamide), is an ingredient in many commercially available repellents. Look for a repellent with at least a 28% concentration of DEET. Note that DEET breaks down plastic, rubber and synthetic fabrics, so be careful what you touch after using it. It poses no danger to natural fibres.

Plenty of vitamin B1 in your system is thought to deter sandflies and mosquitoes. Two NZ dietary icons, kumara and Marmite, are good sources.

Leeches & Ticks Leeches may be present in damp rainforest conditions; they attach themselves to your skin to suck your blood. Trampers often get them on their legs or in their boots. Salt or a lighted cigarette end will make them fall off. Do not pull them off, as the bite is then more likely to become infected. Clean and apply pressure if the point of attachment is bleeding. An insect repellent may keep them away.

You should always check all over your body if you have been walking through a potentially tick-infested area as ticks can cause skin infections and other more serious diseases. If a tick is found attached, press down around its head with tweezers, grab the head and gently pull upwards. Avoid pulling the rear of the body as this may squeeze the tick's gut contents through the attached mouth parts into the skin, increasing the risk of infection and disease. Smearing chemicals on the tick will not make it let go and is not recommended.

Spiders Of NZ's many spiders, the only poisonous one is the retiring little katipo (*Latrodectus katipo*). The katipo's shiny black body, about 6mm long, has a bright red patch on the rear of the abdomen. Males and immature females have white markings alongside the famous red patch. Only mature females are venomous. Although mention of its name strikes fear into the hearts of brave souls, it's very rare to meet anyone who has ever seen a katipo, and its bite is not that dangerous. If you're lucky enough to be bitten by one you'll be a legend among New Zealanders; seek medical assistance when you've finished boasting.

WOMEN TRAVELLERS

New Zealand is an easy and enjoyable country for women travellers, with very few hassles. Women should, however, exercise the same degree of caution as they would in any other country. Observe all the commonsense habits of safety, such as not walking through isolated urban areas (often poorly lit) alone when it's dark, not hitching alone etc.

Check out the following websites for more information: **W** www.womentravel.co.nz and **W** www.womenstravel.co.nz.

GAY & LESBIAN TRAVELLERS

Legislation decriminalising sex between consenting males over 15 was finally passed in 1985 (sex between consenting women was never a criminal act). The Human Rights Act 1993 makes it unlawful to discriminate against a person on the grounds of their sexual orientation, as regards employment, access to public places, provision of goods and services, accommodation and education facilities.

Numerous gay and lesbian organisations are found throughout the country, with the biggest concentration in Auckland. Auckland is also home to the HERO Festival held annually in February. Various cultural events are held and up to 200,000 people line the streets to witness the parade.

NZ has a Gay & Lesbian Tourism Association (☎ 0800-123 429, ☎/fax 09-374 2161, ℮ info@nzglta.org.nz, Ⓦ www.nzglta .org.nz), Private Bag MBE P255, Auckland, that promotes gay and lesbian tourism to NZ. Travel Gay New Zealand (Ⓦ www.gay travel.net.nz) is an information and reservation service covering gay destinations and accommodation. Other good websites include Ⓦ www.gaynz.com, and Ⓦ www.gay nz.net.nz/.

DISABLED TRAVELLERS

New Zealand generally caters well for disabled travellers. Most hostels, hotels, B&Bs etc have wheelchair access and disabled bathrooms, as required by law for new establishments. Many government facilities and tourist attractions are similarly equipped. Disabled travellers usually receive discounts on transport.

Enable New Zealand has a website (Ⓦ www.nzdrc.govt.nz) with links to specific organisations catering to people with disabilities, although its focus is not on travelling with disabilities.

A good contact point is the Disability Information Service (☎ 03-366 6189, fax 379 5939, ℮ dis@disinfo.co.nz) at 314 Worcester St, Christchurch.

Accessible Walks: A Guide to Scenic Walks in the South Island of NZ by Anna & Andrew Jameson is a great guide for people with a disability who want to experience some of NZ's beautiful trails.

SENIOR TRAVELLERS

Senior travellers over the age of 60 receive a discount on most transport; proof of age may be required. Discounts on entry to attractions, activities and other services may also be available, but sometimes only for NZ citizens.

Life for many NZ seniors revolves around the bowling club and the garden, but many seniors are also active. It is not uncommon to meet septuagenarians on the tramping tracks, and many clubs and activities cater for seniors. NZ retirees are out in force touring their country, often pulling a caravan or driving a motor home, and many B&Bs are run by older couples delighted to meet like-minded travellers from overseas.

TRAVEL WITH CHILDREN

NZ is an ideal country to travel with children. Health problems are not a major issue, getting around is easy and many attractions and activities cater for children. Lonely Planet's *Travel with Children* by Cathy Lanigan is a good source of information on this subject.

Family passes are usually available at theme parks and attractions. Children's prices are quoted in this book, but usually apply to children from four to 14 years of age. For children younger than four, admission is often free.

Backpacker hostels rarely cater for children, but also don't discourage them. The YHAs are better set up for families and often have specific family rooms set aside. Holiday parks are kid-friendly, often with a playground and a fenced pool.

B&Bs are mostly for couples and some even ban children. At motels and other accommodation children cost extra on top of double rates, but the charge is usually half the extra adult rate.

DANGERS & ANNOYANCES

Violent crime occurs but is not common in NZ. The newspapers report on murders and bashings in great detail, but this is more a reflection of the lack of crime (or perhaps lack of news). Auckland is the 'crime capital' of the country, but it's very safe by most international city standards. Of course, normal precautions should be taken in rough areas and around drunken yahoos on Saturday nights.

Theft, primarily from cars, can be a big problem. Don't leave any valuables in a car, either outside accommodation or, particularly, at tourist parking areas such as car parks at the start of walks. If you must leave your belongings in the car, make sure they are hidden from view, preferably in the boot.

Remember to take all the recommended precautions when tramping, especially in the mountains; see Tramping in the Activities chapter for advice on tramping safety.

New Zealand is spared from the venomous creatures you find in Australia (poisonous spiders, snakes, jellyfish etc). Sharks exist in NZ waters but are well fed by the abundant marine life and rarely pose a threat to humans. However, attacks do occasionally occur. A greater hazard in the ocean are rips or undertows, which can drag unsuspecting swimmers out to sea and are the cause of many ocean drownings. Take notice of any local warnings when swimming, surfing or diving.

LEGAL MATTERS

Marijuana (AKA 'New Zealand Green', 'electric puha' or 'dac') is widely indulged in but illegal. Don't get caught carrying the stuff – fines can be stiff. Penalties for importing illegal drugs are severe. Police periodically carry out raids on well-known growing areas (forests of the Coromandel, Northland and the East Coast of the North Island).

Despite widespread campaigns, drink-driving still seems to be a national sport, but penalties are tough. The legal drinking age is 18 (lowered from 20 in 1999), and the legal blood alcohol limit is 0.08mg per 100mL of blood. Drivers under 20 face even more stringent penalties than fully licensed drivers.

The legal dictum is pretty much 'buyer beware'. There's been so much deregulation that consumer rights are minimal and regulatory authorities, where they exist, often have little power. Fortunately most Kiwi businesses are honest.

The Commerce Commission, with offices in Auckland, Wellington and Christchurch, oversees the Fair Trading Act and can offer advice. Like most British-based legal systems, lawsuits in NZ are prohibitively expensive and weighted against small complainants – this isn't the USA.

BUSINESS HOURS

Office hours are generally from 9am to 5pm Monday to Friday. Most government offices are open from around 8.30am to 4.30pm Monday to Friday. Shops are usually open from 9am to 5.30pm Monday to Friday plus Saturday morning (9am to 12.30pm), with late-night shopping to 9pm one night of the week – usually Thursday or Friday.

Many small convenience stores (called 'dairies' in NZ) stay open for longer hours and the larger supermarkets are open until 8pm or later daily. There are also 24-hour convenience stores (such as 7-Eleven) in major cities.

PUBLIC HOLIDAYS & SPECIAL EVENTS

Public holidays include:

New Year	1–2 January
Waitangi Day	6 February
Easter	March/April
Anzac Day	25 April
Queen's Birthday	1 June
Labour Day	October
Christmas Day	25 December
Boxing Day	26 December

In addition, each province in NZ has its own anniversary day holiday (a hangover from the old days when each province was separately administered). Provincial holidays (dates can vary) include:

Wellington	22 January
Auckland	29 January
Northland	29 January
Nelson	1 February
Otago	23 March
Southland	23 March
Taranaki	31 March
Hawkes Bay	1 November
Marlborough	1 November
Westland	1 December
Canterbury	16 December

When these holidays fall between Friday and Sunday, they are usually observed on the following Monday; if they fall between Tuesday and Thursday, they are held on the preceding Monday, enabling the great tradition of the 'long weekend' to continue.

Some of the more noteworthy cultural events and festivals include:

January

Auckland Anniversary Day Regatta Auckland's biggest yacht race

Summer City Program Two months of festivals and entertainment around the city of Wellington (beginning of January to end of February)

World Buskers Festival Annual event featuring street performers in Christchurch

February

Marlborough Food & Wine Festival Montana Estate near Blenheim (2nd weekend)

Art Deco Festival Balls, dinners, fancy dress and Art Deco tours of Napier (3rd weekend)

International Festival of the Arts A month of national and international culture, Wellington (even-numbered years only)

Harvest Hawkes Bay Wine and food celebration near Hastings

March

Golden Shears Sheep Shearing Competition A major sheep-related event, Masterton

Ngaruawahia Regatta Maori canoe race, north of Hamilton

Wildfoods Festival Tasty and healthy wild food from the land, sea and air. Held in Hokitika

Pasifika Polynesian Festival Traditional arts, entertainment, sports and food celebrating Auckland's Pacific communities

April

International Trout-fishing Tournaments Held on Lake Taupo on Anzac Day

Highland Games Hastings

June

NZ Agricultural Field Days A major agricultural show at Mystery Creek near Hamilton

September

NZ Trout Festival Fishing contest, Rotorua

World of Wearable Art Award Off-beat fashion show in Nelson

Bay of Islands Wine & food festival held in Paihia and Waitangi

November

Canterbury Show Week Christchurch

December

Festival of Lights Light-up of New Plymouth and Pukekura Park over Christmas

There are smaller annual events held all over NZ. Each town seems to have its annual fair (or show), often involving simple sports like wheelbarrow and sugar bag races, wood chopping and sheep-shearing contests.

COURSES

People from around the world, especially Asia and the Pacific countries, come to NZ to study English. Typically each language school arranges for its students to live with NZ families, so that English is used outside as well as inside the classroom. Schools also arrange a variety of extracurricular evening and weekend activities for students.

Auckland has the highest concentration of language schools, but there are a few in other parts of the country as well. The Auckland Travel & Information Centre keeps a complete, up-to-date list.

Those wishing to learn Maori can do so at polytechnics in the major towns, many of which run evening courses.

Jade (known as greenstone) and hardstone carving is also popular, and an excellent course is run at Tai Poutini Polytechnic in Greymouth. More accessible to travellers is the Just Jade Experience in Hokitika (see The West Coast chapter). One-day courses in bone carving are common around New Zealand, but are more about creating a finished piece than learning a skill. In Kaitaia (Northland) you can do courses in flax weaving as well as bone- and wood-carving at the Maori cultural centre.

WORK

New Zealand has a moderately high unemployment rate, so it's fussy about foreigners taking jobs from its citizens. However, there is quite a bit of casual or temp work around – mainly in the fields of agriculture (fruit picking, farming etc), hospitality, ski resorts and, in Auckland at least, office-based work in IT, banking and finance, and telemarketing.

An ordinary visitor permit or visa does not give you the right to work in NZ. Farmers will often turn a blind eye to this if they're desperate for casual workers, but don't count on it. Apply for a work permit before arriving in NZ or within the country at any NZ Immigration Service office. Generally, you need to be sponsored by an employer with an offer of definite employment in an occupation that is in demand. The exception is with working holiday visas (see Visas & Documents earlier); Australians can work without a visa.

Seasonal fruit picking, thinning, pruning and harvesting is readily available and popular short-term work for visitors. Apples, kiwi fruit and other types of fruit and vegetables are picked in summer and early autumn (December-May); pay rates are low ($8 to $12 an hour) so many New Zealanders won't touch this work, and in many cases farmers are crying out for workers. The main picking season is from around January to April, though there may be some agricultural work year-round on the 'Harvest Trail'. Picking is hard work and you are usually paid according to the amount you pick.

Places where you may find picking work include the Bay of Islands (Kerikeri and Paihia), rural Auckland, Tauranga, Gisborne and Hawkes Bay (Napier and Hastings) in the North Island; Nelson (Tapawera and Golden Bay), Marlborough (around Blenheim) and Central Otago (Alexandra and Roxburgh) in the South Island. The best way to find work is to approach the employers directly, or stay at hostels or camping grounds in the picking areas that specialise in helping travellers to find work.

Working at ski resorts, or in the towns servicing them during the season, is the goal of many travellers. Not only do you get to ski during your time off, but you can immerse yourself in the party atmosphere that inevitably goes with winter sports resorts. Available work includes bar tending, waiting tables, cleaning, working on ski tows and, if you're properly qualified, ski or snowboard instructing. A good place to start looking for work is on the websites of the resorts themselves. Most have a section on availability of work and the requirements for particular jobs. Start inquiring

well before the start of the season – or take your chances just before the season opens and ask around at the resort towns.

Seasonal Work NZ (**W** www.seasonal work.co.nz) is an excellent resource with a database of thousands of casual jobs. It gives the contact details of employers looking for workers, rates of pay and suitable nearby accommodation.

Auckland has several job agencies that can help you find work, including some set up specifically for travellers, such as the Job Search Centre at Auckland Central Backpackers.

WWOOF An economical way of travelling around and doing some voluntary work (for which no visa is required) is joining Willing Workers on Organic Farms (WWOOF). Membership provides you with a list of some 600 organic farms, permaculture farms, market gardens and other environmentally sound cottage industries throughout the country where, in exchange for your few hours of work a day, the owner will provide food, accommodation and some hands-on experience in organic farming. You must contact the farm owner or manager by telephone or letter; you cannot simply turn up at a farm without warning.

WWOOF is an established international organisation represented in Australia, Britain, Europe, Canada and the USA. To join WWOOF and receive the booklet, phone ☎ 03-544 9890, (**e** support@wwoof .co.nz), write to PO Box 1172, Nelson, or complete an online application form (**W** www.wwoof.co.nz). Membership for a year is $30, or $40 a couple.

Bunac For citizens of the USA, where it's not possible to get a normal working holiday visa for New Zealand, Bunac (**W** www .bunac.com) is an alternative. Its *Work New Zealand* programme is similar to the working holiday scheme in that American citizens aged 18 to 30 can apply for a 12-month visa that allows work and travel. The cost is US$450, which includes support such as arrival orientation, help with finding jobs, accommodation (the first two nights are included) and getting the visa in the first place. Apply on-line through their website.

AgriVenture AgriVenture offers farming and horticultural exchanges to people from Australia, Canada, USA, Europe and Japan, for stays of up to 15 months. Visas, jobs (which are regarded as 'traineeships') and accommodation with a host family are arranged in advance and you don't necessarily need an agricultural background to apply. The NZ office for AgriVenture is PO Box 20113 Bishopdale, Christchurch, New Zealand, ☎ 03- 359 0407, fax 03-359 0408, e nz@agiventure.com, W www.agriven ture.com.

ACCOMMODATION

New Zealand is well endowed with accommodation for all budgets but it's essential to book ahead at peak times: the summer holidays from Christmas to the end of January, Easter, and winter in resort towns like Queenstown and Wanaka. At these times prices rise, and finding a room can be difficult.

Accommodation guides are available from visitors centres, and include the free *AA Accommodation New Zealand Guide* (W www.aaguides.co.nz), a 1000-plus-page listing of camping grounds, hotels, motels and guesthouses around the country; *New Zealand Camping Guide*; *Jason's Holiday Parks* (W www.jasons.co.nz); and *B&B Directory of New Zealand*.

Visitor centres have lists of all types of accommodation in their areas, often with illustrations to help in your choice, and can make bookings for you. These places are usually paying members of the local tourist association.

Camping & Cabins

Kiwi commercial camping grounds (sometimes called motor camps but usually 'holiday parks') offer a range of facilities for tent campers, caravans and campervans, plus cabins of varying degrees of luxury.

Holiday parks are found all over the country and often in prime locations. In the major cities they're usually some distance from the centre but in smaller towns they can be very central, or near lakes, beaches, rivers and forests. Most have well-equipped communal kitchens and dining areas and some have games and TV rooms – great places to meet other travellers, both Kiwis and overseas visitors.

Camp or caravan sites are usually charged at a per-person rate, typically around $9 to $12 per adult (half-price for children) but rates may be for a minimum of two people (especially powered sites and definitely during peak periods). Unpowered sites are usually only a dollar or two cheaper than powered sites.

At most sites the kitchen and showers are free but a few have coin-operated hotplates and hot showers. At most sites laundry facilities are coin operated ($2).

DOC Camping Grounds DOC operates over 120 camping grounds around NZ, often in beautiful, isolated locations. Its camping grounds are in reserves and national parks, maritime parks, forest parks and farm parks – DOC offices have lists.

Standard DOC camping grounds are basic, with minimal facilities that include cold running water, toilets and fireplaces, but they also have minimal charges (around $3 to $6 per adult). Informal camping grounds are free, but have almost no facilities, apart from a cold-water tap and places to pitch tents. Some DOC camping grounds are fully serviced and have on-site managers.

Standard and informal camping grounds operate on a first-come, first-served basis, and fees are paid by a self-registration system. Since the low fees are used for the maintenance of the camping grounds, it's important to pay them (usually into an honesty box) even when there's no warden.

The DOC also operates numerous back-country huts, most of which can only be reached on foot. See Tramping in the Activities chapter for more information.

Cabins & Self-Contained Units Many camping grounds and holiday parks also have cabins. Standard cabins are simply freestanding rooms with bare mattresses.

You provide your own sleeping gear (a sleeping bag is fine) or linen can usually be hired. They're cheap enough at around $25 to $30 for two people.

Some motor camps also offer hostel-style bunkrooms, often a cabin with four or more dorm beds, but they are cheap at around $14 per person and often empty. Better-equipped cabins are called kitchen cabins or self-contained units. Closer to motel standard, they have kitchens and/or en suite and may be serviced, with linen provided. On-site caravans (trailer homes in US parlance) are another camping-ground possibility but are not as common these days and are generally old, run-down vans.

Hostels

New Zealand has some of the best back-packer hostels in the world. Several hundred hostels around the country offer dorm beds, usually for around $15 to $20 a night (typically $18). Bunkrooms may be for 10 or more people but most places these days are moving towards smaller dorms or 'share rooms' with three or four beds, and some are mercifully even doing away with the bunks. Some hostels provide bedding (a duvet or blankets) free, but most charge a couple of dollars extra, or you can use your own sleeping bag.

Almost all hostels have at least a few twin or double rooms ($40 to $50) with bedding provided and some even have en suite rooms ($50 to $60). Sometimes single rooms (about $30 to $35) are offered, though they are rare and, unless the place is empty or it's low season, you'll have to pay for a double.

Backpacker hostels usually have a fully equipped kitchen with fridge space for your food, a common lounge area, a reception desk, male and female bathroom facilities, laundry, a phone and Internet access. Many also have spa pools (often free), use of bikes and kayaks, a garden or backyard with barbecue area, TV and video room and some even have an attached cafe or bar. They range from small, homestay-style back-packers with just a few beds, to the enormous multistorey hostels you'll find in central Auckland and Wellington.

If you're a Kiwi travelling in your own country, be warned that some hostel owners only admit overseas travellers. This happens more in the cities where hostels may have had trouble with locals bothering their guests (and, they say, security is another important issue as thefts from rooms do occur). If you encounter this sort of discrimination, you can either try another hostel or insist that you are a genuine traveller and not just looking for a cheap place to crash. Having a YHA/VIP/BBH card might help.

YHA (HI) The Youth Hostels Association (YHA) now goes under the banner of Hostelling International (HI), but the term YHA is still commonly used in NZ. YHA hostels are notionally only open to members, but nonmembers simply pay an extra $3 a night and after 10 nights stay at any hostel you become a full member. You can join the YHA in your home country, or in NZ at any YHA hostel for $30 a year for foreign travellers ($40 for Kiwis, under 17 free). Throughout this guide we quote the rates for *members*.

New Zealand currently has 58 YHA hostels (or associate-YHAs), which are invariably clean and maintain a high standard. The main drawback is office hours, which can be sporadic at best (except in the city YHAs). Rooms are sometimes closed completely during the afternoon.

The head office of the YHA in New Zealand is PO Box 436, Christchurch (☎ 03-379 9970, fax 365 4476, e info@ yha.org.nz, W www.yha.co.nz).

Independent Backpackers Along with Australia, New Zealand has long led the world in the independent backpacker hostel market and nearly every town or tourist area has at least one or two private backpackers – large cities have 20 plus.

These backpackers have similar facilities and prices to YHAs – a communal kitchen, laundry, dining area and lounge area – but they tend to be a little more casual and vary a lot in character. Some have unpowered sites available at $8 to $10 per person.

The biggest group by far is Budget Backpacker Hostels or BBH (☎ 03-379 3014, W www.backpack.co.nz), which is growing as fast as new places are opening up. It has around 300 hostels, including homestays and farmstays under its umbrella. Membership costs $40 (the membership card doubles as a phonecard with $20 worth of calls) and entitles you to stay at any of the member hostels at the set rates advertised in the BBH book. Nonmembers, in theory, pay an extra fee of between $1 and $4, but not all hostel owners bother with this and in some cases you're not even asked if you're a BBH member. We've quoted the full (nonmember) prices throughout this book. If you're planning on staying at backpacker hostels it definitely pays to get a BBH card. The card, and the book, can be picked up at any member hostel.

BBH has an innovative ratings system given to each hostel by travellers. A census-style survey is conducted throughout the country on one night of the year (in January or February), when hostel guests can rate (on a simple scale of 1 to 10) not only the place they are staying in but other hostels they have stayed in. The resulting information is distilled into a percentage figure which, in theory, tells you how good – or at least how popular – a particular hostel is. While the system is generally pretty accurate, our experience has been that some highly rated hostels are not that great, and some lowly rated places are not that bad.

The other major group is VIP Backpackers Resorts (☎ 09-827 6016, W www.vip.co.nz), which represents around 80 hostels, particularly in the cities and major tourist spots. An advantage with VIP is that it's international, with a huge network of hostels in Australia, Southern Africa, Europe, America and some in Fiji. With the $35 VIP card you get $1 off the listed accommodation price and various other discounts. Pick up a copy of the free VIP accommodation book at hostels or visitor centres.

Another group is Nomads Backpackers (W www.nomadsworld.com), which currently has 14 member hostels. Again the discount card ($30) gives you $1 off and membership includes hostels in Australia and Vietnam.

B&Bs & Guesthouses

Bed & breakfast (B&B) accommodation in private homes is by far the biggest category of accommodation, with a wide range of B&Bs found around the country, from isolated hamlets to inner cities.

Although breakfast is part of the deal at genuine B&B places, it may or may not feature at guesthouses. Breakfast may be 'continental' (ie, cereal, toast, tea or coffee) or a substantial cooked meal of eggs, bacon, toast, fruit, tea and coffee. Many guesthouses are in the vein of English B&Bs and pride themselves on the size, quality and 'traditional value' of their breakfasts. If you like to start the day heartily it's worth considering this when comparing prices.

Guesthouses may be spartan, cheap, 'private' (unlicensed) hotels. Most are comfortable, relaxed, low-key places, patronised by people who don't enjoy the impersonal atmosphere of many motels. Others are very fancy indeed and some have self-contained rooms with private en suite and kitchenette, so that you can enjoy privacy and the family-home atmosphere.

Guesthouses and B&Bs usually start at around $40 a single (if available), or $60 a double – that will get you a standard room with a shared bathroom. Doubles with a bathroom start at around $80. Really luxurious B&Bs can cost well over $130.

Farmstays (Farm Holidays)

New Zealand has been called the world's most efficient farm, so farmstays are one way of understanding the real NZ. Many offer guests the chance to 'have a go' at all the typical farm activities and be treated as one of the household. Choose from dairy, sheep, high country, cattle or mixed-farming farms, or even orchards.

Costs vary widely. Some have rooms in the homestead for $100 or more a double, including meals, but most offer B&B for more like $60 to $80 per day. Some farms have separate cottages where you fix your own food. Others have backpacker-style shared accommodation so you can stay cheaply. Information centres have listings, and we include some places in this guide.

Farm Hosting in NZ (FHINZ; ☎ 06-376 4582), at Kumeroa Lodge Stud, RD1 Woodville, produces a booklet ($15) that lists farms throughout NZ providing lodging in exchange for four hours work per day. Rural Holidays NZ (☎ 03-355 6218, W www.ruralhols.co.nz) lists farmstays and homestays throughout the country on its website.

Motels
New Zealand motels are typical of motels throughout the Western world. They are usually made up of ground-floor units with off-street parking and are found in major towns and holiday areas, often lining the highway into and out of town. Many motel units have fully equipped kitchens, though some studio units only have a fridge, and tea- and coffee-making equipment. All have en suite and for a little extra you can usually get one and two-bedroom family units. Some motels have swimming pools and most have a coin-operated laundry.

Some NZ motels date from the 1960s and look like it. Though comfortable enough, they are drab, prefabricated affairs. Newer motels are often cheap constructions but usually brighter with better decor, and some are definitely luxurious.

However, with motels you generally pay for what you get. Old-fashioned no-frills places cost around $50 to $60 a double, then $15 for each extra person. Mid-range motel rooms are around $70 to $90 a double, and the more luxurious places charge from $100 and up. The difference in price between a single or double occupancy, if there is one, is usually minimal (perhaps $5) so they're definitely better value for couples. In tourist towns, motels can really hike prices in the peak season, but often discount in the off season.

Pubs & Hotels
Many traditional, older-style pubs – also called hotels – have rooms upstairs, but they are often just a sideline enterprise and the main emphasis is on the bar. At the cheapest pubs, singles/doubles might cost as little as $25/35 (with a shared bathroom probably a long way down the hall), though $35/50 is more common. Some old pubs, especially in small country towns, have a lot of character; others are noisy, grotty places best avoided, especially by solo women travellers.

At the other end of the scale are the five-star hotels in the big cities – the Hiltons, Novotels, Sheratons et al. There are no surprises here. The only thing to remember is that with weekend specials, seasonal discounts and other deals, you'll virtually never pay the standard quoted 'rack rates'. Rooms in these hotels cost from around $140 to well over $200 a double.

Holiday Homes & Cottages
The basic Kiwi holiday home is called a 'bach' (short for bachelor as they were often used by single men as hunting and fishing retreats). In the deep south of the South Island they're known as 'cribs'. These are simple self-contained cottages that can be rented in many country areas, often well away from more conventional types of accommodation. They can be good for longer stays in one area, although many can be rented for only one or two nights. Prices are usually reasonable – typically $60 to $120, which, for a whole house or self-contained bungalow, is good value.

The popularity of such accommodation has resulted in more upmarket cottages being built in some beautiful locations. They're nowhere near as rustic and are more likely to be rented on a short term basis, but they're great for a splurge – expect to pay from $100 to $400 a double.

There is also the possibility of swapping homes temporarily with people from another country. The contact is Worldwide Home Exchange Club, 18–20 London Rd, Tunbridge Wells, Kent TN1 1YL, England.

FOOD
New Zealand is no longer in culinary no-person's land. The preparation of food was

once ruled by strict adherence to the *Edmond's Cookery Book*, a slavish reflection of Anglo-Saxon stodge. Over the last 10 years the NZ food scene has taken off like a rocket salad – the country is fast approaching the point where it can boast a distinctly Kiwi cuisine. This is often referred to as Pacific Rim, a term as broad in its definition as Mediterranean or Asian.

There's no doubt that the styles of Asia, Europe and other parts of the Pacific have been plundered with abandon. The borrowings, however, have been gloriously applied to New Zealand's fresh produce, especially the abundant and varied seafoods.

Almost every town in a tourist area will have an upmarket brasserie, cafe or restaurant that features Kiwi cuisine, especially towns close to the coastline.

You could expect, depending on the season, such delights as a lamb burger with vegetables and prosciutto, yellow-fin tuna and wasabi caviar salad, pork fillets filled with kumara and apple stuffing accompanied by spinach pilaf, paua risotto with crayfish stock, oysters in seaweed tempura batter, tuatua and pumpkin fritters, feijoa or kiwi-fruit ice cream.

It's not surprising that in these dishes there is more than a smattering of seafood. Green-lipped mussels, available all over NZ, are easily the best in the world and cheap. Oyster fans shouldn't leave NZ without tasting the superb oysters (the best come from Bluff on the South Island). Scallops are also good eating. Crayfish (lobster) is a speciality in some areas, though much of it is exported and it can be hard to find. Kaikoura is the best place in NZ to find fresh crayfish at reasonable prices (about $60 a kilo). Other exotics include the now-rare and expensive shellfish toheroa, or the slightly less pricey tuatua.

Saltwater fish favourites include hoki, hapuka, groper, snapper, John Dory, kingfish and orange roughie. NZ also has good freshwater fish – with incredibly large rainbow and brown trout – in rivers and lakes all over the country. You can't buy trout in the shops but there are many opportunities to catch one yourself. Eels, plentiful in NZ's rivers and creeks, are another local delicacy, especially smoked eel.

Meats such as lamb (a NZ staple), pork and beef are still readily available, but treated with much more flair these days. You can have them with roast vegetables (as Kiwis did in the old days) or embellish them with exotic sauces and accompany them with innovative salads. Cervena (venison) is a regular feature on many menus.

There was also a time when a trip to the supermarket or dairy yielded nothing but white bread, cheddar cheese and instant coffee. These days you don't have to shop around too much to find a French bread stick, brioche, ciabatta or bagel; a fantastic variety of cheeses from Kikurangi creamy blue to Legato goats' cheese (and there are quite a few boutique cheese factories to visit); and cafes serving good coffee abound.

NZ took an obscure fruit, the Chinese gooseberry, and marketed it internationally as 'kiwi fruit'. It's now grown worldwide, but NZ produces the largest and juiciest variety, and it's still a perennial feature on Kiwi cuisine menus. Other exotic fruits, such as nashi, persimmons and the sweet, highly perfumed feijoa, are included in restaurant menus.

One thing you won't see much in New Zealand is Maori or Polynesian restaurants – not even in Auckland. The best way to experience traditional Maori cooking is to attend a *hangi*, usually put on for tourists. The best place is Rotorua.

Takeaway Food

Fish and chips (also known as 'fush and chups' – rest assured the Kiwis have heard that one before!) is an English institution that NZ excels at. Not only can you get some superb fresh fish, deep fried in batter, but fish and chip shops also offer mussels, scallops, oysters, paua fritters and other seafood delights. Try kumara (sweet potato) chips for a variation.

New Zealanders are just about as besotted with the meat pie as Australians but they probably do a better job of them. The NZ meat pie must, by law, have no more than 25% offal content. In Australia up to 75% is permitted. The Kiwis win this one! For variation you can often get venison pies and scallop pies.

The larger towns have pie carts, generally open from late at night to first thing in the morning. Look out for the White Lady in Shortland St, Auckland, and the Roadside Diner in Nelson. They no longer serve pies with pea & 'pud' (mashed potato), the source of their name.

Cities have the usual fast-food suspects, including those symbols of US culinary imperialism: McDonald's, Pizza Hut and KFC.

Cafes & Tearooms

New Zealand's traditional cafes or coffee shops, called tearooms, are nothing to get excited about, and in any case they're on the way out, getting steam-rolled by trendy European-style cafes. If you find a tearoom it will usually be in a small country town and will offer inexpensive fare such as Devonshire teas and sandwiches, possibly served by a little old lady. There will come a time when people will seek these places out as quaint reminders of the past!

The big growth industry in larger cities and tourist areas has been fashionable cafes. These places have proliferated offering steaming espresso machines, enthusiastic young staff and slightly off-beat menus. These cafes serve all types of coffee, fruit smoothies, croissants, salads, baked focaccia with a variety of fillings and sinfully rich desserts. City cafes are also often popular late-night hang-outs for espresso or wine, light meals and music.

Wellington has probably the best cafe scene in New Zealand, with Auckland (Ponsonby) and Dunedin not far behind, but it's amazing the streetside cafe culture you'll find in previously culture-less towns, from the Coromandel to the South Island's West Coast.

The downside is that the cost of eating out in a cafe is going up.

Pubs & Restaurants

Pubs still offer some of the best value for money, but the days of cheap counter meals for $5 have more or less died out. Many pubs have bistro meals – simple but hearty food such as schnitzel, steak, roasts or fish with chips and salad or coleslaw. Average main courses range from $8 to $15 and they are usually good value, though you'll find that pubs are increasingly moving towards more restaurant-style dining and corresponding prices.

If you fancy a night out with a good meal, a bottle of wine and table service, just about every sizable town has one or two decent restaurants. The main cities have a variety of international cuisines and top quality restaurants.

Menus in better NZ restaurants almost invariably feature venison (very much a NZ game meat), lamb, beef and fish dishes. Even in the countryside, you will find some real gems, but expect to pay $18 to $25 or more for a main course in better restaurants. With an entree (appetiser), dessert and drinks, a meal in a good restaurant will cost around $50 per person.

Fully licensed restaurants are the norm, but some restaurants are still BYO, where you 'bring your own' alcohol. In most cases (especially if the restaurant is also licensed) this means wine only, and a corkage charge of $2 usually applies.

Vegetarian New Zealand is traditionally a meat-and-veg society, with the veg being an accompaniment. Consequently, vegetarian restaurants are not particularly widespread, but you'll certainly find a few good ones in the main cities, and in 'alternative' communities such as Golden Bay, west of Nelson, and the Coromandel Peninsula, where there's a tendency towards organic foods.

Auckland, Christchurch and Wellington have several cheap and excellent vegetarian restaurants, including Food for Life, run by the Hare Krishnas.

The website **w** www.vegdining.com has a listing for NZ veg and vegan restaurants, but the best source of information is the New Zealand Vegetarian Society (**☎** 09-523 4686, **w** www.ivu.org/nzvs), based in Epsom, Auckland. The website lists good vegetarian restaurants in NZ.

Self-Catering

As many places to stay provide cooking facilities for guests, buying and cooking your own food will save you a lot of money travelling around NZ.

NZ has several large supermarket chains – Pak N Save, New World and Woolworth's for example – usually open until around 8pm seven days a week. Large supermarkets are found in the cities and towns that serve a large rural community.

DRINKS
Beer

New Zealanders are great drinkers, and both the beer and the pubs are pretty good. Almost all the beer is now brewed by only two companies, New Zealand Breweries and Dominion Breweries (DB). Steinlager, the various types of DB (Bitter, Export etc) and Lion Red are probably the most popular beers. In the deep south, Speights is a popular label, and on the West Coast Monteith's (which, controversially, shifted to Auckland in 2001) is a wonderful brew.

Small boutique breweries or microbrewers are sprouting in many cities and towns, and they make beer sampling around New Zealand a pleasure. Rather than settle for the homogenous styles of the larger breweries, they use a variety of hops, barley and rye to produce more European-style flavours. Probably the best of the boutique beers are from Marlborough and Nelson – Pink Elephant, Mac's, Founders and others. 'Dark' drinkers will appreciate the Black Mac.

If your constitution is up to it seek out Hooker's Ale, a beer with a kick like an enraged moa. Other widely available boutique beers are Emersons (an organic brew from Dunedin), Harringtons (Christchurch), Hawkes Bay Roosters, Miners (West Coast) and Sunshine (Gisborne). Quite often you'll discover a pub that brews its own beer – the Mussel Inn near Takaka, Pines Tavern in the Bay Islands, the Cork & Keg in Renwick, and lots of others. If you're a beer lover it's always worth giving these a go.

In a pub the cheapest beer is on tap. You can ask for a 'seven', originally seven fluid ounces but now a 200mL glass, the closest metric equivalent; a 'twelve' is a 12-fluid ounce glass (350mL); a 'handle' is a half-litre or litre mug with a handle and often called a pint or half-pint (old ways die hard); or a jug, which is just that.

The legal drinking age is 18.

Wine

New Zealand has a thriving wine industry and many wineries have established international reputations, particularly for their whites (the climate is not as good for reds).

The best-known wine-producing regions are Marlborough, noted for its sauvignon blanc, and Hawkes Bay, noted for its chardonnay. Other notable areas are Henderson and Waiheke Island near Auckland, Martinborough in the Wairarapa, Hawkes Bay, Gisborne, Blenheim in the Marlborough region of the South Island (NZ's largest), the Waipara Valley near Christchurch, and Central Otago. Winery visits and tours are popular in these places and most offer free wine tasting or ask a small fee which is waived if you buy wine. New wineries are constantly opening, as NZ wine continues to achieve international recognition and the interest in wine-touring increases – see Wine Touring in the Activities chapter for more information. You can pick up a half-decent bottle of NZ wine in a supermarket or bottle shop for around $12 to $15. At the cellar door, expect to pay closer to $20.

An unusual NZ speciality is kiwi fruit wine. There are lots of different varieties – still and bubbly, sweet and dry – and even a liqueur. You may not like it, but NZ is the best place to try it. Another unusual fruit wine is fejoia.

ENTERTAINMENT

New Zealand has an energetic nightlife scene in the major cities – namely Auckland, Wellington, Christchurch, Dunedin and to a lesser extent Nelson and Napier – but not much in the small towns, where everything seems to shut with a bang after dark (except perhaps the local pub). Tourist resorts also have a party atmosphere during the summer when Kiwis are holidaying, and winter resort towns like Queenstown

ALEXANDER TURNBULL LIBRARY, WELLINGTON NZ

Unknown female rugby team (photographer unknown, circa 1930)

have some of the most debauched nightlife around.

Auckland has a fairly cosmopolitan and sophisticated nightlife with everything from waterfront champagne bars, jazz clubs, comedy venues and rock music venues to dance clubs.

Most sizable towns have a cinema and some are interesting in themselves (eg, Takaka's alternative Village Theatre and Wanaka's fabulous Cinema Paradiso), and the cities have big complexes such as Hoyts, as well as a couple of art-house theatres.

Live theatre is also popular and Wellington has a very active group of professional theatres. Christchurch has a couple, with the Court Theatre in the Arts Centre being the most famous. In the larger cities there are regular performances by the New Zealand Symphony Orchestra, the National Ballet, and operatic and chamber music groups. There are opportunities to see a Maori cultural performance in towns such as Rotorua, Queenstown, Paihia, and at Auckland.

Dunedin, with its large student population, has a vibrant live-music scene and is probably NZ's live music and pubbing capital. Many of Wellington's plethora of cafes also feature live music.

SPECTATOR SPORTS

Rugby union – and the national team, the All Blacks – is practically a national mania (see the boxed text). Cricket takes a distant second place but is the main summer sport. NZ also excels at hockey and netball, although these sports attract fewer spectators.

As you travel you'll see rugby matches played everywhere by teams of all ages and both sexes. In rugby season, when they're not playing, they're inside watching it on television. A variant of the game, rugby league, is also very popular.

All cities have major stadiums, where you can see top national, and sometimes international, rugby and league teams. Just front up to a game (usually on a Saturday or Sunday in winter) and buy a ticket at the gate.

Rugby – A National Obsession

No book about NZ would be complete without mention of the national obsession – rugby union football. It's not exaggerating to say that no other country is as closely associated with the game as NZ, and no other game is as much a part of New Zealanders' lives as rugby!

New Zealand Rugby's Fame Around the world, even countries that don't play rugby know that NZ does, and even people who couldn't name three New Zealanders to save themselves can tell you that the All Blacks are NZ's national rugby team.

So why the All Black's so-very-high profile? They're good – sure. In fact, they're the world's most consistently high-performing team: historically, only South Africa nears NZ's international win rate. Every decade since rugby union's international beginnings in the 1890s, the All Blacks have been placed in the world's top few teams. They're the only team to have played in the semifinals for every rugby union world cup. However the All Blacks are naturally not *always* the world's best team – for the past four years the Wallabies (Australia) have probably held that position. Still, the All Black's fame persists even through those times of poorer performance because of the permanent mystique associated with the team – the *haka*, the fanatical supporters and those blacker-than-black jerseys. As Gareth Edwards (Welsh halfback) once said: 'There is something about the blackness of an All Black jersey which sends a shudder through your heart. Fifteen of them look dark and sinful; eight snorting bulls and seven black panthers'.

Even when the All Blacks aren't playing at their best, even at times that they're ranked internationally as low as third or (gasp) fourth, that mystique and those black jerseys ensure that they're still the team against which every other national team wants to play, and the team against which every team measures their performance.

Rugby in New Zealand Surprisingly, rugby is not NZ's most popular sport for participants – more men play golf or cricket these days and of course netball is the choice for most women (although over 10,000 NZ women do play rugby!). However rugby is still the *dominant* sport in NZ. No other sport pervades NZ culture so deeply or is the topic of so much discussion.

It's often joked that NZ's prime minister holds the country's third-most important position, after the All Blacks' captain and coach. Certainly there would be few New Zealanders who didn't know

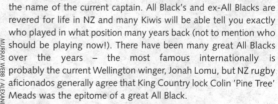

the name of the current captain. All Black's and ex-All Blacks are revered for life in NZ and many Kiwis will be able tell you exactly who played in what position many years back (not to mention who should be playing now!). There have been many great All Blacks over the years – the most famous internationally is probably the current Wellington winger, Jonah Lomu, but NZ rugby aficionados generally agree that King Country lock Colin 'Pine Tree' Meads was the epitome of a great All Black.

When the All Blacks are doing well, NZ's spirits lift, and when the All Blacks are doing poorly, NZ plunges into a mini-depression. That's not mere hyperbole; NZ's economy has actually been known to dip slightly when the Men in Black drop the ball. NZ's semifinal loss to France in the 1999 Rugby World Cup, according to some commentators, even contributed to the change in government in a national election that year.

New Zealanders take their rugby *very* seriously!

MURRAY WEBB / ALEXANDER TURNBULL LIBRARY WELLINGTON NZ

Sean Fitzpatrick

Errol Hunt

If you want to see some really high-quality rugby you should spoil yourself and go watch one of the big games – the All Blacks, a Super-12 match or any top-of-the-first-division clash. The main venues are Eden Park in Auckland, the Caketin (WestpacTrust Stadium) in Wellington, Jade Stadium in Christchurch, Carisbrooke in Dunedin, and Waikato Stadium in Hamilton.

Alternatively, it could be just as much fun, and considerably cheaper, to watch a passionate big-city club match or a third-division game at one of the smaller regional centres – such as West Coast versus North Otago at Greymouth's Rugby Park.

New Zealand hosts an international tennis open, played at Auckland's ASB Bank Tennis Centre in January, though it doesn't attract huge names since it's not a Grand Slam or big money event.

New Zealanders are also big punters and breed fine racehorses. Almost every town worth its salt has a racetrack with weekend meets at various times of year. The main racecourse in Auckland is at Ellerslie.

SHOPPING

You may not go to NZ intending to come back with a backpack full of souvenirs – a photograph of some flawless moment may be your best reminder – but there are some things worth checking out.

Maori Artworks

If you're planning to buy any Maori artwork, have a look at the later 'Maori Culture & Arts' colour section.

Woollen Goods

There are so many sheep in New Zealand that it's hardly surprising that you can find beautiful woollen gear, particularly jumpers (sweaters) made from hand-spun, hand-dyed wool. Hand-knitted jumpers are something of an art form in NZ and although not cheap – around $150 to $300 – they are of the highest quality. Other knitted goods include hats, gloves, scarves and mufflers.

Woollen Swann-Dri jackets, shirts and pullovers are so practical and warm that they're just about the NZ national garment in the countryside, especially for farmers and hunters. Most common are the red-and-black or blue-and-black plaid ones. You can buy Swann-Dris (affectionately called 'Swannies') in outdoor-gear shops and again, though not cheap, they're top quality and should keep you warm for at least the next decade.

Activities

New Zealand is the ultimate Great Outdoors. Not only is there plenty of space and terrain for all sorts of activities – from oceans and lakes to mountains and wilderness forest – but it's compact enough to make all these environments very accessible. Kiwis themselves are great outdoor enthusiasts and there are plenty of facilities and operators to help you get involved in any activity imaginable.

Nothing is off limits, and the Kiwis and their visitors move over or through land, air and water in just about every way possible. They jetboat, white-water sledge, raft, boogie board, canoe, kayak, surf, surf raft, scuba dive and ski through the water; they bungy jump, parapente, skydive, abseil, fly, helicopter and barrel roll through the air; and they tramp, mountain bike, ski, horse ride, rock climb, 'zorb' and ice climb across terra firma. Beneath the surface, caving, cave rafting, *tomo* (hole or entrance to a cave) exploring and hydro-sliding are all pursued.

The various adrenaline-pumping activities do have an element of risk. Perceived danger is part of the thrill and travellers should be aware that adventure sports, particularly rafting and kayaking on fast-flowing rivers, do entail risk. Chances of a mishap are perhaps minuscule, but make sure that the company you choose takes adequate safety precautions. In New Zealand the laws regarding adventure operator liability are not really weighted in favour of the consumer. If an accident occurs and you are injured, the best thing you can hope for is adequate travel insurance.

TRAMPING

Tramping (that's Kiwi talk for bushwalking, hiking or trekking) is the best way to experience NZ's natural beauty. The country has thousands of kilometres of tracks – many well marked, some only a line on the map. Tramping is made easy by NZ's excellent network of huts, enabling trampers to avoid lugging tents and (in some cases) cooking gear.

This section should open your eyes to the possibilities of tramping, however before attempting any track you should consult the appropriate authority (usually the Department of Conservation, or DOC) for the latest information. The so-called Great Walks are the most popular tracks. Their beauty does indeed make them worth experiencing, but please don't go and then be disappointed that they are crowded. Of *course* these tracks are sometimes crowded, especially in summer, when people from all over the world come to tramp. On the Milford Track the number of walkers is restricted and you have to book your tramp for specific days well in advance.

The most walked tracks in NZ are the Abel Tasman Coastal Track, the Routeburn, Milford, Tongariro Northern Circuit (and the one-day Tongariro Crossing), the Kepler and Lake Waikaremoana. Surprisingly, most people on these tracks are from outside NZ. Kiwis do tramp, but they tend to avoid the popular tracks, making use of local knowledge rather than posted tracks, or seeking the really wild and untouched regions.

If you want to avoid the crowds, DOC (W www.doc.govt.nz) offices and park headquarters can advise and help you plan some enjoyable walks on lesser known tracks. DOC offices are in every city and in dozens of towns, and give free information about tramping in their areas.

When to Go

The busiest season is during the school summer holidays, two weeks before Christmas until the end of January – a good period to avoid if you can. The best weather is from January to March, though most tracks can be walked enjoyably any time from about October to April. June and July, mid-winter, is not the time to be out on the tracks, especially at altitude – some are closed in winter because of avalanche danger.

NEW ZEALAND PARKS

THE 9 GREAT WALKS OF NEW ZEALAND

North Island
Lake Waikaremoana Track
Tongariro Northern Circuit
Whanganui Journey

South Island
Abel Tasman Coastal Track
Heaphy Track
Kepler Track
Milford Track
Routeburn Track
Rakiura Track

Kaitaia

Bay of Islands
Maritime &
Historic Park

Poor Knights
Islands Marine
Reserve

Northland
Forest Park

Whangarei

Hauraki Gulf
Maritime Park

Coromandel
Forest Park

Raukumara

Auckland

Kaimai-Mamaku
Forest Park

Whakarewarewa
Forest Park

Hamilton   Tauranga

Pirongia
Forest Park

Rotorua

Whirinaki
Forest Park

TE UREWERA
NATIONAL
PARK

TONGARIRO
WORLD
HERITAGE
AREA

Pureora
Forest Park

Tongariro
Northern
Circuit

Taupo

Gisborne

Lake
Waikaremoana
Track

Sugar Loaf Islands
Marine Park

New
Plymouth

Kaimanawa Forest Park

Kaweka Forest Park

EGMONT
NATIONAL
PARK

TONGARIRO
NATIONAL
PARK

Napier

WHANGANUI
NATIONAL
PARK

Ruahine Forest Park

Wanganui

TASMAN
SEA

Whanganui
Journey

Palmerston
North

ABEL TASMAN
NATIONAL PARK

Marlborough
Sounds
Maritime
Park

Rimutaka
Forest
Park

Tararua
Forest
Park

Abel Tasman Coastal Track

Heaphy Track

Takaka

Rimutaka
Forest
Park

Haurangi
Forest Park

KAHURANGI
NATIONAL PARK

Nelson

WELLINGTON

Victoria
Forest
Park

Mt Richmond
Forest Park

PAPAROA NATIONAL PARK

NELSON LAKES NATIONAL PARK

Lewis Pass
National Reserve

Lake Sumner Forest Park

Hanmer Forest Park

WESTLAND
TAI POUTINI
NATIONAL
PARK

ARTHUR'S PASS NATIONAL PARK

Craigeburn
Forest Park

Christchurch

SOUTH
PACIFIC
OCEAN

TE WAHIPOUNAMU
WORLD HERITAGE
AREA

AORAKI
MT COOK
NATIONAL
PARK

Banks
Peninsula

MT ASPIRING
NATIONAL
PARK

Timaru

Routeburn Track

Milford Sound

Milford Track

Otago Goldfields Park

Queenstown

Kepler Track

Dunedin

Otago Peninsula

FIORDLAND
NATIONAL
PARK

Catlins
Forest
Park

Invercargill

Rakiura Track

Oban

RAKIURA
NATIONAL
PARK

Stewart Island (Rakiura)

0   100   200km

0   50   100mi

What to Bring

For an enjoyable tramp the primary considerations are your feet and shoulders. Make sure your footwear is adequate and that your pack is not too heavy. Having adequate, waterproof rain gear is also very important, especially on the South Island's West Coast, where you can get drenched to the skin in minutes if your rain gear is not up to the challenge.

If you're camping, or if staying in huts where there are no stoves (for example, on the Abel Tasman Track), you'll need a camping stove. These, along with fuel and any other camping gear you'd care to mention, can be purchased from outdoor shops around New Zealand.

Books

DOC produces very good books with detailed information on the flora and fauna, geology and history of NZ's national parks. DOC leaflets outline thousands of walking tracks throughout the country. These generally cost $1 to $1.50 each.

Lonely Planet's *Tramping in New Zealand,* by Jim DuFresne, describes nearly 50 walks of various lengths and degrees of difficulty in all parts of the country. *101 Great Tramps,* by Mark Pickering and Rodney Smith, has suggestions for two- to six-day tramps around the country. Also worth a scan is John Cobb's *Walking Tracks of NZ's National Parks*.

Tramping in North Island Forest Parks by Euan and Jennie Nicol, and *Tramping in South Island Forest Parks* by Joanna Wright, are good for shorter walking and tramping possibilities, from half-hour walks to tramps taking several days.

Maps

Land Information New Zealand's (LINZ; W www.linz.govt.nz) topographical maps are the best, but bookshops don't usually have a good selection. LINZ has map-sales offices in the main cities and towns, and DOC offices will often sell LINZ's maps of the tracks in the immediate area. LINZ has various map series. Park maps cover national, state and forest parks, and Trackmaps cover some of the more popular walking tracks. The most detailed are the Topomaps series of topographical maps, but you may need two or three maps to cover one track.

Track Classification

Tracks are classified according to their level of difficulty and many other features. In this chapter we loosely refer to the level of difficulty as one of the following: easy, medium, hard or difficult. The widely used track classification system is:

Path Easy and well formed; allows for wheelchair access or constructed to 'shoe' standard (ie, walking boots not required). Suitable for people of all ages and fitness levels.

Walking Track Easy and well formed; constructed to 'shoe' standard. Suitable for people of most ages and fitness levels.

Tramping Track Requires skill and experience; constructed to 'boot' standard. Suitable for people of average physical fitness.

Route Requires a high degree of skill, experience and route-finding ability. Suitable for well-equipped trampers.

Track Safety

It's very important that you learn and follow some basic rules of safety when tramping in NZ. Thousands of Kiwis and overseas visitors tramp in NZ every year without incident, but every year a few die in the mountains. Most fatalities could have been avoided if simple safety rules had been observed.

Some trails are only for the experienced and well-equipped, and weather conditions are changeable, making high-altitude walks subject to snow and ice even in summer. Always check weather conditions before leaving.

Consult and register your intentions with a DOC office before heading off on the longer walks. Above all, heed their advice.

The Great Walks

All nine of the Great Walks are described in this book. The walks (one is actually a river trip) are covered in detail in the pamphlets provided by DOC offices (and visitors centres) and in Lonely Planet's *Tramping in New Zealand*.

New Zealand's Environmental Care Code

Toitu te whenua – Care for the land

• **Protect plants and animals** Treat NZ's unique forests and rare birds with care and respect.

• **Remove rubbish** Litter is unattractive, harmful to wildlife and can increase vermin and disease. Plan your visits so as to reduce rubbish, and carry out what you carry in.

• **Bury toilet waste** In areas without toilet facilities, bury your toilet waste in a shallow hole well away from waterways, tracks, camp sites and huts.

• **Keep streams and lakes pure** When cleaning and washing, wash well away from water sources. Because soaps and detergents are harmful to water life, drain used water into the soil to allow it to be filtered. If you suspect the water may be contaminated, boil it for at least three minutes, filter it or chemically treat it.

• **Take care with fires** Portable fuel stoves are less harmful to the environment and are more efficient than fires. If you do use a fire, keep it small, use only dead wood and make sure it is out by dousing it with water and checking the ashes before leaving.

• **Camp carefully** When camping, leave no trace of your visit.

• **Keep to the track** By keeping to the track, you lessen the chance of damaging fragile plants.

• **Consider others** People visit the back country and rural areas for many reasons. Be considerate of other visitors who also have a right to enjoy the natural environment.

• **Respect cultural heritage** Many places in NZ have spiritual and historical significance. Treat them with consideration and respect.

• **Look** Take a last look before leaving an area: Will the next visitor know that you have been there?

• **Enjoy your visit** Enjoy your outdoor experience. Protect the environment for your own sake, for the sake of those who come after you and for the environment itself.

All Great Walks require a special Great Walks Pass, sold at DOC offices and visitors centres in the vicinity of each walk. Prices differ between the walks (up to $35 a night for huts on Milford and Routeburn). They allow you either to use the huts or to camp in the designated camping grounds, whichever you prefer.

The Great Walks are:

Abel Tasman Coastal Track An easy, two- to three-day walk along the coast and close to beaches and bays in Abel Tasman National Park (South Island). NZ's most popular walk is inundated with people (including sea kayakers), and a booking system operates in summer.

Heaphy Track A four- to five-day, medium to hard tramp of 77km through the forest and limestone (karst) landscape of Kahurangi National Park (South Island). The last day includes a magnificent beach walk.

Kepler Track This 67km, four- to five-day walk in Fiordland National Park (South Island) is a medium to hard tramp. It climbs to the top of a mountain and includes alpine, lake and river-valley scenery.

Lake Waikaremoana Track A three- to four-day, easy to medium tramp in Te Urewera National Park (North Island), with great views of the lake and surrounding bush-clad slopes.

Milford Track This 54km, four-day walk in Fiordland National Park (South Island) is one of the best known in the world. It includes views of river valleys, glaciers, waterfalls and an alpine pass crossing.

Rakiura (Stewart Island) Track A three-day tramp, mostly on duckboards, for which medium fitness is required. The track goes along the coast and through forest.

Routeburn Track A medium, 40km, three-day walk through the stunning alpine scenery of Mt Aspiring and Fiordland National Parks (South Island).

Tongariro Northern Circuit A four-day, medium to hard tramp through the active volcanic landscape of Tongariro National Park (North Island). Part of this tramp can be done as the one-day Tongariro Crossing.

The Whanganui Journey A canoe trip down the Whanganui River in Whanganui National Park (North Island). It's obviously not a walk but it, too, is one of the Great Walks.

Paragliding over Queenstown

Jet boating on the Shotover River near Queenstown

Abseiling at Port Hills

Mountain biking across a creek near St Bathans, Otago

Windsurfing at Otago Harbour

PHOTO COURTESY OF WWW.WELLINGTONNZ.COM

ANDREW PEACOCK

Ice cave, Fox Glacier

PHOTO COURTESY OF DESTINATION LAKE TAUPO

Bungee jumper

DAVID WALL

Fly by Wire, Paekakariki

Luge in Queenstown, Otago

GRANT SOMERS

Snowboarding on Cardrona ski fields in Canterbury

Hut & Camping Fees DOC has a huge network of back-country huts (over 950) in the national, maritime and forest parks. Hut fees range from $4 to a maximum of $35 per night for adults, paid with tickets purchased in advance at any DOC office or park visitors centre. You can buy $4 tickets in booklets and they are valid for 15 months. Children under 11 years of age can use all huts free of charge. Children 11 and older are charged half-price and use a special 'youth ticket'. If you plan to do a lot of tramping, DOC also sells an annual hut pass, available at all huts except the Great Walks huts.

Huts are classed into four categories and, depending on the category, a night's stay may use one or two tickets, except on Great Walks where special passes are needed. When you arrive at a hut, date the tickets and put them in the box provided. Accommodation is on a first come, first served basis. A list of all huts and their categories is available at any DOC office.

The Milford and Routeburn tracks operate on a system of their own and can be booked through DOC in Te Anau (e greatwalks booking@doc.govt.nz). The booking centre for the Abel Tasman Track is the Motueka visitors centre (☎ 528 6543, e mzpvin@ xtra.co.nz).

Other Tracks
In addition to the Great Walks there are numerous other tramping possibilities in all forest and national parks. Most of the following walks are *not* described in detail in this book:

North Island
Coromandel Track An easy to medium, three-day walk in the Kauaeranga Valley in the Coromandel Forest Park, Coromandel Peninsula.

Mt Holdsworth Circuit & Totara Flats Track Two three-day tramps in Holdsworth and Tararua Forest Park respectively. The first is a medium to hard walk over the top of alpine Mt Holdsworth. The second is a medium tramp mostly along the Totara River Valley.

Ninety Mile Beach–Cape Reinga Walkway A 50km, three-day, easy beach tramp (camping only) in Northland.

Round the Mountain, Mt Taranaki (Egmont) A 55km walk of four days or more in Egmont National Park. It is medium to hard tramping through mountainous country.

Tongariro Crossing A brilliant 17km one-day, medium tramp through Tongariro National Park.

South Island
Arthur's Pass tramps There are many walks to choose from in Arthur's Pass National Park, most of which are rated difficult.

Banks Peninsula Walk A two-day (medium) or four-day (easy) walk over the hills and along the coast of Banks Peninsula, crossing private and public land near Akaroa.

Greenstone & Caples Tracks These two tracks are on stewardship land, just outside Fiordland National Park. They're close to the Routeburn and a good way to start or finish this popular track.

Hump Ridge Track NZ's newest walking track (opened 2001) is a three-day, 53km circuit that begins and ends at Bluecliffs Beach on Te Wae Wae Bay, 20km from Tuatapere.

Inland Pack Track A 30km medium tramp in Paparoa National Park, following river valleys through the karst landscape near Punakaiki on the West Coast.

Kaikoura Coast Track A three-day walk over private and public land along the spectacular coast 50km south of Kaikoura.

Matukituki Valley walks There are good walks in the Matukituki Valley, Mt Aspiring National Park, near Wanaka.

North-West Circuit This eight- to 10-day route is just one of the many possibilities on Stewart Island (Rakiura). The whole island has wilderness possibilities.

Queen Charlotte Track A three- to four-day medium walk in Marlborough Sounds from which you get great views of the sounds and pass many historic places. There's accommodation and water transport on this track.

Rees-Dart Track A 70km, four- to five-day hard walk in Mt Aspiring National Park, through river valleys and traversing an alpine pass.

St James Walkway This 66km, five-day medium walk in Lake Sumner Forest Park/Lewis Pass Reserve passes through excellent subalpine scenery.

Wangapeka & Leslie-Karamea Tracks The Wangapeka is a four- to five-day medium tramp through river valleys and overpasses. The Leslie-Karamea is a 90km to 100km, five- to seven-day tramp for the experienced only, which includes river valleys, gorges and passes.

Getting There & Away

Getting to and from tracks can be a real problem, except for the most popular, which are serviced by trampers' transport. Having a vehicle only simplifies the problem of getting to one end of the track. Otherwise you have to take public transport or hitch in, and if the track starts or ends at the end of a dead-end road, hitching will be difficult.

Of course, tracks that are easily accessed by public transport – such as Abel Tasman – are also the most crowded. An alternative is to arrange private transport, either with a friend or by chartering a vehicle to drop you off at one end and pick you up at the other. If you intend to leave your own vehicle at a track-head car park and come back for it later, don't leave anything of value in it – thefts from cars in these isolated areas is a real problem.

SKIING & SNOWBOARDING

New Zealand is one of the most popular places in the southern hemisphere for skiing and snowboarding. In addition to downhill (alpine), there is cross-country, ski touring and ski mountaineering.

Heli-skiing is another popular, though pricey, attraction. In winter, helicopters are used to lift skiers up to the top of long, isolated stretches of virgin snow.

Unlike Europe, America or even Australia, New Zealand's commercial ski areas are generally not set up as resorts with chalets, lodges or hotels. Accommodation and après-ski nightlife is usually in surrounding towns, and there are daily shuttles to/from the main ski areas.

Club ski areas are open to the public and are much less crowded than commercial ski fields. Although non-members pay a slightly higher rate, they are still usually a cheaper alternative. Many have lodges you can stay at, subject to availability. Winter holidays and weekends will be fully booked, but mid-week you'll have no trouble.

The variety of resorts and conditions makes it difficult to rate the ski fields in any particular order. Some people like to be near the party scene of Queenstown, others prefer the high slopes and quality runs of Mt Hutt, the less crowded Rainbow Valley or the many club skiing areas. And for class NZ scenery, it's hard to beat the volcanic slopes of Ruapehu.

At the major ski areas, lifts cost from $30 to $68 a day (roughly half for children and two-thirds for students). Lesson-and-lift packages are available at most resorts. All the usual equipment can be bought or hired in NZ (rental from $30 a day). Snowboard with boots hire starts at $45. (Prices are lower if the hire is over a longer period). It makes sense to hire equipment close to where you'll be skiing, so that you can return your gear if there's a problem with the fit.

The ski season is generally from June to October, although it varies considerably from one ski area to another and can go as late as November.

Information centres in NZ, and the NZ Tourism Board (NZTB) internationally, have brochures on the various ski areas and packages, and can make bookings. The *NZ Ski & Snowboard Guide*, published by Brown Bear, is an excellent annual reference ($2).

The useful snowphone services provide prerecorded information on weather, access conditions and snow levels. On the Internet, check out **W** www.snow.co.nz for ski field reports, employment, Web cams and virtual tours; and the equally informative **W** www.nzski.com. Some resorts have their own website (see the following listings) and these are packed with the most up-to-date info, including lift prices, snow reports and even job vacancies.

North Island

The North Island is dominated by volcanic cone skiing. The impressive active volcano Mt Ruapehu is the premier ski area.

Whakapapa & Turoa These twin ski resorts *(information 07-892 3833, snowphone, ☎ 0900 99333,* **W** *www.whakapapa .co.nz)*, on either side of Mt Ruapehu, easily form the largest ski area in NZ. Whakapapa, 6km above Whakapapa Village in Tongariro National Park, has over 30 groomed runs. It includes a downhill course dropping nearly 722m over 4km, and the highest lift access in NZ. There are plenty of possibilities for snowboarding, including excellent pipes off the far western T-bar, cross-country, downhill and ski touring. You can drive yourself up to the slopes or you can take a shuttle minibus from Whakapapa Village, National Park township or Turangi.

Turoa has a 4km run, a beginners' lift, snowboarding and cross-country skiing. There is no road toll or parking fee and daily ski area transport is available from Ohakune, 17km away, which has the liveliest après-ski scene in the North Island.

Day lift passes (covering all lifts) are $54/27 for adults/children (five-day specials are $215/110). For accommodation see the Central Plateau chapter.

Tukino This club-operated ski area (☎ 06-387 6294, W www.tukino.co.nz) is on the eastern side of Mt Ruapehu, 50km from Turangi. It's quite remote – 14km of gravel road from the sealed Desert Rd (SH1), and you need a 4WD vehicle to get in (or make a prior arrangement to use the club transport). Because access is so limited the area is uncrowded, but most runs are beginner or intermediate.

Accommodation at the lodges must be arranged in advance: contact either *Desert Alpine Club* (☎ 07-856 1361) or *Aorangi Club* (☎ 04-234 7453). Lift passes are cheap at $20/10 for adults/children.

Manganui Ski Area There's more volcano-slope skiing on the eastern slopes of Mt Taranaki in the Egmont National Park, at the Manganui club ski area (*information 765 5493, snowphone ☎ 06-765 7669*), 22km from Stratford. For accommodation see the Taranaki chapter.

Skiing is possible off the summit of Mt Taranaki; when conditions permit, it's an invigorating two-hour climb to the crater with an exhilarating 1300m descent.

Lift passes are $30/15 for non-member adults/children.

South Island

New Zealand's best known – and top rated – skiing is in the South island, most of it re-

volving around the resort towns of Queenstown and Wanaka.

Coronet Peak The oldest ski field in this region is Coronet Peak (*information 03-442 4620, snowphone ☎ 0900 99766*). The season here is reliable because of a multimillion dollar snow-making system. Access is from Queenstown, 18km away, and there are shuttles in the ski season.

The treeless slopes and good snow provide excellent skiing – the chairlifts run to altitudes of 1585m and 1620m. The consistent gradient and the many undulations make this a snowboarder's paradise. Lift passes cost $68/34 for adults/children.

For accommodation see Queenstown and Arrowtown in the Otago chapter.

The Remarkables The visually impressive Remarkables ski area is near Queenstown (23km away), with shuttle buses running from Queenstown during the season. It, too, has beginner, intermediate and advanced runs, with chairlifts and beginners' tows. Look out for the sweeping run, Homeward Bound. Contact details are the same as for Coronet Peak. Lift passes are $65/32 for adults/children.

Treble Cone This area, 29km from Wanaka, has been improved with the extension of snow-making to the top of the Deliverance Chair. The highest of the southern lake areas, Treble Cone (*information 03-443 7443, snowphone ☎ 0900 34444, W www.treblecone.co.nz*) is spectacularly situated, overlooking Lake Wanaka. Slopes are steep and best for intermediate to advanced skiers. It has a natural half-pipe for snowboarding. For accommodation, see Wanaka in the Otago chapter. Lift passes are $61/31 for adults/children and first-timer packs are $50.

Cardrona Some 25km from Wanaka, Cardrona has three chairlifts, beginners' tows and a radical half-pipe for snowboarders. Buses run from Wanaka during the ski season, and from Queenstown, about 1½ hours away.

Cardrona *(snowphone ☎ 0900 47669, information 03-443 7341, ⓦ www.cardrona .com)* has acquired a reputation for the services it offers to disabled skiers, and it is the first resort in the South Island to have an on-field creche. In summer it attracts mountain bikers. Winter lift passes are $60/30 for adults/children.

Waiorau Nordic Area New Zealand's only commercial Nordic ski area *(☎ 03-443 7542)* is 26km from Wanaka, on the Pisa Range, high above Lake Wanaka. There are 25km of groomed trails and thousands of hectares of open rolling country for the ski tourer. Huts with facilities are dotted along the top of the Pisa Range.

Day passes are $20/10 for adults/children and executive passes, giving access to 55km of groomed trails, are $30/15.

South Canterbury Region There are three fields in the region; for accommodation see the Canterbury and Otago chapters. The most distant from Christchurch, the **Ohau** commercial ski area, is on Mt Sutton, 52km from Twizel. It has the longest T-bar lift in NZ. It has a large percentage of intermediate and advanced runs, plus excellent terrain for snowboarding, cross-country and ski touring to Lake Dumb Bell.

Contact the Ohau ski area *(snowphone ☎ 03-438 9885, PO Box 51, Twizel)*. Lift passes are $40/14 for adults/children ($35/12 for lodge guests).

With a 3km-wide basin, **Mt Dobson** *(information 03-685 8039, snowphone ☎ 0900 39888, ⓦ www.dobson.co.nz)*, a commercial ski area 26km from Fairlie, caters for learners and has NZ's largest intermediate area. From the summit of Mt Dobson, on a clear day, you can see Mt Cook and the Pacific Ocean. Lift passes are $40/14 for adults/children.

Fox Peak (information 685 8539, snowphone ☎ 03-688 0044), a club ski area, is 29km from Fairlie in the Two Thumb Range. Fox Peak has four rope tows and the learners' tow is free. There is good ski touring from the summit of Fox Peak and parapenting is also popular here. There is

accommodation at Fox Lodge, 3km below the ski area. Lift passes are $30/20 for members/non-members.

Mt Hutt One of the highest ski areas in the southern hemisphere, as well as one of the best in NZ, is Mt Hutt. It's 118km west of Christchurch, close to Methven, and can be reached by bus from Christchurch.

Mt Hutt *(information 03-302 8811, snowphone ☎ 0900 99766)* has beginner, intermediate and advanced slopes, with a quad and a triple chairlift, three T-bars, various other lifts and heli-skiing from the car park to slopes farther afield. The wide open faces are good for those learning to snowboard. Lift passes are $65/32 for adults/children.

For accommodation see Methven and Ashburton in the Canterbury chapter.

Mt Potts The former Erewhon club ski area *(☎ 03-309 0960, ⓦ www.mtpotts.co .nz)* has got to be one of the best little gems in NZ, though it's not cheap since it's the base for a snow cat and heli-skiing operation. Based on Mt Potts, above the headwaters of the Rangitata River, it's about 75km from Methven. Accommodation and meals are available from a lodge at Mt Potts, 8km from the ski area (B&B with dinner $60 per person). It has a good mix of beginner, intermediate and advanced slopes, with snowboarding and cross-country also popular here. Transport by 4WD is essential, and can be arranged through the club.

A day of skiing from the snow cat, including heli access, is $245, and a one week all-inclusive deal is $1890.

Porter Heights The closest commercial ski area to Christchurch, Porter Heights *(information 03-318 4002, snowphone ☎ 0900 34444, ⓦ www.porterheights.co.nz)* is 96km away on the Arthur's Pass road. The 720m-long Big Mama is the steepest run in NZ. There's a half-pipe for snowboarders, plus good cross-country areas, and ski touring out along the ridge. There is a $6 toll on the access road. Lift passes are $46/23 for adults/children.

Arthur's Pass & Craigieburn Regions
There are five ski areas in the Arthur's Pass and Craigieburn regions. For accommodation see the Methven, Springfield and Arthur's Pass sections in the Canterbury chapter.

Temple Basin *(information 377 7788, snowphone ☎ 03-366 7766)* is a club area just 4km from the Arthur's Pass township. It is a 45-minute walk uphill from the car park to the lift area. At night there's floodlit skiing. There are good back-country runs for snowboarders. Lift passes are $34/25 for adults/children.

The **Craigieburn Valley** ski area *(information 379 2514, snowphone ☎ 03-366 7766, W www.craigieburn.co.nz)*, centred on Hamilton Peak, is 40km from Arthur's Pass. It is one of NZ's most challenging club areas, with intermediate and advanced runs and a shredder's 'soggy dream'. It is a pleasant 10-minute walk through beech forest from the car park to the ski area. Lift passes are $38/20.

Another good club area in the Craigieburn Range is **Mt Cheeseman**, 112km from Christchurch. The ski area *(☎ 379 5315)*, based on Mt Cockayne, is in a wide, sheltered basin. Lift passes are $42/24.

Hard to find, but worth the search, **Mt Olympus** *(☎ 03-366 6644 ext 1108)* is 66km from Methven and 12km from Lake Ida. This club area has four tows which lead to intermediate and advanced runs. Snowboarding is allowed, there are good cross-country areas and ski-touring trails to other areas. 4WD is advisable from the bottom hut. Lift passes are $30/15.

Hanmer Springs Region There are three ski areas near Hanmer Springs. Accommodation is on-field, or you can stay in Hanmer Springs.

Hanmer Springs Ski Area *(information 03-315 7233, snowphone ☎ 366 7766,)*, a field based on Mt St Patrick, is 17km from Hanmer Springs and has mostly intermediate and advanced runs. Lift passes are $34/17 for adults/children.

Mt Lyford *(information 03-315 6178, snowphone ☎ 366 7766,)* is about 60km from Hanmer Springs or Kaikoura, and 4km from Mt Lyford Village, where accommodation is available. The Lake Stella field has skiing at all levels, basin and off-piste cross-country skiing, 15km of groomed trails for ski touring, and a natural pipe for snowboarding. A $5 toll applies on the access road.

The nearby **Terako Basin** ski field has advanced skiing and is linked by rope tow to Mt Lyford. Lift passes are $40/20 for adults/children.

Nelson Region In the north, near St Arnaud in Nelson Lakes National Park, there are two ski areas. The closest accommodation is in St Arnaud but there is also transport to and from Nelson and Blenheim.

The **Rainbow Valley** commercial ski area *(information 03-521 1850, snowphone ☎ 0900 34444)* is just outside the park. There's a double chair and T-bar to lift skiers to the top of a spacious bowl and two learners' tows, and there's good cross-country ski touring. Lift passes are $44/24 for adults/children (learners' pack $61/45).

Inside the park, 15km from St Arnaud, **Mt Robert** *(snowphone ☎ 03-548 8336)* is a club area, but it's a two-hour walk from the car park, 7km from St Arnaud, to reach it. This area is known for its powder and many cross-country opportunities, but only for those suitably equipped. Lift passes are $20/15.

Heli-Skiing & Glacier Skiing
New Zealand is an excellent place to try heli-skiing. From July to October, operators cover a wide area of off-piste all along the Southern Alps.

Heli-skiing companies include: ***Harris Mountains Heli-skiing*** *(☎ 03-443 7930, W www.heliski.co.nz, 99 Ardmore St, Wanaka)*; ***Fox and Franz Heliservices*** *(☎ 0800 800 732)*; ***Mt Hutt Heli-Ski*** *(☎ 03-302 8401)*; ***Heli-Guides Heli-ski*** *(☎ 03-442 7733, e heliski@flynz.co.nz, Queenstown)*; and ***Hanmer Heli-ski & Heli-board*** *(☎ 0800 888 308)*. The cost is from $395 for a half day (three runs), or $650 to $830 for a full day (four to seven runs).

MOUNTAINEERING

New Zealand has a rich history of mountaineering, and has proved an ideal training ground for greater adventures overseas (remember this is the home of Sir Edmund Hilary, the first person, with Tenzing Norgay, to climb Mt Everest). The Southern Alps offer many challenging climbs, and are studded with a number of impressive peaks. This very physical and highly challenging pursuit is not for the uninitiated, and contains a number of dangers – fickle weather, storms, winds, extreme cold, loose rock, rock falls and equipment failure. In late 2001, the bodies of two Swiss climbers were discovered on Mt Cook – 38 years after they had disappeared.

But if you have to climb 'because it's there', proper instruction and training will enable you to make commonsense decisions that will enhance your safety and get you up among those beautiful mountain peaks.

The Mt Cook region is only one of many outstanding climbing areas in the country. The others extend along the spine of the South Island from Tapuaenuku (in the Kaikoura Ranges) and the Nelson Lakes peaks, in the north, to the rugged mountains of Fiordland.

Beyond the Cook region is Mt Aspiring National Park, centred on 'the Matterhorn of the South', Mt Aspiring, and the Volta, Therma and Bonar ice fields which cling to its sides. This is the second centre of mountaineering in NZ, with possibilities for all levels of climbs. To the south, in the Forbes Mountains, is Mt Earnslaw, flanked by the Rees and Dart Rivers.

The NZ Alpine Club (☎ 03-377 7595, W www.nzalpine.org.nz), Level 6, Manchester Courts, on the corner of Manchester and Hereford Sts, Christchurch, provides information and publishes the annual *NZ Alpine Journal* and *NZ Climber*.

For those seeking to learn the necessary skills, there are companies in Wanaka, Mt Cook, Tekapo and at the Fox and Franz Josef glaciers that provide expert instruction, mountaineering courses and private guiding (see the relevant chapters).

ALEXANDER TURNBULL LIBRARY, WELLINGTON NZ

Sir Edmund Hilary (photographer unknown)

ROCK CLIMBING

In the North Island, popular climbing areas include the Mt Eden Quarry in Auckland, Whanganui Bay and Motuoapa in the vicinity of Lake Taupo and Piarere, near Cambridge. Wharepapa, about 20km south-east of Te Awamutu, is regarded as one of the best places in the country for climbing.

In the South Island the Port Hills area above Christchurch has many climbs, and 100km away on the road to Arthur's Pass is Castle Hill, with great friction climbs. West of Nelson, the marble and limestone mountains of Golden Bay and Takaka Hill provide prime climbing, and north of Dunedin is Long Beach.

Several companies take beginners out for their first climbs, with all attention paid to safety. A good rock climbing website is Climb New Zealand, at W www.climb .co.nz.

CAVING

Caving opportunities abound, and this is another NZ speciality. Auckland, Westport and Waitomo are all areas where you'll find both active local clubs and organised tours. A spectacular caving experience is the

100m abseil into the Lost World tomo near Waitomo.

For more information about caving in the area, contact the NZ Speleological Society (NZSS; ☎ 07-850 8548), PO Box 18, Waitomo Caves.

MOUNTAIN BIKING & CYCLE TOURING

With its great scenery and off-road possibilities, New Zealand is great biking country. At any given time, but especially in summer, you'll see plenty of pannier-laden cycle tourists cruising the highway and backroads. Most towns have some sort of bike for hire, either at backpacker hostels or specialist bike shops, but you'll really only find quality mountain bikes for hire in major towns or adventure sports centres such as Queenstown, Nelson, Picton, Taupo and Rotorua. Service and repair shops can be found in most big towns, and there are excellent cycling books available (see the Bicycle section in the Getting Around chapter), including Lonely Planet's *Cycling New Zealand*.

For downhill fans, various companies will take you up to the tops of mountains, hills and volcanoes (Mt Ruapehu, Christchurch's Port Hills, Cardrona, The Remarkables) so that you can hurtle down without the usual grunt of getting uphill beforehand. The Redwood Forest and Rotorua is a noted place for mountain biking, as is the 42nd Traverse near National Park and Twizel near Mt Cook.

Some of the traditional tramping tracks are open to mountain bikes, but DOC has restricted access in many cases due to track damage and the inconvenience to walkers, especially at busy times. *Never* cycle on walking tracks in national parks unless it's permitted (check with DOC). There are fines if you're caught. The Heaphy Track was closed to mountain-bikers some years ago but there is a strong push to allow bikes out of season. The Queen Charlotte Track is a good one to bike, but part of it is closed in summer.

Contact the NZ Mountain Bike Association (NZMBA; ☎ 07-377 4328, W www .mountainbike.co.nz/nzmba), PO Box 371,

Taupo. A good website is W www.moun tainbike.co.nz.

WATER ACTIVITIES
Jetboating

New Zealand is the home of the amazing jetboat, invented by Kiwi CWF Hamilton in 1957. An inboard engine sucks water into a tube in the bottom of the boat, and an impeller driven by the engine blows it out a nozzle at the stern in a high-speed stream. The boat is steered simply by directing the jet stream.

The boats are ideal for use in shallow water and white water because there are no propellers to damage, there is better clearance under the boat and the jet can be reversed instantly for quick braking. The instant response of the jet enables the boats to execute 360° spins almost within the length of the boat.

The Shotover and Kawarau Rivers near Queenstown and the Buller near Westport are renowned jetboating rivers in the South Island; the Dart River is less travelled but also good, and the Waiatoto River near Haast is a superb wilderness experience.

In the North Island, the Whanganui, Manganui-a-te-Ao, Motu, Rangitaiki, Kaituna and Waikato Rivers are excellent for jetboating, and there are sprint jets at the Agrodome in Rotorua and at Waitomo. The Wairoa River near Dargaville is the main place in Northland.

Half-hour trips costs from $50 to $70 and sprints from $25. Like many activities it seems to be marginally cheaper in the North island than the South.

Whitewater Rafting & Kayaking

There are almost as many white-water rafting possibilities as there are rivers in NZ. And there is no shortage of companies to take you on a heart-pounding, drenching, exhilarating ride down some wild, magnificent rivers. The Shotover and Kawarau Rivers in the South Island are popular rafting venues. Canterbury has the Rangitata River, considered one of the country's best.

The north of the South Island has great rafting possibilities, such as the Buller,

Karamea, Mokihinui and Gowan Rivers. Westport and Murchison are the best bases to take on these rivers. The West Coast has endless possibilities, including the Hokitika, Perth, Landsborough, Arnold and Waiho Rivers.

In the North Island there are plenty of rivers too, such as the Rangitaiki, Wairoa, Motu, Tongariro, Rangitikei and Ngaruroro, that are equally as good. There is also the Kaituna Cascades near Rotorua, with the 7m Okere Falls as its highlight.

Rivers are graded from I to VI, with VI meaning 'unraftable'. The grading of the Shotover canyon varies from III to V+, depending on the time of year, the Kawarau River is rated IV, and the Wairoa River III to V. On the rougher stretches there's usually a minimum age limit of 12 or 13 years. All safety equipment is supplied.

Full day or multi-day rafting trips cost between about $120 and $250 per person per day, depending on whether or not helicopter access is involved. Half-day trips cost from $85.

Whitewater kayaking is popular among enthusiasts but, unlike rafting, it's a solo activity requiring skills and training. The New Zealand Kayak School (☎ 523 9611, W www.nzkayakschool.com) in Murchison offers intensive four-day courses for introductory to advanced levels ($550 including accommodation).

Cave Rafting
This is a variation on the rafting theme and not true rafting at all, but it's very unusual and exciting. It's known as 'tumu tumu toobing' and 'black-water rafting' at Waitomo in the North Island, as 'underworld rafting' at Westport and as 'adventure caving' at Greymouth in the South Island.

It involves donning a wet suit, a lighted hard hat and a black inner tube and floating on underground rivers through some spectacular caves with glow-worms.

Canoeing & Kayaking
An open two-person canoe is called a 'Canadian canoe' in NZ. A smaller, narrower one-person craft that's covered except for a hole in which the paddler sits, is often called a 'kayak' but it can also be called a 'canoe', especially if it's the sit-on-top style. Specify whether you mean a 'Canadian canoe' or a 'kayak' when talking about river trips in NZ.

Canoeing is especially popular on the Whanganui River in the North Island, where you can hire a canoe for days at a time. It's also popular on lakes, notably Lake Taupo and many lakes in the South Island.

Many backpacker hostels close to any body of water will have kayaks for hire or for free, and there are loads of commercial guided trips (for those without equipment or experience) offered on rivers and lakes throughout the North and South Islands. Many trips combine an eco aspect such as bird-watching – a good example is the beautiful Okarito Lagoon on the West Coast of the South Island.

Contact the NZ Recreational Canoeing Association (NZRCA; ☎ 04-560 3590, W www .rivers.org.nz), PO Box 284, Wellington.

Sea Kayaking Equally popular is sea kayaking. Renowned areas are the Hauraki Gulf, including Waiheke and Great Barrier islands, the Bay of Islands and Coromandel in the North Island and, off the South Island, the Marlborough Sounds and along the coast of Abel Tasman National Park, where sea kayaking has become almost as big as walking (see the Marlborough & Nelson chapter for further details). Fiordland is also a great destination. Tour operators in Te Anau, Milford and Manapouri arrange spectacular trips on the lakes and fiords.

River Sledging
Discard the raft, kayak, canoe, water mattress or inflated inner tube if you think they lack manoeuvrability. Instead, grasp a responsive polystyrene sled or a modified boogie board, flippers, wet suit, helmet and a positive attitude, and go for it.

In the South Island, rivers around Queenstown and Wanaka offer this thrill, and in the North Island, Rotorua is the place (it includes a 7m waterfall drop on the Kaituna River).

In Taranaki, there is a new variant called 'dam dropping', the highlight of sledging on the Waingongoro River.

Sailing

Auckland is appropriately named the City of Sails – the island nation throws up the world's best mariners and Kiwis have swept the world before them in international yachting races. It's possible to wander around to the various sailing clubs and ask if you can help crew on local race competitions, such as Ponsonby Cruising Club's 'Rum Race' (see the Auckland chapter). Otherwise there are plenty of sailing operators who charge around $70 a day for sailing, whether you just laze around on deck or help with the sailing.

The Bay of Islands (and Whangaroa to the north), the southern lakes (Te Anau and Wakatipu) and the cities of Auckland and Dunedin are good venues to experience the thrill of the wind in your sails.

Scuba Diving

The Bay of Islands Maritime & Historic Park, the Hauraki Gulf Maritime Park in the North Island, and the Marlborough Sounds Maritime Park in the South Island, are obvious attractions but both islands have many more diving possibilities. Even Invercargill, with its notoriously cold water, has a club!

NZ has two marine parks offering interesting diving. The Poor Knights Islands, off the coast near Whangarei, is reputed to have the best diving in NZ and the late Jacques Cousteau rated it one of the top 10 diving spots in the world. Nearby is the diveable wreck of the Greenpeace flagship *Rainbow Warrior* (see the boxed text in the Northland chapter). The interesting Sugar Loaf Islands reserve is off Back Beach in New Plymouth, not far from the city centre.

Marlborough Sounds has some interesting dives, including the *Mikhail Lermontov*, the largest diveable cruiseship wreck in the world.

Fiordland in the South Island is most unusual because the extremely heavy rainfall and mountain run-off leaves a layer of freshwater, often peaty brown, over the saltwater.

You descend through this murky and cold freshwater into amazingly clear and warmer saltwater. The freshwater cuts out light, discouraging the growth of seaweed, and this provides ideal conditions for the growth of black coral *(Antipathes fiordensis)*.

For more information, pick up a copy of Lonely Planet's *Diving & Snorkeling New Zealand* or contact the NZ Underwater (☎ 09-849 5896, ℮ nzu@iconnz.co.nz), PO Box 875, Auckland.

Surfing

NZ has plenty of surfing possibilities. Swells come in from every angle and, while different beaches have better surfing at different times of the year, there's good surfing to be found *somewhere* in NZ at any time of the year.

Raglan's 2km-long left-hander is NZ's most famous wave – this is the place to learn to surf with the **Raglan Surfing School** *(☎ 07-825 7573,* W *www.raglan surfingschool.co.nz)*. There's another surf school (Aloha) based at Piha, west of Auckland. Other spots in the North Island recommended by surfers include: Auckland area (Muriwai, Piha); Matakana Island and Tauranga; Mt Manganui; Whangamata, on the Coromandel; Gisborne (city beaches and Mahia Peninsula); Taranaki (Greenmeadows Point, Puniho Rd and Stent Rd); and Wellington region (Castlepoint, Palliser Bay and Titahi Bay).

Dunedin is one of the best spots in the South Island, especially in summer and autumn, but other South Island locations include: Greymouth (Blaketown and Cobden breakwater); Kaikoura (Mangamanu Reef, Mangawhau Point and Meatworks); and Westport (local beaches and Tauranga Bay).

Among the guidebooks on surfing in NZ, look out for *The New Zealand Surfing Guide* by Mike Bhana, and *A Guide to Surf Riding in New Zealand* by Wayne Warwick.

Windsurfing

Windsurfing has thousands of Kiwi adherents and plenty of popular spots to catch the wind. The lakes of both main islands are popular.

NEW ZEALAND SKI, SURF & DIVE SPOTS

COMMERCIAL SKI AREAS
1 Whakapapa
3 Turoa
6 Rainbow Valley
7 Mt Lyford, Terako Basin
8 Hanmer Springs
13 Porter Heights
14 Mt Hutt
15 Mt Potts
17 Mt Dobson
18 Ohau
19 Treble Cone
20 Cardrona
21 Coronet Peak
22 Waiorau Nordic Area
23 The Remarkables

CLUB SKI AREAS
2 Tukino
4 Manganui
5 Mt Robert
9 Temple Basin
10 Craigieburn Valley
11 Broken River
12 Mt Cheeseman &
   Mt Olympus
16 Fox Peak

Heli-Skiing & Glacier Skiing
(See text for contact details)

Kaitaia

Bay of Islands Maritime & Historic Park

Poor Knights Islands

Dargaville
Whangarei

Hauraki Gulf Maritime Park

Great Barrier Island

Muriwai Beach
Piha
Auckland
Whangamata

Raglan
Hamilton
Mt Maunganui, Matakana Island

Manu Bay
Tauranga

Rotorua

Greenmeadows Point, Puniho Rd, Stent Rd
Taupo
Gisborne

Sugar Loaf Island Reserve
New Plymouth
Turangi

Mahia Peninsula

4
3
2
Napier
Ohakune
Hastings

Wanganui

Palmerston North
Castlepoint

Marlborough Sounds Maritime Park

Takaka
Titahi Bay
Masterton

WELLINGTON

**T A S M A N
S E A**

Nelson
Blenheim

Palliser Bay

Tauranga Bay
Westport

Palliser Bay

5
6
Mangamauna Reef

Blaketown
Cobden Breakwater
Greymouth
7
8
Kaikoura

Hanmer
Mangawhau Point, Meatworks

Hokitika
9

Hanmer Heli-Ski & Heli-board

10

Franz Josef
Fox Glacier
12
11

**SOUTH
PACIFIC
OCEAN**

Fox and Franz Heliservices
15
13
Christchurch

14
Hanmer Heli-Ski & Heli-board

Mt Cook
Tekapo
16

Mt Hutt Heli-Ski

18
17

Harris Mountains Heli-Skiing
Twizel
Timaru

19
20
Wanaka

21
22
23

Queenstown

Doubtful Sound

Te Anau

Heli-Guides Heli-Ski

Dusky Sound

Dunedin
St Clair Beach
Akatore Reef

Balclutha

Invercargill
Long Point

Oban

Stewart Island (Rakiura)

0   100   200km
0   50   100mi

Scuba Diving Areas
(See Scuba Diving section in Activities for contact details within New Zealand)

Recommended Surfing spots
(See Surfing section in Activites and individual regional sections for more details)

Auckland harbour and the Hauraki Gulf, the Bay of Islands, Oakura near New Plymouth and 'windy' Wellington are just some outstanding coastal locations. There are many places where you can hire boards and receive NZ Windsurfing Association-approved instruction.

Kiteboarding is the next big thing (where a mini parachute drags you along on a surf board) – try it at Paihia.

Fishing

New Zealand is renowned as one of the great recreational fishing countries of the world, thanks largely to the introduction of exotic rainbow trout, brown trout, quinnat salmon, Atlantic salmon, perch, char and a few other fish.

The lakes and rivers of central North Island are famous for trout fishing, especially Lake Taupo and the rivers that feed it. Turangi is a top base for trout fishing (see the boxed text 'It's a Trout's Life' in the Central Plateau chapter). The rivers and lakes of the South Island are also good for trout, notably the Mataura River, Southland, and Lake Brunner and the Arnold River on the West Coast. The rivers of Otago and Southland also have some of the best salmon fishing in the world.

Saltwater fishing is also a big attraction for Kiwi anglers, especially in the warmer waters around the North Island where surf-casting or fishing from boats can produce big catches of grey mullet, trevally, mao mao, porae, John Dory, snapper, gurnard, flounder, mackerel, hapuku, tarakihi, moki and kahawai.

Ninety Mile Beach (Northland) and the beaches of the Hauraki Gulf are good for surfcasting. The Bay of Islands, Whangaroa, Tutukaka near Whangarei (all also in Northland), Whitianga on the Coromandel and Mayor Island in the Bay of Plenty are noted big-game-fishing areas.

The colder waters of the South Island, especially around Marlborough Sounds, are good for snapper, hake, hapuku (groper), trumpeter, butterfish, ling, barracouta and blue cod. The Kaikoura Peninsula is great for surfcasting.

Fishing gear can be hired in areas such as Taupo and Rotorua, and at a few sports outlets in other towns, but serious enthusiasts may wish to bring their own. Rods and tackle may have to be treated by NZ quarantine officials, especially if they are made with natural materials such as cane or feathers.

A fishing permit is required to fish on inland waters. They cover particular regions and are available for a day, a month or a season; these are sold at sport shops. Local visitors centres and DOC offices have more information about fishing licences and regulations.

Many books have been written about fishing in NZ. John Kent has written the *North Island Trout Fishing Guide* and the *South Island Trout Fishing Guide*. Tony Orman, a renowned NZ fisherman and author, has written *21 Great New Zealand Trout Waters* as well as *Fishing the Wild Places of New Zealand*, telling not only how to catch fish but also relating some of the author's adventures fishing in many of NZ's wilderness areas.

Marine-Mammal Watching

Kaikoura, on the north-eastern coast of the South Island, is the NZ centre for marine-mammal watching. The main attraction is whale-watching tours but these are dependent on weather conditions, so don't expect to be able to turn up and go straight out on a boat. The sperm whale, the largest toothed whale, is seen from October to August. Most of the other mammals are seen year-round.

Kaikoura is also the best place for swimming with dolphins. Pods of up to 500 playful dusky dolphins can be seen on any given day. Dolphin swimming is common across NZ, with dolphins in the North Island at Whakatane, Paihia, Tauranga, Whitianga and the Hauraki Gulf (from Auckland), and at Akaroa near Christchurch. Seal swimming is possible at Kaikoura and Abel Tasman National Park.

Swimming with sharks is also popular, but thankfully it is done with a protective cage. It can be done at Tutukaka, near Whangarei, and at Kaikoura.

AERIAL ACTIVITIES
Bungy Jumping
Bungy jumping was made famous by Kiwi AJ Hackett's bungy dive from the Eiffel Tower in 1986. He teamed up with NZ's champion speed skier, Henry van Asch, and looked for a way to make commercial jumping safe. This company alone has sent many thousands of people hurtling earthward from bridges over the Shotover and Kawarau Rivers near Queenstown with nothing between them and kingdom come but a gigantic rubber bungy cord tied to their ankles.

The jump begins when you crawl into the preparation area, get your ankles strapped up with a towel for padding, and have adjustments made to the cord depending on your weight. You then hobble out to the edge of the jumping platform, stand looking out over thin air, and get ready to jump. The crew shout out 'five, four, three, two, ONE!' and you dive off, dropping like a stone before rebounding upwards again on the bungy.

It's a daredevil sport, and the adrenaline rush can last for days. But it's all very well organised, with every possible precaution and attention to safety. And for exhibitionist backpackers, the days of bungying nude for free are over – though you do get a discount.

The historic Kawarau Suspension Bridge near Queenstown attracts the most jumpers; it's 43m above the Kawarau River. Another spectacular bungy spot is The Pipeline (102m), over the Shotover River in Skippers Canyon. The Ledge (47m) is an urban jump in Queenstown, where you can also jump at night. Highest of the lot, also near Queenstown, is the 134m Nevis Highwire (see the boxed text 'Nervous on the Nevis' under Queenstown in the Otago chapter). There's another bungy jump at the Waiau River Bridge near Hanmer Springs.

Jumping is also done in the North Island at Taupo (45m), above the scenic Waikato River, and from a bridge over the Rangitikei River near Mangaweka (80m).

A new variation is the bungy rocket (or reverse bungy) – zoom up and bounce around in a tandem capsule in Auckland, Tauranga, Wellington and Queenstown.

Yet another variation to take off in Auckland is the Sky Jump from the landmark Skytower. It's a 20-second freefall using a cable and 'fan descenders' (of the type used by movie industry stunt actors) and at 192m it's the world's highest tower-based jump.

Parapenting & Paragliding
This is perhaps the easiest way for humans to fly. After half a day of instruction you should be able to do limited solo flights. Before you know it you could be doing flights from a height of 300m.

The best place to learn the skills necessary to operate your parapente/paraglider is the Wanaka Paragliding School (see Wanaka and Queenstown in the Otago chapter). Initial instruction is conducted at Mt Iron, just outside the town, and the long jumps are from the road up to the Treble Cone ski field. This is a sport where you should be confident in the qualifications and safety record of your instructor – we've had some complaints from readers about substandard operators.

Tandem flights, where you are strapped to an experienced paraglider, are offered all over the country. Perhaps the most popular is from the top of the gondola hill in Queenstown or from Te Mata Peak in Hawkes Bay.

Aerial Sightseeing
All over NZ planes and helicopters offer sightseeing trips (called 'flightseeing' by the locals), a great way to see the incredible contrast in scenery and the spectacular mountain ranges.

Some of the best trips are around the Bay of Islands, the Bay of Plenty, Tongariro National Park and Mt Taranaki in the North Island, and Mt Cook and the West Coast glaciers and fiords in the South Island.

Aerial sightseeing companies operate from local aerodromes, and a flight can often be arranged on the spot. Ask at the local visitors centre for information.

A far more sedate way to see the countryside is from a **hot-air balloon**. A company operating from near Methven (Aoraki Hot Air Balloon Safaris, see the Canterbury chapter) takes you up to an altitude where you get spectacular views of the Southern Alps and contrasting Canterbury Plains, and there are early morning balloon trips from Queenstown, Taupo, Auckland and Wellington (from around $230).

Skydiving

Skydiving is another thing a lot of travellers choose to do in NZ. There are plenty of professional operators and at most drop zones the views on the way up, and on the way down, are breathtaking. Some operators or clubs offer static-line jumps and Accelerated Free Fall (AFF) courses, but for most first-timers the tandem skydive is the way to go. You're attached to a fully-qualified instructor and you get to experience up to 45 seconds of high-speed freefall before the chute opens. It's not cheap, from $170/215 for a 9000/12,000ft jump (in Taupo) to $225/295 (in Wanaka and Queenstown), but the thrill is worth every dollar.

Tandem skydiving can be tried in the North Island at Parakai near Auckland, Paihia, Taupo, Rotorua and Napier. In the South Island there's tandem skydiving at Nelson, Christchurch, Fox Glacier, Methven, Wanaka and Queenstown.

OTHER ACTIVITIES

New Zealand is the home of invention when it comes to activities. The unique **zorbing** (rolling downhill in a transparent plastic ball) can be experienced in Rotorua (the original) and Paihia on the Bay of Islands. **Fly By Wire** (a self-drive flying machine dangling from a wire) can be tested by the brave at Paekakariki in the Wellington region or Queenstown. There are more traditional **flying foxes** at Buller Gorge near Murchison and Riwaki near Motueka, and **high ropes courses** at Whitianga in the Coromandel and near Taupo.

A variation on a traditional theme, **quad bikes** (four-wheel farm bikes) are a fun way to traverse the countryside and are popping up everywhere (see the Rotorua, Taupo, Nelson, Ahipara, Bay of Islands, Queenstown, Wanaka, Te Anau, Kaikoura and Hanmer Springs sections).

Horse Riding

Horse riding is offered almost everywhere, and unlike some other parts of the world where beginners only get led around a paddock, in NZ you really can get out into the countryside on farm, forest and beach rides. Horse rides range from one-hour jaunts (around $30) to 12-day fully catered treks.

In the South Island, all-day adventure rides on horseback are a great way to see the surrounding country in Kaikoura, around Mt Cook, Hanmer Springs, Wanaka, Queenstown Glenorchy and Dunedin. There are many treks offered in West Coast national parks.

In the North Island, Taupo has options for wilderness horse trekking and for rides in the hills overlooking the thermal regions. The Coromandel Peninsula, Waitomo, South Kaipara, Pakiri, Ninety Mile Beach (from Ahipara) and the East Cape are also good places for horse trekking. Horse-riding operators are covered throughout this book.

Where to Ride In New Zealand, a pamphlet produced by the International League for the Protection of Horses (ILPH; ☎ 07-849 0678), PO Box 10-368, Pukete Rd, Te Rapa, is available from visitors centres. Hamilton (Waikato, in the North Island) has Riding for the Disabled (☎ 07-849 4727, Formon Rd).

Bird-watching

New Zealand is a twitcher's paradise – in a relatively small area it has many unique endemic species, interesting residents and wave upon wave of visitors. Sadly, NZ is as famous for extinct and point-of-extinction species as it is for common species.

The flightless kiwi is probably the species most sought after by bird-watchers and you are almost guaranteed to see the Stewart Island subspecies at all times of the year. Elsewhere, wild sightings of this increasingly rare nocturnal species are difficult but there are quite a few kiwi-houses in NZ. Other sought-after birds are the royal albatross, white heron, Fiordland crested penguin, yellow-eyed penguin, Australasian gannet and wrybill.

The Firth of Thames, particularly Miranda, is a haven for migrating birds, while the Wharekawa Wildlife Refuge at Opoutere in the Coromandel is a breeding ground of the endangered NZ dotterel and the variable oystercatcher. There's a very accessible Australasian gannet colony at Muriwai west of Auckland.

For more information on birdwatching in NZ, see the colour 'Watching Wildlife' section – it lists locations where species are likely to be seen.

Two good guides are *A Field Guide to New Zealand Birds* by Geoff Moon, and *Birds of New Zealand – Locality Guide* by Stuart Chambers.

Golf

New Zealand has more golf courses per capita than any other country (which, given the population, is not all that surprising).

Included among the more than 400 courses here are some in spectacular settings – Howick in Auckland, the swanky Formosa and Gulf Harbour just outside Auckland, Wairakei near Taupo, Paraparaumu near Wellington (where Tiger Woods famously swung his clubs in 2002), and Arrowtown and Millbrook near Queenstown.

The average green fee in NZ varies from $25 to $30.

Wine-touring

Wine touring may not seem synonymous with New Zealand in the same way as, say, France, Germany or Australia, but the country has some wonderful wine regions and a growing international reputation for the quality of its wines.

As the interest in NZ wines has increased, so have the opportunities for touring wine regions. From the far north (there's a winery near Kaitaia and a cluster around Kerikeri) to the south (vineyards of Central Otago are among the most southerly in the world, at 45°S), you can cycle or drive and taste at the cellar door. As is the trend these days, many wineries have fine cafes, restaurants, associated businesses such as cheese-making or preserves, and even accommodation. Getting around the main regions is easy since half and full-day tours operate regularly – see the relevant chapters for details.

The best regions for touring are Marlborough (near Blenheim in the South Island); Nelson; Martinborough in the Wairarapa; Hawkes Bay and Napier; Gisborne; Henderson (near Auckland); Waiheke Island (in the Hauraki Gulf); and Central Otago (near Queenstown). Marlborough, Hawkes Bay and Martinborough all host big wine and food festivals.

Getting There & Away

WARNING

The information in this chapter is particularly vulnerable to change: prices for international travel are volatile, routes are introduced and cancelled, schedules change, special deals come and go, and rules and visa requirements are amended. Airlines and governments seem to take a perverse pleasure in making price structures and regulations as complicated as possible. You should check directly with the airline or a travel agent to make sure you understand how a fare (and tickct you may buy) works. In addition, the travel industry is highly competitive and there are many lurks and perks.

The upshot of this is that you should get opinions, quotes and advice from as many airlines and travel agents as possible before you part with your hard-earned cash. The details given in this chapter should be regarded as pointers and are not a substitute for your own careful, up-to-date research.

AIR

New Zealand has six airports that handle international flights: Auckland, Wellington, Palmerston North and Hamilton in the North Island, and Christchurch and Dunedin in the South Island. Most international flights go through Auckland, and this is generally the cheapest port to fly in and out of. Wellington airport has limited runway capacity and international flights are mainly to Australia, as they are from Christchurch, although there are some connections from Christchurch to other countries.

Buying Tickets

Since New Zealand is on the other side of the world from most places (except Australia), a long haul flight is required, which usually means an expensive air ticket. With a bit of research – ringing around travel agents, checking Internet sites, perusing the travel ads in newspapers – you can often get yourself a good travel deal. Start early as some of the cheapest tickets need to be bought well in advance and popular flights can sell out.

Full-time students and people under 26 years (under 30 in some countries) have access to better deals than other travellers. You have to show a document proving your date of birth or a valid International Student Identity Card (ISIC) when buying your ticket and boarding the plane.

Many travel agencies around the world have websites, which can make the Internet a quick and easy way to compare prices. There is also an increasing number of online agents which operate only on the Internet. Some useful sites include:

Cheapest Flights Cheap worldwide flights from the UK, although you've got to get in early for the bargains. **W** www.cheapestflights.co.uk

Cheap Flights A very informative site with specials, airline info and flight searches from the UK. **W** www.cheapflight.com

Expedia Microsoft's travel site, this is for the US but has links to sites for Canada, the UK and Germany. **W** www.expedia.msn.com

Flight Centre International A respected operator for straight flights with sites for Australia, New Zealand, UK, USA and Canada.
W www.flightcentre.com

Flights.com A truly international site for flight-only tickets; cheap fares and easy-to-search database. **W** www.tiss.com

STA The leader in world student travel but you don't necessarily have to be a student. This also has links to worldwide STA sites.
W www.statravel.com

Travel.Com A good Australian site – you can look up fares and flights into and out of the country. **W** www.travel.com.au

Travelocity This US site allows you to search fares from/to practically anywhere (in US$).
W www.travelocity.com

Travel Online A good site to check worldwide flights from New Zealand. **W** www.travelonline .co.nz

Round-the-World & Circle Pacific Tickets

If you're flying to New Zealand as part of a bigger trip, especially from Europe or the UK, Round-the-World (RTW) tickets can be real bargains – sometimes not much more than a standard return fare and you get four or more stopovers. They are usually put together by a combination of two airlines and permit you to fly anywhere you want on their route systems so long as you do not backtrack. There may be restrictions on how many stops you are permitted and usually the tickets are valid up to a year. An alternative type of RTW ticket is one put together by a travel agent using a combination of discounted tickets.

A good UK agent like Trailfinders can put together interesting London-to-London RTW combinations that include New Zealand from £800. Or try the excellent website W www.roundtheworldflights.com that allows you to build your own trips with up to six stops from the UK. A four-stop trip including Asia, Australia, New Zealand and the USA costs from £700.

Airbrokers (W www.airbrokers.com) is a US company specialising in cheap RTW tickets. A South Pacific trip from Los Angeles, including New Zealand, Australia and some Pacific island stops, costs around US$1300.

Circle Pacific tickets use a combination of airlines to circle the Pacific – combining Australia, NZ, North America and Asia. As with RTW tickets, there are advance purchase restrictions and limits to how many stopovers you can take. These fares are likely to be around 15% cheaper than RTW tickets.

Travellers with Specific Needs

If they're warned early enough, airlines can often make special arrangements for travellers such as wheelchair assistance at airports or vegetarian meals on the flight. Children under two years travel for 10% of the standard fare (or free on some airlines) as long as they don't occupy a seat. They don't get a baggage allowance. 'Skycots', baby food and nappies should be provided by the airline if requested in advance. Children aged between two and 12 can usually occupy a seat for half to two-thirds of the full fare, and do get a baggage allowance.

The disability-friendly website W www.everybody.co.uk has an airline directory that provides information on the facilities offered by various airlines.

Australia

New Zealand cities with flights to and from Australia are Auckland, Christchurch, Wellington, Dunedin, Palmerston North and Hamilton (the last three have Freedom Air flights only). Air New Zealand and Qantas Airways are the main carriers, though quite a few international airlines include Australia and NZ on their Asia-Pacific routes.

Freedom Air (☎ 1800 122 000, W www.freedomair.com), a no-frills budget airline, flies from the Gold Coast and Newcastle to Auckland (around A$400 return) and from Sydney, Brisbane and Melbourne to Dunedin, Palmerston North and Hamilton for similar fares. To get these fares you need to book at least 14 days in advance and they're not available during the peak season (15 December to 19 January). One-way fares are only marginally cheaper than return. Virgin Blue (W www.virginblue.com.au) plan in 2003 to start flying trans-Tasman routes at prices comparable to Freedom Air.

Typical rock-bottom fares from a travel agent specialising in discount tickets from Sydney cost from A$450 return to Auckland, and $550 to Christchurch or Wellington. From Melbourne the equivalent fare is around A$650 to Auckland, Christchurch or Wellington. Return fares in peak season cost around A$200 more, while tickets valid for two months or longer are also more expensive. It's possible to fly into Auckland and out of Christchurch to save backtracking, but again you won't get the cheapest fares with this type of ticket.

Two agents good for cheap fares are STA Travel and Flight Centre. STA Travel (☎ 1300 360 960; W www.statravel.com.au) has an office at 222 Faraday St, Carlton, in Melbourne, and offices in all major cities and on many university campuses.

Flight Centre (☎ 13 31 33 Australiawide; W www.flightcentre.com.au) has a central

Air Travel Glossary

Alliances Many of the world's leading airlines are now intimately involved with each other, sharing everything from reservations systems and check-in to aircraft and frequent-flyer schemes. Opponents say that alliances restrict competition. Whatever the arguments, there is no doubt that big alliances are the way of the future.

Courier Fares Businesses often need to send urgent documents or freight securely and quickly. Courier companies hire people to accompany the package through customs and, in return, offer a discount ticket which is sometimes a bargain. However, you may have to surrender all your baggage allowance and take only carry-on luggage.

Fares Airlines traditionally offer 1st class (coded F), business class (coded J) and economy class (coded Y) tickets. These days there are so many promotional and discounted fares available that few passengers pay full fare.

Lost Tickets If you lose your airline ticket, an airline will usually treat it like a travellers cheque and, after inquiries, issue you with another one. Legally, however, an airline is entitled to treat it like cash and if you lose it then it's gone forever. Take very good care of your tickets.

Onward Tickets An entry requirement for many countries is that you have a ticket out of the country. If you're unsure of your next move, the easiest solution is to buy the cheapest onward ticket to a neighbouring country or a ticket from a reliable airline which can later be refunded if you do not use it.

Open-Jaw Tickets These are return tickets where you fly out to one place but return from another. If available, this can save you backtracking to your arrival point.

Overbooking Since every flight has some passengers who fail to show up, airlines often book more passengers than they have seats. Usually excess passengers make up for the no-shows, but occasionally somebody gets 'bumped' onto the next available flight. Guess who it is most likely to be? The passengers who check in late. If you do get 'bumped', you are normally offered some form of compensation.

Reconfirmation Some airlines require you to reconfirm your flight at least 72 hours prior to departure. Check your travel documents to see if this is the case.

Restrictions Discounted tickets often have various restrictions on them – such as needing to be paid for in advance and incurring a penalty to be altered or cancelled. Others are restrictions on the minimum and maximum period you must be away.

Round-the-World Tickets RTW tickets give you a limited period (usually a year) in which to circumnavigate the globe. You can go anywhere the carrying airlines go, as long as you don't backtrack. The number of stopovers or total number of separate flights is decided before you set off and they usually cost a bit more than a basic return flight.

Ticketless Travel Airlines are gradually waking up to the realisation that paper tickets are unnecessary encumbrances. On simple one-way or return trips, reservations details can be held on computer and the passenger merely shows ID to claim their seat.

Transferred Tickets Airline tickets cannot be transferred from one person to another. Travellers sometimes try to sell the return half of their ticket, but officials can ask you to prove that you are the person named on the ticket. On an international flight, tickets are compared with passports.

office at 82 Elizabeth St, Sydney, and there are dozens of offices throughout Australia.

The USA

Most flights between the USA and NZ are to/from the USA's West Coast. Most travel through Los Angeles but some are through San Francisco. If you're coming from some other part of the USA, your travel agent can arrange a discounted 'add-on' fare to get you to the city of departure.

Excursion (round-trip) fares are available from various airlines but are more expensive than those from travel agents. Cheaper 'short life' fares are frequently offered for limited periods. Discount travel agents in the USA are known as consolidators. San Francisco is the ticket consolidator capital of America, although some good deals can be found in Los Angeles, New York and other major cities.

Council Travel (☎ 800 226 8624, **W** www .counciltravel.com) is the USA's largest student travel organisation, with 60 offices in the USA. STA Travel (☎ 800 777 0112, **W** www.statravel.com) has offices in Boston, Chicago, Miami, New York, Philadelphia, San Francisco and other major cities.

At the time of writing competition on this route had dropped considerably and a struggling Air New Zealand had cut back flights so fares were not cheap. Standard return fares from Los Angeles or San Francisco start at about $1200 to US$1600 with Qantas, Air New Zealand or United Airlines. From New York it's about US$1700 to US$2200. In low season and with restructured tickets, you should be able to find fares lower than these.

If you want to visit other Pacific destinations on your way to or from NZ, compare carefully the stopover possibilities offered by each airline. Air New Zealand offers an excellent variety of stopover options on its route between Los Angeles and Auckland. You can tack on stopovers in Honolulu, Tahiti, Rarotonga, Samoa, Tonga and Fiji quite cheaply. Other airlines fly to NZ for the same price, or sometimes cheaper, but with more limited stopover options.

Canada

Canadian discount air ticket sellers are also known as consolidators and their air fares tend to be about 10% higher than those sold in the USA; at the time of writing you could pick up cheap fares from Vancouver to Auckland from C$1400 and from Toronto for C$1800.

Travel CUTS (☎ 800-667-2887, **W** www .travelcuts.com) is Canada's national student travel agency and has offices in all major cities. STA Travel (☎ 1888-427-5639) and Flight Centre (☎ 1888-967-5331) are also represented.

The UK

London's bucket shops are among the cheapest places in Europe to buy international air tickets. Depending on which airline you travel with, flights to New Zealand go via Asia or the USA. If you come across Asia you can often make stopovers in countries like India, Thailand, Singapore and Australia; in the other direction, stopover possibilities include New York, Los Angeles, Honolulu or a variety of Pacific islands. Stopover options vary depending on the airline you use.

Trailfinders (☎ 020-7628 7628, **W** www .trailfinders.co.uk), with two branches in London and more around the country, produces a lavishly illustrated brochure which includes air fare details. STA Travel (☎ 08701-600 599, **W** www.statravel.co.uk) and Flight Centre (☎ 08708-908 099, **W** www.flightcentre.co.uk) also have many branches in the UK.

Discount return flights from London to Auckland can be found for around £550 to £650. Airfares.co.uk (**W** www.airfares.co .uk) is a good online resource.

Advertisements for many travel agencies appear in the travel pages of the weekend broadsheet newspapers, in *Time Out*, the *Evening Standard* and in the free magazine *TNT*.

Continental Europe

Frankfurt is the major arrival and departure point for flights to and from NZ, with connections from there to other European cities. Recommended agencies in Germany include STA Travel (☎ 030-311 0950), Goethestrasse 73, 10625 Berlin, plus branches in major cities across the country.

In France, try OTU Voyages (☎ 01 40 29 12 12, W www.otu.fr), 39 av Georges-Bernanos, 75005 Paris, with branches across the country. Other recommendations include Voyageurs du Monde (☎ 01 42 86 16 00), 55 rue Ste-Anne, 75002 Paris, and Nouvelles Frontières (nationwide number ☎ 08 25 00 08 25, Paris ☎ 01 45 68 70 00, W www.nouvelles-frontieres.fr), 87 blvd de Grenelle, 75015 Paris, with branches across the country.

Recommended travel agents in Italy include CTS Viaggi (06-462 0431), 16 Via Genova, Rome, a student and youth specialist with branches in major cities, and Passagi (☎ 06-474 0923) Stazione Termini FS, Galleria Di Tesla, Rome.

Nouvelles Frontières (☎ 91-547 42 00, W www.nouvelles-frontieres.es) has an office at Plaza de España 18, 28008 Madrid, plus branches in major cities.

Asia

Most Asian countries offer fairly competitive air-fare deals with Bangkok, Singapore and Hong Kong the best places to shop around for discount tickets. Hong Kong's travel market can be unpredictable, but some excellent bargains are available if you are lucky.

DEPARTURE TAX

There's a $20 departure tax from Auckland, Wellington and Dunedin airports, and a $25 tax from Christchurch, Hamilton and Palmerston North, payable at the airport.

SEA

Cruise ships aside, there are no regular passenger ship services to NZ. Even arranging to work your way across the Pacific as crew on a yacht is much more difficult than it used to be. There are many yachts sailing around the Pacific, but nowadays they're usually only willing to take on experienced yachties as crew.

To try your luck finding a yacht, you have to go to the appropriate port at the appropriate time. There are lots of favourite islands, ports and harbours where you're likely to find yachts, such as: Sydney and Cairns in Australia; Bali in Indonesia; various ports in Fiji or Tahiti; and Hawaii, San Diego or San Francisco in the USA. In NZ, popular yachting harbours include the Bay of Islands and Whangarei (both in Northland), Auckland and Wellington.

There are certain times when you're more likely to find yachts. From Fiji, October to November is a peak departure season as cyclones are on their way. March to April is the main departure season for yachts heading to Australia; be prepared for rough seas and storms when crossing the Tasman Sea.

Getting Around

New Zealand has extensive air services, reasonable bus networks and a limited passenger train system. The main cities and tourist areas are well covered and easy to reach. Smaller communities and many interesting out-of-the-way places are not so easy, or often impossible, to reach by public transport.

Transport can be expensive, especially if you pay as you go, but discounts are almost always available. The rules for cheaper travel are: always assume a discount is available, book as far in advance as possible, and get yourself a discount card.

The most readily available discounts are for backpackers and students. Cards issued by backpacker associations, such as Youth Hostel Association (YHA), International Student Identity Cards (ISIC), VIP Backpackers Resorts International (VIP), Budget Backpackers Hostels (BBH) and Nomads, can bring reductions of around 25% to 50% on some services.

Flexibility and the ability to reach so many delightful places away from the tourist hordes make car travel the best way to see NZ. Competition between the many small rental car operators means cheap car hire, but beware of insurance policies and the bond requirement. For stays of a couple of months or more, it is worth considering buying a car and reselling it when you leave. NZ is also very well set up for cyclists.

AIR

Flying can be a good option, particularly if you've already done the same journey by land. Discounted flights can make flying in NZ reasonable value and there are some great views to be had, particularly over the mountains or volcanoes.

Domestic Air Services

New Zealand's major domestic airline, and the only true national carrier, is Air New Zealand (☎ 0800 737 000, Ⓦ www.airnew zealand.co.nz). With a host of connecting flights, the Air New Zealand network just about covers the entire country. Smaller airlines, such as Eagle Air and Air Nelson, are partly owned or booked by Air New Zealand and come under its Air New Zealand Link umbrella.

Origin Pacific (☎ 0800 302 302, Ⓦ www .originpacific.co.nz) is the next biggest with services to all major centres between Auckland and Christchurch and also from Christchurch to Queenstown. It's an efficient regional airline with some attractive fares.

Freedom Air (☎ 0800 600 500, 09-912 6801, Ⓦ www.freedomair.co.nz) is a no-frills, budget airline with cheap domestic flights between Auckland, Wellington and Christchurch – Auckland to Christchurch costs $109 if booked on the Internet.

Qantas New Zealand (☎ 0800 737 000, Ⓦ www.qantas.co.nz) maintains routes between Auckland, Wellington, Christchurch, Rotorua and Queenstown, mostly using other airlines' planes.

Apart from the major operators, there are many local and feeder airlines, such as Stewart Island Flights (between Invercargill and Stewart Island), Great Barrier Airlines and Air Chathams. If you go all green at the thought of taking a ferry across the Cook Strait, flights between the North and South Islands are a popular and cheap alternative to ferry services – Soundsair does the short hop for $68.

Discount Fares

Air New Zealand, Qantas New Zealand and Origin Pacific have regular listed economy fares, but also regular discounts – which make it virtually unnecessary to ever pay the full fare.

Some discounts apply for domestic tickets bought before arrival in NZ. Air New Zealand's Visit New Zealand fares, which can only be bought outside the country, offer a 15% discount from 1 October to 30 April and 25% during the other months. However, better discounts often apply to tickets bought in conjunction with an international flight (on any airline), depending on the country you are flying from; ask your travel agent.

On the other hand, the various discount fares available in NZ are up to 50% cheaper than the regular fare, although restrictions apply – no-refund rules may apply for cancellations and the fares may not be available at peak times, such as school holidays.

Other discounts and one-off specials may be available. Always ask about discounts when booking domestic tickets at airline offices, or go through a travel agent.

Air Passes

Air New Zealand offers an Explore New Zealand Pass for residents of other countries. Valid for all Air New Zealand and Link flights, it can be bought overseas or in New Zealand on presentation of an international ticket, but in NZ a 12.5% GST is added.

The tickets are in the form of coupons and represent one sector (ie, a single flight with just one flight number). Flights use between one and three coupons, depending on how many transfers are involved. The pass can be excellent value for long-distance, direct or through flights, eg, Auckland to Dunedin, but shorter hops involving transfers make it less attractive. Passes are issued in conjunction with an international ticket (with any airline) and are valid for the life of that ticket.

The cost of passes varies according to the number of coupons involved:

pass	price (NZ$)
three coupons	515
four coupons	686
five coupons	858
six coupons	1030
seven coupons	1201
eight coupons	1373

BUS

Bus travel in NZ is relatively easy and well organised, but can be expensive and time consuming. The main bus companies are InterCity (☎ 09-913 6100, 03-379 9020, W www.intercitycoach.co.nz) and Newmans (☎ 0800 777 707, W www.newmanscoach .co.nz), which InterCity operates. Guthrey's Express (☎ 0800 759 999, W www.nz here.com) is a growing competitor with a number of routes in the North Island and using private operators to cover South Island routes. Shuttle bus companies also cover many routes – see that section later.

InterCity buses go to almost all bigger towns and the main tourist areas. Newmans operates in the North Island (but not Northland) and from Christchurch to Milford via Mt Cook and Queenstown. The Northland route is admirably covered by Northliner Express (☎ 09-307 5873, W www.nz info.com/northliner).

Buses on major routes usually run at least daily, although on weekends on some routes they may run less frequently or not at all.

Discount Fares

Fares vary only slightly between companies. Knowing the discounts available can cut travel costs by as much as 50% – you should never have to pay full fare. All bus companies have free timetable booklets detailing discounts and schedules. Most of the following discounts apply only to trips that would otherwise cost $20 or more.

InterCity and Newmans offer a 25% discount to seniors (over 60), 33% discount to children under 12, 20% discount to card-carrying students, and 15% to anyone with recognised backpackers cards (VIP, YHA, BBH, Nomads). These discounts are easy to get and have no special restrictions.

InterCity also has Saver/Super Saver fares offering a 25% to 50% discount on some services, but you need to book ahead as seats are limited. Discounts for return fares are usually 20%.

On standard fares you get a full refund if you cancel more than two hours before departure, otherwise the penalty is 50%. On Saver and Super Saver fares you can forget the refund if you cancel within two hours of departure.

[Continued on page 112]

BUS & TRAIN ROUTES

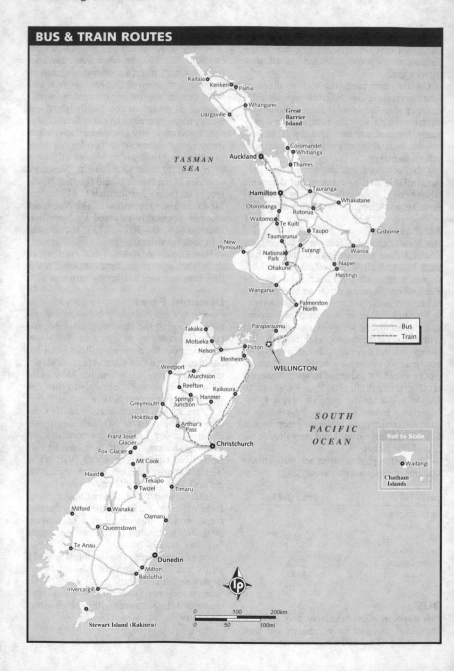

Air Fares

from	to	one way (NZ$)	from	to	one way (NZ$)
Auckland	Wellington	100	Christchurch	Nelson	69
Auckland	Christchurch	118	Christchurch	New Plymouth	138
Auckland	Dunedin	299	Christchurch	Queenstown	300
Auckland	Hamilton	39	Christchurch	Rotorua	140
Auckland	Napier	107	Christchurch	Hokitika	190
Auckland	Nelson	137	Wellington	Christchurch	100
Auckland	New Plymouth	96	Wellington	Gisborne	275
Auckland	Palmerston North	158	Wellington	Dunedin	159
Auckland	Rotorua	215	Wellington	Hamilton	103
Auckland	Kaitaia	230	Wellington	Nelson	77
Auckland	Kerikeri	245	Wellington	Westport	250
Auckland	Whangarei	175	Wellington	Blenheim	85
Auckland	Great Barrier Island	576	Wellington	Napier	240
Auckland	Whakatane	210	Wellington	Whakatane	310
Auckland	Queenstown	590	Wellington	Palmerston North	180
Auckland	Taupo	218	Wellington	Rotorua	247
Christchurch	Dunedin	99	Wellington	Chatham Is (return)	576
Christchurch	Hamilton	143			
Christchurch	Napier	146			

Bus Fares

from	to	one way (NZ$)	from	to	one way (NZ$)
Auckland	Hamilton	18	Paihia	Kaitaia	29
Auckland	New Plymouth	53	Picton	Kaikoura	15
Auckland	Paihia	44	Picton	Nelson	15
Auckland	Rotorua	45	Queenstown	Dunedin	30
Auckland	Taupo	51	Queenstown	Greymouth	80
Auckland	Tauranga	38	Queenstown	Invercargill	43
Auckland	Thames	32	Queenstown	Milford	81
Auckland	Wellington	99	Queenstown	Mt Cook	63
Christchurch	Dunedin	30	Queenstown	Te Anau	35
Christchurch	Greymouth	30	Queenstown	Wanaka	25
Christchurch	Kaikoura	15	Rotorua	Gisborne	39
Christchurch	Nelson	35	Rotorua	Taupo	21
Christchurch	Picton	30	Te Anau	Dunedin	61
Christchurch	Queenstown	45	Te Anau	Invercargill	40
Dunedin	Invercargill	43	Wellington	Napier	62
Nelson	Greymouth	40	Wellington	New Plymouth	61
New Plymouth	Wanganui	30	Wellington	Rotorua	78

Train Fares

from	to	one way (NZ$)	from	to	one way (NZ$)
Auckland	Palmerston North	104	Picton	Kaikoura	42
Auckland	Wellington	128	Picton	Christchurch	77
Wellington	Palmerston North	30	Kaikoura	Christchurch	44
Picton	Blenheim	20	Christchurch	Greymouth	87

[Continued from page 109]

Travel Passes

The major bus lines offer discount travel passes valid from around 14 days to three months. InterCity, with the biggest network, has the most options. As with any unlimited travel passes, you have to do lots of travelling to make them pay and there's no backtracking except on dead-end routes (ie, Milford Sound). Book ahead to be sure of a seat.

InterCity, in conjunction with the Tranz Scenic rail network and the *Interislander* ferry, offers a Best of NZ pass (**W** www.best pass.co.nz) covering bus/train/ferry travel that allows you to save up to 30% if you plan your itinerary well enough. You have three points options (600 points for adult/child $462/308, 800 for $598/402 and 1000 for $725/486) and can purchase top-up points when you need them (100 points costs $77/52).

A 1000-point ticket could include Auckland to Wellington by train and coach, the *Interislander* and a fair whack of the South Island by train (including the *TranzAlpine*) and coach.

The main travel passes (available at visitor information centres and bus depots) include:

InterCity Passes InterCity has numerous passes, either covering the whole country, or the North and South Islands separately. If you're planning to cover a lot of ground, the passes can work out cheaper than paying as you go, but they lock you into using Inter-City buses (rather than, say, the convenient shuttle buses that cover much of the country). Combo passes include:

Pathfinder A seven-day pass from Auckland to Christchurch, including most of the South Island as far as Milford Sound (adult/child $408/273).
Trail Blazer A 10-day pass Auckland-Auckland, including South Island loop and Northland (adult/child $524/351).
Total Experience A 12-day pass Auckland-Auckland, covers most of the country except Northland (adult/child $588/394).
North Island passes include: Coromandel Trail from Auckland with onward travel to Rotorua ($101/68). Auckland-Wellington via Waitomo, Rotorua and Taupo ($125/84); Auckland-Wellington via Napier, Rotorua and the east coast ($209/140); Auckland, Northland, Great Barrier Island, Whitianga, Rotorua, Taupo, Wellington (or Waitomo with return to Auckland; $341/228)
South Island passes include: Nelson to Queenstown via the West Coast ($129/86); Christchurch to Milford via Queenstown and Mt Cook ($149/100); Picton to Queenstown or Te Anau via Christchurch and Dunedin ($149/100); Greymouth-Christchurch loop via Queenstown, Milford and Mt Cook ($282/188).

There may be a reservation charge of $3 per sector (depending on the agent), or check to see if stand-by seats are available.

Northliner Express Northliner offers discount backpackers passes for Northland, which provide unlimited travel on various routes. The Bay of Islands ($53), Northland Freedom ($115), Loop ($83) and Top Half ($80) passes are valid for one month from date of purchase.

Shuttle Buses

Small shuttle-bus companies offer useful services throughout the country. Typically these buses are smaller, cheaper and have a friendlier atmosphere than the regular buses.

Some of these services are designed with foreign travellers and/or backpackers in mind and have lots of little extras that make them attractive. Some will pick-up and drop-off at your accommodation or leave from central destinations, and make photo-stops along the way. The South Island, between Picton/Nelson and Christchurch, Greymouth and Queenstown, is particularly well covered by these buses, with many competing on the same runs. Atomic Shuttles is the biggest South Island operator.

Following are a few examples of the more useful or extensive services in New Zealand – these are not hop-on-hop-off tours such as those operated by Kiwi Experience, but genuine shuttles. North Island services are listed first:

Alpine Scenic Tours (☎ 07-386 8918) Services between Turangi and National Park, with useful stops for trampers in Tongariro National Park and extension services up to Taupo and Rotorua.
Call-a-Bus (☎ 0800 100 550) Services between Auckland to Tauranga.

Go Kiwi Shuttles (☎ 0800 446 549) Coromandel Peninsula.

Hot Water Beach Connexions (☎ 06-866 2478) Whitianga to Hahei and Hot Water Beach on the Coromandel Peninsula.

Waitomo Shuttle (☎ 0800 808 279) Otorohanga to Waitomo.

Waitomo Wanderer (☎ 0800 924 866) Loops between Waitomo-Rotorua-Taupo.

South Island shuttle bus companies include:

Atomic Shuttles (☎ 03-322 8883) Daily services between Christchurch, Dunedin, Invercargill, Picton, Nelson, Greymouth and Queenstown/Wanaka.

Alpine Coaches (☎ 0800 274 888) Christchurch to Hokitika/Greymouth via Arthur's Pass.

Alpine Shuttles (☎ 03-443 7966) Services from Wanaka to Cardrona and Treble Cone ski fields.

Coast to Coast (☎ 0800 800 847) Christchurch to Hokitika/Greymouth via Arthur's Pass.

Cook Connection (☎ 025 583 211) Mt Cook to Timaru three times a week.

East Coast (☎ 03-789 6251) Christchurch to Westport and return daily.

Hanmer Connection (☎ 0800 377 378) Daily from Hanmer to Christchurch and Kaikoura.

High Country Shuttles (☎ 0800 435 050) Twizel to Mt Cook three times daily.

Kahurangi Bus (☎ 03-525 9434) Services all the towns between Nelson and Collingwood, and the Abel Tasman and Heaphy Tracks.

Karamea Express (☎ 03-782 6617) Westport to Karamea for the southern end of the Heaphy Track.

Kiwilink (☎ 0800 802 300) Picton and Nelson to Invercargill via Christchurch and Dunedin.

Knightline (03-547 4733) Picton to Motueka via Blenheim and Nelson.

Knightrider (☎ 03-342 8055) Christchurch to Invercargill via Dunedin.

Lazerline (☎ 0800 220 001) Christchurch to Nelson via Lewis Pass daily.

Southern Link Shuttles (☎ 03-358 8355) Christchurch to Queenstown, Picton and Dunedin.

Spitfire Shuttle (☎ 03-214 1851) Daily between Invercargill and Te Anau.

Wanaka Connexions (☎ 03-443 9122) Daily between Wanaka and Queenstown.

Backpackers Buses

Bus companies catering for backpackers offer hop-on-hop-off passes lasting from several days to weeks for various parts of the country. The passes offer a degree of flexibility, some more than others, allowing you to get off the bus for independent travel and then catch the next bus. In summer it can be difficult to get a seat on a crowded bus, so advance bookings are necessary.

The buses are comfortably fitted, their atmosphere is casual, drivers provide some commentary and there are plenty of sightseeing and activity stops along the way.

If you have limited time, can't be bothered arranging transport connections, want to see a number of spots en route and sample a wide variety of activities, these buses may be ideal. Probably the biggest advantage is meeting other travellers. If you're travelling solo, this is a great way to meet travelling companions. The downside is the feeling that you're really on tour, and the party aspect doesn't appeal to some travellers.

The best-known companies are Kiwi Experience and Magic Travellers Network, which runs the Magic Bus, and at the time of writing there were rumoured to be two new backpacker buses starting up. A few others run specialised routes with varying degrees of flexibility. We get lots of feedback about Kiwi and Magic, most of it positive. The best thing is to compare passes and companies when you arrive in NZ and talk to other travellers – you're bound to see them piling out of one or both buses at hostels.

All companies have pamphlets detailing itineraries, departure times and costs; they require advance booking and usually a deposit. Be sure you understand the refund policy in case you decide to cancel. The main companies (and their routes, prices and details) include:

Flying Kiwi (☎ 0800 693 296, **e** flying.kiwi@ xtra.co.nz, **w** www.flyingkiwi.com) The Flying Kiwi is a tour rather than a bus service. With an emphasis on outdoor activities, its 'rolling travellers' home' includes hot shower and kitchen and carries mountain bikes, a Canadian canoe, a windsurfer, fishing gear and more. Accommodation is camping – you can bring you own tent or hire one. There's an additional food fund and the group takes turns at cooking. South Island trips include eight-day ($395) and 10-day ($795) trips. North Island options include nine-day comprehensive ($465) and two-day Northern Express ($99) trips. A 27-day, all-NZ tour costs from $1195.

Kiwi Experience (☎ 09-366 9830, e enquiries@ kiwiex.co.nz, W www.kiwiexperience.com, 170 Parnell Rd, Auckland). The biggest of the hop-on-hop-off backpacker/tour buses, the familiar pea-green bus operates a very comprehensive service on the North and South Islands. There are 17 routes, and most passes are valid for one year. Trips include: North Island Loop ($265, seven-day minimum) or South Island Loop ($360, eight-day minimum); all-NZ tours ($470 to $615, from a minimum 12 to 18 days); and the Whole Kit & Caboodle trip ($925, minimum 25 days). Useful small loops where other services are limited include Awesome Adventures & Top Bit around Northland, the Bottom Bus along the Catlins and Southern Scenic Route, East Cape Escape, Milford Sound Overland Adventure and the Ghost Train loop, which includes the *TranzAlpine* ($310).

Magic Bus (☎ 09-358 5600, e info@magicbus .co.nz, W www.magicbus.co.nz) Magic Bus is another hop-on-hop-off bus operating an extensive network on the North and South Islands, with 13 main trips from a minimum of four days to 23 days. Trips range from the basic North ($185) or South ($195) to all NZ tours (minimum 23 days) for $985.

West Coast Express (☎ 03-546 5007, W www .cyberskink.co.nz/westcoastexpress) This hop-on-hop-off bus does a six-day Nelson to Queenstown route via the West Coast for $115; you can depart from either end of the line.

TRAIN

Sadly, New Zealand's privately owned rail network is on the wane as far as passenger services go. It now covers just a few main routes; most of the North Island services ended in October 2001 when the company's new owner, West Coast Railways, rejected them as being unprofitable. They included the *Bay Express* (Wellington-Napier) and the *Geyserland Express* (Auckland-Rotorua).

Fortunately, what remains includes some of the most scenic rail journeys in the southern hemisphere. In NZ you travel on the train for the journey – not in order to get anywhere. Best known is the stunning *TranzAlpine*, from Christchurch to Greymouth via Arthurs Pass. Also good is the *TranzCoastal* from Picton to Christchurch, and there's the *Northerner* from Auckland to Wellington.

Tranz Scenic has a nationwide central reservations centre (☎ 0800 802 802, W www.tranzscenic.co.nz) which is open from 7am to 9pm daily (from overseas call ☎ 64-4-498 3303). Reservations can also be made at most train stations, travel agents and visitor centres. The Tranz Scenic fares and timetables booklet is available at most train stations and visitor centres.

As with the buses, there are discounts for trains. YHA and VIP card holders get a 20% discount, students 20%, seniors 30% and disabled travellers 50%. A limited number of other discounted seats are set aside on each train – advance booking is required. Discount fares are: Super Saver (50% discount), Saver (30%) and Economy Fare (15%).

CAR & MOTORCYCLE

Without doubt, the freedom of your own vehicle is the best way to explore New Zealand in depth. Driving around NZ is quite easy. Distances between towns are short, traffic is light and the roads are usually in good condition, though there are very few multilane highways in the country. Petrol (gasoline) is relatively expensive at about $1.05 a litre (around $4 a US gallon); prices vary slightly from station to station and from city to countryside, but only by a few cents.

Driver courtesy is reasonably good in the towns, but the highways are full of cowboys. Driving 20km/h over the speed limit and aggressive tailgating are common, despite the forever twisting and narrow roads. There are brief stretches of motorway heading outwards from Auckland, Wellington and Christchurch. Elsewhere in the country, apart from the occasional overtaking lane, highways are single-lane in either direction and pass through the towns. Traffic is generally light, especially in the South Island, but it is easy to get stuck behind a truck or campervan. Count on covering about 80km for every hour of driving on the highways.

Unsealed, backcountry roads are another hazard for the uninitiated. Many visitors lose control by moving onto the loose gravel verges and skidding into ditches.

Kiwis drive on the left, as in the UK, Australia, Japan and much of Asia. For those used to driving on the right – take care. Every year serious or fatal accidents involve foreign drivers, many of them driving on the wrong side of the road.

A 'give way to the right' rule applies. This is interpreted in a rather strange fashion when you're turning left and an oncoming vehicle is turning right into the same street. Since the oncoming vehicle is then on your right you have to give way to it.

Speed limits on the open road are generally 100km/h; in built-up areas the limit is usually 50km/h. An LSZ sign stands for Limited Speed Zone, which means that the speed limit is 50km/h (although the speed limit in that zone is normally 100km/h) when conditions are unsafe due to bad weather, limited visibility, pedestrians, cyclists or animals on the road, excessive traffic, or poor road conditions. Speed cameras and radars are used extensively. At single-lane bridges (of which there are a surprisingly large number), a smaller red arrow pointing in your direction of travel means that *you* give way, so pull a little to the side if you see a car approaching the bridge from the other end.

Pick up a copy of *The Road Code*, a wise investment that will tell you all you need to know. It's available at the NZ Automobile Association (AA; ☎ 0800 500 444) offices and bookshops. There is a similar book for motorcyclists.

A valid, unrestricted driver's licence from your home country is required to rent and drive a car in NZ. The AA staff can advise if you wish to obtain an NZ driver's licence. To ride a motorcycle you must have a motorcycle licence or special endorsement on your home-country driver's licence.

Members of an equivalent automobile association overseas may qualify for reciprocal benefits from the AA in NZ; remember to bring your card. Otherwise AA membership is good insurance if you buy a car. Apart from free maps and publications, membership entitles you to free emergency breakdown service, free advice on traffic tickets and accidents, and discounts on services and accommodation.

Rental

Car Usually you must be at least 21 years old to rent a car in NZ (sometimes 26) and under 26s often incur a larger insurance excess.

The major car hire companies offer new cars, countrywide networks (with one-way drop-offs), more reliability, better insurance and high prices. The many smaller companies are much cheaper, have mostly older cars, and contracts and insurance policies have to be looked at closely, but most are reasonably reliable and are certainly more attractive to backpackers.

Because rental-car accidents (usually minor) are so common in NZ, insurance premiums are high. Bigger companies will remove the excess (up to $1500) for around $15 a day extra, but smaller operators offering cheap rates often have a compulsory insurance excess, taken as a credit-card bond, of around $700. Some but not all travel-insurance policies will cover your car-rental insurance excess themselves if there's an accident – in which case there's no need to pay the extra fee. But check it out in advance! Insurance coverage for all hire cars is invalid on certain roads, typically beaches (such as the Ninety Mile Beach) and unsealed roads in major tourist areas.

The big operators – Avis (W www.avis .com), Budget (W www.budget.co.nz), Hertz (W www.hertz.co.nz) – have extensive fleets of cars with offices in most cities and at major airports. Unlimited kilometres rental of a small car (a late-model Japanese car of 1600cc or less) starts at around $70 per day, more for rental of only a few days. Medium-sized cars are typically around $100 per day with unlimited kilometres. A drop-off fee may apply if you're not returning the car to the city of hire; however, on rental of a month or more this should be waived between Auckland and Wellington or Christchurch. On the other hand, an operator in Christchurch may need to get a vehicle back to Auckland and will offer an amazing one-way deal (Budget lists relocation specials on their website). Overseas travel agents can often get better deals in hiring new cars through major operators than you can hunt out yourself in NZ.

A huge number of smaller companies undercut the big operators, but there may be more restrictions on use and one-way rentals may not always be possible. On the other hand, an operator in Christchurch may need to get a vehicle back to Auckland and will offer a good one-way deal. Ring around and find out what specials are on. Some budget operators, such as Pegasus (☎ 0800 803 580, W www.rental cars.co.nz) and Shoestring (☎ 0800 746 378, W www.carhire.co.nz/shoestring) have national networks.

Car rental is competitive in Auckland, Christchurch, Wellington and also in Picton since it's a gateway to the South Island, but Auckland is still the cheapest place to rent. The surplus of operators means that you can often get special deals for longer rentals, especially outside the peak summer months. Shop around by phone – quoting a competitor's rates may bring a reduction, even from the major companies. In peak season you may get a good, reasonably current model for $55 a day (all inclusive) for rentals of more than four days.

Many smaller operators have old second-hand cars, advertised for as little as $25 per day, but you get what you pay for. Advertised rates (and even quotes over the phone) are often misleading, and business practices can leave a lot to be desired. Always check kilometre rates, if the price includes GST, minimum-hire periods, the age of the car, bonds and insurance coverage. Always read the rental agreement before you sign.

Insurance from the cheaper rental agencies is usually subject to a $700 excess for any accident or damage to the car (some even include tyre replacement and puncture repairs), even if it is not your fault. Most, however, will cash your bond but refund it later if the other driver's blame can be proved and they have insurance (don't count on it).

If you are prepared to risk the insurance excess, second-hand car hire can be good value. By shopping around, you can hire a 10-year-old Japanese import for a month in the off season for as little as $25 a day or a more recent model for $40 a day (sometimes less). Prices are up to 50% higher in the peak season.

Campervan Campervans (also known as mobile homes, motor homes or, in US parlance, RVs) are an enormously popular way of getting around NZ. In tourist areas of the South Island almost every other vehicle seems to be a campervan. Campervans combine transport, accommodation and cooking facilities. The only drawback is that you might feel a little isolated in your self-contained bubble, although holiday parks are great places for meeting other travellers.

Many companies rent out campervans and their costs vary with the type of vehicle and the time of year. A small van, suitable for two people, typically has a sink, hot and cold water, gas cooker, 12V fridge and 240V heater. The dining table and seats fold down to form a double bed. Slightly larger varieties may have their own toilets and showers.

Four- to six-berth campervans are of light-truck size and usually contain the works. They are very comfortable, with an extra double sleeping cabin at the front, microwave, toilet, shower etc. Fuel consumption is about the same as for the smaller vans but they may run on much cheaper diesel fuel. The only drawback is their size – they're not much fun to drive in the cities and sluggish on the hills.

Campervans usually have 240V AC power systems (just plug them in at a motor camp) with backup 12V DC systems, so you can still camp in luxury out in the wild or at basic camp sites. Dispose of waste water properly; toilets must be emptied at designated dumping stations, found at motor camps or provided by some councils.

Peak season (December to February) rates through the main companies for two/four/six-berth vans are around $170/ 250/300 a day, dropping to as low as $70/ 110/125 in winter (May to September) and slightly less again for more than three weeks' hire. But price wars have sometimes seen rates drop to as low as $65 a day for a four-berth van. Overseas travel agents can also get good discounts.

Maui (☎ 0800 651 080, 09-255 0620, W www.maui.co.nz) and Britz (☎ 0800 831 900, 09-275 9090, W www.britz.co.nz) are two of the biggest operators. Other (cheaper) operators include Kea Campers (☎ 09-444 4902, W www.kea.co.nz) and the budget Backpacker Campervans (☎ 03-358 4159, 09-255 0620, W www.back packercampervans.com). Smaller operators' rates start at around $40 per day for kitted-out minivans.

Motorcycle New Zealand is a great country for motorcycle touring, despite the changeable weather. Most of the country's motorcycle hire shops are in Auckland, but Christchurch has a few too. You can hire anything from a little 50cc moped (nifty-fifty) for zipping around town to a big 750cc touring motorcycle. To hire a regular motorcycle (rental bikes are usually from 250cc to 750cc) you need a valid motorcycle licence.

NZ Motorcycle Rentals (☎ 09-377 2005, W www.nzbike.com), 31 Beach Rd, Auckland, has Yamahas, BMWs, touring and enduro bikes from $79 to $375 a day. You can climb on a Harley 1450cc for $350 a day. It also has a buy-back option, and a branch at 166 Gloucester St, Christchurch (☎ 03-377 0663).

Purchase

Car For a longer stay and/or for groups, buying a car and then selling it at the end of your travels can be one of the cheapest and best ways to see NZ. You can often pick up a car as cheap as (or cheaper than) a one- or two-month rental, and you should be able to get back most of your money. The danger is, of course, that you'll buy a lemon and it will break down every five minutes.

Auckland is the easiest place for travellers to buy a car, followed by Christchurch. An easy option for a cheap car is to scour the notice boards of backpacker places, where other travellers sell their cars before moving on. You can pick up an old car for only a few hundred dollars.

Some backpackers specials are so cheap it may be worth taking the risk that they will finally die on you.

Other good options in Auckland and Christchurch are the car markets, or car auctions. There are three weekly car markets in Auckland (see that chapter for details), the Canterbury Car Fair in Christchurch and a smaller market in central Wellington. Auctions are interesting events where you can pick up cheap cars from around $1000 to $4500, but you don't have the luxury of a test drive. Turners Auctions (☎ 587 1400, 0800 282 8466, W www.turners.co.nz) is the largest in the country with 11 locations, including Auckland, Christchurch and Wellington. It's worth checking its website. Otherwise, cars are advertised in the newspapers just like anywhere else in the world.

Another option is the 'buy-back system', where the dealer guarantees to buy the car back from you at the end of your travels. The buy-back amount varies, but may be 50% less than the purchase price. Hiring or buying and selling it yourself (if you have the time) is usually much better value.

Make sure any car you buy has a WOF (Warrant of Fitness) and that the registration lasts for a reasonable period. A WOF certificate, proving that the car is roadworthy, is valid for six months but must be less than 28 days old when you buy a car. To transfer registration, both you and the seller fill out a form which can be filed at any post office. Papers are sent by mail within 10 days. It is the seller's responsibility to transfer ownership and pay the costs involved. If needed, registration can be purchased for either six months or a year (around $200 per year). Third-party insurance, covering the cost of repairs to another vehicle in an accident that is your fault, is also a wise investment.

Car inspections are highly recommended and the cost may well save you in repair bills later. Various car inspection services will check any car you intend to buy for around $85. They stand by at car fairs and auctions for on-the-spot inspections, or will come to you. The AA also offers a mobile inspection service – it is slightly cheaper if you bring the car to an AA-approved mechanic. AA checks are thorough, but most garages will look over the car for less.

Another wise precaution before you buy a car is to ring for a credit check (☎ 0800 658 934). If you have the licence plate and chassis numbers, the ownership of the car can be confirmed and you can find out if any outstanding debts remain on it.

BICYCLE

Many cyclists call NZ a pedaller's paradise. The country is clean, green, uncrowded, friendly, there are numerous camping options and cheap accommodation, plenty of fresh water, the climate is not too hot or too cold, and the roads are good. Hills make for hard going at times, but it's a compact country with plenty of variety. You'll spot touring cyclists almost everywhere in NZ, especially in summer. Bikes and cycling gear (to rent or buy) are readily available in the main centres, as are bicycle repair services.

By law you must wear an approved safety helmet (or risk a fine) and it's also good to have reflective gear for cycling at night or on dull days.

Lonely Planet's *Cycling New Zealand* is a comprehensive guide with detailed maps, route descriptions and elevation profiles, plus tips on what to see and do along the way and where to stay and eat. The *Pedallers' Paradise* booklets by Nigel Rushton cover the North and South Islands.

Classic New Zealand Mountain Bike Rides by the Kennett brothers, Paul, Simon and Jonathan, suggests a wide variety of short and long rides all over NZ.

Occasionally a cyclist may resort to public transport. The major bus lines and trains only take bicycles on a 'space available' basis (meaning bikes may not be allowed on) and charge up to $10. Some of the shuttle or backpackers buses, on the other hand, make sure they always have storage space for bikes and often carry them for free.

Many international airlines will carry your bicycle at no additional cost as 'sporting equipment'. Except on the smallest planes, domestic airlines take bicycles for $20.

Rental

Many bicycle rental operators offer daily and weekly bicycle hire, with negotiable monthly rates. Costs vary widely – rates can be anywhere from around $15 to $50 a day, or $80 to $150 a week. They depend on what kind of bike you get and where you get it from.

Backpacker hostels often have cheap bikes for rent, but they range from clapped out to standard, rigid-fork mountain bikes.

Purchase

Bicycles can be readily bought in NZ's larger cities, but prices are high for new bikes. For a decent hybrid bike or rigid mountain bike you'll need to pay from $800 to $1200, though you can get a cheap one for around $500. You're better off bringing your own or buying a used one.

Backpacker hostel notice boards frequently have signs offering mountain bikes for sale. Alternatively, check adverts in the local newspapers.

HITCHING

Hitching is never entirely safe in any country in the world, and we cannot recommend it. Travellers who decide to hitch should understand that they are taking a small but potentially serious risk. People who do choose to hitch will be safer if they travel in pairs and let someone know where they are planning to go. The well-publicised murder of two Swedish hitchers a few years ago highlights the fact that even in relatively safe NZ hitching can be a risky undertaking.

That said, NZ is a great place for hitching, and although almost anybody who does a fair amount of hitching will get stuck somewhere uncomfortable for an uncomfortably long time, most travellers rate it highly. It's pretty safe and the roads are not crowded, but there are just enough cars on the main routes to make things fairly easy and the locals are well disposed towards hitchhikers.

Hitching on the main North Island routes is generally good. In the South Island hitching down the east coast from Picton through Christchurch to Invercargill is mostly good. Elsewhere in the South Island, hundreds of kilometres of main roads have very little traffic. Expect long waits – even days – in some places. If it gets too much (eg, you find yourself hurling abuse at drivers who don't stop), catch a bus, but you may have to get into the next town first.

It's easier hitching alone if you are male, or better still with a female companion. Unfortunately, even though NZ is basically a safe country for women, a woman on her own may experience some tricky – if not dangerous – situations. It is better to hitch with someone else if possible. Many backpacker places have local hints for hitching (such as what bus to get out of town and where to hitch from) on their notice boards.

BOAT
Inter-island Ferries

The *Interislander* and *Lynx* services, operating between Wellington in the North Island and Picton in the South Island, are covered in the Wellington Region chapter.

Other regularly scheduled inter-island ferry services include those to the various islands in the Hauraki Gulf off Auckland (see the Auckland chapter). A ferry also connects Stewart Island with the South Island at Bluff, near Invercargill.

Other Water Transport

Transport can be more convenient by water than by land, especially in the Marlborough Sounds where many of the places to stay can only be reached by boat. Regular launch and water-taxi services also operate along the coast of Abel Tasman National Park.

Other convenient ferry services include the ferries in the Bay of Islands, such as the Russell-Paihia passenger ferry and the car ferry crossing over from Opua.

In other places, such as Wakatipu, Taupo and Waikaremoana, transport over lakes is a good way to get around and see things.

URBAN TRANSPORT
Bus & Train

Most of the urban buses have been privatised and only operate on profitable runs, ie, hardly at all. Larger cities have bus services but, with a few honourable exceptions, they are mainly daytime, weekday operations and departures are infrequent. On weekends, particularly on Sunday, bus services can be hard to find or may stop altogether. Central Auckland has a good Link bus service.

The only city with a good suburban train service is Wellington.

Taxi

The main cities have plenty of taxis and even small towns may have a local service. Taxis cruise the busy areas in Auckland, Wellington and Christchurch, but elsewhere you usually either have to phone for one or go to a taxi rank.

An interesting variation on the taxi is the tuk-tuk (or autorickshaw), a three-wheeled Asian contraption which you might find operating in Auckland and the Bay of Islands (Paihia and Russell).

ORGANISED TOURS

Tours can sometimes be a useful way of getting around, especially in otherwise hard-to-reach areas, when your time is limited or when you want the benefit of commentary. For instance, the trip to Cape Reinga along the Ninety Mile Beach in the country's far north is best done on a tour from Kaitaia or the Bay of Islands. Throughout this book, organised tours are listed under the relevant sections.

Backpackers often use the 'alternative' buses as a sort of informal tour (see Backpackers Buses under Bus earlier in this chapter). For instance, Kiwi Experience has a number of short 'add-ons' that can be taken as stand-alone tours, so check out their itineraries.

New Zealand Nature Safaris (☎ 0800 697 232, **W** www.nzsafaris.co.nz) has small-group tours with an emphasis on hiking, wildlife and wilderness areas. A North Island safari, the West Coast Wilderness and Secret South tours are all 10 days and cost

$920, plus a food kitty. Accommodation (camping, huts or cabins) costs extra.

More conventional tours include Thrifty Tours (☎ 09-478 3550, www.tourmasters .co.nz), which uses a combination of tour buses and public transport to create a variety of short and long tours all over NZ.

The organisation Bushwise Women (☎ 03-332 4952, W www.bushwise.co.nz) specialises in trips for women only. The trips range from working on conservation projects to tramping and kayaking, but all provide a good opportunity to meet other women travellers.

NORTH ISLAND

Auckland cityscape

Te Papa Tongarewa (Museum of New Zealand)

Te Papa Whakahiku (Auckland Museum)

Modern sculpture on Queen St

Auckland Region

☎ 09 • pop 1.2 million

The name Auckland (in Maori, 'Tamaki Makaurau') refers both to a region, stretching roughly from the Bombay Hills in the south to the Whangaparaoa Peninsula in the north; and to a city, nestled between the Waitemata and Manukau Harbours.

Auckland

It may not be the nation's capital, but Auckland is New Zealand's largest, most vibrant and far and away most happening city. By international standards it's quite small – some would say more of a village than a metropolis – but it's also one of the world's most exciting waterside cities. To really appreciate it, you have to take to the waters, sailing on the harbour or ferrying out to the nearby islands of the Hauraki Gulf.

Dubbed the 'City of Sails', Auckland has plenty of enthusiastic yachties and the America's Cup defence of 2000 – and preparations for the 2003 Cup – have breathed new life into the swish Viaduct area in central Auckland.

On land, Auckland is covered in volcanic hills, replete with *pa* (fortified Maori villages). So many islanders from NZ's Pacific neighbours have moved to the city that it now has the largest concentration of Polynesians in the world, most living in the southern suburbs. More recently it has attracted immigrants from Asia, and it's these foreign influences that help give Auckland a much more cosmopolitan feel than other NZ cities.

Administratively, Auckland city consists of four cities and three districts, which form one vast urban sprawl. Auckland City proper lies between Waitemata and Manukau Harbours. North Shore City, centred on Takapuna, is just over the harbour bridge. Manukau City is to the south of Auckland, around the airport, and Waitakere City is to the west. Rodney District is

Highlights

- Cruising the Waitemata Harbour by yacht or ferry
- Exploring the exhibitions at Auckland War Memorial Museum, and catching a Maori cultural show
- Dining or stopping for coffee on Ponsonby or Parnell Rds
- Day-tripping to historical Devonport on the ferry
- Visiting the islands of the Hauraki Gulf, particularly volcanic Rangitoto, vineyard-laden Waiheke and the wild Great Barrier Island
- Tramping through the rugged forest of the Waitakere Ranges

on the North Shore and borders the Kaipara Harbour; Papakura and Franklin Districts are south of Manukau City. Some 30% of New Zealand's population calls the Auckland region home.

Being the international gateway to the country, Auckland has plenty of accommodation, a reasonably good transport system and the best of New Zealand's restaurants and entertainment venues.

GREATER AUCKLAND

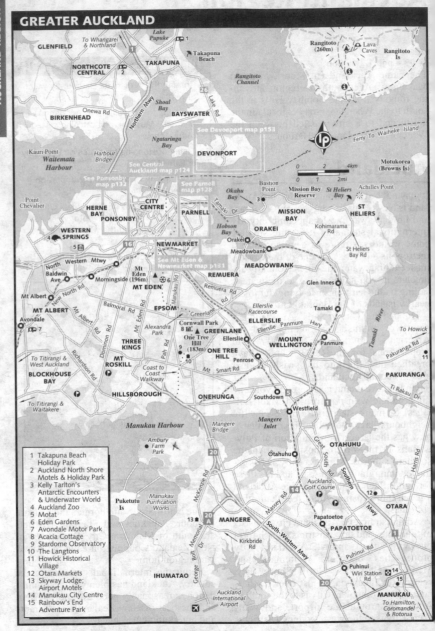

1 Takapuna Beach
  Holiday Park
2 Auckland North Shore
  Motels & Holiday Park
3 Kelly Tarlton's
  Antarctic Encounters
  & Underwater World
4 Auckland Zoo
5 Motat
6 Eden Gardens
7 Avondale Motor Park
8 Acacia Cottage
9 Stardome Observatory
10 The Langtons
11 Howick Historical
  Village
12 Otara Markets
13 Skyway Lodge;
  Airport Motels
14 Manukau City Centre
15 Rainbow's End
  Adventure Park

HISTORY

Maori settlement in the Auckland area dates back at least 800 years. Initial settlements were concentrated on the coastal regions of the Hauraki Gulf islands, but gradually the fertile isthmus became settled and land was cleared for gardens. From the 17th century tribes from outside the region challenged the local Ngati Whatua tribe for this desirable place. The locals in response built fortified villages, or pa, on Auckland's numerous volcanic cones. But when the first Europeans arrived in the area in the 1830s they reported a land largely devoid of inhabitants. The Auckland isthmus (Tamaki Makaurau – literally, 'Tamaki Desired by Many') had largely been forsaken: ravaged by war, or the threat of it.

From early colonial times the administrative centre of the country had been at Russell in Northland, but after the signing of the Treaty of Waitangi in 1840 Captain William Hobson, NZ's first governor, moved the capital south to a more central position. The site of Auckland was chosen principally for its fine harbour (Waitemata, meaning 'Sparkling Waters'), fertile soil and central location. In September 1840 officials came down from Russell to formally proclaim Auckland the NZ capital. Hobson named the settlement after his commanding officer, George Eden (Lord Auckland). Beginning with just a few tents on a beach at Official Bay, the settlement grew quickly. Twenty years after its establishment it was extensively farmed, with its port kept busy exporting the region's produce, including kauri. Yet it lost its capital status to Wellington after just 25 years.

Since the beginning of the 20th century Auckland has been NZ's fastest-growing city and its main industrial centre. Political deals may be done in Wellington, but Auckland is the dominant commercial centre.

ORIENTATION

The commercial heart of the city is Queen St, which runs from Queen Elizabeth II Square (QEII Square) near the waterfront up to Karangahape Rd (K Rd). On the way it passes Aotea Square, and comes within a few blocks of the landmark Skytower.

While the commercial district has accommodation, restaurants and nightlife, it suffers from the 'dead heart' syndrome of many cities. K Rd, with its artists' enclaves, ethnic restaurants and nightclubs is a lively, bohemian alternative. Parnell, just east of the city centre, is a fashionable area of renovated wooden villas. Parnell Rd is lined with restaurants and boutiques, and continues to fashionable Broadway in Newmarket. Just west of the city centre are Ponsonby and Jervois Rds, packed with cafes and bars. Further out of town, Mt Eden, Kingsland, Takapuna and the eastern beaches are residential suburbs with more restaurants and cafes. Devonport, easily reached by ferry across the harbour, is a quaint waterside suburb on the southern end of the residential North Shore.

INFORMATION
Tourist Offices

There are two visitors centres in downtown Auckland: the busy Auckland Travel & Information Centre (☎ 09-979 2333, fax 979 2334, ℯ visitor@auckland.tourism.co.nz, ⓦ www.aucklandnz.com) is at 287 Queen St. It's open from 8.30am to 5.30pm Monday to Friday and 9am to 5pm Saturday and Sunday. Bookings for transport, accommodation or tours can be made via email (ℯ reservations@aucklandnz.com).

At the Viaduct Harbour, the New Zealand Visitor Centre (☎ 09-979 7005, ℯ nzvc@ aucklandnz.com), near the corner of Quay and Hobson Sts, is a more spacious and less hectic place, open from 9.30am to 5.30pm daily.

If you manage to get lost in the city centre, or you just need a chat, look out for the **Auckland City Ambassadors** wandering around in bright red and yellow jackets and boy scout hats. They're around the streets daily and you can collar them for any information – beats asking strangers or looking for a policeman.

The Visitor Information Centre (☎ 09-275 6467), at the international airport, is open daily from the first flight to the last. At the domestic airport, the Visitor Information Centre (☎ 09-256 8480) is open from 7am to 7pm daily.

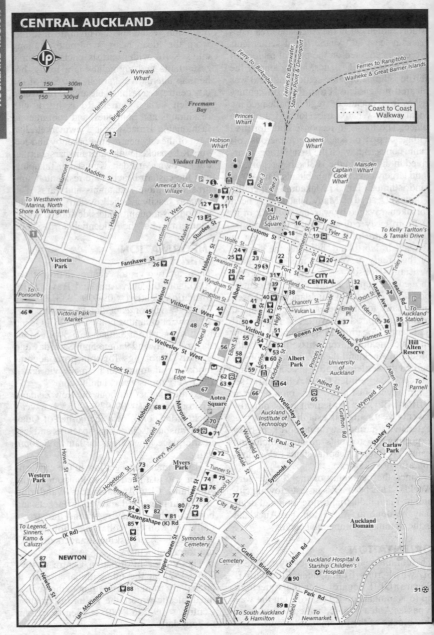

CENTRAL AUCKLAND

CENTRAL AUCKLAND

PLACES TO STAY

1	Hilton Hotel
21	Fat Camel Backpackers
22	Queen St Backpackers
23	Stamford Plaza Hotel
27	The Heritage Auckland
32	Aspen Lodge
35	Auckland City Hotel
36	Darlinghurst Quest Inn
37	Hyatt Regency Hotel
41	City Life Auckland
47	Albion Hotel
52	Downtown Backpackers Albion Park
55	Auckland Central Backpackers; Auckland Travel Centre
57	First Imperial Hotel & Apartments
60	Central City Backpackers; Embargo
68	YWCA
73	YMCA
75	Auckland International YHA
78	Auckland City YHA
89	Grafton Hall of Residence
90	Huia Residence

PLACES TO EAT

3	Princes Wharf Restaurants & Cafes
10	Loaded Hog
12	Milano
16	Daikoku; Daikoku Ramen
24	Food Alley
31	White Lady
38	Cafe Melba
39	Khymer; Raw Power; Occidental Belgian Beer Cafe
43	Colombus
44	Mai Thai; Cafe Midnight Express
45	Toto
51	Wofem Bros Bagelry
53	Sierra; City
54	Alba
59	280 Centre (food hall)
74	Japanese & Korean Restaurants
77	No.5 Wine Bistro
80	Food for Life
81	Verona; Departure Lounge
83	Rasoi; Little Turkish Cafe
85	Brazil

PUBS & CLUBS

5	Lenin Bar; Coast Bar; Leftfield
8	Danny Doolans
11	Bubbles Champagne Bar
20	Rose & Crown
25	The Ministry
26	The Immigrant
28	Shakespeare Tavern
40	The Box; Papa Jack's Voodoo Lounge
42	Fu Bar
58	London Bar; STA Travel
76	The Temple
79	The Khuja Lounge
86	Galatos
87	Dogs Bollix
88	The Kings Arms Tavern

OTHER

2	Subritsky Ferry Terminal
4	Soren Larson
6	NZ National Maritime Museum
7	NZ Visitor Centre
9	Harbour Tours & Water Taxi
13	Tepid Baths
14	Downtown Shopping Centre
15	Ferry Building; DOC; Fullers; Cin Cin on Quay
17	Magic Travellers Network
18	Air New Zealand; Mercure Hotel
19	Downtown Bus Terminal
29	American Express
30	Travellers Contact Point
33	NZ Motorcycle Rentals
34	Car Rental Companies
46	New World Supermarket
48	Skytower; Sky City Hotel; Sky City Coach Terminal; Tamarind; Orbit; Sky City Theatre
49	Automobile Association (AA); Sky Screamer
50	Qantas Travel Centre
56	Atrium on Elliot
61	New Gallery; New Cafe
62	The Civic
63	Force Entertainment Centre (IMAX; Planet Hollywood; Borders; Cybermax); Auckland Visitors Centre
64	Auckland Art Gallery
65	Maidment Theatre
66	Central City Library
67	Aotea Centre
69	Silo Theatre
70	Auckland Town Hall
71	Classic Comedy Club
72	Real Groovy Records
82	St Kevins Arcade (Alleluya; Calibre)
84	Pride Centre
91	Wintergarden

There are several regional tourism offices, including the Arataki Visitor Centre in the Waitakere Ranges. There are also centres at Devonport, Orewa (on the Hibiscus Coast) and on both Waiheke and Great Barrier Islands (see those sections for details).

The Department of Conservation (DOC) has an information centre (☎ 09-379 6476) at the ferry building in downtown Auckland.

The free tourist information booklets *Auckland A-Z Visitors Guide* and Jason's *Auckland – What's On* contain maps of the city and various listings.

The Automobile Association (AA; ☎ 09-377 4660) is at 99 Albert St. Members of an overseas auto club have reciprocal rights, and it has accommodation directories and excellent maps. The office is open from 8.30am to 5pm Monday to Friday and 9am to 3pm Saturday.

Money

There are plenty of moneychangers, banks and ATMs on Queen St. The exchange rates offered at private moneychangers are similar but it pays to shop around. Thomas Cook

(☎ 0800 200 232) has bureaux de change at 34 and 159 Queen St. American Express (☎ 09-367 4422) is at 105 Queen St.

The Bank of New Zealand branch at the airport is open for all international arrivals and departures.

Post

Poste restante (general delivery) is held at the main post office in the Bledisloe building on Wellesley St West, near the corner of Queen St. There are several NZ post offices throughout the city – office hours are from 9am to 5pm Monday to Friday.

Email & Internet Access

Rates vary slightly from place to place, but generally expect to pay from $4 to $6 an hour. There are so many Internet cafes that it's not worth listing them, and most backpacker places have access. Two better ones in the city are Cyber Max, 291 Queen St and PC Com Cyber Centre, 109 Queen St.

Internet Resources

The following sites are useful for tracking down information about Auckland:

Auckland Live Gig guide, events guide, activities and exhibitions.
  W www.aucklandlive.co.nz
Auckland Regional Council Facts and information about Auckland's environment parks and transport.
  W www.arc.govt.nz
Out & About For restaurant listings, what to do and local events.
  W www.outandabout.co.nz

Travel Agencies

For international air tickets, try STA Travel (☎ 0800 874 773, 09-309 0458), and Flight Centre (☎ 09-358 0074, 377 4655). Both have several offices in Auckland.

Backpacker travel centres offer good deals and discounts on activities, but remember if activities are cancelled you may have to return to Auckland to collect your refund. The biggest is Auckland Central Travel (☎ 09-358 4874) in Auckland Central Backpackers.

Travellers Contact Point (TCP; ☎ 09-300 7197), at 87 Queen St, is another good

agency that provides plenty of budget travel services and has branches in Australia and London.

Bookshops

Whitcoulls, on the corner of Queen and Victoria Sts, is a huge bookshop with good NZ, travel and fiction sections. Unity Books at 19 High St has an excellent selection of fiction and nonfiction. Parsons Bookshop, on the corner of Lorne and Wellesley Sts, specialises in books on art and culture.

Auckland has many second-hand bookshops. Among the best is the Hard to Find (But Worth the Effort) Secondhand Bookshop at 171–173 The Mall, Onehunga. There's a branch on Victoria Rd, Devonport.

Libraries

The Central City Library (☎ 09-377 0209) is at 44–46 Lorne St. It's open from 9.30am to 8pm Monday to Thursday, until 9pm Friday and from 10am to 4pm Saturday.

Medical Services & Emergency

Vaccinations for onward travel are available at:

Travelcare (☎ 09-373 4621) 5th floor, Dingwall building, 87 Queen St
Traveller's Health & Vaccination Centre (☎ 09-520 5830) 21 Remuera Rd, Newmarket
Traveller's Medical and Vaccination Centre (TMVC; ☎ 09-373 3531, fax 373 3732) Level 1, Canterbury Arcade (off Queen St)

There are also many private accident and emergency clinics. See the *White Pages* telephone directory under 'Hospitals' and other health service providers for contact details. Public hospitals, such as the following, have accident and emergency clinics:

Auckland Hospital (☎ 09-379 7440) Park Rd, Grafton
Middlemore Hospital (☎ 09-270 4799) Hospital Rd, Otahuhu
North Shore Hospital (☎ 09-486 1491) Shakespeare Rd, Takapuna

In the case of an emergency, the police can be contacted on ☎ 111.

America's Cup 2003

On 15 February 2003, the 31st America's Cup yacht race will begin, and Auckland – which has already spent four years in the planning and anticipation – will go nuts.

The America's Cup (affectionately known as the 'Auld Mug') has a long and illustrious history. In 1851 the *America* sailed to England, participated in and won the Round the Isle of Wight Race. A silver pitcher was presented to the skipper of *America* who took it back to the USA. In 1857, it was entrusted to the New York Yacht Club (NYYC). It was first challenged for (unsuccessfully) in 1870–71 by the British.

Challenge after challenge was mounted but the cup seemed to be cemented safely in its case at the NYYC. The Australians had been peppering away until, in 1983, *Australia II*, with its now legendary winged keel, beat the NYYC's *Liberty* 4–3, taking the cup out of the USA for the first time. US defence stalwart Dennis Conner, skipper of the unsuccessful defender, was flabbergasted and vowed to get it back. In 1987 he wrested the cup from the Aussies off Fremantle, Western Australia.

New Zealand's first real challenge was mounted in 1988 in San Diego. Amid legal wrangling, the defender's *Stars and Stripes* beat challenger *KZ1* (now on display outside the maritime museum). In 1992 the cup was again successfully defended by the San Diego Yacht Club.

On 14 May 1995 NZ's *Black Magic*, skippered by Russell Coutts, won the fifth straight race against *Young America*, skippered by Conner. The remarkable 5–0 victory in this final challenge series off San Diego entitled the Kiwis to take the America's Cup out of the USA for only the second time in 144 years. And it was only NZ's third cup challenge.

After *Black Magic*'s 1995 win, the defence of the cup fell to Team New Zealand/Royal NZ Yacht Squadron. After some indecision, Auckland and the Hauraki Gulf were chosen as the defence site, and regatta courses were sited in the East Coast Bays between Rangitoto Island and the Whangaparaoa Peninsula.

The Viaduct Basin was totally redeveloped and 12 challenger syndicates settled into the Cup Village in 1999. Many new bars and restaurants opened up to cater for the influx of spectators and accommodation prices went sky high. The world had come to Auckland.

Challenging syndicates from Spain, Japan, Italy, Switzerland, France and Australia sailed in the Louis Vuitton Challenger Series from October 1999 to February 2000 to earn the right to challenge the defending Team New Zealand. Italy's *Luna Rossa* went through to compete against NZ's *Black Magic* (the first time in history that the Yanks were not involved in the finals).

The Italian and New Zealand boats raced in February and March 2000. *Black Magic*, skippered by Russell Coutts and buoyed along by a nation clad in red socks, trounced *Luna Rossa* conclusively, 5–0 in a possible nine race series.

With the right to defend and host the international event again in 2003, Auckland is brimming with Cup fever and the Viaduct Basin has never been busier. The nine-race series (the challenger is decided in October 2002) will take place during February and early March 2003. Accommodation will be tight, but this will be a great time to be in the City of Sails.

Gay & Lesbian

The Out! Bookshop (☎ 09-377 7770) at 45 Anzac Ave and the Pride Centre (☎ 09-302 0590, W www.pride.org.nz) at 281 K Rd are both good contact points for the gay and lesbian community. The fortnightly gay magazine *Gay Express* (W www.gayexpress.co.nz) boasts a complete guide to gay Auckland. The city also hosts the very popular HERO Festival every February. The flamboyant street parade follows a week of gay and lesbian cultural events.

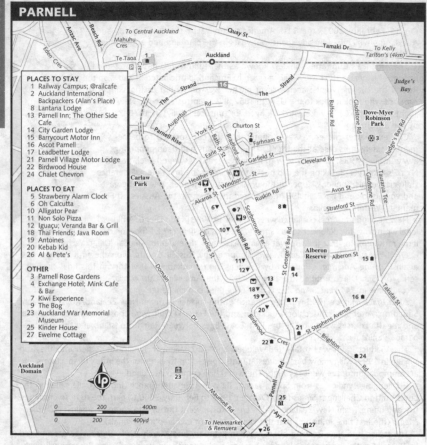

PARNELL

PLACES TO STAY
1 Railway Campus; @railcafe
2 Auckland International Backpackers (Alan's Place)
8 Lantana Lodge
13 Parnell Inn; The Other Side Cafe
14 City Garden Lodge
15 Barrycourt Motor Inn
16 Ascot Parnell
17 Leadbetter Lodge
21 Parnell Village Motor Lodge
22 Birdwood House
24 Chalet Chevron

PLACES TO EAT
5 Strawberry Alarm Clock
6 Oh Calcutta
10 Alligator Pear
11 Non Solo Pizza
12 Iguaçu; Veranda Bar & Grill
18 Thai Friends; Java Room
19 Antoines
20 Kebab Kid
26 Al & Pete's

OTHER
3 Parnell Rose Gardens
4 Exchange Hotel; Mink Cafe & Bar
7 Kiwi Experience
9 The Bog
23 Auckland War Memorial Museum
25 Kinder House
27 Ewelme Cottage

THINGS TO SEE & DO
Skytower

The imposing Skytower (☎ 09-363 6400, Ⓦ www.skycity.co.nz, cnr Federal & Victoria Sts; tickets $15; open 8.30am-11pm Mon-Thur, 8.30am-midnight Fri & Sun) is part of the Sky City complex – a 24-hour casino with revolving restaurant, cafes, bars and the sky lounge. At 328m it is the tallest structure in the southern hemisphere. A lift takes you up to the observation decks in 40 seconds; in a 200km/h wind the top of the building sways up to 1m. It costs $3 extra to catch the skyway lift to the ultimate viewing level: the spectacular views, better viewing windows and fewer observers make it well worth while. Late afternoon is a good time to go up, when you can see the sun set over the horizon and the city lights come on.

The **Sky Jump** (☎ 0800 759 586, Ⓔ bookings@skyjump.co.nz) brings New Zealand's obsession with death-defying activities to the big smoke. At 192m it's the world's highest tower-based jump, but this is not your standard bungy. It's a 20-second freefall using a cable and 'fan descenders' used by movie industry stunt actors. A jump costs $195.

New Zealand National Maritime Museum

This museum (☎ 0800 725 897, 09-373 0800, W www.nzmaritime.org; adult/child $12/6; open 9am-6pm daily) on the downtown waterfront is dedicated to one of NZ's national obsessions – sailing. It's a well-designed, extensive display area exploring 1000 years of NZ's seafaring history. Dozens of sailing craft and displays are exhibited, including the huge 25m (76ft) outrigger canoe *Taratai* constructed using 1000-year-old methods by navigator Jim Siers, who later sailed it across the Pacific. Outside is *KZ1*, the 1988 America's Cup challenger.

Other exhibits illuminate the Maori and European discoveries of and migrations to NZ. There's a re-creation of an old immigrant ship, complete with swaying movement and creaking floorboards. There are exhibits on navigation, fishing, oral history and even a NZ seaside dairy and classic kiwi bach (holiday home), not to mention the Hall of NZ Yachting, and the world's first jetboat (the Hamilton Jet) invented in NZ in 1957. There's also a replica of the America's Cup and history of the event.

Moored in the harbour is the *Ted Ashby*, a replica of an old trading scow which does heritage cruises on Waitemata Harbour most days (adult/child $15/7, or $19/12 with museum admission).

Auckland War Memorial Museum

The museum (Te Papa Whakahiku; Parnell map; ☎ 09-309 0443, W www.akmuseum .org.nz; adult/child $5/free; open 10am-5pm daily) sits at the apex of a sweeping expanse of lawn that forms part of the Auckland Domain, one of Auckland's oldest parks. Completely refurbished, the museum has a comprehensive display on Pacific Island and Maori cultures on the ground floor, including the historic 25m-long war canoe *Te Toki a Tapiri*. The 1st floor is dedicated to the natural world. There is a first-class activities centre here for children. The 2nd floor focuses on New Zealanders at war – from the 19th century to the peace-keeping assignments of today. It includes a re-creation of 19th-century Auckland.

For many, a highlight of a visit to the museum is the performance of Maori culture, song and dance by **Manaia** (☎ 09-306 704; adult/child $10/7.50). It's an informal show and a good introduction to Maori culture. Afterwards the performers are happy to explain aspects of Maori culture as it relates to museum exhibits. The shows are at 11am, noon and 1.30pm.

Although admission to the museum is by donation, the cashier encourages $5 per adult. The United Airlines Explorer Bus (see the Organised Tours section later in this chapter) passes the museum's front door every 30 minutes. It's about a 25-minute walk from Queen St through the domain or you can catch either the Link or Explorer Bus to Parnell Rd, from where it's a short walk.

Kelly Tarlton's Antarctic Encounter & Underwater World

This unique aquarium (☎ 0800 805 050, 09-528 0603, 23 Tamaki Drive; adult/child/family $24/10/49; open summer 9am-8pm daily, winter 9am-6pm daily) is housed in old stormwater holding tanks. It is designed to re-create the experience of scuba diving around the NZ coast. A transparent acrylic tunnel runs through the centre of the aquarium, through which you travel on a moving footpath – the fish, including sharks, swimming all around you. You can step off at any time to take a better look. The aquarium was the inspiration of the late Kelly Tarlton, himself a diver.

The big attraction, however, is the Antarctic Encounter. It includes a walk through a replica of Scott's 1911 Antarctic hut; a ride aboard a heated Snow Cat through an environment where a colony of king penguins lives at sub-zero temperatures; and a very cold below-the-ice aquarium. There's also a visit to an Antarctic scientific base of the future and exhibits on the history of Antarctica.

One ticket gives you entry to all parts of the complex. Check for the shark feeding times. Get there on bus Nos 746, 750, 755–57 or 767–69 from the Downtown Bus Terminal, or on the Explorer Bus.

Auckland Art Gallery

The Auckland Art Gallery *(Toi o Tamaki; ☎ 09-379 1349)* has two parts, both open from 10am to 5pm daily. The **main building** *(cnr Wellesley St East & Kitchener St; admission free, except special exhibitions)* is two blocks east of Queen St, below Albert Park. The art gallery houses an extensive collection of NZ art, including many works by painters Colin McCahon and Frances Hodgkins. **The New Gallery** *(cnr Wellesley & Lorne Sts; adult/child $4/free)* is for contemporary art and special exhibitions. Entry is free on Monday.

Motat (Museum of Transport & Technology)

This museum *(☎ 09-846 0199, Great North Rd; adult/child $10/5; open 10am-5pm daily)* is at Western Springs near the zoo. Motat is in two parts. **Motat I** has exhibits on transport, communications and energy, including one about pioneer aviator Richard Pearse. This eccentric South Island farmer may have flown even before the Wright brothers, and during his life he produced a steady stream of inventions and devices. Also at Motat I is the infotainment Science Centre, with hands-on exhibits.

Motat II, at nearby Sir Keith Park Memorial Airfield, features displays of rare and historic aircraft. Exhibits include a V1 flying bomb and Lancaster bomber from WWII, but pride of place goes to the huge Solent flying boat that ran a Pacific islands loop in the days of luxury flying.

Electric trams run regularly from Motat I to both the zoo and Motat II.

Auckland Zoo

The Auckland Zoo *(☎ 09-360 3819, Motions Rd; adult/child $12/7; open 9.30am-5.30pm daily)*, though not large, is beautifully landscaped and a continuing renovation programme has replaced many of the old animal houses with more spacious, naturalistic compounds. The **primate exhibit** is particularly well done, and the African animals' enclosure, **Pridelands**, is also excellent, as is the meerkat enclosure, which can be explored through tunnels. There's also a nocturnal house with native birds such as the kiwi. The latest addition to the zoo is a sealion and penguin enclosure.

Last admission to the zoo is at 4.15pm. The Explorer Bus or the Pt Chevalier bus (No 045) from Customs St East will get you to both Motat and the zoo.

Auckland Bridge Climb

Get a unique perspective of the city by climbing the girder bridge that spans the Waitemata Harbour and link the city with the North Shore. The 2½-hour climb involves walking to one of the support pylons (Pier 2), into which you descend, then climbing the arch itself up to the summit and back down the other side. You wear a climb suit with a harness attached to a static line. Day climbs are arranged on demand, with the first climb at 9am and the last at 3pm Monday to Thursday, 6pm Friday to Sunday, plus a night climb at 7.40pm on Saturday. Bookings are essential *(☎ 0800 000 808, 09-625 0445, W www.aucklandbridgeclimb.co.nz, 70 Nelson St)*.

Historic Buildings

There are numerous restored and preserved colonial-era buildings in the city. The oldest of these is **Acacia Cottage** in Cornwall Park at the foot of One Tree Hill. Built in 1841, the cottage was originally where Shortland St is today.

Built in 1862, **Highwic** *(Mt Eden & Newmarket map; ☎ 09-524 5729, 40 Gillies Ave, Epsom; adult/child $5/free; open 10.30am-noon & 1pm-4.30pm Wed-Sun)* and **Alberton**, *(☎ 09-846 7367, 1 Kerr-Taylor Ave, Mt Albert; adult/child $5/free; open 10.30am-noon & 1pm-4.30pm Wed-Sun)* were both large houses of wealthy Victorian New Zealanders.

Ewelme Cottage *(Parnell map; ☎ 09-379 0202, 14 Ayr St; adult/child $3/free; open 10.30am-noon & 1pm-4.30pm Fri-Sun)* was built from fine native kauri by a clergyman in the 1860s. Just five doors from Ewelme, the restored 1857 **Kinder House** *(2 Ayr St; adult/child $2/50c; open 11am-3pm Tues-Sun)* is a fine example of early New Zealand

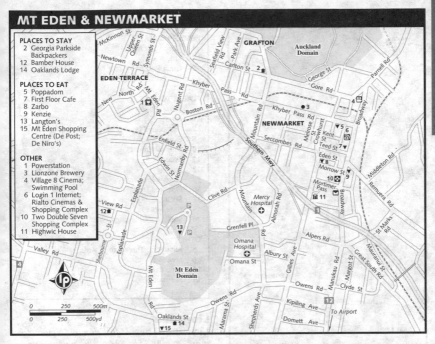

MT EDEN & NEWMARKET

PLACES TO STAY
2 Georgia Parkside
   Backpackers
12 Bamber House
14 Oaklands Lodge

PLACES TO EAT
5 Poppadom
7 First Floor Cafe
8 Zarbo
9 Kenzie
13 Langton's
15 Mt Eden Shopping
   Centre (De Post;
   De Niro's)

OTHER
1 Powerstation
3 Lionzone Brewery
4 Village 8 Cinema;
   Swimming Pool
6 Login 1 Internet;
   Rialto Cinemas &
   Shopping Complex
10 Two Double Seven
   Shopping Complex
11 Highwic House

architecture and has two galleries of the art and memorabilia of the Rev Dr John Kinder.

In southeast Auckland, **Howick Historical Village** (☎ 09-576 9506; *Bells Rd, Pakuranga; adult/child $9/7; open 10am-5pm daily*), in Lloyd Elsmore Park, is a restored village on the old military settlement of Howick. The restored buildings, dating from 1840 to 1880, include a thatched sod cottage, forge, village store and settlers' houses.

Mt Eden & One Tree Hill

Auckland is punctuated by some 48 volcanoes, many of which provide parkland retreats and great views.

The view from Mt Eden (Maungawhau), the highest volcanic cone in the area, at 196m, is superb. You can see the entire Auckland area – all the bays and the land between Manakau Harbour and Hauraki Gulf – and look 50m down into the volcano's crater. The summit crater is sacred to the Maori and known as Te Ipu a Mataaho (meaning 'The Bowl of Mataaho') after the god of volcanoes. You can drive to the top or take bus Nos 274 to 277 from Customs St East and then walk.

The 183m Maungakiekie ('Mountain of the Kiekie Tree'), or One Tree Hill, is a distinctive bald hill, topped only by a huge obelisk and, until recently, a lone Monterey pine. It was the largest and most populous of the Maori pa, and the terracing and dugout storage pits are still visible. It was named after a sacred totara tree that stood here until 1876 and was then replaced by the pine tree.

The pine tree was braced with steel cables after a Maori protester attempted to fell it a few years back in retribution for the felling of the original tree. It was attacked again with a chainsaw in 1999 and a year later the council decided to remove the damaged tree. Hundreds of Aucklanders crowded onto One Tree Hill to farewell the 125 year old city landmark.

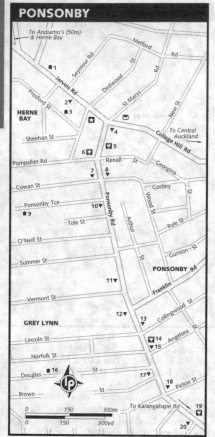

PONSONBY

Stardome Observatory

The Stardome Observatory (☎ 09-624 1246, Ⓦ www.stardome.org.nz; adult/child $12/6) is in the One Tree Hill Domain, off Manukau Rd. At the observatory, as well as viewing the sky inside the planetarium, on clear nights it is possible to view the night sky and stars through a 50cm telescope (adult/child $5/3). The observatory is open every day but the most popular attraction, the **Stardome Show**, is held Tuesday to Saturday evenings (phone the observatory for scheduled times); Sunday is a family day (adult/child $9/6).

Lionzone

Lion Breweries (Mt Eden & Newmarket map; ☎ 09-358 8366, Ⓦ www.lionzone .co.nz, 380 Khyber Pass Rd, Newmarket; adult/ child $15/7.50), NZ's largest multinational brewer, has turned its plain old brewery tours into an interactive 'beer experience'. Two-hour tours are held daily at 9.30am, 12.15pm and 3pm and include a history of brewing, an audiovisual presentation, a virtual tour of the brewing process and, of course, some quality time spent sampling Steinlager and Lion Red beers in a replica brewhouse.

Markets

Opposite Victoria Park is the large **Victoria Park Market** (☎ 09-309 6911, 210 Victoria St West; open 9am-6pm daily). It mostly sells crafts, souvenirs and clothes, but also has outdoor cafes, entertainers and a concentration of eclectic New Age goods. It's a 20-minute walk west from the city centre, or you can take the Link or Explorer buses.

Aotea Square Market is held at Aotea Square on Friday and Saturday from 10am to 6pm. It's a good central market with all sorts of stalls, including food stalls, arts and crafts and entertainment.

Auckland also has traditional markets that sell fruit, vegetables and everyday goods. The biggest and most interesting are the **Otara Markets** *(Newbury St; open 6am-noon Sat)* held in the car park between the Manukau Polytech and the Otara town centre, and the **Avondale Market**, held every Sunday at the Avondale Jockey Club raceway; get off at Avondale Station.

K Rd & Ponsonby

Just south of the central city area, straight up the hill from Queen St, is Karangahape Rd – known simply as **K Rd**. After WWII, the area around K Rd was a popular inner suburb for Maori and then Polynesian residents. In recent years artists have moved in and established studios, and the street has a distinctly bohemian flavour. The strip clubs that gave the street its notoriety are clustered in the slightly seedy western end, towards the junction with Ponsonby Rd. The eastern end has a growing number of cafes and ethnic restaurants.

K Rd runs southwest to Ponsonby Rd and the fashionable suburb of **Ponsonby**. Behind historic shopfronts, Ponsonby Rd's many restaurants are abuzz with the chatter of diners, the hiss of cappuccino machines and the bleep of mobile phones. Ponsonby has many fine old houses, and the adjoining **Herne Bay**, right on the harbour, has some of Auckland's best Victorian homes.

Tamaki Drive

Starting at the Auckland train station, Tamaki Drive crosses Hobson Bay and first reaches **Orakei**, which contains some of Auckland's most expensive real estate. Paratai Drive in Orakei is millionaires' row, with great views across the city. Tamaki Drive continues on to **Bastion Point**. A fort was built here in the 19th century to protect the entrance to the harbour. It now protects the remains of former prime minister Michael Joseph Savage, who in the 1930s introduced the notion of a welfare state. In 1978 Bastion Point became the focus of a land occupation by members of the Ngati Whatua tribe in protest at a proposed development. The protesters were eventually evicted in a huge police operation.

Tamaki Drive leads further around to **Mission Bay**, where there is a park by the beach with an attractive fountain (floodlit at night), and plenty of sidewalk cafes. Further on, **St Heliers Bay** is smaller and more relaxed, with good dining opposite the beach. Further east along Cliff Rd, the **Achilles Point lookout** has dramatic views of the city, harbour and Hauraki Gulf.

Rainbow's End Adventure Park

This large amusement park *(☎ 09-262 2030, cnr Great South Rd & Wiri Station Rd; super pass adult/child $35/25; open 10am-5pm daily)* at Manukau has enough rides (including a corkscrew rollercoaster and the 'fear fall'), shows and interactive entertainment to keep the kids happy all day. Super passes allow unlimited rides while an entry-only pass is $10.

Parks & Gardens

Covering about 80 hectares, the **Auckland Domain**, right near the centre of the city, is a lovely public park that contains the War Memorial Museum and the **Wintergarden**, with its hothouse and fernery.

On Gladstone Rd in Parnell is the **Parnell Rose Gardens**. There are harbour views and the roses are in bloom from November to March.

Popular for jogging, picnics and walks, **Cornwall Park** adjoins One Tree Hill on Greenlane Rd and is an extensive pastoral retreat only 6km south of the city centre. It has sportsgrounds, fields of grazing sheep, a visitors centre (Huia Lodge), Acacia Cottage (see Historic Buildings earlier) and a restaurant.

The **Eden Gardens**, on the slopes of Mt Eden, are noted for camellias, rhododendrons and azaleas – July and August are the best months for viewing camellias.

The extensive **Auckland Regional Council Botanical Gardens** are 27km south of the city. Take the Southern Motorway to the Manurewa turn-off (the one past Rainbow's

End). NZ's most important horticultural fair, the Ellerslie Flower Show, is held here annually in mid-November.

ACTIVITIES
Walking
The visitors centres and the DOC office have pamphlets on walks in and around Auckland. DOC's *Auckland Walkways* pamphlet has a good selection of forest and coastal day walks outside the metropolitan area.

The **Coast to Coast Walkway** is a 16km north-south walk between the Viaduct on Waitemata Harbour and Onehunga Bay on Manukau Harbour. The four-hour walk encompasses Albert Park, the university, the domain, Mt Eden, One Tree Hill and other points of interest, keeping as much as possible to reserves rather than city streets. Starting from the Viaduct and heading south it's marked by yellow markers and milestones – heading north from Onetunga there are blue markers. The visitors centre has a detailed brochure and map showing the walk and describing sights along the way.

Swimming & Surfing
Auckland is known for its fine and varied beaches dotted around its harbours and the coast.

The east coast beaches along Tamaki Drive, including Mission and St Heliers Bays, are popular and can get crowded in summer. At most east coast and harbour beaches swimming is best at high tide. Popular North Shore beaches include Takapuna, Cheltenham and Milford.

For good surf less than 50km from the city, try Te Henga (Bethells Beach), Piha or Muriwai, on the west coast, where the water is often very rough. Most of the surfing beaches have surf clubs and lifeguards. The Aloha Surf School (☎ 09-489 2846) conducts lessons at Piha, and trips south to Raglan for lessons with the excellent Raglan Surfing School (see the Waikato & King Country chapter) can also be arranged from Auckland.

You can hire windsurfers ($25 an hour) and take windsurfing lessons ($75 for level one) at Mission Bay Watersports (☎ 09-521 7245) on the beach at Mission Bay.

The **Tepid Baths** *(☎ 09-379 4754, 100 Customs St; admission $4.50; open 6am-9pm Mon-Fri, 7am-7pm Sat & Sun)* have two undercover pools, a gym, sauna, spa and steam rooms.

Sea Kayaking
Fergs Kayaks *(☎/fax 09-529 2230, 12 Tamaki Drive)*, at Okahu Bay, hires out a variety of kayaks from $12/25 per hour for single/double sea kayaks, or $25/50 for half-day. Sit-on-top kayaks (easier for beginners) are a bit cheaper. Fergs also hires out inline skates ($10 an hour or $25 a day).

Dolphin Swimming
Although Kaikoura (South Island) and Paihia (Bay of Islands) are better known for their resident dolphins, the Hauraki Gulf is a fine habitat for common and bottlenose dolphins, as well as orca and various species of whale. **Dolphin Explorer** *(☎ 09-237 1466, Ⓦ www.dolphinexplore.com; adult/child $90/45)* has daily dolphin swimming trips departing from Pier 3 in downtown Auckland. From April to September there is one trip at 9.30am, and from October to March there are trips at 6am and noon (around five hours). Wetsuits, masks and fins are provided for swimming, and if no dolphins or whales are sighted you can take another trip free. The success rate for whale sightings is around 60%.

These trips could be regarded as ecotours – university dolphin and whale research takes place on board, and some of the proceeds go towards marine research.

Skydiving
You can do tandem skydives, static line jumps and accelerated freefall (AFF) courses with the Mercer Skydiving Centre (☎ 0800 865 867, Ⓦ www.skydiveauckland.com) at Mercer, about 50km south of central Auckland; or Skydive Parakai (☎ 0800 425 867) near Helensville, about 45km northwest. They cost around $250/220 for a 12,000/10,000ft tandem jump and transport can be arranged from Auckland.

Gone Sailing

Nothing gets you closer to the heart and soul of Auckland than sailing on the harbour, and there are plenty of opportunities to give it a go.

One option, particularly if you have some experience, is to wander down to the marina on the weekend (or on weekday evenings) and ask around at the sailing clubs to see if anyone needs a hand crewing. Westhaven Marina is the closest to the city centre and there you'll find the historic **Ponsonby Cruising Club** (☎ 09-376 0245, **W** www.pcc.org.nz), which hosts the social 'Rum Race' every Thursday. You'll need to register beforehand and, although it's free to participate, the club is considering a small entry fee for nonmembers. The race is so called because the winning yacht receives a bottle of rum – but more alcohol is likely to be consumed back at the club afterwards!

There are also commercial operations. **NZL40** (☎ 0800 724 569, 09-359 5987, **W** www.sail newzealand.co.nz) is a $3.5 million grand prix racing yacht originally built for the 1995 America's Cup. It didn't make that event but was used as a trial boat during Auckland's 2000 Cup defence. It now earns its keep as a pleasure craft and passengers are encouraged to help crew. A two-hour spin costs adult/child $85/75 and leaves from the Viaduct Harbour.

Gulfwind Charters (☎ 09-521 1564, **W** www.gulfwind.co.nz, half/full day $75/150 per person), based at Westhaven Marina, can get you out on the water cruising or racing on a 34ft yacht. It also runs sailing courses. **Penny Whiting Sailing** (☎ 09-376 1322, **W** www.tickit.com/nz/sail ing/penny) has a ton of experience and runs highly regarded courses for those serious about learning to sail. The full course (October to March) consists of five three-hour practical lessons for $475.

Other Activities

Ocean Rafting (☎ 0800 801 193, 09-577 3194) is a fast inflatable boat that can whip you around the harbour and further into the gulf. A 45-minute trip costs adult/child $40/20 and a two-hour jaunt around Waiheke and Rangitoto islands is $125/62.50 (Tuesday and Thursday only). It's based in the Viaduct Basin.

Scuba-diving trips and PADI courses are organised by the **Dive Centre** (☎ 09-444 6948, 128 Wairau Rd) in Takapuna, or **Orakei Scuba Centre** (☎ 09-524 2117, 234 Orakei Rd) in Remuera. The best diving is in Northland off Goat Island and the Poor Knight's Islands; see the Northland chapter.

Cliffhanger Adventures (☎ 09-827 0720, **W** www.cliffhanger.co.nz; half/full day trips $95/125) runs abseiling and rockclimbing trips to the Waitakere Ranges and around the west coast. **Balloon Safaris** (☎ 09-415 8289) and **Balloon Expedition Company of NZ** (☎ 09-416 8590) do early morning hot-air balloon flights for around adult/child $220/150.

One of the best places for a round of **golf** is the spectacular 18-hole Howick Golf Course (☎ 09-535 1001, 32 Musick Point) at Bucklands Beach at the mouth of the Tamaki River. The course is on a peninsula that juts out into the Hauraki Gulf and some of the holes are placed alongside sheer cliffs.

The **Sky Screamer** is a three-seater 're-verse bungy' ride set up near the Skytower on Victoria St. One ride costs $35, subsequent rides are $15.

Language Courses

People from around the globe, especially Asia and the Pacific, come to NZ to study English. Auckland has the highest concentration of **language schools** in NZ, and the visitors centre keeps a complete, up-to-date list (check also in Auckland A-Z). Starting Point NZ (☎ 09-813 3735, **W** www.start ingpointnz.com) gives information and advice on universities and language schools, and offers a daily guided tour of six registered language schools ($20).

ORGANISED TOURS

You can spend a day touring the major Auckland attractions in the hop-on-hop-off **United Airlines Explorer Bus** (☎ 0800 439 756,

09-486 8670, W *www.explorerbus.co.nz)* for
$25. It departs daily from the ferry building
every half-hour from 9am to 4pm in summer
and every hour from 10am to 4pm in winter
(May to October). It goes to Mission Bay,
Kelly Tarlton's, Parnell Rose Gardens,
Auckland Museum, Parnell Village, Sky
Tower, Victoria Park Market, Viaduct Harbour and back to the ferry building. At the
museum you can pick up its Satellite Link
(summer only) to Mt Eden, St Lukes Shopping Mall, Auckland Zoo, Motat, IMAX,
Auckland Art Gallery and back to the museum. This service also offers free pick-up
from the airport.

Auckland has plenty of tour operators.
Three-hour bus tours will typically take you
around the city centre, over the harbour
bridge and out along Tamaki Drive, including stops at Mt Eden, the Auckland
Museum and Parnell, for about $40. *ABC
Tours (☎ 0800 222 868, 025 921 145)* also
has an afternoon tour covering Devonport,
the Henderson wine region, Scenic Drive
and the Waitakere Ranges, and Manakau
Harbour ($48). A full-day tour ($85) gives
a good picture of the Auckland region.

*Scenic Pacific Tours (☎ 0800 698 687,
09-634 2266)* and *Great Sights (☎ 0800
744 487, W www.greatsights.co.nz)* are
other major operators with city tours as well
as tours to the Bay of Islands, Waitomo and
Rotorua. Free hotel pick-up and drop-off is
usually included with city tours.

*Auckland Adventures (☎ 09-379 4545;
W www.aucklandadventures.co.nz; tours
$60-89)* is a backpacker-oriented company
with three good-value tours including a
trip out to the wine region and beaches
of the west coast, and a similar trip that
adds a two-hour mountain bike ride to the
itinerary.

If you want to visit the wineries west of
Auckland in style, *Wine Trail Tours (☎ 09-
630 1540, W www.winetrailtours.com;
half/full day tours $75/115)* has small-group
tours, as well as trips further afield to the
Matakana wineries ($119/139). *Fine Wine
Scenic Tours (☎/fax 09-849 4519; tours
$95-149)* has half-day tours visiting three
wineries and the gannet colony at Muriwai,

and longer trips combining wine tasting
with bushwalks or a picnic lunch.

*Geotours (☎ 09-525 3991, W www.geo
tours.co.nz; half-/full-day tours $69/99)*
offers more cerebral trips led by a geologist
who can explain Auckland's volcanic cones
and other geological features, as well as
flora and fauna.

Numerous companies take trips to west
Auckland, including the Waitakere Ranges,
Murawai gannet colony and the beaches.
*Bush & Beach (☎ 09-575 1458, W www
.bushandbeach.co.nz; tours $65-110)* has
several options and will pick-up and drop-
off in the city centre.

Harbour Cruises

Fullers Cruises (☎ 09-367 9111) has the
largest selection of cruises and operates almost all the ferries. Fullers has popular
tours around the inner harbour, including a
daily two-hour harbour cruise (adult/child
$30/15), on which you can visit the Amer-
ica's Cup village and Devonport. Ferries go
to many of the nearby islands in the gulf;
Rangitoto and Waiheke are easy to reach
and make good day or half-day trips from
Auckland.

*Pride of Auckland (☎ 09-373 4557,
W www.prideofauckland.com)*, based at the
NZ National Maritime Museum, operates a
fleet of four monohulls and a catamaran (all
with distinctive blue and white sails).
Cruises range from a 45-minute sail
(adult/child $45/25) to lunch ($65/35) and
dinner ($90/55) cruises.

For one of the best experiences on the
water, take a trip on the tall ship *Soren
Larsen (☎ 09-411 8755, W www.soren
larsen.co.nz)*, a square-rigged, 19th-century
brigantine beauty with 12 sails. The *Soren
Larsen* was built out of oak in Nykøbing
Mors in Denmark and achieved fame as
the star of the TV series *The Onedin Line*.
Day sails in the Hauraki Gulf cost $89 and
that price includes lunch; three-hour
cruises are $49 and overnight voyages are
also scheduled. The ship is based at
Princes Wharf.

There are 45-minute **harbour tours**
(☎ 0508 86872, adult/child $20/10), that

take in the Cup Village, on the hour from 10am to 6pm, leaving from the Viaduct Basin (outside the Loaded Hog).

Plenty of other companies offer cruises; the visitors centre has details. If you're a sailor yourself, most charter companies offer skippered, skippered and crewed, or bareboat (skipper the boat yourself) charters, as well as instruction. Fishing charters are also available.

SPECIAL EVENTS

The visitors centre keeps a list of the many annual events held in Auckland and will provide precise dates. Some of these events are:

January
Open Tennis Championships; Opera in the Park; Auckland Anniversary Day Regatta

February
Devonport Food & Wine Festival; HERO Festival; Aotearoa Maori Performing Arts Festival; America's Cup (2003)

March/April
Waiheke Jazz Festival; Pasifika Polynesian Festival; Royal NZ Easter Show; Asian Lantern Festival; Vintage Alfresco

May
NZ Boat Show

October
Auckland to Russell Yacht Race; Wine Waitakere; Spring Into Art

November
Ellerslie Flower Show

December
Auckland Cup

PLACES TO STAY – BUDGET
Camping & Cabins

Unsurprisingly, camping grounds are outside the city centre and by no means cheap, but the North Shore is not a bad place to stay.

Auckland North Shore Motels & Holiday Park (☎ 09-418 2578, 0508 909 090, e info@nsmotels.co.nz, 52 Northcote Rd, Takapuna) Single/double camp site $22/30, bunkroom $33, cabin $55-67, motel rooms from $94. Situated 4km north of the Harbour Bridge, this pricey five-star holiday park has loads of facilities, including an indoor pool, and it's surprisingly handy to the city.

Takapuna Beach Holiday Park (☎ 09-489 7909, e takabeach@xtra.co.nz, 22 The Promenade, Takapuna) Powered/unpowered sites $26/24 for 2 people, cabins $42-65, motel units $95. Takapuna Park is 8km north of the city centre and right on the beach, with a good view of Rangitoto. Aside from the good location, it's quite cramped and the cabins are pokey for the price.

Avondale Motor Park (☎ 0800 100 542, 09-828 7228, e avondalemotorpark@ xtra.co.nz, 46 Bollard Ave) Powered/ unpowered sites $12/10 per person, on-site vans $40 per double, cabins $50-55 per double, self-contained units $60. Avondale is off New North Rd, 9km southwest of central Auckland and close to Motat and the zoo. It's in a leafy setting and cabin prices are very reasonable.

Hostels

Auckland has plenty of hostels in the city centre and inner suburbs, but you'll still need to book ahead in summer, especially if you want a private room. If you have a car or van, parking is a big problem at the inner-city places. For easier parking, and if you're after a quieter time, try the hostels in Parnell or Mt Eden. If you're after a party, head downtown. All hostels have kitchens; some have cafes and even bars.

City Centre The city centre has the biggest hostels in town, mostly on or just off Queen St. They're all well-equipped and secure, and several are good party places.

Auckland Central Backpackers (☎ 09-358 4877, w www.acb.co.nz, Strand Arcade, Queen St) Dorm beds $20-22, singles/doubles $42/57. Auckland's, indeed New Zealand's, largest hostel recently became even larger when it moved to a new, renovated premises in Queen St. With around 600 beds, a travel centre, job centre, basement bar, 24-hour reception and 40-terminal Internet cafe, it's got everything that opens and shuts as well as friendly, efficient staff.

Fat Camel Hostel & Cafe (☎ *0800 220 198, 09-307 0181,* e *bookings@nomads world.com, 38 Fort St)* Dorm beds $20-21, singles/doubles $40/45, apartments $65. The 200-bed Nomads backpackers has been refurbished; clean apartment-style backpacker rooms open onto a kitchen and lounge area. There's a good bar and cafe downstairs.

Queen St Backpackers (☎ *09-373 3471, 4 Fort St)* Dorm beds $21, twins & doubles $50. For an inner-city place, Queen St is a bit less hectic than some and has a good atmosphere. It has three- and four-bed dorms, private rooms and a big first-floor reception with a beach-theme bar and pool tables.

Auckland International YHA (☎ *09-302 8200,* e *yhaakint@yha.org.nz, 5 Turner St)* Dorm beds $22, twins & doubles $56, en suite double $72. Just off Queen St, this relatively new place has spotless rooms, beds with duvets, a travel centre and a bright ground-floor common area.

Auckland City YHA (☎ *09-309 2802,* e *yhaauck@yha.org.nz, cnr City Rd & Liverpool St)* Dorm beds $22, twins & doubles $56. This eight-storey place is one of Auckland's biggest hostels, but it's in a reasonably quiet spot. There's a ground-floor cafe (Tommy's Bistro) and an outdoor area with good city views on the 3rd floor. It's open 24 hours and has a shop and luggage lockers.

Downtown Backpackers Albert Park (☎ *09-309 0336,* e *bakpak@albertpark .co.nz, 27-31 Victoria St East)* Dorm beds $19-20, singles $40, twins/doubles $45/50. Albert Park is in a good location and has made-up beds in 12-bed and six-bed dorms as well as the usual facilities. The Beam Bar is next door and there's a rooftop garden.

Central City Backpackers (☎ *09-358 5685,* e *ccbnz@xtra.co.nz, 26 Lorne St)* Dorm beds $20-22, singles/doubles $38/50. This is another good, clean hostel which manages to maintain a homey feel despite its size. There's a travel agency and downstairs is the popular Embargo bar.

Georgia Parkside Backpackers (*Mt Eden & Newmarket map;* ☎ *09-309 8999, 0508 436 744,* e *bacpacgeorgia@xtra.co.nz, 189 Park Rd)* Dorm beds $20, singles/doubles $35/46. This backpacker place is a big, old double-storey house in Grafton, overlooking the domain. It has a pleasant courtyard and big balcony but is unfortunately looking decidedly tired and rundown these days.

rocca backpackers auckland (☎ *09-300 9999,* w *www.roccabackpackers.com, 16–20 Fort St)* is due to open in December 2002 in the historic Wrights Building. It will come with all the trimmings, including Internet and a cafe-bar. Dorm beds in four- and six-bed dorms start at $18, and en suite doubles start at $75.

The YWCA and YMCA are both big, centrally located places and often have rooms in summer when everything else is full. Both take men and women.

YWCA (☎ *09-377 8763,* e *ywca@akywca .org.nz, 103 Vincent St)* Singles/twins $25/35, weekly rates $90/125. The YWCA has a friendly, relaxed atmosphere. There is a fully equipped kitchen, a cafe and laundry. Linen is included and there's secure parking.

YMCA (☎ *09-303 2068, cnr Pitt St & Greys Ave)* Singles/doubles $35/55, weekly rates $210/330. The YMCA is another big place with recreation facilities and a gym.

Parnell Stylish Parnell is a good alternative to the city, with plenty of good restaurants and a residential feel. It's a 30-minute walk to downtown or you can take the Link bus.

Auckland International Backpackers (☎ *09-358 4584,* e *international.bp@xtra .co.nz, 2 Churton St)* Dorm beds $19, twins & doubles $46. Also known as Alan's Place, this is the former Parnell YHA and it has a range of rooms in a rambling, slightly ageing but comfortable building. Although close to Parnell Rd, this is a quiet residential location. There's a big kitchen (with walk-in fridge) and a garden/barbecue area.

City Garden Lodge (☎ *09-302 0880, 25 St Georges Bay Rd)* Dorm beds $18-19, twins $42-46, doubles $48. City Garden is a fine hostel in an elegant old two-storey home originally built for the queen of

Tonga. It has a TV-less lounge, separate ladies dorm and a bright upstairs double with views over Neil Finn's home and recording studio.

Lantana Lodge *(☎ 09-373 4546, 60 St Georges Bay Rd)* Dorm beds $19, twins & doubles $46. Lantana Lodge is in a quiet spot right at the end of the northern half of St Georges Bay Rd. It's a friendly, neat and well-run house with made-up beds.

Leadbetter Lodge *(☎ 09-358 0665, 17 St Georges Bay Rd)* Dorm beds $18, doubles $44. Leadbetter is a bit older and pretty grim, compared with others in this street, but it's friendly enough and has a small garden.

Mt Eden A pleasant residential area 4km south of the city centre, Mt Eden is away from the action but has some of the most relaxing hostels in Auckland. Bus Nos 274 and 275 run from the Downtown Bus Terminal to Mt Eden Rd.

Bamber House *(☎ 09-623 4267, ℮ bamber@ihug.co.nz, 22 View Rd)* Dorm beds $20-22, twins & doubles $52. Bamber House is in a huge colonial-era home surrounded by gardens – easily one of the most comfortable and impressive hostels in the city. The rooms are bright and spacious, the house has large and pleasant communal areas (even the TV is huge). There's a swimming pool and trampoline and children are welcome. Buses stop on the corner of Mt Eden and View Rds.

Oaklands Lodge *(☎ 0800 222 725, 09-638 6545, ℮ backpacker@ak.planet.gen.nz, 5A Oaklands Rd)* Dorm beds $19-21, singles $40, twins & doubles $52. Tucked away down a quiet, tree-lined street around the corner from the Mt Eden shops, Oaklands is another laid-back place setting a high standard. The two-storey house has a backyard, clean rooms and the remodelled bathrooms even have wall-mounted hair dryers.

Ponsonby Groovy Ponsonby is a very happening area as far as cafes and bars go, but unfortunately it lacks good budget accommodation and parking is hard to find.

Brown Kiwi *(☎ 09-378 0191, ℮ bookings@brownkiwi.co.nz, 7 Prosford St)* Dorm

beds $19-20, doubles $46. The Brown Kiwi is a well-kept, homey place in a good location. It's a bit cramped and you need a pole vault to get to the top bunks but it has a good courtyard at the back.

Airport With 24-hour shuttles running between the airport and the city centre, it's hardly necessary to spend a night near the airport. If you do, ***Skyway Lodge*** *(☎ 09-275 4443, ℮ skyway@ihug.co.nz, 30 Kirkbride Rd, Mangere)* is the best option for budget accommodation. It has dorm beds for $18, singles/doubles for $45/65, a communal lounge and kitchen and a pool.

University & Student Accommodation

There are several options for travellers to use off-campus student accommodation in the inner city, particularly during the long summer break.

Railway Campus *(Parnell map; ☎ 0800 8644678, 09-367 7100, ℮ railcamp@auckland.ac.nz, 26-48 Te Taou Crescent)* Studios from $77, 2-bedroom apartments $139. In the imposing old railway station, this new apartment complex is the best of the student accommodation (though not cheap) and apartments are generally available year-round. As well as comfortable en suite rooms, there's a huge industrial kitchen, games room, library, funky cafe-bar and good security. The original station concourse has been beautifully renovated.

Huia Residence *(☎ 09-377 1345, fax 377 4871, 110 Grafton Rd)* Singles/doubles $30/40, weekly rates $125/160. Huia has quality rooms in a high-rise building near the Domain. Friendly, safe and highly organised, the reception is open 24 hours and facilities include laundry and Net access.

Grafton Hall of Residence *(☎ 09-373 3994, ℮ graftonhall@auckland.ac.nz, 40 Seafield View Rd)* B&B $40 per person. This large, well-equipped hostel is open to travellers from mid-June to the second week of July and from mid-November to late-February. There's off-street parking, a tennis court, and you can get dinner there for only $13 extra.

PLACES TO STAY – MID-RANGE
B&Bs & Guesthouses

B&Bs and guesthouses are more common in Devonport and residential suburbs than in the city centre, but there are a few good central choices.

Aspen Lodge (☎ *09-379 6633,* W *www .aspenhouse.co.nz, 62 Emily Place)* Singles/ doubles $50/70. In a prime inner-city location, Aspen Lodge is small and comfortable with a convivial dining/common area. Breakfast is included.

The fashionable Parnell district has several excellent guesthouses.

Ascot Parnell (☎ *09-309 9012,* W *www .ascotparnell.com, 36 St Stephens Ave)* Singles $95, doubles $145-185. Ascot is a longstanding favourite, with 11 guest rooms in a restored historic home. It's a very welcoming place with many a homely touch provided by the owners, and the suite rooms ($185 to $220) are huge.

Chalet Chevron (☎ *09-309 0290, fax 373 5754,* e *chaletchevron@xtra.co.nz, 14 Brighton Rd)* Doubles $90-125. Chalet Chevron is a double-storey house down a quiet street. All rooms have en suite and some (the more expensive ones) have harbour views. It's a well-kept place and reasonable value.

Birdwood House (☎ *09-306 5900,* e *info@birdwood.co.nz, 41 Birdwood Crescent)* Singles $130-150, doubles $155-175. Birdwood House is a lovingly restored 1914 home with a peaceful garden at the back. The elegant rooms all have en suite (one has separate private bathroom) and some have old claw-foot bath tubs. Gourmet breakfast is included.

Great Ponsonby B&B (☎ *09-376 5989,* e *great.ponsonby@xtra.co.nz, 30 Ponsonby Terrace)* En suite doubles from $145-155, studios $155-245. This modestly named guesthouse is a tastefully decorated old villa, where the owners make you feel at home. The studios are self-contained.

Ponsonby Potager (☎ *09-378 7237, 43 Douglas St)* Singles/doubles $90/120, cottage $160. Down a quiet street off Ponsonby Rd, this self-contained cottage has two double rooms and DIY breakfast is supplied.

The Langtons (Greater Auckland map; ☎ *09-625 7520, fax 624 3122,* e *thelang tons@xtra.co.nz, 29 Haydn Ave, One Tree Hill)* Doubles $240-260. If you can afford it, The Langtons is a beautiful two-storey 1920s home at the foot of One Tree Hill. There are four suites, a garden room separate from the main house and a pool.

Motels

Auckland has over 100 motels and costs start at around $80 to $100 for a studio double, though they can be considerably higher. Good motel areas close to the city include Parnell, Newmarket and Herne Bay.

Parnell Village Motor Lodge (☎ *09-377 1463,* e *parnellvillage@clear.net.nz, 2 St Stephens Ave)* Studio units from $88, apartments $125 and $135 per double. This motel has a bit of character and is reasonably priced for the good location. It's in a converted and appended double-storey house with retro furnishings and decor. The apartments have kitchenettes.

Parnell Inn (☎ *09-358 0642,* e *parnell in@ihug.co.nz, 320 Parnell Rd)* Studio doubles $85-110. Also well located, this is a more modern motel with studio units and a two-bedroom flat for $120. It's behind The Other Side cafe.

Barrycourt Motor Inn (☎ *0800 504 466, 09-303 3789,* e *barrycourt@xtra.co.nz, 10-20 Gladstone Rd)* Rooms $112-350. Barrycourt is a large motel with a wide selection, including double or twin rooms, studio apartments and suites.

There are a number of motels on, or just off, Jervois and Shelly Beach Rds in fashionable Herne Bay, close to the southern end of the Harbour Bridge.

Sea Breeze Motel (☎ *0800 473 227, 09-376 2139, 213 Jervois Rd)* Studio/1-bed units $109/115. The Sea Breeze is a small, comfortable motel with self-contained units. It's close to beaches, fishing areas, restaurants and shops.

Abaco Spa Motel (☎ *0800 220 066, 09-360 6850,* e *abacospa@xtra.co.nz, 59 Jervois Rd)* Studio units $75-105, spa units $135. The Abaco is one of the closest motels to Ponsonby Rd and it has off-street parking. The cheaper units are small and showing their age but the spa units are fine.

Remuera, just past Newmarket, 5km from the city, has a motel row along Great South Rd, starting at around No 70. *Hansen's* (☎ 09-520 2804, fax 524 7597, 96 Great South Rd) and the *Tudor Court* (☎ 09-523 1069, e stay@tudor.co.nz, 108 Great South Rd) are two of the cheapest, with units from $70 to $95. Hansen's has a pool.

Out near the airport, Mangere has dozens of motels, particularly along Kirkbride and McKenzie Rds. They're competitively priced and all provide free airport transfers. *Pacific Inn* (☎ 0800 504 800, e info@ pacific-inn.co.nz, 275 1129, 210 Kirkbride Rd) and *Gateway Hotel* (☎ 0800 651 110, 09-275 4079, e gatewayhotel@xtra.co.nz, 206 Kirkbride Rd) both charge $90 a double.

Hotels & Apartments
It's not difficult to find a hotel in the city centre, though they're mostly pretty anonymous places.

Auckland City Hotel (☎ 0800 569 888, 09-303 2463, e aucklandcityhotel@xtra .co.nz, 131 Beach Rd) Singles/doubles with bath $60/75. This old multistorey hotel (formerly the Harbourview) doesn't look like much but it's good value for such a central location, and fills up fast. All rooms have en suite.

Albion Hotel (☎ 09-379 4900, cnr Hobson & Wellesley Sts) Doubles/triples $85/120. The Albion is a city centre pub with restored hotel rooms upstairs, all with en suite.

First Imperial Hotel & Apartments (☎ 0800 687 968, 09-355 1500, e res@ firstimperial.co.nz, 131–139 Hobson St) Hotel rooms $160, studio units $195. More expensive than other hotels, but an excellent place with spacious rooms, the First Imperial has refurbished hotel rooms and studio and two-bedroom units.

Darlinghurst Quest Inn (☎ 09-366 6500, w www.questdarlinghurst.co.nz, 52 Eden Cres) Studios $144, 1-/2-bedroom apartments $175/210. Every room is this modern

hotel has en suite, laundry and private balcony. There are good discounts available for weekends and long stays.

PLACES TO STAY – TOP END
Auckland's best business hotels charge from around $200 per room, but substantial discounts are usually available so you'll rarely pay the quoted rack rates.

Hilton (☎ 09-978 2000, fax 978 2001, e rm_auckland@hilton.com, Princes Wharf, 147 Quay St) Doubles $310-385. Auckland's newest luxury hotel doesn't get any closer to the waterfront – it's at the end of Princes Wharf. As well as 160 rooms (most with king-size beds), the hotel has serviced apartments, conference facilities, a top-class restaurant, cocktail bar, pool and leisure centre.

Sky City Hotel (☎ 0800 759 2489, 09-363 6000, fax 363 6210, w www.skycity.co.nz) Doubles from $290. Auckland's best-known city landmark, the Skytower, has a big luxury hotel with all the trimmings.

Hyatt Regency (☎ 09-355 1234, fax 303 2932, e auckland@hyatt.co.nz, w www .hyatt.co.nz, Princes St) Doubles $170-320. The large, elegant Hyatt has rooms well equipped for business travellers, and a gym.

Stamford Plaza Hotel (☎ 09-309 8888, fax 379 6445, e sales@spak.stamford, Albert St) Another top business hotel, the luxury Stamford boasts a heated rooftop swimming pool, champagne bar and cigar lounge.

The Heritage Auckland (☎ 09-379 8553, 35 Hobson St) Doubles $179-360. The Heritage is a restored department store, but it has a bit of character and spacious suites with separate bedroom.

City Life Auckland (☎ 09-379 9222, e res .citylifeakl@dynasty.co.nz, 171 Queen St) Doubles $177-299. City Life is one of the cheaper luxury hotels, if you get a weekend special. It's right in the centre of town and has Zest restaurant on the 1st floor.

PLACES TO EAT
Because of its size and ethnic diversity, Auckland has the best range of dining options in the country.

For good-value fast food, you can't beat the sushi and noodle places that sell ready-made lunch packs for $3.50 to $6 – there's a string of them on Queen St, especially at the top end between City Rd and Tunner St, where you'll also find sit-down Japanese and Korean restaurants. Cheap takeaway kebab places are also common in downtown Auckland.

Aucklanders have really taken to cafe culture, and there is a huge choice of places. In the city, Lorne St, High St and Vulcan Lane are lined with cafes of all shapes, sizes and philosophies. West of the city, Ponsonby Rd is by far the trendiest cafe strip. It has some great restaurants and bars, which attract a hip, young crowd who come to drink and dine before heading off to the clubs on K Rd.

Parnell has a more refined and compact eating scene, with a strip of good (some quite pricey) restaurants mingling with the boutique fashion shops along Parnell Rd, particularly at the eastern 'village' end. Other inner suburbs, such as Newmarket, Mt Eden, Herne Bay and Mission Bay, have smaller clusters or eateries. Devonport (see the Around Auckland section), which bubbles with cafes and bars, is only a short ferry ride from the city centre.

The redeveloped Princes Wharf and Viaduct area is where some of the fanciest and most expensive restaurants have sprung up, as a result of the America's Cup frenzy. This area is popular with the 'after-five' crowd and is heaving on Friday and Saturday evenings, but tends to be bit dead later in the night.

If you're looking for a late-night feed, the *White Lady* mobile hamburger stand is an Auckland institution. It's on Shortland St just off Queen St and is open in the evenings until around 3am during the week and 24 hours on weekends and holidays.

Central Food Halls & Supermarkets

Food halls in central Auckland are mostly open during shopping hours only – because they're usually located in shopping centres. The *280 Centre (280 Queen St)*, down from

Wellesley St, has an international food hall with kebabs, fish and chips, Chinese, Japanese and traditional cafes. *Atrium on Elliot (Elliot St)* has a range of international outlets.

For Asian fare, you can't beat *Food Alley (9 Albert St)*, opposite the Stamford Plaza Hotel. Thai, Chinese, Malay, Korean and Japanese meals mostly cost under $10. It's open 10.30am to 10pm daily.

There is a *New World supermarket (College Hill Rd)* near Victoria Park Market, open from 8am to 10pm daily, and a *mini supermarket* in the basement of *Deka (48 Queen St)*.

City Centre

Food for Life (☎ 09-300 7585, 423 Queen St) Open noon-3pm Mon-Fri. For cheap vegetarian meals, you can't beat the Hare Krishnas. For $5 you get a plate heaped with rice, dhal and a pappadam. There's another branch on Ponsonby Rd.

Good downtown cafes in Lorne St include the understated *City*, a tiny place and easy to miss, but popular among those who have discovered it (courtyard dining in summer), and the stylish *Alba*, which is open until 10pm most nights. High St is virtually lined with cafes popular with the lunch-time work crowds. They include the modern *Wofem Bros Bagelry* and the seriously-dedicated-to-coffee *Colombus*, with a wide range of coffee blends from NZ and around the world.

Cafe Melba (☎ 09-377 0091, 33 Vulcan Lane) Meals $4-14. In tiny Vulcan Lane, Melba is a small but very busy place with covered outdoor tables, bagels, croissants and breakfast (half serves of breakfast available).

@railcafe is a student hang-out in the cavernous old train station (now off-campus student accommodation), with reasonably priced food and alcoholic drinks.

Rose & Crown (☎ 09-373 2071, Customs St) Lunch $6, pizzas $8. This pub has a range of ready-made lunches that are hard to beat for value.

There's a cluster of restaurants along Victoria St, almost opposite the Skytower.

Mexican Cafe (☎ 09-373 2311, 67 Victoria St West) This cafe has a fun, casual atmosphere and the usual burritos and enchiladas.

Cafe Midnight Express (☎ 09-303 0312, 59 Victoria St West) Open until 11pm. This is a busy little restaurant serving authentic Turkish and Middle Eastern food.

Mai Thai (☎ 09-366 6258, cnr Albert St & Victoria St West). Mains $18-22. This is a long-running and reliable Thai restaurant in the heart of the city. It has that old-fashioned Asian elegance and is not particularly cheap – the chilli rating on the menu will help you decide what to avoid. It's closed on Sunday.

Raw Power (☎ 09-303 3624, 10 Vulcan Lane) Raw Power serves healthy food from free-range eggs to tofu, soups, salads and fresh juices. Downstairs, *Khmer* dishes up steaming bowls of Cambodian-style noodle soup from $5, as well as satay and fried noodles.

Occidental Belgian Beer Cafe (☎ 09-300 6226, 6-8 Vulcan Lane) Mains $8-20. This busy Belgian bar is the best place for a steaming pot of mussels ($12 to $15) or pomme frites ($4.50), washed down with real Belgian beer.

Auckland has many Japanese restaurants. Good ones include *Daikoku* (☎ 09-302 2432, 148 Quay St), a teppanyaki restaurant with mains from $22 to $29, and *Daikoku Ramen* (Tyler St), behind the main restaurant, where you can get a steaming bowl of ramen noodles for $10.

Toto (☎ 09-379 7385, 53 Nelson St) Mains $20-32. Toto has good Italian food and a great atmosphere, including live opera on Saturday and Thursday.

No.5 Wine Bistro (☎ 09-309 9273, 5 City Rd) $20-26. Open Tues-Sat from 5.30pm. An intimate atmosphere, a wide range of NZ wines by the glass, and simple but high-quality dishes mean this restaurant is usually very busy.

Skytower (☎ 09-363 6000) has several restaurants, including the revolving *Orbit*, which offers great 360-degree views (minimum charge for lunch or dinner is $25 per person), and the excellent *Tamarind*,

specialising in modern Pacific Rim cuisine (mains $28 to $30).

K Rd

One of Auckland's most interesting and culturally diverse streets, K Rd offers some unusual dining options, but it's more of a night-time place.

Rasoi (☎ 09-377 7780, 211 K Rd) Mains from $4. Rasoi specialises in authentic thalis and Indian sweets; eat well for under $10 or go for the huge Maharaja thali ($13.50).

Little Turkish Cafe (☎ 09-302 0353, 217 K Rd) Kebabs $9. This cafe is brisk and bright and has inexpensive food such as kebabs and moussaka.

Verona (☎ 09-307 0508, 169 K Rd) Verona uses organic fare and has a good vegetarian selection, but it's also a pleasant low-key place for a drink.

Departure Lounge (☎ 09-307 6873, 173 K Rd) Breakfast & lunch $9-14. This modern place is a chilled cafe by day and a small club with house and soul music by night.

Brazil (☎ 09-302 2677, 256 K Rd) Mains $4-12. This is a small cafe with a dark, industrial interior, and an interesting barrel-shaped roof that arcs over the sitting area upstairs. Crepes, eggs and bagels are on the agenda for breakfast.

St Kevins Arcade is a rather dismal shopping area on K Rd, but the city views through the huge windows of *Alleluya*, make it a reasonable place for lunch or coffee.

Viaduct Harbour & Princes Wharf

The Viaduct Basin and Princes Wharf are awash with restaurants and bars. It has a very international flavour with tables sprawling out the front and hovering black-tie waiters armed with menus. You can't beat the location – and this will be the place to be seen during the 2003 America's Cup campaign – though none of these places is cheap.

Wildfire (☎ 09-353 7595) Mains $19-34, dinner buffet $40. On the eastern side of Princes Wharf, closest to Quay St, Wildfire is a Brazilian 'churrascaria', where barbecued and char-grilled meats are the order of the day. Tapas and pizzas are also featured.

The Wharf (☎ 09-358 1284) Mains $18-25. This Belgian cafe-bar has snacks such as frites from $4.50, mussels for $15 and Belgian beers such as Hoegaarden and Leffe on tap.

Euro Restaurant & Bar (☎ 09-309 9866) Mains $25-35. Euro is one of the priciest and most stylish places along the wharf; it is an award-winning restaurant suitable for a splurge.

Cin Cin on Quay (☎ 09-307 6966, 99 Quay St) Mains $22-33. In the ferry building, Cin Cin is an oyster bar (oysters from $2.50 each) and seafood and pizza restaurant with a good reputation and great views from the outside deck.

Loaded Hog (☎ 09-366 6491, 204 Quay St) Mains $12.50-20. For something a bit more down to earth, the Loaded Hog is a brash and busy brewery pub with a range of meat-heavy bistro meals (lots of pork). There are tables facing out to the Viaduct.

Milano (☎ 09-377 2720, 95-97 Customs St) Mains $18-30. This highly rated restaurant (not to be confused with the pizzeria of the same name in Parnell) has two levels facing the Viaduct and some of Auckland's best Italian food.

Parnell

East of the city centre, Parnell Rd heads uphill and is lined with bars, cafes and restaurants. Parnell Village, a labyrinth of shops near the top of the rise, has some good medium-priced restaurants, several with tables in open courtyards.

Strawberry Alarm Clock Mains $8.50-13. Open from 7am. This neat little open-fronted cafe is a good spot for breakfast, coffee, smoothies and bagels, and the blackboard menu features pasta dishes.

Kebab Kid (363 Parnell Rd) Kebabs from $8.50. This small place does great doner kebabs and shwarmas (including vegetarian).

Al & Pete's (☎ 09-377 5439, 496 Parnell Rd) Burgers $3.50-9. Al & Pete's is an unassuming takeaway shop with a legendary reputation for gourmet burgers (such as chicken and camembert, and scotch fillet), as well as fish and chips and sandwiches. It's at the southern end of Parnell Rd.

Thai Friends (☎ 09-373 51247, 311 Parnell Rd) Mains $17-22. This is a convivial, authentic Thai restaurant with a great courtyard dining area. The food is tasty, and soups, such as tom yum, are all $7.50.

Java Room (☎ 09-366 1606, 317 Parnell Rd) Mains $16.50-21. Specialising in Indonesian, Malaysian, Thai and Indian cuisine, the Java Room is a hidden gem. There are vegetarian selections from $7 to $10.

Oh Calcutta (☎ 09-377 9099, 151 Parnell Rd) Mains $15-19. Oh Calcutta is said to be the best Indian restaurant in Auckland. It's a tandoori favourite but has a wide-ranging Indian menu from Kashmiri rogan josh to Goan fish curry.

Alligator Pear (☎ 09-307 2223, 211 Parnell Rd) Mains $15-23. Tucked downstairs between the shop fronts, the Alligator Pear is a long-running BYO restaurant with reasonably priced pasta dishes, along with an à la carte menu.

Non Solo Pizza (☎ 09-379 5358, 259 Parnell Rd) Pizzas $20-24, pasta $16-24. This popular pizzeria has a great little semi-open air dining area, a bar and a big range of pizzas (large only) and Italian dishes.

The Other Side (☎ 09-366 4426, 320 Parnell Rd) Mains $10-19. This cafe is open from 7am for breakfast and it has a pleasant sunny deck set back from the street a little so you can observe Parnell from a distance. It also has a bar.

Iguaçu (☎ 09-358 4804, 269 Parnell Rd) Lunch $16-25, dinner $20-28. This is a perennially popular place and a good spot for lunch, with salads, pasta, burgers and tables at the front. There's a regular live jazz slot on Sunday (brunch and in the evening).

The Mink Cafe & Bar (☎ 09-377 7035, 99 Parnell Rd) Mains $14-24. Part of the Exchange Hotel, this corner cafe is a trendy place serving breakfast (from 7.30am), pasta and wood-fired pizzas.

Antoines (☎ 09-379 8756, 333 Parnell Rd) Mains $28-39. For fine dining, Antoines is one of Auckland's best. In a renovated house, it's one of those silver service, gold credit-card places where the best local produce is tantalisingly presented in the French way. Bookings are essential.

Ponsonby

This is Auckland's busiest restaurant district, strung out over many blocks along Ponsonby Rd. You can walk along and see what captures your fancy, but on Saturday night get here early or else book. The road even has its own website: **W** www.ponsonbyroad.co.nz.

Ponsonby Pies (134 Ponsonby Rd) is an institution with many imaginative fillings on offer, such as smoked fish or Thai chicken curry, as well as more traditional fare.

Expresso Love (☎ 09-376 2433, 265 Ponsonby Rd) is one of the many loungy cafes on Ponsonby Rd, where you can linger over coffee and a light meal.

One Red Dog (☎ 09-360 1068, 151 Ponsonby Rd) Pizza $17-25. One Red Dog is a popular, casual place specialising in innovative pizzas (with names like Sum Yum Thai and Daffy Duck), calzones and pasta. The bar has a good atmosphere and there's live jazz on Sunday afternoons.

Cafe India (☎ 09-360 4113, 107 Ponsonby Rd) Main $14-18. Cafe India has an all-you-can-eat buffet for $20 and cheap lunch specials.

Sponge (☎ 09-360 0098, 198 Ponsonby Rd) Mains $16-28. With its orange plastic seats and trendy bar, Sponge is one of the 'be seen' new places on Ponsonby Rd. The tasting platters ($13.50) are an interesting introduction to the cuisine here – things like duck and pistachio nut terrine.

SPQR (☎ 09-360 1710, 150 Ponsonby Rd) Mains $18-26. A gothic wrought iron front gives way to stylish classical decor at SPQR, a trendy wine bar that's open late. The initials stand for (in Latin) the Senate and People of Rome – the food is mostly Italian. It's another of the places to be seen in Ponsonby.

Surrender Dorothy (☎ 09-376 4460, 175 Ponsonby Rd) This gay and lesbian-friendly cafe does wraps and espresso, but is as much an evening venue.

Stella (☎ 09-738 7979, 118 Ponsonby Rd) Meals $12-22. Stella is a popular place with a Mediterranean brasserie-style menu. Start with a bloody mary oyster shot ($4.50).

Musical Knives (☎ 09-376 7354, 272 Ponsonby Rd) Lunch $12.50, mains $23.50. This place has stylish although not cheap vegetarian food, including organic soba and organic vegetables with tofu.

Estasi (☎ 09-378 7888, 222 Ponsonby Rd) Mains $18-27. Open for breakfast, lunch and dinner, Estasi has an extensive Pacific Rim and Mediterranean menu, including oven-baked salmon and pumpkin gnocchi.

There are numerous cafes and restaurants along Jervois Rd, at the northwestern end of Ponsonby Rd. One of the most popular places for breakfast, brunch and lunch is *Andiamo (194 Jervois Rd)* although *Fusion* and *Sierra* are also fine cafes.

Other Suburbs

The busy **Newmarket** shopping district has numerous restaurants and cafes.

Zarbo (☎ 09-520 2721, 24 Morrow St) Situated right in the heart of Newmarket, this is an excellent fine-food delicatessen and cafe where you can get great bagels and pick up gourmet picnic fare.

Poppadom (☎ 09-529 1897, 471 Khyber Pass Rd) Mains $12-18. Poppadom is a reliable Indian restaurant with reasonably priced North Indian curries and tandooris, and a $10 lunch special (between 11am and 2pm).

Mt Eden has a much more compact shopping district with several restaurants, including the *Occidental Belgian Beer Cafe*, *De Post* (for details of both see Entertainment) and *De Niro's Italian Restaurant (☎ 09-623 3450, 448 Mt Eden Rd)*.

Langton's (☎ 09-630 2670) at the foot of Mt Eden itself, is an elegant restaurant that does Devonshire teas and light lunches, and a buffet dinner (bookings essential).

Along **Tamaki Drive** there are plenty of places to recharge on caffeine or idle away a summer evening over a drink and a meal. At Okahu Bay, not far from Kelly Tarlton's, is *Hammerheads (☎ 09-521 4400, 19 Tamaki Drive)*, a fine seafood restaurant with an expansive deck for outdoor dining. Mains such as roasted John Dory and baked salmon are around $28.

At **Mission Bay** there is a string of cafes with outdoor seating – stroll along and take your pick. Recommended is *Bluefins (☎ 09-528 4551, cnr Tamaki Drive & Atkin Ave)* for seafood (mains $23 to $28); **Bar Comida** (☎ 09-521 7000, 81 Tamaki Drive), has Spanish-style tapas and pizza ($12 to $24); and, for the sweet tooth, **Death By Chocolate** (☎ 09-521 4783, 91 Tamaki Drive).

ENTERTAINMENT

To find out what's happening in the city try the NZ Herald's entertainment pages and Saturday 'What's On' supplement, and 7 Days which comes out on Thursday. What's Happening is a free monthly magazine that lists major events. It's available from visitors centres and other places.

The giveaway events calendar The Fix is available at record and music shops (try Real Groovy Records at 438 Queen St). It comes out on Thursday. Re-Mix (free) and Lava ($2.50 from bookshops) also have gig guides. For an online gig guide try W www .roadworks.co.nz/roadworks/gigguide.

Pubs & Bars

Auckland's nightlife tends to be quiet during the week. On weekends the popular spots are full to overflowing and dress standards apply at many of the fancier bars. Most pubs and bars are open till about 1am.

The best places for backpacker-oriented bars, which offer cheap drinks, pool competitions, and general debauchery practically every night of the week, are the big hostels. The **Globe** at the new Auckland Central Backpackers is a big party place, and **Embargo** bar, below Central City Backpackers, is also good.

Down on the waterfront you'll find several good watering holes that get pretty crowded at lunch time and after work.

Loaded Hog (☎ 09-366 6491, 204 Quay St) This huge microbrewery has a good range of beers, food and tables spilling out towards the Viaduct. Next door, **Danny Doolan's** (☎ 09-358 2554) is one of the better inner-city Irish theme pubs, and well located to take in the waterfront action.

Lenin Bar (☎ 09-377 004) At Princes Wharf, this bar specialises in 'infused vodka' drinks and is open late on weekends.

Coast Bar (☎ 09-300 9966) Also on Princes Wharf (above the Hewlett Packard

building), this lounge-bar is a good place for an early evening drink, if only for the view.

Leftfield (☎ 09-307 9500) This is the place to indulge the NZ passion for watching sport – especially rugby. With a giant screen that can be seen from two levels, and mini-stadium seating, Leftfield packs out when there's a big game on. It's also a popular nightclub with a state-of-the-art laser light show.

The Immigrant (☎ 09-373 2169, 104 Fanshawe St) This is a good, traditional Irish bar with live northern-hemisphere sports telecasts and bands on Friday and Saturday.

Other options in the downtown area include the **Rose & Crown** (☎ 09-373 2071, Custom St), with live music on weekends; **Shakespeare Tavern** (☎ 09-373 5396, 61 Albert St), a microbrewery; and the central **London Bar**.

Dogs Bollix (☎ 09-376 4600, 582 K Rd) Slightly removed from the city, near the corner of K Rd and Newton St, this is a busy Irish Pub with live music nightly, except for Monday when it's quiz night. Tuesday and Wednesday are acoustic jam and open mike nights.

Along Ponsonby Rd, the line between cafe, restaurant and entertainment gets a little blurred. A lot of food places also have live music or become clubs later on. The long-running **Java Jive** (☎ 09-376 5870) has live music every night and focuses mainly on blues and roots music. Also on Ponsonby Rd and featuring live music are the **Safari Lounge** (☎ 09-378 7707, 116 Ponsonby Rd), which mixes styles including R&B, ska and house; and **Alhambra** (☎ 09-376 2430, 283 Ponsonby Rd), a Spanish restaurant tucked away in the Three Lamps Arcade, with live pop, jazz and blues.

Garage Bar (☎ 09-360 5453, 152 Ponsonby Rd) Next to SPQR, this bar has a peculiar glass floor, a good selection of drinks and DJs on the weekend.

St Arnou (☎ 09-376 6373, 43 Ponsonby Rd) This place is an unusual brewery pub and French restaurant with an imposing facade and cavernous interior – worth a visit to try out the constantly changing European-style beers.

One of the hottest places on Ponsonby Rd is also one of the smallest: it's easy to miss the entrance to the *Lime Bar* (☎ *09-360 7167, 167 Ponsonby Rd*) but it's an intimate music bar and very popular.

Parnell is more a place for dining than drinking but there are a few entertainment options, including the *Exchange Hotel*, which lures in students and backpackers with $5 jugs of beer.

The Bog (☎ *09-377 1510, 196 Parnell Rd*) This is a new Irish pub, next door to the Kiwi Experience in Parnell. It's a popular night out for travellers, with plenty of Guinness, hearty Irish stodge and a quiz on Tuesday.

If you consider yourself a connoisseur of beer, it's hard to go past the Belgian beer cafes, of which there are three in Auckland. The best are the usually crowded *Occidental Belgian Beer Cafe* (☎ *09-300 6226, 6-8 Vulcan Lane*) in the city centre, and *De Post* (☎ *09-630 9330, 466 Mt Eden Rd*), a more spacious place in the former post office in Mt Eden. At both places you will be served beers, such as Leffe and Hoegaarden, properly poured into the appropriate glasses by well-instructed bar staff.

For the last word in chic, *Bubbles Champagne Bar* at the Viaduct Harbour pretty much sums up the yachting, jet-setting fraternity – champagne is from $20 a glass or from $65 to infinity a bottle.

Nightclubs & Live Music

K Rd, High St and Ponsonby Rd are the places to find late-night clubs. Most clubs have a cover charge depending on the night and the event.

The Khuja Lounge (☎ *09-377 3711, 536 Queen St*) Open Wed-Sun from 7pm. Located above the Westpac building, this is a laid-back venue with plenty of variety in musical style, including latin, hip-hop, jazz and reggae, and a mix of DJ and live music.

Calibre (☎ *09-303 1673, 179 K Rd*) Calibre, in the basement of St Kevins Arcade, is a consistently popular club with dance and house music from 11pm to 8am Friday and Saturday.

The Box (☎ *09-303 1336, 33-35 High St*) Open Wed-Sun 11pm-6am. This central

club is popular for drum and bass, garage and retro (Wednesday).

Galatos (☎ *09-303 1928, 17 Galatos St*) Open Wed-Sat from 8pm. This small, funky club has dance, funk and soul DJ music. It's one block south of K Rd in Newton.

Ministry (☎ *09-373 3664, 17 Albert St*) Ministry is a place for hard house and trance, and it has a recovery session on Sunday morning.

In Vulcan Lane *Papa Jack's Voodoo Lounge* (☎ *09-358 4847*) turns up the volume, attracting a mixed crowd.

Fu Bar (☎ *09-309 3079, 166 Queen St*) Open Tues-Sun. This innovative basement dance club has house and techno DJ's with some drum and bass and hip-hop, plus pool tables.

The Temple (☎ *09-377 4856*, **W** *www .temple.co.nz, 486 Queen St*) If you want to see original Kiwi musicians, the Temple is the place. It showcases everything from solo acoustic to fully plugged bands – all original. Singer-songwriters come here to perform, and so can you; Monday is open mike night.

The Kings Arms Tavern (☎ *09-373 3240, 59 France St, Newton*) Thur-Sun. This is the most popular small venue for live acts, with emerging bands, rock and alternative rock.

For big international bands and major local bands, the main venues in Auckland are the *Powerstation* (☎ *09-377 7666, 33 Mt Eden Rd*) and the *North Shore Events Centre (Torana Rd, Glenfield)*. Big dance venues are at Alexandra Park and Ellerslie Racecourse.

Gay & Lesbian Venues

Auckland's gay and lesbian scene is fairly low key. Cafes and clubs with a gay and lesbian following are mainly found in Ponsonby and the western end of K Rd. They include the popular cafe-bar *Surrender Dorothy* (☎ *09-376 4460, 175 Ponsonby Rd*); *Atlas* (☎ *09-285 Ponsonby Rd*); *Kamo (382 K Rd*); and *Caluzzi (461 K Rd*), which has good food and a lively atmosphere.

K Rd clubs with a gay and lesbian following include *Sinners* (☎ *09-309 9985*) at No 373 and **Legend** at No 335. Also try *GA.Y (5 High St*).

Cinema, Performing Arts & Casino

Aotea Square, and the buildings that surround it, comprise Auckland's main arts and entertainment complex. The *Force Entertainment Centre (☎ 09-979 2405)*, facing Queen St and Aotea Square, boasts a giant 460-seat Imax theatre (☎ 09-979 2400; adult/child $15/9), and the 12-screen Village Force Hoyts Cinemas (☎ 09-979 2400), *Planet Hollywood (☎ 09-308 7827)* and numerous cafes, bars and shops.

The Edge (☎ 09-309 2677, W www .the-edge.co.nz) is the collective name given to the other venues around Aotea Square: the Town Hall, Civic and Aotea Centre.

The restored *Auckland Town Hall* hosts concert performances in its Great Hall (home to the NZ Symphony Orchestra and Auckland Philharmonia) and Concert Chamber. The *Aotea Centre* is Auckland's main venue for theatre, dance, ballet and opera. It houses a number of venues, the main one being the 2250-seat ASB Theatre. The Auckland Theatre Company performs regularly in the Herald Theatre at the Aotea Centre.

The Civic, on the corner of Queen St and Wellersley St West, is a grand theatre which reopened in early 2000. It's worth a peak inside just to see the lavishly restored Eastern-fantasy interior. It is now the venue for major touring productions including opera, musicals, cinema and live theatre, as well as the Auckland International Film Festival.

Other performing arts venues include the *Maidment Theatre (☎ 09-308 2383, 8 Alfred St)*, at the University of Auckland, and the *Sky City Theatre* at Sky City, which both host musical and theatre performances. *Silo Theatre (☎ 09-373 5151, Lower Greys Ave)* specialises in fringe theatre.

The Classic Comedy Club (☎ 09-373 4321, W www.comedy.co.nz, 321 Queen St) This is Auckland's top venue for comedy. The main shows are from Thursday to Sunday from 8pm and there's an open mike night most Mondays. A bimonthly calendar of events is available at the door or check the website.

The *NZ Herald* carries listings of what's on. Most theatrical and major musical events at the venues above can be booked through Ticketek (☎ 09-307 5000, W www.ticketek .co.nz), and you can search online to find out what's on.

Sky City (☎ 0800 759 2489, cnr Victoria & Hobson Sts) This is Auckland's biggest single entertainment venue in terms of diversity. As well as restaurants, bars, the observation deck and a 700-seat theatre, it has two casinos – the huge 24-hour Sky City Casino (Level 2) and the smaller Alto Casino (Level 3). If you're over 20 years of age and sufficiently well dressed you can gamble to your heart's content here.

GETTING THERE & AWAY

Air

Auckland is the major gateway to NZ, and a hub for domestic flights. See the Getting There & Away chapter in the front of this book for information on international flights.

Domestic airlines operating to/from Auckland include:

Air New Zealand (☎ 09-357 3000, W www .airnewzealand.co.nz) Cnr Customs and Queen Sts
Great Barrier Airlines (☎ 0800 900 600, 09-256 6500, W www.greatbarrierairlines.co.nz) Auckland Domestic Terminal
Mountain Air – Great Barrier Xpress (☎ 09-256 7025, W www.mountainair.co.nz) Auckland Domestic Terminal
Origin Pacific (☎ 0800 302 302, W www .originpacific.co.nz) Trent Drive, Nelson Airport, Nelson

Bus

The main bus company in Auckland, as for the rest of NZ, is InterCity, in combination with Newmans. With a few exceptions, these buses go to almost all bigger towns and the main tourist areas.

There are services from Auckland to just about everywhere in NZ, and these operate from the Sky City Coach Terminal at 102 Hobson St (reservations ☎ 0800 777 707, 09-913 6100).

Northliner Express (☎ 09-307 5873) services Northland, with buses heading north from Auckland to Whangarei, the Bay of Islands and Kaitaia.

Backpacker buses operate in and from Auckland and have their main offices here; both Kiwi Experience (☎ 09-366 9830, 170 Parnell Rd) and Magic Travellers Network (☎ 09-358 5600, 136–138 Quay St) offer a door-to-door service with pick-ups and drop-offs at any Auckland hostel.

Train

Trains arrive at and depart from the Auckland Station (☎ 0800 802 802, W www .tranzscenic.co.nz) on Beach Rd, about 1km east of the city centre. Several readers have written saying they felt intimidated when visiting the station at night as it's in a rather isolated location. The booking office is open from 7am to 6pm Monday to Friday and 7.15am to 12.15pm Saturday and Sunday.

There are only two trains operating out of Auckland – the *Overlander* and the *Northerner* – and both go to Wellington via Hamilton and Palmerston North. The *Overlander* runs daily, departing from Auckland at 8.30am and arriving in Wellington at 7.30pm (return times are almost identical). The *Northerner* is an overnight train operating Sunday to Friday, departing from Auckland at 8.40pm (arriving 7.35am) and from Wellington at 7.50pm (arrives 7am). There are no sleeper carriages. The standard Auckland-Wellington adult fare on the *Overlander* is $102, and on the *Northerner* it's $90.

Hitching

Getting out of Auckland by thumb can be hard work. The only legal ways to hitch out of town are either to stand by the ramps leading on to the motorway or take a bus to Mercer or Albany and start from there.

GETTING AROUND
To/From the Airport

Auckland airport (☎ 09-256 8899) is 21km southwest of the city centre. It has an international terminal and a domestic terminal, each with a tourist information centre. A free shuttle service operates between the terminals and there's also a signposted footpath between them.

At the international terminal there's a freephone for accommodation bookings. Both terminals have left-luggage facilities and car-rental desks, though you get better rates from companies in town.

The AirBus shuttle (☎ 09-375 4702, 0508 247 287) runs every 20 minutes (roughly from 6am to 10pm) between the international and domestic terminals and the city, stopping outside several accommodation places and Aotea Square; reservations are not required: you buy a ticket from the driver. The trip takes about 50 minutes one way (longer during rush hour) and costs $13/22 one way/return ($11/18 with a backpackers card).

Convenient door-to-door shuttles run to and from the airport, and competition is cutthroat. The two main operators are Super Shuttle (☎ 09-306 3960) and Johnston's Shuttle Link (☎ 09-275 1234). The cost between the airport and the city centre is around $18 one way ($12 if booked through your hostel); various discount deals are available.

A taxi to the airport from the city will cost around $40 one way.

Bus

The city bus service is run by Stagecoach Auckland (Rideline; ☎ 09-366 6400, W www .stagecoach.co.nz). The Downtown Bus Terminal is on Commerce St, between Quay St and Customs St East, but not all buses leave from there. As with any city bus service, it takes a while to work out where to pick up the right bus, but local bus route timetables are available from the bus terminal, newsagents and the visitors centres. Single-ride fares in the inner city are adult/child 50c/30 (you pay the driver when you board) but if you're travelling further afield there are fare stages from $1.20/70c to $7.90/4.70. A standard one-day pass (which includes downtown ferries) costs $8, a three-day pass costs $19.

The Link is a handy bus service that travels clockwise and anticlockwise around a loop which includes Queen St, Skytower, Victoria Park Market, Ponsonby Rd, K Rd, the university, Newmarket, Parnell, the train station and QEII Square. It runs every

10 minutes (every 20 minutes on weekday nights and Sundays) and costs $1.

The Night Rider bus service departs from the intersection of Queen St and Wellersley at 1am, 2am and 3am Saturday and Sunday mornings, but with a flat fare of $4 it's hardly worth the hassle unless you're staying well out of the city and can't afford a taxi.

Train

There's a limited Tranz Metro (Rideline; ☎ 09-366 6400) train service, with just two main lines running west to Waitakere and south to Papakura. The Auckland Station is on Beach Rd, behind the imposing former Auckland central railway station.

Car & Motorcycle

Parking is a big problem in downtown Auckland – there's very little of it, time limits are short and the city's parking inspectors and 'towies' are rabid. There's a car park outside the old Auckland train station where you can park for 24 hours for $5.

Auckland is crawling with car-hire operators and is the best city in which to hire (or buy) a vehicle for touring NZ. Some good deals can be had for long-term hire, but be warned that cheapest is not necessarily the best.

A whole swag of car-hire companies can be found conveniently grouped together along Beach Rd, opposite the old train station. The major companies – Avis, Budget, Hertz and Thrifty – are reliable, offer full insurance and have offices at the airport and all over the country. They are expensive, but rates are often negotiable for longer rentals.

If you are prepared to take limited insurance and risk losing an excess of around $700, then the cheaper operators offer some pretty good deals. Prices vary with the season, the age of the car and length of rental. Ignore prices quoted in brochures and shop around by phone. Always read the rental agreement thoroughly before you sign.

Auckland has more than 60 rental operators. They include:

A2B	☎ 0800 222 929, 09-377 0825
Ace*	☎ 0800 502 277

Alternative Rental Cars	☎ 09-373 3822
Avis	☎ 09-526 2800
Britz NZ*	☎ 0800 831 900
Budget*	☎ 0800 652 227, 09-375 2270
Hertz	☎ 0800 654 321, 09-309 0989
Maui*	☎ 0800 651 080, 09-255 0620
Thrifty	☎ 0800 737 070, 09-309 0111

* Rents out sleepervans or campervans as well as cars

You can rent a small scooter for $24 for 24 hours; only a car driver licence is needed. New Zealand Motorcycle Rentals (☎ 09-377 2005), 31 Beach Rd, has one-day hire starting at $80.

Buying a Car For stays of two months or more, many people look at buying a car. You can buy through dealers on the buy-back scheme at car fairs or through ads in the newspapers. Backpacker hostels in Auckland also have notice boards where travellers leaving the country advertise their cars.

For newspaper listings, cars are advertised in the *NZ Herald* on Wednesday, the *Trade & Exchange* on Monday and Thursday, and the *Auto Trader* magazine.

Buy-backs, where the dealer agrees to buy back your car for an agreed price, are not usually a great deal but offer some piece of mind. Dealers who work on this system include:

Budget Car Sales	☎ 09-379 4120
Downtown Rentals	☎ 09-303 1847
Rex Swinburne Motors	☎ 09-620 6587
Rock Bottom Rentals	☎ 09-622 1592

The most popular way to buy a car is through the car fairs, where people bring their cars to sell them. Manukau is the biggest and the best, but the Ellerslie Racecourse car fair is also good. Arrive between 8.30am and 9.30am for the best choice; car fairs are over by about noon. For a credit check (☎ 0800 658 934) quote chassis and licence-plate numbers. Mechanical inspection services, credit agencies and Auto Check details are all on hand at the car fairs, which are listed here:

Ellerslie Racecourse (☎ 09-810 9212) Ellerslie is near the Greenlane roundabout and is open from 9am to noon on Sunday. It costs $20 to register your vehicle.

Manukau (☎ 09-358 5000) Manukau is in the car park of the giant shopping mall of the Manukau City Centre, Manukau City, South Auckland, near the Manukau motorway off-ramp, and is open from 8.30am to 1pm on Sunday.

Old Oriental (Beach Road) Markets (☎ 09-524 9183) Old Oriental is on Beach Rd in the city centre, and open from 9am to noon on Saturday.

Alternatively, you could try the car auctions for a good deal. Two of the best known car auctions in Auckland are:

Hammer Auctions (☎ 09-579 2344) 830 Great South Rd, Penrose. Auctions are held several times a week. Visit 6pm Monday, Wednesday and Friday for budget vehicles.

Turner's Car Auction (☎ 09-525 1920, Ⓦ www.turners.co.nz) McNab St, Penrose. Auctions several times a week. Visit 11.30am Wednesday for budget vehicles.

Taxi
Auckland's many taxis usually work from ranks, but they also cruise popular areas. You often have to phone for a taxi; Auckland Taxi Co-Op (☎ 09-300 3000) is one of the biggest.

Taxi companies are listed in the *Yellow Pages*. Flagfall is $2 and then around $1.60 per kilometre.

Bicycle
Adventure Cycles (☎ 09-309 5566), at 104 Quay St, hires out mountain bikes for around $25 a day and carries out repairs. Hedgehog Bikes (☎ 09-489 6559, Ⓦ www .hedgehog.co.nz), at Takapuna, has touring and mountain bikes for hire and offers a buy-back option.

Tuk-Tuk
Located on the city side of the harbour bridge Auckland City Tuk Tuks (☎ 09-309 4823) will take you on short trips in an Asian three-wheeler around the city centre, or for longer trips such as pub crawls. The tuk-tuks can generally be found outside the ferry building in summer.

Boat
Fullers (☎ 09-367 9111) operates passenger ferries between the city and Devonport, Stanley Bay, Birkenhead and Bayswater on the North Shore, the gulf islands and Half Moon Bay near Howick. Fullers' website, at Ⓦ www.fullers.co.nz, lists timetables and fares. Ferries to Devonport take 12 minutes and run frequently.

Around Auckland

REGIONAL PARKS
The Auckland Regional Council (ARC) administers 21 regional parks around the Auckland region, all within 15km to 90km of the city. There are several coastal and beach parks with swimming and surfing beaches, plus bush parks, a kauri park, the Waitakere Ranges west of Auckland, the Hunua catchment southeast of Auckland and a gannet colony at Muriwai. The parks have good walking and tramping tracks, ranging from 20 minutes to several hours to walk, and camping is allowed in several of the parks.

An Auckland Regional Parks pamphlet, with a list of facilities in each park, is available from the Auckland Travel & Information Centre, or the DOC office in the ferry building in Auckland.

Auckland Regional Council has *camping grounds* in the regional parks, many in coastal areas. Some are accessible by vehicle, others are reached by tramping. Most tend to be heavily booked in summer; contact *Parksline* (☎ *09-303 1530*) for information and bookings.

DEVONPORT
Devonport is a quaint suburb on the tip of Auckland's North Shore peninsula, easily reached by ferry from downtown Auckland. One of the earliest areas of European settlement, it retains a 19th-century atmosphere with many well-preserved Victorian and Edwardian buildings. Since it makes such an easy day trip from the city, it's touristy and has lots of small shops, art and craft galleries and cafes. There's a great

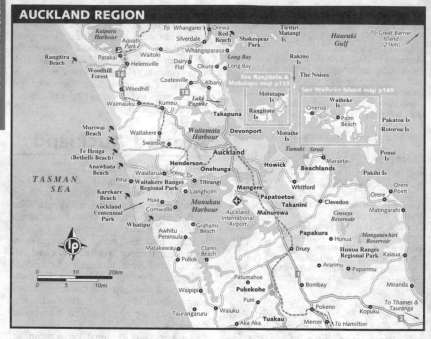

AUCKLAND REGION

view of the Auckland city skyline from the foreshore here, especially in the evening.

The friendly Devonport visitors centre (☎ 09-446 0677, ℮ visitorinfo@nthshore .govt.nz, ⓦ www.tourismnorthshore.org.nz) on Victoria Rd is open from 9am to 5pm daily. The *Old Devonport Walk* pamphlet guides you around the many historic buildings in this antique port.

Things to See & Do

Two volcanic cones, Mt Victoria and North Head, were once Maori *pa* – you can see the terracing on the sides of the cones. **Mt Victoria** is the higher of the two, with a great 360-degree view and at the top, a map of all the landmarks and giving the names of the many islands you can see. Walk or drive to the summit of Mt Victoria; the road is open at all times except from 6pm to 7am on Thursday, Friday and Saturday.

North Head, on the other cone, is a historic reserve riddled with old tunnels built

at the end of the 19th century in response to fears of a Russian invasion. The fortifications were extended and enlarged during WWI and WWII, but dismantled after the latter. Some of the old guns are still here. The reserve is open to vehicles from 6am to 6pm daily and to pedestrians until 10pm.

Walk west from the wharf along the promenade (left as you exit the wharf building) for about five blocks, until you reach the navy base, then turn right into Spring St. At the end of the street is the small **Naval Museum** (☎ *09-445 5186, Spring St; admission free; open 10am-4.30pm daily*).

The **Devonport Museum** (☎ *09-445 2661, 31A Vauxhall Rd; open 2pm-4pm Sat & Sun*), in the Mt Cambria Reserve, chronicles Devonport's history. **Bryan Jackson's Muzeum** (☎ *09-446 3236; adult/child $5/2*) is an eccentric collection of NZ historical memorabilia – a true testament to one man's passion for collectables! The museum is located in the original post

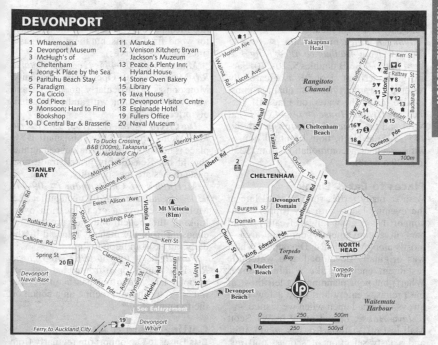

DEVONPORT

1 Wharemoana
2 Devonport Museum
3 McHugh's of Cheltenham
4 Jeong-K Place by the Sea
5 Parituhu Beach Stay
6 Paradigm
7 Da Ciccio
8 Cod Piece
9 Monsoon; Hard to Find Bookshop
10 D Central Bar & Brasserie
11 Manuka
12 Venison Kitchen; Bryan Jackson's Muzeum
13 Peace & Plenty Inn; Hyland House
14 Stone Oven Bakery
15 Library
16 Java House
17 Devonport Visitor Centre
18 Esplanade Hotel
19 Fullers Office
20 Naval Museum

office building on Victoria Rd (now the Venison Kitchen).

Just north of the foot of North Head, **Cheltenham Beach** is a lovely little beach with a superb view of Rangitoto.

Organised Tours

Devonport Tours (☎ *09-357 6366; tours $25-45*) has one-hour hop-on-hop-off tours of the main sights, and two-hour tours that include a buffet lunch. Tour prices include return ferry from Auckland.

Devonport Tuk Tuk (☎ *0800 428 858; tours $15-20 per person*) offers a different way of touring the sights – aboard an Asian three-wheeled autorickshaw.

Places to Stay

Devonport has more B&Bs than any other Auckland suburb, many of them lovingly restored Victorian or Edwardian villas. If your budget doesn't run to overpriced boutique accommodation, Devonport is best treated as a day trip. The nearest motels and motor camps are a little way north in Takapuna or Bayswater. The visitors centre has a list of all accommodation in the area.

Esplanade Hotel (☎ *09-455 1291, 1 Victoria Rd*) Doubles from $175. This historic hotel directly opposite the ferry wharf has simple but stylish rooms, with TVs and phones and large en suite bathrooms. You *really* pay for this location, though.

Ducks Crossing Cottage (☎/*fax 09-445 8102, 58 Seabreeze Rd*) B&B doubles $85-100. Ducks Crossing is a lovely, modern cottage and one of the more affordable B&Bs. The owners also offer free tours of Devonport.

Wharemoana (☎ *09-445 7549,* ✉ *whare moana@win.co.nz, 4a North Avenue*) Singles/doubles $50-80. Just north of Cheltenham Beach, this is another good value B&B.

Parituhu Beachstay (☎/*fax 09-445 6559, 3 King Edward Parade*) Doubles $80. This place is a small (two-room) but gay-friendly homestay in a great location.

Jeong-K Place by the Sea (☎ 09-445 1358, e jeong-k@ihug.co.nz, 4 King Edward Parade) B&B doubles $220-240. Facing the waterfront, Jeong-K is a carefully restored Edwardian villa with quality rooms.

Also facing the water, on Flagstaff Terrace, are *Hyland House* (☎ 09-445 9917) at No 4 and the *Peace & Plenty Inn* (☎ 09-445 2925) at No 6, both beautiful houses with excellent accommodation from $230 to $320 a double.

Places to Eat & Drink

With so many ferries running until late in the evening laden with day-trippers, Devonport has a great range of eateries and bars in a conveniently compact area – mostly along Victoria Rd. Devonport Wharf was originally developed as a waterside restaurant enclave (like a mini Princes Wharf) but poor planning has left most of the premises empty and only a few takeaways remained open when we visited.

Java House, tucked away in WJ Scott Mall just off Victoria Rd, has good coffee and a tasty selection of scones, muffins, cakes and light meals. *Cod Piece (26 Victoria Rd)* is a good takeaway place for fish and chips and hamburgers.

Stone Oven Bakery (☎ 09-445 3185, 5 Clarence St) Breakfast $4-15. The busy Stone Oven is the place for breakfast with fresh bread and generous servings. There's plenty here for lunch too, with filled rolls or panini (around $5).

Venison Kitchen (☎ 09-446 3236, 10 Victoria Rd) Meals $5-10. If you like venison, this deli and cafe is the place. You can get pies, gourmet burgers, lasagne, steak and other light meals, all using lean deer meat. It's licensed and there are tables out the front.

D Central Bar & Brasserie (☎ 09-445 3010, 14 Victoria Rd) Meals $10-22. D Central, the former Bankers Arms pub, has been turned into a trendy brasserie serving salads, burgers and pasta dishes for lunch and dinner. The al fresco tables are good for people-watching.

Manuka (☎ 09-445 7732, 49 Victoria Rd) Meals $18-21. Manuka is the top place for wood-fired pizzas, but there's also pasta (including half serves).

Monsoon (☎ 09-445 4263, 71 Victoria Rd) Mains $13-20. Open from 5pm daily. Monsoon is a particularly good Thai and Malaysian restaurant, with authentic, sensibly priced food.

Da Ciccio (☎ 09-445 8133, 99 Victoria Rd). Mains around $18. This small BYO place is how you imagine Italian restaurants should be. Reasonably priced traditional pasta dishes are the speciality.

McHugh's of Cheltenham (☎ 09-445 0305, 46 Cheltenham Rd) Lunch buffet $22. McHugh's enjoys a great location overlooking the beach and the pressure of choosing from the menu is relieved by the daily buffet from noon to 2pm.

Paradigm (☎ 09-466 0967, 48 Victoria Rd) This loungy, open-fronted bar and cafe is open late and often has acoustic live music. You can even recline on a couch on the footpath.

Getting There & Away

Bus Buses to Devonport run regularly from the Downtown Bus Terminal in Auckland, but you have to pass through Takapuna and traffic can be slow. The ferry crossing is quicker and far more enjoyable.

Boat The 10-minute ferry ride departs from the Auckland ferry building every 30 minutes from 6.15am to 11pm (till 1am Friday and Saturday and 10am on Sunday). The last ferries back from Devonport are at 11.30pm Monday to Thursday, 1.15am Friday and Saturday, and 10.30pm Sunday. The fare is adult/child $5/2 for a one-way ticket, $8/4 for an open return.

Fullers has ferries to Waiheke and Rangitoto Islands that call in at Devonport – see the Hauraki Gulf section later in this chapter.

WEST OF AUCKLAND

No more than an hour's drive from the city, West Auckland has a dramatic, rugged coastline with iron-sand beaches backed by regenerating bush. There are some fine surf beaches and more than 130 bushwalks, making this an important recreational zone for Auckland city dwellers.

West Auckland is also the place to go for vineyards and craft outlets. Enterprise Waitakere (☎ 09-837 1855) puts out a map called *Art out West*, available from the Auckland and Arataki visitors centres, which provides information on galleries and studios.

Wineries

The area west of Auckland, particularly around Henderson and Kumeu, is a major wine-producing region. Although there are quite a few vineyards in this region, grapes are drawn from vineyards all over New Zealand for use here. The glossy map *Winemakers of Auckland*, available from Auckland visitors centres, details the vineyards, their addresses and opening hours.

Some places, such as **Delegat's** (☎ 09-836 0129, Hepburn Rd) and **Corbans** (☎ 09-837 6773, 448 Great North Rd), are within walking distance of Henderson, which can be reached by bus or the Tranz Metro train from downtown Auckland. If you're driving, there are 10 vineyards in the Henderson area.

Other large and well-known vineyards, such as **Matua Valley** (☎ 09-411 8301, Waikoukou Valley Rd), **House of Nobilo** (☎ 09-412 9148, Station Rd) and **Coopers Creek** (☎ 09-412 8560) are further out near Kumeu, most not far off SH16.

Some of the wineries have very good restaurants.

Hunting Lodge (☎ 09-411 8259) is a 130-year old villa in a beautiful setting at Matua Valley. It's open Wednesday to Sunday for lunch and dinner.

Alley House (☎ 09-412 7206, Old North Rd), at Selaks Wines in Kumeu, has an à la carte garden restaurant open for lunch and dinner daily. It's surrounded by extensive grounds.

Pleasant Valley Wines (☎ 09-838 8857, 322 Henderson Valley Rd), at Henderson, has a good cafe open weekends from 11.30am to 4pm.

Half- and full-day tours of the Henderson and Kumeu wineries run out of Auckland daily – see Organised Tours under Auckland earlier.

There are a couple of annual festivals out this way – **Vintage Alfresco** (mid-March) and **Wine Waitakere** (October).

Waitakere Ranges

These scenic ranges once supported important kauri forests, but they were logged almost to extinction in the 19th century. A few stands of kauri and other mature trees, such as rimu, survive.

The **Centennial Memorial Park** now protects many native plants in the regenerating forest. Bordered to the west by the beaches on the Tasman Sea, the park's sometimes rugged terrain with steep-sided valleys is the most significant forest area close to Auckland. It is popular for picnics and walks (there are some 143 tracks). The website W www.waikatereranges.org.nz has information.

Scenic Drive (SH24) winds its way from Titirangi to Swanson, passing numerous falls and lookouts. The **Arataki Visitor Centre** (☎ 09-817 7134; open 9am-5pm daily) is 6km west of Titirangi along this road and is a good starting point for exploring the ranges. As well as providing a host of information on the area, this impressive centre with its Maori carvings and spectacular views is an attraction in its own right. The giant carving that greets visitors at the entrance depicts the ancestors of the Kawerau iwi. Inside there is a theatre showing a 20-minute video (adult/child $2/1) on the park and its wildlife. A 1.6km nature trail opposite the centre takes visitors past labelled native species, including mature kauri.

The centre has numerous pamphlets and maps for walking over 200km of trails in the ranges. Noted walks are the **Karamatura Loop Walk** (one hour return) near Huia, leading to the waterfalls and northern rata forest; and the Cascade/Kauri area to the north, which has three good walks: **Auckland City Walk**, the **Upper Kauri Track** and **Pukematekeo Track**.

There are a couple of miniature train rides through the ranges but both must be booked in advance. **Waitakere Tramline Society** *(☎ 09-836 0900 evenings)* has weekend trips (adult/child $8/4) leaving from East Portal (near Titirangi), which pass through tunnels filled with glowworms.

The **Rain Forest Express** *(☎ 0800 788 788; adult/child $16/8)* departs from Jacobsons' Depot (off Scenic Drive) at 2pm on Sunday, and there's a twilight special trip at 5.30pm in summer. It runs along the 6km Nihotupu line.

Go Wild *(☎ 09-278 1937; half-/full-day tours $50/90)* has guided tours in the ranges, and transport from Auckland can be arranged.

de Vines *(☎ 09-832 4178, 1012 Scenic Drive)*, just past the Te Henga turn-off, is a pleasant garden restaurant open from 8.30am for breakfast and lunch ($14 to $18) on weekends, and for dinner on Friday and Saturday nights (bookings essential). Wood-fired pizzas cost $16.50 and there's also a bar.

Whatipu & Karekare

In the 19th century, steam trains hauled huge kauri logs from Karekare along the surf-pounded coast to the wharf at Paratutai Island, just off Whatipu. Many ships have foundered on the treacherous sand bars near here, the most famous and tragic being the *Orpheus* which went down in 1863 with the loss of 189 lives. Scenes from Jane Campion's *The Piano* were filmed at Karekare.

Piha & Te Henga (Bethells Beach)

Piha, with its rugged, iron-sand beach, has long been a favourite with Auckland holiday-makers and surfers, as well as with artists and alternative types. The view of the coast as you drive down on Piha Rd is quite spectacular. The distinctive **Lion Rock** (101m), which you can climb, sits just off the beach.

In summer, the beach and small town fill up and there's lots of partying. Surfing competitions are held at Piha and there are horse races along the beach towards the end of summer. You can hire surfboards and wet suits from *Lush*, opposite the camping ground, and the Aloha Surf School (☎ 09-489 2846, W www.alohasurfschool.com) conducts most of its lessons here.

Some 8km north of Piha (but accessed by a circuitous route back around via Scenic Drive) is Te Henga, or Bethells Beach, with its windswept sand dunes. Although much less visited than Piha, Te Henga has a surf club and there's a walkway (part of the NZ Walkway system) that starts at the freshwater Lake Wainamu.

Note that swimming on the west coast beaches can be very dangerous because of strong undercurrents. Surf lifesaving clubs patrol the main beaches – always swim between the flags where lifeguards can provide help if you get into trouble.

Places to Stay Right on the beach, *Piha Domain Motor Camp* *(☎ 09-812 8815)* is a basic but popular camping area with plenty of tent space. Camp sites are $10, and single/double caravans $25/38.

Piha Lodge *(☎ 09-812 8595,* e *piha lodge@xtra.co.nz, 117 Piha Rd)* Units $120 a double. Piha Lodge has two self-contained units with good views from its hillside location. There's a pool, and breakfast is included.

Bethells Beach Cottages *(☎ 09-810 9581, fax 810 8677, 267 Bethells Rd)* Cottages from $200. Bethells Beach comprises three lovely, self-contained cottages.

Muriwai Beach & Gannet Colony

Muriwai Beach, reached by turning off SH16 at Waimauku, is home to the **Takapu Refuge**, an Australasian gannet colony in the Muriwai Regional Park. The colony was once confined to a nearby rock stack but has now overflowed to the shore cliffs, even past the barriers erected to keep observers out. There's an easy walking trail to two viewing platforms and this is a great opportunity to see (and smell) these beautiful birds at close range.

There's also a renowned **surf beach** stretching away into the distance, north of the refuge. You can go horse riding on the beach with **Muriwai Beach Riding Centre**

(☎ 09-411 8480), and there's also camping at *Muriwai Beach Motor Camp* (☎ 09-411 9262, Motutara Rd).

Helensville & Kaipara Harbour

Less than an hour's drive from Auckland, Helensville is 4km inland from the southern end of Kaipara, NZ's biggest harbour.

The small visitors centre (☎ 09-420 8060) at Helensville is on the main street opposite Kaipara Tavern.

Helensville itself is no great attraction, but you can take interesting **cruises** (☎ 09-420 8466) on the Kaipara Harbour. There are three-hour trips at 1pm on Saturday, Sunday and Monday (adult/child $15/7), which cover some historical aspects of the old kauri timber trade; there are also day trips on Sunday ($25/12).

There's a **Pioneer Museum** (*Porter Crescent; open 1pm-3.30pm daily*) in the town centre.

Four kilometres northwest of Helensville, **Parakai Aquatic Park** (☎ 09-420 8998, Parkhurst Rd; adult/child $10/7; open 10am-10pm daily) is a huge hot pool and swimming complex with indoor and outdoor hot mineral pools and various waterslides. There's **camping** here for $15, which includes entry to the complex.

MacNuts Farms (☎ 09-420 2853), 11km past Parakai, is a large macadamia farm. There's a cafe, shop and guided tours of the orchard.

Many travellers are drawn here from Auckland for tandem skydiving at **Parakai Parachute Centre** (☎ 09-420 8064). Jumps cost $250/220 from 12,000/10,000ft. You can arrange in advance to be picked up from Auckland city.

Places to Stay & Eat A late 19th-century kauri villa, *Malolo House* (☎/fax 09-420 7262, 110 Commercial Rd) is a lovely place to stay. As well as tidy backpacker accommodation, there are stylish en suite rooms in a separate part of the house and you can have B&B here for an extra $10. Camp sites are $12 per person, dorm beds $19, singles $35, twins/doubles $50 and en suite singles/doubles $75/90.

Kaipara House B&B (☎ 09-420 7462, cnr SH16 & Parkhurst Rd) Singles/doubles $50/100. Kaipara House is an attractive 1890s villa with two guest rooms and two self-contained summer houses.

Helensville's main street has plenty of takeaways, including the *Fish Country Cafe* for fish and chips and seafood. The *Kaipara Tavern* (☎ 09-420 8343) has cheap bistro meals.

No 88 Bar & Restaurant (☎ 09-420 8894, 88 Commercial Rd) is Helensville's top restaurant, with imaginatively prepared steaks, chicken, seafood and pasta.

Hauraki Gulf Islands

The Hauraki Gulf, off Auckland, is dotted with islands (in Maori, *motu*). Some are only minutes from the city and make popular day trips. Waiheke, a favourite weekend escape, really should not be missed.

Great Barrier, once a remote and little-visited island, still feels like a million miles from anywhere, and it can be used as a stepping stone to the Coromandel. The islands are accessible by ferry or light aircraft.

There are 47 islands in the Hauraki Gulf Maritime Park, administered by DOC. Some are good-sized islands, others are no more than rocks jutting out of the sea. The islands are loosely put into two categories: recreation and conservation. The recreation islands can easily be visited; transport is available, and their harbours are dotted with yachts in summer. The conservation islands, however, have restricted access. Special permits are required to visit some, and others cannot be visited at all as they are refuges for the preservation of plants and animals, especially birds, that are often extremely rare or even endangered species.

For information on Kawau Island and Goat Island, see the Northland chapter.

Information

The DOC information centre in Auckland's ferry building has the best information about natural features, walkways and camping. The Auckland Travel & Information Centre is where you can find out about the more commercial aspects of the islands, such as hotels, ferry services etc. Trampers should get hold of the 1:50,000 Topomaps for Waiheke and Great Barrier. For information on the islands, visit W www.islands.co.nz.

RANGITOTO & MOTUTAPU ISLANDS
pop 105

About 600 years ago, Rangitoto (260m) erupted from the sea and was probably active for several years before settling down. It's now believed to be extinct. Maori living on nearby Motutapu Island, to which Rangitoto is now joined by a causeway, certainly witnessed the eruptions. Human footprints have been found here, embedded in the ash thrown out during the course of the mountain's creation. It is the largest and youngest of Auckland's volcanic cones.

Rangitoto literally means 'Blood Red Sky', although this is generally thought to allude not to the eruptions but to a battle in which the commander of the *Awara* canoe, Tamatekapua, was badly wounded. Rangitoto is an abbreviation of Nga Rangi i Totongia a Tamatekapua, meaning 'The Days of Tamatekapua's Bleeding'.

Ten kilometres northeast of downtown Auckland, Rangitoto is a good place for a picnic. It has many pleasant walks, barbecues, a surprising amount of flora (including flowering pohutukawa in summer) and a great view from the summit of the cone. There's an information board at the wharf with maps of the walks. The DOC pamphlet *Rangitoto* ($1) has a useful map and descriptions of good walks.

The hike from the wharf to the summit takes about an hour. Up at the top, a loop walk goes around the crater's rim. The walk to the lava caves branches off the summit walk and takes 30 minutes return. As the basalt surface can get hot in summer, you'll need good shoes and plenty of water.

Motutapu, in contrast to Rangitoto, is mainly covered in grassland grazed by

sheep and cattle. Archaeologically, this is a very significant island – the traces of some 500 years of continuous human habitation are etched into its landscape.

There's an interesting three-hour round-trip walk between the wharf at Islington Bay and the wharf at Home Bay. Islington, the inlet between the islands, was once known as Drunken Bay because sailing ships would stop here to sober up crews who had hit the bottle in Auckland.

There's a *DOC camping ground (adult/child $5/2)* at Home Bay. Facilities are basic, with only a water tap and toilet provided. Bring cooking equipment, as open fires aren't permitted. For information contact the senior ranger (☎ 09-372 7348) or DOC in Auckland.

Getting There & Away
The ferry trip to Rangitoto Island from the ferry building in Auckland takes about half an hour. Fullers (☎ 09-367 9111) has ferries leaving at 9am and 11am daily with extra sailing at 1pm during summer and weekends. The return fare is adult/child $20/10.

Fullers also has one-day tours to Rangitoto. On the Volcanic Explorer you ride in a canopied trailer, towed by a 4WD tractor, to a 900m boardwalk leading to the summit. It costs adult/child $49/25, including the return ferry.

WAIHEKE ISLAND
pop 8000

Waiheke is the most visited of the gulf islands and, at 93 sq km, is one of the largest. Though only a little over half an hour by ferry from Auckland, Waiheke enjoys the slow pace of island life and a fine climate; its many picturesque bays and beaches make it a great place to relax. Much of the rolling hills on the western half of the island are cloaked with vineyards, and there are wineries scattered all around.

The island attracts artistic types who exhibit their work in galleries and craft shops on the island. There is also an increasing number of retirees and commuters. While it is slowly becoming an Auckland suburb, it is still a relaxed, rural retreat that deserves

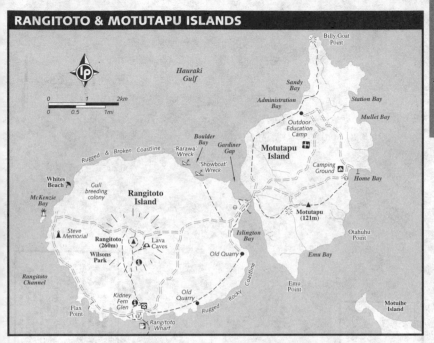

RANGITOTO & MOTUTAPU ISLANDS

more than one day. To experience Waiheke at its best, try to visit on a weekday.

Waiheke has been populated since about AD 950; legends relate that one of the pioneering canoes landed on the island. Traces of an old fortified *pa* can still be seen on the headland overlooking Putiki Bay. Europeans arrived with the missionary Samuel Marsden in the early 1800s and the island was soon stripped of its kauri forest.

The biggest event on the island is the annual **Waiheke Jazz Festival** (**W** www .waihekejazz.co.nz), which draws up to 30,000 people over Easter. Another biggie is the **Spring Into Art** festival in October.

Orientation & Information
The main settlement is Oneroa, at the western end of the island. From there the island is relatively 'built-up' through to Palm Beach and Onetangi in its middle. Beyond Onetangi, the eastern half of the island is lightly inhabited.

The Waiheke Island visitors centre (☎ 09-372 1234, **e** waiheke@iconz.co.nz), at the Artworks complex on Ocean View Rd, 1km from the ferry wharf, is a useful first stop. It's open from 9am to 5pm daily (closes earlier in winter).

Oneroa has a post office, banks and 24-hour ATMs. You can access the Internet at the Lazy Lounge Cafe in Oneroa, or at Surf.com in Surfdale.

Things to See & Do
The **Artworks complex** (*cnr Ocean View Rd & Kororoa Rd; open 10am-4pm daily*) is home to a variety of art and craft galleries, a library and bookshop, a cafe and a community theatre. If you're interested in visiting the many art and craft **galleries** and studios dotted around the island, the visitors centre has a brochure.

Whittaker's Musical Experience (*☎ 09-372 5573; adult/child & senior $10/7; open 10am-noon & 2.30pm-4pm*), also located in

AUCKLAND REGION

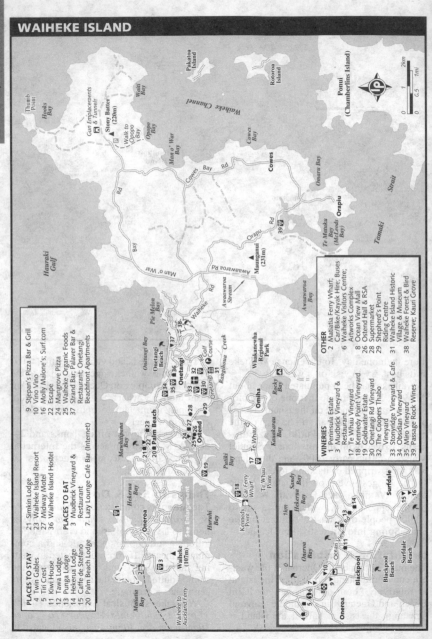

WAIHEKE ISLAND

PLACES TO STAY
4 Twin Gables
5 Tiri Crest
11 Kiwi House
12 Tawa Lodge
13 Punga Lodge
14 Hekerua Lodge
15 Caffe de Stefano
20 Palm Beach Lodge

21 Simkin Lodge
23 Waiheke Island Resort
27 Midway Motel
36 Waiheke Island Hostel

PLACES TO EAT
3 Mudbrick Vineyard &
   Restaurant
7 Lazy Lounge Café Bar (Internet)

9 Stepan's Pizza Bar & Grill
10 Vino Vino
16 Molly Malone's; Surf.com
22 Escape
24 Mangrove Pizza
25 Waiheke Organic Foods
37 Strand Bar; Palaver Bar &
   Restaurant; Onetangi
   Beachfront Apartments

OTHER
2 Matiatia Ferry Wharf;
   Car/Bike/Kayak Hire; Buses
6 Waiheke Visitors Centre;
   Artworks Complex
8 Ocean View Mall
26 Ostend Hall & RSA
28 Supermarket
29 Shepherd's Point
   Riding Centre
31 Waiheke Island Historic
   Village & Museum
38 Waiheke Forest & Bird
   Reserve; Kauri Grove

WINERIES
1 Peninsula Estate
3 Mudbrick Vineyard &
   Restaurant
17 Te Whau Vineyard
18 Kennedy Point Vineyard
19 Goldwater Estate
30 Onetangi Rd Vineyard
32 The Coopers Thabo
   Vineyard
33 Stonyridge Vineyard & Cafe
34 Obsidian Vineyard
35 Miro Vineyard
39 Passage Rock Wines

the Artworks centre, has a 1½-hour show daily at 1pm, featuring a range of antique concert instruments. There's also a museum of instruments which you can visit by donation.

On the road to Onetangi, next to the golf club, is the small **Waiheke Island Historic Village and Museum** *(open noon-4pm Mon, Wed, Sat & Sun)*. Entry is by donation.

The colourful *Ostend market* is held at the RSA hall on Belgium St from 8am to 3pm Saturday in summer (closing earlier in winter). Here you can find local preserves and jams, second-hand books and clothes, handicrafts, plants and more.

It's possible to drive right around the scenic loop road at the eastern end of the island. At the end of Man o' War Bay Rd there's a car park and a 1.5km walk to **Stony Batter** where you can explore WWII tunnels and gun emplacements built in 1941 to defend Auckland's harbour.

Wineries

At last count Waiheke had 27 vineyards, 11 of which you can visit for tasting and sales. Some of these also have restaurants or accommodation. Because of the relatively small quantities produced (grapes are often bought in from elsewhere) and a growing demand for Waiheke's boutique wines, the wine here is generally pretty expensive and most places charge for tastings – you might find the snob factor here is higher than wine regions elsewhere in NZ, but some of the wineries are spectacularly located and well worth a visit.

The greatest concentration of vineyards is in the western half of the island, particularly around Onetangi, but they are spread as far as Stony Batter in the far east and Passage Rock Wines on the Orapiu Loop Road. Pick up a copy of the *Waiheke Winegrowers Map* from the visitors centre.

Wineries worth a visit include: *Mudbrick* *(☎ 09-372 9050, Church Bay Rd)*, which has a fine restaurant and is open daily year-round; *Te Whau (☎ 09-372 7191, 218 Te Whau Drive)*, perched out on the end of Te Whau peninsula with superb views, and with a restaurant open from 11am to 5pm

daily (except Tuesday) in summer; *Stonyridge (☎ 09-372 8822, 80 Onetangi Rd)*, one of Waiheke's oldest vineyards, with a pleasant al fresco restaurant overlooking the vines; *Onetangi Road (☎ 09-372 6130, 82 Onetangi Rd)*, which has tours by appointment of its winery and microbrewery; and *Goldwater Estate (☎ 09-372 7493, 18 Causeway Rd)* in Putiki Bay, which has casual lunch (platters) in summer.

Beaches

Popular beaches with good sand and swimming include Oneroa Beach and the adjacent Little Oneroa Beach. Palm Beach is in a lovely little cove, and there's a long stretch of sand at Onetangi Bay. A number of the beaches have shady pohutukawa trees.

There are nudist beaches at Palm Beach and on the west end of Onetangi Bay. Surf Skis and boogie boards can be hired on Onetangi and there's snorkelling at Hekerua Bay.

Activities

Walking Waiheke has a good system of walkways outlined in the *Waiheke Islands Walkways* pamphlet, available on the island or at the DOC office in Auckland.

In Onetangi there's a **forest and bird reserve** with several good walks. For coastal walks, a good, well-marked track leads right around the coast from Oneroa Bay to Palm Beach. It's about a two-hour walk; at the Palm Beach end you can jump on a bus back to town. Another good coastal walk begins at the Matiatia ferry wharf.

The best walks are in the less-developed eastern part of the island. The **Stony Batter Walk**, leading through private farmland, derives its name from the boulder-strewn fields. From there you can continue north to Hooks Bay or south to Opopo Bay.

Sea Kayaking Waiheke's many bays and central position in the Hauraki Gulf make it an ideal spot for sea kayaking. *Ross Adventures (☎ 09-372 5550)* is based at Matiatia and offers trips from half-day paddles ($60) to four-day camping excursions and night kayaking. *Kayak Waiheke (☎ 09-372 7262)* also has daily guided tours.

Horse Riding The **Shepherd's Point Riding Centre** (☎ 09-372 8104, 91 Ostend Rd), between Ostend and the airstrip, has guided horse treks starting at $45 an hour.

Organised Tours

Fullers (see the Getting There & Away section later in this chapter) has a host of tours in conjunction with its ferry service.

With **Ananda Tours** (☎ 09-372 7530; tours $40 per person) you can visit artists and their studios, or local wineries. The informal tours (about four hours) can be customised to suit your needs.

Beyond & Back Tour (☎ 09-367 9111, e waiheke_tours@hotmail.com; tours adult/child ex-Waiheke $25/15, ex-Auckland $47/25) is a half-day trip including a tour of Stony Batter and the WWII tunnels. This bus tour can be started from Auckland or the Matiatia Wharf on Waiheke. A barbecue lunch or light meal at Passage Rock winery is extra.

Places to Stay

Waiheke has more than 130 homestays, farmstays, B&Bs, baches or flats for rent, costing anything from $20 to $250 a night. Prices at most places jump from mid-December to the end of January and at Easter (when you'd be lucky to get a bed anywhere). If you're on a budget there are some great backpackers, but if you want to splash out, there are some real treats.

Staff at the Waiheke Island visitors centre in Oneroa will match you with the type of place you seek. The Auckland Travel & Information Centre also lists Waiheke accommodation.

Camping The only *camping ground* on the island is at Rocky Bay, at the far end of the beach off Gordon's Rd in the Whakanewha Regional Park. You need to book a camp site (adult/child $5/2) through Parksline (☎ 09-303 1530) in order to get a combination to open the chain gate. There are limited camp sites at *Hekerua Lodge* and *Simkin Lodge*.

Hostels Nestled in serene bush near Oneroa, *Hekerua Lodge* (☎ 09-372 8990,

e hekerua@ihug.co.nz, 11 Hekerua Rd) is a pleasure to stay in. The small but spotless lodge has a pool and the owner is very laid back. Camp sites cost $15 per person, dorm beds $19 to $22, and singles/doubles $35/59.

Simkin Lodge (☎ 09 372 8662, e simkin lodge@xtra.co.nz, 54 Palm Rd) Camp sites from $12, dorm beds $20, twins/doubles $55, en suite doubles $135. Formerly Palm Beach Backpackers, and once an Anglican school camp, this place was receiving major renovations when we visited, including new self-contained units and recreation areas. It's in a great spot right across from the beach.

Waiheke Island Hostel (☎ 09-372 8971, e www.waiheke.cjb.net, 419 Seaview Rd) Dorm beds $19, singles/doubles $30/44-48, en suite doubles $65. This colourful associate-YHA at Onetagi is another tidy place with a big garden and a good location overlooking Onetangi Bay.

B&Bs & Guesthouses There are plenty of lovely guesthouses on the island.

Kiwi House (☎ 09-372 9123, e kiwi house@clear.net.nz, 23 Kiwi St) Singles/doubles $40/75, en suite doubles $85. Kiwi House is a friendly B&B with pleasant outdoor decks and a communal kitchen.

Twin Gables (☎ 09-372 9877, 17 Tiri Rd) B&B doubles $100. Twin Gables is a welcoming, modern place built to get the best out of the lovely views. Some rooms have decks.

Punga Lodge (☎/fax 09-372 6675, 223 Ocean View Rd) B&B doubles $110-145, apartments $130-200. Close to Oneroa town, Punga Lodge is set in tranquil bush surroundings with lots of outdoor decking to enjoy it from. There are B&B rooms in the main house and three comfortable timber apartments.

Tawa Lodge (☎ 09-372 9434, 15 Tawa St) B&B $100, cottages $140-175. Tawa Lodge is a similar set up (same owners) but with an exposed hilltop location offering sea views over Oneroa Bay.

Motels & Apartments One of the few standard motels on the island, *Midway*

Motel (☎ 09-372 8023, 1 Whakarite Rd, Ostend) has studio and one-bedroom units ($85 to $120 per double), a heated swimming pool and spa.

Tiri Crest (☎ 09-372 5423, 16 Tiri Crescent) Flat $90, cottage $110, house $140. Tiri Crest is great value if you can get it. There's a neatly kept, fully furnished house (minimum two nights), as well as a flat and a cute little cottage with polished floorboards. Prices are for two people.

Waiheke Island Resort (☎ 0800 372 0011, 09-924 4353, Palm Rd) Chalets $199, villas $225-250. This upmarket resort near Palm Beach has a full range of facilities including a swimming pool, tennis court and a restaurant. The villas are fully self-contained and have sea views.

Palm Beach Lodge (☎ 09-372 7763, ⓔ plambch@orcon.net.nz, 23 Tiri View Rd) Apartments $190-260. This lodge, set high above the beach, has three self-contained apartments with an unusual modern design, decks, sea views and barbecues. Each apartment has two double bedrooms.

Onetangi Beachfront Apartments (☎ 09-372 7051, ⓔ info@onetangi.co.nz, 27 The Strand) Studios $85-140, apartments from $185. This is a well-situated complex on Onetangi Beach. The studio units are reasonably priced but you pay for the beach-facing apartments.

Places to Eat

The main centre for cafes and restaurants is Oneroa's main street, but there are other places in Surfdale, Palm Beach, Ostend and Onetangi. A number of wineries also have restaurants, with limited opening hours. The *Ocean View Mall* in Oneroa has a couple of cafes and an ice-creamery with outdoor tables.

Lazy Lounge Cafe Bar (☎ 09-372 5732, 139 Ocean View Rd) Mains $8-19. In Oneroa, the Lazy Lounge is an arty place that lives up to its name with comfy furniture and a garden overlooking the bay. It's open from 8.30am for breakfast.

Vino Vino Cafe & Wine Bar (☎ 09-372 9888, 3/153 Ocean View Rd). Tucked away below street level, this popular licensed restaurant has good food and a regular programme of live music. There are great ocean views from the deck (bookings advised).

Stjepan's Pizza Bar & Grill (☎ 09-372 8209, 124 Ocean View Rd) Mains $18-24. Stjepan's has tasty pizzas, pasta and seafood.

Surfdale, between Oneroa and Ostend, has a small enclave of cafes and shops.

Caffe de Stefano (☎ 09-372 5309, Surfdale) Dishes $15-25. Stefano's is a locally recommended place for cheap Italian pizza, pasta, focaccia and even gelati. It's BYO, which makes for an inexpensive night out.

Molly Malone's (☎ 09-372 8011, 6 Miami Ave) Lunch $8.50-15, dinner $12-23. Open 11am-11pm. An ambient place for a drink or hearty bistro meal. There's a big beer garden at the front and live music in summer.

In the centre of Ostend, the *RSA* has little character but serves good pub food and the cheapest beer on the island. Also at Ostend is a large *supermarket*, which is the place to head if you're self-catering, and *Waiheke Organic Food,* where you can get bulk wholefoods.

In Ostend, *Mangrove Pizza (☎ 09-372 8789, 14 Belgium St)* is a popular takeaway pizza place open from 5pm. Pizzas are $10.50 to $18.

Mudbrick Vineyard & Restaurant (☎ 09-372 9050, Church Bay Rd) Mains $24-33. Open lunch & dinner daily. This is probably the best place for fine dining on Waiheke. From the patio you look across the rows of vines towards the harbour and Auckland city. It's not hard to while away an afternoon here over chardonnay and a cheese platter. The seasonal à la carte menu features Pacific and Mediterranean flavours.

Stonyridge Veranda Cafe (☎ 09-372 8822, 80 Onetangi Rd) $7.50-26. Open 11.30am-5pm weekends. Another winery with a beautiful setting and an al fresco cafe, Stonyridge offers on interesting Pacific Rim lunch menu and a party atmosphere complete with music and spa pool.

Escape (☎ 09-372 3068, 39 Palm Rd) Mains $10-21. Open for lunch and dinner Wed-Sun. Down at Palm Beach, next to the general store, this cafe and bar is a great place for an evening drink or a meal of seafood or steak.

The **Strand Bar**, on the beachfront at Onetangi, is a good place for a beer, and **Palaver Bar & Restaurant** (☎ 09-372 7583) hosts live bands and has a nightclub in summer.

Getting There & Away

Waiheke Air Services (☎ 0800 372 5000, 09-372 5000) has flights between Waiheke and Auckland ($90), Coromandel ($90) and Great Barrier Island ($150) in summer but these are not scheduled – call ahead to check.

Fullers (☎ 09-367 9111) runs frequent daily ferries between downtown Auckland and Matiatia Wharf. From Monday to Friday they operate roughly hourly from 5.30am to 11.30pm, on Saturday it's 6.30am to 11.30pm and on Sunday 7am to 9.30pm. Four daily ferries go via Devonport, the rest are direct. The return fare is $23.60/11.60 adult/child ($20/10 if you go via Devonport). Auckland to Matiatia takes about 35 minutes.

You can take your car over to Waiheke with Subritzky Line (☎ 09-534 5663), which has regular daily departures from Half Moon Bay in Pakuranga to Kennedy Point on Waiheke, and on Friday at 5.30pm from Wynyard Wharf in Auckland. Ferries ply between Half Moon Bay and Kennedy Point roughly every two hours between 6am and 6pm (45 minutes one way, bookings essential). The return trip costs $106/31 for a car/motorcycle, plus $24/12/55 per adult/child/family. You can also travel on this ferry as a foot passenger.

Getting Around

Bus Fullers operates four bus routes on the island, connecting with the arriving and departing ferries. All buses go from Matiatia Wharf to Oneroa, then depending on the route you can get to Little Oneroa, Palm Beach, Ostend and Rocky Bay; or Blackpool, Surfdale, Ostend and Onetangi. A short trip costs $1, complete route is $3 and an all-day bus pass is $7. You can buy a bus and boat pass from Fullers in Auckland for $26/12 adult/child.

Car, Scooter & Bicycle Waiheke is small enough (and the roads good enough) to make cycling or scootering around the western half a breeze. For longer trips around the Loop Road a car is the go and car hire is reasonably priced. Minimum age for car hire is 21 years.

Waiheke Rental Cars (☎ 09-372 8635) and Waiheke Auto Rentals (☎ 09-373 8998) are both based at Matiatia Wharf. Cars cost from $45 a day, soft-top jeeps from $60 and you can even rent a convertible sports car from Waiheke Auto Rentals for $80 a day (just the thing for winery touring). Hourly rentals may also be possible. There's an additional charge of 50c a kilometre, which can add up if you do a full circuit of the island (around 65km).

Waiheke Rentals also has 50cc scooters (for which you only need a valid driver licence) for around $40 a day and motorbikes from $60 a day, both with unlimited mileage.

Attitude Rentals (☎ 09-372 7897) has motor-assisted mountain bikes for hire (minimum two hours; $25). You will need to pick up the bike from Surf & Rock on Ocean View Rd in Oneroa.

Ordinary mountain bikes can be rented at various places, including Wharf Rats Bike Hire (☎ 09-372 7937) at Matiatia Wharf, and the visitors centre ($15/25 a half/full day at both). Get a copy of the *Bike Waiheke* pamphlet; the route takes you past most of the sights and usually takes four to six hours at a leisurely pace – count on eight hours if you include the loop at the eastern end of the island and Stony Batter.

Taxi For taxi service on the island ring Waiheke Taxis (☎ 09-372 8038), Dial-a-Cab (☎ 09-372 9666) or Waiheke Island Shuttle Service (☎ 09-372 7756).

GREAT BARRIER ISLAND
pop 1200

Great Barrier, 88km from the mainland, is the largest island in the gulf. It is a rugged scenic island, resembling the Coromandel Peninsula to which it was once joined.

Great Barrier has hot springs, historic kauri dams, a forest sanctuary and a network of tramping tracks. Because there are no possums on the island, the native bush is lush.

It could be said the island's main attractions are its beautiful beaches and its fine tramping, but the sheer isolation is also an appealing factor – Great Barrier has none of the hype or resort-feel of Waiheke. The west coast has safe sandy beaches; the east coast beaches are good for surfing. Mountain biking, swimming, fishing, diving, boating, sea kayaking and just relaxing are other popular activities on the island.

Named by James Cook, Great Barrier Island later became a whaling centre. The island implemented the world's first airmail postal service in 1897 (using pigeons). The centenary of the service was celebrated with the release of hundreds of birds. Great Barrier has also been the site of some spectacular shipwrecks, including the SS *Wairarapa* in 1894 and the *Wiltshire* in 1922. There's a cemetery at Katherine Bay, where victims of the *Wairarapa* wreck were buried. There is a signposted NZ Walkways track from Whangapoua Beach (20 minutes from Port Fitzroy by taxi) to the mass graves on the Tapuwai headland.

Although easily reached from Auckland, Great Barrier Island is a world – and a good 20 years – away. The island has no electricity supply (only private generators), most roads are unsealed, most of the cars look like refugees from the mainland, and there are only a handful of shops in a few scattered settlements. Still, the great god Internet has found its way here – practically everyone has their own website!

From around mid-December to Easter the island is a busy holiday destination, especially during the Christmas holidays until the end of January, Easter and the Labour Day long weekend. At these times make sure you book transport, accommodation and activities in advance.

Orientation

Tryphena is the main settlement and nearest arrival point for the ferries (at Shoal Bay 5km away). Strung out along several kilometres of coast road, it consists of a few dozen houses, a cardphone, toilets, a school and a handful of accommodation places dotted around the harbour. From the wharf it is a couple of kilometres to Mulberry Grove, and then another 1km over the headland to Pa Beach and the Stonewall Store.

The airport and visitors centre are at Claris, a small settlement with a store, laundry, fuel and a good cafe, about 16km north of Tryphena. Whangaparapara is an old timber town and the site of the island's 19th-century whaling activities. Port Fitzroy is the other main harbour on the west coast, about a one hour drive from Tryphena (roads are unsealed beyond Claris).

Information

The Great Barrier Island visitors centre (☎ 09-429 0033, W www.greatbarrier .co.nz) is on the main road at Claris, opposite the airfield. It's very helpful – this must be one of the few places where staff know the names and phone numbers of just about everyone on the island off by heart! You can get an accommodation list here, book activities and get details on walks and camping. It's open from 9am to 5pm Monday to Friday and 9am to 1pm Saturday and Sunday in summer (shorter hours in winter). The free *Great Barrier Island* booklet is full of useful info and you can also pick up a walking trails brochure here.

The main DOC office (☎ 09-429 0044) is in Port Fitzroy, a 15-minute walk (1km by road) from the Port Fitzroy jetty. It has information and maps on the island, collects fees and sells hut tickets and operates the adjacent Akapoua Bay camping ground. It's open from 8am to 4.30pm Monday to Friday.

Because there's no power on the island, make sure you bring a torch (flashlight) – there are no streetlights anywhere. There are public telephones in the main centres but no mobile phone reception. There are no ATMs.

Things to See & Do

Beaches & Surfing Medlands, with its wide sweep of white sand, is one of the best beaches on the island and is easily accessible from Tryphena. Remote Whangapoua requires more effort to get to but it's a fine surfing beach, while Kaitoke, Awana Bay

GREAT BARRIER ISLAND

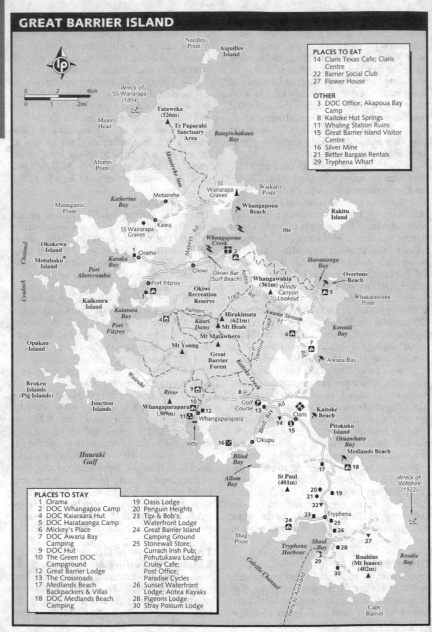

PLACES TO EAT
14 Claris Texas Cafe; Claris Centre
22 Barrier Social Club
27 Flower House

OTHER
3 DOC Office; Akapoua Bay Camp
8 Kaitoke Hot Springs
11 Whaling Station Ruins
15 Great Barrier Island Visitor Centre
16 Silver Mine
21 Better Bargain Rentals
29 Tryphena Wharf

PLACES TO STAY
1 Orama
2 DOC Whangapoa Camp
4 DOC Kaiaraara Hut
5 DOC Harataonga Camp
6 Mickey's Place
7 DOC Awana Bay Camping
9 DOC Hut
10 The Green DOC Campground
12 Great Barrier Lodge
13 The Crossroads
17 Medlands Beach Backpackers & Villas
18 DOC Medlands Beach Camping
19 Oasis Lodge
20 Penguin Heights
23 Tipi & Bob's; Waterfront Lodge
24 Great Barrier Island Camping Ground
25 Stonewall Store; Currach Irish Pub; Pohutukawa Lodge; Cruisy Cafe; Post Office; Paradise Cycles
26 Sunset Waterfront Lodge; Aotea Kayaks
28 Pigeons Lodge
30 Stray Possum Lodge

and Harataonga are also good. Okiwi Bar has an excellent right-hand break, while Awana has both left- and right-hand breaks. Tryphena's bay, lined with pohutukawa, has sheltered beaches.

Walking Many people come here just for the walks – be aware they are often not well signposted. The best tramping trails are in the Great Barrier Forest north of Whangaparapara, where there has been a great deal of reforestation.

The most spectacular short walk is from Windy Canyon to Hirakimata (Mt Hobson). **Windy Canyon**, only a 15-minute walk from the main Port Fitzroy–Harataonga (Aotea) road, has spectacular rock outcrops and affords great views of the island. From Windy Canyon, an excellent trail continues for another 1½ hours through scrubby forest to **Hirakimata** (621m), the highest point on the island, with views across to the Coromandel and Auckland on a fine day. Near the top of the mountain are lush forests and a few mature kauri that survived the logging days. From Hirakimata it is two hours through forest to the hut closest to Port Fitzroy and then 45 minutes to Port Fitzroy itself. Another popular walk is the **Tramline Track** that also starts on Aotea Rd and follows old logging tramlines to Whangaparapara Harbour (five hours). It also joins up with the **Kaitoke Hot Springs Track**. The hot pools can be reached from Whangaparapara Rd (45 minutes).

Many other trails traverse the forest, taking between 30 minutes and five hours – pick up a copy of *Great Barrier Island Walking Tracks* from the visitors centre.

The Stray Possum Lodge has a good trampers bus service that will drop you at the start of a trail and pick you up at the other end – see Getting Around later in this chapter.

Mountain Biking With rugged scenery and little traffic on the unsealed roads, mountain biking is a popular and not too difficult activity here. A good ride is from Tryphena to Whangaparapara: cycle about an hour to Medlands Beach where you can

Pigeon Post

MW

Great Barrier's first pigeon postal service took flight in 1897, a year after an enterprising Auckland newspaper reporter had used a pigeon to file a report from the island. From small beginnings the service expanded to include a good part of the Hauraki Gulf: shopping lists, election results, mine claims and important pieces of news winged their way across land and sea bound to the legs of the canny birds. The arrival of the telegraph in 1908 grounded the service, but it was resurrected in 1993 as a novelty for visitors. Twenty dollars buys a pigeon pack, which includes a leaflet on the history of the service, a pigeon-gram form and a triangular stamp. (The original stamps used are now worth a small fortune.)

Your message will be flown by pigeon to Auckland and forwarded to you by more conventional means. Postal centres in Tryphena, Claris and Port Fitzroy all sell the packs. The service depends somewhat on the ferries, since the pigeons need to be ordered in from Auckland (they only fly home, not to the island) – so it doesn't operate daily outside summer.

stop for a swim, then cycle another hour to the hot springs, from where it's another half-hour to accommodation in Whangaparapara. Spend another day cycling through the forest up to Port Fitzroy, stopping on the way for a hike up to the kauri dams on a good, well-marked 4WD track.

You can hire bikes at Paradise Cycles (☎ 09-429 0474) next to the Stonewall Store in Tryphena, or from Stray Possum Lodge.

Sea Kayaking There are plenty of secluded bays around Great Barrier's coastline and kayaking is a great way (often the only way) to explore them. **Aotea Kayak Adventures** (☎ 09-429 0664) hires out kayaks for $35 per person a day, and has several short guided paddles including a two-hour cruise around Tryphena Harbour ($30), a sunset paddle ($35) and a night trip ($50) on which you can see phosphorescence dancing around your paddles. Fully catered overnight trips from three to seven days can be arranged for $125 per person per day – including a circumnavigation of the island. **Great Barrier Island Kayak Hire** (☎ 09-429 0520) in Tryphena also hires out kayaks. **Blue Water Safaris** (☎ 09-429 0171) has boat-based kayaking trips around outlying islands off Whangaparapara Harbour for $175.

Horse Treks Guided horse treks from can be arranged through **Adventure Horse Treks** (☎ 09-429 0274) in Claris for about $30 for an hour. Trips include a beach ride on Kaitoke Beach, and a ride from Claris to Okupu following a historic 'cream trail'.

Fishing & Diving Boat tours of all descriptions are on offer around Great Barrier, particularly fishing charters. **Mokum Fishing Charters** (☎ 09-429 0485) is a recommended operator with half-day trips for $65. **Tipi & Bob's** (☎ 09-429 0550) has half-day trips for $55.

Great Barrier has some of the most varied scuba diving in NZ. There's pinnacle diving, shipwreck diving, lots of fish and over 33m visibility at some times of the year; February to April is probably the best time. **Tryphena Mobile Dive Centre** (☎ 09-429 0654), at Tryphena Wharf, hires out gear and fills tanks.

Places to Stay
Most accommodation is in and around Tryphena, but there are places scattered all over the island, so it's easy to head somewhere more remote if you don't like the 'Big Smoke'. Prices can be steep in summer, but rates drop dramatically outside the peak period. Summer prices are quoted here.

Great Barrier Island has loads of baches, all privately owned and maintained. The going rate is $100-plus a double, and many sleep four or more. The visitors centre can give you a list of contacts.

Camping & Huts There are DOC *camping grounds* at Harataonga Bay, Medlands Beach, Akapoua Bay, Whangapoua, The Green (Whangaparapara) and Awana Bay, all with basic facilities, including water (cold shower) and pit toilets. Only Akapoua Bay has a barbecue; you are not allowed to light fires elsewhere. Camping is not allowed outside the camping grounds without a permit. Camping costs adult/child $7/3.50.

As well as the camping grounds, DOC has the *Kaiaraara Hut* in the Great Barrier Forest, a 45-minute walk from Port Fitzroy wharf. The hut sleeps up to 24 in bunkrooms, and facilities include cold water, pit toilets and a kitchen with a wood stove. Bring your own sleeping bag and cooking equipment. The cost is $10 for adults (children $5) and you can camp outside for $5/2.50. From November to January the hut and camping grounds are very busy. There's another hut north of Whangaparapara. Bookings are essential at all DOC camp sites (☎ 09-429 0044). The hut is on a first-come, first-served basis.

There are two camping grounds on private property: *Mickey's Place* (☎ 09-429 0140) near Awana Bay has sites for adult/child $5/2; the *Great Barrier Island Campground* (☎ 09-429 0184, Schooner Bay Rd) at Puriri Bay has sites for adult/child $8.50/4.50 with toilets, barbecue sites and cold-water showers.

Hostels Great Barrier has a surprising number of backpacker places.

Stray Possum Lodge (☎ 0800 767 786, 09-429 0109, e straypossum@acb.co.nz) Camp sites $12 per person, dorm beds $19, doubles $55, chalets $120 per couple. Not far from the ferry wharf but hidden away in a lovely bush setting, the Stray Possum is a great spot for backpackers and trampers. As well as camping and a comfortable backpackers section, there are two self-contained bush chalets sleeping up to six. There's a restaurant and bar (open 6pm to 11pm), which can get pretty lively. The Stray Possum also organises trampers transport – see the Getting Around section later.

Pohutukawa Lodge (☎ 09-429 0211, e plodge@xtra.co.nz) Camp sites $12 per person, dorm beds $17, singles/doubles $30/60, en suite units $95. This friendly lodge, attached to the Currach Irish Pub (see Places to Eat) in Tryphena, has a big back garden, bunkrooms and three modern en suite rooms.

The Crossroads (☎ 09-429 0889, e xroads@ihug.co.nz, 1 Blind Bay Rd) Dorm beds $20, singles/doubles $30/50. Crossroads, a comfortable purpose-built backpackers, is well-placed at the junction of the roads to Whangaparapara and Port Fitzroy 2km from Claris. It has a large common area and separate units, a bar and Internet access.

Penguin Heights (☎ 09-429 0628, e bileve@penguinheights.co.nz, 41 Medland Rd) Dorm beds $18 (with linen $23), double unit $115. Penguin Heights is a small place just out of Tryphena with a rustic backpacker cottage sleeping six (although there are plans to expand) and a modern self-contained unit next door. The Rafts Gift Shop here is packed with penguin paraphernalia and 10% of proceeds goes towards nesting boxes for blue penguins.

Medlands Beach Backpackers & Villas (☎ 09-429 0320, e info@medlandsbeach .com, 9 Mason Rd) Dorm beds $20, doubles/triples $50/70, villa $200. Just off the main road from lovely Medlands Beach, this place has a relatively basic and well-worn range of accommodation in the main house and an outbuilding. There's also a fully-equipped two-bedroom house that can sleep six. Boogie boards, bikes and snorkelling gear are available.

Sunset Waterfront Lodge in Tryphena has backpackers beds at $20, *Great Barrier Lodge* at Whangaparapara has backpacker accommodation at a steep $30, and *Orama* has beds in bunkrooms for $12 per person (see following).

Guesthouses, Lodges & Motels Behind the Tryphena shopping centre at Mulberry Grove, *Sunset Waterfront Lodge* (☎ 09-429 0051, W www.sunsetlodge.co.nz) has a variety of accommodation including self-contained A-frame chalets sleeping five ($150), nice new studios with kitchenette ($120 a double) and a backpackers lodge ($20).

Oasis Lodge (☎ 09-429 0021, e barrier oasislodge@xtra.co.nz) B&B $250 a double, cottage $170. Oasis Lodge is pricey but has three bright, luxury en suite rooms, plus a self-contained unit, on a property that includes a vineyard. The restaurant here is worth a visit (see Places to Eat).

Pigeons Lodge (☎ 09-429 0437, e info@ pigeonslodge.co.nz, Shoal Bay Rd) Twins & doubles $95-120. This lodge, on the beach-front at Shoal Bay, is in a peaceful bush setting and has a restaurant and bar. There are four en suite rooms, two self-contained units and a big deck overlooking the water.

Tipi & Bob's Waterfront Lodge (☎ 09-429 0550, W www.waterfrontlodge.co.nz) Units $135-150, cottage $150. Tip & Bob's, a short drive west of Tryphena, has casual one- and two-bedroom units overlooking the sea, as well as a neat little cottage sleeping six. Most of the units have sea views and there's a fine garden bar and restaurant here.

Great Barrier Lodge (☎ 09-429 0488, W www.greatbarrierlodge.com) Dorm beds with linen $30, units $130 a double, cottage $140. At Whangaparapara, this is a big place on the water's edge overlooking the inlet. It has modern self-contained units, a restaurant and bar (open in summer), and a small general store. There's also a backpacker lodge. In summer the Fullers ferry may drop-off at the wharf here.

Orama (☎ 09-429 0063, W www.orama .org.nz) Camping $8 per person, dorm beds $12, guest rooms $25 per person, flats $100. At Karaka Bay, just north of Port Fitzroy, Orama is a Christian community with a variety of accommodation, including camping. It has good facilities, including a swimming pool (open in summer) and a general store, and it's in a quiet bush setting.

Places to Eat & Drink

Eating out is understandably limited on the Barrier, but the few options are quite good, sociable places for a meal and a number of accommodation places have their own licensed restaurants.

There is a well-stocked grocery store at the *Claris Centre*, near the airport and the *Stonewall Store* at Tryphena, and there are *general stores* at Port Fitzroy, Great Barrier Lodge and Mulberry Grove in Tryphena. The *Cruisy Cafe*, next to the Stonewall Store, is a bakery with fresh breads, cakes and pies.

Currach Irish Pub (☎ 09-429 0211) Meals $8-20. Next to the Stonewall Store at Tryphena, this lively pub is not just another mock Irish theme bar. It's Irish-owned (and usually staffed) and there's Guinness, Murphy's Kilkenny and Bulmer's cider on tap, as well as the locally produced John Mellars red wine and Island Mead. As well as bar snacks and burgers, there's a changing menu of seafood, steak and Asian influenced dishes. There's a regular music night on Thursday at which you can sing (or perform) for your supper. The Shipwreck Gallery features work by local artists.

Claris Texas Cafe (☎ 09-429 0811) In the Claris Centre, this is a pleasant cafe serving cakes, salads, pies and light meals daily.

Tipi & Bob's (☎ 09-429 0550) Mains $8.50-23.50. At the Waterfront Lodge near Tryphena, this is a great casual restaurant and bar open for breakfast, lunch and dinner. There's an inviting deck overlooking the harbour and fresh fish is a regular dinner speciality.

Flower House (☎ 09-429 0464) Lunch & Garden Tour $23 per person. For a vegetarian, organic lunch in a lovely setting try the Flower House. The meal includes homemade organic bread, freshly picked salad, home-made cheeses, pickles, chutneys and jams. Bookings are essential (for a minimum of two people).

Oasis Lodge (☎ 09-429 0021). Lunch $25, dinner $55. At Tryphena, Oasis is a good place for a night of fine dining with a set three-course dinner and fresh, local seafood a speciality. There's also a set lunch daily.

There are several sports and social clubs on Great Barrier where you can get reasonably priced bistro meals and cheap bar prices. They include the *Barrier Social Club* (☎ 09-429 0421) in Tryphena, and the *Great Barrier Island Sports & Social Club* at Claris, which is attached to the golf club.

Getting There & Away

Air Two airlines currently service the island: Great Barrier Airlines (☎ 0800 900 600, 09-275 9120) and Mountain Air (Great Barrier Xpress; ☎ 0800 222 123, 09-256 7025). They each schedule three to four flights a day. It takes about 35 minutes to reach Great Barrier from Auckland's domestic airport. The standard one way/ return fare with Mountain Air is $89/169; Great Barrier Airlines has a same-day return fare of $165, otherwise it's $115/189. You can also go by ferry one way and fly the other way for $115 with either airline.

Great Barrier Airlines also has flights from Auckland's North Shore, from Whangarei in Northland and from Whitianga on the Coromandel Peninsula.

Boat Sealink (Subritzky; ☎ 09-373 4036, W www.subritzky.co.nz) is the main passenger service, operating daily from Subritzky's terminal at Wynyard wharf in Auckland to the Shoal Bay wharf at Tryphena. There's one ferry at 8am but more services in summer. The return fare is adult/child $75/45. Fullers has scaled down its services and now operates only during busy holiday periods (Labor weekend, January-February and Easter). The standard fare is adult/child $89/50. When Fullers is operating you may be able to take the ferry to Whangaparapara or Port Fitzroy.

Travel Passes There are various passes aimed mostly at backpackers that mean it's possible to take in the Great Barrier (including flights), as part of a wider trip around northern New Zealand, at a pretty reasonable cost.

Great Barrier & Coromandel ($155) This includes the ferry to Great Barrier, flight to Whitianga and bus to Auckland.

Great Barrier & Bay of Islands ($185) Similar, but with a flight from Great Barrier to Whangarei and a bus to Paihia and back to Auckland.

Forests, Islands & Geysers ($325) Offered by InterCity (☎ 09-913 6100) This enables you to travel by bus to the Bay of Islands via Waipoua Kauri Forest, then fly to Great Barrier and on to Whitianga, from where you travel by bus to Rotorua.

'Top 3' ($235) This combines the first two, with a bus to Paihia, flight to Great Barrier then on to Whitianga in the Coromandel, then a bus back to Auckland.

All these passes are available from visitors centres, or contact the Stray Possum Lodge on Great Barrier (☎ 0800 767 786).

Getting Around

From Tryphena in the south to Port Fitzroy in the north is 47km by (mostly) unsealed road, or 40km via Whangaparapara using the walking tracks. The roads are sealed – but narrow and winding – from Tryphena to Claris. Elsewhere they are graded but quite rough.

Stray Bus Service (☎ 09-429 0109) runs between the Stay Possum Lodge and Claris (via Tryphena and Medlands Beach) five times daily, with two services continuing on to the hot pools and White Cliffs. It also offers an excellent trampers transport service, which can drop you off at any of the main trail heads and pick you up at the other end. A one-day pass that includes trampers transport or scheduled services is $25, a three-day pass (valid over five days) is $45. This pass includes free use of mountain bikes, boogie boards, snorkels and wet suits.

Aotea Transport (☎ 09-429 055) has airport and wharf transfers ($12 from Claris to Tryphena) and a daily bus service from Tryphena to Port Fitzroy ($15).

Many of the accommodation places will pick you up from the airport or wharf if notified in advance.

You can hire a car, generally an old rattler, from Better Bargain Rentals (☎ 09-429 0092) in Tryphena from around $70 a day. Cars can also be hired from Aotea Transport (☎ 09-429 055) and Te Motu Rentals (☎ 09-429 0046) in Port Fitzroy.

Barrier Taxis (☎ 09-429 0527) and Bob's Island Tours (☎ 09-429 0988) provide a taxi service between the main settlements and beaches.

MOTUIHE ISLAND

Named for an ancestor of the Arawa tribe, Motuihe contains much evidence of pre-European occupation: pa, storage pits and gardens. There are picnic grounds, barbecue sites, changing sheds and toilets on the northern end of the island where the old wharf is. Also in this area is a kiosk where you can get food, fishing supplies and information. It's open daily in summer and whenever there is a demand in winter. *Camping (☎ 09-534 5419)* costs adult/child $5/2. The DOC pamphlet *Motuihe* has a map of the island, and a description of three walks.

Fullers (☎ 09-367 9111) runs ferries to Motuihe on Friday and Sunday, with an extra sailing in summer adult/child $30/15.

TIRITIRI MATANGI ISLAND

Tiritiri Matangi was at one time occupied by Maori; there are remains of a *pa* site here. In 1841 it was bought by the Crown and eventually leased and farmed; its forests were mostly cleared. The historic and well-preserved 30m-high lighthouse was completed in 1865 and donated to Auckland city by the wealthy brewer Sir Ernest Davis. The island has been part of the Hauraki Gulf Maritime Park since 1971. Since 1984 volunteers have planted many thousands of native trees, and as the forest has regenerated, endangered native birds have been reintroduced. The island is now an open sanctuary with boardwalks through the bush.

Fullers (☎ 09-367 9111) has ferries from Auckland (adult/child $45/23) and Gulf Harbour on the Whangaparaoa Peninsular ($25/15) from Thursday to Sunday.

OTHER ISLANDS

Dotted around Rangitoto, Motutapu and Waiheke, and further north, are many smaller islands.

South of Rangitoto is the small island of **Motukorea** (Island of the Oystercatcher), also known as Browns Island. The island had three fortified Maori *pa* on the volcanic cones in 1820; it was purchased from Maori by John Logan Campbell and William Brown in 1839, before the founding of Auckland, and used as a pig farm. It's now part of the Hauraki Gulf Maritime Park; access is unrestricted.

Rotoroa, a Salvation Army alcohol rehabilitation clinic, is just south of Pakatoa. **Ponui**, also known as Chamberlins Island, is a larger island just south of Rotoroa. It has been farmed by the Chamberlin family ever since they purchased it from Maori in 1854. Further south is **Pakihi**, or Sandspit Island, and tiny Karamuramu Island.

Little Barrier, 25km northeast of Kawau Island, is one of NZ's prime nature reserves, and the only area of NZ rainforest unaffected by humans, deer or possums. Several rare species of birds, reptiles and plants live in the varied habitats on the volcanic island. Access to the island is highly restricted and a DOC permit, which is very difficult to obtain, is required before landing can be made on this closely guarded sanctuary.

Motuora Island is halfway between Tiritiri Matangi and Kawau. There is a wharf and *camping ground* on the west coast of the island, but there is no regular ferry service. Get a camping permit from the ranger (☎ 09-422 8882) on Kawau, or from the caretaker on Motuora.

The most remote islands of the Hauraki Gulf Maritime Park are the **Mokohinau Islands**, 23km northwest of Great Barrier. They are all protected nature reserves and visitors require landing permits.

Northland

☎ 09 • pop 141,900

Northland is the cradle of New Zealand history: it was one of the first regions settled from eastern Polynesia, and was where Europeans first made permanent contact with the Maori. The first squalid sealers' and whalers' settlements were established here and the Treaty of Waitangi between the settlers and the Maori was signed here. To this day Northland has a greater proportion of Maori in its population than almost anywhere else in NZ.

Northland's tourist magnet is the beautiful Bay of Islands and although most visitors make a beeline for this popular region, there are scenic, sheltered bays and beaches all along the east coast.

The west coast is a long stretch of sand pounded by the surf of the Tasman Sea. It also has scenic harbours, such as Hokianga, but the main attraction is the Kauri Coast, where the best remaining stands of NZ's once mighty kauri forests can be seen.

Kaitaia and the Far North feature some great beaches – including Ninety Mile Beach – and are home to Maori communities, offering travellers the chance to learn about Maori lifestyle and culture.

Getting Around

There are two main routes – east and west – through Northland to Cape Reinga at the top of New Zealand, and these can be travelled as a loop.

The west coast route is longer, but it passes along the Kauri Coast through Matakohe, Dargaville, the beautiful Waipoua Kauri Forest and the remote and scenic Hokianga Harbour.

This chapter describes a clockwise (west coast) route, but the direction you take may depend on the prevailing weather – if it's fine in the Bay of Islands, take advantage of it and head there first.

The two main bus lines serving Northland are Northliner Express (☎ 09-307 5873 in Auckland, 09-438 3206 in Whangarei)

Highlights

- Sailing and cruising the Bay of Islands, with the most beautiful of Northland's wonderful coastal scenery
- Visiting the ancient kauri forests of the Kauri Coast, particularly Waipoua with its enormous trees
- Travelling across the desolate landscapes of Ninety Mile Beach to sacred Cape Reinga
- Deep-sea fishing anywhere on the coast, but especially Tutukaka, the Bay of Islands and Whangaroa
- Diving in the Poor Knights Islands Marine Reserve and on the wreck of the *Rainbow Warrior*

and InterCity (☎ 09-913 6100). These services have identical fares and follow the east coast from Auckland to Whangarei, Bay of Islands and Kaitaia, but connect with the West Coaster service for the west coast. Northliner has bus passes for backpackers with ID (YHA, VIP or BBH card), including the Northland Freedom Pass ($115), which gets you anywhere on the Northland loop.

NORTHLAND

NORTHLAND

North of Auckland

While many visitors, in their haste to get to the Bay of Islands, do this trip along SH1 in just a few hours, the east coast, north of Auckland, has many delightful bays and beaches that are well worth taking the time to check out. A multi-lane motorway takes you as far as Orewa, to the Hibiscus Coast between Whangaparaoa and Warkworth. This is a popular holiday area for Aucklanders and international jetsetters. Heading further north, the coast is less developed but no less beautiful.

WHANGAPARAOA PENINSULA

The Whangaparaoa (pronounced fa-nga-pa-ro-a) Peninsula – just north of Auckland off SH1 – is a heavily developed spit of land with a suburban feel and the **Shakespear Regional Park** at its tip. It's good for water-based activities; windsurfers flock to Manly Beach; boaties leave from the Weiti River and Gulf Harbour; swimmers and walkers find great beaches around the park. Many native bush birds and waders can be seen here, and the native forests of the park contain karaka, kowhai and old puriri trees. A number of walking tracks traverse it.

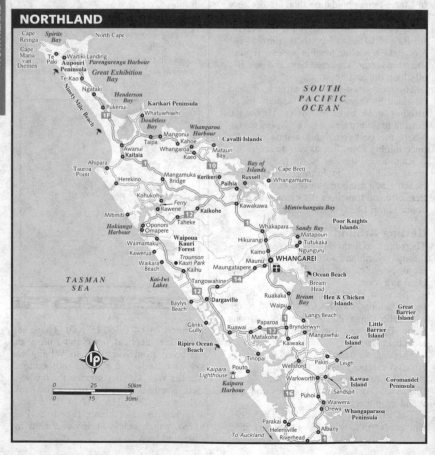

NORTHLAND

The park is just beyond the huge Gulf Harbour Marina development, which boasts a resort golf course and country club. Gulf Harbour Ferries (☎ 09-424 5561) stops here to and from Tiritiri Matangi Island on the regular service from downtown Auckland; this is a good option for cyclists wanting to skip the boring road trip out of Auckland.

The **Whangaparaoa Steam Railway** (☎ 09-424 5018, 400 Whangaparaoa Rd; $3.50) is at Stanmore Bay on the main road into the peninsula. There are steam-train rides, tramps and an animal park open from 10am to 5pm, Saturday and Sunday only.

OREWA & WAIWERA
pop 4900

Orewa is the main town on the Hibiscus Coast. The attraction here is the great stretch of **beach** that runs next to the highway and faces Whangaparaoa Harbour. The town also has a statue of mountaineer Sir Edmund Hillary in the main shopping centre (Hillary Square).

The Hibiscus Coast Information Centre (☎ 09-426 0076) is on the highway south of town, next to KFC. It has information on a wide area of the coast from Whangaparaoa to Warkworth and is open from 9am to 5pm Monday to Saturday and 10am to 4pm Sunday.

The **Alice Eaves Scenic Reserve**, off the Old North Rd near the north end of the beach, has some good walks through native kauri, matai and rimu forest, and an old Maori *pa* site.

Orewa Cycle Works (☎ 09-426 6958, 278 Main Rd) hires out bikes and is handy for spares and repairs. You can kayak to Warkworth and back on the Mahurangi River with **Auckland Canoe Centre Adventures** (☎ 09-426 5369); guided tours cost from $60 – book at the Wairewa thermal pools.

About 6km north of Orewa, the coastal village of **Waiwera** (literally 'Warm Waters'), is noted for its hot pools. It's dominated by the huge **Waiwera Thermal Resort** (☎ 0800 924 9372, **W** www.waiwera.co.nz; adult/child $16/10; open 9am-10pm Sun-Thur, 9am-10.30pm Fri & Sat), a fun park of hot pools, spa pools, waterslides, plus a luxury private spa and gym. Private spas cost from $20 and massage from $40.

Just north of Waiwera is **Wenderholm Regional Park**, a coastal farmland park with a good beach, estuary and walks. Couldrey House, the original homestead, is now a **museum** (☎ 09-303 1530; adult/child $2/50c; open Labour weekend-Easter 1pm-4pm Sat, all-year 1pm-4pm Sun). Bus No 895 from Auckland goes into the park.

Places to Stay

Puriri Park (☎ 09-426 4648, 0508 478 7474 Puriri Ave) Powered/unpowered sites $10 per person (minimum $15), double cabins from $40-45, self-contained double units $60. Puriri Park is a well-equipped family park (with pool) in a quiet bush setting, complete with resident peacocks.

Pillows Travellers Lodge (☎ 09-426 6338, **e** pillows.lodge@xtra.co.nz, 412 Hibiscus Coast Hwy) Dorm beds $16-17, singles/doubles $39/40, en suite singles/doubles $50/65. This tidy and friendly backpackers is just north of the shopping centre. Rooms are arranged around a courtyard and there's a good kitchen and off-street parking.

Marco Polo Backpackers Inn (☎ 09-426 8455, **e** marcopolo@clear.net.nz, 2D Hammond Ave, Hatfields Beach) Camp sites $12 per person, dorm beds $18-19, twins & doubles $45-50. Nestled in native bush just off the highway on the northern outskirts of Orewa, this is a peaceful, spotless hostel. The Dutch owners are helpful and can arrange trips. Buses from Auckland stop on the highway nearby.

Most of Orewa's motels line the Hibiscus Coast Highway on either side of town. They include the **Orewa Motor Lodge** (☎ 0800 267 392, 09-426 4027, **e** orewamotor lodge@xtra.co.nz, 290 Hibiscus Coast Hwy) with studio units for $99 and larger one- or two-bedroom units. On the beachfront is the **Golden Sands Beachfront Motel** (☎ 0800 800 467, 09-426 5177, **e** goldensands@ xtra.co.nz, 381 Hibiscus Coast Hwy) with studios at $95 and one-bedroom units from $110, some with spas.

Muritai Guest House (☎ 09-426 1996, **e** cc.white@ihug.co.nz, 242 Hibiscus Coast

Hwy) Doubles \$50-70, self-contained apartments \$80-120. Muritai is a reasonably priced guesthouse on the highway, close to the town centre.

Waiwera Holiday Park *(☎ 09-426 5270, e camp@waiwera.co.nz, 37 Waiwera Place)* Powered & unpowered sites adult/child \$13/9, 2-person cabins \$40. This park is mainly set up for campers and campervanners. It's right next to the thermal resort and guests receive discount entry.

Places to Eat
Farmhouse Cafe, in the main shopping centre, is a good place for breakfast or for a light lunch with toasted sandwiches, rolls and fish and chips from \$3 to \$10. ***Kai Zen Coffee House***, on the highway below Rock Salt, is a chic spot for coffee.

Thai Orewa *(☎ 09-426 9711, 328 Main Rd)* Lunch \$6-9, dinner \$12-18. This licensed Thai restaurant has inexpensive rice and noodle dishes.

Creole's Bar & Brasserie *(☎ 09-426 6254, 310 Main Rd)* Mains \$10-18. Open 11am-1am. The Creole Bar has good seafood, Mexican and Asian meals and is a popular nightspot, usually with some sort of live entertainment on Saturday and Sunday.

Rock Salt *(☎ 09-426 5379, 350 Hibiscus Hwy)* Mains \$20-27. Open from 6pm daily. This 2nd-floor restaurant around the corner from the shopping area has sea views and a reputation for good steak and seafood. It's licensed and BYO.

Walnut Cottage *(☎ 09-427 5570, 498 Main Rd)* Mains \$20-27. Open lunch from noon Fri-Sun, dinner from 6.30pm Tues-Sat. Walnut Cottage, tucked away off the main road beside Orewa's oldest house, is an atmospheric spot for a light lunch and it has an interesting dinner menu.

Woody's Bar & Grill *(☎ 09-426 4029)* \$3-10. At Waiwera, there's Woody's for burgers, toasted sandwiches, mussels and oysters.

Getting There & Away
Stagecoach buses (Nos 893, 894, 895 and 897) run between Auckland and Orewa/Waiwera via Takapuna, Albany and Silverdale. There are local Hibiscus Coast buses between Orewa and Army Bay at the end of the Whangaparaoa Peninsula via Red Beach approximately every hour.

PUHOI
North of Waiwera, 1km west of SH1, Puhoi is a picturesque historic village that claims to be NZ's first Bohemian (Czechoslovakian) settlement.

The main point of interest is the historic (and legendary) local pub, the **Puhoi Hotel**. It's a rough-edged place dripping with rusty old artefacts – pots, kettles, old boots, miner's lamps, saw blades, trophy heads, a lone one-armed bandit and a couple of old bar-room pianos. It's open daily from 11am to 10pm (for a drink – no food).

The small **Puhoi Bohemian Museum** *(\$1 donation; open 1pm-4pm Sat & Sun)*, opposite the pub, also has its share of historical memorabilia.

You can kayak down the Puhoi River as far as the Wenderholm Regional Park. **Puhoi River Canoe Hire** *(☎ 09-422 0891)* has single/double kayaks from \$15/20 an hour, as well as guided moonlight trips.

Puhoi Cottage, 500m past the Puhoi Store, has Devonshire teas and home-cooked goodies (open Thursday to Tuesday).

The ***Art of Cheese Cafe*** *(☎ 09-422 0670, 275 Ahuroa Rd)*. Open Tues-Sun 9am-5pm. About 3km past the pub, this busy licensed cafe is part of the Puhoi Valley Cheese complex. Gourmet platters cost from \$9.50 to \$16 and there are salads and light lunches.

WARKWORTH
pop 2450
Just off the main highway, beside the Mahurangi River, this pretty town was once connected to Auckland by steamships that docked at the town's old wharf. Today Warkworth is a busy little place crammed with arcades, cafes, galleries, antique and arts and crafts shops.

The helpful Warkworth visitors centre *(☎ 09-425 9081, w www.warkworth-information.co.nz)*, 1 Baxter St, is near the river and bus station and can book transport and accommodation. There's Internet access at the library next door.

NORTHLAND

Things to See & Do

Apart from wandering around local shops and galleries, most of the attractions are a little way outside Warkworth.

Just south of town, the **Parry Kauri Park** has short forest boardwalks and a couple of monstrous old kauri, including the 800-year-old McKinney kauri. Also at the park, the small **Warkworth Museum** (☎ 09-425 7093, *adult/child $5/1; open 9am-4pm daily)*, features well-preserved pioneer-era exhibits.

About 6km south of Warkworth, the **Honey Centre & Cafe** (☎ 09-425 8003; *open daily 9am-5pm)* has glass-fronted hives where you can see bees at work. The shop sells all sorts of bee-related products from honey to beeswax candles. Next door is **Greg's Sheep-n-Show** which has sheep and dog shows at 11am and 1.30pm daily.

Agriculturally, NZ has always ridden on the sheep's back and the biggest touristy sheep-related attraction is 4km north of Warkworth on SH1. **Sheepworld** (☎ 0800 227 433, 09-425 7444, **W** *www.sheep world.co.nz, open 9am-5pm daily)* demonstrates many aspects of NZ sheep farming – there is shearing plus things you can try for yourself, such as carding, spinning and feeding tame sheep and lambs. It also has the largest woollen arts and crafts cooperative in NZ, a cafe and shop. Shows are held at 11am, 1pm and 3pm in summer (one show in winter) and cost $10/5 adult/child, but you can feed the animals for free.

Further north on SH1, the **Dome Forest** is a regenerating forest that was logged about 90 years ago. A walking track to the Dome summit (336m) and its great views across the Mahurangi Peninsula leads from the car park and takes about 1½ hours return. A three-hour return walk leads beyond the Dome summit to the **Waiwhiu Kauri Grove**, a stand of about 20 mature kauri trees. The start of the walkway is some 6km north of Warkworth and *Top of the Dome Cafe* (☎ 09-425 7794)*, open from 7am, is also here.

Places to Stay & Eat

Sheepworld Caravan Park (☎/fax 09-425 9962) Powered & unpowered sites $12.50 per person, dorm beds $20, cabins $50-80.

Set on a large farm next to Sheep World, this park has six backpacker beds and good family cabins. The owners will pick up from Warkworth.

Warkworth Inn (☎ 09-425 8569, **e** *ww inn@maxnet.co.nz, Queen St)* Dorm beds $16, singles/twins $30/50. Warkworth's historic kauri pub (1862) offers typical old pub rooms with shared bathroom, as well as backpacker bunkrooms and kitchen facilities.

Bridge House Lodge (☎ 09-425 83510, *16 Elizabeth St)* Singles/doubles $75/85. This lodge, next to the river, has older-style en suite rooms. At the time of writing a new bar and restaurant were being constructed alongside.

Ducks Crossing in Riverview Plaza, has a patio with a fine view over the river and the old wharf, while *Pukeko Cafe*, hidden away inside the Riverside Arcade is a good place for breakfast (open from 7am), and light lunches such as wraps.

Burgers from off this Planet, on Queen St, at least knows what it's making and how good they are – gourmet burgers cost $6.50 to $10.

Thai Warkworth (☎ 09-422 2511, 6 *Wharf St)* Mains $12-18. This is a good South-East Asian restaurant with cheap curries and stir-fries, some with interesting Anglicised names ('Drunken Chef', 'Lion Milk' and the classic 'Jungle Curry').

Getting There & Away

Warkworth can be reached from Auckland or Whangarei on Northliner or InterCity buses. If you're catching a bus out of Warkworth, book ahead because they don't automatically stop here. Mainline (☎ 09-278 8070) stops in Warkworth on its Auckland-Dargaville route daily except Saturday.

There is no bus from Warkworth to Sandspit for Kawau Island; the only option is a taxi which costs about $15 one way.

KAWAU ISLAND
pop 105

East of Warkworth is the scenic Mahurangi Peninsula and **Sandspit**, from where ferries depart for Kawau Island. The island's main

NORTHLAND

attraction is **Mansion House** (☎ *09-422 8882, adult/child $4/2; open 9.30am-3.30pm daily)*, an impressive historic house rebuilt from an earlier structure by Sir George Grey, a former governor of NZ, who purchased the island in 1862. It was a hotel for many years before being restored and turned into a museum. Inside is a collection of Victorian memorabilia including items once owned by Sir George.

Kawau has many beautiful walks, starting from Mansion House and leading to beaches, the old copper mine and a lookout. The *Kawau Island Historic Reserve* pamphlet ($1) published by DOC has a map of walking tracks.

Every year, in the last week of February, the four-day Furuno fishing competition, one of the world's biggest, is held off Pah Farm's stretch of coast.

Places to Stay

There are a couple of places to stay at Vivian Bay, on the north side of Kawau Island, and a *camping ground* and a couple of *cottages* on Bon Accord Harbour.

There is one self-contained *DOC cottage* for rent at Sandy Bay (contact Mansion House on ☎ 09-422 8882). It sleeps five and costs $60 per night.

Pah Farm Restaurant & Lodge (☎ *09-422 8765)* Camp sites $10, dorm beds $20, rooms $45. Open 9am-late daily. On Bon Accord Harbour, Pah Farm also has camping and budget accommodation.

The *Beach House* (☎ *09-422 8850,* e *beachhouse@paradise.net.nz)* Chalet with full board from $270 per double. The Beach House is an upmarket place offering beachfront units with all meals.

For a meal or a drink try the *Kawau Island Yacht Club* (☎ *09-422 8845)* on Bon Accord Harbour.

Getting There & Away

Two ferry companies operate trips to Kawau from Sandspit (1hr) year-round. Departures from central Auckland run between October and April only.

The Kawau Kat (☎ 0800 888 006, 09-425 8006, w www.kawaukat.co.nz) has a Royal Mail Run daily at 10.30am which stops at Mansion House and many coves, bays and inlets (adult/child $39/15, $49/18 with lunch). A coffee cruise departing at the same time is $24/12. There's also the Shipwreck Cruise at 11.30am and direct sailings to Mansion House at 8am, 10am and 2pm – contact Kawau Kat to confirm. The Paradise Cruise departs from central Auckland on Saturday and Sunday at 9.30am, visiting the *Rewa* shipwreck en route ($45/15, or $55/20 with a barbecue lunch).

Matata Cruises (☎ 0800 225 292, e mat ata.cruises@xtra.co.nz) has a coffee cruise to Kawau for $25 at 10am daily (returning 2pm) and a combined three-hour Mansion House lunch cruise ($40).

WARKWORTH TO BREAM BAY

Less frequented than the main highway to Whangarei is the scenic route from Warkworth out to Leigh on the east coast, and then north via Mangawhai and Waipu to Bream Bay. This route has a number of attractions including wineries, craft galleries and Goat Island.

Wineries along the Matakana Rd include **Ascension Vineyard & Cafe** (☎ *09-422 9601)* and **Matanka Estate** (☎ *09-425 0494)*, which offers wine tastings daily from 10am to 5pm. **Heron's Flight** (☎ *09-422 7915, 49 Sharp's Rd; open 10am-6pm daily)*, further north and just off Matakana Rd, has a cafe.

Morris & James Cafe & Bar (☎ *09-422 7116, Tongue Farm Rd)* has a pleasant courtyard for summer dining but it's also worth visiting for a poke around the large pottery showroom. Colourful, practical ceramics are on show and sale and you can also see potters and artists at work. It's worth looking at the 'imperfect' pieces for a bargain.

Matakana Backpackers (☎ *09-422 9264, 19 Matakana Valley Rd)* Dorm beds & twins $15 per person. This is a straightforward house catering to travellers and people harvesting capsicum and harvest crops from November to March.

The first good beach, **Omaha**, is only a short detour from Leigh Road, and has a sweeping stretch of white sand, good surf and a lifesaving club. For a sheltered beach, try **Mathesons Bay**, just before you enter the small town of **Leigh**, perched above a picturesque harbour dotted with fishing boats.

Leigh Sawmill Cafe & Accommodation (☎ 09-422 6019, 142 Pakiri Rd) has a considerable reputation, certainly as far afield as Auckland. It is indeed a converted sawmill and as well as great food (mains $18 to $25) served in a stylish bar/dining room supported by huge timber beams, it's popular as a funky nightspot with DJ and live music in summer. There's clean, modern backpacker accommodation next door at $25 per person, and upmarket en suite doubles at $120.

Further north, around the cape from Leigh, **Goat Island** is the site of the Cape Rodney-Okakari Point Marine Reserve. The reserve is teeming with fish that can be hand-fed in the water or viewed from a glass-bottomed boat, the *Habitat Explorer* (☎ 09-422 6334). The popular 45-minute around-the-island trips cost adult/child $18/12, departing from the mainland, opposite Goat Island, daily year-round, weather permitting.

Snorkelling and diving gear can be hired at **Seafriends** (☎ 09-422 6212), 1km before the beach. Seafriends also has an inexpensive restaurant, a small aquarium and a marine education centre. **Goat Island Dive** (☎ 0800 348369, 09-422 925), just past the Sawmill Cafe, is a professional outfit hiring out gear and running diving trips to Goat Island (from $50 for one dive).

Goat Island Camping & Backpackers (☎ 09-422 6185) Powered/unpowered sites $12/10 per person, bunk beds $15, caravans $40, cabins $40-60 a double. Almost at the end of the road, this camp has a remote feel, plenty of space for camping and a barn-sized common room.

Continuing along the coast, a gravel road leads to **Pakiri**, a tiny rural settlement with a white-sand beach. A good way of seeing the unspoilt beach and the forests behind is on horseback. **Pakiri Beach Horse Rides** (☎ 09-422 6275, W www.horseride-nz.co.nz) offers superb rides along the beach ranging from a one-hour ($35) or one-day ($155)

ride to the great 'Northern Coast to Coast' ride (seven days; $2595).

From Pakiri, the gravel road via Tomatara eventually meets up with the sealed road to Mangawhai. You can rejoin the coast at **Mangawhai Heads**, a rapidly developing summer resort town with a great surf beach. The **Mangawhai Cliffs Walkway** (1½ to two hours one way) starts at the beach and affords extensive views inland and out to the Hauraki Gulf islands. For an insight into local history there's the **Mangawhai District Museum** (*Moir Rd; open 10am-noon Sat*). Mangawhai has *motels*, *caravan parks* and some lovely *guesthouses*.

Milestone Cottages (☎ 09-431 4018, 27 Moir Rd) Apartments $95-185. Milestone is located at Mangawhai Heads, and has self-contained accommodation set in pretty gardens.

Mangawhai Lodge (☎ 09-431 5311, 4 Heather St) B&B singles/doubles $80/110. Mangawhai is a boutique B&B with a commanding position and great views.

Smashed Pipi Cafe & Gallery (☎ 09-431 4849, 40 Moir Rd) The Smashed Pipi looks a bit out of place in tiny Mangawhai – it's a nightclub-sized, modern bar and cafe with a small, contemporary ceramics gallery next door.

From Mangawhai, a particularly scenic part of the road goes over the headland to Langs Beach and then on to Waipu.

WAIPU & BREAM BAY
pop 1980
Near the mouth of the Waipu River is an estuary which provides a refuge for many species of wader birds, including the rare NZ dotterel, variable oyster-catchers and fairy terns.

Ebb & Flow Backpackers (☎/fax 09-432 1288, Johnson Point Rd) Dorm beds $16-18, twins & doubles $40. Ebb & Flow is beautifully situated overlooking the Waipu River estuary and a world away from anywhere. There's plenty of space here, cosy common areas, a laid-back feel and free bikes and kayaks.

Waipu Wanderer Backpackers (☎ 09-432 0532, 25 St Marys Rd) Dorm beds $15,

NORTHLAND

doubles $17.50. Waipu Wanderer is a clean, simple backpackers in town, with a self-contained unit behind the owners' house.

The Stone House (☎ 09-432 0432) B&B doubles $80-100. This place is built in the style of a Cornish cottage. The delightful guest accommodation here has a pretty lounge area with a patio. Adjacent to the main cottage is a small outdoor loft with backpacker accommodation at $10 per person (no kitchen).

Waipu Cove Cottages & Camping (☎ 09-432 0851, e covecottages@xtra.co.nz, Cove Rd) Camp sites $20 for 2 people, cottages $100-110. A pleasant camping area with easy beach access, kitchen, common facilities and neat self-contained two-bedroom cottages make this a comfortable option.

Close to the beach on Bream Bay at Uretiti is a DOC ***camping ground*** ($6); book on ☎ 09-430 2133.

Waipu was originally settled by Scottish Highlanders, by way of Nova Scotia (Canada), in the 19th century. The **House of Memories** (☎ 09-432 0746; admission $4; open 9.30am-4pm daily), an unusual local museum, tells the story of the Nova Scotian settlers and doubles as a visitor information service. Also worthwhile is a visit to the **Waipu Art Gallery** (☎ 09-432 0797, open 10am-4pm daily) in the old firehouse, to see the acclaimed Waipu tiles. The **Waipu Herbal Apothecary** (☎ 09-432 1000, 43 The Centre) has an intriguing collection of tonics, lotions, balms and salves.

Pizza Barn 'n' Bar (☎ 09-432 1011, 2 Cove Rd) is one of Waipu's few good places for a meal, mainly pizza and other light fare.

The biggest annual event in Waipu is the **Highland Games** held at Caledonian Park in town on 1 January (or the 2nd if the 1st falls on a Sunday).

About 10 minutes' drive west of Waipu is **North River Treks** (☎ 09-432 0565), offering a variety of horse rides along rivers, through farmland and on beaches.

There are many **walks** including the McKenzie walking track (starts near Waipu Caves), the Brynderwyn Walkway and the Mangawhai Coastal Walkway. All these walks are outlined in the pamphlet *Bream Bay Northland* available from the visitors centre and from most places to stay.

From Waipu, it's about 38km north along the highway to Whangarei, Northland's major city.

Kauri Coast

Many people skip the west coast of Northland, but it's well worth including in a loop trip which takes you through rolling farmland (this is kumara country) and the area known as the Kauri Coast. The kauri forests are a natural highlight in this part of NZ.

Turn off SH1 at Brynderwyn and travel west along SH12. You pass through several unremarkable rural towns (such as Maungaturoto, which bills itself as a 'real NZ town!') on the way to the west coast. From the northern end of Kaipara Harbour, extending along the west coast to Hokianga, the Kauri Coast is so-called because of the kauri timber and gum industry that flourished here in the 19th century, generating much of NZ's wealth. Those massive kauri forests are all but gone now, but the **Waipoua Kauri Forest** has untouched kauri stands and is the best place in NZ to see these magnificent trees.

MATAKOHE

At Matakohe, the superb **Kauri Museum** (☎ 09-431 7417; adult/child $9/2.50; open 9am-5.30pm daily, 9am-5pm winte) will probably leave you surprised at how interesting wood can be. There's a scale exhibit of a working pioneer sawmill, clever static displays showing the lives of kauri bushmen, tradesmen and their families, and a gallery with a huge vertical cross section of kauri. But perhaps the most fascinating aspect is the **Gum Room**, a weird and wonderful collection of kauri gum, the amber substance that can be carved, sculpted and polished to a jewel-like quality. The museum shop has some excellent items crafted from kauri wood and gum.

Facing the museum is the **Matakohe Pioneer Church**, built in 1867 of local kauri. The tiny church served both Methodists and

Anglicans, and also acted as the town hall and school for the pioneer community.

Kauri Country Eco-tours (☎ *0800 246 528, 09-4316007,* ⓦ *www.kauricountry .co.nz; tours $65/40 adult/child)* A descendant of one of the area's original pioneering families provides explanations of the history of kauri logging and an insight into conservation efforts today. You can also dig for kauri gum. The three-hour trips leave from the museum daily (10am and 1.30pm). Bookings (essential) can also be made at Matakohe House Cafe.

Places to Stay

Matakohe Motor Camp (☎*/fax 0800 431 6431, 09-431 6431, Church Rd)* Powered & unpowered sites $10 per person, double cabins $38, tourist flat $60, self-contained motel $75. This friendly camp has modern amenities, plenty of space, good views and is only about 350m from the museum.

Matakohe House (☎ *09-431 7091,* ⓔ *mat house@xtra.co.nz, Church Rd)* Singles/ doubles with breakfast $90/115. This lovely B&B and attached cafe, a short walk from the museum, is built in colonial style. Rooms feature antique furnishing and open out onto a veranda deck. The licensed cafe is a good spot for a light meal (open 7.30am to 5pm, and for dinner with prior booking).

Old Post Office Guesthouse (☎*/fax 09-431 6444, Oakley Rd)* Dorm beds without/with linen $20/25, B&B doubles & twins $70. Back in Paparoa, 7km east of Matakohe, this homely place has shared accommodation (no bunks) and B&B rooms with shared facilities. Paparoa has a store, pub and fuel.

Ruawai Travellers Lodge (☎ *09-439 2283, 64 Jellicoe Rd)* Camp sites $8 per person, twins & doubles without/with linen $15/20 per person. West of Matakohe on the main road to Dargaville, this simple but clean house in the tiny town of Ruawai is a handy stop for cyclists.

DARGAVILLE

pop 4530

Founded in 1872 by Joseph McMullen Dargaville, this once-important river port thrived on the export of kauri timber and gum. As the forests were decimated, it declined; today it is a quiet backwater servicing the agricultural Northern Wairoa area.

It's the main town on the Kauri Coast and the access point for the Waipoua kauri forests to the north. Dargaville's only other claim to fame is its title as the Kumara Capital of NZ (the winner of the local beauty competition is named the Kumara Queen).

The helpful visitors centre (☎ 09-439 8360, ⓔ info@kauricoast.co.nz, ⓦ www .kauricoast.co.nz.) is on the corner of Normanby and Poto Sts and has Internet access.

Dargaville Museum & Harding Park

On a hill overlooking the town and the sweeping (muddy) Wairoa River, Harding Park is the site of an old Maori *pa* Po-tu-Oterangi. Tucked into the bottom of the hill is an early European cemetery.

On top of the hill, the **Dargaville Museum** (☎ *09-439 7555; adult/child $5/1; open 9am-4pm daily)* has an eccentric collection of anything over 50 years old, including settlers' items and local memorabilia. Of more interest is the **Kauri Gum Diggers Exhibition Hall**, which has a good gum collection and a display showing the collection and processing of gum. The maritime section has models of ships built or repaired in Kaipara Harbour, notorious for its shipwrecks, and a massive Maori war canoe. Nearly 18m long, the 18th-century canoe is the only surviving example of pre-European times. In front of the museum are the masts from the *Rainbow Warrior*, the Greenpeace flagship bombed by the French in 1985.

Organised Tours & Jetboat Trips

The information centre has details on tours to Waipoua Kauri Forest, Trounson Kauri Park, Kai-Iwi Lakes, and 4WD tours along the beach to Kaipara Lighthouse. A recommended operator is **Taylor Made Tours** (☎ *09-439 1576)*.

Kaipara Kapers (☎ *09-431 7493)* takes half-day jetboat trips ($35) down the northern Wairoa River to Kaipara Harbour, and organises quad-bike safaris.

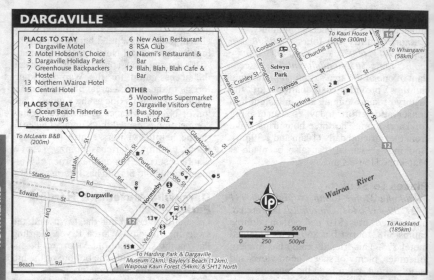

DARGAVILLE

PLACES TO STAY
1 Dargaville Motel
2 Motel Hobson's Choice
3 Dargaville Holiday Park
7 Greenhouse Backpackers
   Hostel
13 Northern Wairoa Hotel
15 Central Hotel

PLACES TO EAT
4 Ocean Beach Fisheries &
   Takeaways

6 New Asian Restaurant
8 RSA Club
10 Naomi's Restaurant &
   Bar
12 Blah, Blah, Blah Cafe &
   Bar

OTHER
5 Woolworths Supermarket
9 Dargaville Visitors Centre
11 Bus Stop
14 Bank of NZ

Places to Stay

Dargaville Holiday Park (☎ 09-439 8296, ℮ dargavilleholidaypark@xtra.co.nz, 10 Onslow St) Powered & unpowered sites $10 per person, dorm beds $19, cabins $38-45, tourist flats/motel units $65/70 per double. Right in the middle of town, this small but tidy park caters to a wide range of travellers.

Greenhouse Backpackers Hostel (☎ 09-439 6342, 13 Portland St) Dorm beds $18, singles $27, twins & doubles $42. Greenhouse Backpackers is in the town's original school (1921), complete with asphalt playground out the front. It's a big place with a large partitioned dorm (no bunks) but it's very comfortable with a nice feel.

Basic pub accommodation (shared bathrooms) on Victoria St is available at the ***Northern Wairoa Hotel*** (☎ 09-439 8923) and the ***Central Hotel*** (☎ 09-439 8034).

Dargaville Motel (☎/fax 09-439 7734, 217 Victoria St) Doubles from $79. This is a welcoming motel with river views, kitchenettes in units and a lock-up for bicycles.

Motel Hobson's Choice (☎ 0800 158 786, 09-439 8551, ℮ hobsonschoice@xtra.co.nz, 212 Victoria St) Studio $92, 1-/2-bedroom units $110/165. Almost opposite, Hobson's Choice is more upmarket with a pool and nicely furnished villa-style units.

McLeans B&B (☎ 09-439 5915, ℮ westendnursery@xtra.co.nz, 136 Hokianga Rd) Singles/doubles $40/75. This very friendly and homely place was originally built for one of Dargaville's mayors. It has three guest bedrooms and a large lounge on the upper floor.

Kauri House Lodge (☎/fax 09-439 8082, Bowen St) Doubles $175-185. The top place to stay in Dargaville, this lovely colonial homestead is furnished with antiques and has an extensive garden (set on 40 hectares) and a swimming pool. All rooms have en suite and breakfast is included, but booking is a must.

Places to Eat & Drink

A good meal is not so easy to find in this working town. For atmosphere or a night out, consider heading down to the ***Funky Fish*** at Baylys Beach (see Around Dargaville).

Ocean Beach Fisheries & Takeaways (☎ 09-439 8055, 164 Victoria St) does the best fish and chips in town. The ***Northern Wairoa Hotel*** (☎ 09-439 8923) has cheap pub food, and the ***RSA Club*** (☎ 09-439

8164) on Hokianga Rd has a good-value three-course meal for $12 on Thursday, Friday and Saturday from 6pm to 8pm.

Blah, Blah, Blah Cafe & Bar *(☎ 09-439 6300, 101 Victoria St)* Open 9am-11pm. Meals $5-12. This is the pick of the cafes for breakfast or lunch, and is a laid-back place for a drink in the evening. You can get a range of snacks and good pizza and pasta.

New Asian Restaurant *(☎ 09-439 8388, 114 Victoria St)* Mains $7-9.50. Open 11am-10pm Mon-Sat, 4pm-10pm Sun. New Asian serves up cheap Chinese fare, eat-in or takeaway, including a smorgasbord selection from $5 to $8.50.

Naomi's Restaurant & Bar *(☎ 09-439 5777, 17 Hokianga Rd)* Naomi's was a trendy new place just about to open at the time of writing, with a bar, à la carte restaurant and a nightclub on Friday and Saturday nights.

Getting There & Away

The bus stop is on Kapia St. Main Coachlines (☎ 09-278 8070) has a bus to/from Auckland via Matakohe every day except Saturday. InterCity does the same run every day except Sunday.

The West Coaster bus service runs from Paihia to Dargaville (via Kaikohe) on Monday, Wednesday and Friday, and from Dargaville to Paihia on Tuesday, Thursday and Saturday. Twin Coast Tours has a student/backpacker bus direct between Dargaville and Whangarei Monday to Friday (departs Dargaville at 7.30am) for $10.

AROUND DARGAVILLE
Baylys Beach & Ripiro Ocean Beach

Baylys Beach, 12km from Dargaville off the SH12, lies on the 100km-long Ripiro Ocean Beach, which is backed by high sand dunes. This stretch of surf-pounded coast is the site of many shipwrecks, including a French man o' war and an ancient Portuguese ship.

Ripiro Ocean Beach is a gazetted highway and you can drive along its hard sands at low tide, although it is primarily for 4WD vehicles – several tour companies do it. It's NZ's longest drivable beach and less crowded than

the Ninety Mile Beach further north. Ask locals about conditions before venturing out onto the sands. There is also access at Glinks Gully, Mahuta Gorge and Omamari.

Horse rides on Baylys Beach are popular. **Baylys Beach Horse Treks** (☎ 09-439 4531) offers regular half-day beach rides for $35.

Baylys Beach Holiday Park *(☎/fax 09-439 6349,* e *motorcamp@baylysbeach .co.nz, 22 Seaview Rd)* has good facilities and powered/unpowered sites for $10/9 per person, single/double cabins from $20/30, en suite double cabins for $50 to $60 and self-contained units for $70.

There are several holiday houses and baches (huts) to rent here. The ***Seaview Cafe*** *(☎/fax 09-439 4549)* rents out four very liveable and fully equipped houses, sleeping between six and eight people, for only $100 a night.

Funky Fish Cafe *(☎ 09-439 8883, 34 Seaview Rd)* Lunch $5-12, dinner $12-23. The Funky Fish is a real find in this quiet holiday spot. With great food, a trendy cafe and garden bar (open till 1am Thursday to Saturday), this is worth a detour off the highway for lunch or dinner, and takeaways are available.

Kaipara Lighthouse

If you have the time, a worthwhile trip from Dargaville is the 71km run southeast to the remote Kaipara Lighthouse (built in 1884) at Pouto Point; it's a rugged trip on unsealed roads and for the last 6.5km you go on foot along the foreshore.

Kaipara Action Experience (☎ 09-439 1401; $135) has an interesting adventure tour involving a boat trip down the Kaipara Harbour, a quad-bike ride across the dunes to the lighthouse, and a 4WD drive truck trip up Ripiro Beach back to Dargaville.

Lighthouse Lodge *(☎ 0800 439 515, 09-439 5150)* Four-share $50 per person, twins & doubles $150. Perched on Pouto Point, this is a real getaway. The comfortable en suite rooms all have an unbeatable view and there's a bar and dining room (dinner $25). You can get here by car from Dargaville, or by boat from Helensville at the southern end of Kaipara Harbour.

NORTHLAND

DARGAVILLE TO HOKIANGA

The highlights of the Kauri Coast are the forests north of Dargaville – apart from several massive kauri trees, there are many walks in Waipoua Kauri Forest and the smaller reserves. Get the DOC brochure *Waipoua & Trounson Kauri Forests* ($1) from the Dargaville visitors centre.

There are a couple of distractions along the coast en route to the big trees. If you're planning to overnight along here, bring your own food as there are no supermarkets and few restaurants between Dargaville and Opononi.

Kai-Iwi Lakes

Only 34km north of Dargaville, and 12km off the highway, are three freshwater lakes known as Kai-Iwi Lakes (Taharoa Domain), which are popular for swimming, trout fishing and boating. The lakes are Kai-Iwi, Taharoa and Waikere. The largest, Taharoa, has deep-blue water fringed with gleaming white-sand beaches and pine groves. You can rent kayaks at Lake Taharoa.

A three-hour return **walk** from the lakes leads to the coast, then north along the beach to the base of Maunganui Bluff. You can also climb the summit (three hours return) or continue north for the three-day walk to Omapere.

There are two rustic camping grounds at Kai-Iwi Lakes, one at *Pine Beach* right on the main lake and another at *Promenade Point* (these can be booked at Dargaville's visitors centre). They have toilets, cold showers, fireplaces, but no power, and cost adult/child $8/4.

Waterlea (☎ 09-439 0727) Double unit $85, 4-person house $150. Waterlea is a farm with self-contained accommodation right at the entrance to the lakes; costs vary, depending on the season. The owners organise trout-fishing tours (from $45 per hour for two).

There are several other guesthouses close to the lakes – the Dargaville visitors centre has a list.

Trounson Kauri Park

The 573-hectare Trounson Kauri Park, 40km north of Dargaville (turn off the highway at Kaihu), has an easy half-hour walk leading from the parking and picnic area by the road. It passes through a beautiful forest with streams and some fine kauri stands, a couple of fallen kauri trees and the Four Sisters – two trees each with two trunks. There's a ranger station and camping grounds.

Guided night-time **nature walks** *(adult/ child $15/9)*, organised by the Kauri Coast Holiday Park, explain the flora and nocturnal wildlife that thrives here. Trounson is a mainland refuge for threatened bird species.

Places to Stay There's a DOC *camping ground* (☎ 09-439 3011) at the Trounson Kauri Park but it's open only from the Labour Day weekend to Easter. It's a beautiful place, ringed by superb kauri trees. Sites are adult/child $7/5, with or without power, and there's a basic camp kitchen.

Kauri Coast Holiday Park (☎/fax 09-439 0621, 0800 807 200, e kauricoast.top10@ xtra.co.nz) Powered & unpowered sites adult/child $10/5, dorm beds $17, double cabins $32-45, self-contained units $70-80. On the side road to the park, this impressive camping ground is in a lovely riverside spot central to the lakes and the kauri forest. Tramps, horse rides, fishing and (in summer) quad-bike trips are among the activities on offer. There's plenty of camping space and a couple of modern motel units.

Kaihu Farm Backpackers (☎ 09-439 4004) Camp sites $12 per person, dorm beds $18, singles $27, twins & doubles $42. This small (18 beds), farm-based hostel is on SH12, 2km north of the Trounson turn-off. It's a cosy and well kept and a perfect stop for cyclists. There are tramps, a glow-worm dell and you can rent a mountain bike or go horse riding.

Waipoua Kauri Forest

The highlight of the west coast, this superb forest sanctuary – proclaimed in 1952 after much public pressure and antagonism towards continued milling – is the largest remnant of the once extensive kauri forests of northern NZ.

The road through the forest passes some magnificent huge kauri trees – a fully grown

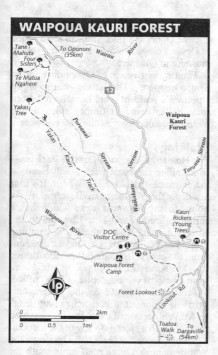

WAIPOUA KAURI FOREST

is believed to be the oldest in NZ (possibly 4000 years). This massive tree, a 20-minute walk from the car park, must be seen to be believed. It presides over a clearing surrounded by mature trees that look like matchsticks in comparison. Close by are the **Four Sisters** (not to be confused with the kauri siblings of the same name in Trounson Kauri Park), a graceful stand of four tall trees clumped together.

From the same access path you can follow a half-hour walking track to the large **Yakas Tree**. At the time of writing the popular two-hour forest trek from here to the visitors centre was closed due to track damage – check with the visitors centre.

Further north up the highway is **Tane Mahuta**, named for the Maori god of the forests. It's the largest kauri tree in NZ, standing close to the road and estimated to be between 1200 and 2000 years old. At 51m, it's much taller than Te Matua Ngahere but doesn't have the same impressive girth – although its volume is greater.

Places to Stay In the heart of the forest, next to the Waipoua River and just past the visitors centre, *Waipoua Forest Camp* (☎ 09-439 3011) has camping for $7 per person, single cabins for $10, two-berth cabins with kitchen for $14 per adult and four-berth cabins for $10 per person. There are showers, toilets and a separate kitchen. You can book and pay at the visitors centre; bookings aren't required for camping, but in summer you should call ahead for cabins.

Waipoua Lodge (☎ 09-439 0422) B&B doubles $125-145. On the highway at the southern edge of the forest, 48km north of Dargaville, this fine old colonial homestead has three unique converted units – they were originally the stables, the woolshed and the calf-rearing pen! They each have an en suite and are spacious with imaginative decor. Two-course dinner is available at the house restaurant for $45.

Solitaire Homestay (☎ 09-405 4891) Singles/doubles $50/90. At Waimamaku, just north of the forest, this pleasant, well-restored old kauri house is set in a pretty garden. Dinner is available for guests at $25.

kauri can reach 60m and have a trunk 5m or more in diameter. Turn off to the forest lookout just after you enter the park – it was once a fire lookout and offers a spectacular view. A little further north, the park visitors centre (☎ 09-439 3011), open from 8.30am to 6pm Monday to Friday and 9am to 6pm on Saturday and Sunday, has plenty of information and interpretive displays on kauri trees, the gum industry, native birds and wildlife.

From the visitors centre, the highway meanders and winds through this lush forest of ferns and native trees for about 8km before the signposted turn-off to the kauri walks, where several giant trees are easily reached. The car park here is guarded voluntarily – theft from cars has been a problem – and a $2 donation is appreciated. There are four main trees reached by well-marked paths and boardwalks. **Te Matua Ngahere** (The Father of the Forest) has a trunk over 5m in diameter, believed to be the widest girth of any kauri tree in NZ, and

NORTHLAND

Hokianga

North of the Kauri Coast, the road winds down to Hokianga Harbour and the tiny twin towns of Omapere and Opononi. Hokianga is a depressed rural area with no industry and little development, but the harbour is beautiful, and the area is unspoilt – much less commercial than the Bay of Islands. For that reason alone it's a good place to take time out and drift for a while, as plenty of alternative lifestylers have discovered.

As you come up over the hill from the south, the lookout on **Pakia Hill** has a great view of the harbour and is worth a stop.

Further down the hill, 2km west of Omapere, Signal Station Rd leads out to **Arai-Te-Uru Recreation Reserve**, on the South Head of Hokianga Harbour. It's about a 30-minute walk from Omapere or, if you're driving, a five-minute walk from the car park to Signal Station Point. This overlooks the harbour entrance, the massive sand dunes of North Head and the turbulent confluence of the harbour and the open sea. There's a swimming beach, and it's also the northern end of the superb Hokianga-Waipoua Coastal Track.

OMAPERE & OPONONI
pop 630

These two sleepy towns, on the southern shore of the Hokianga Harbour, more or less run into one another.

The Hokianga visitors centre (☎ 09-405 8869) at Omapere is open daily from 8.30am to 5pm. In the same building is the tiny local **museum**, much of which is devoted to the late 'Opo the friendly dolphin'. Back in 1955 a lone dolphin began following local fishing boats and then started visiting the harbour and communing with locals. Opo, as she came to be known, played with children and learned to perform tricks with beach balls, turning tiny Opononi into a national attraction. The nation almost went into mourning when Opo was found dead less than a year later – possibly killed accidentally by illegal dynamite fishers, although theories include accidental stranding, stress, suicide and even foul play. Opo's **grave** is outside the war memorial hall and there's a sculpture nearby outside Opononi's pub. You can see a video of Opo – a classic piece of 1950s film – at the museum in Omapere.

The tiny settlement of Opononi is 3.5km past Omapere. The stone walls along Opononi's seafront were constructed from rock ballast used in timber ships which were sailed out from Sydney by convicts.

Walking

The **Hokianga-Waipoua Coastal Track** leads south along the coast from South Head, at the entrance of Hokianga Harbour. It's four hours to the Waimamaku Beach exit; six hours to the Kawerua exit, which has a camping ground and hut; 12 hours to the Kerr Rd exit, where there's a camping ground at Waikara Beach. Or you can continue the entire 16 hours (allow about three days) to Kai-Iwi Lakes. Pick up a brochure from any local visitors centre or DOC office.

From Cemetery Rd on the eastern outskirts of Opononi, a half-hour climb leads up **Mt Whiria**, one of the oldest unexcavated *pa* sites, with a splendid view of the harbour.

Two kilometres east of Opononi the Waiotemarama Gorge road turns south for 6km to the **Waiotemarama bush track**, the best short walk from Opononi. This track climbs to Mt Hauturu (680m). It's a four-hour walk to the summit (six hours return), but there's a shorter two-hour loop walk starting from the same place, passing kauri trees and a picturesque waterfall.

The **Six Foot Track** at the end of Mountain Rd (near Okopako Lodge) gives access to many Waima Range walks.

Other Activities

The steep dunes on the north side of Hokianga Harbour are the perfect place for **sandboarding**. To get there take the regular **Hokianga Express** (☎ 09-405 8872), a water taxi which leaves hourly from the wharf opposite the Opononi Resort Hotel. It costs $18 for board hire and the return fare. The Express is also available for charters.

Fishing and **shellfishing** are excellent around Hokianga Harbour and trips are easily arranged. The **Alma** (☎ 09-405 7704) is a 78-foot, solid kauri boat built in 1902. Originally a twin-masted scow, it's now powered by twin diesel motors. Regular fishing trips on this working museum are run December to April on Friday, and there's a cruise from Rawene during summer (Thursday at 10am). At other times it goes when there is a sufficient demand (a minimum of 10 for fishing trips).

Okopako Pony Trekking (*☎ 09-405 8815*) at Okopako Lodge has two-hour horse treks ($40) and longer rides through the bush of the Waima Hills.

Places to Stay

Omapere Overlooking the harbour, *Globe Trekkers* (*☎ 09-405 8183,* e *globe trekkers@hotmail.com*) is a pleasant backpackers on the main road in Omapere. Dorm beds cost $16, twins & doubles $40 and there's a self-contained unit (kitchenette, bathroom, double bed and single bed), and ample space for tents ($8 per person).

Omapere Tourist Hotel & Motel (*☎ 09-405 8737,* e *icesam@ihug.co.nz*) Camp sites $9 per person, motel units $100-120, double apartments $135. The hotel here is historic and sits on the water's edge, but there's a wide range of accommodation from camping to modern motel units.

Baxters B&B (*☎ 09-405 8727, 255 SH12*) Singles/doubles $30/57, self-contained unit $70. Near the information centre, this homely old-fashioned place is run by a lovely old lady. The large self-contained unit is great value.

Opononi The waterfront *Opononi Holiday Park* (*☎/fax 09-405 8791*) has powered and unpowered sites for $10 per person and various double cabins from $30 to $55.

House of Harmony (*☎/fax 09-405 8778,* e *harmony@igrin.co.nz*) Dorm beds $18, twins/doubles $40 per person. Near the wharf, House of Harmony is a small self-contained backpackers lodge with good facilities and a veranda deck.

Opononi Resort Hotel (*☎ 0800 116565, 09-405 8858, fax 405 8827*) Dorm beds $12, hotel singles/doubles $25/35, motel double units $90-120. Opposite the wharf,

this hotel complex dominates little Opononi. It has plain but clean hotel rooms, including backpacker bunk rooms, and modern motel units at the back.

Opononi Dolphin Lodge (*☎ 09-405 8451,* e *shirley@xtra.co.nz, cnr Fairlie Cres & SH12*) B&B singles/doubles $55/65, en suite doubles $85. This new place is a comfortable converted house with a big deck on which to sit and admire the harbour. There are some dorm beds at $16 and powered campervan sites at $8 per person.

Okopako Lodge (*☎/fax 09-405 8815, Mountain Rd*) Camping $9 per person, dorm beds $17, doubles & twins $42. Nestled in bush 5km east of Opononi, this is a cosy YHA associate where you can go horse trekking ($20 per hour), walking (eg, along the Six Foot Track) or join in farm activities. The lodge is clean and comfortable with made-up beds, and farmhouse breakfast ($9) and dinner ($25) are available. The owners will pick you up from the highway (where buses drop you off).

Places to Eat

Calypso Cafe (*☎ 09-405 8708*) Meals $4-20. On the road into Omapere from Dargaville, this cafe is perched up on a hill with great harbour views from its deck. The outlook is more spectacular than the food, which ranges from pies and cakes to simple seafood and steak meals. It's open late (till 11pm) from Thursday to Sunday and is BYO and licensed.

Harbourmaster's Restaurant Mains $21.50-23.50. At the Omapere Tourist Hotel & Motel, this is a fancy restaurant that overlooks the harbour, and it's open for lunch and dinner.

The *Opononi Resort Hotel* (*☎ 09-405 8858*). Bistro meals $7-16, mains $22-24. The hotel, with a pub, bistro and restaurant, is the hub of this town for food and entertainment. The bar meals, such as nachos or steak and vegies, are good value.

Getting There & Away

West Coaster buses stop off at Omapere and Opononi, on the route between Paihia and Dargaville, daily except Sunday.

NORTHLAND

RAWENE
pop 515

Rawene is a tiny settlement on a point on Hokianga Harbour, from where ferries cross to Kohukohu to connect to the pleasant (and quicker) back route to Kaitaia. The shallow waters around Rawene become mudflats at low tide but it's Rawene's historical points of interest, rather than its location, that make it worth a stop. Notable structures include **Clendon House** (☎ 09-405 7874; adult/child $3/free; open 10am-4pm Sat-Mon Nov-Apr), built in the late 1860s by James Clendon, the resident magistrate.

At the end of Russell Esplanade, the **Wharfhouse** (originally the Harp of Erin Hotel) is the oldest building in Rawene. (The intriguing musical public toilets are opposite).

Further up Hokianga Harbour, 3km west of Horeke, **Mangungu Mission** dates from 1839. The Hokianga chiefs signed the Treaty of Waitangi here in 1840.

If you opt to continue on the main highway heading towards the Bay of Islands, you'll pass through **Kaikoke**, a centre for the Ngapuhi tribe and the scene of bloody battles during the Northland Land War (1844–46). Hone Heke eventually settled in Kaikohe and died there in 1850.

Places to Stay & Eat

Rawene Motor Camp (☎ 09-405 7720, 1 Marmon St) Powered/unpowered sites $9/8 per person, cabins $18 per person. This small park is just off the main road into Rawene and offers backpacker accommodation in cabins.

Masonic Hotel (☎ 09-405 7822) Singles/doubles $30/40. The local pub is just up from the ferry landing and has a restaurant as well as rooms with shared bathroom.

Old Lane's Store Homestay (☎/fax 09-405 7554, 9 Clendon Esplanade) Doubles with breakfast $110. This is a delightful, modern self-contained extension of a historic 1885 villa, on the waterfront near Clendon House. It has a large lounge area and patio.

Boatshed Cafe (☎ 09-405 7728, 8 Clendon Esplanade) For good coffee, panini, quiche, pizza, focaccias and imaginative lunches, this waterfront cafe is top notch. There's also a gallery featuring flax kits, colourful textiles, jewellery, bone carving, paintings and more – all by local artists.

The **Ferry House** (☎ 09-405 7676, Russell Esplanade) Lunch $6-20, dinner $20-23. This is an antique and curio shop and an informal cafe where you can relax with a coffee on Chesterfield couches. There's also a restaurant for evening meals such as flounder and steak, and a bar.

You can stock up on the locally grown organic fruit and vegies at **Hokianga Wholefood**, which also has cheese, yogurt, health shakes, dried fruits, essential oils, soaps and so on.

Getting There & Away

Ferries run daily between Rawene and the Narrows on the north side of the harbour roughly every hour from 7.30am to 7.30pm. The crossing takes 15 minutes, and fares are cars/passengers $14/2 ($19/4 return). Visitors centres have timetables or you can call ☎ 09-405 2602. You buy your ticket on board. The InterCity bus stops outside the Wharf House.

KOHUKOHU
pop 220

This somnolent town is in a very quiet backwater on the north side of Hokianga Harbour, about 4km from the ferry landing. It's beautifully preserved, with a number of historic kauri villas over 100 years old and other fine buildings including the Masonic Lodge, the Anglican Church and an old school.

Kohukohu Tree House (☎ 09-405 5855, ℮ tree.house@xtra.co.nz) Camp sites $12 per person, dorm beds $19, singles/twins/doubles $31/44/48. For the pure indulgence of doing as little as possible, this is one of the finest backpackers in the country and a good reason to detour off the main road. Constructed of wood and stained glass, there's a main house and various cabins, and you can even sleep in a bus. It's 2km from the northern ferry terminus (turn sharp left as you come off the ferry).

Harbour Views Guest House (☎ 09-405 5815, Rakautapu Rd) B&B $40 per person. Harbour Views is a restored kauri home. There are two rooms (one with a queen-sized bed, one twin), and a large guest bathroom. Both guestrooms open onto a veranda from which there are expansive harbour views. Dinner is available for $18.

The *Palace Flophouse & Grill* is an alternative cafe on the main road and as good a place as any to flop for a coffee, muffin or a burger.

MITIMITI

About 45km west of Kohukohu, via Panguru on a rugged, wild stretch of coast, is the isolated Maori settlement of Mitimiti, which offers seclusion and another cool backpackers hostel.

Manaia Hostel & Treks (☎ 09-409 5347, West Coast Rd) Singles & doubles $20 per person. This comfortable hostel rates highly among travellers who make the effort to get out here. You can arrange trips over the North Head sand dunes on an all-terrain vehicle, and there is horse trekking, fishing off the rocks and drag netting. There is lots of scope for great walks, including Warawara Forest (NZ's second-largest kauri forest).

PUKETI & OMAHUTA FORESTS

North of Kaikohe, the Puketi and Omahuta Forests consist of one large forest area with kauri sanctuaries and other native trees, camping and picnic areas, streams and pools. Kauri milling in Puketi was stopped some years back to protect not only the kauri trees but also the rare kokako bird.

The two forests are reached by several entrances and contain a network of walking tracks varying in length from 15 minutes (the Manginangina Kauri Walk) to two days (the Waipapa River Track). A pamphlet detailing the tracks and features of the forests is available from any DOC office. Camping is permitted and there are basic trampers huts and a *camping ground* ($6) at Puketi Recreation Area on Waiare Rd, 28km north of Kaikohe. Book at DOC in Kerikeri (☎ 09-407 8474).

The Far North

KAITAIA
pop 5630

Kaitaia is mainly the jumping-off point for trips up Ninety Mile Beach to Cape Reinga. It's also a good place to learn about and participate in aspects of Maori culture.

Entering Kaitaia you'll see a welcome sign in three languages – welcome, *haere mai* (Maori) and *dobro dosli* (Serbo-Croatian) – as both Maoris and Dalmatians live in the area. Both groups are culturally active, with a Maori *marae* and a Dalmatian Cultural Club the focus of activities.

Each year in March a special marathon, the Te Houtawea Challenge, is conducted along the length of Ninety Mile Beach, celebrating the legend of Te Houtaewa. This great runner ran the length of the beach from Te Kao to Ahipara to steal kumara (sweet potatoes) from the Te Rarawa people, returning with two full baskets after

NORTHLAND

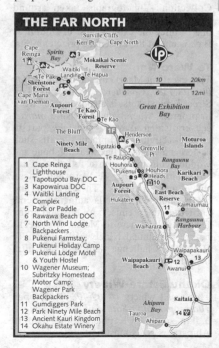

THE FAR NORTH

1 Cape Reinga Lighthouse
2 Tapotupotu Bay DOC
3 Kapowairua DOC
4 Waitiki Landing Complex
5 Pack or Paddle
6 Rawana Beach DOC
7 North Wind Lodge Backpackers
8 Pukenui Farmstay; Pukenui Holiday Camp
9 Pukenui Lodge Motel & Youth Hostel
10 Wagener Museum; Subritzky Homestead Motor Camp; Wagener Park Backpackers
11 Gumdiggers Park
12 Park Ninety Mile Beach
13 Ancient Kauri Kingdom
14 Okahu Estate Winery

being angrily pursued. The marathon celebrates the return of the kumara – reconciliation for a past deed.

Information

The helpful Far North Information Centre (☎ 09-408 0879, e fndckta@xtra.co.nz) in Jaycee Park on South Rd has information on Kaitaia and the region, and books accommodation, tours and activities. It is open from 8.30am to 5pm daily (to 1pm on winter weekends).

There's Internet access at the visitors centre and at Hackers Internet Cafe in Commerce St.

Far North Regional Museum

This museum (☎ 09-408 1403; adult/child $1.50/1; open 10am-5pm Mon-Fri, 10am-4pm Sat), near the information centre, houses an interesting collection, including a giant moa skeleton, various bits and pieces from shipwrecks and the Northwood Collection – photographs taken around 1900. The giant 1769 de Surville anchor, one of three the explorer lost in Doubtless Bay, is one of the museum's prize exhibits.

Te Wero Nui

This excellent Maori **cultural centre** (☎/fax 09-408 4884, Commerce St), next to Main Street Backpackers, is a cooperative 'work in progress' where you can visit a marae, see craftsmen at work, and take part in cultural activities and practical crafts such as herbal medicines, flax weaving, bone and woodcarving ($50 with a full day of instruction). Its name, Te Wero Nui, mean 'the ultimate challenge'. There's an arts and crafts shop which sells authentic items crafted on the premises. An arts and crafts festival is held here in March, two weeks before the annual Ninety Mile Beach Te Houtawea Challenge (half, full and ultra marathon).

Okahu Estate Winery

This small winery (☎ 09-408 0888; open 10am-6pm Mon-Sat, daily in summer), 3.5km south of Kaitaia on the road to Ahipara, is NZ's most northerly winery. It

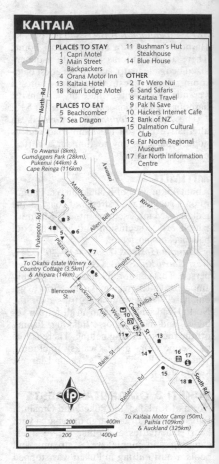

KAITAIA

PLACES TO STAY
1 Capri Motel
3 Main Street Backpackers
4 Orana Motor Inn
13 Kaitaia Hotel
18 Kauri Lodge Motel

PLACES TO EAT
5 Beachcomber
7 Sea Dragon

11 Bushman's Hut Steakhouse
14 Blue House

OTHER
2 Te Wero Nui
6 Sand Safaris
8 Kaitaia Travel
9 Pak N Save
10 Hackers Internet Cafe
12 Bank of NZ
15 Dalmation Cultural Club
16 Far North Regional Museum
17 Far North Information Centre

has a great selection for a boutique winery and tastings are free.

Activities & Organised Tours

Blue Sky Scenics (☎ 09-406 7320), based at Awanui, operates a number of scenic flights in the Far North, including to Cape Reinga ($135) and Kari Kari Peninsula ($65).

Jayar Horse Treks (☎ 09-409 2055) at Ahipara, and **Heather's Horse Treks** (☎ 09-406 7133) in Awanui, both offer rides along Ninety Mile Beach, farmland and sand hills (around $45 for two hours).

Kaitaia is a centre for tours to surrounding areas, notably Cape Reinga and the gumfields of Ahipara.

Places to Stay

Camping & Hostels The only camping ground in town is *Kaitaia Motor Camp* (☎ *09-408 1212, 69a South Rd*) with powered and unpowered sites for $10 per person (small tents cost only $6 per person), although there are others at Ahipara and north along Ninety Mile Beach.

Main Street Backpackers (☎ *09-408 1275,* e *mainstreet@xtra.co.nz, 235 Commerce St*) Camp sites $13 per person, dorm beds $17-20, singles/doubles $39/42. Main Street is a comfortable, central YHA-associate backpackers and a good place to get involved in local cultural activities. The live-in owner, Peter, is active in the Maori community and takes visitors on tours of the local *marae*. You can do your own bone carving here ($20, equipment supplied).

Motels & Hotels Kaitaia has plenty of motels, mostly along North Rd, but there are a few in the town centre.

Kauri Lodge Motel (☎ *09-408 1190, 15 South Rd*) Units $65. One of the cheaper motels in town, Kauri Lodge is conveniently located opposite the visitors centre.

Capri Motel (☎ *0800 422 774, 09-408 0224, 5 North Rd*) Doubles $65-80. Just north of the town centre, the Capri has clean comfortable rooms, including smoke-free units.

Orana Motor Inn (☎ *0800 267 262, 09-408 1510, 238 Commerce St*) Doubles from $85. Orana is one of the better central motels. It has a pool, a range of studios and suites, and a very good restaurant and bar.

Kaitaia Hotel (☎ *09-408 0360, 15-33 Commerce St*) Singles/doubles with bath $38/52. This central hotel (established 1837) is a Kaitaia institution. It's not luxurious and it can get pretty boisterous and loud on the weekends.

Okahu Country Cottage (☎ *09-408 0888,* e *okahuestate@xtra.co.nz, Ahipara Rd*) Cottage $180-220 for 2. This lovely self-contained cottage on the edge of the Okahu vineyard is a great place to pamper

yourself. It's tastefully furnished with two double bedrooms and an inviting veranda deck. Price includes a bottle of wine and breakfast basket; and rates are reduced after the first night.

Places to Eat

The gigantic *Pak N Save* in West Lane is the cheapest place for self-caterers. The best of the main street cafes, the *Blue House* (☎ *09-408 4935, 14 Commerce St*) is open at 8am daily and does all-day breakfasts on weekends. The *Kaitaia Hotel* has $7 roasts on Sunday.

Beachcomber (☎ *09-408 2010, 222 Commerce St*) Mains $19-25. Open Mon-Sat. This is Kaitaia's top restaurant, with a good range of steak and seafood dishes. It's licensed and offers dial-a-meal takeaways.

The *Bushman's Hut Steakhouse* (☎ *09-408 4320, 7 Bank St*) Mains $18.50-28. Open Tues-Sun from 5pm. This rustic steakhouse specialises in barbecueing big pieces of meat. It's also open for lunch from Wednesday to Friday and there's a carvery on Sunday night.

Sea Dragon (☎ *09-408 0555, 185 Commerce St*) $6.50-10. This is an inexpensive Chinese restaurant with a buffet ($10) and takeaways.

Getting There & Away

Air Kaitaia (☎ 0800 222 123, 09-256 7025) has flights Monday to Friday between Auckland and Kaitiai (via Whangarei), and Air New Zealand Link (☎ 09-408 0540) has flights between Kaitaia and Auckland, and the Bay of Islands, daily except Saturday. The standard one-way fare is $226 but discounted fares are available.

InterCity (☎ 09-408 0540) and Northliner (☎ 09-408 0540) leave from Kaitaia Travel on Blencowe St. Buses go daily to Auckland via Paihia and Whangarei.

AROUND KAITAIA
Ahipara

Ahipara is a small community at the southernmost section of Ninety Mile Beach, only 14km southwest of Kaitaia. It's popular with locals and visitors and makes a good alternative to staying at Kaitaia. Activities include fishing, surfing, horse riding and quad-biking, but the area is best known for the massive gumfield sand dunes. Sand tobogganing, beach safaris and quad-bike rides are popular activities on the dunes above Ahipara and further around the Tauroa Peninsula.

Tua Tua Tours *(☎ 09-409 4875,* W *www .ahipara.co.nz/tuatuatours)* operates guided quad-bike trips along the gumfields and Ninety Mile Beach. A 1½-hour tour costs $80 per bike ($90 with a passenger), a three-hour tour is $145 ($165 with a passenger).

You can tour alone by hiring a quad bike from **Adriaan Lodge** (see Places to Stay & Eat) at $50 for the first hour and $30 for each subsequent hour. Each bike takes only one person. To minimise damage to the environment, stay below the high tide line and formal tracks. Sandboards can also be hired for $10 a day.

Ahipara has a decent 18-hole links **golf course** at the end of Takahe Rd.

Places to Stay & Eat Ahipara has quite a few places to stay, many of them facing the beach.

Pine Tree Lodge Motor Camp *(☎ 09-409 4864,* e *pinetree@xtra.co.nz, Takahe St)* Powered & unpowered sites $9 per person, cabins $28-50 per double. Pine Tree Lodge isn't fancy but it is located in a great position, close to the beach and the golf course.

Bay Links Lodge *(☎ 09-409 4694,* e *bay links@xtra.co.nz, 115 Takahe St)* Doubles from $70. Opposite the motor lodge and right next to the golf course, this comfortable motel has seven units.

Adriaan Lodge Motel *(☎ 0800 906 453, 09-409 4888,* e *adriaan@ahipara.co.nz, 22 Reefview Rd)* Dorm beds $20, units $60-90. Adriaan Lodge has a cramped backpackers section (there are beds in the lounge area) with a nice sundeck, older-style studios and modern self-contained units.

Coastal Cabins *(☎ 09-409 4839, 267 Foreshore Rd)* Cabins $40 a double. These beachfront cabins are great value. The bathroom facilities are shared and there's a

barbecue and gas cooking outside, but each unit has its own fridge and microwave.

Bayview Restaurant, at Adriaan Lodge, has steak and seafood ($19 to $25) on its à-la-carte menu and a two-course set menu for $22.50.

Herekino

This remote spot, 29km south of Kaitaia, is a typical Northland rural outpost which you'll pass through if driving the scenic backroad between Kohukohu and Kaitaia. Its attractions are its isolation and country pub (known for drinkin', and talkin' of shearin', crutchin' and dockin').

Tui Inn Farmstay *(☎ 09-409 3883, Puhata Rd)* Camp sites $6 per person, beds $12. The Tui Inn, about 1km south of the pub, is a self-contained cottage on a farm with activities including horse-riding and hunting. Rooms are pretty basic and toilets and showers are outside, but it has a rustic charm.

Kaitaia Region Walks

The **Kaitaia Walkway**, on the edge of the Herekino Forest, makes a good day trip and has excellent views. The track has a gentle gradient along its 9km and you should allow four hours to walk it. To get there head south from Kaitaia on SH1 for 3km, then turn right into Larmers Rd and follow it to the end.

More challenging is the **Mangamuka Walkway**, which connects the Takahue Valley south of Kaitaia with the Mangamuka Gorge. The 9km track through the Raetea and Maungataniwha Forests requires good bush skills to negotiate and could take up to six hours. You can best reach the walk from SH1 at the Top of the Range picnic area.

Gumdiggers Park

Part of the enigma of the Far North is the mystery of what happened to the ancient kauri forests that once covered the region (most of them vanished 35,000 years ago, long before human intervention). The **Gumdiggers Park** *(☎ 09-406 7166, Heath Rd; adult/child $5/2.50; 9am-5pm daily)* offers some explanations and shows the history

NORTHLAND

GRANT DIXON

Cape Reinga lighthouse

of the kauri gum industry. The site contains an original gumdigger's hut, evidence of ancient buried kauri forests and shafts from where gum was extracted. The park is 25km north of Kaitaia and 3km off the highway (signposted). If the site is unattended you can wander around on your own.

Ancient Kauri Kingdom

This impressive workshop and gallery (☎ 09-406 7172, open 9am-5pm daily) on the highway at Awanui is well worth a visit. Here 30,000- to 50,000-year-old kauri stumps, which have been dragged up from swamps, are fashioned into furniture and woodcraft products, with some superb (and expensive) results. Check out the kauri sofa for $35,000! There's even a huge upright kauri log with a spiral staircase carved into it to take you to the mezzanine level.

CAPE REINGA & NINETY MILE BEACH

At the tip of the long Aupouri Peninsula, Cape Reinga is at the northern tip of NZ. As such it is a pilgrimage site for those who want to travel from one end of the country to the other. Contrary to popular belief, Cape Reinga is not the northernmost point of the country – that's Surville Cliffs on North Cape, 30km to the east. Nor is it the most western part of the North Island. Cape

Maria van Diemen, just one bay around, claims that title. But standing at the windswept **Cape Reinga lighthouse** and looking out over the endless South Pacific Ocean and Tasman Sea (they converge here) certainly has an end-of-the-world feel to it. The lighthouse is still in use, though the original 1000-watt lamp has been replaced by a solar-powered 50-watt beacon (visible from 38km). Directly below the lighthouse is the Columbia Bank maelstrom, where the waters of the Tasman Sea and Pacific Ocean meet, generating waves up to 10m high in stormy weather.

Still visible on the very tip of Cape Reinga is the 800-year-old pohutukawa tree whose roots hide the entrance to the mythical Maori Underworld; see Ancestors (Tipuna) in the special section 'Maori Culture & Arts'. This point is known in Maori legend as Te Rerenga Wairua, where the spirits of the dead depart the earth.

The Aupouri Peninsula is known to the Maori as Te Hiku o te Ika a Maui (The Tail of Maui's Fish) from the creation legend that tells of how Maui hauled a great fish from the sea, which became the North Island (see 'And Then Came Aotearoa...' in the 'Maori Culture & Arts' special section). The peninsula is a rugged, desolate landscape dominated by high sand dunes and flanked by Ninety Mile Beach. If they were to metricate it to Ninety Kilometre Beach the name would be less romantic but more accurate. Cape Reinga is about 116km by road from Kaitaia.

The **Aupouri Forest**, about 75km long and 5km wide, covers two-thirds of the western side of the peninsula. It's an exotic forest, mostly pine, planted for timber. Kauri forest used to cover the area; in fact, traces have been found of three separate growths of kauri that were buried and then grew up again. No-one is quite sure what caused the demise of the forests – climate change, volcanic eruption or some other natural disaster – but the forests ended up covered in sand and peat bogs and this became a fruitful area for gumdiggers.

On the northern edge of the Aupouri Forest, a volcanic rock formation called **The Bluff** is part of a private reserve used for fishing by the Aupouri tribe living in nearby Te Kao. A colony of white-fronted terns can be seen just past the Bluff on a prominent sandspit.

North of the Bluff, Te Paki Reserves are public land with free access; just leave the gates as you found them and don't disturb the animals. There are about 7 sq km of giant sand dunes on either side of where Te Paki Stream meets the sea. A stop to take flying leaps off the dunes is a highlight of locally operated tours.

Bus tours (see Organised Tours later in this chapter) travel along the hard sands of Ninety Mile Beach on their way from Kaitaia to Cape Reinga, or vice versa, depending on the tides. Private vehicles can also do the beach trip but all hire-car agreements prohibit driving on the beach. The usual access point for vehicles is Waipapakauri, just north of Kaitaia. Tours go as far as Te Paki Stream, though most cars only go as far as the Bluff. The beach 'road' is only for the well prepared with rugged vehicles. Cars have hit soft sand and been swallowed by the tides – you may see the roof of an unfortunate vehicle poking through the sands. Check tide times before setting out and avoid it 2½ hours either side of high tide – and watch out for 'quicksand' on Te Paki Stream (keep moving).

Motorcycling on the beach is OK, but take it slowly and be extra careful – a few bikers have been killed by riding into washouts or soft sand.

Wagener Museum

This museum (☎ 09-409 8850, adult/child $6/2; open 8.30am-5.30pm daily) at Houhora, 40km north of Kaitaia, houses an unrelated collection of oddities but the sheer number of items makes it astonishing. Exhibits include stuffed animals and birds, Maori artefacts, antique gramophones and washing machines, a commode collection, pianolas and other musical instruments that the guide will play for you.

The museum has a cafe and there's a bush motor camp next door. All Cape Reinga tours stop here, but the entry fee is not usually included. For an extra adult/child $3/1.50 you can visit the **Subritzky Homestead** next door. The 1862 homestead is constructed of local swamp kauri, and set in a pretty cottage garden.

Walking

The coastline is scattered with beautiful beaches, connected by a network of tracks. You can walk the **Ninety Mile Beach**, but you'll need to carry camping gear as there are no huts.

From Cape Reinga you can walk along Te Werahi Beach to **Cape Maria van Diemen** in about five hours return. Beautiful **Tapotupotu Bay** is a two-hour walk east of Cape Reinga, via Sandy Bay and the cliffs. From Tapotupotu Bay it is about an eight-hour walk to **Kapowairua** at the eastern end of Spirits Bay. Both Tapotupotu Bay and Kapowairua have camping grounds and road access.

Organised Tours

Bus tours go from Kaitaia, Mangonui (Doubtless Bay) and the Bay of Islands. If possible it makes sense to take the tour from Kaitaia or Doubtless Bay since they're much closer to Cape Reinga.

In Kaitaia, **Sand Safaris** (☎ 0800 869 090, 09-408 1778, 221 Commerce St) and **Harrison's Cape Runner** (☎ 0800 227 373,

09-408 1033, 123 North Rd) have small buses for day trips that take in the main features of the cape and sand tobogganing. The trips are pretty much identical and cost adult/child $40/20, including a picnic lunch.

Far North Outback Adventures *(☎ 09-408 0927,* e *outbackadventure@actrix .co.nz)* has full-day 4WD trips up to the cape with side trips to the east coast beaches and the Ahipara gumfields.

Paradise Connexion *(☎ 0800 494 392, 09-406 0460)* operates from Mangonui, while Fullers, King's Tours & Cruises, Dune-Rider, Northern Exposure and Awesome Adventures operate long day trips from the Bay of Islands (see that section later in this chapter for details).

Pack or Paddle *(☎ 09-409 8445; half-day/day trips $80/125)*, at Tom's Landing, offers combined sea kayaking and fishing trips around the superb Parengarenga Harbour. Guided walks to fishing spots cost $90 a day (including lunch) and you can hire kayaks for $55 a day. There's also backpacker accommodation here.

Places to Stay & Eat

There are several DOC *camping grounds* in the Cape Reinga area. There's a site at *Kapowairua* on Spirits Bay ($5 per person), with cold water and limited toilet facilities, and another at *Tapotupotu Bay* ($6), with toilets and showers; neither has electricity. Bring a cooker as fires are not allowed. Both bays have mosquitoes and biting sandflies, so come prepared with repellent. The *Rarawa Beach camping ground* ($6), at the end of Rarawa Beach Rd, 3km north or Ngataki or 10km south of Te Kao, has water and toilet facilities only (no prior bookings, no open fires; open September to April).

Waitiki Landing Complex (☎/fax 09-409 7508) Powered/unpowered sites $18/14, dorm beds $13, double cabin $50. At Waitiki Landing, the last settlement before the cape, this complex is the northernmost accommodation in NZ. There is a camp kitchen, laundrette and hot (metered) showers. Waitiki Landing is also the last stop for fuel, and it has a shop, liquor store and a restaurant that does good pizzas ($14.50)

and ostrich burgers. Sandboard hire is $8 a day here.

North Wind Lodge Backpackers (☎ 09-409 8515, Otaipango Rd) Dorm beds $17, twins $36. North Wind Lodge is a real retreat, 6km down an unsealed road at Henderson Bay on the peninsula's east side. It is spacious and modern, and near a great stretch of beach. There are two shared rooms and one twin. Boogie boards and sand toboggans are available to guests.

Pukenui village, on the highway about 45km north of Kaitaia, is situated on the Houhora Harbour, a good spot for fishing and boating. There are several budget places to stay here.

Pukenui Lodge Motel & Youth Hostel (☎ 09-409 8837, e *pukenui@igrin.co.nz)* Dorm beds $16, doubles & twins $40, double studio units $99, double 1-bedroom units $109. This lodge has a lovely setting overlooking Houhora Harbour, a pool, spa and a range of accommodation. The YHA-associated backpacker accommodation (no bunks) is in historic Thomson House (built in 1891). The rates for motel units depend on the season.

Pukenui Holiday Camp (☎ 09-409 8803, e *pukenuiholidays@xtra.co.nz, Lambs Rd)* Powered & unpowered sites $10 per person, cabins $45-50 per double, self-contained units $60. About 500m from the highway down Lambs Rd, this is a small, shady camping ground.

Pukenui Farmstay (☎ 09-409 7863, Lambs Rd) Camp sites $8, dorm beds $13, doubles $34. Pukenui Farmstay is about 2km down the mostly unsealed Lambs Rd. It's a modern, comfortable cottage with a six-bed dorm, a twin and double, and a veranda from which you see memorable sunsets. The owners will pick up from the Pukenui shop and let visitors collect their own eggs and vegetables.

Wagener Park Backpackers (☎ 09-409 8564, e *wagener.park@xtra.co.nz)* Bed in a bunkroom/quad $12.50/17.50, doubles $38. Next to the Wagener Museum at Houhora Heads, this new backpackers has a waterfront location, a cafe and bar next door and kayaking, golf and swimming.

Park Ninety Mile Beach (☎ 0800 367 719, 09-406 7298, e ninetymilebeach@ xtra.co.nz) Powered & unpowered sites $22 for 2 people, double cabins $45, self-contained double cabins $60. This modern park is 18km north of Kaitaia on the Cape Reinga road at Waipapakauri Ramp. It has a restaurant and bar.

KARIKARI PENINSULA

Remote Karikari Peninsula forms the north-western end of Doubtless Bay. Roads are mostly unsealed (although the development of a resort golf course at Rangiputa has resulted in sealed roads there) and facilities are limited, but the peninsula's beaches are among Northland's finest.

Rangiputa has lovely white-sand beaches that are easy to reach. A turn-off on the road to Rangiputa takes you to remote **Puheke Beach** with white sand dunes and long, lonely windswept beaches. On the east coast of the peninsula, **Matai Bay**, with its tiny 'twin coves', is the loveliest of the beaches.

There is a DOC *camping ground* (☎ 09-408 6014) at Matai Bay. During the Christmas holidays it's very busy, but at other times is usually not full ($6).

Whatuwhiwhi Holiday Park (☎ 0800 282 444, 09-408 7202, e whatuwhiwhi@ xtra.co.nz, Whatuwhiwhi Rd) Powered & unpowered sites $12 per person, cabins $40-50, motel units $65-120. At the end of the road and a short walk from the beach, this is a well-equipped park with boat and kayak hire and facilities for backpackers.

Reef Lodge (☎ 09-408 7100, e reef lodge@clear.net.nz) Studios & units $70-180 per double. Reef Lodge has units facing the beach.

DOUBTLESS BAY

The bay gets its unusual name from an entry in Captain Cook's logbook, where he wrote that the body of water was 'doubtless a bay'. Lying between the Bay of Islands and Kaitaia, Doubtless Bay has picturesque bays, coves and beaches. The whole area is great for fishing and shellfishing, boating, swimming and other water sports.

The principal town, Mangonui, is a charming historic waterside village. Stretching west around the bay are the modern beach resorts of Coopers Beach, Cable Bay and Taipa. With its glorious climate and beautiful beaches, Doubtless Bay is a go-ahead area, attracting moneyed retirees and other rat race escapees, and it competes with Kaitaia as a good base for exploring the Far North.

Mangonui

Mangonui is a small, picturesque fishing village – the name means 'Great Shark' – with numerous old kauri buildings lining the shallow harbour.

The Mangonui Information & Booking Centre (☎ 09-406 2046), at the waterfront shopping centre, can book local tours and accommodation. It's open from 8am to 6pm daily in summer. There's Internet access in the newsagency next door. You'll find more information at w www.doubtlessbay.co.nz.

The surrounding area attracts many craftspeople and Doubtless Bay has plenty of craft outlets. In Mangonui you'll find the Flax Bush Sea Shell Shop, the Wharf Store, and Arterior. The **Mangonui Courthouse** is a historic reserve. Pick up a copy of the free *Mangonui Heritage Trail* from the visitors centre.

Also at Mangonui is attractive **Mill Bay**, dotted with tiny boats; you can take Silver Egg Rd out to Mill Bay's Mangonui Cruising Club and an assortment of historical markers. This was the spot where Mangonui's first European settler made his base, and whaling ships replenished their water from the stream.

Between Mangonui and Coopers Beach is the **Rangikapiti Pa Historic Reserve**, with ancient Maori terracing and a spectacular, sweeping view of Doubtless Bay. There's a walkway from Mill Bay, west of Mangonui, to the top of the *pa*.

At Hihi, about 10 minutes' drive from Mangonui, is **Butler Point**, site of an 1847 homestead built by whaler turned MP, Captain William Butler. Near the house is a **museum** (☎ 09-406 0006; admission to *museum & grounds $7.50, grounds only $5)*

NORTHLAND

dedicated to whaling. You can only visit by appointment.

Beaches

The first beach west of Mangonui is **Coopers Beach**, a fine sweep of sand lined with pohutukawa trees. Coopers Beach is quite developed and has a small shopping centre. The next bay along, less-developed **Cable Bay**, was once a terminus of the world's longest cable, stretching 3500 nautical miles from here to Queensland, Australia. It was in use from 1902 to 1912 when another cable was laid between Sydney and Auckland.

Across the river from Cable Bay, **Taipa** is another popular summer destination. According to local legend, Taipa is the place where Kupe first set foot on the mainland. Today it has a fine beach, a harbour where the Taipa River meets the sea, and several motels and motor camps.

Activities & Organised Tours

Dolphin Encounters (☎ *09-406 0914; adult/child $80/60)* runs two dolphin swimming trips daily (weather permitting) from Mangonui. The 4-hour trips leave at 8am and 2pm and include commentary on the flora, fauna and history of the Karikari Peninsula and Doubtless Bay.

Hooked on Fishing (☎ *0800 466 533)* and **Clypso Charters** (☎ *09-406 0914)* have boats for charter and fishing trips (from $60).

Crystal Coast Seabed Safaris (☎ *09-408 5885; boat dives $95-135)* does dives in Doubtless Bay, and to the *Rainbow Warrior* further out near the Cavalli Islands.

Paradise Connexion (☎ *09-406 0460)* has trips up to Ninety Mile Beach and Cape Reinga for adult/child $55/25, with lunch.

Places to Stay

Camping & Hostels There are no camping grounds in Mangonui town. *Hihi Beach Holiday Camp* (☎*/fax 09-406 0307, 58 Hihi Rd)* is 13km from Mangonui at the unattractive Hihi Beach. It has good facilities, including a fish smokehouse. Powered/unpowered sites are $12/10 per person, cabins $30-55. The *Taipa Caravan Park* (☎ *09-406 0995, Taipa Point Rd)* is much

more basic but has a better beachfront location.

Old Oak Inn (☎ *09-406 0665, 66 Waterfront Rd)* Bed in a dorm room/quad $20/25, en suite doubles/twins $55/60, upstairs doubles $80. The Old Oak Inn in Mangonui is a nicely restored 1861 kauri pub with cute upstairs rooms. It's part-backpackers, part-guesthouse and still functions as a pub, with an atmospheric bar and restaurant.

Taipa Backpackers Beach Resort (☎ *09-406 0789, 4 Taipa Point Rd)* Bed in a 4-bed room $25. This new resort is a series of self-contained units (each with kitchen, bathroom and lounge), which can be rented as a whole ($100) or shared by backpackers. It's a short walk from the beach.

Guesthouses & Apartments There are numerous B&Bs and homestays, plus a few self-contained apartments. The visitors centre in Mangonui has details.

Waterfront Apartments (☎ *09-406 0347, fax 406 1347)* Double apartments $90-150. These elevated self-contained apartments, looking right over the water, have loads of character. Each one is different but they all have an old world charm and interesting furniture.

Mac 'n' Mo's (☎ *09-406 0538,* e *mac nmo@xtra.co.nz, Main Rd)* Singles/doubles $40/65, with en suite $60/75. On the highway in Coopers Beach, Mac 'n' Mo's is a friendly B&B with tidy units and views over the harbour from the breakfast balcony.

Motels & Hotels There are many motels in the area costing around $70 to $80 a double, but most charge $100 or more from Christmas to the end of January and are generally booked solid then anyway.

Driftwood Lodge (☎ *09-406 0418)* in Cable Bay is a standard motel but right on the beach.

Mangonui Motel (☎ *0800 462 646, 09-406 0346,* e *info@mangonuimotel.co.nz, 1 Colonel Mould Drive)* Doubles from $75. On the hill on the way down to Mangonui, this motel has fine harbour views and self-contained one-bedroom units. Rates double in the high season.

NORTHLAND

Mangonui Hotel (☎ *09-406 0003)* Singles/
doubles $40/80. This historic waterfront
hotel has comfortable rooms upstairs.

Places to Eat

The licensed *Mangonui Fish Shop* (☎ *09-
406 0478)*, sitting on stilts over the water, is
beloved of tour groups and probably a little
more popular than it deserves to be. Still,
it's a great spot to eat your fish and chips (or
ready-made seafood salads and smoked
fish) on tables overlooking the bay.

Waterfront Cafe (☎ *09-406 0850)* Mains
$15-30. Open 8am-late. This is a cosy little
licensed cafe in Mangonui, with good pizzas
and seafood.

The *Slung Anchor* (☎ *09-406 1233, 10
Beach Rd)*. Mains $22-27. This is a recom-
mended place for seafood, with a pleasant
courtyard dining area. There's a cheaper
lunch-time menu and a bar.

Flame Tree Restaurant & Bar (☎ *09-406
0656)* Lunch $7-10, dinner $23-27. Open
Tues-Sat. At the Taipa Resort Hotel, this
flash restaurant is a good place for a splurge,
with fresh local seafood a speciality and waterfront views. Reasonably priced lunches
are available from Thursday to Saturday.

DOUBTLESS BAY TO BAY OF ISLANDS

From Mangonui it's 44km to Kerikeri via
the main highway (SH10), but about
halfway along you can make a scenic detour,
following the eastern side of Whangaroa
Harbour and continuing around to Matauri
Bay before rejoining the highway.

Whangaroa Harbour

Whangaroa Harbour is a picturesque inlet
of small bays and bright green water, surrounded by high, rugged cliffs. The small
town of **Whangaroa**, 6km off the main road,
is a popular game-fishing centre and has a
number of water-based activities, but otherwise it's a very sleepy place. **Totara North**,
on the other side of the bay, is even sleepier
and has an old timber mill.

The Boyd Gallery (☎ 09-405 0230), the
general store in Whangaroa, is also an informal tourist information office.

Things to See & Do Between December
and May, game fishing is the main event
here. At the **Big Gamefish Club** you can see
the marlin being weighed in.

For **walks**, the domed, bald summit of St
Paul's offers fine views. It is a half-hour
walk to the south of Whangaroa. The
Wairakau track north to Pekapeka Bay (90
minutes) begins near the church hall on
Campbell Rd in Totara North and passes
through farmland, hills and shoreline
before arriving at DOC's *Lane Cove
Cottage* ($8 per night); book through DOC
in Kerikeri on ☎ 09-407 8474. The 16-bed
hut has showers and flush toilets, but you
have to bring your own cooker.

Snow Cloud (☎ *09-405 0523; day trip
$65)*, a 36ft yacht operating out of
Whangaroa Harbour, sails to the Cavalli Islands, where there are excellent beaches,
diving spots (including the wreck of the
Rainbow Warrior), snorkelling and walks.
This is a great day trip and much less commercial than operators in the Bay of Islands.

The calm waters and bays around
Whangaroa Harbour are ideal for sea
kayaking. **Northland Sea Kayaking** (☎ *09-
405 0381;* e *northlandseakayaking@xtra
.co.nz; tours $60 per day)* is based on the
coast past Tauranga Bay (pick-up from
Kaeo can be arranged). The kayak tours
'comb' this magical coastline of bays, sea
caves and islands; accommodation is available for $10 extra.

Places to Stay & Eat About 2.5km before
the wharf, the *Whangaroa Harbour Retreat* (☎*/fax 09-405 0306)* has powered/
unpowered sites for $15/12 per person, cab-
ins from $38 to $80 and facilities for
backpackers. Fishing and diving trips can
be arranged here.

Sunseeker Lodge (☎ *09-405 0496)* Dorm
beds $19, twins & doubles $44, double
motel units $80. Sunseeker is up on a hill
about 500m beyond the wharf, with a great
view of the harbour and an outdoor spa to
boot. There's a comfortable backpackers
section and kayaks are available.

Kahoe Farm Hostel (☎ *09-405 1804,*
e *mjoh@igrin.co.nz)* Dorm beds $18,

doubles & twins $46-52. Legendary on the backpacker circuit for its nightly pizzas and pasta prepared by an Italian chef ($15) and impromptu soccer competitions, Kahoe Farm is a homely backpackers just west of the Totara North turn-off (17km back from Whangaroa). The enthusiastic owners organise activities like walks to kauri dams, kayaking and sailing.

Marlin Hotel (☎ 09-405 0347) Singles/twins/doubles $45/50/55. The Marlin is located opposite the wharf and is the social centre of the town. Most of the rooms have shared bath. You can also get meals here in summer.

Tauranga & Matauri Bays

For a drive passing many beautiful bays and fine beaches, head back out of Whangaroa and continue east towards Tauranga Bay. The road was being sealed at the time of writing and the coastal scenery across to Matauri Bay makes it worth the effort.

The first settlement you reach is **Tauranga Bay**, with a fine sweeping surf beach and accommodation. From there you pass **Mahinepua Bay**, **Wainui Bay** and on to **Te Ngaire**, a small settlement with a lovely, quiet beach. The road climbs up to a headland with superb views looking down to **Matauri Bay**, an area owned by the Ngati

NORTHLAND

The *Rainbow Warrior* Trail

In 1985, a tragic, explosive event in Auckland Harbour made world headlines and put New Zealand on the map.

The Greenpeace flagship *Rainbow Warrior* lay anchored in Auckland Harbour, preparing to sail to Moruroa near Tahiti to protest against French nuclear testing.

The *Rainbow Warrior* never left Auckland. French saboteurs, in the employ of the French government, attached explosives to the side of the ship and sank her, killing one green campaigner, Fernando Pereira.

It took some time to find out exactly what had happened, but in inquisitive, rural NZ the comings and goings of foreigners are not easily forgotten. Two of the saboteurs were captured, tried and found guilty, while the others have never been brought to justice.

The incident caused an uproar in France – not because the French government had conducted a wilful and lethal act of terrorism on the soil of a friendly nation, but because the French secret service had bungled the operation and been caught. The French used all their political and economic might to force NZ to release the two saboteurs, and in a farcical turn of events the agents were imprisoned on a French Pacific island as if they had won a trip to Club Med. Within two years, and well before the end of their sentence, they returned to France to receive a hero's welcome.

Northland was the stage for this deadly mission involving several secret service agents. Explosives for the sabotage were delivered by a yacht (which had picked them up from a submarine) from Parengarenga Harbour in the Far North. They were driven to Auckland in a Kombi van by French agents posing as tourists. Bang! An innocent man dead, and international outrage – Auckland Harbour was in the news.

The skeletal remains of the *Rainbow Warrior* were taken to the waters of Northland's beautiful Cavalli Islands, where it can now be explored by divers. The masts of this oceanic crusader were sent to the museum in Dargaville. The memory of the Portuguese photographer and campaigner who died endures in a peaceful bird sanctuary in Thames. A haunting memorial to the once-proud boat sits atop a Maori *pa* site at Matauri Bay, Bay of Islands.

Attention again focused on the *Rainbow Warrior* in 1995. Ten years after the sinking the French announced they were resuming nuclear testing in the Pacific, and Greenpeace's new flagship bearing the name of its ill-fated predecessor set sail for the Moruroa test site. It entered the exclusion zone and was stormed by French marines.

Kura tribe. The view from the ridge above the bay is spectacular with the beach, Cavalli Islands and headland way down below. At the top of the headland in Matauri Bay is a monument to the *Rainbow Warrior*. The sunken boat itself lies offshore in the waters of the Cavalli Islands and dives can be arranged at Matauri Bay Holiday Park (from $95 including gear) or in Paihia – for background information see the boxed text 'The *Rainbow Warrior* Trail' in this chapter.

Places to Stay The *Tauranga Bay Holiday Park* (☎/fax 09-405 0436), on the beach at Tauranga Bay, has a large camping area with sites at $12 per person but not a lot of shade. There are cabins and units from $35.

Tauranga Bay Motel (☎ 09-405 0222) Doubles $60-100. This is a plain but comfortable motel – the higher rate applies in peak season.

Matauri Bay Holiday Park (☎/fax 09-405 0525, ☻ matauribayhp@actrix.co.nz) Powered/unpowered sites $23/20 for 2 people, on-site caravans $45. The road down to the beach is narrow and rough in places, but this is a good spot to pitch a tent. There's a full-size Maori war canoe under a shelter outside the park.

Oceans Holiday Village (☎/fax 09-405 0417, ☻ oceans@matauribay.co.nz) Off-peak/peak units from $85/145. At the end of the beach road at Matauri Bay, this place has its own little beachfront and a range of self-contained lodges and units that are reasonable value outside the peak summer months. There's also a licensed restaurant and bar, as well as boat and kayak hire.

There is a very basic DOC *hut* (sleeps eight) at Papatara Bay on Motukawanui Island, one of the Cavallis; book through DOC in Kerikeri.

Bay of Islands

Long famed for its stunning coastal scenery, the Bay of Islands is one of NZ's major attractions. The bay is punctuated by dozens of coves and when the sun is shining its clear waters range in hue from turquoise to deep blue. Although a hugely popular tourist and sailing destination, the 150 or so islands have thankfully escaped development; townships are all on the mainland.

The Bay of Islands is also of enormous historical significance. As the site of NZ's first permanent English settlement, it is the cradle of European colonisation. It was here that the Treaty of Waitangi was drawn up and first signed by 46 Maori chiefs in 1840; the treaty remains the linchpin of race relations in modern-day NZ (see History in the Facts about New Zealand chapter).

Paihia is the hub of the Bay of Islands. Though only a small town, its population swells dramatically in summer and it has all the trappings of a thriving tourist centre. Waitangi Reserve is within walking distance.

Only a short passenger ferry ride away, Russell has all the character that Paihia lacks. Though also a popular side trip for Bay of Islands tourists, historic Russell is a smaller, sleepier town with many fine old buildings and a delightful waterfront.

To the north is Kerikeri, more of a working town, much less touristy, but still with a few attractions and a great deal of history.

Special Events

In January there is a **Tall Ships Race** at Russell. February has **Waitangi Day** on the 6th and a 10-day arts festival, with exhibits of touchable art, plays, music, comedy and dance.

There is a **Country Music Festival** in early May and a **Jazz & Blues Festival** in mid-August. September is 'foodies' month, with Russell's **Oyster Festival** and the very popular **Wine & Food Festival** in Paihia, on the Waitangi foreshore.

In October, the Auckland to Bay of Islands **Weekend Coastal Classic** – NZ's largest yacht race – is held.

Activities & Organised Tours

The Bay of Islands has a mind-boggling array of activities and tours and it seems like everyone is willing and able to sell you one. Many are water-based to make the most of the natural surroundings. It's a

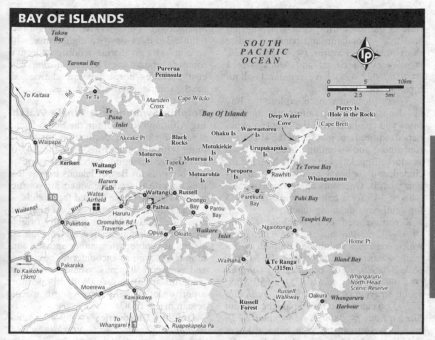

BAY OF ISLANDS

NORTHLAND

competitive business and backpacker discounts are available for many activities and tours. Hostels can book all tours and can generally arrange cheap deals. Most of the following depart from Paihia, but pick-ups from Kerikeri can be arranged and most of the cruises call in at Russell.

Cruises & Sailing You can't leave the Bay of Islands without taking some sort of cruise and there are plenty of operators keen to get you on board. They are dominated by the 'big two': Fullers (☎ 09-402 7422, W www .fullers-bay-of-islands.co.nz) and King's Tours & Cruises (☎ 0800 222 979, 09-402 8288, W www.kings-tours.co.nz). There are also smaller operators, as well as sailing boat charters.

Best known is Fullers' 'Cream Trip' (adult/child $85/45), which started back in 1920 when one Captain Lane picked up dairy products from the many farms around the bay. As more roads were built and the

small dairy farms closed, the service became more of a tourist trip. It's now part of the 'Supercruise', which incorporates the Hole in the Rock and a one-hour stopover on Urupukapuka Island. It leaves Paihia at 10am daily from September to May, and Monday, Wednesday, Thursday and Saturday the rest of the year.

Other Fullers cruises include the Hole in the Rock (passing through it) off Cape Brett (adult/child $60/30) and the R Tucker Thompson tall sailing ship cruise (adult/ child $89/45). Most tours stop at Otehei Bay on Urupukapuka Island, where Westerns writer Zane Grey went big game fishing, and a tourist submarine, the Nautilus, is submerged. To go underwater costs adult/ child $12/6).

Kings has a Day in the Bay cruise for $83/45, which combines the Cream Trip route and Hole in the Rock with dolphin swimming. It also has a Hole in the Rock cruise for $58/28.

Also very popular are the high-speed Hole in the Rock trips, neck-snapping jet-boat ride – good fun and handy if you're short on time. *Excitor* (☎ *09-402 7020,* W *www.excitor.co.nz)* and *Mack Attack* (☎ *0800 622 528)* have regular 1½-hour trips for $60/30.

A very pleasant way to explore the Bay of Islands is on a day **sailing** trip. In most cases you can help crew the boat (no experience required), or just spend the afternoon sunbathing and swimming. Activities such as snorkelling, kayaking and fishing are included, and the boats usually call in at various islands. Operators charge similar rates – about $45 for a half-day and $70 to $75 for a full day, including lunch.

Recommended boats include *Carino* (☎ *09-402 8040; adult/child $69/35 a day)*, which combines sailing and dolphin swimming; *Phantom* (☎ *0800 224 421; adult/child $70/30)*, a 50ft ocean racer; *Gungha* (☎ *0800 478 900; adults $75)*, a 65ft Maxi yacht; *Straycat* (☎ *09-402 6130; adult/child $72/45)*, a catamaran for 16 passengers; and *She's a Lady* (☎ *0800 724 584; adult $72)*, on which you can try your hand at kneeboarding or tubing. The *Iron Butterfly* (☎ *0800 787 367; adult/child $75/45)* has a 'late riser cruise' (for those with hangovers?) departing Paihia at 10.30am.

If you're interested in learning to sail, **Great Escape Yacht Charters** (☎ *09-402 7143; 1-/2-day courses $140/260)*, based in Opua, has courses with only two people on each boat.

Overnight Cruises The cheapest way to spend a night on the water is aboard **The Rock** (☎ *0800 762 527,* W *www.rockthe boat.co.nz; 24-hour cruise $125)*, an unlikely-looking vessel set up for backpackers. The Rock was a vehicle ferry in a former life but now it's a comfortable floating hostel with four-bed dorms, twins and double rooms, and (of course) a bar. The cruise departs at about 5pm and includes an excellent barbecue and seafood dinner, then a full day spent cruising the islands, fishing and swimming. You can stay on board another night (and day) for $48.

Ecocruz (☎ *0800 4326 278,* W *www.big blueandgreen.co.nz; cruise $375)* is a recommended three-day/two-night cruise, with an emphasis on marine wildlife and environment, aboard the 72ft *Manawanui*. The cost includes dorm accommodation, all meals, sailing and other activities.

Dolphin Swimming & Whale Watching Although Kaikoura in the South Island is still the premier destination for swimming with dolphins, trips from the Bay of Islands are becoming increasingly popular. The big plus for Bay of Islands trips is that they operate all year, the waters are warmer and you get to cruise around the islands.

The Bay of Islands trips have a high success rate, and operators generally offer a free trip if dolphins are not sighted. Dolphin swims are subject to weather and sea conditions. As well as encountering bottlenose and common dolphins, whales, orcas and penguins are often seen. With all operators a portion of the cost goes towards marine research, via DOC.

Dolphin Discoveries (☎ *09-402 8234,* e *dolphin@igrin.co.nz; adult/child $95/48)* was the first to do dolphin-swimming trips in the bay. It takes out small groups twice daily and provides all equipment. **Awesome Dolphin Adventures** (☎ *09-402 6985,* W *www.awesomeadventures.co.nz)* has similar trips (same price) with an option to spend the day on Urupukapuka.

Fullers (☎ *09-4027421; adult/child $95/48)* and **Kings** (☎ *09-402 8288; adult/child $83/45)* run dolphin-swimming trips daily. The Kings trip offers boom netting if you're uneasy about swimming in deep water.

Sea Kayaking There are plenty of opportunities for kayaking around the bay, either on a guided tour or by renting a kayak and going it alone. **Coastal Kayakers** (☎ *09-402 8105,* W *www.coastalkayakers.co.nz)* and **New Zealand Sea Kayak Adventures** (☎ *09-402 8596)* both have trips ranging from half-day to longer expeditions. A half-day guided tour with Coastal Kayakers costs $45 per person ($65 for a full day), and a two-day budget harbour wilderness tour is $110 (minimum two people). New Zealand Sea Kayak Adventures has multi-day kayak-camping trips for $125 per day including meals. Longer 'outer island' trips cost $750 for six days or $1200 for 10 days. Kayak hire starts from $12 an hour or $40 a day.

Island Kayaks (☎ *09-402 7111, 18 Kings Rd)* and **Bay Beach Hire** (☎ *09-402 6078, Marsden Rd)* also have half-day guided trips.

Bay Beach Hire, on the waterfront south of the town centre, rents out all sorts of gear including kayaks, boogie boards and wake boards, windsurfers, wetsuits, snorkelling gear, boats and bikes.

Scuba Diving The Bay of Islands offers some fine subtropical diving and local operators all go out to the wreck of the *Rainbow Warrior* off the Cavalli Islands, about an hour from Paihia by boat.

Paihia Dive (☎ *09-402 7551,* **W** *www.divenz.com, Williams Rd; dives with/without gear supplied $150/90)* offers two boat dives. Rainbow Warrior trips are $160 (including gear). It also offers five-day PADI courses ($450), tank filling, scuba gear servicing and snorkelling for nondivers.

Dive North (☎ *09-402 7079)* also has trips to the *Rainbow Warrior* and other popular dive sites such as Deep Water Cove and Cape Brett.

Other Activities The Bay of Islands is noted for its fishing, particularly snapper and kingfish. Fishing charter boats abound and can be booked at the Maritime Building in Paihia or at Russell wharf.

Salt Air (☎ *09-402 8338,* **W** *www.saltair.co.nz)* has scenic flights ranging from a 30-minute tour of the Bay of Islands ($95 per person) to a five-hour flight-and-4WD tour to Cape Reinga and Ninety Mile Beach ($285). Helicopter flights out to the Hole in the Rock and Cape Brett cost $150.

Sky-Hi Tandem Skydive (☎ *0800 427 593)* operates from the Watea (Haruru Falls) airport; the cost is $205/255 from 9000/12,000ft and a jump video is $110.

Flying Kiwi Parasail (☎ *09-402 6078,* **W** *www.parasail-nz.co.nz),* at Bay Beach

Hire, does one-hour parasailing trips leaving from Paihia wharf hourly during summer. A 600ft (ie, 600-foot rope, which determines how high you go) flight costs $60 per person and 1000ft is $70. The same outfit runs **Air Torn Kiteboarding**, where the drag from a kite (a mini-parachute really) propels you on a surfboard. Described as the next big thing after windsurfing, you get a full day of instruction on how to fly the kite and control the board for $150.

If you tire of cruising the open water, **Bay of Islands Mini Cruises** (☎ *09-402 7848)* has relaxing evening barbecue cruises up the Waitangi River to Haruru Falls ($45) and 2½-hour day cruises for $28.

There are a couple of **horse riding** operators. With **Big Rock Springs Trail Rides** (☎ *09-405 9999; day trip $70)* you swim the horses.

Zorbing (☎ *025 208 1319; $35),* that curious Kiwi activity where you roll downhill inside a clear plastic sphere, has come to the bay. The site is on the road out to the highway (towards Kerikeri) about 4km from Paihia.

Bush 'n' Bike Adventures (☎ *09-402 1142, Tirohanga Rd; 1½hr tours $65),* based near Kawakawa about 15km south of Paihia, has quad-bike tours over scenic farm property. The cost is $85 with a passenger. Pick-up from Paihia can be arranged.

Cape Reinga Tours It's easier to do trips to Cape Reinga and Ninety Mile Beach from Kaitaia or Doubtless Bay if you're heading up that way. However, if you're short on time, it's possible to do a long day trip (10 to 12 hours) from the Bay of Islands with several operators. They're all pretty similar bus tours, driving one way along Ninety Mile Beach.

Awesome Adventures (☎ *09-402 6985, Maritime Building; trips $79)* has backpacker-oriented trips with sandboarding on the dunes, swimming at Tapotupotu Bay and a visit to Puketi kauri forest.

4X4 Dune Rider (☎ *09-402 8681,* **W** *www.dunerider.co.nz; adult/concession $77/69)* is popular among backpackers and younger travellers. The smaller group trips make plenty of stops for sandboarding and swimming.

Fullers *(☎ 09-402 7421)* has all-day trips departing from Paihia and Kerikeri for adult/child $89/45 ($99/55 with lunch), but more interesting is the Heritage trip ($110/65 including lunch) which features a Maori guide and explanations of the history and culture of this important peninsular.

King's Tours & Cruises *(☎ 09-402 8288)* has coach tours for $85/44 with stops at the Puketi kauri forest and Wagener Museum.

Getting There & Away
Air Air New Zealand Link (☎ 09-407 8419) has daily flights to Kerikeri from Auckland.

Bus All buses serving Paihia arrive at and depart from the Maritime Building by the wharf.

InterCity and Northliner have buses daily from Auckland to the Bay of Islands, via Whangarei. The trip takes about four hours to Paihia and goes to Kerikeri before continuing north to Kaitaia. Northliner has a backpackers Bay of Islands pass ($53) that gets you from Auckland to Kerikeri via Paihia and back, with unlimited free travel between Paihia and Kerikeri.

Getting Around
Passenger ferries connect Paihia with Russell, running from around 7am to 7pm (to 10pm from October to June). Ferries operate on average every 20 minutes from Russell to Paihia in summer. The fare is $6/3 one way/return.

To get to Russell with your car, cross from Opua to Okiato Point using the car ferry (see Getting There & Around under Russell later in this chapter).

There's also a water taxi (☎ 09-403 8823) for getting around the bay islands. For bicycle hire try Bay Beach Hire (☎ 09-402 6078) on Marsden Rd.

BAY OF ISLANDS MARITIME & HISTORIC PARK
The park consists of some 40 different sites extending all the way from Mimiwhangata

Bay in the south to Whangaroa Harbour in the north. Marked walks of varying levels of difficulty take anywhere from 10 minutes to 10 hours and include tramps around islands, *pa* sites and other historical sites, scenic, historic and recreational reserves, and the Mimiwhangata Marine Park.

The Bay of Islands Maritime & Historic Park Visitor Centre (☎ 09-403 9005) at Russell can provide information on walks and camping in the park. Development of islands is limited, though **Urupukapuka Island** has camping facilities.

Places to Stay
The *Cape Brett Hut* is a very popular destination. You can arrange to walk there and stay in the hut by ringing DOC in Russell (☎ 09-403 9005; bookings essential). It costs $8 per adult per night.

Camping is only permitted at two bays on Urupukapuka Island. Cable and Urupukapuka Bays have water supplies and cold showers but you need food, a stove, fuel, and a portable chemical toilet, which, let's face it, most travellers don't keep in their backpack. The cost is $6 per person. To get to Urupukapuka Island, take a water taxi or a tour boat, get off at Otehei Bay and arrange to catch the tour boat back on the day you want to return.

Camping is also possible at the Mimiwhangata Coastal Park ($6); book through DOC in Russell.

PAIHIA & WAITANGI
pop 7250

Paihia was settled by Europeans as a mission station in 1823 when the first *raupo* (bullrush) hut was built for the Reverend Henry Williams. Paihia has a very pretty setting but the missionary zeal has been replaced with an equally rampant tourist industry. It's the centre of the Bay of Islands tourist activity but is basically an accommodation, eating and tours centre.

Adjoining Paihia to the north is Waitangi, the site of the historic signing on 6 February 1840 of the treaty between the Maori people and the representatives of Queen Victoria's government.

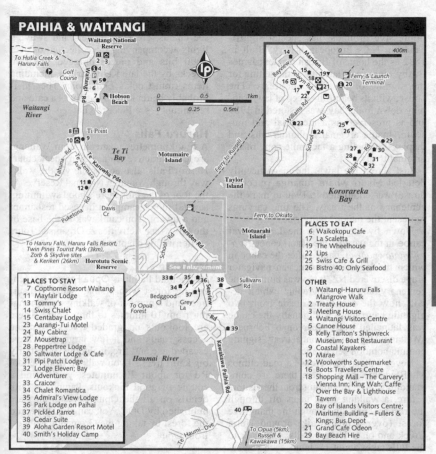

PAIHIA & WAITANGI

PLACES TO STAY
7 Copthorne Resort Waitangi
11 Mayfair Lodge
13 Tommy's
14 Swiss Chalet
15 Centabay Lodge
23 Aarangi-Tui Motel
24 Bay Cabinz
27 Mousetrap
28 Peppertree Lodge
30 Saltwater Lodge & Cafe
31 Pipi Patch Lodge
32 Lodge Eleven; Bay Adventurer
33 Craicor
34 Chalet Romantica
35 Admiral's View Lodge
36 Park Lodge on Paihai
37 Pickled Parrot
38 Cedar Suite
39 Aloha Garden Resort Motel
40 Smith's Holiday Camp

PLACES TO EAT
6 Waikokopu Cafe
17 La Scaletta
19 The Wheelhouse
22 Lips
25 Swiss Cafe & Grill
26 Bistro 40; Only Seafood

OTHER
1 Waitangi-Haruru Falls Mangrove Walk
2 Treaty House
3 Meeting House
4 Waitangi Visitors Centre
5 Canoe House
8 Kelly Tarlton's Shipwreck Museum; Boat Restaurant
9 Coastal Kayakers
10 Marae
12 Woolworths Supermarket
16 Boots Travellers Centre
18 Shopping Mall – The Carvery; Vienna Inn; King Wah; Caffe Over the Bay & Lighthouse Tavern
20 Bay of Islands Visitors Centre; Maritime Building – Fullers & Kings; Bus Depot
21 Grand Cafe Odeon
29 Bay Beach Hire

NORTHLAND

Information

The Bay of Islands visitors centre (☎ 09-402 7345, e visitorinfo@fndc.govt.nz), at the start of the wharf, is open from 8am to 6.30pm daily (to 8pm in peak times). There's a vast amount of information on the region abailable here. Opposite is the Maritime Building where you'll find Fullers, King's and other offices for cruises and tours, fishing boat bookings, and the bus terminal. Staff here are friendly but competition is hot and there's a subtle hard sell. There are many other places in Paihia that will book tours.

Internet access is available at the visitors centre, in the Maritime Building and at Boots Travellers Centre (☎ 09-402 6632) on Selwyn Rd.

Waitangi National Reserve

A visit to the Waitangi National Reserve (☎ 09-402 7437; adult/child $9/free; open 9am-6pm daily) is definitely a must for the itenary. The visitors centre here has an interesting short audiovisual that is played every half-hour from 9am. The centre also has a gallery of portraits, Maori weaponry and a gift shop.

The **Treaty House**, the centrepiece of the impressive grounds, has special significance in NZ's European history. Built in 1832 as the home of British resident James Busby, eight years later it was the setting for the signing of the Waitangi treaty. The house, with its beautiful sweep of lawn running down to the bay, was restored in 1989 and is preserved as a memorial and museum. Inside are many photographs and displays, including a facsimile copy of the original treaty.

Just across the lawn, the magnificently detailed Maori **whare runanga** (meeting house) was completed in 1940 to mark the centenary of the treaty. The fine carvings represent the major Maori tribes.

Down by the cove is the largest **war canoe** in the world – the Maori canoe *Ngatokimatawhaorua*, named after the canoe in which the legendary Polynesian navigator Kupe discovered NZ. It too was built for the centenary, and a photographic exhibit details how the canoe was made from two gigantic kauri logs. Traditionally the canoe was launched every year on 6 February (Waitangi Day) for the annual treaty-signing commemoration ceremonies.

Beyond the Treaty House a road climbs Mt Bledisloe, from where there are commanding views. Beginning from the visitors centre, a **walking track** takes off through the reserve, passing through the mangrove forest (over a boardwalk) around Hutia Creek and on to Haruru Falls. The walk to the falls takes about 1½ hours each way.

A high-tech **Sound & Light Show** (☎ 09-402 5990; adult/child $45/23) is held at the Waitangi Treaty Grounds on Monday, Wednesday, Thursday and Saturday from 8pm to 9.15pm. The show includes a live performance of Maori customs and dance. Bookings are essential.

Kelly Tarlton's Shipwreck Museum

The Shipwreck Museum (☎ 09-402 7018; adult/child $7/2.50; open 10am-5.30pm daily) is on board the old barque *Tui*, beached beside the bridge on the Paihia side of the Waitangi River. The sailing ship has been imaginatively fitted out with recorded sea chants, creaking timbers and swaying lights accompanying the collection of over 1000 bits and pieces dragged up from wrecks by the late Kelly Tarlton, including items from Cook's *Endeavour*. The *Tui* is probably better known locally as a cafe and restaurant – see Places to Eat.

Haruru Falls

A few kilometres upstream from Waitangi are the attractive (rather than spectacular) Haruru Falls, also accessible via the walkway through Waitangi National Reserve. At the foot of the falls there's good swimming, several motor camps, a licensed restaurant and a tavern. You can kayak to the base of the falls – see Activities & Organised Tours earlier in this chapter.

Walking

Just behind Paihia is **Opua Forest**, a regenerating forest with a small stand of kauri trees and a number of walking tracks ranging from 10 minutes to three hours. There are lookouts up graded tracks from the access roads and a few large trees have escaped axe and fire, including some fairly big kauri trees. If you walk up from School Rd for about 20 minutes, you'll find a couple of good lookouts. Pamphlets with details on all the Opua Forest walks are published by DOC. You can also drive into the forest by taking the Oromahoe Rd west from Opua.

Places to Stay

Camping & Cabins There are several camping spots around Paihia and Waitangi, including three near pretty Haruru Falls.

Haruru Falls Resort (☎ 0800 757 525, 09-402 7525, ℮ resort@onenz.co.nz, Old Wharf Rd) Powered & powered sites $12.50 per person, double studio units $99, double self-contained units $119-159. This well-equipped park is in a beautiful spot by the river and has a pool, bar and restaurant.

Twin Pines Tourist Park (☎/fax 09-402 7322, ℮ enquiries@twinpines.co.nz, Puketona Rd) Powered/unpowered sites $12/11.50, self-contained double units $70, double cabins $55. Overlooking the falls, Twin Pines has good amenities and A-frame cabins. Next door, the Pines pub and restaurant is good for a night out (see Entertainment).

Park Lodge on Paihia (☎ *09-402 7826,* e *parklodge@xtra.co.nz, Seaview Rd)* Powered sites $12 per person. In Paihia town, this hotel complex has powered sites and facilities for campers (it's better for campervanners than tent campers as there's not much lawn). Guests can use the hotel facilities, including the pool.

Smith's Holiday Camp (☎ *09-402 7678)* Powered sites $12.50 per person, cabins & flats $60-90, double motel units $100. Smith's occupies a lovely waterside spot, 2.5km south of Paihia towards Opua.

Hostels Paihia has the greatest concentration and arguably the highest standard of backpacker hostels in Northland; all make discount bookings for activities. Most are on Kings Rd, Paihia's 'backpackers row'.

Saltwater Lodge (☎ *0800 002 266, 09-402 7075,* e *saltwater.lodge@xtra.co.nz, 14 Kings Rd)* Dorm beds $20-22, doubles & twins $90 ($75 off season). This spotless new purpose-built place sets a very high standard for backpacker accommodation – as the price indicates. All rooms, including four- and six-bed dorms, have large en suite bathrooms and made-up beds. There are spacious, modern common areas, undercover parking, free bikes and kayaks and even a small gym.

Pipi Patch Lodge (☎ *09-402 7111,* e *pipipatch@acb.co.nz, 18 Kings Rd)* Dorm beds $20, doubles & twins $47-65. The Pipi Patch has long been popular, and each room has a basic kitchen and en suite. There is also a pool, spa, and a great backpackers bar with an outdoor patio.

Mousetrap (☎ *09-402 8182, 11 Kings Rd)* Dorm beds $18, doubles & twins $40. Mousetrap is not flash but, with a warren of little rooms and corridors, and strange pictures and ornaments on the walls, it has a bit more character than most backpackers in Paihia. The all-round nautical theme includes a veranda shaped like a ship's bridge.

Peppertree Lodge (☎ *09-402 6122,* e *peppertree.lodge@xtra.co.nz, 15 Kings Rd)* Dorm beds with en suite $19-21, doubles $57. The Peppertree is another well-equipped place, with a modern kitchen, games room with table soccer, spotless rooms and friendly hosts. You can rent mountain bikes for $10 a day, and kayaks and luggage storage are free.

Lodge Eleven (☎/fax *09-402 7487, cnr Kings & MacMurray Rds)* Dorm beds $18-22, twins & doubles $48-52. This YHA associate hostel at the end of Kings Rd is a converted motel, so each room has an en suite. There's a smallish lounge and kitchen and the four-bed dorms are heated in winter.

Pickled Parrot (☎ *09-402 6222,* e *the parrot@paradise.net.nz, Greys Lane)* Dorm beds $20, twins & doubles $48. The Pickled Parrot, just around the corner from Kings Rd, is a laid-back place in a nice setting with a pleasant outdoor area and a little stream running past. Breakfast is included in the price. There's no sign of the parrot.

Centabay Lodge (☎ *09-402 7466,* e *centabay@xtra.co.nz, 27 Selwyn Rd)* Dorm beds $19, twins & doubles $47, en suite double $57, self-contained studios $60-85. Centabay, just behind the shops, is part-backpacker, part-tourist lodge. The friendly owners maintain a high standard with plenty of facilities, including a spa pool and free kayaks.

Tommy's (☎/fax *09-402 8668,* e *tom mys@xtra.co.nz, 44 Davis Crescent)* Dorm beds $19-21, twins & doubles $46. Tommy's is a clean, spacious two-storey house down at the Waitangi end of Paihia. There's a nice lounge and kitchen and an upstairs balcony.

Mayfair Lodge (☎ *09-402 7471,* e *may fair.lodge@xtra.co.nz, 7 Puketona Rd)* Camp sites $12, dorm beds $19, twins/ doubles $44/47. Mayfair Lodge is a little away from action on the road into Paihia. It's a small, quiet place with a back courtyard and spa pool.

At the time of research a new backpackers, *Bay Adventurer* (☎ *09-402 5162,* e *bayadventurer@xtra.co.nz, 28 Kings Rd)* was being built between Lodge 11 and Pipi

Patch. It promises to be another good place – let us know what you think.

B&Bs, Guesthouses & Apartments Numerous B&Bs are found around Paihia and the Bay of Islands; the visitors centre makes referrals and bookings.

Cedar Suite (☎ 09-402 8516, fax 402 8555, 5 Sullivans Rd) Studio suite from $81, B&B $95, self-contained suite with spa $120. Cedar Suite has a range of relaxing self-contained and B&B accommodation in a lovely, secluded bush setting.

Craicor (☎ 09-402 7882, fax 402 7883, 49 Kings Rd) Doubles $120. Craicor is another place in among the trees, and the units (Garden Suite and Tree House) have pleasant decks to sit out on.

Chalet Romantica (☎/fax 09-402 8270, e chalet-romantica@xtra.co.nz, 1 Bedggood Close) Rooms $105-200. This Swiss-owned guesthouse brings a touch of the alpine to Paihia, and it's high enough to offer fine views of the bay. There's an indoor pool and spa and the units are one and two bedroom.

Admiral's View Lodge (☎ 09-402 6263, e admiralsview@actrix.gen.nz, 2 McMurray St) B&B doubles $75 ($95 peak season). This lodge has three good-value rooms with en suite and kitchenette and an elevated outlook over to the bay.

Bay Cabinz (☎ 09-402 8534, fax 402 8536, 32-34 School Rd) Cabins $78-120. Back from the waterfront, this is a group of comfortable self-contained cabins, each with a veranda. Good discounts are available in winter.

Motels & Hotels In Paihia motels stand shoulder to shoulder along the waterfront; doubles are around $120 (or more) during the peak summer season, dropping to $80 or so during the low season. The following is a tiny sample.

Aarangi-Tui Motel (☎ 0800 453 354, 402 7496, 16 Williams Rd) Doubles from $70. This is one of Paihia's cheaper motels. Even though it's as old fashioned as they come, it's clean and in a quiet location that is close to the shops.

Aloha Garden Resort Motel (☎ 0800 425 642, 09-402 7540, e alohamotel@xtra .co.nz, 32-36 Seaview Rd) Doubles from $95, 2-bedroom apartments from $155. Aloha Garden is a large place with one- and two-bedroom self-contained apartments, a pool and spa.

Swiss Chalet (☎ 09-402 7615, e swiss .chalet@xtra.co.nz, 3 Bayview Rd) Units $95-160. Swiss Chalet has a variety of self-contained units (studio, one-/two-bedroom, executive) and a spa.

Copthorne Resort Waitangi (☎ 09-402 7411, Tau Henare Drive) Rooms $166-223. This resort is in a nice setting, north across the bridge, with an excellent restaurant, bar and heated pool. Room rates vary depending on whether you have garden view or sea view, and regular discounts are offered.

Places to Eat
True to its status as tourist capital of Northland, Paihia has quite a few good restaurants, though some are not cheap and reservations should be made for dinner in summer. For cheap eats, the shopping mall (with a lane running through it) is the place to start.

The Carvery whips up hot roast-meat rolls ($5), roast dinners (from 4.30pm, $8.95), baked potatoes and fruit smoothies. *Caffe over the Bay*, upstairs on Marsden Rd, is not particularly cheap but it's a good spot to enjoy breakfast ($9.50 to $13.50), coffee or a light lunch if you can get a spot on the balcony. Adjacent to the wharf, the *Wheelhouse* (☎ 09-402 6281) is nothing special for food, but it's the home of the old aquarium, so you can watch the fish swim while you eat (or drink – there's a bar).

King Wah (☎ 09-402 7566) Dishes $17-22, buffet $22. In the mall, this licensed Chinese restaurant is pricey by Chinese standards but the banquets and buffets are reasonable.

Saltwater Cafe & Bar (☎ 09-402 7783, 14 Kings Rd) Pizzas $13.50-23.50. Popular with backpackers and locals alike, this lively revamped bar does good pizzas.

Vienna Inn (☎ 09-402 7867) Mains $18-23. Next to the Carvery, Vienna Inn specialises in Austrian food, naturally, including stuffed schnitzels, Berner Wurstel and crepes.

La Scaletta (☎ 09-402 7035, Selwyn Rd) This casual pizzeria, one street back from the waterfront, has tables out on its veranda. Below is the more formal **La Scala**.

Lips (☎ 09-402 7185, 14 Selwyn Rd) On the same street, this is a cosy cafe open for breakfast and lunch. Later on it's an intimate spot for a quality evening meal.

Only Seafood (☎ 09-402 6066, 40 Marsden Rd) Mains $20-27. Open from 5pm. In a converted old seafront home with indoor and outdoor dining areas, this is the place to go for seafood, including mussels, oysters and scallops. In the same house, below Only Seafood, **Bistro 40** (☎ 09-402 7444) has an interesting menu of venison, chicken and steak.

Swiss Cafe & Grill (☎ 09-402 6701, 48 Marsden Rd) Mains from $16. This European cafe has an eclectic menu that includes a hearty Swiss farmhouse plate, pizza, pasta, soups and salads, and a garden dining area.

The Boat Restaurant (☎ 09-402 7018, 1 Tau Henare Drive) $15-22. Aboard Rosemary Tarlton's Tui, the Boat is a bay experience, without actually going on the water. Seafood is a speciality, but there are steak, salad and chicken dishes. During the day there's an informal cafe here.

At Waitangi, near the visitors centre car park, is the excellent **Waikokopu Cafe** (☎ 09-402 6275) with light meals from $10. You can sit inside or out – outside has a deck that borders a little pond.

Entertainment

The evening entertainment generally begins at the **Saltwater Cafe & Bar** and/or **Pipi Patch** on Kings Rd. Saltwater has a tabletop shuffleboard – put your name on the blackboard.

Also good for a drink is the **Grand Cafe Odeon** (☎ 09-402 6677, 9 Williams Rd) in the shopping centre. It has cocktails and a jumping happy hour from 4.30pm to 6pm.

The **Lighthouse Tavern** (☎ 09-402 8324), upstairs in the shopping mall on Marsden Rd, is where the ragers kick on. It has a nightclub with occasional live bands (a small cover charge usually applies).

At Haruru Falls, the **Pines** (☎ 09-402 7195) is a tavern brewing its own draught beers. It's a convivial place with an open fire, a restaurant and entertainment on Saturday and Sunday. A courtesy coach operates to and from Paihia, if there are enough passengers.

RUSSELL
pop 1140

Historic Russell is directly across the bay from Paihia. It was originally a fortified Maori settlement which spread over the entire valley, then known as Kororareka ('sweet penguin').

Russell's early European history was turbulent. In 1830 it was the scene of the War of the Girls, when two Maori girls from different tribes each thought they were the favourite of a whaling captain. This resulted in conflict between the tribes, which the Maori leader, Titore, who was recognised as the ariki (high chief) of the area, resolved by separating the two tribes and making the border at the base of the Tapeka Peninsula. A European settlement quickly sprang up in place of the abandoned Maori village.

In 1845, during the Northland Land War, government soldiers and marines garrisoned the town after the Ngapuhi leader Hone Heke threatened to chop down the flagstaff, a symbol of Pakeha authority, again – he had already chopped it down three times. On 11 March 1845 the Ngapuhi staged a diversionary siege of Russell. It was a great tactical success, with Chief Kawiti attacking from the south and another Ngapuhi war party attacking from Long Beach. While the troops rushed off to protect the township, Hone Heke felled the hated symbol of European authority on Maiki (Flagstaff Hill) for the fourth and final time. The Pakeha were forced to evacuate to ships lying at anchor off the settlement. The captain of HMS Hazard was wounded severely in the battle and his replacement ordered the ships' cannons to be fired on the town – most of the buildings were razed.

NORTHLAND

NORTHLAND

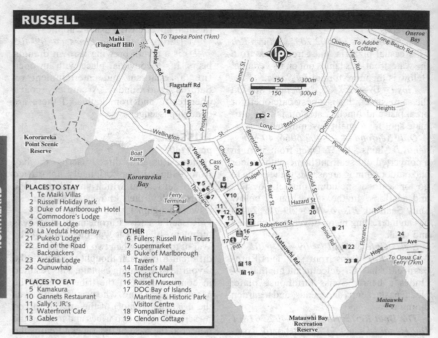

RUSSELL

To Tapeka Point (1km)
Maiki (Flagstaff Hill)
Tapeka Rd
James St
Queens View Rd
To Adobe Cottage
Long Beach Rd
Oneroa Bay
Flagstaff Rd
Queen St
Prospect St
Russell Heights
1
2
Kororareka Point Scenic Reserve
Wellington
Long Beach Rd
Beresford St
Onerou Rd
Pomare Rd
Boat Ramp
York Street
Cass St
Church St
Chapel St
Ashby St
Gould St
Kororareka Bay
3
4
9
Ferry Terminal
The Strand
8
5
6
7
10
Baker St
Hazard St
20
11
12
13
14
15
Robertson St
21
24
Ave
16
17
Pitt St
Matauwhi Rd
Bind Rd
22
Florance
Hope
23
To Opua Car Ferry (7km)
18
19
Matauwhi Bay
Matauwhi Bay Recreation Reserve

0   150   300m
0   150   300yd

PLACES TO STAY
1 Te Maiki Villas
2 Russell Holiday Park
3 Duke of Marlborough Hotel
4 Commodore's Lodge
9 Russell Lodge
20 La Veduta Homestay
21 Pukeko Lodge
22 End of the Road Backpackers
23 Arcadia Lodge
24 Ounuwhao

PLACES TO EAT
5 Kamakura
10 Gannets Restaurant
11 Sally's; JR's
12 Waterfront Cafe
13 Gables

OTHER
6 Fullers; Russell Mini Tours
7 Supermarket
8 Duke of Marlborough Tavern
14 Trader's Mall
15 Christ Church
16 Russell Museum
17 DOC Bay of Islands Maritime & Historic Park Visitor Centre
18 Pompallier House
19 Clendon Cottage

In its early days Russell was a magnet for rough elements like fleeing convicts, whalers, prostitutes and drunk sailors. Charles Darwin described it in 1835 as full of 'the refuse of society'.

Russell today is a peaceful and pretty little place, which justifiably calls itself 'romantic' in promotional material. It's a marked contrast to the hustle of Paihia across the bay. Most Bay of Islands water-based tours pick up from here, so it's certainly a suitable alternative base.

Information

There's a small information kiosk on the end of the pier where the passenger ferry drops off. The excellent DOC Bay of Islands Maritime & Historic Park visitors centre (☎ 09-403 9005) is in Russell. The *Russell Heritage Trails* pamphlet ($1.20) includes walking and driving tours.

There's Internet access at Innovation (☎ 09-403 8843) in the Trader's Mall.

Russell Museum

The Russell Museum (☎ 09-403 7701, 2 York St; adult/child $3/50c; open 10am-4pm daily) was built for the bicentenary of Cook's Bay of Islands visit in 1769. It's small but houses maritime exhibits, displays relating to Cook and his voyages, and a fine 1:5 scale model of his barque *Endeavour* – a real working model – in addition to a collection of early settlers' relics.

Pompallier House

Close by, and on a lovely waterfront site, is Pompallier House (☎ 09-403 7861; tours $5; open 10am-5pm daily), built to house the printing works for the Roman Catholic mission founded by the French missionary Bishop Pompallier in 1841. In the 1870s it was converted to a private home. One of the oldest houses in NZ, it has been restored to its original state. It is closed on weekends from June to October. Guided tours are conducted five times a day (ring for times).

Maiki

Overlooking Russell is Maiki (Flagstaff Hill), where Hone Heke made his attacks – this, the fifth flagpole, has stood for a lot longer than the first four. The view is well worth the effort to get up there, and there are several routes to the top. By car take Tapeka Rd; if on foot, take the track west from the boat ramp along the beach at low tide, or up Wellington St at high tide. Alternatively, simply walk to the end of Wellington St and take the short track up the hill, about a 30-minute climb.

Long Beach

About 1km behind Russell, to the east is Oneroa Bay, with a beautiful beach known variously as Oneroa Bay Beach, Donkey Bay Beach or Long Beach. There is an interesting **adobe cottage** here. It's about a 15-minute walk from the Russell wharf, heading over the hill on Long Beach Rd. When you reach the hill's summit, at the intersection with Queen's View Rd, there's a tiny graveyard with benches and a good view of Oneroa Bay. Turn right here and go about one block up Queen's View Rd to where it meets Oneroa Rd and the view is even better – a sweeping vista of the peninsula. There's also an unofficial nudist beach past the rocky outcrops at the northern end of the beach.

Historic Buildings

Russell lays claim to some of NZ's oldest buildings, including **Christ Church** (1847), the oldest church in NZ; it's suitably scarred with musket and cannonball holes, and has an interesting graveyard.

Clendon Cottage was built by James Clendon, US Consul in 1839, who later moved to Rawene as resident magistrate.

Organised Tours

Russell Mini Tours (*☎ 09-403 7866; adult/child $16/8*) departs from the Fullers office, fronting Russell Wharf, several times daily and visits local sites of interest. Many of the cruises out of Paihia pick up passengers at Russell about 15 minutes after their Paihia departure.

Places to Stay

Camping, Cabins & Hostels Of the two camping grounds in town, *Russell Holiday Park* (*☎ 0800 503 889, 09-403 7826, e russelltop10@xtra.co.nz, Long Beach Rd*) has plenty of lawn and a kid's playground. It has powered and unpowered sites from $11 per person, cabins from $40/55 a double and self-contained units $75 to $85. Rates are higher from Christmas to end of January.

Russell Lodge (*☎ 0800 478 773, 09-403 7640, cnr Beresford & Chapel Sts*) Dorm beds $20, doubles $55, self-contained units $105. The centrally located Russell Lodge is an odd combination of motel and backpackers. The four-bed backpacker units each have their own bathroom and there's a fully equipped kitchen and TV lounge.

End of the Road Backpackers (*☎ 09-403 7632, 24 Brind Rd*) Dorm beds $20, doubles $44. End of the Road is a small but comfortable backpackers with good views out over the marina.

Pukeko Cottage (*14 Brind St*) Dorm beds $18. Another very small hostel with just a handful of beds, this is a homely little place with an artistic owner.

B&Bs, Motels & Hotels Russell has some fine B&Bs, some of them atop the hill overlooking the town and harbour, while the waterfront is a good location for a motel or hotel room.

La Veduta Homestay (*☎ 09-403 8299, e laveduta@xtra.co.nz, cnr Gould & Hazard Sts*) Doubles $130-150. This nicely furnished B&B is run by a lovely family who ensure you feel at home. There's a good view from the front deck, a billiard room and all rooms have en suite or private bath.

Arcadia Lodge (*☎ 09-403 7756, e arcadialodge@xtra.co.nz, Florance Ave*) B&B doubles $135-200. Arcadia Lodge is a historic home (1890) full of antique furniture and with fine views over Matauwhi Bay. There's a variety of atmospheric rooms, most with en suite.

Te Maiki Villas (*☎ 09-403 7046, Flagstaff Rd*) Doubles high/low season $199/159. The fading, free-standing Te

Maiki Villas, halfway up Flagstaff Hill, have awesome views of Russell Harbour. They're not cheap but each sleeps six ($22.50 per extra person).

Ounuwhao (Harding House) (☎ 09-403 7310, fax 403 8310, ⓔ ounuwhao@bay-of-islands.co.nz, Hope Ave) B&B doubles $120-150. This is another fine period home about 1.5km from the town centre. There are four guest rooms in the main house and a self-contained cottage at the back.

Commodore's Lodge (☎ 09-403 7899, ⓔ commodores.lodge@xtra.co.nz, 28 The Strand) Studio units $120, 1-bedroom units $130-190. This motel has a good waterfront location and self-contained rooms arranged around a pleasant courtyard and swimming pool. The rooms with an aspect (waterfront or pool) are more expensive.

Duke of Marlborough Hotel (☎ 09-403 7829, ⓔ info@theduke.co.nz, 35 The Strand) Singles/doubles $95/125, superior doubles $175-280. This fine old hotel, right on the waterfront, has real old-fashioned charm although the standard rooms are not particularly special. The harbour-facing rooms are the best (and most expensive).

Places to Eat

There are a couple of decent cafes on the Strand overlooking the water. ***Waterfront Cafe*** and ***Sally's Restaurant & Cafe*** are virtually side by side and both do sandwiches, burgers, breakfast and light meals from $4 to $12. Sally's is also good for evening meals. Separating the two, ***JR's*** specialises in delicious lamb pitta bread rolls and felafels ($9).

There are several stylish upmarket restaurants on the waterfront that blend nicely with Russell's romantic character. The historic ***Duke of Marlborough Hotel*** (☎ 09-403 7829) has a dining room and bar with a fine covered veranda overlooking the water. Dinner mains are from $16.50 to $28.50. This was the first pub in NZ to get a licence, way back on 14 July 1840. Its three predecessors all burnt down.

Gables (☎ 09-403 7618, The Strand) Lunch $18, dinner $25-32. Said to be NZ's oldest operating restaurant (established 1847), the Gables is a fancy waterfront place for a stylish dinner. The à la carte menu has an international flavour.

Kamakura (☎ 09-402 7771) Mains $13-37. This is a stylish, modern and quite pricey place with a wide-ranging Pacific Rim menu. It's open for dinner from Wednesday to Sunday and lunch on Saturday and Sunday.

Gannets Restaurant (☎ 09-403 7990, cnr York & Chapel Sts) $18-29. Gannets is a quality brasserie with a blackboard menu specialising in seafood dishes such as scallops, crab and bouillabaisse, as well as steak and venison. Most dishes are available as an entree or half serve.

Getting There & Around

From Paihia, the quickest and easiest way to get to Russell is on the regular passenger ferry (adult/child $6/3 each way). Otherwise you can drive or hitch in via the Opua car ferry.

The car ferry runs continuously during the day from Opua to Okiato Point, about 8km from Russell. It operates from 6.50am to 9pm (10pm on Friday). The one-way/return fare is $8/15 for a car and driver, $4/7 for a motorcycle and rider, plus $1/2 for each additional passenger. There's a much longer dirt road to Russell, but it's a very long haul.

Russell Tuk Tuk is a Bangkok-style three-wheeler autorickshaw that can whizz you around for between $3 and $7 per person. It's usually found at the end of the town wharf.

KERIKERI
pop 4290

At the northern end of the Bay of Islands, Kerikeri is a relaxed provincial town. It has plenty of accommodation and can be used as a base for exploring the region, but is primarily a service town for the surrounding agricultural district.

The word *kerikeri* means 'to dig'; the Maori grew large crops of kumara here before the Pakeha arrived, and it was here, in 1820, that the first agricultural plough was introduced to NZ. Today it is still primarily an agricultural region, with kiwi

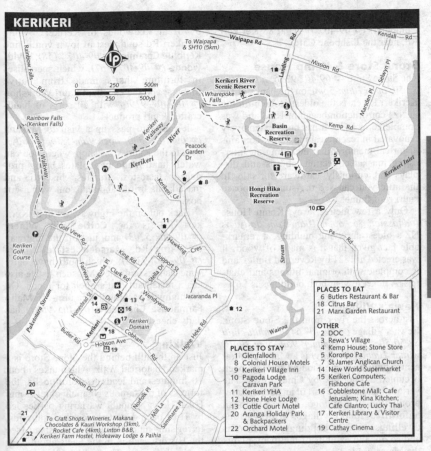

KERIKERI

NORTHLAND

PLACES TO EAT
6 Butlers Restaurant & Bar
18 Citrus Bar
21 Marx Garden Restaurant

OTHER
2 DOC
3 Rewa's Village
4 Kemp House; Stone Store
5 Kororipo Pa
7 St James Anglican Church
14 New World Supermarket
15 Kerikeri Computers;
   Fishbone Cafe
16 Cobblestone Mall; Cafe
   Jerusalem; Kina Kitchen;
   Cafe Cilantro; Lucky Thai
17 Kerikeri Library & Visitor
   Centre
19 Cathay Cinema

PLACES TO STAY
1 Glenfalloch
8 Colonial House Motels
9 Kerikeri Village Inn
10 Pagoda Lodge
   Caravan Park
11 Kerikeri YHA
12 Hone Heke Lodge
13 Cottle Court Motel
20 Aranga Holiday Park
   & Backpackers
22 Orchard Motel

fruit, citrus and other orchards. Large numbers of itinerant farm workers congregate in Kerikeri for the six-week kiwi fruit harvest beginning in early May, but orchard work of one kind or another is usually available year-round.

Kerikeri is significant in NZ history. It became the site of the country's second mission station when the Reverend Samuel Marsden chose the site at the head of the Kerikeri inlet under the protection of the Ngapuhi chief, Hongi Hika. In November 1819 the Reverend John Butler arrived at the site and set up the mission headquarters.

New Zealand's oldest building made of wood, Kemp House, and its oldest stone building, the Stone Store, were established as part of this mission.

Information
An informal visitors centre (☎ 09-407 9297) is in the library on Cobham Rd, open from 9am to 5pm Monday to Friday and 10am to noon on Saturday. You can also get local information at Rewa's Village and on the Internet at **W** www.kerikeri.co.nz. Get information on walks in the area from DOC (☎ 09-407 8474) at 34 Landing Rd.

Internet access is available at Kerikeri Computers (☎ 09-407 7941) at 88 Kerikeri Rd, near the Fishbone Cafe.

Stone Store & Kemp House

The Stone Store (☎ 09-407 9236; admission $2.50; open 10am-5pm), on the banks of the Kerikeri River, is the oldest stone building in NZ; construction began in 1833 and was completed in 1836. It has been extensively renovated in recent years and now contains historical memorabilia, including an interesting musket collection, photos and displays and, curiously, hardware for sale. In the attic you can see the superb exposed kauri roof frame.

Only a few metres away, Kemp House (admission $5; open 10am-5pm daily) is NZ's oldest surviving building, a remarkable fact given that it is made of wood. It was erected in 1821 by Reverend Butler, and is complete with original fittings and chattels. A ticket to visit both buildings is $6.

Rewa's Village

Just across the river from the Stone Store, Rewa's Village (☎ 09-407 6454; adult/child $2.50/50c; open summer 9am-5pm daily, winter 10am-4pm daily) is a Maori cultural centre built on a site thought to have been occupied at one time by Chief Rewa. The various buildings are part of an authentic reproduction of a kainga, a pre-European unfortified Maori village, with various dwellings, kitchen buildings, storerooms and so on, and exhibits of the many plants the Maori used.

Arts, Crafts, Food & Wine

The Kerikeri area is home to many artists and craftspeople. Several shops display their work, and in most you can see work in progress, especially pottery. You can also spend an enjoyable afternoon tasting wines, cheese and chocolate.

On the highway (SH10) there are several good shops, including the Origin Art & Craft Cooperative (☎ 09-407 1133), with its many different kinds of local, including stained glass, leatherwork and paintings; Akatere Wool Craft (☎ 09-407 6199), near

Pungaere Rd; and Moonpotz (☎ 09-407 6446) at Redwoods of Kerikeri. Along Kerikeri Rd southwest of town you'll find Keriblue Ceramics (☎ 09-407 7158); Wyldwoode (☎ 09-4079767), which specialises in furniture that's made from native timbers; and the excellent Kauri Workshop (☎ 09-407 9196) with all sorts of handcrafted kauri products.

It's hard to pass up a visit to Makana (☎ 09-407 6800; open 9am-5.30pm daily), next to the Kauri Workshop, where you can watch hand-made chocolates being produced, taste-test truffles, biscotti and macadamia brittle and walk out with a gift box.

Back out on the highway, south of Kerikeri Rd is the Cottle Hill Winery (☎ 09-407 5203) and, just off the highway on Wiroa Rd, Marsden Estate Winery (☎ 09-407 9398), which both have daily wine tastings and sales. Marsden Estate also has a restaurant that's open for lunch. On the highway past the Paihia turn-off, Maho Farmhouse Cheese (☎ 09-405 9681) has daily cheese tastings.

Walking

Just up the hill behind the Stone Store is a marked Historical Walk, which takes about 10 minutes and leads to Kororipo Pa, the fortress of the famous Ngapuhi chief Hongi Hika. Huge Ngapuhi warfaring parties led by Hika once departed from here on raids, terrorising much of the North Island (see the History section in the Facts about New Zealand chapter). The walk finally emerges near the St James Anglican church, which was built in 1878.

Across the river from the Stone Store is a scenic reserve with several marked tracks. There's a 4km Kerikeri River track leading to Rainbow Falls, passing by the Wharepoke Falls (Fairy Pools) along the way. Alternatively, you can reach the Rainbow Falls from Waipapa Rd, in which case it's only a 10-minute walk to the falls. The Fairy Pools are great for swimming and picnics and can be reached from the dirt road beside the YHA hostel, if you're not up to the hike along the river.

Places to Stay

Camping & Cabins There are several camping grounds near town, catering to a mix of tourists and workers.

Aranga Holiday Park & Backpackers *(☎ 09-407 9326, Kerikeri Rd)* Powered/unpowered sites $10/9 per person, dorm beds $15, double cabins $34-38, self-contained double units $58-68. Aranga Park is the closest park to town and is in a lovely setting beside the Puketotara Stream, and a mere five minutes' walk from town. There's a decent range of accommodation styles here, cheap weekly rates and impressive facilities, including a brilliant, covered barbecue area featuring a spa pool and a retractable roof!

Pagoda Lodge Caravan Park *(☎ 09-407 8617, Pa Rd)* Powered sites $12 per person, cabin $45, self-contained double units $65-75. Pagoda Lodge is located at the inlet across from the Stone Store, but to reach it by vehicle requires the long drive around Inlet Rd. The historic waterfront Jade Cottage (sleeps two) is popular here ($85).

Hostels Kerikeri has a couple of good backpacker places, and two that are popular with itinerant workers, with cheap weekly rates and contacts for finding orchard work.

Kerikeri YHA *(☎ 09-407 9391,* e *yha keri@yha.org.nz, 144 Kerikeri Rd)* Camp sites $11, dorm beds $16-18, doubles $40-44 per person. This place has a big garden leading down to the river and a bit more character than some YHAs, with a funky common room and 'earthy' atmosphere.

Kerikeri Farm Hostel *(☎ 09-407 6989,* e *kkfarmhostel@xtra.co.nz)* Dorm beds $17, singles $25, twins & doubles $40, self-contained unit $65. This comfortable lodge, 1.5km north of the Kerikeri turn-off on SH10, is on a pleasant family farm and orchard where the owners encourage you to participate in farm and orchard activities.

Hone Heke Lodge *(☎/fax 09-407 8170,* e *honeheke@xtra.co.nz, 65 Hone Heke Rd)* Dorm beds $15, singles/doubles $28/36, en suite doubles $44. Hone Heke is in a quiet residential area, although it can get pretty loud with partying workers. It's a good place to set up for a while if you're looking for work.

Hideaway Lodge *(☎ 0800 562746, 09-407 9773, Wiroa Rd)* Camp sites $9 per person, dorm beds $14, singles/doubles $25/35. Hideaway Lodge is another good place to stay at, if you're looking for work. It's a spacious place with cheap weekly rates and the owners are on the ball when it comes to helping you to find work. It's 4km out, west of the SH10 junction, but there are free rides to town. The lodge has a pool and games room and a lively atmosphere.

B&Bs & Guesthouses About 500m north of the Stone Store, ***Glenfalloch*** *(☎/fax 09-407 5471,* e *glenfall@ihug.co.nz, Landing Rd)* is a relaxing homestay B&B with a pleasant patio and garden pool. There's one single for $55, and comfortable en suite doubles for $85 and $90.

Kerikeri Village Inn *(☎ 09-407 4666,* e *kerikeri.village.inn@xtra.co.nz, 165 Kerikeri Rd)* Rooms $145-165. This is a stylish contemporary B&B with a Mediterranean flavour and fine views over the inlet and valley. There are three large en suite rooms.

Linton B&B *(☎ 09-407 7654, Kerikeri Rd)* B&B single/double $40/60, family room $120. Linton is a no-frills family-run B&B with separate en suite units. It's set on a large garden property.

Motels A cut above your average motel, ***Colonial House Motels*** *(☎ 0800 242 555, 09-407 9106,* e *colonial.lodge@xtra.co.nz, 178 Kerikeri Rd)* has one- and two-bedroom cottages, apartments and family units in a lovely garden setting from $95 to $140.

Cottle Court Motel *(☎ 09-407 8867, Kerikeri Rd)* 1-bedroom units $90. Cottle Court is as central as you can get and has spacious modern units and a heated outdoor pool.

Orchard Motel *(☎ 0508 808 869, 09-407 8869,* e *orchardmotel@xtra.co.nz, Kerikeri Rd)* Doubles from $72. About 1km south of the town centre, the Orchard has well-kept rooms, plenty of space and an outdoor pool and spa.

Places to Eat & Drink

Kerikeri's main street has quite a few cafes and takeaways. The *Fishbone Cafe* (☎ 09-407 6065) is the place for good espresso, light meals, soups and salads.

The Cobblestone Mall has several good choices. *Lucky Thai* (☎ 09-407 1127) has eat-in/takeaway Thai dishes for around $10. *Cafe Jerusalem* (☎ 09-407 1001), an Israeli/Middle Eastern café, does genuine felafel, shwarma and even sticky sweet baklava, eat in or takeaway ($7.50 to $15).

Kina Kitchen (☎ 09-407 7669) Mains $23. Also in the mall, Kina has a limited menu of pasta, *cervena* (venison) and seafood, but the quality is high and servings generous.

Rocket Cafe (☎ 09-407 3100, *Kerikeri Rd*) Near the intersection with SH10, Rocket is an excellent cafe and deli specialising in fresh local produce.

Citrus Bar (☎ 09-407 1050) Meals $8-22. Citrus is a sports-music bar and the most popular nightspot in town. You can get bagels and wraps in the afternoon, and a blackboard dinner menu which includes pizza and nachos.

Butler's Restaurant & Bar (☎ 09-407 8479, *Stone Store Basin*) Lunch $9.50-20, dinner $18-25. Opposite the Stone Store, Butler's is a good spot for breakfast or lunch, especially out on the veranda overlooking the inlet. In the evening it's an atmospheric à la carte restaurant.

Marx Garden Restaurant (☎ 09-407 6606, *Kerikeri Rd*) Mains $25-29. For fine dining, Marx is among Kerikeri's best. Set back off the road, the converted house is in a leafy garden, with an à la carte menu including steak and pasta dishes. It's open for dinner Monday to Saturday and lunch Tuesday to Saturday.

Getting There & Away

Both InterCity and Northliner Express buses arrive at and depart from Cobham Rd, just off Kerikeri Rd in the centre of town. Both companies have buses departing from Kerikeri in the morning for the half-hour trip to Paihia. The return bus service is in the evening.

Paihia to Whangarei

There are two scenic routes out on the east coast: the back road from Russell to SH1, and the drive out to Tutukaka from Hikurangi on SH1, which loops around to Whangarei. Out to sea are the Poor Knights Islands, a paradise for divers.

RUSSELL ROAD

The back road from Russell skirts around the coast before joining SH1 at Whakapara. The scenic road is long, unsealed and rough for most of the way – strictly for those with their own transport, plenty of time and a desire to get off the beaten track.

From Russell, the road starts near Orango Bay and skirts along the Waikare Inlet before reaching the Waikare Rd to Waihaha. This turn-off eventually leads back to the

Artistic Relief

If you take the main highway between Paihia and Whangarei, you'll pass (or pass through) Kawakawa, a quiet town with little of interest to the traveller – except for a peek at the public toilets.

Designed in 1997 by the late Austrian-born artist Friedensreich Hundertwasser, the unique earth-canopy toilet block, fronted by colourful ceramic columns, is certainly an interesting sight. Hundertwasser was no stranger to unusual building projects. As a renowned architect, designer and artist in Vienna he worked on such radical projects as an industrial incinerator, a block of flats, and the innovative KunstHausWien gallery, using his trademark uneven lines, patchwork coloured ceramics and grassed roofs.

Hundertwasser moved to the Kawakawa area in the 1970s and although leading something of a reclusive life, he was keen to take on the project, using local artists, labour and materials. He died in February 2000, but certainly left his mark on Kawakawa.

highway and Paihia. It's about a 90-minute drive from Russell.

Continuing along Russell Road past the Waihaha turn-off, there's access to the **Ngaiotonga Scenic Reserve**, which conserves the mixed forest that once prevailed throughout Northland. There are two short walks: the 20-minute **Kauri Grove Nature Walk** and the 10-minute **Twin Bole Kauri Walk**.

Further on is the turn-off to isolated **Rawhiti**, a small Ngapuhi settlement where life still revolves around the *marae*. Rawhiti is also the starting point for the trek to **Cape Brett**, a hard 7½-hour walk to the top of the peninsula, where overnight stays are possible in the Cape Brett Hut. You can book the hut and get information on the walk at the Bay of Islands Maritime & Historic Park visitors centre (☎ 09-403 9005) in Russell.

Closer to the Rawhiti turn-off, a shorter one-hour walk leads through tribal land and over the headland to Whangamumu Harbour. At the main beach on the harbour, the **Whangamumu Scenic Reserve** has camping. There are over 40 prehistoric sites on the peninsula and the remains of an unusual whaling station. A net, fastened between the mainland and Net Rock, was used to ensnare or slow down whales so the harpooners could get an easy shot in.

Further south, another side road leads to the **Whangaruru North Head Scenic Reserve**, which has beaches, camping grounds, walks and fine coastal scenery in a farmland park setting.

Whangaruru Beach Camp (☎ 09-433 6806) and, further south at Oakura, *Oakura Motels and Caravan Park* (☎ 09-433 6803) both have camping, cabins and motel units.

At Helena Bay, Russell Road returns to tarseal and leads back to SH1. About 8km from Helena Bay along a rough, winding side road is the **Mimiwhangata Coastal Park**. This is a truly scenic part of the coastline, with coastal dunes, pohutukawa, jutting headlands and picturesque beaches. There is a luxurious *lodge* run by DOC, and a simpler but comfortable *cottage*; both sleep eight people. Camping is also possible ($6). Book and inquire about fees with

DOC in Russell (☎ 09-403 9005) or the Whangarei visitors centre.

TUTUKAKA COAST

At Hikurangi on SH1 you can turn off for the scenic route to Whangarei via the Tutukaka Coast. The first place on the coast is **Sandy Bay** surf beach, followed by a succession of idyllic bays where you can surf, swim, walk and, most popularly, fish.

Whananaki Trail Rides (☎ 09-433 8299) has farmhouse dorm accommodation for $15 and free camping if you're participating in horse rides ($40 for two hours, or $200 for a two-day trek).

Tiny, exclusive **Tutukaka** is the home of the Whangarei Deep Sea Anglers Club and the beautiful harbour is cluttered with yachts and fishing boats. The yacht club here launched an ambitious multimillion dollar challenge for the 1995 America's Cup, eventually won by Auckland-based *Black Magic*.

Tutukaka is best known as a premier game-fishing destination, and late in the day marlin and other catch are weighed in. It's also a base for diving trips to the Poor Knights Islands.

Tutukaka Charter Boat Association (☎ 09-434 3818) is a well-organised group at the marina that handles fishing, diving and cruise charters. This is also the place to go **shark-cage diving** (☎ 09-434 3233). Mako and blue sharks are found in these waters from December to May.

If you love seafood, Tutukaka has a couple of fine restaurants right on the marina. The casual *Schnappa Rock Cafe* (☎ 09-434 3774) is a great place for lunch, and the more fancy *Blue Marlin Restaurant* (☎ 09-434 3909) at the Whangarei Deep Sea Anglers Club, is just right for an evening splurge.

Ngunguru, located a few kilometres on from Tutukaka, is more of a service centre than anything else, with shops, motels and other facilities. The *Ngunguru Holiday Camp* (☎ 09-434 3851, Papaka Rd) has accommodation such as camping ($25 for two), cabins ($35 to $55) and dorm beds ($15 per person).

NORTHLAND

POOR KNIGHTS ISLANDS MARINE RESERVE

This marine reserve, 24km off Northland's east coast near Tutukaka, was established in 1981. It is reputed to have the best scuba diving in NZ and has been rated as one of the top diving spots in the world.

The two large islands, Tawhiti Rahi and Aorangi, were once home to members of the Ngati Wai tribe but, since a raiding-party massacre in the early 1800s, the islands have been *tapu* (sacred). You're *not* allowed to land on the islands but you can swim near them.

Since the northern islands are bathed in a subtropical current, varieties of tropical and subtropical fish not seen in other coastal waters are observed here. The waters are clear and there are no problems with sediment. The underwater cliffs drop steeply (about 70m) to a sandy bottom, where there is a labyrinth of archways, caves and tunnels, packed with a bewildering variety of fish. For a comprehensive coverage of the islands and surrounding marine life, check out *Poor Knights Wonderland* ($25.95) by Glen Edney, available from local dive shops.

As the islands are relatively isolated from the mainland they have acted as a sanctuary for flora and fauna – the most famous example is the prehistoric tuatara (see the special colour section 'Watching Wildlife').

You can organise diving trips to the islands from Whangarei and Tutukaka. A sightseeing day trip on the boats costs around $60 to $80. Divers should count on about $150 to 175 for full diving equipment and two dives ($95 for dives only).

Recommended operators in Tutukaka are **Dive! Tutukaka** (☎ *0800 288 882, 09-434 3867,* W *www.diving.co.nz*), next to the Schnappa Cafe; and **Dive Poor Knights** (☎ *0800 564 4487,* W *www.nzdive.com*).

There are a number of operators based in Whangarei, including: **Pacific Hideaway** (☎ *09-437 3632,* W *www.divenz.co.nz, 13 Moody Ave*); **Knight Diver Tours** (☎ *0800 766 756,* W *www.poorknights.co.nz*); **Dive Connection** (☎ *09-430 0818, 140 Lower Cameron St*); and **Dive HQ** (☎ *09-438 1075,* W *www.divenow.co.nz*).

There are also opportunities for diving on the wrecks of the naval boats *Tui* and *Waikato*, both scuttled in the reserve for recreational diving. Dive! Tutukaka has guided dives on both wrecks for $95 ($175 with full gear). A five-day PADI open-water course with Dive! Tutukaka costs $550, which also includes two days of diving around the islands.

The MV ***Wairangi*** (☎ *09-434 3350)* has interesting ecotourism trips along the coast and to the islands.

WHANGAREI

pop 45,800

Whangarei is the major city of Northland and a haven for yachts. It's a pleasant enough city with an equable climate, but with the Bay of Islands just up the road, most travellers don't find a pressing reason to stay here long. Most of the attractions are in the surrounding area – the beaches at Whangarei Heads, about 35km east of town, and diving around the Poor Knights Islands.

The climate and soil combine to make Whangarei a gardener's paradise – many parks and gardens thrive in this city; there's an interesting collection of dry-stone walls just north of the city.

Information

The Whangarei visitors centre (☎ 09-438 1079, e whangarei@clear.net.nz) is at Tarewa Park, Otaika Rd (SH1), at the southern entrance to town. It's open from 8.30am to 5pm Monday to Friday and 10am to 4pm Saturday and Sunday (8.30am to 6.30pm daily in January).

Also here is the DOC office (☎ 09-438 0299), with information on camping, recreational activities, maps and hut tickets, as well as an environmental shop with souvenirs. The AA office (☎ 09-438 4848) is on the corner of Robert and John Sts.

Internet access can be found at the visitors centre and at the post office on the Town Basin.

Things to See & Do

Boats from around the world are moored in the **Town Basin**, an attractive area right on

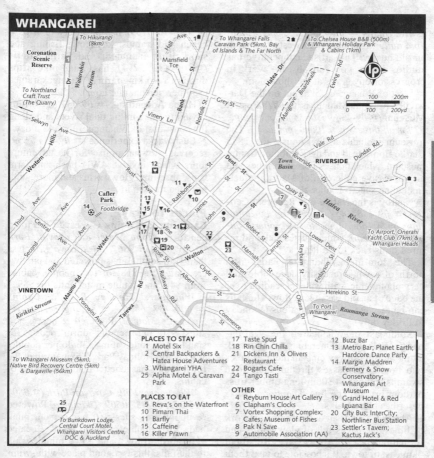

WHANGAREI

NORTHLAND

PLACES TO STAY
1 Motel Six
2 Central Backpackers & Hatea House Adventures
3 Whangarei YHA
25 Alpha Motel & Caravan Park

PLACES TO EAT
5 Reva's on the Waterfront
10 Pimarn Thai
11 Barfly
15 Caffeine
16 Killer Prawn
17 Taste Spud
18 Rin Chin Chilla
21 Dickens Inn & Olivers Restaurant
22 Bogarts Cafe
24 Tango Tasti

OTHER
4 Reyburn House Art Gallery
6 Clapham's Clocks
7 Vortex Shopping Complex; Cafes; Museum of Fishes
8 Pak N Save
9 Automobile Association (AA)
12 Buzz Bar
13 Metro Bar; Planet Earth; Hardcore Dance Party
14 Margie Maddren Fernery & Snow Conservatory; Whangarei Art Museum
19 Grand Hotel & Red Iguana Bar
20 City Bus; InterCity; Northliner Bus Station
23 Settler's Tavern; Kactus Jack's

the edge of the town centre along Quay St. The waterfront along the river has been smartened up and has a number of attractions including **Clapham's Clocks** (☎ *09-438 3993; adult/child $5/3; open 9am-5pm daily*), in a modern building with a striking mural on the facade and an awesome 1300 timepieces inside, all ticking away furiously. Admission includes a guided tour.

Also at the Town Basin is the **Museum of Fishes** (☎ *09-438 5681; adult/child $5/2; open 10am-4pm daily*). Fishing enthusiasts will appreciate the stuffed game fish – otherwise forget it. There are several

Edwardian-style shops, galleries and cafes here, including the Vortex complex, *New Zealand Fudge*, and the busy *Mondo's Cafe*.

Spanning a stream in the centre of town, **Cafler Park** (*admission free; open 10am-4pm daily*) has well-tended flowerbeds, and the **Margie Maddren Fernery & Snow Conservatory** (*admission free; open 10am-4pm daily*), an all-native fernery. Also here is the **Whangarei Art Museum** (☎ *09-430 7240, admission by donation; open 10am-4.30pm Tues-Fri, noon-4.30pm Sat & Sun*) which showcases arts and crafts from Northland.

The Northland Craft Trust, known simply as **The Quarry** (☎ *09-438 1215; open 10am-4pm daily*), is about 500m west of town in an old quarry. This artists' cooperative has studios where you can observe work in progress or buy crafts at the showroom.

West of Whangarei, 5km out on the Dargaville Road at Maunu, is the **Whangarei Museum** (☎ *09-438 9630; $3 for one venue, $7 for all three; open 10am-4pm daily*). The museum includes a kiwi house, the 1885 Clarke Homestead and the Exhibition Centre museum, which houses European relics and an impressive collection of Maori artefacts (including superb feather cloaks).

Nearby is the **Native Bird Recovery Centre** (☎ *09-438 1457; admission by donation; open 10am-4pm Mon-Fri, afternoons only Sat & Sun*), which nurses sick and injured birds back to health.

The 26m-high **Whangarei Falls**, 5km north of town, are easily accessible and very photogenic, with water cascading over the edge of an old basalt lava flow. The falls can be reached by Tikipunga bus (Monday to Friday only).

Southeast of Whangarei, the **Waimahanga Walkway** in Onerahi is an easy walk along an old railway embankment. It takes two hours and passes through mangrove swamps and over a 300m-long timber truss harbour bridge. The free *Whangarei Walks* describes more walks.

Abbey Caves is an undeveloped network of limestone caves full of glowworms and formations just off Abbey Caves Rd, about 4km east of town. It's possible to visit them alone for free (take a torch and strong shoes), but you'll get further with a guided tour. **Hatea Adventures** (☎ *09-437 6174*), at Central Backpackers, has 1¼ hour trips into the caves for $15 and more adventurous 2½ hour tours for $35. **Bunkdown Lodge** also offers evening glowworm trips to the caves.

Activities

Whangarei is a popular centre for diving and fishing, mostly organised out of Tutukaka.

Northland Districts Aero Club (☎ *09-436 0890*) has scenic flights and tandem skydiving; **Northland Coastal Adventures** (☎ *09-436 0139*) has a variety of trips – beach and tramps, kayaking, fishing and snorkelling included; and **Farm Safaris** (☎ *09-432 3794*) has quad-bike trips through a working farm at Maungakaramea ($50 per person, one hour).

Hatea Adventures (☎ *09-437 6174*) runs kayaking tours in the tidal rivers and along the coast east of Whangarei for $45 a day.

Bushwacka Experience (☎ *09-434 7839*) receives glowing praise for its adventure tours which involve 4WD bush and farm trips, abseiling, glowworms and more, with billy tea thrown in.

Places to Stay

Camping & Cabins Closest to the town centre is *Alpha Motel & Caravan Park* (☎/*fax 09-438 9867, 34 Tarewa Rd*), less than 1km south. It has powered and unpowered sites for $18 for two people, cabins from $40, and double motel units for $59.

Whangarei Holiday Park & Cabins (☎ *09-437 6856,* e *whangarei@actrix .co.nz, 24 Mair St*) Powered & unpowered sites $10 per person, dorm beds $15, standard/en suite cabins $36/46 per double. Whangarei Holiday Park, 2.5km north of the town centre, has a better than average set of cabins.

Whangarei Falls Caravan Park (☎ *0800 227 222, 09-437 0609, Tikipunga*) Powered & unpowered sites $10 per person, bunk beds $15, double cabins $32-38. Located 5km north of town and a two-minute walk to the falls, this is a good place with swimming and spa pools and cheap backpacker accommodation.

Hostels On the highway just south of the city centre, *Bunkdown Lodge* (☎ *09-438 8886,* w *www.bunkdownlodge.co.nz, 23 Otaika Rd*) is a comfortable place with well-equipped communal areas, a garden aviary and a homely atmosphere. Dorm beds are $17 to $20, twins/doubles $44/50.

Whangarei YHA (☎ *09-438 8954,* e *yhawhangarei@hotmail.com, 52 Punga Grove Ave*) Dorm beds $18, twins & doubles $36-42. This is a small, easygoing hostel with good views from the hilltop location. It's a short walk from town, but the final climb is up a steep hill – take the signposted short cut from Dundas Rd if walking.

Central Backpackers (☎ *09-437 6174,* **e** *centralback@xtra.co.nz, 67 Hatea Dr)* Dorm beds $18, singles $32-40, doubles $40, double cabins $47. Close to the town centre, this long-running backpackers is in an ageing but cosy home. The owners know a lot about the area and organise caving and kayaking trips.

Motels & Guesthouses Whangarei has plenty of motels, particularly along the highway (SH1) on the north and south approaches into town.

Motel Six (☎ *0800 668 356, 09-438 9219, 153 Bank St)* and **Central Court Motel** (☎*/fax 09-438 4574, 54 Otaika Rd)* are good budget choices with doubles from $60 to $80.

Also good is colonial-style **Stonehaven** (☎ *09-437 6898,* **e** *stonehaven-motel@ xtra.co.nz, 30 Mill Rd)* with studios and self-contained units from $75 to $95.

Chelsea House B&B (☎ *0508 243573,* **e** *mel.clarke@clear.net.nz, 83 Hatea Dr)* Twins/doubles $70/90. Just north of the town centre, Chelsea House is peaceful and set back from the road. The two rooms have en suites and the double has a kitchen.

Places to Eat

For cheap eats, **Taste Spud** (☎ *09-438 1198, Water St)* has about 20 different kinds of filled baked potatoes ($5) and a few Mexican and Indian snacks. There's a second branch called **Tango Tasti Food** at 99 Cameron St.

Caffeine (☎ *09-438 6925, 4 Water St)* Meals $8-12. Caffeine is Whangarei's top cafe for good coffee, atmosphere and ready-made snacks such as bagels, pizza slice and quiche ($5 to $8).

Reva's on the Waterfront (☎ *09-438 8969, Town Basin)* Mains $18-28. Whangarei's most famous restaurant and bar, Reva's sits right on the water overlooking the basin. It gets busy with yachties and others on weekends. The food is less

exciting than the location, with burritos, pizza, pasta and steaks dominating.

Killer Prawn (☎ *09-430 3333, Bank St)* Mains $22-29, prawn dishes all $27.50. You know what you're in for when you dine at Killer Prawn – and they do it well. With 19 different prawn dishes and other seafood options (sashimi, chowder, crab etc) on the menu, this restaurant and bar is one of Whangarei's hot spots.

Rin Chin Chilla (☎ *09-438 5882, 6 Vine St)* Meals $6.50-9.50. Trendy Rin Chin Chilla is all orange and black with cheap kebabs, tacos and Tex-Mex dishes.

Bogart's (☎ *09-438 3088, cnr Cameron & Walton Sts)* $15-28. Bogarts is a fashionable little corner cafe serving better than average pizzas, pasta, nachos and salads.

Pimarn Thai (☎ *09-430 0718, 12 Rathbone St)* $13-18. Pimarn is a centrally located, authentic Thai place with quite inexpensive eat-in or takeaway food.

Barfly (☎ *09-438 8761, 13 Rathbone St)* A trendy bar with pizza and other light meals, Barfly usually has live music on weekends and tables out the front.

There's no shortage of pub food in Whangarei. In the town centre, **Dickens Inn & Olivers Restaurant** (☎ *09-430 0406, cnr Cameron & Quality Sts)* is a busy place open for breakfast, lunch and dinner and offers the best of pub-style dining.

Entertainment

Unlike, say, Paihia, much of Whangarei's nightlife is aimed at locals rather than tourists, and there are quite a few hip bars and nightclubs. Local advice is to start with a drink at the Killer Prawn and follow the crowds!

Most of the late-night action is along the southern end of Bank St, where you'll find the **Metro Bar**, **Planet Earth** and the **Hardcore Dance Company**.

Kactus Jack's, a nightclub behind the Settler's Tavern, is popular and features local bands.

The **Red Iguana Bar** in the Grand Hotel has live music on weekends, and **Reva's on the Waterfront** is a casual place for live music on most weekdays in summer.

NORTHLAND

Getting There & Away

Air Air New Zealand Link has daily flights between Auckland and Whangarei, with onward connections. Great Barrier Airlines (☎ 0800 900 600) flies thrice weekly between Whangarei and Great Barrier Island.

The Whangarei Airport Shuttle (☎ 09-437 0666) has a door-to-door service for $8.

Bus The InterCity bus depot (☎ 09-438 2653) is on Rose St. InterCity has frequent buses between Auckland and Whangarei, continuing north to Paihia, Hokianga Harbour and Kaitaia, with another route to Dargaville.

Northliner stops here on its Auckland-Kaitaia service via the Bay of Islands and operates from the Northliner Terminal (☎ 09-438 3206), 11 Rose St.

AROUND WHANGAREI
Whangarei Heads

From Whangarei, Heads Rd winds its way around the northern shore of Whangarei Harbour, passing picturesque coves and bays on its way to the heads at the harbour entrance. This drive (there is no bus) has magnificent scenery and passes small settlements such as Parua Bay, McLeod Bay and McKenzie Bay. There are great views from the top of 419m **Mt Manaia**, a sheer rock outcrop above McLeod Bay, but it is a hard, steep climb.

Urquharts Bay near the heads has good views (somewhat blighted by the oil refinery on the other side), and from adjoining Woolshed Bay it is a 30-minute walk over the headland to the delightful beach at Smugglers Bay.

You can also make a detour from Parua Bay to beautiful **Pataua**, a sleepy fishing settlement that lies on a shallow inlet. A footbridge leads to the small offshore island, which has a surf beach.

Marsden Point Refinery Model

New Zealand's only oil refinery is at Marsden Point, across the harbour from Whangarei Heads.

At the information centre (☎ 09-432 8194) on Marsden Point Rd, Ruakaka, open 10am-5pm daily, there is a 130 sq m scale model of the refinery, accurate down to the last valve and pump.

Coromandel Region

The Coromandel is a rugged, densely forested peninsula where rivers force their way through gorges and pour down steep cliffs to the sea. With its beautiful coastal scenery and fine beaches, the peninsula is a bit of a summer playground for New Zealanders; from Christmas onwards it gets very busy in the small coastal towns and holiday resorts. The Coromandel Forest Park stretches almost the entire length of the peninsula, getting more rugged and isolated the further north you go.

South of the Coromandel Peninsula are the pancake-flat Hauraki Plains and, to the west, the bird-watchers' heaven, the Firth of Thames.

Getting There & Away

Air Great Barrier Airlines (☎ 0800 900 600, 09-256 6500) services the Coromandel Peninsula. Flights operate twice daily in summer between Auckland and Whitianga.

There are also flights between Whitianga and Great Barrier Island (Claris) via Pauanui and Matarangi. In summer there are flight departures from Whitianga on Friday and Sunday at 10am and from Great Barrier at 2pm.

Bus Thames is the transport hub of the Coromandel. InterCity (☎ 09-913 6100) has daily buses from Auckland to Thames (two hours), from where you can continue on to Paeroa, Waihi, Tauranga and Rotorua.

The Coromandel Loop pass ($54/36 adult/child) allows you to travel around the peninsula from Thames to Coromandel Town and Whitianga, then back to Thames. The Coromandel Trail pass ($101/68) starts from Auckland, includes the Coromandel Loop, and goes on to Rotorua.

A third pass, the suitably named Forests, Islands and Geysers ($341/228), combines parts of Northland (Waipoua Kauri Forest and the Bay of Islands) with a flight to Great Barrier Island and then another on to

Highlights

- Sailing, swimming, windsurfing and kayaking around Mercury Bay and Cathedral Cove
- Digging a natural spa bath in the sand at Hot Water Beach
- Driving or cycling along the peninsula's dramatic coastal scenery
- Trekking from Fletcher Bay to Stony Bay in the far north
- Walking in the rugged Coromandel Forest Park, especially the Pinnacles walk
- Exploring the historic goldmining towns of Thames and Waihi
- Bird-watching at the Firth of Thames

Whitianga, before finally doing the bus journey on to Rotorua.

Go Kiwi Shuttles (☎ 0800 446549, 09-866 0336) operates a door-to-door service from Auckland city and Auckland airport to Whitianga via Thames, Coromandel and Whangamata. Auckland to Whitianga costs $52, Auckland to Thames $38. There are discounts of around 15% for backpackers.

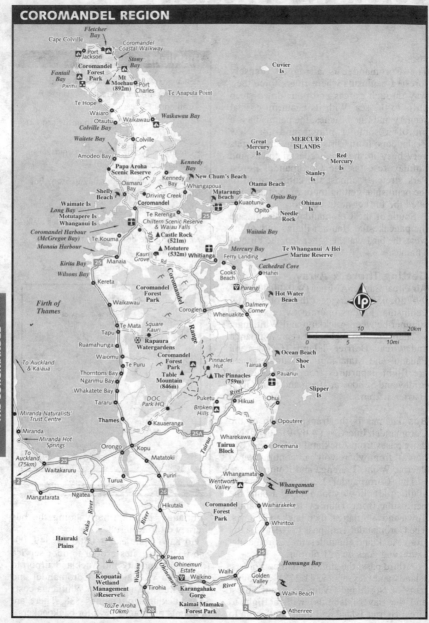

COROMANDEL REGION

Fletcher Bay
Cape Colville
Port Jackson
Coromandel Coastal Walkway
Stony Bay
Fantail Bay
Coromandel Forest Park
Parifu
Mt Moehau (892m)
Port Charles
Te Anaputa Point
Te Hope
Waiaro
Otautu
Waikawau
Waikawau Bay
Colville Bay
Waitete Bay
Colville
Amodeo Bay
Papa Aroha Scenic Reserve
Kennedy Bay
New Chum's Beach
Whangapoua
Otama Beach
Oamaru Bay
Kennedy Bay
Matarangi Beach
Opito Bay
Shelly Beach
Driving Creek
Kuaotunu
Ohinau Is
Waimate Is
Coromandel
Opito
Needle Rock
Long Bay
Motutapere Is
Te Rerenga
Whanganui Is
Chiltern Scenic Reserve & Waiau Falls
Coromandel Harbour (McGregor Bay)
Te Kouma
Castle Rock (521m)
Waitaia Bay
Manaia Harbour
Motutere (532m)
Whitianga
Mercury Bay
Te Whanganui A Hei Marine Reserve
Kirita Bay
Kauri Grove
Ferry Landing
Cathedral Cove
Wilsons Bay
Manaia
Cooks Beach
Hahei
Kereta
Parangi
Coromandel Forest Park
Coroglen
Hot Water Beach
Firth of Thames
Waikawau
Whenuakite
Dalmeny Corner
Te Mata
Square Kauri
Rapaura Watergardens
Ocean Beach
Ruamahunga
Shoe Is
Waiomu
Te Puru
Coromandel Forest Park
Pinnacles Hut
Tairua
Pauanui
Thorntons Bay
Table Mountain (846m)
The Pinnacles (759m)
Ngarimu Bay
Slipper Is
Whakatete Bay
DOC Park HQ
Puketu
Ohui
Tararu
Broken Hills
Hikuai
To Auckland & Kaiaua
Thames
Kauaeranga
Opoutere
Miranda Naturalists' Trust Centre
Wharekawa
Miranda
Orongo
Kopu
Onemana
Miranda Hot Springs
Matatoki
Tairua Block
To Auckland (75km)
Waitakaruru
Turua
Puriri
Whangamata
Wentworth Valley
Whangamata Harbour
Mangatarata
Ngatea
Hikutaia
Waiharakeke
Coromandel Forest Park
Whiritoa
Hauraki Plains
Kopuatai Wetland Management Reserve
Paeroa
Ohinemuri Estate
Waikino
Waihi
Homunga Bay
Tirohia
Karangahake Gorge
Waihi
Golden Valley
To Te Aroha (10km)
Kaimai Mamaku Forest Park
Waihi Beach
Athenree

Cuvier Is

MERCURY ISLANDS
Great Mercury Is
Red Mercury Is
Stanley Is

THE COROMANDEL

0   10   20km
0   5   10mi

Coromandel Peninsula

The Coromandel Peninsula juts out into the South Pacific Ocean, bordered on the west by the Hauraki Gulf. As well as boasting some of the North Island's finest coastal scenery and beaches, it's a haven for those seeking an alternative lifestyle away from the city bustle, a serenity only briefly punctuated by the hordes of Christmas and New Year holiday-makers.

The west coast of the peninsula contains the historical towns of Thames and Coromandel, with remote settlements and rugged coastline further north. The best of the coastal scenery and beaches are over on the east coast, which also has the main resorts (including the famed Hot Water Beach) and consequently most of the tourists.

Although it's compact, the narrow, winding roads mean it can take a surprisingly long time to get around the peninsula. It takes about an hour to drive from Thames to Coromandel Town, another hour from Coromandel to Whitianga, another from Whitianga to Tairua and 40 minutes from Tairua back to Thames. Those planning on 'doing' the peninsula in a day should think again! Cyclists should be prepared for some winding roads and a fair bit of hill climbing.

History

Maori have lived on the peninsula since well before the first settlers arrived; the sheltered areas of the east coast supported a large population. This was one of the major moa-hunting areas of the North Island, although other subsistence practices included fishing, sealing, bird-hunting and horticulture.

The history of European colonisation of the peninsula and plains to the south is steeped in gold-mining, logging and gumdigging. Gold was first discovered in NZ at Coromandel in 1852, but the rush was short-lived once miners found it was not alluvial gold but gold to be wrested from the ground by pick and shovel. More was discovered around Thames in 1867, and over the next few years, other fields were proclaimed at Coromandel Town, Kuaotunu and Karangahake. It is also rich in semi-precious gemstones, such as quartz, agate, amethyst, jasper, chalcedony and carnelian.

Kauri logging was big business on the peninsula for around 100 years. Allied to the timber trade was shipbuilding, which took off after 1832 when a mill was established at Mercury Bay. By the 1880s Kauaeranga, Coroglen (Gumtown) and Tairua were the main suppliers of kauri to Auckland mills. Things got tougher once the kauri around the coast became scarce due to indiscriminate felling, and loggers had to penetrate deeper into the bush for the timber. Kauri dams were built in order to use water power to get the timber to the coast. By the 1930s the logging of kauri on the peninsula had all but finished.

THAMES
pop 6810

Thames is the western gateway to and main town of the Coromandel, lying on the shallow Firth of Thames. Its streets are lined with old wooden houses and pubs from the 19th century, when the gold rush and kauri trade made it one of the biggest towns in NZ.

Although most visitors pause only briefly in Thames on their way to villages and bays further around the peninsula, it's an interesting historic town and a good base for tramping in the Coromandel Forest Park.

Information

The Thames visitors centre (☎ 09-868 7284, ℮ thames@ihug.co.nz) is at 206 Pollen St. It's open from 8.30am to 5pm Monday to Friday and 9am to 4pm Saturday and Sunday. You can pick up the *Thames Heritage Trail* and *Coromandel Craft Trail* pamphlets, and it's also an agent for AA, InterCity and Tranz Rail. United Video, 456 Pollen St, has Internet access, 9am to 9pm daily.

Things to See & Do

The **gold mine and stamper battery** (☎ 09-868 8514; admission $6; open 10am-4pm daily), at the northern end of Pollen St, offers a look at the town's gold-mining history with

THE COROMANDEL

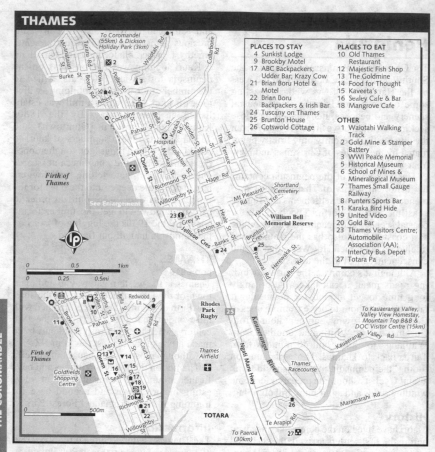

THAMES

PLACES TO STAY
4 Sunkist Lodge
9 Brookby Motel
17 ABC Backpackers;
   Udder Bar; Krazy Cow
21 Brian Boru Hotel &
   Motel
22 Brian Boru
   Backpackers & Irish Bar
24 Tuscany on Thames
25 Brunton House
26 Cotswold Cottage

PLACES TO EAT
10 Old Thames
   Restaurant
12 Majestic Fish Shop
13 The Goldmine
14 Food for Thought
15 Kaveeta's
16 Sealey Cafe & Bar
18 Mangrove Cafe

OTHER
1 Waiotahi Walking
   Track
2 Gold Mine & Stamper
   Battery
3 WWI Peace Memorial
5 Historical Museum
6 School of Mines &
   Mineralogical Museum
7 Thames Small Gauge
   Railway
8 Punters Sports Bar
11 Karaka Bird Hide
19 United Video
20 Gold Bar
23 Thames Visitors Centre;
   Automobile
   Association (AA);
   InterCity Bus Depot
27 Totara Pa

displays, photographs and mine tours by appointment.

The **School of Mines & Mineralogical Museum** (☎ 09-868 6227, cnr Brown & Cochrane Sts; $3.50; open 11am-3pm Wed-Sun) has a full collection of NZ rocks, minerals and fossils. The local **historical museum** (cnr Cochrane & Pollen Sts; adult/child $2.50/1; open 1pm-3pm daily) has pioneer relics, rocks and old photographs of the town.

Kids will enjoy a **train ride** on the tiny 900m-loop narrow-gauge train, operated by the Thames Small Gauge Railway Society

(☎ 09-868 6678; $1; Sunday only, 11am-3pm). The little station is a replica of the original railway station (1898) that served the Auckland-Thames line.

The **Karaka Bird Hide** is a great bird-watching hide that's easily reached by a boardwalk through the mangroves just off Brown St. It overlooks the Firth of Thames; the best viewing time is two hours either side of high tide.

There is an interesting produce and handicraft **market** every Saturday morning at the northern end of Pollen St (an area known as Grahamstown), starting at 9am.

Places to Stay

Camping & Hostels In a quiet valley beside a stream 3km north of Thames, *Dickson Holiday Park (☎ 09-868 7308)* is a camping ground and YHA associate. Unpowered/powered sites cost $10/11 per person, dorm beds $16, cabins $41-62 a double, and motel units $84. There's also a tropical butterfly and orchid house and a cafe here.

Sunkist Lodge (☎ 09-868 8808, ⓔ sunkist@xtra.co.nz, 506 Brown St) Dorm beds $16-18, twins & doubles $37. This relaxed place is in a historic building, the former Lady Bowen Hotel (1868 to 1952). It's said to have a resident ghost, but LP has been unable to confirm its presence. You can pitch a tent in the pleasant garden for $12 per person. There's loads of information on the Coromandel here, as well as bike hire and luggage storage.

Brian Boru Backpackers (☎ 09-868 5330, ⓔ brianboru@xtra.co.nz, 330 Pollen St) Singles/doubles $20/40. Right in the centre of town, this 'boutique' backpackers had just opened when we visited. It has no dorms as such, just one triple room at $15 a bed – the rest are nice doubles and twins with shared bathroom. There's a well-equipped kitchen, lounge/dining area and a large balcony over Pollen St. There's also an Irish bar and cafe downstairs. The owner is renowned for her murder-mystery nights – see Entertainment.

ABC Backpackers Thames (☎ 0800 868 6200, 09-868 6200, ⓔ abc.thames@xtra .co.nz, 476 Pollen St) Dorm beds $14, singles $24, twins/doubles $36/38, double with en suite $44. In the Art Deco former Imperial Hotel, this place has been fully renovated and has spacious former pub rooms and a large lounge. It can get noisy on Friday and Saturday nights due to its position over the the Krazy Cow nightclub.

B&Bs & Guesthouses There are some charming guesthouses in Thames and a couple of relaxing homestays further out in the lush, peaceful Kauaeranga Valley.

Brunton House (☎ 09-868 5160, 210 Parawai Rd) B&B singles/doubles $60/95. Brunton House, a large two-storey home encircled by verandas, has plenty of historical charm, as well as a pool and tennis court.

Cotswold Cottage (☎ 09-868 6306, Maramarahi Rd) Singles $50, doubles $80-100. This beautiful villa was moved here all the way from Epsom, Auckland, and now occupies a prime spot overlooking the Kauaeranga River. The separate guest wing has comfortable en suite rooms.

Valley View Homestay (☎ 09-868 7213, 53 Kauaeranga Valley Rd) B&B singles/doubles $50/70. The bright and spotless Valley View has a separate guest area with two rooms and a thriving organic garden outside. Dinner is available by arrangement.

Mountain Top B&B (☎ 09-868 9662, 452 Kauaeranga Valley Rd) Twin/double $90/95. This is another organic farm with a couple of B&B rooms and great views over the valley from the back deck.

Motels & Hotels The *Brookby Motel (☎ 09-868 6663, 102 Redwood Lane)* is plain but one of the cheapest in town at

Historic Brian Boru Hotel, Thames

THE COROMANDEL

DAVID WALL

$50/60 for singles/doubles, and it's in a quiet location a couple of blocks east of Pollen St.

Brian Boru Hotel (☎ 09-868 6523, 200 Richmond St) Singles/doubles with shared bathroom $25/50, motel doubles $125. This is one of the town's original hotels and has simple pub rooms with shared bathroom upstairs and better (though overpriced) motel rooms in an adjacent section.

Tuscany on Thames (☎ 09-868 5099, e tuscanyonthames@xtra.co.nz, Jellicoe Crescent) Studio units $110-135, 1-/2-bedroom units $125-135/150-200. Thames' newest and most stylish motel, Tuscany on Thames has a modern Mediterranean feel with large, tastefully furnished rooms, all with spa. There's a pool and free laundry.

Places to Eat

Pollen St has plenty of takeaways and coffee lounges. Try *Food for Thought* for cake, quiche and sandwiches, and *Mangrove Cafe* for good coffee. The Goldfields Shopping Centre, on Queen St, has a big Pak N Save supermarket, food court and cinema.

Majestic Fish Shop (☎ 09-868 6204, 640 Pollen St) $11.50-19. This local favourite has a fish and chip takeaway at the front and serves good seafood meals in the BYO restaurant around the back.

Kaveeta's (☎ 09-868 7049, 518 Pollen St) $6-12. This genuine, inexpensive Indian curry place has eat-in or takeaway. They even do kulfi (Indian icecream).

Old Thames Restaurant (☎ 09-868 7207, 705 Pollen St) Mains $12-18. This restaurant isn't as old as the facade would suggest (70s booth seating inside) but it's good value for pizzas, steak and seafood.

Sealey Cafe & Bar (☎ 09-868 8641, 109 Sealey St) Breakfast/lunch $5.50-13.50, dinner $20-25. This is a fine place for a meal or just a drink, with reasonably priced lunches including pasta and burgers and a pleasant courtyard out the front.

The Goldmine (☎ 09-868 3180) Meals $9-18. The Goldmine has a range of burgers, steaks and fish dishes at lower-than-average prices.

About 8km from Thames, on SH26 en route to Paeroa, is *Matatoki Farm Cheese*

(☎ 09-868 1284), where you can taste and buy cheeses handmade from milk produced by the farm's cows. It's open daily from 10am to 4pm.

Entertainment

Barbara Doyle, the owner of Brian Boru Backpackers, is well known in NZ for her murder-mystery weekends. They begin with a meeting and introductions on Friday night, a bus tour of the Coromandel on Saturday and a dinner and 'murder' that evening. Someone in the group is the murderer and you have to guess who through clues dropped over the weekend. The cost is $290 per person, and includes all accommodation and meals.

Popular places for an evening drink include the *Gold Bar*, *Punters Sports Bar* and the *Krazy Cow* nightclub.

COROMANDEL FOREST PARK

There are over 30 walks and tramps through Coromandel Forest Park, covering the area from the Maratoto Forest, near Paeroa, to Cape Colville. The most popular region is the Kauaeranga Valley, which cuts into the Colville Range behind Thames. There are old kauri dams in the valley, including the Tarawaere Waterfalls, Dancing Camp, Kauaeranga Main, Moss Creek and Waterfalls Creek Dams. Do not climb on them!

Walks in the Kauaeranga Valley, have become so popular, especially on weekends, that DOC has built an 80-bed hut at the Pinnacles to accommodate trampers. Hut tickets ($15 per night) *must* be prebooked via the DOC visitors centre in Kauaeranga. The most popular walk is the three- to four-hour hike through regenerating forest to the jagged limestone outcrop known as the **Pinnacles**, from which there are fine views.

Information

The DOC visitors centre (☎ 09-867 9080), in the Kauaeranga Valley about 15km from Thames, is the place for information on tramping and mountain-biking in the park. It is open from 8am to 4pm daily and has a small interpretive display as well as slide shows on the history of kauri logging in the park ($1). There's also a one-third scale model of a kauri dam.

The headquarters and main entrance to the park are reached from the southern edge of Thames, along the partly unsealed Kauaeranga Valley Rd. Sunkist Lodge in Thames has a bus going into the park on demand for $25/35 one way/return.

Places to Stay

There are *DOC camping grounds* scattered throughout Coromandel Forest Park. You'll find them around the northern tip of the peninsula at Fantail Bay, Port Jackson, Fletcher Bay, Stony Bay and Waikawau Bay. In southern Coromandel there are *camping grounds* at Broken Hills and Wentworth Valley. Fees are $7 per night and bookings are required for Waikawau Bay over Christmas and New Year (☎ *09-866 1106*). Elsewhere sites are available on a first-come first-served basis. There are resident site managers during summer.

Remote camping spots include *Moss Creek*, beside the Pinnacles Hut, and *Billygoat Clearing* (both $7.50 per night). *Pinnacles Hut* itself ($15) must be prebooked through DOC (see earlier).

THAMES TO COROMANDEL TOWN

As you travel north from Thames, SH25 snakes along the coast for 32km past lots of pretty little bays and calm beaches. Fishing and shellfishing are excellent all the way up the coast and the landscape turns crimson when the pohutukawa, or 'Christmas tree', blooms in summer.

You can go searching for quartz crystals washed down from the hills on the beach at **Waiomu**.

The **Rapaura Watergardens** (*Tapu-Coroglen road; adult/child $5/1; open summer 10am-5pm daily*) are 6km inland from Tapu, and there are tearooms here.

At Wilsons Bay the road leaves the coast and climbs over several hills and valleys before dropping down to Coromandel Town. Cyclists should count on taking the best part of a day to do the ride from Thames to Coromandel.

Plant a Kauri

Coromandel Peninsula once supported magnificent stands of the long-lived kauri tree, but after logging in the 19th and early 20th centuries little remains. In 1999, Kauri 2000 was launched to organise and encourage long term replanting. For $10 you can have a kauri seedling planted on your behalf by Kauri 2000 volunteers. You receive a voucher, explaining the project's vision and operation and, after the seedling is planted (June/July), a certificate indicating its exact location. If you were to return to the Coromandel, you could check on your little kauri tree, which you can identify by an inscribed commemorative marker.

For more information contact the Kauri 2000 Trust (☎/fax 09-866 2656), Box 174, Whitianga, New Zealand.

Places to Stay

There are holiday parks with camping and cabins at regular intervals along the highway, including: *Boomerang Motor Camp* (☎ *09-867 8879*) in Te Puru; *Waiomu Bay Holiday Park* (☎ *09-868 2777*) in Waiomu, which also has backpacker bunkrooms at $12 per person; and *Tapu Motor Camp* (☎ *09-868 4837*) at Tapu, 22km north of Thames.

Te Puru Coast View Lodge (☎ *09-868 2326*) Doubles $125-150. About 11km north of Thames, this is a luxurious Mediterranean-style villa on a hill overlooking the Firth of Thames.

Te Mata Lodge (☎ *09-868 4834*) Camping $10 per person, share room $17, cabins $40 a double. This lodge has a variety of accommodation in a quiet, riverside bush setting. There are cabins and a self-contained unit. It's at the end of Te Mata Creek Rd, 1.5km past Tapu.

Te Kouma Farmstay (☎ *09-866 8747*, ℮ *tekouma@xtra.co.nz*) Share unit $18 per person, self-contained unit $70 a double. Set on a cattle and deer farm on Te Kouma harbour, this farmstay has modern units and kayaking and bushwalking opportunities in a secluded environment.

COROMANDEL TOWN

pop 1620

Coromandel, 55km north of Thames, was named after HMS *Coromandel*, which visited in 1820 to pick up a load of kauri spars for the navy. It was here, on Driving Creek, 3km north of the township, that Charles Ring discovered gold in 1852. At the height of the gold rush the town's population rose to over 10,000, but today it's a sleepy little township noted for its crafts, alternative lifestylers and mussel fishing.

The Coromandel visitors centre (☎ 09-866 8598) is in the District Council building at 355 Kapanga Rd. It's open from 9am to 5pm daily (10.30am to 2.30pm on weekends in winter). It has Internet access and you'll also find the DOC field centre here with information on parks and walks in the area.

Things to See & Do

The small **Coromandel Mining & Historic Museum** (*Rings Rd; adult/child $2/50c; open summer 10am-1pm daily, winter 1.30pm-4pm Sat & Sun*) provides a glimpse of life in the old, gold days. Behind the main hall is the century-old solid kauri jailhouse. The cell now on display was declared *tapu* (taboo) after a man was asphyxiated in it in 1913 when he set his mattress on fire.

The **Coromandel Stamper Battery** (*☎ 025 246 4898, Buffalo Rd; adult/child $6/3; open summer 10am-5pm daily, winter Sat & Sun or by appointment*) demonstrates the process of crushing ore, the first step in extracting gold, and shows various amalgamation processes.

The **Driving Creek Railway** (*☎ 09-866 8703; train trips $15/7 adult/child*), 3km north of Coromandel, is the remarkable life's work of one of Coromandel's leading artists, Barry Brickell. The potter and brickmaker discovered workable clay on his land, but he needed a way of moving it down the hill to his kiln. So he built his own railway! The miniature train travels up steep grades, across four high trestle bridges, along two spirals and a double switchback, and through two tunnels, finishing at the 'Eyefull Tower'. The hour-long round trip runs at 10.15am and 2pm daily, and at 11.30am,

12.45pm, 3.15pm and 4.30pm in summer. A shop at the 'station' sells ceramics.

Coromandel has interesting **craft shops** along Kapanga Rd; pick up a copy of the *Coromandel Craft Trail* pamphlet from the information centre.

Good **walks** around Coromandel include the loop kauri walk at the Long Bay Recreation Reserve.

Places to Stay

Camping & Cabins At the Long Bay Recreation Reserve, 3km west of Coromandel, the beachfront *Long Bay Motor Camp* (*☎ 09-866 8720, e lbmccoromandel@paradise.net.nz*) has unpowered/powered sites for $11/12 per person, good cabins at $35-60 a double, and the secluded Tuck's Bay camping area.

Tidewater Tourist Park (*☎ 09-866 8888, e tidewater@world-net.co.nz, 270 Tiki Rd*) Tent sites $9 per person, dorm beds $16, twins/doubles $36/38, self-contained units $95-110 a double. This tidy place near the harbour is a YHA-associate hostel and also has camping and good motel units. Bicycles and kayaks can be hired.

North of Coromandel are: *Shelly Beach Motor Camp* (*☎ 09-866 8988*) at Shelley Beach (5km); *Oamaru Bay Tourist Flats & Caravan Park* (*☎ 09-866 8735*) on Oamaru Bay (7km north); *Papaaroha Motor Camp* (*☎ 09-866 8818*) at Papaaroha (12km); and *Angler's Lodge & Motor Park* (*☎ 09-866 8584*) at Amodeo Bay (18km).

Hostels The *Lion's Den* (*☎/fax 09-866 8157, 126 Te Tiki St*) perfectly fits the 'alternative' mould of Coromandel. It's a cosy country house with a vegie garden out back and eels to be fed in the stream behind the property. Tent sites are $12 per person, dorm beds $18, doubles $38; the garden's 'Hippy House' is popular ($36 a double).

Tui Lodge (*☎ 09-866 8237, 600 Whangapoua Rd*) Tent sites $10 per person, dorm beds $17, twins & doubles $38, en suite double $55. Tui Lodge is a lovely backpackers set in an orchard, 10 minutes' walk from town on the road to Whitianga. There's a sauna and free bikes.

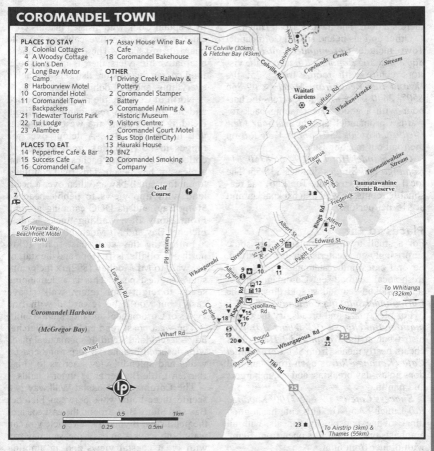

COROMANDEL TOWN

PLACES TO STAY
3 Colonial Cottages
4 A Woodsy Cottage
6 Lion's Den
7 Long Bay Motor
   Camp
8 Harbourview Motel
10 Coromandel Hotel
11 Coromandel Town
   Backpackers
21 Tidewater Tourist Park
22 Tui Lodge
23 Allambee

PLACES TO EAT
14 Peppertree Cafe & Bar
15 Success Cafe
16 Coromandel Cafe

17 Assay House Wine Bar &
   Cafe
18 Coromandel Bakehouse

OTHER
1 Driving Creek Railway &
   Pottery
2 Coromandel Stamper
   Battery
5 Coromandel Mining &
   Historic Museum
9 Visitors Centre;
   Coromandel Court Motel
12 Bus Stop (InterCity)
13 Hauraki House
19 BNZ
20 Coromandel Smoking
   Company

THE COROMANDEL

Coromandel Town Backpackers (☎ 09-866 8327, 732 Rings Rd) Dorm beds $16, doubles $34. This is a small, clean but nondescript hostel.

B&Bs, Motels & Hotels Coromandel has a good range of B&B and motel accommodation. Motels charge from $70-110 a double.

A Woodsy Cottage (☎/fax 09-866 8111, e gaiacot@wave.co.nz, 2 Oxford Terrace) B&B doubles $75, self-contained cottage $95-110. Tucked away off Alfred St, A Woodsy Cottage has a couple of delightful self-contained timber cottages nestled in the

bush. One is a converted pottery, another is a large cottage with polished floorboards and a loft. There are also B&B rooms in the main house.

Allambee (☎ 09-866 8011, fax 866 8611, 1680 Tiki Rd) B&B singles/doubles from $50/80. Allambee is a small homestay B&B on the main road into Coromandel. There's also a separate self-contained unit for $85.

Colonial Cottages (☎/fax 09-866 8857, e coromandel_colonial_cottages@xtra.co .nz, 1737 Rings Rd) 1- & 2-bedroom units $85-155. A cut above your average motel in the style department, these self-contained cottages are set in a pleasant garden and there's a pool. The owners speak Dutch.

Other options in and around Coromandel Town include: *Coromandel Court* (☎ 09-866 8402, 365 Kapanga Rd) next to the visitors centre with rooms from $75; the *Wyuna Bay Beachfront Motel* (☎ 09-866 8507, 2640 Wyuna Bay Rd), across the harbour with a good aspect facing back towards Coromandel; and the *Harbour View* (☎ 09-866 8690, 25 Harbour View Rd) on the road out to Long Bay.

Coromandel Hotel (☎ 09-866 8760, 611 Kapanga Rd) Singles/doubles $35/55. The local pub (known as the Top Pub) has reasonable rooms, as well as a backpacker unit at $15 per person.

Places to Eat
For a small town, Coromandel has some surprisingly good eateries on its main street. Several cafes and restaurants specialise in fresh local seafood, eg, Coromandel mussels. Smoked seafood is sold direct at the *Coromandel Smoking Company* on Tiki Rd.

For pies, pizza and breads, try the *Coromandel Bakehouse* (92 Wharf Rd). The bistro bar at the *Coromandel Hotel* does cheap, hearty meals (from $8). *Coromandel Cafe* (Kapanga Rd) is open from 8am and does an all-day breakfast and cheap burgers and panini.

Success Cafe (☎ 09-866 7100, Kapanga Rd) Lunch $3.50-10. This cafe has a good range of inexpensive light meals, with an emphasis on seafood. It's open from 10am, with dinner from 6pm.

Assay House Wine Bar & Cafe (☎ 09-866 7397, 2 Kapanga Rd) Assay House is an interesting, colourful little cafe. For brunch you can enjoy bagels and pancakes, for dinner pasta is the speciality ($18-20).

The *Peppertree* (☎ 09-866 8211, 31 Kapanga Rd) $8.50-24.50. Perhaps the pick of Coromandel's restaurants, the licensed Peppertree is open for breakfast, lunch and dinner and has a large courtyard dinner area.

FAR NORTH COROMANDEL
The road north is sealed up to the tiny town of **Colville**, 85km north of Thames. Colville was formerly known as Cabbage Bay, named by Captain Cook who insisted that his crew eat the leaves of native cabbage trees to guard against scurvy. These days it's home to alternative lifestylers; there is a small wholefood *cafe*, a quaint store that sells just about everything, and a Buddhist retreat.

North of Colville, the roads are unsealed and narrow but in reasonable condition. Heading north along the west coast takes you to Fletcher Bay. A detour over the ranges to **Port Charles**, goes to a small collection of holiday baches (cottages) on a pleasant bay beach. This road continues to another small bay and then over a headland with fine views to pebble-beached **Stony Bay**, and its DOC camping ground. From Stony Bay, walking tracks lead to Fletcher Bay and Mt Moehau.

Following the west coast road, 12km north of Colville, is Te Hope and the start of the walk to **Mt Moehau** (892m), the peninsula's highest peak. This is a demanding seven to eight-hour return walk (leave early) but you'll be rewarded with fine views of Coromandel and the Hauraki Gulf.

The west coast road ends up at **Fletcher Bay** – a real land's end. It's a magical place with deserted beaches, a forest and coastal walks and splendid views across to Great Barrier, Little Barrier and Cuvier Islands.

The **Coromandel Coastal Walkway** is a scenic three-hour walk between Fletcher Bay and Stony Bay, around the east coast of the peninsula. If you have a vehicle you can walk both ways – an easy, pleasant day trip with great coastal views and an ambling section across open farmland. *Coromandel Bus Services* (☎ 09-866 8045) can drop you off at Fletcher Bay and pick you up from Stony Bay three or four hours later. The return trip from Coromandel Town is $65.

Mountain bikers must use the longer and tougher, marked stock route that runs along the flank of Mt Moehau.

Places to Stay There are DOC *camping grounds* at Waikawau Bay and Stony Bay on the eastern side of the peninsula, and at Port Jackson, Fantail Bay and Fletcher Bay on the western side.

Colville Farm (☎/*fax 09-866 6820*) Camp sites $7-9 per person, dorm beds $16, bush lodge $65 a double. This is a working farm with a backpackers house and some rustic bush cottages. You can join in with activities such as milking cows and there's horse trekking and bushwalks on offer.

Mahamudra Centre (☎ *09-866 6851,* **W** *www.mahamudra.org.nz*) Beds $15 per person. Also at Colville, this is a Buddhist retreat with basic accommodation, a meditation centre and regular visits by Buddhist teachers and lamas. Courses are open to anyone interested in Buddhism.

Fletcher Bay Backpackers (☎ *09-866 6712,* **e** *js.lourie@xtra.co.nz*) Camping $12, dorm beds $14. This quiet, comfortable 16-bed cottage is on a farm property right at the end of the road. It has all facilities but you must bring food.

COROMANDEL TOWN TO WHITIANGA

There are two routes from Coromandel Town south-east to Whitianga: the main road is the longer SH25 (1hr, 32km) and although there are still some gravel sections, it's the more scenic route, following the coast and offering exquisite beach views. The other road is the unsealed 309 Rd.

First stop on the SH25 east of Coromandel is Te Rerenga, almost on the shore of Whangapoua Harbour. The road forks at the harbour; if you head north you come to Whangapoua, from where you can walk along the rocky foreshore to the isolated and pristine **New Chum's Beach** (30 minutes).

Also at Te Rerenga is the *Castle Rock Winery* (☎ *09-866 4542*), which produces a wide range of fruit wines (including feijoa and guava) and has tastings from 9am to 6pm daily.

Continuing east you can detour to the beachside settlements of Matarangi, Kuaotunu, Otama and Opito before heading south to Whitianga. This whole stretch has lovely beaches, though there's little of interest in the 'towns' themselves. **Matarangi** is a good example of a beach backed by a dull real-estate development, which seems to be the fate of parts of the Coromandel.

Kuaotunu is a quaint settlement with a delightful beach and a camping ground, the *Kuaotunu Motor Camp* (☎ *09-866 5628, 33 Bluff Rd*).

Black Jack Backpackers (☎ *09-866 2988,* **W** *www.black-jack.co.nz*) Tent sites $12 per person, dorm beds $20, double $50, en suite double $70. On the highway at Kuaotunu, this new backpackers was just about to open at the time of writing. As well as modern facilities and a large deck, it has kayaks, dinghies and meals by arrangement.

Heading off the highway at Kuaotunu takes you around to **Otama** and **Opito**, a more remote area with some of the finest stretches of sand, this part of the coast. At the end of Opito Beach there's a walk up to the headland, providing good views.

Highway 309

Highway 309 (known locally as the 309 Rd) is the shorter route to Whitianga (45mins, 26km), and all but a few kilometres at either end is gravel. It's a bush road and is not as scenic as SH25, although there are some good forest walks en route, including the **Chiltern Scenic Reserve**, **Waiau Falls** and a two-hour return walking track to the summit of **Castle Rock** (521m). The **kauri grove**, 8km in from SH25, is particularly interesting as there is a Siamese kauri, which forks just above the ground.

The **Waiau Waterworks** (*$8/4 adults/ children; open 9am-5pm daily*) is a family theme park with water-powered sculptures, swimming holes and other things to keep kids occupied.

309 River Lodge (☎ *09-866 5151*) Tent sites $12 per person, cottage $17 per person. About 12km from Whitianga, this is a lovely old kauri cottage beside a river with swimming holes. It's a relaxing place surrounded by bush and farmland. The owners live in a separate house.

WHITIANGA
pop 3580

The pleasant Whitianga area of Mercury Bay has a long history by NZ standards. The Polynesian explorer Kupe landed near here around AD 800 and the area was called

THE COROMANDEL

Te Whitianga-a-Kupe (The Crossing Place of Kupe). At that time the land abounded with moa but subsequent Polynesian settlers soon whittled them down.

Mercury Bay was given its modern name by Captain Cook when he observed the transit of Mercury across the face of the sun while the *Endeavour* anchored in the bay in November 1769.

Whitianga is the main town on Mercury Bay and has a busy marina crammed with yachts and fishing boats. Buffalo Beach, the principal frontage onto the bay, takes its name from HMS *Buffalo*, wrecked there in 1840. There are a string of better beaches to the north and across Whitianga Harbour.

The town is a big game-fishing base for tuna, marlin, mako (blue pointer shark), thresher shark and kingfish. It is very much a tourist town so there's a good range of accommodation, but its small population swells to mammoth proportions during the December–January holidays.

The Whitianga visitors centre (☎ 09-866 5555, e whitvin@ihug.co.nz), 66 Albert St, is open from 8am to 6pm daily during the peak summer season. At other times it opens from 9am to 5pm Monday to Friday, 9am to 1pm Saturday and Sunday.

Internet access is available at the Cyber Surf Shop on Coghill St, or at the visitors centre.

Things to See & Do

The little **museum** *(adult/child $2.50/50c; open summer 10am-4pm daily, winter 11am-3pm Tues-Thur & Sun)* opposite the ferry wharf has historical photos of Mercury Bay and the kauri-logging era; exhibits on mining, blacksmithing and the colonial era; Maori carvings; and HMS *Buffalo* and other shipwrecks. The jaws of a 1350kg white pointer shark caught in the Hauraki Gulf in 1959 hang on the wall, overlooking it all.

Whitianga is a good place to try your hand at bone carving, and there are two bone carving studios, both offering a similar experience. Maurice Aukett of **Bay Carving** *(☎ 09-866 4021, Esplanade)*, next to the museum, can help you whip up a simple piece in a few hours – even less if he

cuts the basic design and you just sand it into shape ($35). More complex designs take four to five hours or longer (up to $70). At the **Bone Studio** *(☎ 09-866 2158, 16 Coghill St)* watch craftspeople at work and spend a day creating your own piece ($60).

Purangi Winery *(☎ 09-866 3724)*, 6km south on the back road to Hahei, has wine tasting, including kiwi-fruit wine, and it operates cruises on the Purangi River. **High Zone** *(☎ 09-866 2113, 49 Kaimarama Rd)*, 7km south of Whitianga just off the main highway, is a high ropes course where you can swing above the ground or try a 14m freefall from $15 to $56.

Ferry Landing

From the Narrows, on the southern side of town, a passenger ferry crosses over to **Ferry Landing**, site of the original township on the southern side of Mercury Bay. The wharf at Ferry Landing was built in 1837 and the stone from which it is constructed came from Whitianga Rock, a *pa* (fortified Maori village) site, of which Captain Cook said 'the best engineers in Europe could not have chosen a better site for a small band of men to defend against a greater number'. The view from **Shakespeare's Lookout**, on top of the white cliffs above Ferry Landing, is lovely and a great spot to see all of Mercury Bay with its many beaches and coves.

The five-minute ferry crossing costs $1 each way (children and bicycles 50c) and it runs continuously from 7.30am to 10.30pm in summer, from 7.30am to 6.30pm in winter. The ferry does not take cars, which have to take the circuitous route around the bay to the south, via Coroglen.

Walk, cycle or drive to scenic spots on this side, including Cook's Beach, Lonely Bay, Front Beach and Flaxmill Bay (where Cook is believed to have careened the *Endeavour*), and further on to Hahei. A bus service also runs from Ferry Landing (see Getting There & Around in this chapter).

Activities

Whitianga is a base for many activities on land and water – the visitors centre has more details.

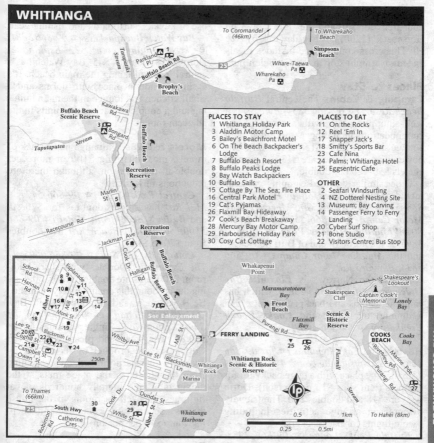

WHITIANGA

PLACES TO STAY
1 Whitianga Holiday Park
3 Aladdin Motor Camp
5 Bailey's Beachfront Motel
6 On The Beach Backpacker's Lodge
7 Buffalo Beach Resort
8 Buffalo Peaks Lodge
9 Bay Watch Backpackers
10 Buffalo Sails
15 Cottage By The Sea; Fire Place
16 Central Park Motel
19 Cat's Pyjamas
26 Flaxmill Bay Hideaway
27 Cook's Beach Breakaway
28 Mercury Bay Motor Camp
29 Harbourside Holiday Park
30 Cosy Cat Cottage

PLACES TO EAT
11 On the Rocks
12 Reel 'Em In
17 Snapper Jack's
18 Smitty's Sports Bar
23 Cafe Nina
24 Palms; Whitianga Hotel
25 Eggsentric Cafe

OTHER
2 Seafari Windsurfing
4 NZ Dotterel Nesting Site
13 Museum; Bay Carving
14 Passenger Ferry to Ferry Landing
20 Cyber Surf Shop
21 Bone Studio
22 Visitors Centre; Bus Stop

Dolphin Quest (☎ *09-866 5555; swims $98, safari $80*) organises swims with dolphins in summer, dependent on definite sightings. Wetsuits, snorkels and flippers are supplied. The three-hour Seven Island Seafari is a popular alternative when the dolphins are not around.

Paddle around this interesting coastline in a sea kayak with **Coromandel Safaris** (☎ *09-866 2850, 025 394 597*). A one-day safari with equipment and lunch is $90. For windsurfer hire and lessons, **Seafari Windsurfing** (☎ *09-866 0677*) is set up on Brophy's Beach, just north of Buffalo Beach.

There are plenty of opportunities to go out sailing or fishing from Whitianga's marina. **Sailfish Charters & Sailing School** (☎ *09-866 5267*) can organise a day's crewing for visitors, from around $70.

The **Cave Cruzer** (☎ *0800 427 893*) is a rigid-hull inflatable boat doing trips from Whitianga to Cathedral Cove with commentary and music thrown in for atmosphere. There's a variety of trips from $40.

For horse trekking, the **Twin Oaks Riding Ranch** (☎ *09-866 5388*) is 9km north of Whitianga on the Kuaotunu Rd; **Ace Hi Ranch** (☎ *09-866 4897*) is 8km south of

Whitianga on the highway. Both have two-hour treks for $30 and the 'Pub Crawl on Horseback' ($200) is a two-day trek by Ace Hi. This cross-country ride includes meals and an overnight stop at the Coroglen pub.

Places to Stay

Camping & Cabins The central *Buffalo Beach Resort* (☎ 09-866 5854, Eyre St) is a well-equipped place with a range of accommodation, including a three-bedroom cottage sleeping nine ($15 per person). Unpowered/powered sites are $13 per person, chalets $50-120 per double.

Other similarly priced camping grounds include: *Harbourside Holiday Park* (☎ 09-866 5746, 135 Albert St); *Mercury Bay Motor Camp* (☎ 09-866 5579, 121 Albert St); *Whitianga Holiday Park* (☎ 09-866 5896) at the northern end of Buffalo Beach; and the *Aladdin Motor Camp* (☎ 09-866 5834, Bongard Rd).

Across the Narrows is *Flaxmill Bay Hideaway* (☎/fax 09-866 2386), which has camping, cabins and backpacker huts ($35 a double) available; and *Cooks Beach Breakaway* (☎ 09-866 5469).

Hostels The *Cat's Pyjamas* (☎/fax 09-866 4663, e catspjs@ihug.co.nz, 4 Monk St) is a small, cosy place with a huge backyard for campers (tent sites $12 per person). Dorm beds are $18 and doubles $40. The friendly owners can arrange activities including scenic flights for backpackers.

Buffalo Peaks Lodge (☎ 09-866 2933, e whitiangabuffpeaks@xtra.co.nz, 12 Albert St) Dorm beds $18, doubles $48. Buffalo Peaks is a neat place with a spa and patio and lots of colourful murals. The same people also run the quieter *Buffalo Sails* (20 Mill Rd) which has the same prices.

On The Beach Backpackers Lodge (☎ 09-866 5380, e enquiries@coromandelbackpackers.com, 46 Buffalo Beach Rd) Dorm beds $20, twins/doubles $48. This bright blue and yellow YHA associate is a converted motel and the progressive owners are expanding it to include adjacent buildings, so there'll be plenty of beds. Most of the dorms have an en suite, there are plenty

of common areas (four kitchens), and free use of kayaks, surfboards and fishing gear.

Bay Watch Backpackers (☎ 09-866 5481, e kristorb@ihug.co.nz, 22 Esplanade) Dorms $18, doubles $45. Bay Watch has a central location facing the main beach. It's a simple enough place with dorms and a small kitchen and lounge in the main building and a couple of backpacker units in the adjacent motel.

Motels & B&Bs Whitianga has a stack of motels, most charging $100 or more per double in peak season, although there are reductions in winter.

Central Park Motel (☎ 09-866 5471, 6 Mill Rd) has singles/doubles for $70/80, and *Bailey's Beachfront Motel* (☎ 09-866 5500, 66 Buffalo Beach Rd) has doubles from $70 to $140.

Cottage By The Sea (☎ 09-866 0605, 11 The Esplanade) Doubles with share bathroom $100, en suite doubles $130-150. Facing the harbour, this quaint, nicely furnished B&B was once a radar station in Opito Bay.

Cosy Cat Cottage (☎ 09-866 4488, 41 South Highway) Singles/doubles from $50/80. The small and pleasant Cosy Cat Cottage is the product of its cat-loving owner, with cats portrayed on everything from the sheets to the place mats at the dinner table and literally hundreds of cat figurines. As well as rooms in the house there's a separate self-contained unit sleeping four ($40 per person).

Places to Eat

For takeaway fish & chips and seafood, *Snapper Jacks* (☎ 09-866 5482, Albert St) is a local favourite that has returned after being burnt down. It also has a sit-in restaurant featuring seafood dishes.

Palms (☎ 09-866 5818) Mains $13.50-24. Attached to the Whitianga Hotel and overlooking the marina, Palms specialises in Thai food and does a reasonable job of it. Mains such as green curry and pad thai are around $15.

Cafe Nina (☎ 09-866 5440, 20 Victoria St) Dishes $3.50-$10.50. Open from 8am to 5pm. Tucked away in a cottage behind the library, Cafe Nina is worth searching out, especially for an afternoon coffee with one of the delicious cakes. There's also quiche, pasta and seafood dishes.

Smitty's Sports Bar (☎ 09-866 4647, 37 Albert St) $4.50-21. Smitty's is the place for burgers, nachos and big steaks.

Whitianga has plenty of places where you can dine al fresco overlooking the water.

Reel 'Em Inn (The Esplanade) $12-20. This is a seafront place with outdoor seating and pizza. To top it off, there's an adjoining ice-cream parlour.

Fire Place (☎ 09-866 4828, 9 The Esplanade) Mains $17.50-26. Facing the waterfront on the marina side, the Fire Place is good spot for gourmet pizzas and has an inviting timber deck at the front.

On the Rocks (☎ 09-866 4833, 20 The Esplanade) Mains $21-32. This is one of the better upmarket waterfront restaurants, specialising in fresh seafood such as has succulent scallops and mussels. It's open for dinner from 5pm.

Eggsentric Cafe (☎ 09-866 0307, 1047 Purangi Rd) Lunch $7-11, dinner $18-25. Across the harbour at Flaxmill Bay, this unassuming cafe has Coromandel written all over it. As well as an innovative menu (with dishes such as wasabi-glazed South Island salmon) there's live music most nights in summer, and a very laid back vibe.

Getting There & Around

Go Kiwi (☎ 09-866 0336) has a daily bus from Whitianga to Thames and Opoutere, and Intercity passes through on its Coromandel Loop daily in summer (daily except Saturday in winter). Hot Water Connections has a regular bus from Ferry Landing to Hahei – see the following Hahei & Hot Water Beach section.

The Bike Man (☎ 09-866 0745) in Coghill St is the best place to hire a bike ($15 for first hour, $20 for two hours) and you can get spare parts and repairs here.

HAHEI & HOT WATER BEACH

This popular section of coast is accessible from the Stone Steps Wharf at Ferry Landing and from the highway. The offshore

---

Beach Warning

Hot Water Beach has dangerous currents (also known as rips or undertows) year-round. These are particularly strong on the seaward side of the rocks that jut into the ocean near the spot where people looking for hot water dig holes in the sand. Several tourists have drowned at this beach in the past 10 years. There are warning signs posted on the cliffs near the digging place, and there is a locally funded life-saving patrol operating between Christmas (mid-December) and Easter (March/April). But you should be aware that swimming here isn't safe.

---

islands and rock stacks dotting the shoreline protect the beaches around Hahei, and these waters form the **Te Whanganui-a-Hei Marine Reserve**.

At the eastern end of Hahei Beach is a former Maori *pa*, **Te Pare Point**, which still has much evidence of the elaborate terracing used as fortifications. Just north of Hahei is the impressive **Cathedral Cove** (Te Whanganui a Hei), accessible only at low tide through a gigantic arched cavern that separates it from Mares Leg Cove. This is also a former *pa* site. There's a walking track from the Cathedral Cove car park through forest to Mares Leg Cove (30mins), or you can walk from Hahei Beach (1hr).

To the south of Hahei is the famous **Hot Water Beach**, where thermal waters brew just below the sand. You can join the crowds down on the beach two hours each side of low tide, dig a hole in the sand (use a shovel as the water and sand really are hot) and sit in your own little natural spa pool; allow about 15 minutes to prepare your pool. If you want to take a cooling dip in the ocean afterwards, be very careful (see the boxed text 'Beach Warning').

Organised Tours & Activities

The **Hahei Explorer** (☎ 09-866 3910), based near the store in Hahei, is a rigid inflatable boat making daily scenic trips from Hahei to Cathedral Cove and Hot Water Beach;

landings are made whenever the sea allows. They also organise snorkelling trips.

Cathedral Cove Sea Kayaking (☎ 09-866 3877, W www.seakayaktours.co.nz; half/full day trips $55/95) has guided kayaking trips around the superb coastline of the marine reserve. They're based at Hahei but free pick-up is available from Whitianga.

The reserve is particularly good for diving and **Cathedral Cove Dive** (☎ 09-866 3955, 3 Margaret Place) has dives from $40 (own gear) to $80 (including all gear). They also do four-day PADI courses for $390 plus gear hire, and introductory scuba courses (to 10m).

Places to Stay & Eat

Hot Water Beach Holiday Park (☎ 09-866 3735) Unpowered/powered sites $10/15 per person, on-site vans $35. This basic park is right on Hot Water Beach so it gets pretty crowded in summer.

Auntie Dawn's Place (☎ 09-866 3707, e auntiedawn@mercurybay.co.nz, Radar Rd) Dorm beds $20, doubles $75-85. Close to Hot Water Beach, the self-contained units here are comfortable and there are backpacker beds available in summer.

Hahei Holiday Resort/Cathedral Cove Lodge Backpackers (☎ 09-866 3889, e in fo@haheiholidays.co.nz) Unpowered/powered sites $10/11 per person, dorm beds $16, cabins $36-49, studio units $73, family units $85. This large, well-equipped park is right on the beach. Exception for the small backpackers lodge, prices rise sharply over Christmas/January.

Tatahi Lodge (☎ 09-866 3992, e tatahi_lodge@xtra.co.nz, Grange Rd) Dorm beds $20, doubles $45, 2-bedroom units $125 per double. Tatahi Lodge, located behind the Hahei Store, is a motel with high standard, purpose-built backpacker accommodation. The self-contained, two-bedroom units are reasonable value for a group of four. The lodge lends out shovels for Hot Water Beach and arranges transport.

Fernbird (☎ 09-866 3080, 24 Harsant Ave) Dorms $18, doubles $46. On the same street as the camping ground, Fernbird is a small hostel with a homely touch.

The Church (☎ 09-866 3533, 87 Beach Rd) Studios $105, cottages $125, 1-bedroom cottages $140. In a pleasant garden behind the Church Restaurant are these lovely timber cottages, with en suites and modern furnishings. The **restaurant** (☎ 09-866 3797) is the best in Hahei. Housed in a beautifully rebuilt former church, the a la carte menu (mains $18-26) has a Mediterranean and Pacific Rim flavour.

The tiny Grange Court Shopping Centre has a general store. There are also a couple of good places to eat including the **Luna Cafe** (☎ 09-866 3016) and **Breakers Restaurant** (☎ 09-866 3502).

Getting There & Around

The easiest way to get from Whitianga to Hahei is by using the ferry crossing. Hot Water Beach Connections runs a bus from Ferry Landing at 7.15am, 9.30am, 12.30pm, 2.30pm and 4.30pm to Cook's Beach ($3), Hahei and Hot Water Beach ($10), with some services continuing to Dalmeny Corner on the highway for connections with buses to Auckland and Whitianga. The $35 explorer pass allows you to use the service as much as you like over a three-day period. You can pick up a timetable and make booking at the Whitianga visitors centre.

TAIRUA & PAUANUI
pop 2600

This schizophrenic twin-town is separated by Tairua Harbour. A passenger ferry links the two, otherwise it's a long, worthless drive. Tairua, the original settlement, lies on the highway and has the wider choice of accommodation, especially in the budget range. The main attraction here is the climb to the top of **Paku** (an old *pa* site), which provides great views. If you climb Paku, legend has it that you will return in seven years. The ranges away from the coast also offer a number of **walks**, including the Broken Hills and Puketui Valley.

Pauanui, on the other hand, is an upmarket suburban development of canal-side homes for the rich and (at least in NZ) famous. The ferry service (☎ 09-864 8133 before 6pm, 025 970 316 after hours) from the Paku marina makes regular crossings between 9am and 5pm (till 7pm on Saturday; $2 one way, children $1).

The Tairua visitors centre (☎ 09-864 7575) on SH25 is open from 9am to 4pm daily (shorter hours in winter). The Pauanui visitors centre (☎ 09-864 7101) is at the Pauanui shopping centre.

Off the coast, the privately-owned **Slipper Island**, has camping ($10 per person) and expensive lodge accommodation an a *resort* (☎ 09-298 8459, W *www.slipper.co.nz)*. It's a beautiful little retreat, but the problem for independent travellers on a budget is actually getting out there: There are no scheduled boat services. It's possible to charter a boat for around $90, or join a group. Enquire through the resort or at **Tairua Dive & Fishing** (☎ 09-864 8054), on the Paku Marina, which also organises kayak tours on the estuary and dive trips.

For nature and wilderness walks in this area, **Kiwi Dundee Adventures** (☎ 09-865 8809) has built up quite a reputation over the years. Guide, Doug Johansen, has been called NZ's answer to Crocodile Dundee, and he'll lead you on informative day-long adventure walks. They're not cheap, at $178, but you pay for experience.

Places to Stay

Tairua Estuary Holiday Park (☎ 09-864 8551, 116 Pepe Rd) Unpowered/powered sites $10, cabins from $45. This park is well situated on the estuary at the end of Pepe Rd, about 10 minutes' walk from town.

Tairua Backpackers Lodge (☎ 09-864 8345, 200 Main Rd) Tent sites $12.50 per person, dorm beds $20, twins/doubles $46. This is a top-notch backpackers in a Spanish-style villa overlooking the harbour. Friendly and well run, it's also a windsurfing school ($10 a session for guests), with gear (eg, windsurfers, canoes and wave skis) available free. The owners can advise on walking in the Puketui Valley and furnish you with an interesting 'survival kit'.

Pinnacles Backpackers (☎ 09-864 8448, 305 Main Rd) Tent sites $12 per person, dorm beds $18, twins/doubles $44. Formerly known as the Flying Dutchman, Pinnacles is

on the highway just north of the shopping strip. It's pretty basic but clean and has a balcony leading off the recreation room.

There are at least 10 motels or lodges in Tairua and Pauanui. A cheapish option is *Blue Water Motel* (☎ 09-864 8537, Main Rd South) on the highway, which has rooms for $75 outside peak season.

Pacific Harbour Lodge (☎ 09-864 8581, Main Rd). Doubles $110. Rates rise to $160 in summer. This is a more upmarket 'island-style' resort with the very good *Shells Restaurant* (☎ 09-864 8811).

Places to Eat

In Tairua, *Out of the Blue Cafe* on the main road has decent coffee and a range of light meals.

Punters Cafe & Bar, on the highway opposite Pacific Harbour Lodge, has cheap fare such as burgers and pizzas and does meal deals for backpackers.

Upper Deck Restaurant & Bar (☎ 09-864 7499, 1 Paku Marina) Mains $16-24. In the grounded SS *Ngorio*, this almost-floating restaurant is a former Auckland steamer ferry. It's an atmospheric place for a meal or a drink (open from 6pm) with occasional live entertainment in summer.

OPOUTERE

Secluded Opoutere has 5km of fine beach and, about a 15 minutes' walk from the road, the **Wharekawa Wildlife Refuge**, a breeding ground of the endangered NZ dotterel and the variable oystercatcher.

Opoutere YHA (☎ 09-865 9072) Tent sites $12 per person, dorm beds $15-17, doubles $46. This long-running YHA is a brilliant place to get away from it all. It's in a pretty setting, almost encircled by native bush and overlooking Wharekawa Harbour. Take one of the hostel's kayaks and paddle around, and there are plenty of bushwalks in the area. There are small dorms separate from the main house, or you can bunk down in the larger former schoolhouse. The management is friendly and informative.

Opoutere Park Beach Resort (☎ 09-865 9152), just down the road from the Opoutere YHA, has camping, cabins and beach access.

THE COROMANDEL

A local bus (☎ 09-863 8627) runs between Opoutere and Waihi ($23), where you can connect with Intercity services to Auckland or Rotorua.

WHANGAMATA
pop 3880

Whangamata (pronounced fa-nga-ma-ta) has a great 4km surf beach with an excellent break by the bar, which attracts a big influx of surfers and NZ holiday-makers in summer. It's not a particularly attractive town by Coromandel standards and is a major service centre, but there are some interesting **craft** outlets on Port Rd, the main shopping strip.

Whangamata can serve as a base for plenty of activities (eg, horse riding, game fishing, kayaking, windsurfing and mountain biking) and the region has some excellent walks. The most popular is the **Wentworth Falls walk**, which takes one hour (one way) through beautiful bush. To get to the track, follow the highway south for 3km to the turn-off and then 4km to the camping ground. From the falls, a harder trail (get advice at the camping ground) leads to the top of the ranges and on to Marakopa Rd.

The Whangamata visitors centre (☎ 09-865 8340) on Port Rd is open from 9am to 5pm Monday to Saturday, 10am to 2pm Sunday. Bartley Internet & Graphics, next to the cinema on Port Rd, has Internet access.

Places to Stay

As well as the places listed below, there are quite a few homestays and lodges in the area – the visitors centre has a list.

Pinefield Holiday Park (☎ 09-865 8791, e *pinefield@xtra.co.nz, 207 Port Rd*) Unpowered/powered sites $10/12, cabins $35-150. Just south of town, Pinefield is a well-equipped park with a large pool and limited backpacker accommodation.

Garden Tourist Lodge (☎/fax 09-865 9580, e *gardenlodge@xtra.co.nz, cnr Port Rd & Mayfair Ave*) Dorm beds $20, twins/doubles $47, motel units $75-85 ($110-130 peak season). This spotless motel complex, about 1km south of the shopping centre, has a good backpackers with a well-equipped kitchen and common areas.

Whangamata Backpackers Hostel (☎/fax 09-865 8323, 227 Beverley Terrace) Dorm beds $18, doubles $35. This basic backpackers occupies the bottom half of a tatty house just a few minutes from the beach. It's popular with surfers.

Whangamata Motel (☎ 09-865 8250, 106 Barbara Ave) Doubles from $70. Well-located a block east of the main street, this standard motel has one- and two-bedroom units and a pool.

Wentworth Valley Campground (☎ 09-865 7032) Camp sites $7. This DOC-owned campground is in a beautiful valley at the start of the trek to Wentworth Falls, 7km from Whangamata. It has gas barbecues and hot showers.

Bushland Park Lodge (☎ 09-865 7468, e *bushparklodge@xtra.co.nz*) Doubles from $175-290. The upmarket Bushland Lodge is also in Wentworth Valley, but it's in the seriously-pamper-yourself category, with luxurious rooms, saunas, spas and massages, and a winery-style restaurant. Breakfast is included.

Places to Eat

Whangamata has a surprising number of decent cafes and restaurants, mostly on or just off Port Rd, along with the usual takeaways.

Vibes Cafe is a relaxed, trendy place, and *Neros*, across the road, specialises in wood-fired pizzas.

Caffe Rossini (☎ 09-865 6117, 646 Port Rd) Dishes $14-29. Almost next door to Vibes, Rossini is more refined with a Mediterranean menu. Lunchtime fare (eg, panini, burgers and salads) is all under $10.

Cafe 101 (☎ 09-865 6301, Casement Rd) Mains $14-16, open Thur-Sun. Cafe 101, off Port Rd, has a musical theme and regular live performances.

Oceana's (☎ 09-865 7157, 328 Ocean Rd) Mains $12-27. Away from the main restaurant strip, this is a good spot for dinner with seafood featuring heavily on the menu.

WAIHI
pop 4700

Once a booming gold-mining town, Waihi is at the foot of the Coromandel Forest Park on the main highway to Tauranga. Gold was first discovered here in 1878 and Martha Mine became the richest gold mine in NZ. It closed in 1952 but has since reopened with a lookout over part of the enormous pit from the pumphouse next to the Waihi visitors centre (☎ 09-863 6715) on Seddon St.

Things to See & Do

The interesting **Waihi Arts Centre & Museum** (*☎ 09-863 8386, Kenny St; adult/child $3/1; open summer 10am-4pm Mon-Fri, 1.30pm-4pm Sat & Sun*) explains the region's goldmining history with models and displays relating to the Martha Mine.

Tours of the **Martha Mine** (*☎ 09-863 9880*) are available on weekdays. There is no charge, but donations are welcome and the money given to non-profit community organisations. Bookings are essential.

Railway buffs have repaired 8km of track between Waihi and Waikino and run the **Goldfields Vintage Train** (*☎ 09-863 8251; $10/4 adult/child return*) between the towns. To get to Waihi train station turn off SH2 at Wrigley St and proceed to the end. Trains depart Waihi daily at 11am, 12.30pm and 2pm. Around Waikino there are several walks and points of historical interest – see the Karangahake Gorge section later.

Waihi Beach, 11km east, is a small, expanding town with a fine surf beach. The town is technically in the Bay of Plenty and gets packed over Christmas and New Year. There's local information at Waihi Beach Natural Health (☎ 09-863 4350) on Wilson Rd. Continuing south along the coast takes you to Bowentown and Athenree, smaller beachside communities.

Places to Stay

Waihi Motor Camp (*☎ 09-863 7654, 6 Waitete Rd*) Unpowered/powered sites $20, cabins $30-40 per double, self-contained flats $55. This is close to town, though the parks at Waihi Beach are better located.

Golden Cross (*☎ 09-863 6306, cnr Rosemount & Kenny Sts*) Dorm beds $15, rooms $20 per person. Golden Cross is an old pub offering backpacker beds in shared rooms, as well as singles, doubles and twin rooms.

The **Palm Motel** (*☎ 09-863 8461, Parry Palm Ave*) and **Waihi Motel** (*☎ 09-863 8095, Tauranga Rd*) on SH2, both have single/double rooms starting at $65/75.

Westwind B&B (*☎ 09-863 7208, 22 Roycroft St*) Singles/doubles $35/65. Westwind, about 500m from the visitors centre, is a guesthouse set in a lovely garden.

The visitors centre has an up-to-date list of more B&Bs and homestays in the area.

Waihi Beach The **Waihi Beach Holiday Park** (*☎ 09-863 5504, 15 Main Rd*) is a very slick park with a couple of backpacker cabins ($19 per person). Campers have the option of an staying in area closer to the beach, with their own kitchen and amenities (unpowered/powered sites $12 per person). There are also cabins for $40-60 per double and self-contained units for $70. Surfboards, boogie boards, bikes and kayaks can be hired here.

Waihi Beach Backpackers (*☎ 09-863 4587, 8 Scarborough Rd*) Dorm beds $16, doubles $32. This small, unpretentious backpackers doesn't look like much but it has a homely ambience. Pick-ups can be arranged from Waihi and a surfing instructor is usually on hand. You can pitch a tent for $8 per person.

Waterfront Homestay (*☎/fax 09-863 4342, 17 The Esplanade*) Singles/doubles $50/75. This is one of several B&Bs close to the beach. It offers comfortable homestay accommodation.

Athenree Hot Springs & Holiday Park (*☎ 09-863 5600, Athenree Rd*) Unpowered/powered sites $12 per person, cabins $40-65 a double, motel units $80 a double. This small park, 10km from Waihi Beach, has ageing cabins but the big attraction is the thermal-fed hot pool (free to guests).

Places to Eat

Miners Arms (*☎ 09-863 8591, 65 Seddon St*) Open 8.30am-3pm Mon-Sat. The Miners Arms is a licensed cafe that has loads of character as well as the usual line-up of burgers, wedges, salads and quiche.

The **Farmhouse Cafe** (*☎ 09-863 7649, 14 Haszard St*) This pleasant garden cafe,

THE COROMANDEL

just off Seddon Ave, has a range of sandwiches and home-made pies.

Chambers Wine Bar & Restaurant (☎ *09-863 7474, 22 Haszard St*) Lunch $9.50-16, dinner $22-28. This classy licensed place in the former council chambers has an interesting dinner menu – venison, kangaroo and ostrich steak – and inexpensive meals and snacks available during the day.

Grandpa Thorn's (☎ *09-863 8708, 4 Waitete Rd*) Mains $20-26. Open Tues-Sun from 6pm. Grandpa Thorn's is a rustic log cabin restaurant in a rural setting a couple of kilometres from town. Steak and seafood are the specialities.

Jellyfish & Custard Restaurant & Bar (☎ *09-863 5840, 21 Shaw Rd*) $8.50-14.50. At Waihi Beach, this intriguingly named restaurant specialises in gourmet pizzas and has a hip bar with happy hour from 4.30pm to 6.30pm.

Hauraki Region

pop 21,100

The pancake-flat Hauraki Plains are drained by the Piako and Waihou Rivers, which flow into the Firth of Thames.

The main drawcard here is the superb bird-watching on the firth at Miranda. The hot springs at Miranda and Te Aroha may also help slow the traveller down. Between the rural centre of Paeroa and the mining town of Waihi is the historic Karangahake Gorge, with numerous walks.

MIRANDA & KAIAUA

Avid bird-watchers love this area – one of the most accessible for studying birds. It's off the Thames-Pokeno road, an hour's drive from Auckland. The vast mudflat on the western side of the Firth of Thames is teeming with aquatic worms and crustaceans, which attract thousands of Arctic-nesting shore birds over the winter. The two main species seen are the bar-tailed godwit and the lesser knot, but it isn't unusual to see turnstones, curlew sandpipers, sharp-tailed sandpipers and the odd vagrant red-necked stint and terek sandpiper.

Miranda also attracts internal migrants after the godwits and knots have departed, including the pied oystercatcher and the wrybill from the South Island, and banded dotterels and pied stilts from both main islands. First stop should be the **Miranda Shorebird Centre** (☎ *09-232 2781,* e *shorebird@ xtra.co.nz*), 7km south of Kaiaua, open 9am to 5pm daily. There are interpretive displays here and binoculars for hire, and you can pick up a copy of the useful *Shore Bird Migration to and from Miranda.*

The **Miranda Hot Springs complex** (☎ *09-867 3055; adult/child $8/5; open 8am-9pm Mon-Thurs, 8am-10.30pm Fri-Sun*) is the country's largest mineral pools complex. It has open and covered thermal hot pools, private spas, saunas, play areas and a holiday park next door.

Places to Stay & Eat

Miranda Naturalists' Trust Centre (☎ *09-232 2781*) Bunk beds non-members/ members $15/10, self-contained units $45/35 per double. This place has clean and modern rooms at its education centre. Membership of the trust is $30 per year.

Bayview Hotel (☎ *09-232 2717, East Coast Rd*) Doubles $65. The pub in Kaiaua has motel-style en suite rooms. This is also a good place for a drink or a bistro meal, with a big beer garden out the back.

Miranda Holiday Park (☎ *09-867 3205,* e *mirandaholidaypark@xtra.co.nz*) Unpowered/powered sites $14, backpacker beds $25, motel units $100 per double. Not far south of the centre, next to the hot springs, is this tidy park – the main advantage of staying here (in the middle of nowhere) is that the hot pools are free.

Kaiaua Fisheries (☎ *09-232 2776*) This is a very popular takeaway fish-and-chip shop (mainly with bus tour groups) with a licensed seafood restaurant attached. Tuck into a serve of hoki and chips for $3.50.

PAEROA
pop 4000

The Maori name for the Coromandel range was Te Paeroa-o-Toi (The Long Range of Toi) and local Maori are descendants of the

Arawa and *Tainui* canoe crews. In the early colonial period, before the plains were drained, Paeroa was a thriving port, and evidence of this can be seen at the otherwise drab **Paeroa Historical Maritime Park** (*☎ 09-862 7121; adult/child $4/2; open 10am-4pm daily*), about 3km north-west of town. The double-paddle steamer *Kopu* once operated between Paeroa and Auckland.

Paeroa's only claim to fame these days is that New Zealand's own 'internationally famous in NZ' soft drink, Lemon & Paeroa, had its beginnings here. A couple of giant L&P bottles are the only reminders.

The Paeroa visitors centre (*☎/fax 09-862 8636*), on Belmont Rd (SH2), is open from 9am to 5pm Monday to Friday, 10am to 3pm on Saturday and Sunday during summer. The town has a small **museum** (*open 10.30am-3pm Mon-Fri*) and is a popular centre for antique and second-hand junk shops.

Karangahake Gorge
The 4.5km Karangahake Gorge Historic Walkway, along the Ohinemuri River, was created when the Paeroa to Waihi railway line was closed in 1979.

At the western end of the gorge, about 5km from Paeroa, is a car park and a swingbridge leading to numerous walkways and tunnels which pass by the remains of ore-crushing plants. It takes about 1½ hours to walk to Waikino, at the eastern end of the gorge. The **visitors centre** in Waikino, now the terminus of the 6km Waihi to Waikino vintage railway, has information on the history and walks of the area. The DOC pamphlet *Karangahake Gorge Historic Walkway* also outlines several walks.

Three highlights of the walkway are the **Owharoa Falls** and the Talisman and Victoria **gold battery sites**. There's a small **museum** in Waikino and the **goldfield train** that runs between Waikino and Waihi (see the earlier Waihi section).

Ohinemuri Estate Winery & Cafe (*☎ 09-862 8874, Moresby St, Karangahake*), on SH2 about 6km east of Paeroa towards Waikino, serves Mediterranean-style food and has wine tastings. It's open daily in summer from 10am-5pm.

Places to Stay & Eat
It's hard to think of a good reason to stay in Paeroa, but there are plenty of motels and cheap rooms in the local pubs if you do.

Criterion Hotel (*☎ 09-862 7983, 145 Normanby Rd*) Singles $20. The Criterion, on the main street near the Hamilton turn-off, has pub rooms with shared bath.

Casa Mexicana (*☎ 0800 654040, 862 8216, 71 Puke Rd*) Singles/doubles $58/70. North of the visitors centre on the highway, Casa Mexicana has reasonably priced units.

World Famous in New Zealand Cafe Bar (*☎ 09-862 7773, Belmont Rd*) $8.50-14.50. Cashing in on the L&P brand name, this is part dull cafeteria, part fancy bar, with an L&P merchandising shop next door! Pizzas costs $14.50 and there's a range of ready-made snacks.

The Lazy Fish (*☎ 09-862 8822, Belmont St*) This trendy little cafe with Mediterranean flavour is the pick of the places for a coffee or light meal in Paeroa.

TE AROHA
pop 3800
Te Aroha, 31km south of Paeroa and 55km north-east of Hamilton on SH26, is just far enough off the tourist trail to discourage most express tourists. But a combination of some good walks followed by therapeutic spa treatment makes it worth the detour if you have time.

Te Aroha is at the foot of the mountain of the same name. The name (literally 'The Love') comes from a story of a chief who sat here filled with love for his people and the land.

In the late 19th century, Te Aroha became a favourite spa resort with people who flocked down from Auckland hoping a soak in the waters could cure anything from gout to asthma. The hot mineral and soda pools in the domain are still a great place to relax and rest any aching muscles.

Information
The Te Aroha visitors centre (*☎ 09-884 8052*), 102 Whitaker St, is open from 9am to 5pm Monday to Friday and 10am to 3pm Saturday and Sunday (shorter hours in

winter). It sells maps and provides information on Mt Te Aroha and the Kaimai-Mamaku Forest Park, and has a small display on the region's history.

Internet access is available at Air Quay Cyber Cafe (☎ 09-884 9228) on Whitaker St.

Things to See & Do

The main attraction is a soak in the **Te Aroha Mineral Pools** (☎ 09-884 8717) in the Domain, which have two types of thermal water: soda and mineral. The Edwardian bathhouses have private pools and you can choose between the roomier wooden baths or the stainless steel tubs – to which you can add soaps or aromatherapy oils. A half-hour spa costs $7 between 10am and 4pm Monday to Friday, $8 between 4pm and 10pm Monday to Friday and $9 Saturday and Sunday. Towel hire is $3.

Also here is the outdoor **Wyborn Leisure Pool** ($4) and a health spa and **massage** centre ($25/40 for half-/one-hour massage).

Behind the pools is the 3.5m-spouting **Mokena Geyser**, said to be the only soda-water geyser in the world. It's quite active, erupting every half-hour or so.

The **Te Aroha Museum** (*admission by donation; open 26 Dec-31 Mar 11am-4pm daily*), located in the Cadman building in the domain, occupies the town's original bathhouse building and has exhibits on the mining and agricultural development of the town. From April to December it's open weekends only from 1pm to 3pm.

History or music buffs might be interested in NZ's oldest organ, the 1712 **Renatus Pipe organ** in St Mark's Church.

Walking

The walking tracks up **Mt Te Aroha** start at the rear of the domain, from behind the hot pools. It takes about an hour on a relatively easy track to ascend to the Bald Spur Lookout (350m), also called the Whakapipi Lookout; it's a further two hours' steep climbing to reach Te Aroha's summit (950m). The view is magnificent. For a two-day tramp, walk all the way to Karangahake Gorge via Daley's Clearing Hut. The visitors centre has details.

Places to Stay & Eat

Te Aroha Holiday Park (☎ 09-884 9567, 217 Stanley Rd) Unpowered/powered sites $8/9 per person, backpackers beds $13, cabins from $30 per double, motel units $52. About 3km south-west of town, this simple park is in a pleasant rural setting with shady camping areas.

Te Aroha YHA (☎ 09-884 8739, e tearoha.yha@xtra.co.nz, Miro St) Dorm beds $14, doubles $32. Above the town this small, TV-free cottage is not fancy but it's a pleasure to stay in. Separate sex shared rooms have their own bathroom. Bicycles are available free and the walking and mountain biking track up Mt Te Aroha starts right outside the door.

Te Aroha Motel (☎ 09-884 9417, 108 Whitaker St) Singles/doubles $58/70. This standard motel next to the visitors centre is good value, with self-contained studio units.

Aroha Mountain Lodge (☎/fax 09-884 8134, 5 Boundary St) Single/double B&B $110/150. Right next to the Domain spa entrance, this comfortable B&B has four en suite rooms (each with a different theme).

Ironique Cafe & Bar (☎ 09-884 8489, 159 Whitaker St) Lunch $5-12.50, dinner $15-24. This stylish cafe features a hand-crafted totara (a native tree) interior, good food and massive cups of coffee. As well as burgers, panini and pastas, there's a vegetarian menu with such kiwi cuisine as kumara and camembert ($8.50).

Caffé Banco (☎ 09-884 7574, 174 Whitaker St) Lunch $8-16, dinner $22-26. Open for lunch Tues-Sun, dinner Thur-Sun. Behind the impressive facade of the old 1922 town bank is a trendy licensed cafe.

Domain House Restaurant (☎ 09-884 9675, 1 Wilson St) This restaurant is housed in a lovely Edwardian heritage building. It's a bit formal, but a perfect spot for lunch overlooking the croquet lawns.

Getting There & Away

Turley-Murphy Buses (☎ 09-884 8208) has a service between Hamilton and Te Aroha ($10, 1hr) and from Te Aroha to Thames ($14.60, 40mins) on Monday to Friday only. These connect with InterCity services.

Waikato & the King Country

The Waikato, one of the world's richest dairy, thoroughbred and agricultural areas, is about one hour's drive from central Auckland. It includes four fertile plains, quiet coastal towns such as Raglan and Kawhia, and Hamilton, New Zealand's fifth-largest city, as its major centre. The region also encompasses the central and lower reaches of New Zealand's longest river, the Waikato, which starts in central North Island, flows out from Lake Taupo and meets the sea on the west coast.

Further south is a historic region known as the King Country, extending roughly from the towns of Otorohanga in the north to Taumarunui in the south, and from Lake Taupo west to the coast. The feather in the region's cap is Waitomo Caves, famous for its glowworms and underground activities.

Waikato

☎ 07 • pop 236,200

The Waikato region was cultivated by the Maori in pre-European times; archaeological evidence shows that thousands of hectares were under cultivation with kumara (sweet potatoes) and other crops.

When the Europeans settled in Auckland in 1840, relations with the local Maori were peaceful at first; missionaries in the 1830s introduced European crops and farming methods to the Waikato region, and by the 1840s the Maori were trading their agricultural produce with the European settlers in Auckland.

Relations between the two cultures soured during the 1850s, largely due to the Europeans' eyeing of Maori land for settlement. By the early 1860s the Waikato Maori had formed a 'King Movement' and united to elect a king. The movement probably stemmed both from a need for greater organisation of Maori tribes against the Pakeha and from a desire to have a Maori leader equivalent to the British queen when dealing with the Pakeha.

Highlights

- Experiencing adventure activities at Waitomo Caves
- Surfing at Raglan beaches
- Exploring the coastal backwaters of Kawhia, Marokopa and Mokau
- Enjoying the rich agricultural lands of the Waikato, the English-style settlements of Cambridge and the secluded reaches of the Waikato River

Potatau Te Wherowhero was a paramount high chief of the Waikato tribes when he was made the first Maori king in 1858. He died in 1860 aged about 85 and was succeeded by his son, the second and most widely known Maori king, Matutaera Te Wherowhero – known as King Tawhiao – who ruled for the next 34 years until his death.

The King Movement was a nationalistic step for the Maori, who were unwilling to sell or otherwise lose their homeland to the Europeans. The Europeans, however, were equally unwilling to take no for an answer. In July 1863 they sent a fleet of gunboats and small craft up the Waikato River to put down what they regarded as the 'open rebellion' of

WAIKATO & THE KING COUNTRY

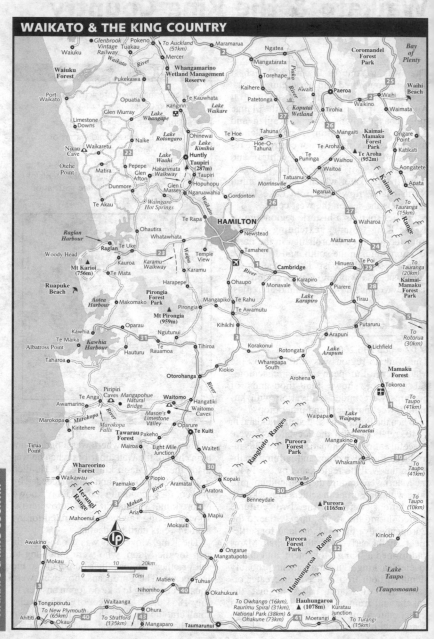

the Maori King Movement. After almost a year of warfare, known as the Waikato Land War and involving many historic battles, the Pakeha finally won in April 1864 and the Kingites retreated south to what became known as the King Country, where Europeans dared not venture for several more decades.

AUCKLAND TO HAMILTON

The trip to Hamilton by road from Auckland takes about 1½ hours and there are a few points of interest along the way. Steam train enthusiasts pause at the **Glenbrook Vintage Railway** (☎ 09-235 8924, adult/child $10/5), where 12km steam train rides run on Sunday and public holidays between late October and early June. There are plans to extend the track into the heart of Waiuku. To get there follow the yellow signs west after leaving the Southern Motorway at Drury, 31km south of Auckland, and head for Waiuku.

The Waiuku visitors centre (☎ 09-235 8924) at 2 Queen St has information on the sailing scow *Jane Gifford* (undergoing maintenance at the time of writing) and other attractions in the Waiuku area.

Mercer, 55km south of Auckland, is a good petrol/food stop where you can buy bacon and pork produced locally at Pokeno, and locally produced cheese and wine.

Te Kauwhata, 67km south of Auckland and just off SH1, is home to a couple of wineries, including **Rongopai Wines** (☎ 07-826 3981, Wayside Rd) and **Cooks Landing** (☎ 07-826 0004, Paddy Rd). A few kilometres south on SH1 is the **Rangiriri Battle Site Heritage Centre** (☎ 07-826 3663; open 9am-4pm daily). New Zealand is a little bereft in representing the history of the land wars between European and Maori – this is a small attempt to redress the imbalance. Wander over the battleground, including cemetery and redoubts, where a small group of warriors made a stand against the British forces in November 1863.

From Rangiriri the road follows the Waikato River all the way to Hamilton. Along the way, **Huntly** is a coal-mining town with its large power station. The visitors centre (☎ 07-828 6406) is at 160 Great South

Rd. There is also the **Huntly Mining & Cultural Museum** (☎ 07-828 8128, 26 Harlock Place; adult/child $3/1; open 10am-3pm Mon-Fri, 1pm-3pm Sat). If you're looking for more steam train action, **The Bush Tramway Club** (☎ 07-828 4859, Glen Afton; tickets $8/4; open 10.30am-3.30pm Apr-Dec) operates steam train rides from Pukemrio Junction, 8km west of Huntly.

South of Huntly the road enters Taupiri Gorge, a gap through the ranges. On the left, as you emerge from the gorge, is the sacred mountain Taupiri, and a Maori cemetery on the hillside where past Maori kings are buried.

Ngaruawahia, 19km north of Hamilton on SH1, is an important centre for the Waikato Maori people and the home of the present Maori queen, Te Arikinui Dame Te Atairangikaahu. The Ngaruawahia Regatta is held here every March. About 300m east of SH1, beside the river on River Rd, is the impressive **Turangawaewae Marae**.

If you're fit, the top of Taupiri Mountain has excellent views (a sign on the track explains the appropriate etiquette near graves), and the **Hakarimata Walkway** on the opposite side of the river also has good views. The northern end leads off Parker Rd, which can be reached by crossing the river at Huntly and following the Ngaruawahia-Huntly West Road. The southern end meets the Ngaruawahia-Waingaro Road just out of Ngaruawahia. To walk the length of the track takes seven hours.

A shorter walk, and easier to get to if you have no transport, is the three-hour return trek from Brownlee Ave, Ngaruawahia, to Hakarimata Trig (371m). The top part is fairly steep but the view is rewarding. Tracks from each access point meet at the trig.

If you detour west, off SH22, you'll find **Nikau Cave** (☎ 09-233 3199, 1779 Waikaretu Rd, RD5 Tuakau; 1-hr tours up to 2 adults & 1 child $50, additional adult/child $20/10), where you can see glowworms, limestone formations and subterranean streams. The cave lies beneath a farm and the farm owners will happily take you on tours. Hats and torches are supplied, just bring sturdy shoes with a decent tread.

Te Arikinui Dame Te Atairangikaahu

The Maori King Movement, in which local chief Te Wherowhero was elected as the first Maori king in 1859, is still very much alive among the Waikato tribe. Te Arikinui Dame Te Atairangikaahu, 'the Maori queen', is sixth in the line of succession.

Her father, Koroki Mahuta, was the fifth Maori king. When he died in 1966, there was widespread concern over his successor, since he had no sons but two daughters, Tura and Piki, and there had never been a Maori queen.

According to Tainui tradition, if an *ariki* (first-born of a noble family) died and had no sons, office would be passed on to a close male relation. This posed a major question: should it be passed on to one of Koroki Mahuta's female descendants or bestowed upon someone else?

After much discussion and debate, the Waikato chiefs and elders decided that the office should pass to his daughter Piki. Princess Piki became the first Maori queen on 23 May 1966. In 1970 Queen Elizabeth II gave her the title of Dame Commander of the British Empire, and her official title became Te Arikinui Dame Te Atairangikaahu.

Many Westerners misunderstand her position, believing her to be queen of all New Zealand Maori; in fact Te Arikinui Dame Te Atairangikaahu is queen only of the tribes who united to form the Maori King Movement in the 1850s. She is head of the Tainui tribal confederation, which consists of four major tribes: the Waikato, Maniapoto, Hauraki and Raukawa – all descended from those who arrived in NZ on the *Tainui* canoe (see the boxed text 'The *Tainui* Canoe' later in this chapter). Tainui is one of NZ's largest Maori confederations.

Te Arikinui Dame Te Atairangikaahu's *marae* is the magnificent Turangawaewae Marae, beside the Waikato River in Ngaruawahia. If you are travelling through Ngaruawahia on SH1, you can see the marae as you cross the bridge over the river. The queen has houses in various places significant to her people – for example, there is a house for the Maori queen beside the Maketu Marae in Kawhia, where the *Tainui* canoe is buried.

HAMILTON

pop 132,100

New Zealand's largest inland city, Hamilton is 129km south of Auckland. Built on the banks of the Waikato River, it is the Waikato region's major centre and in the past few decades has undergone spectacular growth.

Archaeological evidence shows that the Maori had long been settled around the Hamilton area but when Europeans arrived, the site was deserted. European settlement was initiated by the Waikato Militia, who were persuaded to enlist with promises of an acre in town and another 50 in the country. The advance party, led by Captain William Steele, travelled up the Waikato River on a barge drawn by a gunboat and on 24 August 1864 went ashore at the deserted Maori village of Kirikirioa. The township built on that site was named after John Fane Charles Hamilton, the popular commander of HMS *Esk,* who had been killed in Tauranga at the battle of Gate Pa four months earlier.

The Waikato River was once Hamilton's only transport and communication link with other towns including Auckland, but it was superseded by the railway in 1878 and later by roads.

Orientation & Information

Running north to south a block from the Waikato River, Victoria St is the main commercial thoroughfare with most essential services.

The Hamilton Visitor Information Centre (☎ 07-839 3580, W www.waikatonz.com), is at the Hamilton Transport Centre on the corner of Bryce and Anglesea Sts. It's open 8.30am to 5pm Monday to Friday, 9am to 4pm Saturday and 10am to 4pm Sunday. It has information on the Hamilton, Waitomo and Waikato regions and also sells bus and train tickets and has Internet access.

DOC (☎ 07-838 3363) is at 18 London St near the river. The Map Shop (☎ 07-856 4450), 361 Grey St, has maps of NZ and most of the world. The Automobile Association (AA; ☎ 07-839 1397) is at 295 Barton St and there's a post office on Bryce St.

Waikato Museum of Art & History

This museum (☎ 07-838 6606, 1 Grantham St; open 10am-4pm daily) is in a modernistic building overlooking the river. It has a good Maori collection, with carvings and the impressively large and intricately carved Te Winika war canoe, dating from 1836. The canoe has been beautifully restored, a project displayed in photos along the wall. Entry fees vary depending on what exhibition is currently running. The attractive *Museum Cafe* is good for a snack.

Also at the museum is **Exscite** (☎ 07-838 3470; adult/child $5/3), the Science and Technology Exhibition Centre which has science exhibits and hands-on activities.

Close by is **ArtsPost** (☎ 07-839 2315, 120 Victoria St; admission free; open 10am-4.30pm), an art gallery focusing on local artists.

Mormon Temple

This temple at Tuhikaramea, 12km southwest of the city centre, is worth visiting, if just for pondering how and why it became the first to be established by the Church of Latter-Day Saints in the South Pacific. The best time to visit the temple is at night over Christmas; it has a visitors centre (free guided tours; open 9am-9pm daily).

Parks & Gardens

The huge **Hamilton Gardens** (☎ 07-856 3200, Cobham Dr; free; open 7.30am-sunset) complex contains a multitude of different theme gardens – rose gardens, a riverside magnolia garden, a scented garden, cacti and succulents, vegetable and glasshouse gardens, carnivorous plants, and many more, with new ones still under construction. The complex is about 3km southeast of the city centre, and can be reached by following the river upstream along the river walkway, or by taking the SH1 out of town.

Other relaxing spots are **Hamilton Lake (Rotoroa)** and the **Waikato River**. Walkways pass through verdant parks and bushy areas on both sides of the river, through the city, all the way south to Cobham Bridge. The area below the Bridge St bridge, on the east bank, is particularly attractive. Embedded in the riverbank walkway are the remains of the gunboat SS *Rangiriri*, which was used in the Waikato Land War.

Hamilton Zoo

More natural pens, walkways and a programme to house endangered species from around the world make this zoo (☎ 07-838 6720, Brymer Rd; adult/child $7.50/4; open 9am-5pm daily, last entry 3.30pm) one of NZ's best. It is well laid out with spacious grounds and the largest walk-through aviary in the southern hemisphere. It is 8km from the city – take Norton Rd then SH23 west towards Raglan, turn right at Newcastle Rd and then left onto Brymer Rd.

Activities

The historic paddleboat MV *Waipa Delta*, which made its first voyage on the Waikato River in 1877, runs popular **river cruises** (☎ 0800 472 3353; cruises Thur-Sun) from Memorial Park, on the riverbank opposite the town centre. Cruises range from afternoon tea ($20) to dinner cruises (adult/child $49/24.50). Reservations are recommended.

The visitors centre supplies a free map of the walkways around the lake, along the river and down to Hamilton Gardens. Information on other walks in and around Hamilton can be obtained from DOC.

Waterworld Te Rapa (☎ 07-849 4389, Garnett Ave, Te Rapa; adult/child $3.50/1.50; open 6am-9pm Mon-Fri, 7am-9pm Sat, 9am-9pm Sun), located 4km north of the centre, is large with several indoor and outdoor pools and waterslides.

Archies Tours (☎ 07-855 2860) has informative three-hour tours of Hamilton ($35) and places such as Waitomo ($105), Rotorua ($110) and Taupo ($105).

Places to Stay

Camping & Cabins Hamilton has a couple of camping grounds on the eastern side of the river, 2km or 3km from the city centre.

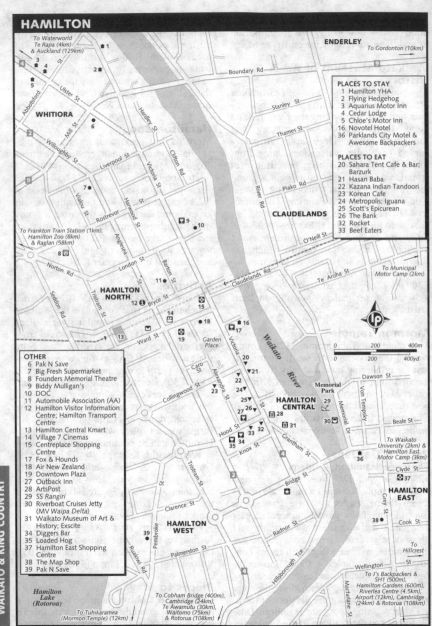

HAMILTON

PLACES TO STAY
1 Hamilton YHA
2 Flying Hedgehog
3 Aquarius Motor Inn
4 Cedar Lodge
5 Chloe's Motor Inn
16 Novotel Hotel
36 Parklands City Motel & Awesome Backpackers

PLACES TO EAT
20 Sahara Tent Cafe & Bar; Barzurk
21 Hasan Baba
22 Kazana Indian Tandoori
23 Korean Cafe
24 Metropolis; Iguana
25 Scott's Epicurean
26 The Bank
32 Rocket
33 Beef Eaters

OTHER
6 Pak N Save
7 Big Fresh Supermarket
8 Founders Memorial Theatre
9 Biddy Mulligan's
10 DOC
11 Automobile Association (AA)
12 Hamilton Visitor Information Centre; Hamilton Transport Centre
13 Hamilton Central Kmart
14 Village 7 Cinemas
15 Centreplace Shopping Centre
17 Fox & Hounds
18 Air New Zealand
19 Downtown Plaza
27 Outback Inn
28 ArtsPost
29 SS Rangiri
30 Riverboat Cruises Jetty (MV Waipa Delta)
31 Waikato Museum of Art & History; Exscite
34 Diggers Bar
35 Loaded Hog
37 Hamilton East Shopping Centre
38 The Map Shop
39 Pak N Save

ENDERLEY

To Gordonton (10km)

Boundary Rd

Stanley St

Thames St

Piako Rd

River Rd

CLAUDELANDS

O'Neill St

To Waterworld
Te Rapa (4km)
& Auckland (129km)

Ulster St

Abbotsford St

Mill St

WHITIORA

Willoughby St

Hardley St

Clifton Rd

Liverpool St

Victoria St

Harwood St

Vialou St

Rostrevor St

Anglesea St

To Frankton Train Station (1km),
Hamilton Zoo (8km)
& Raglan (58km)

Norton Rd

London St

Barton St

Seddon Rd

Tristram St

HAMILTON NORTH

Bryce St

Claudelands Rd

Te Aroha St

To Municipal Motor Camp (2km)

Ward St

Garden Place

Waikato River

Memorial Park

Dawson St

Von Tempsky St

Beale St

Caro St

Alexandra St

Collingwood St

Hood St

Knox St

HAMILTON CENTRAL

Grantham St

Memorial Dr

To Waikato University (2km) &
Hamilton East Motor Camp (3km)

Clyde St

HAMILTON EAST

Grey St

Cook St

To Hillcrest

Tristram St

Clarence St

HAMILTON WEST

Pembroke St

Palmerston St

Ruakiwi Rd

Bridge St

Radnor St

Hillsborough Tce

Wellington St

To J's Backpackers &
SH1 (500m),
Hamilton Gardens (600m),
Riverlea Centre (4.5km),
Airport (12km), Cambridge
(24km) & Rotorua (108km)

Macandrew St

Macdarlane St

Hamilton Lake (Rotoroa)

To Tuhikaramea
(Mormon Temple) (12km)

To Cobham Bridge (400m),
Cambridge (24km),
Te Awamutu (30km),
Waitomo (75km)
& Rotorua (108km)

0   200   400m
0   200   400yd

Municipal Motor Camp (☎ 07-855 8255, fax 855 3865, 14 Ruakura Rd) Powered/unpowered sites $18/15 for 2 people, cabins $36, tourist cabins $46. This place is 2km east of town. The staff are friendly and there is plenty of tree-shade.

Hamilton East Motor Camp (☎/fax 07-856 6220, e tourist.court@clear.net.nz, Cameron Rd) Powered/unpowered sites $17/14 for 2 people, cabins $30-38, tourist flats $48. This plain camp is 3km east of town.

Hostels Hamilton is not on the backpackers' route so there should be no problem finding a bed.

Flying Hedgehog (☎ 07-839 2800, e maxfield@centralcity.co.nz, 1157 Victoria St) Dorm beds $19, doubles & twins $50. The Flying Hedgehog is a converted motel in a quiet part of town. All rooms have TV.

Hamilton YHA (☎ 07-838 0009, e yha hamil@yha.org.nz, 1190 Victoria St) Dorm beds $16, singles $26, doubles $38. This large, welcoming YHA is beside the river a few blocks north of the centre, a pleasant 15-minute walk along the river.

J's Backpackers (☎ 07-856 8934, e admin@jsbackpackers.co.nz, 8 Grey St) Dorm beds $17, twins $40. This cosy hostel is in a suburban house, about 1.5km south of the Hamilton East shops. J's also offers a free pick-up service.

Farmstays, Homestays & B&Bs The visitors centre lists farmstays, homestays and B&Bs in the Waikato region.

Motels & Hotels There are many motels, particularly along Ulster St, the main road from the north.

Cedar Lodge (☎ 0800 105 252, 07-839 5569, 174 Ulster St) Units from $70. Cedar Lodge has cheap and spacious units.

Chloe's Motor Inn (☎ 0800 245 637, 07-839 3410, e chloes@ihug.co.nz, 181 Ulster St) Units from $89. Chloe's is a friendly place with well-kept units.

Aquarius Motor Inn (☎ 0800 839 244, 839 2447, e bookings@aquarius-motor-inn.co.nz, 230 Ulster St) Units from $90. This modern motel has an indoor heated pool.

Parklands City Motel & Awesome Backpackers (☎ 07-838 2461, e parklands_motel@hotmail.com, 24 Bridge St) Dorm beds $20-25, units from $70. The Parklands is on a busy road, but is handy to the city and the river. Dorms are spartan, units comfy.

Novotel (☎ 07-838 1366, e hamilton@novotel.co.nz, 7 Alma St) Rooms $110-190. This is quite a large, plush hotel, with a health club and spa. Rates increase Monday to Friday.

Places to Eat

Restaurants & Cafes Hamilton has plenty of good places to eat, with a wealth of choice along the southern end of Victoria St.

Rocket (cnr Hood & Victoria Sts) Dishes $6.50-8.50. This retro cafe has big glass windows for people-watching, and it serves good food.

Scott's Epicurean (181 Victoria St) Lunch $6-10. This very popular cafe has quite an international menu at reasonable prices.

Hasan Baba (228 Victoria St) Mains around $13.50. Hasan Baba has Turkish, Greek and Middle Eastern food.

Metropolis (211 Victoria St) Mains $8-14. This excellent cafe, with its distinctive black-and-white tiled entrance, artwork and upstairs dining area, is a good place for a glass of wine and some international cuisine.

Korean Cafe (Collingwood St) Mains $8-13. This cafe serves a mixture of Korean and Japanese food.

Kazana Indian Tandoori (☎ 07-839 3939, 237 Victoria St) Mains around $16. This tandoori restaurant serves all your favourites.

Sahara Tent Cafe & Bar (☎ 07-834 0409, 254 Victoria St) Mains $15.50-21. This one does a good job of impersonating a back-street Istanbul cafe. The food ain't bad either.

Barzurk (☎ 07-834 2363, 250 Victoria St) Pizzas $16-25. This place specialises in creating unusual and tasty gourmet pizzas.

The Bank (☎ 07-839 4740, cnr Victoria & Hood Sts) Mains $14-20. This converted historic building has a convivial atmosphere, good food, and a pleasant garden bar.

Iguana (☎ 07-834 2280, 203 Victoria St) Pizzas $17-23. Gourmet pizzas must be big in Hamilton when you consider that Iguana is the second restaurant specialising in them on Victoria St.

Fast Food The modern Centreplace shopping centre is good for a quick and cheap meal. On the ground floor is an *international food hall* with a variety of cuisines, including Indian, Chinese and Turkish. The Downtown Plaza also has a busy *food hall* with a variety of foods.

Beef Eaters (☎ 07-839 5374, 5 Hood St) Burgers from $3.15. If you are in need of a feed in the wee small hours of the morning, Beef Eaters will almost certainly be open.

Entertainment

Music, Dancing & Pubs Hamilton has a decent-sized student population which means it has plenty of lively nightspots on weekends. Pick up a copy of the student rag *Nexus* from the Waikato University campus for information on venues, or head to Hood St, where there are many bars.

Outback Inn (Hood St) Outback Inn is a favourite with students; it also has a lounge dance floor.

Diggers Bar (☎ 07-834 2228, 17B Hood St) This bar has Mac's Ales on tap and occasional bands.

Loaded Hog (27 Hood St) Next door to Diggers is this generic bar with a large garden bar that proves popular.

The Bank (☎ 07-839 4740, cnr Victoria & Hood Sts) This is a trendy bar and is always busy.

Fox & Hounds (cnr Victoria & Alma Sts) Fox & Hounds is an English-style pub with many types of imported beer, and Newcastle Brown, Guinness and cider on tap.

Biddy Mulligan's (☎ 07-834 0306, 742 Victoria St) Biddy Mulligan's is an Irish pub where live bands play regularly.

Cinema & Theatre The *Village 7 Cinema (☎ 07-834 1222, Ustairs Ward St)* has 10 movie theatres showing latest releases.

Live theatre venues in the city include the *Founders Memorial Theatre (☎ 07-838 6603, Tristram St)*, and the *Riverlea Centre (☎ 07-856 5450, Riverlea Rd)*, south of the city off Cambridge Rd.

Getting There & Away

Air Near Victoria St, Air New Zealand (☎ 07-839 9835), 25 Ward St, has direct flights daily to Auckland, Nelson, Palmerston North and Wellington, Friday to Sunday to Christchurch and on Sunday to Dunedin, with onward connections. Origin Pacific (☎ 0800 302 302) has direct flights from Hamilton to Auckland, Wellington and Nelson with connections to Christchurch. Freedom Air (see the Getting There & Away chapter) flies from Hamilton to Sydney, Brisbane, the Gold Coast and Melbourne.

Bus All local and long-distance buses arrive at and depart from the Hamilton Transport Centre on the corner of Anglesea and Bryce Sts. InterCity (☎ 07-834 3457) and Newmans (☎ 07-838 3114) are both represented.

Frequent buses make the connection between Hamilton, Auckland ($20, 2hrs) and Rotorua ($27, 1½hrs). Buses also leave for Thames ($24, 1¾hrs), Tauranga ($33, 2hrs), Whakatane ($33, 3½hrs), Opotiki ($33, 4¼hrs), Gisborne ($50, 6¾hrs), Taupo ($33, 2½hrs), New Plymouth ($33, 4¼hrs) and Wellington (from $67, 8¼hrs). Guthreys (☎ 0800 759 999) runs between Hamilton, Auckland ($18, 2hrs), Rotorua ($20, 1½hrs), Taupo ($26, 3hrs) and Waitomo ($38, 1¾hrs). Dalroy Express (☎ 0508 465 622) operates a service between Auckland ($18, 2hrs) and Hawera ($55, 4¾hrs) via Hamilton, stopping at most towns, including New Plymouth ($42, 3½hrs) and Te Kuiti ($14, 1¼hrs).

A number of local bus companies offer regular services to nearby towns including Raglan, Huntly, Te Awamutu, Morrinsville, Te Aroha and Thames. Magic Bus stops at Hamilton.

Train Hamilton is on the main rail line between Auckland and Wellington. Trains stop at Hamilton's Frankton train station (☎ 07-846 8353) on Queens Ave, 1km west of the city centre. Tickets can be bought at the Frankton train station, or conveniently at the Hamilton Transport Centre or the visitors centre. Buses run between the visitors centre and the train station ($5).

Hitching Hamilton is spread out and it's a long walk to good hitching spots in any direction on the outskirts of town.

Heading south to Waitomo or New Plymouth, catch a Glenview bus to the outskirts. For hitching to Rotorua, Taupo, Tauranga or Wellington, catch a Hillcrest bus and get off by the Hillcrest School. Hitching north to Auckland is easiest if you take a Huntly bus to the outskirts.

Getting Around

To/From the Airport Hamilton Airport is surrounded by farmland, 12km south of the city. The Super Shuttle (☎ 07-843 7778) offers a door-to-door service to/from the airport for $10 per person.

Bus Hamilton's city bus system operates Monday to Friday with a limited service on Saturday; services start around 7am and finish around 5.45pm (until 8.45pm on Friday). All local buses arrive at and depart from the Hamilton Transport Centre.

For information and timetables of local city bus routes and local buses travelling further afield (to Huntly, Te Aroha, Thames, Raglan) consult the Hamilton Visitor Information Centre (☎ 07-839 3580) which has timetables, or call the Busline (☎ 0800 4287 5463).

Car The many car rental agencies include:

Budget Rent-A-Car (☎ 07-838 3585)
Rent-a-Dent (☎ 07-839 1049)
Waikato Car Rentals (☎ 07-855 0094)

WAINGARO HOT SPRINGS

A popular day trip from Hamilton is a visit to the Waingaro Hot Springs (☎ 07-825 4761; adult/ child $6/3; open 9am-10pm daily), which has three thermal mineral pools, private spa pools, giant waterslides, children's play areas and barbecues. Kids love it! There's also a *motel & caravan park* here, with powered sites for $14 per person, on-site vans $48, and motel units $85. To get there, turn west at Ngaruawahia, 19km north of Hamilton, and travel for 23km; it is clearly signposted.

RAGLAN

pop 2700

On the coast 48km west of Hamilton, Raglan is Hamilton's closest and most popular beach. Raglan is world famous for its surf and attracts top surfers from around the world to Manu Bay and Whale Bay, especially in summer when surfing competitions are held. It is named after Lord Raglan, a British officer who seriously wiped out at the Charge of the Light Brigade.

Relaxed little Raglan, with its art and craft shops and cafes, lies on a beautiful sheltered harbour, good for windsurfing, boating and swimming. The famous black-sand surfing beaches are west of town.

There is a small, interesting **museum** (Wainui Rd; admission free; open 1pm-3.30pm Sat & Sun) dealing mainly with local European history.

Information

The Raglan visitors centre (☎ 07-825 0556, W www.raglan.net.nz) at 4 Wallis St opens from 10am to 5pm Monday to Friday and 10am to 4pm Saturday and Sunday.

Surfing & Beaches

You can attempt to catch 'Hang Ten' with the **Raglan Surfing School** (☎ 07-825 7573, W www.raglansurfingschool.co.nz) on their soft surfboards which make it easier to stay upright. Lessons last two hours and cost $70 (all equipment is provided); if you're already experienced you can rent surfboards ($10 per hour), boogie boards ($5 per hour) and wet suits ($5 per hour) from them.

Te Kopua beach, a five-minute walk over the footbridge from town, is a safe, calm estuary popular with families. On the other side of the tiny peninsula is a popular windsurfing beach, reached via the Raglan Kopua Holiday Park ($2 day-usage fee).

Other sheltered inner-harbour beaches close to town include **Cox's Bay**, reached by a walkway from Government Rd or from Bayview Rd, and **Puriri Park**, towards the end of Wallis St, a safe swimming spot at high tide.

Ngarunui (Ocean) Beach, about 5km west of town, is a popular surf beach. Swim

RAGLAN

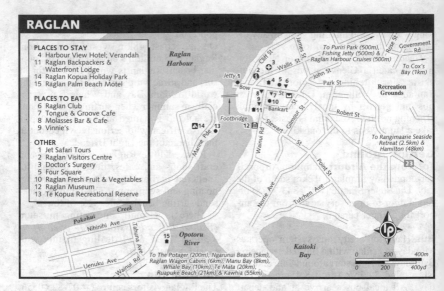

PLACES TO STAY
4 Harbour View Hotel; Verandah
11 Raglan Backpackers &
   Waterfront Lodge
14 Raglan Kopua Holiday Park
15 Raglan Palm Beach Motel

PLACES TO EAT
6 Raglan Club
7 Tongue & Groove Cafe
8 Molasses Bar & Cafe
9 Vinnie's

OTHER
1 Jet Safari Tours
2 Raglan Visitors Centre
3 Doctor's Surgery
5 Four Square
10 Raglan Fresh Fruit & Vegetables
12 Raglan Museum
13 Te Kopua Recreational Reserve

Raglan Harbour

*To Puriri Park (500m),
Fishing Jetty (500m) &
Raglan Harbour Cruises (500m)*

*To Cox's
Bay (1km)*

*Recreation
Grounds*

*To Rangimaarie Seaside
Retreat (2.5km) &
Hamilton (48km)*

*Opotoru
River*

*Kaitoki
Bay*

*To The Potager (200m), Ngarunui Beach (5km),
Raglan Wagon Cabins (6km), Manu Bay (8km),
Whale Bay (10km), Te Mata (20km),
Ruapuke Beach (21km) & Kawhia (55km)*

0 200 400m
0 200 400yd

on the left side, away from the riptides, where lifeguards are posted in summer.

Manu Bay, a further 3km west of Raglan, is a world-famous surfing beach, said to have the longest left-hand break in the world. It was featured in the 1966 cult surfing film *Endless Summer*, where a surfer rode what seemed like endless waves. The very long, uniform waves at Manu Bay are created by the angle at which the ocean swell from the Tasman Sea meets the coastline. **Whale Bay**, a couple of kilometres further west, is another excellent surfing spot. There are some **tattooed rock faces** nearby; they aren't easy to find so ask for directions.

Ruapuke Beach, a rugged stretch of coastline still further past Whale Bay, is good for surfcasting but not so good for swimming, due to treacherous crosscurrents; it can be reached from Ruapuke Rd.

Activities

Contact the information centre for details on fishing charters, kayaking, paragliding, skydiving and other activities.

Raglan Harbour Cruises (☎ 07-825 0300; *adult/child $20/7.50*) has 1½-hour cruises in summer. It also arranges fishing charters.

Jet Safari Tours (☎ 07-825 0556; *trips $35-45*) takes groups to see Okete Falls and nearby Sugar Loaf Islands.

Midway between Hamilton and Raglan, the **Karamu Walkway** goes through the Four Brothers Scenic Reserve. It's worth a short walk for the scenery.

Places to Stay

Camping, Cabins & Hostels Raglan has some very laid-back places to stay.

Raglan Kopua Holiday Park (☎ 07-825 8283, e *raglanholidaypark@xtra.co.nz*) Powered/unpowered sites $9/8 per person, bunk dorms $12, cabins $40, tourist flats $50. The beachside Raglan Park is on a sheltered, sandy inner-harbour beach across the estuary from town, popular for swimming and windsurfing.

Raglan Wagon Cabins (☎ 07-825 8268, 611 Wainui Rd) Camp sites $10 per person, cabins $40, units $80. On a hill with magnificent coastal views, 6km west of Raglan this place has comfortable cabins (constructed from restored railway carriages), self-contained units, camping, a kitchen and TV lounge. The friendly owner has a video copy of *Endless Summer*.

WAIKATO & KING COUNTRY

Raglan Backpackers & Waterfront Lodge (☎ 07-825 0515, 6 Nero St) Dorm beds $16, doubles & twins $38. The superb Raglan is on the water's edge and has fine views. This purpose-built hostel, with its central outdoor recreation area, has excellent standards. Kayaks are free for guests.

B&Bs, Motels & Hotels The visitors centre has lists of homestays and farmstays.

The Potager (☎ 07-825 8722, 78 Wainui Rd) Singles/doubles $35/85. The Potager has comfortable rooms, some with balcony. Breakfast is included.

Harbour View Hotel (☎ 07-825 8010, Bow St) Singles/doubles $50/70. This older-style hotel is very central.

Rangimaarie Seaside Retreat (☎ 07-825 7567, Greenslade Rd) Singles/doubles $65/85, self-contained flats $85 per double. Rangimaarie is about five minutes' drive east of town.

Raglan Palm Beach Motel (☎/fax 07-825 8153, e raglanmotels@paradise.co.nz, 50 Wainui Rd) Units from $75. This peaceful motel is 1½km south-west of town, across the bridge spanning Opotoru River.

Places to Eat

Tongue & Groove Cafe (19 Bow St) Meals $7-20. This excellent cafe serves soups, salads, panini, pasta, burgers, wedges and other scrumptious fare. Check out the surfboard tables.

Molasses Bar & Cafe (Bow St) Mains $6-13. Molasses Bar is good for coffee, snacks, light meals and people-watching. The blueberry fritters are something special.

Vinnie's (☎ 07-825 7273, 7 Wainui Rd) Mains $12.50-25. Vinnie's serves an incredible selection of seafood, pastas, pizzas, curries, wraps and much more.

The Harbour View Hotel on Bow St has the *Verandabah* serving snacks, drinks and light meals with dining inside or outside. It also has bands on Friday nights – the well-known blues musician Midge Marsden and his band are regulars.

The *Raglan Club* may not look like much, but it reputedly has the best fish and chips ($4) for miles around.

Getting There & Away

Pavlovich Coachlines (☎ 07-847 5545) operates a return service to Hamilton at least three times daily on weekdays (adult/child $5.50/3.50). It departs from the Raglan visitors centre.

RAGLAN TO KAWHIA

The back roads between Raglan and Kawhia, 55km south on the coast, are slow and winding, but scenic, enjoyable and off the beaten track. The gravel roads take at least 1½ hours of driving time, not counting stops. Traffic is light.

There are two routes between Raglan and Kawhia. From Raglan you can head west along the coast, out past Ngarunui Beach, Manu Bay and Whale Bay, and keep following the coast road until it turns inland and meets the interior road at Te Mata, 20km south of Raglan. Along the way is the *Ruapuke Motor Camp* (☎ 07-825 6800) near the beach at Ruapuke. Or, from Raglan, head towards Hamilton and take the signposted Te Mata-Kawhia turn-off.

Near Te Mata are the **Bridal Veil Falls**. From the car park it's an easy 10-minute walk through native bush to the top, with a further 10-minute walk leading to the pool at the bottom, where it's possible to swim.

Magic Mountain Farmstay (☎ 07-825 6892, w www.magicmountain.co.nz, Houchen Rd) Singles/doubles including breakfast $90/120. The self-contained lodge at Magic Mountain has everything, including a log fire and stunning views (from the height of 328m). Horse-riding is also available (from $30). It's at the end of the road, 4km off the main road just north of Te Mata.

About 12km south-west of Raglan is **Mt Karioi**. You can drive around the mountain on mostly gravel roads in a couple of hours. Along this route **Te Toto Track**, starting from Te Toto car park on Whaanga Rd (the coast road) on the western side of Mt Karioi, is strenuous but scenic, ascending steeply to a lookout point (2½ hours) followed by an easier stretch up to Karioi summit (one hour). From the east side of the mountain, the **Wairake Track** is a steeper 2½-hour climb to the summit and meets the Te Toto Track.

Mt Karioi is in one part of the Pirongia Forest Park; a much larger part lies within the triangle formed by the towns of Raglan, Kawhia and Te Awamutu, with the 959m summit of **Mt Pirongia** clearly visible from much of the Waikato region. Tracks going through the forest park lead to the summit of Mt Pirongia – the mountain is usually climbed from Corcoran Rd on the Hamilton side. There's a hut near the summit if you want to spend the night. Maps and information about Pirongia Forest Park are available from DOC in Hamilton. The township of **Pirongia** is 32km south-west of Hamilton.

You can go horse-riding on the slopes of the mountain with **Mt Pirongia Horse Treks** (☎ 07-871 9960) – a one-hour ride is $20.

KAWHIA
pop 670

Kawhia is a sleepy little port on pretty Kawhia Harbour. The harbour is large, with many extensions, but its entrance is narrow – the occupants of the *Tainui* canoe missed it on their first trip down the coast in the 14th century and Captain Cook also missed it when he sailed past in 1770, naming Albatross Point on the southern side of the harbour but failing to note the harbour itself.

Today Kawhia (pronounced 'kar-fee-a') is still easy to miss, though it gets a few fishing enthusiasts and bathers during summer.

Things to See & Do

The **Kawhia Museum** (☎ 07-870 0161; admission free; open 11am-4pm Wed-Sun) is in the historic former Kawhia County Building right near the wharf. It has interesting exhibits as well as pamphlets and information on the town.

From the museum and the wharf, a pleasant **walk** extends along the coast to the **Maketu Marae** with its impressively carved meeting house, Auaukiterangi. Through the *marae* grounds and behind the wooden fence, two stones, Hani and Puna, mark the burial place of the Tainui. You need permission from a local elder to visit this *marae*.

Three kilometres behind the town and through the Tainui Kawhia Pine Forest is windswept **Ocean Beach** and its black dunes; swimming can be dangerous. Two hours either side of low tide you can find the **Puia Hot Springs** in the sands – just dig a hole for your own little natural spa. It is a lot less crowded than Hot Water Beach near Hahei on the Coromandel. There's a driveable track over the dunes.

Places to Stay & Eat

Kawhia's camping grounds fill up at busy periods in summer, so plan ahead.

Forest View Motor Camp (☎/fax 07-871 0858, Waiwera St) Powered/unpowered sites $16/12 for 2 people, cabins $25-30. This place can arrange fishing trips and harbour cruises.

Kawhia Beachside S-Cape (☎ 07-871 0727, fax 871 0217, 225 Pouewe St) Powered/unpowered sites $14/10 per person, on-site caravans $34, cabins $36. This camping ground is right on the harbour's waters edge. There are bikes for use and kayaks for hire ($6 to $10).

Rosamond House (☎ 07-871 0681, Rosamond Terrace) B&B singles/doubles $55/75. Rosamond is a historic colonial-style house. It's a quiet retreat with a pool.

Kawhia Motel (☎ 07-871 0865, fax 871 0165, cnr Jervois & Tainui Sts) Singles/doubles $59/69. This is a friendly place offering accommodation in units.

Kawhia has two general stores, a *pub*, a *fish and chip shop* and *Annie's Cafe & Restaurant* (☎ 07-871 0198), which is next door to the *Wee Knot Inn* watering hole.

Getting There & Away

Kawhia Bus & Freight (☎ 07-871 0701) takes passengers (adult/child $6/3) on the freight run to Te Awamutu daily except Sunday.

The 50-minute drive to Kawhia from Te Awamutu or Otorohanga is a scenic route offering fine views of the harbour. Along the way is Te Kauri Park Nature Reserve, with a one-hour walk from the road to a kauri grove – the harbour probably marks the southernmost 'boundary' of where kauri grow naturally. Kawhia has a petrol station.

Drive or cycle down the mostly unsealed coastal back roads all the way from Raglan in the north to Awakino and Mokau in the

The *Tainui* Canoe

Though it's only a small town, Kawhia has an illustrious history. It was here that the *Tainui* canoe – one of the ancestral canoes that arrived here in the 14th century from the Maori homeland Hawaiki, – made its final landing.

Before the *Tainui* canoe departed from Hawaiki, the priests there prophesied that the departing canoe would eventually come to a favourable place where its people would make a new home, have a good life and prosper. The priests told the leaders of the *Tainui* canoe which landmarks to look for so they would know they had arrived at the new home they were destined to find.

The *Tainui* canoe left Hawaiki, stopping at Rarotonga in the Cook Islands as it crossed the Pacific. It landed in NZ at Maketu in the Bay of Plenty, accompanied by the *Arawa* canoe. The *Arawa* canoe stopped there, its people becoming the Arawa people, a large Maori tribe that still lives in the Bay of Plenty and Rotorua areas today.

The leaders of the *Tainui* canoe – Hoturoa, the captain, and Rakataura, the *tohunga* or high priest – knew that the Tainui's home was destined to be on the west coast. So they continued on, seeking a way to get to the west coast. They finally dragged their canoe overland at Manukau Harbour, near Auckland. Setting off southwards in search of the prophesied landmarks, they journeyed all the way to the South Island. They turned around and came north again, still searching, and finally recognised their prophesied new home at Kawhia Harbour.

When they landed the canoe, they tied it to a pohutukawa tree on the shore, naming the tree Tangi te Korowhiti. Though the tree is not marked, it still grows with a few other pohutukawa trees on the shoreline between Kawhia town and the Maketu Marae; you can easily see them. At the end of its long voyage, the *Tainui* canoe was dragged up onto a hill and buried. Hoturoa and Rakataura placed sacred stones at either end to mark its resting place. Hani, on higher ground, is the stone marking the bow of the canoe, and Puna, the lower stone, marks the stern. You can walk up behind the *marae* and see the stones behind a wooden fence.

The prophecy that this place would be a good home for the long-journeying Tainui people did come true. Kawhia Harbour was abundant with shellfish, fish and food. Today the Tainui tribes extend over the entire Waikato region, over the Coromandel Peninsula, north to Auckland and south to Lake Taupo and south past Mokau on the coast. Kawhia, the Maketu Marae and the burial place of the *Tainui* canoe are supremely sacred to all the Tainui people.

Another point of historical significance for Kawhia is that it was once the home of Te Rauparaha, the great warrior of the Ngati Toa tribe. When pushed out of Kawhia by warring Waikato tribes in 1821, Te Rauparaha moved southwards, making his base on Kapiti Island off the west coast near Wellington, from there making raids all the way down to the South Island. For more on Te Rauparaha, see the boxed text 'Haka' in the 'Maori Culture & Arts' special section.

south, finally coming to New Plymouth (or vice versa). It's slow going but scenic.

TE AWAMUTU
pop 9340

Te Awamutu is a service town for the local dairy-farming community. It is noted for its rose gardens, hence its title 'the Rose Town of New Zealand'. Brothers Tim and Neil Finn of the popular band Split Enz (and later of Crowded House) came from here.

Te Awamutu was an important site in the Waikato Land War – you can still see the flat-topped hill where there was a fort. After the war, it became a frontier town. The name Te Awamutu means 'The River Cut Short', since the river above this point was unsuitable for canoes.

Te Awamutu visitors centre (☎ 07-871 3259, Ⓦ www.teawamutu.co.nz) on the corner of Gorst Ave and SH3, opposite the Rose Garden, is open from 9am to 4.30pm

Monday to Friday and 9.30am to 3pm Saturday and Sunday.

Things to See & Do

Te Awamutu Rose Garden has over 2000 rose bushes. The garden is on the main road, opposite the visitors centre. The roses are at their best from November to April; a rose show is held at the beginning of every November.

Beginning behind the Rose Garden, the Pioneer Walk goes beside the river for about 1.5km to Memorial Park and the **Te Wananga Centre** (☎ *07-871 4257, 1 Factory Rd*), where there's a Maori carving and weaving institute.

Te Awamutu Museum (☎ *07-871 4326, Roche St; admission free; open 10am-4pm Mon-Fri, 10am-1pm Sat & Sun*), in the Civic Centre, has a fine collection of Maori *taonga* (treasures). The centrepiece is Uenuku, a totara carving that once housed a tribal god said to have been brought to NZ on the *Tainui* canoe from Hawaiki. There is also an exhibit of Finn brothers memorabilia and a video on their rise to fame.

The **Wharepapa Outdoor Centre** (☎ *07-872 2533, 1424 Owairaka Valley Rd*), 23km south-east of Te Awamutu at Wharepapa South, is one of the best places for rock climbing in the North Island. There's indoor climbing walls at their **Bouldering Cafe** ($5 entry) where you can hire gear. Only two minutes away from the centre is Froggate Edge, a rock climbing Mecca with over 115 climbs. There's *accommodation* available at the centre ($15 per person), or you can *camp* at the primary school next door ($2). For more information on rock climbing in New Zealand check out Ⓦ www.climb.co.nz.

Places to Stay & Eat

The visitors centre has lists of B&Bs, homestays and farmstays.

Road Runner Motel & Holiday Park (☎ *07-871 7420, fax 871 6664, 141 Bond Rd*) Powered/unpowered sites $105 per person, cabins $35, motel units $65. This basic holiday park is the closest to town.

Rosetown Motel (☎ *0800 767 386, Ⓔ bryants@ihug.co.nz, 844 Kihikihi Rd*)

Blind Date with Destiny

Fans of Split Enz or Crowded House, NZ's two most famous pop music exports, can trace the early lives of the bands' best-known members – the Finn brothers, Neil and Tim. They allude to their beginnings in this humble NZ town in songs such as Crowded House's *Mean to Me* and keen fans of the bands can analyse the brothers' roots by taking a walk through Te Awamutu (the information centre even provides a keyed map!).

Included on the walk is 588 Teasdale St where the brothers lived when they were young; St Patrick's School, which both attended; Te Awamutu College, which Neil attended from Form 4; Martins Electrical Store, where Neil worked (and played piano outside on Friday nights); Craft Shop Pot Pourri (now Trade Aid Shop), where Neil often played guitar; Hammond, Finn & Chaplin, the firm in which their father Dick was a partner (he and his wife now live in Cambridge); and Albert Park, where the brothers performed for the Te Awamutu Centennial in 1984.

Singles/doubles $65/75. The Rosetown is on the main road towards Otorohanga, and has a pool.

Albert Park Motor Lodge (☎ *07-870 2995,* Ⓔ *albert.park@xtra.co.nz, 299 Albert Park Dr*) Units from $90. This is Te Awamutu's most modern motel, which has double rooms with spa baths and two wheelchair-accessible units.

Te Awamutu's Arawata St is your best bet for cafes and restaurants.

Robert Harris Coffee Shop (*39 Arawata St*) Sandwiches $2-4. This chain cafe has a good selection of sandwiches, cakes and pastries.

Rose & Thorn (*32 Arawata St*) Mains $6-20. For a fuller meal, head to this quiet restaurant, which doubles as a bar in the evenings.

The Redoubt Bar & Eatery (☎ *07-81 4768, cnr Rewi & Alexandra Sts*) Mains $10-15. This popular eatery has daily specials, and kiwi memorabilia adorning the walls.

Getting There & Away

Buses and trains (☎ 0800 802 802) between Auckland and Wellington stop at Te Awamutu. Hodgson Motors (☎ 07-871 6373) runs a shuttle between Te Amamutu and Hamilton five times daily (adult/child $5/3).

CAMBRIDGE

pop 11,300

On the Waikato River, 20km south-east of Hamilton, Cambridge is a small town with a charming rural English atmosphere. Cricket is played on the village green in the town centre and the avenues are lined with broad, shady European trees, at their best in autumn. The Cambridge region is famous for the breeding and training of thoroughbred horses. One well-known Cambridgebred horse is Charisma, which won the Olympic three-day event in 1984 and 1988, (ridden by New Zealander Mark Todd).

Information

The Cambridge visitors centre (☎ 07-827 3456, e cvc@wave.co.nz) on the corner of Victoria and Queen Sts is open from 9am to 5pm Monday to Friday and 10am to 4pm Saturday and Sunday. Get the free *Cambridge and Heritage Tree Trails* pamphlet or join a guided walk of heritage sites ($6 for a 1½ hour walk); book at the visitors centre.

Things to See

Cambridge has a number of arts and crafts and antiques shops, adding to the town's twee atmosphere. Best known is the award-winning **Cambridge Country Store** *(☎ 07-827 8715, 92 Victoria St)*, in an old church on SH1. The town hosts an annual **antiques fair** in September.

Another old church worth seeing, also on SH1, is the 100-year-old **St Andrew's Anglican Church** *(cnr Victoria St West & Hamilton Rd; open 9am-noon Mon-Fri, 1pm-3pm daily)*, a white church with a beautiful wooden interior, fine stained-glass windows and a high steeple sheathed in copper. The outside is beautiful but it's still a surprise to see the beauty of the interior.

The stuffy **Cambridge Museum** *(☎ 07-827 3319, Victoria St; donations welcome; open 10am-4pm Tues-Sat)*, occupies the former Cambridge Courthouse building (built in 1909).

Te Koutu Lake in the centre of town is a peaceful bird sanctuary.

The **Cambridge Thoroughbred Lodge** *(☎ 07-827 8118; shows $12; 10.30am Tues-Sun)*, 6km south of town on SH1, is a magnificent horse stud, ideal for horse lovers. The thoroughbreds are brought out on show with commentaries and there are show-jumping and dressage exhibitions.

Activities

Other attractions in Cambridge include **jet-boat rides** on the Waikato River and walking on tracks along both sides of the river and around Te Koutu Lake.

There are also **walks** further afield. From SH1 take the turn-off north at Cambridge and after about a five-minute drive you'll reach the Maungakawa Scenic Reserve, a regenerating forest with some exotic timber species and a fairly easy short bush walk. From the eastern side of Mt Maungakawa, a track suitable for experienced trampers ascends from Tapui Rd; it takes half a day to walk there and back.

Also about a five-minute drive south from town, **Mt Maungatautiri** is another good walking spot; it takes about 1½ hours to climb to the summit.

Places to Stay

Cambridge Motor Camp (☎ 07-827 5649, 32 Scott St, Leamington) Powered/unpowered sites $10 per person, cabins $30, tourist flats $65. This camp site is about 1.5km from town.

Cambridge Country Lodge Backpackers (☎ 07-827 8373, Peake Rd) Camp sites $9 per person, dorm beds $16-18, twins & doubles $38, units $60. This is a pleasant hostel in a rural setting on a small farm 200m down the road, a turn-off from the SH1 1.5km north of Cambridge. It provides courtesy transport.

Cambrian Lodge Motel (☎ 0800 886 886, 827 7766, e cambrian@clear.net.nz, 63 Hamilton Rd) Units from $75. The Cambrian Motel has a good array of units.

The Mews (☎ 07-827 7166, e themews motorinn@clear.net.nz, 20 Hamilton Rd) Units from $120. The Mews is a very tidy motel with better-than-average units.

Cambridge also has good B&Bs and farmstays; the visitors centre has details.

Places to Eat

Cambridge is a popular lunch spot.

All Saints Cafe (92 Victoria St) Lunches from $3. All Saints is upstairs in the atmospheric Cambridge Country Store. Try the home-made quiches.

The Gallery (☎ 07-823 0999, 64c Victoria St) Light meals $5-10. The Gallery is a relaxed cafe that has nice cakes, coffee and artwork adorning the walls.

Prince Albert Tavern (☎ 07-827 7900, Victoria Plaza, Halley's Lane) Mains $7-15. This old English-style pub, off Duke St, has open fires and an outdoor garden area, and serves pub meals.

Alphaz Restaurant (☎ 07-827 6699, 72 Alpha St) Mains $19-24. Alphaz Restaurant is a pleasant restaurant that does good brunches on weekends (10am to noon).

Souter House (☎ 07-827 3610, 19 Victoria St) Mains $21-28. Souter House is situated in a stately Victorian house and is by far and away the best place in town.

Getting There & Away

Lying on SH1, Cambridge is well connected to by bus. Most long-distance buses from Hamilton to Rotorua or the Bay of Plenty stop in Cambridge.

Cambridge Travel Lines (☎ 07-827 7363) has weekday services between Cambridge and the Hamilton Transport Centre (adult/child $5/3).

KARAPIRO

Karapiro, the furthest downstream of a chain of hydroelectric power stations and dams on the Waikato River, is 28km southeast of Hamilton, 8km past Cambridge, just off SH1. The side road passes over the dam and the lake is popular for aquatic sports.

Karapiro Lake Domain (☎ 07-827 4178) Camp sites $7 per person, powered sites $8 per person, chalets $40. Located on the western side of the lake, this place is a quiet camping spot. The chalets are with en suite.

The Boatshed Cafe (☎ 07-827 8286) Open 10am-5pm Wed-Sun. Right by the lake, this cafe makes a good stop for a bite to eat and a bit of exercise. Hire a kayak for a trip on the lake; a half day costs $10 to $15, while a full day costs $15 to $30.

MATAMATA
pop 7800

This town, 23km north-east of Cambridge and nestled beneath the Kaimai Range, is the apotheosis of NZ rural living. It is one of the premier thoroughbred training and breeding centres in the world, producing many great champions.

There is a visitors centre (☎ 07-888 7260, W www.matamata-info.co.nz), at 45 Broadway, open from 8.30am to 5pm Monday to Friday and 10am to 3pm Saturday and Sunday. It can provide a list of places to stay (especially homestays and farmstays). You can also access the Internet here.

Things to See & Do

Of particular interest in town is the **Firth Tower** (☎ 07-888 8369, Tower Rd; adult/child $5/1; open 10am-4pm daily), built in 1882 by Yorkshireman Josiah Clifton Firth. Firth spoke Maori fluently and was respected by the regional Maori leaders with whom he negotiated during the Waikato Land War. He must have had some doubts about his standing, however, as the tower, with its 24-rifle loopholes and 45cm-thick walls, was built long after the war had ended.

Opal Hot Springs (☎ 0800 800 198, 888 8198, Okuia Springs Rd; adult/child $4.50/1.50), 6km north-east of the town centre, has private mineral pools, a public swimming pool and camping.

The visitors centre has details on **tandem skydiving**, **gliding** and the many **walking tracks** through the Kaimai-Mamaku Ranges, including the Wairere Falls Scenic Reserve.

Places to Stay & Eat

Opal Hot Springs (☎ 0800 800 198, 888 8198, Okuia Springs Rd) Powered/unpowered sites $12.50/$10 per person, cabins

$35-48, tourist flats $58, motel units $78. This place has the added advantage of soothing hot pools on your doorstep.

Southern Belle B&B (*☎ 0800 244 233, 888 6804, 101 Firth St*) Singles/twins/doubles $50/60/70. The Southern Belle, built in 1936, is a pleasant place to stay. There are three guestrooms, a separate guest lounge and bathroom facilities. Surprisingly, breakfast is extra ($4 to $10).

Maple Lodge (*☎/fax 07-888 8764, 11 Mangawhero Rd*) Single/double units from $62/72. This slightly dated motel is within walking distance of the town centre and has a swimming pool and spa.

There are plenty of places to eat on Broadway, the main drag, including the cool retro cafe **Workman's**. For a drink and a game of pool pop into **Cue Bar**, also on Broadway.

TIRAU

The small rural town of Tirau, 54km southeast of Hamilton at the junction of SH1 and SH5, has fallen in love with corrugated iron. The building material has been used to construct a **Dog and Sheep**, which are both bigger than most buildings in town and are used to house the visitors centre and a wool shop (no prizes for guessing which holds the wool shop). It's amazing how many people stop to get a photo of themselves swinging on the dog's big red tongue. Both are open from 9am to 5pm daily.

The King Country

☎ 07 • pop 53,000

The King Country is named after the Maori King Movement, which developed in the Waikato region in the late 1850s and early 1860s. When King Tawhiao and his people were forced to move from their Waikato land after the Waikato Land War of 1863 to 1864 against British troops, they came south to this region, which was as yet unaffected by European encroachment. Legend has it that King Tawhiao placed his white top hat, symbol of the kingship, on a large map of NZ and declared that all the land it covered would be under his *mana,* or authority.

The area coincided roughly with the present-day districts of Otorohanga, Waitomo and Taumarunui, extending west to the coast and eastwards as far as Lake Taupo.

For several decades the King Country remained the stronghold of King Tawhiao and other Maori chiefs, who held out against the Europeans longer than other Maori in NZ. This area was forbidden to the Europeans by Maori law until the 1880s, and was even then not much penetrated by Europeans until, with the consent of the Maori chiefs, the Auckland-Wellington Main Trunk Railway line arrived in 1891. The earliest Europeans to settle in Otorohanga were timber millers, the first arriving in 1890. The laying of the railway to form a continuous line from Auckland to Wellington in 1908 marked the end of the region's isolation, though even today a powerful Maori influence pervades.

From 1884, when Pakeha were allowed into the district, until 1955, the King Country was 'dry' (alcohol was prohibited). This condition was apparently imposed by Maori chiefs when they agreed to the Europeans building the railway through their country, opening it up even more to the outside world.

OTOROHANGA
pop 2590

Otorohanga, in the upper Waipa basin, is on SH3, 58km south of Hamilton and 16km from Waitomo. Traditionally a dairy and sheep-farming community, Otorohanga is attempting to reinvent itself as the 'Kiwiana' capital of NZ by displaying typical kiwi icons all over town, including buzzy bees, gumboots, Maori totem poles and of course, kiwis (including Wiki the Kiwi, a big cuddly kiwi that wanders the streets greeting passers-by). Otorohanga's biggest attraction, though, is its impressive kiwi house.

For rural atmosphere, the local stock and farm auction, the Otorohanga Sale – is held every Wednesday at the saleyards on Otewa Rd from around 10am to 2pm. The Otorohanga County Fair is held on the second Saturday in February.

On the corner of Maniapoto St and Wahanui Crescent, there is a useful visitors centre

(☎ 07-873 8951, 🌐 www.otorohanga.co.nz) open from 9am to 5.30pm Monday to Friday and 10am to 4pm Saturday and Sunday. It is the AA agent, and sells bus, ferry and train tickets. There is a small **museum** *(Kakamutu Rd; open 2-4pm Sun)* covering local history. If you're looking to take home a bit of ki-wiana, try the **Kiwiana Shop** *(50 Maniapoto St)*, which sells a plethora of kiwi bits and bobs, including the irrepressible buzzy bee.

Otorohanga Kiwi House

'Not another kiwi house' *(☎ 07-873 7391, Alex Telfer Dr; adult/child $8/3; open 9am-5pm daily, last entry 4.30pm)*, you may groan – but this one is worth a visit. In a kiwi house night and day are reversed, so you can watch the nocturnal kiwi in day-time under artificial moonlight. There are also various other native birds, including some kea, which more than live up to their reputation for being inquisitive. Other birds include morepork owls, hawks and weka. Tuatara are also on display. It's also possi-ble to partake in a night-time kiwi watch; here you spend up to a couple of hours in an enclosure observing kiwis going about their nightly business (adult/child $15/6).

Places to Stay

Otorohanga Kiwitown Caravan Park *(☎ 07-873 8279, Domain Dr)* Powered/un-powered sites $8/7 per person. This small park is adjacent to the kiwi house – you can hear the kiwi calling at night. There's a 10% discount for entry to the kiwi house when staying here.

Oto-Kiwi Lodge *(☎ 07-873 6022,* 📧 *oto-kiwi@xtra.co.nz, 1 Sangro Crs)* Camp sites $8.50 per person, dorm beds $17, twins/doubles $42/40. Oto-Kiwi is a well-equipped backpackers near the kiwi house. It hires out mountain bikes ($10 per day) and arranges kayak trips ($30).

Palm Court Motel *(☎ 07-873 7122,* 📧 *pa lmcourt@xtra.co.nz, cnr Clarke & Mani-poto Sts)* Units from $80. The units at this new modern motel all have spa baths. Two are wheelchair accessible.

The visitors centre keeps a list of B&Bs and farmstays in the area.

Places to Eat

Toni's *(Maniapoto St)* Light meals around $5. Toni's is an exceptionally popular lunch-time spot, with lovely sandwiches and filling meals.

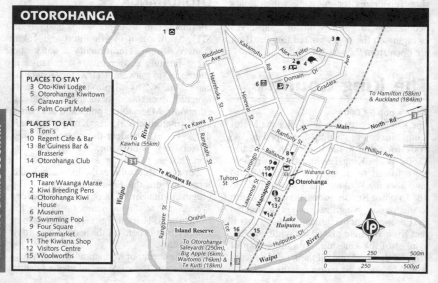

OTOROHANGA

PLACES TO STAY
3 Oto-Kiwi Lodge
5 Otorohanga Kiwitown Caravan Park
16 Palm Court Motel

PLACES TO EAT
8 Toni's
10 Regent Cafe & Bar
13 Be'Guiness Bar & Brasserie
14 Otorohanga Club

OTHER
1 Taare Waanga Marae
2 Kiwi Breeding Pens
4 Otorohanga Kiwi House
6 Museum
7 Swimming Pool
9 Four Square Supermarket
11 The Kiwiana Shop
12 Visitors Centre
15 Woolworths

To Hamilton (58km) & Auckland (184km)

To Kawhia (55km)

To Otorohanga Saleyards (250m), Big Apple (6km), Waitomo (16km) & Te Kuiti (18km)

0   250   500m
0   250   500yd

WAIKATO & KING COUNTRY

Regent Cafe & Bar *(Maniapoto St)*
Sandwiches $1.40-4. This is a pleasant
place that is large and open.

Otorohanga Club *(☎ 07-873 6543, Man-iapoto St)* Mains $12.50-17. This is one of
the best and cheapest places in town; the
menu includes steaks and seafood and the
desserts are mountainous.

Be'Guiness Bar & Brasserie *(☎ 07-873
8010, Maniapoto St)* Mains $17-22. This is
another good option, with a large selection
of steaks.

The *Big Apple*, a barn-like complex with
a large restaurant, is on the highway south
of town just before the Waitomo turn-off.

Getting There & Away
InterCity buses arrive at and depart from the
visitors centre, which sells tickets. There
are several buses a day in each direction in-cluding services to Rotorua ($40) and
Auckland ($41), both via Hamilton ($18).

To get to Waitomo, change buses in
Otorohanga. The Waitomo Shuttle (☎ 0800
808 279) runs to and from Waitomo for $7
one way; book through the visitors centre.

The train station is in the centre of town.
The day and evening Auckland-Wellington
trains (☎ 0800 802 802) stop at Otorohanga.

WAITOMO
The name Waitomo, which comes from *wai*
(water) and *tomo* (hole or shaft), is rather
appropriate: dotted throughout the country-side are a number of shafts dropping
abruptly through the surface of the ground
into underground cave systems and streams.
These limestone caves and accompanying
limestone formations make up one of the
premier attractions of the North Island.

Tours through the Glowworm Cave (also
known as the Waitomo Cave) and the
Aranui Cave have been feature attractions
for decades, but in typical kiwi fashion, the
list of things to do has grown and lately be-come more daring. Now you can abseil, raft
and tube through the caves, or try your hand
at a number of activities above ground.

Most people do Waitomo as a day trip
and don't stay overnight, which makes it a
great place to chill out if you decide to.

DAVID WALL
Aranui Cave

Information
There is a visitors centre located at the
Museum of Caves (☎ 07-878 7640, ℮ waito
moinfo@xtra.co.nz), which has Internet ac-cess, a book shop, acts as a post office and
a booking agent for all activities and has an
ATM. It's open 8am to 5.30pm Monday to
Friday (until 5pm in winter from Easter to
the end of October, and until around 8pm in
January and February).

Serious cavers can get more information
from the HTG Lodge (07-878 7442).

Waitomo Caves
Glowworm Cave This cave had been
known to the local Maori for a long time,
but the first European to explore it was Eng-lish surveyor Fred Mace, who was shown
the cave in December 1887 by Maori chief
Tane Tinorau. Mace prepared an account of
the expedition, a map was made and
photographs given to the government, and
before long Tane Tinorau was operating
tours of the cave.

WAITOMO CAVES

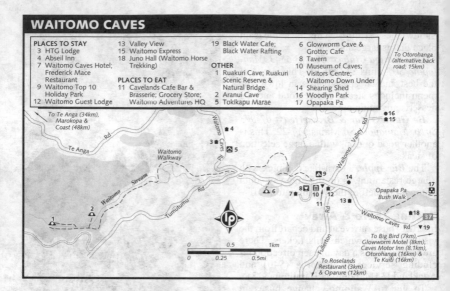

PLACES TO STAY
3 HTG Lodge
4 Abseil Inn
7 Waitomo Caves Hotel;
    Frederick Mace
    Restaurant
9 Waitomo Top 10
    Holiday Park
12 Waitomo Guest Lodge

13 Valley View
15 Waitomo Express
18 Juno Hall (Waitomo Horse
    Trekking)

PLACES TO EAT
11 Cavelands Cafe Bar &
    Brasserie; Grocery Store;
    Waitomo Adventures HQ

19 Black Water Cafe;
    Black Water Rafting

OTHER
1 Ruakuri Cave; Ruakuri
    Scenic Reserve &
    Natural Bridge
2 Aranui Cave
5 Tokikapu Marae

6 Glowworm Cave &
    Grotto; Cafe
8 Tavern
10 Museum of Caves;
    Visitors Centre;
    Waitomo Down Under
14 Shearing Shed
16 Woodlyn Park
17 Opapaka Pa

The Glowworm Cave is just a big cave with the usual assortment of stalactites and stalagmites – until you board a boat and swing off onto the river. As your eyes grow accustomed to the dark you'll see a Milky Way of little lights surrounding you – these are the glowworms. You can see them in other caves and other places around Waitomo, and in other parts of NZ, but the ones in this cave are really something special; conditions for their growth in this cave are just about perfect, so there is a remarkable number of them.

The Glowworm Cave is the most popular cave, crammed with tourists being shuttled through, one tour after the other. The big tour buses peak at around lunch time; try to go on the first tour of the day.

Aranui Cave   Three kilometres west from the Glowworm Cave is the Aranui Cave. This cave has no river running through it and hence no glowworms. It is a large cave with thousands of tiny, hollow 'straw' stalactites hanging from the ceiling. Various scenes in the formations are pointed out and photography is permitted. Transport to the cave is not included with the tour ticket.

Nearby **Ruakuri Cave** is open only for black-water rafting (see Cave Activities later in this chapter).

Tours & Tickets   The Glowworm and Aranui Caves (☎ 07-878 8227) can be visited individually or with a combined ticket. Tickets are sold at the entrance to the Glowworm Cave. Entry to the Glowworm or Aranui Cave is adult/child $24/12, or a combined two-cave ticket costs $40/20.

A 'museum-cave special' includes the Glowworm Cave tour and the Museum of Caves for $25/12.

The 45-minute tours of the Glowworm Cave leave daily on the half-hour from 9am to 5pm. From late October to Easter there's also a 5.30pm tour, with more at the height of the summer season. Aranui Cave tours go at 10am, 11am, 1pm, 2pm and 3pm, and also take about 45 minutes.

Museum of Caves

This museum (☎ 07-878 7640; *adult/child $5/free; open 8.15am-5pm daily, summer 8.15am-5.30pm*) has some excellent exhibits that helpfully explain exactly how caves are formed, the flora and fauna that

WAIKATO & KING COUNTRY

thrive in them, the history of the caves and cave exploration.

Displays include a cave model, fossils of extinct birds and animals that have been discovered in caves, and a cave crawl for the adventurous. There are also audiovisual presentations about caving, glowworms and the many other natural attractions in the Waitomo area.

Free entry is often included with various activities or you can get a 'museum-cave special' (see Tours & Tickets under Waitomo Caves earlier).

Cave Activities

If it's underground adventure you're after, then Waitomo is the place to be. The caves offer many challenging activities, from abseiling and rock climbing to cave tubing. You can pick and choose from a number of operators.

Waitomo Adventures The people at Waitomo Adventures (☎ 0800 924 866, 07-878 7788, ⓦ www.waitomo.co.nz, Cavelands Cafe) offer a range of cave adventures.

With 100m (330ft) of abseiling to get into the Lost World Cave, its **Lost World** trip is one of the most amazing things you can do in this country. And you don't even need prior abseiling or caving experience. The principal trip to Lost World is an all-day one ($300; trips leave at 10.30am). First you abseil 100m down into the cave (accompanied by your guide), then, by a combination of walking, rock climbing, spider-walking, inching along narrow rock ledges, wading and swimming through a subterranean river, you take a three-hour journey through a 30m-high cave to get back out, passing glowworms, amazing rock and cave formations, waterfalls and more. The total price includes lunch (underground) and dinner.

The other option is a four-hour trip ($195) that involves a 100m abseil into the cave, with a guide right beside you on another rope. At the bottom, you walk for half an hour into the cave, and exit via another vertical cavern back to the surface, without doing the underground river trip. The trips depart at 7am and 11.30am.

The **Haggas Honking Holes** four-hour caving trip ($135) includes professional abseiling instruction followed by a caving trip with three abseils, rock climbing, and travelling along a subterranean river with

Glowworms

Glowworms are the larvae of the fungus gnat, which looks much like a large mosquito without mouth parts. The larvae glowworms have luminescent organs which produce a soft, greenish light. Living in a sort of 'hammock' suspended from an overhang, they weave sticky threads which trail down and catch unwary insects attracted by their lights. When an insect flies towards the light, it gets stuck in the threads and becomes paralysed – the glowworm reels in the thread and eats the insect.

The larval stage lasts for six to nine months, depending on how much food the glowworm gets. When the glowworm has grown to about the size of a matchstick it goes into a pupa stage, much like a cocoon. The adult fungus gnat emerges about two weeks later.

The adult insect does not live very long because it does not have a mouth; it emerges, mates, lays eggs and dies, all within about two or three days. The sticky eggs, laid in groups of 40 or 50, hatch in about three weeks to become larval glowworms.

Glowworms thrive in moist, dark caves, but they can survive anywhere if they have the requisites of moisture, an overhang to suspend from, and insects to eat. Waitomo is famous for its glowworms but you can see them in many other places around NZ, both in caves and outdoors.

When you come upon glowworms, don't touch their hammocks or hanging threads, try not to make loud noises and don't shine a light right on them. In daylight their lights fade out, and if you shine a torch right on them they will dim their lights. It takes the lights a few hours to become bright again, during which time the glowworm will catch no food. The glowworms that shine most brightly are the hungriest.

waterfalls. Along the way you see glow-worms and a variety of cave formations – stalactites, stalagmites, columns, flowstone and cave coral. It's a good way to see real caving action, using caving equipment and going through caverns of various sizes, squeezing through tight, narrow passageways as well as traversing huge caverns.

The name of the adventure derives from a local farmer, 'Haggas', and characters in a Dr Seuss story, 'honking holers'. Trips depart 11.15am and 4.15pm. The 'Gruesome Twosome' combines this with the four-hour Lost World trip ($310).

Tumu Tumu Toobing is a more physical four-hour tubing trip ($70) for the adventurous traveller. Trips leave at 11am and 3.30pm. 'Blackwater Fever', a combination of this trip and the Haggas Honking Holes adventure, costs $185. Combining the Lost World and Tumu Tumu trips saves you $20.

Black-Water Rafting Peter Chandler and John Ash, the founders of Black Water Rafting (☎ 0800 228 646, 878 6219, W www .blackwaterrafting.co.nz, Black Water Cafe) introduced the sport of cave tubing to the unsuspecting traveller in 1987. Also known as black-water rafting, it soon became one of NZ's most popular adventures. The cost of each trip includes admission into the Museum of Caves.

Black Water Rafting I is a three-hour trip ($69) on an inner tube floating down a subterranean river that flows through Ruakuri Cave. The high point is leaping off a small waterfall and then floating through a long, glowworm-covered passage. The trip ends with hot showers, soup and toast. You wear a wetsuit which will keep you warm, but having something hot to eat or drink before the trip will make you feel more comfortable.

The five-hour 'Mark II' version of Black Water Rafting I is **Black Water Rafting II** ($140). It's more adventurous and involves a 30m abseil into Ruakuri Cave, more glowworms, tubing and cave climbing. Food consumed in the cave is included.

If you're not keen on getting wet then **Black Water Dry** ($35; one hour underground including boat trip) could be an option. This guided tour goes through parts of the Mangawhitiakau cave system at Oparure, 12km south of Waitomo. During the three-hour tour you will learn all about the life cycle of glowworms, and gain an insight into other things that inhabit the caves. Moa bones were discovered in this cave back in 1849. Bookings are essential; transport from the Museum of Caves in Waitomo, tea/coffee and biscuits are included in the price.

Waitomo Down Under Next door to the Museum of Caves is Waitomo Down Under (☎ 0800 102 605, 07-878 6577, e wdu@ xtra.co.nz). They operate 'float through' caving adventures. In its **Adventure I** ($75), you go through Te Ana Roa (Long Cave) in inner tubes, going over *two* waterfalls (one on a slide) and getting a good close-up view of some glowworms along the way. Its **Adventure II** ($75) is a 50m abseil down into the 'Baby Grand' *tomo* (you can do it at night as well for $85). Waitomo Down Under's **Adventure III** ($35) is a two-hour trip purely involving caving.

Rap, Raft n Rock The five-hour **trip** ($75) with Rap, Raft n Rock (☎ 0800 228 372) starts with a 27m abseil into a natural cave, and then involves floating along a subterranean river on an inner tube. How fast you float will depend on the season; in winter the water moves more swiftly. But whatever time you do it, one of the outstanding features of this trip is the magnificent glowworm display here. After some caving you do a belayed rock climb up a stepped 20m pitch to the surface.

Walking

The Museum of Caves has free pamphlets on various **walks** in the area. The walk from the Aranui Cave to the Ruakuri Cave is an excellent short walk. From the Glowworm Cave ticket office, it's a 15-minute forest walk to a grove of California redwood trees. Also from here, the 5km three-hour **Waitomo Walkway** takes off through farmland and follows Waitomo Stream to the Ruakuri Scenic Reserve, where a half-hour return walk passes by the river, caves and a natural limestone bridge. This last section of the walk is magical at night when glowworms blaze away (bring a torch).

A one-hour return walk, the **Opapaka Pa Bush Walk** leads up to a pre-European *pa* (fort) site on a hill. Plaques along the way describe traditional Maori medicines found in the forest, traditional forest lore and the pa site itself.

Many other good walks are west of Waitomo on the Marokopa Road; see the following Marokopa Road section.

Things to See & Do

Woodlyn Park (☎ 07-878 6666, W *www .woodlynpark.co.nz; adult/child $13/7; shows 1.30pm daily*) is the realisation of a fair-dinkum Kiwi's dream. Barry Woods, ex-shearer, puts on a helluva show, in which he cleverly integrates a history lesson into his inimitable humorous piece of theatre. It is a New Zealand farm show with a difference, featuring many introduced, trained animals. A sheepdog, cows, bulls, sheep, a dancing pig and a 'kiwi bear' (possum) work in cohorts with Barry. The shows are riotous fun and the audience are deliberately involved in all sorts, including shearing a sheep and exploding a log. It is well worth the entry fee. You can also drive a powerful jetboat, capable of 100HP, around a specially designed course – this is the only operation of its type in NZ and a thrilling experience. Eight laps will cost you $42 and it is open 9.30am to 6.30pm November to April and 9.30am to 5pm May to October.

The **Shearing Shed** (☎ 07-878 8371; admission free; open 9am-4.30pm daily) has an exhibition of products made with the fibre of Angora rabbits. Rabbit shearing takes place at 12.45pm daily.

Waitomo Caves Horse Treks (☎ 07-878 5065; 1-/2-/4-hr rides $40/50/90) offers a variety of different rides through the Waitomo wilderness areas.

Big Red (book at the visitors centre; $65 for 2 hours) takes self-drive quad bike trips through bush and countryside.

Rap, Raft n Rock (☎ 0800 228 372; rope course $50, rope course & cave trip $110) has constructed a rope course to test your skills and to get your adrenaline pumping. The course, set amongst pine trees, includes, a trapeze, rope bridge, and big swing.

Places to Stay

Camping, Cabins & Hostels Opposite the museum is the *Waitomo Top 10 Holiday Park* (☎/fax 07-878 7639, e *stay@waitomo park.co.nz*) with powered/unpowered sites for $11/10 per person, cabins $32 to $35 and tourist flats for $80. It has modern communal facilities, including Internet access.

Juno Hall (☎ 07-878 7649) Camp sites $10 per person, dorm beds $18, twins & doubles with shared/private bath $44/54. Juno Hall is on the main road in from the highway to the caves, about 1km before the Museum of Caves. Its communal area has the feel of a ski lodge and it has good accommodation. Activities include horse trekking, hunting and fishing trips. There's a pool.

HTG Lodge (☎ 07-878 7442) First/successive nights $12/10. Situated 2km further on past the Glowworm Cave, this is the clubroom of the Hamilton Tomo Group, which is the largest caving club in NZ. It welcomes visitors, and the cost helps to support the club. The hut is quite 'rustic' but has good lounge and kitchen areas, even if beds in the shared rooms are hard. Bring your own sleeping bag. The helpful caretaker can tell you about walks and free activities in the area or, if you're lucky, you may be invited on a caving trip, particularly on weekends when the caving isn't too difficult.

Guesthouses & Farmstays Conveniently situated just 100m from the Museum of Caves, *Waitomo Guest Lodge* (☎ 07-878 7641, fax 878 7466, Waitomo Caves Rd) is a pleasant, friendly B&B, and all rooms have a bathroom. Singles/doubles are $50/70.

Waitomo Express (☎ 07-878 6666, e *bil ly@woodlynpark.co.nz*) Doubles $80 plus $10 per extra person. At Woodlyn Park (see Things to See & Do earlier this chapter) you can stay in this converted railcar which has all mod cons – kitchen, shower, toilet, three bedrooms and comfortable lounge. A kitchen is available to picnickers for lunch in summer.

Abseil Inn *(☎ 07-878 7815,* **e** *abseil inn@xtra.co.nz, 709 Waitomo Caves Rd)* Singles/doubles $80/100. This very modern and comfortable B&B has spacious en suite rooms, and a large communal lounge.

Valley View *(☎/fax 07-878 7063,* **e** *val ley123@xtra.co.nz, 168 Te Anga Rd)* Self-contained unit $70. As the name suggests, this place has views across the Waitomo valley. The unit is spacious and has everything you need.

Big Bird *(☎ 0800 733 244, 873 7459,* **e** *bigbird.bb@xtra.co.nz, 17 Waitomo Caves Rd)* Singles/doubles with breakfast $40/65, self-contained cottage $80. It is near the turn-off to Te Kuiti and Otorohanga (7km east of the visitors centre). Farmstays and free tours of the adjacent ostrich farm and glowworm caves are available.

Motels & Hotels There are a couple of motels on SH3 at Hangatiki, at the Waitomo turn-off, 8km from Waitomo.

Glowworm Motel *(☎ 07-873 8882, fax 873 8856)* Units from $73. This motel has an outdoor swimming pool and spa.

Caves Motor Inn *(☎ 07-873 8109,* **e** *glow .worm@xtra.co.nz)* Lodge $20, unit singles/doubles $69/79. Caves Motor Inn is about 100m south of Glowworm Motel on SH3, and has a bar and restaurant. The lodge has shared bathrooms.

Waitomo Caves Hotel *(☎ 07-878 8227, fax 07-878 8205)* Dorm beds $20, singles $25, hotel rooms $40-130. This hotel, high on the hill in the centre of the village, was built in 1908 and was *the* place to stay. It retains a certain charm. From here it's a five-minute walk to the glowworm caves. There are occasional specials.

Places to Eat

The grocery store beside the Museum of Caves is open daily, but there is better selection at Otorohanga or Te Kuiti.

Cavelands Cafe Bar & Brasserie *(Main Rd)* Meals $8.50-13. This large place has inexpensive meals to takeaway or eat in.

Black Water Cafe *(Waitomo Caves Rd)* Light meals $5-8. The Black Water Cafe has good vegie pizzas and quiche, hearty breakfasts, Internet access, a pool table and both indoor and patio seating.

There is also a *cafe* at the entrance to the Glowworm Cave.

The Waitomo Caves Hotel has the ***Frederick Mace Restaurant***, which has an a la carte menu (mains around $25).

Roselands Restaurant *(☎ 07-878 7611, Fullerton Rd)* Set menu $22. Open 11am-2pm. This upmarket place is open for lunch, and puts on an ample barbecue of steak or fish, a salad buffet, dessert and coffee. It is in an attractive setting with garden, veranda or indoor seating. From Waitomo village, go 400m east towards SH3, then follow the signs for 3km.

The ***Tavern*** near the Museum of Caves is excellent value for meals and snacks ($8.50 to $13), and is the place where everyone migrates to for a drink after a hard day spelunking.

Getting There & Away

The Waitomo Shuttle (☎ 0800 808 279) operates between Waitomo and Otorohanga ($7 one way).

InterCity (☎ 09-913 6100) has round-trip bus services to the Glowworm Cave from Auckland and Rotorua ($114). You only get to spend an hour at the caves so it's a very rushed trip. Magic Bus and Kiwi Experience also come to Waitomo.

The Waitomo Wanderer (☎ 0800 924 866) operates a useful daily loop around central North Island. It departs from Waitomo at 4pm, and Rotorua at 6pm. Otherwise there is an overnight stop at Rotorua and you can pick up the bus again at 7.30am for the trip back to Waitomo (arriving 9.30am). The trip costs $25. They also offer discounts on Waitomo attractions, if you use their services.

Hitching to Waitomo from the turn-off on SH3 is usually pretty easy, as is hitching around Waitomo once you're there. Hitching out towards Te Anga and Marokopa can be more difficult because there's so little traffic.

MAROKOPA ROAD

Heading west from Waitomo, you start to enter a little-visited corner of NZ. Te Anga Road becomes Marokopa Road, and follows a rewarding and scenic route with a couple of natural beauties worth visiting. The useful *West to Marokopa* pamphlet ($1) is produced by DOC; or get a copy of *A Trip Through Time* by Peter Chandler ($6.50), available from the Waitomo Museum of Caves, which outlines a geological driving tour of the 53km road from Waitomo to Kiritehere on the coast, with suggestions for walks.

The **Tawarau Forest**, about 20km west of Waitomo village, has various walks outlined in a DOC pamphlet, including a one-hour walk to the Tawarau Falls from the end of Appletree Rd. The track was closed at the time of writing.

The **Mangapohue Natural Bridge Scenic Reserve**, 26km west of Waitomo, is a 5.5 hectare reserve with a giant natural limestone bridge formation; this is a 20-minute round-walk from the road on a wheelchair-accessible pathway. You can easily walk to the summit. On the far side, big rocks full of oyster fossils jut up from the grass. At night you'll see glowworms.

About 4km further west is **Piripiri Caves Scenic Reserve**, where a 5-minute track leads to a large cave containing fossils of giant oysters. Bring a torch and be prepared to get muddy.

The impressive 36m **Marokopa Falls** are 32km west of Waitomo. A short track (10 minutes return) from the road leads to the bottom of the falls.

The falls are near **Te Anga**, where you can stop for a drink at the pleasant *Te Anga Tavern*. From Te Anga you can turn north to Taharoa or Kawhia, 53km away, or southwest to **Marokopa**, a small village on the coast, 48km from Waitomo. The whole Te Anga-Marokopa area is riddled with caves. The bitumen ends just past Marokopa at Kiritehere, but it is possible to continue, on a difficult but scenic road, 60km further south until you meet SH3 at Awakino (see Te Kuiti to Mokau). About 20km south of Marokopa is the **Whareorino Forest**, which has forest walks and overnight accommodation at *Leitch's Hut* (inquire at DOC in Te Kuiti; $7).

On weekdays Perry's Bus (☎ 07-876 7595) runs from Taharoa on the coast along the Marokopa Road to Te Kuiti via Te Anga and Waitomo (one way/return $6/12). The bus departs from the Te Kuiti train station at 1pm for the return trip. There are no petrol stations on the Marokopa Rd.

Places to Stay
Marokopa Camping Ground *(☎ 07-876 7444, Rauparaha St)* Powered/unpowered sites $9/7 per person. This camping ground at Marokopa is close to the coast and has a small shop.

Hepipi Farm *(☎ 07-876 7861)* B&B & dinner $50 per person, self-contained units $50. About 10km south of Te Anga on the road to Marokopa is this friendly farmstay. Hepipi Farm also manages three self-contained units at the beach in Marokopa, each of which sleep up to four people.

TE KUITI
☎ 07 • pop 4540
This small, provincial town, south of Otorohanga, is another base for visiting Waitomo, 19km away. Te Kuiti probably comes from Te Kuititanga, meaning 'the narrowing in', referring not only to the narrowing of the Mangaokewa Valley here but also to the confiscation of Maori property after the Waikato Land War. Locals will proudly tell you, however, that the town is named for Te Kooti, a prominent Maori rebellion leader who settled here in 1872, seeking refuge from the Pakeha, and stayed for a number of years (see the boxed text 'Te Kooti' in the East Coast chapter).

The magnificently carved Te Tokanganui -o-noho Marae, overlooking the south end of Rora St, was Te Kooti's grateful gift to his hosts, the Ngati Maniapoto people, once he had accepted the Maori king's creed of pacifism.

Te Kuiti, home to many champion sheep shearers, is known as 'the Shearing Capital of the World'. A 'big shearer' statue is the most prominent feature of the town.

Information
The Te Kuiti visitors centre (☎ 07-878 8077, ✉ tkinfo@voyager.co.nz) on the main drag, Rora St, is open from 9am to

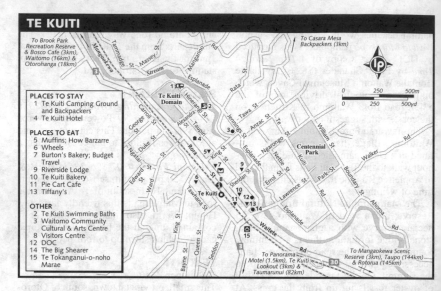

TE KUITI

To Brook Park
Recreation Reserve
& Bosco Cafe (3km),
Waitomo (16km) &
Otorohanga (18km)

To Casara Mesa
Backpackers (3km)

Te Kuiti
Domain

Centennial
Park

Te Kuiti

0   250   500m
0   250   500yd

PLACES TO STAY
1 Te Kuiti Camping Ground
   and Backpackers
4 Te Kuiti Hotel

PLACES TO EAT
5 Muffins; How Barzarre
6 Wheels
7 Burton's Bakery; Budget
   Travel
9 Riverside Lodge
10 Te Kuiti Bakery
11 Pie Cart Cafe
13 Tiffany's

OTHER
2 Te Kuiti Swimming Baths
3 Waitomo Community
   Cultural & Arts Centre
8 Visitors Centre
12 DOC
14 The Big Shearer
15 Te Tokanganui-o-noho
   Marae

To Panorama
Motel (1.5km), Te Kuiti
Lookout (3km) &
Taumarunui (82km)

To Mangaokewa Scenic
Reserve (3km), Taupo (144km)
& Rotorua (145km)

5pm Monday to Friday (from 10am to 4pm on Saturday and Sunday in winter). It has information on homestays and farmstays and does bus and train bookings.

The DOC office (☎ 07-878 1050) is at 78 Taupiri St.

Things to See & Do
Apart from the big shearer, Te Kuiti's main attraction is the **Te Kuiti Muster**, held on the first weekend in April (or the following weekend, if Easter falls then). This popular event includes sheep- and goat-shearing championships, a parade, arts and crafts, live music, sheep races, Maori culture groups, barbecues and *hangi*, a duathlon and a town-wide bargain day.

Te Kuiti has some fine gardens and parks. If you're a garden fan, ask at the visitors centre for its *King Country Gardens* brochure, which gives details on 11 private gardens you can visit in the region.

The **Mangaokewa Stream** winds through the town, with a pleasant riverside walkway. Beside the stream, the **Mangaokewa Scenic Reserve**, 3km south of town on SH30, has picnic and barbecue areas, a waterhole for safe swimming and overnight camping.

On the north-western boundary of Te Kuiti, the attractive **Brook Park Recreation Reserve** has walking tracks leading to the summit of the Ben Lomond Hill. Besides affording a fine view, the hill is the site of the historic Matakiora Pa, constructed in the 17th century by Rora, son of Maniapoto. Camping is permitted.

Te Kuiti Lookout *(Awakino Rd, SH3)*, on the road as it climbs out of town heading south, provides a great view over the town, especially at night with the sparkling lights stretching out below.

Places to Stay
Te Kuiti Camping Ground and Backpackers (☎ 07-878 6761, ℮ tewaka@hotmail .com, Hinerangi St) Powered/unpowered sites $7 per person, bed with linen $15, on-site vans $23, cabins $27. On the north side of town beside the Mangaokewa Stream, about 800m north of the visitors centre, is this peaceful camping ground. There is also accommodation in a cosy house, and breakfast ($5 to $8).

Camping is also permitted at the **Brook Park Recreation Reserve** on the north-western boundary of Te Kuiti, and at the

Mangaokewa Scenic Reserve beside the stream (see Things to See & Do); both have barbecues, picnic areas and toilets, but no other facilities. Payment is by donation.

Casara Mesa Backpackers (☎ 07-878 6697, e casara@xtra.co.nz, Mangarino Rd) Beds with linen $17.50, doubles & twins $40, doubles with bath $45. Situated 3km north of town, this farmstay has great views over the town from its veranda and is well worth the price. The owner picks up and drops off in Te Kuiti.

Te Kuiti Hotel (☎ 07-878 8172, Rora St) Singles/doubles with bath $35/50. This hotel is located in the town centre.

Panorama Motel (☎ 07-878 8051, e gl ow.worm@xtra.co.nz, 59 Awakino Rd) Unit singles/doubles $75/80. This motel, on SH3 about 1.5km south of the visitors centre, has a pool and partial views of town.

Places to Eat

Bosco Cafe (Te Kumi Rd) Light meals around $5. This excellent cafe, out by Brook Park, has delectable delights on offer, including fantastic custard squares.

Te Kuiti has daytime cafes and bakeries on Rora St, including the *Te Kuiti Bakery* and *Burton's Bakery*. *Pie Cart Cafe*, in a refurbished train carriage, is open until very late.

Muffins (King St) Light meals around $5. This pleasant cafe has snacks and light meals.

Tiffany's (☎ 07-878 8872, Rora St) Meals from $15. This place also does sandwiches and burgers, and opens late.

Wheels Restaurant (☎ 07-878 6790, Carroll St) Meals $8-15. This friendly and casual restaurant has both Western and Chinese food, and also a takeaway section.

Riverside Lodge (☎ 07-878 8027, Sheridan St) Mains $20-30. This restaurant is a bit more upmarket, with fine dining by the Mangaokewa Stream.

Te Kuiti's one nightspot, *How Barzarre (cnr King & Taupiri Sts)*, serves snacks (from $3.50) such as nachos before it transforms into a late-night venue.

Getting There & Away

InterCity buses arrive at and depart from Tiffany's restaurant at the south end of Rora St; book and buy your tickets from the visitors centre. Long-distance buses stopping at Te Kuiti include those to New Plymouth, Taumarunui or north to Hamilton and on to Auckland.

Buses also operate in the local region. On weekdays the Perry's bus (☎ 07-876 7596) runs between Taharoa on the coast and Te Kuiti, passing through Waitomo, Te Anga and the other scenic attractions along the Waitomo-Marokopa Road. The Waitomo Wanderer (see Waitomo earlier in this chapter) operates a loop between Rotorua and Waitomo via Te Kuiti.

The Auckland-Wellington trains stops (☎ 0800 802 802) in Te Kuiti at the Rora St station. Get tickets from the visitors centre or Budget Travel (☎ 07-878 8184).

TE KUITI TO MOKAU
☎ 06

From Te Kuiti, SH3 runs south-west to Mokau on the rugged west coast before continuing on to New Plymouth in Taranaki. The road runs through a lightly populated farming area and is partly very scenic. InterCity buses between Hamilton and New Plymouth take this route, as does Dalroy Express (☎ 0508 465 622; see Getting There & Away under Hamilton later in this chapter).

The road passes through the small town of **Piopio**, which has a small museum, and then tiny **Mahoenui**, from where the road follows the Awakino River. The road along the river is the most spectacular part of the route. Through a short road tunnel you enter the steep **Awakino Gorge**, lined with dense bush and giant ponga.

The road follows the river all the way to **Awakino**, a small settlement on the coast where boats shelter on the river estuary, away from the windswept coast. Awakino can also be reached via the Marokopa Road from Waitomo. Just south of Awakino is the **Manioroa Marae**, which contains the anchor stone of the *Tainui* canoe, whose descendants populated Waikato and the King Country. Ask at the organic farm opposite the *marae* on SH3 for permission to enter. Marae protocol should be observed (see Visiting a Marae in the 'Maori Culture & Arts' special section).

Five kilometres further south, the little town of **Mokau** is at the border of King Country and Taranaki. The town's **Tainui Museum** *(open 10am-4pm)* has a fascinating collection of old photographs from the time when this once-isolated outpost was a coal and lumber shipping port for Pakeha pioneer settlements along the Mokau River.

Mokau River Cruises *(☎ 06-752 9775; adult/child $30/15)* has good three-hour trips up the river in the historic *Cygnet*. Reservations are essential.

Mokau is otherwise just a speck on the map, but it does have a fine stretch of wild beach and good fishing. The river mouth hides some of the best whitebait in the North Island.

Places to Stay & Eat

Palm House *(☎ 06-752 9081, e palm house@taranaki-bakpak.co.nz)* Dorm beds $16, twins/doubles $38/40. Palm House in Mokau, is a good little backpackers on SH3 and close to the beach. Inquire at the house next door if no-one is around.

Seaview Holiday Park *(☎ 06-752 9708)* Powered/unpowered sites $9 per person, cabins $35, tourist flats $55. This holiday park just north of Mokau is right on the beach. There's a shop.

Awakino Hotel *(☎ 06-752 9815)* Singles/doubles $30/60. This is a basic but friendly place.

Mokau Inn Motel *(☎ 06-752 9725)* Twins/doubles $60/70. Some units here have full cooking facilities.

There are a couple of little stores selling a limited range of goods, and a butcher. The **Whitebait Inn** has takeaway and sit-down meals, with the area's famous whitebait on the menu in various forms.

TAUMARUNUI
☎ 07 • pop 4500

Taumarunui is a quiet little town on SH4, 82km south of Te Kuiti and 43km north of the township of National Park. Its name means 'Big Screen' and is from the town's history. Maori chief, Pehi Taroa, was dying and asked for a screen *(taumaru)* to shade him from the sun. They say that he died

before the screen was in place, still asking for it with his final words – *taumaru nui*.

In winter Taumarunui operates as a ski town, but is really too far from the snow to be convenient. In summer it is one of the main access points for canoeing on the Whanganui River; five-day trips on the river start from here (see Whanganui National Park in the Whanganui & Manawatu chapter for details).

History

At the confluence of the Whanganui and Ongarue Rivers, both major transport waterways, Taumarunui was already an important settlement in pre-European days. It was also significant as the historical meeting place of three important Maori tribes: Whanganui, Tuwharetoa and Maniapoto.

Pakeha did not settle in the area until the 1880s, but even then their influence was minimal until the Main Trunk Railway Line came south from Te Kuiti in 1903. In the same year, the riverboat service coming from the coast at Wanganui was extended up the Whanganui River to Taumarunui. Taumarunui flourished as the rail link, running all the way to Auckland, became a much-travelled route and timber from the area's sawmills was freighted out.

Information

The Taumarunui visitors centre (☎ 07-895 7494, e taumarunui.vic@xtra.co.nz) is at the train station on Hakiaha St in the town centre. It's open from 9am to 4.30pm Monday to Friday and 10am to 4pm Saturday and Sunday. It's the agent for AA and for bus, train and ferry tickets. It also books river trips and stocks DOC brochures. It's worth a stop just for a look at the operating model of the Raurimu Spiral.

The DOC office (☎ 07-895 8201) at Cherry Grove, has information on the Whanganui National Park and canoeing the river. It is open from 8am to 5pm, Monday to Friday, but may not always be manned.

Raurimu Spiral

The Raurimu Spiral is a feat of rail engineering that was declared a 'wonder of the

WAIKATO & KING COUNTRY

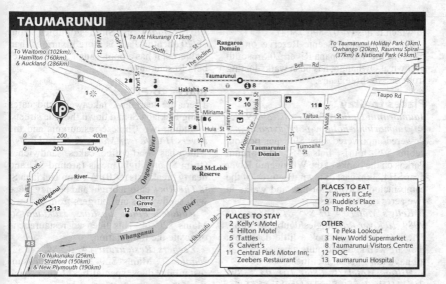

TAUMARUNUI

PLACES TO STAY
2 Kelly's Motel
4 Hilton Motel
5 Tattles
6 Calvert's
11 Central Park Motor Inn;
    Zeebers Restaurant

PLACES TO EAT
7 Rivers II Cafe
9 Ruddie's Place
10 The Rock

OTHER
1 Te Peka Lookout
3 New World Supermarket
8 Taumarunui Visitors Centre
12 DOC
13 Taumarunui Hospital

world' when it was completed in 1908. The spiral's three horseshoe curves, one complete circle and two short tunnels, allowed the Main Trunk Railway coming south from Auckland and north from Wellington to finally be joined (at Horopito). The visitors centre has an excellent working model of the spiral, and pamphlets explaining its construction. At Raurimu, 37km south of Taumarunui, you can see the real thing from a lookout just off the highway.

Rail buffs can experience the spiral on any train between Wellington and Auckland. For a day trip, take the train from aumarunui to National Park township and return to Taumarunui the same day ($28 return). It leaves at 1pm, and returns at 3.10pm. Book at the visitors centre.

Nukunuku Museum
This private museum (☎ 07-896 6365; *admission by donation; open by appointment only*), also known as Erceg's museum, is devoted to the Whanganui River and the area around it with Maori and pioneer artefacts, and pioneer buildings. The museum is at Nukunuku, 25km down the Whanganui River from Taumarunui and it can either be

reached by river or via Saddlers Rd, off the Whanganui River Road.

Stratford-Taumarunui Heritage Trail
See the Taranaki chapter for details on this route between Taumarunui and Stratford (note that 19km of this is unsealed).

Walking
The visitors centre has suggestions for several enjoyable walks around Taumarunui. A pleasant walkway extends east along the Whanganui River from Cherry Grove Domain to the Taumarunui Holiday Park, about 3km away. Another track leads to the Rangaroa Domain with a good view over the town, its rivers and mountains; go over the train line, up The Incline and through the native bush behind the scout den to reach the domain. Te Peka Lookout across the Ongarue River on the western side of town is another good vantage point.

For even better views extending to Tongariro National Park in the south, climb flat-topped Mt Hikurangi (771m), north of the town. This curious hill can be seen from far and wide. Before climbing, you must

WAIKATO & KING COUNTRY

ask permission from the owner of the farm in which it lies (☎ 07-896 7804).

The Ohinetonga Scenic Reserve on the banks of the Whakapapa River, 20km south of town at Owhango, has bush walks lasting from one to three hours.

Places to Stay

Taumarunui Holiday Park *(☎ 07-895 9345,* e *taumarunui-holiday-park@xtra.co.nz)* Powered/unpowered sites $9/8 per person, cabins $29, tourist flats $45. Taumarunui Park is on the banks of the Whanganui River near SH4, 3km east of town. Features of the camp include kayaks for hire and walks in five acres of native bush.

Kelly's Motel *(☎ 07-895 8175, fax 895 9089, 10 River Rd)* Singles/doubles $50/65. The units here may look a little dated but they are well kept and quite a bargain. They all have full kitchen facilities.

Hilton Motel *(☎ 0800 101 942, 895 7181, Hakiaha St)* Singles/doubles $55/65. The Hilton doesn't quite live up to *other* Hiltons' standards, but then again neither does the price.

Tattles *(☎/fax 07-895 8063, 23 Marae St)* Singles/doubles from $56/68. Tattles has good, cheap units and also hires out canoes for trips on the river.

Calvert's *(☎ 07-895 8501, 6 Marae St)* Singles/doubles with breakfast $60/70. Calvert's has units that are both upstairs and downstairs.

Central Park Motor Inn *(☎ 07-895 7132, Maata St)* Singles/doubles from $6/70. Central Park is more luxurious than Calvert's; it has a pool, sauna, spa and Zeebers Restaurant.

Places to Eat

There are tearooms, takeaways and cafes along Hakiaha St and down the side streets, including two Chinese restaurants and the ***Rivers II Cafe*** *(cnr Marae & Hakiaha Sts)*, which has good coffee, cakes, sandwiches (from $3.50), light meals (around $6) and hearty breakfasts ($10). Also on Hakiaha St is *The Rock* cafe, a bright and bouncy place with sandwiches and burgers from $3.

Ruddie's Place *(upstairs, Hakiaha St)* Mains $20-24. This licensed restaurant is opposite the train station.

Zeebers Restaurant *(☎ 07-895 7132, Maata St)* Mains $20-25. This pleasant restaurant does specialities like ostrich steak in a red wine sauce.

Getting There & Away

Buses and trains that are travelling between Auckland and Wellington all stop at the train station at Taumarunui. This train station also houses the visitors centre, where you can buy tickets.

Hitching is easy if you are heading north or south on SH4. It's a lot harder hitching a ride on the lightly trafficked Stratford-Taumarunui Road.

Taranaki

☎ 06 • pop 107,600

The Taranaki region juts out into the Tasman Sea on the west coast of the North Island, about halfway between Auckland and Wellington. The region is named after the Mt Taranaki volcano, also called Mt Egmont, the massive cone of which dominates the landscape. Conditions are excellent for agriculture, with rich volcanic soil and abundant rainfall. The 'big smoke' for the area is New Plymouth.

The names Taranaki and Egmont are both widely used in the region. Taranaki is the Maori name for the volcano and Egmont is the name James Cook gave it in 1770, after the Earl of Egmont, who had encouraged his expedition. Today the region is called Taranaki, the cape is called Cape Egmont, and the waters on either side of the cape are called the North and South Taranaki Bights. Egmont National Park retains the name of the national park but Taranaki and Egmont are *both* official names for the volcano.

In addition to the obvious attraction of Taranaki – the 'most climbed' mountain in NZ – the region is popular for its world-class surfing and windsurfing beaches along SH45 – the surf highway.

NEW PLYMOUTH
pop 49,100

A coastal city backed by towering Mt Taranaki and surrounded by rich agricultural and dairy lands, New Plymouth is a good base for visiting Egmont National Park. It has some fine parks and the spectacular backdrop of Mt Taranaki, but near the sea the city's industrial installations blight the landscape.

History

Archaeological evidence shows that the region was settled by the Maori from early times. In the 1820s the Taranaki Maori fled to the Cook Strait region to avoid a threatened attack by the Waikato tribes, but it was not until 1832 that the Waikato attacked and

Highlights

- Walking, mountain climbing or skiing on the awe-inspiring Mt Taranaki volcano
- Visiting significant Maori and European historical sites
- Windsurfing or surfing the beaches along the surf highway
- Driving along the Stratford-Taumarunui Heritage Trail
- Dam dropping over the edge at Hawera

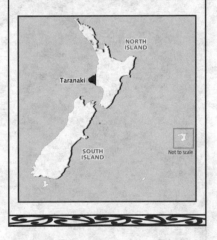

subdued the remaining Te Ati-awa tribe. The Te Ati-awa remained only at Okoki Pa (New Plymouth), where whalers had joined in the battle. Thus when the first European settlers arrived in the district in 1841 the coast of Taranaki was almost deserted. Initially it seemed there would be no opposition to land claims, so the New Zealand Company managed to buy extensive tracts from the Te Ati-awa who had stayed.

When other members of Te Ati-awa and other tribes returned after years of exile and slavery, they objected strongly to the sale of their land. Their claims were substantially upheld when Governor Fitzroy ruled that the

275

TARANAKI

TARANAKI

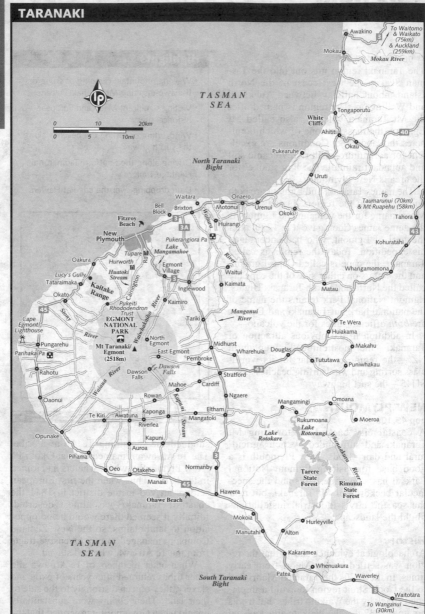

NZ Company was only allowed to retain just over 10 sq km around New Plymouth of the 250 sq km it had claimed. The Crown slowly acquired more land from the Maori, who became increasingly reluctant to sell. At the same time the European settlers became increasingly greedy for the fertile land around Waitara, just north of New Plymouth.

The settlers' determination finally forced the government to abandon its policy of negotiation, and in 1860 war broke out. For 10 years the Maori kept them engaged in guerrilla warfare. During this time, settlers mov-ed in on Waitara and took control, but the Maori did as they pleased throughout the rest of the province. The Taranaki chiefs had not signed the Treaty of Waitangi and did not recognise the sovereignty of the British queen, so they were treated as rebels. By 1870 over 500 hectares of their land had been confiscated and much of the rest acquired through dubious transactions.

The Taranaki province experienced an economic boom with the discovery of natural gas and oil at Kapuni in 1959 and more recently at the Maui natural gas field off the coast in the South Taranaki Bight.

Orientation & Information

Devon St (East and West) is the city's hub. The New Plymouth visitors centre (☎ 06-759 6080, ⱳ www.newplymouthnz.com), currently on the corner of Liardet and Leach Sts, is open from 8.30am to 5pm Monday to Friday and 9am to 5pm on Saturday and Sunday. Plans are afoot to move the centre into Pukeariki (Ariki St), a new museum and library complex under construction at the time of writing and due for completion mid-2003. Call ahead to confirm its whereabouts if you arrive after this date. The staff are helpful and the informative brochure *Options* is good.

For information on the region pick up the *Taranaki* guide or check out the website ⱳ www.taranakinz.org. The Department of Conservation (DOC) office (☎ 06-758 0433), 220 Devon St West, is open from 8am to 4.30pm Monday to Friday.

The Automobile Association (AA) office (☎ 06-759 4010) is at 49–55 Powderham St and the main post office is on Currie St.

Internet access is available at the visitors centre, Flick's Cafe (125 Devon St East) and at most backpackers.

Museums & Galleries

At the time of writing the Taranaki Museum was closed and its extensive collection of Maori artefacts, wildlife and colonial exhibits was in storage awaiting the completion of **Pukeariki** (*Ariki St*). This new museum and library complex, named after a New Plymouth Maori Pa, will open mid-2003. Contact the visitors centre for details.

The **Govett-Brewster Art Gallery** (☎ 06-758 5149, cnr Queen & King Sts; admission free except during special exhibitions; open 10.30am-5pm daily) is a renowned contemporary art gallery with a good reputation for its adventurous shows. Fans of abstract animation should seek out the films of Len Lye, pioneer animator of the 1930s, whose works are held here and shown from time to time.

Bone and wood carvings from local students are on display at the **Rangimarie Maori Arts & Crafts Centre** (☎ 06-751 2880, 80 Centennial Dr; admission free; open 9am-4pm Mon-Fri), 3km west of town at the foot of Paritutu Hill. Some of the smaller pieces are also for sale.

Historic Places

The free *Heritage Walkway* leaflet, obtainable from the visitors centre, outlines an interesting self-guided tour of 30 historic sites around the city.

Richmond Cottage (*cnr Ariki & Brougham Sts; adult/child $1/0.20*) was built in 1853. Unlike most early cottages, which were made of timber, Richmond Cottage was sturdily built of stone. It is currently closed and will reopen along with Pukeariki.

St Mary's Church (*Vivian St*) between Brougham and Robe Sts, built in 1846, is the oldest stone church in NZ. Its graveyard has headstones of early settlers and of soldiers who died during the Taranaki Land Wars (1860–61 and 1865–69). Impressed by their bravery, the British also buried several Maori chiefs here.

On Devon St at the eastern end of the city is the **Fitzroy Pole**, erected by the Maori in

TARANAKI

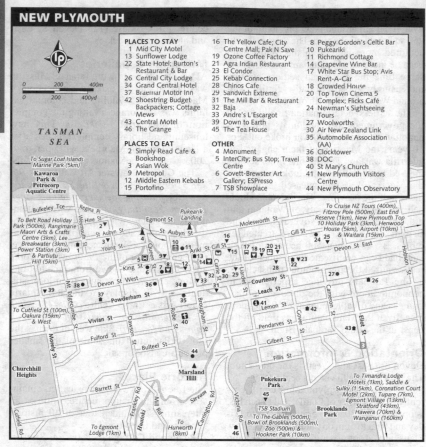

NEW PLYMOUTH

PLACES TO STAY
1 Mid City Motel
13 Sunflower Lodge
22 State Hotel; Burton's Restaurant & Bar
26 Central City Lodge
34 Grand Central Hotel
37 Braemar Motor Inn
42 Shoestring Budget Backpackers; Cottage Mews
43 Central Motel
46 The Grange

PLACES TO EAT
2 Simply Read Cafe & Bookshop
3 Asian Wok
9 Metropol
12 Middle Eastern Kebabs
15 Portofino

16 The Yellow Cafe; City Centre Mall; Pak N Save
19 Ozone Coffee Factory
21 Agra Indian Restaurant
23 El Condor
25 Kebab Connection
28 Chinos Cafe
29 Sandwich Extreme
31 The Mill Bar & Restaurant
32 Baja
33 Andre's L'Escargot
39 Down to Earth
45 The Tea House

OTHER
4 Monument
5 InterCity; Bus Stop; Travel Centre
6 Govett-Brewster Art Gallery; ESPresso
7 TSB Showplace

8 Peggy Gordon's Celtic Bar
10 Pukeariki
11 Richmond Cottage
14 Grapevine Wine Bar
17 White Star Bus Stop; Avis Rent-A-Car
18 Crowded House
20 Top Town Cinema 5 Complex; Flicks Café
24 Newman's Sightseeing Tours
27 Woolworths
30 Air New Zealand Link
35 Automobile Association (AA)
36 Clocktower
38 DOC
40 St Mary's Church
41 New Plymouth Visitors Centre
44 New Plymouth Observatory

1844 to mark the point beyond which Governor Fitzroy had forbidden settlers to acquire land. The carving on the bottom of the pole depicts a sorrowful Pakeha topped by a cheerfully triumphant Maori.

Marsland Hill & Observatory

The New Plymouth Observatory (☎ 06-753 2358, Marsland Hill; donations welcome; open 7.30pm-9pm Tues Mar-Oct, 8pm-9.30pm Tues Nov-Mar) is off Robe St. Public nights include a planetarium programme and viewing through a 6-inch refractor telescope, if the weather is clear.

Paritutu & Other Viewpoints

Above the power station is Paritutu, a steep hill with a magnificent view from the top. The name means 'rising precipice' and it's worth the tiring but quick scramble to the summit. Not only do you look down on the power station but also out over the city and the rocky Sugar Loaf Islands looming just offshore.

Another good viewpoint is Churchill Heights, with a trig marker on top showing distances to places near and far. You can walk up from Morley St or drive up from the entrance on Cutfield St.

Parks

New Plymouth is renowned for its superb parks. **Pukekura Park**, a 10-minute walk from the city centre, is worth a visit, with 49 hectares of gardens, bushwalks, streams, waterfalls, ponds and a kiosk. There are **display houses** *(admission free; open 8am-4pm daily)* with orchids and other exotic plants. Rowing boats on the lake can be hired on weekends, holidays and summer evenings ($5 per half hour). The lights and decorations in Pukekura Park from late December to early February are worth making a special trip to see. The park also has a delightful cricket oval in the English tradition.

Adjoining Pukekura is the lovely **Brooklands Park** and, between them, the Bowl of Brooklands, an outdoor sound-shell in a bush and lake setting. Brooklands Park was once the land around an important early settler's home; the fireplace and chimney are all that remain of the house after the Maori burnt it down. Highlights include a 2000-year-old puriri tree, a rhododendron dell with over 300 varieties, a great children's **zoo** *(admission free; open 8.30am-5pm daily)*, which has a new walk-through monkey enclosure, and **The Gables** *(admission free; open 1pm-4pm weekends)*, one of the oldest hospitals in NZ, now converted into an art gallery and medical museum.

On the waterfront is **Kawaroa Park**, with green areas, squash courts and the Petrocorp Aquatic Centre, which has a waterslide, an outdoor pool and an indoor pool (open all year). Also on the waterfront in the central city area is **Pukeariki Landing**, a historic area with sculptures.

Sugar Loaf Islands Marine Park

This marine park, established in 1986, includes: the rocky islets offshore from the power station; Back Beach on the west side of Paritutu; and the waters up to about 1km offshore. The islands, eroded volcanic remnants, are a refuge for sea birds, NZ fur seals and marine life; the greatest number of seals is from June to October but some are there all year round.

Activities in the park include boating and sailing, diving, bird-watching, pole fishing, surfing and beach walks. Boat trips to this islands are popular in summer. **Happy Chaddy's Charters** *(☎ 06-758 9133; charters adult/child $20/10)* has boats departing from Lee Breakwater, tide and weather permitting.

Walking

The visitors centre has leaflets on good walks around New Plymouth, including coastal, local reserve and park walks, in addition to the Heritage Walkway already mentioned. Te Henui Walkway, extending from the coast at East End Reserve to the city's southern boundary, is one of the most interesting and varied walks.

Huatoki Valley Walkway, following Huatoki Stream, makes an attractive walk to the city centre.

There are many tramps on Mt Taranaki; the **New Plymouth Tramping Club** (contact the visitors centre for details) may help.

Surfing & Windsurfing

Besides being beautiful, the Taranaki coastline is a world-class surfing and windsurfing area. In this area, Fitzroy and East End beaches are both at the eastern end of the city. Fitzroy is a good surfing beach and can be reached by bus from New Plymouth. There's also good surf at Back Beach, by Paritutu at the western end of the city, and at Oakura, about 15km west of New Plymouth. There are no buses to Oakura but hitching is easy. There are surf beaches all along SH45.

Vertigo (☎ 06-752 8283), on the Main Rd in Oakura, hires out surfboards and sailboards and offers instruction. **Tangaroa Adventures** *(☎ 021 701 904, ℮ tangaroa@ adventures.co.nz)* and **Taranaki Coastal Surf Charters** *(☎ 025 592 306)* both provide guided surf tours of the area, and the inexperienced can try **Tandem Surfing** *(☎ 06-752 7734)* – they guarantee you'll stand up. **Carbon Art** *(☎ 06-752 4485, ℮ carbonart@ xtra.co.nz)* specialises in windsurfing hire and lessons.

Aerial Sightseeing

Several operators offer scenic flights around the area, including flights over the snow-capped summit of Mt Taranaki – superb if

TARANAKI

the weather's clear. Operators include **Air Taranaki** (☎ *06-754 4375)*, **New Plymouth Aero Club** (☎ *06-755 0500)* and **Beck Helicopters** (☎ *06-764 7073)*.

Organised Tours

Cruise NZ Tours (☎ *06-758 3222, 8 Baring Terrace; full day tour adult/child $90/60)* takes tours around the city and out into the surrounding area.

Neuman's Sightseeing Tours (☎ *06-758 4622, 78–80 Gill St)* has a variety of tours, ranging from a $30 half-day scenic city tour to a three-quarter-day tour around Mt Taranaki ($40) or down the Stratford-Taumarunui Heritage Trail ($60; minimum of eight persons).

Places to Stay

Camping & Cabins Camping can be found not far from the city centre.

Belt Road Holiday Park (☎ *0800 804 204, ☎/fax 06-758 0228, 2 Belt Rd)* Powered & unpowered sites $9 per person, cabins $25-55. This pohutukawa-covered Holiday Park is on a bluff overlooking the port, 1.5km west of the town centre. Cabin prices depend on facilities.

New Plymouth Top 10 Holiday Park (☎/fax *06-758 2566,* e *new.plymouth .topten@xtra.co.nz, 29 Princes St)* Camp sites $10 per person, cabins $39, tourist flats $50-55, motel units $69. New Plymouth Park is in Fitzroy, 3.5km east of the centre. The camping area has plenty of tree shade.

Hookner Park (☎ *06-753 6945,* e *hook ner park@paradise.net.nz, 885 Carrington Rd)* Powered & unpowered sites $8.50 per person, on-site vans $15 per person, cabins without/with en suite $28/$40. This is a quiet, peaceful camp on a commercial dairy farm 10km south of the town centre. Campers are more than welcome to join in with the farm life.

Hostels New Plymouth has its fair share of backpackers.

Egmont Lodge (☎ *06-753 5720,* e *egm ontlodge@taranaki-bakpak.co.nz, 12 Claw ton St)* Camp sites $10, dorms $16, singles $25, twins & doubles $40. This YHA

Associate is a tranquil hostel in large, park-like grounds with a stream running through it. It's a fair way from town – a 15-minute walk south on a pleasant streamside walkway or phone for a free pick-up from the bus station. It's well set up for information on walks and other activities.

Shoestring Budget Backpackers (☎ *06-758 0404, 48 Lemon St)* Dorm beds $16, singles $25, twins & doubles $38. The central Shoestring Backpackers is in a large, stately old home. It's a well-equipped, friendly place with huge communal areas and very comfy rooms.

Central City Lodge (☎ *06-758 0473,* e *centralcity@xtra.co.nz, 104 Leach St)* Dorm beds without/with linen $15/20, singles/twins $30/40. This place is on a busy road, but has off-street parking.

Sunflower Lodge (☎ *06-759 0050,* e *jr sanders@xtra.co.nz, 25 Ariki St)* Dorm bed $17, singles $32-40, doubles $45-50. Sunflower Lodge is an old converted hotel with rather spartan rooms but it has a fantastic balcony that overlooks both the ocean and the centre of town.

B&Bs The visitors centre has details on numerous other homestays and B&Bs.

The Grange (☎ *06-758 1540,* e *cath yt@clear.net.nz, 44b Victoria Rd)* Singles/doubles with bath & breakfast $70/90. The Grange is a lovely, welcoming, contemporary home with decks and bush views. It's also opposite beautiful Pukekura Park.

Henwood House (☎/fax *06-755 1212,* e *henwood.house@xtra.co.nz, 314 Henwood Rd)* Singles/doubles from $100/120. Henwood House is 5km east of town. This beautifully restored Victorian home with lovely grounds has five rooms (three of them have an en suite). The tariff includes breakfast.

Motels & Hotels New Plymouth has plenty of motels, charging from around $70/80 for singles/doubles.

Mid City Motel (☎/fax *06-758 6109, cnr St Aubyn & Weymouth Sts)* Singles/doubles $60/70. This motel is five minutes' walk to the centre.

Central Motel (☎ 06-758 6444, 86 Eliot St) Units $60-80. The Central Motel is a few blocks east of the centre; it's small but convenient and the units are tidy.

Timandra Lodge Motels (☎ 06-758 6006, e timandra@xtra.co.nz, 31B Timandra St) Singles/doubles $68/78. This secluded motel in a large colonial style house south of town backs onto bush. There's lawn tennis and meals available (on request).

Cottage Mews (☎/fax 06-758 0403, 50 Lemon St) Rooms from $65. Cottage Mews, next door to the Shoestring Budget Backpackers, is good value with well-kept units.

Braemar Motor Inn (☎ 0800 242 779, 06-758 0859, e braemarmotorinn@xtra .co.nz, 152 Powderham St) Singles/doubles from $77/88. The Braemar has modern units with cooking facilities.

Coronation Court Motel (☎ 0800 246 811, 06-757 9125, fax 757 9123, 226 Coronation Ave) Singles/doubles $69/79. Most of the roomy units in this place south of town come with cooking facilities.

Saddle & Sulky (☎/fax 06-757 5763, 188 Coronation Ave) Singles/doubles $70/74. The imaginatively named Saddle & Sulky (it's right next to the racetrack, south of town) has clean, accommodating rooms.

There are several old-style hotels around central New Plymouth.

State Hotel (☎ 06-758 5373, cnr Devon St East & Gover St) Singles/doubles $55/70. This hotel has a family restaurant.

Grand Central Hotel (☎ 06-758 7495, e office@grandcentralhotel.co.nz, 42 Powderham St) Rooms from $111. The Grand Central is relatively new and close to the centre of town.

Places to Eat

Cafes & Restaurants Like so many of New Zealand's towns and cities, New Plymouth has embraced the coffee culture.

Yellow Cafe (City Centre Mall, Ariki St) Sandwiches $5.50. The cosy Yellow Cafe has good espresso, cakes, hefty sandwiches and soups.

Sandwich Extreme (☎ 06-759 6999, 52 Devon St East) Dishes $4.50-7. This funky little eatery makes fresh, filling sandwiches, toasties and baked potatoes for eat-in or takeaway.

Simply Read Cafe & Bookshop (cnr Dawson & Hine Sts) Dishes $7.50-8.50. Simply Read is a popular bookshop/cafe and an ideal place for a coffee and snack during the day with views across the sea. Its blackboard menu changes regularly.

Other good cafes are *ESPresso* in the Govett-Brewster Art Gallery, *Ozone Coffee Factory* (Devon St East), and the *tea house* (AKA the Kiosk) in Pukekura Park.

Baja (☎ 06-757 8217, 17 Devon St) Mains $8-13. This restaurant/bar has a definite Mexican theme running through its menu and decor. It also serves sandwiches and isn't bad for a drink or two.

El Condor (☎ 06-757 5436, 170 Devon St East) Pizzas $10.50-24. Open for dinner Tues-Sun. El Condor, near the corner of Gover St, is a trendy little pizza and pasta place with a difference – it's Argentinean.

Chinos Cafe (☎ 06-758 6843, 146 Devon St East) Mains $16.50-23. Informal Chinos has an imaginative (cheaper-by-day) menu and a pleasantly relaxed atmosphere.

Asian Wok (☎ 06-758 1828, cnr St Aubyn & Dawson Sts) Mains $10-20. Open evenings only. Asian Wok has great-value smorgasbords of Chinese, Thai and Indonesian food. It also does takeaway.

Agra Indian Restaurant (☎ 06-758 0030, 151 Devon St East) Mains $13.50-18. Try this place for authentic Indian food.

Portofino (☎ 06-757 8686, 14 Gill St) Pizza & pasta $15-19. This Italian restaurant has a huge selection of pasta dishes and many pizzas to boot.

Metropol (☎ 06-758 9788, cnr King & Egmont Sts) Mains $19-24. This is the place to taste NZ and Pacific Rim dishes with a hint of international flavours. Again, this place does cheaper meals during the day.

Andre's L'Escargot (☎ 06-758 4812, 37-39 Brougham St) Mains $23-30. This is a 'genuinely French' restaurant that has fine dining in a historical building.

Pub Food The licensed *Burton's Restaurant & Bar* in the State Hotel (see Places to Stay) is open daily for all meals.

TARANAKI

The Mill Bar & Restaurant (☎ *06-758 1935, 2 Courtenay St*) Burgers & mains $8.50-25. The Mill specialises in Stonegrill – a piping hot stone (supposedly heated to 400°C!) is used to cook your meat selection at your table. This way you get to cook your steak just the way like it.

Fast Food In the City Centre Mall on Gill St there's a *food hall* with Chinese and Italian food, seafood, wholefood, sandwich and dessert counters, and a *Robert Harris Coffee Shop* upstairs (with superb sea views). Also in the City Centre shopping mall is the large *Pak N Save* supermarket for groceries. *Woolworths* is between Leach and Courtenay Sts.

Middle Eastern Kebabs (*Devon St West*) Kebabs $7-9. Tasty kebabs are served at this ever-reliable takeaway bar.

Down to Earth (*cnr Devon St West & Morley St*) Sandwiches from $3.50. This bulk wholefood grocery specialises in organic foods.

Entertainment
The Mill Bar & Restaurant (☎ *06-758 1935, 2 Courtenay St*) This large bar is a popular place for a night out, and often has live bands on weekends.

Peggy Gordon's Celtic Bar (☎ *06-758 8561, cnr Devon St West & Egmont St*) This relaxed Irish bar has bands on weekends.

Baja (see Places to Eat) Baja has a fine selection of shooters and cocktails, and has street-side seating.

Some other popular nightspots include *Crowded House* (*Devon St East*), popular with all ages, and the *Grapevine Wine Bar* (*cnr Currie & Devon Sts*), catering largely to a more mature crowd.

The *Bowl of Brooklands*, at the entrance to Brooklands Park, is a large outdoor theatre; the visitors centre will have current concert schedules and prices. The *TSB Showplace* (*Devon St West*) stages a variety of performances.

Getting There & Away
Air Air New Zealand Link (☎ 06-737 3300), 12–14 Devon St East, has daily direct flights to Auckland, Nelson and Wellington, with onward connections. Origin Pacific (☎ 0800 302 302) has direct flights to Nelson and Auckland, and onward connections.

Bus InterCity (☎ 06-759 9039) stops at the Travel Centre on the corner of Queen and King Sts. One bus daily heads to Hamilton ($33, 4hrs) and Auckland ($53, 6hrs), and two buses daily (three on Friday and Sunday) to Wanganui ($16, 3hrs), Palmerston North ($42, 4hrs) and onto Wellington ($61, 6¾hrs). Dalroy Express (☎ 0508 465 622) operates a daily service between Auckland ($65, 5½hrs) and Hawera ($6, 1¼hrs) via New Plymouth and Hamilton ($42, 3½hrs).

White Star (☎ 06-758 3338) buses for Wanganui ($22, 2½hrs), Palmerston North ($30, 3¾hrs), Wellington ($43, 6¼hrs) and many small towns in between depart from the Budget Rent-A-Car office at 25 Liardet St. Buses leave at 7.50am and 5pm Monday to Friday, and 2.05pm on weekends.

Bookings and ticketing for InterCity can be done at the visitors centre.

Hitching A good spot to hitch north from is on Courtenay St, about 1.5km east of the town centre; anywhere from about Hobson St eastwards is good, the further out the better. A good hitching spot for south towards Wanganui is on the corner of Coronation Ave and Cumberland St, about 1.5km south of the town centre down Eliot St. To hitch west around the Taranaki coast towards Oakura, head west out of town on Devon St West, which becomes South Rd.

Getting Around
New Plymouth's airport is 11km east of the centre. Withers (☎ 06-751 1777) operates a door-to-door shuttle to and from the airport ($10).

Okato Bus Lines (☎ 06-758 2799, 32 Queen St; timetables 50c) serve the city and its surrounding suburbs Monday to Saturday. The main bus stop is outside the City Centre Mall.

For details of shuttle services from New Plymouth to Mt Taranaki, see Mt Taranaki/ Egmont later in this chapter.

AROUND NEW PLYMOUTH

Egmont National Park, of course, is the primary attraction of the New Plymouth area, but there are several other places of interest, all within about 20km of New Plymouth.

Tupare

Tupare (☎ 06-764 6544, 487 Mangorei Rd; adult/child gold coin donation/free; garden open 1 Sept-31 Mar 9am-5pm daily), 7km south of New Plymouth, is a fine three-storey Tudor-style house surrounded by 3.6 hectares of lush English garden. It's part of the National Trust; look for it on the Waiwhakaiho River.

Hurworth

This early homestead (☎ 06-753 3593, 759 6080, 906 Carrington Rd; open by appointment only), about 8km south of New Plymouth, dates from 1856. Its pioneer builder and first occupant, Harry Atkinson, was to become New Zealand premier four times. The house was the only one at this site to survive the Taranaki Land Wars and is today owned by the Historic Places Trust.

Pukeiti Rhododendron Trust

This is a 4 sq km garden (☎ 06-752 4141, 2290 Carrington Rd; adult/child $8/free; open 9am-5pm Oct-Mar, 10am-3pm Apr-Sept) surrounded by native bush and internationally renowned for its collection of rhododendrons and azaleas. Peak flowering of rhododendrons generally takes place from September to November, though the garden is worth seeing at any time of year.

Pukeiti is 20km south of New Plymouth. To get there, just keep following Carrington Rd all the way from town. The road passes between the Pouakai and Kaitake Ranges, both part of Egmont National Park, but separated by the trust.

Lake Mangamahoe & the Tatatm

If you're heading out towards Stratford or North Egmont on SH3, stop at Lake Mangamahoe, 9.5km south of New Plymouth. It's a great setting for photographs of Mt Taranaki (when it shows itself), reflected in the waters of the lake.

Opposite the lake, on the corner of SH3 and Kent Rd, is the Taranaki Aviation, Transport & Technology Museum (Tatatm; ☎ 06-758 0686; adult/child $4/50c; open 10.30am-4pm Sun & public holidays), with vehicles, railway and aviation exhibits, farm equipment and household items.

Inglewood

The small town of Inglewood, 13km southeast of New Plymouth, is handy for daytrippers to Egmont National Park.

Forrestal Lodge (☎ 06-756 7242, ⓔ forrestallodge@xtra.co.nz, 23 Rimu St) Dorm beds $18, B&B singles/twins $30/60. This large house occupies a quiet corner in town.

Macfarlanes Caffé (☎ 06-756 6665, 1 Kelly St) Mains $19-25. Macfarlanes is situated in a charming colonial-style building dating from the late 1800s. Alongside its well-prepared mains, cheaper light meals are available.

North via SH3

Heading north towards Waikato from New Plymouth, SH3 is a scenic route. This is the route for Waitomo, and buses heading north go this way to Hamilton. Get the free Scenic 3 Highway pamphlet from the Otorohanga or New Plymouth visitor centre.

Waitara is 13km north-east of New Plymouth on SH3. If you turn off SH3 at Brixton, just before Waitara, and head 7km south, you'll reach the site of the Pukerangiora Pa. It's beautifully situated on a high cliff by the Waitara River, but historically it was a particularly bloody battle site. Rafting and canoeing on the Waitara and Mokau Rivers are popular local activities. For operators, telephone the New Plymouth visitors centre.

Just beyond Waitara, on SH3 heading east from New Plymouth, is the Methanex NZ's Motunui Plant (☎ 06-754 9700; admission free; open 8am-8pm summer, 8am-5pm other times). Opened in 1986, it was the world's first plant to convert natural gas to petrol (gasoline) and remains the world's largest methanol production facility. Natural gas is piped here from the Maui natural gas field, 34km offshore from Cape

Egmont. The synthetic fuel produced here meets a third of NZ's petrol needs. You can stop by the unmanned visitors centre near the plant's main entrance to see exhibits.

Heading north the highway follows the west coast, with its high sand dunes and surf beaches. **Urenui**, 16km past Waitara, is a popular beach destination in summer. *Urenui Beach Motor Camp (☎/fax 06-752 3838, 148 Beach Rd)* has a variety of accommodation options (unpowered/powered sites $15/17) right next to the beach and sand dunes.

About 5km past Urenui, you can sample natural beers at the **White Cliffs Brewing Company** *(open 9.30am-6pm daily)*, a boutique brewery.

The brewery is near the turn-off to Pukearuhe and the **White Cliffs**, huge cliffs resembling their namesake in Dover. The cliffs dominate the coastal landscape and contain two-million-year-old marine sediments. A walkway along the cliffs leads from Pukearuhe to Tongaporutu via a tunnel from the beach, accessible only at low tide. On a fine day the full-day walk has superb views of the coastline and of Mts Taranaki and Ruapehu.

SH3 continues further north from Tongaporutu to Mokau, on the border of Taranaki and Waikato. Mokau has backpackers and other accommodation (see Waikato & the King Country chapter).

Oakura
pop 1218

If you're starting round the mountain from New Plymouth, on the coast road SH45, the first settlement is tiny Oakura, 15km west of New Plymouth. It's known for its beautiful **beach**, which is great for swimming, surfing and windsurfing. Oakura has a craft shop called *Crafty Fox* which is open daily, and **Vertigo** *(☎ 06-752 8283, e surf@ blackdiamondssafaris.co.nz)*, a surfing and windsurfing shop which hires out gear and gives lessons.

Oakura Beach Camp (☎ 06-752 7861, fax 752 7286, 2 Jans Terrace) Unpowered/powered sites $15/17 for 2 people, cabins $40 for 2 people. This basic camping ground is right on the beach with great views back towards the Sugar Loaf Islands.

Wave Haven (☎ 06-752 7800, e wave .haven@clear.net.nz, 1518 Main Rd) Dorm beds $15, singles/doubles $25/40. Wave Haven is a very chilled out and well-kept house with a deck on the corner of Ahu Ahu and Main South Rds. It isn't far from the beach and is extremely popular with wave riders.

Ahu Ahu Beach Villas (☎ 06-752 7370, e holiday@ahu.co.nz, 321 Ahu Ahu Rd) Units $135 per double. At the beach end of Ahu Ahu Rd are these fantastic villas with views back towards New Plymouth. Recycled materials were used to construct the two villas and the result is rustic yet elegant, with large bay windows, stone floors and wood-beam ceilings.

Butler's Bar & Cafe (South Rd) Bar meals $7.50-10. This local bar has an attractive beer garden and small conservatory facing SH45.

Malaysian Restaurant & Cafe (☎ 06-752 1007, South Rd) Mains $15-25. This Malaysian place is housed in a former railway carriage behind the Crafty Fox.

Lucy's Gully

Lucy's Gully, 25km from New Plymouth on SH45, is one of the few places where exotic trees are being maintained in a national park. A pleasant picnic area, it is also the start of a couple of tracks into the Kaitake Ranges. Further along SH45, turn west at Pungarehu onto Cape Rd to reach **Cape Egmont Lighthouse** – it's closed to visitors.

MT TARANAKI/EGMONT

The Taranaki region is dominated by the massive cone of 2518m Taranaki, a dormant volcano that looks remarkably like Japan's Mt Fuji or the Philippines' Mayon.

Geologically, Mt Taranaki is the youngest of a series of three large volcanoes on one fault line, the others being Kaitake and Pouakai. Mt Taranaki last erupted 350 years ago, and is considered dormant rather than extinct. The top 1400m is covered in lava flows and a few descend to 800m above sea level. An interesting feature is

View of comet above Mt Taranaki
(photographer unknown, 4 October 1882)

the small subsidiary cone on the flank of the main cone and 2km south of the main crater, called Fantham's Peak (1962m).

There's a saying in Taranaki that if you can see the mountain it's going to rain and if you can't see the mountain it's already raining! The mountain is one of the wettest spots in NZ, with about 7000mm of rain recorded annually at North Egmont (compared with about 1500mm in New Plymouth), as it catches the moisture-laden winds coming in from the Tasman Sea and sweeps them up to freezing heights. Still, it doesn't *always* rain there and the volcano is a spectacular sight on a clear day.

History

Mt Taranaki was supremely sacred to the Maori, both as a burial site for chiefs and as a hide-out in times of danger.

According to legend, Taranaki was once a part of the group of volcanoes at Tongariro. He was forced to leave rather hurriedly when Tongariro caught him with the beautiful Pihanga, the volcano near Lake Taupo who was Tongariro's lover.

So angry was Tongariro at this betrayal that he blew his top (as only volcanoes can) and Taranaki took off for the coast. The defeated Taranaki gouged a wide scar (the Wanganui River) in the earth as he fled south in anger, pain and shame, meeting the sea at Wanganui and then moving still further west to his current position, where he's remained in majestic isolation ever since, hiding his face behind a cloud of tears.

The Maori did not settle the area between Taranaki and Pihanga very heavily, perhaps because they feared the lovers might be reunited with dire consequences. Most of the Maori settlements in this district were clustered along the coast between Mokau and Patea, concentrated particularly around Urenui and Waitara.

Egmont National Park was created in 1900 and is the second-oldest national park in the country.

Information

If you plan to tramp in Egmont National Park, get hold of some local information about current track and weather conditions before you set off. DOC operates two visitors centres on the mountain, that both offer maps and advice on weather and track conditions. The revamped North Egmont visitors centre (☎ 06-756 0990, fax 756 0991) is the closest to New Plymouth and therefore the most visited. It has interactive displays on the mountain, an informative video and a small cafe. It opens from 8am to 4.30pm daily (extended hours in December and January). On the other side of the mountain, the periodically staffed one at Dawson Falls (☎ 025 430 248) is open from 8am to 4.30pm Wednesday to Sunday (daily during the school summer holidays). It also has displays and screens an audiovisual.

Other places for maps and information on the mountain include DOC's Stratford Area Office (☎ 06-765 5144) on Pembroke Rd, coming up the mountain from Stratford, and the DOC office in New Plymouth (☎ 06-758 0433). There are also visitors centres around the mountain in New Plymouth

TARANAKI

(☎ 06-759 6080), Stratford (☎ 06-765 6708) and Hawera (☎ 06-278 8599).

Tramping & Skiing

In winter the mountain is popular with skiers, while in summer it can be climbed in one day. There are a number of excellent tramping possibilities, including hikes to the summit or right round the mountain. Shorter tracks ranging from easy to difficult, and in length from 30 minutes to several hours, start off from the three roads heading up the mountain.

Due to its easy accessibility, Mt Taranaki ranks as the 'most climbed' mountain in NZ. Nevertheless, tramping on this mountain holds definite dangers and should not be undertaken lightly. See the boxed text 'The Deceptive Mountain' for more details. If you intend to walk or climb for any distance or height then get the relevant Infomap (No 273-09; $13.50).

Trips to North Egmont, Dawson Falls and East Egmont are worthwhile for the views, and there are numerous long and short tracks and tramps as well. Pick up a copy of the DOC pamphlet *Short Walks in Egmont National Park* ($2.50) which outlines many of the walks you can do. Other walks include the York Loop Track, which follows part of a disused railway line (DOC produce a leaflet on the walk). York Rd provides access to the walk.

The round-the-mountain track, accessible from all three mountain roads, goes 55km around the mountain and takes from three to five days to complete. You can start or finish this track at any park entrance and there are a number of huts on the mountain. Purchase hut tickets and the handy *Around the Mountain Circuit* DOC pamphlet ($1) at visitor centres or through DOC.

There is one main route to the summit, which starts at the North Egmont visitor centre; it's a pole route and you should allow about six to eight hours for the return trip. This route on the north side of the mountain loses its snow and ice earliest in the year – it's advisable not to make the climb in snow and ice conditions if you're inexperienced. Another route to the summit, taking off from the Dawson Falls visitor centre, requires more technical skill and keeps its ice longer; it's best attempted with an experienced guide.

If you are an inexperienced climber, want other people to climb or tramp with or want to try your hand at rock climbing, DOC can put you in contact with tramping clubs and guides in the area. Reliable operators include **MacAlpine Guides** (☎ *025 417 042*), **Mountain Guides** (☎ *025 474 042*, W *www .mountainguides.co.nz*) and **Top Guides** (☎ *0800 448 433, 021 838 513*, W *www .topguides.co.nz*).

At the top of Pembroke Rd is Stratford Plateau, and from there it's a mere 1.5km walk to the small Manganui ski area. You can purchase ski passes for the day (adult/child $30/15), and skiing equipment can be hired at the Mountain House Motor Lodge in Stratford. The Stratford visitors centre has useful daily weather and snow reports and there's also a snow phone service on ☎ 06-765 7669.

The Deceptive Mountain

To many, Mt Taranaki may look for all intents and purposes an easy climb, but the mountain has claimed almost 60 lives. The principal hazard is the erratic weather, which can change from warm and sunny to raging gales and white-out conditions unexpectedly quickly; snow can come at any time of year on the mountain, even in summer. There are also precipitous bluffs and steep icy slopes. Don't be put off, but don't be deceived.

In good conditions, tramping around the mountain, or even to the summit, can be reasonably easy. January to March is the best time for this. Be sure that you have up-to-date maps and consult a conservation officer for current weather and track conditions before you set off. It's also a very good idea to register your tramping intentions and some emergency contact numbers with a DOC office. For a low-down on more safety tips pick up the DOC leaflet *Taranaki: The Mountain* from DOC offices or local information centres.

Places to Stay
Camping, Cabins & Backpackers There are many tramping huts scattered about the mountain, administered by DOC and reached only by trails. Most cost $10 a night (for two tickets, purchased from DOC offices), but two cost $5 (Syme and Kahui huts). You provide your own cooking, eating and sleeping gear, they provide bunks and mattresses, and no bookings are necessary. It's all on a first-come, first-served basis, but you must purchase tickets before starting the walks. Camping is permitted in the park, though it is not encouraged; you're supposed to use the tramping huts.

For DOC places (the first two places in the following list) bookings are essential, and you must carry out *all* your rubbish. You must also bring your own sleeping bag, food and cooking utensils.

Konini Lodge (☎ 025 430 248) Dorm beds adult/child $15/7.50. Located by the Dawson Falls visitors centre, this lodge offers bunkhouse accommodation.

The Camphouse (☎ 06-756 0990) Bunk beds adult/child $15/7.50. The Camphouse is located at North Egmont.

Eco Inn (☎ 06-752 2765, e ecoinn@ xtra.co.nz, 671 Kent Rd) Camp sites $10 per person, singles/twins & doubles $22/40. About 6.5km further south from Tatam, this ultra-eco, friendly place is small and made from recycled timber. A mixture of solar, wind and waterpower provides hot water and electricity. A hot tub is available for use. Eco Inn is 3km from the border to Egmont National Park and they provide transport to the mountain (for a price).

The Missing Leg (☎ 06-752 2570, e jo .thompson@xtra.co.nz, 1082 Junction Rd) Camp sites $8 per person, dorm beds $16, doubles $37. The Missing Leg is in Egmont Village. There's a swimming hole here.

Guesthouses For something a bit more plush try the following:

Dawson Falls Mountain Lodge (☎ 0800 695 6343, ☎/fax 06-765 5457, e dawson falls@paradise.net.nz, Upper Manaia Rd) Dinner, bed and breakfast singles/doubles $150/250. Dawson Falls is located beside the visitors centre, and is an attractive alpine-style lodge with lots of carved wood, good views, sitting rooms and a spacious dining room. All rooms have en suite and are individually decorated. There is fine three-/four-course dining for $36.50/42.50.

Mountain House Motor Lodge (☎ 0800 668 682, ☎/fax 06-765 6100, e mountain house@xtra.co.nz, Pembroke Rd) Rooms from $105. This lodge, on the east side of the mountain, about 15km from Stratford, has rooms and chalets with kitchens. There's a restaurant, and you can hire skis in winter for use at the Manganui ski area.

Andersons Alpine Lodge (☎ 0800 668 682, 06-765 6620, fax 765 6100, 922 Pembroke Rd) Rooms $125-155. The same management that runs Mountain House Motor Lodge also runs this place, further down the mountain not far from the DOC office. It's a modern place in pleasant surroundings.

Getting There & Away
There are several points of access to the park, but three roads lead almost right up to where the heavy bush ends. Closest to New Plymouth is Egmont Rd, turning off SH3 at Egmont Village, 12km south of New Plymouth, and heading another 14km up the mountain to the North Egmont visitors centre. Pembroke Rd enters the park from the east at Stratford and ascends 15km to East Egmont, Mountain House Motor Lodge, the Plateau car park and Manganui ski area. From the south-east, Upper Manaia Rd leads up to Dawson Falls, 23km from Stratford.

Public buses don't go to Egmont National Park but shuttle buses from New Plymouth to the mountain include Cruise NZ Tours (☎ 06-758 3222) and Withers (☎ 06-751 1777). A return journey costs between $28 and $35 (minimum of 2 people). Central Cabs (☎ 06-765 8395) provide a taxi service from Stratford.

AROUND MT TARANAKI
Mt Taranaki is the main attraction but there are also other places of interest around the Taranaki region.

There are two principal highways around the mountain. SH3, on the inland side of the mountain, is the most travelled route, heading south from New Plymouth for 70km until it meets the coast again at Hawera. The coast road, SH45 (also known as the surf highway), heads 105km around the coast from New Plymouth to Hawera, where it meets up again with SH3. An around-the-mountain trip on both highways is 175km, though short cuts can be taken. Get a *Taranaki Heritage Trails* booklet, free from visitor centres and DOC offices.

Stratford
pop 9730
Stratford, 40km south-east of New Plymouth on SH3, is named after Stratford-upon-Avon in England, Shakespeare's birthplace, and almost all of its streets are named after Shakespearian characters.

The town has an excellent visitors centre (☎ 06-765 6708, W www.stratfordnz.co.nz) at the corner of Miranda St and Prospero Place (it's also the AA agent). It stocks a heap of brochures on walks in the area, including guided tramps and tours. It's open 8.30am to 5pm Monday to Friday and 9.30am to noon Saturday. The DOC field centre (☎ 06-765 5144) is 8km up Pembroke Rd, on the way to Mt Taranaki.

On SH3, 1km south of the centre, the **Taranaki Pioneer Village** (☎ 06-765 5399, *adult/child $7/3; open 10am-4pm daily)* is a four-hectare outdoor museum with 50 historic buildings.

At Stratford is the turn-off for Pembroke Rd, heading up the mountain for 15km to East Egmont, the Mountain House Motor Lodge and the Manganui ski area. Stratford is also the southern end of the Stratford-Taumarunui Heritage Trail.

Places to Stay & Eat Stratford has a couple of cheap accommodation possibilities.

Stratford Holiday Park (☎ 06-765 6440, 10 Page St) Unpowered/powered sites $9/10, dorm beds $16, cabins & motel units $28-75. Stratford Park has an indoor heated pool. Bike hire costs $5 per hour, $12 per half day or $20 for a full day.

Taranaki Accommodation Lodge (☎/fax 06-765 5444, e mttaranakilodge@hotmail

.com, 7 Romeo St) Dorm beds $18, singles/doubles $22/37. This large, friendly, pink place has good kitchen facilities, but the rooms are rather bare.

The main street has numerous fast-food places. Good cafes include *Urban Attitude*, which doubles as a wine bar, and the excellent *Backstage Cafe*, both on Broadway.

Stratford-Taumarunui Heritage Trail
From Stratford, the Whangamomona–Tangarakau Gorge route (SH43) heads off towards Taumarunui in central North Island. This has been designated a Heritage Trail, passing many historic sites, including **Whangamomona village**, **Maori pa sites**, **small villages**, **waterfalls**, **abandoned coal mines** and small **museums**. You can pick up a free Heritage-Trail booklet from visitors centres or DOC offices in Stratford, Taumarunui or New Plymouth that give details of places of interest along the way; keep an eye out for the blue-and-yellow Heritage Trail signs, with explanatory plaques.

It takes a minimum of 2½ to three hours to drive the 150km from Stratford to Taumarunui (or vice versa), as the road winds through hilly bush country and 19km of it is unsealed. Nevertheless it's a good trip if you can put up with the road. It's best to start early in the day; allow at least five hours for the trip if you plan to make stops to see the historic sites. Fill up with petrol at either Stratford or Taumarunui, as petrol stations are limited once you're on the road. This road is definitely off the beaten track.

Kaieto Cafe (☎/fax 06-762 5858) Dorm beds $28 per person, sandwiches and pies from $2.70, meals $14-20. This cafe, situated high on the Tahora Saddle 73km from Stratford, has panoramic views of the surrounding countryside. The food is mainly NZ orientated, but with Russian influences (try the pie). Accommodation consists of small but cosy cabins.

Eltham & the Lakes
About 10km south of Stratford is Eltham, well known for its cheeses. You can get information from the Eltham Public Library

(☎ 06-764 8838) on the High St. It's open 9.30am to 5.30pm Monday, Wednesday and Friday, to 6.30pm Thursday.

Eleven kilometres south-east down the Rawhitiroa Rd is **Lake Rotokare** (Rippling Lake), the largest stretch of inland water in Taranaki. There's a 1½- to two-hour walk around the lake through native bush. The nearby artificial **Lake Rotorangi**, 46km long, is popular for boating and fishing.

On Manaia Rd, 4km north of Kaponga, which is about 13km west of Eltham on the road to Opunake, is **Hollard Gardens** (☎ 06-764 6544; adult/child gold coin donation/ free; open 9am-5pm daily), administered by the National Trust. It's most colourful from September to November when the rhodo-dendrons bloom, but many other plants pro-vide colour year-round. The vast array of rare plants makes it a horticulturist's de-light, with posted half- and one-hour walks through various gardens.

Hawera
pop 8740

Hawera is on the coast, 70km south of New Plymouth and 90km from Wanganui. It's the largest town on the southern coast of Taranaki. Information South Taranaki (☎ 06-278 8599, ℮ visitorinfo@stdc.govt.nz) can be found at 55 High St, beside the dominat-ing water tower (which is currently under-going renovation and should be climbable late 2003). It opens 8.30am to 5pm Monday to Friday and also 10am to 3pm weekends November to March. The AA office (☎ 06-278 5095) is at 121 Princes St.

Things to See & Do Elvis fans might want to visit the **Kevin Wasley Elvis Presley Memorial Room** (☎ 06-278 7624, 025 982 942, 51 Argyle St; admission by donation), which has a collection of Elvis records (over 2000) and souvenirs. Please phone before you arrive.

The excellent **Tawhiti Museum** (☎ 06-278 6837, 401 Ohangai Rd; adult/child $5/1; open 10am-4pm Fri-Mon Sept-May (daily Jan), 10am-4pm Sun only June-Aug) houses a private collection of remarkable exhibits, models and dioramas covering many aspects

of Taranaki heritage. The lifelike human figures were modelled on real people around the region; it's quite an unusual museum. A bush railway at the museum operates on the first Sunday of each month and every Sun-day during school holidays. It is near the corner of Tawhiti Rd, 4km from town.

One of the most exciting activities around is dam dropping and white-water sledging with **Kaitiaki Adventures** (☎/fax 06-278 4452, 025 249 9481, ☒ www.kaiti aki.co.nz; 3-hr trips $80 per person, night trips available). The trips, which centre on the Waingongoro River, include sliding down a seven- metre dam on a board (more than once if you're game enough), then sledging a further 5km on the river (Grade II to III). This is one activity that rain can't spoil; in fact it can be more fun if it's rained hard the night before. Also included is a journey past Okahutiti Pa, birthplace of the Maori prophet Tohu Kakahi, an advocate of passive resistance following the Taranaki Land Wars of the 1860s (see Parihaka later in this chapter). All gear is provided. This group also does river trips in Rotorua (see the Bay of Plenty chapter for details).

Two kilometres north of Hawera, on Turuturu Rd, are the remains of the pre-European **Turuturumokai Pa**. The reserve is open to the public daily. The **Tawhiti Mu-seum** has a model of the *pa*.

Dairyland (☎ 06-278 4537, cnr SH3 & Whareroa Rd; adult/child $3/2; open 9am-5pm daily, plus evenings Thur-Sat), is 2km south of Hawera. It has interactive and au-diovisual displays (including a simulated dairy tanker ride) covering all aspects of the dairy industry. The licensed *cafe* revolves, simulating a rotary cowshed floor.

Places to Stay Hawera has two farm back-packers places past the Tawhiti Museum:

Ohangai Farm Backpacker (☎ 06-272 2878, Urupa Rd) Quads $14 per person, or singles $16, doubles & twins $30. This place in Ohangai is a 350-cow dairy farm with a well-equipped backpackers in the paddocks. German and French are spoken. Free pick-up from Hawera is offered, or take the Tawhiti Rd from Hawera, turn right in front of the museum and follow the signs for 8km.

Wheatly Downs (☎ *06-278 6523*, **e** *whe atlydowns@taranaki-bakpak.co.nz, 46 Ararata Rd)* Dorm beds $16, twins & doubles $38. This is another good farmstay backpackers in the area, also past the Tawhiti Museum – don't turn right but keep going straight on the Ararata Rd (the extension of Tawhiti Rd) for 5.5km beyond the museum. There is also a free pick-up from Hawera.

Try either **Rough Habits Sports Bar and Cafe** *(79 Regent St)* or the more upmarket **White Elephant** *(☎ 06-278 7424, 47 High St)* for reliable eating options.

Parihaka

Inland 2km from Pungarehu is the Maori village of Parihaka, formerly the stronghold of the prophets Te Whiti and Tohu, and once one of the largest and most-successful Maori villages in NZ.

Te Whiti and Tohu led a passive resistance campaign against the government's confiscation of land after the Taranaki Land Wars, but the two were jailed (without trial) in 1881 and Parihaka was razed. The heavily armed troops were opposed only by dancing children.

The spirit of Te Whiti lives on; his descendants and followers meet at Parihaka annually. Parihaka is not open to the public.

Opunake
pop 1500

Opunake is the largest town on the west side of the mountain. There's a fine beach in the sheltered Opunake Bay, a peaceful place good for swimming and surfing even on the windiest of days.

The visitors centre (☎ 06-761 8663) is in the Egmont Public Library & Cultural Centre on Tasman St.

Opunake Beach Camp *(☎ 0800 758 009, ☎/fax 06-761 7525)* Camp sites $9 per person, on-site caravans $17.50 per person. This resort is a stone's throw from the water's edge.

Opunake Motel & Backpackers Lodge *(☎ 06-761 8330,* **e** *opunakemotel@xtra .co.nz, 36 Heaphy Rd)* Lodge rooms $15, cottage $50 for 2 people, single/double motel units $55/70. This place has a range of good accommodation options that should suit most travellers.

Opunake's main street hosts a couple of pleasant cafes, including the **Volcanic Cafe** *(☎ 06-761 8848)*, which doubles as a surf shop (surf boards can be rented here).

Wanganui & Manawatu

The Wanganui region and its southern neighbour Manawatu make up much of the south-western corner of the North Island, collectively running from Tongariro National Park to the Wellington region. The area is generally bypassed by the tourist hordes travelling from Taupo to Wellington, but it does have attractions worthy of attention. Dominating Wanganui is Whanganui National Park, which in turn is overshadowed by the Whanganui River, historically one of the most important rivers in New Zealand. Manawatu's allure is the rural nature of much of the region.

Wanganui and Palmerston North are the major centres of Wanganui and Manawatu respectively.

Wanganui Region

☎ 06 • pop 45,300

The Wanganui region's main artery is the Whanganui River, and its main highlight is Whanganui National Park, based around the river and the parallel River Rd. The estuary, over 30km long, was known to the early Maori as Whanganui, meaning 'Great Harbour' or 'Great Wait'.

The spelling difference between Whanganui and Wanganui causes much confusion. Both town and river were originally spelt Wanganui, because in the local dialect *whanga* (harbour) is pronounced 'wha-nga' not (as in the rest of the country) 'fa-nga'. However to indicate that the 'wh' sound is aspirated the 'h' was officially restored to the name of the river and national park, but not to the city or the region as a whole (the pronunciation of the two spellings is identical). The Pakeha-dominated town and region retain the old spelling, while the river area – very much Maori territory – takes the new spelling. The difference in spellings is in many ways a reflection of the split in attitudes over Maori issues, which came to a head at Moutoa Gardens in Wanganui

WANGANUI & MANAWATU

Highlights

- Canoeing and jetboating on NZ's longest navigable river, the Whanganui
- Walking in the wilderness of Whanganui National Park
- Driving along the Whanganui River Rd to Pipiriki
- Visiting the attractive and historic riverport city of Wanganui
- Exploring the rich farming region of the Manawatu and its largest centre, Palmerston North

(see Parks & Gardens in the Wanganui section later in this chapter).

WHANGANUI NATIONAL PARK

Whanganui National Park's main attraction is the Whanganui River, which winds its way 329km from its source on the flanks of Mt Tongariro in central North Island to the Tasman Sea at the city of Wanganui. The river is not the longest in the country – that honour goes to the Waikato River – but the fact that it is the longest *navigable* river in the country has been shaping its destiny for

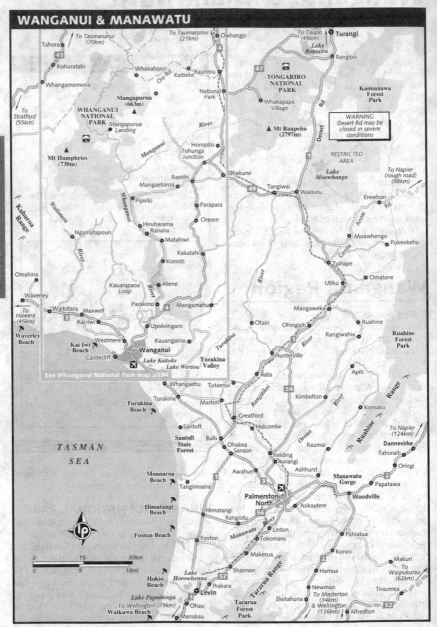

WANGANUI & MANAWATU

centuries. Historically a major link between the sea and the interior of the North Island, first for the Maori and then for the Pakeha, the route was eventually superseded by rail and road. Many recreational canoe, kayak and jetboat enthusiasts now use it to reach the isolated interior of the Whanganui National Park.

The stretch of the river from Taumarunui south to Pipiriki has been added to the NZ Great Walks system (see the Activities chapter) and called the 'Whanganui Journey'. A Grade II river, the Whanganui is easy enough to be enjoyed by people of any age, whether they have previous canoeing experience or not, yet there are enough small-sized rapids and movement to keep it interesting. A canoe trip down the river is a great way to relax in one of NZ's last great wilderness areas.

Other attractions of the park include two excellent walks, the Matemateaonga Track and Mangapurua Track. Fishing and hunting are also popular.

History

In Maori legend, the Whanganui River was formed when Mt Taranaki, after his fight with Mt Tongariro over the lovely Mt Pihanga, fled the central North Island and headed for the sea, leaving a long gouge in the earth in his wake. When he reached the sea he turned westwards, finally coming to rest in the place where he stands today. Mt Tongariro sent cool water from his side, to flow down and heal the wound in the earth – and the Whanganui River was born.

The river was settled from very early on in NZ's history. The great Polynesian explorer Kupe explored some distance upriver from the river's mouth in around AD 800. Maori genealogy traces a group of people living on the river from about 1100. Major settlement began along the river around 1350 and flourished along this major route from the sea to the interior. The group's motto was and still is: 'I am the river and the river is me'.

The first European to travel the river was Andrew Powers, who made the trip in 1831. However he didn't do so of his own free will – he was brought up the river as a captive of the Ngati Tuwharetoa tribe.

European influence only arrived here with the missionaries in the 1840s. The missionary settlements of Hiruharama (Jerusalem), Ranana (London), Koriniti (Corinth) and Atene (Athens) survive today, though the population along the river has dwindled. A French Catholic missionary established the Daughters of Our Lady of Compassion in Jerusalem in 1892. St Joseph's church is still the most prominent feature of the town and the large, white wooden convent stands in a beautiful garden.

Steamers first voyaged up the river in the mid-1860s, when, encouraged by Maori from the Taranaki region, some of the river tribes joined in the Hauhau Rebellion – a Maori movement seeking to oust Pakeha.

In 1886 the first commercial steamer transport service was established by a Wanganui company. Others soon followed, connecting parts of the river all the way from Wanganui to Taumarunui. They serviced the river communities and grew in importance as a transport link from the sea to the interior of the island, especially after 1903, when the Main Trunk Railway reached Taumarunui from the north.

Tourism was another major development on the river. Internationally advertised tourist trips on the 'Rhine of Maoriland' became so popular that by 1905 12,000 tourists a year were making the trip upriver from Wanganui or downriver from Taumarunui to Pipiriki House (which burnt down in 1959).

The engineering feats and skippering ability required to operate the steamboats and paddle steamers on the Whanganui River became legendary, spawning something like the lore that Mark Twain made famous on the Mississippi River. Some places required some imaginative engineering, eg, cables and channelling of the river's currents.

Around 1918, land along the river above Pipiriki was granted to returning WWI soldiers. This rugged area was a major challenge to clear – some families struggled for years to make a go of their farms, but by the early 1940s only a few remained.

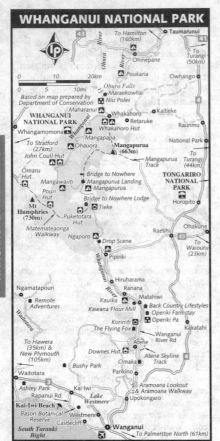

WHANGANUI NATIONAL PARK

operates on the river: the *Waimarie* makes river cruises on the lower reaches of the river from Wanganui. Another of the old fleet, the MV *Ongarue*, is usually on display at Pipiriki, but is off limits for safety reasons.

Information

Maps, brochures and information about the park are available at Department of Conservation (DOC) offices in Wanganui (☎ 06-345 2402), Taumarunui (☎ 06-895 8201) and Pipiriki (☎ 06-385 4631). Visitor centres at Taumarunui, Ohakune, Raetihi and Wanganui also have information on the park.

Books about the river include the *Guide to the Whanganui River* ($9) by the NZ Canoeing Association (good for canoe trips). *In and Around Whanganui National Park,* ($2.50) a DOC booklet, is good if you want to do some walking or tramping; alternatively, pick up a copy of *Walking Opportunities in the Wanganui Area* ($5) by the Wanganui Tramping Club.

Whanganui River

The native bush is thick podocarp-broadleaf forest, with many types of trees and ferns. Occasionally you will see poplar and other introduced trees along the river, evidence of settlements that have long since vanished.

There are also traces of former Maori settlements along the river in various places, with *pa* (fortified village) sites, old *kainga* (village) sites, and the unusual Hauhau *niu* poles of war and peace at Maraekowhai, at the confluence of the Whanganui and Ohura Rivers. The Ratakura, Reinga Kokiri and Te Rerehapa Falls, all near Maraekowhai on the Ohura River, were popular places for Maori to come to catch small *tuna riki* eels (river, or freshwater, eel found in the Whanganui). Several of the landings marked along the Whanganui River's banks were once riverboat landings.

Canoeing & Kayaking The most popular section of the river for canoeing and kayaking is between Taumarunui and Pipiriki. Enter the river at Taumarunui, Ohinepane and Whakahoro (Wades Landing). The DOC

One of the most famous features of the river, the Bridge to Nowhere, was built in 1936 as part of a road from Raetihi to the river. It stands as mute testimony to the failed efforts to settle the region. The track from the Mangapurua Landing to the bridge, though now only a walking track, used to be a 4.5m-wide roadway leading down to the riverboat landing.

The Auckland-Wellington Main Trunk Railway line and improved roads gradually superseded the riverboats, the last of which made its final commercial voyage in 1959. Today only one vessel of the old fleet still

leaflet *Whanganui Journey* has information on canoeing the river.

Taumarunui to Pipiriki is a five-day/four-night trip, Ohinepane to Pipiriki is a four-day/three-night trip, and Whakahoro to Pipiriki is a three-day/two-night trip. Taumarunui to Whakahoro is a popular overnight trip, especially for weekenders, or you can do a one-day trip from Taumarunui to Ohinepane or Ohinepane to Whakahoro. From Whakahoro to Pipiriki, 88km downstream, there's no road access so you're committed to the river for a few days. This is the most popular trip. Most canoeists stop in Pipiriki.

The season for canoe trips is usually from around September to Easter (from October to Easter a Great Walks pass must be purchased for hut and campsite use; see Places to Stay later). Up to 5000 people make this trip each year, the majority of them doing it over the summer holidays from Christmas to the end of January. During winter the river is almost deserted, with good reason. The cold weather and shorter days deter most people, and the winter currents are swifter.

Canoe and kayak operators will provide you with everything you need for the journey, including life jackets and waterproof drums – essential if you capsize in the rapids. Prices range from about $35 per day for single-person kayaks to $40 per day for two-person Canadian canoes (transport not included). Transport in and out can be just as costly as the canoes themselves; the cost may be around $50 per person. Quite often operators include the transport fee in the cost of canoe or kayak hire for multi-day trips. Three-day hire costs between $115 and $125 per person, and five-day hire $130 to $165.

Another option is a fully guided canoe or kayak trip – prices start at $260 per person for a two-day guided trip and $650 per person for a five-day trip.

Operators that offer independent hiring and/or guided trips include:

Blazing Paddles (☎ 0800 252 946, e ebrey@xtra.co.nz, Taumarunui) Canoe hire
Canoe Safaris (☎ 0800 272 335, W www.canoesafaris.co.nz, Ohakune) Guided trips and hire
Plateau Outdoor Adventure Guides (☎ 0508 752 832, Raurimu) Guided trips and hire
Rivercity Tours (☎ 0800 377 311, e rivercity-tours@xtra.co.nz, Wanganui) Guided trips and hire
Taumarunui Canoe Hire (☎ 06-895 8063, Taumarunui) Canoe hire
Wades Landing Outdoors (☎ 06-895 5995, Owhango) Guided trips and hire
Wairua Hikoi Tours (☎ 06-342 8190, Jerusalem) Guided trips
Yeti Tours (☎ 0800 322 388, W www.canoe.co.nz, Ohakune) Guided trips and hire

Jetboat Trips Jetboat trips give you a chance to see in just a few hours parts of the river that would take you days to cover in a canoe or kayak. Jetboats depart from Pipiriki, Taumarunui and Whakahoro. All operators provide transport to the river ends of the Matemateaonga Track and the Mangapurua Track.

Departing from Pipiriki, you can take a number of trips including a four-hour return trip to the Bridge to Nowhere for $80 with **Bridge to Nowhere Jet Boat Tours** (☎ 06-385 4128, e *bridgetonowhere@paradise.net.nz*) or **River Spirit** (☎ 06-342 1718, W *www.riverspirit.co.nz*).

From Taumarunui you can do anything from a short 15-minute jetboat tour to a two-day run to Wanganui with **Pioneer Jetboat Tours** (☎ 06-895 8528). Whakahoro is a bit off the beaten track – it's a long drive down an unsealed road to get there, whichever way you come – but Wades Landing Outdoors conducts from one- to three-day trips that take in this area. See Canoeing & Kayaking earlier for details.

Tramping

Probably the most famous and best-travelled track in Whanganui National Park is the 40-minute bush walk from the Mangapurua Landing to the Bridge to Nowhere, 30km upstream from Pipiriki.

The Matemateaonga Track and the Mangapurua Track are excellent for longer tramps. Both are one-way tracks beginning (or ending) at remote spots on the river, so you must arrange for jetboat transport to or from these points. Any jetboat operator on the river will do this; from the Matemateaonga Track it costs $55 per person and from the Mangapurua Track it costs $70 per person.

The DOC offices in Wanganui, Pipiriki and Taumarunui have information and maps, including the excellent *In and Around Whanganui National Park* ($2.50).

Matemateaonga Track Taking four days to complete, the 42km Matemateaonga Track has been described as one of NZ's best walks. Nevertheless it is not widely known and, probably due to its remoteness, does not attract the crowds that can form on some of NZ's more famous tracks.

Penetrating deep into bush, wilderness and hill country, the track follows an old Maori track and a disused settlers' dray road between the Wanganui and Taranaki regions. It traverses the Matemateaonga Range along the route of the Whakaihuwaka Rd, started in 1911 to create a more direct link from Stratford to Raetihi and the Main Trunk Railway. The outbreak of WWI interrupted the plans and the road was never completed.

The track passes through thick and regenerating bush. Much of it follows the crest of the Matemateaonga Range. On a clear day, a 1½-hour side trip to the summit of Mt Humphries affords a panoramic view of the Wanganui region all the way to Mt Taranaki and the volcanoes of Tongariro. There's a steep section between the Whanganui River (75m above sea level) and the Puketotara Hut (427m), but much of the track is easy walking. There are three huts along the way.

Mangapurua Track The Mangapurua Track is a 40km track between Whakahoro and the Mangapurua Landing, both on the Whanganui River. The track runs along the Mangapurua and Kaiwhakauka Streams, both tributaries of the Whanganui River, passing through the valleys of the same names. Between these valleys a side track leads to the Mangapurua Trig, at 663m the highest point in the area, from where you can see all the way to the volcanoes of the Tongariro and Egmont National Parks on a clear day. The route passes through land that was cleared for farming by settlers earlier

this century and later abandoned. The Bridge to Nowhere is 40 minutes from the Mangapurua Landing end of the track.

The track takes 20 hours and is usually walked in three to four days. Apart from the Whakahoro Hut at the Whakahoro end of the track, there are no huts, but there are many fine camping spots. Water is available from numerous small streams. There is road access to the track at the Whakahoro end and from a side track leading to the end of the Ruatiti Valley–Ohura Rd (from Raetihi).

Places to Stay

The park has several huts, a lodge and numerous camping grounds.

During the summer season, from October to April, a Great Walks Pass is required for boat trips on the river involving overnight stays in the park between Taumarunui and Pipiriki; the rule applies only to this stretch of the river. The pass is valid for six nights and seven days and allows you to stay overnight in the huts, in camp sites beside the huts or in other designated camp sites along the river. Along this section are three Category 2 huts classified as Great Walks Huts: the *Whakahoro Hut* at Whakahoro, the *John Coull Hut* and the *Tieke Marae/hut*, which has been revived as a marae; you can stay here, but full *marae* protocol must be observed (see the 'Maori Culture & Arts' special section).

The Great Walks Pass costs $25 in advance ($35 otherwise). Children aged 11 and over are half price (under 11 free). Canoeists spending a night camping between Taumarunui and Whakahoro pay $6 (children $3); jetboaters pay $10 (children $5). Passes are available at all DOC offices and visitors centres in the region, and some canoe operators also sell them. During summer, hut wardens are on duty and the river is patrolled by conservation officers, so bring your pass.

Great Walks Passes are not required in the off season from May to September. During this time, the cost is $10 in huts, $5 for camping beside the huts, and free for camping at designated river camp sites. Annual hut passes are acceptable during this time.

Bridge to Nowhere Lodge (☎ *025 480 308,* **e** *bridge2nowhere-lodge@clear.net .nz*) Camp sites $5 per person, cabin beds $20, self-catering accommodation $30, room and meals $85. On the other side of the river, opposite the Tieke Marae, this lodge has a range of accommodation options. The lodge can arrange jetboat transfers. It's quite remote, 21km upriver from Pipiriki, near the Matemateaonga Track; the only way to get there is by river or by tramping.

Along the Matemateaonga Track are three huts, all Category 2. The others are simpler, with only two bunks. On the lower part of the river, ***Downes Hut*** is on the west bank, opposite Atene.

Getting There & Away

If you're going on a canoe or kayak trip, the canoe company will make some arrangement for transport to get you and the canoe to and from the river.

There's road access to the river at Taumarunui, Ohinepane and Whakahoro. Whakahoro is a long drive through a remote area along a road that is unsealed for much of its distance; roads leading to Whakahoro take off from Owhango or Raurimu, both on SH4. There isn't any further road access to the river until you reach Pipiriki. From Pipiriki, the Whanganui River Rd heads south for 79km to Wanganui and east for 28km to Raetihi.

The only public transport to any part of the river is at Taumarunui (buses and trains) and at Pipiriki, where the mail bus makes a round trip from Wanganui Monday to Friday. See the Wanganui section in this chapter and the Taumarunui section in Waikato & the King Country chapter for details.

WHANGANUI RIVER ROAD & PIPIRIKI

The Whanganui River Rd, running along the Whanganui River most of the way from Wanganui to Pipiriki, is a scenic and historic area worth making the detour to see. The road meets SH4, the highway from Wanganui to the centre of the North Island, 14km north of Wanganui and again at Raetihi, 91km north of Wanganui.

It takes about 1½ to two hours to drive the 79km between Wanganui and Pipiriki – that's not counting stops. If you come on the mail-run bus from Wanganui to Pipiriki the trip will take most of the day, but you'll have the benefit of lots of social and historical commentary. The full circle from Wanganui to Pipiriki to Raetihi and back down SH4 through the scenic Paraparas and the Mangawhero River Gorge to Wanganui takes about four hours.

Information

The Pipiriki DOC office (☎ 06-385 5022) is open from 8am to 5pm Monday to Friday, but is not always staffed.

Things to See

The main attractions of the drive are the scenery and the lovely views of the Whanganui River. Notable sights include the historic **Catholic church** at Jerusalem, the restored **Kawana Flour Mill** near Matahiwi, the **Operiki Pa** and other *pa* sites, **Aramoana hill**, from where there's a panoramic view, and **Pipiriki**. The Maori villages of **Atene**, **Koriniti**, **Ranana** and **Jerusalem** (Hiruharama) along the road are generally not open to visitors.

Pipiriki is beside the river at the north end of Whanganui River Rd. It was once a bustling place served by river steamers and paddleboats. An interesting relic, the **MV Ongarue**, is a 20m, 65-passenger riverboat that once plied the river, now on display on land (off limits for safety reasons), about 50m from the turn-off to the DOC office.

The **Colonial House** (☎ *06-385 5022; adult/child $1/50c; open 1 Nov-Easter 10am-noon & 1pm-4pm*) in Pipiriki is a historic house now converted into a museum with many interesting exhibits on the history of Pipiriki and the river.

Beside the Colonial House, some old steps and foundations are all that remain to mark the site of the old **Pipiriki House**, a glamorous hotel once popular with tourists.

Pipiriki is the ending point for canoe trips coming down the Whanganui River, and for jetboat rides (see the Whanganui National Park section earlier).

Walking

Branching off from the road, there are a couple of walks that provide a glimpse of the wilderness of the Whanganui National Park. The DOC booklet *In and Around Whanganui National Park* ($2.50) has details on these walks.

The Atene Skyline Track begins at Atene, on the Whanganui River Rd about 22km north of where it meets with SH4. The 18km track takes six to eight hours and features native forest, sandstone bluffs and the Taumata Trig (523m), with its broad views as far as Mt Ruapehu, Mt Taranaki and the Tasman Sea. The track ends back on the river road, 2km downstream from the start.

From the Pipiriki DOC field centre a 1km track cuts its way through native bush to the top of Pukehinau, a hill that affords panoramic views of the surrounding valleys.

Places to Stay

Omaka (☎ 06-342 5595, e omakaholiday@ xtra.co.nz) Camp sites $8 per person, wool-shed beds $12, homestay with meals $60. Omaka, about 12km north of Parikino, is a delightful, friendly homestay. A bed in the spacious woolshed includes mattresses, bathroom and kitchen, and there's camping. You can also do canoeing (1½/3hrs $25/40).

The Flying Fox (☎ 06-342 8160, e the flyingfox@paradise.net.nz) Camp sites $8, cottage with self-catering/meals $35/70. The Flying Fox is a superb little getaway on the right bank of the river across from Koriniti. You can stay in The Brewhouse or the James K, both self-contained cottages, and self-cater, or you can get dinner, bed and breakfast. You can also camp in a secluded bush clearing. Cableway access is $2.50.

Koriniti Marae (☎ 0800 783 2637) Beds $10 per person. This *marae* on the east bank takes prebooked visitors; you should offer *koha*, or a donation, as well as the fee – see the 'Maori Culture & Arts' special section. Call Sunny Teki at the Whanganui River-boat Centre to make a booking.

Operiki Farmstay (☎ 06-342 8159) Adult/child $55/25. At this friendly place, you can get all meals and accommodation. It's about 3km north of Koriniti Marae.

Back Country Lifestyles (☎ 06-342 8116) $20 per person. This place, on the Wanganui side of Matahiwi, has horse riding and jet-boating. Accommodation is in restored shearers' quarters with linen and breakfast included. There's a kitchen and a barbecue.

Kauika Camp Site (☎ 06-342 8061) Camp sites $6, powered sites $10, $5 per person to camp. Beside the river at Ranana, this privately owned site has hot showers, a kitchen and a laundry.

The nuns at the *Catholic church* in Jerusalem take in travellers (you should book ahead on ☎ 06-342 8190). A large room has been divided by curtains into cubicles; the cost is around $10.

At Pipiriki there's an informal *camping ground* with toilets and cold water.

Getting There & Away

One of the most convenient and congenial ways of travelling the Whanganui River Rd is with the mail-run bus, which goes from Wanganui to Pipiriki Monday to Friday and takes passengers along with the mail for an interesting tour. See under Organised Tours in the Wanganui section.

If you're travelling by car, petrol is available at Raetihi (north) and at Upokongaro and Wanganui (south), but not in between. Despite the steep hills and gravel road, this route is also popular with cyclists.

WANGANUI
pop 40,700

Midway between Wellington and New Plymouth, Wanganui is an attractive city on the banks of the Whanganui River. The town has many fine old buildings and the centre has been rejuvenated by the restoration of historic buildings on the main street (Victoria Ave) and down by the river. The block from Taupo Quay and Ridgway St has many restored reminders of Wanganui's days as a prominent port.

History

Kupe, the great Polynesian explorer, is believed to have travelled up the Whanganui River for about 20km around AD 800. There were Maori living in the area around 1100, and they fully established themselves soon after the larger migration from Hawaiki in the 14th century. By the time the first European settlers came to the coast around the late 1830s there were numerous Maori settlements scattered up and down the river.

European settlement at Wanganui was hurried up when the New Zealand Company was unable to keep up with the demand for land around Wellington. In 1840 many Wellington settlers moved to Wanganui and founded a permanent settlement there; the deed was signed on the site now known as Moutoa Gardens. Initially called

Petre, after one of the directors of the New Zealand Company, in 1844 the town's name was changed to Wanganui (the name Kupe had given the river).

When the Maori understood that the gifts the Pakeha had given them were in exchange for the permanent acquisition of their land, seven years of bitter opposition followed. The Pakeha brought in thousands of troops to occupy Queen's Park, and the Rutland Stockade dominated the hill. Ultimately, the struggle was settled by arbitration and, in the Taranaki Land Wars, the Wanganui Maori assisted the Pakeha.

WANGANUI & MANAWATU

WANGANUI

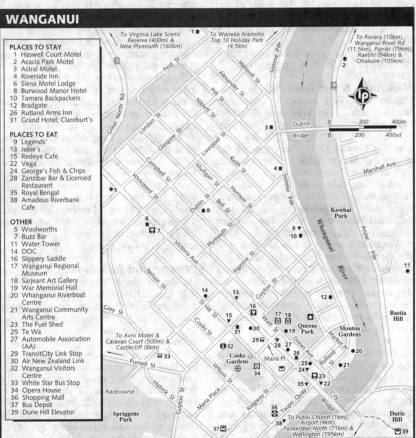

PLACES TO STAY
1 Haswell Court Motel
2 Acacia Park Motel
3 Astral Motel
4 Riverside Inn
6 Siena Motel Lodge
8 Burwood Manor Hotel
10 Tamara Backpackers
12 Bradgate
26 Rutland Arms Inn
31 Grand Hotel; Clareburt's

PLACES TO EAT
9 Legends'
13 Jabie's
15 Redeye Cafe
22 Vega
24 George's Fish & Chips
28 Zanzibar Bar & Licensed Restaurant
35 Royal Bengal
38 Amadeus Riverbank Cafe

OTHER
5 Woolworths
7 Buzz Bar
11 Water Tower
14 DOC
16 Slippery Saddle
17 Wanganui Regional Museum
18 Sarjeant Art Gallery
19 War Memorial Hall
20 Whanganui Riverboat Centre
21 Wanganui Community Arts Centre
23 The Fuel Shed
27 Automobile Association (AA)
29 TransitCity Link Stop
30 Air New Zealand Link
32 Wanganui Visitors Centre
33 White Star Bus Stop
34 Opera House
36 Shopping Mall
37 Bus Depot
39 Durie Hill Elevator

The town today is still very much a centre for re-emergent Maori consciousness.

Information

The very helpful Wanganui visitors centre (☎ 06-349 0508, W www.wanganuinz.com) is on Guyton St between St Hill and Wilson Sts. It's open from 8.30am to 5pm Monday to Friday and 10am to 2pm on Saturday and Sunday (9am to 3pm during summer). It has a great model of the area from Wanganui right up to Tongariro National Park, as well as Internet access ($1.50 for 10 minutes).

The DOC office (☎ 06-345 2402), on the corner of Ingestre and St Hill Sts, is a good resource for maps, pamphlets and information on Whanganui National Park and the river road.

The Automobile Association (AA) office (☎ 06-348 9160) is at 78 Victoria Ave.

Museums & Art Galleries

Opposite the War Memorial Hall, near Maria Place, is the **Wanganui Regional Museum** (☎ 06-345 7443, Watt St; adult/child $2/0.60; open 10am-4.30pm Mon-Sat, 1pm-4.30pm Sun), one of the largest and best regional museums in NZ, with excellent Maori exhibits. The collection includes the magnificently carved Te Mata-o-Houroa war canoe, other fine carvings and some mean-looking mere (elegant but lethal greenstone clubs). The museum has good colonial and wildlife collections.

Wanganui's art scene has blossomed in the past few years, partly due to a local polytech art course. There are numerous small art galleries scattered around town and many cafes and restaurants proudly display works by local artists. On the hill beside the museum is the neo-classical **Sarjeant Art Gallery** (☎ 06-349 0506, Queen's Park; admission free; open 10.30am-4.30pm Mon-Fri, 1pm-4.30pm Sat & Sun) which has an extensive permanent exhibition, as well as frequent special exhibits. **Te Wa** (☎ 06-348 7790, 25a Drews Ave; admission free; open noon-4pm Tues-Sat) and the **Wanganui Community Arts Centre** (☎ 06-345 1551, 19 Taupo Quay; admission free; open 10am-4pm Mon-Sat,

1pm-4pm Sun) are well-known for their support of local and NZ artists. The visitors centre has a comprehensive list of galleries.

Parks & Gardens

Wanganui has several parks right in the city centre, including the pleasant **Queens Park**, in which the museum and gallery are situated. The visitors centre has a bunch of brochures on parks scattered around the area.

Wanganui's most famous park is **Moutoa Gardens**, claimed as Maori land and subject to a four-month Maori occupation in 1995. The occupation signalled a new chapter in Maori-Pakeha relations and caused great acrimony in the town. The city council, abandoned by Wellington, fought the claim in the High Court, while some angry Pakeha counter-demonstrated under the banner of 'One New Zealand'; police raids further inflamed Maori anger. When the claim was eventually rejected by the High Court, the country looked on, expecting violence, but the occupation was peacefully abandoned after a moving night-long meeting addressed by Maori leaders. The gardens have acquired a sacred status in the eyes of many Maori.

The **Virginia Lake Scenic Reserve** (Rotokawau; winter gardens open 9am-5pm daily, aviary open 8.30am-5pm daily), about 1km north from the top end of Victoria Ave, is a beautiful reserve with a lake, theme gardens, a walk-in aviary, statues and the Higginbottom Fountain. The rest of the reserve is always open.

Whanganui Riverboat Centre

On the riverbank beside Taupo Quay, the Whanganui Riverboat Centre (☎ 0800 783 2637, 1a Taupo Quay; admission free; open 9am-4pm Mon-Fri, 10am-4pm Sat, 1pm-4pm Sun) houses the Waimarie side-paddle steamer. This vessel's long history began in 1900, when it was shipped in pieces from England and reassembled at Murrays Foundry in Wanganui. After plying the Whanganui River for 50 years it sank in 1952 at its original berth. It remained submerged for 40 years until it was raised and finally relaunched, restored and proud, on the first day of the 21st century.

Durie Hill

Across the river from the town centre is the carved gateway to the Durie Hill **elevator** *(adult/child $1/50c; open summer 7.30am-6pm Mon-Fri, 9am-5pm Sat, 10am-5pm Sun)*. You can follow a tunnel into the hillside and then ride up through the hill to the summit 65m above.

There are two viewpoints at the top: a lower one on the top of the lift machinery room and the higher War Memorial Tower, from which there's a fine view over the town all the way to Mt Taranaki, Mt Ruapehu, or the South Island if the weather is clear. Once you have climbed the tower and returned to the elevator building there is a path around the front which takes you back to your starting point at street level.

Putiki Church

If you turn right after crossing the City Bridge and continue for 1km you come to Putiki Church, also called St Paul's Memorial Church. It's a plain little place from the outside but the interior is magnificent, completely covered in **Maori carvings** and **tukutuku** (wall panels). The church is usually closed during the day; you can ask for the key at the caretaker's house on the corner of Anaua St and SH3.

Activities

The best way to get a feel for the Whanganui and its history is to take a **river cruise** on the 30.6m *Waimarie* **paddle steamer** *(☎ 06-347 1863; adult/child $25/15)*. Excursions are for one hour and leave from the Whanganui Riverboat Centre most days; check with the centre for times.

Other river trips by canoe, kayak, jetboat or motorised vessel are possible, starting further up the river in Whanganui National Park. **Rivercity Tours** *(☎ 06-344 2554)* offers additional tours up the Whanganui River Rd and on to the Drop Scene or the Bridge to Nowhere by jetboat, returning to Wanganui via SH4. See the Whanganui National Park section earlier for more details on river activities.

If you prefer sightseeing from the air, **Wanganui Aero Work** *(☎ 06-345 3994)* has

Tiger Moth flights, and **Remote Adventures** *(☎ 06-346 5747)* has scenic flights in a five-passenger Cessna.

Organised Tours

A very interesting trip up the Whanganui River Rd can be made with the weekday mail run, going up the river from Wanganui to Pipiriki Monday to Friday. You get picked up around 7.30am for an all-day trip along the river, stopping at many interesting and historic sites, including the **Kawana Flour Mill**, **Jerusalem church** and **Koriniti Marae**; the river's past and present is related along the way. Coffee and tea are provided, but bring lunch (you return to town around 3pm or 4pm). The cost is $30 per person, with an optional half-hour jetboat trip from Pipiriki to Drop Scene for another $45 or to the Bridge to Nowhere ($80, minimum of three people). Contact **Rivercity Tours** *(☎ 06-344 2554)* for bookings.

Places to Stay

Camping & Cabins There are no camping grounds in the centre of Wanganui.

Avro Motel & Caravan Court (☎ 06-345 5279, e avro_nz@hotmail.com, 36 Alma Rd) Camp sites $8 per person, powered sites $19 per double, motel units singles/doubles from $67/72. This place is closest to the city centre, 1.5km west of the centre. There's an indoor spa pool and swimming pool but no kitchen facilities.

Aramoho Top 10 Holiday Park (☎ 0800 272 664, ☎/fax 06-343 8402, e aramoho .holidaypark@xtra.co.nz, 460 Somme Parade) Unpowered/powered sites $19/20 per double, cabins from $30, tourist flats $55, chalets $70. Aramoho Park, 6km north of the Dublin St Bridge, is a peaceful, parklike camp on the town-side bank of the Whanganui River. Local Aramoho buses run there Monday to Saturday.

Castlecliff Motor Camp (☎ 0800 254 947, 06-344 2227, cnr Karaka & Rangiora Sts) Unpowered/powered sites $16/18 per double, cabins $26-50. Castlecliff Camp is by the beach, 8km north-west of Wanganui. Local buses run to Castlecliff from Monday to Saturday.

WANGANUI & MANAWATU

Hostels Two good backpacker options present themselves.

Riverside Inn (☎/fax 06-347 2529, 2 Plymouth St) Camp sites $10, dorm beds $16, doubles & twins $36, cabins $32, guest-house singles/doubles with breakfast $35/50. Opposite the river is the friendly, pink Riverside Inn. It's a bit of a chameleon: part YHA associate, part guest-house and with cabins out the back.

Tamara Backpackers (☎ 06-347 6300, e tamarabakpak@xtra.co.nz, 24 Somme Parade) Dorm beds $17, singles $27, doubles & twins $38-48. Also overlooking the Wanganui River is this rambling old guest-house-turned-hostel. It's a well-run, friendly place with large recreational areas and a great garden. You can organise all sorts of activities here, both on the river and elsewhere, and there are free bikes to use.

Motels, Hotels & Guesthouses There are plenty of motels, hotels and guesthouses to choose from.

Haswell Court Motel (☎ 0800 809 107, ☎/fax 06-343 9848, 59 Halswell St) Singles/doubles from $65/89. This motel is attractively situated on a quiet, tree-lined street at the foot of St John's Hill.

Astral Motel (☎ 06-347 9063, fax 347 8653, 45 Somme Parade) Units from $65. Astra has cheap, pleasant motel units.

Acacia Park Motel (☎/fax 06-343 9093, 140 Anzac Parade) Singles/doubles from $68/75. Most of Acacia Park's units are set back from the road and sheltered by trees.

Burwood Manor Motel (☎ 06-345 2180, 63 Dublin St) Studio units $80, luxury spa units $99. Eight units at this inn have their own spa.

Siena Motor Lodge (☎ 0800 888 802, 06-345 9009, fax 345 9935, 335 Victoria Ave) Units from $98. Siena Lodge has good, modern units with spas. All are non-smoking.

Rutland Arms Inn (☎ 0800 788 5263, 06-347 7677, e enquiries@rutland-arms .co.nz, cnr Victoria Ave & Ridgway St) Rooms $115-160. The Rutland Arms has tastefully appointed rooms in a beautifully restored building in the heart of the city.

Grand Hotel (☎ 06-345 0955, fax 345 0953, 99 Guyton St) Singles/doubles $65/77. This is about the only hotel of the old school still surviving in Wanganui; all rooms have private facilities.

Bradgate (☎/fax 06-345 3634, 7 Somme Parade) Singles/doubles from $40/70. Bradgate is a grand old home, overlooking the Whanganui River, with three comfortable guestrooms: one single, one queen-sized and one double. Breakfast is included.

Places to Eat

Jabie's (☎ 06-347 2800, 168 Victoria Ave) Kebabs $4.50-10. For superb eat-in or take-away kebabs that fill a large hole in the stomach, head to Jabie's.

Amadeus Riverbank Cafe (☎ 06-345 1538, 69 Taupo Quay) Mains from $10. This cafe is an excellent place for a meal or snack and a drink. Seafood, steaks, chicken and pasta are all on the menu, along with snacks and cakes.

Redeye Cafe (☎ 06-345 5646, 96 Guyton St) Mains $12-14. This fresh and funky cafe has good light meals and snacks, and colourful art.

Zanzibar Bar & Licensed Restaurant (☎ 06-345 5900, Victoria Court, Victoria Ave) Meals $10-27. Zanzibar's pleasant courtyard seating area is quietly tucked away from busy Victoria St.

Clareburt's (cnr Guyton & St Hill Sts) Bar meals $8.50-10. For pub food try Clareburt's, tucked away in the recesses of the Grand Hotel, a block from Victoria Ave.

Royal Bengal (☎ 06-348 7041, 9 Victoria Ave) Mains $12-13. Good Indian food at very reasonable prices can be found at the Royal Bengal.

Vega (☎ 06-345 1082, 49 Taupo Quay) Mains $25-30. Vega is a more upmarket restaurant/bar with excellent food, cool atmosphere and dark decor.

Legends' (☎ 06-348 7450, 25 Somme Parade) Mains $19-29, sandwiches & pastries $2-6. Next to Tamara Backpackers, in a beautifully restored Victorian house, is this convivial restaurant. The menu has international flair and delicious sandwiches and such to take away. Book for dinner.

Riviera (☎ 06-345 6459) Mains $15-25. At Upokongaro, on SH3, about 12km north of Wanganui, is this authentic Italian restaurant. It's well worth the trip out of town.

George's Fish & Chips (☎ 06-345 7937, 40 Victoria Ave) Fish & chips from $3.50. George's has great fresh fish.

Entertainment

The Fuel Shed (cnr Taupo Quay & Victoria Ave) This large, popular place doesn't get going till around 11.30pm, when resident DJs quickly fill the bar's dance floor.

Slippery Saddle (cnr Guyton St & Victoria Ave) Competing with the Fuel Shed in the popularity stakes is the Slippery Saddle. It also has a dance floor that gets jumping late in the evening.

Vega (See Places to Eat) For something a little more sophisticated, drop into Vega for a drink. They sometimes have live jazz on a Sunday afternoon.

Buzz Bar (321 Victoria Ave) This is a good spot for a quiet drink and a game of pool.

Rutland Arms Inn (48 Ridgway St) The Rutland is a pleasant, family-style pub in a magnificently restored historic building.

Getting There & Away

Air Air New Zealand (☎ 06-348 3500) at 133 Victoria Ave has daily direct flights to Auckland and Wellington, with onward connections.

Bus InterCity and Newmans buses operate from the top end of Ridgway St. Both have buses to Auckland ($38, 8hrs) via Taumarunui, and to New Plymouth ($16, 2½hrs). Heading south, buses go to Palmerston North ($10, 1¾hrs) and on to Wellington ($18, 3hrs). For services north to Tongariro, Taupo and Rotorua, you have to transfer at Bulls, although some buses call into Palmerston North. For Napier, Hastings and Gisborne change at Palmerston North.

White Star buses (☎ 06-347 6677) operate from in front of Budget Rent A Car, 161 Ingestre St, with buses to New Plymouth, Palmerston North and Wellington (see the Taranaki chapter for prices).

The mail-run bus (☎ 06-344 2554) heads up the Whanganui River Rd to Pipiriki and back Monday to Friday (it picks up from hostels); see under Organised Tours earlier in this section.

Car & Motorcycle Between Wanganui and the centre of the North Island the windy highway (SH4) passes through the Paraparas, an area of interesting *papa* (large blue-grey mudstone) hills with some beautiful views, and also passes close by the impressive Raukawa Falls and along Mangawhero River Gorge.

Alternatively you can take the Whanganui River Rd (see Whanganui River Rd & Pipiriki).

Getting Around

To/From the Airport The airport is about 4km south of town, across the river towards the sea. Ash's Transport Services (☎ 025 958 693) operates a shuttle to the airport ($8), bus station and other points in town.

Bus TransitCity Link (☎ 06-343 5555) operates a limited local bus service Monday to Friday, including routes to Castlecliff and to Aramoho, all departing from the bus stop on Maria Place near Victoria Ave. Single adult/child fares cost $2/1.20.

AROUND WANGANUI

Heading north-west from Wanganui on SH3 as if you were going to New Plymouth, after about 5.5km you reach Rapanui Rd. Turn towards the sea on this road and you come to some pleasant spots.

First is the **Westmere Reserve & Wildlife Refuge**, where there's lots of bird life and a 40-minute walk around Lake Westmere. Next along, **Bason Botanical Reserve** *(open 9am-dusk daily; conservatory open 9am-4.30pm daily)* is a 25-hectare reserve with a lake, conservatory, gardens of many kinds, lookout tower and an old homestead.

At the end of Rapanui Rd, 9km from the SH3 turn-off, the black-sand **Kai Iwi Beach** is beautiful. The Mowhanau Creek meets the sea here and provides a safe place for children to swim, and there's a small motor camp and scenic papa cliffs. You can walk back to Castlecliff along the coast (two to three hours).

Bushy Park

Bushy Park *(Whanganui National Park map; ☎/fax 06-342 9879, adult/child $3/1; open 10am-5pm daily)*, 24km north-west of Wanganui, is a 220-acre scenic reserve owned by the Royal Forest & Bird Protection Society. It has spacious grounds, picnic and barbecue areas, bush walks and a 1906 homestead with period furniture and fittings. To get there take SH3 to Kai Iwi, turn off north where you see the signs and go 9km further on a sealed side road.

Accommodation is available in the ***homestead***; it's like staying in a well-preserved museum. Bunk beds cost $18, caravan and Camp sites $25 per double, B&B singles $65 to $100 and doubles $85 to $130. A three-course dinner is available for $35.

Ashley Park

Ashley Park *(Whanganui National Park map; ☎ 06-346 5917, fax 346 5861; adult/child $3/1; open 9am-5pm daily)* at Waitotara, 34km north-west of Wanganui on SH3, is another attractive park, with gardens and trees surrounding a picturesque lake. Activities include fishing, eeling, bird-watching and kayaking.

Accommodation is available and you can join in the farm activities, or go boating on the lake or hunting. ***Motel units*** overlooking a small lake cost $75, ***farmstays*** $40 and ***tent/powered sites*** $7/13.

Remote Adventures *(☎ 06-346 5749, ☒ www.remoteadventures.co.nz)* Self-contained cottage $18 per person, B&B and dinner $84. Remote Adventures is a wilderness farmstay which organises bushwalks, jetboating and scenic flights near Waitotara. It's 57km north of Waitotara.

Lake Wiritoa

About 12.5km south-east of Wanganui, off SH3, Lake Wiritoa is popular for swimming and water-skiing. To get there, turn left at Lake Kaitoke and keep going past it to get to Lake Wiritoa.

Manawatu

☎ 06 • pop 147,400

The rich sheep- and dairy-farming district of Manawatu is centred around the provincial city of Palmerston North, dominated by Massey University, and includes the districts of Rangitikei to the north and Horowhenua to the south.

PALMERSTON NORTH

pop 67,400

On the banks of the Manawatu River, Palmerston North is the principal centre of the Manawatu region and a major crossroads. With Massey University, the second-largest university in NZ, and several other colleges, Palmerston North has the relaxed feel of a rural university town. Though not really a tourist destination, it is well ordered and pleasant.

Orientation & Information

The wide open expanse of The Square, with its gardens and fountains, is very much the centre of town. You can get your bearings from a lookout on top of the Civic Centre building on The Square, open Monday to Friday.

The Destination Manawatu visitors centre (☎ 06-354 6593, ☒ www.manawatunz.co.nz), 52 The Square, has plenty of information on the area. It's open from 9am to 5pm Monday to Friday and 10am to 3pm on Saturday and Sunday.

The DOC office (☎ 06-350 9700) is at 717 Tremaine Ave, on the north side of town.

The AA office (☎ 06-357 7039) is at 185 Broadway Ave, near Amesbury St.

Internet access is available for $5 per hour at *i* Cafe (☎ 06-353 7899), on the corner of The Square and Fitzherbert Ave.

Things to See & Do

The **Science Centre & Manawatu Museum** *(☎ 06-355 5000, cnr Church & Pitt Sts, entrance off Main St; museum free; Science Centre adult/child/family $6/4/15; open 10am-5pm daily)* has a museum specialising in the history of the Manawatu region,

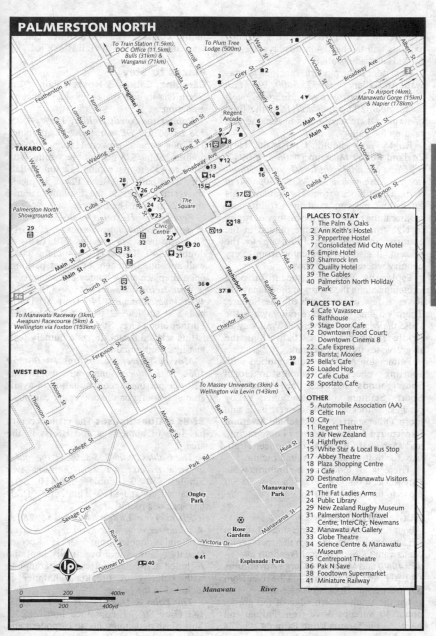

PALMERSTON NORTH

PLACES TO STAY
1 The Palm & Oaks
2 Ann Keith's Hostel
3 Peppertree Hostel
7 Consolidated Mid City Motel
16 Empire Hotel
30 Shamrock Inn
37 Quality Hotel
39 The Gables
40 Palmerston North Holiday
Park

PLACES TO EAT
4 Cafe Vavasseur
6 Bathhouse
9 Stage Door Cafe
12 Downtown Food Court;
Downtown Cinema 8
22 Cafe Express
23 Barista; Moxies
25 Bella's Cafe
26 Loaded Hog
27 Cafe Cuba
28 Spostato Cafe

OTHER
5 Automobile Association (AA)
8 Celtic Inn
10 City
11 Regent Theatre
13 Air New Zealand
14 Highflyers
15 White Star & Local Bus Stop
17 Abbey Theatre
18 Plaza Shopping Centre
19 i Cafe
20 Destination Manawatu Visitors
Centre
21 The Fat Ladies Arms
24 Public Library
29 New Zealand Rugby Museum
31 Palmerston North Travel
Centre; InterCity; Newmans
32 Manawatu Art Gallery
33 Globe Theatre
34 Science Centre & Manawatu
Museum
35 Centrepoint Theatre
36 Pak N Save
38 Foodtown Supermarket
41 Miniature Railway

including its Maori history, culture and art. The Science Centre has rotating science exhibits and the hands-on displays are fun for kids and adults alike.

Next door is the modern, spacious **Manawatu Art Gallery** (☎ *06-355 5000, 398 Main St West; admission free, donations welcome; open 10am-5pm daily*). At the time of writing there were plans to rename and revamp the gallery.

Rugby fans shouldn't miss the **New Zealand Rugby Museum** (☎ *06-358 6947, 87 Cuba St; adult/child $4/1; open 10am-noon & 1.30pm-4pm Mon-Sat, 1.30pm-4pm Sun*), a few blocks from The Square. This interesting museum contains exhibits and memorabilia relating to the history of rugby in NZ, from the first game played in the country, in Nelson in 1870, up to the present. It also has mementos from every country where rugby is played.

Esplanade Park is a beautiful park stretching along the shores of the Manawatu River, a few blocks south of The Square. There's a small **miniature railway** for the kids; the Manawatu Riverside Walkway & Bridle Track, extending 10km along the river, passes through the park.

Palmerston North is well supplied with sporting venues. The **Palmerston North Showgrounds** includes the Manawatu Sports Stadium, other stadiums, rugby pitches, a stockcar track, concert halls and more. Other sports venues include **Awapuni Racecourse** for thoroughbred horse racing, and **Manawatu Raceway** on Pioneer Highway for trotting and greyhound racing.

There is an indoor rock-climbing wall, **City Rock** (☎ *06-357 4552, 38a Grey St; $8*) close to the centre of town.

Manawatu Gorge

About 15km north of Palmerston North the SH2 to Napier runs through the spectacular Manawatu Gorge. **Physical Freedom** (☎ *06-329 4060*) and **Manawatu Gorge Adventures** (☎ *0800 746 688*) offer trips on the river from $55 per person. Booking is essential.

On the south-eastern edge of the gorge, about 40 minutes drive from Palmerston North, is the **Tararua Wind Farm** (☎ *06-574 4800, Hall Block Rd*), the largest of its kind in the country. The 48 turbines can be viewed from the top of Hall Block Rd.

Places to Stay

Camping, Cabins & Hostels Palmerston North has its fair share of budget accommodation.

Palmerston North Holiday Park (☎ *06-358 0349, 133 Dittmer Drive*) Camp sites $10 per person, powered sites $20 per double, cabins $28 per double, cabins with kitchens $35, tourist cabins $42, tourist flats $55. This park, off Ruha Place, is pleasantly situated beside the Esplanade Park, about 2km from The Square.

Peppertree Hostel (☎ *06-355 4054*, @ *peppertreehostel@clear.net.nz, 121 Grey St*) Dorm beds $17, singles $30, twins & doubles $40. This YHA associate has a well-appointed kitchen, off-street parking, open fireplace and a homey atmosphere.

Ann Keith's Hostel (☎ *06-358 6928*, @ *ak1@clear.net.nz, 146 Grey St*) Dorm beds $20, singles $32, twins & doubles $47. Further along Grey St from the Peppertree is this relaxed hostel. It has a homely feel, just like your grandma's.

Massey University campus (☎ *06-350 5056*, @ *k.l.macey@massey.ac.nz*) Rooms $30 per person. Accommodation is available year-round on the university campus.

B&Bs & Guesthouses The visitors centre has lists of homestays and B&Bs in the area.

The Gables (☎ *06-358 3209*, @ *thegables .pn.nz@xtra.co.nz, 179 Fitzherbert Ave*) Singles $50-80, doubles $80-110, self-contained cottage $110. This comfy B&B has spacious rooms.

Plum Tree Lodge (☎ *06-358 7813*, @ *plumtreelodge@xtra.co.nz, 97 Russell St*) Singles/doubles from $95/115. Accommodation here is in a beautifully kept and secluded self-contained cottage, complete with balcony. A breakfast hamper is included in the price.

The Palm & Oaks (☎/*fax 06-359 0755, 183 Grey St*) Self-contained house $250. This plush two-storey house is modern and elegant and has everything you could possibly need, including a spa pool, dishwasher, garage, balcony, garden and even the use of a tennis court.

Motels & Hotels Palmerston North has a huge array of motels to choose from. There's even a 'motel row' on Fitzherbert Ave, south of The Square.

Consolidated Mid City Motel (☎ 06-357 2184, e *consolidated-mid-city-motel@xtra .co.nz, 129 Broadway Ave*) Singles/doubles from $63/70. This motel is very handy to the town centre. All units have cooking facilities.

Empire Hotel (☎ 06-357 8002, fax 357 7157, cnr Princess & Main Sts*) En suite singles/doubles $70/75. The Empire has the convenience of a bar and restaurant, and off-street parking.

Shamrock Inn (☎ 06-355 2130, fax 358 3782, 267 Main St West*) Singles/doubles $30-45/40-55. The Shamrock is a restored building with good budget rooms.

Quality Hotel (☎ 06-356 8059, e *qual ity.palmerston@cdlhms.co.nz, 110 Fitzherbert Ave*) Rooms from $69. This large complex has 151 rooms, a gym, spa and sauna. Guests receive a complimentary game of golf.

Places to Eat
Palmerston North has its fair share of cafes and bar/restaurants serving inexpensive fare to cater for the town's student population.

Cafe Express (*The Square*) Meals $12-24. Apart from the normal cafe fare, Cafe Express serves larger meals such as fettuccini and Thai green curry.

Bella's Cafe (*2 The Square*) Lunch mains $12-16. This popular lunch spot has a heavily weighted Italian menu with plenty of pasta dishes.

Barista (☎ 06-357 2614, George St*) Mains around $25. The supremely popular Barista's has an international (cheaper-by-day) menu and a range of coffees.

Moxies (*Cnr George & Main Sts*) All day menu $5-9. This friendly cafe has an unusual range of freshly squeezed juices.

Cafe Cuba (☎ 06-356 5750, cnr George & Cuba Sts*) Meals $7-12. Choose from a selection of pastas and sandwiches at this nicely chilled out cafe.

Stage Door Cafe (*Regent Arcade*) Meals $6-18. This place is good for just hanging out. It has great coffee and juices.

Loaded Hog (☎ 06-356 5417, Coleman Place*) Mains $15-25. The Loaded Hog is busy both at lunch and dinner.

Spostato Restaurant (☎ 06-355 5505, upstairs 213 Cuba St*) Mains $25-28. Open 6pm-late daily. Great Italian dishes are served in a graceful setting at Spostato.

Bathhouse (☎ 06-355 0051, 161 Broadway Ave*) Mains $24-28. Bathhouse is a stylish restaurant with a couple of big open fires for winter and sometimes has jazz.

Cafe Vavasseur (☎ 06-359 3167, 201 Broadway Ave*) Mains $20-30. This upmarket restaurant has equally upmarket food.

On Broadway Ave, *Downtown Food Court* offers Chinese, fish and chips, coffee, ice cream etc. It's open late to cater to movie-goers. For self-caterers, the *Foodtown* supermarket is on Ferguson St at the rear of the Plaza shopping centre. *Pack N Save* is a little further along.

Entertainment
Nightlife fluctuates according to the student year and is quieter during the holidays. The cafes and bars along Broadway Ave and George St (see Places to Eat) are also popular drinking spots.

Celtic Inn (☎ 06-357 5571, Regent Arcade*) Located between Broadway Ave and King St is this small, pleasant, low-key Irish pub with live music on weekend nights.

Fat Ladies Arms (*cnr Church & Linton Sts*) This is a popular student watering hole.

Highflyers (*cnr The Square & Main St*) This bar is for a more mature crowd.

Theatre and music performances are staged at the *Centrepoint Theatre* (☎ 06-354 5740, Church St*), *Globe Theatre* (☎ 06-358 8699, Main St*) and the *Abbey Theatre* (☎ 06-355 0499, Church St*). The revamped *Regent Theatre* (☎ 06-350 2100, Broadway Ave*) hosts big events. The large *Downtown Cinema 8* complex, upstairs in the Downtown Arcade, shows the latest films and art-house selections.

WANGANUI & MANAWATU

WANGANUI & MANAWATU

Getting There & Away

Air The international airport is on the northern outskirts of town; planes often get diverted here when the weather at Wellington is bad.

Air New Zealand (☎ 06-351 8800), at 30 Broadway Ave, offers daily direct flights to Auckland, Christchurch, Hamilton and Wellington, with onward connections. Freedom Air (☎ 0800 600 500) flies to Brisbane, Sydney, the Gold Coast and Melbourne in Australia. Origin Pacific (☎ 0800 302 302) has direct flights to Auckland, Napier and Nelson with connections to other centres.

Bus InterCity, Newmans and Tranzit Coachlines buses operate from the Palmerston North Travel Centre (☎ 06-355 4955) on the corner of Main and Pitt Sts. InterCity and Newmans buses go from Palmerston North to most places in the North Island; Tranzit Coachlines operates one route – Palmerston North via Masterton to Wellington ($27).

White Star (☎ 06-358 8777) operates from a bus stop at the Tranzit bus stop, on Main St near The Square, with buses to Wellington, Wanganui and New Plymouth.

Some direct services between Auckland and Wellington bypass Palmerston North, stopping instead at the nearby township of Bulls.

Train The train station (☎ 0800 802 802) is off Tremaine Ave, about 12 blocks north of The Square. Trains between Auckland and Wellington stop here.

Getting Around

Tranzit City Link (☎ 06-355 4955) minibuses operate from the bus stop in the middle of Main St, on the east side of The Square. They operate Monday to Friday from 6.45am to 5.50pm, Saturday and Sunday from 8.30am to 2.55pm; all rides cost $1.80. The No 12 bus goes to Massey University but none go to the airport. One of the minibuses stops near the airport at the Milson shopping centre; from the terminal to the shopping centre is a 10- to 15-minute walk. The visitors centre has timetables. A taxi costs $9 to the centre, or $11 to Massey.

RANGITIKEI

The Rangitikei region stretches from Taihape (the self-styled 'gumboot' capital of NZ) in the north to Bulls in the south (west of Palmerston North) and also includes the towns Hunterville and Marton. Most tourists only catch a glimpse of this region from their bus or car window as they race from Tongariro National Park to Wellington. However, the region does have a few attractions that may tempt some to stop, especially along the banks of the untamed Rangitikei River. The Rangitikei visitors centre (☎ 06-388 0350) on Hautapu St, Taihape, has more information and a free pamphlet *Rangitikei: The Undiscovered Secret*. It's open 9am to 5pm daily.

River Valley Lodge (☎ 06-388 1444, e *thelodge@rivervalley.co.nz)* Dorm beds $16-18, B&B $27, twins & doubles $50. Thirty kilometres east of Taihape is this lodge on the banks of the Rangitikei. It is quite remote, in a pristine valley, and there are many activities to engage in: whitewater rafting ($95); abseiling ($25); kayaking (from $40); horse trekking (two hours $45); and walking (free). The lodge has a huge communal area with an open fire and is popular with some tour group buses.

Mangaweka

Located north on SH1, 52km south of Waiouru, Mangaweka's most noticeable attraction is the *Aeroplane Cafe (open daily)*, a cafe in an old DC-3 plane right beside the highway. Beside the plane, **Rangitikei River Adventures** *(☎ 0800 655 747)* offers a number of Rangitikei River trips, including jetboating, kayaking and rafting, and can arrange accommodation. Bookings are absolutely essential for all activities.

At 80m, the **High Time Bungy** *(☎ 0800 802 8649, 06-388 9109; jump $99)* off the Mokai bridge over the Rangitikei river is the North Island's highest. The bungy site is 15 minutes' drive east of SH1; the turn-off is signposted just north of Utiku.

Gardens

The **Cross Hills Gardens** *(☎ 06-328 5797; adult/child $4/free; open 10.30am-5pm* *daily Sept-May)* with one of NZ's largest and most varied collections of rhododendrons and azaleas, is 5km north of Kimbolton, on SH54 about a 45-minute drive north of Palmerston North.

Ohakea

Ohakea is a whistle-stop town, west of Palmerston North on SH1 near Bulls. It is dominated by a large air-force base, where you'll find the **Ohakea Museum** *(☎ 06-351 5020; adult/child $8/3; open 9.30am-4.30pm daily)*. This small museum of air-force memorabilia is dedicated to the exploits of the tiny Royal New Zealand Air Force. There's also a *cafe* on the premises.

HOROWHENUA

The Horowhenua region extends south from Foxton to Waikawa Beach, and is bordered by the Tasman Sea to the west and the rugged Tararuas to the east. In the region are the provincial centre Levin, the beautiful Papaitonga and Horowhenua Lakes, and Himatangi, Foxton, Waitarere and Hokio Beaches.

Levin

pop 19,000

Levin is a sizeable town (by NZ standards) in the centre of the fertile Horowhenua agricultural region, 50km south of Palmerston North.

The Horowhenua visitors centre (☎ 06-367 8440), 93 Oxford St, opens from 9am to 5.30pm Monday to Friday and 10am to 3pm on Saturday and Sunday. It can do bookings for InterCity, Newmans, White Star, Tranzrail and the Interislander ferry, and has DOC information. It can also provide details on B&Bs, homestays and farmstays, and activities in the area. The AA (☎ 06-367 8430) is at 212 Oxford St.

Bentons Motel *(☎ 06-367 8282, ⓔ m.j .benton@xtra.co.nz, 2 York St)* Singles/doubles from $75/85. This modern and comfortable motel has the added advantage of a bistro bar on the premises.

The Fantails *(☎ 06-368 9011, ⓔ fan tails@ xtra.co.nz, 40 MacArthur St)* Singles $60-80, doubles $90-120, self-contained cottages from $100. Fantails is a serene homestay set amongst a cared-for garden. There's also a cafe that serves organic food.

Italian Flame *(☎ 06-367 0110, 104 Oxford St)* Mains $18-24. Open for dinner from 6pm Mon-Sat. Italian Flame has a fireplace and couches, and a good wine list.

Cafe Club *(7 Bath St)* Light meals $8.50-11. Relaxed Cafe Club has a good range of light meals, sandwiches and coffee.

Lake Papaitonga, a few kilometres south of Levin and reached by Buller Rd, is a serene, beautiful place. Follow the boardwalk to the sacred lake, which features heavily in the story of the Maori chief Te Rauparaha.

Tokomaru Steam Engine Museum

The Tokomaru Steam Engine Museum *(☎ 06-329 8867; adult/child $8/4; open 9am-3.30pm Mon-Sat, 10.30am-3pm Sun)*, in Tokomaru on SH57 about 30km north of Levin, exhibits a large collection of working steam engines and locomotives. On the occasional Sunday there is a 'steam up' day *(adult/child $10/5; open 1.30pm-4pm)*, where one or more of the engines provide rides for the public.

Central Plateau

☎ 07 • pop 41,741

New Zealand's main volcanic area, the Taupo Volcanic Zone, stretches in a line from White Island, north of the Bay of Plenty, through Rotorua and down to Tongariro National Park. The Central Plateau, at the heart of the North Island, is the centre of the country's volcanic activity.

The Central Plateau was at its most active some 2000 years ago. The remaining volcanoes do not match the destructive fury of some of the world's other hot spots, but still put on spectacular shows from time to time. Since 1995, Mt Ruapehu, the tallest mountain in the North Island, has had a series of eruptions, spewing forth rock and clouds of ash and steam.

Taupo, on Lake Taupo, is the main resort town of this volcanic plateau. The plateau extends southwards to the majestic, snow-capped volcanoes in Tongariro National Park, one of NZ's premier parks, with many fine walks during summer and pristine skiing over winter.

Tongariro National Park

Established in 1887, Tongariro was NZ's first national park. The three peaks were given to the country in September 1887 by Horonuku Te Heuheu Tukino, a far-sighted paramount chief of the Ngati Tuwharetoa people, who saw it as the only way to preserve an area of such spiritual significance. The name Tongariro originally covered the three mountains of the park (Tongariro, Ngauruhoe and Ruapehu) and comes from *tonga* (south wind) and *riro* (carried away). The story goes that the famous *tohunga* (priest) Ngatoro-i-rangi was stuck on the summit and had almost perished from the cold. He called to his sisters in Hawaiki for fire, saying he was being 'carried away by the south wind'. As the sisters approached

Highlights

- Visiting Tongariro National Park, dominated by smoking Mt Ruapehu
- Walking the famous Tongariro Crossing and the Northern Circuit
- Trout fishing or boating at Lake Taupo
- Exploring Wairakei Park and its thermal regions, and the Huka Falls
- Skiing at Whakapapa and Turoa
- Tandem skydiving or bungy jumping at Taupo

they stopped at Whakaari (White Island), Tarawera, Rotorua and Taupo, igniting the fires that still burn in those places.

With its mighty, active volcanoes, Tongariro is one of NZ's most spectacular parks. In summer it has excellent walks and tramps, most notably the Tongariro Northern Circuit and the Tongariro Crossing. In winter it's an important ski area.

Information

The Whakapapa visitors centre (☎ 07-892 3729, fax 892 3814) in Whakapapa (pronounced 'fa-ka-pa-pa') Village, on the

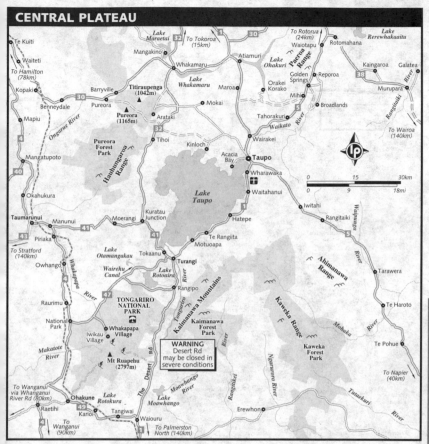

CENTRAL PLATEAU

CENTRAL PLATEAU

north-western side of the park, is open from 8am to 5pm daily (till 6pm December to mid-April). It has maps and lots of information on the park, including walks, huts and current skiing, track and weather conditions. Audiovisuals (one video adult/child $3/1, both videos $5/1.50) and the many displays on the geological and huma history of the park, plus a small shop, make the centre an interesting place to visit. The detailed *Tongariro National Park* map ($14.95) is worth buying before you go tramping. DOC produces a number of handy brochures on all walks in the park.

DOC centres serving the park are in Ohakune and Turangi. From late December to late January DOC offers an excellent array of guided walks in and around the park; ask the park centres for brochures and information.

If you are visiting the park, remember that much of the Tongariro National Park experiences alpine conditions, which means that weather can change faster than you can say 'Where did all those clouds come from?' See the boxed text 'Track Safety' later in this chapter for safety tips before setting out on your adventure.

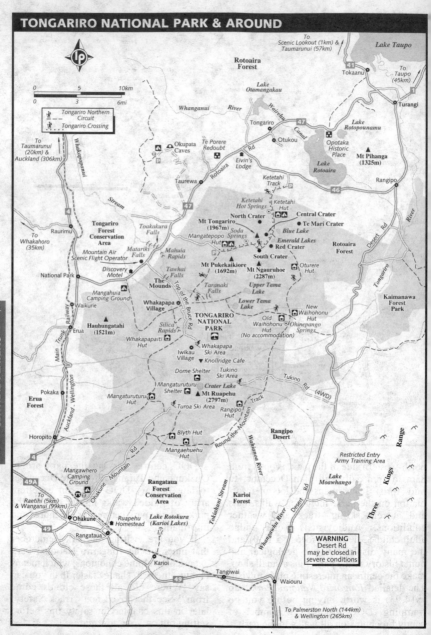

TONGARIRO NATIONAL PARK & AROUND

To Scenic Lookout (1km) & Taumarunui (57km)

Lake Taupo

Rotoaira Forest

Whanganui River

Waikato Canal

Tokaanu

41

To Taupo (45km)

Turangi

Lake Otamangakau

Tongariro

Otukou

47

Lake Rotopounamu

Opotaka Historic Place

Mt Pihanga (1325m)

Lake Rotoaira

Rangipo

46

Eivin's Lodge

Okupata Caves

Te Porere Redoubt

Taurewa

Ketetahi Track

Ketetahi Hot Springs

Ketetahi Hut

Central Crater

North Crater

Mt Tongariro (1967m)

Soda Springs

Te Mari Crater

Blue Lake

Emerald Lakes

Red Crater

Rotoaira Forest

To Whakahoro (35km)

To Taumarunui (20km) & Auckland (306km)

Raurimu

Tongariro Forest Conservation Area

Mountain Air Scenic Flight Operator

Toakakura Falls

Matariki Falls

Mahuia Rapids

Tawhai Falls

Discovery Motel

Mangatepopo Hut

South Crater

Mt Pukekaikiore (1692m)

Mt Ngauruhoe (2287m)

Oturere Hut

National Park

The Mounds

Top of the Bruce Rd

Taranaki Falls

Upper Tama Lake

Kaimanawa Forest Park

Mangahuia Camping Ground

Waikune

Whakapapa Village

TONGARIRO NATIONAL PARK

Lower Tama Lake

New Waihohonu Hut

Old Waihohonu Hut (No accommodation)

Ohinepango Springs

Hauhungatahi (1521m)

Erua

Silica Rapids

Whakapapaiti Hut

Iwikau Village

Whakapapa Ski Area

Knollridge Cafe

Dome Shelter

Tukino Ski Area

Tukino Rd (4WD)

Pokaka

Mangaturuturu Shelter

Crater Lake

Mt Ruapehu (2797m)

Rangipo Hut

Erua Forest

Mangaturuturu Hut

Turoa Ski Area

Rangipo Desert

Round the Mountain Track

Wahianoa River

Restricted Entry Army Training Area

Horopito

Blyth Hut

Mangaehuehu Hut

Lake Moawhango

Three Kings Range

Mangawhero Camping Ground

49A

To Raetihi (5km) & Wanganui (99km)

Ohakune

Ruapehu Homestead

Rangataua Forest Conservation Area

Lake Rotokura (Karioi Lakes)

Tokiahuru Stream

Karioi Forest

Whangaehu River

Desert Rd

1

WARNING
Desert Rd may be closed in severe conditions

49

Rangataua

Karioi

Tangiwai

49

Waiouru

To Palmerston North (144km) & Wellington (265km)

Ohakune Mountain Rd

Main Trunk Railway

Auckland–Wellington

Stream

Whakapapanui

Turangi

Wairehu Canal

Desert Rd

Tongariro River

Kings Range

CENTRAL PLATEAU

Legend
Tongariro Northern Circuit
Tongariro Crossing

0 — 5 — 10km
0 — 3 — 6mi

Volcanoes

Mt Ruapehu The long, multi-peaked summit of Mt Ruapehu (2797m) is the highest and most active of the volcanoes. The upper slopes were showered with hot mud and water in the volcanic activity of 1969 and 1975, and in December 1988 the volcano threw out some hot rocks. These were just tame precursors to the spectacular eruptions of September 1995, when Ruapehu sprayed volcanic rock and emitted massive clouds of ash and steam. From June to September the following year the mountain rumbled, groaned and sent ash clouds high into the sky. The 1996 ski season was pretty much a write-off, and local businesses really felt the pinch. The locals in Ohakune set up deck chairs at the end of their main street, sipped wine and observed the mountain's antics.

These eruptions were not the worst of the century, however. Between 1945 and 1947 the level of Crater Lake rose dramatically when eruptions blocked the overflow. On Christmas Eve 1953 the overflow burst and the flood led to one of NZ's worst natural disasters. The volcanic mudflow (known as a lahar) swept away a railway bridge at Tangiwai (between Ohakune and Waiouru) moments before a crowded express train arrived and 153 people lost their lives in the resulting collision.

The 1995–96 eruption has once again blocked the overflow of Ruapehu's Crater Lake and has caused it to fill once more. Scientists recently predicted that if the lake continues to fill at its current rate, a lahar will occur sometime between late 2002 and 2005. A major lahar has the potential to cause damage to the road and rail bridges at Tangiwai, parts of State Highway 1 (SH1) and possibly spill over into the headwaters of the Tongariro River. This is the worst case scenario; the Crater Lake may just leak through the dam and trickle away. DOC has set up alarm systems at the Crater's Lake's edge to monitor its build-up so that locals and emergency teams have plenty of warning should it decide to burst its banks.

Mt Tongariro Another old, but still active, volcano is Mt Tongariro (1967m). Red Crater last erupted in 1926. It has a number of coloured lakes dotting its uneven summit as well as hot springs gushing out of its side at Ketetahi. The Tongariro Crossing (see later), a magnificent walk, passes beside the lakes, right through several craters, and down through lush native forest.

Mt Ruapehu, Tongariro National Park

PAUL KENNEDY

CENTRAL PLATEAU

Mt Ngauruhoe Much younger than the other volcanoes in the park is Mt Ngauruhoe (2287m) – it's estimated to have formed in the last 2500 years and the slopes to its summit are still perfectly symmetrical. In contrast to Ruapehu and Tongariro, which have multiple vents, Ngauruhoe is a conical, single-vent volcano. It can be climbed in summer, but in winter (under snow) it is definitely only for experienced mountaineers. It's a steep but rewarding climb.

Tongariro Northern Circuit

Classed as one of NZ's Great Walks (see The Great Walks in the Activities chapter), the Northern Circuit, which starts and finishes at Whakapapa Village (you can begin at Mangatepopo car park), normally takes three to four days to complete. The walk embraces Ngauruhoe and Tongariro and much of the famous one-day Tongariro Crossing.

Highlights of the circuit include tramping through several volcanic craters, including the **South Crater**, **Central Crater** and **Red Crater**; brilliantly colourful volcanic lakes including the **Emerald Lakes**, **Blue Lake** and the **Upper** and **Lower Tama Lakes**; the cold **Soda Springs** and **Ohinepango Springs**; and various other volcanic formations including **cones**, **lava flows** and **glacial valleys**.

There are several possibilities for side trips that take from a few hours to overnight. The most popular side trip from the main track is to Ngauruhoe summit (3 hours), but it is also possible to climb Tongariro from Red Crater (2 hours) or walk to Ohinepango Springs from New Waihohonu Hut (30 minutes).

Walking the Track The safest and most popular time to walk the track is December to March. The track is served by four huts: Mangatepopo, Ketetahi, Oturere and New Waihohonu. These have mattresses, gas heating (cookers in summer), toilets and water. Camping is allowed near all the huts.

During the full summer season (from late October to early June) a Great Walks Pass is required and must be bought in advance, whether you stay in the huts or camp beside them. Ordinary backcountry hut tickets and annual passes (see Hut & Camping Fees in the Activities chapter) cannot be used during these months. All park visitors centres sell passes ($14/18 per night prebook/at the track; $10/12 camping).

At other times, ordinary backcountry hut passes or annual passes may be used ($5/10 per night for half-ticket huts and camping). However, this track is quite different in winter, when it is covered in snow, and becomes a tough alpine trek.

Estimated walking times are:

route	time
Whakapapa Village to Mangatepopo Hut	3 hrs
Mangatepopo Hut to Emerald Lakes	3 to 4 hrs
Emerald Lakes to Ketetahi Hut	2 to 3 hrs
Emerald Lakes to Oturere Hut	1 to 2 hrs
Oturere Hut to New Waihohonu Hut	2 to 3 hrs
New Waihohonu Hut to Whakapapa Village	5 to 6 hrs

Tongariro Crossing

Often called the finest one-day walk in NZ, the Tongariro Crossing covers many of the most spectacular features of the Tongariro Northern Circuit between the Mangatepopo and Ketetahi Huts. On a clear day the views are magnificent. This is what many trampers do as day two of the Northern Circuit, with the extra walk along the Ketetahi track. Because of its popularity, shuttles are available to both ends of the track.

There are a couple of steep spots, but most of the track is not terribly difficult. However it is a long, exhausting day's walk. It's billed as a six- to seven-hour walk, but expect it to take longer if you're not in top condition. Some prefer to do it as a two-day walk, especially if side trips are included.

The track passes through vegetation zones ranging from alpine scrub and tussock, to places at higher altitudes where there is no vegetation at all, to the lush podocarp forest as you descend from Ketetahi Hut towards the end of the track.

Worthwhile side trips from the main track include ascents to the summits of Mt Ngauruhoe and Mt Tongariro. Mt Ngauruhoe can be ascended most easily from the Mangatepopo Saddle, reached near the beginning of the track after the first steep climb. The summit of Tongariro is reached by a poled route from Red Crater.

Walking the Track The Mangatepopo Hut, reached via Mangatepopo Rd, is near the start of the track, and the Ketetahi Hut is a couple of hours before the end. To stay at or camp beside either hut in summer you must have a Great Walks Pass, purchased in advance and valid from the end of October until the Queen's Birthday weekend.

The Ketetahi Hut is the most popular in the park. It has bunks to sleep 24 people, but regularly has 50 to 60 people trying to stay there on Saturday night and at the busiest times of year (summer and school holidays). As bunks are claimed on a first-come, first-served basis, it's not a bad idea to bring camping gear, just in case. Campers can use all the hut facilities (except for bunks), which can make the kitchen crowded, especially at peak times.

Estimated walking times are:

route	time
Mangatepopo Rd end to	
Mangatepopo Hut	15 mins
Mangatepopo Hut to	
Mangatepopo Saddle	1½ hrs
(Side trip) Mangatepopo	
Saddle to summit	
of Mt Ngauruhoe	3 hrs return
(Side trip) Red Crater to	
Tongariro summit	1½ hrs return
Mangatepopo Saddle to	
Emerald Lakes	1½ to 2 hrs
Emerald Lakes to	
Ketetahi Hut	2 hrs
Ketetahi Hut to road end	2 hrs

Crater Lake

When Ruapehu is volcanically active the area within 1.5km of Crater Lake is off

Track Safety

The weather on the mountains is extremely capricious – it can change from warm, brilliant sunshine to snow, hail or wind within a few minutes. Be sure to check with one of the DOC offices for current track and weather conditions before setting out. Bring a raincoat and warm woollen clothing. Take local advice seriously: they know the mountains best and it's their time, money and effort that's going to be expended getting you back safe and sound.

Accidents occur on tracks when people misjudge loose rocks or go sliding down the volcanic slopes – watch your step! On Ngauruhoe, watch out for loose scoria, and be careful not to dislodge rocks onto people coming up behind.

Essential equipment for walking in the park include:

  waterproof raincoat and overtrousers
  warm clothing
  tramping boots
  food and drink
  first aid kit
  suncream and sunglasses
  sunhat and warm hat

In winter, alpine or mountaineering experience is essential if you are walking many tracks, especially climbing peaks. If you don't know how to use ice axes, crampons and avalanche gear, do not attempt the summits.

limits; check with DOC park offices for the latest information.

The walk to Crater Lake in the crater of Ruapehu begins at Iwikau Village, at the end of the Top of the Bruce Rd above Whakapapa Village, and takes about seven hours return (four hours up, three hours down). It's definitely not an easy stroll and the track isn't marked. Even in summer there may be ice and snow to get through; in winter, forget it unless you are an experienced mountaineer. Check with the Whakapapa visitors centre for current weather conditions before you set off. Boots, sunglasses and windproofs are always essential, while ice axes and crampons may be needed.

From December to April you can use the chair lift (adult/child $15/8) at the Whakapapa Ski Area to get you up the mountain, cutting about three hours off the walk. **Guided walks** (☎ 07-892 3738 for reservations; adult/child $45/20, including lift pass) to Crater Lake go from the chair lift.

You can reach Crater Lake from the Ohakune side, but the track is steeper and ice axes and crampons are always necessary (to ascend a steep glacier). From this side, allow five hours to go up and three to go down.

Other Walks

The visitor centres at Whakapapa, Ohakune and Turangi have maps and information on interesting short and long walks in the park as well as track and weather conditions.

Keen trampers can do the entire Round-the-Mountain Track (four to six days), which circumnavigates Ruapehu. It's one of the least tramped in the park, and the terrain varies from beech forest to desert. Be sure to get a good map (such as Parkmaps No 273-04) before walking this track.

Both the Tongariro Northern Circuit and Tongariro Crossing can be reached from Mangatepopo Road off SH47.

From Whakapapa Village

A number of fine walks begin at or near the Whakapapa visitors centre and from the road leading up to it. Several other good walks take off from the road leading from Ohakune to the Turoa Ski Area (see Ohakune later). *Whakapapa Walks* ($1), published by DOC, lists walks from the visitors centre, including:

Ridge Track A 30-minute return walk, which climbs through beech forest to alpine shrub lands for views of Ruapehu and Ngauruhoe.

Silica Rapids A 2½-hour, 7km loop track to the Silica Rapids, named for the silica mineral deposits formed here by the rapids on Waikare Stream. The track passes interesting alpine features and, in the final 2½km, passes down the Top of Bruce Rd above Whakapapa Village.

Tama Lakes A 17km track to the Tama Lakes (five to six hours return). On the Tama Saddle between Ruapehu and Ngauruhoe, the Tama

Lakes are great for a refreshing swim. The upper lake affords fine views of Ngauruhoe and Tongariro (beware of winds on the saddle).

Taranaki Falls A two-hour, 6km loop track to the 20m Taranaki Falls on Wairere Stream.

Whakapapa Nature Walk A 15-minute loop track suitable for wheelchairs, beginning about 200m above the visitors centre and passing through beech forest and gardens typical of the park's vegetation zones.

North of Whakapapa Village Still more tracks take off from SH47, on the national park's north side, including:

Lake Rotoaira On the shores of Lake Rotoaira, on the northern side of the park, are excavations of a pre-European Maori village site.

Mahuia Rapids About 2km north of the turn-off leading to Whakapapa, SH47 crosses the Whakapapanui Stream just below the rapids.

Matariki Falls A 20-minute return track to the falls takes off from SH47 about 200m from the Mahuia Rapids car park.

Skiing

The two main ski areas are the Whakapapa Ski Area (1630m), above Whakapapa Village, and the Turoa Ski Area, to the south near Ohakune. The Tukino Ski Area is on the eastern side of Ruapehu, only accessible by a 4WD road. The only accommodation at the ski fields is in private lodges, so most skiers stay at Whakapapa Village, National Park township or Ohakune. One pass is valid for both Whakapapa and Turoa. See Skiing in the Activities chapter or check **w** www.whakapapa.co.nz.

Other Activities

The Grand Chateau in Whakapapa has a public nine-hole golf course and tennis courts and hires out golf clubs, tennis rackets etc. Even if you can't afford to stay at the hotel, stop in for a drink in the lobby just to savour the atmosphere.

Mountain Air (☎ 0800 922 812; flights from $70), with an office on SH47 near the SH48 turn-off to Whakapapa, has flights over the volcanoes.

Plateau Outdoor Adventure Guides (☎ 0508 752 832), based at Raurimu 6km north of National Park township, offers a wide variety of activities around Tongariro and the Whanganui River. These include canoeing, white-water rafting, horse riding, mountaineering, tramping and ski-touring.

Places to Stay

Within the park, Whakapapa Village has an expensive hotel, a motel and a motor camp. Also in the park are two DOC camping grounds (near National Park and Ohakune) and huts, accessible only by walking tracks. Prices quoted here are for summer; rates are much higher in winter. National Park, Ohakune and Turangi are towns near the park (see those sections later in this chapter).

Camping & Cabins There are two basic DOC camping grounds in the park with cold water and pit toilets; the cost is low ($4) and you place your money in an honesty box.

The *Mangahuia Camping Ground* is on SH47, between National Park and the SH48 turn-off heading to Whakapapa. The *Mangawhero Camping Ground (Ohakune Mountain Rd)* is near Ohakune.

Whakapapa Holiday Park (☎/fax 07-892 3897) Unpowered/powered sites $8/10 per person, backpacker's lodge $16.50 per person, cabins $35, tourist flats $55. This popular park is up the road from the Grand Chateau, opposite the visitors centre. It's in a pretty spot and couldn't be more conveniently located.

Scattered around the park's tramping tracks are nine *huts*, with foot access only. It costs $10 to stay in huts, $5 for camping beside the huts, with backcountry hut tickets and annual hut passes both acceptable. However, in the summer season a Great Walks Pass is required for the four Tongariro Northern Circuit huts: Ketetahi, Mangatepopo, New Waihohonu and Oturere. Pre-booked huts/camping cost $14/10, non pre-booked cost $18/12.

All park visitor centres have information on huts and can sell hut tickets or Great Walks Passes. Howard's Lodge at National Park sells DOC hut tickets.

Motels & Hotels Both these accommodation options are at Whakapapa Village.

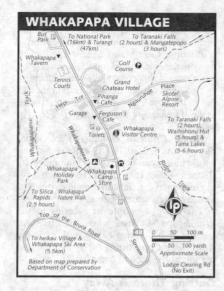

Skotel Alpine Resort (☎ 07-892 3719, e skotel@clear.net.nz) Beds in hostel rooms $20-35, standard rooms $70-110, chalets $90-175, deluxe rooms $90-135. This hotel is well equipped with a communal kitchen for the regular rooms (you provide crockery and cutlery), as well as a sauna, spa pool, gym, games room and a licensed restaurant and bar. Prices increase during peak winter and summer periods.

Grand Chateau Hotel (☎ 07-892 3809, e reservations@chateau.co.nz) Economy rooms $125, standard rooms $155, premium rooms $195, suites $450, single/double chalets $147/175. This is indeed a grand hotel, with 63 rooms, an executive suite and nine chalets. Apart from the Hermitage at Mt Cook, it is the best-known hotel in NZ. Built in 1929 in an opulent style, it has been well preserved and is priced accordingly. Discount packages are sometimes available.

Places to Eat

Whakapapa Village is your best bet for food.

The *Whakapapa Camp Store* sells a range of takeaway snacks and food for self-catering. As usual it's more expensive from a store than a supermarket.

CENTRAL PLATEAU

Ferguson's Cafe Light meals $7.50. Open 8am-3pm. Ferguson's is reasonably priced for snacks, light meals and coffee.

Pihanga Cafe Mains $13.50-19. Tucked away in the side of the Grand Chateau by the main road is this convivial establishment.

The *Skotel* has a licensed restaurant and bar in the evenings only, and the restaurant at the *Whakapapa Tavern* only does food in winter.

Grand Chateau Hotel (*see Places to Stay*) Mains $23-30. If you prefer something a little more grandiose, this is your place. Its Ruapehu Room is an elegant restaurant serving expensive a la carte meals; the $20 Sunday lunch buffet is good value.

There are a couple of eateries at the Whakapapa Ski Area, where the lifts start, but the high point of eating options is the *Knollridge Cafe*, sitting pretty at 2020m at the top of the second chair lift.

Getting There & Away
Bus & Train Trains and InterCity buses stop at National Park, the main gateway to Tongariro.

Alpine Scenic Tours (☎ 07-386 8918) has an inexpensive shuttle departing from Taupo (6.30am) to Whakapapa Village (arriving 8.25am) via Turangi (7.30am), Ketetahi car park (end of the Tongariro Crossing) and Mangatepopo car park (for the Tongariro Crossing). There are various shuttles running between Turangi, Whakapapa Village and National Park township during the day, and it goes up to the ski area at the Top of the Bruce by request. Since seats are limited, book in advance to guarantee a spot. Tongariro Expeditions (☎ 07-377 0435, **W** www.thetongarirocrossing.co.nz) is another option, specialising in the Tongariro Crossing and with buses departing from Taupo and Turangi.

From National Park township other shuttles run to Whakapapa, Mangatepopo and Ketetahi for the Tongariro Crossing (see the National Park section). Transport is also available from Ohakune (see that section).

Car & Motorcycle The park is encircled by roads. SH1 (at this point it's called the Desert Road) passes down the eastern side of the park, SH4 passes down the western side, SH46 and SH47 cross the northern side and SH49 crosses the southern side. The main road up into the park is SH48, which leads to Whakapapa Village, continuing further up the mountain to the Top of the Bruce and the Whakapapa Ski Area. Ohakune Mountain Rd leads up to the Turoa Ski Area from Ohakune in the south-west.

For the Tongariro Crossing, access is from the end of Mangatepopo Rd off SH47, and SH46 from the end of Ketetahi Rd off National Park Rd (between SH1 and SH47). Theft from parked vehicles is a problem at both ends: don't leave valuables in the car.

NATIONAL PARK
pop 460
At the gateway to Tongariro, this small settlement is at the junction of SH4 and SH47, 15km from Whakapapa Village. It caters to the ski season crowds, with plenty of accommodation but little else apart from great views of Ruapehu. In the summer season it's one of the best bases for the walks and attractions of the park. Several daily shuttles leave from here to the start of the Tongariro Crossing and the Whakapapa Village in summer, and the ski area in winter. It is also a base for other ventures, such as canoe trips on the Whanganui River.

A few kilometres south on SH4 at Horopito is a monument to the Last Spike – the spike that marked the completion of the Main Trunk Railway Line between Auckland and Wellington in 1908.

Activities
Howard's Lodge, Pukenui Lodge and the Ski Haus hire out tramping boots and other gear for the Tongariro Crossing and other treks. The spa pools at Ski Haus and Pukenui Lodge can be hired by non-guests as well.

Howard's Lodge takes **guided mountain bike tours** (*see Places to Stay later; from $30 for 2 hours*) and also provides transport and bike hire for the **42nd Traverse**, an excellent 46km mountain-bike trail through the Tongariro Forest, classed among the best one-day rides in NZ.

Go For It Tours *(☎ 07-892 2705; tours $85)*, at the Petticoat Junction building, which is also the train station, does guided off-road motorcycle tours. **Pete Outdoors** *(☎ 07-895 4445; 1-hr bike hire $10, guided trips from $25)* rents mountain bikes and will take guided bike trips.

Horse trekking can be arranged through **Tussock Trekkers** *(☎ 07-892 2711)* or **John Smythe** *(☎ 07-895 4401, Owhango; 2-hr trek $35)*. Treks range from one hour rides to overnight excursions.

For those rainy days there's an 8m-high indoor **climbing wall** *(☎ 07-892 2870, Finlay St; entry $10, $8 with own gear; open 9am-9pm daily)* at National Park Backpackers.

See Whanganui National Park in the Wanganui & Manawatu chapter for details on canoe hire and operators on the Whanganui River.

Places to Stay

Prices increase dramatically in the ski season, when accommodation is tight and bookings are essential, especially on weekends. The prices below are for the summer.

Hostels Backpackers in National Park are well set up for walkers and skiers.

Howard's Lodge (☎/fax 07-892 2827, e howards.nat.park@xtra.co.nz, Carroll St) Dorm beds $18, quads $19, doubles & twins $50, deluxe doubles & twins $70, triples $65, 4-person suites $100. Howard's Lodge is an excellent place with a spa pool, ski hire, comfortable lounge and spotless, well-equipped kitchens. Standard rooms have made-up beds, and deluxe rooms have their own bathrooms. Breakfast is available from $7 (continental) to $12 (fully cooked).

Pukenui Lodge (☎ 0800 785 368, 07-892 2882, e pukenuilodge@xtra.co.nz, Millar St) Tent & campervan sites $8 per person, quads $16-20, doubles & twins $50-65, chalets $80. The modern Pukenui has a variety of rooms and campers are also catered for. There is a spa, a kitchen and a restaurant, as well as Internet access. The lodge sells lift passes and organises Tongariro track transport, Whanganui River canoeing and trout fishing.

Ski Haus (☎ 07-892 2854, e skihaus@ xtra.co.nz, Carroll St) Tent sites $10 per person, dorms $15, doubles & twins $40. Ski Haus has a spa pool, billiards table and a sunken fireplace in the large lounge. There is also a house bar, a restaurant and a kitchen. Rooms are simple but comfortable.

Plateau Lodge (☎ 0800 861 861, 07-892 2993, e plateaulodge@xtra.co.nz, Carroll St) Dorm beds $15, twins & doubles $40, motel units from $60 per double. This older-style ski lodge has a large lounge area and comfortable rooms.

National Park Backpackers (☎/fax 07-892 2870, e nat.park.backpackers@xtra .co.nz, Finlay St) Dorm beds $15, quads $18, en suite doubles $40. This welcoming backpackers is next to Schnapps. The big attraction is the climbing wall (see Activities earlier).

Bushline Lodge (☎ 07-895 4518, fax 895 4581, Owhango Rd) Beds from $18. This lodge, 21km north of National Park on SH4 at Owhango, has comfortable accommodation with full kitchen and laundry facilities.

Chalets, Motels & Hotels Motel and hotel accommodation options are rather limited in the area.

Mountain Heights Lodge (☎/fax 07-892 2833, e mountainheights@xtra.co.nz) Motel units single/double $55/70, B&B per double from $90. This welcoming lodge on SH4, 2km south of National Park, has self-contained motel units and also does B&B. Meals are available by arrangement, and there's a cosy licensed cafe on the premises.

Discovery Motel (☎ 07-892 2744, fax 892 2603) Campsites $10, cabins from $25, units from $66. This park is on SH47, between National Park and Whakapapa. It has a spa pool, a restaurant and bar.

Places to Eat

All the places to stay in National Park provide either meals, kitchens or both for their guests.

Schnapps (☎ 07-892 2788, Findlay St) Burgers $5-8, pizzas $7-12, meals $11-16. Schnapps is a congenial place for a drink and/or a meal. There are excellent pizzas, burgers, steaks, seafood and more. There are often bands on Saturday night in winter.

The bar and restaurant at the *Ski Haus* are open to guests and non-guests in winter; and there is a licensed cafe at *Mountain Heights Lodge*.

Getting There & Away

Bus InterCity buses arrive at and depart from outside Ski Haus on Carroll St daily except Saturday. Buy tickets at Ski Haus and Howard's Lodge. Journeys north to Auckland via Hamilton or south to Wellington via Palmerston North take about five hours.

Alpine Scenic Tours (☎ 07-386 8918) has several daily shuttles making a round trip between Turangi and National Park, with stops at Whakapapa Village, Whakapapa Ski Area by request, the Mangatepopo and Ketetahi car parks (Tongariro Crossing), and on from Turangi to Taupo. For the track ends, make sure you arrange transport beforehand, as there are no phones at the trail heads.

Tongariro Track Transport (☎ 07-892 3716) operates a daily shuttle from National Park to the Mangatepopo car park, stopping at Whakapapa Village on the way ($15 return). Howard's Lodge (see Places to Stay) also runs a shuttle for the Crossing. Bookings are essential.

Train Some trains (☎ 0800 802 802) running between Auckland and Wellington stop at National Park. *Interislander* ferry tickets and train tickets are sold not from the train station, but from Ski Haus or Howard's Lodge, both on Carroll St.

Air Mountain Air (☎ 0800 922 812) flies between Auckland airport and Mt Ruapehu (from around $200 same-day return per person) during the ski season.

OHAKUNE
☎ 06 • pop 1490
Pretty Ohakune is the closest town to the Turoa Ski Area, on the southern side of Ruapehu. During the ski season a lot of effort goes into catering for those who've come to enjoy the snow, but visitors are discovering that there is plenty to do at

other times, including hiking, canoeing, white-water rafting and horse riding.

Ohakune's main commercial district is to the south of the town on the highway. The northern end of town by the train station (known as the 'junction') comes alive during the ski season but is quiet otherwise.

Check out the Big Carrot on SH49, paying homage to the town's primary product. Kids like the tank in the Clyde St park.

Information
The Ruapehu visitors centre (☎ 06-385 8427), 54 Clyde St, has an excellent 3-D model of Tongariro National Park – great for tracing where you're going to walk. The staff make bookings for activities and accommodation, for InterCity buses, the *Interislander* ferry, and for the train. It's open from 9am to 5pm Monday to Friday and until 3.30pm on weekends.

The Ohakune Field Centre (☎ 06-385 0010) is on Ohakune Mountain Rd, which leads to Turoa. It's open from 8am to 3pm daily and from 8am to 5pm during school holidays and public holiday weekends. It has maps, weather reports and advice about this side of the Tongariro National Park.

The Turoa Ski Area operates a phone line (☎ 06-385 8456) with information on ski and road conditions.

Walking
Ohakune Mountain Rd travels 17km from the northern end of Ohakune to the Turoa Ski Area on Ruapehu. Several walking tracks lead off it into the national park. Stop by the Ohakune Field Centre for maps and information about the tracks. Weather on the mountains is highly changeable, so be prepared and let someone know your itinerary.

Two of the most delightful walks are the short 15-minute **Rimu Track** and the longer one-hour **Mangawhero Forest Walk**, both departing from opposite the Field Centre and both passing through a lovely section of native forest. The Rimu Track is marked with plaques pointing out various features of the forest.

Other popular tracks leading from Ohakune Mountain Rd include a 1½-hour

CENTRAL PLATEAU

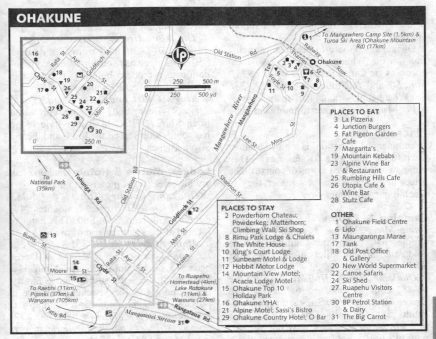

OHAKUNE

PLACES TO EAT
3 La Pizzeria
4 Junction Burgers
5 Fat Pigeon Garden Cafe
7 Margarita's
19 Mountain Kebabs
23 Alpine Wine Bar & Restaurant
25 Rumbling Hills Cafe
26 Utopia Cafe & Wine Bar
28 Stutz Cafe

PLACES TO STAY
2 Powderhorn Chateau; Powderkeg; Matterhorn; Climbing Wall; Ski Shop
8 Rimu Park Lodge & Chalets
9 The White House
10 King's Court Lodge
11 Sunbeam Motel & Lodge
12 Hobbit Motor Lodge
14 Mountain View Motel; Acacia Lodge Motel
15 Ohakune Top 10 Holiday Park
16 Ohakune YHA
21 Alpine Motel; Sassi's Bistro
29 Ohakune Country Hotel; O Bar

OTHER
1 Ohakune Field Centre
6 Lido
13 Maungaronga Marae
17 Tank
18 Old Post Office & Gallery
20 New World Supermarket
22 Canoe Safaris
24 Ski Shed
27 Ruapehu Visitors Centre
30 BP Petrol Station & Dairy
31 The Big Carrot

return walk to the **Waitonga Falls**, beginning 11km past the Field Centre, and the five-hour return walk to **Lake Surprise**, beginning 4km further on. If you continue past the falls on Waitonga Falls track, you join the Round-the-Mountain Track (see the Tongariro National Park section later). Other tracks taking off from Ohakune Mountain Rd include a 10-minute return walk to the **Mangawhero Falls** and a four- to five-hour walk on the **Old Blyth Track**. Pick up the handy DOC brochure *Ohakune Walks and Mountain Rd* ($1) from the Ruapehu visitors centre or Field centre.

Transport up the mountain can be arranged through **Snowliner Shuttle** (☎ 06-385 8573) or **Snow Express** (☎ 06-385 9280; winter only). Expect to pay about $8 one way or $12 return. Or you could go to the top with a bicycle (see Cycling) and do some tramping on your way down. Transport to Tongariro Crossing can be arranged through the **Ohakune Top 10 Holiday Park**

(☎ 0800 825 825; $25 return, minimum 2 people) or the **Ski Shed** (☎ 06-385 8887).

Cycling

Hire bikes at the **Powderhorn Ski Shop** (☎ 06-385 8888; bike hire per hr/½ day/day $10/25/35), at Powderhorn Chateau. The **Ski Shed** (☎ 06-385 8887, Clyde St) hires out mountain bikes for the same prices. A highly enjoyable way to do some cycling in Ohakune is to go with **Ron Rutherford** (☎ 06-385 8257). In summer you go by van to the ski area at the top of Ohakune Mountain Rd and are set loose with a bicycle, helmet and all the gear you'll need ($30).

Bicycles are not allowed on any trails in the national park.

Other Activities

Ask at the visitors centre about activities around Ohakune – horse trekking, golf, white-water rafting, fishing, canoeing, kayaking and jetboat trips on the nearby

Whanganui River, and more. You can swim in the Powderkeg restaurant-bar's indoor hot pool.

Ohakune is a base to organise canoeing trips on the Whanganui River. Two local operators are **Canoe Safaris** (☎ *06-385 9237, Miro St*), and **Yeti Tours** (☎ *0800 322 388*). See Whanganui National Park in the Wanganui & Manawatu chapter for more details.

Places to Stay

In summer the 'junction' is a bit of a ghost town, so it may pay to stay near SH49 (unless you like ghost towns of course). The prices listed below are for summer; they're much higher in winter.

Camping & Cabins The *Mangawhero Camp Site (Ohakune Mountain Rd)* is a simple DOC camp site. Facilities include cold water and pit toilets. Camp sites cost adult/child \$4/2.

Ohakune Top 10 Holiday Park (☎/*fax 06-385 8561*, e *ohakune_holiday_park@ xtra.co.nz, 5 Moore St)* Sites \$10 per person, cabins \$35-46, units \$50-75. This is a pleasant camp beside a gurgling stream, with plenty of trees and green areas and a comfortable TV lounge/dining room. There's also a mini golf course.

Hostels Places fill up quickly over winter, so it pays to book ahead.

Ohakune YHA (☎/*fax 06-385 8724, Clyde St)* Dorm beds \$19, doubles & twins from \$46. This hostel is near the bus stop and visitors centre. It's a good place with twins, triples and bunkrooms; guests have their own room key. It's only open from June to October.

Rimu Park Lodge & Chalets (☎/*fax 06-385 9023*, e *rimulodg@ihug.co.nz, 27 Rimu St)* Dorms \$16-30, doubles \$36-70, cabins \$40-70, chalets & units \$75-260. This is a comfortable, restored 1914 villa in a secluded spot just two minutes' walk from the train station, restaurants and nightlife. It's quiet and restful in summer and very popular with skiers in winter. There are also chalets and units next to the house (all sleep 10). The three quaint restored train

carriages cost the same as the chalets. Rates vary depending on the season.

The White House (☎/*fax 06-385 8413, 22 Rimu St)* Dorm beds from \$25, doubles \$50. This place has comfortable accommodation in a modern building. Breakfast is available, and there's a nice spa.

King's Court Lodge (☎ *06-385 8648, Rimu St)* Dorm beds with own/provided linen \$17/27. This old, Tudor-style lodge has rooms with shared facilities, and there's also a kitchen.

Lodges, Motels & Hotels Ohakune has a wide selection of motels and hotels.

Ohakune Country Hotel (☎ *06-385 8268, 72 Clyde St)* Singles & doubles \$40, doubles with bath from \$60. This hotel is located at the southern end of town.

Alpine Motel (☎/*fax 06-385 8758*, e *alp ine.motel@xtra.co.nz, 7 Miro St)* Dorm beds \$15, double units \$75. The Alpine is a popular place, with studio units, family units, and a good backpackers in the rear, plus a spa pool and a popular restaurant-bar.

Mountain View Motel (☎ *0800 688 439, 06-385 8675*, e *mountain-view@xtra.co .nz, 2 Moore St)* Cabins \$15 per person, units from \$50. This motel also has cabins (no linen) with shared communal facilities. It is also located at the southern end of town.

Acacia Lodge Motel (☎ *0800 888 385, 06-385 8729, fax 385 8347, 4 Moore St)* Units without/with kitchens \$70/80. Acacia is next door to the Mountain View. The owner is very knowledgeable about walks in the National Park.

Hobbit Motor Lodge (☎ *0800 843 462, 06-385 8248, fax 385 8515, cnr Goldfinch & Wye Sts)* Bunk beds \$20, motel units \$65-95. This place is located between the southern and northern ends of town. It has a licensed restaurant.

Sunbeam Motel & Lodge (☎ *06-385 8470, fax 385 8662, 4 Foyle St)* Units from \$65. Sunbeam's units have kitchen facilities, and there are spa pools.

Powderhorn Chateau (☎ *06-385 8888*, e *powderhorn@xtra.co.nz, cnr Thames St & Mangawharo St)* Chalet doubles \$135. Top of the heap is the Powderhorn, *the* place to be for apres-ski, with a bar, restaurant and heated pool.

***Ruapehu Homestead** (☎/fax 06-385 8799, 1 Piwari St)* Singles/doubles $60/80. Four kilometres east of Ohakune on SH49 at Rangataua is Ruapehu Homestead. It has a variety of fancy rooms, a licensed restaurant and a pleasant, rural setting; it also organises horse riding (from $25) through the Rangataua Forest.

Places to Eat

The 'junction' is active during the winter with the apres-ski crowd, but little is open in summer. Many places to stay also open restaurants during the ski season.

***Stutz Cafe** (Clyde St)* Breakfast $7, pizzas up to $12. On the south side, this pleasant cafe has European food, pizza and takeaways. Nearby, the *O Bar* at the Ohakune Country Hotel is also open for long hours and has a better class of pub food.

***Utopia Cafe & Wine Bar** (☎ 06-385 9120, 47 Clyde St)* Light meals around $9. This relaxed cafe serves focaccia, panini, bagels, cake, big breakfasts and good coffee.

***Rumbling Hills Cafe** (☎ 06-385 9292, Clyde St)* Light meals from $5. This large, open cafe has a good selection of sandwiches and cheap lunches.

***Mountain Kebabs** (☎ 06-385 9047, 29 Clyde St)* Kebabs from $7. For filling takeaway kebabs head here, unless it's summer, when it's closed.

***Alpine Wine Bar & Restaurant** (☎ 06-385 9183, cnr Clyde & Miro Sts)* Mains $9-28. Alpine is open for wining and dining every evening.

***Sassi's Bistro** (See Alpine Motel in Places to Stay)* Mains around $20. Open for dinner daily. Sassi's is a pleasant place with a varied, changing menu and welcoming owners.

There are many popular restaurants along Thames St that are open over winter, including *La Pizzeria*, which does reasonable pizza, *Junction Burgers*, for a late-night hunger buster (about $7), and *Margarita's*, with Tex-Mex food on the go.

The *Powderkeg* and the *Matterhorn*, both restaurant-bars on the corner of Thames St and Mangawhero Terrace within the Powderhorn Chateau, are favourite apres-ski hang-outs.

***Fat Pigeon Garden Cafe** (☎ 06-385 9423, 2 Tyne St)* Mains $16-25. A renovated house is home to this quality cafe. It has pleasant seating indoor or outside in the garden, and plenty of choice on the menu.

Entertainment

Ohakune is known as a good-fun nightlife place during the ski season; the rest of the year it's quiet. Get hold of the gig guide, available from the visitors centre and most lodges.

***Lido** (Thames St)* This nightclub is a popular spot, open every night during the ski season, with live music on weekends and disco music on other nights (in winter it attracts some big-name bands).

Other places that present live music in the ski season include the eternally popular *Powderkeg*, *Margarita's* at the 'junction', and the *O Bar (Clyde St)* at the Ohakune Country Hotel, in the southern part of town.

Getting There & Away

InterCity buses serve Ohakune daily except Saturday; they arrive at and depart from outside Mountain Kebabs. The town is on the bus route from Auckland to Wellington via Taumarunui.

Auckland-Wellington trains (☎ 0800 802 802) stop at Ohakune. Buy tickets at the Ruapehu visitors centre, not at the station.

Getting Around

In winter several companies have transport between Ohakune and the Turoa Ski Area, charging around $12 for return door-to-door transport from wherever you're staying.

Snowliner Shuttle (☎ 06-385 8573) and Snow Express (☎ 06-385 9280) offer a variety of transport around the area.

RAETIHI

☎ 06 • pop 1070

Only 11km west of Ohakune and 26km east of Pipiriki, the small town of Raetihi makes a handy base for both the Tongariro and Whanganui National Parks. The enthusiastic Raetihi visitors centre (☎ 06-385 4805), at

48 Seddon St, has details on activities and a list of farmstays and B&Bs to suit all budgets. It's open from 9.30am to 4.30pm Monday to Friday and 1pm to 4.30pm on Sunday.

Kiwi Encounters (☎ *025 535 456; adult/child $35/20*) arrange night excursions to the Waimarino Forest in an attempt to spot the elusive kiwi from late October to mid-April. Bookings are essential.

Raetihi Holiday Park (☎ *06-385 4176, Parapara Rd*) Sites $10 per person, cabins $50. This camp ground has only a small number of cabins.

NZ Police Ski Club (☎ *06-385 4003, 35 Queen St*) Beds $12. Backpackers will like this comfortable lodge, which has a spa in winter. There are four doubles, one single and dorms. Duvets and pillows are supplied.

Country Classic Lodge (☎ *06-385 4511, 14 Ameku Rd*) Rooms with breakfast $50 per person. This lovely Victorian villa has a restaurant and bar.

LAKE ROTOKURA

About 11km south-east of Ohakune, on SH49, is Lake Rotokura, at Karioi in the Karioi Forest. It's called Lake Rotokura on the map and the sign but it's actually two lakes not one – the locals call them the Karioi Lakes (Karioi means 'places to linger'). It's a beautiful spot. The round-trip walk only takes an hour: be aware that the top lake is *tapu* (sacred) to Maori which means no eating, fishing or swimming at the lake.

WAIOURU
☎ 06 • pop 2600

At the junction of SH1 and SH49, 27km east of Ohakune, Waiouru is primarily an army base. In a large, grey concrete building with tanks out the front, the **Army Museum Waiouru** (☎ *06-387 6911; adult/child $8/5; open 9am-4.30pm daily*) tells the history of the NZ army in times of war and peace, with an extensive collection of artefacts from early colonial times to the present, and an audiovisual presentation.

SH1 from Waiouru to Turangi is known as the Desert Road and is often closed in winter because of snow, but it can also close at other times of the year. It runs through the Rangipo Desert east of Ruapehu. It's not a true desert, but was named because of its desert-like appearance, caused by a cold, exposed and windswept location.

Lake Taupo Region

New Zealand's largest lake, Lake Taupo, is in the very heart of the North Island. Some 606 sq km in area and 357m above sea level, the lake was formed by one of the greatest volcanic explosions of all time (see the boxed text 'Bang!' later in this chapter). The surrounding area is still volcanically active and, like Rotorua, has thermal areas.

Today, serene Lake Taupo is proclaimed as the world's trout-fishing capital. If you thought those trout in the Rotorua springs looked large and tasty, they're nothing compared to the monsters found in Lake Taupo. All NZ's rainbow trout descend from a single batch of eggs brought from California's Russian River nearly a century ago. International trout-fishing tournaments are held on Lake Taupo each year on the Anzac Day long weekend (on or around 25 April).

TAUPO
pop 21,040

Taupo lies on the north-eastern corner of Lake Taupo and has scenic views across the lake to the volcanic peaks of Tongariro National Park. With a long list of attractions in close proximity to the town and a plethora of activities (ranging from fishing and boating on the lake to adrenaline-pumping bungy jumping and skydiving) it's no wonder Taupo is on most travellers' itineraries.

Lake Taupo is also the source of NZ's longest river, the Waikato, which leaves the lake at the township, flows through the Huka Falls and the Aratiatia Rapids, and then through the heart of the northern part of North Island to the west coast just south of Auckland.

History

Back in the mists of time, the Maori chief Tamatea-arikinui visited the area, noticed that the ground felt hollow and his footsteps

CENTRAL TAUPO

PLACES TO STAY
2 190 Spa Rd
3 Berkenhoff Lodge
4 Continental Motel
5 Rainbow Lodge
7 Burke's Backpackers
13 Taupo Motor Camp
28 Go Global
30 Taupo Central Backpackers
38 Action Down Under
39 Bradshaw's B&B
40 Dunrovin Motel
41 Chandlers Lodge

PLACES TO EAT
6 Walnut Keep
11 Santorini
19 Villino Restaurant & Wine Bar; Starlight Cinema Centre
21 Pasta Mia
23 Verdi's
25 Replete Deli & Cafe
26 Italian Cafe; Rockefeller Cocktail Bar & Brasserie; Hobler; Wildflame & Kazbar
31 Holy Cow; Nonni's; Taupo Rod & Tackle; Asian Noodle House

32 JJ's Cafe;Aqaba
35 Finch's Brasserie & Bar
36 Cajun-Kiwi
37 Seoul House Korean Restaurant
43 The Brantry

OTHER
1 Taupo Bungy
8 Pak N Save
9 Taupo Travel Centre
10 Dive Inn
12 Woolworths
14 Launch Office & Harbour

15 Taupo Regional Museum & Art Gallery
16 Taupo Visitors Centre; Great Lake Centre
17 Automobile Association (AA)
18 James Holiday Shoppe
20 Budget Travel
22 Super Loo
24 Fly & Gun Shop
27 Finn MacCuhal's
29 Sugar Club; Gravity
33 Internet Outpost
34 Top Cabs
42 Taupo Mini-golf

CENTRAL PLATEAU

seemed to reverberate, and called the place Tapuaeharuru (Resounding Footsteps). Another source of the name comes from the story that Tia, who discovered the lake, slept by it draped in his cloak, and it became known as Taupo-nui-a-Tia (The Great Cloak of Tia). Taupo, as it became known, was first occupied by Europeans as a military outpost during the East Coast Land War (1868–72). Colonel JM Roberts built a redoubt in 1869 and a garrison of mounted police remained there until the defeat of the rebel warrior Te Kooti (see the boxed text in the East Coast chapter) later that year.

In the 1870s the government bought the land from the Maori. Taupo has grown slowly and sedately from a lakeside village of about 750 in 1945 to a large resort town, with the population swelling considerably at peak holiday times. The town is on the lakefront where SH1, the main road from the north, first meets the lake.

Information

The Taupo visitors centre (☎ 07-376 0027, W www.laketauponz.com), on Tongariro St, handles bookings for all accommodation, transport and activities in the area. It has a

Bang!

The Taupo region's *really* big eruption was about 25,000 years ago – that was the one that actually created the huge basin now filled by Lake Taupo. The eruption produced an estimated 800 cubic kilometres of ash. The North Island would have been devastated, coated with hot, poisonous ash tens of metres thick. Even the Chatham Islands (800km downwind) copped a 10cm-deep layer!

More recently, in AD 181, accounts of darkened skies and spectacular sunsets were recorded in China and Rome – the effects of another Taupo explosion. This was the world's most powerful eruption in historical times and it's bloody lucky NZ was still uninhabited: about 30 cubic kilometres of ash and pumice was ejected in just a few minutes, shooting out across the land at speeds up to 900km/h and laying waste to the unfortunate fauna and flora as far away as Rotorua, Gisborne and Napier.

good, free town map as well as Department of Conservation (DOC) maps and information. The centre is open from 8.30am to 5pm daily.

The Super Loo nearby is a large shower-toilet complex, with showers for $1 (for four minutes) and towels for $1.

The Automobile Association (AA; ☎ 07-378 6000) is at 93 Tongariro St. The post office is on the corner of Horomatangi and Ruapehu Sts – it exchanges money on Saturday mornings.

Internet access is available at Internet Outpost on Tuwharetoa St.

Things to See

Taupo's main attractions, such as Wairakei Park and thermal regions, are north of town. In town, near the visitors centre, the **Taupo Regional Museum & Art Gallery** (☎ *07-378 4167, Story Place; admission by gold coin donation; open 10.30am-4.30pm daily)* has many historical photos and memento's of the 'old days' around Lake Taupo, including Maori carvings, a moa skeleton and a rundown on the trout industry.

In the middle of the Waikato River, off Spa Rd and not far from the centre of town, **Cherry Island** (☎ *07-378 9028; adult/child $8.50/3; open 9am-5pm daily)* is a small, low-key trout and wildlife park with a cafe. The wildlife consists of a few goats, pigs, pheasants, ducks etc. The kids might like it but admission is steep. The island is reached by a footbridge.

Further out, on Spa Rd next to the Spa Hotel, **Spa Dinosaur Valley** *(Taupo & Wairakei map;* ☎ *07-378 4120; adult/child $5/3; open 10am-4pm daily)* is Taupo's answer to Jurassic Park, with giant, concrete dinosaurs.

Acacia Bay, a pleasant, peaceful beach, is a little over 5km west of Taupo.

Activities

Thermal Pools & Climbing Walls The **AC Baths** at the Taupo Events Centre *(Taupo & Wairakei map;* ☎ *07-376 0350; adult/child $4/2; 8am-9pm daily)* at the top of Spa Rd, about 2km east of town, has a big, heated pool with a waterslide, private mineral pools and a sauna. Use of the saunas/waterslide costs $4/3. There is also a **climbing wall** *(adult/child $13/11; open 5pm-9pm Mon-Fri, noon-6pm Sat & Sun).* The cost includes a harness and ropes.

The **Taupo Hot Springs** *(Taupo & Wairakei map;* ☎ *07-377 6052, Taupo-Napier Highway (SH5); adult/child $8/2.50, private pools $9 per person; open 7.30am-9.30pm daily)* is 1km from the lake. There are large outdoor pools, a big, hot waterslide, private pools, massages and beauty therapies to relax with.

Fishing The Taupo region is world famous for its trout fly fishing. Fly fishing is the only fishing you can do on all rivers flowing into the lake, and within a 300m radius of the river mouths. Spin fishing is allowed on the Waikato River (flowing *out* of the lake) and on the Tokaanu tailrace, flowing into the lake from the Tokaanu Power Station. Several fly-fishing guides operate around Taupo, some of whom are very good. The price of around $250 a day, everything included, is reasonable when you consider you are paying for years of local knowledge.

An alternative way to experience the thrill of catching your own dinner is to take a boat out on the lake. A number of fishing guides and charter boats operate in Taupo; check with the visitors centre or head to the **launch office** (☎ 07-378 3444), where boats can be hired. Trips generally start at $65 per hour for a boat taking up to six people and going up to around $130 per hour for the larger boats. A minimum of two to three hours is required. Both spin fishing and fly fishing are allowed on the lake.

The backpackers also book fishing-boat trips. Count on a fishing trip lasting around two or three hours. If you go on a boat trip they'll supply all the gear and organise a fishing licence.

If you're going to do it on your own, **Taupo Rod & Tackle** (☎ 07-378 5337, 7 Tongariro St) by the waterfront, and the **Fly & Gun Shop** (☎ 07-378 4449, 34 Heu Heu St), have fishing tackle for hire.

Fishing licences are available from the visitors centre or the launch office. Licences for fishing on Lake Taupo and the nearby rivers cost $12.50/27/37/58 per day/week/month/year.

Make sure you always have your fishing licence and obey the rules listed on it when fishing – there are huge fines for violations. See the boxed text 'It's a Trout's Life' later in this chapter.

Water Sports The **Acacia Bay Lodge** (☎ 07-378 6830, 868 Acacia Bay Rd; motorboat hire $24 per hour, row boat, canoe & kayak hire $12 per hour), 5km west of Taupo in Acacia Bay, hires out motorboats, rowing boats, canoes and kayaks. It takes an hour from there in a motorboat to reach the Maori rock carvings.

The **Sailing Centre** (☎ 025 967 350) at Two Mile Bay, south of Taupo, hires out Canadian canoes and kayaks ($20), windsurfers (from $25), catamarans and sailboats (both from $40) in summer.

Kayaking is a popular way to enjoy the lake and river; **Kayak New Zealand** (☎ 0800 529 256, W www.kayaknz.com) has two-

hour guided trips ($20) on the Waikato River, while **Kayaking Kiwi** (☎ 0800 529 255, W www.kayakingkiwi.com) does half-day trips ($75) on the lake, including a launch cruise.

During summer there are lots of activities on Lake Taupo, including swimming, water-skiing, windsurfing, paragliding and sailing. The visitors centre has details. Gear can be hired at the lakefront.

Several white-water rafting companies offer one-day trips on the Tongariro and Rangitaiki Rivers, and longer trips on other rivers (from grades II to IV). Book these trips through the hostels or the Taupo visitors centre. (See Other Activities in the later Turangi section for details of rafting companies.) The float trips on local rivers such as the Waikato are ideal for children.

Popular and a little different is drift scuba diving, which provides the chance to let the current of the Waikato River do the work, and let you swim with the trout. Contact the **Dive Inn** (☎ 07-378 1926, 26 Spa Rd) for more details; it charges $85, including gear hire. This one's for certified divers only.

Bungy Jumping Right near Cherry Island is the **Taupo Bungy** (☎ 0800 888 408, 07-377 1135; single/tandem jump $100/160; open 9am-7pm daily, shorter hours in winter). It's the most popular on the North Island, largely due to its scenic setting on the Waikato River. Jumpers leap off a platform jutting 20m out over a cliff and hurtle down towards the Waikato River, 45m below. If you don't want to jump, it's a picturesque spot with plenty of vantage points. Cheap deals are available, combining a bungy, skydive with Taupo Tandem and jetboat ride with Huka Jet; contact one of the operators for details.

Tandem Skydiving This is one of the popular Taupo adrenaline rushes. In addition to the skydiving itself, at the cheapest rate in NZ, you get a brilliant view over Lake Taupo and the entire region. Both **Great Lake Skydive Centre** (☎ 0800 373 335, 07-378 4662, W www.freefly.co.nz) and **Taupo Tandem Skydiving** (☎ 0800 275 934, W www.tts.net .nz), at Taupo Airport, do tandem skydives for around $170. If that's not gung-ho enough for you then you can move up to a 12,000 feet (from $215) jump or the mind-boggling 15,000 feet oxygen-assisted jump (from $345).

Aerial Sightseeing & Gliding You can go for a scenic flight on the **floatplane** (☎ 07-378 7500; flights from $60-180) next to Taupo Boat Harbour.

Taupo Air Services (☎ 07-378 5325; flights $50-150) at Taupo Airport also does scenic flights ranging from a 15-minute flight to flights across Lake Taupo, Tongariro, Ngauruhoe and Ruapehu.

Balloons Over Taupo (☎ 025 787 919, flights from $135), at Taupo Airport, will take you up in a Grumman G164A radial engine biplane and can also arrange hot-air balloon trips ($275 if you book and pay in advance; otherwise $255).

Helistar Helicopters (Taupo & Wairakei map; ☎ 0800 435 478, 07-374 8405, **w** www .helistar.co.nz, Huka Falls Rd; flights from $55), about 3km north-east of town, offers a variety of scenic helicopter flights, ranging from five minutes to over an hour.

The **Taupo Gliding Club** (Taupo & Wairakei map; ☎ 07-378 5627; flights from $70) goes gliding on Saturday, Sunday and Wednesday afternoons (when the weather is suitable) at Centennial Park on Centennial Drive, about 5km up Spa Rd from the town centre.

Horse Trekking Running off-road treks, **Taupo Horse Treks** (Taupo & Wairakei map; ☎ 07-378 0356, Karapiti Rd; 1-/2-hr rides $25/40) has a good reputation. Its treks go through some fine forest with good views over the Craters of the Moon.

Cycling If you don't make it to Arataki (see Arataki & Pureora Forest Park later) then **Taupo Quad Adventures** (☎ 07-377 6404; bike hire 1 hr-full day $50-225) has fully guided off-road mountain-bike trips. It's at the turn-off to Orakei Korako on SH1 (see the Central Plateau map).

For self-propelled motion, all of the following rent bikes for around $20 per day:

Rainbow Lodge, **Go Global** (see Places to Stay); **Rent-a-Bike** (☎ 025 322 729); or **Rapid Sensations** (☎ 0800 227 238).

Lake Taupo is the location of the 160km Great Lake Cycle Challenge, held in November each year.

Rock 'n' Ropes The masochist from Rock 'n' Ropes (☎ 0800 244 508, 07-374 8111; swing $15, adrenaline combo (swing, high beam & trapeze) $35, ½-day blast $59; free pick-up from Taupo) who dreamt up this diabolical confidence course, must lurk furtively in bush near Taupo. Obviously he/she led a Tarzan/Jane-like existence as a kid. Enough said. Leap to your death (only to be saved by a rope), swing into oblivion, be a 'flying fox' and generally have a fantastic time. The cost depends on how daring you are. What did these guys do before kern-mantel ropes? Rock 'n' Ropes is at **Crazy Catz Adventure** (☎ 0800 462 7219, 374 8223; activities $5-20; open 9am-4.30pm daily, 9am-6pm in summer) on SH5, 13km north of Taupo, which has go-carts, quad bikes and gravity ride, among other things.

Paintball Try out pump-action paintmarkers with **Ultimate Challenge** (Taupo & Wairakei map; ☎ 025 908 964, **e** topgun paintball@hotmail.com), which can be found just off the road that leads to the Craters of the Moon, or **Commando Paintball** (☎ 025 294 7144, Caroline Rd) off SH5 leading to Napier. You'll need a team of at least six to play, and sandshoes (overalls, masks and paintmarkers supplied). The markers fire small gelatine balls filled with coloured vegetable oil. It costs $25 to $50 a head (including 40 rounds of paintballs per person). Bookings are essential.

Walking An enjoyable, easy walk runs from **Taupo to Aratiatia** along the east bank of the Waikato River. The track follows the river to Huka Falls, crossing a hot stream and riverside marshes en route. It's about a one- to 1½-hour walk from the centre of Taupo to Huka Falls. From the falls continue straight ahead along the 7km Taupo Walkway to Aratiatia (another two-plus hours). There are good views of the river, Huka Falls and the power station across the river. From the centre of town, head up Spa Rd, passing the Taupo Bungy site. To reach the start of the walk turn left at County Ave and continue through Spa Thermal Park till the end of the street. The path heads off to the left of the car park, up over a hill and down to the hot springs by the river. Alternatively, drive out to the falls and car park, cross the bridge and walk out to Aratiatia.

Another walk goes to **Mt Tauhara**, with magnificent views from the top. Take the Taupo-Napier Highway (SH5) turn-off, 2km south of the Taupo town centre. About 6km along SH5, turn left into Mountain Rd. The start of the track is signposted on the right-hand side. It will take about two hours to the top, walking slowly.

A pleasant **walkway** goes from the Taupo lakefront to Five Mile Bay. It's a flat, easy walk along public-access beaches. Heading south from Taupo, there's a hot-water beach on the way to Two Mile Bay. At Two Mile Bay the walkway connects with the Lions Walk, going from Two Mile Bay (4.2km south of Taupo) to Five Mile Bay (8km). Anywhere along here you can easily get back to SH1, the lakeside road.

There are plenty of other good walks and tramps in the area; the visitors centre has the relevant DOC pamphlets ($1).

Organised Tours

Paradise Tours *(☎ 07-378 9955; tours adult/child $25/12)* does three-hour tours to the Aratiatia Rapids, Geothermal Centre, Craters of the Moon and Huka Falls. It also offers tours to Orakei-Korako, Rotorua and Waitomo.

Wilderness Escapes *(☎ 07-378 3413; walks from $40, kayak trips from $50)* has a number of trips; guided walks and full-day kayak trips.

Taupo Volcano Tours *(☎ 0800 529 255, 025 2233 524; tours $80-190)* runs tours with an interesting, informed commentary on the regions' geology and vulcanology. Half day and full-day tours are available, ranging from trips on and around the lake to flights over Tongariro National Park.

With **Discover Taupo** *(☎ 07-377 0774; tours adult/child 4-15 yrs $5/2.50)* you can do a 20-minute tour of central Taupo's main sights in a 1951 Bristol double-decker bus. The bus departs every half-hour from 10am till 3pm (bus stops behind the Super Loo and at the town end of the lakefront). How did this bus get to Taupo? New Zealand was the last stop on a 40,000-mile world tour.

Lake Cruises & Jetboating Five boats specialise in cruises on the lake: the *Barbary,* the *Ernest Kemp,* the *Cruise Cat,* the *Super-jet* and the *Alice.* The *Barbary ($25, 10am & 2pm daily; $20, 5pm summer only),* built in 1926, is a 15m ocean-going racing yacht once owned by actor Errol Flynn. 'Barbary Bill', the skipper, is much loved by tourists and locals and his trip is probably the most popular.

The *Ernest Kemp ($22, 10am & 2pm daily; 1pm departure $11),* built to resemble a 1920s steamboat, is named for Alfred Ernest Kemp, whose family occupied the house that still bears their name in Kerikeri, Northland. There are written commentaries for its trips in various languages.

Another steamboat plying Lake Taupo's waters is the *Alice ($25, 2pm Sat).*

For something with a little more zip try the *Cruise Cat ($26, 11.30am daily; $40, 10.30am Sun bubbly brunch),* which is a large, modern launch.

The *Superjet ($29, 10.30am & 3.30pm 1hr sailing; $59, 1pm 2hr sailing)* is a fast, twin-jet catamaran.

All the boats offer similar trips, including visiting a modern Maori rock carving beside the lake. The carving is on private land so it cannot be reached by foot; the only way to see it is by boat. Trips take between one and 2½ hours.

All the boats leave from the wharves at the Taupo Boat Harbour, off Redoubt St. Bookings can be made at the visitors centre or at the launch office *(☎ 07-378 3444)* by the wharves.

Places to Stay

Camping & Cabins Most of these places are just a little out of town (see the Taupo & Wairakei map).

CENTRAL PLATEAU

Camping is free beside the river at *Reid's Farm*, about 1.5km south of Huka Falls towards Taupo; it is popular, and colourful house trucks are often parked there.

Taupo Motor Camp (*☎/fax 07-377 3080, 15 Redoubt St*) Unpowered & powered sites $11 per person, cabins $44, on-site caravans $60-66. This camp is in a nice spot beside the river and handy to the town centre.

Taupo All Seasons Holiday Park (*☎ 07-378 4272, e reservations@allseasons.nzl .com, 16 Rangatira St*) Unpowered & powered sites $11 per person, bunk beds $20, cabins $42-48, self-contained units $62-72. This park is about 1.5km from the town centre. It has a hot thermal pool.

De Bretts Thermal Resort (*☎ 07-378 8559, e debrett@xtra.co.nz, SH5*) Unpowered & powered sites $11 per person, cabins from $40, motel units from $75, lodges from $80. De Bretts is next to Taupo Hot Springs on the road heading to Napier.

Hilltop Thermal Holiday Park (*☎ 07-378 5247, e hilltopthermal@firm.tc, 39 Puriri St*) Powered & tent sites $12 per person, caravans $40, cabins $42. A few kilometres from the town centre is Hilltop Park. It has plenty of shelter and hot mineral spas.

Lake Taupo Top 10 Holiday Park (*☎ 0800 332 121, ☎/fax 07-378 6860, e off ice@ taupotop10.co.nz, 28 Centennial Dr*) Unpowered & powered sites $12 per person, cabins from $50, self-contained units from $68, motel units from $84. This park is opposite the Taupo Golf Course, 5km from town.

Great Lake Holiday Park (*Central Taupo map; ☎ 07-378 5159, Acacia Bay Rd*) Powered & tent sites $9 per person, cabins $30-40, tourist flats $58-78. Great Lake Park is 3km west of town.

Windsor Lodge (*☎ 07-378 6271, fax 378 6246*) Unpowered/powered sites $12/15, cabins from $25. The Windsor is at Waitahanui, 12km south on SH1.

Hostels The backpackers selection in Taupo ranges from party spots to quiet retreats.

Rainbow Lodge (*☎ 07-378 5754, e rain bowlodge@clear.net.nz, 99 Titiraupenga St*) Dorm beds $17-19, singles $32, doubles &

twins $42-48. Rainbow Lodge is the pick of the crop and popular with travellers. It has a large communal area, a sauna and a games area, and is on the ball with activities, tours and travel information. Rooms are spotless and spacious. Mountain bikes, fishing tackle and camping gear are available for hire, and there's free luggage storage.

Taupo Central Backpackers (*☎ 07-378 3206, e taupocentral@xtra.co.nz, 7 Tuwharetoa St*) Dorm beds $21, doubles & twins $50. This is a bit of a party-central backpackers with a rooftop bar that is packed on weekends and a barbecue/meeting area with superb views of the lake and the Central Plateau area. All of the rooms here have an attached bathroom.

Go Global (*☎ 07-377 0044, e easy street@clear.net.nz, cnr Tongariro & Tuwharetoa Sts*) Dorms $21, singles $32, twins $46, en suite doubles $50. Go Global, across the road from Taupo Central and another party backpackers, is a friendly place with decent facilities. It's situated above Sugarclub nightclub, so some rooms can be rather loud on weekends – but at least the staff warn you of the fact before checking in.

Action Down Under (*☎ 07-378 3311, e yhataupo@xtra.co.nz, 56 Kaimanawa St*) Dorms from $17, twins & doubles from $42. This YHA associate has bright rooms, good views of the lake and roomy outside deck areas. It has three- and five-bed dorms and other rooms.

Sunset Lodge (*Taupo & Wairakei map; ☎ 07-378 5962, 5 Tremaine Ave*) Dorms from $15, doubles & twins from $34. Sunset Lodge, 2km south of town, is a small, quiet backpackers. It has a comfortable atmosphere and free services including pickup and shuttles to attractions. To get there, turn off from Lake Terrace into Hawai St, then into Pipi St – it's on the corner.

Burke's Backpackers (*☎ 07-378 9292, e jananddoug@hotmail.com, 69 Spa Rd*) Dorms $18, twins & doubles $40, doubles with bath $50. Burke's is a quiet, friendly hostel with good communal facilities, central garden and picnic area, and personal lockers in each room. There's a games room and well-equipped kitchen, and free pick-up.

Berkenhoff Lodge (☎/*fax 07-378 4909, 75 Scannell St)* Dorms $19, twins & doubles $44. Berkenhoff Lodge is a rambling old place with a bar/games room, dining room (with $7 steak meals) and a spa. Each room has its own bathroom.

B&Bs & Guesthouses The visitors centre has lists of B&Bs and farmstays in and around Taupo.

Bradshaw's B&B (☎ *07-378 8288, fax 378 8282, 130 Heu Heu St)* Singles/doubles from $35/50. Bradshaw's is a friendly, clean B&B but breakfast is extra.

190 Spa Rd (☎ *07-377 0665, 190 Spa Rd)* Singles/doubles $55/75. This homely B&B has en suite rooms with magnificent views of Cherry Island and the Waikato River.

Chandlers Lodge (☎/*fax 07-377 0555,* e *chandlertaupo@xtra.co.nz, 135 Heu Heu St)* Singles/doubles $55/65. Chandlers is another inexpensive B&B, run by a friendly and accommodating couple.

There are several top-end guesthouses around the lake where you can bask in beautiful surroundings. Ask at the visitors centre for details.

Motels & Hotels Taupo is packed with plenty of motels for you to choose from and the competition tends to keep prices down, though many of them have minimum rates during holiday periods.

Dunrovin Motel (☎/*fax 07-378 7384, 140 Heu Heu St)* Singles/doubles from $55/68. This 1950s-style economical motel has basic rooms.

Continental Motel (☎/*fax 07-378 5836, 9 Scannell St)* Doubles from $75. Continental Motel is another value-for-money accommodation option.

On the lakeside, along Lake Terrace, are numerous upmarket places.

Boulevard Waters (☎ *0800 541 541, 07-377 3395,* e *inquiries@boulevardwaters .co.nz, 215 Lake Terrace)* Units $138 for 2. All units at Boulevard overlook the lake.

Copthorne Manuels Resort (☎ *07-378 5110,* e *m.corry@clear.net.nz, 243 Lake Terrace)* Rooms from $189. Copthorne has units facing the lake and the busy SH1.

Huka Lodge (☎ *07-378 5791,* e *reser vations@hukalodge.com, Huka Falls Rd)* From $600 per person. If money is no object and you're looking for the height of understated luxury, one of NZ's most celebrated hotels is just outside Taupo. Near Huka Falls, Huka Lodge is internationally renowned for the quality of its accommodation and cuisine. Fishing, hunting, golf, boating, horse riding and sailing are some of the activities that can be arranged.

Places to Eat
European and Asian cuisine is very well represented in Taupo.

Italian Cafe (☎ *07-377 6293, 28 Tuwharetoa St)* Pasta & pizza from $15. This BYO cafe has a good selection of pizza and pasta. It also does takeaway.

Verdi's (*Heu Heu St)* Sandwiches & quiches $2-5. Verdi's is a sunny cafe with an inviting array of cakes, quiches, sandwiches and pasta dishes.

Hobler (*42 Tuwharetoa St)* Meals from $17. Hobler is a funky cafe-style eatery with an open fire and a good selection of light meals and larger mains.

JJ's Cafe (☎ *07-377 1545, 10 Roberts St)* Light meals $8-15. JJ's has a cheap, daytime menu and outdoor seating.

Pasta Mia (☎ *07-377 6495, 5 Horomatangi St)* Mains from $7.50. Relaxed Pasta Mia makes fresh pasta to eat in or take away, and accompanying sauces.

Replete Deli & Cafe (*45 Heu Heu St)* Dishes $4.50-12. This excellent cafe, with its imaginative menu, is a great place for breakfast or brunch.

Villino Restaurant & Wine Bar (☎ *07-377 4478, 45 Horomatangi St)* Mains $19-33. Villino is excellent and extremely popular. It has German and Italian cuisine, plus a smattering of Asian dishes.

Aqaba (☎ *07-377 0086, Roberts St)* Mains $15-23. A pleasant and popular Mediterranean-style brasserie.

Nonni's (☎ *07-378 6894, 3 Tongariro St)* Mains from $20. Nonni's is a good Italian place with pasta and speciality breads.

Santorini (☎ *07-377 2205, 133 Tongariro St)* Mains $13-25. Seat yourself at

Santorini's first-floor balcony and enjoy the likes of moussaka, ravioli, chicken souvlaki and lamb kofta.

Cajun-Kiwi (☎ *07-378 5276, cnr Roberts & Titiraupenga Sts)* Mains around $25. Taupo and Louisiana come together at Cajun-Kiwi, where you'll find the likes of jambalaya and gumbo, and occasional live music.

Seoul House Korean Restaurant (☎ *07-377 3344, 100 Roberts St)* Mains $15-25. This place has the authentic barbecue-style Korean dishes, along with Japanese cuisine.

Finch's Brasserie & Bar (☎ *07-377 2425, 64 Tuwharetoa St)* Mains $14.50-29. Finch's is a fine-dining restaurant serving up mainly kiwiana dishes.

Walnut Keep (☎ *07-378 0777, 77 Spa Rd)* Mains $20-25. The upmarket Walnut has superb beef and lamb dishes.

The Brantry (☎ *07-378 0484, 45 Rifle Range Rd)* Mains $20-30. The Brantry is another refined dining choice, serving a selection of NZ dishes.

Gravity (*Cnr Tongariro & Tuwharetoa Sts)* Breakfasts $9-13.50. From 8am to 3pm Gravity does great breakfasts that take the edge off a hangover.

Asian Noodle House (☎ *07-377 6449, 9 Tongariro St)* Mains $7.50-14. A large selection of vegetarian dishes, friendly service and generous portions makes this place a good takeaway or eat-in option.

For self-caterers, *Pak N Save* and *Woolworths* (open 24 hours) are open daily.

Entertainment

Holy Cow (*11 Tongariro St)* Located upstairs, the Holy Cow absolutely heaves after 11pm with much dancing and partying, mostly on table tops. People generally gravitate to the Holy Cow once other places close.

Finn MacCuhal's (*Tuwharetoa St)* This lively Irish pub packs in the punters, with DJs on weekends and a large outdoor patio.

Sugar Club (*cnr Tongariro & Tuwharetoa Sts)* Sugarclub is a more traditional nightclub, with a younger crowd and cheesy music.

Other popular places are *Rockefeller Cocktail Bar & Brasserie*, *Wildflame* and *Kazbar*, all on Tuwharetoa St and catering to a more sedate crowd.

Great Lake Centre (☎ *07-376 0340, Tongariro St)* has a theatre and hall for performances, exhibitions and conventions. The visitors centre has the current schedule.

For movies, there's the *Starlight Cinema Centre* (☎ *07-378 7515, Horomatangi St)*.

Getting There & Away

Air Air New Zealand (☎ 07-378 5428) has daily direct flights to Auckland and Wellington, with onward connections.

In Taupo, ticketing is handled through travel agencies including AA Travel Centre (see Information earlier), Budget Travel (☎ 07-378 9799), at 37 Horomatangi St, and the James Holiday Shoppe (☎ 07-378 7065) at 28 Horomatangi St.

Bus Taupo is about halfway between Auckland and Wellington. InterCity, Newmans and Alpine Scenic Tours arrive at and depart from the Taupo Travel Centre (☎ 07-378 9032) at 16 Gascoigne St. The travel centre also sells tickets for trains, the *Interislander* ferry and Tranz Rail.

InterCity and Newmans have several daily buses to Turangi ($27, 45mins), Auckland ($52, 4½hrs), Hamilton ($33, 2¾hrs), Rotorua ($25, 1hr), Tauranga ($44, 2¾hrs), Napier ($38, 2hrs), Palmerston North ($45, 4¼hrs) and Wellington ($69, 5¾hrs).

Shuttle services operate all year-round between Taupo, Tongariro National Park and the Whakapapa Ski Area, a 1¼-hour trip. Transport to the Tongariro Crossing costs $25. During winter shuttles travel daily and may include package deals for lift tickets and ski hire. Bookings can be made at the visitors centre or at any backpackers. Tongariro Expeditions (☎ 0800 828 763) depart from Taupo at 6am and 6.20am, and return at 4.30pm.

Getting Around

Taupo's Hot Bus does an hourly circuit of all the major attractions in and around Taupo. It leaves from the visitors centre every hour on the hour from 10am to 6pm (each stop $2).

Taxi services in Taupo are provided by both Taupo Taxis (☎ 07-378 5100) and Top Cabs (☎ 07-378 9250).

Bikes are forbidden on the track from Spa Park to Huka Falls due to track damage.

AROUND TAUPO
Wairakei Park

Crossing the river at Tongariro St and heading north from town on SH1, you'll arrive at the Wairakei Park area, also known as the Huka Falls Tourist Loop. Take the first right turn after you cross the river and you'll be on Huka Falls Rd, which passes along the river. At the end, turn left back to the highway and you'll pass other interesting spots on your way back to town.

There's no public transport but tours go to a few places along here; otherwise walk or hire a mountain bike for the day.

En route look out for **Honey Hive New Zealand** (☎ 07-374 8553; admission free; open daily), for all you ever wanted to know about bees, and **New Zealand Woodcraft** (admission free; open daily), where you can buy wood-turned items made from native timbers.

Huka Falls Along Huka Falls Rd are the spectacular Huka Falls, known as Hukanui in Maori, meaning 'Great Body of Spray'. A footbridge crosses the Waikato River above the falls – a great torrent of water, more like a giant rapid that plunges through a narrow cleft in the rock. The water here is clear and turquoise, particularly on a sunny day.

Volcanic Activity Centre Budding vulcanologists will love this activity centre and bookshop (☎ 07-374 8375; adult/child $5/2.50; open 9am-5pm Mon-Fri & 10am-4pm Sat & Sun). The observatory monitors volcanic activity in the volatile Taupo Volcanic Zone, and the visitors centre has some excellent displays on NZ's geothermal and volcanic activity.

Exhibits include a large relief map with push-button highlighters to show the volcanic regions, and old documentaries about the eruptions of Ngauruhoe and Ruapehu in 1945, the largest NZ eruptions last century. Pick up a monitoring report to tell you about recent earthquakes or to see if Ruapehu is about to erupt.

The Huka Jet & Prawn Park On the banks of the Waikato River is Prawn Park and next door, the office for the Huka Jet.

Partly inspired by the engineering of riverboats like the *Waireka*, which has a draught of only 30.5cm laden, Kiwi CWF Hamilton was inspired to invent the jetboat. In the *Huka Jet* (☎ 0800 485 2538, 07-374 8572; trips adult/child $59/30) you can take a 25-minute ride down to the Aratiatia Dam and up to Huka Falls. Trips run all day (price includes transport from Taupo).

Prawn Park is the world's only geothermally heated freshwater prawn farm (☎ 07-374 8474; tours adult/child $6/1.50). There are tours on the hour from 11am to 4pm, more frequently in summer. There's a restaurant where you can try the prawns prepared various ways.

Aratiatia Rapids Two kilometres off SH5 are the Aratiatia Rapids, a spectacular part of the Waikato River until the government, in its wisdom, plonked down a power house and dam, shutting off the water. To keep the tourists happy they open the control gates at various times: from 1 October to 31 March at 10am, noon, 2pm and 4pm; from April to September at 10am, noon and 2pm. You can see the water flow through from three good vantage points (entry is free).

Rapids Jet (☎ 0800 727 437, 07-378 5828; adult/child $65/35) shoots up and down the lower part of the Aratiatia Rapids. It's a sensational 45-minute ride, rivalling the trip to Huka Falls. The jetboats depart from the end of the access road to the Aratiatia lookouts. Go down Rapids Rd; look for the signpost to the National Equestrian Centre.

The paddle steamer **Otunua** (☎ 0800 278 336, 07-378 5828; day time cruise or glowworm cruise adult/child $30/20) makes cruises daily to Huka Falls, at 10.30am and 2.30pm from the Aratiatia dam. The Moonlight Glowworm Cruise goes at 5.30pm in winter and 9pm in summer.

Wairakei Thermal Valley This thermal valley, like Orakei Korako, gets its name from the water having once being used as a mirror (see Orakei Korako later). It is the

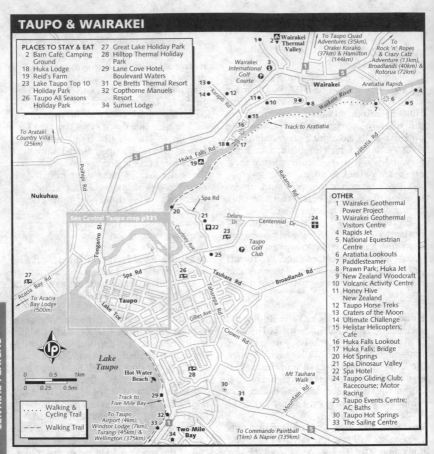

TAUPO & WAIRAKEI

PLACES TO STAY & EAT
2 Barn Café; Camping Ground
18 Huka Lodge
19 Reid's Farm
23 Lake Taupo Top 10 Holiday Park
26 Taupo All Seasons Holiday Park
27 Great Lake Holiday Park
28 Hilltop Thermal Holiday Park
29 Lane Cove Hotel, Boulevard Waters
31 De Bretts Thermal Resort
32 Copthorne Manuels Resort
34 Sunset Lodge

OTHER
1 Wairakei Geothermal Power Project
3 Wairakei Geothermal Visitors Centre
4 Rapids Jet
5 National Equestrian Centre
6 Aratiatia Lookouts
7 Paddlesteamer
8 Prawn Park; Huka Jet
9 New Zealand Woodcraft
10 Volcanic Activity Centre
11 Honey Hive New Zealand
12 Taupo Horse Treks
13 Craters of the Moon
14 Ultimate Challenge
15 Helistar Helicopters; Cafe
16 Huka Falls Lookout
17 Huka Falls; Bridge
20 Hot Springs
21 Spa Dinosaur Valley
22 Spa Hotel
24 Taupo Gliding Club; Racecourse; Motor Racing
25 Taupo Events Centre; AC Baths
30 Taupo Hot Springs
33 The Sailing Centre

Walking & Cycling Trail
Walking Trail

remains of what was once known as Geyser Valley. Before the geothermal power project started in 1959 it was one of the most active thermal areas in the world, with 22 geysers and 240 mud pools and springs. The neighbouring geothermal project has sucked off the steam, and only eight or so mud pools remain active. There's a 30-minute **bushwalk** *(adult/child $6/2; open from 9am daily)* taking in the thermal attractions, but the pools are better seen after heavy rain when they are most active.

The quaint *Barn Cafe* is here. Be sure to buy one of the Weta eggs on sale. There's also

a *camping ground* (☎ 07-374 8004); powered/unpowered sites are $15/9 per person.

Wairakei Geothermal Power Project

New Zealand was the second country in the world to produce power from natural steam. If you dive into all that steam you will find yourself at the Wairakei Geothermal Power Project, which generates about 150MW, providing about 5% of NZ's electricity.

The **visitors centre** *(open 9am-5pm daily in summer; 9am-4.30pm in winter)* is close to the road. You can make an educational stop there. Information on the bore field and power house is available and an audiovisual is shown (from 9am-4pm). You can drive up the road through the project and from a look-out see the long pipes, wreathed in steam.

Just south of here is the big Wairakei Resort and its golf course.

Craters of the Moon Craters of the Moon *(admission free, donations appreciated; open dawn-dusk)* is an interesting and unexploited thermal area. It's run by DOC, so it is less touristy than other commercially exploited thermal areas. Don't miss the lookout just before the car park – it's the best place for photos.

This thermal area sprang up in the 1950s. The power station lowered underground water levels, reducing the pressure of the heated water, and causing more vigorous boiling and steam. New mud pools and steam vents appeared, and you can wander through them on a plank-walk.

There is a small kiosk staffed by volunteers at the car park (they will keep an eye on your car).

Craters of the Moon is signposted on SH1 about 5km north of Taupo.

Broadlands

This beautiful and often unseen stretch of the mighty Waikato River, equidistant (40km) from Rotorua and Taupo, is worth visiting. To get there turn off SH5 onto Homestead Rd, just south of Reporoa.

The stunning scenery of the region is best seen by **NZ Riverjet** *(☎ 07-333 7111, W www .riverjet.co.nz; trips $55-125)*. You can travel downstream by jetboat to the Orakei Korako thermal region through some magnificent steamy gorges or head upstream through the exciting Full James Rapids to Aratiatia.

Near the township of Reporoa is **Butcher's Pool** *(admission free; open daily)*, a natural thermal spring in the middle of a farmer's paddock. It's well set up, with a small parking area, changing sheds and wooden decking around the water's edge. To get there from Reporoa head south on Broadlands Rd for 2km and look for a row of trees lining a gravel driveway off to your left. This leads to the pool.

Arataki & Pureora Forest Park

The dominating western ramparts of Lake Taupo largely comprise the huge Pureora Forest. Logging was eventually stopped in the park in the 1980s after long campaigns by conservationists.

There are long and short forest treks, including tracks to the summits of Mt Pureora (1165m) and the rock pinnacle of Mt Titiraupenga (1042m). Pamphlets, maps and information on the park are available from the DOC offices in Taupo and Te Kuiti. The north section of the park is designated for recreational hunting, but you must obtain a permit from park headquarters.

Arataki Country Villa (☎ 07-882 8857, 025 819 145) Self-contained cottage $50 per double. This villa, nestled beside the picturesque Mangakino Stream, is one of those rare gems. There are activities galore here, including horse trekking ($50 for two hours), mountain biking, tramping, and trout fishing on a secluded section of the stream. The house, surrounded by a working farm (where you can participate in some of the daily activities), is well equipped with comfortable beds. On the balcony is a barbecue and heated spa pool – enjoying the sunsets from here is a pure delight. There is a minimal fee charged for the many activities held. Phone ahead for directions on how to get there.

Orakei Korako

Between Taupo and Rotorua, Orakei Korako *(☎ 07-378 3131; adult/child $19/6; open 8am-5pm daily)* receives fewer visitors than other thermal areas because of its remote location, but since the destruction of the Pink and White Terraces by the Tarawera eruption it has been possibly the best thermal area left in NZ, and one of the finest in the world. Although three-quarters of it now lies beneath the dam waters of Lake Ohakuri, the quarter that remains is the best part and still very much worth seeing.

A walking track takes you around the large, colourful silica terraces for which the park is famous, as well as geysers and Ruatapu Cave – a magnificent natural cave with a pool of jade-green water. The pool may have been used by Maori as a mirror during hairdressing ceremonies: Orakei Korako means 'the place of adorning'.

Entry includes a boat ride across Lake Ohakuri. Canoes and dinghies are available for hire ($5 per hour) and there are two hot tubs.

Geyserland Resort Lodge (☎ *07-378 3131,* e *ok@reap.org.nz)* Bunk beds $20, self-contained lodge $80. Right on the river at Orakei Korako is Geyserland. There's accommodation available in a self-contained lodge (it sleeps up to seven people), or in a communal lodge.

To get to Orakei Korako from Taupo, take SH1 towards Hamilton for 23km, and then travel for 14km from the signposted turn-off. From Rotorua the turn-off is on SH5, via Mihi.

TURANGI
pop 3900
Developed for the construction of the nearby hydroelectric power station in 1973, Turangi is Taupo's smaller cousin at the southern end of Lake Taupo. The town itself is 4km inland from the lake, access to which is from nearby Tokaanu.

Turangi's main attractions are its excellent trout fishing (on the Tongariro River) and access to the northern trails of nearby Tongariro National Park.

Information
The Turangi visitors centre (☎ 07-386 8999, e turangivc@laketauponz.com), just off SH1, has a detailed relief model of Tongariro National Park and is the best place to stop for information about the park, Kaimanawa Forest Park, trout fishing, walks, and general snow and road conditions. The office also issues hut tickets, ski passes and hunting and fishing licences, and acts as the AA agent for that area. It is open from 8.30am to 5pm daily.

You will find the DOC (☎ 07-386 8607) near the junction of SH1 and Ohuanga Rd. The nearest post office and banks are located in the Turangi shopping mall, opposite the visitors centre. Plenty of places in town have Internet access.

TURANGI

PLACES TO STAY
1 Bellbird Lodge
9 Extreme Backpackers; Climbing Wall
10 Sportsman's Lodge
12 Club Habitat & Brew Haus
13 Parklands Motor Lodge
14 Turangi Cabins & Holiday Park
16 Anglers Paradise Resort Motel
17 Creel Lodge

PLACES TO EAT
5 Valentino's
6 Hong Kong Chinese Restaurant
7 Mustard Seed Cafe
8 Grand Central Fry

OTHER
2 Turangi Bus & Travel Centre
3 Turangi Shopping Mall; Post Office; Banks
4 New World Supermarket
11 Turangi Visitors Centre; Automobile Association (AA)
15 DOC
18 Tongariro Hike 'n' Bike
19 Rafting Centre; Tongariro Eco Tours

Tongariro National Trout Centre
About 5km south of Turangi on SH1 is the last DOC-managed trout hatchery/centre (☎ 07-386 9254, admission free; open 10am-3pm daily). This landscaped centre has a self-guided walk to an underwater viewing area, keeping ponds and a picnic area. You can fish for trout in the Tongariro River, which runs close by.

Tokaanu
On the lake, about 5km west of Turangi, this settlement has a collection of motels and fishing lodges and there's plenty to do

It's a Trout's Life

The first brown trout eggs arrived in NZ from Tasmania in 1867. They had originally come to Australia from England. Rainbow trout eggs first arrived from California in 1883. Hatcheries were established at that time to rear the young fish and, while many fish are hatched naturally nowadays, there is still a need for artificial hatcheries. This is because some of NZ's lakes and rivers, while ideal for adult trout, have insufficient spawning grounds. In addition, there's a lot of fishing going on (although there are tight limitations on the number of fish that can be caught). Nationwide the need for hatcheries is dropping, however.

In the wild, fully grown trout migrate each winter to suitable spawning beds. This usually means gravel beds in the upper reaches of rivers and streams. Here a female fish makes a shallow depression (redd) and deposits eggs that are quickly fertilised by an attendant male. The female then sweeps gravel over the eggs. Over two or three days this process is repeated to create a redd with several pockets of eggs. During this process the fish do not feed – a female fish may lose one-third of her body weight by the time she returns to the lake. Male fish are in even worse shape because they arrive at the spawning grounds before the females and leave afterwards.

Less than 1% of the eggs survive to become mature fish. The eggs may be damaged or destroyed by gravel movement, and once hatched the tiny fish may be eaten by other fish, birds, rats or even other trout.

Because there were only a few shipments of eggs, from which all of today's trout are descended, NZ's rainbow trout are considered to be a very pure strain. The hatchery eggs are collected by capturing fish during their spawning run. Eggs are gently squeezed from a female fish and milt from males added and stirred together in a container. Incubator trays containing about 10,000 eggs are placed in racks and washed over by a continuous flow of water.

After 15 days the embryos' eyes start to appear and by the 18th day the embryos, previously very sensitive and frail, have become quite hardy. They need to be because on that day the eggs are poured from a metre height into a wire basket. Any weak eggs are killed off by this rough treatment, ensuring that only healthy fish are hatched out. The survivors are now placed 5000 to a basket and about 10 days later the fish hatch out, wriggle through the mesh and drop to the bottom of the trough. They stay there for about 20 days, living off the yolk sac.

When they have totally absorbed their yolk sac they are known as fry; although they can be released at this stage they are normally kept until they are nine to 12 months old. By this time they are 10cm to 15cm long and are known as fingerlings. They are moved outside when they are about 4cm long and reared in ponds. Fingerlings are transported to the place where they will be released in what looks rather like a small petrol tanker, and simply pumped out the back down a large pipe!

For more information on all things trout, visit the Tongariro National Trout Centre, just south of Turangi.

in the way of outdoor activites, especially for thrillseekers and nature lovers.

The **Tokaanu Thermal Pools** (☎ 07-386 8575, Mangaroa St; admission public pools adult/child $4/2, private pools $6/2.50 for 20 mins; sauna $7/4; open 10am-10pm daily) is an interesting thermal area with hot baths, a sauna and exhibits. A 15-minute walk down a boardwalk (free) leads around the mud pools and thermal springs.

Walking

The DOC Turangi Walks ($1) leaflet outlines notable walks, such as the Tongariro River Walkway (three hours return), which is also suitable for mountain bikes, Tongariro River Loop Track (one hour), Hinemihi's Track near the top of Te Ponanga Saddle (15 minutes return), a walk on Mt Maunganamu (40 minutes return) and a walk around Lake Rotopounamu. This lake abounds in bird life and has some great little beaches, perfect for a summer's day picnic and swim (20 minutes to the lake, 1½ hours around it). The leaflet also lists walks in the nearby Kaimanawa Forest Park.

Trout Fishing

February and March are the best months for brown trout and June to September are the best for rainbow trout, but the fishing is good almost year-round. Don't forget that you need a fishing licence.

The visitors centre has over 20 fishing guides on file who charge from around $45 to $50 per hour (generally a minimum of three hours), including all gear (excluding the fishing license). The other option is to hire your own gear from sports stores around town – rods cost $10 and waders $15 – but unless you're an experienced fisherman it's best to hire a guide.

Boats can be hired for lake fishing: aluminium dinghies cost $20 per hour from Braxmere Lodge (☎ 07-386 7513), just before Waihi, which also rents out fishing gear ($5 for rods), and from Motuoapa Marina (☎ 07-386 7000), at Motuoapa.

Other Activities

River rafting is popular, and the Tongariro River has grade III rapids or, for families, grade I on the lower reaches in summer. The **Rafting Centre** (☎ 0800 101 024, 07-386 6409, Atirau Rd; rafting $85 per person; family floats $140 for 4 people) is the home of Tongariro River Rafting; you have the option of a four-hour trip on grade III (half that time spent on the river), the more gentle family floats or raft fishing (only in summer). The Rafting Centre also hires out bikes for $20 for two hours.

Rock 'N' River (☎ 0800 865 226, 07-386 0352, 203 Puanga St, Tokaanu) has various trips. The Tongariro River trip (grade III) includes a visit to the Puketarata Falls topped off by a soak in a thermal pool. There is also a two-hour float trip (grade II) on the Lower Tongariro, and three more exhilarating river trips (the Wairoa, Rangitikei and Mohaka Rivers – the latter is an overnight trip).

Rapid Sensations (☎ 0800 227 238, 07-378 7902, W www.rapids.co.nz) has trips on the Tongariro (grade III, and a more gentle trip), raft fishing, white-water rafting on the Rangitaiki, Wairoa and Mangahao Rivers, and multi-day trips on the Upper and Lower Mohaka Rivers.

Highly recommended is the wetlands ecotour with **Tongariro Eco Tours** (☎ 0800 101 024, 07-386 6409; tours $40 per person), based at the Rafting Centre. You will have the chance to see some 40 species of bird life in the wetlands environment as you cruise around the lake edge on the Delta Queen (binoculars supplied). Trips leave at 8am and 6pm and last two hours.

Kiwi Outback Tours (☎ 07-386 6607) does quad-bike trips from three hours to a full day.

Tongariro Hike 'n' Bike (☎ 07-386 7588, 203 Taupahi Rd; ½-/full-day bike hire $30/40) has guided walks, mountain biking and scenic tours, and will arrange track transport.

On those wet days, head to the **climbing wall** (☎ 07-386 8949, Ngawaka Place; admission $15) run by Extreme Backpackers. There's also a licensed cafe.

Contact the visitors centre for details on horse riding (approximately $30 per hour) in the area.

Places to Stay

Camping & Cabins Most camping grounds are not in Turangi township.

Turangi Cabins & Holiday Park (☎/fax 07-386 8754, Ohuanga Rd) Unpowered/powered sites $9/10 per person, cabins $32, on-site vans $40. This place, close to town, was once the power station construction workers' quarters, which explains all the cabins. The staff are very friendly and accommodating.

Oasis Motel & Caravan Park (☎ 07-386 8569) Unpowered/powered sites $9/10 per person, cabins $32, studios $50, family units $65. Oasis is at Tokaanu, on SH41. It also has hot pools and spa pools.

Tauranga-Taupo Fishing Lodge (☎ 07-386 8385, fax 386 8386) Camp sites $10 per person, cabins $35, tourist flats $65, units

$85. This place is 11km north of Turangi on the SH1 towards Taupo.

Motutere Bay Caravan Park (☎/fax 07-386 8963) Camp sites $10 per person, on-site caravans $25, tourist flats $55. This camp ground is located in a pleasant spot right next to the lake, about 17km north of Turangi on SH1.

Eivin's Lodge (☎ 07-386 8062, e eivins@xtra.co.nz) Unpowered/powered sites $8/9 per person, beds without/with linen from $20/25. Eivin's lodge is on SH47 about halfway between Turangi and the Grand Chateau at Whakapapa (approximately 24km from either; see Tongariro National Park map). It has 40 heated rooms, a kitchen, a lounge and ski hire in winter.

Hostels Turangi's backpackers are popular all year round.

Extreme Backpackers (☎ 07-386 8949, e ebpcltd@xtra.co.nz, 26 Ngawaka Place) Tent sites $10 per person, bunk beds $18, singles $30, twins & doubles $42 (including linen), doubles with bath $52. This backpacker place is an excellent, spotless, friendly lodge. There's a pleasant lounge with an open fire, an inner courtyard with hammocks and barbecue and the rooms are spacious. They also run their own Tongariro crossing bus.

Bellbird Lodge (☎ 07-386 8281, 3 Rangipoia Place) Dorm beds $18, singles, twins & doubles $40. Bellbird is a small, friendly place with a spacious lounge area and kitchen. Fishing licences and tackle can be arranged. There's a freezer and you can arrange to have your catch smoked.

Club Habitat (☎ 07-386 7492, fax 386 0106, Ohuanga Rd) Camp sites $8 per person, campervan sites $20 per double, dorm beds $16, singles $23, twins & doubles $40, rooms with bath & tourist cabins $64, motel units $74, 4-person family units $99. This is a huge complex (220 beds) with rooms scattered around the grounds. There is a big restaurant/bar complex (see Places to Eat), a sauna and spa.

Motels The visitors centre has a list of B&Bs and homestays in the area.

Sportsman's Lodge (☎ 07-386 8150, fax 386 8180, 15 Taupehi Rd) Singles/doubles from $40/50, self-contained unit $80. This place backs onto the river. The rooms have en suites and there's a shared kitchen and TV lounge.

Creel Lodge (☎/fax 07-386 8081, 183 Taupehi Rd) Singles/doubles from $55/75. This lodge also backs onto the river, but each room has its own kitchen facilities.

Parklands Motor Lodge (☎ 07-386 7515, e prklands@reap.org.nz, cnr SH1 & Arahori St) Singles/doubles from $70/75. This is quite a large complex. The units have all the standard amenities you'd expect.

Anglers Paradise Resort Motel (☎ 07-386 8980, e anglers@reap.org.nz, cnr SH41 & Ohuanga Rd) Studio & 1-bedroom units from $95. Anglers Paradise has studio or one-bedroom units; it also has a restaurant and heated pool and spa.

Places to Eat

Mustard Seed Cafe (Ohuanga Rd) Light meals $3-10. This modern, new cafe has a large selection of cafe-style food and good coffee.

Hong Kong Chinese Restaurant (☎ 07-386 7526, Ohuanga Rd) Mains $14-22. Takeaway meals $10. Head here for sit-down or takeaway Chinese.

Valentino's (☎ 07-386 8821, Ohuanga Rd) Mains $18-28. Open from 6pm Wed-Mon. This is a good Italian restaurant and a reminder of the many Italian construction workers here when the power station was built.

Brew Haus Restaurant mains $15-25, bar burgers $4-11. The Brew Haus is situated in Club Habitat (see Places to Stay). There's a pleasant restaurant and a popular bar serving light meals and beer that is brewed on the premises.

Grand Central Fry (☎ 07-386 5344, Ohuanga Rd) Burgers and toasted sandwiches $3-5. This takeaway stand's burgers and fish and chips are good value.

Getting There & Away

Both InterCity and Newmans buses arrive at and depart from the Turangi Bus &

Travel Centre. Auckland-Wellington and Rotorua-Wellington buses that travel along the eastern side of the lake to and from Taupo, all stop at Turangi.

Alpine Scenic Tours (☎ 07-386 8918) runs a shuttle several times daily between Turangi and National Park township, stopping at the Ketetahi and Mangatepopo trail heads, Whakapapa and, in winter, the Whakapapa ski area. This is an excellent service for skiers and trampers. It also has services to and from Taupo.

Tongariro Expeditions (☎ 0800 828 763) runs shuttles from Turangi, Taupo and Whakapapa for the Tongariro Crossing and the Northern Circuit. Bellbird Lodge, Club Habitat and Extreme Backpackers also provide shuttles for the Tongariro Crossing ($20 return), and sometimes for the Whakapapa ski area.

Bay of Plenty

☎ 07 • pop 230,500

The sweeping Bay of Plenty, like its name, is blessed with a good climate and fine beaches, and has a thriving agricultural sector most noted for its kiwi fruit. The bay stretches from the main city of Tauranga in the west, to Whakatane and Opotiki, the main focal points of the Eastern Bay.

Just inland in this region is one of NZ's premier tourist attractions, Rotorua. The Rotorua region is world famous for its geysers, hot springs, mud pools, shimmering lakes, trout fishing, tramping and a host of other activities.

The region is also of great significance to the Maori, whose presence dates back to their discovery and exploration of the area in the 14th century.

Captain Cook sailed into the Bay of Plenty on the *Endeavour* in October 1769, naming it for the number of thriving settlements of friendly Maori he encountered (and the amount of supplies they gave him). It was a sharp contrast to the 'welcome' he received from the Maori of Poverty Bay several weeks earlier, when lives were lost and no food was available.

Rotorua

pop 56,900

Rotorua is the most popular tourist area of the North Island. Nicknamed 'Sulphur City', it has the most energetic thermal activity in the country, with bubbling mud pools, gurgling hot springs, gushing geysers and evil smells. Rotorua also has a large Maori population, whose cultural activities are among the most interesting and accessible in NZ.

The city itself is thriving, buoyed by the huge influx of tourists (earning it another local nickname, 'Roto-Vegas'). It's scenically located 280m above sea level on the shores of Lake Rotorua, which teems with trout. The area surrounding Rotorua has a

Highlights

- Visiting the many geothermal areas in and around Rotorua
- Cruising the lakes around Rotorua – Rotomahana, Rotorua and Tarawera
- Feasting at a Maori *hangi* and taking in a concert at Rotorua
- Easing into one of Rotorua's thermal spas
- Taking an adrenaline joyride on the Luge or inside the zorb
- Visiting Whakaari (White Island), NZ's most active marine volcano
- Soaking up the rays on the Bay of Plenty's sandy beaches

number of serene lakes, trout springs, wildlife parks, farm shows and adrenaline activities.

History

The Rotorua district was first settled in the 14th century when the canoe *Te Arawa*, captained by Tamatekapua, arrived from Hawaiki at Maketu in the central Bay of Plenty. The settlers took the tribal name Te Arawa to commemorate the vessel that had

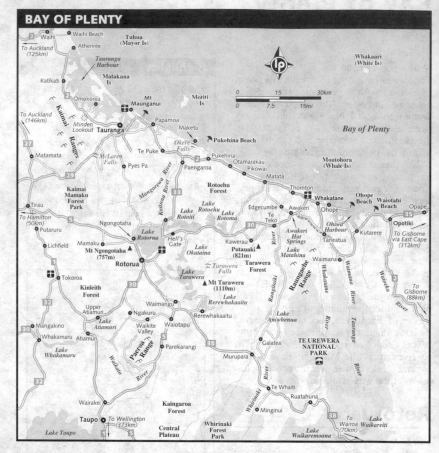

BAY OF PLENTY

brought them safely so far. Much of the inland forest was explored by Tamatekapua's grandson, Ihenga, who also named many geographical features of the area. The name Rotorua means 'The Second Lake' (*roto* means 'lake' and *rua* 'two'), as it was the second lake that Ihenga discovered.

In the next few hundred years, various sub-tribes spread through the area and, as they grew in number, split into more sub-tribes and conflicts broke out over territory. In 1823 the Arawa lands were invaded by the Ngapuhi chief, Hongi Hika, of Northland, in the so-called Musket Wars. Both the

Arawa and the Northlanders suffered heavy losses and the Ngapuhi eventually withdrew.

During the Waikato Land War (1863–67) the Arawa tribe threw in their lot with the government against their traditional enemies in the Waikato, gaining the backing of its troops and preventing East Coast reinforcements getting through to support the Maori King Movement.

With the wars virtually over in the early 1870s, European settlement around Rotorua took off with a rush. The army and government personnel involved in the struggle helped broadcast the scenic wonders of the place. People came to take the waters in the hope of cures for all sorts of diseases, and Rotorua's tourist industry was thus founded. The town's main attraction was the fabulous Pink and White Terraces, formed by the sinter deposits of silica from volcanic activity. Touted at the time as the eighth natural wonder of the world, they were destroyed in the 1886 Mt Tarawera eruption (see the boxed text later in this chapter).

Orientation & Information

The main shopping area is down Tutanekai St, the central part of which is a parking area and pedestrian mall. Running parallel, Fenton St starts by the Government Gardens near the lake and runs all the way to the Whakarewarewa ('Whaka') thermal area 2km away. It's lined with motels for much of its length.

The office of Tourism Rotorua (☎ 07-348 5179, W www.rotoruanz.co.nz), at 1167 Fenton St, is open from 8am to 5.30pm daily (to 6pm October to April). It makes bookings for everything around Rotorua and has a travel agency and DOC office. There is also a money changing bureau (open 8am to 5.30pm daily), a cafe and other services for travellers, including showers, luggage storage and public telephones (buy your phonecard from the money changing bureau).

The Automobile Association (AA; ☎ 07-348 3069) is on Amohau St. The American Express agent is Galaxy United Travel (☎ 07-347 9444), at the corner of Amohau and Tutanekai Sts. Thomas Cook has a forex desk in the Air New Zealand office and there are plenty of banks that will change foreign currencies.

The post office is on Hinemoa St, between Tutanekai and Amohia Sts, and a laundry is at 1209 Fenton St, opposite the police station.

The Arthritis Centre (☎ 07-348 5121) can arrange a wheelchair for disabled people. Call them between 10am and 3pm Monday to Friday. Rotorua Taxis (☎ 07-348 1111) has a taxi with a wheelchair hoist.

The weekly magazine *Thermal Air* is a useful and free tourist publication while the annual free *Rotorua Visitors Guide* is a more basic affair. Tourism Rotorua sells a good map, *Gateway to Geyserland* ($1), of the city and surrounding area.

There are plenty of Internet cafes around town, all charging around $5 to $6 per hour, including Contact Cyber Cafe (1217 Fenton St), Cyber World (1174 Haupapa St) and Cybershed (1176 Pukuatua St).

If you're planning to stick around Rotorua for a while, consider purchasing the *Rotorua Good Time Card* ($20), which gives you discounts on quite a few activities. It's available from the visitors centre.

Lake Rotorua

Lake Rotorua is the largest of 12 lakes in the Rotorua district. It was formed by an eruption and subsequent subsidence of the area. Two cruises on the lake depart from the Rotorua lakefront jetty, at the northern end of Tutanekai St.

The **Lakeland Queen paddle steamer** *(☎ 0800 862 784)* does one-hour breakfast cruises ($28), luncheon ($30), afternoon tea ($20) and dinner cruises ($50) on the lake. Children are half-price.

The motorised catamaran **Scatcat** *(☎ 07-347 9852; 1-hr cruise adult/child $25/free)* does a one-hour circuit of Mokoia Island. There are longer cruises available.

Ohinemutu

Ohinemutu is a lakeside Maori village. Its name means 'Place of the Young Woman who was Killed' and was given by Ihenga in memory of his daughter.

The historic Maori **St Faith's Anglican Church** *(open 8am-5pm daily)* by the lakefront has a beautiful interior decorated with Maori carvings, *tukutuku* (weaved panels), painted scrollwork and stained-glass windows. An image of Christ wearing a Maori cloak is etched on a window so that he appears to be walking on the waters of Lake Rotorua. Seen from this window, it's surprising how much Lake Rotorua does resemble the Sea of Galilee.

Opposite the church is the impressive **Tamatekapua Meeting House**, built in 1887. Named for the captain of the *Arawa*

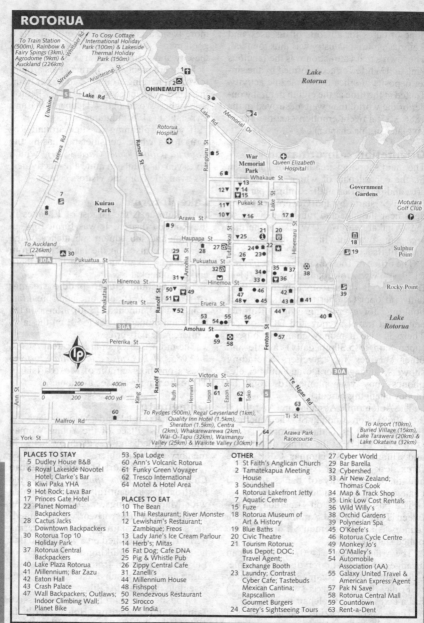

ROTORUA

PLACES TO STAY	53 Spa Lodge	OTHER	27 Cyber World
5 Dudley House B&B	60 Ann's Volcanic Rotorua	1 St Faith's Anglican Church	29 Bar Barella
6 Royal Lakeside Novotel	61 Funky Green Voyager	2 Tamatekapua Meeting	32 Cybershed
Hotel; Clarke's Bar	62 Tresco International	House	33 Air New Zealand;
8 Kiwi Paka YHA	64 Motel & Hotel Area	3 Soundshell	Thomas Cook
9 Hot Rock; Lava Bar		4 Rotorua Lakefront Jetty	34 Map & Track Shop
17 Princes Gate Hotel	PLACES TO EAT	7 Aquatic Centre	35 Link Low Cost Rentals
22 Planet Nomad	10 The Bean	15 Fuze	36 Wild Willy's
Backpackers	11 Thai Restaurant; River Monster	18 Rotorua Museum of	38 Orchid Gardens
28 Cactus Jacks	12 Lewisham's Restaurant;	Art & History	39 Polynesian Spa
Downtown Backpackers	Zambique; Freos	19 Blue Baths	46 O'Keefe's
30 Rotorua Top 10	13 Lady Jane's Ice Cream Parlour	20 Civic Theatre	48 Rotorua Cycle Centre
Holiday Park	14 Herb's; Mitas	21 Tourism Rotorua;	49 Monkey Jo's
37 Rotorua Central	16 Fat Dog; Cafe DNA	Bus Depot; DOC;	51 O'Malley's
Backpackers	25 Pig & Whistle Pub	Travel Agent;	54 Automobile
40 Lake Plaza Rotorua	26 Zippy Central Cafe	Exchange Booth	Association (AA)
41 Millennium; Bar Zazu	31 Zanelli's	23 Laundry; Contrast	55 Galaxy United Travel &
42 Eaton Hall	44 Millennium House	Cyber Cafe; Tastebuds	American Express Agent
43 Crash Palace	48 Fishspot	Mexican Cantina;	57 Pak N Save
47 Wall Backpackers; Outlaws;	50 Rendezvous Restaurant	Rapscallion	58 Rotorua Central Mall
Indoor Climbing Wall;	52 Sirocco	Gourmet Burgers	59 Countdown
Planet Bike	56 Mr India	24 Carey's Sightseeing Tours	63 Rent-a-Dent

BAY OF PLENTY

canoe, this is an important meeting house for all Arawa people. The Magic of the Maori Concert is held here (see Maori Concerts & Hangi later in this section).

A good **craft market** is held in Ohinemutu every second Sunday at the Soundshell.

Rotorua Museum of Art & History

This impressive museum (☎ 07-349 4350; adult/child $9/3; open 9.30am-5pm daily winter, 9.30am-6pm daily summer), better known as the Bath House, is in a Tudor-style building in the Government Gardens. The building was an elegant spa retreat, built in 1908; it also serviced as a rehabilitation centre for soldiers during WWI. Tour through some of the reconstructed spa rooms and marvel at the seemingly odd therapies practised therein.

The museum has a very good exhibition (Te Ohaaki O Houmaitahiti) of the taonga (treasures) of the local Arawa people. Opposite, a small theatre houses a Tarawera exhibition that includes a rousing video (every 20 minutes) on the 1886 Mt Tarawera eruption, with great sound effects and simulated quakes. Another rather less dramatic video on the eruption (running on a continuous loop) can be viewed in the main exhibition area, where there is plenty about Tarawera before and after the eruption. The survivors' stories have been preserved, as has the strange tale of the ominous, ghostly war canoe that appeared before a boatload of astonished tourists hours before the eruption. There is a pleasant cafe with good coffee.

In the **gardens** around the Bath House are typical English touches, eg, croquet lawns, rose gardens, steaming pools and a pétanque ring. There's also a nine-hole **golf course** (☎ 07-348 9126; golf 9/18 holes $10/15). You can hire trundlers, clubs and motorised golf carts; bookings are essential. There is also a 27-bay **driving range** (50/110 balls $6/11; open 7.30am-9pm daily).

Orchid Gardens

The Orchid Gardens (☎ 07-347 6699, Hinemaru St; adult/child $10/4; open 8.30am-5.30pm daily) contain an extensive hothouse of orchids that bloom year-round as well as a Micro-world display where you can get a microscopic view of living reptiles and insects. There is also a big **water organ**, really a huge fountain with over 800 jets. It's a magnificent 15-minute show of water that swirls, leaps and generally makes graceful, balletic movements up to 4m high. It plays every hour on the hour from 9am to 5pm.

Te Whakarewarewa

This is Rotorua's largest and best-known thermal reserve and a major Maori cultural area. It's pronounced 'fa-ka-re-wa-re-wa' – most call it simply 'Whaka'. However, even Whakarewarewa is a shortening of its full name, Te Whakarewarewatanga o te Ope Taua a Wahiao, which means 'The Gathering Together of the War Party of Wahiao'.

Entry to Whakarewarewa's geyser area is through the **NZ Maori Arts & Crafts Institute** (☎ 07-348 9047, Hemo Rd; adult/child 5-15 yrs $18/9; open 8am-5pm daily winter, 8am-6pm daily summer). It's most spectacular geyser is **Pohutu** (Maori for 'Big Splash' or 'Explosion'), an active geyser that usually erupts between 10 and 20 times a day. Pohu-tu spurts hot water about 20m (sometimes over 30m) into the air. The average eruption lasts about five to 10 minutes, though the longest is reputed to have lasted for 15 hours! You get a warning because the Prince of Wales' Feathers geyser always starts off shortly before Pohutu. The institute also has working craftspeople, an art gallery, a replica Maori village, kiwi house, a Maori concert held daily at 12.15pm and access to the thermal reserve.

Thermal Village (☎ 07-349 3463, Tryon St; adult/child $18/9, admission includes tours & concerts; open 8.30am-5pm daily) is on the eastern side of Whaka. There are concerts in the meeting house at 11.15am and 2pm, and regular guided tours through the village, with its souvenir shops and cafe, and the thermal area (try sweetcorn cooked in a hot pool for $2) between 9am and 4pm daily. There's plenty of thermal activity in the village but no access to the geysers. On weekends and school holidays, usually during summer, kids dive for coins in the river

Hinemoa & Tutanekai

The story of Hinemoa and Tutanekai is one of NZ's most well-known lovers' tales. It is not a legend but a true story, though you may hear one or two variations. The descendants of Hinemoa and Tutanekai still live in the Rotorua area today.

Hinemoa was a young woman of a sub-tribe that lived on the western shore of Lake Rotorua. Tutanekai was a young man of the sub-tribe that lived on Mokoia Island, on the lake.

The two sub-tribes sometimes visited one another; that was how Hinemoa and Tutanekai met. But though both were of high birth in their respective tribes, Tutanekai was illegitimate and so,

Hinemoa & Tutanekai (George Woods, circa 1940)

ALEXANDER TURNBULL LIBRARY, WELLINGTON NZ

while the family of Hinemoa thought he was a fine young man and could see that the two young people loved one another, they were not in favour of them marrying.

At night, Tutanekai would play his flute on the island, and sometimes the wind would carry his melody across the water to Hinemoa. In his music she could hear his declaration of love for her. Her people, meanwhile, took to tying up the canoes at night to make sure she could not take off and go to him.

Finally, one night, as she heard Tutanekai's music wafting over the waters, Hinemoa was so overcome with longing that she could stand it no more. She peeled off her clothes to rid herself of the weight and swam the long distance from the shore to the island.

When she arrived on Mokoia, Hinemoa was in a quandary. She had to shed her clothing in order to swim, but now on the island she could scarcely walk into the settlement naked! She sought refuge in a hot pool to figure out what to do next.

Time passed and eventually a man came to fetch water from a cold spring beside the hot pool. In a deep man's voice, Hinemoa called out, 'Who is it?' The man replied that he was the slave of Tutanekai, come to fetch water. Hinemoa reached out of the darkness, seized the slave's calabash gourd and broke it. This happened a few more times, until finally Tutanekai himself came to the pool and demanded that the interloper identify himself. He was amazed when it turned out to be Hinemoa.

Tutanekai stole Hinemoa into his hut. In the morning, when Tutanekai was sleeping very late, a slave was sent to wake him and came back reporting that someone else was also sleeping in Tutanekai's bed. The two lovers emerged, and when Hinemoa's efforts to reach Tutanekai had been revealed, their union was celebrated.

that flows beneath the bridge leading to the village. This is an old tradition at Whaka.

Whaka is 2km south of the city centre, straight down Fenton St. City buses drop you near Tryon St, or Sightseeing Shuttle buses will drop you at the Maori Arts & Crafts Institute.

Close to town is **Kuirau Park**, an area of volcanic activity (it's most recent eruption, early 2001, covered most of the park in mud) that you can wander around for free. It has a crater lake, pools of boiling mud and small mineral baths.

Maori Concerts & Hangi

Maori culture is a major attraction in Rotorua and, although it has been commercialised, it's worth investing in the experience. The two big activities are concerts and *hangi* (meals cooked in an earth oven). Often the two are combined.

The concerts are put on by locals. Chances are, by the evening's end you'll have been dragged up on stage, experienced a Maori *hongi* (nose-to-nose contact), have joined hands for a group sing-in, and harboured notions of freaking out your next-door neighbour with a *haka* (war dance) when you get home. Other features of a Maori concert are *poi* dances, action songs and hand games.

Elements of the performances you are likely to see here are described in the Maori Culture & Arts colour section.

There are plenty of options available to catch a concert and hangi. Concerts take place at 8pm daily at **Tamatekapua Meeting House** *(tickets adult/child $18/5)* in Ohinemutu, opposite St Faith's Church down by the lake. You can show up at the door for the Magic of the Maori Concert or book directly *(☎ 0800 000 445)* or through **Tourism Rotorua**.

Another option is the daily concerts at **Whakarewarewa thermal village**, which are included in the entry fee, or the Mai Ora concert and hangi during summer evenings ($65/35; see that section earlier).

For a combined concert and hangi one of the best options is **Tamaki Tours** *(☎ 07-346 2823; tours adult/child $70/35)*, which does an excellent Twilight Cultural Tour to a *marae* and Maori village complex 15km south of Rotorua. It provides transport and on the way explains the traditional protocol involved in visiting a marae. A 'chief' is chosen among the group to represent the visitors. The concert is followed by a hangi.

Big hotels that also offer Maori concerts and hangi are listed below with prices for adults/children:

Centra (☎ 07-348 1189) Froude St
Concert Only: $20/10 (8pm)
Concert & Hangi: $49/24.50 (6.30pm)
Lake Plaza Rotorua (☎ 0800 801 440) Eruera St
Concert Only: $20/10 (8pm)
Concert & Hangi: $47/23.50 (6.30pm)
Millennium (☎ 07-347 1234) Eruera St
Concert Only: $16/8 (8pm)
Concert & Hangi: $35/17 (6.30pm)

NZ Maori Arts & Crafts Institute
(☎ 07-348 9047) Hemo Rd
Concert & Hangi: $65/35 (6.15pm)
Quality Inn Hotel (☎ 07-348 0199) Fenton St
Concert Only: $15.50/7.75 (8pm)
Concert & Hangi: $35/17.50 (7pm)
Rotoiti Tours (☎ 07-348 8969) Rakeiao Marae
(includes pick-up/drop-off)
Concert & Hangi: $63/31.50
Royal Lakeside Novotel Hotel
(☎ 07-346 3888) Tutanekai St
Concert Only: $27.50/13.75 (7pm)
Concert & Hangi: $55/27.50 (6.30pm)
Sheraton Rotorua (☎ 07-349 5200) Fenton St
Concert Only: $22/12 (8pm)
Concert & Hangi: $49/25 (7.15pm)

Times and prices are subject to change, so check with the tourist office or with the hotel offering the service before you book.

Thermal Pools

The popular **Polynesian Spa** *(☎ 07-348 1328, off Hinemoa St; admission main pools $10 adults only, private pools adult/child $10/4 per half-hr; open 6.30am-11pm daily, last tickets 10.15pm)* is in the Government Gardens. A bathhouse was opened at these springs in 1886 and people have been swearing by the health-giving properties of the waters ever since.

Remember to take off anything you are wearing that has silver in it; silver will instantly turn black on contact with the water. It's advisable to put all valuables in a safe-deposit box at the ticket office. The modern complex has several pools at the lake's edge that range in temperature from 34°C to 43°C, and a main pool at 38°C. An Aix massage (which includes entry to the luxury lakeside spa) costs $60. Aix massage (appointment required) involves a relaxing half-hour during which you lie under jets of warm water while a masseur gets to work with oil. Towels and swimsuits can be hired, and there is a licensed cafe.

For swimmers, the historical **Blue Baths** *(☎ 07-350 2119; adult/child $7/4; open 10am-6pm Sun-Fri, 10am 8pm Sat)* a heated swimming pool in the government gardens, has been beautifully renovated.

There are two open-air natural pools with medicinal mineral waters (more than 39°C)

Pokarekare Ana

Pokarekare ana is NZ's most cherished traditional song. Though most people think its origin is more ancient, the song was actually adapted from a poem by Paraire Henare Tomoana (1868–1946) of the Ngati Kahungunu tribe. His original lyrics were not about Rotorua, but rather Waiapu. Nevertheless, the words seemed to fit the story of Hinemoa and Tutanekai so perfectly that in popular song the lake's name was changed to Rotorua.

Almost anyone from NZ can sing this song for you. Often you will hear only the first verse and the chorus sung, but there are several verses. If you want to sing along, the first verse and chorus go like this:

Pokarekare ana nga wai o Rotorua.
Troubled are the waters of Rotorua.
Whiti atu koe, e hine, marino ana e.
If you cross them, maiden, they will be calm.

E hine e, hoki mai ra,
Come back to me, maiden,
Ka mate ahau i te aroha e.
I will die for love of you.

at the **Waikite Valley Thermal Pools** (☎ 07-333 1861; adult/child $5/2.50; open 10am-10pmdaily). To get there, go 30km south on SH5 (the highway to Taupo) to a signposted turn-off opposite the Wai-o-Tapu turn-off. The pools are another 6km down this road. There's a **camp site** nearby; tent and powered sites cost $10 per adult ($5 per child), including entry to the pools.

Those wishing to swim in hot water can visit **Kerosene Creek**, out on SH5. Turn left on the unsealed old Waiotapu Rd and follow it for 2km. This is one of the few places where the public can bathe in natural thermal pools for free (see also Butcher's Pool in the Central Plateau chapter).

Walking

Check in at the Map & Track Shop for pamphlets and excellent maps outlining the many fine walks in the area. A handy booklet is DOC's *Walks in the Rotorua Lakes area* ($2.50).

All these walks are shown on the Around Rotorua map.

On the south-east edge of town, **Whakarewarewa Forest Park** was planted early in the 20th century as an experiment to find the most suitable species to replace NZ's rapidly dwindling and slow-growing native trees. The **Fletcher Challenge Visitor Information Centre** (☎ 07-346 2082; open 8.30am-6pm Mon-Fri (to 5pm Apr-Sept), 10am-4pm Sat & Sun) in the park has a woodcraft shop, displays and audiovisual material on the history and development of the forest. Check in here if you want to go walking. Walks range from half an hour to four hours, including some great routes to the Blue and Green Lakes. Several walks start at the visitors centre, including a half-hour walk through the **Redwood Grove**, a grove of large Californian redwood trees.

Other walks in the Rotorua area are the 22.5km **Western Okataina Walkway**, through native bush from Lake Okareka to Ruato, on the shores of Lake Rotoiti. There's public transport past the Ruato end only; the whole walk takes about seven hours and you need good boots or stout shoes.

The **Eastern Okataina Walkway** goes along the eastern shoreline of Lake Okataina to Lake Tarawera – about a three hour, 10.5km walk. The 6km **Northern Tarawera Track** connects to the walkway and makes it possible to do a two-day walk from either Lake Okataina or Ruato to Lake Tarawera and camp overnight at a DOC camping ground ($6 per site), from where you can walk another two hours to the Tarawera Falls.

For tramping on **Mt Tarawera**, the easiest access is from Ash Pit Rd at the northern end of Lake Rerewhakaaitu, but there is no public transport. Mt Tarawera is on private land, so firstly you need to pay the extortionate fee of $23 per person before entering the area. From the parking area it is a two-hour walk along a 4WD track to the crater chasm and Ruawhaia dome. From here, most walkers return along the same route, but it is possible to follow another track leading to Lakes Rotomahana and Tarawera.

It is essential to take water and wear good tramping shoes with ankle support – it's easy to slip on the volcanic scoria. The weather on Mt Tarawera can be very changeable, so bring warm and waterproof clothing to protect against wind and rain.

The **Okere Falls** are about 16km north-east of Rotorua on SH33 – the turn-off is well signposted. It's about a 30-minute walk through native podocarp forest to the falls. These are the 7m falls that the rafting companies take people over (see White-Water Rafting under Rotorua earlier). There are several other walks, including those up the Kaituna River to Hinemoa's Steps and to some caves.

Just north of Wai-o-Tapu on SH5, a good trail leads to **Rainbow Mountain**, with its small crater lakes and fine views. It's a short, but fairly strenuous 1½-hour walk to the top at Maungakakatamea Lookout.

Other short walks can be made around Lake Okataina, Mt Ngongotaha (just north of Rotorua) and Lake Rotorua.

White-Water Rafting

Several rafting companies organise white-water rafting trips on the Rangitaiki River (grade III to IV). Day trips with a barbecue lunch cost around $89. There are also trips to the fast flowing Wairoa River (grade IV to V; from $72), Motu River (grade IV to V) and multi-day trips to the Upper Mohaka (grade III to IV). Companies include:

Great Kiwi White Water Co (☎ 07-348 2144)
Kaituna Cascades (☎ 0800 524 8862)
Raftabout (☎ 0800 723 822)
River Rats (☎ 0800 333 900,
   W www.riverrats.co.nz)
Wet 'n' Wild Rafting (☎ 0800 462 7238,
   W www.wetnwildrafting.co.nz)
The Whitewater Excitement Co
   (☎ 07-345 7182, W www.raftnz.co.nz)

Most popular are the shorter and more dramatic rafting trips on the Kaituna River, off SH33 about 16km north-east of Rotorua. Time on the river is about 40 minutes and you go over the 7m Okere Falls, then over another 3m drop and various rapids (around $65). All Rotorua's rafting companies do a

Kaituna trip. Kaituna Cascades also does an extreme tandem kayak trip, in which a passenger, weighing less than 85kg with no prior experience can negotiate a series of grade V drops on the Kaituna. Book well ahead for ($95). Kaituna Kayaks (☎ 021 465 292) also offers tandems.

White-water Sledging

Kaitiaki Adventures (☎ 0800 338 736, 025 249 9481) does white-water sledging on the Rangitaiki River and on the Kaituna. You zoom along on a sledge especially designed for manoeuvrability on the river. The 1½-hour, grade II to III trip on the Rangitaiki costs $100 per person and the 2½-hour, grade II to V trip on the Kaituna, costs $115. The Kaituna trip includes one of the biggest buzzes you'll ever get in adventure tourism – going over the 7m Okere Falls. All the necessary equipment is supplied.

Fishing

You can hire guides to trout fish or go it alone but a licence is essential and there are various regulations. Guided fishing trips cost about $70 per hour per person (minimum 2 persons) but you are almost guaranteed to catch a fish. Plan to spend about two to three hours on the trip. Ask at Tourism Rotorua or at the Rotorua lakefront for fishing operators.

You can wander down to the Rotorua lakefront and fish if you have a licence. Not all lakes can be fished year round; check with the tourist office first before fishing other lakes. Get your fishing licence directly from a fishing guide or the **Map & Track Shop** (☎ 07-349 1845, 1225 Fenton St; licences per day/week/season $15/ 30/75). Fishing gear can also be hired at **O'Keefe's** (☎ 07-346 0178, 1113 Eruera St; rod & reel $15, waders $15).

Other Activities

The Whakarewarewa State Forest Park has some of the best **mountain bike trails** in the country. There are 10 tracks within the forest that will keep mountain bikers of all skill levels happy. **Planet Bike** (☎ 07-348 9971) hires out bikes and gear ($30 2 hours, $50 full day), does drop-offs and pick-ups,

BAY OF PLENTY

and also organises guided trips. For more information about the forest contact the **Fletcher Challenge Visitor Information Centre** (☎ 07-346 2082) in the forest.

For a bit of indoor exercise try the **indoor climbing wall** (☎ 07-350 1400, 1401 Hinemoa St; open 10am-10pm daily). The $20 fee includes all gear; it is $12 with your own gear.

You can go **tandem skydiving** (☎ 07-345 7520; dives $190-225) from the Rotorua airport. The initial flight includes some amazing views over the lakes and volcanoes of the region.

Adventure Kayaking (☎ 07-348 9451) has half-day kayaking trips on Lake Rotorua ($50); full-day trips on Lake Tarawera ($75) or Lake Rotoiti ($70); a twilight lake paddle with a soak in a hot pool ($60); and two- and three-day trips starting at $250. **Sunspots Go Kayaking** (☎ 07-362 4222) offers white-water and lake kayaking. The company also rents kayaks and gear.

Operators doing horse treks include **Farmhouse** (☎ 07-332 3771) and **Peka** (☎ 07-346 1755). It costs about $25 for the first hour and less for consecutive hours.

For 4WD experiences try: **Mountain Action** (☎ 07-348 8400) for tours through farm and bush (they also offer horse treks); **Mt Tarawera 4WD Tours** (☎ 07-349 3714) for tours to Mt Tarawera's summit; and **Off Road NZ** (☎ 07-332 5748) for self-drive tours through bush at Amoore Rd, 20km north of Rotorua. Prices start at around $60 for one hour (more for self drive).

Off-Road Luge (☎ 035 907 907, Tarawera Rd) has a sport luge that you ride down a gravel track ($25 per ride, including a helmet). Bookings can be made at Blue Lake Holiday Park (see Places to Stay).

Action New Zealand (☎ 07-348 3531, cnr Te Ngae Rd & Sala St) has a bunch of activities you can try, including axe and knife throwing, archery ($10), clay target shooting ($6) and a short nine-hole golf course ($10).

Organised Tours

Rotorua offers a mind-boggling array of tours. Tourism Rotorua can book any tours, as can hostels and hotels.

Carey's Sightseeing Tours (☎ 07-347 1197, 1108 Haupapa St; tours $28-145) is the largest outfit in Rotorua. It visits most of Rotorua's favourite volcanic and thermal attractions, with a dip in an isolated hot-water stream along the way (from $65 for a half-day tour to the Wai-o-Tapu and Waimangu thermal areas). Its 'world-famous' Waimangu Round Trip, well known here since 1902, is one of the best. Focusing on the 1886 Mt Tarawera eruption, it includes the Waimangu Volcanic Valley, a cruise on Lake Rotomahana past the site of the Pink and White Terraces, a cruise on Lake Tarawera, a visit to the Buried Village (formerly Te Wairoa), and a dip in the Polynesian Spa (adult/child $145/80, full day). The budget version is $130/70, without the spa.

InterCity (☎ 07-348 0366), **Newmans** (☎ 07-348 0999), and **Taylor's** are established companies while **Tekiri Trek** (☎ 035 391 288) comes locally recommended; Tourism Rotorua provides details of them and other companies.

Slim's East Cape Escape (☎ 07-345 6645, e slim@wave.co.nz; tour $250, accommodation extra $15-20 per night) is a four-day journey from Rotorua, right around the East Cape, and then heading back to Rotorua via Lake Waikaremoana. Pick-up from Rotorua backpackers is included.

Waitomo Wanderers (☎ 0800 924 866) does return trips to Waitomo.

Scenic Flights Flights over the city and the lake start at around $50, Tarawera flights around $130. Otherwise you can fly further afield to Whakaari (White Island) and even down to Mts Ruapehu and Ngauruhoe in Tongariro National Park.

Volcanic Wunderflites (☎ 0800 777 359; flights $70-480) is particularly popular for flights over the awesome chasm of Mt Tarawera.

Volcanic Air Safaris (☎ 0800 800 848; flights $50-725) has fixed-wing and helicopter flights, including a combined flight and jetboat experience.

Another operator that does flights over Tarawera ($120) and Taupo ($190) is **Lakeside Aviation** (☎ 07-345 4242).

Adventure Aviation (☎ 07-345 6780; flights $120-295) has a Boeing Stearman WWII open-cockpit biplane; trips include nice easy 'cotton wool cruises' ($120) over the lake and city, and more challenging looping, rolling, turning, stalling, 'gravity-grabber' tours ($150) for those who like to see things from all different perspectives.

Helicopter-tour specialists include **Helipro** (☎ 07-357 2512), which is based at Agrodome Leisure Park and Skyline Skyrides, **New Zealand Helicopters** (☎ 07-348 1223), based at Whakarewarewa, and **Heli-Kiwi** (☎ 07-366 6611), based at Wai-o-Tapu. They all fly over Mt Tarawera (New Zealand Helicopters is the only to land) and Whakaari and link up to other activities, such as 4WD tours and jetboating.

Places to Stay
Camping & Cabins Rotorua has a number of good camp grounds close to its centre.

Rotorua Top 10 Holiday Park (☎ 07-348 1886, e stay@rotoruatop10.co.nz, 137 Pukuatua St) Powered & unpowered sites $11 per person, cabins $40, tourist flats $55-60, motel units $70. This holiday park is beside Kuirau Park and has a solar-heated swimming pool in summer.

Cosy Cottage International Holiday Park (☎ 07-348 3793, fax 347 9634, 67 Whittaker Rd) Camp sites $11 per person, cabins $44, tourist flats $68. This park may be the only place in the world with heated camp sites – the ground warmth gradually warms your tent at night. It also has a mineral pool and a heated swimming pool, as well as canoes, bicycles and fishing tackle for hire.

Lakeside Thermal Holiday Park (☎/fax 07-348 1693, e relax@lakesidethermal .co.nz, 54 Whittaker Rd) Camp sites $10 per person, cabins $40, tourist flats $55-65. Lakeside Park has hot mineral pools and spas, and, as the name suggests, a lakeside position.

There are also many places a little out of the township (see the Around Rotorua map).

Holdens Bay Holiday Park (☎ 07-345 9925, e admin@holdensbay.co.nz, 21 Robinson Ave) Camp sites $12 per person,

cabins $28-48, tourist flats $58-72, motel units $70-88. Located about 500m from Lake Rotorua, and 6.5km from central Rotorua on SH30, this holiday park has a huge range of accommodation options.

All Seasons Holiday Park (☎/fax 07-345 6240, e janb@wave.co.nz, Lee Rd, Hannahs Bay) Camp sites $9 per person, on-site caravans $28, cabins $28-35, tourist flats $45-55. All Seasons is another kilometre on from Holdens Bay, off SH30.

Blue Lake Top 10 Holiday Park (☎ 07-362 8120, e bluelake@xtra.co.nz, Tarawera Rd) Unpowered/powered sites $10/11, cabins $39-47, tourist flats $68, motel units $84-88. Blue Lake Park is 10km from town, near the shores of Blue Lake. Kayaks, canoes, fishing boats and bicycles are available for hire. Prices increase over school holidays.

Lake Rotoiti Lakeside Holiday Park (☎ 07-362 4860, e lakerotoiti@xtra.co.nz, Okere Rd, Okere Falls) Powered sites $12.50 per person, cabins $40-55, self-contained units $75. This camping ground has a great spot on the shores of beautiful Lake Rotoiti, 21km north-east of Rotorua.

Redwood Holiday Park (☎ 07-345 9380, 5 Tarawera Rd, Ngapuna) Unpowered/powered sites $9.50/10 per person, bunk bed in lodge $16, cabins $50-60, tourist flats $60-70. Redwood is very handy to Whakarewarewa forest, 3km from the city centre at the intersection with Te Ngae Rd.

Other possibilities scattered around the lake include *Rainbow Resort* (☎ 07-357 4289, e k.a.bryan@xtra.co.nz, 22 Beaumonts Rd, Ngongotaha) 8km from the city centre and *Waiteti Trout Stream Holiday Park* (☎ 07-357 5255, 14 Okona Crescent, Ngongotaha) beside Waiteti Stream.

Hostels Backpackers are well catered for in Rotorua.

Funky Green Voyager (☎ 07-346 1754, 4 Union St) Dorms from $18, doubles & twins $41, doubles with en suite $45. This place is one of the smallest and nicest of Rotorua's backpackers. In a tranquil residential neighbourhood, close to the centre, the hostel is comfortable and casual with a spacious backyard and a pleasant sunny conservatory.

There's plenty of personal touches, such as heated towel rails, personal lockers and a welcoming sweet on your pillow.

Rotorua Central Backpackers (☎/fax 07-349 3285, e rotorua.central.bp@clear.net.nz, 1076 Pukuatua St) Dorms $19-20, twins & doubles $44. This place has spacious, tidy rooms and a spa pool in a classic older building. It's very clean, comfortable and quiet and centrally located.

Wall Backpackers (☎ 07-350 2040, fax 350 3020, e info@thewall.co.nz, 1140 Hinemoa St) Dorms $18-20, twins & doubles $45-60. This new kid on the block is modern and spacious, with large communal areas, personal lockers and a games room on the top floor. There's a climbing wall and bar within the complex.

Crash Palace (☎/fax 07-348 8842, 1271 Hinemaru St) Dorm beds $18-19, twins $45, doubles $46-38. This quiet and comfortable two-storey hostel, handy to central Rotorua, has a small but weel-stocked kitchen, a garden area and lounge with games.

Hot Rock (☎ 07-347 9469, e hotrock@acb.co.nz, 1286 Arawa St) Dorm beds from $18, twins $40, doubles $52, with en suite $50. Hot Rock is a former motel with plenty of rooms with good communal areas. There are three hot pools (indoor and outdoor) on the premises. The popular Lava Bar is adjacent.

Planet Nomad Backpackers (☎ 0800 666 237, ☎/fax 07-346 2831, cnr Haupapa & Fenton Sts) Dorms $17, twins & doubles $40. This spic-and-span place is on a busy road near Tourism Rotorua and the bus station. The rooms are a decent size and there is a large lounge.

Spa Lodge (☎ 07-348 3486, e spalodge@wave.co.nz, 1221 Amohau St) Dorm beds $14-16, twins & doubles $35. Spa Lodge is a lived-in hostel with a spa pool and thermally heated rooms.

Cactus Jacks Downtown Backpackers (☎/fax 07-348 3121, e cactusjackpb@xtra.co.nz, 54 Haupapa St) Dorms from $17.50, singles/twins/doubles $28/45/47. As its name suggests, Cactus Jacks has a distinctly Mexican theme. There are also spas for guests to use.

Kiwi Paka YHA (☎ 07-347 0931, e stay@kiwipaka-yha.co.nz, 60 Tarewa Rd) Unpowered/powered sites $9/10.50 per person, dorms $20, singles $27, twins & doubles $46, chalet $54. This efficient, modern associate YHA hostel is 1.2km from the city centre (it runs a transfer service for travellers). There is a thermal pool here as well as a pleasant cafe and a bar, *Under Canvas*.

B&Bs & Guesthouses Tourism Rotorua has listings for nearly 50 homestays and farmstays and can make bookings.

Tresco International (☎ 0800 873 726, 07-348 9611, e johngwyn@xtra.co.nz, 3 Toko St) Singles/doubles with breakfast $50/85. Each room here has its own bathroom and there is a free pick-up from the airport or bus stop.

Eaton Hall (☎/fax 07-347 0366, e eatonhallbnb@xtra.co.nz, 1255 Hinemaru St) Singles with/without bath $50/70, doubles $80/90. This central B&B is a comfortable, homey guesthouse with pleasant rooms.

Dudley House B&B (☎ 07-347 9894, 1024 Rangiuru St) Singles/doubles $40/65. The Tudor-style Dudley House is decorated in traditional English country-cottage style. It's very comfortable, spotless and has a shared bathroom.

Lake Tarawera Lodge (Around Rotorua map; ☎ 07-362 8754, e stay@laketarawera.co.nz) Lodge room $48 per double, cottages $135-155. This lovely lodge has views of Lake Tarawera and is surrounded by native bush.

Waiteti Lakeside Lodge (Around Rotorua map; ☎/fax 357 2311, e waitetilodge@xtra.co.nz, 2 Arnold St, Ngongotaha) Rooms from $125, self-contained bungalow $150. With lakeside views, comfy rooms with balconies, and lake and fishing trips available, Waiteti is a good choice.

Motels Rotorua has more motels than you can shake a stick at. Fenton St, in particular, has wall-to-wall motels as far as the eye can see.

Ann's Volcanic Rotorua (☎ 0800 768 683, 07-347 1007, e volcanic@xtra.co.nz,

107 Malfroy Rd) Units from $79. Ann's is a welcoming and friendly motel with good units, most with private spas.

Ashleigh Court Motel (☎ 0800 337 338, ☎/fax 07-348 7456, 337 Fenton St) Studio units $90, 1-bedroom units from $110. Ashleigh Court has self-contained studio units and self-contained, one-bedroom units. All have private spas.

Baden Lodge (☎ 0800 337 033, ☎/fax 07-349 0634, 301 Fenton St) Units $90-145. Baden Lodge has self-contained, one-bedroom units with private spas.

Birchwood Spa Motel (☎ 07-347 1800, e birchwood.spa.motel@clear.net.nz, cnr Sala St & Trigg Ave) Units from $95. Birchwood has studio, one- and two-bedroom units with private spas.

Hotels Rotorua has some big hotels, including the *Regal Geyserland* (☎ 0800 881 882, e geyserland@silveroaks.co.nz), with rooms from $89, and *Lake Plaza Rotorua* (☎ 07-348 1174), which has rooms from $115. From there it's a jump to the *Centra* (☎ 07-348 1189), *Rydges* (☎ 0800 367 793, e rydges.rotorua@clear.net.nz), the *Sheraton* (☎ 07-349 5200), *Royal Lakeside Novotel Hotel* (☎ 0800 776 677, 07-346 3888) and the *Millennium* (☎ 0800 654 685, 07-347 1234).

Princes Gate Hotel (☎ 07-348 1179, fax 348 6215, 1 Arawa St) Rooms from $130. This is a grand Victorian hotel with crystal chandeliers, canopies over the beds, an elegant restaurant and bar, a health facility and much more.

If expense is no obstacle, the luxurious *Kawaha Point Lodge* (Around Rotorua map; ☎ 07-346 3602, e kawaha.lodge.ro torua@xtra.co.nz, 171 Kawaha Point Rd) has doubles at around $700.

Places to Eat

Restaurants & Cafes Tutanekai St has the widest selection of restaurants and cafes in Rotorua.

The Bean (1149 Tutanekai St) Meals $6.50-11. The Bean makes good sandwiches and hearty cooked breakfasts, along with great coffee.

Zippy Central Cafe (1153 Pukuatua St) Meals $9-13. Zippys is very popular for its bagels and smoothies.

Cafe DNA (Arawa St) Meals $8.50-13. This groovy spot has bruschetta, curry, pasta and the like. It's open late and is popular for a quiet drink.

Fat Dog (☎ 07-347 7586, 1161 Arawa St) Mains $12-20. Fat Dog is a colourful and popular cafe, good for meals at any time of the day.

Freos (☎ 07-346 0976, 1103 Tutanekai St) Mains around $15-25. Freos does lots of pasta, chargrills, salmon fillet, and a venison hotpot.

Zanelli's (☎ 07-348 4908, 1243 Amohia St) Mains from $16. Open evenings Tues-Sun. This is a popular Italian dinner house, with oodles of pasta dishes.

Millennium House (1074 Eruera St) Mains from $10. This is a large and pleasant place serving Korean and Japanese food.

Sirocco (☎ 07-347 3388, 1280 Eruera St) Mains from $15. Sirocco is a popular Mediterranean-style restaurant in a stylish old house.

The Thai Restaurant (☎ 07-348 6677, 1141 Tutanekai St) Meals $19-20. This place offers nicely spicy Thai meals. It also has an extensive wine list.

Mr India (☎ 07-349 4940, 1161 Amohau St) Mains $15-17. Mr India is moderately priced and has all the authentic subcontinent favourites as well as a good selection of vegetarian dishes.

River Monster (☎ 07-346 0792, 1139 Tutanekai St) Mains $18-25. This modern sushi bar has plenty of Japanese dinner choices and cheap lunch deals ($10-12.50).

Rendezvous Restaurant (☎ 07-348 9273, 1282 Hinemoa St) Mains $25-30. For genuine Pacific Rim cuisine, featuring innovative use of local ingredients, try this restaurant.

Lewisham's Restaurant (☎ 07-346 0976, 1099 Tutanekai St) Mains $23-27. Lewisham's food menu ranges from Spanish to Austrian.

Herb's (☎ 07-348 3985, Tutanekai St) Mains $23-32. The steaks at Herb's may not be on the cheap side but they're mighty fine.

BAY OF PLENTY

Zambique (☎ *07-349 2140, 1111 Tutanekai St*) Bar snacks around $10, mains $17-27. Zambique's menu covers a wide spectrum, including kiwiana, Asian and Mediterranean dishes.

Mitas (☎ *07-349 6482, 1114 Tutanekai St*) Mains $24-29. Mitas serves quality Indonesian dishes which have earned loads of local food awards.

Pub Food The best pub in town for food is the ***Pig & Whistle*** (☎ *07-347 3025, cnr Haupapa & Tutanekai Sts*). There's soups and salads, burgers ($12-14) and generous meals, including twice cooked ribs ($14), which comes with pig-tail fries.

Fast Food The Rotorua Central Mall on Amohau St has a *food court* with a good range of eating options.

Tastebuds Mexican Cantina (*1213 Fenton St*) This cheap and cheerful place serves up the usual Tex-Mex fare such as burritos and enchiladas.

Rapscallion Gourmet Burgers (*1207 Fenton St*) Burgers $6.50-10. Rapscallion has a huge array of tasty burgers.

Fishspot (☎ *07-349 3494, 1123 Eruera St*) Mains $17-28. Try this spot for fish and chips and other seafood dishes.

Lady Jane's Ice Cream Parlour, near the lake end of Tutanekai St, is popular with sweet-tooths (ice creams from $1.60).

Entertainment

Many of the cafes in town, such as ***Fat Dog*** and ***Cafe DNA***, turn into popular watering holes after sunset.

At the ***Lava Bar*** in the Hot Rock backpackers (see Places to Stay earlier) you can mix with an international and local crowd, play pool and listen to good sounds.

Outlaws, in the Wall Backpackers (see Places to Stay), is another hostel bar attracting a mix of locals and foreigners.

Pig & Whistle (see the recommendation in the Places to Eat section earlier) is a popular renovated police station with a number of brews on tap, including its own Swine Lager. Guzzle a Swiney and listen to bands on weekend nights.

Other good bars are ***Wild Willy's*** (*1240 Fenton St*) a 'Wild West' bar, and ***O'Malley's*** (*1287 Eruera St*), an Irish pub.

Monkey Jo's (*1263 Amohia St*) is a popular spot that packs them in most nights of the week. It can be rough, though.

Fuze (☎ *07-349 6306, cnr Pukaki & Tutanekai Sts*) is a chilled out bar attracting a more mature crowd. It has a nice ambience, good cocktails and occasional live music.

Bar Barella (*1263 Pukeuatua St*) is good for drum 'n' base on the weekends.

Getting There & Away

Air The Air New Zealand office (☎ 07-343 1100) on the corner of Fenton and Hinemoa Sts is open from 8.30am to 5pm weekdays; it also has a counter at the airport (☎ 07-345 6175) open daily. It offers daily direct flights to Auckland, Christchurch, Nelson, Queenstown and Wellington, with onward connections.

Bus All major bus companies stop at the Tourism Rotorua centre (☎ 07-348 0366, information and bookings) on Fenton St, which handles bookings.

InterCity (☎ 07-348 0366) has daily buses to and from Auckland ($35, four hours), Wellington ($78, 8hrs), Tauranga ($25, 1½hrs) and Hamilton ($19, 1½hrs). On the East Coast routes, InterCity goes daily to Gisborne ($39, 4½hrs) via Opotiki ($18, 2hrs 10mins) and Whakatane ($18, 1½hrs), and to Napier ($57, 3hrs) via Taupo ($25, 1hr).

Newmans (☎ 07-348 0999) go from Rotorua to Auckland ($33, 3½hrs), Hamilton ($19), Taupo ($23, 1¼hrs), Wellington ($78, 6½hrs), Palmerston North ($57, 5½hrs), Tauranga ($23, 1½hrs) and Napier ($55, 4hrs). Magic Bus and Kiwi Experience backpackers buses also stop in Rotorua.

Gutherys Express (☎ 0800 759 999) runs daily buses to Auckland ($35), Hamilton ($20, 2hrs), Taupo ($18) and Waitomo ($30, 2hrs).

Hitching Hitching to Rotorua is generally easy, except on SH38 from Waikaremoana – past Murupara the road is unsealed and traffic is very light. The problem hitching out of Rotorua is often the sheer number of backpackers leaving town. You may have to join the queue and wait.

Getting Around

To/From the Airport The airport is located about 10km out of town, on the eastern side of the lake. Super Shuttle (☎ 07-349 3444) offers a door-to-door service to and from the airport for $10 for the first person and $2 for each additional passenger after that. A taxi from the city centre costs about $18.

Bus There are a multitude of shuttle services to many of the attractions around town. Check with Tourism Rotorua for details.

The Magic of the Maori shuttle (☎ 0800 021 987) does a constant loop service daily, starting at Tourism Rotorua at 8.45am and the the last circuit leaving at 4.15pm. It drops by several hostels, including Ki-wipaka and Hot Rock, as well as all the major attractions, including the Agrodome, Whakarewarewa and Rainbow Springs. It costs $4 for a one-way trip and $12 for an all-day pass. A timetable is available from Tourism Rotorua.

Mt Tarawera Eruption

In the mid-19th century Lake Rotomahana, near Rotorua, was a major tourist attraction. It brought visitors from around the world to see the Pink and White Terraces: two large and beautiful terraces of multileveled pools, formed by silica deposits from thermal waters that had trickled over them for centuries. The Maori village of Te Wairoa, on the shores of nearby Lake Tarawera, was the departure point for visiting the terraces. From here a guide and rowers would take visitors by boat across Lake Tarawera to Rotomahana and the terraces. Mt Tarawera, which had not been active in the 500 years since Maori arrival in the area, towered silently over the lakes.

On 31 May 1886, the principal terrace guide, Sophia Hinerangi, took a party of tourists across Lake Tarawera to see the terraces. Two unusual events occurred that morning: as they boarded the boat a surge of water created a wave on the lake; and as they crossed Lake Tarawera a ceremonial canoe of a kind not seen on the lake for 50 years, glided across its waters. The *waka wairua* (phantom canoe) was seen by all in the tourist boat, both Maori and Pakeha.

To Te Wairoa Maori, the appearance of the canoe was an omen of impending disaster, and Tuhoto Ariki an old *tohunga* (priest) living in Te Wairoa had already told of impending calamity in the community.

In the early hours of 10 June 1886 there were earthquakes and loud sounds, and the erupting Mt Tarawera lit up the sky with exploding fireballs from its three vents. By the time the eruption finished five hours later, over 1500 sq km had been buried in ash, lava and mud. The Maori villages of Te Wairoa, Te Ariki and Moura were obliterated, 153 people were killed, the Pink and White Terraces were destroyed and Mt Tarawera was sliced open along its length as if hit with a huge cleaver. The small Lake Rotomahana swelled to many times its pre-eruption size.

Over the following days excavations were carried out at Te Wairoa to rescue survivors. Guide Sophia became a heroine, having saved many lives by providing shelter in her well-constructed *whare* (house). The old tohunga, however, was not so fortunate. He was trapped inside his buried whare and Maori working to rescue survivors refused to dig him out. They feared he had used his magic powers to cause the eruption: he had claimed that the orientation of the villagers towards tourism and a cash economy were not traditional, and that neglect of the old traditions would anger the fire spirit inside the mountain. After four days had passed, he was dug out alive by Europeans who took him to the Rotorua Sanatorium. He died a week later, aged around 104.

Ritchies Coachlines (☎ 07-345 5694) operates shuttles to many of the attractions in and around Rotorua. An all-day pass costs $7; one stage costs $1.60. They also run suburban buses to Whakarewarewa (route 3) and Rainbow Springs (route 2; Ngongotaha), departing/arriving Rotorua on Pukuatua St.

Car Rotorua has a host of car rental companies. The competition is fierce and all seem to offer 'specials' to undercut the competitors. Rent-a-Dent (☎ 07-349 3993), on 14 Ti St, and Link Low Cost Rentals (☎ 07-349 1629), at 1222 Fenton St, are two economical companies.

Ask about relocating cars to Auckland: you pay only for insurance and fuel.

Bicycle Rotorua is fairly spread out and public transport isn't good, so a bicycle is worthwhile. Bicycle-hire places include Lady Jane's (☎ 07-347 9340), on the corner of Tutanekai and Whakaue Sts, and the Rotorua Cycle Centre (☎ 07-348 6588). Planet Bike (☎ 07-348 9971) operates a drop off and pick-up service from Wall Backpackers. Expect to pay about $15 per hour for a mountain bike; a full day costs around $50.

AROUND ROTORUA
Hell's Gate

Hell's Gate (☎ 07-345 3151, Te Ngae; adult/child $12/6; open 9am-8pm daily) is another highly active thermal area 16km north-east of Rotorua on the road to Whakatane (SH30). George Bernard Shaw visited Hell's Gate in 1934 and said of it, 'I wish I had never seen the place, it reminds me too vividly of the fate theologians have promised me'. The reserve covers 10 hectares, with a 2.5km walking track to the various attractions, including the largest hot thermal waterfall in the southern hemisphere, a spa pool ($10) and mud bath ($25).

Waimangu Volcanic Valley

The valley is another interesting thermal area (☎ 07-366 6137; valley walk adult/child $18/5, boat trip $22/5, walk & boat trip $40/10; open 8.30am-5pm daily) created during the eruption of Mt Tarawera in 1886. Walking through the valley (an easy downhill stroll) you'll first pass many interesting thermal and volcanic features, including the Inferno Crater Lake, where overflowing water can reach 80°C. Waima-ngu means 'Black Water', as much of the water here was a dark, muddy colour. In this valley, the Waimangu Geyser was once active enough to be rated the 'largest geyser in the world'. Between 1900 and its extinction in 1904 it would occasionally spout jets of black water nearly 500m high!

The walk continues down to Lake Rotomahana (meaning 'Warm Lake'), from where you can either get a lift back up to where you started or take a half-hour boat trip on the lake, past steaming cliffs and the former site of the Pink and White Terraces.

Waimangu is approximately a 20-minute drive from Rotorua, 19km south on SH5 (towards Taupo) and then 5km to 6km from the marked turn-off.

Wai-o-Tapu

Also south of Rotorua, Wai-o-Tapu (☎ 07-366 6333; adult/child $15/5; open 8am-5pm daily), meaning 'Sacred Waters', is perhaps the best of the thermal areas to visit. It has many interesting features, including the large, boiling Champagne Pool, craters and blowholes, colourful mineral terraces and the Lady Knox Geyser, which spouts off (with a little prompting) punctually at 10.15am and gushes for about an hour.

Performing to Schedule

How does the Lady Knox Geyser manage to perform so neatly to schedule? Simple – it's blocked up with some rags so the pressure builds up, then a couple of kilos of soap powder is shoved in to decrease the surface viscosity and off it goes.

This scientific principle of the relation of soap powder to surface viscosity of geysers was discovered by some early settlers who thought it would be a great idea to use the hot water in the ground to wash their clothes.

AROUND ROTORUA

To Tauranga via Pyes Pa (45km)

The Farmhouse

To Tauranga (56km)

Kaituna River

33

Okere Falls

Lake Rotoiti Lakeside Holiday Park

Okere Falls

Hamurana Springs

Waiteti Trout Stream Holiday Park

Ohau Channel

Lake Rotorua

Hell's Gate

Tikitere

Lake Rotoiti

Hongi's Track

Lake Rotoehu

Hinehopu

30

To Kawerau (16km), Whakatane (47km) & Gisborne (288km)

Waiteti Lakeside Lodge

To Agrodome, Hamilton & Auckland

Greengrove Holiday Park

Rainbow Resort

Mountain Adventures

Rainbow Springs & Skyline Skyrides

Kawaha Point Lodge

The Happy Homestead

Skyline Gondola

Mt Ngongotaha (745m)

See Rotorua map p344

Mokoia Island

Te Ngae

Te Ngae Park

Lake Rotokawau

Ruato

Lake Rotokawau

Airport

Hedge Maze

Western Okataina Walkway

Lake Okataina

Lake Okataina

Tarawera Forest

Eastern Okataina Walkway

All Seasons Holiday Park; Holdens Bay Holiday Park

30

Redwood Holiday Park

Fletcher Challenge Visitor Information Centre

Tarawera Rd

Lake Okareka

To Paradise Valley Springs

30A

Rotorua

Te Whakarewarewa

Action New Zealand

Whakarewarewa State Forest Park

Off Road Luge

Tarawera Landing; Landing Cafe

DOC Campsite

Northern Tarawera Track

Tarawera Falls

Tarawera River

Tarawera Outlet; DOC Campsite

Peka Horse Treks

30

Blue Lake Holiday Park

Blue Lake

Lake Tarawera Lodge

Lake Tarawera

Green Lake

Te Wairoa (Buried Village)

Waimangu Round Trip

To Te Kuiti (130km)

Whakarewarewa State Forest Park

Crater

Chasm

Mt Tarawera (erupted 1886)

Tamaki Tours (Maori Village)

Hot Water Beach; Te Rata Bay; DOC Campsite

Site of Pink Tces (destroyed 1886)

Patiti Island

Lake Rotomahana

Waimangu Rd

Waimangu Volcanic Valley

0   5   10km
0   3   6mi

Lake Okaro

Lake Rerewhakaaitu

Waikite Valley Thermal Pool

Waikite Valley

Rainbow Mt (743m)

Rerewhakaaitu Rd

Ash Pit Rd

Rerewhakaaitu

Rainbow Mountain Walkway

5

Wai-O-Tapu

Old Waiotapu Rd

Lake Opouri

Mud Pools

Kerosene Creek Thermal Area

Lady Knox Geyser

Wai-O-Tapu Thermal Area

Kaingaroa Forest

Paeroa Range

To Taupo (30km)

To Murupara (19km), Whirinaki Forest Park (44km) & Lake Waikaremoana (113km)

38

BAY OF PLENTY

Last entry to Wai-o-Tapu is at 4pm; it's usually open later in summer. It is 30km south of Rotorua on SH5 (towards Taupo), and a further 2km from the marked turn-off.

Trout Springs

Several springs run down to Lake Rotorua and the trout, lured by the feeds from tourists, swim up the streams to the springs. If you watch you may see a trout leaping the little falls to come up to the springs or returning to the lake.

The **Rainbow Springs Trout & Wildlife Sanctuary** (☎ 07-347 9301; adult/child $19.95/9.50; open 8am-5pm daily; tours 11am & 1pm) is the best known of the trout springs. There are a number of springs (one with an underwater viewer), an aviary and a nocturnal kiwi house. It's a pleasant walk through the ponga trees and native bush to see the trout in the streams. Pick up your bag of trout feed at the entrance and watch the feeding frenzy – unless a tour bus has gone through and the trout have already pigged out. The springs also have a wildlife area with eels, wallabies, deer, birds, sheep, wild pigs and other native and introduced fauna, now all found in the wild in NZ.

Across the road, the **Rainbow Farm Show** is part of Rainbow Springs and has shows at 10.30am, 11.45am, 1pm, 2.30pm and 4pm, with sheep shearing and sheepdogs. Also across the road and part of Rainbow Springs is the **Rainbow World of Bees**, which is devoted to those honey-producing wonders. Shows are at 11.15am and 1.45pm.

Rainbow Springs is 4km north of central Rotorua, on the west side of Lake Rotorua – take SH5 towards Hamilton and Auckland, or catch the Magic of the Maori shuttle bus. Admission to Rainbow Springs includes the farm show, bee show and springs.

Paradise Valley Springs (☎ 07-348 9667; adult/child $15/7.50; open 8am-5pm daily) are similar to Rainbow Springs. Set in an attractive 6-hectare park with various animals, including a pride of lions which are fed at 2.30pm, the springs, 13km from Rotorua on Paradise Valley Rd, are at the foot of Mt Ngongotaha.

Skyline Skyrides

Skyline Skyrides (☎ 07-347 0027; gondola adult/child $13.50/5.50, gondola & 5 luge rides $26/19; open from 9am daily) is on the west side of Lake Rotorua, near the Rainbow and Fairy Springs. Here you can take a gondola ride up Mt Ngongotaha for a panoramic view of the lake area and, once there, fly back down the mountain on one of three concrete tracks on a luge (a sort of toboggan on wheels – it's a lot more fun than it sounds), coming back up again on a chairlift. There is a cafe and restaurant on top of the mountain.

There is also a flight simulator, sky swing (sort of like a reverse bungy) and other attractions to spend your money on at the top, and there are walking tracks around the mountain.

Agrodome

If seeing millions of sheep in rural NZ has stimulated your interest in these animals, visit Agrodome (adult/child $15/7.50, tour $18/9, tour & show $27/13.50). Paying to see a bunch of sheep seems a rather strange thing to do in NZ, but you get an interesting educational and entertaining one-hour show at 9.30am, 11am and 2.30pm daily. There are sheep-shearing and sheepdog displays, and after all that, you may even be able to tell the difference between some of the 19 breeds of sheep on show. There's also a dairy display, farmyard nursery and cow-milking demonstration.

BAY OF PLENTY

You can also hire horses for a guided tour or else take a farm-buggy tour of the 120-hectare farm. Agrodome is 7km north of Rotorua on SH1.

Agrodome Adventure Park As the name suggests, the Adventure Park (☎ 0800 949 888) is a little more exciting than watching sheep being shorn. Here you have the chance to zorb, bungy, swoop and ride the agrojet.

Like the bungy, **zorbing** (dry or wash cycle $40, $35 from three-quarters of the way up) is another of those unusual Kiwi innovations. The rules are simple: climb into an inflated double plastic sphere (the two spheres are held together with shock cords), strap in and then roll downhill for about 150m. You will rotate within the sphere, and eventually the sphere will come to a stop. To cure a hangover (or make it *much* worse), skip the tying in and ask for a couple of buckets of cold water to be tossed inside the sphere – you literally slip downhill. It really is a lot of fun.

If that isn't enough for the adrenaline junkies, move onto a 43m **bungy** ($80), a ride on a rather large swing called the **swoop** ($45), which reaches speeds of up to 130km/h; or go for a spin in the **agrojet** ($35), a supremely speedy jet boat that whips you around a 1km manmade course before you can even catch your breath. Prices decrease if you do two or more rides.

Mazes

Near the airport are a couple of large mazes. The **Hedge Maze** (adult/child $5/2.50; open 9am-6pm daily), opposite the airport, is the largest hedge maze in NZ, with a 1.6km pathway. As well as the maze, there are also gardens, ponds, an orchard, picnic areas, birds and animals.

Te Ngae Park (☎ 07-345 5275; adult/child $5/2.50; open 9am-5pm daily), 3km beyond the airport, is a 3D, 1.7km wooden maze similar to the original Wanaka maze in the South Island.

Buried Village

The Buried Village (☎ 07-362 8287; adult/child $14/4; open 9am-5.30pm daily summer, 9am-4.30pm daily winter), Te Wairoa, is reached by a 15km scenic drive from Rotorua along Tarawera Rd, which passes the Blue and Green Lakes. There's a museum just beyond the ticket counter that has many artefacts and interesting background on the events before and after the eruption. Of particular interest is the story of the *tohunga* Tuhoto Ariki who, according to some, was blamed for the destruction (see the earlier boxed text, 'Mt Tarawera Eruption'). The site of his *whare* (house) has been excavated and the dwelling reconstructed. It is on display in the park along with excavations of other buildings buried by volcanic debris, including one of the hotels. There's a peaceful bush walk through the valley to Te Wairoa Falls, which drops about 80m over a series of rocky outcrops. The last part of the track to the falls is steep and not really suitable for young children to attempt.

Lake Tarawera

About 2km past the Buried Village is Tarawera Landing on the shore of Lake Tarawera. Tarawera means 'Burnt Spear', named by a visiting hunter who left his birdspears in a hut and on returning the following season found both the spears and hut had been burnt.

Tarawera Launch Services (☎ 07-362 8595; adult/child $27/13.50) has a cruise at 11am crossing over Lake Tarawera towards Lake Rotomahana. It stays on the other side for about 45 minutes, long enough for people to walk across to Lake Rotomahana, then returns to the landing. The trip takes 2½ hours.

A shorter 45-minute **cruise** (adult/child $17/9) on Lake Tarawera leaves at 1.30pm, 2.30pm and 3.30pm (the latter two trips operate in summer).

Boats from Tarawera Landing can also provide transport to Mt Tarawera and to Hot Water Beach on Te Rata Bay. The beach has hot thermal waters and a very basic *camping ground* run by the Department of Conservation (DOC).

You can relax on shore near where the launch leaves at the peaceful *Landing Cafe*

& Old Trout Bar (☎ *07-362 8502*). It's open for breakfast, lunch and dinner (around $14) and there is a cosy open log fire.

Whirinaki Forest Park

About 50km south-east of Rotorua, signposted off the main road, is the 609 sq km Whirinaki Forest Park. Access is off SH38 on the way to Te Urewera National Park; take the turn-off at Te Whaiti to Minginui. The park is noted for the sheer majesty and density of its native podocarp forests; it has walking tracks, scenic drives, camping and huts, lookouts, waterfalls, the Whirinaki River and some special areas, including Oriuwaka Ecological Reserve and Arahaki Lagoon. The booklet *Tramping & Walking in Whirinaki Forest Park* from DOC has (rather dated) information about the park.

The best source of information on the park is the DOC Rangitaiki Area Office (☎ 07-366 1080) in Murupara.

Ask for details on the fine Whirinaki Track, an easy two-day walk. This can be combined with Te Hoe Loop Walk for a four-day walk (with seven huts) that starts in some of NZ's finest podocarp forest and proceeds along a series of river valleys.

Places to Stay Down by the Whirinaki River, at Mangamate Waterfall, there is an informal *camping area* with camp sites at $6. The forest has 10 *backcountry huts* costing $5 per person. Murupara has all types of accommodation as well as food outlets.

Western Bay of Plenty

The western Bay of Plenty extends from Katikati and Waihi Beach to Te Puke on the coast and south to the Kaimai Ranges.

The area is not as popular with tourists as the far more commercial Bay of Islands, but in summer it hums along nicely. It enjoys one of the highest proportions of sunny days in NZ, the climate is consistently mild year-round and in summer the coastal beaches are popular.

TAURANGA
pop 58,500

Tauranga is the principal city of the Bay of Plenty and one of the largest export ports in NZ, shipping out the produce of the rich surrounding region. The days of the overnight kiwi fruit millionaires have gone but the area is still thriving economically and draws increasing numbers of retirees, attracted by the temperate climate and a city well endowed with facilities. Tauranga is indeed a pleasant place to live but its tourist attractions are limited mostly to the beaches and headland scenery of Mt Maunganui across the harbour.

Tauranga is Maori for 'Resting Place for Canoes', for this was where some of the first Maori arrived from Polynesian Hawaiki.

As the centre of NZ's principal kiwi fruit region, work is available when the fruit is being picked (May and June) but you may be able to find some orchard or agricultural work at almost any time. Check with the hostels for work contacts.

Information

The Tauranga visitors centre (☎ 07-578 8103, **W** www.tauranga.govt.nz), located at 95 Willow St; opens 7am to 5.30pm weekdays and 8am to 4pm on weekends.

The public library, also at 95 Willow St, has Internet access, and there are plenty of Internet cafes scattered around town.

The DOC office (☎ 07-578 7677) is at 253 Chadwick Rd West, Greerton (about 10 minutes' drive from the centre of Tauranga – follow Cameron Rd).

The AA office (☎ 07-578 2222) is on the corner of Devonport Rd and First Ave.

Things to See

The **Tauranga Community Village** (*☎ 07-571 3700, 155 Seventeenth Ave; admission free; open 8.30am-4.30pm Mon-Fri, 9.30am-4pm Sat & Sun*) features restored period buildings, but it is mainly a location for community organisations.

Te Awanui, a fine replica Maori canoe, is on display in an open-sided building at the top end of The Strand, close to the centre of town. Continue uphill beyond the canoe to

CENTRAL TAURANGA

PLACES TO STAY
2   Roselands Motel
22 Harbour City Motor Inn
23 Tauranga YHA
36 Tauranga Motel

PLACES TO EAT
5   The Old Bond Store
7   Fresh Fish Market
10 Amphora Cafe & Bar
11 Lone Star; Crazy Jack's
13 Soho
14 Tapa Tapa Bar
15 Fish Crazee; Roma
16 Crown & Badger
17 Shiraz
18 New Delhi Cafe & Bar
24 Piccola Italia
26 Stars & Stripes Diner;
     Latino
27 Crowded Muffin
28 Mediterraneo
29 Beach Street
30 Harbourside
     Brasserie & Bar
31 Sushi; Turkish to Go
34 Lava Cafe

PUBS, BARS & CLUBS
9   Grumpy Mole
12 Flannagan's Irish Pub
19 The Bahama Hut

OTHER
1   The Elms Mission
     Station House
3   Robbins Park
4   Monmouth Redoubt
6   Te Awanui Waka
     (Canoe)
8   Bungy Rocket
20 Visitors Centre; Bus
     Terminal; Public Library
21 Baycourt
25 West Plaza
32 Cinema 5
33 Air New Zealand
35 Automobile
     Association (AA)

Monmouth Redoubt, a fortified site during the Maori Wars. Further along is **Robbins Park**, with a rose garden and hothouse.

The **Elms Mission Station House** (☎ 07-577 9772, Mission St; admission $5; open 2pm-4pm Sun & public holidays) was founded in 1835; the present house was completed in 1847 by a pioneer missionary and is furnished in period style.

Walking

There are many walking possibilities around Tauranga and Mt Maunganui. A good number of these are outlined in the free pamphlet *Walkways of Tauranga,* including the fascinating **Waikareao estuary**. For walks further afield pick up a copy of *Short Walks of the Western Bay of Plenty* ($1). Both are available from visitors centres.

The backdrop to the western Bay of Plenty is the rugged 70km-long **Kaimai-Mamaku Forest Park**, with tramps for the more adventurous. More detailed information on walks in this area is provided in the DOC pamphlet *Kaimai Mamaku Forest Park Day Walks* ($1). **McLaren Falls** *(admission free; open 8am-5.30pm, 8am-7.30pm summer)*, found in the Wairoa River

BAY OF PLENTY

valley, 15km south-west of Tauranga just off SH29, is worth a visit. There's good walking, rock pools and the falls.

Sea Activities

During summer, Tauranga comes alive with sea activities of all kinds, including swimming with dolphins, jet-skiing, parasailing, water-skiing, windsurfing, sea kayaking, diving, surfing, swimming, line fishing, deep-sea fishing and sailing. The visitors centre has lots of information on operators. Fishing is a year-round activity: read the centre's *Charter Boats for Hire* brochure.

The **Tauranga Dolphin Company** (☎ *0800 836 574*) and **Dolphin Seafaris** (☎ *0800 326 8747,* W *www.nzdolphin.com*) run dolphin-swimming trips. Even if you don't meet the dolphins it is good value for a day cruise and you get to snorkel on the reefs. Trips cost around $100.

White-Water Rafting

White-water rafting is popular around Tauranga, particularly on the Wairoa River, which has some of the best falls and rafting in NZ. It's definitely a rafting trip for thrill-seekers. One highlight of the trip is a plunge over a 4m waterfall! The water level is controlled by a dam, so it can only be rafted a few days of the year. Contact **Wet 'N' Wild Rafting** (☎ *0800 462 7238*) for more information. It also has trips on other rivers.

Flying & Skydiving

The Tauranga airport at Mt Maunganui is the base for a number of air clubs. Scenic flights can be arranged at the airport. The **Tauranga Glider Club** (☎ *07-575 6768*) flies every weekend, weather permitting.

A 8000ft tandem skydiving starts at $190 with **Tandem Skydiving** (☎ *07-576 7990*).

A different way to fly is on the **Bungy Rocket**. Shoot above The Strand reclamation car park for $35 per person (two at a time); it fires from 10am until late daily.

Places to Stay

Most of the places to stay around Tauranga are a little out of the town centre (see the Tauranga and Mt Maunganui map).

Camping & Cabins There are a couple of camp grounds close to town.

Silver Birch Thermal Holiday Park (☎*/fax 578 4603,* e *silverbirch@xtra.co.nz, 101 Turret Rd*) Unpowered/powered sites $10/11 per person, cabins $27.50-45, tourist flats $55, motel units $65. The Silver Birch is on the Waimapu Estuary, not far from town. It has thermal pools, a boat ramp, dinghies and other recreational facilities.

McLaren Falls Park (☎ *07-577 7000, McLaren Falls Rd*) Camp sites $4 per person, hotel beds $15. This picturesque park has basic camp sites and three accommodating hostels (see the walking section earlier for directions to the park).

Mayfair Tourist Park (☎ *07-578 3323, fax 578 5910, 9 Mayfair St*) Camp sites $12 per person, cabins $40, tourist cabins $70. This park, off busy Fifteenth Ave, is beside the harbour.

Palms Caravan Park (☎ *07-578 9337, 162 Waihi Rd*) Camp sites $10 per person, cabins $38-40. Palms Park is about 4km south of the city centre. Some cabins have their own bathrooms.

Hostels Tauranga has a good selection of backpackers, which fill up in the kiwi fruit picking season.

Tauranga YHA (☎ *07-578 5064,* e *yha taur@yha.org.nz, 171 Elizabeth St*) Camp sites $13 per person, dorms $16, twins $38, doubles $40. Tauranga is a cosy hostel, conveniently close to the city centre. There's a pleasant garden, and lockers for your gear.

Bell Lodge (☎ *07-578 6344,* e *book ings@bell-lodge.co.nz, 39 Bell St*) Camp sites $10 per person, bunk beds $18, twins/doubles with en suite $44, motel units $60. Bell Lodge, 4km west of town, is a newer, purpose-built hostel, pleasantly situated on three hectares of land. This friendly hostel is well equipped, with heating in all the rooms, a big kitchen and a lounge with a fireplace; the motel units are separate from the hostel. Phone for a free pick-up.

Apple Tree Cottage (☎ *07-576 7404, 47 Maxwell St*) Camp sites $8 per person, dorms $15, doubles $36. Apple Tree Cottage, at Pillans Point, Otumoetai, is a small, friendly backpackers in a private house, with a basic bunkroom bungalow at the back with a hot spa. Tours can be arranged here.

Just the Ducks Nuts (☎ 07-576 1366, fax 549 0336, 6 Vale St) Dorms $20, twins & doubles $40. This six-bedroom house has a laid-back atmosphere, good communal areas and comfy rooms. They will drop off and pick up.

Bracewell Lodge (☎ 07-552 4009, 23 Paparoa Rd) Dorms $20, doubles $40. Bracewell Lodge at Te Puna, approximately 9km north of Tauranga, is a self-described 'sports lodge'. It has a kitchen, two lounges with Sky TV, kayaks, volleyball equipment and a swimming pool. Pick-up and drop-off from Tauranga are free.

Motels & Hotels There are over 30 motels around Tauranga. The biggest concentrations are on Waihi Rd and Fifteenth Ave, where you'll find many older motels.

Roselands Motel (☎ 07-578 2294, e pe termarldickson@actrix.gen.nz, 21 Brown St) Singles/doubles from $75/80. Roselands Motel has roomy units and it's located in a central yet quiet spot.

Harbour View Motel (☎ 07-578 8621, e harbview@wave.co.nz, 7 Fifth Ave) Singles/ doubles $75/85. The Harbour View has huge units for a very reasonable price.

Ambassador Motor Inn (☎ 07-578 5665, e ambassador.tga@xtra.co.nz, 9 Fifteenth Ave) Units $80-110. The modern units at the Ambassador are spacious. Some come with spa baths.

Tauranga Motel (☎ 0800 109 007, 07-578 7079, fax 578 0812, 1 Second Ave) Singles $90-110, doubles $105-125. Tauranga Motel offers plush units that feature views of the harbour.

Harbour City Motor Inn (☎ 07-571 1435, e taurangaharbourcity@xtra.co.nz, 50 Wharf St) Units $110. The Harbour City is shiny, new and modern, and very close to downtown.

Guesthouses & B&Bs The *homestay* (☎ 07-576 8895, e rossvale@xtra.co.nz, 8a Vale St), next to Just the Ducks Nuts, is a spic-and-span modern home, with a large twin room and spacious bathroom. It costs $40/70 (single/double).

Places to Eat

Restaurants & Cafes Many good eating options line Devonport Rd and The Strand.

Lava Cafe (130 Devonport Rd) Dishes from $4. This exotic, almost esoteric cafe has good coffee and snacks, and occasional live music.

Mediterraneo (62 Devonport Rd) Dishes from $4. Mediterraneo is a European-style restaurant with great cakes and coffee; it also has occasional live music.

Beach Street (☎ 07-578 0745, 72 Devonport Rd) Mains $18-25. Sandwiched between The Strand and Devonport Rd, this place has an innovative menu and pleasant terrace overlooking the harbour.

Harbourside Brasserie & Bar (☎ 07-571 0520, The Strand) Mains $20-30. There is outdoor dining here overlooking the water at the south end of The Strand. The beef and lamb dishes are your best choice.

Amphora Cafe & Bar (☎ 07-578 1616, 43 The Strand) Mains $16-27. Amphora serves Italian-influenced dishes, and has a lengthy wine list.

Crown & Badger (☎ 07-571 3038, cnr The Strand & Wharf St) Mains $8.50-13. This English-style pub serves up the likes of bangers & mash. It's a popular spot for a drink.

Tapa Tapa Bar (☎ 07-578 8741, 67 The Strand) Mains $18-24. Apart from main dishes, you can sample a variety of small dishes (marinated fish, raw vegies, squid rings and so on) for $4 to $5 a serve, and choose from a cheaper day menu.

Fish Crazee (☎ 07-577 9375, 85 The Strand) Mains $5.50-19. Don't come here looking for steak. The fish selection is huge, and you can personalise your fish and chips.

Soho (☎ 07-577 0577, 59 The Strand) Mains $21-29. Dinner only. Soho is a stylish restaurant serving a combination of French and provincial cuisine.

Lone Star (☎ 07-571 4111, 51 The Strand) Mains $12-25. This place is a little bit of Texas down-under. And like Texas, the servings are huge.

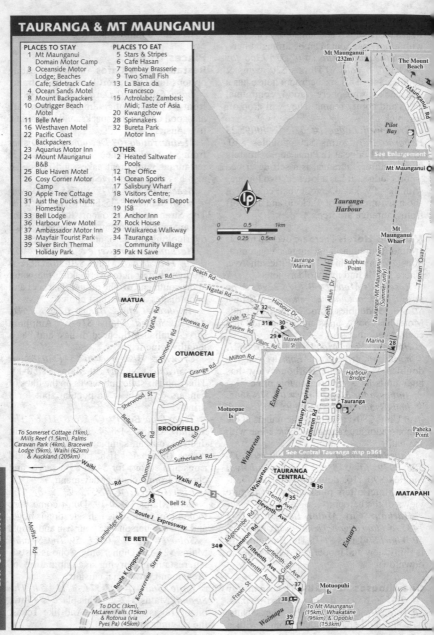

TAURANGA & MT MAUNGANUI

PLACES TO STAY
1 Mt Maunganui Domain Motor Camp
3 Oceanside Motor Lodge; Beaches Cafe; Sidetrack Cafe
4 Ocean Sands Motel
8 Mount Backpackers
10 Outrigger Beach Motel
11 Belle Mer
16 Westhaven Motel
22 Pacific Coast Backpackers
23 Aquarius Motor Inn
24 Mount Maunganui B&B
25 Blue Haven Motel
26 Cosy Corner Motor Camp
30 Apple Tree Cottage
31 Just the Ducks Nuts; Homestay
33 Bell Lodge
36 Harbour View Motel
38 Ambassador Motor Inn
38 Mayfair Tourist Park
39 Silver Birch Thermal Holiday Park

PLACES TO EAT
5 Stars & Stripes
6 Cafe Hasan
7 Bombay Brasserie
9 Two Small Fish
13 La Barca da Francesco
15 Astrolabe; Zambesi; Midi; Taste of Asia
20 Kwangchow
28 Spinnakers
32 Bureta Park Motor Inn

OTHER
2 Heated Saltwater Pools
12 The Office
14 Ocean Sports
17 Salisbury Wharf
18 Visitors Centre; Newlove's Bus Depot
19 ISB
21 Anchor Inn
27 Rock House
29 Waikareoa Walkway
34 Tauranga Community Village
35 Pak N Save

BAY OF PLENTY

The Old Bond Store (☎ *07-571 1559, 1 The Strand*) Mains $22-30. Open Tues-Sun. This place serves up quality Pacific Rim cuisine in the oldest commercial building in Tauranga. The lunchtime special Wednesday to Friday is great value; steak and your choice of drink for $14.

At the ***Bureta Park Motor Inn restaurant*** (☎ *07-576 2221, Vale St*), near Just the Ducks Nuts, you can dine well for $11.

Shiraz (☎ *07-577 0059, 12 Wharf St*) Mains $17.50-20. Shiraz has Mediterranean and Middle Eastern food at a reasonable price.

Piccola Italia (☎ *07-578 8363, 107 Grey St*) Mains $15-25. Piccola has good Italian food and an airy conservatory.

Mills Reef (☎ *07-576 8800, Moffat Rd*) Mains $25-30. Mills Reef is actually a winery first, restaurant second. But the food is by no means second-rate and, unsurprisingly, the accompanying wine list is superb. The winery is 7km from the town centre at Bethlehem.

Somerset Cottage (☎ *07-576 6889, 30 Bethlehem Rd*) Mains $25-30. Situated in a lovely cottage with large garden, this restaurant has a romantic setting along with top-quality food.

Spinnakers (☎ *07-574 4147, Harbour Bridge Marina*) Set menu $25-45. Spinnakers is a fine-dining establishment; it has lovely views of the marina and Tauranga Harbour.

Fast Food For some of the best fish and chips ($4.60) in town, try ***Fresh Fish Market*** (*Dive Crs*), down on the waterfront.

Along Devonport Rd there is a really good mix of inexpensive places to eat at. Try ***Sushi*** and ***Turkish to Go,*** on the corner of Elizabeth St , and further down the street the ***Crowded Muffin*** has a great selection of muffins (from $2.50).

The West Plaza (75 Devonport Rd) has the ***Stars & Stripes Diner*** for burgers, tortillas and other Kiwi Americana, and ***Latino***, a good place for tapas Thursday and Saturday.

The ***New Delhi Cafe & Bar*** (☎ *07-578 5533, 20 Wharf St*) has both dine-in and takeaway options.

BAY OF PLENTY

Entertainment

Venues generally don't start filling up until 11pm or later.

Along The Strand you'll find the *Grumpy Mole*, a large wild-west theme bar with pool tables, and *Crazy Jack's (☎ 07-578 411)*, which has occasional live jazz and rock. Nearby *Lone Star* has a similar decor to the Grumpy Mole, but attracts a more sedated crowd.

The *Crown & Badger (cnr The Strand & Wharf St)* is a quintessential pseudo-English pub, popular with all walks of life. Further up on Wharf St *The Bahama Hut* is one of the more popular joints in town; it has resident DJs, a dance floor and a surfing theme.

On The Strand, *Roma* is good for the electro/techno/trance scene.

The *Baycourt (☎ 07-577 7188 Durham St)* hosts an eclectic mix of highbrow entertainment, including theatre world-music concerts, music festivals, theatre for children and community cultural programs.

Getting There & Away

Air Air New Zealand (☎ 07-577 7300) has an office on the corner of Devonport Rd and Elizabeth St. It has daily direct flights to Auckland, Nelson and Wellington, with connections to other centres. Tauranga's airport is at Mt Maunganui. Origin Pacific (☎ 0800 302 302) flies direct to Wellington and connects to other regional cities.

Bus InterCity (☎ 07-578 7020) tickets and timetables are provided by the Tauranga visitors centre, where buses arrive at and depart from. InterCity connects Tauranga with Auckland ($29, 4½hrs), Hamilton ($24, 2hrs), Thames ($16, 1½hrs), Rotorua ($21, 1½hrs), Taupo ($43, 2½hrs) and Wellington ($88, 9hrs). Gutheries Express (☎ 0800 759 999) has buses to Hamilton ($20) and Auckland ($30).

Supa Travel (☎ 07-571 0583) is a local company with buses on demand to Auckland Airport ($60 one way), as does Tauranga Airport Shuttles (☎ 07-574 6177). Most buslines continue to Mt Maunganui after stopping in Tauranga.

Getting Around

A taxi from downtown Tauranga to the airport costs around $11.

Tauranga's local bus service runs from Monday to Saturday to most locations around the area, including Mt Maunganui, Papamoa and Te Puke.

Several car rental agencies have offices in Tauranga, including Rent-a-Dent (☎ 07-578 1772), Budget (☎ 07-578 5156), Hertz (☎ 07-578 9143) and Avis (☎ 07-578 4204)

The local taxi companies are: Citicabs (☎ 07-577 0999), Tauranga Taxis (☎ 07-578 6086), Coastline (☎ 07-571 8333) and Mount Taxis (☎ 07-574 7555).

The ferry service to Mt Maunganui, which takes about 15 minutes, operates from Boxing Day to Waitangi Day ($4).

MT MAUNGANUI
pop 16,800

The town of Mt Maunganui (the name means 'Large Mountain') stands at the foot of the 232m hill of the same name (also called 'the Mount', or Maumo). It's just across the inlet from Tauranga, and its fine beaches make it a popular holiday resort for Kiwis. Like Tauranga, the town of Mt Maunganui is built on a narrow peninsula.

Information

The Mt Maunganui visitors centre (☎ 07-575 5099) on Salisbury Ave is open 9am to 5pm weekdays and 9am to 4pm weekends October to Easter.

Things to See & Do

Walking trails go around Mt Maunganui and to its top, where there are magnificent views. You can climb around the rocks on **Moturiki Island**, which is actually joined to the peninsula (check out the *Walkways of Tauranga* pamphlet, available from the visitors centre).

The beach between Moturiki and Maunganui is good for surfing and swimming. If you're keen to give surfing a go, or you just want to practise, contact **Ocean Sports** *(☎ 07-575 9133, 96 Maunganui Rd)* or **ISB** *(☎ 07-575 3030, 227 Maunganui Rd)*. Both hire out gear (surf boards $20 for a half day) and give lessons (from $30 per hour).

There are excellent **heated saltwater pools** (☎ *07-575 0868, Adams Ave; adult/child $2.50/1.50; open 6am-10pm Mon-Sat, 8am-10pm Sun)* at the foot of the Mount.

The **Rock House** (☎ *07-572 4920, 9 Triton Ave; open noon-8pm Mon-Fri, 10am-6pm Sat & Sun)* has an indoor climbing wall, which costs $12 for the day.

The **Baypark Speedway** (☎ *07-574 6009; $20)* holds speed-car meetings two times a month in summer, and one in winter. Call for times.

Places to Stay

Camping & Cabins Mt Maunganui is a popular summer resort, so there are plenty of camping grounds.

Mt Maunganui Domain Motor Camp (☎ *07-575 4471,* e *mtdomain@xtra.co.nz, 1 Adams Ave)* Camp sites from $20, cabins $40. This camping ground is located at the foot of the Mount.

Cosy Corner Motor Camp (☎ *07-575 5899,* e *cosycorner@clear.net.nz, 40 Ocean Beach Rd)* Camp sites $11 per person, cabins $45, tourist flats $65. This rather spartan camping ground resides in the suburbs east of the town centre.

Golden Grove Motor Park (☎ *07-575 5821, 73 Girven Rd)* Camp sites $11 per person, cabins with/without bath $50/35, two-bedroom tourist flats $65. Golden Grove is close to the Mount's sandy beaches.

Hostels There are two places and both are on Maunganui Rd.

Pacific Coast Backpackers (☎ *07-574 9601, 432 Maunganui Rd)* Dorms $18-20, singles/doubles $35/45. This is the larger of the two hostels, with good facilities and a colourful decor. The staff are quite happy to book activities for you.

Mount Backpackers (☎*/fax 07-575 0860,* e *action.stations@clear.net.nz, 87 Maunganui Rd)* Dorms $17-19, doubles $45-47. Mount Backpackers is located in the very heart of the Mount's town centre and only a few minutes' walk from the beach. There is also Internet access available for guests.

Motels & Apartments Mt Maunganui has fewer motels than Tauranga and prices spiral outrageously in summer.

Westhaven Motel (☎ *07-575 4753,* e *westhavenmotel@xtra.co.nz, 27A The Mall)* Units $85-95. The Westhaven's huge rooms have views of Tauranga Harbour.

Blue Haven Motel (☎ *07-575 6508,* e *bluehaven@xtra.co.nz, 10 Tweed St)*. Singles/doubles $70/80. The rooms at this motel aren't exactly plush but they have everything you need.

Newer places include the following:

Oceanside Motor Lodge & Twin Towers (☎ *0800 466 868, 07-575 5371,* e *ocean lodge@xtra.co.nz, 1 Maunganui Rd)* Studios from $125. Oceanside has apartments, suites and studios, plus a heated pool, gym and restaurant.

Ocean Sands Motel (☎ *0800 726 371, 07-574 9794,* e *oceansands@thenet.net.nz, 6 Maunganui Rd)* Units from $130. Ocean Sands has self-contained studios, one- and two-bedroom apartments and penthouse suites.

Outrigger Beach Motel (☎ *07-575 4445,* e *outrigger@thenet.net.nz, 48 Marine Parade)* Units $85-110. Outrigger has spacious units a stone's throw to the beach.

Aquarius Motor Inn (☎ *07-572 3120,* e *motorinn@xtra.co.nz, 447 Maunganui Rd)* Studios from $98. Aquarius is another modern place, with a swimming pool, and spa baths in every room.

Belle Mer (☎ *0800 100 235, 07-575 0011,* e *bellemer@xtra.co.nz, 53 Marine Parade)* Apartments $150-240. For a little bit more luxury, try the Belle Mer. The apartments have all the mod-cons, and there's a heated pool and outdoor spa.

There are several B&Bs, including:

Mount Maunganui B&B (☎ *07-575 4013, fax 575 3014,* e *bednbrekkie@ihug .co.nz, 463 Maunganui Rd)* Singles/doubles 445/75. The rooms at this place are a bit small, but they're cheap and a cooked breakfast is included in the price.

Places to Eat & Entertainment

Maunganui Rd has the biggest concentration of eateries in the area.

BAY OF PLENTY

La Barca da Francesco (☎ *07-575 6842, Maunganui Rd*) Mains & pizzas $16-30. This relaxed Italian restaurant has a good selection of pastas and pizzas.

Two Small Fish (☎ *07-575 0096, Maunganui Rd*) Dinner mains around $20. During the day, this place has value-for-money lunch specials ($10), ranging from kiwiana dishes to curries.

Midi (*Maunganui Rd*) Mains $10-22. Midi serves venison, salmon, lamb, roast duck and seafood plus all-day breakfasts. Close by, *Taste of Asia* (☎ *07-575 4555*) is mainly a takeaway place where you can get Vietnamese noodle soup ($7.50) and a good variety of Vietnamese and Thai dishes. *Zambesi* is another good option.

Bombay Brasserie (☎ *07-575 2539, 77 Maunganui Rd*) Mains around $16. This place has all the popular Indian dishes.

Kwangchow (☎ *07-575 5063, 241 Maunganui Rd*) Smorgasbord $14. This relaxed Chinese restaurant packs 'em in with their value-for-money smorgasbord.

Cafe Hasan (☎ *07-574 8200, 16 Pacific Ave*) Mains $14.50-17. This modern and stylish spot deals in Middle-Eastern cuisine.

At the base of the Mount is *Beaches Cafe* and *Sidetrack Cafe*, both serving paninis, sandwiches and the like for around $8.

For cheap burgers (from $5) try *Stars & Stripes* (*cnr Maunganui Rd & Pacific Ave*).

Astrolabe (*Maunganui Rd*) is a classy bar, and is also popular for dining.

The *Anchor Inn* (☎ *07-574 0671, Maunganui Rd*) often has live music and touring bands, and *The Office* (*Maunganui Rd*) is a popular bar.

Getting There & Away

You can reach Mt Maunganui across the harbour bridge from Tauranga or from the south via Te Maunga on SH2. See the Tauranga Getting Around section for public transport details for the Mount. Tauranga airport is at Mt Maunganui.

Newmans, Supa Travel buses and InterCity serve Tauranga stopping at Mt Maunganui visitors centre. Bay Hopper buses run from Wharf St in Tauranga to the Mount, stopping at the visitors centre and hot pools.

AROUND TAURANGA
Matakana Island

Sheltering Tauranga Harbour, this elongated island is a quiet rural retreat just across the harbour from Tauranga. Two-thirds of the island is covered in pine forest, providing the main industry, and the rest, on the western side, is farmland. Matakana Island has 24km of pristine white-sand surf beach on its east shore and is a good place for windsurfing, kayaking and fishing. An ideal way to explore the island is by bicycle, which you can take across on the ferry. There is a general store and social club but not much else, so bring your own supplies.

Getting There & Away The main ferry (☎ 035 927 251) departs from Omokoroa at 7.45am, 2pm and 4pm daily for the western side of the island ($2.50, 15mins). The island has no public transport.

Omokoroa

This town is 22km west of Tauranga, on a promontory which protrudes well into the sheltered harbour and affords fine views of the harbour and Matakana. It is a popular summer destination and has two *caravan parks*. From Omokoroa you can visit Matakana on the regular ferry service.

Katikati
pop 2900

Katikati (known to some as 'Catty-Cat'), on the Uretara River, has become an open-air art gallery with many of its buildings adorned with **murals**. Pick up a map of the town's murals (20c) from the Mural Town Information Centre (☎ 07-549 1658), 36 Main Rd. It's open 9am to 4.30pm daily.

The **Katikati Heritage Museum** (☎ *07-549 0651, cnr SH2 & Wharawhara Rd; adult/child $6/3; open 10am-4pm daily*), 1km south of Katikati, tells the tale of Maori and Pakeha settlement. It also has an extensive collection of pioneering antiques and the largest bottle collection in the Southern Hemisphere.

Morton Estate (☎ *07-552 0795; open 10.30am-5pm daily*) is one of NZ's bigger wineries and it's located on SH2, 8km south

Gulf Harbour Marina, Whangaparaoa Peninsula

Cape Palliser Lighthouse's 252 steps, Wairarapa

Bay of Islands

New Zealand's longest pier is found at Tolaga Bay, on the East Coast

The little Christ Church in Russell

Rainbow Warrior Memorial, Matauri Bay

The geysers of Waiotapu near Rotorua

of Katikati. Wine tastings and door sales are also available.

Places to Stay & Eat Most accommodation is located in the countryside surrounding Katikati.

Sapphire Springs Holiday Park (☎/fax 07-549 0768, Hot Springs Rd) Camp sites $10 per person, lodge bunk beds $12.50, cabins & on-site caravans $30-35, tourist flats $55, motel rooms $65. Sapphire Springs backs onto the Kaimai Ranges. The springs cost $3 for visitors.

Katikati Naturist Park (☎ 0800 456 7567, 07-549 2158, e sampsons@ihug.co.nz, 149 Wharawhara Rd) Day visit $7, tent & powered sites $11 per person, on-site vans $40, cabins/chalets $50/60. Katikati Park is well set up for those who prefer to go as nature intended.

Katikati Motel (☎ 07-549 0385, e kati kati@ihug.co.nz, cnr Main & Fairview Rds) Units $60-80. Conveniently, this motel is close to the centre of town.

The visitors centre has a list of homestays and farmstays in the area. Good choices are:

Colannade Backpackers (☎/fax 07-552 0902, e colannade@actrix.gen.nz, 122 Work Rd, Aongatete) Dorms $14. This tranquil backpackers is 11km east of Katikati, set in the heart of the horticultural area. The rooms are comfy and if you stay three nights or more they'll do your washing.

Jacaranda Cottage (☎/fax 07-549 0616, e jacaranda.cottage@clear.net.nz, 230 Thompson's Track, RD2) B&B singles/doubles $40/70, self-contained cottage $80. Jacaranda Cottage has great views of the coast, walks in the Kaimai Ranges and you can even try your hand at milking a cow. There is also a one-bedroom, self-contained cottage available (two-night minimum stay).

Fantail Lodge (☎ 07-549 1581, e fan taillodge@xtra.co.nz, 117 Rea Rd) Doubles from $500-plus. If you want to push the boat out there's the Fantail Lodge, a stunning Tudor-style mansion.

The *Village Fare (Main Rd)* is a popular local cafe. Also worth trying is *The Landing (Main Rd)*, a licensed restaurant at the Talisman Hotel.

For elegant afternoon teas and fine dining, try the *Twickenham Homestead (cnr SH2 & Mulgan St)*.

Tuhua (Mayor Island)

Beautiful Tuhua, commonly known as Mayor Island, is a dormant volcano about 40km north of Tauranga. The striking features of the island include black obsidian rock and crystal clear water. There are walking tracks through the now overgrown crater valley and an interesting walk around the island. The north-west corner is a marine reserve, but specialist groups can ask for permission to land here.

Tuhua Island Backpackers (☎ 07-579 5655) Camp sites $5 per person, cabin dorm beds $10. This is only place to stay on the island. It's rather basic accommodation but you can't get much more off the beaten track than this. The only cooking facility is a barbecue (wood supplied). You need to bring all your own food and some way of storing it as there are no fridges.

Getting There & Away Blue Ocean Charters (☎ 07-578 9685) runs to the island three or four days a week from late December until around Easter, departing from Coronation Pier in Tauranga, going via Mt Maunganui, at 7am and returning at 4pm. The trip takes about three hours one way and costs $90 return (children $45). You may be able to reach the island from Waihi Beach and Whangamata (see the Coromandel Region chapter) on fishing charters.

Minden Lookout

From Minden Lookout, about 10km west of Tauranga, there's a superb view back over the Bay of Plenty. To get there, take SH2 to Te Puna and turn off south on Minden Rd; the lookout is about 4km up the road.

Papamoa

pop 7460

Papamoa, 13km east of Mt Maunganui, is blessed with miles of beaches and is not quite as urbanised as the Mount. Digging for tuatua (a type of shellfish) is popular when the tide is right.

Papamoa Adventure Park (☎ 07-542 0972, 1162 Welcome Bay Rd), on the road to Welcome Bay, has a list of outdoor activities, including horse riding ($30), target shooting ($30) and a bone-shaking dirt-track luge ($10) – not recommended for those with back problems.

Papamoa Beach Top 10 Holiday Resort (☎/fax 07-572 0816, e resort@papamoa beach.co.nz, 535 Papamoa Beach Rd) Camp sites from $12 per person, cabins $40-48, tourist flats $70, motel units $90, villas $120. This resort has a perfect spot right on the beachfront, with a huge selection of accommodation options. Prices increase over January.

Pacific Palms Resort (☎ 07-572 0035, fax 572 1135, 21 Gravatt Rd) Apartments $125. Pacific Palms has modern one-, two- and three-bedroom apartments a few blocks back from the beach.

Papamoa Beachfront Lodge (☎ 07-542 1900, 127 Karewa Parade) Units $140. Papamoa is a purpose-built lodge with laundry and kitchen facilities.

You can get takeaway food from places on Beach Rd, and the **Blue Biyou** (☎ 07-572 2099, 559 Papamoa Beach Rd) is known for fine meals and enormous Sunday brunches.

Te Puke
pop 6775

Hailed as the 'Kiwi fruit Capital of the World', Te Puke has native bush near the town and it is not far from several good beaches and exciting rivers. Te Puke gets busy in the kiwi fruit picking season when there's plenty of work. The visitors centre (☎ 07-573 9172), at 130 Jellicoe St, has a notice board with fruit picking vacancies. It's open 8am to 4.30pm Monday to Friday and 9am to noon Saturday.

Things to See & Do The Bay of Plenty is kiwi fruit country and here you can learn a little more about the fruit that is so important to NZ's economy. Gardening enthusiasts can visit many private gardens in the area.

Kiwi Fruit Country (☎ 07-573 6340; adult/child $11/5.50; open 9am-5pm daily) is on SH2 at the turnoff for Maketu, 6km east of Te Puke and 36km from Tauranga. You can visit the orchards and the shop, watch a video about kiwi fruit and sample some kiwi fruit or kiwi fruit wine. The complex is also a theme park – it's all quite tacky but the kids will enjoy it, including a 'kiwi-kart' ride through the orchards and an exhibition on how the fruit is grown and packed. Tours of the park run throughout the day.

Next to Kiwi Fruit Country is the **Vintage Auto Barn** (☎ 07-573 6547; adult/child $7/2; open 9am-5pm daily) with over 90 vintage and classic cars on display.

The **Comvita Visitors Centre** (☎ 0800 504 959, Paengaroa; admission free; open daily) represents Comvita healthcare treatments made from honey and other bee products. There's an educational gallery, an auditorium, a shop, and tours at 10am and 2pm daily. The centre is 9km east of Te Puke on the SH33 heading towards Rotorua.

At **Longridge Park** (☎ 07-533 1515, Paengaroa; open 9am-5pm daily, 4pm winter), near Te Puke, you can take a thrilling half-hour jetboat ride (adult/child $59/35) up the winding and bush-clad Kaituna River, or take a tour of a working kiwi fruit farm ($12/6).

Afterwards, you can 4WD over a challenging series of tracks with **Hill Hoppers** (☎ 0800 244 554, Longridge). It only costs $55 (or $25 for the younger unlicensed passengers).

Places to Stay The visitors centre has a list of home and farmstays in the area.

Beacon Motel (☎ 07-573 7825, 173 Jellicoe St) Singles/doubles from $65/85. This is a basic motel not far from the town centre.

Lindenhof Homestay (☎ 07-573 4592, fax 573 9392, 58 Dunlop Rd) Singles/doubles with breakfast $50/90. This place, 2km north of Te Puke, has comfortable rooms in a lovely homestead. There's a spa, tennis court and pool.

Maketu
pop 1000

There's a Maori pa site overlooking the water at Town Point, near the township of Maketu, north-east of Te Puke. Maketu was the landing site of the *Arawa* canoe, more than 600 years ago, and there is a stone monument on the foreshore commemorating this. The name Maketu comes from a place in Hawaiki.

To get to Maketu from Tauranga, take SH2 through Te Puke and turn left into Maketu Rd just past Rangiuru. The visitors centre (☎ 07-533 2343) is on Maketu Rd, and opens noon to 2pm Monday to Friday.

Bay Views Holiday Park & Motels (☎/fax 533 2222, e *sheila@bayviews.co .nz, 195 Arawa Ave)* Camp sites $12 per person, dorms $18, tourist flats $70. Bay Views is 1.5km from the town centre. It is located in a nice rural setting and there are three sandy beaches nearby.

The *Seaside Cafe*, near the lifesaving club on the beach, is a pleasant spot, or try Maketu's famous pies at *Maketu Pies* near the visitors centre.

Eastern Bay of Plenty

The eastern Bay of Plenty extends from Maketu and Pukehina to Opotiki in the far east of the bay, taking in Whakatane and Ohope. The main feature of the region is long stretches of sandy beaches backed by cliffs covered in Pohutukawa trees.

WHAKATANE
pop 17,700

Whakatane (pronounced 'fa-ka-ta-ne') lies on a natural harbour at the mouth of the Whakatane River. When the *Mataatua* canoe landed at the mouth of the river in the 14th century, Whakatane was already an important Maori centre. The *Mataatua* (Face of God) canoe was part of the migration by the Maori people from Hawaiki to New Zealand. It is said that the canoe brought not only people, but soil, kumara and taro for plantation cultivation in the new land. Only around the beginning of the 20th century did Europeans discover the richness of the land and settle there in any significant numbers.

Whakatane today is the principal town for the eastern Bay of Plenty and a service centre for the Rangitaiki agricultural and milling district. It's a pleasant town with a friendly atmosphere, and it enjoys plenty of sunshine year-round. Many visitors are attracted to the nearby beaches, especially in summer. Two of the eastern bay's major attractions are offshore: Whakaari (White Island), NZ's most active volcano; and dolphin-swimming tours.

Information

The visitors centre (☎ 0800 478 647, w www.whakatane.com), at the junction of Quay St and Kakahoroa Dr, is open 8.30am to 5pm weekdays and 10.30am to 3.30pm weekends March to December, and 8am to 6pm weekdays and 9am to 5pm weekends December to February. The staff make tour bookings and also handle general inquiries for DOC. The AA office (☎ 07-308 9556) is on Boon St.

Things to See

The **Whakatane Museum** (☎ 07-307 9805, *Boon St; admission by donation; open 10am-4.30pm Mon-Fri, 11am-1.30pm Sat, 2pm-4.30pm Sun)* is an excellent regional museum. It has photographic and artefact exhibits on early Maori and European settlers as well as on the natural environment, including the smoking Whakaari volcano just offshore. It's also a centre of historical research, with an archive of historical publications. Adjacent is an art gallery featuring mostly local artists.

Just to one side of the traffic circle is **Pohaturoa** *(cnr The Strand & Commerce St)*, a large rock outcrop and important Maori sacred site *(tapu)*. The Treaty of Waitangi was signed here by Ngati Awa chiefs in 1840. The coastline used to come right up to this point and there's a tunnel in the rock where baptisms and other rites were performed. Also here is a monument to the Ngati Awa chief Te Hurinui Apanui.

Muriwai's Cave (partially collapsed), beside Muriwai Rd, once provided shelter to a famous ancestress and seer who arrived from Hawaiki on the *Mataatua*.

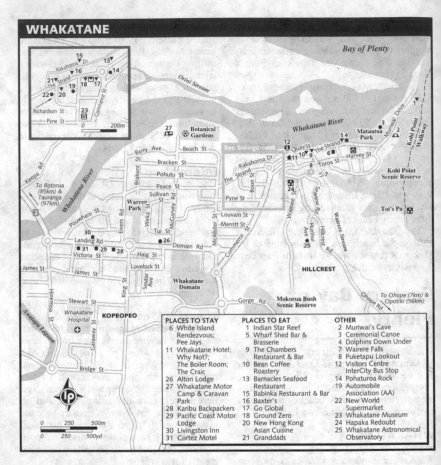

WHAKATANE

PLACES TO STAY
6 White Island Rendezvous; Pee Jays
11 Whakatane Hotel; Why Not?; The Boiler Room; The Craic
26 Alton Lodge
27 Whakatane Motor Camp & Caravan Park
28 Karibu Backpackers
29 Pacific Coast Motor Lodge
30 Livingston Inn
31 Cortez Motel

PLACES TO EAT
1 Indian Star Reef
5 Wharf Shed Bar & Brasserie
9 The Chambers Restaurant & Bar
10 Bean Coffee Roastery
13 Barnacles Seafood Restaurant
15 Babinka Restaurant & Bar
16 Baxter's
17 Go Global
18 Ground Zero
20 New Hong Kong Asian Cuisine
21 Granddads

OTHER
2 Muriwai's Cave
3 Ceremonial Canoe
4 Dolphins Down Under
7 Wairere Falls
8 Puketapu Lookout
12 Visitors Centre InterCity Bus Stop
14 Pohaturoa Rock
19 Automobile Association (AA)
22 New World Supermarket
23 Whakatane Museum
24 Hapaka Redoubt
25 Whakatane Astronomical Observatory

BAY OF PLENTY

A ceremonial **waka** (canoe), named after the original *Mataatua,* sits secure behind a grill in the reserve across the road.

The **Whakatane Astronomical Observatory** (☎ *07-308 7121, Hurunui Crs; admission by gold coin*) in Hillcrest, opens to the public every fine-weather Tuesday evening.

The small **botanical gardens** are at the river end of McGarvey Rd, beside a children's playground.

Dolphin Swimming
Dolphins Down Under (☎ *0800 354 7737, 07-308 4636,* **W** *www.dolphinswim.co.nz;*

trips adult/child $100/75) and **Blue Sky Tours** (☎ *0800 377 878; trips $95)* run popular trips year-round (subject to weather) to swim with the dolphins. There's a high success rate for dolphin spotting (check with local fishing-boat operators at the wharf if you want to make sure there are dolphins around). All necessary equipment, including a wet suit, is supplied.

Walking
The visitors centre stocks a good booklet *Walks Around The Whakatane Area* ($2), which lists walks ranging from 30 minutes

to half a day. An interesting 2½-hour **town centre walk** encompasses a number of scenic and historic spots, including Muriwai's Cave, Wairere Falls, Puketapu Lookout, Hapaka Redoubt, Pohaturoa and a big game-fishing facility.

Other notable walks include the 3½-hour **Kohi Point Walkway**, **Nga Tapuwae-o-Toi** (The Sacred Footsteps of Toi), which extends through the Kohi Point Scenic Reserve, passing many attractive sites including lookouts and Toi's Pa (Kapua te Rangi), reputedly the oldest *pa* site in NZ. Other walkways are the **Ohope Bush Walk**, the **Mokorua Scenic Reserve**, **Latham's Track** and the **Whakatane River Greenway**. The 300m **White Pine Bush Walk**, starting about 10km from Whakatane, is suitable for wheelchairs.

Other Activities

Check with the visitors centre about the wide variety of activities in and around Whakatane. Possibilities include horse treks, bushwalking, trout or sea fishing, diving and kayak trips, windsurfing rafting and jetboating. Most trips to Whakaari leave from Whakatane (see that section later).

Kiwi Jet Boat Tours (☎ *07-307 0663; trips adult/child $60/50)* has a 1¼-hour jetboat trip along the Rangitaiki River from Matahina Dam to Aniwhenua Falls (minimum of four people).

Places to Stay

Camping Beside the Whakatane River is the **Whakatane Motor Camp & Caravan Park** (☎ *07-308 8694, fax 308 2070, McGarvey Rd)*. It has recreational facilities, including a swimming pool and a spa pool. Camp sites are $10 per person, cabins start from $40.

Hostels & B&Bs The visitors centre lists homestays and farmstays in the area.

Karibu Backpackers (☎*/fax 307 8276, 13 Landing Rd)* Dorms $18, twins & doubles $44. This quiet hostel is a converted house, decked out with clean rooms and spacious communal areas.

Motels & Hotels Most motels are on, or just off, Landing and Domain Rds.

Alton Lodge Motel (☎ *07-307 1003,* 🅔 *altonlodge@wave.co.nz, 76 Domain Rd)* Singles/doubles from $75/85. This Tudorstyle place has 11 self-contained units.

Cortez Motel (☎*/fax 07-308 4047, 55 Landing Rd)* Doubles from $75. This is a standard motel, but with the added advantage of a swimming pool.

White Island Rendezvous (☎ *0800 242 299, 07-308 9588,* 🅔 *info@whiteisland .co.nz, 15 The Strand)* Units from $90, 2-bedroom cottage $100. White Island is a modern place with a wide range of accommodation facilities. It also houses a charter to Whakaari and a good cafe.

Livingston Inn (☎ *0800 770 777, 07-308 6400,* 🅔 *livingstoninn@xtra.co.nz, 42 Landing Rd)* Units from $95. The well-kept units have either a spa bath or spa pool.

Pacific Coast Motor Lodge (☎ *0800 224 430, 07-308 0100,* 🅔 *pacific.coast.lodge@ xtra.co.nz, 41 Landing Rd)* Units from $100. Some units at this clean and modern motel have spa baths.

Whakatane Hotel (☎ *07-308 8199, The Strand)* Dorm beds $16, singles/doubles with bath $30/55. This is an old Art Deco hotel – nothing flash, but central and cheap.

Places to Eat

There are quite a few pleasant cafes along Whakatane's Strand.

Bean Coffee Roastery (*54 The Strand)* Coffee from $2.50. This funky little place has some of the best coffee in town.

Pee Jay's (*15 The Strand)* Light meals $7-12. This extremely popular cafe has scrummy paninis, salads, and Cuban coffee.

Baxter's (*The Strand)* Light meals $5-8. Baxter's is another popular cafe with outdoor seating.

Ground Zero (*The Strand)* Light meals $5-10. This cafe has a good selection of sandwiches and paninis.

Why Not? (☎ *07-308 8138, 79 The Strand)* Mains $12.50-20. Why Not serves big portions of pasta, salads, fish and steak and its outdoor seating catches the afternoon and evening sun.

BAY OF PLENTY

Babinka Restaurant & Bar (☎ *07-307 0009, Kakahoroa Dr*) Mains $20-35. Babinka has an interesting menu that includes a variety of north and south Indian dishes.

The Chambers Restaurant & Bar (☎ *07-307 0107, The Strand East*) Mains $18-26. Upmarket Chambers is in the solid former council building. It has a nice garden area.

Wharf Shed Bar & Brasserie (☎ *07-308 5698, Muriwai Dr*) Mains $19-25. The Wharf Shed's menu is heavy on seafood, and there is a smattering of Caribbean dishes.

Go Global (☎ *07-308 9000, The Strand*) Mains $15-24. Go Global has an eclectic menu, including Thai, North African and Texan. Ostrich and kangaroo also feature.

Indian Star Reef (☎ *07-307 0477, The Heads*) Mains $14-22. This Indian restaurant is the perfect spot to watch the sunset. It's out by the Heads.

New Hong Kong Asian Cuisine (☎ *07-308 6864, Richardson St*) Lunch specials from $6. This place has Chinese food, with a separate counter for takeaways, and has cheap lunch specials.

It's toss up between *Barnacles* and *Granddads* for the best fish and chips in town. Both are on The Strand.

Entertainment

Along with *Why Not?* (see Places to Eat), which is a pleasant spot for a tipple, Whakatane has a couple of good pubs that fill up on weekends. *The Craic*, a pseudo Irish pub, is quite new and popular, and next door *The Boiler Room* packs them in with the occasional live band. Both are located in the Whakatane Hotel (see Places to Stay).

Getting There & Around

Air New Zealand (☎ 07-308 8397) has daily flights linking Whakatane to Auckland, with connections to other centres.

A taxi (☎ 0800 421 829) to or from the airport costs $20. There is no bus service.

InterCity buses stop outside the visitors centre. InterCity has buses connecting Whakatane with Rotorua ($18, 1½hrs) and Gisborne ($28, 3hrs), with connections to other places. All buses to Gisborne go via

Opotiki. Courier services around East Cape originate in Opotiki and Gisborne (see East Cape in the East Coast chapter).

WHAKAARI (WHITE ISLAND)

Whakaari, or White Island, is NZ's most active volcano, just 50km off the coast from Whakatane. It's a small island of 324 hectares, formed by three separate volcanic cones, all of different ages. Erosion has worn away most of the surface of the two older cones and the youngest, which rose up between the two older ones, now occupies most of the centre of the island. Hot water and steam continually escape from vents over most of the crater floor and temperatures of 600°C to 800°C have been recorded. The highest point on the island is Mt Gisborne at 321m. Geologically, Whakaari is related to Moutohora (Whale Island) and Putauaki (Mt Edgecumbe), as all lie along the same volcanic trench.

The island is privately owned and the only way you can land on it is with a helicopter or boat tour that has arranged permission. There is no jetty so boats have to land on the beach, which means that landings are not possible in rough seas. A visit to Whakaari is an unforgettable, if disconcerting, experience, but the constant rumblings and plumes of steam do not necessarily mean that it is about to blow up.

History

Before the arrival of Europeans, Maori caught sea birds on the island for food. In 1769 Captain Cook named it White Island because of the dense clouds of white steam hanging above it.

The first European to land on the island was a missionary, the Reverend Henry Williams, in 1826. The island was acquired by Europeans in the late 1830s and changed ownership a number of times after that. Sulphur production began but was interrupted in 1885 by a minor eruption, and the following year the island was hurriedly abandoned in the wake of the Tarawera eruption. The island's sulphur industry resumed in 1898 but only continued until 1901, when production ceased altogether.

In the 1910s, further mining operations were attempted and abandoned, due to mud flows and other volcanic activity, and ownership of the island continued to change. In 1953 White Island was declared a Private Scenic Reserve.

The island was at its most active between 1976 and 1981, when two new craters were formed and 100,000 cubic metres of rock was ejected.

Getting There & Away

Most trips to Whakaari include a one- or two-hour tour on foot around the island. A landing by boat is definitely dependent ion the weather. All trips (except for fixed-wing aerial sightseeing) incur a $20 landing fee, which may be included in the quoted price.

Operators include:

Dive White (☎ 0800 348 394, **W** www.dive white.co.nz) Offers diving and snorkelling trips to White Island from $120 per person.

Pee Jay (☎ 0800 733 529, **W** www.whiteis land.co.nz) Tours on a 60-foot monohull launch, taking six hours with two hours on the island. It costs $110 per person, lunch is included (minimum of 10 people).

Scott Air (☎ 07-308 9558) Aerial sightseeing tours over the island from $135 per person (minimum of two people).

Vulcan Helicopters (☎ 0800 804 354, **W** www .vulcanheli.co.nz) Has 2½-hour helicopter flights at $375 per person (minimum of five people). The pilot will land if conditions are safe.

White Island Adventure Tours (☎ 0800 377 878) Offers a 4½- to six-hour boat trip for $95 per person, including lunch and a bit of dolphin spotting en route. You spend about two hours on the island. The boat used is a 60-foot launch.

MOUTOHORA

Moutohora, or Whale Island, so-called because of its shape, is 9km north off the coast of Whakatane and has an area of 414 hectares. It's another volcanic island, on the same volcanic trench as Whakaari, although it's much less active. Along its shore are hot springs, which can reach 93°C. The summit is 353m high and the island has several historic sites, including an ancient pa site, an old quarry and a camp.

Whale Island was settled by Maori before the 1769 landing of Captain Cook. In 1829 there was a Maori massacre of sailors from the trading vessel *Haweis* while it was anchored at Sulphur Bay. This was followed by an unsuccessful whaling venture in the 1830s. In the 1840s the island passed into European ownership and is still privately owned, although since 1965 it has been an officially protected wildlife refuge administered by DOC.

Whale Island is principally a haven for sea and shore birds, some of which are quite rare. Some of the birds use the island only for nesting at certain times of the year, while others are present year-round. The island has a large colony of grey-faced petrels, estimated to number 10,000.

The island's protected status means landing is restricted. There are only four trips to the island each year (adult/child $40/35) over the Christmas period; bookings can be made through the Whakatane DOC office or visitors centre.

WHAKATANE TO ROTORUA

Travelling along SH30 from Whakatane to Rotorua you'll come to the **Awakeri Hot Springs**, 16km from Whakatane. It has hot springs, spa pools, picnic areas and a *holiday park* (☎ 07-304 9117, fax 304 9290). At the latter, powered sites are $10 per person, cabins $40, tourist flats $55 and motel units $75. The springs cost $3/1.50 for adults/children.

Lying just off SH30, **Kawerau** is a timber town surrounded by pine forest and dependent on the huge Tasman Pulp & Paper Mill. Kawerau has a visitors centre (☎ 07-323 7550) on Plunket St, in the centre of town, and a selection of accommodation, but the only real reason to come here is to visit the waterfalls outside town. You can visit the mill (☎ 07-323 3456) for a 1½-hour tour; bookings are essential.

Tarawera Falls are a half-hour drive from Kawerau, along a well-graded road through the pine forests (watch out for the logging trucks). From the end of the road it is a 15-minute walk through native forest to the falls, which emerge from a hole in the canyon wall. The track continues another two hours up to the top of the falls and on to Lake Tarawera. This is a good walk with views of the lake and Mt Tarawera. You need a permit to visit ($2), which you can obtain from the visitors centre.

Dominating Kawerau is **Putauaki (Mt Edgecumbe)**, a volcanic cone with panoramic views of the entire Bay of Plenty. You need a permit for access ($2) but it closes periodically (generally during times of high fire risk); contact the information centre for permits and the latest news.

On nearby Lake Rotoma, **Kawerau Kayaks** (☎ 035 668 4069; kayak rental & guided tours from $5) offers kayak trips from 10am to 4pm. Bookings are essential.

OHOPE BEACH
pop 3010
The town of Ohope, 7km 'over the hill' from Whakatane, has a great beach, perfect for long walks and lazy days, and is backed by quiet Ohiwa Harbour.

Ohiwa Harbour Tours (☎ 07-308 7837; $55 per person) takes you on a two-hour tour of the harbour, with historical and ecological commentary along the way.

Ohope Beach Holiday Park (☎/fax 312 4460, e ohopebeach@xtra.co.nz, Harbour Rd) Tent & powered sites from $11 per person, cabins from $40, tourist flats from $60. Ohope Park is at the eastern end of the beach overlooking the sea. Prices increase during the summer months.

Surf and Sand Holiday Park (☎ 07-312 4884, e surfandsand@xtra.co.nz, Harbour Rd) Powered sites $15 per person, 1- & 2-bedroom apartments $100-180. The camp sites are generally only open from mid-December to mid-February. This place is next door to the Ohope Beach Park.

Surfs Reach Motels (☎ 07-312 4159, e surfsreachmotels@xtra.co.nz, 52 West End) Units from $80. At the far western end of Ohope Beach is this friendly place. The units are spacious and have views of the sea.

Eating options are limited to a couple of *cafes* at the western end of Ohope. On the main highway heading towards Opotiki is the *Ohiwa Oyster Farm*, a roadside takeaway place. There are tables near the water

where you can consume your fish and chips and oysters (the Pacific variety; $7.50 for a half-dozen).

OPOTIKI
pop 7070
Opotiki, the easternmost town of the Bay of Plenty, is the gateway to the East Cape and the rugged forests and river valleys of the Raukumara and nearby ranges. The town itself might be nothing special, but many visitors stop over on the way to the East Coast and there are some reasonable surf beaches nearby, such as Ohiwa and Waiotahi. Opotiki is a model of Maori tradition – the main street is lined with the works of master carvers.

The Opotiki area was settled from at least 1150, which was 200 years before the larger 14th-century migration. In the mid-1800s Opotiki was a centre for Hauhauism, a Maori doctrine that was grounded in Judaeo-Christian beliefs, and advocated, among other things, an end to Maori oppression.

Known by the local Whakatohea tribe to have acted as a government spy, Reverend Carl Volkner was murdered in 1865 in the Church of St Stephen the Martyr (you can still see the blood stains near the pulpit). This led to the church being employed as a fort by government troops. The murder was used as one justification for land confiscations in the area.

Information
The Opotiki visitors centre (☎ 07-315 8484, w www.eastlandnz.com), on the corner of St John and Elliot Sts, is open 8am to 5pm weekdays mid-February to mid-December and daily the rest of the year. The DOC office (☎ 07-315 6103) is in the same building. The centre does bookings for a range of activities and will attempt to arrange a visit to a local marae.

Internet access is available at the Opotiki Library (cnr King & Church Sts).

Things to See & Do
Just over 7km south of the town centre is the fascinating **Hukutaia Domain** (Woodlands Rd; open daily), which has one of the

finest collections of native plants in NZ, many of them rare and endangered. In the domain's centre a puriri tree, named Taketakerau, is estimated to be over 2000 years old. The remains of the distinguished dead of the Upokorere *hapu* (sub-tribe) of the Whakatohea tribe were ritually buried beneath it. The tree is no longer *tapu* (sacred) as the remains have been reinterred elsewhere.

The **Historical & Agricultural Society Museum** *(☎ 07-315 5193, Church St; adult/child $2/50c; open 10am-3.30pm Mon-Sat, 1.30pm-4pm Sun)* is spilling over with historical items donated by the local community.

Catch the flicks at the not-so-deluxe **Delux Cinema** *(☎ 07-315 6110, Church St)*.

Motu River Jet Boat Tours *(☎ 07-315 8107)* has as many as three trips daily on the Motu River. Trips take 2½ hours and cost $85. **Wet 'n' Wild** *(☎ 0800 462 7238)*, based in Rotorua, rafts the Motu.

Places to Stay

Camping & Cabins For more camping grounds in the area, see the East Coast chapter.

Opotiki Holiday Park *(☎/fax 07-315 6050, ⓔ opotiki.holidays@xtra.co.nz, Potts Ave)* Tent & powered sites $8.50 per person, on-site caravans $32, cabins $36, tourist flats $55. This camping ground is a mere 200m to town.

Ohiwa Family Holiday Park *(☎/fax 07-315 4741, ⓔ ohiwa-holidays@xtra.co.nz, Ohiwa Harbour Rd)* Camp sites $11 per person, on-site caravans $40-55, cabins from $35, tourist flats $50, motel units $75. This park is 15km drive west of Opotiki, and a stone's throw from the sea.

Island View Family Holiday Park *(☎/fax 07-315 7519, Appleton Rd)* Camp sites $11 per person, on-site caravans $35, cabins $45-50, tourist flats $57. Island View is 5km west from town right by the sea at Waiotahi Beach.

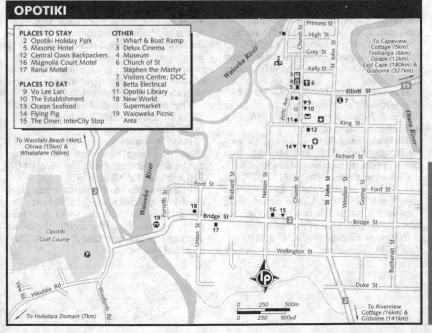

OPOTIKI

PLACES TO STAY
2 Opotiki Holiday Park
5 Masonic Hotel
12 Central Oasis Backpackers
16 Magnolia Court Motel
17 Ranui Motel

PLACES TO EAT
9 Vo Lee Lan
10 The Establishment
13 Ocean Seafood
14 Flying Pig
15 The Diner; InterCity Stop

OTHER
1 Wharf & Boat Ramp
3 Delux Cinema
4 Museum
6 Church of St
   Stephen the Martyr
7 Visitors Centre; DOC
8 Betta Electrical
11 Opotiki Library
18 New World
   Supermarket
19 Waioweka Picnic
   Area

Tirohanga Beach Motor Camp (☎/fax 07-315 7942) Unpowered/powered sites $9/10, cabins $35, tourist flats $45. The friendly Tirohanga Camp is on the East Coast Rd 6km from town.

Also along the East Coast Rd, about 17km from Opotiki, the *Opape Motor Camp* (☎ 07-315 8175) has unpowered/powered sites ($8/8.50) and an on-site caravan ($10 per person).

Hostels Opotiki has two good backpackers.
Central Oasis Backpackers (☎ 07-315 5165, 30 King St) Dorms from $12, twins & doubles $32. This small, friendly backpackers is in the centre of town in an old cottage.
Opotiki Backpackers Beach House (☎ 07-315 5117, Appleton Rd) Dorms $14, on-site caravan $16 per person, doubles $35. On Waiotahi Beach, 5km west of Opotiki, is this place. It has a nice, relaxed air about it, and comfy accommodation. Kayaks, surfboards and boogie boards are available to guests.

Motels & Guesthouses The Opotiki visitors centre has a list of B&Bs and farmstays.
Ranui Motel (☎ 0800 828 128, 07-315 6669, 36 Bridge St) Singles/doubles from $55/60. The Ranui is not flash but it's cheap and adequate.
Magnolia Court Motel (☎ 07-315 8490, e magnolia.crt.motel@xtra.co.nz, cnr Bridge & Nelson Sts) Units from $76. This is a better standard of motel.
Masonic Hotel (☎ 07-315 6115, Church St) Rooms from $25. The Masonic is a cheap option in the centre of town.
Capeview Cottage (☎ 07-315 7877, fax 315 8055, Tablelands Rd) Doubles per night/week $130/800. A little out of town, Capeview Cottage has two bedrooms, hot tubs and lovely views of the coast.
Riverview Cottage (☎ 07-315 5553) Cottage $100. This place, a little way out on

SH2 heading towards Gisborne, is a comfy self-contained cottage nestled in bush and farmland. Kayaks are available to ply the nearby Waioeka River ($39).

Places to Eat
It's slim pickings in Opotiki for places to eat.
Ocean Seafood (*Church St*) Fish & chips from $4.50. This fish and chip shop serves up tasty fresh fish.
Flying Pig (*Church St*) Mains $8-10. The licensed Flying Pig serves kebabs and other delights, and has cheap lunch specials.
The Establishment (*Church St*) Sandwiches $2.50. This cafe may not look like much but the food is good and fresh and very filling.
For Chinese food, check out *Vo Lee Lan* (*Church St*).
The Diner (*Bridge St*) This place does hearty meals (from $5) throughout the day.

Getting There & Away
Travelling east from Opotiki there are two routes. SH2 crosses the spectacular Waioeka Gorge. There are some fine walks that take about a day (some are longer) in the **Waioeka Gorge Scenic Reserve**. The gorge gets progressively steeper and narrower as you travel inland, before the route crosses typically green, rolling hills, dotted with sheep, on the descent to Gisborne.

The other route east from Opotiki is SH35 around the East Cape, described fully in the East Coast chapter.

InterCity buses pick up/drop off at The Diner on Bridge St. Tickets and bookings can be made through Betta Electrical (☎ 07-315 8555) at 115 Church St.

InterCity has daily buses connecting Opotiki with Whakatane ($15, 40mins), Rotorua ($18, 2hrs, 10mins) and Auckland ($45, 6¾hrs). Heading south, the buses connect Opotiki with Gisborne ($18, 2hrs) by a daily service.

The East Coast

The East Coast is an area full of interest, with the sea on one side and the towering forested hills of the hinterland behind. It is also a place of contrasts, from the Art Deco and Spanish Mission-style architecture of bustling Hastings and Napier to the serene, primeval forests that encircle Lake Waikaremoana in Te Urewera National Park.

The area includes three of the North Island's larger cities and their adjoining bays: Gisborne on Poverty Bay and Napier and Hastings on Hawke Bay.

From Opotiki in the eastern Bay of Plenty, circling around to Gisborne, the East Cape is a rugged landscape with stunning coastal scenery and dense inland forest. This long-isolated region has retained its strong Maori influence, and remains largely undeveloped and well off the main tourist routes.

Highlights

- Tramping the Lake Waikaremoana Great Walk and in Te Urewera National Park
- Exploring Napier, with its Art Deco architecture and seaside ambience
- Touring many of the fine wineries of the Hawkes Bay and Gisborne areas
- Leaving the well-trodden tourist trail to visit the rugged, rural East Cape
- Catching the sunrise at East Cape Lighthouse, mainland NZ's most easterly point
- Roaming over wild, windswept Mahia Peninsula
- Surfing at one of the East Coast's many remote beaches

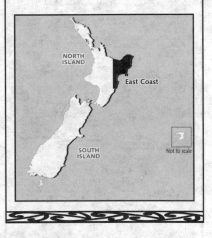

East Cape

☎ 07 & 06 • pop 6700

The East Cape is a scenic, isolated and little-known region of the North Island. The small communities scattered along the coast are predominantly Maori (largely of the Ngati Porou tribe). The pace of life is laid back, the way of life predominantly rural. Geographically, the area has few natural harbours and, until the road network was completed, goods had to be loaded off the beaches onto waiting barges. The interior is still wild bush, with the Raukumara Range extending down the centre of the cape. The western side of the range is divided into several protected forests: Raukumara Forest Park, Urutawa Forest and Waioeka Gorge Scenic Reserve.

The coast is traced by 330km of highway (SH35), which took decades to build and is an excellent road (open year round). The drive is worthwhile, if only for the magnificent views – a wild coast dotted with little bays, inlets and coves that change aspect with the weather. On a sunny day the water is an inviting turquoise, at other times a

layer of clouds hangs on the craggy mountains rising straight up from the beaches and everything turns a misty green. Dozens of fresh, clear streams flow through wild gorges to meet the sea. During summer the coastline turns crimson with the blooming of the pohutukawa trees that line the seashore.

The region is passionate about rugby and especially their rugby team, East Coast, which has had spectacular form in recent

EAST COAST

The Longest Placename in the World
Taumatawhakatangihangakoaua-
uotamateaturipukakapikimaunga-
horonukupokaiwhenuakitanatahu

years. If you're in the area while a match is being played, be sure not to miss it – the atmosphere is electrifying and it seems like the Cape's whole population is there to watch.

Getting There & Around

Travel around the East Cape has been notoriously slow and sometimes non-existent. But transport has firmed up over the past few years and now a couple of transport operators regularly link Hicks Bay with Opotiki and Gisborne. It's essential to book on any of the shuttle services; the service will either pick you up from where you're staying or arrange a place to meet.

The four main transport operators offering their services on the Cape are Matakaoa Coast Line Couriers (☎ 0800 628 252), East Land Couriers (☎ 07-315 6350), Polly's Passenger Courier (☎ 06-864 4728) and Cook's Courier (☎ 06-864 4711).

Three of the four operators travel up and down the west coast of the Cape. Matakaoa departs from Opotiki for Hicks Bay at 1.45pm Monday to Friday (you can also catch them at Whakatane), while Polly's leaves at 2pm Monday to Saturday. East Land only goes as far as Cape Runaway, leaving Opotiki at 2.30pm Monday to Friday. Matakaoa makes the return journey at 6.15am Monday to Saturday, Polly's 6.30am Monday to Friday and 7.30am Saturday, and East Land at 8pm Monday to Friday. One-way tickets cost around $20.

Only Polly's and Cook's operate on the eastern side of the Cape. Polly's departs Gisborne for Hicks Bay at 1pm weekdays and Cook's at 2pm weekdays and 12.30pm Saturday. Polly's then leaves Hicks Bay for Gisborne at 6.30am weekdays, and Cook's at 8am weekdays and half an hour earlier on Saturday. A one way ticket costs around $30. Polly's also offers an unlimited-stops one-way ticket between Gisborne to Whakatane for $60.

For details on Slim's East Cape Escape tour from Rotorua around the Cape see Organised Tours in the Bay of Plenty chapter.

Hitching can be notoriously slow at times due to the general lack of traffic heading around the cape.

OPOTIKI TO EAST CAPE

This trip is well described in *Opotiki & East Cape,* a comprehensive booklet available free from the Opotiki visitors centre. Along the first stretch of road from Opotiki there are fine views across to the steaming Whakaari (White Island) volcano. At the Waiaua River is the turn-off for the road to Gisborne via Toa Toa and the **Old Motu Coach Road**, probably more suited to mountain bikes than cars.

When you are travelling along this stretch of road keep an eye out for the magnificently carved *whakairo* gateway at Torere School.

The beaches at **Torere** and **Hawai** are steeply shelved and covered with driftwood; they're both good spots for seascape photography. Hawai is the boundary of the Whanau-a-Apanui tribe, whose sphere of influence extends north to Cape Runaway. About 45km from Opotiki the road crosses the **Motu River**, famed for jetboating, white-water rafting and kayaking.

Some 25km further on is **Te Kaha**, once a whaling centre but now a small town that's popular for boating and fishing. It has a rocky beach, pub, store, service station and accommodation. At the large *marae*, the Tukaki meeting house is magnificently carved. A succession of picturesque bays, including the beautiful **Whanarua Bay**, are passed before **Whangaparaoa** and Cape Runaway are reached. This is the area where kumara (sweet potato) was supposedly first introduced to NZ. On the way you'll pass the **Raukokore Anglican Church**, nestled under Norfolk pines on a lone promontory, 30km from Te Kaha. Cape Runaway can only be reached on foot; seek permission before going onto private land.

Hicks Bay gets its name from a crew member of Captain Cook's *Endeavour*. It is a magnificent place, complemented by nearby Horseshoe Bay. There are a variety of **horse treks** (☎ *06-864 4634)* at Hicks Bay; one-hour beach rides cost $25, 2½-hour hill treks $50, 4-hour treks $60 and multi-day treks $250-370. There is also horse trekking available at Maungaroa Station (see Places to Stay).

Nearly 10km further on is the sizeable community of **Te Araroa**, which has a visitors centre. At Te Araroa there is a distinct change in geography from the volcanic rock outcrops to the sandstone cliffs standing above the town on the bay. One of NZ's largest **pohutukawa**, Te Waha o Rerekohu, reputed to be over 600 years old, stands in the school grounds.

At Te Araroa you turn off for the **East Cape Lighthouse**, the most easterly tip of mainland NZ. The lighthouse is 21km east of Te Araroa (a 30-minute drive) along a mostly gravel road, and at the end there's a 25-minute climb to the lighthouse itself.

Places to Stay & Eat

Te Kaha, the central point on the western side of the East Cape, makes a good stopping point.

Te Kaha Holiday Park (☎/*fax 07-325 2894)* Unpowered/powered sites $9/10 per person, dorm bunks $15, cabins $65, tourist flats $75, motel units $85. This park is on the main road but it's well tree-lined, making it a peaceful spot. There's a shop, takeaways and post office on site.

Te Kaha Hotel (☎/*fax 07-325 2830)* Singles/doubles from $40/60. This hotel is not the most plush but has fantastic views up and down the coast. Meals are available in the bar, including fresh fish and chips.

Tui Lodge (☎/*fax 07-325 2922, Copenhagen Rd)* Singles/doubles from $65/95. Tui Lodge is a great place to stay. It's a spacious, modern guesthouse – originally intended as a fishing lodge – set in lovely gardens that attracts tuis (parson birds). Some rooms have coastal views. It's a short distance up Copenhagen Rd from SH35.

Maungaroa Station (☎ *07-325 2727, fax 325 2776)* $20 per person. At the end of Maungaroa Access Rd (off Copenhagen Rd) is this timeless station, in the Raukumara Ranges. The accommodation consists of a self-contained lodge. There's the Kereu River to splash about in, native bush to explore and horse trekking (from $25).

Waikawa B&B (☎/*fax 07-325 2070,* e *waikawa.bnb@xtra.co.nz)* Rooms $80-85. Further along towards Whanarua Bay, and signposted on the main road, is Waikawa B&B, set in a delightful little spot overlooking a small bay. There are two comfortable en suite rooms (one double upstairs with a deck and one twin downstairs) in a cottage flanked by a lovely garden. It's an extra $25 for dinner.

Rendezvous on the Coast (☎/fax 07-325 2899, e rotchp@clear.net.nz) Unpowered/powered sites $8/10 per person, bunk dorms $15, cabins $35-50, tourist flats $65. At pretty Whanarua Bay, this place also has mountain bikes and kayaks for hire, and does fishing and diving trips.

Robyn's Place (☎ 07-325 2904, Whanarua Bay) Dorms $17, doubles $40. Staying at friendly Robyn's Place is more like renting your own small beach house; there's only one 4-bed dorm and one double. Beach access and walks are close by.

Maraehako Bay Retreat (☎ 07-325 2648) Dorms $18, doubles $50. This is another great hostel at Whanarua Bay. The double rooms are large and recently renovated. It's right on the water and if you're lucky the owner will take you out in his boat to check his craypots.

Waihau Bay Lodge (☎ 07-325 3804, fax 325 3875) Bunk dorms $20, en suite rooms $75. This old hotel sits opposite the jetty at Waihau Bay. Meals are available.

Waihau Bay Holiday Park (☎ 07-325 3844, fax 325 3980) Unpowered/powered sites $9/10 per person, dorms $10, on-site caravans $30, cabins $40, motel units $100. This place is a bit further on from Waihau Bay, at Oruati Beach.

Lottin Point Motel (☎/fax 06-864 4455, Lottin Point Rd) Units (up to 5 people) $80. This motel is mid-way between Whangaparaoa and Hicks Bay, 4km north of SH35 on the coast. Lottin Point is well known as a top snapper-fishing spot; the motel can organise fishing trips at $60 for four hours.

Hicks Bay Backpackers Lodge (☎ 06-864 4731, Onepoto Beach Rd) Dorm beds $17, twins & doubles $38. Take the dirt road around the peninsula from the Hicks Bay township, to get to this wonderful lodge. It's a small, friendly place with a bunkroom off to one side of the home. It

fronts a beautiful beach, only 50m away. The double and twin are in the main house.

Hicks Bay Motel Lodge (☎ 06-864 4880, fax 864 4708) Units from $80. This motel, also at Hicks Bay, is up on the hill overlooking the bay. There's a restaurant and glow-worm caves on the premises.

Hicks Bay has a *takeaway* and *general store*.

Te Araroa Holiday Park (☎ 06-864 4873, 864 4473) Unpowered/powered sites $8.50/9.50 per person, dorms $12, cabins $35, tourist flats $50. This park, over the hill towards Te Araroa from Hicks Bay, is another lovely spot. In a sheltered 15-hectare parklike setting near the beach, the park has lots of amenities, including a cinema (the most easterly in the world!) and fish and chip shop.

EAST CAPE TO GISBORNE

Heading south from Te Araroa the first place of interest you come to is **Tikitiki**. The Anglican Church is well worth visiting for its Maori architectural design.

A few kilometres off the road is **Ruatoria**, which has powerful Mt Hikurangi as a backdrop. Ruatoria is a very important Maori town – the centre of the Ngati Porou tribe. The politician Sir Apirana Ngata (see History in the Facts about New Zealand chapter) lived here, as did Victoria Cross-winner Lt Moananui-a-Kiwa Ngarimu and All Black George Nepia.

About 25km south is **Te Puia Springs**, a pretty little town with hot springs nearby, and the pleasant **Waipiro Bay**. Another 11km further is **Tokomaru Bay**, a crumbling, picturesque town with a splendid beach and sweeping cliffs at the southern end of the bay. Hiking, swimming, surfing, tennis, fishing and cycling are all popular activities here.

Tolaga Bay, the largest community on the Cape, is next. The attraction here is the beach, 3km south of the town. At the southern end of the beach is a disused **wharf** running 660m out to sea, which is pleasant for a stroll. Close by is the start of the **Cooks Cove Walkway**, a 2½-hour return walk to a cove where Cook landed in 1769. It's a not too strenuous walk across farmland and through native bush; it's closed from August to Labour Day weekend (October) for lambing season. South of Tolaga Bay is the small settlement **Whangara**, the setting for Witi Ihimaera's wonderful novel *The Whale Rider*. It is a great little book to read for a feel of the Maori culture and mythology of the area (see Literature in Facts About NZ).

After passing Tatapouri and Wainui Beaches you reach Gisborne.

Places to Stay

Manutahi Hotel (☎ *06-864 8437, fax 864 8333*) Singles/doubles from $40/50. This old hotel in Ruatoria has standard pub rooms.

Two kilometres south of Ruatoria you can get food at the pleasant *Mountain View Cafe*, and a drink at the adjacent *Blue Boar Tavern*.

Te Puia Springs Motel (☎ *06-864 6828*) Singles/doubles $55/66. This motel is handy to the beach.

The Te Puia visitors centre (☎ 06-864 6894), in the council chambers, can tell you about homestays in the area.

Waikawa Lodge (☎ *06-864 6719, Waikawa Rd*) Doubles $25 per person. Waikawa Lodge is a small, romantic backpackers cottage (with two doubles and a kitchen), ideal for getting away from it all. It's located at Waipiro Bay on the coast. The big plus here is the two-hour horse treks ($40). This place is hard to find. If you are coming from the Opotiki side, turn off at the Kopuaroa Rd sign. If you are coming from the Gisborne side, look for the signposted turn-off to Waipiro Bay. Both roads lead to Waikawa Rd and the lodge is up a farm road at the end of the road. Waikawa Rd is impassable when conditions are very wet so it's essential to ring before you come. The owners will pick you up from Te Puia Springs or Waipiro Bay.

House of the Rising Sun (☎ *06-864 5858, Potae St, Tokomaru Bay*) Dorms $15, twins/doubles $36. This is a small, comfortable and homey hostel about a block from the beach.

Brian's Place (☎ *06-864 5870*) Unpowered sites $10, lofts $16, twins $32, doubles $38. Brian's is in a great spot overlooking the bay, uphill from the House of the Rising Sun. It has a double room, two lofts (can sleep four) and tent sites. You can organise horse treks here (from $30).

Tolaga Bay Holiday Park (☎ *06-862 6716, Wharf Rd*) Camp sites from $9 per person, cabins $36. Further south, this well-equipped camp is located on the beach near the wharf.

Tolaga Bay Inn (☎ *06-862 6856,* ⓔ *bill .kaua@xtra.co.nz, Cook St*) Singles/doubles $40/70. This is a historic place with a bar and restaurant attached.

Tolaga Bay Motel (☎ *06-862 6888, cnr Cook & Monkhouse Sts*) Singles/doubles $60/70. The pleasant units at this motel have cooking facilities.

RAUKUMARA & WAIOEKA

Inland, the Raukumara Range offers tramping (the highest mountain in the range is Hikurangi, at 1752m) and white-water rafting on the Waioeka and Motu Rivers – contact **Wet 'n' Wild Rafting** (☎ *0800 462 7238*) for more information. The most popular way of accessing this rugged, untamed region is via SH2 (the Waioeka Gorge Road), the 144km road which connects Opotiki to Gisborne.

There are many great walks in this region, and the Department of Conservation (DOC) offices in Opotiki and Gisborne can supply you with information. See DOC's *Raukumara Forest Park* and *Waioeka Gorge Scenic Reserve* pamphlets. The rare whio (blue duck) may be seen in Raukumara, and Hochstetter's frog *(Leiopelma hochstetteri)* is quite common in the park. Some parts of the region are penetrable by mountain bike, while others are certainly not. This region is one of NZ's last frontiers, as wild as sections of south Westland.

The *Riverview Cottage* is a great place to stay, only 14km from Opotiki (See Opotiki in the Bay of Plenty chapter for details).

Matawai Hotel (☎ *06-862 4874*) Singles/doubles $35/65. This hotel is 76km from Opotiki on SH2.

Matawai Village Cafe is a convenient place to get a bite to eat.

Poverty Bay

☎ 06 • pop 41,400

This region got its name in 1769 from one of its earliest European visitors, James Cook (on his first expedition). While trying to replenish his ship, there were skirmishes with the local Maori, six of whom were killed. Cook decided the area had little to offer, hence 'poverty'.

The actual bay is quite small, a half-moon stretching from Tuahine Point to Young Nicks Head. The Poverty Bay region includes the coast from Tolaga Bay south to the Mahia Peninsula and west to the hills of the East Cape, the gem of which is Lake Waikaremoana.

GISBORNE

☎ 06 • pop 32,700

Gisborne is NZ's most easterly city, and one of the closest in the world to the International Date Line. The fertile alluvial plains around Gisborne support intensive farming of subtropical fruits, market-garden produce and vineyards. More recently, kiwi fruit and avocados have been important crops in the area.

The city itself is on the coast at the confluence of two rivers: the Waimata and Taruheru (the short stretch below the junction is the Turanganui). Often described as 'the city of bridges', it is also noted for its fine parks. Within easy reach of the city are a number of great surf beaches, making Gisborne a bit of a surfer's mecca.

This part of the East Coast retains a definite Maori character, with a great emphasis on the retention of culture and traditions.

History

The Gisborne region has been settled for over 1000 years. Two skippers of ancestral migratory *waka* (canoes) – Paoa of the *Horo-uta* and Kiwa of the *Takitimu* – made an intermarriage pact which led to the founding of Turanganui a Kiwa (now Gisborne) soon after their arrival from Hawaiki. The newly introduced kumara flourished in the fertile soil and the Maori settlement spread to the hinterland.

Even though Gisborne is the site of Cook's first landing in 1769, European settlement of the region did not occur until the late 19th century. A man of considerable drive, John Williams Harris, was first to purchase a small area on the west bank of the Turanganui River. He set up the region's first whaling venture and in 1839 began farming up the Waipaoa River near Manutuke.

As whaling became increasingly popular, missionaries began to move into the area. Father Baty and Rev William Colenso were the first Europeans to tramp into the heart of Te Urewera and see Lake Waikaremoana.

Gradually more Pakeha arrived but organised settlement was limited due to Maori resistance. When the Treaty of Waitangi was signed in 1840 many chiefs from the east coast did not acknowledge the treaty, let alone sign it.

In the 1860s, numerous battles with the Maori broke out. The Hauhau insurrection that began in Taranaki and spread to the Bay of Plenty and East Coast reached its height here at the battle of Waerenga-a-hika in late 1865. By the following year the government had crushed opposition and transported a number of the survivors, including the charismatic Te Kooti (see the boxed text), to the remote Chatham Islands. This paved the way for an influx of Europeans, who brought sheep. But in 1868 Te Kooti escaped and with an army of 200 exacted revenge on the settlement at Matawhero, killing 33 Europeans and 37 Maori.

Even today, however, much of the pasture land is leased from the Maori and a large part of it is under their direct control. Unfortunately, the pioneer farmers were so anxious to profit from the land that they ripped out far too much forest cover with disastrous results. Massive erosion occurred as the steeply sloping land was unable to hold the soil after heavy rains.

Information

The Gisborne visitors centre (☎ 06-868 6139, 🔲 www.gisbornenz.com) is at 209 Grey St. Look for the fine Canadian totem pole beside it. It's open from 7.30am to 5.30pm Monday to Friday and 9am to 5pm

GISBORNE

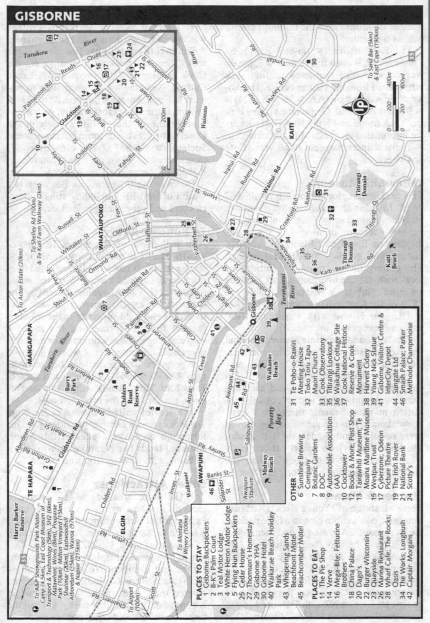

PLACES TO STAY
1 Gisborne Backpackers
2 B-K's Palm Court
3 Teal Motor Lodge
4 White Heron Motor Lodge
5 Flying Nun Backpackers
25 Cedar House
27 Thomson's Homestay
29 Gisborne YHA
30 Gisborne Hotel
40 Waikanae Beach Holiday
   Park
43 Whispering Sands
   Beachfront Motel
45 Beachcomber Motel

PLACES TO EAT
11 The Pie Shop
14 Verve
16 Mega-Bite; Fettucine
   Brothers
18 China Palace
20 Dago's
22 Burger Wisconsin
23 Quayside
26 Marina Restaurant
28 Wharf Cafe; The Rocks;
   Oasis
34 The Works; Longbush
42 Captain Morgans

OTHER
6 Sunshine Brewing
  Company
7 Botanic Gardens
8 DOC
9 Automobile Association
  (AA)
10 Clocktower
12 Books & More; Post Shop
13 Tairawhiti Museum; Te
   Moana Maritime Museum
15 Westpac Trust
17 Cyberzone; Odeon
   Picture Theatre
19 The Irish Rover
21 National Bank
24 Scotty's
31 Te Poho-o-Rawiri
   Meeting House
32 Toko Toru Tapu
   Maori Church
33 Cook Observatory
35 Titirangi Lookout
36 Waikahua Cottage Site
37 Cook National Historic
   Reserve & Cook
   Monument
38 Harvest Cidery
39 Young Nick Statue
41 Gisborne Visitors Centre &
   InterCity Depot
44 Sungate Ltd
46 Smash Palace; Parker
   Methode Champenoise

Saturday and Sunday. Children (and a fair number of adults) love the minigolf course behind the centre.

The DOC office (☎ 06-867 8531), 63 Carnarvon St, is open from 8am to 4.35pm on weekdays; you're requested to first seek information from the visitors centre. The Automobile Association (AA; ☎ 06-868 1424) is at 363 Gladstone Rd. Contact the visitors centre, YHA hostel or Flying Nun Backpackers for information on seasonal fruit picking.

There is Internet access at the Verve Cafe or Cyberzone.

Tairawhiti Museum

This excellent regional museum (☎ 06-867 3832, 18 Stout St; admission by donation; museum complex open 10am-4pm Mon-Fri, 1.30pm-4pm Sat & Sun) has numerous displays on East Coast Maori and colonial history, and geology and natural history. The gallery has changing exhibitions of local, national and international art. Outside are more exhibits – a sled house, stable, the 1870 Wyllie Cottage (first house on the site) and Lysnar House with working artists' studios (not open to the public).

The **Te Moana Maritime Museum** behind the main museum is part of the complex. One wild night in 1912 the 12,000-ton *Star of Canada* was blown ashore on the reef at Gisborne. The ship's bridge and captain's cabin were salvaged, and eventually installed in what became the town's best-known home. This unique house was moved here, restored and made into a museum. There are displays on Maori canoes, early whaling and shipping, Cook's Gisborne visit, and a collection of historic surfboards.

Statues & Views

There's a **statue** of 'Young Nick' (Nicholas Young), Cook's cabin boy, in a little park on the river mouth. A press-ganged member of Cook's crew, he was the first to sight NZ. Across the bay are the white cliffs that Cook named Young Nick's Head.

Across the river at the foot of Kaiti Hill is a **monument** to Cook, near the spot where he first set foot on NZ (9th October 1769 in 'ship time' according to Cook's journal, but really the 8th). It's in the Cook National Historic Reserve. Nearby Waikahua Cottage was once a refuge during the Hauhau unrest.

Titirangi (Kaiti Hill) has fine views of the area. There's a walking track up from the Cook monument, starting near Waikahua Cottage. Near the top is yet another monument to Cook, but it's a fine one. At the 135m summit is the **Cook Observatory**, with a sign proclaiming it the 'World's Easternmost Observatory'. The **Gisborne Astronomical Society** (☎ 06-867 7901; admission $2) meets here at 7.30pm on Tuesday in winter, 8.30pm in summer; all are welcome.

Down on **Kaiti Beach**, low tide attracts a wealth of bird life, including stilts, oystercatchers and other pelagic visitors.

Te Poho-o-Rawiri

Also at the foot of Titirangi is Te Poho-o-Rawiri Maori meeting house, one of the largest in NZ. It has a richly decorated interior and its stage is framed by carved *maihi* (ornamental carved gable boards). The human figure kneeling on the right knee with its right hand held upwards is the *tekoteko* (carved figure) representing the ancestor who challenges those who enter the marae. It is open all the time except when a function is in progress; seek permission before entering (☎ 06-868 5364). A little Maori church, **Toko Toru Tapu**, stands on the side of Titirangi, not far from the meeting house.

The leaflet called *Tairawhiti Heritage Trails: Gisborne District* provides good information on historic sites in this Maori ancestral land. The Ngati Porou tribe has a website at W www.ngatiporou.iwi.nz.

Other Attractions

The Gisborne area has a few attractive gardens that are worth a visit. The huge **Eastwoodhill Arboretum** (☎ 06-863 9003; adult/child $8/free; open 9am-5pm daily), 35km west of town, has NZ's largest collection of northern hemisphere temperate trees, shrubs and climbers. To get there follow the Ngatapa-Rere Road; there's a 45-minute marked track through the trees and budget accommodation in the park. Ask at the visitors centre about other private gardens.

Te Kooti

The enigmatic Te Kooti was born into the Rongowhakaata tribe in Poverty Bay during the early 19th century in the shadow of a prophecy. It was foretold that if, as the second born, he outlived his brother evil would fall upon the land and its people.

Indeed, Te Kooti survived an illness that killed his sibling. Rejected by his father, he was adopted and attended an Anglican mission school. Later, as a young man, he was accused of assisting the Hauhau in Gisborne during a siege by government troops. In 1865 Te Kooti, along with a number of others, was packed off to exile in the Chatham Islands. Here, during a bout of fever, he experienced the visions that were to eventually lead to the establishment of the Ringatu Church. In 1867 he led an escape from the Chathams; more than 200 men, women and children sailed away on a captured supply ship, the *Rifleman*.

They landed at Poverty Bay where during a ceremony of thanks for their safe return, Te Kooti urged his followers to raise their right hands to pay homage to God rather than kneel in submission. This is believed to be the first time the raised hand, from which Ringatu takes its name, was used.

The escapees intended to make their way peaceably into the interior, where Te Kooti hoped to challenge the Maori king, Tawhiao, in the Waikato for spiritual leadership. But resident magistrate Reginald Biggs demanded they give up their arms. They refused, and a series of skirmishes followed, during which the government troops suffered a series of humiliating defeats. But when Te Kooti reached the Waikato he was rejected by Tawhiao.

He turned back to Poverty Bay and attacked Matawhero, killing Biggs and, later, several chiefs, including the father of his first wife. He became both hated and feared, and some of his prisoners decided it would be prudent to become supporters.

For a while he dominated Poverty Bay, but was forced to retreat into the Urewera Ranges in the face of challenges from avenging Maori tribes. There he mustered a fighting force of some 200 warriors and adopted the custom of sallying forth on his various raids astride a white horse.

More fighting took place, during which Te Kooti moved into the King Country, back to the Ureweras and then out again to the King Country, where in 1873 he finally put his fighting days behind him.

From his base in Te Kuiti he formulated the rituals of the Ringatu Church. His reputation as a prophet and healer spread, and he made a series of predictions about a successor. He devoted the rest of his life to making peace with his former enemies and spreading the tenets of his faith. He particularly desired to return to Poverty Bay, but his old foes prevented this.

After his pardon Te Kooti lived near Ohiwa Harbour, and he spent much time visiting other Ringatu centres in the region. He never returned to Poverty Bay and he eventually died at Ohiwa in 1893.

His body was removed by his followers from its original burial place at Maromahue and to this day no-one knows for sure exactly where he was finally laid to rest.

The **Botanic Gardens** are in town beside the Taruheru River.

Gisborne is a major wine-producing area, noted for its chardonnay. Wineries to visit include: **Parker Methode Champenoise** (☎ *06-867 6976, 24 Bank St*); **Matawhero Wines** (☎ *06-868 8366, Riverpoint Rd*); **Millton Vineyard** (☎ *06-862 8680, Manutuke*); **Longbush** (☎ *06-863 0627, The Esplanade*); **Montana** (☎ *06-868 2757, Lytton Rd*); **Pouparae Park** (☎ *06-867 7931, 385 Bushmere Rd*); **Shalimar** (☎ *06-863 7776,*

Ngatapa Rd). The visitors centre has details on opening hours and tours.

Trev's Tours (☎ *06-863 9815; tours $60-250*) does tours to of Gisborne and the surrounding area, including a wine trail.

There is also a natural beer brewery, the **Sunshine Brewing Company** (☎ *06-867 7777, 109 Disraeli St*), and **Bulmer Harvest Cidery** (☎ *06-868 8300, Customhouse St*).

Near the A&P Showgrounds in Makaraka is the **East Coast Museum of Technology & Transport (ECMOT)** (☎ *06-868 8254,*

W *http://ecmot.8m.com/; adult/child $2/ 50c; open 9.30am-4.30pm daily).*

Matawhero is a few kilometres south along SH2. The historic Presbyterian Church here is the only building in town to have survived the conflicts of 1868.

Activities

You can swim at Waikanae Beach in the city. Midway Beach has a surf club and a swimming complex with a big waterslide and children's playground. **Enterprise Pools** *(Nelson Rd)* is an indoor complex open to the public. Wainui Beach also has a surf club where you can safely swim between the flags and do a bit of body surfing.

The Motu and Waioeka Rivers are in the Gisborne district, although they drain into the Bay of Plenty. Ask at the visitors centre about white-water rafting. The centre also has details on walks, horse trekking, fishing, hunting and tours.

Surfing is hugely popular in Gisborne due to a plethora of surf beaches close to the city. Waikanae Beach is good for learners, while more experienced surfers could choose from The Pipe, south of town, or Sponge Bay Island, just to the north. The bays of Wainui and Makrori, on the SH35 heading towards East Cape, also have plenty of breaks.

Sungate Ltd *(☎ 06-868 1673, 55 Salisbury Rd)* hires out an array of water-sports equipment, including surfboards (one hour, $10) and boogie boards (one hour, $5). They also offer surf lessons and hire out bikes (one hr, $6).

Surfing Spit Surfcoaching *(☎ 035-643 9070,* W *www.surf.to/gizzy)* gives lessons from $15 per person.

Te Kuri Walkway is a three-hour (5.6km) walk through farmland and some forest to a commanding viewpoint. The walk starts 4km north of town at the end of Shelley Rd. It's closed from August to October for lambing.

Waimoana Horse Trekking *(☎ 06-868 8218, Wainui Beach; ½-hr treks $30/40)* takes you up over hilly farmland and down onto sandy Wainui Beach.

The adventurous can get close up to mako sharks ('waterborne pussycats') in submersible metal cages with **Surfit Charters**

Dame Kiri Te Kanawa

One of the most internationally famous Kiwis of all time is Dame Kiri Te Kanawa, the serenely beautiful opera diva. (The only equally-well-known Kiwi is perhaps mountaineer Sir Edmund Hillary.)

It's hard to imagine that this lyrical soprano who graces La Scala and Covent Garden with aplomb had her beginnings in this motley neighbourhood – she was born in Gisborne in 1944. Her first major leading role was as the Countess in *Le Nozze di Figaro* at Covent Garden (1971), and she has since embraced the roles of Donna Elvira *(Don Giovanni)*, Marguerite *(Faust)*, Mimi *(La Bohéme)*, Amelia *(Simon Boccanegra)* and Desdemona *(Otello)*. There have been many famous commercial recordings – *West Side Story* with José Carreras, and the haunting calls across the valley of Canteloube's *Songs of the Auvergne*. She also sang at Charles and Diana's wedding in 1981.

(☎ 06-867 2970, W *www.sharks.co.nz; shark trips from $165 per person).* Tamer snorkelling on the reefs around Gisborne can also be arranged.

Places to Stay

Camping & Cabins The *Waikanae Beach Holiday Park (☎ 06-867 5634, Grey St)* has a great spot at Waikanae Beach. Camp sites start at $9 per person, cabins $28 and tourist flats $55.

A&P Showgrounds Park Motor Camp (☎/fax 06-867 5299, e *camp@gisborneshow .co.nz, 20 Main Rd)* Unpowered/powered sites $10.50/12.50 for 2, cabins $30, on-site caravans $30. This park at Makaraka is cheaper than Waikanae Beach Holiday Park, but it's not so conveniently central.

Hostels Finding a bed at one of Gisborne's backpackers shouldn't be too big a problem.

Flying Nun Backpackers (☎ 06-868 0461, e *yager@xtra.co.nz, 147 Roebuck Rd)* Dorms $17-19, singles $27, doubles & twins $44. The Flying Nun (no reference to NZ's independent record label) still awaits the right winds for Sally Fields' Sister

Bertrille. Backpackers with the right equipment (the hat and healthy habits, perhaps) can alight here. This is where Dame Kiri Te Kanawa (see the boxed text) had her early singing lessons.

Gisborne YHA (☎ 06-867 3269, e *yha.gis@clear.net.nz, 32 Harris St*) Dorm beds $16, doubles & twins $38. Situated 1.5km from the town centre across the river, this hostel is in a substantial old home with spacious grounds.

Gisborne Backpackers (☎ 06-868 1000, e *gisbornebp@xtra.co.nz, 690 Gladstone Rd*) Dorms from $17, twins & doubles $42. This large backpackers is about 2km from the town centre. There's a spacious kitchen, games room and backyard garden.

B&Bs & Guesthouses The visitors centre has lists of homestays.

Thomson Homestay (☎ 0800 370 505, 868 9675, 16 Rawiri St*) Singles/doubles $50/70. Thomson's is pleasantly situated in the historic riverfront district, not far from downtown.

Cedar House (☎ 06-868 1902, e *stay@cedarhouse.co.nz, 4 Clifford St*) Singles/doubles $160/180. This Edwardian mansion has been turned into a sumptuous B&B with spacious rooms, enormous beds, immaculate bathrooms and cosy guest lounge.

Motels & Hotels Salisbury Rd, close to the city centre and right near the beach, is a good motel hunting ground, as is Gladstone Rd, the main road south. Note that prices are likely to depend on the season.

Whispering Sands Beachfront Motel (☎ 0800 405 030, 06-867 1319, 22 Salisbury Rd*) Units from $105. Whispering Sands has 14 units right on Waikanae Beach and impressive views of Poverty Bay.

Beachcomber Motel (☎ 06-868 9349, fax 868 6974, 73 Salisbury Rd*) Units from $85. The Beachcomber is across the road from the beach.

B-K's Palm Court (☎ 0800 672 000, 06-868 5601, e *info@palmcourt.co.nz, 671 Gladstone Rd*) Units from $88. B-K's is a well-kept motel, with 15 units, some with their own spa bath.

Teal Motor Lodge (☎ 0800 838 325, 06-868 4019, e *motel@teal.co.nz, 479 Gladstone Rd*) Units from $89. Teal Motor Lodge has modern units and a saltwater swimming pool.

White Heron Motor Lodge (☎ 0800 997 766, 06-867 1108, e *wheron@clear.net.nz, 470 Gladstone Rd*) Units from $100. White Heron is another quality motel. Most units have their own spa.

Gisborne Hotel (☎ 06-868 4109, e *info@gisbornehotel.com, cnr Tyndall & Huxley Rds, Kaiti*) Rooms from $100, suite $150. The Gisborne is a tidy enough place, if a little isolated.

Places to Eat

Gisborne has the usual selection of sandwich places, particularly along Gladstone Rd and Peel St.

Mega-Bite (22 Peel St*) Light meals from $5. This heavily graffitied cafe has good hot lunches (quiche, samosas and the like), sandwiches, rolls and drinks.

China Palace (☎ 06-867 4911, 55 Peel St*) Mains $9-12. China Palace is a popular spot for Chinese takeaways.

Verve (121 Gladstone Rd*) Mains $10-15. This funky cafe has continental meals, Internet connection and a nice ambience.

Quayside (cnr Lowe St & Reads Quay*) Mains $12. Quayside is an attractive cafe with an eclectic menu, ranging from pumpkin and kumara fritatta to Thai soup.

Dago's (☎ 06-867 0543, Gladstone Rd*) Mains $12-17. Don't go past Dago's for takeaways, which is famous for its pizza, pasta, kebabs and Thai cuisine. The food is delicious and the servings are huge.

Burger Wisconsin (26 Gladstone Rd*) Burgers $5.50-9.50. It's hard to beat the variety of burgers at this place: Pumpkin and tofu, satay, and blue cheese, are just some of the flavours on offer.

The Pie Shop (Grey St*) Pies from $2. For a quick pie or sandwich, try here.

Captain Morgans (☎ 06-867 7821, 285 Grey St*) Burgers $4-7. Close to Waikanae Beach is this popular eatery. The burgers are particularly good and particularly large.

Fettucine Brothers (☎ *06-868 5700, 12 Peel St)* Mains $18-28. This is a pleasant Italian restaurant next door to Mega-Bite.

Marina Restaurant (☎ *06-868 5919, 1 Vogel St)* Mains from $25. This place has a fine seafood selection and fine views of town and its rivers.

Down at Gisborne wharf, three waterside restaurants occupy a sunny spot: the *Wharf Cafe* (☎ *06-868 4876)*, *The Rocks* and *Oasis* (☎ *06-867 1103)*.

The Works (☎ *06-863 1285, The Esplanade)* Mains $24-27. Housed in part of the original freezing works of Gisborne, this upmarket winery/cafe serves imaginatively prepared dishes, but is just as good for a glass or two of wine.

Entertainment

The Irish Rover (69 Peel St) This pseudo Irish pub is packed on Friday and Saturday, and there's an over-25 bar upstairs.

Scotty's (☎ *06-867 8173, 35 Gladstone Rd)* Scotty's is popular with all walks of life. The large garden bar fills up on hot summer afternoons and there's the occasional live band.

Smash Palace (☎ *06-867 2769, 24 Bank St)* The most interesting place in town is Smash Palace, set appropriately in the junkyard area of town. A couple of beaten-up old Morris Minor cars and the hulk of a long-grounded aircraft greet you outside, while inside is a veritable Aladdin's cave of junk from all parts of the globe and Kiwi memorabilia. But the place has atmosphere, a good selection of beers and wines, and light bar meals, including good pizzas, which are touched up with a blowtorch.

Sand Bar (☎ *06-868 6828, Oneroa Rd)* The Sand Bar is a friendly and convivial place out at Wainui. Best nights are Thursday to Saturday; a shuttle runs from the bar to downtown at midnight.

During summer, bands, musicians and poets perform in the parks.

Getting There & Away

Air The Air New Zealand office (☎ 06-868 2700) is at 37 Bright St. It has daily direct flights to Auckland and Wellington, with onward connections to places like Rotorua and Hamilton.

Bus The InterCity depot (☎ 06-868 6139) is at the visitors centre. InterCity has one bus daily (leaves at 9am) to Napier ($35, 4hrs) via Wairoa ($20, 1½hrs). From Napier there are connections to Palmerston North ($60, 3hrs) and Wellington ($80, 5¾hrs). InterCity also runs buses (leaves at 8am) between Gisborne and Auckland ($58, 9hrs) via Opotiki ($18, 2hrs), Whakatane ($26, 3hrs) and Rotorua ($39, 4½hrs).

For details on public transport on the much longer, but very scenic, route to Opotiki, via the East Cape, see the East Cape section. Another route from Rotorua to Gisborne is the partly unsealed SH38, which runs through the Te Urewera National Park, past Lake Waikaremoana and joins the Napier route at Wairoa, 97km south of Gisborne; see the Wairoa to Napier section.

Hitching Hitching is OK from the south of the city, and not too bad through Waioeka Gorge to Opotiki – it's still best to leave early. To hitch a ride out, head along Gladstone Rd to Makaraka, 6km west, for Wairoa and Napier, or the turn-off to Opotiki and Rotorua. Hitching from Wairoa to Waikaremoana is hard going.

Getting Around

Gisborne Taxi Buses (☎ 06-867 2222) runs the town's bus service; buses only go on weekdays and the last run is at 5.15pm. Taxis include Gisborne Taxis (☎ 06-867 2222) and Eastland Taxis (☎ 06-868 1133). Link Taxis (☎ 06-868 8385) runs to Gisborne airport ($10 to $12 from town).

For rentals try Hertz (☎ 06-867 9348), Budget (☎ 06-867 9794) or Avis (☎ 06-868 9084).

GISBORNE TO WAIROA

Heading south towards Napier you have two choices: the SH2 follows the coast, while the SH36 skirts inland. The two routes meet in Wairoa.

The **coastal route** runs just inland most of the way south from Gisborne, before it enters the Wharerata State Forest. At the southern edge of the state forest, 56km from Gisborne, Morere is a pretty little town noted for its hot springs. The **hot springs** (☎ 06-837 8856; adult/child $5/2.50; open 10am-6pm Mon-Thur, 10am-7pm Fri, Sat & Sun) are complemented by short walks of up to two hours through the beautiful native forest of the surrounding reserve.

Morere Tearooms & Camping Ground (☎ 06-837 8792, SH2) Unpowered sites $10 per person, cabins $40-50. This place is located opposite the springs alongside native bush and a babbling stream.

Peacock Lodge (☎ 06-837 8824, e pea cocklodge@xtra.co.nz) Dorm beds $16, doubles & twins $32, self-contained cottage $70. Another place to stay in Morere is the delightful old Peacock Lodge, about two minutes' walk from SH2. Follow the road next to the tearooms across the stream. This colonial farmhouse has a spacious lounge, fully equipped kitchen and wide veranda.

SH2 continues south to Nuhaka on the northern end of the sweep of Hawke Bay, where you can head west to Wairoa or east to the superb, windswept and wild **Mahia Peninsula** (said to be named after a place in Tahiti). There are long, curving beaches popular with surfers, clear water for diving and fishing, bird-watching at Mangawhio Lagoon and walks to a number of reserves. Mahia was once an island, but sand accumulation has formed NZ's largest tombolo landform (where a sand or shingle bar ties an island to another island or the mainland). The peninsula is a magical, atmospheric place, majestic in either sun or storm. Facilities are limited and you'll need your own transport to get around.

Blue Bay Holiday Resort (☎ 0800 262 442, 06-837 5867, e blue.bay.holiday.res ort@xtra.co.nz, Opoutama) Unpowered/ powered sites $10/11 per person, on-site caravans $50, cabins $50-90, cottage 490, motel units from $75. This camping ground occupies a nice secluded spot by the beach, 12km east of Nuhaka. There is plenty of tree shelter.

Tunanui Station Cottages (☎ 06-837 5790, e tunanui@xtra.co.nz, 1001 Tuna-nui

Rd) Cottage $165 plus $30 per extra person. Tunanui Station has two fully self-contained cottages on a 3200-acre working farm. It is some 6km north from Opoutama. The views over the peninsula are stupendous.

Along SH36, the **inland route** to Wairoa, there are also several things to see and do. You can climb up **Gentle Annie Hill** for a good view over the Poverty Bay area. **Doneraille Park** (53km from Gisborne), a native bush reserve, is a popular picnic spot with good swimming when the water is clear.

There's fine trout fishing at **Tiniroto Lakes**, 61km from Gisborne, and about 10km further, **Te Reinga Falls** is worth a detour off the main road.

Hawkes Bay

☎ 06 • pop 133,900

The Hawkes Bay region (note that the body of water is 'Hawke Bay') is, sadly, missed by many visitors to NZ. Napier (like Hastings) is one of the best holiday destinations in the country, with fine Art Deco architecture.

The region also offers the 'perfect' village of Havelock North, an abundance of wineries, and natural attractions such as the Cape Kidnappers gannet colony.

WAIROA
pop 5228

The highways SH2 and SH36 meet in Wairoa, 98km south of Gisborne. Wairoa has a reasonable beach and is a gateway to Te Urewera National Park. The relocated **lighthouse** by the river, built in 1877 of solid kauri, used to shine from Portland Island at the tip of the Mahia Peninsula. Ten kilometres east of Wairoa is Whakaki Lagoon, an important wetlands area renowned for its bird populations.

The Wairoa visitors centre (☎ 06-838 7440, e weavic@xtra.co.nz), on the corner of SH2 and Queen St, has information on Te Urewera National Park and sells DOC passes. It opens 9am to 5pm daily (less on winter weekends). The DOC field centre (☎ 06-838 8252) is at 272 Marine Parade, but it generally only opens on Monday.

Places to Stay & Eat

Riverside Motor Camp (☎ 06-838 6301, Marine Parade) Unpowered/powered sites $8.50/9.50 per person, cabins $40. Riverside is a pleasant place on the banks of the Wairoa River.

Clyde Hotel (☎ 06-838 7139, Marine Parade) Dorms $12.50, singles/doubles $25/45. The Clyde is an old-style hotel in the heart of Wairoa.

For food, try the pleasant *Johanna's* (Clyde Court), or *Katz* (Marine Parade) for fuller meals, or the excellent *Oslers Bakery* (Marine Parade), which won *Baker of the Year* award in 2001.

Getting There & Away

All InterCity (☎ 06-838 7440) buses that travel between Gisborne and Napier pass through Wairoa.

WAIROA TO NAPIER

There are some good reserves along this stretch of road that break the twisting drive, all accessible from SH2. Pick up the brochure *Napier to Wairoa: Heritage Trails* at the Wairoa visitors centre; it lists all the following reserves.

Lake Tutira has a farmland setting; there are walkways around the lake and a bird sanctuary. The **Hawkes Bay Coastal Walkway** is 12km from SH2, down Waikari Rd. The walkway is 16km long, goes from the Waikari River to the Aropaoanui River, and involves equal portions of boulder hopping, track walking and beach walking.

Off Waipatiki Rd and 34km from Napier is the **Waipatiki Scenic Reserve**. The **White Pine Bush Scenic Reserve**, 29km from Napier, is notable for the dominant kahikatea (white pine). The **Tangoio Falls Scenic Reserve**, 2km south of White Pine, has Te Ana Falls, stands of ponga and whekiponga, and podocarps. The White Pine and Tangoio Falls Scenic Reserves are linked by the **Tangoio Walkway**, which follows Kareaara Stream.

There's rustic backpacker accommodation at *Bushdale Farm* (☎/fax 06-838 6453, Cricklewood Rd), about 9km from Wairoa heading towards Napier. Pick-up

from Wai-roa can be arranged. Unpowered sites are $8 per person, dorm beds $20, and doubles $40.

Glen-View Farm Hostel (☎ 06-836 6232, fax 836 6067) Dorms $14-15, doubles $40. Glen-View Farm is a hill-country sheep-and-cattle station, where horse riding and walking are popular. You can join in farm activities. The hostel is 31km north of Napier off SH2, 2km along the Arapaoanui Rd towards the sea.

TE UREWERA NATIONAL PARK

Home of the Tuhoe people, one of NZ's most traditional tribes, Te Urewera is rich in history. The army of Te Kooti (see the boxed text, Te Kooti, earlier in this chapter) found refuge here during its battles against the government. Te Kooti's successor, Rua Kenana, led a thriving community at Maungapohatu, beneath the sacred mountain of the same name, from 1905 until his politically inspired arrest in 1916. Maungapohatu never recovered after that and only a small settlement remains. Slightly larger is nearby Ruatahuna, where the extraordinary Mataatua Marae celebrates Te Kooti's exploits.

Te Urewera National Park is one of the country's most attractive parks. It is a marvellous area of lush forests, lakes and rivers, with lots of tramps, ranging from half an hour to several days, and plenty of birds, trout, deer and other wildlife. The main focus of the park is the superbly scenic Lake Waikaremoana (Sea of Rippling Waters). Most visitors to the park come to go boating on the lake or walk the Lake Waikaremoana Track, one of NZ's Great Walks, but other walks are possible.

The park protects part of the largest untouched native forest area in the North Island. The rivers and lakes of the park offer good trout fishing.

Information

The **Aniwaniwa Visitor Centre** (☎ 06-837 3803, ⓔ urewerainfo@doc.govt.nz), within the park on the shores of the lake, is open 8am to 4.45pm daily. It has interesting displays on the park's natural history and supplies information on the walking tracks and accommodation around the park.

The **Rangitaiki Field Centre** (☎ 06-366 1080) near Murupara is the park's other main information centre.

Hut and camping ground passes for the Lake Waikaremoana Track can also be bought at DOC offices and visitor centres in Gisborne, Wairoa, Whakatane and Napier.

For online information about the area check out Ⓦ www.lake.co.nz.

Lake Waikaremoana Track

This three- to four-day tramp is one of the most popular walks in the North Island. The 46km track has spectacular views from the Panekiri Bluff, but all along the walk – through fern groves, beech and podocarp forest – there are vast panoramas and beautiful views of the lake. The walk is rated as easy and the only difficult section is the climb to Panekiri Bluff. Because of its popularity it is very busy from mid-December to the end of January and at Easter.

The walk can be done year-round, but the cold and rain in winter deter most people and make conditions much more challenging. Because of the altitude, temperatures can drop quickly, even in summer. Walkers should take portable stoves and fuel as there are no cooking facilities in the huts. It's not recommended that you park your car at either end of the track – there have been break-ins.

Five huts and five camp sites are spaced along the track. It's essential to book through DOC and if you are intending to do the walk over the Christmas/New Year period, it would be wise to book as far ahead as possible.

Walking the Track The track can be done either clockwise from Onepoto in the south or anticlockwise from Hopuruahine Bridge in the north. Starting from Onepoto, all the climbing is done in the first few hours. Water on this section of the track is limited so make sure you fill your water bottles before heading off. For those with a car, it is safest to leave it at Waikaremoana and then take a boat to the trail heads.

Estimated walking times are:

route	time
Onepoto to Panekiri Hut	5 hrs
Panekiri Hut to Waiopaoa Hut	3-4 hrs
Waiopaoa Hut to Marauiti Hut	4½ hrs
Marauiti Hut to Waiharuru Hut	2 hrs
Waiharuru Hut to Whanganui Hut	2½ hrs
Whanganui Hut to Hopuruahine Bridge	1½ hrs

Other Walks

Other major walks in the park include both the **Whakatane River Round Trip** and the **Manuoha-Waikareiti Track**.

The three- to five-day Whakatane River Round Trip starts at Ruatahuna on SH38, 45km from the Aniwaniwa Visitor Centre towards Rotorua. The five-hut track follows the Whakatane River then loops back via Waikare River, Motumuka Stream and Whakatane Valley. You can walk on north down the Whakatane River and out of the national park at Ruatoki (from where you'll probably have to hitch).

The Manuoha-Waikareiti Track is a three-day walk for experienced trampers. It begins near Hopuruahine and heads up to Manuoha Hut (1392m), the highest point in the park. It then follows a ridge down to pretty Lake Waikareiti via Sandy Bay Hut, before finishing up at Aniwaniwa.

Popular short/day walks include the **Lake Waikareiti Track** (two hours) and the **Ruapani Circuit** (six hours). The DOC booklet *Lake Waikaremoana Walks* ($2.50) lists many good short walks.

Boating

Waikaremoana Guided Tours (☎ 06-837 3729; *kayaks per hr/day $15/35, Canadian canoes $45 per day, dinghies without/with outboard motor $60/80*) is based at the Waikaremoana Motor Camp. The company has kayaks, canoes and dinghies for hire. Plans are afoot to run night trips to a kiwi enclosure near Waiharuru hut; call Waikaremoana for details.

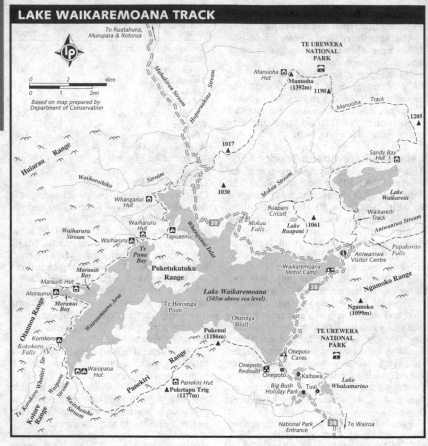

LAKE WAIKAREMOANA TRACK

Places to Stay

There are various camps and cabins along SH38, including a camp, cabins and motel 67km inland from the Wairoa turn-off.

There are more than 50 DOC huts along the walkways throughout the national park. The five Lake Waikaremoana Track *huts* are rated as Great Walks huts and cost $14 per night. There are five DOC *camping grounds*, that cost only $10 to camp. All ranger stations have information on camping.

Waikaremoana Motor Camp (☎ 06-837 3826, ✉ misty@lake.co.nz) Unpowered/ powered sites $7.50/9 per person, dorm bunks $16, cabins $40, chalets $60, tourist flats $60, motel units $85. This camping ground has a wonderful spot right on the shore of Lake Waikaremoana. The camp has a shop.

Big Bush Holiday Park (☎ 06-837 3777, ✉ bigbush@xtra.co.nz) Camp sites $8 per person, dorms $20, chalets $65. This place, between Lake Waikaremoana and Tuai, has its own small lake, cafe and Internet access.

Waikaremoana Homestay (☎ 06-837 3701, ✉ ykarestay@xtra.co.nz, 9 Rotten Row) Singles/doubles $50/80. This comfy homestay is at Tuai, about 5km from Lake Waikaremoana.

Lake Whakamarino Lodge (☎ *06-837 3876,* ⓔ *whakamar@ihug.co.nz)* Singles/doubles $57/69, self-contained units $100. This lodge is at Tuai, and overlooks peaceful Lake Whakamarino.

On the northern edge of the park there is a range of accommodation. There are *motels* at Ruatahuna, Taneatua and Murupara, which also has a *hotel*.

Getting There & Around
Approximately 105km of road between Wairoa and Rotorua remains unsealed; it's a winding and time-consuming drive. Traffic is light, making it slow for hitching. Big Bush Holiday Park (☎ 06-837 3777) runs a shuttle from Wairoa through to Rotorua on Monday, Wednesday and Friday ($30) and from Wairoa to the lake daily ($25).

The Waikaremoana Shuttle or Boat service (☎ 06-837 3729) operates on demand from the motor camp to either Onepoto or Hopuruahine Stream ($15). They also run boats to camping grounds on the western side of the lake ($70-80 return).

NAPIER
pop 55,000
Lying on sweeping Hawke Bay, Napier occupies a fine coastal position and, like most places in the Hawkes Bay area, enjoys its fair share of sunshine all year. But the city's biggest draw card is its architecture; Napier challenges Miami for the title of Art Deco Capital of the World. Much of downtown is blessed with the distinctive Art Deco design.

Napier also joins in on Hawkes Bay's love affair with wine; some of the region's top wineries are a short distance from the city limits.

History
Long before James Cook sighted the area in October 1769, the Maori found a plentiful source of food in the bay and the hinterland. The Otatara Pa, with its barricades now rebuilt, is one of the pre-European sites of habitation. It's on Gloucester St, past the Eastern Institute of Technology.

French explorer Jules Dumont d'Urville used Cook's charts to sail the *Astrolabe* into the bay in 1827. As whalers started using the safe Ahuriri anchorage in the 1830s, a trading base was established in 1839.

The town was planned in 1854, named after the British general and colonial administrator, Charles Napier, and it soon flourished as a commercial regional centre.

In 1931 Napier was dramatically changed when a disastrous earthquake, measuring 7.9 on the Richter scale, virtually destroyed it. In Napier and nearby Hastings over 250 people died, and Napier suddenly found itself 40 sq km larger when the earthquake heaved the seabed above sea level – in some places the land level rose by over 2m. The Napier airport was built on that previously submerged area. The rebuilding program that followed produced one of the world's best examples of an Art Deco city.

Orientation
At the northern end of town looms Bluff Hill, acting as a natural boundary between the centre and the Ahuriri and port areas. The prime commercial streets are Hastings and Emerson Sts. Emerson St has been developed into a pedestrian thoroughfare with paving and street furniture complement its many Art Deco features.

Information
Napier's helpful and well-informed visitors centre (☎ 06-834 1911, Ⓦ www.hawkesbaynz.com, www.napieronline.co.nz) is at 100 Marine Parade. It's open from 8.30am to 5pm daily (extended over summer). The AA office (☎ 06-834 2590) is at 87 Dickens St.

The DOC office (☎ 06-834 3111), at 59 Marine Parade in the Old Courthouse, has information on walkways around Napier, the Cape Kidnappers gannet colony, Te Urewera National Park, and the Kaweka and Ruahine Forest Parks, both 50km west of Napier.

Cybers Internet Cafe is at 98 Dickens St.

Art Deco Architecture
The earthquake and fire of 1931 resulted in the destruction of most of Napier's older brick buildings. Two frantic years of reconstruction from 1931 to 1933 meant that much of the city's buildings date from the

NAPIER

Hawke Bay

Port of Napier

To Portside Inn Backpackers (500m),
Rothman's Building (300m), Ahuriri (500m),
Sri Thai (500m), The Gintrap (600m), Salty
Rock Adventure Centre (600m), Shed 2 (600m),
Pierre sur le Quai (600m), Westshore (2.25km),
Taupo (143km) & Gisborne (215km)

Hardinge Rd

Battery Rd

Hornsey Rd

Breakwater Rd

Bluff Hill
Domain

Bluff Hill
Lookout

BLUFF HILL

Seapoint Rd

Thompson Rd

Lighthouse Rd

Elizabeth Rd

Cobden Rd

Lucy Rd

Priestley Tce

Thompson St

Centennial
Gardens

France Rd

Coote Rd

Childers Rd

Hukarere Rd

Clyde Rd

Marine Pde

Shakespeare Rd

Brewster Tce

Byron St

Madeira Rd

Browning St

Herschell St

Cathedral

Cameron Rd

Tiffen
Park

Milton Rd

Tennyson St

Emerson St

Dickens St

Dalton St

Clive
Sq

May St

Small
Tce

Guys Hill Rd

Chaucer Rd South

Faraday

Carlyle St

Station St

Munroe St

Thackeray St

Vautier St

Raffles St

Bower St

Hastings St

To Westshore (2.5km),
Marineland Motel (3km),
Westshore Holiday Camp (6km),
Riverland Outback Adventures (50km),
Taupo (143km) & Gisborne (215km)

Owen St

Julie St

Kennedy Rd

Nelson Cres

Wellesley Rd

NAPIER
SOUTH

Carnell St

McDonald St

Georges Dr

To Kennedy Park (1km), Onekawa
Complex (2km), Tropicana Motel (2km),
Deco City Motor Lodge (2km),
Snowgoose Lodge Motel (2.5km),
Taradale (6.5km)
& Otatara Pa (8km)

SH50

Edwards St

Sale St

Napier

To National Aquarium
of NZ (200m), Clive (10km)
& Havelock North (21km)

*Hawke
Bay*

0   100   200m
0   100   200yd

PLACES TO STAY
1 Masters Lodge
2 Garden Loft
3 Madeira B&B
4 Toad Hall
9 County Hotel; Anatoles
  & Churchill's
10 Archie's Bunker
18 Provincial Hotel
29 Criterion Art Deco
   Backpackers; Criterion
   Hotel
32 Masonic Establishment;
   Breaker's; Acqua
50 Waterfront Lodge
52 Napier YHA
53 Sea Breeze
55 Stables Lodge
   Backpackers
56 Fountain Court Motor Inn
58 Aqua Lodge
60 Mon Logis

PLACES TO EAT
5 Burger Wisconsin
11 Thorps Cafe
19 Sappho & Heath
20 Rendezvous
21 Trattoria Alla Toscana
   Italia
22 Cafe Aroma
23 Cappa Donna
26 Alfresco's
28 Turkish Delight
30 Ujazi
40 Golden Crown
42 Mossy's
48 Take Five
49 Jade Garden
51 Deano's Steak Bar & Grill
59 Restaurant Indonesia

PUBS & BARS
12 O'Flaherty's Irish Pub;
   Living Room & The
   Orange Room
13 Grumpy Mole Saloon
31 Rosie O'Grady's

OTHER
6 Pania of the Reef Statue
7 DOC
8 Hawkes Bay Museum &
  Cultural Trust
14 Daily Telegraph Building
15 Municipal Theatre
16 Deco Centre & Art Deco
   Tours
17 Napier Cycle & Kart
   Centre
24 Hotel Central
25 Ocean Boulevard Mall;
   Foodcourt
27 Espirit Buildings; Art
   Deco Restaurant
33 Soundshell & Colonnade
34 Napier Visitors Centre;
   Toilets & Showers
35 A&B Building;
   Governors Inn
36 ASB Bank
37 Opossum World
38 Sunken Gardens
39 Air New Zealand
41 Gaiety de Luxe Cinema
43 Cybers Internet Cafe
44 Automobile Association (AA)
45 Clive Square & Carillion
46 Countdown Supermarket
47 Public Library
54 Marineland
57 Napier Travel Centre –
   InterCity & Newmans

peak years of the Art Deco architectural style. Dr Neil Cossons, past president of the British Museums Association, said:

Napier represents the most complete and significant group of Art Deco buildings in the world, and is comparable with Bath as an example of a planned townscape in a cohesive style. Napier is without doubt unique.

The Napier Art Deco Trust promotes and protects the city's architectural heritage. Its excellent **guided Art Deco walks** (tickets $10) leave from the **Deco Centre** (☎ 06-835 0022, **W** www.artdeconapier.com, 163 Tennyson St; open 9am-5pm daily), at 2pm on Wednesday, Saturday and Sunday (daily in the summer months). The walk takes 1½ hours, and is preceded by a half-hour introductory talk (and illustrative slide presentation) ending with a video.

The shop in the Deco Centre sells books, postcards and souvenirs. A **one-hour walk** (tickets $8) starts at the visitors centre at 10am daily during summer and finishes at the Deco Centre (where a video is shown).

Walk leaflets ($2.50; in German also) are available from the visitors centre, Deco Centre or the museum.

There's also an Art Deco Scenic Drive map to the Art Deco and Spanish Mission-style architecture around Napier and Hastings ($2.50). The *Marewa Meander* ($1.50) leads you through a suburb transformed after the quake.

Guided tours in a 1934 Buick can be arranged through **Deco Affair Tours** (☎ 025 241 5279; tours $15-75). Tours last from 20 minutes to 2½ hours.

In the third week of February, Napier holds an Art Deco weekend, when there are dinners, balls and much fancy dress.

See the boxed text 'Decoed Out' for Art Deco examples in Napier.

Marine Parade

Lined with Norfolk pines and some fine old wooden buildings that survived the quake, Marine Parade has retained its air of an old-fashioned English seaside resort complete with pebble beach, but the strong riptide makes for hazardous swimming.

Marine Parade has parks, sunken and scented gardens, swimming pools, an aquarium and a marine park. The statue of **Pania of the Reef**, a sort of Maori equivalent of Copenhagen's Little Mermaid, is at the parade's northern end.

Marineland (☎ 06-834 4027; adult/child $9/4; open 10am-4.30pm daily) has performing seals and dolphins; displays take place at 10.30am and 2pm, with an extra 4pm show in summer. You can also swim with dolphins ($35 to $40, wetsuit hire $10), take a tour of Marineland, which includes touching and feeding dolphins ($15), or tour the penguin recovery workshop, where you'll help feed and care for penguins ($15). Bookings are essential.

Nearby on the parade, the new **National Aquarium of New Zealand** (☎ 06-834 1404; adult/child $7/3.50; open 9am-5pm daily, longer in summer) has sharks (which you can swim with if you're a qualified diver), saltwater crocodiles, piranha, turtles and other animals, including the unique tuatara.

If you want to find out more about the most hated creature in NZ, head to **Opossum World** (☎ 06-835 7697, 157 Marine Parade; admission to displays $3; open 9am-5pm daily). There's also a shop, which sells the possum's incredibly soft pelt.

Hawkes Bay Museum & Cultural Trust

Also on Marine Parade is a well-run art gallery and museum (☎ 06-835 7781, 65 Marine Parade; adult/child $5/free; open 10am-4.30pm daily Apr-Nov, 9am-6pm daily Dec-Mar). Quality artefacts of the East Coast's Ngati Kahungunu tribe are displayed, as well as European antiques and Art Deco items; there's also a dry but informative audiovisual of the 1931 earthquake.

There are exhibitions on Maori art and culture, colonial history, and dinosaurs. The latter display records the struggle of an amateur palaeontologist, Jan Wiffen, who proved university-trained sceptics wrong and found several prehistoric species when they said there were none to be found. There's also a fascinating section on earthquakes including an audiovisual in which

Decoed Out

Art Deco is the name given to a decorative style that hit the headlines in 1925 at the International Exposition of Modern Decorative and Industrial Arts held in Paris. Zigzags, lightning flashes, geometric shapes and rising suns all characterise this distinctive style. Ancient cultures, such as the Egyptian and Mayan, were also drawn upon for inspiration. Soft pastel colours are another Art Deco giveaway, employed by restorers, though many of Napier's buildings were originally monochrome plaster.

Emerson St has some excellent examples of Art Deco, though many of the shopfronts have been modernised and you'll have to look up to the second storeys to see the fine Art Deco detail. Good examples on Emerson St are the **Provincial Hotel**, **Charlie's Art Deco Restaurant**, the **Esprit buildings**, the **Criterion Hotel**, **Criterion Art Deco Backpackers** and the **ASB Bank**. On Dalton St, the **Hotel Central** is a superb example of the style. Round the corner on Dickens St, look for the extravagant Moorish and Spanish Mission-style building which used to be the **Gaiety de Luxe Cinema**. On the corner of Dickens and Dalton Sts is the former **State Cinema** (now a shopping complex).

Tennyson St has fine, preserved buildings. The restored **Municipal Theatre** is a must with its neon light fittings and wall decorations. The **Daily Telegraph building** is one of the finest examples of Art Deco in Napier and the **Deco Centre**, facing Clive Square is also impressive, despite some modifications. At the intersection of Tennyson and Hastings Sts are more fine buildings, particularly the block of **Hastings St** from Tennyson to Browning Sts. On Marine Parade the **Soundshell** is Art Deco, as is the paving of the plaza. From here you can admire the Art Deco **clock tower** (neon-lit at night) of the A&B building and also the **Masonic Hotel**, now the Masonic Establishment.

Napier quake survivors tell their stories. The sound effects as the quake and subsequent fires rip through the town are terrific. The museum shop has good-quality souvenirs.

Bluff Hill Lookout

There's an excellent view over all of Hawkes Bay from Bluff Hill, 102m above the Port of Napier. It's a sheer cliff-face down to the port, however, and rather a circuitous route to the top. It's open daily from sunrise to sunset.

Activities

The visitors centre has full lists of activities in the area.

Although the beach along Marine Parade is too dangerous for swimming, there's great swimming and surfing on the beach up past the port. The pool on Marine Parade is closed in winter. The **Onekawa Complex** (☎ 06-834 4150, Maadi Rd; adult/child $2.50/1.50, waterslide $4 for unlimited rides; open 6am-9pm) has waterslides and other attractions.

At the **Salty Rock Adventure Centre** (☎ 06-834 3500, 58 West Quay, Ahuriri; climb plus harness adult/child $13/9; open 11am-9pm Tues-Fri, 10am-6pm Sat & Sun) there is a climbing wall. It also organises caving and kayaking trips.

More activities can be found at **Riverland Outback Adventures** (☎ 06-834 9756, e riverlnds@xtra.co.nz, horse treks $20-45, rafting $35-80, accommodation $20-40 per person), 50km north of Napier on SH5, where there's horse trekking, white-water rafting and backpacker accommodation.

For tandem skydiving, contact either **Skydive Napier** (☎ 06-835 5563) or **The Beach Drop** (☎ 0800 835 5184). Jumps start at $249 for 9000 ft.

Hawkes Bay Jet Tours (☎ 06-874 9703) organises trips on the scenic Ngaruroro River, which range from 30 minutes to one day.

Hawkes Bay Kayaking Adventures (☎ 06-875 0341) does trips in the inner harbour and out to Cape Kidnappers.

Places to Stay

Camping & Cabins Napier has a number of camping grounds, but none are conveniently central.

Kennedy Park (☎ 0800 457 275, 06-843 9126, e info@kennedypark.co.nz, Storkey Rd)

Unpowered/powered sites from $10/11 per person, cabins from $34, tourist flats $56, motels $65. Closest to the centre, Kennedy Park is in Marewa, 2.5km from town.

Westshore Holiday Camp (☎ 06-835 9456, e ann.david@xtra.co.nz, 1 Main Rd) Unpowered/powered sites $8/9 per person, cabins $25-30, tourist flats $45. This camp is near Westshore Beach, 6km north of town.

Hostels There is a good selection of hostels in and around town.

Criterion Art Deco Backpackers (☎ 06-835 2059, fax 835 2370, e cribacpac@ yahoo.com, 48 Emerson St) Dorms $18-19, singles $12-24, twins & doubles $42. This place is right in the centre of town, upstairs in what was formerly the Criterion Hotel, a classy Art Deco building. It has a large recreation area and well-kept rooms. You can hire bikes for $10 a day.

Stables Lodge Backpackers (☎ 06-835 6242, e stables@ihug.co.nz, 321 Marine Parade) Dorms $14-16, doubles & twins $42. Stables Lodge is a lovely old house with a friendly atmosphere and quiet inner courtyard, complete with hammocks.

Archie's Bunker (☎ 06-833 7990, e archiesbunker@xtra.co.nz, 14 Herschell St) Dorms $18-20, singles $24, doubles $48-50. This modern hostel is quite large with spacious rooms, good communal areas and Internet access. Linen is supplied.

Napier YHA (☎ 06-835 7039, e yha napr@yha.org.nz, 277 Marine Parade) Dorms $18, twins & doubles $42. This large former guesthouse is opposite the beach. There's a courtyard (with barbecue) out the back.

Waterfront Lodge (☎/fax 06-835 3429, e waterfrontlodge@xtra.co.nz, 217 Marine Parade) Dorm beds $17, singles/doubles $35/55. This is another old house opposite the beach. Breakfast is available for $5.

Aqua Lodge (☎ 06-835 4523, e aqua back@inhb.co.nz, 53 Nelson Crescent) Dorms $17, singles $26, doubles $42. Aqua Lodge is a converted suburban house, not far from the bus station.

Toad Hall (☎ 06-835 5555, e toad@ xtra.co.nz, cnr Shakespeare Rd & Browning St) Dorms $15, singles $20, doubles with bath $55. Toad Hall is a former hotel. There's a bar downstairs and a great rooftop garden.

Portside Inn Backpackers Lodge (☎ 06-833 7292, e portside.inn@clear.net.nz, 52 Bridge St) Dorms $14-19, twins & doubles $38. On the other side of Bluff Hill at Ahuriri is this newly built hostel. There's a huge lounge/bar, as well as Internet access, parking and a small garden. It's handy to the bars and restaurants at Ahuriri.

B&Bs & Guesthouses Since it is a summer resort of the old-fashioned variety, Napier has some good guesthouses along Marine Parade. However, as it's a major thoroughfare, it can be quite noisy.

Sea Breeze (☎ 06-835 8067, e seabreeze .napier@xtra.co.nz, 281 Marine Parade) Singles/doubles with breakfast $65/80. This is a friendly, homely place with three attractive rooms individually decorated in Eastern/Asian styles and a comfortable upstairs sun room with sea views.

Mon Logis (☎ 06-835 2125, e monlo gis@xtra.co.nz, 415 Marine Parade) Singles with bath $120, doubles with bath $160. The charming French-style Mon Logis was built in 1915 as a private hotel. It has delightful rooms with en suites or a room with an adjacent bathroom. Breakfast is included.

Madeira B&B (☎ 06-835 5185, e julie ball@clear.net.nz, 6 Madeira Rd) Singles/ doubles $50/75. This fine wooden villa, at the end of a very steep street, is a lovely, spacious house with great bay views.

Garden Loft (☎ 06-835 1527, 29 Cameron Rd) Singles/doubles $50/75. Garden Loft is another fine old villa, with a pleasant guest bedroom and en suite upstairs in a building behind the main house. The price includes breakfast with the family.

Another good hunting ground for **B&Bs** is on Bluff Hill, just a short walk down to the city (but a hard walk back); see the *Napier Hill Homestays* pamphlet.

Masters Lodge (☎ 06-834 1946, e un wind@masterslodge.co.nz, 10 Elizabeth Rd) B&B $540. This sumptuous place is the former home of Gerhard Husheer, the founder of the National Tobacco Company.

Swiss-style meals are served ($120) and German and French are spoken.

Motels & Hotels Napier has plenty of motels, particularly around Westshore, on the Taupo Road.

Marineland Motel (☎ 06-835 2147, fax 835 7710, 20 Meeanee Quay) Units $70-95. Marineland is out near Westshore Beach, 3km from the city centre. There's a heated indoor pool and a licensed restaurant.

Tropicana Motel (☎ 0800 602 000, 06-843 9153, 335 Kennedy Rd) Units from $66. This friendly place has a spa, sauna, and swimming pool.

Snowgoose Lodge Motel (☎ 0800 667 776, 06-843 6083, e snolodge@ihug.co.nz, 376 Kennedy Rd) Units from $80. This lodge has one- and two-bedroom units and executive suites with spas. It's handy for exploring Napier's surrounding area.

Fountain Court Motor Inn (☎ 0508 411 000, 06-835 7387, e accommodation@ fountaincourt.co.nz, 209 Hastings St) Units from $94. Fountain Court is a quality motel with off-street parking, a swimming pool and spa baths.

Deco City Motor Lodge (☎ 0800 536 6339, 06-843 4342, e decocity@xtra.co .nz, 308 Kennedy St) Units from $105. The modern units here sparkle and shine, and some have private spas.

Masonic Establishment (☎ 06-835 8689, e masonic@inhb.co.nz, cnr Marine Parade & Tennyson St) Singles/doubles from $65/ 75. The fine old Masonic Establishment is very central. All rooms have en suites.

County Hotel (☎ 0800 843 468, 06-835 7800, e countyhotel@xtra.co.nz, 12 Browning St) Rooms from $195. For something special, the County is a boutique hotel in a refurbished and converted building. The rooms are individually decorated.

Places to Eat

Emerson St is a good place to hunt for places to eat.

Cappa Donna (Emerson St) Light meals $6-10. This pleasant breakfast and lunchtime cafe does pizza, pasta and rice dishes, and a variety of coffee from which to choose.

Alfresco's (☎ 06-835 1181, 65 Emerson St) Mains $19-21. Alfresco's, located upstairs, has a good range of food and great liqueur coffees.

On lower Emerson St, *Sappho & Heath* is the place for good coffee and panini. Nearby *Rendezvous* has tasty sweet and savoury crepes ($4.50-6) and sundaes ($3.50-6).

Cafe Aroma (Dalton St) Bagels from $2.50. If you're into espresso coffee, bagels and Vespas, this is definitely your place.

Ujazi (Tennyson St) Meals from $13. Ujazi has great coffee and a fresh, innovative menu with lots of choice for vegetarians.

Turkish Delight (☎ 06-835 0474, Market St) Mains $17-24. Open Tues-Sun. Turkish Delight has kebabs and other Turkish fare, including hearty meat/vegie platters for two for $36/32.

Mossy's (☎ 06-835 6696, Dickens St) Mains $12-20. Mossy's has a good range of food, coffees and beers, and has the occasional live band.

Trattoria Alla Toscana Italia (☎ 06-835 6848, 112 Tennyson St) Mains $20-32. Open Tues-Sun. This trattoria has authentic Italian cuisine and a carefully chosen wine list.

Restaurant Indonesia (☎ 06-835 8303, 409 Marine Parade) Mains $18-25. If you are hankering for satay or rendang head to this restaurant.

Jade Garden (☎ 06-835 6061, 201 Marine Parade) Mains around $11.50. Jade Garden offers very reasonably priced Chinese fare (eat in or takeaway).

Take Five (☎ 06-835 4050, 189 Marine Parade) Mains $15-25. Take Five has excellent food (lamb, steaks and seafood) with the added bonus of live jazz on Tuesday and Friday.

Deano's Steak Bar & Grill (☎ 06-835 4944, 255 Marine Parade) Mains from $14. Deano's has a good range of steaks for reasonable prices and special deals on Monday and Wednesday nights.

Acqua (☎ 06-835 8689, Marine Parade) Mains $18-24. This colourful brassiere is situated in the Masonic Establishment.

Anatoles (☎ 06-835 7800, Browning St) Mains $18-23. This highly rated place at the County Hotel is a stylish cafe bar.

JOHN HAY

Nelson, rebuilt after an…

FOKKE MULDER

…earthquake in 1931, is the…

DAVID WALL

Forrester Gallery and National Bank, Oamaru, Otago

FOKKE MULDER

DAVID WALL

…world's most Art Deco city…

Skytower in Auckland

DAVID WALL

Glacier, Southern Alps

DAVID WALL

Mud pools at Whakarewarewa, Rotorua

DAVID WALL

Taranaki countryside

FERGUS BLAKISTON

Potato rows, Orari, Canterbury

SALLY DILLON

Alpine moss

The Ahuriri wharf precinct has a number of trendy eateries.

Shed 2 (☎ 06-835 0029, West Quay) Mains $24-28. This open restaurant/bar overlooks the marina, and concentrates on seafood and meat dishes, but also has pizzas.

Pierre sur le Quai (☎ 06-834 0189, 63 West Quay) Mains $25-30. This place has a touch of class about it and specialises in Mediterranean/French style food.

Sri Thai (☎ 06-835 2299, 60 Bridge St) Mains $17-23. Sri Thai is in the heart of Ahuriri. It does cheap specials Wednesday to Sunday for $13.

There are plenty of Chinese places in Napier. Try the *Golden Crown (Dickens St)*; the Wednesday to Friday lunchtime smorgasbord is good value ($7.50).

Burgers Wisconsin (10 Shakespeare Rd) Burgers $5-9. This place has a good selection of gourmet burgers.

Entertainment

Governors Inn (Cnr Emerson St & Marine Parade) Governors Inn is a sedate drinking pub with pool tables in its back bar.

Rosie O'Grady's (☎ 06-835 8689, Hastings St) Rosie's is part of the Masonic Establishment. It has Guinness on tap and occasional live music.

Mossy's (see Places to Eat) has live music on Friday and Saturday nights.

O'Flaherty's Irish Pub (☎ 06-834 1235, Hastings St) O'Flaherty's is a slightly alternative Irish pub that packs them in with bands Thursday to Saturday night. The chalk drawings adorning the walls are quite the art piece.

Living Room and *Orange Room (Hastings St)* Next to O'Flaherty's, these clubs only open on weekends and play chilled out tunes and techno respectively.

Grumpy Mole Saloon (cnr Hastings & Tennyson Sts) This bar is a popular pick-up joint with a wild-west theme.

The Gintrap (West Quay) This large, open bar has excellent views of the marina. It's good for bar snacks and larger meals.

In the County Hotel there is a cigar bar, *Churchill's*, where you can imitate the great man by sticking a big fat cigar in your face.

Getting There & Away
Air Air New Zealand (☎ 06-833 5400), on the corner of Hastings and Station Sts, offers daily direct flights to Auckland, Christchurch and Wellington, with onward connections. Origin Pacific (☎ 0800 302 302) flies from Napier to Auckland, with connections.

Bus InterCity and Newmans both operate from the Napier Travel Centre (☎ 06-834 2720) on Munro St. InterCity has services to Auckland ($78, 7hrs), Hamilton ($58, 5hrs), Rotorua ($57, 3hrs), Taupo ($38, 2hrs), Tauranga ($78, 5hrs), Gisborne ($35, 4hrs), Palmerston North ($39, 2¾hrs) and Wellington ($62, 4¼hrs). The travel centre is open from 8.30am to 5pm weekdays, from 8am to 11.30am and 12.30pm to 1.30pm on weekends.

Newmans routes head north to Taupo, Rotorua and Tauranga, through Palmerston North and Wanganui to New Plymouth, and to Wellington via Palmerston North.

Hitching If you're heading north catch a bus and get off at Westshore, or try thumbing closer in. If you're heading south stick to SH2. The alternative inland route (SH50) is much harder going, with less traffic.

Getting Around
The airport shuttle bus (☎ 06-844 7333) charges $9 from the airport to Napier city centre, and Napier Taxi Service (☎ 06-835 7777) charges about $12.

Nimbus (☎ 06-877 8133) operates the suburban bus services on weekdays only, with regular buses between Napier and Hastings via Taradale, plus other local services. All local buses depart from the corner of Dickens and Dalton Sts.

Napier Cycle & Kart Centre (☎ 06-835 9528), at the corner of Clive Square and Emerson St, hires out 21-speed mountain bikes at $25/14 for a full-/half-day. Marineland also hires bikes.

HASTINGS
pop 50,200
Hastings, only 20km south of Napier, shared the same fate as Napier in the 1931

earthquake and is also noted for its Art Deco and Spanish Mission-style architecture. The paved Civic Square is particularly attractive, with an Art Deco clock tower as its centrepiece (but watch out for those trains that hurtle through the square!).

Hastings is an agricultural centre. During the apple harvest season, from February to April, it is popular with fruit-pickers (and accommodation is tight at this time). There are many wineries nearby.

The Blossom Festival, a celebration of spring, is held in September/October, with parades, arts and crafts, and visiting artists.

Information
The Hastings visitor centre (☎ 06-873 5526, W www.hawkesbaynz.com), in the Westerman's Building on the corner of Russell and Heretaunga Sts, is open from 8.30am to 5pm on weekdays and 10am until 3pm on weekends. The AA office (☎ 06-878 4101) is at 337 Heretaunga St.

Internet access is available at Internet World on Queen St East.

Things to See & Do
The legacy of the 1931 earthquake is an impressive collection of **Art Deco and Spanish Mission-style buildings**. The *Heritage of Hastings* pamphlet is available from the visitors centre to explore Hastings' architecture in depth.

The highlights are undoubtedly the **Westerman's Building**, with its impressive bronze and leadlight shopfronts that have largely survived modernisation. Then there's the magnificent **Municipal Theatre** *(Hastings St)*, the most imposing example of Spanish-Mission style in the region.

Travelling with children? Head straight for **Splash Planet Waterpark** *(☎ 06-876 9856, Grove Rd; adult/child summer $22/7.50, winter $11/5.50; open 10am-6pm daily summer, 10am-5pm Sat & Sun winter)* in Windsor Park, 2km southeast of the town centre. Splash Planet's facilities include waterslides, hot pools (both closed in winter), a miniature castle, go-karts, minigolf, boats you can take out on the lake, and a paddle steamer.

The **Hawkes Bay Exhibition Centre** *(☎ 06-876 2077, Eastbourne St; open 10am-4.30pm Mon-Fri, 10am-4pm Sat & Sun)* in the Civic Square, hosts a wide variety of changing exhibitions.

Places to Stay
The visitors centre operates a toll-free number (☎ 0800 827 837) for reservations.
Camping & Cabins There are only a few camping options around Hastings.

Hastings Top 10 Holiday Park (☎ 06-878 6692, e holidaypark@hastingstourism.co.nz, Windsor Ave) Unpowered/ powered sites $10/11 per person, cabins $30-48, tourist flats $65, motel units $80. This camping ground has lots of shady areas in Windsor Park, adjacent to Splash Planet.

Raceview Motel & Holiday Park (☎ 06-878 8837, 307 Gascoigne St) Unpowered /powered sites $9/10 per person, cabins $30, on-site caravans $35, tourist flats $60. Next to the racecourse, Raceview fills up quickly during harvest (weekly rates are available).

Hostels Backpackers are very busy in the harvest. All have work contacts during the season.

Rotten Apple (☎ 06-878 4363, e info@hbtv.co.nz, 114 Heretaunga St) Dorms $18, singles $27, twins & doubles $38. This hostel is the pick of the crop, so to speak. It has spacious communal areas, well-kept rooms Internet access and a friendly atmosphere. On Sunday there is a free barbecue at Friend's Bar (See Places to Eat later) for guests.

Hastings Backpackers Hostel (☎ 06-876 5888, 505 Lyndon Rd East) Dorm beds $15, $80 per week, doubles & twins $32. This hostel is in a suburban area, not far from the city centre. The staff organise cheap trips to the region's attractions, including rubber tubing on the Tuki Tuki River ($5).

Travellers Lodge (☎ 06-878 7108, e travellers.lodge@clear.net.nz, 606 St Aubyn St West) Dorm beds $16, $90 per week, twins/doubles $365. This friendly suburban house is well set up for fruit pickers and also has a sauna.

Sleeping Giant Backpackers (☎ 06-878 5393, 109 Davis St) Dorms $15/85 per

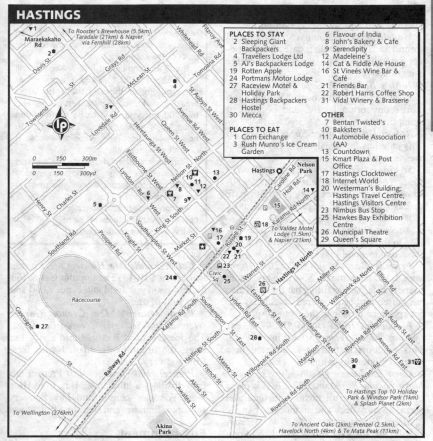

HASTINGS

PLACES TO STAY
2 Sleeping Giant Backpackers
4 Travellers Lodge Ltd
5 AJ's Backpackers Lodge
19 Rotten Apple
24 Portmans Motor Lodge
27 Raceview Motel & Holiday Park
28 Hastings Backpackers Hostel
30 Mecca

PLACES TO EAT
1 Corn Exchange
3 Rush Munro's Ice Cream Garden
6 Flavour of India
8 John's Bakery & Cafe
9 Serendipity
12 Madeleine's
14 Cat & Fiddle Ale House
16 St Vineés Wine Bar & Café
21 Friends Bar
22 Robert Harris Coffee Shop
31 Vidal Winery & Brasserie

OTHER
7 Bentan Twisted's
10 Bakksters
11 Automobile Association (AA)
13 Countdown
15 Kmart Plaza & Post Office
17 Hastings Clocktower
18 Internet World
20 Westerman's Building; Hastings Travel Centre; Hastings Visitors Centre
23 Nimbus Bus Stop
25 Hawkes Bay Exhibition Centre
26 Municipal Theatre
29 Queen's Square

night/week, doubles $38. Sleeping Giant is popular with fruit-pickers. There are dorm beds and doubles in this roomy villa.

AJ's Backpackers Lodge (☎ 06-878 2302, 405 Southland Rd) Dorms $17, twins $38. AJ's is a tidy, well-run place.

Motels & Hotels Within walking distance of the city and Splash Planet is *Mecca* (☎ 06-878 3192, 806 Heretaunga St). Units are $75 to $87. It also has a spa pool and plenty of parking.

Portmans Motor Lodge (☎ 0800 767 862, 06-878 8332, e reservations@port mans.co.nz, 401 Railway Rd) Units from $100. Portmans is a modern motel with a heated pool, and two units designed for people with disabilities.

Valdez Motor Lodge (☎ 06-876 5453, e valdezmotorlodge@xtra.co.nz, 1107 Karamu Rd North) Units from $110. Valdez is 1½km from the city centre. There's a pool and every unit has a spa bath.

Places to Eat

Serendipity (Heretaunga St) Light meals around $5. Hastings is known for its hybrid cafes, which sell furniture, nick-nacks and delicious food. Serendipity is one of them. There is also a great selection of coffee.

Madeleine's (Heretaunga St) Light meals around $5. This is another cafe/store, opposite Serendipity. Again, the food and coffee is a cut above.

John's Bakery & Cafe (cnr Nelson & Heretaunga Sts) Light meals $5. John's is a more conventional cafe, and popular at lunch time.

Robert Harris Coffee Shop (Russell St) This cafe has the usual cafeteria-style pastries and cakes.

St Vineés Wine Bar & Cafe (☎ 06-878 8596, 108 Market St South) Mains $9.50-15. Stylish St Vineés provides both cafe snacks (quiches and vege pies) and more substantial meals.

Ancient Oaks (Havelock Rd) Mains $7-12. On the way to Havelock North, Ancient Oaks makes good salads.

Friends Bar (☎ 06-878 6201, Heretaunga St) Bar meals $3-12. This open, friendly cafe/bar has filling bar meals. It also has a free barbecue at 7pm on Sunday for backpackers staying at the Rotten Apple.

Flavour of India (☎ 06-870 9992, cnr Lyndon Rd & Nelson St) Mains $16-25. This tandoori restaurant is situated in a lovely colonial-style house.

Corn Exchange (☎ 06-870 8333, 118 Maraekakaho Rd) Mains $22-27. This place is open daily for all meals with gourmet pizza, a sunny deck and an intimate bar.

Sileni Estate (☎ 06-879 8768, Maraekakaho Rd; tastings 10am-5pm daily) For a really special experience take a trip out to stunning Sileni Estate, 10 minutes' drive from the centre of Hastings. With its long driveway and striking, rather space-age building, it's hard to miss. The two restaurants, *RD1 (open from 6pm Wed-Sat)* and *Mesa (open from 11.30am Wed-Sun & daily in summer)* are rather expensive but do have cheap lunches ($15). In addition to the fine food you can sample the fine wines (tastings at $2 per glass unless you buy).

Vidal Winery Brassiere (☎ 06-876 8105, 913 St Aubyn St) Mains $20-30. Open lunch & dinner daily. This upmarket brassiere is attached to the Vidal Winery.

There's Work if you Want it

Many overseas travellers come to this region to work so they can extend their trip to other parts of the country.

If you're a competent fruit-picker you will make about $400 to $450 a week either apple-picking or thinning (both are back-breaking work). Top-flight pickers can earn up to $800 but you have to be pretty damn good. Night-packing can earn up to $8.50 an hour. Avoid short-term grape-picking, as it doesn't pay that well.

Farmers are often desperate for workers from November to May. The hostels generally find orchard contracting work if you are staying with them.

For online information check out ⓦ www.hbfruitgrowers.co.nz and ⓦ www.seasonalwork.co.nz.

Cat & Fiddle Ale House (502 Karamu Rd) Mains $10-15. The popular Cat & Fiddle has good pub food and is not a bad spot for a pint of ale.

Rush Munro's Ice Cream Garden (Heretaunga St West) Cones from $1.80. The ice cream at Rush Munro's is a real treat; it's home-made, loaded with fresh fruit and very rich.

Prenzel (108 Havelock Rd) Prenzel is a fruit distillery a little under 1km from Hastings. You can sample and buy liqueurs, schnapps, brandies and sparkling fruit wines.

Entertainment

Bentan Twisted's (211 Eastbourne St) This bar is popular with a mixed crowd.

Bakksters (Nelson St North) Bakksters is a relaxed spot that also serves food.

Roosters Brewhouse (☎ 06-879 4127, 1470 Omahu Rd) This brewhouse, about 10 minutes' drive north-east of Hastings, has its own superbly brewed beer on tap. There's a sunny garden and they do large lunches.

Getting There & Away

Nimbus (☎ 06-877 8133) operates a frequent local bus service from Hastings to Napier and from Hastings to Havelock North; both run on weekdays.

All InterCity and Newmans buses going to Napier continue to Hastings, stopping at the visitors centre.

HAVELOCK NORTH
pop 8510

Havelock North, 5km east of Hastings, is a great holiday destination well worth a visit for its gardens, wineries, village atmosphere and the towering backdrop of Te Mata Peak.

Play spot the queen bee at the **Arataki Honey Shop** *(☎ 06-877 7300, 66 Arataki Rd; free; open 8.30am-5pm Mon-Sat, 9am-4pm Sun)*, 3km east of Havelock North. There's a working beehive, bee products and tours are of the factory (free; 1.30pm Mon-Fri).

If you have kids in tow, there's the **miniature railway** in beautiful Keirunga Gardens; it operates on the first and third Sunday of the month ($1 per ride).

Te Mata Peak

Te Mata Peak is about 11km from Hastings. Dramatically sheer cliffs rise to the Te Mata trig (399m), commanding a spectacular view over the Heretaunga Plains to Hawke Bay. On a clear day you can see all of Hawke Bay across to the Mahia Peninsula and to Mt Ruapehu in Tongariro National Park. You can also see oyster shells in the rocks at your feet!

Te Mata Peak is part of the 98-hectare Te Mata Park, with several walkways. You can drive right up to the trig at the summit.

The peak is naturally a favourite spot for **hang-gliding**. Gliders get remarkable possibilities from the updraughts breezing in from the Pacific Ocean, about 5km away.

Peak Paragliding *(☎ 06-843 4717, 025 512 886)* 15-min trips $120, 4-hr trips $200. Peak Paragliding offers tandem paragliding, weather permitting. There are trips lasting around 15 minutes as well as cross-country flights.

Places to Stay & Eat

There are some superb places to stay, all reasonable considering the high standards and backdrop of vineyards.

Peak Backpackers *(☎ 06-877 1170, fax 877 1175, 33 Havelock North Rd)* Dorms $17/90 per night/week, double $38/118 per night/week. This spacious suburban house caters well for fruit pickers. There's good communal areas, including a large garden.

Telegraph Hill Villa *(☎ 06-877 5140, 334 Te Mata Rd)* Doubles $170. Telegraph Hill is a peaceful hilltop retreat with great views. The villa has two bedrooms each with direct access to the en suite bathroom. There's also a sunny north-facing veranda. Breakfast provisions are supplied (there's a fully equipped kitchen) and barbecue is also available to guests, as are the tennis court and swimming pool.

Providencia *(☎ 06-877 2300, e nfdr .baker@xtra.co.nz, 225 Middle Rd)* Doubles from $195. Providencia is a gracious old building in a picturesque rural setting 2.5km west of the town.

The **Black Barn** and the unbeatable historic **Rush Cottage** *(for both: ☎ 06-877 7985, e lombardi@xtra.co.nz, Black Barn Rd; $290 & $390 respectively)* are situated in the heart of the Lombardi vineyard and have magnificent views over the vineyards, Napier Hill and the bay.

The **Village Court** *(Portere Dr)*, in the centre of town, has a few good eateries, including **Diva** and **Cafe 32**, both of which cater for breakfast and lunchtime crowds.

The **Rose & Shamrock** is a great Irish pub in the centre of the village and the nearby **Turk's Bar** is popular for a drink.

Peak House *(☎ 06-877 8663, Te Mata Rd)* Mains $18-25. Peak House is popular for both the spectacular view and fine food.

AROUND HAWKES BAY
Wineries, Food & Arts and Crafts

The Hawkes Bay area is one of NZ's premier wine-producing regions, with many vineyards. It's very much the chardonnay capital of NZ, but cabernet sauvignon grapes from the area are also highly regarded and many varieties are produced.

The Hawkes Bay Vintners produces the handy *A Guide to the Wineries*, which lists an ever-increasing number of wineries open to visitors. Some of the big vineyards in the area include **Sileni Estate** *(☎ 06-879 8768)*,

Crab Farm Winery (☎ 06-836 6678), Brook-fields (☎ 06-834 4615) at Meeanee, Mission Estate Winery (☎ 06-844 2259) at Taradale (the oldest in the country), Esk Val-ley Estate Winery (☎ 06-836 6411), Vidal Estate (☎ 06-876 8105), Ngatarawa Wines (☎ 06-879 7603) and Church Road Winery (☎ 06-844 2053) in Taradale. Church Road offers a very informative tour of its facili-ties, including a small wine museum, for $5.

Havelock North has a concentration of wineries, especially out on Te Mata Rd. Te Mata Estate Winery (☎ 06-877 4399), Bradshaw Estate Winery (☎ 06-877 5795),

Akarangi Wines (☎ 06-877 8228) and Lom-bardi Wines (☎ 06-877 7985) are all worth a visit. A number of wineries are open for lunch and offer excellent dining.

One of the better wine stores in the Hawkes Bay is Havelock Wines and Spirits (☎ 06-877 8208, Donnelly St, Havelock North), which stocks an extensive range of wine – the staff are very knowledgeable.

Every year around the beginning of Feb-ruary, the Harvest Hawkes Bay puts on a big show to celebrate wine and food. The annual event lasts about six days and in-volves upwards of 30 wineries. For more

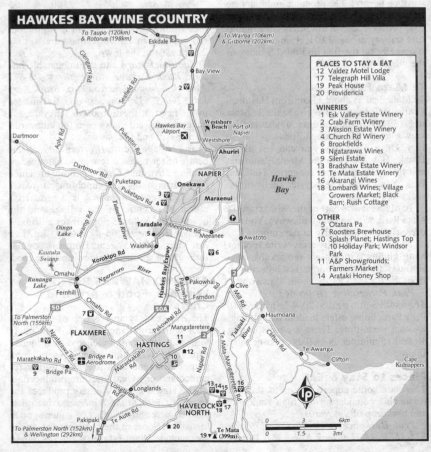

HAWKES BAY WINE COUNTRY

PLACES TO STAY & EAT
12 Valdez Motel Lodge
17 Telegraph Hill Villa
19 Peak House
20 Providencia

WINERIES
1   Esk Valley Estate Winery
2   Crab Farm Winery
3   Mission Estate Winery
4   Church Rd Winery
6   Brookfields
8   Ngatarawa Wines
9   Sileni Estate
13 Bradshaw Estate Winery
15 Te Mata Estate Winery
16 Akarangi Wines
18 Lombardi Wines; Village
    Growers Market; Black
    Barn; Rush Cottage

OTHER
5   Otatara Pa
7   Roosters Brewhouse
10 Splash Planet; Hastings Top
    10 Holiday Park; Windsor
    Park
11 A&P Showgrounds;
    Farmers Market
14 Arataki Honey Shop

information online head to W www.harvest hawkesbay.co.nz.

A fine way of visiting the wineries is by bicycle (you can hire one in Napier), since most of the wineries are within easy cycling distance and it's all flat land. On Yer Bike (☎ 06-879 8735, e info@onyerbike.net.nz) arranges tours on tandems, mountain bikes and even rickshaws.

Motorised tour operators include Bay Tours (☎ 06-843 6953, W www.baytours .co.nz), Vince's Vineyard Tours (☎ 06-836 6705), Vicky's Wine Tours (☎ 06-843 9991), Hawkes Bay in a Glass (☎ 06-843 2478, W www.qualityhb.co.nz), Toast the Bay Wine Tours (☎ 06-844 2375) and Hawkes Bay Tours (☎ 0800 868 742). Tours generally last around four hours and start at $40 per person, which includes a visit to four or five wineries. An all day tour costs around $85. All tour operators will pick up in Napier, Hastings or Havelock North.

Food is also becoming an integral part of many tours to vineyards, and food markets are an extremely popular pastime for locals and tourists alike. Two markets of particular note are the HB Food Group Farmers Market (☎ 06-877 1001, Hawkes Bay Showgrounds, Kenilworth Rd, Hastings), from 8.30am to 12.30pm every Sunday all year round, and the Village Growers Market (☎ 06-877 7985, The Sun Dial, Black Barn Rd, Lombardi Estate, Havelock North), which specialises in organic produce and opens 9am to noon November to March. Pick up a copy of Hawkes Bay Food Trail which lists produce growers in the area, and has a handy map.

Some local craftspeople open their studios to the public. Get the informative Hawkes Bay Arts Trail from the visitor centres.

Cape Kidnappers Gannet Colony

From late October to late April the Cape Kidnappers gannet colony comes to life. Elsewhere these large birds usually make their nests on remote and inaccessible islands but here (and also at Muriwai near Auckland) they nest on the mainland; they are unphased by human spectators.

The gannets usually turn up in late July after the last heavy storm of the month. Apparently, the storm casts driftwood and other handy nest-building material high up the beach, so very little effort is needed to collect it. In October and November eggs are laid and take about six weeks to hatch. By March the gannets start to migrate and by April only the odd straggler will be left.

You don't need a permit to visit the gannet sanctuary. The best time to see the birds is between early November and late February (the sanctuary is closed from June to October).

Several tour operators take trips through Cape Kidnappers (so named because the local Maori tried to kidnap a Tahitian servant boy from Cook's expedition here).

Gannet Beach Adventures (☎ 0800 426 6388, 06-875 0898, W www.gannets.com; rides adult/child $25/17) has rides on a tractor-pulled trailer along the beach, departing from the Clifton Beach carpark. From where they drop you, it's a 20-minute walk to the main saddle colony. The guided return trip takes about four hours.

Gannet Safaris (☎ 0800 427 232, 06-875 0888, W www.gannetsafaris.com; trips adult/child $40/20) has a 4WD overland trip that takes you right to the gannet colonies across farmland. It departs from Sumerlee Station in Te Awanga.

Cape Kidnappers Walks (☎ 06-875 0837, e p.julian@xtra.co.nz; accommodation, walk and transport $150) offers guided walks over Summerlee Station, a 2000-hectare sheep-and-cattle run about 2km from Te Awanga. Accommodation is in renovated shearers quarters.

Alternatively, the 10km walk along the beach from Clifton, just along from Te Awanga, takes about two hours. You must leave no earlier than three hours after high tide and start back no later than 1½ hours after low tide. It's 20km return (at least five hours) and there are no refreshment stops, so go prepared! All trips are dependent on the tides. The tide schedule is available from the Napier visitors centre. No regular buses go to Te Awanga or Clifton from Napier, but Kiwi Shuttle (☎ 027-459 3669) goes on demand for $20 per person. There is a rest hut selling refreshments at the colony.

The Longest Place Name in the World

Hold your breath and then spit this name out as fast as you can:
Taumatawhakatangihangakoauauotamateaturipukakapikimaungahoronukupokaiwhenuaktanatahu.
The name is a shortened form of 'The brow of a hill where Tamatea, the man with the big knees,
who slid, climbed, and swallowed mountains, known as Land Eater, played his flute to his lover'.

Tamatea Pokaiwhenua (Land Eater) was a chief so famous for his long travels across
the North Island that it was said he ate *(pokai)* up the land *(whenua)* as he walked. There
are many other place names in the region also attributed to this ancient explorer.

The reserve is administered by DOC, which produces a handy leaflet and booklets on the colony ($1).

Clifton Reserve Motor Camp (*☎/fax 06-875 0263, Clifton Beach*) Unpowered/powered sites $13/15 per double, cabins $30. Clifton Reserve is conveniently situated right next to the beach and close to the carpark.

Beaches
Two popular surf beaches south of Cape Kidnappers are **Ocean Beach** and **Waimarama Beach**. To get to them, take Te Mata Rd out of Havelock North and continue east past Te Mata Peak.

Inland Ranges
The main populated area of Hawkes Bay is concentrated around Napier-Hastings. Regional Hawkes Bay, however, does extend much further than that, both to the south and inland.

The inland region provides some of the best tramping on the North Island – in the remote, untamed Kaweka and Ruahine Ranges. There is an excellent series of DOC pamphlets on the ranges. See *Central Hawkes Bay, Southern Hawkes Bay, Maraetotara Plateau* and *Puketitiri Reserves* for details.

An ancient Maori track, now a road, runs inland from the bay, heading from Fernhill near Hastings via Omahu, Okawa, Otamauri, Blowhard Bush and the Gentle Annie Rd to Taihape. It is a three-hour return car journey from Fernhill to the top of the Kaweka Ranges.

Central Hawkes Bay
The two main towns of central Hawkes Bay are Waipukurau (almost always called simply 'Wai-puk') and Waipawa. The Waipukurau visitors centre (☎ 06-858 6488, e ch binfo@xtra.co.nz) is in Railway Esplanade and opens 9am to 5pm Monday to Friday and 10am to 2pm Saturday.

The prestigious Te Aute College, about 20km north of Waipukurau, was school to many influential Young Maori Party leaders (see History in the Facts about New Zealand chapter), such as James Carroll, Apirana Ngata, Maui Pomare and Peter Buck.

Many visit this region to see the **longest place name in the world** (yes, longer than Llanfairpwllgwyngllgogerychwyrndrobwllllantysiliogogogoch in Wales – see the boxed text). From Waipukurau, head towards Porangahau on the coast. Follow this road for 40km to the Mangaorapa junction and then follow the 'Historic Sign' indicators. The much-photographed AA road sign is a few kilometres up the hill (on private property) from Mangaorapa station.

Lochlea Farmstay (*☎/fax 06-855 4816, e lochlea.farm@xtra.co.nz, 344 Lake Rd, Wanstead*) Bunks dorms $15, twins/doubles $36-40. After contemplating the name's astronomic length you can stop off at this idyllic, laid-back and friendly farm.

Porangahau Lodge (*☎ 06-855 5386*) Singles/doubles from $35/65. Porangahau Lodge is good value, and is off the beaten track.

In Waipawa stop for tea at the ***Abbotslee Tearooms*** (*34 Great North Rd*) and in Waipukurau try the ***Greenland Bakery*** or ***Cafe Supreme***, both on Ruatauiwha St.

Wellington Region

☎ 04 & 06 • pop 415,700

Wellington, the capital of NZ, is located on a picturesque harbour at the southern tip of the North Island. Approaching it from the north, you'll pass through one of two regions – either the Kapiti Coast on the west side (SH1) or the Wairarapa on the east side (SH2) – before entering the heavily populated Hutt Valley or the city itself.

Wellington

☎ 04 • pop 205,500

Wellington takes part in friendly rivalry with larger Auckland. The city is hemmed in by its magnificent harbour, with wooden Victorian buildings on the steep hills. It prides itself as a centre for culture and the arts, has a plethora of restaurants, cafes, nightlife and activities, and is home to the country's parliament and national treasures. Apart from its importance as the capital, it's a major travel crossroads between the North and South Islands.

The city's harbour was formed by the flooding of a huge valley. An earthquake pushed up Miramar Peninsula in 1460. The city runs up the hills on one side of the harbour, and so cramped is it for space that many of its workers live in two narrow valleys leading north between the steep, rugged hills – one is the Hutt Valley and the other follows SH1 through Tawa and Porirua.

The city's nickname is 'Windy Wellington' and you probably won't need to spend much time here to see that it's a well-deserved moniker. One blustery day back in 1968 the wind blew so hard it pushed the almost-new Wellington-Christchurch car ferry *Wahine* onto Barrett's Reef just outside the harbour entrance. The disabled ship later broke loose from the reef, drifted into the harbour and then sank, causing the loss of 51 lives. The Museum of Wellington City & Sea has a dramatic model and photographic display of the disaster.

Highlights

- Taking in the urban delights of the capital – the multitude of excellent museums, theatres, shops, restaurants, cafes and bars
- Enjoying Wellington Harbour, whether savouring the view from Mt Victoria, cruising across to Days Bay, or walking along the city foreshore
- Taking the cable car to the Botanic Gardens and then walking on trails through stands of native trees
- Spending some time learning about NZ in the city's premier museum, Te Papa
- Discovering mystical Kapiti Island and the scenic Kapiti Coast
- Visiting the vineyards of the Wairarapa and the region's rugged coastline

NORTH ISLAND

Wellington

SOUTH ISLAND

Not to scale

HISTORY

Maori legend has it that the explorer Kupe was the first person to discover Wellington harbour. The original Maori name was Te Whanga-Nui-a-Tara, Tara being the son of a Maori chief named Whatonga who had settled on the Hawkes Bay coast. Whatonga

WELLINGTON REGION

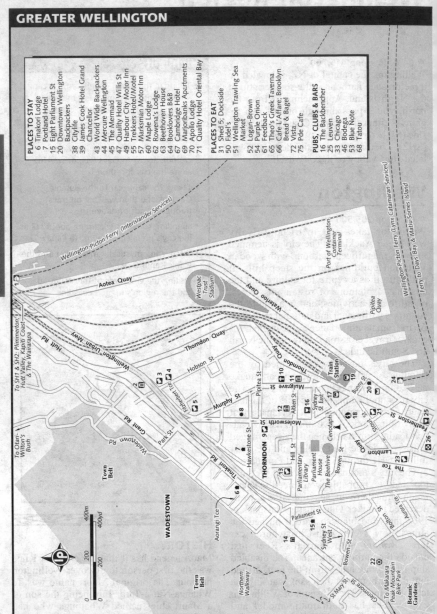

GREATER WELLINGTON

PLACES TO STAY
6   Tinakori Lodge
7   Portland Hotel
15 Eight Parliament St
20 Downtown Wellington
    Backpackers
38 Citylife
39 James Cook Hotel Grand
    Chancellor
43 World Wide Backpackers
44 Mercure Wellington
45 The Mermaid
47 Quality Hotel Willis St
49 Harbour City Motor Inn
55 Trekkers Hotel/Motel
57 Marksman Motor Inn
60 Maple Lodge
62 Rowena's Lodge
63 Beethoven House
64 Booklovers B&B
67 Cambridge Hotel
69 Marjoribanks Apartments
70 Apollo Lodge
71 Quality Hotel Oriental Bay

PLACES TO EAT
31 Shed 5; Dockside
50 Fidel's
51 Wellington Trawling Sea
    Market
52 Logan-Brown
54 Purple Onion
61 Feedback
65 Theo's Greek Taverna
66 Cafe L'Affare; Brooklyn
    Bread & Bagel
72 Vista
75 Pde Cafe

PUBS, CLUBS & BARS
16 The Backbencher
25 Leuven
33 Chicago
46 Bodega
53 Blue Note
68 Tatou

GREATER WELLINGTON

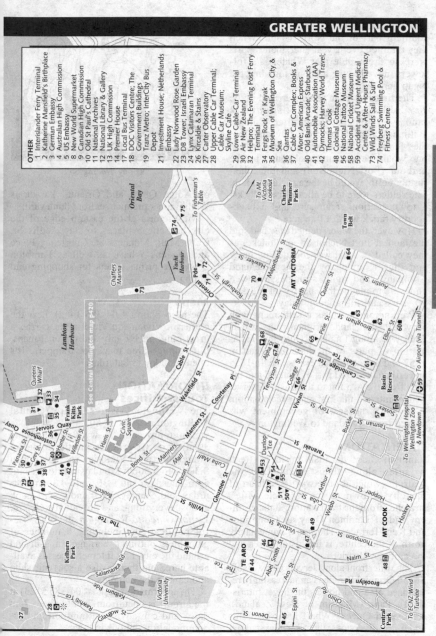

OTHER
1 Interislander Ferry Terminal
2 Katherine Mansfield's Birthplace
3 German Embassy
4 Australian High Commission
5 US Embassy
8 New World Supermarket
9 Canadian High Commission
10 Old St Paul's Cathedral
11 National Archives
12 National Library & Gallery
13 UK High Commission
14 Premier House
17 Local Bus Terminal
18 DOC Visitors Centre; The Government Buildings
19 Tranz Metro; InterCity Bus Depot
21 Investment House; Netherlands Embassy
22 Lady Norwood Rose Garden
23 DB Tower; Israeli Embassy
24 Lynx Catamaran Terminal
26 Kircaldie & Stains
27 Carter Observatory
28 Upper Cable Car Terminal; Cable Car Museum; Skyline Cafe
29 Lower Cable-Car Terminal
30 Air New Zealand
32 Helipro; The Evening Post Ferry Terminal
34 Fergs Rock 'n' Kayak
35 Museum of Wellington City & Sea
36 Qantas
37 Cable Car Complex; Books & More; American Express
40 Old Bank Arcade; Starbucks
41 Automobile Association (AA)
42 Dymocks; Harvey World Travel; Thomas Cook
48 Colonial Cottage Museum
56 National Tattoo Museum
58 National Cricket Museum
59 Accident and Urgent Medical Centre & After-Hours Pharmacy
73 Wild Winds Sail & Surf
74 Freyberg Swimming Pool & Fitness Centre

sent Tara and his half-brother to explore the southern part of the North Island. When they returned over a year later, their reports were so favourable that Whatonga's followers moved to the harbour, founding the Ngati Tara tribe.

The first European settlers arrived in the New Zealand Company's ship *Aurora* on 22 January 1840, not long after Colonel William Wakefield arrived to buy land from the Maori. The idea was to build two cities: one would be a commercial centre by the harbour (Port Nicholson) and the other, further north, would be the agricultural hub. The settlers were to be allotted two blocks: a town section of an acre and a back-country block worth £1 an acre.

However, the Maori denied they had sold the land at Port Nicholson, or Poneke, as they called it. As it was founded on hasty and illegal buying by the New Zealand Company, land rights struggles followed and were to plague the country for the next 30 years, and still affect it today.

Wellington began as a settlement with very little flat land. Originally the waterfront was along Lambton Quay, but reclamation of parts of the harbour began in 1852 and has continued ever since. In 1855 an earthquake razed part of Hutt Rd and the area from Te Aro flat to the Basin Reserve, which initiated the first major reclamation.

In 1865 the seat of government was moved from Auckland to Wellington.

ORIENTATION

Lambton Quay, the main business street, wriggles along almost parallel to the seafront (which it once was). The heart of the city, known as the 'Miracle Mile', stretches from the train station, at the northern end of Lambton Quay, to Cambridge and Kent Terraces. Thorndon, immediately north of the centre, is the historic area and the embassy district.

The waterfront along Jervois Quay, Cable St and Oriental Parade is an increasingly revitalised area and houses the huge, futuristic Te Papa (Museum of New Zealand). Renovated Queens Wharf has restaurants and a few diversions, there's a new stadium

"Windy Wellington"

on Aotea Quay, and Oriental Parade is Wellington's premier seafront boulevard.

Mt Victoria at the eastern edge of the city has cheap places to stay. Willis St, Cuba Mall, Manners St, Courtenay Place and Queens Wharf, as well as Lambton Quay, are prime streets for shopping and dining.

Maps

The Map Shop (☎ 04-385 1462), near the corner of Vivian and Victoria Sts, carries a great range of NZ city and regional maps, plus topographic maps for trampers. It's open Monday to Saturday.

INFORMATION
Tourist Offices

The Wellington visitors centre (Central Wellington map; ☎ 04-802 4860, ℮ info@ wellingtonnz.com, ⓦ www.wellingtonnz .com) is on Civic Square at the corner of Wakefield and Victoria Sts. It's open 8.30am to 5.30pm Monday to Friday (until 5pm Tuesday) and 9.30am to 4.30pm Saturday and Sunday. Its friendly staff book almost everything, and provide the *Official Visitor Guide to Wellington* and other useful publications, including a number of pamphlets outlining heritage trails in and around the city. Fast Internet access is available here, and there's also a souvenir shop and cafe in the complex.

The information desk (☎ 04-385 5123) at the airport is open from 7am to about 7pm daily, and can advise on transport and accommodation options in town.

The Department of Conservation (DOC) visitors centre (☎ 04-472 5821, W www .doc.govt.nz) is in the Government Buildings (enter from Lambton Quay). It has information on walks, parks, outdoor activities, camping in the region and visitor permits for Kapiti Island. It's open 9am to 4.30pm Monday to Friday, 10am to 3pm Saturday and Sunday. Stores selling outdoor equipment are found on Mercer St, including Mainly Tramping (Central Wellington map; ☎ 04-473 5353) at No 39.

The Automobile Association (AA; ☎ 04-470 9999), 342 Lambton Quay, has the usual maps and services as well as NZ travel books.

Free tourist publications with events listings include *Wellington's What's On* and the weekly *City Voice*. The *Dominion* is the city's morning newspaper, while the *Evening Post* comes out in the afternoon. Both are published daily; the best entertainment sections are in Thursday's and Saturday's editions.

Embassies & Consulates

Wellington, as the national capital, houses the consulates and embassies of many countries (see the Facts for the Visitor chapter).

Money

Banks around town exchange foreign currency and are generally open 9.30am to 4.30pm Monday to Friday. Thomas Cook (☎ 04-472 2848) has a foreign exchange office inside the Harvey World Travel branch at 358 Lambton Quay. American Express (☎ 04-473 7766) is inside the Books & More store at the Cable Car Complex, 280–292 Lambton Quay.

A very useful place is City Stop (Central Wellington map; ☎ 04-801 8669) at 107 Manners St, a 24-hour convenience store that will exchange travellers cheques at any hour.

Post & Communications

The main post office (open 7.30am to 5pm Monday to Friday) is on Waterloo Quay near Downtown Wellington Backpackers, however poste restante mail should be collected

The Treasures of Te Papa

Te Papa, the Museum of NZ (*Central Wellington map;* ☎ *04-381 7000,* W *www .tepapa.govt.nz, Cable St; admission free, except special shows; open 10am-6pm Fri-Wed, 10am-9pm Thur*) is in a striking building (its construction took five years and cost $317m) that dominates Wellington's waterfront. Te Papa opened in 1998 and attracted two million visitors in its first year; it quickly gained widespread praise for its innovation and approachability. The museum has become the nation's pride and joy, affectionately called 'Our Place', as it celebrates the essence of NZ and its people.

Among Te Papa's treasures is an extensive Maori collection and its own *marae*. Natural history, the environment, European settlement and many other things New Zealand are presented in impressive gallery spaces with a touch of interactive high tech (eg, a virtual bungy jump and a house shaking through an earthquake). The rest of the world gets a look-in with changing exhibits of international art.

There are a number of hands-on discovery centres designed for children. A store, cafes, an upmarket restaurant and an auditorium round off this impressive complex. Allow yourself plenty of time to explore and enjoy it.

at the post office at 43 Manners Mall (Central Wellington map). More post offices are spread around the centre.

Most backpackers places have Internet facilities. The Wellington visitors centre has high-speed connections, as does Load Cybercafe (Central Wellington map; ☎ 04-384 1871), 115 Cuba St, and Cybernomad (Central Wellington map; ☎ 04-801 5964), 43 Courtenay Place.

Bookshops

Dymocks (☎ 04-472 2080), at 366 Lambton Quay, is one of Wellington's largest bookshops. Unity Books (Central Wellington map; ☎ 04-499 4245), 57 Willis St, is something of an institution with an excellent fiction section, including good NZ literature.

Bellamy's (Central Wellington map; ☎ 04-384 7770), located at 105 Cuba St, is a good second-hand bookshop.

Medical Services
The Accident and Urgent Medical Centre (☎ 04-384 4944) is south of town at 17 Adelaide Rd, Newtown. It's open 24 hours and no appointment is necessary. There's an after-hours pharmacy next door, open 5pm to 11pm Monday to Friday and 9am to 11pm Saturday and Sunday. The Wellington Hospital (☎ 04-385 5999) is further south on Riddiford St in Newtown.

Gay & Lesbian
See Gay & Lesbian Travellers in the Facts for the Visitor chapter for country-wide organisations and useful websites.

The Wellington Gay Switchboard (☎ 04-473 7878, Ⓔe⒠ gayswitchboard@yahoo.com) offers information from 7.30pm to 10pm daily; the Lesbian Line (☎ 04-499 5567, Ⓔe⒠ wgtnlesbianline@hotmail.com) does the same from 7.30pm to 10pm Tuesday, Thursday and Saturday. See also Ⓦ www .gayline.gen.nz and Ⓦ www.wellington .lesbian.net.nz.

Unity Bookshop on Willis St has a good gay and lesbian book section. The fortnightly *express* ($2.50; Ⓦ www.gayexpress .co.nz), a gay community newspaper, is available here and from the YHA.

Pound on Dixon St (see Entertainment later in this chapter) is a popular gay club, but there are few solely gay venues in Wellington.

THINGS TO SEE & DO
The Beehive & Parliament
Three buildings on Bowen St form NZ's parliamentary complex. By far the most distinctive and well known is the modernist executive office building known as the Beehive – because that is just what it looks like. Designed by British architect Sir Basil Spence, its construction began in 1969 and was completed in 1980. Controversy surrounded its construction and, while it's not great architecture, it is the architectural symbol of the country.

Next door to the Beehive is Parliament House, completed in 1922, and beside this is the neo-Gothic Parliamentary Library building, dating from 1899.

Contact the visitors centre (Central Wellington map; ☎ 04-471 9999, Ⓦ www.ps .parliament.govt.nz) in the ground-floor foyer of Parliament House for information on free, one-hour **public tours** of the Parliament buildings, offered on the hour from 10am to 4pm Monday to Friday, 10am to 3pm Saturday and noon to 3pm Sunday. The public can also attend sessions of the House of Representatives and are free to come and go from the public gallery; phone the visitors centre for sitting times (Parliament usually sits from Tuesday to Thursday three weeks of most months).

Historic Buildings
Opposite the Beehive, at the northern end of Lambton Quay, stands the 1876 **Government Buildings**, one of the largest all-wooden buildings in the world. With its block corners and slab wooden planking, you have to look twice to realise that it is not made of stone. The building has been restored and houses the university's law department and various offices, including the DOC visitors centre.

Dating from 1843, **Premier House** on Tinakori Rd is the official prime ministerial residence. An early Labour prime minister, Michael Joseph Savage, spurned such luxury, however, and the house was used for a variety of purposes between 1935 and 1990 until it was restored.

National Library & Archives
Opposite the Beehive, the National Library (☎ 04-474 3000, Ⓦ *www.natlib.govt.nz, cnr Molesworth & Aitken Sts; admission free; open 9am-5pm Mon-Fri, 9am-1pm Sat*) houses by far the most comprehensive book collection in NZ. Also housed here is the Alexander Turnbull Library, an early colonial collection with many historical books, maps, newspapers and photographs.

The library regularly hosts free public lectures and cultural events and the **National Library Gallery** (*open 9am-5pm Mon-Fri,*

9am-4.30pm Sat, 1pm-4.30pm Sun) has changing exhibits.

One block away, the national archives *(☎ 04-499 5595, W www.archives.govt.nz, 10 Mulgrave St; admission free; open 9am-5pm Mon-Fri, 9am-1pm Sat)* displays several significant national treasures, including the original Treaty of Waitangi.

Old St Paul's Cathedral

Completed in 1866, Old St Paul's Cathedral *(☎ 04-473 6722, 34 Mulgrave St; admission by donation; open 10am-5pm daily)* looks quaint from the outside, while the striking interior is a good example of early English Gothic timber design. It features magnificent stained-glass windows and houses displays of Wellington's early history.

Museum of Wellington City & Sea

On the renovated Queens Wharf in the restored 1892 Bond Store (customs house), this museum *(☎ 04-472 8904, W www .bondstore.co.nz, Jervois Quay; adult/child $5/2.50; open 10am-5pm Mon-Fri, 10am-5.30pm Sat & Sun – to 6pm daily Dec–mid-March)* tells the maritime history of the capital as well as its social heritage since Maori settlement. A section is devoted to the inter-island ferry *Wahine*, which sank in Wellington Harbour in 1968; photo and video exhibits document the tragedy.

Katherine Mansfield's Birthplace

This house *(☎ 04-473 7268, 25 Tinakori Rd; adult/child $5.50/2; open 10am-4pm daily)* is where the famous writer was born in 1888. The excellent video *A Portrait of Katherine Mansfield* screens here and the 'Sense of Living' exhibition displays photographs of the period alongside excerpts from her writing. A doll's house has been constructed from details in the short story of the same name. The No 14 Wilton bus stops nearby on Park St.

Other Museums

The **Film Centre** *(Central Wellington map; ☎ 04-384 7647, W www.nzfa.org.nz, cnr Jervois Quay & Cable St; admission free;*

Katherine Mansfield

ALEXANDER TURNBULL LIBRARY, WELLINGTON NZ

Katherine Mansfield is NZ's most distinguished author, known throughout the world for her short stories and often compared to Chekhov and Maupassant.

Born Kathleen Mansfield Beauchamp in 1888, she left Wellington, when she was 19 for Europe, where she spent the rest of her short adult life. She mixed with Europe's most famous writers, such as DH Lawrence, TS Eliot and Virginia Woolf, and married the literary critic and author John Middleton Murry in 1918. In 1923, aged 34, she died of tuberculosis at Fontainebleau in France. It was not until 1945 that her five books of short stories *(In a German Pension, Bliss, The Garden Party, The Dove's Nest* and *Something Childish)* were combined into a single volume, *Collected Stories of Katherine Mansfield*. She spent five years of her childhood at 25 Tinakori Rd in Wellington; it is mentioned in her stories *The Aloe* (which in its final form became *Prelude)* and *A Birthday* (a fictionalised account of her own birth).

---

open noon-5pm Sun-Thur, noon-8pm Fri & Sat) features NZ film, television and video from the 1890s up to the present. The Rialto Cinema, showing mainly art-house films, is located next door.

WELLINGTON REGION

The **Colonial Cottage Museum** (☎ *04-384 9122,* W *www.colonialcottagemuseum .co.nz, 68 Nairn St; adult/child $4/free; open noon-4pm daily Jan-Apr, noon-4pm Wed-Sun May-Dec)* is central Wellington's oldest building, built in 1858 by carpenter William Wallis and lived in by his family until 1977. The museum relates the story of family life in colonial Wellington.

Cricket aficionados will be bowled over by the memorabilia on display at the **National Cricket Museum** (☎ *04-385 6602; adult/child $3/1; open 10.30am-3.30pm daily Nov-Mar, 10.30am-3.30pm Sat & Sun only Apr-Oct)* in the old grandstand at the Basin Reserve.

The brand new **National Tattoo Museum** (☎ *04-385 6444,* W *www.mokomuseum .co.nz, 42 Abel Smith St; admission free; open noon-5.30pm Tues-Sat)* endeavours to showcase traditional and contemporary tattooing, especially Maori *moko* (facial tattoos) and Samoan methods. We were somewhat disappointed when we visited as there were numerous photos of interesting and even freakish tattoos, but little by way of accompanying explanations of cultural context and significance.

Capital E

Kids will love this educational entertainment centre *(Central Wellington map;* ☎ *04-384 8502,* W *www.capitale.org.nz, Civic Square; admission $3; open 10am-5pm daily)* geared especially to them. It has rotating exhibits (usually hands-on), a children's theatre company and television studio, and the huge **Hocus Pocus Toys shop** alone is worth a visit.

City Gallery

The City Gallery *(Central Wellington map;* ☎ *04-801 3952,* W *www.city-gallery.org.nz, Civic Square; admission free except for major international exhibitions; open 10am-5pm daily)* features various changing exhibits, with a reputation for challenging and innovative displays. Pick up a copy of the *Arts Map* brochure from the visitors centre, a guide to the best of Wellington's galleries and museums.

Botanic Gardens

The tranquil, 26-hectare Botanic Gardens (☎ *04-499 1400; open sunrise to sunset daily)* are easily visited in conjunction with a cable-car ride. The large gardens contain native bush and other gardens, including the Lady Norwood Rose Garden with over 100 rose species. There is also a teahouse, visitors centre and the NZ headquarters of World Wide Fund for Nature, with information and displays. You can also access the gardens from the Glenmore St entrance.

The **Carter Observatory** (☎ *04-472 8167,* W *www.carterobs.ac.nz; adult/child $10/6; open 10am-5pm Mon-Fri, noon-5pm Sat & Sun, and 6.30pm-late Tues, Thur & Sat)* is in the gardens near the top cable-car terminal. It has displays and videos about astronomy and is open during the day and some nights, when you can view the night sky through the telescope (weather permitting).

The main entrance to **Otari-Wilton's Bush** (☎ *04-475 3245; open daily)* is north of the city at the junction of Wilton Rd and Gloucester St; get there on the No 14 Wilton bus. Devoted to the cultivation and preservation of indigenous NZ plants, it has a number of walks through densely forested areas and flax clearings, plus picnic areas and an information centre.

Cable Car

A Wellington icon and 'must-do' attraction is the cable car (☎ *04-472 2199, rides one way/return adult $1.50/3, child $1/2)* that runs from an arcade off Lambton Quay up to Kelburn, overlooking the city. The cable-car service began in 1902; the small, well-presented **Cable Car Museum** (☎ *04-475 3578; admission free; open 9.30am-5.30pm daily)* at the top terminus gives information on its history.

The car operates at 10-minute intervals from 7am to 10pm Monday to Friday, 9am to 10pm Saturday and Sunday. The Skyline Cafe (☎ *04-475 8727; open 8am-4pm daily)* at the top offers great vistas. From here, you can stroll back down through the Botanic Gardens or return to town by a series of steps which interconnect with roads (a 30- to 40-minute walk).

Wellington Zoo

The zoo (☎ 04-381 6750, W www.zoo.wcc .govt.nz, Daniel St, adult/child $9/4; open 9.30am-5pm daily) has a wide variety of native and non-native wildlife and has outdoor lion and chimpanzee parks, plus a nocturnal kiwi house which also houses tuatara and giant weta.

The zoo is 4km south of the city centre, at the end of the Newtown Park bus routes No 10 and No 23.

Ferry to Days Bay & Matiu-Somes Island

Trips across the harbour to Days Bay are made on **The Evening Post Ferry** (☎ 04-499 1282, one-way tickets adult/child $7.50/4), departing from Queens Wharf on a daily schedule. It's a 30-minute trip to Days Bay, where there are beaches, a fine park and a boatshed offering canoes and rowboats for hire. There are also a couple of houses that Katherine Mansfield's family kept for summer homes; her story At the Bay recalls summer holidays here. A 10-minute walk from Days Bay brings you to the upmarket settlement of Eastbourne, with good cafes and picnic spots.

At least three Days Bay ferries per day also call in at Matiu-Somes Island (return fare adult/child $16.50/9), a former prisoner -of-war camp and quarantine station that has only recently been opened to the public. Now a reserve managed by DOC, the island has walking trails and beach areas.

Scenic Lookout

The best view of the city, harbour and surrounding region is from the lookout at the top of **Mt Victoria** (196m), east of the city centre. It's a taxing walk but well worth the effort; otherwise take bus No 20 (operating Monday to Friday only). To drive, take Oriental Parade along the waterfront and then Carlton Gore St. Alternatively, head up the hill on Majoribanks St and follow the 'Lookout' signs, turning left onto Hawker St.

Walking

Wellington has many enjoyable walks in the city and surrounds. The visitors centre and DOC (see Information earlier in this chapter) are both good sources of information. See also Organised Tours, later in this chapter, for details on guided city walks.

The easy **Red Rocks Coastal Walk**, south of the city, follows the volcanic coast from Owhiro Bay to Red Rocks and Sinclair Head, where there's a seal colony. Take bus No 1 or 4 to Island Bay, then No 29 to Owhiro Bay Parade (or walk 2.5km along the Esplanade). From the start of Owhiro Bay Parade it's 1km to the quarry gate where the coastal walk starts (two to three hours' duration).

Red Rocks Seal Tours (☎ 04-802 4860) operates excellent, 2½-hour 4WD tours to see the seals and take you off the beaten track – along rugged beach and coastline and up to the wind turbine on Brooklyn Hill for scenic views. Bookings are made at the visitors centre from where tours depart at 10.30am and 1pm (adult/child $50/25).

Mountain Biking

Makarara Peak Mountain Bike Park (W www .makarapeak.org.nz) is a council-run park in the hills of Karori, west of the city centre. The main entrance is on South Karori Rd (accessible on bus routes No 12 and 17). The 200-hectare park has numerous tracks ranging from easy to very difficult. **Mud Cycles** (☎ 04-476 4961, W www.mudcycles .co.nz) is close to the park at 1 Allington Rd, Karori. You can rent bikes from $25/40 halfday/day (inner-city pick-up and drop-off is offered) and get full track information here, plus there are guided tours available, from $65 for a half-day ride.

There are other good opportunities for mountain biking around town – the visitors centre or any of the city's bike stores can give you information.

Other Activities

With all this wind and water, Wellington is a great place for windsurfing – choose from sheltered inlets, rough harbours and wave-beaten coastal areas, all within half an hour's drive of the city. **Wild Winds Sail & Surf** (☎ 04-384 1010, W www.wildwinds .co.nz, Chaffers Marina, Oriental Bay) has

WELLINGTON REGION

windsurfing lessons for beginners ($60 for two-hour lesson including board, rig and wetsuit). **Fergs Rock 'n' Kayak** (☎ 04-499 8898, W *www.fergskayaks.co.nz, Shed 6 Queens Wharf*) rents out kayaks from $9/30 an hour/day. Guided kayaking trips on the bay include three-hour evening trips for $45. You can also rent rollerblades here for $10/25 an hour/day (great for cruising along the waterfront), and the 'rock' part of the name refers to the 14m indoor rock-climbing wall ($12; hire of shoes, harness and karabiner additional).

Good surfing breaks are found at **Lyall Bay** near the airport, and **Palliser Bay**, southeast of Wellington. The visitors centre can help you with fishing and diving charters.

The **Freyberg Swimming Pool & Fitness Centre** (☎ 04-384 3107, *139 Oriental Parade*) has a heated indoor pool plus spa and sauna. It's open 6am to 9pm daily (adult/child $3.50/1.50).

All Track Adventures (☎ 04-477 3374, W *www.alltrack.co.nz*) offers great quad-bike safaris through farmland near Johnsonville and, on longer trips, over rugged coastline and through creeks. A 30-minute beginners tour is $39, the 90-minute trip is ideal for most visitors and costs $99.

Helipro (☎ 04-472 1550, W *www.helipro .co.nz*) is based at Queens Wharf and offers scenic helicopter flights from $75 per person for 10 minutes over the city.

Wellington has few adrenaline activities like those found in abundance in tourist centres such as Queenstown or Rotorua. It does have an incongruous **bungy rocket** (*Central Wellington map;* ☎ 04-382 8438, *cnr Taranaki St & Courtenay Place*), where you sit in a capsule-like device that is flung into the air at high speed ($35). There is also the very cool **Fly by Wire** in Paekakariki (for details see Kapiti Coast later in this chapter).

ORGANISED TOURS

Wally Hammond's City Tours (☎ 04-472 0869) takes a 2½-hour city highlight tour ($25) at 10am and 2pm, including hotel/motel pick-up and drop-off, or from the visitors centre. The half-day Kapiti Coast Tour ($55) runs daily at 9am and

1.30pm. Full-day Wairarapa and Palliser Bay tours ($110) leave at 9am.

From November to March **Walk Wellington** (☎ 04-384 9590) conducts daily tours of the inner city – one walk focuses on the Waterfront (departing 5.30pm Monday, Tuesday and Thursday), the other on the City (10am Wednesday, Friday, Saturday and Sunday). The walks last 90 minutes, cost $20 and depart from outside Starbucks Coffee on Lambton Quay. From April to October, walks are conducted only on Saturday and Sunday at 10am.

Also see Walking earlier in this chapter for information on guided tours to see the seals at Red Rocks, and Other Activities for details on popular quad-bike tours.

SPECIAL EVENTS

Wellington is always celebrating one event or another; the visitors centre has listings, and W www.wellingtonnz.com gives a good rundown. Notable regular events include:

January/February
Summer City Festival A two-month celebration of summer that begins on New Year's Eve and includes many free outdoor events.
W www.feelinggreat.co.nz

February/March
New Zealand Festival A biennial event (held in even-numbered years) involving a month of culture, including theatre, dance, music and opera performances, with many top international artists involved.
W www.nzfestival.telecom.co.nz

The Fringe NZ A month-long festival of visual arts, music, dance and theatre.
W www.fringe.org.nz

April/May
International Laugh Festival National and international comedians perform in venues around town.
W www.laugh.nzoom.com

July
International Film Festival A three-week event showcasing the best of NZ and international cinema.
W www.enzedff.co.nz

October
International Jazz Festival A popular fortnight of jazz concerts, workshops, jazz crawls and street performances.
W www.jazzfestival.co.nz

PLACES TO STAY
Camping & Cabins

Areas for pitching a tent are scarce in Wellington. Rowena's City Lodge can accommodate a few tents or else try the Hutt Valley. All prices quoted here are for two people.

Hutt Park Holiday Village (☎ *0800 488 872, 04-568 5913,* e *info@huttpark.co.nz, 95 Hutt Park Rd, Seaview, Lower Hutt)* Powered/unpowered sites $22/20, cabins $32-45, self-contained units $62, motel units $75-84. This busy park is 13km south-west of the city. It has very good facilities but its industrial location is dreary and inconvenient. It's a 15-minute drive from the ferry, a five-minute walk from the bus stop (take the Eastbourne bus) or a 20-minute walk from Woburn train station.

Harcourt Holiday Park (☎ *04-526 7400,* e *harcourtholidaypark@xtra.co.nz, 45 Akatarawa Rd, Upper Hutt)* Powered/unpowered sites $20/18, cabins $30, tourist flats $63, motel units $75. This well-designed, well-maintained park, only 35km northeast of Wellington, is in native bush just off SH2.

Hostels

Wellington has an ever-increasing number of these, so standards are improving. At the time of research, quite a few places were undergoing expansion and/or refurbishment. However, one hassle may be inner-city parking – some central places offer limited off-street parking spaces, while others have none. Inquire when you book.

Wellington City YHA (*Central Wellington map;* ☎ *04-801 7280,* e *yhawgtn@yha .org.nz, cnr Cambridge Terrace & Wakefield St)* Dorm beds $22, twins & doubles $52, en suite doubles $70. Wellington City is central and well appointed: most rooms have bathrooms and views over the harbour. This well-managed hostel was undergoing expansion at the time of research (its popularity has necessitated a doubling of its capacity) and great new communal areas will be added (including a games room).

Downtown Wellington Backpackers (☎ *04-473 8482,* W *www.downtownback packers.co.nz, 1 Bunny St)* Dorm beds $21,

singles/twins/doubles with shared facilities $30/46/50, en suite twins/doubles $50/55. This huge, busy place is a little further from the central action. It's one of the largest Art Deco buildings in NZ and a young Queen Elizabeth II stayed here in 1953. It has a big-city feel with slightly dingy rooms, but amenities are good: a restaurant serving cheap food; large bar with billiard table; huge kitchen and lounge, and pubs next door.

Trekkers Hotel/Motel (☎ *04-385 2153,* W *www.trekkers.co.nz, 213 Cuba St)* Dorm beds $20-22, singles with shared facilities $49, en suite singles/doubles & twins $65/79. This one is in a lively area among the delights of Cuba St. It's a large hotel, and its rooms are looking pretty tired and worn, especially compared to the newer places. The share backpacker rooms are twins with basins. Extras include the good Parlour Bar & Cafe and some off-street parking.

Cambridge Hotel (☎ *04-385 2503,* W *www.cambridgehotel.co.nz, 28 Cambridge Terrace)* Dorm beds $20, singles/doubles with shared facilities $45/60, en suite twins and doubles $69-85. This newly restored heritage hotel is a big step up from other backpackers-cum-hotels in town. It's a good choice for its location (right by Courtenay Place), newly furnished rooms, and luxurious shared bathrooms There's a bar and restaurant here too.

Wildlife House (*Central Wellington map;* ☎ *04-381 3899, 0508 005 858,* W *www .wildlifehouse.co.nz, 58 Tory St)* Dorm beds $22, doubles & twins $50, en suite doubles $58. You can't miss this large zebra-striped building. Inside are colourful, spacious rooms and good communal areas, such as a reading room, a TV, and video rooms and a big, modern kitchen. There's no parking.

World Wide Backpackers (☎ *04-802 5590,* e *world.wide@paradise.net.nz, 291 The Terrace)* Dorm beds $22, singles $40, twins & doubles $50. This friendly, well-regarded backpackers is small, clean and homely and offers winning free extras like Internet, breakfast and wine in the evening.

Rosemere Backpackers (*Central Wellington map;* ☎ *04-384 3041,* e *rosemerebp@ yahoo.com, 6 MacDonald Crescent)* Dorm

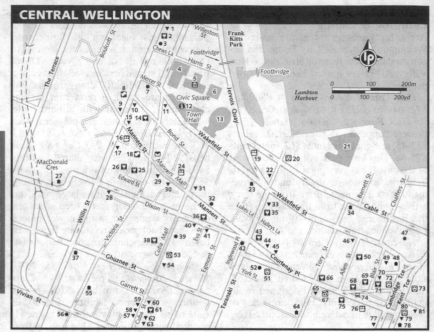

CENTRAL WELLINGTON

beds $20, singles $30, twins $40, doubles $44. Rosemere, under new ownership after being long neglected, is a short walk uphill from the centre. The new owners are doing some serious sprucing up and it's now an OK place to stay. It offers good extras like free city pick-up and free Internet.

There are several backpackers on and near Brougham St in the pleasant Mt Victoria area, a quiet residential suburb close to the city. From the train station catch bus No 2 to Brougham St, or No 1 or 4 to the Basin Reserve stadium. The area is only a five-minute walk from Courtenay Place.

Beethoven House (☎ 04-939 4678, 89 Brougham St) Dorm beds $19, doubles & twins $46. This is one of NZ's original backpackers and many people stay just for the company of the eccentric owner, Alan, who is helpful but straight talking (some find it hard to take). Prices include breakfast in the rambling garden heralded by a classical-music wake-up call.

Rowena's Lodge (☎ 0800 801 414, 04-385 7872, W www.wellingtonbackpackers.co.nz, 115 Brougham St) Camping $10 per person, dorm beds $19, singles $26, doubles & twins $46. This is a large, friendly and well-equipped hostel and the only place in town to offer camping. There are good views over the city and a free shuttle service to ferries, buses and trains.

Maple Lodge (☎ 04-385 3771, 52 Ellice St) Dorm beds $21, singles $28, twins $44, doubles $46. Small, welcoming, Maple Lodge is highly rated, offering good, clean accommodation and safe off-street parking. It's a backpackers that has no TV to encourage guest interaction.

Moana Lodge (☎ 04-233 2010, e moana lodge@clear.net.nz, 49 Moana Rd, Plimmerton) Dorm beds $21-22, singles $28, doubles & twins $44-50. If you'd prefer to stay out of the city this is a great choice. This exceptional backpackers is on the beach in Plimmerton, 25km from town off SH1. It's

CENTRAL WELLINGTON

PLACES TO STAY
23	Duxton Hotel
27	Rosemere Backpackers
34	Museum Hotel de Wheels
37	Quest on Willis
48	Wellington City YHA
55	Victoria Court Motor Lodge
64	Wildlife House
78	Halswell Lodge

PLACES TO EAT
1	BNZ Centre
9	Bouquet Garni
10	Wholly Bagels
11	The Lido
15	Kopi
17	Armadillo's
22	Wellington Market
28	Chevys
29	Kebab Espresso Bar
30	Abrakebabra
31	James Smith Corner
33	Zibbibo
40	Angkor
41	La Casa della Pasta; Diva
44	Espressoholic
45	Catch Sushi
46	Pandoro
49	One Red Dog
54	Tulsi
57	Midnight Espresso
58	Olive Cafe
59	Khmer Satay Noodle House
60	Aunty Mena's Vegetarian Cafe
62	Vegetarian Cafe
63	Sushi Bar
65	Chow
70	Mondo Cucina
77	A Taste of India
79	Deluxe Cafe; Phoenician Felafel
81	Cafe Bastille

PUBS, CLUBS & BARS
2	Malthouse
14	Loaded Hog
25	Tupelo
26	StudioNine
35	Cell
36	Pound
38	Matterhorn
43	Molly Malone's; Dubliner
50	Vespa
61	Indigo
66	Wellington Sports Cafe
68	Kitty O'Shea's
69	CO2 Champagne Bar
71	Amba
75	Coyote; The Grand

OTHER
3	Unity Books
4	Central Library
5	City Gallery
6	Capital E
7	Mainly Tramping
8	Majestic Centre; Japanese Embassy
12	Wellington Visitors Centre
13	Michael Fowler Centre
16	Hoyts Midcity
18	French Embassy
19	The Film Centre; Rialto
20	Circa Theatre
21	Te Papa; Icon Restaurant
24	Hoyts Manners Mall; Fluid
32	City Stop
39	Bellamy's Bookshop
42	Bungy Rocket
47	New World Supermarket
51	WestpacTrust St James Theatre
52	Penny Farthing Cycles
53	Load Cybercafe
56	The Map Shop
67	Cybernomad
72	Downstage Theatre
73	BATS Theatre
74	Bus Stop
76	Paramount
80	Embassy Theatre

WELLINGTON REGION

a well run and luxurious place with friendly, caring owners who are more than happy to share their local expertise and pick you up from the train station (suburban trains between Wellington and the Kapiti Coast stop in Plimmerton). There's free use of kayaks, bikes and gold clubs.

Guesthouses & B&BS
Eight Parliament Street (☎ 04-499 0808, W www.boutique-bb.co.nz, 8 Parliament St) Rooms $120-185. This stylishly renovated house, run by a friendly German host, is in historic Thorndon and offers comfortable accommodation with a choice of three rooms, each with en suite. Access to Parliament St is off Hill St.

Tinakori Lodge (☎ 0800 939 347, 04-939 3478, W www.tinakorilodge.co.nz, 182 Tinakori Rd) Singles/doubles $70/95 with shared facilities, $95/130 with en suite. Tinakori Lodge, also located in Thorndon, is good value. It offers spotless B&B rooms in a grand old house that has a lovely garden area.

The Mermaid (☎ 04-384 4511, W www .mermaid.co.nz, 1 Epuni St) Rooms $68-130 (one en suite room, three with shared facilities). The Mermaid is a small women-only guesthouse in a wonderfully restored villa set among good cafes not far from Cuba St. The villa is colourful and inviting and the facilities, including guest kitchen, lounge and a deck area, are excellent.

Booklovers B&B (☎ 04-384 2714, W www.bbnb.co.nz, 123 Pirie St) Singles/doubles $70/80 with shared facilities, $80/120 with en suite. Booklovers is an elegant old home in the Mt Victoria area run by award-winning NZ author Jane Tolerton. There are four inviting rooms in the house that are filled with books; you can read here or take them with you. You have the best of both worlds in this location, with the option of a bus to the city centre, or a 10-minute bush walk to Oriental Bay.

Motels

Most motels have good off-street parking.

Halswell Lodge (Central Wellington map; ☎ 04-385 0196, **W** www.halswell.co.nz, 21 Kent Terrace) Hotel singles/doubles $75/85, motel units $120-130, lodge units $135-145. Given its great location in the heart of the action, Halswell's prices are reasonable, and there's a good variety of well-maintained accommodation options, from decent hotel rooms to an upmarket lodge suite with spa.

Marksman Motor Inn (☎ 04-385 2499, **e** info@marksmanmotel.co.nz, 44 Sussex St) Units $100-120. Marksman, by the Basin Reserve about 10 minutes walk from Courtenay Place, is well located for airport access. The friendly owners offer clean, comfortable studios plus one-bedroom units.

Apollo Lodge (☎ 0800 361 645, 04-385 1849, **e** accommodation@apollo-lodge.co .nz, 49 Majoribanks St) Units $110-160. Apollo Lodge is close to Courtenay Place and has comfortable, older-style units. The owners also have nearby **Majoribanks Apartments** (☎ 04-385 7305, 38 Majoribanks St), with fully self-contained ex-residential flats sleeping four for $630 per week (or $110-150 per night).

Victoria Court Motor Lodge (Central Wellington map; ☎ 04-472 4297, **e** victoriacourt.nz@xtra.co.nz, 201 Victoria St) Units $135-180. Victoria Court is centrally located and offers new, stylish studios and larger motel units.

Harbour City Motor Inn (☎ 0800 332 468, 04-384 9809, **e** harbourcitymotorinn@xtra.co.nz, 92-96 Webb St) Units $95-160. Harbour City has primarily studio units, normally priced around $110 (although special deals are occasionally available). There's a guest spa and restaurant here.

Hotels

For those on a budget, the popular **Downtown Wellington Backpackers**, **Trekkers Hotel/Motel** and the **Cambridge Hotel** offer budget, hotel-style rooms and are good, central options. The Cambridge is easily the pick of the three, having been newly renovated. See also **Halswell Lodge** in the earlier Motels section.

Otherwise, Wellington is awash with mid-range hotels. It's primarily a business, rather than tourist, destination so there are weekend discounts from Friday to Sunday.

Quest on Willis (Central Wellington map; ☎ 04-916 0500, **e** questonwillis@ clear.net.nz, 219 Willis St) Studios $125, 1-bedroom apartments $175. A centrally located block of mostly studio apartments, each with kitchen facilities, plus a cafe downstairs and some off-street parking make this a good choice.

Museum Hotel de Wheels (Central Wellington map; ☎ 0800 944 335, 04-385 2809, **W** www.museumhotel.co.nz, 80 Cable St) Mon-Fri $180-230, Sat & Sun $135-160. The 'de Wheels' part of this hotel's name refers to its amazing relocation – it was moved 120m in 1993 to vacate the space needed for construction of Te Papa. The comfortable rooms were undergoing a revamp at the time of research; prices vary depending on views (city versus harbour).

Quality Hotel Willis St (☎ 0800 782 548, 04-385 9819, 355 Willis St) and **Quality Hotel Oriental Bay** (☎ 0800 782 548, 04-385 0279, 73 Roxburgh St) Mon-Fri $125-$155, Sat & Sun from $105. These hotels offer good-value weekend rates for their pleasant, well-equipped rooms. During the week, the Oriental Bay hotel is slightly more expensive but has extras such as harbour views from some rooms and a swimming pool. Both hotels have bars and restaurants.

Mercure Wellington (☎ 04-385 9829, **e** reservations@mercurewlg.co.nz, 345 The Terrace) Mon-Fri $165-200, Sat & Sun $129. Nicely tucked away in a quiet but relatively central location and with good facilities such as pool, spa and gym, this is a good choice, particularly on weekends.

Portland Hotel (☎ 04-473 2208, **W** www .portlandhotel.co.nz, 24 Hawkestone St) Mon-Fri $160, Sat & Sun $99. Somewhat distanced from the action in the quieter Thorndon area, Portland's rooms are standard but clean and comfortable. There are cheaper rates if you stay longer than a night.

Top-end hotels, with rooms in the $200 to $300-plus range (although with good weekend rates), include the following:

James Cook Hotel Grand Chancellor (☎ 0800 275 337, 04-499 9500, 147 The Terrace). Mon-Fri $210, Sat & Sun from $130. This is the biggest hotel in Wellington and was undergoing extensive refurbishment at the time of research. Features include spacious rooms, a restaurant and complimentary valet parking.

Citylife (☎ 0800 368 888, 04-922 2800, 300 Lambton Quay) Mon-Fri $255-375, Sat & Sun $149-229. Citylife is affiliated with the upmarket Heritage chain of hotels and has excellent apartment-style accommodation, ranging from studios to two-bedroom rooms. Vehicle entrance to the hotel is off Boulcott St.

Duxton Hotel (Central Wellington map; ☎ 0800 655 555, 04-473 3900, e res@ wellington.duxton.co.nz, 148 Wakefield St) Mon-Fri $250-360, Sat & Sun from $169. Very much a businessperson's hotel during the week, the centrally located Duxton has all the high-quality facilities you'd expect, and prices to match.

PLACES TO EAT
You will find most of the following establishments on the Central Wellington map; where this is not the case please refer to the Greater Wellington map (as indicated).

Restaurants
Courtenay Place is the entertainment centre of Wellington and has a large selection of restaurants to suit most budgets. The Manners Mall-Willis St area and Cuba St also have an interesting range. Slightly out of the centre, Tinakori Rd in Thorndon also has excellent restaurants.

Asian This is the main international cuisine. If you like spicy Malaysian food you're in luck: there are dozens of Malay restaurants and competition keeps prices down. The Indian subcontinent is also well represented. Courtenay Place is traditionally Chinatown and although it has been taken over by fashionable restaurants and bars, many Chinese places remain.

Kopi (☎ 04-499 5570, 103 Willis St) Mains $14-16. Kopi consistently gets voted the city's best Malaysian eatery, and the crowds attest to its popularity. The menu features some good curry options, such as beef rendang and laksa, plus there are old favourites such as mee goreng and nasi lemak as well.

Angkor (☎ 04-384 9423, 43 Dixon Street) Mains $15-25. Angkor's rating as NZ's best Cambodian restaurant comes as little surprise. Here you can sample such delights as *amok trei* (spicy steamed fish) and *yao-horn* (a charcoal broiler steam boat created for sharing).

Catch Sushi (☎ 04-801 9352, 48 Courtenay Place) Dishes $2.50-5. At Catch you make your sushi selection from a revolving conveyer belt; the place is often crowded at lunch time with people enjoying the fresh food, novelty and convenience as well as the reasonable prices.

Tulsi (☎ 04-802 4144, 135 Cuba St) Mains $15-19. Tulsi's bright and colourful decor goes well with its tag of 'contemporary Indian cuisine' and the food, with all the curry and tandoori favourites featured, is fresh and consistently good. There are great lunch-time specials.

Chow (☎ 04-382 8585, 45 Tory St, upstairs) Dishes $9-16. This super-stylish (some might say slightly pretentious) new eatery offers a diverse mix of dishes perfect for sharing with friends. Menu items are plucked from various Asian cuisines and include Japanese *gyoza* (filled dumplings), Vietnamese spring rolls, Cantonese roasted duck and Thai curried chicken.

Tex-Mex A Wellington institution, *Armadillo's* (☎ 04-384 1444, 129 Willis St) is a loud, cowboy-style restaurant-bar that specialises in American food (mains $19-25) such as steaks, ribs, southern chicken and burgers in Texas-size portions.

Chevy's (☎ 04-384 2724, 97 Dixon St) Mains $14-23. Fun, colourful Chevy's is a cheerleader for American-style fare, with hearty Tex-Mex dishes and fancy burgers named after US presidents (the Clinton burger features crumbed chicken breast and other trimmings, for the president 'known to enjoy a tender succulent bird').

Seafood Not surprisingly, most of the seafood restaurants can be found on the city's waterfront.

Fisherman's Table (☎ 04-801 7900, Oriental Bay) Mains $17-25. Built over the water in the old Oriental Bay Sea Baths and with good harbour views, this casual, family-style eatery offers reasonably priced seafood and an excellent $13.95 deal for 'light portions' of their main dishes.

Shed 5 (Greater Wellington map; ☎ 04-499 9069) and *Dockside* (Greater Wellington map; ☎ 04-499 9900) on Queens Wharf are both fine, upmarket restaurants with a great waterside location and quality seafood (mains around $25-30, but lunches are more reasonably priced).

European Many restaurants feature European food with a NZ twist (see Pacific Rim), but the following stay faithful to their roots.

La Casa della Pasta (☎ 04-385 9057, 37 Dixon St) Mains $10-17. Reasonably priced, home-style Italian food is what this no-fuss place does well. Authentic pasta dishes cost only $10.50, and the range includes staples like lasagne, ravioli, tortellini and gnocchi. The popular Diva cafe and bar is downstairs.

Cafe Bastille (☎ 04-382 9559, 16 Majoribanks St) Mains $16-22. Run by the folks behind the award-winning Roxburgh Bistro next door, this French cafe is open for dinner nightly and serves up dishes like pan-roasted salmon and coq au vin, plus Gallic treats such as roast pork belly and braised beef cheeks.

Theo's Greek Taverna (Greater Wellington map; ☎ 04-801 8806, 13 Pirie St) Mains $17-25. Tucked behind KFC is this treat, a whitewashed Mediterranean-style building with outdoor courtyard and live music and dancing (Thursday, Friday and Saturday) to complement the authentic cuisine. The meze platters at $8.50 per person are a great way to sample a variety of tasty appetisers.

Pacific Rim 'Pacific Rim' is a term that is used to describe modern NZ cuisine, which features an innovative use of local produce and imported styles.

Mondo Cucina (☎ 04-801 6615, 15 Blair St) Mains $20-25. Blair St is at the centre of the Courtenay Place restaurant scene, with a string of fashionable eateries. Mondo Cucina, or 'World Kitchen', mixes Californian and Italian styles with a Kiwi twist and offers up imaginative contemporary fare.

One Red Dog (☎ 04-384 9777, 9 Blair St) Meals $8-25. One of Blair St's more casual places, this is a bustling, upmarket brewery pub, popular for late-night drinking on the weekend (with a good selection of domestic and imported bottled beers), and offering excellent gourmet pizzas such as Zorba the Greek (pesto, tomato, feta cheese, olives, capsicum and spinach) and Green Piece (slow-roasted vegetables with feta cheese).

Olive Cafe (☎ 04-802 5266, 170 Cuba St) Meals $15-22. Minimalist decor, a good range of tasty tapas (about $6 per dish) and an array of well-prepared meals – including risotto, pasta, Cajun fish and grilled lamb salad – are the appeal of this relaxed place.

Zibibbo (☎ 04-385 6672, 25-29 Taranaki St) Mains $19-26. With a menu leaning towards Italian and Spanish cuisine, this bright restaurant and bar is a great spot to relax and enjoy the scrumptious tapas or wood-fired pizzas on offer.

Bouquet Garni (☎ 04-499 1095, 100 Willis St) Dinner mains $22-28. An oasis of cool in the bustling centre, this elegant place offers excellent but somewhat pricey bistro meals and a huge wine list. Brunch and lunch are also offered and are easier on the wallet.

Icon (☎ 04-801 5300, Te Papa, Cable St) Dinner mains $24-28, lunch $15-20. It's quite a name to live up to, and Icon certainly tries (it's located in the national icon that is Te Papa, so it has a head start). Brunch, lunch and dinner are served in this bright and breezy restaurant; the food is not quite iconic but certainly very good.

Logan-Brown (Greater Wellington map; ☎ 04-801 5114, cnr Cuba & Vivian Sts) Dinner mains $26-36. For something special, head to stylish and elegant Logan-Brown, which serves superb food in a refurbished 1920s bank chamber. The weekday lunch

Wellington's waterfront cafe scene

Mural detail in Wellington city centre

Playing chess on the 'balcony'

Mural detail in Wellington city centre

CHRISTOPHER GROENHOUT

RICHARD I'ANSON

PHOTO COURTESY OF WWW.WELLINGTONNZ.COM

RICHARD I'ANSON

FERGUS BLAKISTON

FERGUS BLAKISTON

DAVID WALL

DENNIS JOHNSON

Planes, trains & automobiles (clockwise from top): sailing on Waitemata Harbour, Auckland; a train crosses Wingatui Viaduct, near Dunedin; ski-plane at Franz Josef Glacier; 4WDing, Rangitata River

and daily pre-theatre set menus (tables to be vacated by 7.30pm) are excellent value at $29.50. There's an extensive wine selection.

Cafes

Wellington prides itself as a cultural centre and no literati could flourish without a decent cafe scene for a relaxed meal, snack, dessert or coffee. The city boasts more cafes per capita than New York City.

There are several good cafes around the city centre. Cuba St is one of the best strips, favoured by alternative society, and Courtenay Place has more than its fair share of cafe-bars.

Most cafes will offer cheap snacks (eg, cakes and muffins) for under $5, plus breakfast and lunch menus with meals ranging from soup ($6 to $7) to a full cooked breakfast with all the trimmings or lunch meal such as pasta, chicken or fish of the day ($14 to $15). Many restaurants and bars are also cafes by day (also, many cafes serve dinner). Weekend mornings see all these places doing a busy brunch-time trade.

The Lido (☎ 04-499 6666, cnr Victoria & Wakefield Sts) The Lido, a popular corner cafe opposite the civic centre, has big windows and outdoor seating for watching the world go by, and is a good spot for coffee and cake or something more substantial.

Espressoholic (☎ 04-384 7790, 128 Courtenay Place) Near the corner of Taranaki St and with its inside walls splattered with graffiti, Espressoholic's popularity lies in its tasty meals, long hours, cool music and the courtyard out the back.

Midnight Espresso (☎ 04-384 7014, 178 Cuba St) Cuba St has a string of good cafes, including this old favourite, serving up mostly vegetarian fare and proving a popular spot well into the wee hours.

Purple Onion (Greater Wellington map; ☎ 04-384 4344, 203 Cuba St) Slip into a comfy purple booth and choose between the brunch menu, served until 5pm and featuring pancakes, eggs benedict and French toast, or lunch with classic cafe fare such as nachos and pasta of the day.

Fidel's (Greater Wellington map; ☎ 04-801 6868, 234 Cuba St) Fidel's is a cool hang-out for coffee-craving, left-wing subversives, watched over by images of Castro. It features an all-day breakfast and other typical cafe fare.

Vegetarian Cafe (☎ 04-384 2713, 179 Cuba St) A gem for noncarnivores, this cheap, cheerful and inviting place has great vegie and vegan options. Try the Tex-Mex burrito or sate your hunger with a well-priced bowl of chilli or steamed vegetables.

Deluxe Cafe (☎ 04-801 5455, 10 Kent Terrace) A hip little espresso bar beside the Embassy Theatre, this place doesn't offer the hot-food selection of the other cafes but does serve up good-value counter food like sandwiches, panini and muffins.

Cafe L'Affare (Greater Wellington map; ☎ 04-385 9748, 27 College St) and *Brooklyn Bread & Bagel* (Greater Wellington map; ☎ 04-802 4111, 29 College St) These neighbouring cafes are tucked away down an unassuming street and offer great cafe fare and very popular brunches. Part of L'Affare's appeal is its great coffee (it supplies many of the city's cafes), and Brooklyn's bread and bagels are delicious.

Parade Cafe (Greater Wellington map; ☎ 04-939 3935, 148 Oriental Parade) and *Vista* (Greater Wellington map; ☎ 04-385, 7724, 106 Oriental Parade) Two very popular cafes by the water, Parade and Vista both offer mixed menus, great brunch choices, reasonable prices and outdoor seating.

Cheap Eats & Takeaways

You don't have to spend a fortune in Wellington to eat well. There are a number of good, budget eateries, and a wide variety of cuisines on offer. Perhaps the best way to experience the variety is at one of the food courts around town, but these are usually only open during shopping hours.

The food court at the *BNZ Centre* (Willis St) is the biggest in town, full of workers, shoppers and travellers chowing down, particularly at lunch time. The food court on the ground floor of the market at *James Smith Corner* (55 Cuba St) has a good range of fare, while the food court in the *Wellington Market* (Wakefield St) has excellent Asian choices, including Indian and even Nepalese food, but is only open 10am to 5.30pm Friday to Sunday. A speciality here is Maori cuisine; you can buy food prepared in a *hangi*.

Fluid (Manners Mall, next to Hoyts Cinema) sells healthy juices and smoothies from $3.50 to $5.50. *Wholly Bagels (cnr Willis and Bond Sts)* has great fresh bagels, 'naked' ($1.40), with a selection of flavoured cream cheeses ($3 to $4) or filled with the likes of tuna salad or pastrami ($4 to $7). *Pandoro (cnr Allen & Wakefield Sts)* is an upmarket Italian bakery with delicious filled panini and focaccia for $5 to $6.

Khmer Satay Noodle House (148 Cuba St) scores zero for decor but big points for cheap meals, including noodle, soup and rice dishes all under $10. *Aunty Mena's Vegetarian Cafe (165 Cuba St)* has tasty meat-free Malaysian and Chinese dishes for $8 to $12. At 187 Cuba St, a great *sushi bar* does super-fresh Japanese treats for under $10.

There are two bustling kebab places on Manners Mall: *Kebab Espresso Bar (64 Manners St)* has a $9.50 deal for a kebab and house wine or beer; *Abrakebabra (90 Manners St)* has kebabs and burgers ($5 to $9.50) plus a small range of pasta and pizza. *Phoenician Felafel (11 Kent Terrace)*, by the Embassy Cinema, offers felafels, shwarmas and other Lebanese treats for under $10.

It's also worth mentioning that many restaurants offer great value at lunch time. *Tulsi (135 Cuba St)*, for example, is a bright, modern Indian place with lunch meals from $6 to $10, including naan and rice. Head to the Asian restaurants on Allen St for similar lunch deals. *A Taste of India (19 Cambridge Terrace)* offers great tandoori takeaway in the evening.

Wellington Trawling Sea Market (Greater Wellington map; 220 Cuba St) has wonderful fish and chips (a fish fillet dinner with chips and salad is $9). *Feedback (Greater Wellington map; 87 Kent Terrace)* by the Basin Reserve prepares excellent burgers with traditional or gourmet fillings (from steak and egg to tofu with mushrooms), priced from $5.50 to $9.20.

The well-stocked *New World supermarket (cnr Cambridge Terrace & Wakefield St)* is open 7am to 11pm daily. Another large *New World supermarket (Greater Wellington map)* is in Thorndon with entry from Molesworth and Murphy Sts.

ENTERTAINMENT

Wellington is undisputed king of NZ's nightlife with copious clubs, bars and other insomniac refuges. It also has a vibrant performing arts scene. Most venues are on the Central Wellington map.

Pubs

Brewery pubs – and the ubiquitous Irish pubs – are very popular. All offer meals and snacks to accompany their brews.

Loaded Hog (☎ 04-472 9160, 14 Bond St) The lively Hog gets a good crowd and has a friendly atmosphere, a decent menu and there's often live music later in the week.

Malthouse (☎ 04-499 4355, 47 Willis St, upstairs) This place is good for meals but an absolute shrine for the lover of naturally brewed beer. There are some 30 beers available on tap, from lesser-known local ales through to fine international drops like Guinness, Tuborg and Kronenbourg.

Molly Malone's (☎ 04-384 2896, cnr Courtenay Place & Taranaki St) This rousing, popular Irish pub has live music (mostly Irish) nightly. Traditional Irish fare is served upstairs in the *Dubliner* whiskey bar and restaurant (with a scary 100 whiskys to choose from!).

Kitty O'Shea's (☎ 04-384 7392, 28 Courtenay Place) Kitty O'Shea's is yet another convivial Irish pub with live music every night.

Backbencher (Greater Wellington map; ☎ 04-472 3065, cnr Molesworth St & Sydney St East) The Backbencher, opposite the Beehive, does a thriving business at lunch, with large portions. The atmosphere is casual, friendly and fun, greatly enhanced by the excellent puppets of various NZ politicians and satirical cartoons on the walls.

Wellington Sports Cafe (☎ 04-801 5115, cnr Courtenay Place & Tory St) With its big-screen TVs and great-value $12 meals, this place is the perfect spot to watch the big games. There's often a DJ when there's no big sporting contests to televise.

Chicago (Greater Wellington map; ☎ *04-473 4900, Queens Wharf)* Though away from the main nightlife, this large American-sports cafe is popular on a Friday night with after-work office crowds. It often has live music or a DJ, plus there's the requisite big-screen TV for major sporting events.

Leuven (Greater Wellington map; ☎ *04-499 2939, 135 Featherston St)* This 'beer cafe' (their description) is more upmarket than your everyday pub, and it is a great place to sample hearty Belgian cuisine such as mussels and *frites* (fries), washed down by one of a huge selection of international beers, with the emphasis on fine Belgian drops.

Bars & Clubs

For gig guides pick up a copy of the free brochure *The Package,* available at venues, cafes and record stores around town.

Courtenay Place is the nightlife centre of Wellington with numerous bars, and crowds on Saturday and Sunday. *The Grand (*☎ *04-801 7800, 69 Courtenay Place)* is popular and has a ground-level dining area and second-level bar with pool tables, lounge and a balcony. Tex-Mex restaurant-bar *Coyote (*☎ *04-385 6665, 63 Courtenay Place),* next door, has a dance floor that gets going later in the evening on Friday and Saturday.

Blair and Allen Sts, running off Courtenay Place, are fertile hunting grounds for booze and music, but here it's more of the hip and stylish lounge bars where you'll need to dress up to blend in. *CO2 Champagne Bar (*☎ *04-384 1064, 28 Blair St)* bubbles away, *Vespa (*☎ *04-385 2438, 21 Allen St)* has dim lighting, red velvet drapes, cocktails and smooth tunes; in a similar vein is *Amba (*☎ *04-801 5212, 21 Blair St).* A couple of blocks away is laid-back *Cell (*☎ *04-802 5090, 25 Taranaki St),* in the basement next door to Zibibbo, with lounges and a pool table.

Cuba St has its fair share of bars and venues, with the excellent first-floor *Indigo (*☎ *04-801 6797, 171 Cuba St)* hosting DJs and regular live music. The *Blue Note (*☎ *04-801 5007, 191 Cuba St)* has varied live performances including karaoke, open mike and jam sessions, visiting performers and DJs later in the week. The hip *Matterhorn (*☎ *04-*

384 3359, 106 Cuba St) is a local institution, found down a long corridor off Cuba St and offering good food, drink, occasional art showings, DJs and frequent live music.

For original bands, the cool *Bodega (Greater Wellington map;* ☎ *04-384 8212, 286 Willis St)* is the pick of the venues. There's music every night, from around 10pm. DJs play earlier in the week, and live bands on Thursday and Friday. There's a great selection of tap and bottled beers.

Edwards St is a big late-night venue with *StudioNine (*☎ *04-384 9976, 9 Edward St),* a cool dance club hosting international DJs and with a fab lounge area, and *Tupelo (*☎ *04-384 1152, 6 Edward St),* a chic bar.

Tatou (Greater Wellington map; ☎ *04-384 3112, 22 Cambridge Terrace)* allows patrons to flick through musical tastes: upstairs features live bands, downstairs is a dance bar playing lots of techno. Things don't get going here until late and don't finish until very late (on Saturday and Sunday Tatou usually stays open until 6am).

'The straight route is often boring' is written on the façade of *Pound (*☎ *04-384 6024, Dixon St),* and that should leave you in no doubt of the sexual persuasion of Pound's clientele. This is one of Wellington's few solely gay clubs.

Cinemas

Show times for movies are listed in the local newspapers or on W http://film.wellington .net.nz.

Hoyts has two cinemas on Manners St showing the latest Hollywood releases: *Hoyts Midcity (*☎ *04-384 3567)* and *Hoyts Manners Mall (*☎ *04-472 5182).*

The grand *Embassy (*☎ *04-384 7657, 10 Kent Terrace)* screens commercial films and after recent renovations boasts the largest screen in the southern hemisphere. It hosted the Australasian premiere of *The Lord of the Rings* in December 2001.

Paramount (☎ *04-384 4080, 25 Courtenay Place)* shows mainly art-house movies and has $5 tickets all day Monday (normally $12); and the *Rialto (*☎ *04-385 1864, cnr Jervois Quay & Cable St),* next to the Film Centre, screens independent productions.

WELLINGTON REGION

Performing Arts

Wellington is the most active place in NZ for live theatre, supporting a number of professional and quality amateur companies. Tickets are available from Ticketek (☎ 04-384 3840, W www.ticketek.com), with offices at Downstage, the St James Theatre and the Michael Fowler Centre.

Downstage Theatre (☎ 04-801 6946, W www.downstage.co.nz, cnr Cambridge Terrace & Courtenay Place), *Circa Theatre (☎ 04-801 7992, W www.circa.co.nz, 1 Taranaki St)* and *BATS Theatre (☎ 04-802 4175, W www.bats.co.nz, 1 Kent Terrace)* all stage quality productions (Bats is considered the more avant-garde, alternative theatre). Reduced-price, same-day theatre tickets for these three theatres are available at the visitors centre, subject to availability (tickets are on sale from noon).

WestpacTrust St James Theatre (☎ 04-802 4060, W www.stjames.co.nz, 77 Courtenay Place) is a grand old heritage building often used for opera, ballet and major musical shows. It provides a permanent home for the Royal New Zealand Ballet (W www.nzballet.org.nz).

The *Michael Fowler Centre (☎ 04-801 4263)*, part of the Civic Square complex, has its main entrance on Wakefield St. It has great acoustics and hosts all sorts of performances, from popular bands to the New Zealand Symphony Orchestra. Check the newspapers for current shows.

SHOPPING

The useful *Wellington's Shopping Guide* is published twice a year and is available from the visitors centre and around town. Another good publication for shoppers is the *Fashion Map*, which outlines where you'll find hip NZ creations. For second-hand records and books, plus retro clothing and funky off-beat furniture, take a stroll along Cuba St.

Kirkcaldie & Stains (Greater Wellington map; ☎ 04-472 5899, Lambton Quay) is an upmarket department store that was established back in the 1860s and is probably New Zealand's answer to Bloomingdale's or Harrods department stores.

GETTING THERE & AWAY
Air

At Wellington airport (☎ 04-385 5100, W www.wellington-airport.co.nz) there's an information desk (☎ 04-385 5123), open from 7am to about 7pm, located in the check-in hall. There's also a bureau de change, ATMs, storage lockers, car-rental desks, cafes and shops. Those in transit or with early flights are not permitted to stay overnight inside the airport – it's closed from about 2am to 4am. Departure tax on international flights is $25.

Air New Zealand (☎ 0800 737 000, W www.airnz.co.nz) offers direct domestic flights to many places in NZ, with connections to other centres. There are direct flights to and from Auckland, Blenheim, Chatham Islands, Christchurch, Dunedin, Gisborne, Hamilton, Napier, Nelson, New Plymouth, Palmerston North, Rotorua, Taupo, Timaru, Wanganui and Westport. The airline has a large travel centre at the corner of Lambton Quay and Grey St.

Qantas (☎ 0800 808 767, W www.qantas.co.nz) has half-a-dozen daily connections with Auckland and Christchurch. Its Wellington office is at 2 Hunter St.

Freedom Air (☎ 0800 600 500, W www.freedomair.co.nz) has budget-priced connections with Auckland and Christchurch, and Origin Pacific (☎ 0800 302 302, W www.originpacific.co.nz) has daily direct flights to Nelson, where you can connect to Christchurch.

Soundsair (☎ 0800 505 005, W www.soundsair.co.nz) has about six flights daily between Wellington and Picton in the South Island. The flight takes 25 minutes and costs $68/125 one way/return (there are discounts for holders of backpacker and student cards).

Bus

Wellington is an important junction for bus travel, with buses to Auckland and all major towns in between.

Buses from InterCity (☎ 04-472 5111) and Newmans (☎ 04-499 3261), depart from Platform 9 at the train station. Tickets for these buses are sold at the travel reservations and tickets centre in the train station.

White Star City to City (☎ 04-478 4734) buses depart daily from Bunny St, near Downtown Wellington Backpackers opposite the train station, and run along the west coast of the North Island to Palmerston North, Wanganui and New Plymouth. From Palmerston North there are connections with bus services to Masterton, Hastings, Napier and Gisborne.

Train
Wellington train station has a travel centre (☎ 04-498 2058) that can make reservations and sell tickets for trains, buses, ferries, tours and more. It's open from 7.15am to 5.30pm Monday to Friday, 7.15am to 12.15pm Saturday and Sunday. Luggage lockers are also available.

Aside from the Tranz Metro suburban trains (see Getting Around later in this chapter) that leave from here, two long-distance trains operate between Wellington and Auckland daily, running through the central North Island. The daytime *Overlander* departs Wellington at 8.45am, arriving in Auckland at 7.35pm. The overnight *Northerner* departs Wellington at 7.50pm, arriving in Auckland the following morning at 7am. The standard Wellington-Auckland adult fare on the *Overlander* is $102, and on the *Northerner* it's $90.

Hitching
It's not easy to hitch out of Wellington – the highways heading out of the city, SH1 and SH2, are motorways for a long distance and hitching is illegal on motorways. The best option is to catch a bus or train to one of the towns on the Kapiti Coast or to Masterton and hitch from there.

Boat
There are two options for crossing the strait between Wellington and Picton in the South Island by boat. The first is the large Interislander ferry service, which makes the journey in about three hours. The Lynx service is a faster and more expensive option on a high-speed catamaran that makes the journey in 135 minutes. Both services take vehicles. You can make inquiries or bookings for both

on ☎ 0800 802 802. See also the website (W www.interislandline.co.nz) for up-to-date schedules and fares.

It's best to do the crossing in daylight, if the weather's good, to see Wellington Harbour and the Marlborough Sounds. Sailing can be rough in adverse weather but the ferries are large and have lounges, cafes, bars and an information desk (some Interislander ferries even have a movie theatre).

Interislander The Interislander services arrive at and depart from the ferry terminal north of town. Daily sailing times (subject to change) are:

leaves Wellington 1.30am (excluding Sunday and Monday), 9.30am, 2pm, 5.30pm
leaves Picton 5.30am (excluding Monday), 10am (excluding Monday), 1.30pm, 6pm, 9.30pm

One-way standard fares for the Interislander cost $52/31 per adult/child. Passengers transporting a bike or surfboard pay an additional $10. To transport a motorbike costs $52; to take a car or small campervan (up to 5.5m in length) costs $179. A number of discounted fares (from 15% to 50%) are often available – it pays to inquire when you make your reservations.

Lynx The Lynx services are based at Waterloo Quay, not far from the train station. Sailing times are:

leaves Wellington 8am, 3.30pm
leaves Picton 11.30am, 7pm

One-way standard fares are adult/child $68/39. Passengers transporting a bike or surfboard pay an extra $15. To transport a motorbike costs $68; a car or campervan costs $199. Again, it pays to ask about discounted fares when booking.

Children under two years travel for free on all crossings.

All discount fares *must* be booked in advance. Only standard fares are available on the day of departure. Discounts are subject to availability and may not be available during peak travel times.

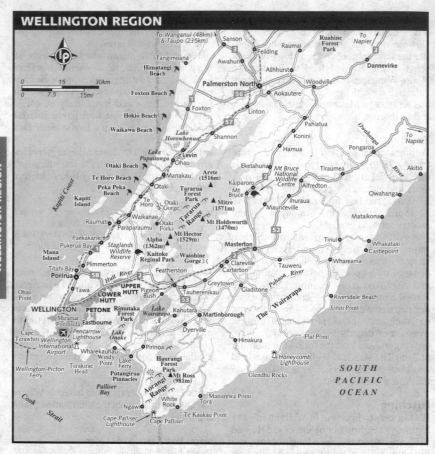

WELLINGTON REGION

You can book up to six months in advance, either directly (☎ 0800 802 802 free call within NZ, or ☎ 04-498 3302) or at most travel agents and visitors centres.

A free ferry shuttle-bus service is provided on both sides of the strait. In Wellington it operates between the ferry and train station (where long-distance buses also depart), departing from the train station 35 minutes before each sailing. A shuttle meets all arriving ferries. On the Picton side, a free shuttle runs between the ferry and the Picton-Christchurch *Tranz Coastal* train.

GETTING AROUND
To/From the Airport

The airport is 7km southeast of the city centre. Super Shuttle (☎ 04-387 8787) and AP Shuttles (☎ 04-477 5059) provide door-to-door shuttle buses at any hour between the city and the airport for $10 to $12.

The Stagecoach Flyer is a local bus running between the airport, Wellington city and Lower Hutt. The fare between the airport and city is $4.50 one way, or you can pay $8 and get a StarPass enabling you to ride most of the local buses. The Flyer runs every half-hour from about 6.30am to

8.30pm Monday to Friday, and every half-hour or hour on Saturday and Sunday.

A taxi between the city centre and airport costs $15 to $20.

Bus

Wellington has a good local bus system, Stagecoach, with frequent buses daily from around 7am to 11.30pm on most routes. Most depart from beside the train station and from the major bus stop on Courtenay Place at the intersection with Cambridge Terrace. Useful colour-coded bus route maps and timetables are available at the visitors centre. Phone Ridewell (☎ 0800 801 7000) for timetable and fare information from 7.30am to 8.30pm Monday to Saturday and 9am to 3pm Sunday. You can also refer to the excellent website W www.wrc.govt.nz/timetables.

Bus fares are determined by zones: there are six zones, and the cheapest fare is $1 for rides in zone one, $2 for two zones and up to $3.50 for rides to sections five and six. A Single Daytripper Pass costs $5 and allows unlimited bus travel for one day (excluding the airport bus, After Midnight buses and services to Hutt Valley). An all-day StarPass for $8 allows unlimited rides on all bus services except the After Midnight buses.

The City Circular is the name given to the distinctive bright yellow buses that take in Wellington's prime inner-city locations, making it very handy for travellers wishing to see the major sights. These buses loop the city every 10 minutes and the fare is $2.

The After Midnight Bus Service (☎ 0800 801 7000) has buses departing from the central entertainment district (Courtenay Place or Cuba St), at 1am, 2am and 3am Saturday and Sunday on a number of routes to the outer suburbs. The flat fare is $3.50.

Train

Tranz Metro operates four suburban electric train routes, with frequent trains daily from around 6am to midnight, leave from Wellington train station. These routes are: Johnsonville, via Khandallah and Ngaio; Paraparaumu, via Porirua and Paekakariki; Melling, via Petone; and Upper Hutt, going on to Masterton. Phone Ridewell (☎ 0800 801 7000), pick up timetables from the train station or visitors centre, or see W www.wrc .govt.nz/timetables.

Taxi

Taxi ranks are conveniently placed around town (eg, Cambridge Terrace, just near Courtenay Place; outside Te Papa). Taxi companies include Wellington Combined Taxis (☎ 04-384 4444) and Wellington Ace (☎ 04-388 8100).

Car

Wellington has a number of hire-car operators (check the *Yellow Pages*), but the prices are not as competitive as in Auckland. Prices start at around $35 a day for longer-term rental of an older car. There are often good deals on car relocation from Wellington to Auckland (most renters travel in the opposite direction) – a few companies offer very cheap rental on this route, with the catch being that you may only have 24 or 48 hours to make the journey. Still, if there are a few of you, the cost of petrol may be cheaper than train or bus tickets. Check noticeboards at backpackers, or call the companies direct.

If you're landing in Wellington and heading to the South Island, it's cheaper and easier to hire a car in Picton. Prices are around the same as in Wellington but you don't have to pay the ferry charges.

For those looking to buy or sell a car, there's a car traders market (☎ 04-499 3322) in the car park near Te Papa on Saturday from 9am to noon. Turners Auctions (☎ 0800 282 8466, 04-587 1400, W www.turners .co.nz), 120 Hutt Park Rd in Lower Hutt (not far from the camping ground), buys and sells used cars by auction.

Bicycle

Penny Farthing Cycles (☎ 04-385 2279), 89 Courtenay Place, rents bikes from $35 per day and offers longer-term rentals at reasonable rates. It also stocks a full range of bicycle gear, clothing, and bicycles for sale.

See Mountain Biking earlier for information on Mud Cycles, a company that rents mountain bikes.

WELLINGTON REGION

Hutt Valley

☎ 04 • pop 130,000

The Hutt River acts as the western boundary for land-starved Wellington's dormitory cities, Lower Hutt and Upper Hutt. Apart from some attractive forest parks for picnics and a few museums, they are fairly suburban. Both cities are easily reached by train or bus from Wellington.

The Hutt City visitors centre (☎ 04-560 4715, W www.huttcity.govt.nz) is at 10 Andrews Ave in Lower Hutt, and the Upper Hutt visitors centre (☎ 04-527 2141, W www.upperhuttcity.com) is at 6 Main St, Upper Hutt.

Lower Hutt is home to the waterfront **Petone Settlers Museum** (☎ 04-568 8373, The Esplanade; admission by donation; open noon-4pm Tues-Fri, 1pm-5pm Sat & Sun), with stories of migration and settlement in the area. The **Dowse Art Museum** (☎ 04-570 6500, 35 Laings Rd, Lower Hutt; admission free; open 10am-4pm Mon-Fri, 11am-5pm Sat & Sun) is a showcase for NZ art, craft and design.

Maori Treasures (☎ 04-939 9630, W www.maoritreasures.com, 56-58 Guthrie St; open 9am-4pm daily), also in Lower Hutt, is a complex of Maori artists and craftspeople that is well worth a visit. You can join one of two tours explaining Maori culture and customs and demonstrating Maori arts and crafts (including weaving, wood and bone carving, and stone sculpting). The 1½-hour tour costs $45, a 2½-hour tour includes a light lunch and costs $85. There is complimentary transport from the visitors centre in Wellington, and staff there can arrange your tour, or you can contact the complex direct.

The drive from Upper Hutt to Waikanae (on the Kapiti Coast) along the scenic Akatarawa road passes the 25-acre **Staglands Wildlife Reserve** (☎ 04-526 7529; adult/child $10/5; open 10am-5pm daily) where the rare blue duck has been successfully bred. It's 17km from SH2, 20km from SH1.

Days Bay and **Eastbourne** are to the south of the Hutt Valley and make a pleasant afternoon excursion. This beachside area is connected to Wellington's centre by The Evening Post Ferry at Queens Wharf. See Things to See & Do under Wellington for details. It's a 7km walk or cycle from Burdans Gate at the end of Muritai Rd in Eastbourne to the 1906 **Pencarrow Lighthouse**, the country's first permanent lighthouse.

Rimutaka Forest Park is 45 minutes' drive east of Wellington. Catchpool Valley, 12km south of Wainuiomata, is the most popular entrance to the park and there's a DOC visitors centre (☎ 04-564 8551), just off Coast Rd. Further on from the visitors centre is a **camping ground** (adult/child $4/2) in a delightful setting. A shower block and barbecues make it better than the usual DOC camp.

There are well-equipped **camping grounds** in both Lower and Upper Hutt. See Places to Stay under Wellington for details.

Kapiti Coast

☎ 04 & 06 • pop 36,700

The Kapiti Coast stretches 30km along the west coast from Paekakariki (45km north of Wellington) to Otaki (75km north of Wellington). Most towns have two settlements – one along the highway and another by the water. The region takes its name from large Kapiti Island, a bird and marine sanctuary 5km offshore.

The coast has fine white-sand beaches and good swimming, and is a summer playground of the city, as well as a suburban extension of Wellington. The other attraction is the Tararua Forest Park in the Tararua Range, which forms a backdrop to the coastline all along its length.

The Kapiti Coast is easily visited as a day trip from Wellington, but also has good accommodation for a few restful days.

Information

If you're coming from the north, the best place for information is the visitors centre at Otaki (☎ 06-364 7620, ⓔ kapiti.info@clear.net.nz), on SH1 just south of the main roundabout. From the south, there's a visitors centre (☎ 04-298 8195, ⓔ kapiti.info@clear.net.nz) in the car park of Paraparaumu's

Coastlands shopping centre on SH1. Both centres are open daily, and offer information and booking services for attractions and accommodation options in the area, including numerous B&Bs and homestays. See also its website at W www.kapititourist.co.nz.

The main DOC office (☎ 04-296 1112) for the Kapiti area is at 10 Parata St in Waikanae (behind the shopping area).

Getting There & Away

Getting to the west coast from Wellington is a breeze – it's on the major route (SH1) north from Wellington. From Wellington it's about 45 minutes to Paraparaumu and an hour to Otaki, much of it by motorway.

Blue Penguin Shuttle Express (☎ 06-364 6899) operates two or three services each Monday to Friday for pre-booked passengers between Otaki and Wellington (and on to the airport). Sample fares are Wellington-Paraparaumu $10, Wellington-Otaki $14. InterCity, White Star, Kiwi Experience and Magic Bus stop at Paraparaumu and Otaki on north-south routes to/from Wellington.

Trains between Wellington and the coast are easier and more frequent than buses. Services between Wellington and Paraparaumu ($7.50, 1hr) run half-hourly in both directions from around 6am to 11pm, stopping at Paekakariki ($6). Monday to Friday off-peak fares (9am to 3pm) are slightly cheaper.

Long-distance trains between Wellington and Auckland stop at Paraparaumu daily, as does the Monday to Friday, peak-hour Tranz Metro *Capital Connection* between Palmerston North and Wellington.

PAEKAKARIKI
☎ 04 • pop 1690

Paekakariki is a quiet seaside village spread out along a lovely stretch of often-deserted beach, just two blocks from the train station and the highway. This little town is a pleasant spot to relax within striking distance of Wellington.

Fly by Wire (☎ 0800 359 259, W www .flybywire.co.nz; 6-min flight $99) provides an adrenaline-buzz activity in the hills just behind Paekakariki. You fly yourself in a bullet-shaped contraption with a turbo fan at the back, hanging from a cable that dangles 55m from an overhead suspension point; you can reach speeds of up to 120km/h. The site is behind the BP service station on the highway; inquire here or telephone direct.

About 5km north of Paekakariki at MacKay's Crossing, just off SH1, the **Tramway Museum** (☎ 04-292 8361; open 11am-4.30pm Sat, Sun & holidays, daily in Jan) has restored wooden trams that ran in Wellington until its tram system was shut down in 1964. A 2km track runs from the museum through **Queen Elizabeth Park** and down to the beach with good swimming, a playground and walking tracks through the dunes. A return ride is adult/child $4/2. There are **horse-riding** opportunities in Queen Elizabeth Park – contact **Stables in the Park** (☎ 04-292 8787) for information.

An alternative way to travel between Wellington and Paekakariki is over the scenic Paekakariki Hill Rd. If you're cycling south, it's a steep climb for about 3km and smooth sailing after that.

Places to Stay & Eat

Paekakariki Holiday Park (☎ 0800 656 699, 04-292 8292) Powered/unpowered sites $20 for 2 people, cabins $39, tourist flats $56. This large, well-maintained ground is about 1.5km north of the township in Queen Elizabeth Park, not far from the beach.

Paekakariki Backpackers (☎ 04-902 5967, ℮ paekakbp@iph.net.nz, 11 Wellington Rd) Dorm beds $18, twins & doubles $44-48 (some with en suite). This excellent backpackers, set high on a hill and close to town and the beach, is a small, friendly and relaxed place with a great outdoor area and views of the sea and sunset. There's free use of boogie boards and bikes; mosquito nets are provided so you can sleep with doors and windows open to enjoy the sea air. At the time of writing, the owners were about to open a second high-quality backpackers, some 15km south of the original. *Stillwater Lodge* (☎ 04-233 6628, 34 Mana Esplanade) is a small, waterside place on SH1 in Mana, not far from the town, Plimmerton. Mana has its own train station with good connections to Wellington and other centres on the Kapiti Coast. Prices here are similar to those at Paekakariki Backpackers.

There are some good eating options in town, including *Paekakariki Cafe* (☎ *04-292 8860, Beach Rd; open Thur-Sun*), with substantial and innovative meals. *Il Gambero* (☎ *04-292 7040, 9 Wellington St; open Wed-Sun*), next to the backpackers, serves up Italian meals for around $15, and there's excellent fish and chips at *Salt-tea-Towers* (☎ *04-292 8890, cnr Cecil & Tilley Rds*). The *Fisherman's Table* (☎ *04-292 8125*) on SH1 in South Paekakariki has $13.95 meal specials.

PARAPARAUMU
☎ 04 • pop 18,900

Paraparaumu is the principal town of the Kapiti Coast, forming almost a suburban satellite of Wellington, which is within commuting distance. This modern town is made up of Paraparaumu on the main highway, Paraparaumu Beach on the coast 3km west, and Raumati Beach further south. The beach is the coast's most developed, and boat trips to Kapiti Island depart from here.

The name Paraparaumu is rather a mouthful, so locally it's usually shortened to 'para-par-**am**', a corruption of the original. The correct pronunciation is 'pah-ra-pah-ra-oo-moo'; the name means 'Scraps From an Oven' and is said to have originated when a Maori war party attacked the settlement and found only scraps of food in the oven.

Things to See & Do

Paraparaumu Beach, with its beachside park, good swimming and other water activities, is the main attraction. The prestigious **Paraparaumu Beach Golf Club** (☎ 04-902 8200, **W** *www.paraparaumubeachgolfclub.co.nz*) is ranked as NZ's best golf course and regularly hosts the NZ Open (in 2002 the special guest was Tiger Woods; his caddie is from the area). Visitors are welcome, with green fees of $60; you can book online.

On SH1, 2km north of Paraparaumu, the **Lindale Centre** (☎ 04-297 0916; open 9am-5pm daily) is a large tourist complex where you'll find the Lindale Farm Park, with Saturday and Sunday farm shows (adult/child $7.50/4) or the opportunity for farm walks

($5/2.50). There is also an outlet for the region's famous cheese and ice cream – it's well worth dropping in for a taste. Craft shops, galleries and cafes complete the scene.

Another kilometre or so north, just off SH1, the **Southward Car Museum** (☎ 04-297 1221; adult/child $5/2; open 9am-4.30pm daily) has one of the largest collections of antique and unusual cars in Australasia. It has over 200 vehicles on display, including motorbikes, antique aircraft and bicycles. See Marlene Dietrich's Rolls Royce, the 1895 Benz 'horseless carriage' and a gull-winged Mercedes Benz from 1955.

Nyco Chocolates (☎ 04-299 8098; open 9am-5pm daily), on SH1 about 1km south of town, has all kinds of chocolates and confections for sale; tours ($1) leave at 10.30am and 2.30pm Monday to Friday.

The airport on Kapiti Rd has a small **aviation museum** (admission free; open 2pm-4pm Sat & Sun), and is home to the Kapiti Aero Club (☎ 04-902 6536, **W** www .kapiti aeroclub.co.nz), which offers Tiger Moth **aerobatic flights** for $165 (20 minutes) plus **scenic flights** (from $90) in four-seater planes or helicopters. Wellington Gliding Club (☎ 04-297 1341) also operates out of here, offering **gliding** from $89.

Places to Stay & Eat

Lindale Motor Park (☎ 04-298 8046) These prices are for 2 people: powered/unpowered sites $20/19, cabins $40. This park is about 2km north of town off SH1, near the Lindale Centre. It offers sheltered sites and cosy, well-equipped cabins.

Barnacles Seaside Inn (☎ 04-902 5856, **e** copp.motel@paradise.net.nz, 3 Marine Parade) Dorm beds $18, singles $30, twins & doubles $40-45. Barnacles is a lovely old hotel opposite the beachside park at Paraparaumu Beach and has views of the sea. Rooms all have basins; dorm rooms usually have twin beds (no bunks, no large dorms).

There are plenty of motels in the area. *Ocean Motel* (☎ 04-298 6458, **e** oceanmo tel@ihug.co.nz, 42-44 Ocean Rd), not far from the beach is situated in a pleasant garden setting, and has comfortable units from $75; *Wrights by the Sea* (☎ 04-298 7646, e *wrights@paradise.net.nz, 387 Kapiti Rd)* is well positioned for both the beach and golf course and also has units from $75.

There are a number of eateries in and around the shopping centre on the highway, but you'll do better heading away from the traffic and down to the beach, where places to eat are plentiful. *Beachcomber Cafe & Bar* (☎ *04-902 8966, 24 Marine Parade)* is open all day for breakfast, lunch and dinner, *Caffé Riviera* (☎ *04-297 2477, 47 Marine Parade)* does good Italian cuisine, and *Burger Wisconsin* (☎ *04-902 8743, 32 Marine Parade)* offers traditional and gourmet burgers from $5.50 to $10.

KAPITI ISLAND

About 10km long and 2km wide, Kapiti Island is the coastline's dominant feature. Since 1897 the island has been a protected reserve – many bird species that are now rare or extinct on the mainland still thrive here. It is maintained by DOC and access is limited to 50 people per day. You must obtain a permit *(adult/child $9/4.50)* from the DOC office in Wellington (☎ 04-472 5821, W www.doc.govt.nz); this can be done up to three months in advance. Transport is booked separately: **Kapiti Tours** (☎ *0800 527 484, 04-237 7965)* and **Kapiti Marine Charter** (☎ *0800 433 770, 04-297 2585)* offer daily services from Paraparaumu Beach for $30 return. Kapiti Tours also does a guided island walk for an extra $10.

It may be easier to let the visitors centre at Paraparaumu's Coastlands shopping centre (see Information earlier for contact details) take care of arrangements for you. Staff there will organise the DOC permit and transportation (at a cost of $39), but you must give them at least a few days' notice.

WAIKANAE

☎ 04 • pop 9340

About 5km north of Paraparaumu, at Waikanae, the **Nga Manu Sanctuary** (☎ *04-293 4131; adult/child $7.50/3.50; open 10am-5pm daily)*, is a 15-hectare bird sanctuary featuring picnic areas, bushwalks and a nocturnal house with kiwi, owls and tuatara. To reach it, turn seawards from SH1

onto Te Moana Rd and then right down Ngarara Rd; follow the signs; the sanctuary is several kilometres from the turn-off.

There's little reason to linger long in town, but Waikanae has a few motels if the need arises, including *Kapiti Gateway Motel* (☎ *04-293 6053)* on the highway with older-style units from $70, and *Toledo Park Motel* (☎ *04-293 6199, 95 Te Moana Rd)*, down towards the beach, with units from $80.

OTAKI

☎ 06 • pop 5600

Otaki is primarily a gateway to the Tararua Range. It has a strong Maori history and influence: the little town has nine *marae* and a Maori college. The historic Rangiatea Church, built under the guidance of Ngati Toa chief Te Rauparaha nearly 150 years ago, was tragically burnt to the ground in 1995 but there are plans for reconstruction. This was the original burial site of Te Rauparaha.

Most services, including the visitors centre and the train station where buses stop, are on SH1. The main centre of Otaki, with the post office and other shops, is 2km seawards. Three kilometres further on the same road brings you to Otaki's windswept beach.

Otaki Forks

Two kilometres south of the town, scenic Otaki Gorge Rd heads inland from SH1 and leads 19km (9km unsealed) to Otaki Forks, the main western entrance to **Tararua Forest Park**. Otaki Forks has picnic, swimming and camping areas (adult/child $4/2), and there are bushwalks from 30 minutes to 3½ hours in the immediate area; longer tracks lead to huts. Ask DOC in Waikanae or Wellington for advice on longer tracks in the park – you can walk across the Tararua Range, but must bring adequate clothing and be well equipped and prepared for adverse weather. Be sure to sign the intentions book.

River Rock (☎ *06-364 3110,* e *riverrock@xtra.co.nz, Otaki Gorge Rd)*, 8.5km from SH1, has guided kayak and rafting trips on the Otaki River (grades II to III) from $75 per person. Night-time rafting trips are their speciality and are very popular. Pre-booking for any of their trips is essential.

Places to Stay & Eat

Byron's Resort (☎ 0800 800 122, 06-364 8121, Ⓦ www.byronsresort.co.nz, 20 Tasman Rd) Powered/unpowered sites $22/20 for 2 people, tourist flats from $65, motels $78-94. This well-maintained resort by the beach, has a licensed restaurant, pool, spa, sauna, gym, tennis and playgrounds. There's also a self-contained cottage ($100), separate from the resort and right on the beach.

Otaki Oasis (☎ 06-364 6860, ⓔ oobackpackers@xtra.co.nz, 33 Rahui Rd) Dorm beds $17, doubles $45. The 'oasis' is a friendly hobby farm on the inland side of the railway tracks. There is a small but adequate backpackers lodge next to the house. Horseriding lessons and treks are available here.

Te Horo Lodge (☎ 0800 483 467, 06-364 3393, ⓔ tehoro.lodge@xtra.co.nz, 109 Arcus Rd) B&B rooms $180-210. For a touch of luxury, this secluded lodge in Te Horo, halfway between Otaki and Waikanae (head inland from SH1 on School Rd), has a great guest lounge with an impressive stone fireplace, plus pool, spa and lovely gardens.

Brown Sugar Cafe (☎ 06-388 1880) on SH1, just south of the township, serves up great coffee, sandwiches and light meals that you can enjoy in their pretty courtyard garden (open until 4pm daily). In the evening, head for **Byron Brown's**, the restaurant at Byron's Resort.

The Wairarapa

☎ 06 • pop 38,700

The large region east and northeast of Wellington is known as the Wairarapa, named after Lake Wairarapa (Shimmering Waters), a shallow but vast 8000-hectare lake.

This region is principally a sheep-raising district – it boasts three million sheep within a 16km radius of Masterton, the region's main town (but not its most appealing). It also features the Mt Bruce National Wildlife Centre, wineries at Martinborough and very good tramping and camping in regional and forest parks.

The route through the Wairarapa, along SH2, is a mountainous, pleasant alternative

to busy SH1 on the west coast. The downside is that budget accommodation is thin on the ground here – surprisingly, the region has no real backpackers hostels. If you're after quality budget accommodation, you'll be better served on the Kapiti Coast.

Information

The main visitors centre in Wairarapa is in Masterton (☎ 06-378 7373, ⓔ masterton@wairarapanz.com) at 5 Dixon St (bordering Queen Elizabeth Park). It's open 9am to 5pm Monday to Friday, 10am to 4pm Saturday and Sunday. A second visitors centre (☎ 06-306 9043, ⓔ martinborough@wairarapanz.com) is at 18 Kitchener St in Martinborough and is open 10am to 4pm daily. There's an information desk (☎ 06-308 8051) inside the courthouse on the highway in Featherston. A comprehensive website for the area is at Ⓦ www.wairarapanz.com.

The main DOC office (☎ 06-378 2061) for the region is on South Rd, 2km south of Masterton by the aerodrome.

Getting There & Away

From Wellington, the Tranz Metro train to Masterton, stopping at Featherston and Carterton, is the only option, with four or five trains daily on weekdays and two daily on weekends. Wellington to Masterton is $11.50 one way; an adult day excursion ticket for return travel is $15. Wairarapa Coach Lines (☎ 06-378 2961, 0800 666 355) operates a weekday bus between Masterton and Martinborough, plus a shuttle service between Featherston and Martinborough (usually meeting trains). Wally Hammond's City Tours (☎ 04-472 0869) has full-day tours of Wairarapa and Palliser Bay out of Wellington ($110).

Tranzit Coachlines (☎ 0800 471 227, 06-377 1227) has a daily bus between Masterton and Palmerston North ($17), plus a few daily services between Featherston and Masterton via Greytown and Carterton.

MASTERTON
pop 19,900
The main town of the Wairarapa, Masterton can be used as a base for the surrounding

area, although Martinborough is a more pleasant option. Masterton's main claim to fame is the international Golden Shears competition held annually during the first week of March, in which sheep shearing is raised to the level of sport and art.

The town's visitors centre and main attractions are conveniently placed close by each other along Dixon St. The 32-hectare **Queen Elizabeth Park** has sports grounds, an aviary, an aquarium, a small lake, minigolf, children's playgrounds and a miniature railway. Opposite the visitors centre is the well-designed **Aratoi: Museum of Art & History** (☎ 06-370 0001, Dixon St; admission free; open 10am-4.30pm Mon-Fri, 11am-4pm Sat & Sun), a brand new museum displaying the art and cultural heritage of the region.

Places to Stay & Eat
Mawley Park Motor Camp (☎ 06-378 6454, ✉ jclark@contact.net.nz, 15 Oxford St) Powered/unpowered sites $18/16 for 2 people, cabins $27-38. Arrowed off SH2 in the northern part of town is this friendly riverside place with sheltered grounds and decent facilities.

Chanel Court Motel & Backpackers (☎ 06-378 2877, ✉ chanelcourtmotel@xtra .co.nz, 14 Herbert St) Dorm beds $17-20, backpacker doubles & twins $40; motel units $65-75. Chanel Court is off Dixon St and offers pretty average backpackers accommodation and reasonably priced older-style motel units.

Mid-range motels line the highway, particularly in the southern part of town, and include *South Park Motel* (☎ 06-378 9749, 55 High St) and *The Highwayman* (☎ 06-377 4144, 46 High St), both with units from around $75 to $85. *Discovery Motor Lodge* (☎ 06-378 7745, 210 Chapel St) is a new complex with a swimming pool and modern units from $90 (studio) to $185 (two-bedroom suites).

Cafe Char Char is part of the new museum complex on Dixon St and serves good lunch fare, eg salads, paninis and pasta ($7 to $12). For something special, head to elegant *Cafe Cecille* (☎ 06-370 1166) in Queen Elizabeth Park and enjoy the park life from its lovely big veranda. Brunch, lunch and dinner is served daily; well-prepared dinner mains cost $20 to $25. In town, *The Slug & Lettuce* (☎ 06-377 3087, 94 Queen St) is an English-style pub and restaurant doing reasonably priced snacks and meals.

MT BRUCE
The **Mt Bruce National Wildlife Centre** (☎ 06-375 8004; adult/child $8/free; open 9am-4.30pm daily), 30km north of Masterton on SH2, is an important sanctuary for native NZ wildlife, mostly birds. Large aviaries and outdoor reserves have some of the country's rarest and most endangered species, as well as more common species. There's an impressive nocturnal house with kiwi (sightings aren't guaranteed), tuatara and other endangered reptiles. Each species has as natural a habitat as possible, so look closely to find them. Tranzit buses between Masterton and Palmerston North can pick up and drop off here ($8 one way).

CARTERTON, GREYTOWN & FEATHERSTON
A number of rural communities line SH2, each with a minor attraction or two and varying degrees of appeal. Greytown is the pick of the three, for its architecture and the high quality of its cafes and restaurants.

Carterton features the **Paua Shell Factory** (☎ 06-379 6777, 54 Kent St; open daily) with shellfish in a live paua aquarium and tacky or tasteful shell souvenirs. **Ballooning NZ** (☎ 06-379 8223) operates from the factory and offers hot-air ballooning trips ($230).

Greytown was the country's first planned inland town and good examples of **Victorian architecture** line the main street. The quaint **Cobblestones Village Museum** (☎ 06-304 9687, 169 Main St; adult/child $2.50/1; open 9am-4.30pm daily) is an early settlers museum.

In Featherston, the **Fell Engine Museum** (☎ 06-308 9379, cnr Lyon & Fitzherbert Sts; entry by donation; open 9.30am-4pm Mon-Fri, 10am-4pm Sat & Sun) houses the only remaining Fell locomotive in the world, which once ran on three rails to climb 265m up the Rimutaka Incline.

WELLINGTON REGION

Places to Stay & Eat

All three towns have a camping ground and at least one motel, but the only backpackers accommodation is at Featherston.

Leeway Motel (☎ *0800 533 929, 06-308 9811, 8 Fitzherbert St, Featherston)* Camping sites $20 for 2 people, dorm beds $20, motel units $78-85. Offering an assortment of accommodation, friendly, well-kept Leeway has limited backpacker lodgings, with most shared rooms sleeping only two.

In Greytown, there's a basic *camping ground* (☎ *06-304 9837)* scenically located in the park on Kuratawhiti St. Powered/unpowered sites are $14/12 for two people. Good accommodation can be found above the pub: *Greytown Hotel* (☎ *06-304 9138, 33 Main St)* is one of the oldest hotels in NZ and offers B&B (cooked breakfast) for $35 to $40 per person. Rooms have a TV and basin but shared bathroom. There's also a new motel complex, *Oak Estate* (☎ *06-304 8187,* e *oak.estate@xtra.co.nz, cnr SH2 & Hospital St)* offering stylish units from $95.

Still in Greytown, *Main St Cafe* (☎ *06-304 9022, 88 Main St)* serves excellent cafe fare, and there's an adjacent deli with lots of takeaway treats. *Salute!* (☎ *06-304 9825, 83 Main St)* opposite has great gourmet pizzas and Mediterranean-inspired meals, with mains in the $14 to $23 price range.

MARTINBOROUGH

pop 1500

Located south of Greytown, off SH2, Martinborough is the centre for tourism in the Wairarapa. Once just a sleepy town (although it still is on weekdays), it has become very popular with Wellingtonians as a weekend retreat because of the many vineyards in the area. On weekends, Gucci replaces gumboots and the town's fashionable dining establishments fill up. There are some great places to stay if your budget is not too tight, but cheap accommodation is all but nonexistent.

An astounding 26 small **wineries** are near the town and outlined in the excellent, free *Martinborough & Wairarapa Wine Trails* pamphlet. The region produces only 3% of NZ's grapes but a broad range of styles. Martinborough is particularly known for its pinot noir. Head to the **Martinborough Wine Centre** (☎ *06-306 9040, 6 Kitchener St)* to learn more about the local produce and sample a few drops. This great complex sells wine and assorted deli produce, and has a cafe serving light meals and wine by the glass. A local-growers market is held here every Saturday morning.

If all the eating and drinking leaves you feeling a little lazy, **Wet n' Wild** (☎ *06-306 8252, 3 Kitchener St)* can definitely help. It offers jetboat tours ($40), kayaking ($35 for two hours) and trout fishing trips ($290 for three hours, with all gear supplied). It also has vineyard tours or scenic tours taking in Cape Palliser and the seal colony ($50).

Bikes are a good way to get around the wineries and can be rented from Martinborough Bike Rental (☎ 06-306 8477), 36 Jellicoe St, for $25/40 half day/full day. Other attractions around Martinborough include the impressive **Patuna Chasm Walkway**, a four-hour walk ($15) through native bush and a limestone gorge. It's partly on private land, so book in advance on ☎ 06-306 9966.

Places to Stay

Martinborough Camp Ground (☎ *06-306 9336, cnr Princes & Dublin Sts)* Powered/unpowered sites $10/12.50 for two people. Facilities are bare-bones at this very basic and not terribly appealing camping ground behind the town pool. The kitchen has two stoves but no cooking equipment or even tables and chairs.

There are only two motels in town. Central *Martinborough Motel* (☎ *06-306 9048, 43 Strasbourge St)* has basic but comfortable studio units for $60, larger one-bedroom units for $75. *Claremont Motel* (☎ *06-306 9162, 38 Regent St)* is slightly out of town in a pretty, peaceful setting off Jellicoe St and has modern two-storey units from $90.

The visitors centre has a long list of B&Bs, farmstays and self-contained cottages in the area, and will book them for you. Cottages are popular and are available in town and in the surrounding area and cost from around $80 to $160 a double.

Margrain Vineyard Villas (☎ *06-306 9292,* w *www.margrainvineyard.co.nz, cnr*

Ponatahi & Huangarua Rds) Villas $150. If you fancy staying on a vineyard, these spacious, modern villa units on Margrain Vineyard will appeal. Extras include provisions for a continental breakfast in the villa's fridge, plus views from the great balcony.

Martinborough Hotel (☎ *06-306 9350,* Ⓦ *www.martinboroughhotel.co.nz, The Square)* B&B rooms $240-295. This grand old hotel on the main square has been magnificently restored and is now home to 16 spacious and luxurious rooms, each individually decorated with great style. All open out onto the fine wrap around veranda or pretty courtyard garden.

Places to Eat
The eating is excellent in Martinborough, with smart cafes and delis and some very good restaurants.

Martinborough Hotel (☎ *06-306 9350, The Square)* Mains $22-28. The hotel includes a classy bistro and wine bar with an innovative menu and an award-winning wine list. The more casual Settlers Bar within the hotel has a small but well-priced menu of pub food.

Ma Maison (☎ *06-306 8388, Jellicoe St)* Ma Maison, a country cottage 4km south of town, is only open Saturday evening for dinner, and it specialises in a nine-course French *degustation* (tasting) menu, priced around $70. Bookings are essential.

Cafe Medici (☎ *06-306 9965, 9 Kitchener St)* Light meals to $10. This cosy and inviting cafe is a great spot for coffee and cake or a simple lunch of soup with homemade bread, salad, calzone or nachos.

Flying Fish Cafe (☎ *06-306 9270, The Square)* Burgers $5.50-9.50, pizzas from $15. There's something for everyone here, from the all-day brunch to pizza and burgers (traditional and gourmet), plus lunch and dinner items from a changing blackboard menu.

WAIRARAPA COAST
The Wairarapa coast from Palliser Bay to Castlepoint is one of the most remote and intriguing coasts in the North Island. The road to Cape Palliser is very scenic, hemmed in by the sea and the mountains of the Aorangi Range. It also offers grand views across to the South Island, a spectacular sight in winter when the far-off hills are cloaked in snow. On the way, you pass the Wairarapa Wetlands and The Spit at Onoke – both good bird-watching sites. The coast is also the best place for surfing around Wellington.

The **Putangirua Pinnacles**, formed by rain washing silt and sand away and exposing the underlying bedrock, stand like giant organ pipes. Accessible by a track near the car park on the Cape Palliser road, it's a one-hour return walk along a stream bed to the pinnacles, or take the three-hour loop track, which takes in the hills and coastal views.

Not far to the south is the archetypal fishing village of **Ngawi**. The first thing you'll notice is the old bulldozers pulling the fishing boats ashore. Continue on to the Cape Palliser **seal colony**, the North Island's largest breeding area. Whatever you do in your quest for a good photo, don't get between the seals and the sea. If you block off their escape route they are likely to have a go at you!

There are 250 steps up to the Cape Palliser **lighthouse**, from where there are even more breathtaking views of the South Island on a clear day.

Castlepoint, 68km from Masterton, with its reef and the lofty 162m-high Castle Rock, is an awesome place, with protected swimming and plenty of walking tracks. There is an easy 30-minute return walk across the reef to the lighthouse, over 70 species of fossil shells are in the rock. Another one-hour walk goes to a huge limestone cave (take a torch), or take the 1½-hour track from Deliverance Cove to Castle Rock. Keep well away from the lower reef when there are heavy seas; many lives have been lost here.

Places to Stay & Eat
Lake Ferry, just a short detour off the road to Cape Palliser, has a couple of accommodation choices. **Lake Ferry Motor Camp** (☎ *06-307 7873)* has powered/unpowered sites at $20/18 for two people and good basic cabins from $35. **Lake Ferry Hotel** (☎ *06-307 7831)* offers backpacker accommodation (bunks in a basic cabin; no kitchen

facilities) for $25 per person, and twin and double rooms for $55 to $65 depending on size and view. All bathroom facilities are shared. The hotel has a cafe, restaurant, bar and good outdoor area overlooking the water

Castlepoint Holiday Park (☎ *06-372 6705,* e *holiday@castlepoint.co.nz)* is a beachside camping ground with sites at $24 for two people, plus a range of cabins priced from $30 to $70.

FOREST PARKS

Good opportunities for tramping in the Wairarapa are in the Tararua, Rimutaka and Haurangi Forest Parks. There are some fine coastal walks too. Maps and information are available from DOC offices in Wellington and Masterton.

A favourite tramping spot is **Holdsworth**, located at the main eastern entrance to the Tararua Forest Park, where mountain streams run through beautiful virgin forest. The park entrance has swimming, picnic and camping areas (adult/child $4/2), and fine walks including: short, easy family walks; excellent one- or two-day walks; and longer, challenging treks for the experienced, as far as the west coast, near Otaki. The resident conservation officer (☎ 06-377 0022) has maps and information about the area, and an intentions book. Ask about the current weather and track conditions before setting off, and come prepared for all types of weather – the Tararua Forest Park has a notoriously changeable climate. The turn-off to Holdsworth is just south of Masterton on SH2; from there it's about 15km to the park entrance.

Closer to Wellington, the 18km **Rimutaka Incline** offers a full-day walk or a few hours' cycle along a historic old railway line that carried trains between Wellington and the Wairarapa between 1878 and 1955. One end is accessed 10km south of Featherston along Western Lake Rd, the other is on SH2 at Kaitoke, 9km north of Upper Hutt. Take a torch for the tunnels.

The **Kaitoke Regional Park**, 16km north of Upper Hutt on SH2, is good for swimming, rafting, camping, picnicking and walking; it has walks ranging from 20 minutes to six hours long.

SOUTH ISLAND

The deep crevasses of the Dart Glacier on Cascade Saddle Route, Mount Aspiring National Park

View of Mount Cook from Hooker Valley

Fox Glacier

Marlborough & Nelson

Crossing Cook Strait from Wellington to Picton – from the North to the South Island – is an exciting prospect and a bit like entering a new country. (Wellington city is actually marginally south of Picton, so you are really moving east to west.) The South Island is less populated than the North and presents a slightly slower pace of life, which is immediately obvious in the sleepy port of Picton. The landscapes and people are similar yet different, and the Maori influence is less apparent. Although many travellers continue on in the direction of Christchurch or Nelson immediately after crossing, there is plenty of interest in this area, in particular the beautiful inlets and bays of Marlborough Sounds.

To the west is the Nelson region, with some of the best tramping and kayaking possibilities in the country. Nelson is a lively, interesting city, as are the towns of Motueka and Takaka further west towards Golden Bay. Continuing on to the far west is the remote and haunting Farewell Spit.

Marlborough Region

☎ 03 • pop 40,200

The convoluted, sheltered waterways of the Marlborough Sounds are the first sight of the South Island for many visitors arriving on the ferry. Picton is the gateway to the South Island and a good base from which to go walking, fishing, sailing, kayaking and exploring the many hideaways in the Marlborough Sounds. Only a short drive to the south of Picton is Blenheim and the nearby vineyards of the Marlborough wine region.

History

The first European to visit the Marlborough district was Abel Tasman, who spent five days sheltering on the eastern coast of D'Urville Island in 1642. It was to be over

Highlights

- Boating, walking and relaxing on the waterways of the Marlborough Sounds
- Walking the many tramping tracks of Kahurangi National Park, including the Heaphy
- Touring the wineries of the Marlborough Region by bicycle
- Chilling out in the alternative towns of Takaka and Motueka
- Kayaking and walking the stunning Abel Tasman Coastal Track
- Tramping the less crowded Queen Charlotte Track in Marlborough Sounds
- Making the trip to the gannet colony and the lighthouse at the end of remote Farewell Spit

NORTH ISLAND

Marlborough & Nelson

SOUTH ISLAND

Not to scale

MARLBOROUGH & NELSON

100 years before the next European, the British explorer James Cook, turned up – in January 1770 – and remained in the area for 23 days. Between 1770 and 1777 Cook made four visits to the stretch of water he named Queen Charlotte's (now Charlotte) Sound. Near the entrance to Ship Cove a monument commemorates the explorer's

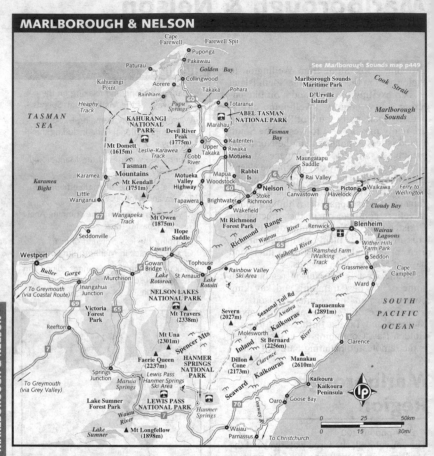

MARLBOROUGH & NELSON

visits. Because of Cook's detailed reports, the area became the best-known haven in the southern hemisphere. In 1827 the French navigator Jules Dumont d'Urville discovered the narrow strait now known as French Pass, and his officers named the island just to the north in his honour.

In the same year a whaling station was set up at Te Awaiti in Tory Channel, which brought about the first permanent European settlement in the district. In June 1840 Governor Hobson's envoy, Major Bunbury, arrived on the HMS *Herald* on the hunt for Maori signatures to the Treaty of Waitangi

and on 17 June he proclaimed the British Queen's sovereignty over the South Island at Horahora Kakahu Island.

Not long after this the Nelson settlers came into conflict with local Maori tribes over ownership of part of the Wairau Plain, which led to an infamous event known as the Wairau Massacre (see the boxed text later). One of the chiefs involved in the conflict, Te Rauparaha, was a formidable man who was, indirectly, a major reason for the British government taking control of New Zealand. He cultivated the captains and crews of visiting whaling ships (they nicknamed him the 'Old

Sarpint') and, with muskets and other weapons he acquired, set out on the wholesale and horrific slaughter of other South Island tribes. In his most gruesome raid he was aided by a Pakeha trader, who transported his warriors and lured the opposing chiefs on board, where they were set upon by Te Rauparaha's men. The ensuing slaughter virtually wiped out the local tribe. When news of this event and the captain's part in it reached Sydney, the British Government finally decided to bring some law and order to NZ and to unruly British citizens operating there.

In March 1847 Wairau was finally bought and added to the Nelson territory. A petition for independence by the settlers then led the colonial government to establish the new region of Marlborough and approve one of the two settlements, Waitohi (now Picton) as the capital. At the same time, the other settlement, known as 'The Beaver', was renamed Blenheim. After a period of intense rivalry between the two towns, including legal action, the capital was transferred peacefully to Blenheim in 1865.

PICTON
pop 3600
Picton, a pretty little port at the head of Queen Charlotte Sound, is not just the marine gateway to the South Island, but also the best base from which to begin exploring the Marlborough Sounds, particularly the Queen Charlotte Track. Picton is a small borough, surprisingly so if you've just come in on the ferry from Wellington. It's a hive of activity when the ferry is in and during the peak of summer, but rather slow and sleepy any other time. The town is built around an enclosed harbour and deep-water port, full of yachts and fishing boats – it's said to be the second-largest marina after Auckland's.

Information
The efficient Picton visitors centre (☎ 03-5737 7477, e pvic@destinationmarlborough .com), 200m from the ferry terminal, has good maps, information on walking in the sounds area and Internet facilities, and can book tours, transport and accommodation. There is a DOC counter here that's staffed during summer. The centre is open 8.30am to 5pm daily.

The Railway Station (☎ 03-573 8857), across the road in the Picton train station, is a private booking office for ferries, trains and buses.

Ferry tickets can be booked directly at the ferry terminal and there's an InterCity booking desk there. The terminal also has conveniences such as a laundrette, public showers, phones and Internet access.

The Marlin Motel (☎ 03-573 6784) at 33 Devon St is the Automobile Association (AA) agent.

Things to See & Do
Between the information centre and the ferry wharf is the battered but still floating hull of the old East Indiaman *Edwin Fox*, now housed under a new shelter. Built of teak in Bengal, the 157ft (48m), 760-ton vessel was launched in 1853. During its long and varied career it carried convicts to Perth (Australia), troops to the Crimean War and immigrants to NZ. The **Edwin Fox Maritime Centre** *(☎ 03-573 6868; adult/child $5/1, open 8.45am-5pm daily)* has a few maritime exhibits and leads through to the vessel, which is gradually being restored.

At the time of writing, a new **aquarium** was being built alongside the Edwin Fox Maritime Centre.

On the eastern side of Shakespeare Bay, across the inlet from the town centre via the footbridge, is the scow (barge) **Echo** *(adult/child $3/1)*, which houses a gallery of historical photographs and a giant crab collection. Built on the Wairau River in 1905, the *Echo* shipped around 14,000 tons of freight a year between Blenheim and Wellington, and was only retired in 1965. Its future appears to be as a cafe-bar, which will be on the upper deck.

The excellent little **Picton Museum** *(☎ 03-573 8283; adult/child $3/50c; open 10am-4pm daily)* is on the foreshore, right below London Quay. Interesting exhibits include whaling items such as a harpoon gun, and a Dursley Pederson bicycle built around 1890.

The visitors centre has a map showing several good **walks** in and around town. An

MARLBOROUGH & NELSON

PICTON

PLACES TO STAY
1 Bay Vista Motel
2 Bayview Backpackers
3 Waikawa Bay Holiday Park
6 Bell Bird Motel
7 Blue Anchor Holiday Park
14 Picton Lodge
15 Atlantis Backpackers;
   Diver's Rest
20 The Villa
21 Bougainvillea Lodge
23 Tourist Court Motel
26 Harbour View Motel
27 Marineland Motels
   & Guesthouse
28 The Gables
29 Wedgewood House
31 House of Glenora
33 Sequoia Lodge Backpackers

34 Picton Campervan Park
35 Juggler's Rest

PLACES TO EAT
13 Toot 'n' Whistle Inn
16 Le Cafe
17 Seaspray Café
18 Kiwi Takeaways
19 Marlborough Terranean;
   Cibo
22 Picton Village
   Bakery
24 Barn Café
25 Settler's Arms

OTHER
4 Cook Strait Ferry Terminal; InterCity
5 Edwin Fox Maritime Centre
8 Echo
9 Town Wharf - Marlborough Sounds
   Adventure Company; Cougar Line; Endeavour
   Express; Beachcomber Cruises; Buzzy Bikes &
   Boat Rentals
10 Picton Museum
11 Picton Visitors Centre; Dolphin Watch Marlborough
12 Railway Station Booking Office
30 Mariners Mall
32 Automobile Association (AA)
   Agent; Marlin Motel

MARLBOROUGH & NELSON

The Snout

Queen Charlotte
Sound

Waikawa
Bay

To Momorangi Bay Motor Camp (15km),
turn-off to Portage (22km) &
Havelock (35km)

Ferry to Wellington

Waikawa
Marina

To Port
Underwood

Mabel
Island

Pine
Bay

Snout Walkway

Beach Rd

Waikawa

Hula St

Waikawa Rd

Weimarama

Shakespeare
Bay

Scenic
Reserve

Bobs
Bay

Endeavour
Park

Ranui St

Booms Valley Rd

Moana View Rd

Port
Shakespeare

Queen Charlotte Dr

Victoria
Domain
Lookout

Bobs Bay Path

Lookout

Picton
Harbour

Breakwater

Picton

Dublin St

Broadway

Buller St

Durham St

Kent St

Wairau Rd

Auckland Rd

Scotland
St

To Koromiko (8km)
& Blenheim
(28km)

Carden Tce

See Enlargement

Lookout

Tirohanga Walkway

Hampden St

Leicester St

Sussex St

Lincoln

Suffolk St

Surrey Rd

Waikawa Rd

Milton

Newgate St

Wairau Rd

Picton

Picton
Harbour

Waitohi
Domain

Picton
Harbour

London Quay

Dublin St

Devon St

York St

Waitohi River

Auckland St

Waikawa Rd

Wellington

High St

Taranaki St

Broadway

Buller St

Otago St

Nelson
Square

Nelson
Square

Canterbury St

Scenic
Reserve

easy 1km track runs along the eastern side of Picton Harbour to Bob's Bay. The **Snout Walkway** carries on along the ridge from the Bob's Bay path and has great views of the length of Queen Charlotte Sound. Allow three hours for the walk.

The **Tirohanga Walkway**, beginning on Newgate St, takes about 45 minutes each way and offers panoramic views of Picton and the sounds.

Organised Tours & Activities
Beachcomber Cruises (☎ *0800 624526, 03-573 6175*) has two-hour Round-the-Bay cruises to the southern part of the sound departing at 10.15am and 2.15pm ($35). Its full-day Mail Boat cruises on Queen Charlotte and Pelorus Sounds are genuine NZ Post rural delivery services. The Queen Charlotte Sound cruise departs daily except Sunday at 1.30pm ($58, 4hrs); the Pelorus Sound cruise visits remote outposts on Tuesday, Thursday and Friday departing from Picton (via Portage) at 10.15am – it actually starts in Havelock at 9.30am ($90, full day). Other options include the Portage Luncheon Cruise ($39, lunch is extra), Ship Cove Cruise ($48) and a variety of 'cruise and walk' options.

There are also a number of cruise and walk opportunities with **Cougar Line** (☎ *0800 504090, 03-573 7926*) and the backpacker-friendly **Endeavour Express** (☎ *03-579 8465*) – see Track Transport in the Queen Charlotte Track section later.

Dolphin Watch Marlborough (☎ *03-573 8040,* **W** *www.dolphinwatchmarlborough .co.nz; trips from $65*), beside the visitors centre, has eco-boat tours visiting the Motuara Island bird sanctuary and spotting seals, sea birds and dolphins with daily departures at 8.45am and 1.45pm.

Sounds Connection (☎ *03-573 8843,* **W** *www.soundsconnection.co.nz, 10 London Quay*) runs various trips including half-day fishing trips ($59) and winery tours by bus to the Marlborough Wine Region ($45/55 half/full day).

Diving opportunities around the sounds include the wreck of the *Mikhail Lermontov*, a Russian cruise ship that sank in Port Gore in 1986. It's said to be the world's biggest diveable cruise shipwreck. There are also some smaller wreck dives. **Diver's World** (☎ *03-573 7323,* **W** *www.picton diversworld.co.nz, London Quay*) has dives on *Mikhail Lermontov*, including transport, gear hire and lunch, for $190 (bookings essential); dives to Karaka Point ($59) and Double Bay ($120); night dives ($79); equipment hire and dive courses.

See the Marlborough Sounds section for sea kayaking options out of Picton, Anakiwa and Havelock.

Places to Stay
Camping & Cabins The *Picton Campervan Park* (☎ *03-573 8875, 25 Oxford St*) is a small park in the middle of town with powered sites at $10 per person, and an amenities building with lounge, kitchen and laundry.

Blue Anchor Holiday Park (☎ *03-573 7212,* **e** *2stay@blueanchor.co.nz, 78 Waikawa Rd*) Unpowered/powered sites $10/11 per person, cabins $35-48 per double, self-contained units $60-80 per double. Located only about 1km from the town centre, the Blue Anchor is a well-kept, modern park with a pool.

Waikawa Bay Holiday Park (☎ *0800 924529, 03-573 7434, 302 Waikawa Rd*) Unpowered/powered sites $9 per person, cabin doubles $30-38, self-contained units $50-75. Waikawa Bay, about 4km from Picton, is a pleasant spot to stay and this park has a good range of accommodation, grassy sites and a courtesy van.

Hostels A popular choice is *The Villa* (☎ *03-573 6598,* **e** *stay@thevilla.co.nz, 34 Auckland St*) with dorm beds for $20, doubles & twins $49. It's quite small and has a buzzy atmosphere so book ahead. Rates include free breakfast and a hot spa.

Bougainvillea Lodge (☎ *03-573 6536,* **e** *bavarian@voyager.co.nz, 42 Auckland St*) Dorm beds $18, twins/doubles $42, budget double $38. Next door to the Villa, the Bougainvillea is not as stylish (or as busy), but it's comfortable enough and breakfast is included. There's also a small budget double.

Sequoia Lodge Backpackers (☎ *0800 222 257, 03-573 8399,* e *stay@sequoia lodge.co.nz, 3a Nelson Square)* Dorm beds $18, en suite doubles $48. Sequoia Lodge, named after one of the enormous trees out the front, is a big place but very comfortable and well run. It has a giant outdoor chess set, fresh bread nightly, and percolated coffee morning and evening.

Atlantis Backpackers (☎ *03-573 7390,* e *diversworld@compuserve.com, London Quay)* Dorm beds $14-18, doubles $44. It's hard to miss this huge new hostel as you wander down from the ferry terminal. Adjacent to Diver's World, it's a big, impersonal place but the facilities, including an indoor heated pool, are good.

Bayview Backpackers (☎ *03-573 7668,* e *bayview.backpackers@xtra.co.nz, 318 Waikawa Rd)* Dorm beds $17, singles $30-36, doubles & twins $40-45. This backpackers is on Waikawa Bay, 4km from central Picton, and has bay views and pleasant porch areas. The friendly owners offer free pick-up and drop-off from town and water sports equipment and bicycles are free for guests. They've built a new, fully-equipped house next door with excellent doubles and a large balcony.

Juggler's Rest (☎ *03-573 5570,* e *jug glers-rest@xtra.co.nz, 8 Canterbury St)* Dorm beds $16, doubles $40. If you're a juggler or even marginally interested in learning, this is the place to be – it's run by professional jugglers and lessons are offered free. Demonstrations of fire juggling/eating and other tricks are part of the fun.

Picton Lodge (☎ *03-573 7788, 0800 223 367,* e *picton.lodge@xtra.co.nz, 9 Auck land St)* Dorm beds $15 per person, doubles & twins $38. This is the closest place to the ferry terminal and although it's a slightly cramped warren of rooms, the facilities are good and there are plenty of free things on offer such as mountain bikes.

Wedgewood House (☎ *03-573 7797,* e *wedgewoodhouse@xtra.co.nz, 10 Dublin St)* Dorm beds $17, twins $40. This YHA associate is in an old converted guesthouse with two, four or six beds to a room. The office opens periodically until 10pm.

B&Bs & Guesthouses *Marineland Motels & Guesthouse* (☎ *03-573 6429,* e *marineland@xtra.co.nz, 26-28 Waikawa Rd)* B&B singles $45, doubles $59-69, self-contained units $79. Marineland has old-fashioned B&B guesthouse rooms, some with shared bath, and modern self-contained units. There's a pool and plenty of parking.

The Gables (☎ *03-573 6772,* e *gables@ mlb.planet.gen.nz, 20 Waikawa Rd)* Doubles $110-135, cottage $150 ($170 with breakfast). The Gables is a bright B&B with three en suite rooms in the home and two cottages with kitchenette at the back.

House of Glenora (☎ *03-573 6966,* e *glenora.house@clear.net.nz, 22 Broadway)* B&B singles/doubles $55/95, with en suite $65/130. This attractive old house has several bright, colour-themed rooms, some with en suite. The owner runs the International Weaving School and you can see her work and studio and even partake in weaving tuition workshops.

Motels Picton has plenty of motels, many of them on Waikawa Rd just east of the city centre. Most are priced at around $70 to $90 for two.

Tourist Court Motel (☎ *03-573 6331, 45 High St)* and **Bell Bird Motel** (☎ *03-573 6912, 96 Waikawa Rd)* are two cheap options in the town centre, with studio units from $60 a double.

Harbour View Motel (☎ *0800 101 133, 03-573 6259, 30 Waikawa Rd)* Units $65-80. Harbour View has an elevated position which offers good views.

Bay Vista Motel (☎*/fax 03-573 6733, 307 Waikawa Rd)* Doubles $90-95. Bay Vista, 4km out at Waikawa Bay, has a waterfront location and good-value one- and two-bedroom self-contained units.

Places to Eat

Self-caterers should head to the **Super Value** supermarket in the Mariners Mall.

The **Picton Village Bakery** *(cnr Auck land & Dublin Sts)* bakes Dutch-style 'dark long-baked rye bread' – good for tramping (as it doesn't break up). **Seaspray Cafe** is a typical small-town cafe with booth seating and cheap cooked breakfasts ($5). **Kiwi Takeaways** *(Wellington St)* is the place for fish and chips.

Most of Picton's cafes and restaurants are on High St or facing the waterfront on London Quay.

Le Cafe *(☎ 03-573 5588, London Quay)* Mains $7-18. With a waterfront location and Bohemian air, Le Cafe is a great place for a lingering breakfast or lunch.

Barn Cafe *(☎ 03-573 7440, 48 High St)* Mains $11.50-20. Hearty serves of pizza, pasta, steak and seafood at reasonable prices are the main trade of this licensed American-style restaurant.

Cibo *(☎ 03-573 7171, 33 High St)* This licensed and BYO cafe offers something different, with things like Spanish tapas for lunch and pancakes for breakfast on Saturday and Sunday.

Toot 'n' Whistle Inn *(☎ 03-573 6086, 7 Auckland St)* Mains $9.50-15. Open 7am-3am. This is classier than most of the pubs in Picton and is handy to the ferry terminal. It's open all day for meals and there are cheap bar snacks.

Settler's Arms *(☎ 03-573 6566, Wellington St)* Mains $13.50-22. Open from 3.30pm daily. The Settler's is a charming little bar and courtyard cafe. It has a good wine selection, locally brewed beer on tap and a range of seafood and meat dishes.

Marlborough Terranean *(☎ 03-573 7122, 31 High St)* Mains $25. This is a sophisticated place with a European, not just Mediterranean-inspired, menu featuring many seafood dishes.

Getting There & Away

Air Soundsair (☎ 0800 505 005, 03-520 3080, W www.soundsair.co.nz) has a regular service across the strait to and from Wellington. The 25-minute flight costs $68/125 oneway/return and operates about six times a day. The courtesy shuttle bus to or from the airstrip at Koromiko, 8km south, is included in the price, and there are discounts available to students and backpackers (YHA/VIP).

Bus There are numerous buses that go south to Christchurch and beyond, and as well, plenty headed west to Nelson, from where there are connections going across to the West Coast.

InterCity (☎ 03-573 7025), at the ferry terminal, has a service to Christchurch ($30, 5hrs) via Kaikoura ($20, 2¼hrs) with connections to Dunedin and Invercargill. Another route goes east to Nelson ($19, 2hrs) via Blenheim and Havelock with connections to Greymouth and the glaciers. At least one bus daily on each of these routes connects with a ferry sailing to and from Wellington.

A profusion of smaller shuttle buses heads south to Christchurch and beyond, usually offering a door-to-door service to central accommodation places. They include Atomic Shuttles (☎ 03-573 7477), South Island Connections (☎ 0508 742 669) and Southern Link Shuttles (☎ 03-573 7477). You can book through the visitors centre.

To Nelson, the main shuttles are Atomic, which continues on to Greymouth, Knightline (☎ 03-547 4733 in Nelson), which continues on to Motueka, and Kiwilink (☎ 03-577 8332). All go via Blenheim.

All buses serving Picton operate from the ferry terminal or the visitors centre.

Train The *Tranz Coastal* is a fine, scenic rail journey between Picton and Christchurch, via Blenheim and Kaikoura. It operates daily in each direction, connecting with the *Interislander* ferry. The train departs Picton at 1.40pm and arrives in Christchurch at 7pm. Going the other way it leaves Christchurch at 7am, arriving in Picton at 12.50pm. A free shuttle service links the train station and ferry terminal on both sides of the strait. The adult fare is $54 but there's an older 'backpackers carriage' for $31. There's also a day return fare to Kaikoura for $62/38 adult/child.

Boat *Interislander* ferries (☎ 0800 802 802; W www.interislandline.co.nz) shuttle back and forth between Wellington and Picton four or five times daily (3hrs). The faster *Lynx* does the crossing three times daily, at 2¼ hours a time – it could go faster but speed is restricted by law. Certain

MARLBOROUGH & NELSON

The Wairau Massacre

One of the most infamous early conflicts between settlers in the Nelson region and Maori tribes occurred in 1843. Around this time the opportunistic and unscrupulous New Zealand Company tried to settle part of the Wairau Plain after buying the alleged rights from the widow of a trader, John Blenkinsopp. He claimed he bought the land from the Maori for a 16-pound cannon, and had obtained a dubious deed signed by Maori chiefs who couldn't read English. The cannon is on display in Blenheim.

By 1843 the pressure for land from the Nelson settlers was so great that it led to conflict with the Maori, who denied all knowledge that any part of Wairau was sold. Two chiefs of the Ngati Toa tribe, Te Rauparaha and Te Rangihaeata, arrived from Kapiti to resist survey operations. The Pakeha sent out a hurriedly co-opted armed party led by Arthur Wakefield and Police Magistrate Thompson to arrest the chiefs. The party was met peacefully by the Ngati Toa at Tuamarina, but the Pakeha precipitated a brief skirmish, during which Te Rangihaeata's wife was shot. The Pakeha were then forced to surrender and Rangihaeata, mad with rage, demanded vengeance. Twenty-two of the party, including Wakefield and Thompson, were clubbed to death or shot; the rest escaped through the scrub and over the hills. The event came to be known as the Wairau Massacre.

Tuamarina, the site of the massacre, is 19km south of Picton. The tree near where the skirmish started still stands on the riverbank. In the cemetery, just above the road, is a Pakeha monument designed by Felix Wakefield, youngest brother of Arthur Wakefield, who was killed in the fray.

ferries may be cancelled if the sea is considered too rough – Lynx are usually the first to be cancelled. The standard one-way passenger fare is $52/31 adult/child on the *Interislander* and $68/39 on the *Lynx*, but if you book at least before you should get the saver fares – $36/23 on the *Interislander*. To take a car across costs $179/129

standard/saver on the *Interislander* and $199/149 on the *Lynx*. See the Wellington Region chapter for more information.

Getting Around

Renting a car in Picton is easy and affordable – most agencies allow drop-offs in Christchurch. Avis, Hertz, Thrifty and Budget have rental offices at the ferry terminal. Cheaper companies include Pegasus (☎ 03-573 7733, 1 Auckland St), and Shoestring (☎ 03-573 7788) at Picton Lodge.

Nifty-fifty (50cc) scooters (for which you need a current car licence) can be hired from Buzzy Bikes (☎ 03-573 7853) at the harbour for $15/45 an hour/day. They also have mountain bikes at $10 a day. A good place to hire quality mountain bikes – recommended for going out on the Queen Charlotte Track – is the Marlborough Sounds Adventure Company (☎ 03-573 6078). They have front or full-suspension machines for $40 a day.

See the Marlborough Sounds section for details of cruises, boat connections and water taxis to the sounds.

MARLBOROUGH SOUNDS

The Marlborough Sounds feature many delightful bays, islands, coves and waterways, which were formed by the sea flooding its deep valleys after the ice ages. Parts of the sounds are now included in the Marlborough Sounds Maritime Park, which is actually many small reserves separated by private land, mostly pastoral leases. To get an idea of how convoluted the sounds are, Pelorus Sound is 42km long but has 379km of shoreline.

The Queen Charlotte Track is the main attraction for trampers, but there are other walks such as the two-day Nydia Track and some fine, secluded accommodation is scattered throughout the sounds.

Information is available in Picton from the visitors centre and DOC, and at Havelock.

Queen Charlotte Track

Those put off by the hordes walking the Abel Tasman Track will love this increasingly popular alternative. It may not have

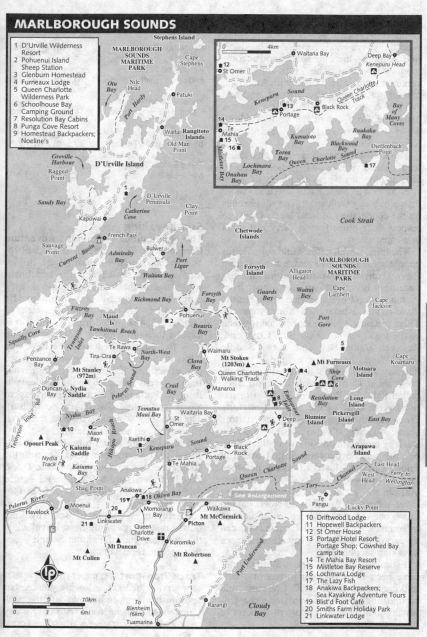

MARLBOROUGH SOUNDS

1 D'Urville Wilderness Resort
2 Pohuenui Island Sheep Station
3 Glenburn Homestead
4 Furneaux Lodge
5 Queen Charlotte Wilderness Park
6 Schoolhouse Bay Camping Ground
7 Resolution Bay Cabins
8 Punga Cove Resort
9 Homestead Backpackers; Noeline's

10 Driftwood Lodge
11 Hopewell Backpackers
12 St Omer House
13 Portage Hotel Resort; Portage Shop; Cowshed Bay camp site
14 Te Mahia Bay Resort
15 Mistletoe Bay Reserve
16 Lochmara Lodge
17 The Lazy Fish
18 Anakiwa Backpackers; Sea Kayaking Adventure Tours
19 Blist'd Foot Café
20 Smiths Farm Holiday Park
21 Linkwater Lodge

MARLBOROUGH & NELSON

the beaches of the Abel Tasman, but it has similarly wonderful coastal scenery, some beautiful coves and – for those who don't like camping – there are some good accommodation options. The 71km-long track connects historic Ship Cove with Anakiwa, passing through privately owned land and DOC reserves. The forest along the coast is lush, and from the ridges you can look down on either side to Queen Charlotte and Kenepuru Sounds.

You can do the walk in sections using local boat services or do the whole three- to four-day journey. There are plenty of camp sites as well as hostels and hotels no more than a half day walk apart. The route relies on the cooperation of local landowners, so respect their property and carry out what you carry in.

The track is well defined and suitable for people of all ages and average fitness. Ship Cove is the usual starting point, mainly because it is easier to arrange a boat from Picton to Ship Cove than vice versa, but the walk can also be started from Anakiwa. There is a public phone at the Anakiwa end of the track, but not at the Ship Cove end. Between Camp Bay and Torea Saddle you'll find the going toughest. About halfway along there's an excellent viewpoint about 15 minutes off the main track called Eatwell's Point. For more information, get a copy of the *Queen Charlotte Track* pamphlet from DOC or the visitors centre in Picton. It's also possible to do the track by mountain bike in two or three days but the section between Ship Cove and Punga Cove is closed to bikers between December 1 and February 28. At this time you can still get dropped by boat at Punga Cove and ride to Anakiwa; fit riders can do this is one day, making it a popular day trip in summer. As with Abel Tasman, you can do part of the trip by sea kayak; see the sea kayaking section later.

Estimated distances and walking times have been revised down in recent years, making some of the DOC literature and signposting somewhat outdated. The following route estimates apply to walkers of moderate fitness:

route	distance	time
Ship Cove to Resolution Bay	4.5km	2 hrs
Resolution Bay to Endeavour Inlet	10.5km	2½ hrs
Endeavour Inlet to Camp Bay/Punga Cove	11.5km	3½ hrs
Camp Bay/Punga Cove to Torea Saddle/Portage	20.5km	6½-7 hrs
Torea Saddle/Portage to Mistletoe Bay	7.5km	3 hrs
Mistletoe Bay to Anakiwa	12.5km	3 hrs

Sea Kayaking

The **Marlborough Sounds Adventure Company** (☎ *0800 283283, 03-573 6078,* **W** *www.marlboroughsounds.co.nz)*, in Picton, organises sea-kayak trips and bushwalks around the sounds. The kayak trips range from a three-hour twilight paddle ($40) to one-day ($85 including lunch) to four-day ($845) guided trips. You can rent kayaks for solo trips for $50 per person (less for multi-day rentals). The three-day Ultimate Sounds Adventure combines one day of walking (Ship Cove to Endeavour Inlet), one day mountain biking (Endeavour Inlet to Portage) and a final day spent kayaking (around Grove Arm to Picton). The cost of $390 includes a guide, transfers, equipment and accommodation.

Sea Kayaking Adventure Tours (☎ *03-574 2765)* operates from Anakiwa, near the southern end of the Queen Charlotte Track. Freedom rentals are $40 a day and guided tours cost from $65 for one day to $280 for three days.

There are a couple of sea kayaking outfits that are operating from Havelock at the southern end of Pelorus Sound – see that section for details.

Track Transport A number of boat operators service the track, allowing you to start and finish where you like and offering pack transfers so you can walk with only a day pack and have your gear waiting for you at your accommodation. The main operators in Picton are Endeavour Express (☎ 03-579 8465, W www.boatrides.co.nz) and Cougar Line (☎ 0800 504 090, 03-573 7925), both at the Town Wharf. Beachcomber Cruises (☎ 0800 624 526, 03-573 6175) also offers the service. Boats from Picton leave around 9am to 10am and again around 1.30pm.

With Endeavour Express you can buy a round-trip ticket for $50, which gives you transport from Picton to Ship Cove, free pack transfers and a pick-up from Torea Bay or Anakiwa. For a day walk, it will drop you off at Ship Cove and pick you up in the afternoon at Furneaux Lodge for $45. Cougar Line also has the round-trip pass for $58 and has a variety of 'cruise and walk' packages. Bikes and kayaks can be carried on the boats.

West Bay Water Transport (☎ 03-573 5597) covers the southern end of the track by boat, leaving from the southern side of the Picton ferry terminal (West Bay jetty) to Anakiwa, Lochmara Bay and Torea Bay. West Bay has good one- and two-day specials with walks from Torea Saddle or Mistletoe Bay to Anakiwa ($30).

Places to Stay & Eat

Accommodation is scattered throughout the sounds; some places are accessible only by boat, and are delightfully isolated. Prices are reasonable and most places offer free use of dinghies and watersports equipment.

Most popular are those on or just off the Queen Charlotte Track – even with people not walking the trail – but there are many other options. Unless you're carrying a tent it's pretty much essential to book these places in summer. Some places close over winter, so again call ahead to check. DOC camp sites cost $5 per adult.

Queen Charlotte Track There are seven different DOC camping grounds on the track and an interesting variety of lodges and guesthouses. Heading south from Ship Cove (where camping is not permitted), the first camp is the beautifully situated DOC *Schoolhouse Bay camping ground* at Resolution Bay.

Resolution Bay Cabins (☎ 03-579 9411) Camping $10, dorm beds $20, cabins $65-85. This is a delightfully rustic place with backpacker beds and old-fashioned cabins with kitchen and attached bathroom. They have real character with pot belly stoves, ageing furniture and no electricity – it's candles and gas cooking out here!

Furneaux Lodge (☎/fax 03-579 8259, W www.furneaux.co.nz) Camping $8.50, dorm beds $18 ($25 with linen), chalets $110 per double. Furneaux Lodge is a century-old place set amid lovely gardens, and a godsend for thirsty trampers – it has a genuine pub, one of the only pubs in NZ accessible only by boat or foot. The backpackers section here is in a lovely old stone cottage with a big open fire, and there are comfortable self-contained one-bedroom chalets. Meals are available in the bar (lunch) or restaurant (dinner).

Glenburn Homestead (☎ 03-579 8048, e glenburn@marlborough.co.nz) Dorm $24, doubles $75. Between Furneaux and Punga Cove, this is a simple homestay place right on the track with some interesting touches such as a golf driving range – straight into the bay.

There's a *DOC camping ground* at Camp Bay on the western side of Endeavour Inlet.

Punga Cove Resort (☎ 03-579 8561, 0800 809 697, W www.pungacove.co.nz) Dorm beds $35 per person, chalets $155-300. Punga Cove has a separate (and pricey) backpacker section overlooking the bay, as well as a range of A-frame chalets and ageing self-contained units. The resort has a pool, spa, shop, bar and an excellent but expensive restaurant.

Homestead Backpackers (☎ 03-579 8373) Dorm beds $20, doubles $40, cottage $60. Open late-Oct–mid-Apr. A 10-minute walk around the bay from Punga Cove, this cosy old farmhouse has a variety of beds, including a romantic unit separate from the main house.

Noeline's (☎ 03-579 8375) Twins $20 per person. Noeline's, five minutes up the hill from the Homestead, is a friendly, relaxed homestay place with a handful of beds and great views.

The Bay of Many Coves has a *DOC camp site* on the saddle above the track. *Black Rock camp site* is further along the trail above Kumutoto Bay.

Portage Hotel Resort (☎ 03-573 4309, ✉ portage.hotel@xtra.co.nz) Dorm beds $25 ($35 with lincn), doubles $140-235. This resort is an old stalwart on Kenepuru Sound. It's quite flash with an a la carte restaurant, as well as a more casual cafe and bar, but there's also a good backpacker section with lounge and cooking facilities. Even if you're not staying, the bar here is a great spot to sit back with a beer. The hotel has sailboats, windsurfers, fishing, a spa, gym and tennis courts. The *Portage Shop* also has backpacker beds ($25) and rents out yachts, dinghies, kayaks and bikes, and has expensive fuel.

The DOC *Cowshed Bay camp site* is just east around the bay from the resort. Portage can easily be reached by road from Picton or Havelock, or by boat to Torea Bay where you can be picked up by a shuttle.

Lochmara Lodge (☎/fax 03-573 4554, ✉ lochmaralodge@xtra.co.nz) Dorm beds $22, doubles $60-80, units $100-120. Lochmara Lodge is a superb and popular retreat on Lochmara Bay, reached by a side track south of the Queen Charlotte Track, or directly by boat from Picton. As well as a homely backpackers lodge with four- and eight-bed dorms, there are stylish en suite rooms and units with kitchenette, all set in lush surroundings.

Mistletoe Bay Reserve (☎ 03-573 7582) Camp sites $5, cottage beds $10. This DOC camping ground also has three farm cottages with share beds.

Te Mahia Bay Resort (☎ 03-573 4089, ✉ temahia@voyager.co.nz) Dorm beds $25, unit doubles $90-110. This resort is north of the track, just off the main road, in a beautiful bay facing Kenepuru Sound. It has dorm beds and very roomy self-contained units looking out over the water. Powered camp sites are $12.50 per person, and there's a store and kayaks for hire.

Anakiwa Backpackers (☎ 03-574 2334) Dorm beds $15. This small place is right at the southern end of the trail. There are only six beds installed in the downstairs self-contained section.

The *Blist'd Foot Cafe* in Anakiwa is the place to rest your feet at the end of the track. It's near the pick-up point for water transport back to Picton.

Other Sounds Accommodation There are almost 30 DOC camping grounds scattered throughout the sounds, providing water and toilet facilities but not a lot else – none have cooking facilities. Pick up a list in Picton. There are numerous places to stay along Queen Charlotte Drive between Picton and Havelock.

Momorangi Bay Motor Camp (☎ 03-573 7865) Unpowered/powered sites $7/8 per person, 1-/2-/3-person cabins $15/25/30. Momorangi Bay, 15km from Picton on the road to Havelock, is one of several motor camps along Queen Charlotte Drive, close to the water.

Smiths Farm Holiday Park (☎/fax 03-574 2806, ⓦ www.smithsfarm.co.nz) Unpowered/powered sites $9/10 per person, cabin doubles $35-60. This is a cut above your average park with lush camping areas and new cabins (shared facilities or self-contained). It's at Linkwater, just before the turn-off to Portage, and is part of a working beef cattle farm.

Linkwater Lodge (☎ 03-574 2507) Dorm beds $15, singles/doubles $45/75. This homestead cafe on Queen Charlotte Drive has backpacker beds and B&B in double and twin rooms.

Hopewell Backpackers (☎/fax 03-573 4341, ⓦ www.hopewell.co.nz) Doubles/twins $40. Hopewell is a comfortable and highly rated backpackers in a remote part of Kenepuru Sound. Access by road is possible but it's a long, tedious and bumpy drive; the best option is a water taxi from Portage.

St Omer House (☎ 03-573 4086, ✉ stomer.house@xtra.co.nz) Tent sites $20 per person, bunkroom $30 per person, cottage doubles $90, rooms with full board $95 per person. St Omer House has cabins, cottages and full board in the old-fashioned main buildings with good homestyle meals.

Lazy Fish (☎ 03-579 9049, e lazyfish@ voyager.co.nz) Dorm beds $20, doubles $55, cabin doubles $125. The Lazy Fish, 12km from Picton and only accessible by boat, has long been popular as a getaway for budget travellers, though it's gradually moving upmarket. There's a secluded beach and free use of watersports equipment. Book and check prices before organising a boat there ($15 each way).

Pohuenui Island Sheep Station (☎ 03-597 8161, e pohuenui.island@xtra.co.nz) Bunkhouse $25 per person, treehouse $60, homestead doubles with full board $380. This place at Pohuenui, 30km north of Havelock and accessible by boat, is a working sheep station and gets good reports.

D'Urville Wilderness Resort (☎ 03-576 5268, e enquiries@durvilleisland.co.nz) Self-contained units $68-88 per double. Accommodation in the Sounds doesn't get any more remote than this beachfront lodge on d'Urville Island. You can rent a unit and self-cater (there's also an attached cafe-bar), or there's fully catered accommodation (including three meals) at $78 per person per day. To get there it's a 1½-hour drive from the highway (SH6) to French Pass (unsealed after Okiwi Bay), then a water-taxi ride across to the lodge.

Queen Charlotte Wilderness Park (☎ 03-579 9025, e wilderness@truenz .co.nz) 2 nights/3 days $230 per person. North of Ship Cove and extending right up to Cape Jackson, this park is a private farming lease which allows you to continue exploring north of the Queen Charlotte Track. The package includes accommodation in the lodge, dinner and transfers from Picton. As well as opportunities for tramping on a virtually deserted track, there's also boating, kayaking and horse riding.

Getting There & Around

The best way to get around the sounds is still by boat, although the road system has been extended. No scheduled buses service the sounds but much of it is accessible by car. Most of the road to Portage is sealed, but beyond that it's nothing but narrow, forever-winding gravel roads. To drive to

Punga Cove from Picton takes about two hours – by boat it takes about 45 minutes.

Scheduled boats service most of the accommodation on the Queen Charlotte Track (see Track Transport earlier) and are the cheapest way to get around.

Arrow Water Taxis (☎ 025 444689) is one well-known operator at Town Wharf in Picton servicing Queen Charlotte Sound.

HAVELOCK
pop 500

Havelock, at the confluence of the Pelorus and Kaiuma Rivers 35km west of Picton, is a good base from which to explore the more remote parts of Marlborough Sounds, particularly Pelorus and Kenepuru. Founded around 1860 and named after Sir Henry Havelock of Indian Mutiny fame, Havelock was once the hub of the timber milling and export trade, and later became the service centre for gold-mining in the area.

Today it's a tiny place with a thriving small-boat harbour – its claim to fame as the 'green-shelled mussel capital of the world' pretty much sums it up. The tiny **museum** on the main street covers local history.

Information

The Havelock Outdoors Centre (☎/fax 03-574 2114) is on the main street. It's open from around 8am to 5pm daily. Almost opposite, Pelorus Enterprises (☎ 03-574 2633) also has information, books tours and is the combined post office, store, pharmacy and hairdresser!

Walking

There's not much to do in the town itself, but good walks include the four-hour return walk to **Takorika Summit** behind the township and the half-hour walk to **Cullen Point** for good views of Havelock and the sunset.

The **Nydia Track** starts at Kaiuma and ends at Duncan Bay (or vice versa). The suggested walking time is two days or 9½ hours. There are DOC *camping grounds* at Nydia Bay and Duncan Bay, and the DOC *Nydia Lodge* ($12), a 50-bed hut. About halfway along, *Driftwood Lodge* (☎ 03-579 8454; dorm beds $15 per person) offers accommodation.

Nydia Bay was originally the site of a Maori *pa* (fortified village) called Opouri, which means 'Place of Sadness', so named after a bloody battle between members of the same tribe. The walk passes through different habitats of various species of birds.

It's best to get dropped off at Shag Point by water taxi as it is only a five-minute trip past the mudflats; you can arrange a water taxi for around $60 at the other end. Pelorus Sounds Water Taxi (☎ 03-574 2151) is one of the main operators; phone the water taxi or shuttle service from Driftwood Lodge.

Sea Kayaking

Havelock Sea Kayaking Company (☎ 03-574 2114, W www.marlboroughadventures .co.nz; kayak trips $70, freedom hire $45) has full-day sea-kayaking trips on the Marlborough Sounds. They also do fully catered overnight kayaking trips staying aboard a luxury launch for $150 per person per day.

The **Wilderness Company** (☎ 03-574 2610) also has guided day trips ($75), multi-day trips (from $95 per day) and rental ($50 a day).

Organised Tours

Beachcomber Cruises (☎ 0800 624 526, 03-573 6175; round trip $90) takes passengers on the Pelorus mail boat, stopping at isolated homesteads to deliver mail and supplies. The trips depart from Havelock at 9.30am on Tuesday, Thursday and Friday, and return between 5pm and 6pm.

The **Mussel Farm Cruise** (☎ 03-574 2144; half-day cruise $55) visits the mussel farms where you can sample the product.

Havelock Sea Charters (☎ 0800 727 002) has overnight cruises on the sounds for $100, aboard the launch *Foxy Lady*. If that's too much, there are good three-hour lunch cruises for $55.Many water taxis operate out of Havelock and nature cruises can be organised to Maud Island, abode of the rare Hamilton frog, takahe and kakapo. Ask at the Havelock Outdoors Centre.

Places to Stay & Eat

Havelock Motor Camp (☎ 03-574 2339, Inglis St) Near the marina, this camp has unpowered/powered sites for $10 per person, and cabins from $30 per double.

Rutherford YHA (☎ 03-574 2104, e stell@xtra.co.nz, cnr Lawrence St & Main Rd) Tent sites $8 per person, dorm beds $16, doubles $40. This well-equipped place is in an 1881 schoolhouse once attended by Lord Ernest Rutherford, who discovered the atomic nucleus. The enthusiastic manager has information on walks and other local activities.

Chartridge Park (☎ 03-574 2129) Camping $8 per person, bunkhouse $12, double cabins $28. Chartridge Park is 6km south of Havelock at Kaiuma Bridge on SH6. Accommodation is basic but it's a rustic spot with a six-hole golf course and a river running through it.

The small, central **Havelock Garden Motel** (☎ 03-574 2387, fax 574 2376, 71 Main Rd) has units for $69-90 per double.

Mussel Boys (☎ 03-574 2824, 73 Main Rd) Open daily from 11am. Mussel Boys specialises in fresh local mussels, especially 'steamers' and 'flats' (half shells) at $14 and chowders for $9; you can't miss the 'mussel' team playing rugby on the roof.

Getting There & Away

InterCity has Picton-Blenheim-Nelson buses daily. Several shuttle bus operators also ply this route, including Kiwilink and Atomic. There are no buses on the more direct 35km back-road to Picton (Queen Charlotte Drive), but this is a scenic route if you're driving or cycling.

AROUND HAVELOCK

Following the SH6 from Havelock to Nelson, there are a couple of interesting stops.

The tiny township of **Canvastown**, in the Wakamarina Valley 8km west of Havelock, got its nickname in the 1860s, when gold was discovered in the river. By 1864 thousands of canvas tents had sprung up as miners flocked to the prosperous working goldfield, one of the richest in the country. By 1865 the boom was over. Nevertheless, gold is still sometimes found in the area and in 1986 a tourist panned a 5g nugget from the river.

The *Pinedale Motor Camp* (☎ *03-574 2349, 820 Wakamarina Rd*), 8km south of Canvastown, has camping and cabins and you can hire gold pans and other fossicking equipment here.

Another 10km west of Canvastown is **Pelorus Bridge**. The Scenic Reserve here has interesting walks of between 30 minutes and three hours on the Pelorus and Rai Rivers, with waterfalls, a suspension bridge and the steel girder Pelorus Bridge itself. Within the reserve are *tearooms*, *camp sites* at $7 per person, and *cabins* from $24. Ask for the ranger at the *Pelorus Bridge Tearoom* (☎ *03-571 6019*).

BLENHEIM
pop 25,900
The largest town in the Marlborough Sounds region, Blenheim is 29km south of Picton on the Wairau Plains, a contrasting landscape to the sounds. The flatness of the town, at the junction of the Taylor and Opawa Rivers, was a problem in the early days – Blenheim grew up around a swamp, now the reclaimed Seymour Square with its attractive lawns and gardens.

Blenheim itself is a modern, characterless place, but it's the main access town to NZ's biggest wine-growing district, and the place where you'll find most of the accommodation and services. Renwick, 10km west and closer to most of the vineyards, is a good alternative to staying in Blenheim.

During the second weekend of every February, Blenheim hosts the now famous **Marlborough Food & Wine Festival** at Montana's Brancott Estate, just south of Renwick. The comprehensive publication *Wineries of Marlborough* ($2) outlines the festival, restaurants and wineries in the festival, and has profiles on the wine makers themselves.

Information
The Marlborough Visitor Information Centre (☎ 03-577 8080, e mvic@destination marlborough.com) is in the refurbished railway station building on Grove Rd. It's a friendly, efficient place, and is open from 8.30am to 5pm daily.

The AA office (☎ 03-578 3399) is at 23 Maxwell Rd, on the corner of Seymour St. There are email facilities at the Blenheim Library (☎ 03-578 2784) in Arthur St, and at Marlborough Copier Services on Scott St.

Things to See & Do
The 5.5-hectare **Brayshaw Museum Park** (*off New Renwick Rd; admission free; open during daylight hrs*) has several attractions, including a reconstructed colonial village of old Blenheim, early farming equipment, a miniature railway and the Museum & Archives Building. As regional museums go, this is a good one.

Near Seymour Square are relics of Blenheim's violent early history. The tiny **Blenkinsopp's cannon** is in front of the council offices on Seymour St. Originally from the whaling ship *Caroline*, which Blenkinsopp captained, this is reputedly the cannon for which Te Rauparaha was persuaded to sign over the Wairau Plains, hence it's one of the causes of the subsequent massacre at Tuamarina.

Opposite Seymour Square, is the **Millennium Art Gallery** (☎ *03-579 2001; admission by donation*), a modern art gallery with changing exhibitions of work by both local and national artists.

In the area are a number of rural retreats with a variety of landforms and flora, such as native broom or prostrate kowhai. The **Robertson Range** and **Whites Bay** near Port Underwood north of Blenheim have great vistas of Cloudy Bay. **Wairau Lagoons**, to the east of Blenheim, is home to more than 70 bird species.

Activities & Organised Tours
Southern Wilderness (☎/*fax 03-578 4531, 0800 266 266,* w *www.actioninmarlborough.co.nz; ½-/1-day trips from $70/110*) has whitewater rafting trips to the Gowan and Buller rivers. Three-day trips on the Clarence River cost $450.

Back Country Safaris (☎ *03-575 7525; 1/2-day trips $210/310*) organises interesting high-country farm trips up to the Molesworth cattle station, via the Awatere and Rainbow valleys.

MARLBOROUGH & NELSON

Horse-trekking operators in the area include **High Country Horse Treks** (☎ 03-577 9424; treks $30-100), which has treks from one to 4½ hours.

The **Ramshead Farm walking track** (☎ 0800 726 743, W www.ramshead.co.nz) in the Waihopai Valley 32km south-west of Blenheim, is a private high-country sheep station with a homestead and three huts, allowing you to walk from one to four days. The cost is $20/50/80/100 for 1/2/3/4 days, plus $15 for a night at the Ramshead Homestead.

For details on the many **winery tours** out of Blenheim, see the 'The Marlborough Wine Trail' boxed text.

Places to Stay

Camping & Cabins The **Blenheim Bridge Holiday Park** (☎ 0800 268 666, 03-578 3667, e grove.bridge@xtra.co.nz, 78 Grove Rd), at the northern end of town has camp sites ($10 per person) by the river, cabins from $40-50 per double and units from $60 per double.

Spring Creek Holiday Park (☎ 03-570 5893, Rapaura Rd) Unpowered/powered sites $10 per person, lodge beds $11, cabins $30-42. Spring Creek is 6km out towards Picton and about 500m off SH1. It's in a peaceful location near a good fishing creek but it's a tired-looking place.

Hostels The **Grapevine** (☎ 03-578 6062, e rob.diana@xtra.co.nz, 29 Park Terrace) Dorm beds $17, doubles $36-40. The Grapevine, in an old maternity home, is a homely place with cot-like dorm beds. The big advantage is the Opawa River running right past the back door – you can borrow canoes for free.

Koanui Backpackers (☎ 03-578 7487, e koanui@xtra.co.nz, 33 Main St) Dorm beds $18, twins & doubles $44. This is a bright, friendly place popular with itinerant fruit-pickers. There's a TV lounge with free videos. The reception and car park is at the back. When it's not busy they offer singles for $35.

Jacks Backpackers (☎ 0800 864 382, 03-578 7375, e hjscott@xtra.co.nz, 144 High St) Dorm beds $20, doubles $50. This is a new backpackers with a spacious lounge/TV area but tiny kitchen. Breakfast is free.

There's a good backpackers at Renwick – see Around Blenheim later.

Guesthouses, Motels & Hotels As well as plenty of varied accommodation in Blenheim itself, there are some lovely places scattered around among the vineyards, particularly along Rapaura Rd.

Stonehaven (☎ 03-572 9730, 414 Rapaura Rd) Singles $90-120, doubles $160-180. Staying at a vineyard is a great way to absorb the atmosphere, and Stonehaven is a lovely B&B with three guest rooms in a solid stone and cedar home.

Vintner's Retreat (☎ 03-572 7420, W www.thevintnersretreat.co.nz, 55 Rapaura Rd) Doubles $173-240. The Vintner's Retreat is a new place in the midst of the Renwick vineyards. There are three types of fully self-contained two- and three-bedroom villas, all very roomy and tastefully decorated. Because the rates are on a sliding scale for the number of guests/nights, a group of six can have the biggest lodge for less than $40 per person.

Ancora Uno Piu (☎ 03-578 2235, e unopiu@iname.com, 75 Murphy's Rd) B&B singles/doubles $125/175, cottage doubles $190. This Italian-run boutique homestead is good for a romantic getaway and there's a separate two-bedroom mud-brick cottage for rent.

Old Saint Marys Convent (☎/fax 03-570 5700, W www.convent.co.nz, Rapaura Rd) B&B doubles $265. Once a convent, this rather exclusive place is set in a lovely garden, reached by a lavender-lined drive, and has it's own chapel. The magnificent interior features a kauri staircase and full-size snooker table.

Chardonnay Lodge (☎/fax 03-570 5194, e chardonnaylodge@xtra.co.nz, 1048 Rapaura Rd) B&B doubles $95. Set in a big, tree-filled garden, this affordable lodge has comfortable self-contained units, a pool and a tennis court.

There are dozens of motels lining the highway (SH6) into Blenheim, most cost

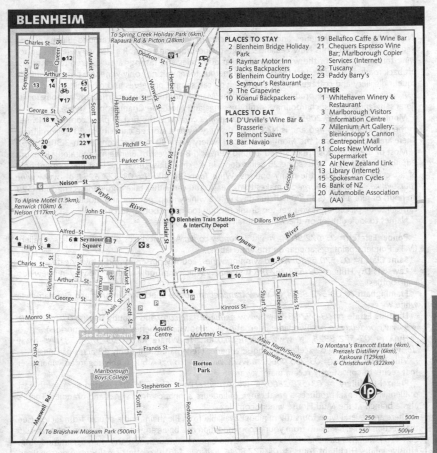

BLENHEIM

To Spring Creek Holiday Park (6km), Rapaura Rd & Picton (28km)

To Alpine Motel (1.5km), Renwick (10km) & Nelson (117km)

Blenheim Train Station & InterCity Depot

To Brayshaw Museum Park (500m)

To Montana's Brancott Estate (4km), Prenzels Distillery (6km), Kaikoura (129km) & Christchurch (322km)

PLACES TO STAY
2 Blenheim Bridge Holiday Park
4 Raymar Motor Inn
5 Jacks Backpackers
6 Blenheim Country Lodge; Seymour's Restaurant
9 The Grapevine
10 Koanui Backpackers

PLACES TO EAT
14 D'Urville's Wine Bar & Brasserie
17 Belmont Suave
18 Bar Navajo
19 Bellafico Caffe & Wine Bar
21 Chequers Espresso Wine Bar; Marlborough Copier Services (Internet)
22 Tuscany
23 Paddy Barry's

OTHER
1 Whitehaven Winery & Restaurant
3 Marlborough Visitors Information Centre
7 Millenium Art Gallery; Blenkinsopp's Cannon
8 Centrepoint Mall
11 Coles New World Supermarket
12 Air New Zealand Link
13 Library (Internet)
15 Spokesman Cycles
16 Bank of NZ
20 Automobile Association (AA)

MARLBOROUGH & NELSON

$70 to $100 a double. Cheap options include **Raymar Motor Inn** (☎ 03-578 5104, 164 High St), and **Alpine Motel** (☎ 03-578 1604, 0800 101 931, 148 Middle Renwick Rd) with units from $60 a double.

Blenheim Country Lodge (☎ 0800 655 079, 03-578 5079, e bclhotel@xtra.co.nz) Doubles $95-165. More upmarket, this hotel-motel has nicely furnished rooms, a pool, spa and an excellent restaurant.

Places to Eat

Blenheim has a compact shopping area with several good cafes and restaurants, or you can dine among the vines at some of the region's vineyards.

For pub food and some occasional live entertainment, **Paddy Barry's** (☎ 03-578 7470, 51 Scott St) is a big, vaguely Irish pub that serves filling meals ($10-14) and it features an outdoor deck.

Belmont Suave (☎ 03-577 8238, 67 Queen St). Bagels from $5.50, Thai dishes $16-18. Belmont Suave is an outstanding little bagelry (by day) and Thai kitchen. This may seem an odd combination, but the food is good and reasonably priced and there's a cosy dining area.

The Marlborough Wine Trail

With more than 50 wineries and countless acres of vineyards scattered around Blenheim and Renwick, Marlborough is New Zealand's biggest wine-producing area. It's also very well set up for wine-touring – many of the wineries with cellar door sales and tastings are clustered together just off back roads that are perfect for cycling. Numerous tours visit not only wineries, but breweries, a liqueur distillery and cottage industries where you can sample preserves and olive oil.

A variety of wines are produced here, but the Marlborough region is particularly famous for its floral sauvignon blancs, chardonnays, fruity rieslings and Methode Champenoise styles.

Montana (☎ 03-578 2099, W *www.montanawines.com*) was the first to plant commercial vines in the region 30 years ago and is NZ's largest winery (with a storage capacity of 20 million litres). There are regular tours of the Montana Brancott winery every 30 minutes from 10am-3.30pm ($5).

Most of the vineyards are clustered around Renwick, 8km west of Blenheim, and along Rapaura Rd, north of Renwick. With some 25 cellar doors in a 5km radius, this is the best place to get hold of a bicycle and explore the many options. **Wine Tours By Bike** (☎ 03-577 6954, W *www.wine toursbybike.co.nz, 55 George St)* makes things easy. You can either take a guided cycling tour ($25 an hour) or hire a bike ($35/50 half/full day) with a winery map, pannier and mobile phone so you can call to be picked up if you get too drunk (or buy too many bottles to carry).

Names to look out for on the wine trail (all open daily) include:

Ponder Estate (☎ 03-572 9034, W *www.ponder.co.nz*) Also produces olive oil and has a gallery (Mike Ponder's paintings appear on the wine labels).

Saint Clair (☎ 03-570 5280) Award-winning wines, country preserves and a lovely cafe.

Lawsons Dry Hills (☎ 03-578 7674) A fine winery which is proudly leading the way in screw-top wine bottles!

Framingham (☎ 03-572 8884, W *www.framingham.co.nz*) Specialises in aromatic German-style white wines.

Nautilus Estate (☎ 03-572 9374, W *www.nautilusestate.com*) and **Cloudy Bay** (☎ 03-520 9040, W *www.cloudybay.co.nz*) Two large internationally renowned wineries (both big exporters).

Huia (☎ 03-572 8326, W *www.huia.net.nz*) and **Te Whare Ra** (☎ 03-572 8581, W *www .te-whare-ra.co.nz*) Two excellent boutique wineries (Te Whare Ra has only 18 acres of vines).

Villa Maria Estate (☎ 03-255 0660, W *www.villamaria.co.nz*) A big, highly regarded winemaker that seems to consistently reel in major awards.

Prenzel Distillery (☎ 03-578 2800, W *www.prenzel.com, Sheffield St*) Located 6km south-east of Blenheim, Prenzel produces a great range of liqueurs, schnapps, fruit wines and brandies. There's also a branch at the Mud House winery complex.

There are several wine tours (by minibus) available from Blenheim and a couple from Picton (see that section earlier). Pick up from your accommodation can be arranged. **Barry's Wine Tours** (☎ 025 264 4704; half/full day $45/70) is one of the more personal tours and Barry is an accommodating, effusive guide. **Highlight Tours** (☎ 03-577 9046; half-day $45) also offers small-group personalised tours.

Deluxe Travel Lines (☎ 0800 500 511, 578 5467, W *www.deluxetravel.co.nz; wine tour $45)* is a bigger operator with a six-hour tour which includes the guided tour at Montana. Departures can also be arranged from Picton.

Bar Navajo (☎ 03-577 7555, 70 Queen St) Mains $12.50-18. This refurbished bar with earthy decor and Indian theme is quite a trendy place for a drink or meal.

On Scott St you'll find a couple of modern, Mediterranean-style places. *Chequers Espresso Wine Bar* is a cool, open-front place with a loungy section and panini and pasta on the menu. *Tuscany* is more traditional, with a nice courtyard garden and pool tables.

D'Urville Wine Bar & Brasserie (☎ 03-577 9945, 52 Queen St) Lunch $5-14, mains $25. Behind an imposing facade, this elegant, highly rated restaurant serves regional produce and a big selection of local wines.

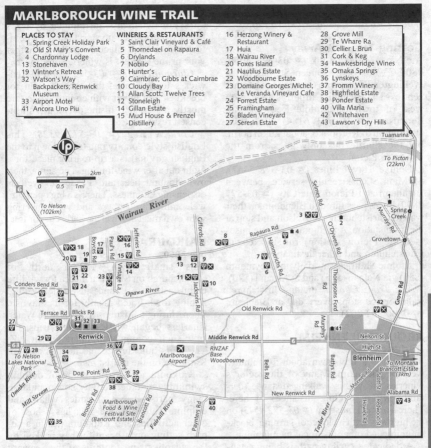

MARLBOROUGH WINE TRAIL

PLACES TO STAY
1 Spring Creek Holiday Park
2 Old St Mary's Convent
4 Chardonnay Lodge
13 Stonehaven
19 Vintner's Retreat
32 Watson's Way Backpackers; Renwick Museum
33 Airport Motel
41 Ancora Uno Piu

WINERIES & RESTAURANTS
3 Saint Clair Vineyard & Café
5 Thornedael on Rapaura
6 Drylands
7 Nobilo
8 Hunter's
9 Cairnbrae; Gibbs at Cairnbrae
10 Cloudy Bay
11 Allan Scott; Twelve Trees
12 Stoneleigh
14 Gillan Estate
15 Mud House & Prenzel Distillery

16 Herzong Winery & Restaurant
17 Huia
18 Wairau River
20 Foxes Island
21 Nautilus Estate
22 Woodbourne Estate
23 Domaine Georges Michel; Le Veranda Vineyard Cafe
24 Forrest Estate
25 Framingham
26 Bladen Vineyard
27 Seresin Estate

28 Grove Mill
29 Te Whare Ra
30 Cellier L Brun
31 Cork & Keg
34 Hawkesbridge Wines
35 Omaka Springs
36 Lynskeys
37 Fromm Winery
38 Highfield Estate
39 Ponder Estate
40 Villa Maria
42 Whitehaven
43 Lawson's Dry Hills

MARLBOROUGH & NELSON

Bellafico Caffe & Wine Bar (☎ 03-577 6072, 17 Maxwell Rd) Lunch \$10-13.50, dinner \$26. Bellafico has an interesting, varied European menu.

Wineries Several vineyards have pleasant cafes or restaurants attached (see the Marlborough Wine Trail map).

Whitehaven (☎ 03-577 6634, Dodson St) Mains \$20-26. Located just north of the town centre, Whitehaven serves up lunch and dinner daily.

La Veranda Vineyard Cafe (☎ 03-572 9177, Vintage Lane), at Domaine Georges Michel, is also recommended for its fine setting and international cuisine.

Twelve Trees (☎ 03-572 9054, Jacksons Rd) Open 9am-5pm daily. This restaurant at Allan Scott's winery, is a recommended cafe with an innovative blackboard menu.

Other winery restaurants include *Gibbs at Cairnbrae* (☎ 03-572 8048, 258 Jacksons Rd), open for lunch and dinner; *Gillan Estate* (Rapaura Rd); *Highfield Estate* (☎ 03-572 8592, Brookby Rd) in the Omaka Valley; the upmarket *Herzog* (☎ 03-572 8770, 81 Jeffries Rd); *Montana Brancott Estate* (☎ 03-578 2099, SH1) with a cafe open from 9am-5pm; and *Wairau River Wines* (☎ *03-572 9800, Rapaura Rd*).

Getting There & Away

Air New Zealand Link (☎ 03-578 4059, 0800 737 000), 29 Queen St, has direct Wellington flights with connections to other centres. The Blenheim airport is about 6km west of town on Middle Renwick Rd. Soundsair (☎ 03-573 6184) flies from Wellington to Korimoko, about 20km north, but the shuttle bus only goes from the airport to Picton.

Deluxe Travel Lines (☎ 03-578 5467), 45 Main St, has regular services between Blenheim and Picton. InterCity (☎ 03-577 2890) buses pass through Blenheim on their way to Christchurch and Nelson and stop at the train station. A plethora of shuttle buses (see the Picton section) run to Nelson, Christchurch and other destinations.

Atomic Shuttles runs daily to Greymouth ($50) via Nelson ($15) and St Arnaud ($20).

The *Tranz Coastal* Picton-Christchurch train service stops every day at Blenheim (☎ 0800 802 802).

AROUND BLENHEIM
Renwick

Renwick is a tiny town about 10 minutes west of Blenheim. Many of the region's wineries are within walking distance (certainly within cycling distance) of here. There's a small **museum** (☎ *03-572 8543*) on the highway with a clutter of farming, blacksmithing and other historical memorabilia.

A dedicated **cycling path** is being established around Renwick town and out through the surrounding vineyards. You can borrow bikes and get more information from Watson's Way Backpackers.

Watson's Way Backpackers (☎/fax *03-572 8228, 56 High St*) Dorm beds $19, doubles $42, en suite doubles $47. This is a great little place to stay. There's a purpose-built section at the back, in a nice garden with small three- and four-bed dorms and nice en suite doubles. Tent camping in the garden costs $10 and there's free bike use.

Airport Motel (☎ *03-572 8767, 0800 767 797, 46 High St*) Doubles $79. Why this motel thinks its proximity to an airport is an attraction when it's surrounded by NZ's finest wineries is a mystery, but it's a comfortable enough place to park – whether your prime interest is wineries or airports.

Clarmont Cafe (☎ *03-572 8934*) In Renwick's town centre, this cafe is open for breakfast and lunch with country-style fare mostly under $10. In the evening it's a licensed restaurant.

Cork & Keg (☎ *03-572 9328*) This English-style country pub (right down to the English guv'na) is a rip-roaring place for a night out after wine-touring. They brew their own draught beer and a cider, as well as dispensing Guinness. There's a big open fire, welcoming atmosphere and you can bring your own meat and use the barbecue for free.

KAIKOURA
pop 3850

This small town, 183km north of Christchurch on SH1, is a mecca for wildlife enthusiasts. It was once just a sleepy little fishing town noted mainly for its crayfish. Then, during Christmas 1987, Nature Watch Charters began whale-watching trips, the first such commercial operation in NZ. The tours quickly became famous and put Kaikoura on the tourist map.

Kaikoura is also the home of dolphin swimming, another activity now popular in many parts of NZ. Besides whale and dolphin watching, the area has a host of other activities and Kaikoura lies in a superb setting on a beautiful bay backed by the steeply rising foothills of the Seaward Kaikouras, snow capped in winter.

History

In Maori legend, the tiny Kaikoura Peninsula (Taumanu o te Waka o Maui) was the seat upon which the demigod Maui sat when he fished the North Island up from the depths of the sea (see the 'Maori Culture & Arts' special section). The area was heavily settled before Europeans came – at least 14 Maori *pa* sites have been identified.

Excavations near the Fyffe House show that the area was a moa-hunter settlement about 800 to 1000 years ago. In 1857,

KAIKOURA

PLACES TO STAY
2 Sunrise Lodge
3 69 Beach Road
   Holiday Park
4 Dusky Lodge
8 Kaikoura Top 10
   Holiday Park
12 A1 Kaikoura Motels
   & Holiday Park
20 Bad Jelly Backpackers
22 Planet Backpackers
26 Topspot Backpackers
28 Dolphin Lodge
30 Nikau Guesthouse
32 Albatross Backpacker Inn

33 White Morph Motor Inn
35 Sierra Beachfront Motel
36 Cray Cottage
37 Anchor Inn Motel
39 Bay Cottages
41 Blue Seas Motels
42 Panorama Motel
43 Maui YHA

PLACES TO EAT
1 Mussel Boys
6 Hislops Cafe
7 Act One
13 Neptunes Fresh Fish
   Shop

21 Craypot
25 Sonic
40 Finz
44 Pacifica Seafoods

OTHER
5 Kaikoura Helicopters
9 Whale Watch Kaikoura
10 Shark Dive Kaikoura
   Office
11 Kaikoura Museum
14 Kaikoura Supermarket
15 West End Motors
16 Photo & Frame
17 InterCity Depot

18 Dolphin Encounter &
   Ocean Wings Office
19 DOC
23 Kaikoura Visitors Centre
24 NZ Sea Adventures (Dive &
   Seal Swim); Walkway
   to Deal St
27 Hospital
29 Garden of Memories
31 Takahanga Domain
34 Four Square Supermarket
38 Nga Niho Pa
45 Fyffe House
46 Seal Colony
47 Start of Peninsula Walk

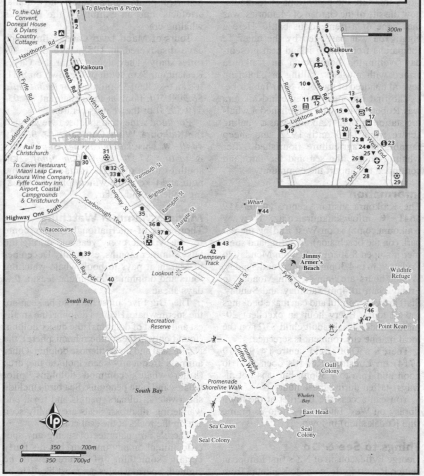

MARLBOROUGH & NELSON

George Fyffe came upon an early moa-hunter burial site near the present Fyffe House. Among other things he found an almost complete moa eggshell, the largest moa egg ever found (240mm long, 178mm in diameter).

James Cook passed by here on 15 February 1770, but did not land. His journal states that 57 Maori in four double-hulled canoes came out from shore towards the *Endeavour,* but 'would not be prevail'd upon to put along side'. In 1828, the beachfront of Kaikoura, now the site of the Garden of Memories, was the scene of a tremendous battle. Here a Ngati Toa war party led by the chief Te Rauparaha from Kapiti Island near present-day Wellington bore down on Kaikoura armed with muskets, killing or capturing several hundred of the local Ngai Tahu tribe.

The first European to settle in Kaikoura was Robert Fyffe, who established a whaling station in 1842. Kaikoura was a whaling centre from 1843 until 1922, and sheep farming and agriculture flourished. After whaling ended, the sea and the farmland continued to support the community.

Information

The Kaikoura visitors centre (☎ 03-319 5641, ℮ info@kaikoura.co.nz, ⓦ www.kaikoura.co.nz) is on West End by the car park (on the beach side). In spring and summer it's open 8.30am to 5.30pm Monday to Friday, 9pm to 4.30pm Saturday and Sunday. Winter hours are 9am to 5pm Monday to Friday, 9am to 4pm Saturday and Sunday. Staff are very helpful and can make bookings for all tours. Every hour an excellent 20-minute audiovisual (adult/child $3/1) on the local marine environment is screened.

There's a DOC field centre (☎ 03-319 5714) on Ludstone Rd. It's open 8am to noon and 1pm to 4.30pm, but it is not always staffed during these hours.

You can access the Internet at the town library on West End or at Photo & Frame (the Kodak shop) in town.

Things to See & Do

George Fyffe, cousin of NZ's first European settler, Robert Fyffe, came to Kaikoura from Scotland in 1854 and built **Fyffe House** (☎ 03-319 5835, *Fyffe Quay; tours adult/child $5/free; open 10am-6pm daily summer, closed Tues & Wed winter)* around 1860. The house, located about 2km east of the town centre, is the only survivor from the whaling days.

The **Kaikoura Museum** (☎ 03-319 7440, *14 Ludstone Rd; admission $3/50c; open 12.30pm-4.30pm Mon-Fri, 2pm-4pm Sat & Sun)* includes the old town jail (1910), historical photographs, Maori and colonial artefacts, and an exhibit on the region's whaling era.

Tours of **Maori Leap Cave**, a limestone cave discovered in 1958, take place six times daily. They depart from the Caves Restaurant, 3km south of the town on SH1. It's an excellent 35-minute **tour** *(adult/child $8.50/3.50)*; book at the restaurant (☎ 03-319 5023) or the visitors centre.

For good wines and great sea views, visit the **Kaikoura Wine Company** (☎ 03-319 4440, ⓦ www.kaikourawines.co.nz; *tours & tasting $7.50; open 10am-5pm),* 2km south of town off SH1. Tours leave on the hour and take in the winery plus the amazing underground cellar.

Marine-Mammal Watching

Thousands of international visitors come for the wildlife every year and during the busy summer months, especially December to March, it pays to book whale-watching tours and dolphin swimming at least a few days ahead.

The 'Big Five' most likely to be seen are the sperm whale, Hectors dolphin (the smallest and rarest of dolphins), the dusky dolphin (found only in the southern hemisphere), the NZ fur seal and the bottlenose dolphin. Other animals frequently seen include the orca (killer whale), common dolphins, pilot whales and blue penguins. Sea birds include shearwaters, fulmars, petrels and royal and wandering albatross. Seals are readily seen out on the rocks at the seal colony.

There's no guarantee of seeing any specific animal on any one tour, but it's fairly certain something of interest will be sighted. Sperm whales are most likely to be seen from October to August and orcas from December to March. Most other fauna is seen year-round.

Marine animals are abundant at Kaikoura because of the currents and continental shelf formation. From land, the shelf slopes gradually to a depth of about 90m, then plunges to over 800m. Warm and cold currents converge here, and when the southerly current hits the continental shelf it creates an upwelling current, bringing nutrients up from the ocean floor and into the light zone. The waters are often red with great clouds of krill, the sperm whale's favourite food, which attract larger fish and squid.

Whale-Watching Based at the old train station is **Whale Watch Kaikoura** *(The Whaleway;* ☎ *03-319 6767, 0800 655 121,* Ⓦ *www.whalewatch.co.nz; tours adult/ child $99.50/60).* It sets out to sea in search of the whales and other wildlife in boats equipped with hydrophones (underwater microphones) to pick up the sounds of whales below the surface. Tours last 3½ hours and operate year-round, daily from early morning to mid-afternoon. It's well worth booking ahead.

For most the tour is a thrilling experience – the main attraction is the sperm whale, and Kaikoura is the most accessible spot on the planet to see one (for more information see the colour 'Watching Wildlife' section). Other whales there may be orcas, the minke, humpback and southern right. Dolphins are also usually spotted, as well as sea birds.

There's one hitch to the whale-watch experience: the weather. Nothing is more dismal than heading out for a special encounter with nature, only to have it stopped by the intervention of uncontrollable elements. Whale Watch depends on its spotter planes to locate the whales at sea and they usually can't find them in foggy or wet conditions. The Whale Watch office then cancels line after line of disappointed customers. The town benefits each time this happens as many people stay on to try the next day. If this trip is a *must* for you, allow a few days.

For aerial whale-watching, **Wings over Whales** *(☎ 03-319 6580, 0800 226 629;* ½-hr flight adult/child $135/75)* is based at the airport south of town. **Kaikoura Helicopters** *(☎ 03-319 6609; 30-40 min flight from $150)* at the old train station also offers flights out over the whales. Both companies guarantee that you see the 'whole whale' as you fly overhead (as opposed to possibly only viewing a tail or flipper from a boat).

Dolphin Swimming Busy **Dolphin Encounter** *(☎ 03-319 6777, 0800 733 365,* Ⓦ *www.dolphin.co.nz, 58 West End; swim adult/child $95/80, observation $48/38)* offers the chance to swim with huge pods of dusky dolphins. It provides wetsuits (essential in this water), masks and snorkels for a three-hour 'dolphin encounter' that most participants rave about. This trip is hugely popular and its well worth booking ahead.

Seal Swimming Seals may appear threatening if approached on land, but under water, in their element, they are completely passive. **Seal Swim Kaikoura** *(☎ 03-319 6182; tours adult/child $50/40)* arranges snorkelling with NZ fur seals from November to April. These two-hour guided snorkelling tours from the shore are a great opportunity to view seals at close hand. **Topspot Backpackers** *(☎ 03-319 5440)* arranges similar trips.

You can also snorkel with the seals from a boat, or kayak in their territory. **NZ Sea Adventures** *(☎ 03-319 6622, 0800 728 223, West End)* organises boat-based seal swimming and supplies all equipment *(adult/ child $60/40, observation $30/20)*, and also offers half-day sea-kayak tours taking in the coastline and fur seals around the peninsula *(adult/child $60/40)*.

Shark Diving

Shark Dive Kaikoura *(☎ 03-319 6888, 0800 225 297; trips $120; Nov-Apr)* takes three-hour trips out to dive with the sharks in the safety of a shark cage (you spend approximately 10 minutes in the cage). All equipment is supplied and scuba experience isn't necessary as air is supplied by a tube connected to the boat.

Bird-Watching

Bird-watchers relish the opportunity to see pelagic species with **Ocean Wings** (☎ *03-319 6777, 0800 733 365,* **W** *www.ocean wings.co.nz, 58 West End; tours adult/child $60/35)* – including albatross, shearwaters, shags, mollymawks and petrels.

Walking

The Kaikoura Peninsula has many good walking opportunities. There are two **walkways**, starting from the seal colony, one along the seashore and one above it along the cliff top; a loop takes 2½ hours. If you go on the seashore trail, check out the tides with the visitors centre beforehand (it's best to go within two hours of low tide). Both walks afford excellent views of the fur seal and red-billed seagull colonies. A trail from South Bay leads over farmland and back to the town (45 minutes). A pamphlet about these walks is available from the visitors centre.

Up on the hill at the eastern end of town is a water tower with a great **lookout**; you can see both sides of the peninsula and all down the coast. Take the walking track up to the tower from Torquay St or drive up Scarborough Terrace.

The **Mt Fyffe Walking Track** centres on Mt Fyffe (1602m), which dominates the narrow Kaikoura plain and the town. Information about history, vegetation, birds and the walking tracks is in the *Mt Fyffe and the Seaward Kaikoura Range* pamphlet.

The **Kaikoura Coast Track** (☎ *03-319, 2715,* **W** *www.kaikouratrack.co.nz)* is a three-day walk through private farmland and along the Amuri coast, 50km south of Kaikoura. The 43km walk has spectacular coastal views and accommodation is in comfortable farm cottages. The cost of $120 includes three nights' accommodation and pack transport; bring your own sleeping bag and food. There's a two-day mountain-bike option also ($60).

Other Activities

In winter, nearby **Mt Lyford** has good skiing (see the Activities chapter). Shuttle buses run from Kaikoura to the mountain daily.

The **beach** in front of the Esplanade has safe swimming and a swimming pool. Other beaches are on the peninsula's north-east (eg, Jimmy Armer's) and at South Bay. The whole coastline, with its rocky formations and abundant marine life, is good for snorkelling and diving. **NZ Sea Adventures** (☎ *03-319 6622, 0800 728 223, West End)* offers scuba-diving opportunities (dives with gear supplied cost $95). Mangamaunu Beach, about 15km north of Kaikoura, has good surfing.

Fishing is popular off the new and old wharves, at the Kahutara River mouth, or by surfcasting on the many beaches. The visitors centre has information on numerous fishing charters. *Victoria Lee* Fishing Charters (☎ *03-319 6478; boat hire $750)* has six- to seven-hour deep sea crayfishing trips (maximum 12 people). Price includes all gear and a crayfish lunch. Shorter trips are available with *Sylver Ann* (☎ *03-319 5710; trips $50 per person),* offering two-hour fishing trips with gear supplied for two to six people.

Four Wheeler Safaris (☎ *03-319 6424; 3-hr/half-day/full-day trip $90/110/150)* operates quad-bike rides on and around Mt Fyffe and the Kowhai River where you drive through rivers, hill country and bush. **Fyffe View Horse Treks** (☎ *03-319 5069)* and **Ludley Horse Treks** (☎ *03-319 5925)* offer two-hour guided horse treks for around $40, both taking in farmland and either riverbeds or the coast.

A novel activity is the chance to **Pilot A Plane** (☎ *03-319 6579; 30-min flight $79),* with no flying experience necessary. The Kaikoura Aero Club takes you on a flight and bravely lets you take the controls.

Places to Stay

Kaikoura gets crowded in the summer months so it's well worth booking ahead if you're travelling at that time.

Camping & Cabins All prices listed in this section are for two people.

69 Beach Road Holiday Park (☎ *03-319 6275,* **e** *69holidaypark@actrix.gen.nz, 69 Beach Rd)* Unpowered/powered sites $18/20, standard cabins $35, cabins with en suite, linen & TV $55. This creek-side park is an excellent newish place right by the bakery. It has friendly, helpful owners and good, clean facilities including a large, well-equipped communal kitchen.

Kaikoura Top 10 Holiday Park (☎ 03-319 5362, e kaikouratop10@clear.net.nz, 34 Beach Rd) Unpowered/powered sites $20/22, cabins & units $35-65, motel units $85. Another busy place, tucked away behind a large hedge, is this well-maintained camping ground with excellent facilities including swimming pool (in summer) and a range of quality cabins.

A1 Kaikoura Motels & Holiday Park (☎ 03-319 5999, e kaimotel@voyager .co.nz, 11 Beach Rd) Unpowered/powered sites $17/20, cabins $33-58, motel units $75-85. This is an older style camping ground but the closest to town. There are a number of comfortable cabins and units and a small, green camping area backing onto a creek.

Kaikoura Coastal Campgrounds (☎ 03-319 5348, e goosebay@ihug.co.nz) This is a collection of several camping grounds spread over a 5km stretch of coastline. *Goose Bay*, 18km south of Kaikoura, is a developed ground offering unpowered/powered sites for $16/20 and basic cabins for $30, as well as facilities such as kitchen, laundry and BBQ. Nearby grounds are *Boat Harbour* (sites $16/20), *Omihi* ($13/17) and *Paia Point* (unpowered sites $10). Facilities at these three places are very basic but the waterfront location compensates.

Hostels One of Kaikoura's newer backpackers is *Sunrise Lodge* (☎ 03-319 7444, 74 Beach Rd), and the enthusiastic owners really make this place. You might be invited to help check craypots, to be taken out on a low-tide beach safari, or out on a rescue mission to pick up injured wildlife. The rooms are bright and comfortable (no bunks). Dorm beds are $19, twins $44. It's closed June and July.

Dusky Lodge (☎ 03-319 5959, 67 Beach Rd) Dorm beds $18, doubles $45. Dusky Lodge is probably the busiest hostel in town (popular with the bus groups), but it has the

facilities to cope. There's a brilliant outdoor deck and spa at the back with mountain views, and a good-sized kitchen and lounge.

Cray Cottage (☎ 03-319 5152, 190 The Esplanade) Dorm beds $19, twins $44. This is a small, friendly place with a self-contained hostel behind the owners' house, about 1km east of the town centre.

There are a couple of places on Deal St, which can be reached by a walking track up past the post office.

Topspot Backpackers (☎ 03-319 5540, e topspot@xtra.co.nz, 22 Deal St) Dorm beds $18, singles $30, twins & doubles $45. Topspot is in a laid-back old house with a big back garden. The attraction here is the backpackers-oriented seal swimming trips run by the owner ($50), and there's free Internet and free fishing rods.

Dolphin Lodge (☎ 03-319 5842, e dol phinlodge@xtra.co.nz, 15 Deal St) Dorm beds $18, twins & doubles $45. Overlooking the bay, Dolphin Lodge is a small, comfortable place with a great outdoor spa and free bikes.

Maui YHA (☎ 03-319 5931, e yhakaikr@ yha.org.nz, 270 The Esplanade) Dorm beds $18-20, doubles & twins $44. The YHA is about halfway between town and the seal colony. The best feature is that the two communal areas (lounge and dining/kitchen) have large windows with great views out over the bay and mountains.

Bad Jelly Backpackers (☎ 03-319 5538, e duskyjack@hotmail.com, 11 Churchill St) Twins/doubles $42/44. Bad Jelly (named after the witch in Spike Milligan's children's book) is as much guesthouse as backpackers. There are no dorms, but it's a welcoming, cosy house with guest kitchen and spa pool.

Planet Backpackers (☎ 0800 687 752, 03-319 6972, 86 West End) Dorm beds $18, singles/doubles $30/40. Right in the centre of town, Planet is an offbeat backpackers with mattresses arranged on the floor in the open upstairs section – not great if you value privacy. There's a big kitchen and a balcony overlooking the street.

Albatross Backpacker Inn (☎ 03-319 6090, e albatrossnz@xtra.co.nz, 1 Torquay

St) Dorms $19-21, singles $32, doubles & twins from $45. This new, high-quality backpackers has a lovely large TV/living area in the main house, plus decks, verandas and even an aviary. Some of the dorms have great 'Turkish-theme' bunks – semi-enclosed beds with a unique design.

B&Bs & Guesthouses There are some excellent B&Bs and guesthouses, but the majority of them are on the outskirts of town, making your own transport an asset.

Old Convent (☎ 03-319 6603, ⊞ www .theoldconvent.co.nz, Mt Fyffe Rd) Singles $75, twins & doubles $130-160. This memorable B&B was formerly a convent and schoolhouse, and many features of the rambling old buildings have been retained. The old chapel is now an inviting guest lounge full of magazines, books and games.

Nikau Guesthouse (☎ 03-319 6973, ⓔ jhughey@xtra.co.nz, 53 Deal St) B&B singles $60-70, doubles & twins $90. This friendly, well-run establishment is a good choice if you want to be close to town (but is closed May to September). All rooms have en suites and some have balconies for enjoying the mountain views. It's hard to miss – look for the blue, two-storey old home set in a colourful, overgrown garden.

Donegal House (☎ 03-319 5083, ⊞ www .donegalhouse.co.nz, Mt Fyffe Rd) Singles/doubles $70/100. Located out of town, Donegal House offers simple B&B in comfortable rooms set in a huge garden, but the real reason to stay here is not the decor, but the proximity to the wonderful pub and restaurant (see Places to Eat).

Dylans Country Cottages (☎ 03-319 5473, ⊞ www.dylanscottages.co.nz, Postmans Rd) B&B cottages $120. Set on the lovely 'Lavendyl' lavender farm, these two private, self-contained cottages make a great spot to escape to. They're set in pretty gardens, and one cottage has a secluded outdoor bath and the other an indoor spa.

Fyffe Country Inn (☎ 03-319 6869, ⓔ fyffe@xtra.co.nz) Doubles from $189-500. Fyffe Country Inn, 5km south of Kaikoura on SH1, is a luxurious lodge set in magnificent gardens. You can choose between studios in the inn or garden, and there's a huge suite available. The hospitable owners can tailor dinner, bed and breakfast packages – well worthwhile, as there's an award-winning restaurant here.

Motels Kaikoura has plenty of motels to choose from, especially along The Esplanade.

Bay Cottages (☎ 03-319 5506, ⓔ baycot tages@xtra.co.nz, South Bay Rd) Cottages $60 for 2, plus $10 per additional person; linen extra. Not technically motels, these are excellent-value tourist flats (with kitchenette and bathroom) capable of sleeping four to six. They're on South Bay, a few kilometres south of town, but are nicely placed for swimming beaches and the excellent Finz restaurant. The friendly owner may take you out crayfishing and often puts on a coffee-and-cray brunch for guests.

Sierra Beachfront Motel (☎ 03-319 5622, 160 The Esplanade) Self-contained units $70-90. This is probably the cheapest motel in town. It's well located and comfortable, although the decor is somewhat dated.

The usual rate for most motels in town is $85 for a studio, $95 to $100 for a larger one-bedroom unit. *Panorama Motel (☎ 03-319 5053, ⓔ panorama.motel@xtra.co.nz, 266 The Esplanade)* and *Blue Seas Motels (☎ 03-319 5441, 222 The Esplanade)* are excellent examples of this mid-range motel genre, offering comfortable, well-equipped units. Panorama wins on the view front, with vistas over the water to the mountains in the distance.

White Morph Motor Inn (☎ 03-319 5014, 92 The Esplanade) Units from $115. Next to the restaurant of the same name, the White Morph is a slightly more upmarket option, with spacious units and all the facilities you'll need.

Anchor Inn Motel (☎ 03-319 5426, 208 The Esplanade) Units $150-225. Anchor Inn is the top choice in town with spacious, immaculate units. Extras include air-con, double-glazed windows and tinted glass, so you can enjoy the great water views without every passer-by seeing you. Rates drop during winter.

MARLBOROUGH & NELSON

Pick Your Poisson

As well as all the marine life you can encounter in Kaikoura, in town you certainly can't avoid one sea creature: the crayfish. The town's name reflects its abundance in these waters – 'kai' in Maori means food, 'koura' means crayfish. In season, crayfish is always featured in Kaikoura restaurants and local takeaways. Unfortunately it's pricey – you'll pay the export price, which at the time of research was hovering around $70 per kilogram. If you're not too keen on the idea of paying $35 to $50 for a restaurant meal of half a cray, you can purchase the fresh, non-garnished variety at **Pacifica Seafoods** (☎ 03-319 5817) on the wharf, or from **Nin's Bin**, a rustic beachside caravan some 20km towards Picton. **Neptunes Fresh Fish Shop** (☎ 03-319 6361, 11 West End) is a takeaway place offering good-value crayfish 'meal deals' – half a crayfish with chips and salad is $25, a whole cray with the same is $45 (there are also cheaper fish-and-chip meals on offer).

And finally, you might strike it lucky and find a local who'll kindly take you out crayfishing with them and allow you to share in their catch. This is an economical way to taste the local produce, not to mention fun.

Places to Eat

If you're not into seafood you might struggle for choice in Kaikoura. If, however, you love crustaceans, bivalves and all things fishy – and if your budget can stretch a little – you'll be in gastronomic heaven. Prices given for main meals here are for dishes not involving crayfish!

Hislops Cafe (☎ 03-319 6971, 33 Beach Rd) Daytime menu $6-15. Hislops is a smart cafe with a god reputation for fresh organic food. Start the morning with their fruit salad, toasted muesli, omelettes or French toast and feel healthy and smug all day. There's also a daytime blackboard menu (salads, pasta, open sandwiches) and evening dining.

Craypot (☎ 03-319 6027, 70 West End) Light meals $10-14, regular mains $20-26.

This is a long-running restaurant and bar serving good feeds of seafood: a half crayfish is $54, or you may wish to order the easier-on-the-pocket mussel chowder ($10). There's not a lot on the menu to appeal to those not into fishy fare.

Finz (☎ 03-319 6688, 103 South Bay Parade) Mains $25-30. Out at South Bay, Finz is widely regarded by locals as the best restaurant in town, and it's not hard to see why. If your budget stretches a little, this is as fine a place as any to try crayfish, or you could settle for the seafood fettuccine, a house speciality. There's much to tempt non-seafood-goers too, with venison, rib eye steak and lamb rump also featuring on the menu. The adjacent bar is an excellent spot for a drink, and there's a small, reasonably priced bar menu (dishes $6-15).

Mussel Boys (☎ 03-319 7160, 80 Beach Rd) Mains $15-24. This bright and cheery, kid-friendly restaurant is a little out of town but well worth the trip, especially if you're into bivalves – you can get them as flats (grilled on the half-shell) or steamers (whole-shell), and with a variety of tempting sauces (eg, roast tomato and chilli, garlic and herb butter, green curry and coconut milk). There are other seafood dishes on offer (pasta, laksa, chowder, scallops, crayfish and fish of the day). Look for the green shells covering the roof.

Act One (☎ 03-319 6760, 25 Beach Rd) Pizzas $19-22. Shock horror – there's only one seafood pizza on the menu! This popular, candlelit restaurant offers good pizza choices, with gourmet toppings such as satay or hot Thai chicken, peppered venison, and assorted vegie options.

Sonic (☎ 03-319 6414, West End) Dinner $10-25. This cafe opposite the visitors centre is a good dining spot and also a popular bar, with a pool table and funky decor featuring a huge metallic fish hanging from the ceiling. Lunch and light meals on offer include gourmet pizza and nachos; dinner mains include beef fillet, Cajun chicken breasts, lamb medallions and seafood.

Donegal House (☎ 03-319 5083, Mt Fyffe Rd) Mains $22-25. Some five minutes' drive west of town is Donegal House, an unexpected 'little Irish pub in the country' and a real gem. Both Guinness and Kilkenny are available on tap and there's regular live music, plus a huge outdoor area. There's a simple menu offering well-prepared staples such as fish and crayfish, steak, chicken and pasta. And if you're a little 'under the influence' and can't get home, B&B is offered here too (see Places to Stay earlier).

Getting There & Around
The daily InterCity bus services operating between Nelson, Picton and Christchurch all stop at Kaikoura. Buses arrive and depart from the town car park; tickets and information are available at the visitors centre next door.

Several shuttle buses service Kaikoura, including Southern Link (☎ 03-358 8355), South Island Connections (☎ 03-366 6633), East Coast Express (☎ 0508 830 900) and Atomic (☎ 03-322 8883). Tickets cost from $15 to $20 to either Christchurch, Blenheim or Picton. The Hanmer Connection (☎ 03-315 7575, 0800 377 378) to Hanmer Springs costs around $25. The visitors centre takes bookings.

One northbound and one southbound *TranzCoastal* train (☎ 0800 802 802) between Picton and Christchurch stop at Kaikoura daily. The northbound departs Kaikoura at 10.25am, and the southbound at 4.05pm.

You can hire bicycles from Westend Motors at the Shell service station (☎ 03-319 5065) at 48 West End (it costs from $5/12/21 per hour/half-day/day).

A taxi (☎ 03-319 6214) costs about $6 from town to accommodation.

Nelson Region

☎ 03 • pop 82,100
The Nelson region is one of the top destinations for travellers to NZ. It boasts an equable climate (with more sunshine than any other part of the country), good beaches, and some of the finest and most popular national parks in the country – Kahurangi, Nelson Lakes and Abel Tasman.

It's also the home of an enthusiastic and progressive community of artists, craftspeople, winemakers and entrepreneurs.

NELSON
pop 52,300
The South Island's second-largest city, Nelson is a bright, active place and an obvious starting point for exploring the wonderful coastal region further west. Nelson is noted for its fruit-growing industry, wineries and breweries and its energetic local arts and crafts community.

History
The Maori began to migrate to the South Island during the 16th century; among the first to arrive in Nelson were the Ngati Tumatakokiri. By 1550 this tribe occupied most of the province, as Abel Tasman (see History in the Facts About New Zealand chapter) found out to his cost when he turned up in 1642 at what he later named Murderers' Bay. Other tribes followed the Tumatakokiri, settling at the mouth of the Waimea River. The Tumatakokiri remained supreme in Tasman Bay until the 18th century, when the Ngati-apa from Wanganui and the Ngati Kahu (or Ngai Tahu) – the largest tribe in the South Island – got together in a devastating attack on the Tumatakokiri, who virtually ceased to exist as an independent tribe after 1800.

The Ngati-apa's victory was short-lived because between 1828 and 1830 they were practically annihilated by armed tribes from Taranaki and Wellington who sailed into the bay in the largest fleet of canoes ever assembled in NZ.

By the time the European settlers arrived no Maori lived at Te Wakatu – the nearest *pa* being at Motueka – and the decimated population that remained in the area put up no resistance. The first Pakeha settlers sailed in response to advertisements by the New Zealand Company, set up by Edward Gibbon Wakefield to systematically colonise the country. His grandiose scheme was to transplant a complete slice of English life from all social classes. In reality 'too few gentlemen with too little money' took up the challenge and the new colony almost foundered in its infancy for lack of money.

The settlement was planned to consist of small but workable farms grouped around central towns. However, the New Zealand Company's entitlement to the land was disputed and it was almost a year before this problem was sorted out. Town land was distributed early, but farmland remained unallocated for so long that landowners and labourers were forced to live in town and whittle away their capital to survive.

The Wairau Massacre (see the boxed text in Marlborough Region section) resulted in the deaths of 22 of Nelson's most able citizens – including Captain Wakefield whose leadership was irreplaceable – and plunged the colony into deep gloom. To make matters worse, the New Zealand Company was declared bankrupt in April 1844. Since nearly three-quarters of the population were dependent on it, particularly for sustenance, the settlement had to endure near-famine conditions. Only the later arrival of hard-working German immigrants saved the region from economic ruin.

Information

The Nelson Visitor Information Centre (☎ 03-548 2304, **W** www.nelsonnz.com) is on the corner of Trafalgar and Halifax Sts. It's open 8.30am to 6pm daily in summer (8.30am to 5pm Monday to Friday and 10am to 4pm Saturday and Sunday in winter). Pick up a copy of the *Nelson Visitor Guide* here.

A DOC officer is at the information centre in summer for inquiries about national parks and walks. The AA (☎ 03-548 8339) is at 45 Halifax St.

There are several good Internet cafes including Aurora (☎ 03-546 6867), next to Nelson Central Backpackers on Trafalgar St, and Boots Off (☎ 03-546 8789) on Bridge St. Rates are about $6 an hour.

Camping gear can be hired from most of the backpackers or from numerous outdoor

Nelson crowd gathered to farewell troops leaving for WWI (Frederick Nelson Jones, 1916)

MARLBOROUGH & NELSON

ALEXANDER TURNBULL LIBRARY, WELLINGTON NZ

NELSON

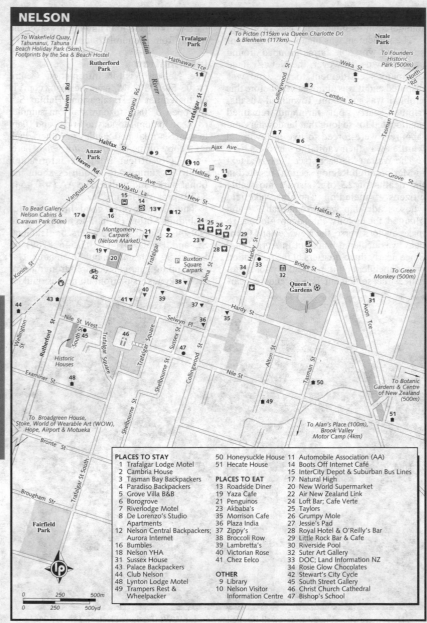

To Wakefield Quay,
Tahunanui, Tahuna
Beach Holiday Park (5km),
Footprints by the Sea & Beach Hostel

To Picton (115km via Queen Charlotte Dr)
& Blenheim (117km)

To Founders
Historic
Park (500m)

To Bead Gallery,
Nelson Cabins &
Caravan Park (50m)

To Green
Monkey (500m)

To Botanic
Gardens & Centre
of New Zealand
(500m)

To Broadgreen House,
Stoke, World of Wearable Art (WOW),
Hope, Airport & Motueka

To Alan's Place (100m),
Brook Valley
Motor Camp (4km)

MARLBOROUGH & NELSON

PLACES TO STAY	50 Honeysuckle House	11 Automobile Association (AA)
1 Trafalgar Lodge Motel	51 Hecate House	14 Boots Off Internet Café
2 Cambria House		15 InterCity Depot & Suburban Bus Lines
3 Tasman Bay Backpackers	PLACES TO EAT	17 Natural High
4 Paradiso Backpackers	13 Roadside Diner	20 New World Supermarket
5 Grove Villa B&B	19 Yaza Cafe	22 Air New Zealand Link
6 Borogrove	21 Penguinos	24 Loft Bar; Cafe Verte
7 Riverlodge Motel	23 Akbaba's	25 Taylors
8 De Lorenzo's Studio	35 Morrison Cafe	26 Grumpy Mole
Apartments	36 Plaza India	27 Jessie's Pad
12 Nelson Central Backpackers;	37 Zippy's	28 Royal Hotel & O'Reilly's Bar
Aurora Internet	38 Broccoli Row	29 Little Rock Bar & Cafe
16 Bumbles	39 Lambretta's	30 Riverside Pool
18 Nelson YHA	40 Victorian Rose	32 Suter Art Gallery
31 Sussex House	41 Chez Eelco	33 DOC; Land Information NZ
43 Palace Backpackers		34 Rosie Glow Chocolates
44 Club Nelson	OTHER	42 Stewart's City Cycle
48 Lynton Lodge Motel	9 Library	45 South Street Gallery
49 Trampers Rest &	10 Nelson Visitor	46 Christ Church Cathedral
Wheelpacker	Information Centre	47 Bishop's School

centres such as Natural High (☎ 03-546 6936), 52 Rutherford St, which also has bicycles, kayaks and ski and snowboarding gear. Hire prices are reasonable at around $8 a day for packs and boots, and $15 a day for tents.

Fruit-picking (nashi pears, apples and grapes) and other agricultural work is available from February to May; berries are picked from December to January – contact the Employment NZ office or individual growers.

Historic Buildings

The traditional symbol of Nelson is its Art Deco **Christ Church Cathedral** (☎ 03-548 1008; open 8am-7pm daily) at the top of Trafalgar St. Work began in 1925 but was delayed and arguments raged in the 1950s over whether the building should be completed according to its original design. Finally completed in 1965 to a modified design, it was consecrated in 1972, 47 years after the foundation stone was laid! There are guides on hand in summer.

Close to the cathedral, **South St** is home to a row of restored workers cottages dating from 1863 to 1867 and is said to be the oldest preserved street in NZ. Of prime interest on the corner of Nile St West is the **South St Gallery**, noted for its extensive collection of fine pottery.

Broadgreen House (☎ 03-546 0283, 276 Nayland Rd; adult/child $3/50c; open 10.30am-4.30pm daily) in Stoke is a historic two-storey cob house built about 1855 and carefully furnished in period style.

World of Wearable Art (WOW)

This eye-popping gallery (☎ 03-548 9299, 95 Quarantine Rd; adult/child $15/7, open 9am-6.30pm daily summer, 10am-5pm winter), opened in 2001, showcases the bizarre but spellbinding 'garments' featured in the annual Wearable Art Awards. The galleries are small but hi-tech, with a carousel

MARLBOROUGH & NELSON

The Wonderful World of Wearable Art

The Nelson and Golden Bay region exudes creativity. Artists, potters, weavers and fashion designers live and work here, so it's hardly surprising that New Zealand's most inspiring and successful art-meets-fashion show was born here.

It began humbly in 1987 when creator Suzie Moncrieff decided to hold an off-beat fashion show in a marquee tent in Wakefield. The concept was not simply to design a dress, but to create a piece of art that could be worn and modelled. Local artists and audiences loved the idea and slowly the NZ Wearable Art Award grew into an annual event with traditional fabrics going out the window in favour of ever more whacky and imaginative designs. Everything from wood, papier mache, paua shell, copper wire, soft drink cans, wine bladders and even food stuffs have been used to create the garments. The show also

features themed entries such as the illumination section and the popular 'Bizarre Bra Award'. Entries are now received from around NZ and overseas, and a look at some of the past winners (and entrants) shows that WOW creativity knows no limits.

The show, now called the Montana World of Wearable Art Award, is held in Nelson's Trafalgar Square every year in September. Even if you can't make it to the show (which attracted around 10,000 people in 2001), check out the new WOW gallery in Nelson.

MARLBOROUGH & NELSON

mimicking the usual catwalk models, and an illumination room. The artworks change every three months and there are plans to display more in future.

Equally enthralling – perhaps more for the boys – is the **Collectable Cars** display, featuring mint condition classics such as a 1959 pink Cadillac, a 1908 Renault made famous as a Parisienne taxi, an E-type Jaguar and an Eldorado Cadillac convertible used by Eisenhower in the 1953 US presidential parade.

There's also a pleasant *cafe* in the foyer of the gallery with cakes, sandwiches and platters ($4-12).

Other Museums & Galleries

The **Suter Art Gallery** (*☎ 03-548 4699, 208 Bridge St; admission $1; open 10.30am-4.30pm daily*) adjoins Queen's Gardens and is named after Bishop Suter, founder of the Bishopdale Sketching Club in 1889. It has a few interesting lithographs and paintings and is the city's main repository of high art, with changing exhibitions, musical and theatrical performances, films, a craft shop and a *cafe*.

The small **Nelson Provincial Museum** (*☎ 03-547 9740; adult/child $2/1; open 10am-4pm Mon-Fri, noon-4pm Sat & Sun*) at Isel Park, 6km south of Nelson in Stoke, has a permanent Maori collection and tries hard with rotating exhibits that occasionally draw on the museum's large photographic collection.

The beautiful **Isel Park gardens** are worth a visit in their own right, and also in the grounds is historic **Isel House** (*adult/child $1/50c; open 2pm-4pm Sat & Sun*). Nelson is famous for its **pottery** and the quality of local clay, but glass-blowing, furniture, woodcarving, paintings and other arts and crafts are also represented. The visitors centre has brochures on the various potters and craft galleries, but if you're really keen on the subject, get hold of a copy of the comprehensive Nelson Regional Guidebook ($20) from the visitors centre.

Founders Historic Park

This replica colonial village (*☎ 03-548 2649, 87 Atawhai Drive; adult/child $5/2; open 10am-4pm daily*) reflects the town's early history with re-created streets and buildings from the late-19th century. It's also home to **Founders Brewery** (*☎ 03-548 4638*), NZ's first certified organic brewery. It produces three styles – Tall Blonde, Red Head and Long Black. There's a bar and cafe here and short tours of the microbrewery are available on request. Founders Park is near the waterfront 1km north-east of the city centre, easily spotted by the large windmill, which is also the entrance hall and gift shop.

Next door to the brewery are the beautiful **Miyazu Japanese Gardens**.

Gardens

Nelson has some fine gardens. The **Botanic Gardens** has a good lookout at the top of Botanical Hill, with a spire proclaiming it NZ's exact geographical centre.

Gardens of the World (*☎ 03-542 3736, 95 Clover Rd East, Hope; adult/child $5/free*) feature, as the name suggests, beautifully landscaped native gardens from the Orient, America, Europe and Australia.

Bone Carving

Nelson is a good place to design and carve your own pendant out of bone. **Nelson Bonecarver** (*☎ 03-546 4275, 87 Green St, Tahunanui; day course $45*) offers instruction and materials. You can also create your own bead necklace at the **Bead Gallery** (*☎ 03-546 7807, 18 Parere St, Nelson*), which has a huge collection of beads.

Tahunanui

Five kilometres west of the town centre, Tahunanui is an old-fashioned Kiwi holiday resort with minigolf, a playground, waterslide and a motley little zoo called Natureland. It's very much a suburb of Nelson these days and has a few fashionable cafes and restaurants. You can get there on a Nelson Suburban bus.

McCashin's Brewery & Malthouse

Better known simply as Mac's Brewery (*☎ 03-547 0526, 660 Main Rd, Stoke*), this is the source of the favourite beer for many

Nelsonites. Black Mac, a dark ale, is legendary but there are five varieties in all. Brewery tours are at 11am and 2pm daily ($5), or just turn up at the bar for a tasting ($3). It's about 6km south of Nelson in Stoke – the Stoke Loop bus runs past.

Nelson Market

The Nelson Market (☎ 03-546 6454) is held in Montgomery Square in the city centre from 8am to 1pm every Saturday. There are produce and food stalls, local crafts and so on. On Sunday, Monty's Market (9am-1pm) is held at the same place but is more of a trash and treasure event.

Activities

There are plenty of activities on offer in this region, and although most take place some way out of the city, the following operators will pick up and drop off in Nelson. For tramping and sea kayaking on the Abel Tasman Track, see that section later.

You can go paragliding with **Adventure Paragliding** (☎ 03-546 6863) or **Nelson Paragliding** (☎ 03-544 1182, 108 Queen St); both charge $110 for a tandem flight, or $150 for a full-day introductory course, then $50 for a solo flight.

For a little extra thrill try a tandem skydive with **Tandem Skydive Nelson** (☎ 03-545 2121, 0800 422 899, ⓦ www.skydive.co.nz). Jumps cost $210 from 9000ft, or $260 from 12,000ft. The cost includes transport out to Motueka airstrip, 10 minutes' instruction and a certificate.

Hang-gliding with **Nelson Hang Gliding Adventures** (☎ 03-548 9151; 20-min flight $130) is another aerial possibility at Takaka Hill and the Richmond Ranges.

Rock climbing on the sheer limestone cliffs of the Golden Bay and Takaka area has long been popular with local outdoor enthusiasts. **Vertical Limits** (☎ 0508 837 842, 28 Halifax St; trips $120) has full-day rock-climbing trips. No experience is necessary.

A popular activity is the **quad-bike tour** through farmland and along high-country trails with **Happy Valley Tours** (☎ 0800 157 300, 03-545 0304, 194 Cable Bay Rd), a 10-minute drive north-west along SH6. Rides range from a one-hour farm-forest ride ($55) to the 'Sundowner' ride ($110).

Horse riding is handled by **Stonehurst Farm Horse Treks** (☎ 0800 487 357, 03-542 4121) which offers one-hour farm rides ($30), two-hour Sundowner treks ($55) and, for experienced riders, the chance to take part in a cattle muster ($80).

There are many opportunities to go **sailing** in Tasman Bay. If you're keen to help out on a yacht, the best option is to join the **Wednesday night races** (☎ 03-548 2754; $25 per person). You get two hours to help crew a boat around the harbour in racing conditions. It's fairly relaxed, a bit of fun and a good learning experience. There are plenty of other sailing, cruising or fishing charters where you'll pay a lot more. Try **Cat 09** (☎ 03-548 0202) or **Sail Tasman** (☎ 0800 157 117, 03-548 2754).

Of the many **walks** and tramps, the riverside footpath makes a pleasant stroll through the city and the Maitai Valley Walkway is particularly restful and beautiful. There are also good **mountain biking** trails around – Natural High can provide maps, information and bikes.

Organised Tours

Many tours around Nelson can be booked through the visitors centre. Popular trips are winery tours in the Richmond and Upper Moutere area and 'craft & scenic tours'. **Bay Tours** (☎ 0800 229 868, 03-544 4494, ⓔ baytours@ts.co.nz, 48 Brougham St) and **JJ's Scenic Tours** (☎ 03-544 7712, ⓔ jjs tours@ts.co.nz, 279 Hill St, Richmond) have half-day wine tours (visiting four vineyards and a brewery) for $55. Both also offer a variety of other tours.

Special Events

With its enthusiastic artistic flair, Nelson stages many noteworthy events throughout the year. The biggest is the **World of Wearable Art Award** in September, and there's the annual **Arts Festival** around the same time. Late December sees the **Nelson Jazz Festival**, and in early February the **Taste Nelson Festival** features locally produced food and beverages.

Places to Stay

Camping & Cabins The most central camp is the basic *Nelson Cabins & Caravan Park* (☎ 03-548 1445, 230 Vanguard St) which has powered sites for $19 but not unpowered sites. There are cabins for $44 and self-contained flats for $55.

Tahuna Beach Holiday Park (☎ 03-548 5159, 70 Beach Rd) Unpowered/powered sites $10 per person, cabin doubles $28-47, unit doubles $60-66, motels $75-80. This is a huge park accommodating thousands – like a mini-village with its own supermarket and minigolf. It's near the beach, 5km from the city centre.

Brook Valley Motor Camp (☎ 03-548 0399, Tasman St) Unpowered/powered sites $16/17, 2-bunk cabins $23, other cabins $39. This place, at the end of Tasman St in the upper Brook Valley, is in a superb forested setting by a stream. It's the same distance from the centre as Tahuna, but smaller and more personal.

Hostels Nelson has a large and ever-increasing number of backpacker hostels (a couple not listed here opened around the time of writing). Many of these are small, homestay places with only a few beds.

Paradiso Backpackers (☎ 03-546 6703, e paradisonelson@hotmail.com, 42 Weka St) Dorm beds $16-17, twins & doubles $38. The most popular backpackers in Nelson, Paradiso is in a lovely old building with spacious grounds. It has a pool, spa, sauna and a cluttered glassed-in dining room: the free 6pm soup and morning breakfast are a hit with travellers. Rooms are nothing special – there are seven- and eight-bed dorms with mezzanines, four-bed dorms and other rooms.

Nelson YHA (☎ 03-545 9988, e yha nels@yha.org.nz, 59 Rutherford St) Dorm beds $20, twins & doubles $50, en suite doubles $70. This spotless place is very central and purpose-built with has good facilities, such as a sound-proof, vault-like TV room and a kitchen opening onto an outdoor terrace.

Palace Backpackers (☎ 03-548 4691, 114 Rutherford St) Dorm beds $18, twins & doubles $45. The Palace is in an early 20th-century villa set above the street with views from the balconies. It doesn't look like much from the street but this is perhaps the nicest of the big backpackers. It has plenty of character, no bunks and lots of little common areas.

Tasman Bay Backpackers (☎ 03-548 7950, e stay@tasmanbaybackpackers.co.nz, 10 Weka St) Dorm beds $18, twins/doubles $46/48. This is a spacious, purpose-built place run by a friendly young couple. Dorms are mostly quads, rooms are bright and there's a big kitchen and barbecue area.

Club Nelson (☎ 0800 425 826, 03-548 3466, e clubnelson@xtra.co.nz, 18 Mount St) Tent sites $12 per person, dorm beds $14 or $18, singles $25, small/large doubles $39/46 with linen. Club Nelson, an uphill walk away from the bus station, is a big, rambling place with plenty of parking, a pool and tennis court.

Nelson Central Backpackers (☎ 03-548 9001, 163 Trafalgar St) Dorm beds $15, doubles $34. Right in the town centre, this place is no frills but clean and roomy enough.

Bumbles (☎ 03-548 2771, e bumbles@ts.co.nz, 8 Bridge St) Dorm beds $16-18, twins & doubles $36, with bath $40. Bumbles is a former hotel turned backpackers, across the road from the bus station. There are large dorms in the main building, converted motel units at the back and an industrial-strength kitchen.

Slightly outside its centre, Nelson has a number of smaller, homestay-style backpackers – perfect if you want to relax away from the usual crowds and ideal for trampers and cyclists. All of these places are in converted houses and most have no bunks.

Trampers Rest & Wheelpacker (☎/fax 03-545 7477, 31 Alton St) Beds $20, doubles $46. Trampers, with just a few beds, is hard to beat for a homely, attentive environment. The enthusiastic owner is a keen tramper and cyclist and provides information as well as free use of bikes.

Alan's Place (☎/fax 03-548 4854, 42 Westbrook Terrace) Dorm beds $18, twins & doubles $38. Alan's Place is a bit further out, but still not far from town. It's an older house but has a good atmosphere and Alan, one of the 'originals' in the backpacker industry, offers pick-up, free bikes and other services. A $1 discount applies to holders of any card (YHA/VIP/BBH).

Honeysuckle House (☎ *03-548 7576, 125 Tasman St*) Dorm beds $18, twins/doubles $42/40. This is another friendly, family-run (10-bed) backpackers house in a quiet part of town.

Hecate House (☎ *03-546 6890,* e *hecate house@xtra.co.nz, 181 Nile St*) Dorm beds $20, single/twins $40/50. This is a women-only hostel in a lovely old house. It has a warm atmosphere, an outdoor hot tub and gets rave reviews from women travellers.

Green Monkey (☎ *03-545 7421,* e *the greenmonkey@xtra.co.nz, 129 Milton St*) Dorm beds $20, doubles $48. This small, relatively new place has a funky atmosphere, made-up beds and a big backyard.

Beach Hostel (☎ *03-548 6817,* e *nelson beachhostel@xtra.co.nz, 25 Muritai St*) Dorm beds $18, doubles $44. Out at Tahunanui, this is a slightly worn but friendly and laid-back hostel with a balcony deck. Free pick-up and bikes are offered.

Footprints by the Sea (☎ *03-546 5441,* e *info@footprints.co.nz, 31 Beach Rd*) Dorms $18-20, single $22, twins/doubles $44/48. This new, purpose-built place is close to Tahunanui Beach and has a variety of clean rooms.

B&Bs & Guesthouses Nelson has plenty of B&Bs, but they may be full in the high season.

Borogrove (☎ *03-548 9442, 27 Grove St*) Singles/doubles $60/85. Borogrove is an Edwardian villa with self-contained rooms.

Grove Villa B&B (☎ *0800 488 900, 03-548 8856, 36 Grove St*) Singles $75-115, doubles $85-140. In the same street, this is another lovely historic villa with six rooms with en suite or share bathroom.

The Sussex (☎ *03-548 9972,* e *reserva tions@sussex.co.nz, 238 Bridge St*) Singles $100-130, doubles $120-150. In a historic family home, the Sussex has four lovely en suite rooms and a fifth with private bath-

room – all named after famous composers (the owners are musicians). The Strauss room has the best views. There's a pleasant garden and buffet breakfast is included.

Cambria House (☎ *0800 548 4681, 03-548 4681,* e *cambria@cambria.co.nz, 7 Cambria St*) Singles/doubles $145/185, deluxe double suites $235. The popular Cambria House, located in a 130-year-old homestead, is as superb as ever. The larger suites are huge and come with complementary drinks.

Motels Many of Nelson's motels, mostly of higher standard, are near the beach at Tahunanui on Beach Rd and Muritai St. There are also plenty on the highway in from Richmond.

Lynton Lodge Motel (☎ *03-548 7112, 25 Examiner St*) Doubles $70-90. Lynton Lodge looks and feels more like a guesthouse than a motel, with pleasant common areas and comfortable self-contained rooms.

Riverlodge Motel (☎ *03-548 3094,* e *riv erlodge.nelson@xtra.co.nz, 31 Collingwood St*) Studio units from $79, apartments $105. This place is central, with a heated pool.

Trafalgar Lodge Motel (☎/*fax 03-548 3980, 0800 000 051, 46 Trafalgar St*) B&B $55 per person, unit doubles $68-88. Trafalgar Lodge has comfortable units, as well as B&B in the guesthouse.

De Lorenzo's Studio Apartments (☎ *0508 335673, 03-548 9774, 51-55 Trafalgar St*) Doubles $120-170. De Lorenzo's is central, luxurious and has fully self-contained apartments that are worth the price if you want that little bit extra.

Places to Eat

The wealth of local produce, particularly seafood, makes dining out in Nelson a pleasure. Deep-sea fish such as orange roughie and hoki, scallops from the bays, and mussels and oysters are available, complemented by local wines and beers.

Rosy Glow Chocolates (☎ *03-548 3383, 20 Harley St*) This is a sibling of the original Rosy Glow in Collingwood (see the Golden Bay section later). If you're not heading that far, this is your chance to try these mega homemade chocolates. It's in the pink house opposite the police station.

Penguinos, in the arcade between Montgomery's car park and Trafalgar St, is a good place for icecream, with Italian gelati, sundaes and milkshakes.

Cafes & Takeaways At *Akbaba's (☎ 03-548 8825, 130 Bridge St)*, a tiny Turkish kebab house, you dine at low tables surrounded by rugs and carpets. Kebabs cost $6-12.

Chez Eelco (☎ 03-548 7595, 296 Trafalgar St) Meals $4-12. Open 7am-7pm daily. Chez Eelco, near the cathedral, is a Nelson institution. The spacious, arty cafe has plenty of newspapers and magazines to read and serves a range of breakfast staples and light meals. There's a small gallery at the back and Internet facilities.

Yaza Cafe (☎ 03-548 2849) Meals $4-11. Yaza's, in Montgomery car park (where the weekend markets are held), is a cosy cafe with all-day breakfast and occasional live acoustic and jazz music.

Zippy's (☎ 03-546 6348, 276 Hardy St) Zippy's specialises in vegetarian and vegan selections; it opens early in the evening, and stays open until late.

Morrison Cafe (☎ 03-548 8110, 244 Hardy St) This cafe-gallery is in a beautiful heritage building, and there is a delightful outdoor area where breakfast is served on sunny days.

The *Roadside Diner* is a big white pie cart that has been serving fast food since 1933 and is reputed to have the 'biggest burgers in NZ'. It's parked on Trafalgar St near Bridge St after 6pm daily, except Sunday, and is open until late most nights (until 3.30am on Friday and Saturday).

Pubs & Restaurants *Victorian Rose (☎ 03-548 7631, 281 Trafalgar St)* Mains $7-15. This place is a pastiche of English/Irish pub styles in airy premises. The Guinness is served with care and there is a large selection of beers. Meals are cheap and backpackers specials are offered.

Lambretta's (☎ 03-545 8555, 204 Hardy St) Dishes $12-23, small/large pizzas $12/21. Named after the Italian scooter, this predominately pizza and pasta restaurant has great, reasonably priced food and a busy but casual atmosphere. There are no run-of-the-mill toppings here – all are interesting gourmet combinations.

Broccoli Row (☎ 03-548 9621, 5 Buxton Square) Lunch $3-6.50, mains $20-25. Closed Sunday. Vegetarian and seafood dishes are the speciality here, including soups, tapas platters ($24.50) and spinach and potato gnocchi ($19.50). It's a lovely little cafe, tucked away off Buxton Square, and it's BYO.

Plaza India (☎ 03-546 9344, 132 Collingwood St) Mains $13-15. Specialising in North Indian and tandoori (although Goan fish curry appears temptingly on the menu), this is an authentic and reasonably priced place.

For excellent seafood by the sea and a touch of the Cote d'Azur in sunny Nelson, head to Wakefield Quay for the *Quayside Brasserie (☎ 03-548 3319, 309 Wakefield Quay)* or the casual *Harbour Light Store (☎ 03-546 6685, 341 Wakefield Quay)*.

Boat Shed (☎ 03-546 9783, 350 Wakefield Quay) Lunch $16-18, dinner $24-27. The Boat Shed is an ambient seafood restaurant sitting on stilts over the sea. The food here is undeniably good but it's pricey. There's an interesting menu, including a range of 'breakfast cocktails' ($8) – perfect for a hangover.

Entertainment

Nelson has a reasonable, if rather parochial, local nightlife scene. Backpackers (and locals) often start with a meal and a few drinks at the popular *Victorian Rose*, which also has regular live bands (jazz on Tuesday, blues on Thursday). By 10pm or so the action is starting to build on Bridge St, where most of the late-night pubs and bars are located.

Places worth checking out include *Little Rock*, a bar and cafe that turns into a dance club later on; the *Grumpy Mole*, a cavernous theme bar with 'dinosaur rock' exploding from the sound system, young people knocking back shooters, and a table for dancing on (open until 3am); *Taylor's*, a party place popular with backpackers; and the *Loft Bar (☎ 03-545 7576)*, a smaller place next to *Cafe Verte*.

For live music, *O'Reilly's*, in the Royal Hotel, has pop, blues and occasionally a Celtic jam session; *Yaza's* has jazz and acoustic music; and *Jessie's Pad*, next to the Grumpy Mole, is a small, laid-back jazz and blues bar.

The *Suter Art Gallery* has theatre, music and dance, and its *Stage Two theatre* shows a selection of art films.

Getting There & Away

Air The Air New Zealand Link office (☎ 0800 737 000) is on the corner of Trafalgar and Bridge Sts. Direct flights go to Wellington, Auckland and Christchurch, with connections to other cities.

Origin Pacific (☎ 0800 302 302), which is based in Nelson, has direct connections to several major centres including Auckland, Christchurch, Wellington and Hamilton.

Bus The main depot for InterCity (☎ 03-548 1538) is at 27 Bridge St. InterCity buses run daily to Picton (2hrs), Christchurch (9hrs) and to Greymouth (6hrs) via Murchison and Westport, with connections to the Franz Josef and Fox Glaciers.

Numerous shuttle buses operate out of Picton, dropping off and picking up at the visitors centre. Atomic Shuttles goes to Picton ($15) and down the West Coast to Greymouth ($40), where you have to wait until the following day to continue to the glaciers or Queenstown.

Lazerline (☎ 0800 220 001) has a reliable shuttle service to Christchurch daily via Murchison and Hanmer Springs, with onboard videos. Coast Shuttles (☎ 03-789 6837) goes from Nelson to Westport ($34) via Murchison and St Arnaud (Nelson Lakes).

The main shuttles to Picton and Blenheim are Kiwilink (☎ 0800 802 300), and Knightline (☎ 03-528 7798).

Abel Tasman Coachlines (☎ 03-548 0285), at 27 Bridge Rd, provides transport from Nelson, Motueka and Takaka to the Abel Tasman Track (see the Abel Tasman National Park section later for details) and to the Heaphy Track. Kahurangi Bus (see Takaka later in this chapter) provides transport to the tracks and as far as Collingwood ($32). Knightline also goes to Motueka from Nelson.

Getting Around

To/From the Airport Super Shuttle Nelson (☎ 03-547 5782) offers door-to-door service to and from the airport (6km southwest) for $10. A taxi to the airport costs about $15.

Bus Nelson Suburban Bus Lines (☎ 03-548 3290) operates local services from its terminal on Lower Bridge St. Buses run out to Richmond via Tahunanui and Stoke until about 5pm or 6pm Monday to Friday, and until 2pm or 3pm on Saturday. These connect with two loop services in Stoke, which will get you to Isel park, Broadgreen House and Mac's Brewery

The Bus (☎ 03-547 5912) is a central bus service running every hour or so on four routes, all starting from the bus depot. A single trip costs $4.

Bicycle Bicycles can be hired from Stewart Cycle City (☎ 03-548 1666) at 114 Hardy St and Natural High (☎ 03-546 6936), 52 Rutherford St. It costs around $20 a day for a road bike, $35 for a quality mountain bike.

NELSON LAKES NATIONAL PARK

Nelson Lakes National Park is 118km southwest of Nelson. Two beautiful glacial lakes are fringed by beech forest and flax, with a backdrop of forested mountains. Part of the park, east of Lake Rotoiti, is classed as a 'mainland island' and is part of an aggressive conservation scheme to eradicate introduced pests such as possums and stoats, and recover native flora and fauna. There's good tramping – without the crowds found in more well-known tramping spots – including short walks, lake scenery and also winter skiing at the Rainbow Valley and Mt Robert ski fields.

MARLBOROUGH & NELSON

The park is accessible from two different areas: Lakes Rotoiti and Rotoroa. St Arnaud village, at Lake Rotoiti (on the highway between Murchison and Blenheim) is a tiny place that's the main centre. Rotoroa, about 7km off the highway, gets far fewer visitors (mainly trampers and fishing groups).

All sorts of park information, including weather reports and hut tickets, is available from the DOC **Park Visitors Centre** (☎ 03-521 1806, ⓔ starnaudao@doc.govt.nz, Lake Rd, St Arnaud; open 8am-4.30pm daily) also has an interesting interpretive display.

If you're interested in photography, Phototrek South (☎ 03-521 1023) runs a variety of tours into the park and further afield with the emphasis on taking better pictures, with help from a professional photographer.

Walking

An excellent three-day tramp from St Arnaud takes you south along the eastern shore of Lake Rotoiti to Lake Head Hut, across the Travers River and up the Cascade Track to Angelus Hut on beautiful alpine Lake Angelus. The trip back to St Arnaud goes along Roberts Ridge to the Mt Robert ski field. On a clear day this ridge walk affords magnificent alpine views all along its length. The track descends steeply to the Mt Roberts car park, from where it's a 7km road walk back to St Arnaud.

Other walks at Rotoiti, most starting from the car park and camping area at Kerr Bay, include the Bellbird Walk (15mins), Honeydew Walk (45mins), Peninsula Nature Walk (1½hrs), Black Hill Track (1½hrs return), St Arnaud Range Track (5hrs), Loop Track (1½hrs return) and Lake Circuit (6hrs).

Short walks around Lake Rotoroa include the Short Loop Track (20mins), while medium-length ones include Porika Lookout (2-3hrs return) at the north end of the lake, and Braeburn Walk (2hrs return) on the western side. The long and arduous track along the eastern shore of the lake connects with the Travers-Sabine and Speargrass tracks to Lake Rotoiti. The visitors centre has pamphlets on all of these walks and can provide current information on track conditions.

Places to Stay & Eat

Lake Rotoiti There are well-equipped **DOC camping grounds** (☎ 03-521 1806) on the lakeshore at West Bay and Kerr Bay. Unpowered/powered sites cost $8/9 per person ($5/6 in winter) and they each have toilets, hot showers and a kitchen.

St Arnaud has quite a few accommodation options, but there's not much happening here after about 8pm.

Yellow House (☎ 03-521 1887, ⓦ www .nelsonlakes.co.nz, Main St) Dorm beds $19, doubles & twins $46. A well-maintained and well-equipped YHA associate has a spa pool, big kitchen and pleasant sun deck. You can also hire tramping equipment and store luggage here.

Alpine Chalet (☎/fax 03-521 1869) Dorm beds $16, doubles/twins $45. This is a large, clean European-style 'alpine' building, part of the more expensive Alpine Lodge next door. Guests are pretty much left to themselves, but a list of house rules in the foyer specifies 'Absolutely no parties'. Mountain bikes can be hired here for $25 a day.

St Arnaud Log Chalets (☎ 03-521 1887, 0800 867 468) Studio units $75, 1-bedroom units $90. Next door to the Yellow House (and run by the same people), these chalets are stylish timber en suite units. The larger one-bedroom units feature full kitchen facilities.

Top House (☎ 03-521 1848) B&B $40 per person, self-contained cottage doubles $90. Perched on a hill, 8km from St Arnaud, the Top House dates from 1887 when it was a hotel. Now it's a lovely B&B with a cosy fireplace, superb views of the St Arnaud range and even a chance for a round of golf on the hillside nine-hole course. As well as rooms in the historic house, there are modern units out the back. Dinner is available for $25.

Nelson Lakes Homestay (☎ 03-521 1191) B&B singles/doubles $60/95. This pleasant B&B is on a property about 4km from St Arnaud on the road to Blenheim. The en suite rooms are comfortable and good value evening meals are available.

The **Alpine Lodge** has a monopoly on eating out in St Arnaud. It has a bar with average bistro meals ($13.50-17.50), a more upmarket licensed restaurant (dinner $22-29), and the *Alpine Cafe* (☎ *03-521 1869)*, which is a good option for breakfast and lunch ($8-13).

Across the road is the *Nelson Lakes Village Centre* (☎ *03-521 1854)* with a general store, fish and chips and fuel.

Lake Rotoroa There's not much budget accommodation here. A basic *DOC camping ground* ($4 per person) by the lake has only a toilet and water point.

Gowan River Holiday Camp (☎/fax 03-523 9921, Gowan Valley Rd) Unpowered/powered sites $7/8, cabins $25-30. This small, scenic camp is 5km from SH6 on the road to Lake Rotoroa.

Getting There & Around

Atomic Shuttles passes through St Arnaud twice daily in each direction on its Picton-Greymouth run (one is an express service). Fares include Picton ($25), Nelson ($20), Blenheim ($25) and Greymouth ($35).

Nelson Lakes Shuttles (☎ 03-521 1023) provides transport from St Arnaud to Mt Robert car park ($10 per person), Lake Rotoroa ($20) and Rainbow Ski field ($15).

Water taxis operate on Lakes Rotoiti (☎ 03-521 1894) and Rotoroa (☎ 03-523 9199). At Lake Rotoiti, there's also kayak and fishing boat hire ($20/30 half/full day).

NELSON TO MOTUEKA

From Richmond, south of Nelson, SH60 heads west to Motueka. The region fringing Tasman Bay is all the rage with local holiday-makers, so there's plenty of accommodation, art and craft outlets, vineyards, yacht charters, fishing and swimming.

About 20km west of Nelson is the turn-off to **Rabbit Island**, which boasts great swimming beaches, boating, fishing and forest walks. The island has 13km of undeveloped, unspoilt beach backed by plantation forest. The bridge to the island is closed after 9pm daily and camping is not allowed.

Further along, the picturesque Waimea Inlet and the twin villages of **Mapua** and **Ruby Bay** are at the mouth of the Waimea

River. Mapua has numerous arts and crafts outlets and down on the wharf there's a small aquarium, **Touch the Sea**.

Mapua Jet & Mapua Adventures (☎ *03-540 3770*, W *www.mapuaadventures.co.nz; rides from $30)*, at the end of the wharf, has jetboat rides. A one-hour tour of Rabbit Island and the Waimea Inlet costs $49. They also offer an eco-tour with an ecologist/ornithologist explaining the diverse birdlife of the inlet ($119). Mapua Adventures has mountain biking tours on Rabbit Island ($20) and kayaking trips around it ($35), away from the crowds further west on the Abel Tasman.

The Smokehouse (☎ *03-540 2280, Shed 3, Mapua Wharf)*, right on Mapua waterfront, is a great cafe with delicious wood-smoked fish such as groper, tarakihi, moki and snapper. It's not cheap, and the dishes are rather small at around $20-24.

Nearby, the *Wharf Cafe* (☎ *03-540 2028)* is a casual licensed bar and restaurant with the added attraction of an aquarium and a display of local history.

Wineries

The Nelson region has a growing wine-making industry and although it doesn't rival the Marlborough region in size, there are more than enough wineries to keep you busy for a day or two (19 open at last count). Many vineyards on the **Nelson Wine Trail** can be visited by doing a loop from Nelson through Richmond to Motueka, following the SH60 coast road in one direction and the inland Moutere River road in the other. Many of the wineries are open for tastings and sales, and several have cafes and restaurants. Check out W www .nelsonwines.co.nz for more information.

The **Grape Escape** (☎ *03-544 4054, McShane Rd)* is a complex housing two wineries, Richmond Plains (certified organic wine) and Te Mania, as well as a cafe-bar and an art & craft gallery. It's on the wine tour itineraries and is open 10am-4.30pm Monday to Friday, 10am-5pm Saturday and Sunday.

Other wineries worth a visit include: **Denton Winery** (☎ *03-540 3555, Awa Awa Rd)*, which has a cafe open 11am-5pm daily; **Seifrieds** (☎ *03-544 1555, Redwood Rd*), one of the region's biggest wineries and with a good restaurant; **Ruby Bay Winery** (☎ *03-540 2825, Korepo Rd*), open daily from December to Easter, Saturday and Sunday only from October to November; **Moutere Hills Winery** (☎ *03-543 2288, Sunrise Valley*), open daily from November to Easter; **Neudorf Vineyards** (☎ *03-543 2643, Neudorf Rd*).

See Organised Tours in the Nelson section for information on wine tours.

Places to Stay

Mapua Leisure Park (☎ *03-540 2666*, @ *leisure.park@mapua.gen.nz, 33 Toru St*) Unpowered/powered sites $22/24 per double, cabin doubles $38, chalets $55-60. This park is 'NZ's first clothes-optional leisure park'. You don't *have* to bare all (many don't) and the position (next to the beach and river) and facilities are superb – tennis and volleyball courts, pool, sauna and spa, and a waterfront cafe.

McKee Memorial Reserve Camp sites $3.50 per person. McKee Memorial, 2km north of the leisure park, is a very basic camping ground located at the water's edge. Water, toilets and barbecue pits are the only amenities.

There are many homestays and farmstays in the region, including *Rerenga Farm* (☎ *03-543 3825, Dovedale-Woodstock Rd*), a rural retreat at Thorpe. The 85-year-old homestead has B&B ($95 a double) and dinner is $25.

MOTUEKA
pop 6610

Motueka is the centre of a green tea, hops and fruit-growing area. The main picking season for apples, grapes and kiwi fruit is from March to June. For most travellers, Motueka is not much more than a base or stopover en route to the Abel Tasman and Kahurangi National Parks and Golden Bay. In summer it's a bustling place, but in winter it's comatose. The inhabitants here are very cosmopolitan and there's a solid community of craftspeople.

Information

The Motueka visitors centre (☎ 03-528 6543, @ mzpvin@xtra.co.nz, W www .motueka.net.nz) in Wallace St (just off the main road) sells tickets for most things, including tours, kayaking, hut bookings for Abel Tasman and transport. It's open 8am to 5pm daily (until 7pm in summer).

On the corner of High and King Edward Sts there's a DOC field office (☎ 03-528 9117) that can provide information on the Abel Tasman and Kahurangi National Parks. However, the visitors centre handles hut bookings for the Abel Tasman Track and is generally a more accessible source of park information.

Internet access ($6 an hour) is available at Cyberworld, opposite the visitors centre in Wallace St. It's open 9am to 9pm daily.

Coppins Great Outdoor (☎ 03-528 7296), at 255 High St, hires out tents, backpacks and camping gear for use on the tracks.

Things to See & Do

The small **Motueka District Museum** (☎ *03-528 7660; adult/child $2/50c, open 10am-3pm Mon-Fri, 10am-1pm Sat*) has displays re-creating the region's colonial past, as well as a changing exhibition.

The **Riwaka Flying Fox**, north of Motueka at the turn-off to Kaiteriteri, is supposedly NZ's longest flying fox. You shoot down the hillside in an enclosed cabin. Unfortunately it was out of action at the time of research.

Places to Stay

Camping & Cabins At the southern entrance to town, *Fernwood Holiday Park* (☎/fax *03-528 7488, 519 High St South*) is a well-kept place with unpowered/powered sites for $8/9 per person and good cabins from $32-50.

Fearon's Bush Holiday Park (☎ *03-528 7189, 0800 668 835, 10 Fearon St*) Unpowered/powered sites $20/21 per double, self-contained units $60-80. Fearon's is a spacious place at the northern end of town. It has grassy camp sites, comfortable cabins and motel units.

Plenty of NZ wine at Hawkes Bay Wine Festival

Montana Winery, NZ's biggest, near Blenheim

Barrel racing at Hawkes Bay Wine Festival

The Coleraine vineyard, a participant in the yearly Hawkes Bay Wine Festival, Napier

OLIVER STREWE

Ice cave, Fox Glacier

DAVID WALL

Spirit of New Zealand, Marlborough Sounds

GARETH McCORMACK

Silver beech forest, Kahurangi National Park

CHRIS MELLOR

The flat plains of the Christchurch region, Canterbury

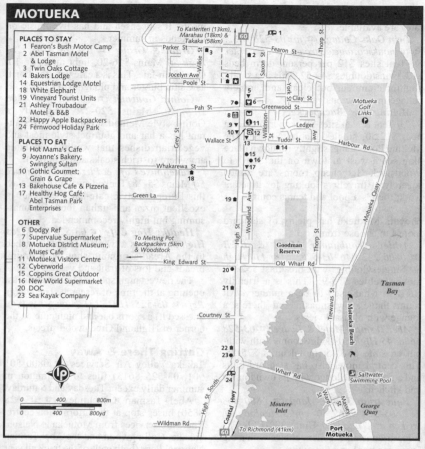

MOTUEKA

PLACES TO STAY
1 Fearon's Bush Motor Camp
2 Abel Tasman Motel & Lodge
3 Twin Oaks Cottage
4 Bakers Lodge
14 Equestrian Lodge Motel
18 White Elephant
19 Vineyard Tourist Units
21 Ashley Troubadour Motel & B&B
22 Happy Apple Backpackers
24 Fernwood Holiday Park

PLACES TO EAT
5 Hot Mama's Cafe
9 Joyanne's Bakery; Swinging Sultan
10 Gothic Gourmet; Grain & Grape
13 Bakehouse Cafe & Pizzeria
17 Healthy Hog Café; Abel Tasman Park Enterprises

OTHER
6 Dodgy Ref
7 Supervalue Supermarket
8 Motueka District Museum; Muses Cafe
11 Motueka Visitors Centre
12 Cyberworld
15 Coppins Great Outdoor
16 New World Supermarket
20 DOC
23 Sea Kayak Company

MARLBOROUGH & NELSON

Vineyard Tourist Units (☎ 03-528 8550, 328 High St) On-site vans $30, cabins $45, units with kitchen & bath $60-65. Bordering a local vineyard, this park is very small and has a variety of ageing but good-value accommodation.

Hostels The YHA-associate *Bakers Lodge* (☎ 03-528 0102, ⓦ www.bakerslodge.co .nz, 4 Poole St), in a carefully renovated former bakery, is the pick of Motueka's hostels. It's spacious, immaculate and has plenty of common areas including a large kitchen and outdoor barbecue area. Dorm

beds are $17-18, singles $30, doubles/twins $40 and en suite doubles $50-55.

White Elephant (☎ 03-528 6208, fax 528 0110, 55 Whakarewa St) Tent sites $10, dorm beds $17-18, doubles with linen $40. This is a good backpackers in a big, comfortable old house with a couple of outside units.

Happy Apple Backpackers (☎/fax 03-528 8652, ⓔ happyapple@xtra.co.nz, 500 High St) Tent sites $11 per person, dorm beds $17, twins/doubles $40. The Happy Apple is a friendly hostel with a number of rooms separate from the main house. There's a huge backyard for tents and it has the facilities to handle the numbers. Weekly rates are available.

Twin Oaks Cottage (☎/fax 03-528 7882, e twinoakscottage@xtra.co.nz, 25 Parker St) Tent sites $12 per person, dorm beds $17, twins/doubles $44-52. This is a small, slightly cramped, but clean and homely cottage in a spacious garden.

Melting Pot Backpackers (☎ 03-528 9423) Tent & van sites $8 per person, dorm beds $12.50, singles/doubles $18/36. The Melting Pot is a big, slightly rundown place 4km south-west of town on the SH61 to Woodstock. Its cheap rooms are aimed squarely at travellers looking for itinerant work; there's a pool and tennis court.

Motels Motueka has plenty of standard motels to choose from.

Ashley Troubadour Motel & B&B (☎ 0800 222 046, 03-528 7318, 430 High St) Singles/doubles with breakfast $52/75, motel doubles $75-95. This is a friendly B&B in what used to be a nunnery. All rooms have a washbasin and there's a lounge with pleasant views.

Abel Tasman Motel & Lodge (☎ 03-528 6688, 45 High St) Lodge rooms with/without en suite $75/45, motel units $75-85. This central motel also has standard units and a good-value lodge with its own lounge and kitchen.

Equestrian Lodge Motel (☎ 0800 668 782, 03-528 9369, e equestrianlodge@xtra.co.nz, Tudor St) Units $90-120. The Equestrian is an excellent choice with a big lawn, spa pool and tidy units.

Places to Eat

Motueka's seemingly endless main street (High St) has the usual string of takeaways and sandwich bars, including ***Joyanne's Bakery***, and the tiny ***Swinging Sultan***, which does great kebabs ($6-9) and coffee.

Muses (☎ 03-528 8696), in the museum building, is a cafe and art gallery, with dining inside or out on the covered patio. It has good salads, desserts and coffee.

Hot Mama's Cafe (☎ 03-528 7039, 105 High St) Mains $9.50-17.50. Open from 8am. Hot Mama's is a hip little open-fronted cafe with good coffee, pancakes and light meals. It's licensed and has live music on weekends in summer.

Grain & Grape (☎ 03-528 6103, 218 High St) Mains $16-20, light meals $6-10. Open 8am-late. This is a cafe with food such as Cajun burger and ploughman's lunch.

Gothic Gourmet (☎ 03-528 6699, 208 High St) Mains $20-27. Originally a Gothic-style Methodist church, this restaurant has a bar and gourmet-style meat and vegetarian dishes that would be notable anywhere (ostrich steaks and scallops).

Bakehouse Cafe & Pizzeria (off Wallace St) Mains $5-28. Tucked away in a laneway, this European-style cafe-bar specialises in excellent pizza and Italian food. It's unassuming but highly recommended.

Healthy Hog Cafe (☎ 03-528 7840, 265 High St) This is a wholefood cafe attached to the Arcadia organic shop with grainy breads and lots of fruit and vegies.

The newest nightspot in Motueka was just opening at the time of research. The ***Dodgy Ref*** (☎ 03-528 4101, 121 High St) is (you guessed it) a sports bar and nightclub on the corner of High and Greenwood streets.

Getting There & Away

Takaka Valley Air Services (☎ 0800 501 901, 03-525 8613) flies to Wellington in summer daily except Tuesday and Saturday.

Abel Tasman Coachlines (☎ 03-528 8850) buses stop at the information centre. There are services from Motueka to Nelson, Takaka, Collingwood and the Abel Tasman National Park (both ends of the track all year round). It also operates a charter service to the Heaphy Track. Buses also link Motueka and Nelson with Kaiteriteri and Marahau.

Knightline (☎ 03-528 7798) has a Motueka-Picton service at 6.15am and 2pm daily (3hrs). These services arrive back in Motueka at 1.30pm and 8.45pm.

Kahurangi Bus Services (☎ 03-525 9434) has daily buses to Takaka and Nelson via Motueka; they pick up at the visitors centre. Buses also run to and from Totaranui and Marahau. See the Abel Tasman National Park section for more information on transport to and from the Abel Tasman Track.

MOTUEKA TO ABEL TASMAN
Kaiteriteri Beach

This is one of the most popular resort beaches in the area, 13km from Motueka on a sealed road (which continues on to Marahau). The beach has genuine golden sand and clear, green waters. Behind the camping ground is **Withells Walk**, a 45-minute excursion into native bush from where great views look out across the bay. Otherwise walk to Kaka Pah Point at the end of the beach and explore some of the secluded little coves and hideaways.

Launch and kayak trips run to the Abel Tasman National Park from Kaiteriteri, though Marahau is the usual base.

Places to Stay & Eat Summer brings many holiday-makers, mainly locals, to Kaiteriteri, but bed-space is limited.

Kaiteriteri Beach Camp (☎ 03-527 8010) Unpowered/powered sites $9.50 per person, cabins $26-34, en suite cabins $50. This well-equipped camp, across from the beach, is large enough to cater to some of the summer crowds.

Kimi Ora Spa Resort (☎ 03-527 8027, 0508 546 4672, ☒ www.kimiora.com, Martin Farm Rd) Single/double units $129-163, spa suites $169/223. Kimi Ora is above the town and is a place to really pamper yourself with spa units, an indoor and outdoor pool complex, sauna, massage, as well as tennis courts, gym and a bush fitness track. Excellent units have balconies and views over the bay. There's also a very good vegetarian *restaurant* here, open to all.

Marahau

Further along the coast from Kaiteriteri, tiny Marahau, 18km north of Motueka, is the main gateway to the Abel Tasman National Park. From here you can book water taxis, hire kayaks, swim with seals or just head off on foot into the park. There are regular bus connections here (see the Abel Tasman National Park section).

Places to Stay For its size, Marahau has quite a few accommodation possibilities but the camping grounds still fill up in summer.

Marahau Beach Camp (☎ 0800 808 018, 03-527 8176, Franklin St) Unpowered/powered sites $9/10 per person, dorm beds $15, cabin doubles $40. This camp has a shop, kayaks hire ($55 a day) and a water-taxi service. There's also a cramped self-contained backpackers lodge.

Southern Exposure Backpackers (☎ 03-527 8424, ☒ info@southern-exposure.co.nz, Moss Rd) Tent sites $8 per person, dorm beds $18, singles/doubles $30/40. Sitting on a hill in a patch of native bush above Marahau, this small backpackers is run by Southern Exposure Kayaking. The buildings are new, the surroundings rustic and it's well run.

Barn Backpackers (☎ 03-527 8043, Harvey Rd) Tent sites $10, dorm beds $17, twins & doubles $42. This is a comfortable, homely place with a big loft bunkroom, spacious lawn area, house truck and a tepee.

Old MacDonald's Farm (☎ 03-527 8288, ☒ oldmacs@xtra.co.nz, Harvey Rd) Unpowered/powered sites $10/12 per person, on-site vans $35-40 per double, backpacker beds $15-16, self-contained unit doubles $120. Towards the end of Harvey Rd, this 100-acre property has llamas, alpacas, deer and cows, as well as backpacker huts, camping and the semi-open air *Gum Drop Cafe*, with meals from $6-15 (open noon-4pm in summer).

Ocean View Chalets (☎ 03-527 8232, ☒ o.v.ch@xtra.co.nz) Studio units $91, chalets $109-165. Ocean View has stylish cypress cottages on the hill overlooking Sandy Bay, and self-contained chalets. Prices drop in the off season.

Marahau Lodge (☎ 03-527 8250, ☒ jan@abeltasmanmarahaulodge.co.nz) Doubles from $120. This lodge, on the main waterfront road, has modern comfortable studios and self-contained units, and there's a guest kitchen.

Park Cafe (☎ 03-527 8270) Mains $10-24. Open breakfast, lunch & dinner. Near the start of the Abel Tasman Track and the park information kiosk, this cafe has good food and atmosphere. Gorge on cakes, muffins, blueberry crumble and milkshakes before heading out on the track. Lunch is reasonably priced but the evening menu is fairly upmarket. It's also a licensed bar.

ABEL TASMAN NATIONAL PARK

The coastal Abel Tasman National Park is a very accessible and popular tramping area. The park is at the northern end of a range of marble and limestone hills extending from Kahurangi National Park, and the interior is honeycombed with caves and potholes. There are various tracks in the park, including an inland track, although the coastal track is the most popular – just beware of the sandflies.

Abel Tasman Coastal Track

This 51km, three- to four-day track is one of the most beautiful in the country, passing through pleasant native bush that overlooks beaches of golden sand, which is lapped by gleaming blue-green water. The numerous bays, small and large, are like a travel brochure come to life.

Once little known outside the immediate area, this track has well and truly been 'discovered' and in summer (December to late February) hundreds of backpackers and trampers may be on the track at any one time – far more than can be accommodated in the huts, so bringing a tent is a good idea. Track accommodation works on a booking system, similar to the Routeburn and Milford Tracks. If you don't have a prebooked hut ticket for a particular night in season (September to May), you may be refused entry to a hut – check with DOC. In winter you don't need to book but you still need to purchase a ticket.

Information The track operates on a Great Walks Pass system – the cost is $14 per adult in the huts and $7 for camp sites (from May to September hut tickets cost $10). Children pay half price (free under 11 years). The Abel Tasman Coastal Track booking desk (☎ 03-528 0005) is at the Motueka visitors centre, but you can obtain hut passes from DOC or information centres in Nelson and Takaka.

There's also a National Park Visitors Centre at Totaranui, open seasonally from late November to February; at other times the latest bus and boat schedules are posted there.

Walking the Track Several sections of the main track are tidal, with long deviations during high tides, particularly at Awaroa. As the tidal stretches are all just on the northern side of huts, it is important to do the track in a southerly direction if the low tides are in the afternoons, and from south to north if they are in the mornings. Check the newspaper, subtracting 20 minutes from the Nelson tidal times. Tide tables and advice are available at the DOC office or visitors centre in Motueka.

Take additional food so you can stay longer should you have the inclination. Bays around all the huts are beautiful but the sandflies are a problem, except at the tiny, picturesque beach of Te Pukatea near the Anchorage Hut.

Many visitors combine walking and kayaking on the track – see the boxed text 'Paddling the Abel Tasman'.

Many walkers stop at Totaranui, the final stop for the boat services and a pick-up point for buses, but it is possible to keep walking around the headland from Totaranui to Whariwharangi hut (2hrs) and then on to Wainui (1½hrs), where buses service the car park.

Estimated walking times are as follows, south to north: Marahau to Anchorage Hut (3½hrs), Anchorage Hut to Bark Bay Hut (3hrs), Bark Bay Hut to Awaroa Hut (3hrs), and Awaroa Hut to Totaranui (1½hrs).

Seal Swimming

An off-shore section of the park, from Bark Bay to Awaroa Head, is classified as the **Tonga Island Marine Reserve** and is home to a seal colony and visiting dolphins. Tonga Island itself is a small rock outcrop out from Onetahuti Beach. **Abel Tasman Seal Swim** (☎ 0800 527 8136; adult/child $75/55) organises trips to the seal colony, departing from Marahau at 8.45am and again at 1pm. You can also choose to be dropped off in the park and walk back from there after the swim.

ABEL TASMAN NATIONAL PARK

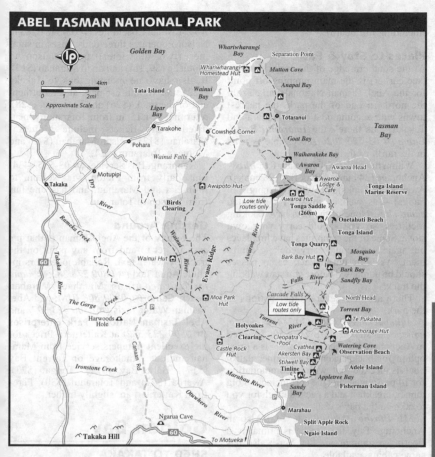

Golden Bay
Whariwharangi Bay
Separation Point
Whariwharangi Homestead Hut
Mutton Cove
Anapai Bay
Tata Island
Wainui Bay
Totaranui
Ligar Bay
Tasman Bay
Tarakohe
Cowshed Corner
Goat Bay
Pohara
Waiharakeke Bay
Wainui Falls
Awaroa Bay
Awaroa Head
Motupipi
Awapoto Hut
Awaroa Lodge & Cafe
Takaka
Tonga Island Marine Reserve
Birds Clearing
Low tide routes only
Awaroa Hut
Tonga Saddle (260m)
Onetahuti Beach
Wainui Hut
Wainui River
Evans Ridge
Awaroa River
Tonga Quarry
Tonga Island
Bark Bay Hut
Mosquito Bay
Falls River
Bark Bay
Sandfly Bay
Moa Park Hut
Cascade Falls
Low tide routes only
North Head
The Gorge
Creek
Torrent River
Torrent Bay
Te Pukatea
Harwoods Hole
Holyoakes Clearing
Cleopatra's Pool
Anchorage Hut
Castle Rock Hut
Cyathea
Akersten Bay
Watering Cove
Observation Beach
Ironstone Creek
Canaan Rd
Stilwell Bay
Tinline
Adele Island
Marahau River
Appletree Bay
Fisherman Island
Sandy Bay
Ngarua Cave
Marahau
Split Apple Rock
Takaka Hill
To Motueka
Ngaio Island

MARLBOROUGH & NELSON

Organised Tours

Abel Tasman National Park Enterprises (☎ 03-528 7801, W www.abeltasman.co.nz; cruises from $36) has launch services from Kaiteriteri, which can be used as trampers transport or a day cruise. The full 5½-hour return cruise to Totaranui is $49/22 adults/children, and the 3½-hour cruise to Torrent Bay is $36/18. You can easily combine a walk along part of the Abel Tasman Track with the cruise, getting dropped off at one bay and picked up later at another. Other water taxi operators provide a similar service – see Getting Around later.

The launch operates scheduled routes all year, but cancellations occur and they are not 100% reliable. All trips should be booked in advance. Abel Tasman Coachlines has a bus service from Nelson and Motueka which connects with the launch, making it an easy day trip from either town.

Abel Tasman National Park Enterprises also has a range of upmarket guided walks and walk-kayaking trips from $900 for a three-day trip in high season.

Sailing is a popular way to explore the coastline. Try **Centresail** (☎ 03-545 0548, W www.centresailcharters.co.nz) with its multiday trips from $140 per person per day (including full board).

Places to Stay & Eat

At the southern edge of the park, Marahau (see earlier) is the main jumping-off point for the Abel Tasman National Park. From the northern end of the park, the nearest towns with accommodation are Pohara and Takaka, plus there's the *Totaranui Beach Camp* (☎ 03-525 8026), accessible by road in the north of the park.

Within the park itself there are four *huts* – Anchorage (24 bunks), Bark Bay (28 bunks), Awaroa (22 bunks) and Whariwharangi (20 bunks) – as well as some 21 designated *camp sites*. None of the huts have cooking facilities, so you should carry your own stove. Some of the camp sites have fireplaces but again you should carry cooking equipment. As with hut tickets, camp passes should be purchased before you start walking the track.

There are also several other options in the park.

Aquapackers (☎ 0800 430 744, e chris@aquapackers.co.nz) DB&B $50. Moored in Anchorage Bay, the MV *Parore* is a great option for backpackers. The former patrol boat is decked out with accommodation for 14 passengers and the cost includes a big dinner, breakfast and a packed lunch for you to take on the day's walk.

MV Etosha (☎ 0800 386 742) Also in Anchorage Bay, the Etosha is primarily a floating restaurant and bar, but it also has some cabins available.

Kanuka Hill Lodge (☎ 03-548 2863) DB&B $285. Kanuka Hill at The Anchorage is surrounded by native bush. There are three en suite rooms, and the rate includes a three-course meal.

Awaroa Lodge & Cafe (☎ 025 433 135). Doubles $85-155. This lodge, at Awaroa Bay, is only about 300m from the water and 200m off the track. There are doubles with shared facilities as well as en suite units. The *cafe* here offers a range of health food and the proprietors will also pack lunches for daytrippers. Awaroa is accessible by road, water taxi or on foot.

Getting There & Away

Abel Tasman Coachlines (☎ 03-548 0285 in Nelson) operates three daily buses in summer (two in winter) from Nelson to Motueka ($9, 1hr) and on to Marahau ($13). It also has one morning bus to Takaka ($22), the Wainui car park at the northern end of the track ($26) and Totaranui ($28), returning at 1.15pm from Totaranui. Open-dated return tickets include Motueka-Marahau ($12), Nelson-Marahau ($23) and Motueka-Totaranui ($24).

Kahurangi Bus Services (☎ 03-525 9434) runs daily from Picton, via Nelson, to Motueka and Marahau, and has one bus from Nelson to Totaranui.

Getting Around

The beauty of the Abel Tasman is that it's easy to get to and from any point on the track by water taxi. Reliable operators include **Aqua Taxi** (☎ 0800 278 282; e aqua taxi@xtra.co.nz) in Marahau; **Marahau Beach Camp** (☎ 0800 808 018); and **Abel Tasman Water Taxis** (☎ 0800 423 397) and **Abel Tasman National Park Enterprises** (☎ 0800 223 582) at Kaiteriteri. Prices for the excellent trampers service from Marahau include: Anchorage or Torrent Bay ($17), Bark Bay ($21), Tonga ($23), Awaroa ($27) and Totaranui ($30). Fares from Kaiteriteri are slightly higher.

Golden Bay

SH60 TO TAKAKA

From Motueka, SH60 continues over Takaka Hill to Takaka and Collingwood.

Takaka Hill (791m) separates Tasman Bay from Golden Bay. Near the summit are the **Ngarua Caves** (☎ 03-528 8093; *adult/child $11/4; open Sept-mid June*) where you can see moa bones. You can only enter the caves on a 40-minute guided tour, leaving on the hour between 10am and 4pm. Just before the Ngarua Caves is the Hawkes Lookout, from where there are great views of the Riwaka River headwaters.

Also in the area is the biggest *tomo* (entrance, or cave) in the southern hemisphere,

Paddling the Abel Tasman

The Abel Tasman Track has long been famous among trampers, but its main attractions – the scenic beaches, coves and bays – make it an equally alluring spot for sea kayaking.

Many travellers choose to kayak around at least part of the park, cruising around the relatively safe, sheltered waters and calling in at those impossibly pretty beaches. You can easily combine kayaking, walking and camping here. It's not necessarily a matter of hiring a kayak and looking after yourself (although it is possible to do that) – a string of professional outfits can get you out on the water and the possibilities and permutations for guided or freedom trips are virtually endless. You can kayak from half a day to three days, camping or staying in huts. You can kayak one day, camp overnight and walk back, or walk further into the park and catch a water taxi back. Trips can be fully catered or you can arrange to stay in huts or accommodation such as Aquapackers in Anchorage Bay. A popular choice if your time is tight is a guided kayak trip to Anchorage, where you stay overnight, walk unguided to Onetahuti Beach and catch a water taxi back – it costs around $110 plus camping or hut fees. Most companies offer a three-day trip where you get dropped at the northern end of the park and paddle back (or vice versa) for around $290 ($380 with food included). What you decide to do may depend on your own time (and financial) constraints – pick up the brochures, look at the options and talk to other travellers.

Instruction is given to first-timers and double-kayaks are used by all outfits unless you can demonstrate that you're competent enough to control and keep up in a single kayak. If you're on your own you'll be matched with someone else in the group.

Freedom rentals (kayak and equipment hire) are around $55 per person per day; some companies require a minimum of two days hire and do not allow solo hires.

The peak season in the park is from November to Easter but you can paddle year-round. December to February is by far the busiest time, so it's worth timing your visit earlier or later. Winter is a good time as you will see more bird life and the weather is surprisingly calm and mild.

Most of the sea kayaking operators have plenty of experience and all offer similar trips at similar prices. Marahau is the closest base but trips are also run out of Motueka, Kaiteriteri and even Nelson.

Abel Tasman Kayaks (☎ *0800 527 8022, 03-527 8022,* Ⓦ *www.kayaktours.co.nz, Marahau Beach)* Day trip $99, two-day kayak/walk $150, three-day guided tour $295 ($385 with food).

Kaiteriteri Kayaks (☎ *0800 252 925, 03-527 8383,* Ⓦ *www.seakayak.co.nz, Kaiteriteri Beach)* Sunset paddle $45, half-day guided trips $50, full day $80, kayak/walk from $95.

Kiwi Kayaks (☎ *0800 695 494)* One-day kayak/walk from $65-120, guided trips $89 per day (freedom rentals $55 per person per day); three-day tour $285 ($375 catered).

Ocean River Adventure Company (☎ *0800 732 529, 03-527 8266,* Ⓦ *www.seakayaking.co.nz, Main Rd, Marahau),* One-day ($95) to three-day ($250) trips, catered packages which include lodge accommodation from $365.

Sea Kayak Company (☎ *0508 252925, 03-528 7251,* Ⓦ *www.seakayaknz.co.nz, 506 High St, Motueka)* One-day tour ($95) up to five-day tour ($550), which includes a trip down Awaroa estuary.

Southern Exposure Sea Kayaking (☎ *0800 695 292, 03-527 8424,* Ⓦ *www .southern-exposure.co.nz, Moss Rd, Marahau)* One-day trips $80-99, two- and three-day catered trips $290/445. They have a backpackers hostel in Marahau.

MARLBOROUGH & NELSON

Harwood's Hole. It is 400m deep and 70m wide. It's a half-hour walk one way from the car park at the end of Canaan Rd, off SH60. Exercise caution as you approach the lip of the hole – accidents have occurred.

As you cross the crest of the hill, **Harwood Lookout** has fine views down the Takaka River Valley to Takaka and Golden Bay. The lookout has interesting explanations of the geography and geology of the area, from the north-west Nelson peneplain to the Anatoki Ranges. A peneplain, you ask? It's an area worn almost flat as a result of erosion.

From the lookout you wind down through the beautiful Takaka Hill Scenic Reserve to the river valley. The nearby Cobb Valley is notably the site of New Zealand's biggest annual dance (rave) party, **The Gathering**, held over the New Year period. If you're interested in going, check out Ⓦ www.gathering.co.nz.

TAKAKA
pop 1230
Takaka is the main centre for the beautiful Golden Bay area and the last town of any size as you head towards the north-west corner of the South Island. It's a bustling place in summer and quite a hip little community – full of 'Woodstock children' and artistic types and all the galleries, craft shops and trendy organic cafes that go with it.

Information
The Golden Bay Information Centre (☎ 03-525 9136), on the main road into town from Motueka, is open 9am to 5pm daily.

DOC (☎ 03-525 8026), on Commercial St, has information on Abel Tasman and Kahurangi National Parks, the Heaphy and Kaituna Tracks, Farewell Spit, Cobb Valley and the Aorere goldfields. It's open 8am to 4pm Monday to Friday.

There's Internet access at the Golden Bay Net Cafe, in The Avenue, down a side street near Wholemeal Cafe.

The Quiet Revolution Cycle Shop (☎ 03-525 9555) hires mountain bikes from $15 to $25, has local track information and also does repairs and service.

Things to See & Do
The **Golden Bay Museum & Gallery** (☎ 03-525 9990, Commercial St; adult/child $2/50c, open 10am-4pm daily) is a well-presented jumble of historical memorabilia, but the stand-out exhibit is the diorama depicting Abel Tasman's 1642 landing in Golden Bay, when four of his crew were killed by Maori warriors. Visitors can take a look around the attached gallery for free.

Many artists and craftspeople are based in the Golden Bay area, including painters, potters, blacksmiths, screenprinters, silversmiths and knitwear designers. The large **Artisans' Shop** (30 Commercial St), a cooperative next to the Village Theatre, displays their wares. Many other artists and craftspeople are tucked away all around the bay. The *Arts of Golden Bay* leaflet provides directions to all the galleries and workshops in the area.

Bencarri Farm (☎ 03-525 8261, McCallums Rd; admission $5), on the Anatoki River 6km from town, has a variety of farm animals (including llamas) and a cafe, but the prime attraction at this farm is feeding the tame eels down at the river. Next door, you can fish for salmon at the **Anatoki Salmon Farm** (☎ 03-525 7251) or buy fresh or smoked fish.

Waikoropupu Springs
These springs (simply called 'Pupu') are the largest freshwater springs in NZ and reputedly the clearest in the world. About 14,000 litres of water a second is thrown up from a number of underground vents dotted around the Pupu Springs Scenic Reserve, including one with 'dancing sands' thrown upwards by the great volume of incredibly clear water emerging from the ground.

Walking tracks through the reserve take you to the springs and a glassed viewing area, passing by **gold-mining works** from the 19th century – gold was discovered in Golden Bay in 1856. There is a good DOC leaflet describing the reserve. To reach Pupu from Takaka, head 4km north-west on SH60, turn inland at Waitapu Bridge and continue for 3km.

Organised Tours

Kahurangi Guided Walks (☎ 03-525 7177, W www.kahurangiwalks.webnz.co.nz) covers just about every track in the park, including a five-day walk along the Heaphy Track ($800 with transport and gourmet food). It also has day walks on the Upper Cobb, Sylvester Lakes and Aorere Goldfields ($80) and various catered three- to four-day walks at $130 per day.

Golden Bay Sailing Charters (☎ 0800 370 017; trips $35-210) has day sailing and scalloping trips.

Places to Stay

Takaka has some good accommodation, though the nearby beach resort of Pohara is also popular and has the closest camping ground (see the Pohara section later).

Annie's (☎ 03-525 8766, 25 Motupipi St) Dorm beds $18, doubles $46. Close to the town centre on the road to Pohara, Annie's is a small, peaceful haven with a homely atmosphere. There's a separate shared room at the bottom of the organic garden.

Golden Bay Barefoot Backpackers (☎ 03-525 7005, 114 Commercial St) Dorm beds $19, doubles $40. This is a comfortable renovated house with open lounge and kitchen areas and a garden out the back – a good place for meeting other travellers.

River Inn (☎ 03-525 9425, e riverinn@xtra.co.nz) Singles, twins & doubles $18 per person. The River Inn, 3km west of town on the road to Collingwood, is a big old two-storey pub with backpacker rooms upstairs and a big bar below.

Shambhala Beach Farm Hostel (☎ 03-525 8463) Dorm beds $17, twins & doubles $38. Closed June-Nov. Located about 15km west of the River Inn this rustic retreat is spectacularly set overlooking Onekaka Beach. If you're driving take the right turn 50m before the Mussel Inn (coming from Takaka), but it is then about 3km along a dirt road. Rooms are in the house and cottages around.

Motels in Takaka include the **Golden Bay Motel** (☎ 0800 401 212, 03-525 9428, 132 Commercial St) with doubles from $70 to $100, and the **Anotaki Lodge** (☎ 0800 262 333, 03-525 8047, 87 Commercial St), with a solar-heated pool and spacious self-contained rooms from $95 to $120.

Places to Eat

Golden Bay's popularity and Takaka's arty community have helped ensure that this small town is no culinary wasteland.

Wholemeal Cafe (☎ 03-525 9426, 60 Commercial St) Mains $18-23. Open 7.30am-8.30pm. This is a local institution and the stand-out place to eat in Takaka. It's a bohemian cafe, restaurant and art gallery which also sells bulk natural foods and sometimes has live music in the evenings. The curries ($12.50/16 small/large, including venison and organic veg varieties) are outstanding and there are croissants, bagels and free-range eggs for breakfast.

The Dangerous Kitchen (☎ 03-525 8686, 48 Commercial St) Dedicated to Frank Zappa, the Dangerous Kitchen specialises in whacky gourmet pizzas ($10/17/24 small/medium/large), and does great coffee and cakes as well.

The Big Fat Moon Cafe (☎ 03-525 7490, 1 Commercial St) Mains $13.50-15.50. Open 8am-9pm Mon-Sat. This is a casual Asian cafe-restaurant dabbling in Indian, Thai, Malaysian and Indonesian dishes. Lunch dishes and takeaways (such as laksa) are only $5-9.50.

Milliways (☎ 03-525 9636, Commercial St) Mains $20-28. Open daily summer. Milliways is a fancier licensed restaurant with a relaxed atmosphere. There are roast dinners ($14.50) on Sunday and Monday.

Bencarri Farm & Cafe (☎ 03-525 8261) Mains $7-22. Bencarri Farm, in a pleasant bush setting on the Anatoki River 6km from town, has a cafe serving bagels, baguettes and country-style lunches and dinners.

Entertainment

Watching a movie ($10) at the **Village Theatre** (☎ 03-525 8453) is a good night out. Otherwise, the **Telegraph Hotel** (☎ 03-525 9308) and the **Mussel Inn** (☎ 03-525 9241), about 15km away on the road to Collingwood, often have live bands performing on weekends.

MARLBOROUGH & NELSON

Getting There & Away

Kahurangi buses (☎ 03-525 9434) go from Takaka to Collingwood ($12), the beginning of the Heaphy Track ($20), and to Nelson ($22) daily. Abel Tasman Coachlines also operates from Nelson to Takaka. Both have daily services to Totaranui at the northern end of the Abel Tasman National Park, passing Pohara on the way.

POHARA

Pohara is a small but popular summer resort, 10km north-east of Takaka. The beach is on the way to the northern end of the Abel Tasman Track. The unsealed road to the park is scenic and passes by **Ligar Bay**, which has a lookout and a memorial that is dedicated to Abel Tasman, the first European to enter Golden Bay. Tasman anchored here in December 1642 but didn't stay long after one of his shore parties was rammed by a Maori canoe and four crewmen were killed. Tasman originally named this 'Murderer's Bay'.

The **Rawhiti Caves** near Pohara have the largest entrance of any cave in NZ, well worth a look. There is an enjoyable three-hour return guided tour of the caves run by **Kahurangi Guided Walks** (☎ 03-525 7177; adult/child $25/15).

Golden Bay Kayaks (☎ 03-525 9095) rents out kayaks ($55 a day, with discounts for multiple days) and has half-day guided tours ($50). Although not as picturesque as Abel Tasman, Golden Bay's waters are a lot less crowded.

Places to Stay & Eat

Pohara Beach Holiday Park (☎ 03-525 9500, Abel Tasman Dr) Unpowered/powered sites $11 per person, cabin doubles $40-50, motel units $95. Right on the beach in the middle of the village, this friendly park has self-contained units and basic but clean cabins sleeping four. There's also a well-equipped camp kitchen.

The Nook (☎ 03-525 8501, e nook@clear.net.nz, Abel Tasman Dr) Tent sites $12, dorm beds $18, twins & doubles $42. The Nook is a casual backpackers place, close to the beach between Clifton and Pohara.

Behind the main house is a very nice self-contained straw-bale cottage (sleeps 6) at $90 for two and $10 for each extra person.

Sans Souci Inn (☎/fax 03-525 8663, e reto@sanssouciinn.co.nz, Richmond Rd) Singles/doubles with shared bath $50/75. Just off Abel Tasman Drive at Pohara Beach, Sans Souci Inn has seven stylish mud-brick rooms, done in a bright, breezy Mediterranean style. It's very chic and superb value even if you don't normally like the idea of a shared bathroom. There's a good licensed restaurant open for breakfast and dinner (from 7pm; bookings essential) and guests can use the kitchen.

The Sandcastle (☎ 03-525 9087, 0800 433 909, e sandcastle@xtra.co.nz, Haile Lane) Doubles $84. This is a pleasant eco-friendly place with a wood-fired sauna and outdoor spa pools. There are six fully self-contained and individual chalets set in native bush surroundings.

COLLINGWOOD & AROUND
pop 250

Tiny Collingwood is the last town in this part of the country and it certainly has that end of the road feel. It gets pretty busy in summer, but for most it's simply one jumping-off point for the Heaphy Track in the Kahurangi National Park or a base for trips to the natural wonderland of Farewell Spit.

No visit to Collingwood would be complete without dipping into the original **Rosie Glow Chocolate House** (☎ 03-524 8348; open Sat-Thur) on Beach Rd. Chocoholics will go nuts here, where handmade chocolates are lovingly produced (though not cheap). There's also the local **museum** on Tasman St ($2 donation).

As befits a frontier town, this is a place where you can get a horse: **Cape Farewell Horse Trekking** (☎ 03-524 8031) based in Puponga has one-hour rides and a three-hour trip to Wharariki.

Guided kayaking trips in the Whanganui Inlet are organised by the **Inn-let Backpackers** (☎ 03-524 8040). Full day trips cost around $70 and kayaking/tramping trips are $95. You can also hire kayaks for $40/60 for a half/full day.

Farewell Spit

Farewell Spit is a wetland of international importance and a renowned bird sanctuary. It's the summer home to thousands of migratory waders from the Arctic tundra. On the 26km beach run there are huge crescent-shaped sand dunes from where you get panoramic views of the Spit, Golden Bay and, at low tide, the vast salt marsh.

The **Farewell Spit Visitor Centre & Cafe** (*☎ 03-524 8454; open 9am-8pm daily Jan, 9am-6pm Dec & Feb, 10am-4pm winter, closed June-Aug)*, 24km from Collingwood, provides information on the region as well as a cafe with a view and reasonable food. There are coin-op binoculars set up to view the wetlands and the many species of wading birds. On the track leading down from the visitors centre is the assembled skeleton of a pilot whale, a species which often beaches here. You can walk down and look out over the eel grass flats and see many waders and sea birds such as pied and variable oystercatchers, turnstones, Caspian terns, eastern bar-tailed godwits, black and white-fronted terns, and big black shags.

The crossing to the northern side of the Spit is made by the tour companies. The trucks grind up over the beach to about 1km from Cape Farewell. Down towards the start of the sand are a number of fossilised shellfish. From this point it is 27km to the end of the sandy spit. Again many species of birds are seen along the way. The normal trip ends at the old lighthouse compound.

Further east, up on the blown shell banks which comprise the far extremity of the Spit, are colonies of Caspian terns and Australasian gannets.

Two companies offer guided tours to the remarkable Farewell Spit region, departing from Collingwood (both have offices on Tasman St). These are the only vehicles allowed to visit the Spit. Scheduled tours leave daily, but departure times are dependent on the tides (departure at low tide).

Farewell Spit Safari (*☎ 0800 808 257, 03-524 8257, W www.farewellspit.co.nz; tours from $55)* pioneered travel up the sandy beach and offers four different trips.

The original five-hour lighthouse safari takes you up the beach in a 4WD vehicle and costs $60/35 adult/child. They are also licensed by DOC to visit the gannet colony, a 1km walk from the lighthouse. The 5½-hr tour costs $75. The wader-watch tour ($55, 3-4hrs) on the inside of the sandy spit (the estuarine side) is a must for twitchers. The Cape Farewell Tour ($70, 6½hrs) takes you in another direction, to the South Island's northernmost point at the rocky headland of Cape Farewell.

Farewell Spit Nature Tours (*☎ 03-524 8188, 0800 250 500, W www.farewell-spit .co.nz; adult/child $75/45)* also goes to the lighthouse. Prices include lunch.

Wharariki Beach

This isolated beach is a further 6km from the visitors centre along an unsealed road, and then a 20-minute walk from the car park over farmland (part of the Puponga Farm Park, administered by DOC). It is a wild introduction to the West Coast, with unusual dune formations, two looming, rock islets just out from shore, and a seal colony at its eastern end. What a way to get away from the 'rat race' of Collingwood! As inviting as a swim at this usually deserted spot may seem, resist the temptation – there are strong undertows that make the sea very dangerous along this stretch.

Places to Stay

There's accommodation in Collingwood itself and more places scattered along the road to Farewell Spit.

Collingwood Motor Camp (*☎ 03-524 8149, William St)* Unpowered & powered sites $9 per person, huts $18 per person, self-contained cabin doubles from $50. This friendly camp is at the end of Tasman St and has a range of accommodation including a house. The house sleeps up to 11; the tarrif begins at $100 for four people.

Skara Brae (*☎ 03-524 8464, e skara brae@xtra.co.nz, Elizabeth St)* B&B $100, motel units $85. This comfortable, centrally located guesthouse has en suite B&B rooms in the main house and two self-contained units at the back.

Beachcomber Motel (☎ 03-524 8499, *Tasman St*) Studio unit doubles $72-94, family units $105. Beachcomber is a tidy set of units on the main street. The larger units have a mezzanine floor and full cooking facilities.

Pakawau is hardly a spot on the map, halfway between Collingwood and Farewell Spit, but there are a few places here.

Inn-let (☎ 03-524 8040, e jhearn@xtra .co.nz) Tent sites $7 per person, dorm beds $18.50, twins & doubles $45-55, cottage $110. The Inn-let, on the way to Pakawau about 10km from Collingwood, is a top-notch backpackers. The renovated main house is comfortable, with an inviting pot-belly stove in the lounge, and there are various huts outside. The owners, Jonathan and Katie, are attuned to their environment and offer kayak hire and guided kayaking and tramping trips.

Continuing along you come to the end of the main road at Puponga near Cape Farewell.

World's End Backpacker Lodge (☎ 03-524 8037) Dorm beds $16, doubles $38. World's End is a small, no-frills house in a great location at Puponga, close to Farewell Spit.

Golden Bay Holiday Park (☎ 03-525 9742) Unpowered/powered sites $10/11 per person, cabin doubles $52 ($18 per person outside high season). About 8km south of Collingwood on Tukurua Beach, this is a nice little retreat – the cabins are booked solid in December and January, but it's not a big park so retains some charm.

Places to Eat

Collingwood Cafe is your standard country town cafe with a blackboard menu of sandwiches and greasy food; try the homemade scallop pies for $3.50. The *Collingwood Tavern* has bar snacks from $6-10 and more substantial meals in its bistro.

Courthouse Cafe & Gallery (☎ 03-525 8472, *cnr Haven Rd*) Meals $6-25. This historic cafe prepares delicious a la carte meals from locally grown organic produce and fresh seafood. There's a nice outdoor seating area for enjoying a long lunch.

Mussel Inn (☎ 03-525 9241, *Onekaka*) Lunch $3-10.50, dinner $14-19.50. Open 11am-late. About halfway between Takaka and Collingwood, this tavern-cafe-brewery was modelled on an early 1900s establishment. The food is good and reasonably priced (a big bowl of steamed mussels is $10.50) and they brew their own beer – four draught beers, plus a draught cider, and two bottled varieties, including the sledge-hammer Monkey Puzzle (10% alcohol). The Mussel Inn is also doing its bit for the local wildlife – they offer a free beer for every fresh possum's tail brought in! Evening meals are served 6pm-9pm and there's live entertainment in summer.

Old School House Cafe (☎ 03-524 8457) Mains around $20. Found in Pakawau, this restaurant has a good local reputation. The building's decor matches its former calling, and scallops and other local seafood are featured on the menu.

Getting There & Away

Kahurangi Bus (☎ 03-525 9434) has a daily bus service between Collingwood and Nelson via Takaka and Motueka. The same bus goes to the Inn-let and the Heaphy Track car park.

Abel Tasman National Coachlines (☎ 03-528 8850) also has daily services from Nelson to Motueka, Takaka and Collingwood (and the Heaphy Track in summer).

KAHURANGI NATIONAL PARK

This is the second-largest of NZ's national parks and undoubtedly one of the greatest. Its 500,000 hectares comprise an ecological wonderland – over 100 bird species, 50% of all NZ's plant species, 80% of its alpine plant species, a karst landscape and the largest known cave system in the southern hemisphere. Kahurangi means 'treasured possession'. Few keen trampers will disagree, as the many fine tracks and rugged country attract them in droves, mostly to walk the Heaphy Track.

Information

Detailed information, park maps and Great Walks Passes for the Heaphy Track are available from the following DOC offices or visitors centres:

Golden Bay Area Office (☎ 03-525 8026),
62 Commercial St, Takaka
Karamea Information Centre
(☎ 03-782 6652), Market Cross, Karamea
Motueka Area Office (☎ 03-528 1810),
corner of King Edward and High Sts, Motueka
Nelson Visitor Information Centre
(☎ 03-548 2304), corner of Trafalgar and
Halifax Sts, Nelson

Heapy Track

Named after Major Charles Heaphy, the painter and soldier who was awarded the Victoria Cross during the Waikato Land Wars (1864), the Heaphy Track is one of the best-known tracks in NZ. The four- to six-day 77km track doesn't have the spectacular scenery of the Routeburn or Milford, but it certainly has its own beauty.

The track lies almost entirely within the Kahurangi National Park. Highlights include the view from the summit of Mt Perry (two-hour return walk from Perry Saddle Hut) and the coast, especially around the Heaphy Hut. It's worth spending a day or two resting at the Heaphy Hut, something appreciated by those travelling south from Collingwood. It is possible to cross the Heaphy River at its mouth at low tide.

There are seven huts set up for 20 or more people, and beds are on a first-come-first-served basis. All have gas stoves, except Heaphy and Gouland Downs which need wood. Nightly *hut* fees are $14/7 for adults/children, or $18/9 if they are purchased at the time of walking. Camping ($8/6 booked/unbooked, children half) is only allowed at three sites on the coastal part of the track – the Heaphy Hut, Katipo Shelter and Scotts Beach. You can camp outside the other huts if they are full, but you must purchase hut tickets for those sites.

Walking the Track Most people travel south-west from Collingwood to Karamea. From Brown Hut the track passes through beech forest to Perry Saddle (but don't take the short cut uphill, unless you are fit). The country opens up to the swampy Gouland

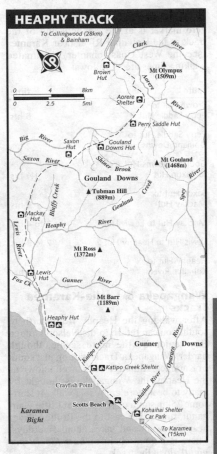

HEAPHY TRACK

Downs, then closes in with sparse bush all the way to Mackay Hut. The bush becomes more dense towards the Heaphy Hut with the beautiful nikau palm growing at lower levels.

The final section is along the coast through heavy bush and partly along the beach. Unfortunately, the sandflies can be unbearable along this, the most beautiful part. The climate here is surprisingly mild, but do not swim in the sea as the undertows and currents are vicious. The lagoon at Heaphy Hut is good for swimming, and fishing is possible in the Heaphy River.

MARLBOROUGH & NELSON

The Heaphy has kilometre markers; the zero marker is at the southern end of the track at the Kohaihai River near Karamea (see the West Coast chapter). Estimated walking times are as follows:

route	time
Brown Hut to Perry Saddle Hut	5 hrs
Perry Saddle Hut to Gouland Downs Hut	2 hrs
Gouland Downs Hut to Saxon Hut	1½ hrs
Saxon Hut to Mackay Hut	3 hrs
Mackay Hut to Lewis Hut	3 to 4 hrs
Lewis Hut to Heaphy Hut	2 to 3 hrs
Heaphy Hut to Kohaihai River	5 hrs

Wangapeka & Leslie-Karamea Tracks

After walking the Heaphy from north to south, you can return to the Nelson/Golden Bay region by the more scenic, though harder, Wangapeka Track starting just south of Karamea. Although not as well known as the Heaphy, the Wangapeka is thought by many to be a more enjoyable walk. It starts some 25km south of Karamea at Little Wanganui, runs 52km east to the Rolling River near Tapawera and takes about five days. There is a good chain of *huts ($5-10 per night)* along the track.

The 90km Leslie-Karamea Track is a medium to hard tramp of five to seven days. It connects the Cobb Valley near Takaka with Little Wanganui, south of Karamea, on the West Coast (thus including part of the Wangapeka Track on the final two days).

Cobb Valley & Mt Arthur Tablelands

The Cobb Valley and Mt Arthur Tablelands offer plenty of scope for walkers. The Cobb Valley is 28km from the Upper Takaka turn-off. You first drive up to the power station and from there it's another 13km drive to the

valley. Once in the valley there are a number of walks to choose from. These range from the 45-minute Mytton's Forest Walk to others of a few hours' duration, eg, Cobb Ridge to Peat Flat and Trilobite Hut to Chaffey Hut.

To get to the Mt Arthur Tablelands, drive from Motueka south to Pokororo. Take the Graham Rd into the Flora car park, and from here there are a great number of walking possibilities. Walks in the area include Mt Arthur Hut (3km, 1hr), Mt Arthur (8km, 3hrs), Mt Lodestone (5km, 2hrs) and Flora Hut (2km, 30 minutes).

Aorere Goldfield

The Aorere goldfield was the first major goldfield in NZ. In February 1857 five ounces (142g) of Collingwood gold were auctioned in Nelson, precipitating a gold rush which lasted three years, although various companies continued to wrest gold from the soil by sluicing and stamping batteries right up until WWI. The old goldfields are now overgrown but terraces, water races and mine shafts can still be seen.

The DOC office in Takaka has an excellent pamphlet, *Aorere Goldfields/Caves Walk*, detailing the history of the goldfield and guiding you on a historical walk, beginning from Collingwood. It takes most of the day to complete.

Getting There & Away

Abel Tasman Coachlines (☎ 03-528 8850, 03-548 0285) has a service from Nelson to the Heaphy Track entrance in summer ($44), going via Takaka and Collingwood; in winter it runs on demand and is expensive.

Kahurangi Bus (☎ 03-525 9434) provides transport to either end of the Heaphy Track on demand, with a regular service from October to April. Return transport from Nelson to the Heaphy is $92. There's a phone at the trail head to call buses.

Wadsworths Motors (☎ 03-522 4248) services the Wangapeka and Leslie-Karamea Tracks. For details on the Karamea end of the tracks see the Karamea section in The West Coast chapter.

Hitchhiking to either the Karamea or Bainham end of Heaphy Track is difficult.

The West Coast

☎ 03 • pop 22,000

The West Coast (Westland) is a rugged land of wild, pebbled and rocky beaches and bush-clad hills sweeping up to towering icy peaks. Often the narrow coastal strip is nothing but *pakihi* (dried-up swamp) or second-class farmland.

The hills are still largely untamed, and scattered throughout the thick bush and by the rivers is the rusted debris of 100 years of exploitative industry: gold- and coal-mining and timber milling.

The two glaciers, Fox and Franz Josef, framed by the dominating peaks of Mts Cook and Tasman, are the big drawcards, but the full stretch from Karamea to Jackson Bay is well worth exploring. The West Coast is historically a major source of greenstone and Hokitika is the best place in New Zealand to see it being crafted.

Most people visit the region in summer, December to February, but from May to September the days can often be warm and clear, with views of snow-capped peaks, no crowds and off-peak accommodation rates. With average annual rainfall of around 5m (200 inches), Westland could aptly be called 'Wetland'. When it rains it pours, but the West Coast receives as many sunshine hours as the Christchurch region and when it's raining over on the east coast it's just as likely to be sunny here.

MURCHISON
pop 850

Murchison, on the Buller Gorge Heritage Highway some 125km south of Nelson, is the gateway to the West Coast if you are coming from the north. It's an important service centre for the surrounding region and the starting point for adventure activities in the Upper Buller Gorge.

The Murchison visitors centre (☎/fax 03-523 9350) on Waller St is open from 10am to 6pm daily from October to April. The small **museum** (☎ *03-523 9335, open 10am-4pm daily)* on Fairfax St has photographs

Highlights

- Heli-hiking or glacier walking on spectacular Franz Josef and Fox Glaciers
- Kayaking and watching birdlife on the mirror-calm waters of the Okarito Lagoon
- Shopping for or, better still, carving your own greenstone pendant in Hokitika
- White-water and black-water rafting in the rivers and caves near Westport
- Driving the coastal road from Westport to Greymouth, and overnighting near the Pancake Rocks at Punakaiki
- Visiting the white heron *(kotuku)* colony near Whataroa

NORTH ISLAND

The West Coast

SOUTH ISLAND

Not to scale

and displays from the damaging earthquakes of 1929 and 1968. Admission is by donation.

The main event of the year is the **Buller White Water River Festival** on the first weekend in March.

Activities

Murchison is a major centre for outdoor activities, including fishing, tramping, gold panning, boating, mountain biking, caving, rafting and kayaking. Hundreds of kayakers

WEST COAST

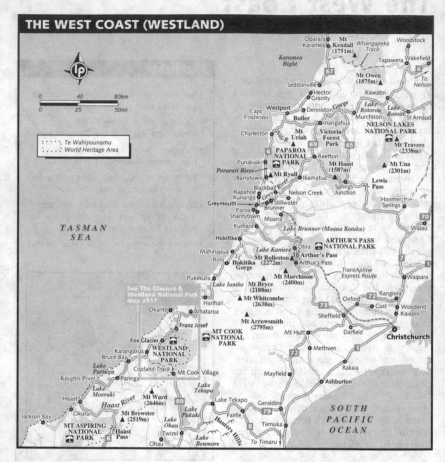

THE WEST COAST (WESTLAND)

See The Glaciers & Westland National Park map p517

descend on Murchison in summer to kayak the Buller and its tributaries.

New Zealand Kayak School (☎ 03-523 9611, W www.nzkayakschool.com, 111 Waller St) rents out kayaks including gear ($40 a day), and offers intensive four-day courses from introductory to advanced levels ($550 including accommodation).

Whitewater Action Rafting Tours (☎ 0800 100 582, 03-523 9581, half-/full-day trips $85/125) has a variety of river adventures including Buller Big Water, Ariki Falls with its big-volume 3m drop, and 'funyaks' (inflatable kayaks).

Ultimate Descents (☎ 0800 748 377, 03-523 9899, W www.rivers.co.nz, 51 Fairfax St) is a highly regarded company that offers a range of whitewater rafting and kayaking trips on the Buller, starting from $90/155 for a half/full day. They can also put you in 'riverbugs' – individual inflatable rafts that add an extra thrill. Both rafting companies offer full day or multi-day heli-rafting trips to the West Coast from $275 a day.

Buller Experience (☎ 03-523 9880) offers 20-minute jetboating trips on the Buller River for adult/child $65/45.

WEST COAST

Mountain-bike trails dot the area and popular rides include the west bank of the Matakitaki (16km return) and the Upper Matakitaki (76km return). Bikes can be hired from Riverview Holiday Park or Ultimate Descents.

The Tutaki Valley has good horse trekking and **Tiraumea Horse Treks** (☎ 03-523 9341) runs trips from one hour to a full day.

The fishing in the scenic rivers nearby is regarded as superb, but a guided day out flyfishing for trout is not cheap – from $550. The visitors centre lists guides.

Gold panning in Lyell Creek, the Buller River and the Howard Valley is popular. The information centre rents out pans and shovels for $5 with a $20 bond.

Places to Stay

The ***Riverview Holiday Park*** (☎ 03-523 9591, e riverview.hp@xtra.co.nz) has powered/unpowered sites for $16/12 for two people, single/double cabins for $15, self-contained cabins for $55, and motel units for $65. This park is right by the river, 1.5km from town on the road to Nelson.

Kiwi Park Motels (☎ 03-523 9248, e kiwipark@xtra.co.nz, 170 Fairfax St) Powered/unpowered sites $18/16 for 2 people, cabins $15-20 per person, tourist flats from $60, motel units $100. Kiwi Park has camping, basic cabins and good modern motel units. There's a camp kitchen and a pool.

Commercial Hotel (☎ 03-523 9696, 37 Fairfax St) and ***Hampden Hotel*** (☎ 03-523 9008), diagonally opposite each other on the main street, both have standard pub rooms for $25/40 a single/double.

Motels include the ***Mataki*** (☎ 0800 279 088, 03-523 9088, 34 Hotham St) with units from $55; and the more upmarket ***Murchison Motels*** (☎ 0800 166 500, ☎/fax 03-523 9026, 53 Fairfax St) from $80.

Coch-y-Bondhu Lodge (☎ 03-523 9196, e cochybondhu@xtra.co.nz, 15 Grey St) B&B singles/doubles $75/95-105, cottage $115. This is a delightful, two-storey homestay with a separate cottage outside. Rooms have en suite or private bathroom and it's set in a pleasant garden near the Buller River.

About 38km from Murchison, but of interest to cyclists, is *Hu-Ha Bikepackers* (☎ 03-548 2707). It's a small homestay on SH6 just north of Kawatiri where the highway splits to Nelson and St Arnaud.

Places to Eat

In the Ultimate Descents headquarters on Fairfax St, ***Rivers Cafe*** (☎ 03-523 9899) serves up a variety of reasonably priced organic meals, such as sandwiches ($5) and curries ($6.50). It's licensed and there's seating out the front.

Beechwoods Wayside Restaurant (☎ 03-523 9571, 32 Waller St) Meals $3-16. This is a busy place when the buses pull in and to that end it's a bit like a roadhouse with a range of ready-made food from sandwiches and burgers to cakes and pasta. There's an outdoor eating area and it's open from 6am until about 11pm.

Getting There & Away

A number of bus services pass through Murchison on the way to the West Coast, Nelson, St Arnaud, Blenheim and Picton. These include Atomic Shuttles (Picton-Greymouth), InterCity (Nelson-Fox Glacier), Southern Link Shuttles and Lazerline (Christchurch-Nelson). These buses stop either at Collins Tearooms on Fairfax St or outside Beechwoods Wayside Restaurant on SH6.

BULLER GORGE

The road from Murchison to the coast via the Buller Gorge is scenic, though the area is still scarred from the 1929 Murchison and 1968 Inangahua earthquakes. The prime attraction in the gorge itself is the watersports available – white-water rafting, kayaking and jetboating (see Murchison for information).

About 14km from Murchison and 4km west of O'Sullivan's Bridge is the **Buller Gorge swingbridge** (☎ 03-523 9809; adult/child $5/2). It's NZ's longest swingbridge (110m) and it leads to some interesting short walks on the other side of the gorge, including the epicentre of the 1929 earthquake. To get back you can ride the

WEST COAST

thrilling Comet Line flying fox, either seated in a harness (adult/child $25/15) or flying Superman-style ($35/20). It's open daily from 8.30am to 8pm in summer (till 6.30pm in winter).

Further along is Inangahua Junction, where you can head through the lower Buller Gorge to the coast, or south via Reefton to Greymouth on the inland route. The coastal route has more to offer but is longer.

The Buller Gorge itself is dark and forbidding, especially on a murky day – primeval ferns and cabbage trees cling to steep cliffs, and toi toi (a tall native grass) flanks the road between gorge and river. The road at **Hawks Crag**, an overhang just high enough to fit a bus under, has been literally hacked out of the rock. It is named after a gold-miner, Robert Hawks, who prospected in the area.

Inwood Farm Backpackers (☎ 03-789 0205, Inwoods Rd) is a small farmhouse at Inangahua Junction with beds for $14 and twins for $32. This is a cosy stopover and a good option for cyclists.

There's a *DOC camping ground* on SH6 at Lyell, Upper Buller Gorge, 10km north of Inangahua.

WESTPORT
pop 4845

Westport, the main town at the northern end of the West Coast, where the Buller River drains into the sea, lies close to some interesting coastline. On the surface it's a dull working town, but Westport makes a reasonable base for a number of outdoor adventure activities, particularly in the Buller Gorge and Charleston ranges, and is an obvious stopover on the way to Karamea (for the Heaphy Track). Its prosperity is based on coal mining, although most mining takes place some distance from town at Stockton.

Information

The Westport visitors centre (☎ 03-789 6658, e westport.info@xtra.co.nz, w www .westport.org.nz), at 1 Brougham St, is open from 9am to 7pm daily in summer (in winter 9am to 5pm on weekdays, 9am to 4pm on Saturday, 9am to 3pm Sunday). It has information on the many tracks and walkways in the area, handles bookings for tours and transport, and sells DOC (Department of Conservation) hut tickets for the Heaphy and Wangapeka Tracks.

The Buller Region office of the DOC (☎ 03-788 8088) at 72 Russell St is open from 8am to 4.30pm Monday to Friday (closed from noon to 1pm). The Automobile Association (AA; ☎ 03-789 8002) is at the Seal Colony Tourist Park on Marine Parade, Carters Beach.

Internet access is available at Web Shed (☎ 03-789 5131), 208 Palmerston St, for $6 an hour.

Seal Colony & Cape Foulwind

Depending on the time of year, anything from 20 to over 100 NZ fur seals may be down on the rocks at the Tauranga Bay seal colony, 15km from Westport. Pups are born from late November to early December and for a month afterwards the mothers stay on the rocks to tend the young before setting off to sea on feeding forays.

The 90-minute **Cape Foulwind Walkway** extends along the coast 4km past the seal colony to Cape Foulwind, passing a replica of Abel Tasman's astrolabe (a navigational aid) and a lighthouse site. The northern end of this walk can be accessed by car from Cape Foulwind Rd.

The Maori knew the cape as Taringa, meaning 'a sheltered anchorage or landing place'. The first European to reach the cape was Abel Tasman, who sighted it in December 1642 and named it Glyphaygen Hock (Rocky Point). When James Cook anchored in March 1770 his ship, the *Endeavour*, was rocked by a furious storm, so he gave it the apt name it retains today.

From the Taringa Bay car park it's a five-minute walk to the seal colony lookout, though you can often see them playing in the surf anywhere along this walk. The cliffs can be dangerous, so stick to marked areas.

Burning Mine Adventures *(☎ 0800 343 337)* has two-hour tours to the seal colony including a scenic drive for $25.

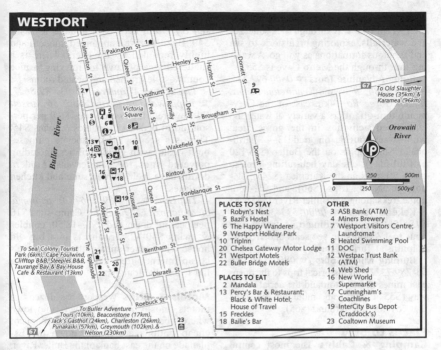

WESTPORT

PLACES TO STAY
1 Robyn's Nest
5 Bazil's Hostel
6 The Happy Wanderer
9 Westport Holiday Park
10 TripInn
20 Chelsea Gateway Motor Lodge
21 Westport Motels
22 Buller Bridge Motels

PLACES TO EAT
2 Mandala
13 Percy's Bar & Restaurant;
   Black & White Hotel;
   House of Travel
15 Freckles
18 Bailie's Bar

OTHER
3 ASB Bank (ATM)
4 Miners Brewery
7 Westport Visitors Centre;
   Laundromat
8 Heated Swimming Pool
11 DOC
12 Westpac Trust Bank
   (ATM)
14 Web Shed
16 New World
   Supermarket
17 Cunningham's
   Coachlines
19 InterCity Bus Depot
   (Craddock's)
23 Coaltown Museum

Coaltown Museum

This well laid-out museum (☎ 03-789 8204, Queen St; adult/child $6/3; open 9am-4.30pm daily) reconstructs aspects of coal-mining life, including a walk through a simulated mine complete with sound effects and videos. As well as original coal- and gold-mining artefacts, a brewery display and some excellent photographic exhibits, there's a whole section devoted to the dredging of Westport's harbour, including a huge operational steam engine (that is now running on electricity).

Miners Brewery

This locally owned brewery (☎ 03-789 6201), found on Lyndhurst St, was established in 1993 and has tours from Monday to Friday at 11.30am and 1pm ($5). The beer that's made here (Miners Draught, Miners Dark and Barracuda Pilsner) is not bad, but you could skip it if you're going to Monteith's in Greymouth.

Special Events

The **Buller Gorge Marathon** culminates in Westport with a big party on the second weekend in February. The **Cape Classic** surf contest is another big event on the Labour Day weekend in October.

Activities & Organised Tours

From Charleston, south of Westport, **Norwest Adventures** (☎ 0800 116 686, 03-789 6686, ⓦ www.caverafting.com; trips $105) runs underground **cave rafting** trips into what could easily be the reaches of Xanadu on Coleridge's sacred river (the Nile actually). In the lower levels of Metro Cave you walk through ancient limestone formations and paddle rubber rafts through caverns filled with glowworms. The trip ends in the rapids of the Nile River. There are two trips from Westport daily in summer at 9am and 2.30pm.

Norwest Adventures also does four-hour **adventure caving trips** ($220), starting with

WEST COAST

a 30m abseil into Te Tahi *tomo* (hole). You then worm your way through rock squeezes and waterfalls, exploring prehistoric fossils and fabulous formations as you go. A walking tour through the Metro Cave is $55.

Buller Adventure Tours (☎ *0800 697 286, 03-789 7286,* **W** *www.adventuretours.co.nz, Buller Gorge Rd)*, 4km east of the Greymouth turn-off, offers a variety of water and land-based activities in the gorge area: white-water rafting on grade 3–4 'Earthquake Slip' rapids on the Buller ($85/120 half/full day); one-day heli-rafting trips to grade 5 rapids on the Karamea ($245); 1½-hour jetboating trips ($60); and 2½-hour horse treks along the Buller River ($45).

Kekeno Tours (☎ *0800 535 366; trips $45-95)* takes surf-rafting trips, from a half hour to 1½ hours, to see seals and Hectors dolphins at Taringa Bay.

Burning Mines Tours (☎ *0800 343 337, 03-789 7277)* has historical trips to the opencast mines at Stockton and the aerial cableway ($55, 4 hours), and mountain-bike trips that cover similar ground ($65).

Places to Stay

Camping & Cabins The most central camping option is *Westport Holiday Park* (☎ *03-789 7043,* **e** *westportholidaypark@xtra.co.nz, 31-37 Domett St)* with powered/unpowered sites $20/17 for two people, dorm beds $13.50 and double chalets $32 to $44. It has compact A-frame chalets and very basic (old) bunkrooms.

Seal Colony Tourist Park (☎ *03-789 8002, 0508 937876, Marine Parade, Carters Beach)* Powered & unpowered sites $11 per person, cabins $45, motel units $85. This well-maintained park is 6km from Westport, on the way to the seal colony. It's near a fairly ordinary beach.

Hostels Just north of town, *Robyn's Nest* (☎ *03-789 6565, fax 789 8015, 42 Romilly St)* is a nicely restored two-storey house with loads of character. Rooms are bright, airy and spacious, and most of the dorms have no bunks. You can pitch a tent for $8 per person, dorm beds are $17, and doubles and twins are $37.

Bazil's Hostel (☎ *03-789 6410, 54 Russell St)* Dorm beds $18, doubles & twins $40. Bazil's is well appointed, modern and highly regarded by travellers. There is a sheltered area of lawn for relaxing, a nice country-style kitchen and heated rooms.

The Happy Wanderer (☎ *03-789 8627,* **e** *happywanderer@xtra.co.nz, 56 Russell St)* Powered/unpowered sites $8/9 per person, dorm beds $18, doubles & twins $45. This is a secure YHA-associate purpose-built hostel with good facilities, including powered sites for campervans. Modern dorms have their own en suite and kitchen facilities.

TripInn (☎ *03-789 7367,* **e** *tripinn@clear.net.nz, 72 Queen St)* Camp sites $10 per person, dorm beds $17-18.50, doubles & twins $40-42. TripInn is in a big old house with newer units at the side. There's cheap Internet, free bikes and linen, and a log fire in the lounge.

Motels & B&Bs Wesport has dozens of motels, mostly on the highway into town where it becomes Palmerston St. A couple of cheap options are hiding down the Esplanade on the east bank of the Buller River.

Westport Motels (☎ *0800 805 909,* ☎*/fax 03- 789 7575, 32 The Esplanade)* Studio singles/doubles $65/80, one/two bedroom units $90/100. This friendly motel is good value with spa and pool.

Buller Bridge Motels (☎ *0800 500 209, 03-789 7519,* **e** *bullerbridge@clear.net.nz, The Esplanade)* Studio $75, 1-bedroom unit $85. This older-style motel is also reasonably priced and all rooms are self-contained.

Chelsea Gateway Motor Lodge (☎ *03-789 6835, cnr Palmerston & Bentham Sts)* Units from $90, with spa bath $160. One of Westport's top motels, Chelsea Gateway has a range of fully self-contained units.

There are some excellent B&Bs and homestays out towards Taringa Bay, most with just a few rooms.

Clifftop B&B (☎ *03-789 5472, Clifftop Lane)* Doubles $90. As the name suggests this home has a beautiful location overlooking the sea and offers two comfortable double rooms.

Steeples B&B *(☎ 03-789 7876, e steep leshomestay@xtra.co.nz, Cape Foul wind Rd)* Doubles $80. Another lovely home with a huge garden running down to the clifftops, there are two rooms here with shared bathroom.

Places to Eat

Palmerston St has several garden-variety takeaways and sandwich shops, but Westport isn't really blessed with many great eating spots.

Freckles, on Palmerston St, is a pleasant little cafe serving espresso, muffins and wholesome burgers and sandwiches from $5 to $8. ***Mandala*** *(☎ 03-789 7931, 110 Palmerston St)* has standard fare, but is a good choice for breakfast.

Percy's Bar & Restaurant *(☎ 03-789 6648, 198 Palmerston St)* Mains $14-23. In a town of few outstanding restaurants, this is the best central option. The pan-fried turbot (a local fish) is particularly recommended. It's in the Black & White Hotel and is open for breakfast, lunch and dinner.

Bailie's Bar *(☎ 03-789 7289, 187 Palmerstown St)* Open 11.30am-1.30pm & 5pm-9pm daily. Meals $5-27. This is a popular bar with occasional live entertainment, Guinness and a vague Irish theme. Dinner mains are a little overpriced but you can get a range of reasonable snacks, pizzas, roasts and barbecue meals for around $10 to $15.

Bay House Cafe & Restaurant *(☎ 03-789 7133, Beach Rd, Taringa Bay)*. Mains $23-28. Undoubtedly the best restaurant for miles around, the Bay House is stylish, has a superb ocean-view location, and backs it up with fine food and an extensive list of wine, ciders and beers – you'll certainly need to book for dinner. Lunch is reasonable at $8 to $16 for dishes including pasta, flounder and Thai curry. It's open from 9am for breakfast.

Getting There & Away

Air New Zealand Link has daily direct flights to Wellington (except Saturday). Flights can be booked through House of Travel (☎ 03-788 8120) on Palmerston St. A taxi to the airport costs around $15.

InterCity buses leave daily from Craddock's Service Station (☎ 03-789 7819) on Palmerston St to Nelson (3½ hours), Greymouth (2 hours) and Franz Josef (6½ hours). Atomic Shuttles stops at Westport on its daily Picton-Greymouth run. Fares from Westport include: Picton ($45), Nelson ($30), Greymouth ($20). Both InterCity and Atomic have a stopover in Punakaiki.

Southern Link Shuttles, based at the Cunningham depot, has a Westport-Christchurch service (via Springs Junction and Lewis Pass) daily except Saturday ($35).

East-West Express has a shuttle to Christchurch ($44) at 8am from the visitors centre. The return shuttle leaves Christchurch station at 1.30pm.

Heading north to Karamea, the Karamea Express (☎ 03-782 6617) makes the return trip from Monday to Friday (and Saturday in summer), leaving Karamea at 8.20am and returning from Westport at 11.30am ($15).

WESTPORT TO KARAMEA

This trip north along SH67 passes through a few mildly interesting towns and close to some good coastal scenery. The first along the way is Waimangaroa and the turn-off to **Denniston**. This town was once the largest producer of coal in NZ and can be reached via the Denniston Walkway. The track follows the original path to the town and has great views of the Denniston Incline. In its day this was a great engineering feat, as empty coal trucks were hauled back up the incline by the weight of the descending loaded trucks, sometimes at a gradient of one in one. Four kilometres north of Waimangaroa is the **Britannia Track**, a six-hour return walk to the Britannia battery and other remnants of the gold-mining era.

At **Granity**, head uphill for 5km to the semi ghost towns of Millerton and Stockton. The area has quite a community of alternative lifestylers these days, curiously sharing in NZ's largest operational coal mine. The **Millerton Incline Walk** is 40 minutes return and takes in the old railway, a tunnel and an old dam.

The Old Slaughter House *(☎ 03-782 8333)*, just north of Hector (which is just north of Granity), is a rustic backpackers on a hill above the highway. Dorm beds cost $17 ($22 with bedding).

Further north is another interesting walk at **Charming Creek**. This all-weather, five-hour return track follows an old coal line through the picturesque Ngakawau River Gorge. You can also walk along the track all the way to **Seddonville**, a small town surrounded by bush-covered hills on the Mohikinui River.

Turning off the highway, 3km along the gravel De Malmanche Rd, brings you to the wild **Gentle Annie Beach** at the mouth of the Mohikinui. This secluded spot has rustic accommodation at *Gentle Annie Coastal Enclave* (☎ 03-782 1826) with lodge beds for $18 per person and holiday houses from $63 to $85 a double. You can camp for $8 per person, but there's no kitchen. Also here is the charming *Cowshed Cafe*, which was indeed once a cow shed but now offers a range of muffins, salads and steaks.

Between Mohikinui and Little Wanganui you pass over the **Karamea Bluff**, a slow, winding but magnificent drive through rata and matai forest with views of the Tasman Sea below.

KARAMEA
pop 685
Karamea is very much an end-of-the-road town (at the end of SH67) near the southern end of the Heaphy and Wangapeka Tracks. Information, local maps and DOC hut tickets are available at the Karamea Information & Resource Centre (☎ 03-782 6652, e karamea .info@xtra.co.nz) on Market Cross. It's open daily from 9am to 5pm (closed Sunday and Saturday afternoon in winter).

There's a small supermarket here (open 8.30am to 6pm Monday to Friday, 9am to noon Saturday and Sunday) and some good accommodation options for weary trampers.

Oparara Basin & Honeycomb Caves
North of Karamea, there are spectacular limestone arch formations and the unique Honeycomb Caves, ancient home to the moa. Of equal interest is the primitive rainforest growing over the karst landscape.

Moss-laden trees droop over the tannin-coloured Oparara River, illuminated by light filtering through the dense forest canopy.

Halfway along the road to the start of the Heaphy Track, turn off just before McCallum's Bridge and go 15km past the sawmill along a winding gravel (sometimes rough) road to the arches. It's an easy 20-minute walk, through primeval old-growth forest, to the huge **Oparara Arch** spanning the Oparara River – you can scramble through to the other side of the 200m long and 37m high arch. The smaller but equally beautiful **Moria Gate** is a harder 40-minute walk along a muddy track that is not always easy to follow. Another arch, the Honeycomb, can only be reached by canoe.

Other interesting formations are the **Mirror Tarn**, the **Crazy Paving** and **Box Canyon Caves** at the end of the road. Beyond these are the magnificent **Honeycomb Caves**, with bones of moa and other extinct species. See the bones of three of the five moa species: slender *Megalapteryx didinus;* small *Pachyornis elephantopus;* and giant *Dinornis giganteus*. This is also where bones of the now-extinct giant Haast eagle, the world's largest, were discovered. This eagle, with a 3m to 4m wingspan, preyed on the moa.

Access to the cave is restricted and it can only be visited on a tour. The Last Resort (see Places to Stay) organises 5½-hour tours to the cave and other features for $60 (minimum four people). Bus only to the Oparara Basin is $30.

Activities
The Karamea River is good for swimming, fishing and canoeing. Canoe trips are organised by the **Last Resort** (☎ 03-782 6617) at $30/50 for a single/double kayak. The Little Wanganui, Oparara and Kohaihai Rivers also have good swimming holes. Tidal lagoons, 1km north and 3km south of Karamea, are sheltered and good for swimming at high tide; otherwise swimming in the open sea is dangerous. The only drawback to the beautiful beaches around Karamea are the millions of sandflies. Plenty of repellent or wind will save your sanity.

Many good day walks are found in this area, including the five-hour Fenian Track into **Adams Flat**, the eight-hour return trek to 1084m **Mt Stormy** and the walk to **Lake Hanlon**. The first leg of the Wangapeka Track also makes a good day walk.

If you're not keen on walking the whole **Heaphy Track**, or if you have a vehicle and want to get back to it, you can walk all or part way to the Heaphy Hut and return. This takes in the walk along the beach, considered by many to be the best part. Scotts Beach is 1½ hours return and passes beautiful nikau palm groves. It's about five hours to the Heaphy Hut where you can stay overnight then return. For more information on the Heaphy and Wangapeka Tracks, see Kahurangi National Park in the Marlborough & Nelson chapter.

Places to Stay & Eat

Karamea Holiday Park (☎ *03-782 6758)* Powered/unpowered sites $18/16 for 2 people, small/large double cabins $20/29, single/double units $45/55. The main motor park is on the road into Karamea about 3km back from Market Cross.

You can also camp at the *Domain Camping Ground* (☎ *03-782 6719)* at the sports reserve on Waverly St (powered and unpowered sites $8 for two people).

Last Resort (☎ *03-782 6617,* e *last.re sort@xtra.co.nz, Waverly St)* Dorm beds $20, lodge doubles with shared/private bathroom $60/75, studio units $90, 2-bedroom cottages for 4 people $180. This beautiful complex has a range of rooms connected by walkways to the impressive central building. The buildings have sod roofs and feature massive beams made of local timbers. There are modern lodge rooms and cottages, all set in a pleasant native garden. If you're staying in the backpackers accommodation, there's no kitchen. However, there is a fine licensed restaurant (open from 7.30am for breakfast and from 5.30pm for dinner) and a lively cafe-bar serving cheaper meals (open from 10am till late).

Karamea Village Hotel (☎ *03-782 6800, Waverly St)* Dorm beds $18, motel units from $95. The local pub has modern en suite

motel units next door, as well as a fully-equipped backpackers house across the road. It also does good, cheap meals.

Punga Lodge Backpackers (☎ *03-782 6667, Waverly St)* Dorm beds $17, doubles with linen $40. A bit rough around the edges, this is a casual backpackers house and they offer free pick up from the end of the Heaphy Track.

Bridge Farm Motel (☎ *03-782 6955, Bridge Rd)* Self-contained double units $75-95. The rooms in this motel are bright, comfortable and spacious and most have separate bedrooms. Outside are playful deer and alpacas.

Getting There & Away

The Karamea Express (☎ 03-782 6617, 782 6916) operates Monday to Friday all year and on Saturday in summer. It leaves Karamea at 8am for Westport and returns at 11.30am ($15, 1½ hours). Cunningham's Motors (☎ 03-789 7177) has an evening service to Westport at 6.15pm. It leaves Westport for Karamea at 3pm ($15, $7 for bicycles).

The ends of the Heaphy and Wangapeka Tracks have phones to arrange transport out to Karamea. From the Labour Day weekend (mid-October) to Easter, the Karamea Express runs to the southern end of the Heaphy Track (Kohaihai) daily at 1.45pm, returning at 2pm ($5 per person). At any other time it runs on demand for $25.

For Wangapeka, the Karamea Express runs on demand ($30 for up to five passengers, $5 each extra person).

It's also possible to fly from Karamea to Takaka (from $90) and then walk back on the Heaphy Track – contact the Karamea Information & Resource Centre for details.

WESTPORT TO GREYMOUTH

The coastal road offers some fine views of the Tasman Sea and surf-pounded coastline, as well as a few interesting diversions. The main attraction along here is Punakaiki and the strange Pancake Rocks.

From Westport to Punakaiki there are a number of very small towns (10 or so inhabitants) but it was a different story 130 years ago, when the gold rush was in full swing.

WEST COAST

Charleston was a booming town with shanties all along the pack route and gold-diggers staking their claims on the Nile River. Today, the raucous pubs are all gone – except for the **Charleston Cavern** – but you can stay at the **Motor Camp** (☎ 03-728 6773) or **Charleston Motel** (☎ 03-728 7599), which has comfortable units for $65.

Beaconstone (☎ 025 310 491) Dorm beds $17-20, doubles & twins $40. This back-to-nature 'eco-backpackers' is 1km off the highway and about 17km south of Westport. The comfortable 12-bed timber lodge has an equipped kitchen, cosy lounge and no phone or TV. Solar power and composting toilets complete the picture – come here to get away from it all. It's open from October to mid-June only.

Jack's Gasthof (☎ 03-789 6501) Camp sites $6 per person, motel units $35. There's camping and basic units on this farm property, found on the Little Totara River near Charleston, but it's also a great little licensed restaurant. Mains cost from $13.50 for pasta to $21.50 for seafood and steak, or $7.50 to $18.50 for pizzas. It's open for breakfast, lunch and dinner and you can eat out in the garden.

The coast from Fox River to Runanga is rugged and the road will remind West Coast Americans of California's Big Sur. Woodpecker Bay, Tiromoana, Punakaiki, Barrytown, Fourteen Mile, Motukiekie, Ten Mile, Nine Mile and Seven Mile are all beaches sculpted by the relentless fury of the Roaring Forties.

Coastal Experience (☎ 03-789 7830) Doubles $50-60. This small place consists of a couple of rustic baches nestled right on the beach at Woodpecker Bay. There's good fishing in the sea or Fox River and you'll feel a million miles from anywhere with the sea crashing outside your door.

Punakaiki & Paparoa National Park

Almost midway between Westport and Greymouth, the small settlement of Punakaiki has some of the finest coastal scenery on the West Coast. In December 1987 many years of public pressure bore fruit when the area was declared a national park and the 30,000-hectare Paparoa National Park became NZ's 12th national park.

Punakaiki is best known for the weird **Pancake Rocks and Blowholes**. These limestone rocks at Dolomite Point have formed into what looks like stacks of thin pancakes, through a layering and weathering process known as stylobedding. When a good tide is running, the water surges into caverns below the rocks and squirts out in impressive geyser-like blowholes. A 15-minute loop walk from the road goes around the rocks and blowholes. It's best to go at high or king tide, when the blowholes perform (check at the visitors centre for times).

In addition to the rocks at Punakaiki, the park has many other natural attractions: mountains (the Paparoa Range), rivers, wilderness areas, limestone formations including cliffs and caves, diverse vegetation and a Westland black petrel colony – the world's only nesting area of this rare sea bird.

Interesting walks in the park include the 30km **Inland Pack Track**. This is a two-day track along a route established by miners around 1867 to circumvent the more rugged coastal walk. Also worthwhile is the **Croesus Track**, a full-day or two-day tramp over the Paparoa Range from Blackball to Barrytown, passing through historic goldmining areas (see the Blackball section later in this chapter). There are also many shorter river and coastal walks. If you're planning on walking, register your intentions at the park's visitors centre. Many of the inland walks are subject to river flooding and other conditions, so check before setting out.

The **Paparoa National Park visitors centre** (☎ 03-731 1895, e *punakaikivc@doc.govt.nz*), open summer 9am to 6pm daily, winter 9am to 4.30pm, is next to the highway. It has interesting displays on the park and can supply information on activities, accommodation and current conditions throughout the park. There's a 15-minute audiovisual ($2) shown on request.

Activities & Organised Tours Visit the only breeding colony of the Westland black petrel, the largest burrowing petrel, with

Paparoa Nature Tours (☎ 03-322 7898; tours $25 per person); trips start 30 minutes before sunset.

Kiwa Sea Adventures (☎ 03-768 7765; adult/child $100/50) combines natural history and geology – Hectors dolphins, seals and spotted shags may be seen on the two-hour trip to Seal Island. Swimming with dolphins is also possible. You can book at Punakaiki Beach Hostel.

Punakaiki Guides (☎ 03-731 1839) has horse trekking in the Paparoa National Park at $60 for two-hour treks, but longer rides can also be arranged. They also have an all-terrain amphibious vehicle that can take you further into the valley.

Punakaiki Canoes (☎ 03-731 1870; canoe hire $15 for first hour plus $5 per extra hour), based near the bridge over the Pororari River, hires out canoes and kayaks.

Places to Stay & Eat Next to the beach, *Punakaiki Beach Camp* (☎ 03-731 1894, Owen St) has powered/unpowered sites $20/17 for two people, double cabins $28 to $33, nice lawn areas and good communal facilities.

Te Nikau Retreat (☎ 03-731 1111) Dorm beds $16-18, doubles/twins $35/55, double cabins $55. Te Nikau Retreat is a superb and aptly-named bush lodge in a thick forest setting. As well as the main house (with dorms and private rooms), a variety of rustic cabins and self-contained lodges are hidden among the Nikau palms. Te Nikau is 3km north of Punakaiki.

Punakaiki Beach Hostel (☎ 03-731 1852, fax 731 1852, Webb St) Dorm beds $19, doubles & twins $48. This hostel is in a comfortable converted motel with spa, 1km from the visitors centre and only a stone's throw from the beach. You can sleep in the house truck outside for $46 a double. There's also a separate house (the Seaside House) on Owen St where dorm beds are $17 and doubles $42.

Hydrangea Cottage (☎ 03-731 1839, Ⓦ www.pancake-rocks.co.nz) Doubles $125-180. These lovely self-contained cottages are situated on a hillside, backed by rainforest and overlooking Pancake Rocks.

Punakaiki Cottages Motels (☎ 03-731 1008, Dickinson Parade) Double studio & family units $88-110. Standard units here are good value for their beachfront location.

Wild Coast Cafe (☎ 03-731 1873), next to the visitors centre, opens early for breakfast, when you can indulge in a stack of pancakes with fruit and maple syrup ($10) and coffee. There's also a range of light meals and Internet access.

Punakaiki Tavern (☎ 03-731 1188) Bar snacks $2-8, mains $13-22. On the highway near the Pororari River, this is the local watering hole, with a beer garden and big open fire. Meals are simple but hearty.

Getting There & Away InterCity buses and the Atomic Shuttle between Westport and Greymouth stop at Punakaiki daily, allowing enough time to see the Pancake Rocks.

The Coast Road

The scenic coast road from Punakaiki to Greymouth is flanked by white-capped breakers and rugged rocks out at sea, and the steep, bush-clad Paparoa Ranges. There are a number of accommodation possibilities along this coastline.

Barrytown Tavern (☎ 03-731 1812) Dorm beds $15, doubles $50. At Barrytown, 16km south of Punakaiki, the local pub has backpacker accommodation, hotel rooms and meals. There's also a kitchen for guests. It's opposite the western end of the Croesus Track, which is handy for trampers coming from Blackball and desperate for a beer and a bed!

Hexagon (☎ 03-731 1827, Golden Sands Rd) Beds $14, cabins $18-22 per person. Located about 2km south of the tavern, is this hexagonal building on an organic farm, where you get a mattress on the floor. It's quite basic but in a beautiful setting, and you can help yourself to the vegies.

Darcy's Buffalo Steak House (☎ 03-731 1875) Meals $8-18.50. Perched up on a hill in Barrytown, this restaurant is set on a buffalo farm and that's what makes up the bulk of the menu – buffalo burgers, sausages, steak and kebabs are all available. It's also a bar (open till 3am) with good views and live entertainment in summer.

THE GREY VALLEY

From Murchison, an alternative route to the West Coast is to turn off at Inangahua Junction and travel inland via Reefton, then over the mountains into the Grey Valley. Despite the best efforts of a century of plunderers, abundant rainfall has fuelled regenerating bush on the green-cloaked hills and the paddocks have fast become overgrown. The small towns provide a reminder of those futile attempts to tame the land and of the gold that brought diggers flooding into this area in the 19th century.

Reefton

pop 1050

Reefton is a pleasant little town in the heart of great walking country. Its name comes from the gold-bearing quartz reefs in the region. As early as 1888, Reefton had its own electricity supply and street lighting, beating all other towns in NZ. If you've crossed the Lewis Pass from Christchurch, this is the first town of any size you come to.

There are quite a few heritage buildings in and around Reefton – the *Historic Reefton* leaflet ($1) explains all.

The modern **Reefton visitors centre** (☎ 03-732 8391, e reeftoninfo@paradise .net.nz, 67 Broadway) is open from 8.30am to 6pm in summer (to 4pm in winter). It has lots of information, an interesting re-creation of the Quartzopolis Mine (50c), historical displays and Internet access.

About 2km east of town, on the road to Christchurch, is **Blacks Point**, where'll you'll find a small museum and the Golden Fleece Gold Battery ($1), both open Wednesday to Sunday 1pm to 4pm (museum is also open 9am to noon).

The surrounding area has many fine walks and great possibilities for mountain biking on the Big River Track. The walks include short ones around town such as the **Powerhouse Walk**, **Reefton Walkway** and the historic **Reefton Walk**. The **Blacks Point Walk** (two to three hours) goes to abandoned coal mines.

There is a wealth of walking in **Victoria Forest Park**, the largest forest park in the country. The two-day Big River and the three-day Kirwans, Blue Grey River and Robinson Valley Tracks are all exciting possibilities. The visitors centre has maps and information.

Places to Stay & Eat There's a DOC *camping ground* ($5) at Slab Hut Creek, on SH7, 7km southwest of Reefton.

Reefton Motor Camp (☎ 03-732 8477, 1 Ross St) Powered/unpowered sites $18/14, double cabins $32. The motor camp is on the Inangahua River at the western end of the main street.

The Old Bread Shop (☎ 03-732 8420, e lorettar@chc.quik.co.nz, 155 Buller Rd) Dorm beds $16, doubles & twins $20 per person. This small, homely backpackers is in an old bakery. It has been brightly restored and the friendly owners live next door.

Reefton Backpackers (☎/fax 03-732 8183, 64 Shiel St) Dorm beds $16. This is a well-equipped (unstaffed) house with comfortable rooms, kitchen and lounge.

Reef Cottage (☎ 0800 770 440, ☎/fax 03-732 8440, e reefton@clear.net.nz, 51 Broadway) Double with shared bathroom/ ensuite $75/95-130. Befitting Reefton's historic character, this charming B&B was once a solicitor's office. One of the rooms uses the old vault as its en suite, complete with the original heavy vault door! There's a neat little cafe attached, serving breakfast and light lunches.

Quartz Lodge (☎ 0800 302 725, 03-732 8383, 78 Shiel St) Singles/doubles $40/80. Quartz Lodge is a pleasant, good-value B&B which specialises in hearty breakfasts.

Broadway, the main street, has a proliferation of takeaways and tearooms. The *Electric Light Cafe* in Dawsons Hotel is a busy eatery with $6 bar meals and mains from $12 to $20. The *Reefton Hotel*, across the road, has good old-fashioned roast dinners for $7.

Al Fresco's (☎ 03-732 8513, Broadway) As its name suggests, this is exclusively an outdoor eatery (open summer only) and a great spot to sit for lunch or dinner on a fine day. The speciality is pizza but you can also get cakes, coffee, salads and light meals.

Getting There & Away Southern Link Shuttles and East-West Express both stop in Reefton on their daily services between Westport and Christchurch.

Atomic Shuttles also stops here on its Greymouth-Picton express run.

SH7 to Greymouth

At Hukarere, 21km south of Reefton, turn east to visit **Waiuta**, an overgrown ghost town, once the focus of a rich gold mine. A reef of gold was discovered at this lonely spot in 1905, and by 1906 the Blackwater Mine had been sunk. The town grew to a population of around 500 but in 1951 the mine collapsed and Waiuta was abandoned virtually overnight. The drive through beech forest to Waiuta is scenic, though the winding dirt road is narrow and rough in places. The interpretive walks and views are well worth it and this is not the sort of place that tour buses visit, so you may have it to yourself. If you feel like bedding down in a ghost town, the *Waiuta Lodge* is a 30-bunk lodge with kitchen facilities at $15 per person – book and pick up a key at the Reefton visitors centre.

Blackball Off the highway and north of the Grey River (take the Blackball-Taylorville Rd) about 25km north of Greymouth is the historic town of Blackball. This working town was established in 1866 as a service centre for the gold-diggers and developed into a coal-mining centre from the late 1880s until 1964. The national Federation of Labour (an organisation of trade unions) was born here after two cataclysmic strikes in 1908 and 1931.

Blackball is the recommended starting point for the 18km **Croesus Track**, which crosses the Paparoa Range and ends at Barrytown on the West Coast. It can be done in a long day, or you can plan an overnight stop at the DOC *Ces Clark Hut* ($10), roughly halfway along.

Formerly the Blackball Hilton (☎ 03-732 4705, e bbhilton@xtra.co.nz) Dorm beds $18, doubles $57, DB&B $65 per person. Once a hotel, this pub and hostel is full of character and designated a New Zealand Historic Place. The 'formerly' has been added as the giant hotel chain mounted a challenge to force a change of name. There's a range of accommodation, meals, a small gym and spa, and the friendly owners provide lots of information on the area. Organised activities include tramping over the Croesus Track, gold panning, horse riding and walking the historic trail.

Blackball Salami Co (☎ 03-732 4111, 11 Hilton St) The Salami brothers of the Blackball Salami Co lovingly produce low fat venison and beef salami.

Lake Brunner At Stillwater you can detour to Lake Brunner (also known as Moana Kotuku, 'Heron Sea'). Locals reckon Lake Brunner and the Arnold River which feeds it are among the best spots in the world to catch a trout (you hear that about quite a few rivers and lakes in NZ). Fishing guides can be hired in Moana (ask at the Moana Hotel) or just collar a local for advice.

Lake Brunner Boat Hire (☎ 03-738 0291) at the end of Koe St in Moana, hires out fishing boats and kayaks from $15 an hour (single/double kayaks $40/60 a day).

The **Moana Kiwi House & Conservation Park** (☎ 03-738 0405; adult/child $8/3) has kiwi viewing and a large area devoted to indigenous bird species such as the white heron (*kotuku*).

Short walks include the 20-minute **Velenski Walk**, which starts near the camping ground and leads through a remarkable tract of native bush consisting of totara, rimu and kahikatea, and the **Arnold River Walk** which crosses a swingbridge over the river.

Lake Brunner Motor Camp (☎ 03-738 0600, Ahau St) Powered/unpowered sites $20/16 for 2 people, double cabins $36-45. Near the end of the road in Moana township, this camp is on the shores of Lake Brunner. It has a general store which also sells fishing gear.

Moana Hotel (☎ 03-738 0083, Ahau St) Cabins $14-16 per person, hotel rooms $60-75, motel units $70-90. The local pub has a

WEST COAST

range of accommodation, including shared cabins and self-contained motel units. You can also get bistro meals here and hook up with a fishing guide.

The *Station House Cafe* (☎ 03-738 0158) On a hillside opposite the Moana Railway Station, this is a recommended cafe open from 10.30am till late. It does hot drinks and cakes as well as meals under $20. The *TranzAlpine* train pulls in here daily.

GREYMOUTH
pop 13,500
Greymouth was once the site of a Maori *pa* and known as Mawhera, meaning 'Widespread River Mouth'. To the Ngati Kahu people, the Cobden Gap to the north of the town is where their ancestor Tuterakiwhanoa broke the side of *Te Waka o Aoraki* (The Canoe of Aoraki), releasing trapped rainwater to the sea.

Greymouth has a long gold-mining history and, though not much more than a small provincial town, it's easily the largest town on the West Coast. It's at the mouth of the Grey River – hence its name – and despite the high protective wall along the Mawhera Quay the river still manages to flood the town after periods of heavy rain.

Being at the other end of the coast-to-coast route from Christchurch (by road or rail), Greymouth gets a fair bit of tourist traffic, but there's not much to do in the town itself. As with Westport, plenty of adventure activities can be organised from here.

Information
The Greymouth visitors centre (☎ 03-768 5101, ⓔ vinin@minidata.co.nz, Ⓦ www.westcoastbookings.co.nz) is in the Art Deco Regent Theatre on the corner of Herbert and Mackay Sts. In summer it's open from 9am to 7pm daily; in winter, it's open to 5pm Monday to Friday and from 10am to 4pm Saturday and Sunday. There's Internet access here and the cinema screens movies in the evening.

The best Internet cafe in town is at the DP One Coffee House (see Places to Eat) on Mawhera Quay.

Things to See
High on the list of things to do in Greymouth is a tour of the **Monteith's Brewing Co** (☎ 03-768 4149; tours 10am, 11.30am, 2pm; admission $5). Monteith's, the original West Coast brewery, distributes its beers – original ale, golden lager, Celtic Red, pilsner, Monteith's black and the perky Summertime Ale – throughout the country, though part of the brewing operation has shifted to Auckland. The tours end with a free beer or four.

History House Museum (☎ 03-768 4028, adult/child $3/1; open 10am-4pm Mon-Fri) has a fabulous photo collection and other bric-a-brac detailing the town's history.

Original jade sculpture and jewellery is crafted at the pricey but impressive **Jade Boulder Gallery** (☎ 03-768 0700, 1 Guinness St). There's a workshop and cafe here, and a fascinating display of jade boulders, showing the raw state of the precious *pounamu*. Also good is the **Left Bank Art Gallery** (☎ 03-768 0038, 1 Tainui St; open winter 10am-5pm daily, summer 10am-7.30pm; admission $2) with its permanent jade collection.

Activities & Organised Tours
Good walks in the region include the three-hour return **Point Elizabeth Track**, 6km north of Greymouth, which passes through the Rapahoe Range Scenic Reserve. The short **quay walk** from Cobden Bridge towards Blaketown is also well worth doing.

White-water rafting is possible in many of the coast rivers. **Eco-Rafting Adventures NZ** (☎ 03-768 4005, Ⓦ www.ecorafting.co.nz, 108 Mawhera Quay), based at the DP One Coffee House, has half-day trips on the Arnold ($70) and two-day trips on the Upper Grey Rivers ($300), and runs heli-rafts (from $210) to further afield.

Wild West Adventures (☎ 0800 123 724, 03-768 6649) operates a variety of trips, including white-water rafting ($95 for a three-hour trip to $335 for a full-day heli-raft) and the Dragons Cave Rafting subterranean adventure into the Taniwha Cave ($105, 5½-hours) where you float on inflated tubes down through a subterranean glowworm

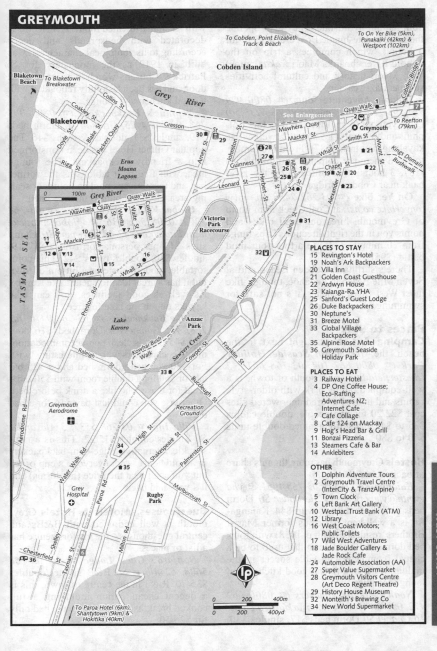

GREYMOUTH

To Cobden, Point Elizabeth
Track & Beach

To On Yer Bike (5km),
Punakaiki (42km) &
Westport (102km)

Cobden Island

Blaketown
Beach

To Blaketown
Breakwater

Blaketown

Grey River

Cobden Bridge

Quay Walk

See Enlargement

Mawhera Quay

Greymouth

To Reefton
(79km)

Mackay St

Smith St

Kings Domain
Bushwalk

TASMAN SEA

Erua Moana
Lagoon

Gresson

Johnston

Guinness St

Leonard St

Victoria
Park
Racecourse

Chapel St

Grey River

Quay Walk

Mawhera Quay

Custom St

Albert
Mackay

Tainui St

Werita St

Waite St

St

Guinness St

Whall St

Lake
Karoro

Kowhai Bush
Walk

**Anzac
Park**

Sawyers Creek

Cowper St

Franklin St

Tunumaha St

Preston Rd

Raleigh

Greymouth
Aerodrome

Buccleugh St

Recreation
Ground

High St

Shakespeare St

Palmerston St

Aerodrome Rd

Water Walk Rd

Paroa Rd

Grey
Hospital

Shelley St

Milton Rd

Chesterfield St

Tasman St

**Rugby
Park**

Marlborough St

To Paroa Hotel (6km),
Shantytown (9km) &
Hokitika (40km)

PLACES TO STAY

15 Revington's Hotel
19 Noah's Ark Backpackers
20 Villa Inn
21 Golden Coast Guesthouse
22 Ardwyn House
23 Kaianga-Ra YHA
25 Sanford's Guest Lodge
26 Duke Backpackers
30 Neptune's
31 Breeze Motel
32 Global Village
   Backpackers
35 Alpine Rose Motel
36 Greymouth Seaside
   Holiday Park

PLACES TO EAT

3 Railway Hotel
4 DP One Coffee House;
  Eco-Rafting
  Adventures NZ;
  Internet Cafe
7 Cafe Collage
8 Cafe 124 on Mackay
9 Hog's Head Bar & Grill
11 Bonzai Pizzeria
13 Steamers Cafe & Bar
14 Anklebiters

OTHER

1 Dolphin Adventure Tours
2 Greymouth Travel Centre
  (InterCity & TranzAlpine)
5 Town Clock
6 Left Bank Art Gallery
10 Westpac Trust Bank (ATM)
12 Library
16 West Coast Motors;
   Public Toilets
17 Wild West Adventures
18 Jade Boulder Gallery &
   Jade Rock Cafe
24 Automobile Association (AA)
27 Super Value Supermarket
28 Greymouth Visitors Centre
   (Art Deco Regent Theatre)
29 History House Museum
32 Monteith's Brewing Co
34 New World Supermarket

WEST COAST

gallery and end the trip by sliding down a 30m natural hydroslide. They also operate the more sedate Jungle Boat cruise ($95 for 3 hours), which combines a trip on the Arnold River aboard a Maori *waka* (canoe) with Maori history and cultural activities such as flax-weaving.

Dolphin Adventure Tours (☎ *0800 929 991, 03-768 9770; adult/child $67/33.50*) takes you out to spot the rare Hectors dolphins and fur seals (1½ hours), a well as sea kayaking day trips ($87). From November to April there are dolphin swimming trips ($87, 3 hours). The office is on the river bank near Cobden Bridge.

On Yer Bike (☎ *03-762 7438,* W *www .onyerbike.co.nz)*, at Coal Creek 5km north of Greymouth, hires out quad bikes and points you in the right direction. Trips range from 20 minutes ($25) to a two-hour mud battle ($95).

There's **surfing** at Cobden Beach and at Seven Mile Beach in Rapahoe, though, like most West Coast beaches, it's not safe for swimming.

Places to Stay
Camping & Cabins Right next to the beach, the *Greymouth Seaside Holiday Park* (☎ *0800 867 104, 03-768 6618, 2 Chesterfield St)*, 2.5km south of town, is a well-equipped family park with older-style cabins and units. Powered/unpowered sites cost $22/20 for two people, double cabins $35 to $45 and self-contained double units $60 to $80.

Hostels Greymouth has more than its share of backpacker places.

Kaianga-Ra YHA (☎ *03-768 4951,* e *yha gymth@yha.org.nz, 15 Alexander St)* Dorm beds $16-18, doubles & twins $44. Kaianga-Ra is a well-kept, spacious former Marist Brothers' residence (built in 1938) with four-bed dorms, a 10-bed dorm that used to be a chapel (complete with table soccer in the middle of the room), and good kitchen and lounge facilities.

Noah's Ark Backpackers (☎ *0800 662 472, 03-768 4868,* e *noahsark@xtra.co.nz, 16 Chapel St)* Dorm beds $17, singles $30,

doubles & twins $42. Noah's is a big hit with its animal-themed rooms – each one is decorated with bedspreads and decor according to its zoological character. It was built in 1912 as the monastery for St Patrick's Church, which was once next door, and has been tastefully renovated with a good kitchen and lounge.

Neptune's Backpackers (☎ *0800 003 768, 03-768 4425, Gresson St)* Dorm beds $19, singles $31, doubles & twins $46. The popular Gilmer Hotel has been transformed into a friendly backpackers. The lounge area, with free pool table, was the former bar, and there's a spa pool and outdoor seating area. Beds (no bunks) include linen.

Global Village Backpackers (☎ *03-768 7272, 0508 542 636,* e *globalvillage@ minidata.co.nz, 42-54 Cowper St)* Camp sites $13 per person, dorm beds $17-19, singles $30, doubles/twins $42. This comfortable, modern hostel is a bit out of town but it has a great location near Lake Karoro. As well as good facilities, you can take kayaks out on the lake for free.

Duke Backpackers (☎ *03-768 9470, fax 768 7471, Guinness St)* Dorm beds $16, doubles $45. This is clean pub-accommodation-meets-backpackers with an interesting twist. For $30 you get a dorm bed and a $25 bar tab, or $60 for a double room with $50 tab – great for those who like a drink before bed! Otherwise you could just pay $16 for a bed only.

Villa Inn (☎ *03-768 5537, 3 Alexander St)* Singles/doubles $15/22. This is a ramshackle, alternative lodge-cum-backpackers in an old house – not everyone's cup of tea but you can't beat the price (no dorms) and it's very laid back.

Guesthouses, Motels & Hotels Greymouth is well endowed with B&Bs and central guesthouses – the visitors centre has a list of places.

Sanford's Guest Lodge (☎/*fax 03-768 5608, 62 Albert St)* B&B singles/doubles $35/70. Right in the centre of town, this is a decent cheap option including a full cooked breakfast, or you can have bed only for $25/50.

Golden Coast Guesthouse (☎ 03-768 7839, 10 Smith St) B&B singles/doubles $50/75. Near the train station, the good value Golden Coast overlooks the river.

Ardwyn House (☎ 03-768 6107, 48 Chapel St) Singles/doubles $45/75. Reached via a steep drive, Ardwyn House has a homely character and is set in a pleasant garden.

There are scores of motels, most of them lining the highway south of the town centre, and north of the river.

Breeze Motel (☎ 0800 523 524, 03-762 5068, e info@breezemotel.co.nz, 125 Tainui St) Units from $90. This central motel has standard ground-floor units.

Alpine Rose Motel (☎ 03-768 7586, 139 High St) Units from $85-120. Alpine Rose is one of Greymouth's best with nicely furnished, fully self-contained rooms, some with spa bath. The family rooms are huge.

Revington's Hotel (☎ 03-768 7055, e accom@revingtons.co.nz, 46 Tainui St) Singles/doubles/triples $60/70/85. This once-grand hotel (Queen Elizabeth II stayed here) is still the best of the central pubs to stay in. There are bright en suite rooms and a few older-style rooms, and at the time of writing parts of it were being renovated into a new backpacker section.

Places to Eat

Standard cafes, takeaways and sandwich places include: *Anklebiters* (☎ 03-768 5026, 33 Albert St) with all-day breakfast, crepes, baked potatoes and Mexican ($9 to $12); the *Jade Rock Cafe (cnr Guinness & Tainui Sts)* in the Jade Boulder Gallery; and the *Bonzai Pizzeria* (☎ 03-768 4170, 31 Mackay St), a pleasant place with 20 varieties of pizza, a blackboard menu and a good selection of wines and beers.

Railway Hotel (☎ 03-768 7023, Mawhera Quay) Near the railway station, this pub is hard to beat for its nightly barbecue – sausages cost $3, vegie burgers $5 and steaks $8, with buffet salad. Karaoke nights are popular here too.

DP One Coffee House (☎ 03-768 4005, 108 Mawhera Quay) A bohemian feel and arty decor make this a great place to lounge around over coffee and cake. It also has an Internet cafe, and there are live bands and DJs here on weekend evenings.

Hog's Head Bar & Grill (☎ 03-768 4093, 9 Tainui St) Lunch $5-10, mains from $15. Hog's Head has a good selection of steaks and seafood. Its speciality is whitebait in season.

Steamers Cafe & Bar (☎ 03-768 4193, 58 Mackay St) Meals $11.50-18.50. This is a carvery with hearty roasts and grills for lunch and dinner.

Cafe 124 on Mackay (☎ 03-768 7503, 124 Mackay St) Lunch $7-13, dinner mains $19-28. Cafe 124 is a good place for lunch with delicious bacon-and-egg pie, risotto, sandwiches and several varieties of coffee.

Cafe Collage (☎ 03-768 5497, 115 Mackay St) Mains $22-30. Open Tues-Sat from 6pm. This highly regarded cafe, located upstairs, is quite pricey although there are specials for around $13 to $16 and it's licensed and BYO (wine).

Getting There & Away

The Greymouth Travel Centre (☎ 03-768 7080) at the train station on Mackay St books all forms of transport, including the TranzScenic trains and inter-island ferries. This is also the depot for bus services.

InterCity has daily services north to Westport (2¼ hours) and Nelson (6 hours) and south to the glaciers (3 hours). Atomic Shuttles has daily buses from Greymouth to Queenstown (10½ hours, $80) at 7.30am, as well as a separate service to Fox Glacier ($30), and a Greymouth-Picton bus ($50) via either Westport or Reefton. Atomic also has a Christchurch-Hokitika service via Greymouth.

The Coast to Coast Shuttle (☎ 0800 800 847) and Alpine Coaches (☎ 0800 274 888) operate between Greymouth and Christchurch ($35) via Arthur's Pass ($20 from Greymouth, $25 from Christchurch) and also go to Hokitika.

The spectacular *TranzAlpine Express* (☎ 0800 802 802) runs daily between Christchurch and Greymouth, departing from Greymouth at 2.25pm (see the boxed text 'The *TranzAlpine*' in this chapter). It's

The *TranzAlpine*

One of the great rail journeys of the world is the traverse of the Southern Alps between Christchurch and Greymouth – it begins near the Pacific Ocean and ends by the Tasman Sea.

Not so long ago, this popular rail journey, now made in the comfort of specially designed carriages, was undertaken in a ramshackle railcar. In times of bad weather and road closure, it was often the only means that West Coasters had to get to the eastern side of the Divide.

The *TranzAlpine* crossing offers a bewildering variety of scenery. It leaves Christchurch at 9am, then speeds across the flat, alluvial Canterbury Plains to the foothills of the Alps.

In the foothills it enters a labyrinth of gorges and hills known as the Staircase, and the climb here is made possible by a system of three large viaducts and most of the tunnels, which will be encountered along the line.

The train emerges into the broad Waimakariri and Bealey Valleys, and (on a good day) the surrounding vista is stupendous. The river valley is fringed with dense beech forest which eventually gives way to the snow-capped peaks of Arthur's Pass National Park.

At the small alpine village of Arthur's Pass the train enters the longest of the tunnels, the 'Otira' (8.5km), and heads under the mountains to the West Coast.

There are several more gems on the western side – the valleys of the Otira, Taramakau and Grey Rivers, patches of podocarp forest, and the pleasant surprise of trout-filled Lake Brunner (Moana Kotuku), fringed with cabbage trees.

The train arrives in Greymouth around 1.25pm. (It departs for Christchurch an hour later, arriving at 6.35pm.)

Few travellers who make this rail journey will have regrets, except when the weather is bad. Chances are if it's raining on one coast it'll be fine on the other.

possible to do the trip as a day return from Christchurch, but not from Greymouth. If you can get it (numbers are limited, so book early), a Super Saver will cost $61 one way but there are special fares as low as $44, otherwise it's a hefty $87.

AROUND GREYMOUTH

Greymouth to Hokitika has great views of the wild West Coast. If you deviate from the main road to the beach you will see kilometres of salt spray and endless lines of driftwood.

Shantytown (☎ 03-762 6634, **W** *www .shantytown.co.nz; open 8.30am-5pm daily*), 8km south of Greymouth and 3km inland from the main road, does a good job of re-creating an 1880s West Coast town in the gold rush. For many the prime attraction is a ride on the 1897 steam locomotive. You can also try gold panning; everyone is assured of coming up with at least a few flakes of gold to take away. Re-created buildings include the jail, schoolhouse, blacksmith shop, bank and lolly shop. The admission price of adult/child/family $13.50/7/31.50 includes gold panning and train ride, or $11/2.50 without panning.

Paroa Hotel & Motel (☎ 03-762 6860, **e** *bkmonk@xtra.co.nz, 508 Main South Rd*) Singles/doubles $70/85, budget rooms $65. You can't beat the Paroa, opposite the turn-off to Shantytown, for good old-fashioned West Coast hospitality. There are motel units, and hearty meals are available from *Ham's* restaurant. Just 100m away is the unspoilt Paroa Beach.

HOKITIKA
pop 4000

Hokitika, or 'Hoki' for short, is 40km south of Greymouth. It was settled in the 1860s, after the discovery of gold, and became a busy town.

Hokitika is the country's major centre for the working of greenstone – the main attraction for many visitors – but the region offers more to do than just look at stone being mass produced into bookends of *tiki* and *taniwha* images. Hoki is rich in history and nearby is a wealth of native forests,

Crossing the footbridge into Mount Aspiring National Park, Matukituki Valley

'No Horses Allowed' in this 'long drop' toilet at Pioneer Hut, upper Fox Glacier, Southern Alps

DAVID WALL

St Clair Beach, Dunedin

DAVID WALL

Lake Tekapo, Mackenzie Country, Canterbury

ANDREW PEACOCK

Ice mushroom, Mount Cook National Park

DAVID WALL

Church of the Good Shepherd, Lake Tekapo

lakes and rivers. Although smaller and quieter than Greymouth, it makes for a more interesting overnight stop.

In mid-March Hokitika hosts the increasingly popular Wildfoods Festival in Cass Square. This major West Coast event attracts up to 20,000 people.

Information

The Westland visitors centre (☎ 03-755 6166, e hkkvin@xtra.co.nz), in the Carnegie Building, is open 8am to 6pm daily in summer (otherwise 9am to 5pm weekdays and 10am to 2pm weekends).

Internet access is available at Aim West Sports on Weld St ($10 an hour).

If heading south, do your banking in Hokitika, as there are no banks or ATMs until you reach Wanaka.

Things to See & Do

Westland's Water World (☎ 03-755 5251, Sewell St; adult/child $8/3; open summer 9am-5.30pm daily, winter 9am-4.30pm) is a small aquarium with a variety of fish and other West Coast marine life, including giant eels and whitebait. The main attraction is at 10am, noon, 3pm and 5pm, when

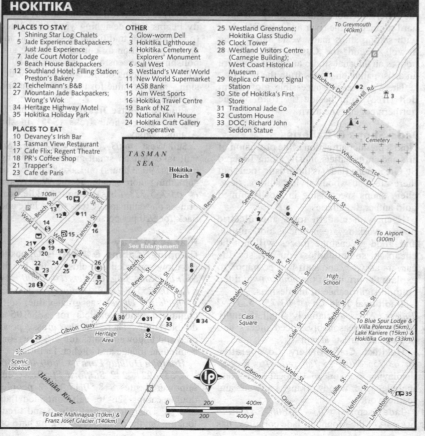

HOKITIKA

PLACES TO STAY
1 Shining Star Log Chalets
3 Jade Experience Backpackers; Just Jade Experience
7 Jade Court Motor Lodge
9 Beach House Backpackers
12 Southland Hotel; Filling Station; Preston's Bakery
22 Teichelmann's B&B
27 Mountain Jade Backpackers; Wong's Wok
34 Heritage Highway Motel
35 Hokitika Holiday Park

PLACES TO EAT
10 Devaney's Irish Bar
13 Tasman View Restaurant
17 Cafe Flix; Regent Theatre
18 PR's Coffee Shop
21 Trapper's
23 Cafe de Paris

OTHER
2 Glow-worm Dell
3 Hokitika Lighthouse
4 Hokitika Cemetery & Explorers' Monument
6 Sail West
8 Westland's Water World
11 New World Supermarket
14 ASB Bank
15 Aim West Sports
16 Hokitika Travel Centre
19 Bank of NZ
20 National Kiwi House
24 Hokitika Craft Gallery Co-operative

25 Westland Greenstone; Hokitika Glass Studio
26 Clock Tower
28 Westland Visitors Centre (Carnegie Building); West Coast Historical Museum
29 Replica of Tambo; Signal Station
30 Site of Hokitika's First Store
31 Traditional Jade Co
32 Custom House
33 DOC; Richard John Seddon Statue

TASMAN SEA

Hokitika Beach

See Enlargement

To Greymouth (40km)

Cemetery

To Airport (300m)

High School

Cass Square

Heritage Area

Scenic Lookout

Hokitika River

To Lake Mahinapua (10km) & Franz Josef Glacier (140km)

To Blue Spur Lodge & Villa Polenza (5km); Lake Kaniere (15km) & Hokitika Gorge (33km)

WEST COAST

a diver descends into the eel tank to feed the voracious giant eels.

The **National Kiwi Centre** *(☎ 03-755 8904, 86 Revell St; adult/child $6/3, open 9am-7pm daily)* is a nocturnal kiwi house, where you can dimly see these flightless birds foraging, and there's a small aquarium.

The **West Coast Historical Museum** *(☎ 03-755 6898, Hamilton St; adult/child $5/1; open 9.30am-5pm daily)*, in the same building as the visitors centre, has many gold-mining relics and the usual mish-mash found in regional museums, as well as an audiovisual presentation about the gold rush.

Pick up a copy of the *Hokitika Heritage Walk* from the visitors centre and explore the waterfront along **Gibson Quay** – it's not hard to imagine the river and wharf choked with sailing ships many years ago. At the Sewell St end, the **Custom House** now houses an unusual studio and gallery where an artist paints on stones from the beach.

There's an easily accessible **glowworm dell** (free) right beside the road on the northern edge of the town.

Jade Shops & Galleries

Hoki's premier attraction is the profusion of arts and crafts outlets, mostly along Tancred St. Greenstone (jade) is the artistic focus but there are also wood-carving studios, jewellery shops specialising in locally mined gold and craft galleries.

Even with modern tools and electric power, working greenstone is not simple, and good greenstone pieces will not be cheap. In some studios you can see the carvers at work, and staff will be happy to explain the origins of the *pounamu* and the cultural significance of the designs.

Traditional Jade Co *(☎ 03-755 5233, 2 Tancred St)* is a relatively small, friendly studio with reasonably priced pieces and you can see artists at work.

Hokitika Craft Gallery Co-operative *(☎ 03-755 8802, 25 Tancred St)* is a coop displaying the work of 19 local artists and includes jade, woodworking, knitwear and leatherwork.

Jade Factory *(☎ 03-755 8007, 41 Weld St)*, part of the Mountain Jade complex, has a big range of well-presented jade sculpture (including golf putters from $225), as well as gold-nugget jewellery (at the Heart of Gold shop within the complex).

Another Hokitika speciality is glass-blowing and there are a couple of studios where you can see glass-blowers at work and browse (and buy) the finished product. **Hokitika Glass Studio** *(☎ 03-755 7775, 28 Tancred St)* is the best known, but there's also **Schroder's Handblown Glass** at the Mountain Jade complex.

Activities

You can try your hand at **jade carving** in Hokitika at the Just Jade Experience *(☎ 03-755 7612, 197 Revell St)*. The all-day activity begins with designing your own piece (or choosing a traditional design), and includes instruction on cutting, working and polishing the greenstone. The cost of $80 to $120 – depending on the complexity of design – is great value for the experience and finished product.

Blue Spur Horse Treks *(☎ 03-755 6603)* has guided 1½-hour treks ($45) in the Arahura Valley.

Sail West *(☎ 03-755 6024, 14 Park St)* will take you on small-group day sailing cruises ($90, 3 hours) on Lake Kaniere. For something more sedate, **Scenic Waterways** *(☎ 03-755 7239)* has 1½-hour paddle boat cruises on Mahinapua Creek to the lake and back for $20 per person.

Places to Stay

Camping, Cabins & Hostels Opposite the glowworm dell and close to the beach, *Shining Star Log Chalets (☎ 0800 744 6464, 03-755 8921,* e *shining@xtra.co.nz, 11 Richards Drive)* has great-value, self-contained timber chalets for $88/105 a double/family. There are also grassy powered and unpowered sites for $10 a person, communal lounge and kitchen facilities.

Hokitika Holiday Park (☎ 0800 465 436, 03-755 8921, 242 Stafford St) Powered/ unpowered sites $18.50/17 for 2 people, double cabins $26-36, self-contained flats $56-78. This park is pretty bare and tired-looking but the owners are working hard on improvements. There's a wide range of accommodation and some of the self-contained units are new and well equipped.

Jade Experience Backpackers (☎ 03-755 7612, 197 Revell St) Dorm beds $16, double $38. This small, homestay-style place is run by jade-carver Gordon Wells and is home to the Just Jade Experience (see Activities). There's just a handful of beds and you can pitch a tent out the back for $10 per person.

Mountain Jade Backpackers (☎ 0800 838 301, 03-755 8007, e mtjade@minidata .co.nz, 41 Weld St) Dorm beds $18, doubles $45. This spacious, open-plan place is very centrally located above the jade shop of the same name. It's spotless and sets a high standard (despite the small kitchen and large dorms), though it lacks personality. There are also self-contained units sleeping five for $80.

Beach House Backpackers (☎ 03-755 6859, 137 Revell St) Camp sites $10 per person, dorm beds $19 ($15 for subsequent nights), doubles $43 ($35 for subsequent nights). This backpackers is in an old and fading house.

Blue Spur Lodge (☎/fax 03-755 8445, e bluespur@xtra.co.nz) Dorm beds $19, doubles/twins $42/46. This cosy, peaceful lodge is only 5km east of town but seems miles from anywhere. It has clean, modern rooms, a large kitchen/lounge with open fire and a separate cottage ($110 or $55 per double room). There's free pick-up from Hokitika, free bikes and for $60 (two people, including transport) you can take a kayak out to Lake Kaniere or Lake Mahinapua. To get there follow Cement Lead Rd via Hau Hau Rd.

Motels & B&Bs The well-kept, friendly *Jade Court Motor Lodge* (☎ 0800 755 885, 03-755 8855, 85 Fitzherbert St) has spacious self-contained units from $85-105, and spa units for $95.

Heritage Highway Motel (☎ 0800 465 484, 03-755 8098, 12 Fitzherbert St) Units from $88. This is one of Hoki's newest motels and it offers attractive units and a spa for guests.

Teichelmann's B&B (☎ 0800 743 742, 03-755 8232, e teichel@xtra.co.nz, 20 Hamilton St) Singles/doubles $100/110-130. Teichelmann's is a lovely homestay B&B in an historic house opposite the museum and visitors centre. There's a variety of bright en suite rooms and friendly hosts.

Villa Polenza (☎ 0800 241 801, 03-755 7801, e villapolenza@xtra.co.nz, Brickfields Rd) Suite doubles with breakfast $250-350. This fine boutique guesthouse is modelled on a classical Italian villa and has a wonderful hilltop position overlooking the town and ocean, 5km east of Hokitika.

Places to Eat

For snacks and sandwiches try historic *Preston's Bakery* on Revell St, or *PR's Coffee Shop* (☎ 03-755 8379, Tancred St). *Wong's Wok* (☎ 03-755 6444, 41 Weld St), next to Mountain Jade, does cheap Chinese (lunch from $6).

Cafe Flix (☎ 03-755 8581, 23 Weld St) Meals $3.50-16.50. Open 6am-4pm daily. Next to the Regent Theatre, this is an ambient little cafe offering everything from toasted sandwiches to gourmet burgers ($6 to $8.50) and pizzas ($14 to $16.50).

Tasman View Restaurant (☎ 03-755 8344, Beach St) Meals $19.50-27.50. Part of the Southland Hotel, this á la carte restaurant overlooks Hokitika's windswept, grey beach. The menu includes ostrich salad, venison and whitebait. Also part of the hotel, the *Filling Station* on Revell St is a casual, inexpensive cafe with outdoor seating.

Cafe de Paris (☎ 03-755 6859, Tancred St) Mains $21-30. Hokitika's top restaurant and easily the busiest evening dining place in town, Cafe de Paris is recommended for its French-influenced food – crepes, venison, lamb, mussels and pasta. There's a cheaper lunch and breakfast menu.

Trapper's (☎ 03-755 5133, 79 Revell St) This is a locally recommended West Coast themed restaurant with 'wild food' game dishes on the menu and hunting trophies on the wall. There's a rustic bar here too.

Devaney's Irish Bar, found on Revell St, is a good place for a night out and also does good pizza.

Getting There & Away

Air New Zealand Link (☎ 0800 652 881) has daily direct flights to Christchurch with connections to other centres. Book at the Hokitika Travel Centre.

From Hokitika there are daily InterCity services to Greymouth (40 minutes), Nelson (7 hours) and south to Fox Glacier (3 hours). Atomic Shuttles has two services daily to Fox Glacier ($30) and Greymouth ($10), and one to Queenstown (10 hours, $70). The Coast to Coast Shuttle and Alpine Coach run to Christchurch via Arthur's Pass ($35).

AROUND HOKITIKA

A scenic drive or cycle of about 33km brings you to **Hokitika Gorge**, a small but stunning gorge filled by the turquoise blue glacial waters of the Hokitika River. There's a swingbridge across the gorge and several forest walkways.

A loop road takes you around the scenic **Lake Kaniere**, passing by **Dorothy Falls**, **Kahikatea Forest** and **Canoe Cove**. The visitors centre and DOC have detailed brochures on other walks in the area, including the 13km **Lake Kaniere Walkway** which follows the western shore of the lake (four hours). The **Mahinapua Walkway** (5.5km, three hours return) goes through the scenic reserve on the northeast side of Lake Mahinapua to a swamp teeming with wildlife.

There are *DOC camping grounds* at Goldsborough (17km from Hoki) on the 1876 'gold trail', Hans Bay on the east side of Lake Kaniere (19km) and Shanghai Bay at Lake Mahinapua (10km). The turn-off to the latter is opposite the legendary *Lake Mahinapua Hotel (☎ 03-755 8500)*, a classic West Coast pub with accommodation at the rear.

HOKITIKA TO THE GLACIERS

It's about 140km south from Hokitika to the Franz Josef Glacier and while many travellers pass straight through, there are a few interesting stops for walking, kayaking, watching birdlife and delving into West Coast history. The InterCity and Atomic Shuttle buses from Greymouth to the glaciers will stop anywhere along the highway.

Ross

Ross, 30km south of Hokitika, is a small, historic gold-mining town where gold is still mined today. NZ's largest gold nugget, the 99oz 'Honourable Roddy', was found here in 1907. Grimmond House which, in the gold-rush era was home to the Bank of New South Wales, is now the **Ross Gold-fields Information & Heritage Centre** *(☎ 03-755 4077, open 8.30am-5.30pm daily in summer)* which features a scale model of the town at its goldmining peak.

Just up from the visitors centre is a small, furnished **Miner's Cottage museum**, complete with old piano and cast-iron stove.

The cottage stands at the beginning of two historic goldfield **walkways**, the Jones Flat Walk and the Water Race Walk. Each takes about one to two hours and passes by interesting features from the gold rush era.

Behind the visitors centre is the relatively new **Birchfields Mine**, an open-cast alluvial gold mine, where you can look down on the operations. Nearby you can try your hand at gold panning ($6).

Empire Hotel (☎ 03-755 4005, 19 Aylmer St) Dorm beds $15, double cabins $30, rooms with shared/private bathroom $30/55. The local pub has budget accommodation and atmospheric old hotel rooms, as well as inexpensive bar meals.

Roddy Nugget Cafe (☎ 03-755 4245, 5 Moorhouse St) This classic country cafe is licensed and does great homemade pies (venison, beef satay etc) and whitebait sandwiches.

Ross to Okarito

Heading southwards the rainforest becomes more dense and, in many parts, looks as if it would be easier to walk over the top of the rainforest than to find a way through.

Pukekura Just north of Lake Ianthe, is this tiny place that is pretty much run by one family.

The **Bushmen's Centre** *(☎ 03-755 4144)*, easily recognised by the giant sandfly hanging out the front, consists of a shop selling West Coast crafts and bush clothing, a cafe and the Bushmen's Museum. Admission to

THE GLACIERS & WESTLAND NATIONAL PARK

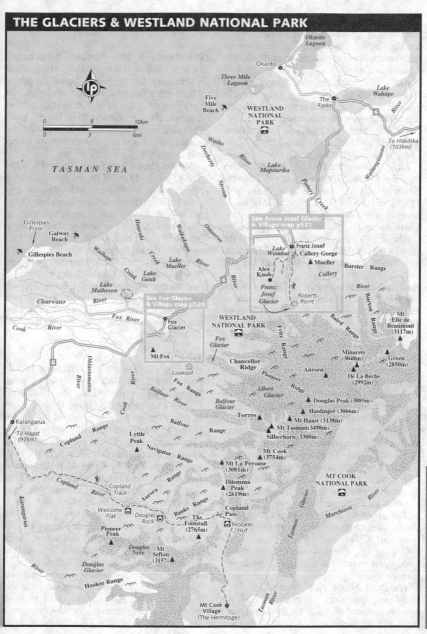

Okarito Lagoon

Okarito

Three Mile Lagoon

Five Mile Beach

WESTLAND NATIONAL PARK

The Forks

Lake Wahapo

River

To Hokitika (103km)

Waiho

Dockery Stream

River

Lake Mapourika

Potters Creek

Waitangitaona

TASMAN SEA

Hauraki Creek

Waikukupa River

Omoeroa

Waihopi Creek

Creek

See Franz Josef Glacier & Village map p521

Lake Wombat

Franz Josef

Callery Gorge

Mueller

Burster Range

River

Gillespies Point

Galway Beach

Gillespies Beach

Lake Mueller

Lake Gault

Alex Knob

Callery

Burton Range

Mt Elie de Beaumont (3117m)

Lake Matheson

Clearwater River

River

See Fox Glacier & Village map p524

Franz Josef Glacier

Roberts Point

Baird Range

Fox River

Fox Glacier

WESTLAND NATIONAL PARK

Green (2850m)

Cook River

River

Mt Fox

Fox Glacier

Minarets (3048m)

Aurora

De La Beche (2992m)

Ohinetamatea River

Lookout

Fox Range

Chancellor Ridge

Pioneer Ridge

Fritz Range

Albert Glacier

Douglas Peak (3085m)

Balfour River

Balfour Glacier

Torres

Haidinger (3066m)

Mt Haast (3138m)

Karangarua

To Haast (97km)

Copland Range

Balfour Range

Lyttle Peak

Navigator Range

Mt Tasman(3498m)

Silberhorn (3300m)

Copland River

Copland Track

Aurora

Range

Mt La Perouse (3081m)

Mt Cook (3754m)

MT COOK NATIONAL PARK

Welcome Flat

Douglas Rock

Banks Range

The Footstall (2765m)

Dilemma Peak (2619m)

Copland Pass

Hooker Hut

Karangarua River

Pioneer Peak

Douglas Neve

Mt Sefton (3157m)

Murchison River

Tasman Glacier

Douglas Glacier

Hooker Range

River

Tasman River

Mt Cook Village (The Hermitage)

0   5   10km
0   3   6mi

WEST COAST

the museum is $2 ('$3 if you want the possum out') or $4 with a guided tour. Among the displays is historical information on NZ's destructive introduced animals and the venison industry.

Across the road, the charmingly named *Puke Pub* is like stepping into an old bushy's shack. The rustic timber bar adjoins the *Wild Foods Restaurant*, which specialises in game dishes such as venison, wild pork and rabbit (mains $20 to $25). There's also a set of hot pools out the back.

Lake Ianthe Cabins & Backpackers (☎ 03-755 4088) Camp sites $7.50-10, powered sites $20 for 2 people, dorm beds $15, doubles $40. This comfortable backpackers is opposite the Bushman's Centre. There's also a house for rent for $60.

About 100m south of Lake Ianthe, on the eastern side of the highway, is a giant **matai tree**, thought to be over 1000 years old.

Harihari This small town is 22km south of Lake Ianthe. Harihari made headlines in 1931, when Australian Guy Menzies completed the first solo flight across the Tasman Sea from Sydney. The landing was anything but smooth as he crash-landed *Southern Cross Junior* in the La Fontaine swamp. The aircraft turned over and when he undid his safety straps he fell head-first into the mud. He had made the trip in 11¾ hours, 2½ hours quicker than fellow Australian Charles Kingsford Smith and his crew in 1928.

The two- to three-hour **Hari Hari Coastal Walkway** (also called the Doughboy Walk or Coastal Pack Track) is a popular loop taking in the Poerua and Wanganui Rivers. The start of the walk is about 16km from the main highway – follow Wanganui Flats Rd then La Fontaine Drive.

Tomasi Motel & Backpackers (☎ 03-753 3116) Twins $20 per person, double motel units $70. This friendly place is a favourite with passing cyclists – the share rooms are good value as they have en suite, and there's a small kitchen.

Harihari Motor Inn (☎ 03-753 3026, e hhmi@xtra.co.nz) Camp sites $7.50 per person, powered sites $20 for 2 people, dorm beds $16.50, motel units $70. Backpackers

can use the basic twin rooms. There's no kitchen but a bar and restaurant.

Whataroa & the Kotuku Sanctuary

Near Whataroa, 35km south of Harihari, is a sanctuary for the white heron (kotuku), which nests from November to the end of February. It is the only NZ nesting site of this species. The herons then fly off individually to spend winter throughout the country. Access is possible only with a permit from DOC.

White Heron Sanctuary Tours (☎ 0800 523 456, 03-753 4120, e info@whiteheron tours.co.nz; adult/child $89/40) has 2½-hour trips into the sanctuary from late October to March. This is a 'jetboat eco-tour' to the kotuku colony – a strange combination, but don't panic bird lovers, the jetboat does not enter the nesting area. You walk along a boardwalk to the hide, where you spend 30 to 40 minutes. The cost includes a permit.

Sanctuary Tours Motel Cabins $35-40, motel units from $75. Owned by the tour company, this motel has standard units, cabins and powered and unpowered sites (but no kitchen).

Okarito

Another 15km south of Whataroa is The Forks and the turn-off to peaceful Okarito, 13km away on the coast. Much of Keri Hulme's bestseller, *The Bone People*, is set in this wild, isolated region and the author is one of the 16 permanent residents in the tiny community. There are lots of walks along the coast from Okarito – try the one-hour return walk to **Three Mile Lagoon** at low tide or the 30-minute walk to the **Trig**, which offers fine views of the southern Alps and back across the lagoon.

Okarito Nature Tours (☎/fax 03-753 4014, W www.okarito.co.nz) rents kayaks for trips into the beautiful and safe **Okarito Lagoon**, a feeding ground for the kotuku and a good place for watching all kinds of birds. The lagoon is NZ's largest unmodified wetland and consists of shallow open water and tidal flats. The lake is surrounded by rimu and kahikatea rainforest. A half-day trip can take you deep into the Okarito River delta

Advance & Retreat

Glaciers always advance, they never really retreat. Sometimes, however, the ice melts even faster than it advances, and in that case the terminal, or end face, of the glacier moves backwards up the mountain and the glacier appears to be retreating.

The great mass of ice higher up the mountain pushes the ice down the Fox and Franz Josef Valleys at prodigious speeds but – like most glaciers in the world – this past century has been a story of steady retreat and only the odd short advance.

The last ice age of 15,000 to 20,000 years ago saw the glaciers reach right down to the sea. Then warmer weather came and they may have retreated even further than their current position. In the 14th century a new 'mini ice age' started and for centuries the glaciers advanced, reaching their greatest extent around 1750. At both Fox and Franz Josef, the terminal moraines from that last major advance can be clearly seen. In the 250 years since then, the glaciers have steadily retreated and the terminal face is now several kilometres back from its position in the late 19th century or even in the 1930s.

From 1965 to 1968 the Fox and Franz Josef Glaciers made brief advances of about 180m, and in 1985 they once again started to advance and have been moving forward steadily and fairly dramatically until about 1996 when they began to slow down. The reason for this advance could be cooler or more overcast summers, but it most likely the result of heavy snowfalls 10 or 15 years ago, which are now working their way down to the bottom of the glacier.

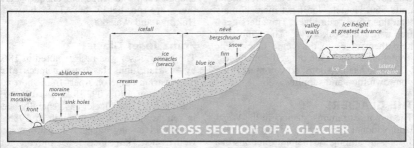

CROSS SECTION OF A GLACIER

Useful Terminology

ablation zone – where the glacier melts

accumulation zone – where the snow collects

bergschrund – large crevasse in the ice near the headwall or starting point of the glacier

blue ice – as the accumulation zone or névé snow is compressed by subsequent snowfalls, it becomes firn and then blue ice

crevasse – cracks in the glacial ice as it crosses obstacles and moves down the mountain

dead ice – as a glacier retreats, isolated chunks of ice may be left behind (sometimes these can remain for many years)

firn – partly compressed snow on the way to becoming glacial ice

glacial flour – the river of melted ice that flows off glaciers is a milky colour from the suspension of finely ground rocks

icefall – when a glacier descends so steeply that the upper ice breaks up in a jumble of iceblocks

kettle lake – lake formed by the melt of an area of isolated dead ice

moraine – walls of debris formed at the glacier's sides (lateral moraine) or end (terminal moraine)

névé – snowfield area where firn is formed

seracs – ice pinnacles formed, like crevasses, by the glacier passing over obstacles

terminal – the final ice face at the end of the glacier

along mirror-calm channels. Kayak rental costs $40/50 for a half/full day, including maps, gear and instruction, or you can take a fully guided trip for $65. It's also possible to go out overnight ($80) and camp on deserted North Beach or Lake Windemere.

In the middle of the village is a very basic *camping ground* with barbecues, toilets and showers. Sites cost adult/child $5/1, payable to the honesty box, and hot showers cost $1.

Okarito YHA Hostel (☎ 03-753 4124, Palmerston St) Dorm beds $15. This tiny 16-bed hostel is a classic YHA 'original' – the kitchen, lounge and some of the bunks are all in one room! It was originally a schoolhouse, built in the 1890s when Okarito was a thriving gold town. Hot showers are available at the camping ground across the road.

Royal Hostel (☎ 03-753 4080, Strand) Dorms $20, doubles & twins $48, motel units $60. Hostels don't get more homely than this family-run place. Travellers get a free pancake breakfast at 'The Club' and help themselves to the vegie patch. The 'motel units' are rustic but self-contained.

Okarito has no shops, so you must bring your own food and supplies.

THE GLACIERS

The two most famous glaciers in the Westland National Park – the Fox and the Franz Josef – are among the major attractions in a country full of natural wonders. Nowhere else in the world, at this latitude, have glaciers advanced so close to the sea. Unlike the Tasman Glacier, on the other side of the dividing range in Mt Cook National Park, these two are just what glaciers should be – mighty rivers of ice, tumbling down a valley towards the sea.

The reason for the glaciers' development is threefold. The West Coast is subject to the prevailing rain-drenched westerlies which fall as snow high up in the névés. The snow crystals fuse to form clear ice at a depth of about 20m. Secondly, the zones where the ice accumulates on the glacier are very large, so there's a lot of ice to push down the valley. Finally, the glaciers are very steep – the ice can get a long way before it finally melts.

The rate of descent is staggering: wreckage of a plane that crashed on the Franz Josef in 1943, 3.5km from the terminal face, made it down to the bottom 6½ years later – a speed of 1.5m per day. At times the Franz Josef can move at up to 5m a day, over 10 times as fast as glaciers in the Swiss Alps. Generally, it moves at the rate of about 1m a day.

Heavy tourist traffic – most people stay only one or two nights – is catered for in the twin towns of Franz Josef and Fox, 23km apart. These small, modern tourist villages have accommodation and enough facilities at higher than average prices. Franz is definitely the busier of the two, with more nightlife and accommodation options, but Fox has more of an Alpine village charm. Although it's possible to change cash and travellers cheques here, there are no banks or ATMs between Hokitika and Wanaka.

Franz Josef Glacier

The Franz Josef was first explored in 1865 by Austrian Julius Haast, who named it after the Austrian emperor. Apart from short advances from 1907–09, 1921–34, 1946–59 and 1965–67, the glacier has generally been in retreat since 1865, although in 1985 it started advancing again. It has progressed well over 1.7km since 1985, moving forward by about 70cm a day, although it is still several kilometres back from the terminal point Haast first recorded and since 1996 it has again been retreating.

The glacier is 5km from the town. From the car park it is a 20-minute walk to the terminal face. Hope for a fine day so that you will have great views to the snow-capped peaks behind. The glaciers are roped off to stop people getting close to where there is a risk of icefall; if you want to venture further it's best to take a guided walk.

Information The Franz Josef DOC visitors centre (☎ 03-752 0796, fax 752 0797) is open from 8.30am to 6pm daily in summer (until noon and 1pm to 5pm in winter). It has an excellent interpretive display and information on walks in the area.

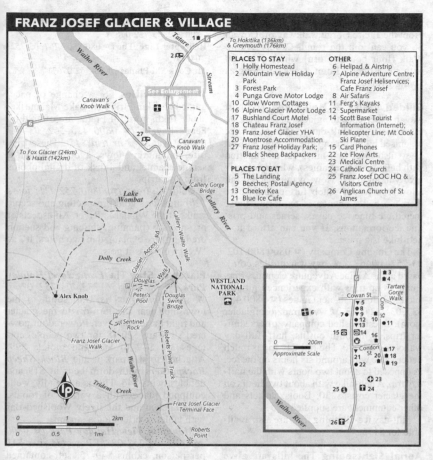

FRANZ JOSEF GLACIER & VILLAGE

PLACES TO STAY
1 Holly Homestead
2 Mountain View Holiday Park
3 Forest Park
4 Punga Grove Motor Lodge
10 Glow Worm Cottages
16 Alpine Glacier Motor Lodge
17 Bushland Court Motel
18 Chateau Franz Josef
19 Franz Josef Glacier YHA
20 Montrose Accommodation
27 Franz Josef Holiday Park; Black Sheep Backpackers

PLACES TO EAT
5 The Landing
9 Beeches; Postal Agency
13 Cheeky Kea
21 Blue Ice Cafe

OTHER
6 Helipad & Airstrip
7 Alpine Adventure Centre; Franz Josef Heliservices; Cafe Franz Josef
8 Air Safaris
11 Ferg's Kayaks
12 Supermarket
14 Scott Base Tourist Information (Internet); Helicopter Line; Mt Cook Ski Plane
15 Card Phones
22 Ice Flow Arts
23 Medical Centre
24 Catholic Church
25 Franz Josef DOC HQ & Visitors Centre
26 Anglican Church of St James

The Alpine Adventure Centre (☎ 0800 800 793) is a major booking agent for activities and also screens the 20-minute *Flowing West* movie on a giant Helimax screen (adult/child $10/5).

Internet access is available at the backpacker places and at the Scott Base Tourist Information Centre on the highway.

Walking There are several good glacier viewpoints that are close to the road leading from the glacier car park, including Sentinel Rock (10 minutes) or the Ka Roimata o Hine Hukatere walk (50 minutes

one way), which takes you towards the terminal face.

Other walks require a little worthwhile footslogging. The **Douglas Walk**, off the Glacier Access Rd, is an hour's stroll by the terminal moraine from the 1750 advance and Peter's Pool, a small 'kettle lake'. It's a longer walk (five hours return) over more rugged terrain to **Roberts Point**, which overlooks and is quite close to the terminal face.

The **Terrace Track** makes a pleasant one-hour round trip. It starts on the old Callery Track, a former gold-mining area, and leads up onto a terrace at the back of the village

WEST COAST

with pleasant views of the Waiho River. From the Tatare Gorge walkway off Cowan St, you can join the rough **Callery-Waiho Walk** (four hours return) which joins up with the Roberts Point Track at Douglas Swing Bridge.

Guided Walks & Heli-hikes The best way to experience the glaciers is to walk on them. Half- and full-day guided walks are organised by two companies at Franz Josef. They also offer heli-hikes (in conjunction with helicopter companies), which not only give you an aerial view of the glacier, but allow you to get much further up where there's a better chance of exploring those incredible blue ice caves, seracs and pristine ice formations. If you can afford it, a heli-hike is a must.

The Guiding Company (☎ 0800 800 102, 03-752 00467, W www.nzguides.com), based at the Alpine Adventure Centre, offers small group trips with experienced guides; and Franz Josef Glacier Guides (☎ 0800 484 337, 03-752 0763, W www.franzjosefglacier .com), an established company, offers similar trips. With both outfits, half-/full-day walks cost $45/90. The full-day trip is much better value with around six hours on the ice, as opposed to about two hours with the half-day trip. A heli-hike with about two hours on the glacier costs $230. Boots, jackets and other equipment are supplied.

Full-day **ice-climbing** trips are also available for $175.

Aerial Sightseeing The hills are alive with the sound of buzzing helicopters and planes doing runs over the glaciers and Mt Cook. Many flights include a snow landing. Flights are expensive but they're a superb experience – particularly the helicopters which can fly right in and bank close to the glacier face. A 20-minute flight to the head of the Franz Josef or Fox is $155, a full tour including Mt Cook is around $300.

Companies include:

Air Safaris (☎ 03-752 0716)
Franz & Fox Heliservices (☎ 0800 800 793, 03-752 0793)

Glacier Southern Lakes Helicopters (☎ 0800 800 732, 03-752 0755)
Helicopter Line, The (☎ 0800 807 767, 03-752 0767)
Mt Cook Ski Planes (☎ 03-752 0767)

Other Activities For a change of pace, guided kayaking trips on Lake Mapourika, about 10km north of Franz, are offered by **Ferg's Kayaks** (☎ 0800 423 262, 03-752 0230, Cron St; 3-hr trip $45). These trips offer mountain views, a detour down a serene channel and a disk of digital photos from your trip.

Gold 'n' Trees (☎ 0800 752 111; tours $20) organises gold prospecting and scenic walks at the Whataroa River. All aspects of prospecting (panning, sluicing and suction dredging) are explained in two hours. It's as 'West Coast' as it gets.

Places to Stay The *Franz Josef Holiday Park* (☎ 0800 4356 733, 03-752 0766, W www.fjhp.co.nz) is 1km south of the township, near the turn-off to the glacier and right beside the river. Powered/un-powered sites are $20/18 for two people, cottages are $49 to $69 and motels $99. Attached to the park is the *Black Sheep Backpackers* with dorm beds at $19 and doubles/twins $46. This is a friendly, well-equipped place with a variety of rooms, large kitchen and the lively Woolshed Bar with tables overlooking a stream.

Mountain View Holiday Park (☎ 0800 467 897, 03-752 0735) Powered sites $11 per person, cabins $49-75, self-contained units from $79. Just north of town, this is a tidy park with spa, children's playground and very good motel units.

Forest Park (☎ 03-752 0220, Cron St) Powered/unpowered sites $11/10 per person, dorm beds $20, self-contained cabins $75-130. This is something of a gem – right in town, but surrounded by rainforest, this camping area has individual log cabins, some raised on stilts. The surroundings give it a very private feel and there's a camp kitchen.

All of Franz Josef's backpacker hostels are on Cron St, one block east of the highway.

Glow Worm Cottages (☎ 0800 151 027, 03-752 0172, e glowwormcottages@ hotmail.com, 27 Cron St) Dorm beds $18-20, doubles/twins $45, double motel units $85. For cosiness and atmosphere, this is the best of Franz Josef's backpackers. Each of the four-bed dorms has an en suite and there's an inviting lounge/kitchen area. Like most Franz Josef backpackers, there's a free spa house.

Franz Josef Glacier YHA (☎ 03-752 0754, e yhafzjo@yha.org.nz, 2-4 Cron St) Dorm beds $20, doubles $44, en suite doubles $52. The YHA was getting a complete (and much-needed) refit at the time of research and looks like it will provide a high standard of accommodation with 10 new en suite twin/doubles, a large, open common area and spotless kitchen.

Chateau Franz Josef (☎ 0800 472 856, fax 03-752 0738) Dorm beds $18-19, doubles & twins $45. Chateau Franz, next door to the YHA, has a warren of rooms and is showing its age, but it's well equipped with a neat spa pool.

Montrose Accommodation (☎ 03-752 0188) Dorm beds $18, twins $40, doubles $44. This large, refurbished house is comfortable and well kept, but a bit nondescript. There's a nice deck on the upper floor and the usual facilities such as a spa pool and large kitchen.

Punga Grove Motor Lodge (☎ 0800 437 269, 03-752 0001, e pungagrove@xtra .co.nz, Cron St) Units $118-180. Punga Grove is a quality motel in a nice rainforest setting. Self-contained rooms include split level two-bedroom family units and spacious studios.

Bushland Court Motel (☎ 0800 757 111, 03-752 0757, e alpine.glacier@xtra.co.nz, 10 Cron St) Units $65-85. The Bushland Court is one of the best value motels in town. The same people own the more upmarket *Alpine Glacier Motor Lodge* across the road where large self-contained units cost from $110 to $145 including spa.

Holly Homestead (☎ 03-752 0299, e hol lyhomestead@xtra.co.nz) Double with shared bathroom/en suite $98/150. This pleasant two-storey home has four tastefully furnished rooms and a cooked breakfast is included in the rates.

Places to Eat & Drink Franz Josef has a busy little shopping centre along the highway with a decent **supermarket** open from 7.45am to 8.30pm daily.

The *Cheeky Kea* is a cheap place (BYO) with roast dinners for $12, fried chicken and whitebait sandwiches. *Cafe Franz Josef* in the Alpine Adventure Centre is a bright cafe serving breakfast, lunch and dinner, including gourmet burgers and sandwiches.

Beeches (☎ 03-752 0721) Mains $21.50-29.50. Beeches is the pick of Franz Josef's restaurants with a good range of wines and NZ cuisine (salmon, lamb and venison). Lunches are reasonably priced at $6 to $15 and pasta dishes are $14.50.

The Landing (☎ 03-752 0229) Dishes $10.50-25. The Landing is a new restaurant and bar open from noon till late with everything from nachos to seafood and steak dishes.

Blue Ice Cafe Pizzas $12-26. The Blue Ice has a cafe and restaurant downstairs and the upstairs bar is the happening place for a night out in Franz Josef.

Getting There & Around North and southbound InterCity buses cross between the two glaciers with daily buses south to Fox Glacier and Queenstown, and north to Nelson. You can also get to Franz Josef from Christchurch (via Arthurs Pass) in a day. In the high season (summer) these buses can be heavily booked, so plan and book well ahead or be prepared to wait until there's space.

Atomic Shuttles has daily services to Queenstown ($50, 7½ hours) and Greymouth ($30, 3½ hours). A ticket on the bus to Fox costs $10.

Kamahi Tours (☎ 03-752 0699) runs a variety of shuttles and trips including to the terminal face of the glacier, Lake Matheson ($45) and Okarito ($40)

Bikes can be hired from Ice Flow Arts (☎ 03-752 0144) near the Blue Ice Cafe for $6 an hour or $35 a day, or from hostels.

WEST COAST

Fox Glacier

Even if you've already visited Franz Josef Glacier, it's worth stopping to see Fox, 25km down the road. If nothing else you should pause for the walk around Lake Matheson and Fox village has more of a quaint, Alpine feel than Franz. The same activities are offered at both glaciers – glacier walks, flights and so on.

Despite consistent retreat throughout much of this century, Fox Glacier, like Franz Josef, began advancing around 1985. In the last 10 years it has advanced almost 1km but again appears to be on the retreat. It was named in 1872 after a visit by the NZ prime minister, Sir William Fox.

Information The DOC Fox Glacier visitors centre (☎ 03-751 0807, fax 751 0858) is open from 8.30am to 6pm daily in summer, from 9am to 4.30pm in winter (with a break between noon and 1pm). The centre has a small display on the glaciers and the natural environment as well as leaflets on a number of short walks around the ice.

Alpine Guides (☎ 03-751 0825) dominates the village and books most activities and bus services. It's also the local postal agency and money exchange – cash and travellers cheques – but rates are poor.

There's a petrol station in the village – the last fuel stop until you reach Haast, 120km further south.

Walking The shortest walk at Fox Glacier village is the two-minute stroll from the centre to the **glowworm dell** ($2 at honesty box). Of course, you have to go at night (open until 11pm) to see them glowing.

About 6km down Cook Flat Rd is the turn-off to **Lake Matheson** and one of the most famous panoramas in NZ. It's an hour's walk around the lake and at the far end are those unforgettable postcard views of Mt Tasman and Mt Cook reflected in the lake. On a fine day the best time to see it is

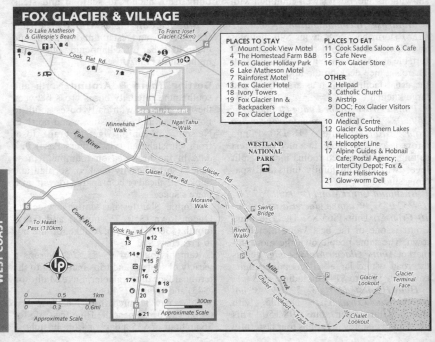

FOX GLACIER & VILLAGE

PLACES TO STAY
1 Mount Cook View Motel
4 The Homestead Farm B&B
5 Fox Glacier Holiday Park
6 Lake Matheson Motel
7 Rainforest Motel
13 Fox Glacier Hotel
18 Ivory Towers
19 Fox Glacier Inn & Backpackers
20 Fox Glacier Lodge

PLACES TO EAT
11 Cook Saddle Saloon & Cafe
15 Cafe Neve
16 Fox Glacier Store

OTHER
2 Helipad
3 Catholic Church
8 Airstrip
9 DOC; Fox Glacier Visitors Centre
10 Medical Centre
12 Glacier & Southern Lakes Helicopters
14 Helicopter Line
17 Alpine Guides & Hobnail Cafe; Postal Agency; InterCity Depot; Fox & Franz Heliservices
21 Glow-worm Dell

To Lake Matheson & Gillespie's Beach

To Franz Josef Glacier (25km)

Cook Flat Rd

Minnehaha Walk

Ngai Tahu Walk

Fox River

WESTLAND NATIONAL PARK

Glacier View Rd

Glacier Rd

Moraine Walk

Swing Bridge

River Walk

To Haast Pass (130km)

Cook River

Mills Creek

Chalet Lookout Track

Glacier Lookout

Glacier Terminal Face

Chalet Lookout

See Enlargement

Cook Flat Rd

Sullivan Rd

0   0.5   1km
0   0.3   0.6mi
Approximate Scale

0   300m
Approximate Scale

very early in the morning, when the lake is at its most mirror-like calm, but late afternoon, when the setting sun illuminates the mountains, is also a great time.

At the car park, *Cafe Lake Matheson* (☎ 03-752 0124) is a good place for the mountain views, not so much for the quality of food or service.

Other than from the air, the best view of Fox Glacier and the mountains is from further down Cook Flat Rd (towards Gillespie Beach). **Mt Fox** (1021m), off SH6 3km south of Fox Village, is another excellent viewpoint but the rugged walk is recommended only for equipped trampers – it's a three-hour walk one way.

Other interesting walks around the glacier include the **moraine walk**, over the advance of 200 years ago, the short **Minnehaha Walk** or the **River Walk**. The 1½-hour return Chalet Lookout Track takes you to a lookout over the terminal face.

It's 1.5km from Fox to the turn-off and the glacier is another 5km back from the main road. From there you can follow the marked track from the car park to the glacier, but just like at Franz Josef it's roped off before you get to the terminal face.

Glacier Walks & Helihikes Most activities can be booked at **Alpine Guides** (☎ 0800 111 600, 03-751 0825, W www .foxguides.co.nz; half-day tours adult/child $42/39, full-day walk $70), with guided walks leaving at 9.30am and 2pm daily and a full-day walk at 9.30am; boots and other equipment are provided. If you're of reasonable fitness it's well worth doing the full-day walk, which takes you much further up the glacier. Pack your own lunch.

Alpine Guides also has three-hour ($195) and full-day heli-hikes ($385), as well as an overnight trip to Chancellor Hut. The overnight trip includes hut fees, food and the flight up for $545 each for three people, $645 each for two.

You can try you hand at **ice climbing**, with a full-day introductory course ($180) or a three-/five-/eight-day guided mountain climbing trip for $1175/1575/1995, including accommodation in a mountain hut.

Skydiving & Aerial Sightseeing With a backdrop of the Southern Alps, glaciers, rainforest and the ocean, it's hard to imagine a better place to jump out of a plane than Fox Glacier. **Skydive NZ** (☎ 0800 751 0800, 03-751 0080) is a small but professional outfit offering jumps from 12,000 feet ($265) and $9000 feet ($225). Jump videos cost $170.

For aerial sightseeing, the following have much the same flights and prices as at Franz Josef. Some trips include flights over Mt Cook and Franz Josef. If you're doing a heli-hike or skydive, you get the aerial experience thrown in.

Franz & Fox Heliservices (☎ 0800 800 793, 03-751 0866) $130 to $295
Glacier Southern Lakes Helicopters (☎ 0800 800 732, 03-751 0803) $135 to $210
Helicopter Line (☎ 0800 807 767, 03-752 0767) $160 to $300
Mountain Helicopters (☎ 0800 369 423, 03-751 0045) $90 to $260

Places to Stay The well-equipped *Fox Glacier Holiday Park* (☎ 03-751 0821) is a short way down Cook Flat Rd from the township. It has powered/unpowered sites for $11/10 per person, dorm bed $13, double cabins for $35 to $45 and motel units for $70 to $80.

Ivory Towers (☎ 03-751 0838, E ivory towers@xtra.co.nz, Sullivans Rd) Dorm beds $18, singles from $27, doubles & twins $40. Ivory Towers is as a backpackers should be: tidy, well equipped, laid-back and most of the dorms have single beds (rather than bunks) with duvets supplied. There's also a spa.

Fox Glacier Inn & Backpackers (☎ 03-751 0022, fax 751 0024, 39 Sullivans Rd) Dorm beds from $17, singles $40, doubles & twins $45. This is primarily a bar and restaurant with a backpackers tacked on the back. It's clean enough but a bit cramped, especially in the kitchen.

The Homestead Farm B&B (☎ 03-751 0835, Cook Flat Rd) Doubles with bathroom $120. There are three rooms in this 100-year-old farmhouse set on a large working property. It's very home-style with fresh scones baked each morning (as well as breakfast).

Fox Glacier Hotel (☎ 03-751 0839, e foxresort@xtra.co.nz, Cook Flat Rd) Shared rooms $25 per person, singles/doubles with en suite $70/90. The shared budget rooms in this hotel complex have two or three beds in each but are available summer only (October to May). The better annexe has presentable motel-style doubles with TV and en suite.

Motels in Fox village charge around $80 to $100 a double and include: **Lake Matheson Motels** (☎ 0800 452 2437, e lake.matheson.motel@xtra.co.nz, Pekanga Drive); **Mount Cook View Motel** (☎ 0800 828 814, 03-751 0814, Cook Flat Rd); and **Rainforest Motel** (☎ 03-751 0140, e rain forest@xtra.co.nz, Cook Flat Rd).

Fox Glacier Lodge (☎ 03-751 0888) Powered sites $22, double units $160-180. This lodge has five excellent upmarket units (some have double spa baths) and campervan sites (no kitchen).

Places to Eat The **Fox Glacier Store** in the town centre has a reasonable (though pricey) selection of essentials, including takeaway wine and beer, and is open from 8am to 9pm daily.

Cafe Neve (☎ 03-751 0110) Lunch $7.50-13.50, dinner $20-30. Cafe Neve serves the best food in town and has outdoor seating. It's licensed with pizzas and good coffee in a variety of cup sizes – a latte in something resembling a soup bowl costs $5.

Cook Saddle Saloon & Cafe (☎ 03-751 0700) Mains $16-27. This bar and bistro is very popular with locals. You can get all-day breakfast, snacks and burgers from $5 to $15 with main meals of seafood, steak and venison.

The **Fox Glacier Inn** and **Fox Glacier Hotel** both have bars with open fires and bistro meals. The latter has a buffet dinner for $30.

Getting There & Away The InterCity bus services overlap – southbound services from Greymouth go to Fox Glacier, while northbound ones from Queenstown continue on

---

Whitebait

Whitebait are small, translucent, elongated fish – the imago (immature) stage of the river smelt. They swarm up the West Coast rivers in dense schools and are caught in set seine-net traps or large, round scoop nets. Many an argument has been had along a riverbank or near a river mouth about the best rock to position yourself on to catch the biggest haul.

The season has been limited in recent years in an attempt to allow the declining stocks to breed. Usually it is from September to mid-November, but may vary from year to year. Cooked in batter, these small fish are delicious and highly prized by locals.

One of the West Coast's doyennes of culinary expertise provided this perfect recipe for whitebait patties:

Take a pint of whitebait (about half a litre – yes, the fish are measured as a liquid rather than a solid, as they used to be loaded into glass pint milk bottles for sale) and pour it into a bowl. For the batter take one egg, about three tablespoons of flour, a pinch of salt and a little milk to make a smooth paste. Mix this and then pour over the whitebait. Cook in smoking hot fat until golden brown and serve straight away with mint sauce and hot potato chips. Pickled onions are a fine accompaniment.

---

to Franz Josef. Both north and southbound services from Fox village depart at 8.45am daily. Services run to and from Nelson (10½ hours) and Queenstown (8 hours). There's also a service to Christchurch via Arthur's Pass (9 hours) with a change at Hokitika.

Atomic Shuttles also runs between Queenstown and Greymouth daily. Fares include Queenstown ($40), Greymouth ($30) and Franz Josef ($10). There's an additional northbound service to Punakaiki ($40).

SOUTH TO HAAST

Just 26km south of Fox Glacier is the **Copland Valley**, at the end of the Copland Track, coming over from Mt Cook. The full walk should be done east to west (ie, from Mt Cook) but it's a very pleasant six-hour walk up the valley from the highway here to the last hut at Welcome Flat, where there are hot springs. A sign on the road marks the entrance to the valley and the track. The modern hut at Welcome Flat sleeps 40 and should be paid for at the DOC visitors centre in Haast or Fox village. Buses pass by the Copland Valley entrance.

Pinegrove Motel (☎ *03-751 0898,* e *pine_grove@xtra.co.nz, Jacobs River)* Powered sites $16 for 2 people, dorm beds $18, singles $20, double motel units $70. Pinegrove is 8km south of the start of the Copland Track (owners can arrange transport) and it's also close to a decent sandy beach. There's a range of accommodation as well as a kitchen and laundry.

Lake Paringa, about 70km south of Fox Glacier and 50km north of Haast, is a tranquil little trout-filled lake surrounded by forest, right beside the road. There's a free DOC *camping area* with basic facilities (toilets and picnic areas) on the lakefront just off the highway.

The historic **Haast-Paringa Cattle Track** starts from the main road 43km north of Haast (just south of Lake Paringa) and comes out at the coast by the Waita River, a few kilometres north of Haast. Before the Haast Highway was opened in 1965 this trail was the main stock route between Haast and the markets at Whataroa. The first leg of the track to Blowfly Hut and back makes a pleasant day hike but the full walk takes three days with stops at Maori Saddle Hut and Coppermine Creek Hut. Information on the track is available from the visitors centre in Haast.

Off the highway just north of the Paringa River, **Salmon Farm Cafe** (☎ *03-751 0837),* part of South Westland Salmon Farm, specialises in fresh and smoked salmon dishes and home-cooked food ($10 to $22.50).

Lake Moeraki, 31km north of Haast, is another peaceful forest lake with good fishing. It's also close to the coast – a 40-minute walk along a stream brings you to **Monro Beach**, where there's a breeding colony of Fiordland crested penguins (from July to November) and fur seals.

Wilderness Lodge Lake Moeraki (☎ *03-750 0881, fax 750 0882,* e *lakemoeraki@ wildernesslodge.co.nz),* right on the highway and just 20m from the lakeside, is a beautifully situated place where visitors can fully enjoy a wilderness experience, at a price – B&B rooms cost from $160/230 per person low/high season.

About 5km south of Lake Moeraki is the much-photographed **Knight's Point**, which is the coastal region where the Haast road was eventually opened in 1965; there is an information shelter here. And who was Knight? He was a surveyor's dog.

THE HAAST REGION

The Haast region is the centre of a major wildlife refuge, where some of the biggest stands of rainforest survive alongside some of the most extensive wetlands. The kahikatea swamp forests, sand dune forests, seal and penguin colonies, kaka, Red Hills and vast sweeps of beach have ensured the listing of this hauntingly beautiful and remote place as a World Heritage area.

In the forests you will see the flaming red rimu in flower and kahikatea thriving in swampy lagoons. Bird life abounds and the observant twitcher might see fantail, bellbird, NZ pigeon *(kereru),* falcon, kaka, kiwi and morepork.

Haast
pop 295

The tiny community of Haast is on the coast where the wide Haast River meets the sea, 120km south of Fox Glacier. After the magnificent scenery of the glaciers or Haast Pass, this modern little service town is hardly a place to get excited about, but it makes a convenient stop and base for the surrounding World Heritage area.

The DOC **Haast visitors centre** (☎ *03-750 0809, fax 750 0832),* at the junction 3km from the village, has comprehensive displays and information on the area. The brief *Edge of Wilderness* film *(adult/child $3/free)* gives an overall view of the Haast landscape. It's open daily from 9am to 6pm November to March and 9am to 4.30pm the rest of the year.

WEST COAST

Like many places on the West Coast, Haast is a big whitebaiting centre. Between September and November the rivers are lined with whitebaiters making the most of the brief season.

The InterCity and Atomic Shuttle buses stop on Pauareka Rd on their way between Fox and Wanaka.

Jetboating Exhilarating two-hour jetboat trips along the true wilderness of the Waiatoto River are organised by **River Safaris** (☎ 0800 865 382, 🖥 www.riversafaris .co.nz; adult/ child $109/69), based at the Red Barn between Haast township and the visitors centre. They fully detail the Maori history and legends of the region, and include an optional bushwalk. Trips depart at 9am, noon and 3pm daily.

Places to Stay & Eat Accommodation is divided between Haast township, 3km east of the visitors centre, and the road to Jackson Bay.

Wilderness Backpackers (☎ 0800 750 029, 03-750 0029, Pauareka Rd) Dorm beds $18, doubles & twins $40, en suite doubles $55. This comfortable backpackers lives up to its name with a lovely, rustic naturally lit common room.

Haast Highway Lodge (☎ 03-750 0703) Dorm beds $16, doubles & twins $38. This is a spacious YHA-associate with good facilities, including a large kitchen and store open till 10pm. The same owners run the *Aspiring Court Motel* (☎ 0800 500 703) next door, with doubles from $78 to $110.

Haast Beach Holiday Park (☎ 0800 843 226, 03-750 0860) Powered/unpowered sites $10/9.50 per person, dorm beds $15, double cabins $30-55, double motel units $90. This park is 11km south of Haast township on the road to Jackson Bay. It has new recreation facilities and two fully equipped kitchens.

McGuires Lodge (☎ 0800 624 847, 03-750 0020, 🖥 www.mcguireslodge.co.nz) Twin/double units $100/110, family (sleeping five) $150. Between the town and visitors centre, McGuire's is a new place with modern, comfortable self-contained units, cosy lounge, spa pool and good restaurant.

Haast World Heritage Hotel (☎ 0800 502 444, 03-750 0828, 🖂 info@world-her itage-hotel.com) Singles/doubles $79-89, family units $140-150. The hotel with the grandiose name has a wide range of accommodation from ageing motel units to modern suites and even backpacker accommodation at $20 per person. There is a public bar next door, a house bar and restaurant with a good selection of á la carte dishes. It's just before the Haast River bridge on the road to Jackson Bay.

Okuru Beach Homestay (☎ 03-750 0722, 🖂 okurabeach@xtra.co.nz) Doubles & twins $70-75 with breakfast. This is a friendly, family-run place tucked away in a remote hamlet, 14km south of Haast.

The *supermarket* is open daily from 9am to 7pm in summer. *Smithy's Tavern* is the cheapest place in town for lunches and dinners (bar snacks $2 to $6, meals $11 to $18). The best restaurant around is at *McGuires Lodge* (mains $22 to $25).

Haast to Jackson Bay & the Cascade

South from the SH6 at Haast, the road heads to the Arawhata River and Jackson Bay with numerous wilderness walks along the way.

Near Okuru (opposite the Haast Beach Holiday Park) is the 20-minute **Hapuka Estuary Walk** which takes you on a boardwalk loop through this tidal estuary.

On the southside of the Arawhata Bridge, turn off onto the gravel road that follows the Jackson River to Martyr Saddle, with its views of the incredible **Red Hills** and Cascade River valley. The distinctive colour of the Red Hills is due to high concentrations of magnesium and iron in the rock forced up by the meeting of the Australo and Pacific tectonic plates at this point. Continue on from Martyr Saddle to the flats of the Cascade River, a true wilderness region.

The main road continues west from the bridge to the remote fishing hamlet of **Jackson Bay**, a real end-of-the-road town. The views across to the Southern Alps are memorable and there are colonies of Fiordland crested penguins close to the road. Migrants settled here in 1875 under an assisted

WEST COAST

immigration programme that was doomed. Dreams of establishing a farming district were shattered by rain and the lack of a wharf, which was not built until 1938. Today, fishing boats seek lobster, tuna, tarakihi, gurnard and grouper.

Interesting short **walks** here include the three-hour Smoothwater Bay Track, and the 20-minute Wharekai Te Kau Walk, which leads to 'Ocean Beach', a secluded bay with interesting rock formations. Keen, fully-equipped trampers can walk to Stafford Bay Hut, which is a long day walk or an easier two-day walk with an overnight stop at the hut. Check hut bookings (free) and tidal information with the Haast visitors centre.

Round About Haast (☎ 03-750 0890) has bus and boat tours between Haast and Jackson Bay from $60 to $100.

The *Cray Pot* is a classic mobile sit-in cafe parked by the wharf. It offers whitebait pattie sandwiches (in season, $6), along with fish and chips ($8), venison ($22) and snacks. It's open from 9am to 6.30pm daily.

HAAST PASS

Turning inland at Haast, the road snakes along beside the wide Haast River and climbs up the pass, entering Mt Aspiring National Park. Here the scenery changes again – further inland the vegetation becomes more sparse until beyond the 563m summit, when you reach snow country covered only in tussock and scrub. Along the Haast Pass en route to Wanaka (145km; 2½ hours) are several picturesque waterfalls, most just a couple of minutes' walk off the road. They include the **Fantail** and **Thunder Creek** waterfalls, and there's a bridle path track near the pass itself. See the DOC booklet *Haast Pass Highway: Short Walks*.

The present roadway over Haast Pass (Tioripatea or 'clear path' in Maori) was opened in 1965. Prior to that the only southern link to the West Coast was by the Haast-Paringa Cattle Track, walking or on horseback. The original route was used by Maori carrying greenstone from the West Coast to the Makarora River in Otago. In 1863, geologist Julian Haast led a party over the pass.

There are food and fuel stops at Makarora and Lake Hawea. If driving north, check your fuel gauge: the petrol station at Haast is the last before Fox Glacier, 120km north.

WEST COAST

Canterbury

☎ 03 • pop 473,300

Canterbury is the hub of the South Island and contains its largest city, Christchurch. The region extends from Kaikoura in the north to near Oamaru in the south, and from the Pacific Ocean to Arthur's Pass and Mt Cook in the Southern Alps. (We have included Kaikoura in the Marlborough & Nelson chapter due to its proximity to Blenheim and Picton, and the ease of travelling between these coastal towns.)

This is one of the driest and flattest areas of New Zealand. The moisture-laden westerlies from the Tasman Sea hit the Southern Alps and dump their rainfall on the West Coast before reaching Canterbury, which has an annual rainfall of only 0.75m compared with 5m on the West Coast.

The region is dominated by the expansive Canterbury Plains, dead-flat farming land that's backed by the Southern Alps. The Alps contain NZ's highest mountains – Mts Cook (Aoraki), Tasman and Sefton. This striking geographical contrast is the NZ of postcards – rural, sheep-strewn fields backed by rugged, snow-capped mountains.

Christchurch

pop 331,400

Christchurch is often described as the most English of NZ's cities. Punts glide down the picturesque Avon River, a grand Anglican cathedral dominates the city square and trams rattle past streets with oh-so-English names.

To the west, tranquil suburbs contain the exquisite gardens Christchurch is famous for – geraniums, chrysanthemums and carefully edged lawns with not a blade of grass out of place.

Away from the Avon River and the gardens, much of Christchurch is a flat, typical NZ city. Though it still has the Gothic architecture and wooden villas, it has strayed somewhat from the vision of its

Highlights

- Experiencing the picturesque city of Christchurch and its excellent museums and restaurants
- Exploring the Port Hills and Banks Peninsula region, including the charming settlement of Akaroa
- Walking in the fabulous mountainscapes of Arthur's Pass National Park
- Being amazed by the grandeur of Mt Cook (Aoraki) and the glaciers in Mt Cook National Park
- Discovering the Lewis Pass region and the getaway town of Hanmer, with its hot springs
- Seeing scenic Lake Tekapo – an azure blue lake surrounded by mountains

founders: the settlement of Christchurch in 1850 was an ordered Church of England enterprise, and the fertile farming land was deliberately placed in the hands of the gentry. Christchurch was meant to be a model of class-structured England in the South Pacific, not another scruffy colonial outpost. Churches rather than pubs were built, and wool made the elite of Christchurch

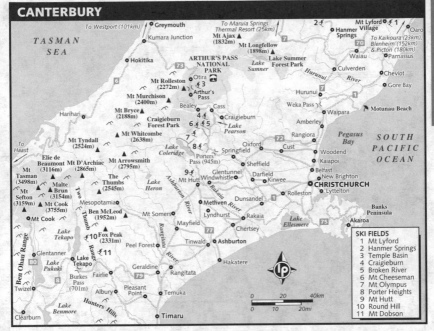

CANTERBURY

SKI FIELDS
1 Mt Lyford
2 Hanmer Springs
3 Temple Basin
4 Craigieburn
5 Broken River
6 Mt Cheeseman
7 Mt Olympus
8 Porter Heights
9 Mt Hutt
10 Round Hill
11 Mt Dobson

wealthy. In 1862 it was incorporated as a very English city, but its character slowly changed as other migrants arrived and new industries followed.

ORIENTATION

Cathedral Square is the centre of town – to find it, just look for the spire. Once there, you can climb to the top of the tower to get your orientation. The western half of the city centre is dominated by the Botanic Gardens.

Christchurch is compact and walking around is easy, although it's slightly complicated by the river which twists and winds through the centre and crosses your path in varied directions. If you're driving, the network of one-way streets adds more confusion.

Colombo St, running north-south through the square, is the main shopping street. Oxford Terrace is the prime street for dining, and New Regent St is well worth a look for its pretty Spanish mission-style architecture.

Maps

Map World (☎ 03-374 5399), on the corner of Manchester and Gloucester Sts, is an excellent shop carrying a wide range of NZ city and regional maps, plus topographic maps for trampers.

INFORMATION
Tourist Offices

The busy Christchurch & Canterbury visitors centre (☎ 03-379 9629, e info@christchurchnz.net, w www.christchurchnz.net) is on Cathedral Square. It's open 8.30am to 5pm Monday to Friday (8.30am to 4pm on Saturday and Sunday). The helpful staff at the centre, give out loads of information and make bookings for just about everything, including transport, activities and accommodation. They can also provide you with a number of helpful publications, including the free pamphlet *Today & Tonight Christchurch & Canterbury*. A Starbucks coffee shop and Internet cafe are also

CANTERBURY

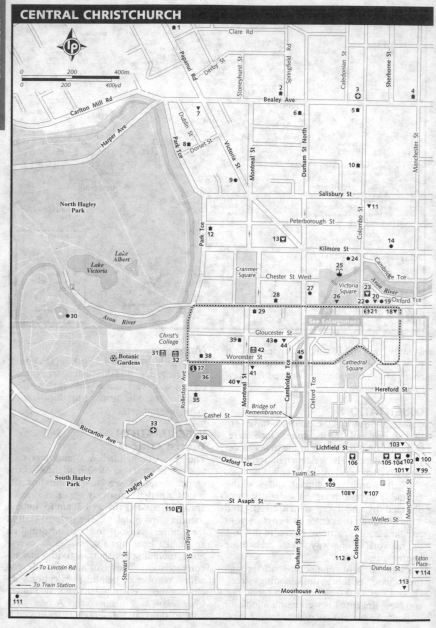

CENTRAL CHRISTCHURCH

See Enlargement

To Lincoln Rd

To Train Station

CANTERBURY

CENTRAL CHRISTCHURCH

PLACES TO STAY
1 Casino Court
2 Hambledon
4 Bella Vista
5 Avenue Motor Lodge
6 Turret House
8 Dorset House
10 Colombo in the City
12 The George Hotel
15 Foley Towers
16 Chester Street Backpackers
28 Croydon House
29 Windsor Hotel
35 YMCA
38 Rolleston House YHA
39 Orari B&B
49 Central City YHA; Wheels n' Deals
53 Warners on the Square
54 Camelot Cathedral Square Hotel
59 Rydges Hotel
62 The Heritage
80 Hotel Grand Chancellor
89 Charlie B's
90 Stonehurst
91 Latimer Hotel
92 Vagabond
93 Frauenreisehaus Women's Hostel
94 Dorothy's Boutique Hotel
96 Occidental Backpackers; Chat's Bar
100 New Excelsior Backpackers

PLACES TO EAT
7 Saggio di Vino
11 Main Street Cafe & Bar
18 Daily Grind
20 Matsu Sushi
26 Ice Cream Van
40 Dux de Lux
41 Le Bon Bolli
44 Santorini
48 City Seafood Market
55 Mum's 24; Netopia Internet Cafe
58 Sala Sala; Vesuvio; Caffe Roma
63 Penang Noodle House
64 Blue Jean Cuisine
65 Coffee d'Fafo
71 Daily Grind
72 Barcelona; Sticky Fingers
74 Viaduct; di lusso
75 Mythai; Ebisu
76 Dimitris
77 New Zealand Natural Ice Cream
78 Topkapi
82 Tap Room; Coyote; All Bar One
99 Two Fat Indians
101 Zydeco
103 Java Coffee House
107 Hare Krishna Food For Life
108 Lotus Heart
113 Pak'n Save Supermarket
114 Lone Star

PUBS, BARS & CLUBS
13 The Jolly Poacher
23 The Vic & Whale
70 Holy Grail
79 Sullivans
83 The Bog
86 Base
87 Grumpy Mole Saloon
88 The Loaded Hog
97 Sammy's Jazz Review
98 Southern Blues Bar
104 Da Box
105 Lichfield St Clubs
106 eye spy

OTHER
3 Accident & Acute Medical Care Centre (24 Hours)
9 DOC
14 Pegasus Rental Cars
17 Centennial Leisure Centre
19 Qantas House
21 American Express
22 Thomas Cook
24 Town Hall
25 Dandelion Fountain
27 Floral Clock
30 Information Centre; Cafe
31 Robert McDougall Art Gallery
32 Canterbury Museum
33 Christchurch Hospital
34 Antigua Boatsheds
36 Arts Centre
37 Information Centre for Arts Centre
42 Site for New Christchurch Art Gallery
43 Centre of Contemporary Art
45 Punting on the Avon
46 Theatre Royal
47 New Regent Street Mall
50 Map World
51 New Zealand Motorcycle Rentals
52 InterCity Bus Terminal
56 Vadal Internet Fone Shop
57 NZ Independent Travel
60 Christchurch & Canterbury Visitors Centre; PC Bang; Starbucks; Southern Encounter Aquarium
61 Christ Church Cathedral; Cafe Cathedral
66 Bank of New Zealand
67 Guided Walks Kiosk
68 ANZ Bank
69 Regent on Worcester
73 Scorpio Books
81 Whitcoulls
84 Ballantynes
85 Bus Exchange
95 Automobile Association (AA)
102 Smith's Bookshop
109 Renny Rentals
110 Canterbury Brewery
111 Turners Auctions
112 Air New Zealand; New World Supermarket
115 Science Alive!; Hoyts Cinema Complex
116 Roman Catholic Cathedral

housed in the complex, as is the Southern Encounter Aquarium (see Things to See & Do later in this chapter).

There are information desks at the airport in both terminals (☎ 03-353 7774) that can advise on and book transport and accommodation options in town.

The Department of Conservation (DOC; ☎ 03-379 9758), at 133 Victoria St, has leaflets and information on most national parks and walkways in the South Island.

The Automobile Association (AA; ☎ 03-379 1280) is at 210 Hereford St and provides maps and touring advice.

Another good source of information is NZ Independent Travel (☎ 03-377 3155, ⓔ nzitravel@yahoo.com) at 7 Chancery Lane, off Cathedral Square. The friendly staff here make bookings and offer advice to independent travellers. Bike rental is also available.

Money

Hereford St has a collection of banks; opening hours are usually 9.30am to 4.30pm Monday to Friday. Thomas Cook (☎ 03-366 2087) is inside the Harvey World Travel branch on the corner of Armagh and Colombo Sts. American Express (☎ 03-365 7366) is at 773 Colombo St.

Post & Communications

You'll find the main post office and pay phones in the southwest corner of Cathedral Square.

Most hostels have Internet facilities. Many cybercafes are clustered around Cathedral Square and include Vadal Internet Fone Shop (☎ 03-377 2381), opposite the visitors centre, and PC Bang, adjacent to the centre. Netopia (☎ 03-365 2612) is at 728 Colombo St, behind Mum's 24 Korean restaurant, and the E-caf at the Arts Centre (☎ 03-372 9436) is above the Boulevard Bakehouse. The going rate is about $5 an hour.

Bookshops

Smith's Bookshop (☎ 03-379 7976), 133 Manchester St, is a classic second-hand bookshop with over 80,000 volumes on three floors. Whitcoulls (☎ 03-379 4580) on

Cashel St is one of the biggest bookshops in Christchurch. Scorpio Books (☎ 03-379 2882), 79 Hereford St, also has a wide range. The Arts Centre Bookshop (☎ 03-365 5277) at the Arts Centre has a good range of NZ titles.

Medical Services

The Accident & Acute Medical Care Centre (☎ 03-365 7777) is on the corner of Bealey Ave and Colombo St. It's open 24 hours and no appointment is necessary. The Christchurch Hospital (☎ 03-364 0640, emergency department 364 0270) is on Riccarton Ave.

THINGS TO SEE & DO
Cathedral Square

Cathedral Square is the heart of Christchurch and the best place to start exploring the city. The square is dominated by **Christ Church Cathedral** *(☎ 03-366 0046; open 8.30am-5pm Mon-Fri, 9am-5pm Sat, Sun & holidays)*, consecrated in 1881. For $4 you can climb 134 steps to the viewing balconies 30m up the cathedral's 63m-high spire.

One of the city's most-visited attractions, the church has embraced tourism and the free market with secular zeal. The cathedral has a visitors centre-cum-souvenir shop that screens videos ($2), charges for cameras (another $2.50) and has a good cafe. What would the pious founding fathers say? But the proceeds all go to helping to maintain this wonderful Gothic building.

About the only aberration in this sea of order is the **Wizard**, a local eccentric and soap-boxer who trots out the same diatribe daily in front of the cathedral.

Guided Walks runs informative, two-hour walks of the city, departing from the kiosk in the southwestern section of the Cathedral Square. The tours of the city are conducted by knowledgeable volunteers and cost $8 per person. Tours depart at 10am and 1pm daily, from October to April; at 1pm only from May to September. The kiosk is not open during winter months so inquire and make tour bookings at the visitors centre instead.

Southern Encounter Aquarium

This pseudo-landscaped warehouse in Cathedral Square (enter through the visitors centre) has touch tanks, divers feeding the eels and other oddities, including a re-creation of a fishing lodge. The aquarium (☎ 03-377 3474; adult/child $10/5; open 9am-4.30pm daily) is well presented but quite small and nothing to get excited about.

The Banks of the Avon

The picturesque **Avon River** is a delight just to walk along. Head to the historic green-and-white **Antigua Boatsheds** (☎ 03-366 5886, 2 Cambridge Terrace) by the foot-bridge at the southern end of Rolleston Ave, where you can rent canoes, paddle boats and rowing boats for river exploration. Or you can relax and be punted along the river: **Punting in the Park** (☎ 03-366 0337) is based at Antigua Boatsheds and offers a 30-minute trip costing $12.50 per person. The punts ply the river 10am to dusk daily (10am to 4pm in winter) and can accommodate up to six people.

You can also take a punting trip with **Punting on the Avon** (☎ 03-379 9629), at the landing stage at Worcester St bridge, from 9am until dusk in summer, 10am to 4pm in winter. A 20-minute punting trip costs $10 per person.

The **Botanic Gardens** (☎ 03-379 1660; open 7am-1 hr before sunset) are 30 hectares of pretty greenery beside the Avon River. There's a cafe and information centre by the Armagh St car park; 20-minute tours on a small electric vehicle ($6) leave from here between 10am and 4.30pm daily September to May, weather permitting.

Mona Vale (Greater Christchurch map; ☎ 03-348 9660, 63 Fendalton Rd) is an Elizabethan-style riverside homestead set in 5.5 hectares of landscaped gardens, ponds and fountains. There's a cafe inside the homestead, open 9.30am to 3.30pm daily – the perfect place for morning or afternoon tea. From November to March there are guided tours of the gardens (inquire at the homestead), and from October to April there is punting on the Avon. Mona Vale is 1.5km west of the city (take bus No 9).

Canterbury Museum

This excellent museum (☎ 03-366 5000, Rolleston Ave; admission by donation; open 9am-5pm daily) is at the entrance to the Botanic Gardens. Particularly interesting are the early colonist exhibits and the Antarctic discovery section (Christchurch is the HQ for 'Operation Deep Freeze', the supply link to Antarctica). The Maori gallery is good, as is the slightly repugnant but informative collection of stuffed birds, right across NZ's species list. The museum has a cafe on the 4th floor with views of the gardens, and a hands-on Discovery Centre for kids (admission $2).

Art Galleries

The **Robert McDougall Art Gallery** (☎ 03-365 0915, ⓦ www.mcdougall.org.nz; free admission; open 10am-4.30pm daily in winter, 10am-5.30pm daily in summer), in the Botanic Gardens (behind the Canterbury Museum), has an extensive collection of NZ and international art. At the time of writing the flash new **Christchurch Art Gallery** was under construction, due for completion in early 2003. It will replace the Robert McDougall Art Gallery and will provide an auditorium, cafe and increased exhibition spaces. The new gallery site is on the corner of Worcester St and Montreal St.

The **Centre of Contemporary Art** (CoCA; ☎ 03-366 7261, ⓦ www.coca.org.nz, 66 Gloucester St; free admission; open 11am-5pm Tues-Fri, noon-4pm Sat-Sun) exhibits and sells contemporary art by NZ artists. It recently opened 'Art Zone', a gallery dedicated to showing art produced by kids.

Arts Centre

The former University of Canterbury town site has been transformed into the excellent **Arts Centre** (☎ 03-366 0989, ⓦ www.arts centre.org.nz), on Worcester St opposite the Botanic Gardens. The beautiful old Gothic buildings are now an arts, craft and entertainment complex with a good selection of cafes and restaurants thrown in. Gothic Revival Tours ($5) are conducted by the Christchurch town crier at 11am Monday to Friday – get your tickets at the Arts Centre's information centre (near the corner of Worcester St and Rolleston Ave).

The **Galleria** has dozens of craft shops and art galleries with everything from pottery, jewellery, woollen goods and Maori carvings to handmade toys – not cheap but one of the best craft centres in NZ, and in some cases you can see the craftspeople at work. A bustling craft market is also held on Saturday and Sunday, and there are often buskers performing.

International Antarctic Centre

Near the airport, this centre *(Greater Christchurch map; ☎ 03-358 9896, W www .iceberg.co.nz, Orchard Rd; adult/child $18/9; open 9am-8pm daily Oct-Mar, 9am-5.30pm Apr-Sep)* is part of a huge complex built for the administration and warehousing of the NZ, US and Italian Antarctic programmes. You can reach it on an airport bus.

The centre has hands-on exhibits, video presentations and the 'sights and sounds' of the vast continent. The Snow and Ice Experience allows you to freeze while you slide down a snow slope and explore a snow cave. You can also ride in a Hägglund Antarctic snowmobile through an outdoor adventure course ($10 per person). It's all fun and educational family stuff, but it is pricey; the Canterbury Museum also has historical exhibits on Antarctic exploration and is a lot cheaper.

Other Museums

Air Force World *(☎ 03-343 9532, Main South Rd; adult/child $10/5; open 10am-5pm daily)* is exceptionally well presented. On display are aircraft used by the NZ Air Force over the years, with figures and background scenery as well as archival footage. Antarctic aircraft sit in the snow, a Canberra bomber of the 1950s taxis out at night, a WWII fighter is hidden in the jungle. The museum is at the former Wigram air base, a 15-minute drive south of the city (bus No 51 or 81).

Six kilometres Southeast of the city centre is **Ferrymead Historic Park** *(Greater Christchurch map; ☎ 03-384 1970, 269 Bridle Path Rd; adult/child $6/3 Mon-Fri, $8/4 Sat & Sun; open 10am-4.30pm daily)*. This historical village is a working museum of transport and technology, with electric and steam locomotives, old household appliances, cars and machinery. Trams operate on Saturdays, Sundays and holidays.

In the old train station, **Science Alive!** *(☎ 03-365 5199, W www.sciencealive.co.nz, 392 Moorhouse Ave; admission $6; open 9am-5pm Mon-Fri, 10am-6pm Sat-Sun)* has lots of interactive and kid-friendly science exhibits.

National Marae

The largest marae *(☎ 03-388 7685, 250 Pages Rd)* in NZ is 6km east of the city centre. Nga Hau e Wha (The Four Winds) is a multicultural facility open to all people. You can see the carvings, weavings and paintings in the whare nui (meeting house) and the whare wananga (house of learning). Evening tours and concert cost $30, or $65 with a hangi, and begin at 6.45pm (bookings essential).

Canterbury Brewery

This *brewery (☎ 03-379 4940, 36 St Asaph St)* is Canterbury's largest and is the brewer of Lion beers. There are two-hour tours at 10.30am Monday to Thursday ($10); bookings are essential as minimum numbers are required. You'll first visit the Brewing Museum showing the history of brewing in NZ, and after the tour there is the requisite sampling of the produce.

Tramway

Trams were first introduced to Christchurch streets in 1905 but only lasted as a means of transport for 50 years. Restored trams have been reintroduced and operate a 2.5km inner-city loop around many of the city's best features and shopping areas.

The **trams** *(☎ 03-366 7830)* operate 9am to 9pm daily November to March, to 6pm April to October. Tickets cost $10 per person, but last for the duration of your stay (for residents they're good for one year). One tram was recently fitted out as a *restaurant (☎ 03-366 7511)*, which means you can dine while sightseeing.

Gondola

The gondola *(Greater Christchurch map; ☎ 03-384 0700, Bridle Path Rd; adult/child $15/7)* whisks visitors up from the Heathcote Valley terminal on a five-minute ride to a point above the Lyttelton Rd tunnel. There are great views at the top (Mt Cavendish, around 500m) right across to the Southern Alps on a fine day. It operates 10am until late daily; take the No 28 Lyttelton bus.

At the top, there's a cafe, shop and heritage show. Paths lead to the Crater Rim Walkway (see Walking). You can also mountain bike down with the **Mountain Bike Adventure Company** *(☎ 0800 424 534)*; $40 gets you a one-way gondola ride plus the pedal down; pre-booking is essential.

Wildlife Reserves

Orana Wildlife Park *(☎ 03-359 7109, W www.oranawildlifepark.co.nz, McLeans Island Rd; adult/child $12/6; open 10am-5pm daily)* has an excellent walk-through aviary of native birds and a nocturnal kiwi house, as well as prehistoric tuatara. Most of the extensive grounds, however, are devoted to the 'African Plains' with lions, rhinos, giraffes, zebras, oryx and cheetahs. Animal feeding times are scheduled daily. Entry includes a 'safari' shuttle-bus tour. The park is in Harewood, beyond the airport, and about 25 minutes from the city.

The very well-maintained **Willowbank Wildlife Reserve** *(☎ 03-359 6226, W www.willowbank.co.nz, Hussey Rd; admission adult/child $15/7; open 10am-10pm daily)* has exotic and local animals, including a variety of domestic animals, and there's a large nocturnal kiwi house. It's 20 minutes north of the city centre; take Main North Rd.

Walking

The visitors centre has details and leaflets about walks around Christchurch. Starting in the city are the **Riverside Walk** and various historical walks.

For great views of the city, there's a walkway from the **Sign of the Takahe** on Dyers Pass Rd. The various 'Sign of the...' places in this area were originally roadhouses built during the Depression as rest

stops. Now they vary from the impressive tearooms at the Sign of the Takahe to a simple shelter at the Sign of the Bellbird and are referred to primarily as landmarks. This walk leads up to the **Sign of the Kiwi** through Victoria Park and then along the Summit Rd to Scotts Reserve, with several lookout points along the way.

You can walk to Lyttelton on the **Bridle Path**. It starts from Heathcote Valley (take bus No 28) and takes one to 1½ hours at an easy pace. The **Godley Head Walkway** is a two-hour round trip from Taylors Mistake, crossing and recrossing Summit Rd with beautiful views on a clear day.

The **Crater Rim Walkway** around Lyttelton Harbour goes some 14km from the Bridle Path to the Ahuriri Scenic Reserve, passing through a number of scenic reserves along the way, plus the Sign of the Bellbird and the Sign of the Kiwi. The walkway can easily be done in several short stages.

Other Activities

There are diverse activities within Christchurch or just on its fringe. Ballooning ($200), fishing (half a day for around $300), horse trekking (from $45 per hour), jetboating ($45), tandem skydiving ($245), biplane flights (from $195) and golf tours (from $80) are all possible; ask at the visitors centre.

There's very good **rafting** on the Rangitata River in Peel Forest, and Rangitata Rafts has a courtesy bus to/from Christchurch. See Peel Forest later in the chapter.

There are several ski areas within a two-hour drive of Christchurch. For more information see Skiing & Snowboarding in the Activities chapter, plus the Hanmer Springs, Craigieburn Forest Park and Methven sections in this chapter.

Queen Elizabeth II Park *(Greater Christchurch map; ☎ 03-383 4313, Travis Rd)*, 8km northeast of the centre in New Brighton, is a huge sports complex, with indoor pools, waterslides, gym and sports facilities, and was the venue for the 1974 Commonwealth Games. Take bus No 43. Closer to town, the **Centennial Leisure Centre** *(☎ 03-372 2853, Armagh St)* has a heated indoor pool ($4/1.50 adult/child).

The closest **beaches** to the city are Waimairi, North, New Brighton and South Brighton, east and northeast of the city and all accessible by bus (take No 5 or 60). Sumner to the southeast is popular – take bus No 30 or 31. Taylors Mistake, beyond Sumner, is a popular spot for surfing but doesn't have bus services.

ORGANISED TOURS

There are a number of companies offering tours of Christchurch, and also day trips to nearby towns (Lyttelton, Akaroa) and places further afield (Arthur's Pass, Hanmer Springs, the wineries of the Waipara). The visitors centre is a good place to get details. See also the earlier listing for Cathedral Square for more information on guided city walking tours.

Christchurch Sightseeing Tours *(☎ 03-366 9660)* offers comprehensive 3½-hour city tours ($30) daily, plus tours to the city's leading gardens in spring and summer ($25, two tours weekly) and tours of heritage homes ($25, five tours weekly).

Canterbury Leisure Tours *(☎ 0800 484 485,* W *www.leisuretours.co.nz)* has loads of options. You can tour the city for three hours ($38), participate in activities like jet-boating (from $55), horse trekking (from $55) and golf ($110) in the surrounding area, or take a day trip to Akaroa (from $60). There's even day trips to Mt Cook ($235) and Kaikoura (with whale watching for $180) – such tours are OK if you're short on time, but if possible these areas warrant more than just a couple of hours.

Walkaway Tours *(☎ 03-365 6672,* W *www.walkaway.co.nz)* has interesting day trips to Akaroa, the Banks Peninsula, Arthur's Pass and Hanmer Springs (tours priced from $125). The trips incorporate a few hours of walking.

Canterbury Wine Trails *(☎ 03-381 5320)* offers a full day out to the Waipara wineries, about an hour's drive north of Christchurch. The tour costs $95, and this includes lunch.

Canterbury Vin de Pays *(☎ 03-357 8262,* W *www.canterburyvindepays.co.nz)* has a five-hour tour of Waipara for $70, or

a six-hour scenic tour to Akaroa taking in a winery and cheese factory en route ($90).

PLACES TO STAY
Camping & Cabins

All prices given in this section are for two people.

Meadow Park Holiday Park *(☎ 0800 396 323, 03-352 9176,* e *meadowpark@ xtra.co.nz, 39 Meadow St)* Unpowered & powered sites $22, basic cabins $36, cottages & tourist flats $52-70, motels $85. Well-maintained Meadow Park is off Main North Rd, 5km north of the city centre. The excellent facilities here include a heated swimming pool, spa, sauna, gym and children's playground. There's also a wide variety of good accommodation options. Take bus No 4.

Russley Park Motor Camp *(☎ 03-342 7021, 372 Yaldhurst Rd)* Unpowered/powered sites $18/20, chalets from $35, tourist flats $56. Small, neat Russley Park, opposite Riccarton Racecourse, is about 10km northwest of the Cathedral Square or 2km from the airport (not far from the pick-up offices of the major campervan-rental agencies). Take bus No 84.

South Brighton Motor Camp *(Greater Christchurch map;* ☎ *03-388 9844, 59 Halsey St)* Unpowered/powered sites $18/20, cabins $30-46. This motor camp is off Estuary Rd, 10km northeast of Cathedral Square, and is an attractive park in a sheltered waterside setting, very close to the beach. Take bus No 5.

Amber Park *(Greater Christchurch map;* ☎ *03-348 3327, 308 Blenheim Rd)* Unpowered/powered sites $20/22, cabins with bathroom $46-56. This pleasant park is only 4km west of the square in well-kept grounds. Take bus No 5.

North South Holiday Park *(☎ 0800 567 765, 03-359 5993,* e *northsouth@par adise.net.nz, 530 Sawyers Arms Rd)* Unpowered/powered sites $17/19, cabins $35-56. This large park is located on the North-South Bypass, 2.5km from the airport. There are good facilities here, including a pool, sauna and playground, and airport transfers can be arranged as well.

Hostels

Christchurch has many popular backpackers places, most concentrated within the Bealey, Moorhouse, Fitzgerald and Rolleston Aves grid.

Latimer Square Area Several stalwarts are found in the region of Latimer Square, and there are some excellent small, homely backpackers in the area too.

Stonehurst (☎ 03-379 4620, W www .stonehurst.co.nz, 241 Gloucester St) Dorm beds $19, singles/doubles or twins with shared facilities $40/50, en suite doubles & twins $55-65. Catering to all budgets, classy, well-run Stonehurst is a large hotel and backpackers complex close to the city centre. Guests can use the bar, lounge or pool in the main building. All attention is on the guests here, and there's even a TV and seating in the laundry. There are also fully self-contained tourist flats for longer stays ($500 per week, minimum stay one week), and stylish motel units (see Motels later).

Foley Towers (☎ 03-366 9720, e foley .towers@backpack.co.nz, 208 Kilmore St) Dorm beds $16-18, twins & doubles without/with bath $42/48. One of the original backpackers, friendly Foley Towers is spacious, laid-back and run by the compiler of the BBH *Blue Book*. Its well-maintained accommodation is in a number of small buildings set around inviting courtyards.

Vagabond (☎ 03-379 9677, 232 Worcester St) Dorm beds $17-19, singles $30, twins & doubles $44. With a sunny outdoor area and a relaxed, homely feel, this small and well-run place, 10 minutes' walk from Cathedral Square, is a good choice.

The Old Countryhouse (☎ 03-381 5504, 437 Gloucester St) Dorm beds from $17, twins & doubles from $44. This excellent small hostel is a little further east of the others but it is well worth travelling the extra distance (and it's still only a 15-minute walk to the square). Accommodation is inside an attractively restored old home – the decor is great, with lots of colour on the walls and timber furniture made by the owner, and there is a warm and relaxed atmosphere.

Chester Street Backpackers (☎ 03-377 1897, e chesterst@free.net.nz, 148 Chester St East) Dorm beds $19, twins & doubles $46. Tucked away on a suburban street is the welcoming Chester Street, Christchurch's smallest backpackers. Check out the funky, novel car-b-que and E-van and play with the resident pets.

Frauenreisehaus Women's Hostel (☎ 03-366 2585, 272 Barbadoes St) Dorm beds $17, singles $27, twins $42. Frauenreisehaus is a wonderfully well-equipped, women-only backpackers east of Latimer Square. It's a welcoming place with full kitchen and laundry, herb garden, TV and video, library, comfortable lounge with fire and free bikes for use.

Charlie B's (☎ 03-379 8429, W www .charliebs.co.nz, 268 Madras St) Dorm beds $14-18, singles $35, twins & doubles $42. Located on the corner of Gloucester St, this large, bustling backpackers has pretty tired rooms but all the facilities you'd need, including a games room, videos, barbecue and off-street parking. The infamous big dorm (beds $14) is open summer only and sleeps up to 38 people; it has partitions but offers little privacy.

Occidental Backpackers (☎ 03-379 9284, W www.occidental.co.nz, 208 Hereford St) Dorm beds $17, singles $35, twins/doubles $42/47. The friendly Occidental is in a large heritage hotel opposite Latimer Square and is home to the very popular Chats backpackers bar (with dirt-cheap meals). There's free breakfast on offer and all the expected facilities.

City Centre Most Christchurch backpackers are less than a 10-minute walk from Cathedral Square, but some are more central to the action.

Central City YHA (☎ 03-379 9535, e yhachch@yha.org.nz, 273 Manchester St) Dorm beds $22, singles $40, twins & doubles with shared facilities/en suite $50/64. This clean, modern hostel is northeast of Cathedral Square. It's a large and well-equipped place with a spacious common room, excellent kitchen facilities and helpful staff.

Warners on the Square (☎ 03-377 0550, ✉ bailies@xtra.co.nz, 50 Cathedral Square) Dorm beds $18, twins & doubles (some with en suite) $45-50. Warners is in a prime location on the main square (the backpackers' entrance is next to the Press building). At the time of research its accommodation was undergoing a complete overhaul – the result should be high-quality backpacker and budget accommodation, with the added bonus of *Bailie's Bar* and beer garden beneath. **New Excelsior Backpackers** (☎ 0800 666 237, 03-366 7570, ✉ newexcel@ihug.co.nz, cnr Manchester & High Sts) Dorm beds $17-21, singles $38, doubles without/with en suite $50/55. This family-run, revamped pub is a good, central backpackers, with facilities including modern kitchen, dining room, lounge and great outdoor deck.

Parkside There are a couple of good choices by the gardens.

Dorset House (☎ 03-366 8268, ⓦ www .dorsethouse.co.nz, 1 Dorset St) Dorm beds $22, doubles & twins $53. Well positioned by the gardens, this highly rated backpackers is in a restored 1870s home. It's a warm and well-run place with good facilities, including pretty outdoor area, a couple of kitchens and a large, inviting guest lounge with a fire and pool table.

Rolleston House YHA (☎ 03-366 6564, ✉ yhachrl@yha.org.nz, 5 Rolleston St) Dorm beds $19, doubles & twins $46. West of Cathedral Square, pleasant Rolleston House is in an excellent position on the tramline, opposite the Arts Centre and across from the Botanic Gardens.

YMCA (☎ 03-365 0502, ✉ accom@ym cachch.org.nz, 12 Hereford St) Dorm beds $18, singles $40-65, doubles & twins $55-90. Lacking the atmosphere of most backpackers but with a great location and good facilities, the large, modern Y isn't a bad choice for clean and comfortable budget accommodation. The cheaper prices given here are for basic rooms with shared facilities, the upper end of the range includes bathroom, TV, phone and tea- and coffee-making facilities. Apartments are also available from $120.

B&Bs & Guesthouses

There are two central guesthouses on Armagh St, both in old buildings with lots of character. **Croydon House** (☎ 03-366 5111, ⓦ www.croydon.co.nz, 63 Armagh St), run by a German-speaking couple, offers comfortable B&B rooms. Singles are from $85 to $99, twins and doubles are from $115 to $135. (prices are $10 to $20 cheaper from May to October). The nearby **Windsor Hotel** (☎ 0800 366 1503, 03-366 1503, ⓦ www .windsorhotel.co.nz, 52 Armagh St) has B&B singles/doubles and twins for $66/98; facilities here are shared.

Turret House (☎ 03-365 3900, ⓦ www .turrethouse.co.nz, 435 Durham St North) B&B en suite singles/doubles from $65/95. Turret House, originally built in 1905, has been elegantly restored and offers comfortable accommodation in a good position.

Orari B&B (☎ 03-365 6569, ⓦ www .orari.net.nz, 42 Gloucester St) Singles/doubles from $130/150. Orari is in a lovely old home that has been stylishly refurbished to offer spacious, light-filled rooms and inviting guest areas.

Dorothy's Boutique Hotel (☎ 03-365 6034, ⓦ www.dorothys.co.nz, 2 Latimer Square) B&B rooms $130-160. This historic mansion is rich in character and features a lovely courtyard area and bar with *Wizard of Oz* mementos. The rooms are attractive and inviting and there's an award-winning restaurant here too.

Hambledon (☎ 03-379 0723, ⓦ www .hambledon.co.nz, 103 Bealey Ave) B&B rooms $195-270. This impressive heritage mansion has been immaculately restored and features antiques, art and oriental rugs. The breakfasts are noteworthy and the rooms are spacious and sumptuous – some feature four-poster beds.

Motels

Christchurch has over 120 motels, most of them charging from around $75 for a studio. The visitors centre will help find one that suits your needs.

As well as its budget accommodation, **Stonehurst** (see Hostels earlier in this chapter) has excellent motel rooms. Studio units sleep up to three people and cost $75, a one-bedroom unit costs $125. The two-bedroom units sleep up to six and cost $135 for two people, with each additional person costing $15.

Colombo in the City (☎ *0800 265 662, 03-366 8775,* e *info@motelcolombo.co.nz, 863 Colombo St)* is a new, central motel complex offering luxurious units priced from $95 to $115.

Bealey Ave, north of the centre, is a good hunting ground for motels, including the new *Bella Vista* (☎ *0800 235 528, 03-377 3445,* e *bella_vista_motel@xtra.co .nz, 193 Bealey Ave)*, with studios from $75 and one-bedroom units for $110. *Avenue Motor Lodge* (☎ *03-366 0582,* e *avenue motorlodge@xtra.co.nz, 136 Bealey Ave)* is another good choice, with comfortable units from $75. On Papanui Rd, north off Bealey Ave, there are also several motels, including *Casino Court* (☎ *0800 109 388, 03-355 6863,* e *casino@ihug.co.nz, 76 Papanui Rd)*, which has studio, one- and two-bedroom units priced from $85 to $140.

Riccarton Rd, west of town beyond Hagley Park, is another spot for motels of varying price and quality. *Clyde on Riccarton* (☎ *0800 280 282, 03-341 1280,* e *clyde motel@xtra.co.nz, 280 Riccarton Rd)* is comfortable, well-equipped units from $75.

Close to the airport, *Airport Lodge Motel* (☎ *0800 256 343, 03-358 5119,* e *airport lodge@clear.net.nz, 105 Roydvale Ave)* has units from $79 and is well placed if you need to catch an early flight. There are a number of motels in this area catering to airport traffic.

Hotels

Camelot Cathedral Square Hotel (☎ *0800 258 858, 03-365 2898,* e *camelot.cathe dral@xtra.co.nz, 66 Cathedral Square)* Rooms $95-150. This is a surprisingly affordable hotel in a central location on the main square. Staff are friendly and service is good, plus the rooms are well equipped, modern and quite spacious – ask for one with a view of the square.

Latimer Hotel (☎ *0800 176 176, 03-379 1180,* e *enquiries@latimerhotel.co.nz, 30 Latimer Square)* Rooms $145-155. This large hotel and conference centre offers well-priced accommodation only a few minutes' walk from town. Facilities include gym, sauna, restaurant and off-street parking.

The Heritage (☎ *0800 936 936, 03-377 9722,* e *res.heritagechc@dynasty.co.nz, 28-30 Cathedral Square)* Rooms from $260, suites from $330. On the main square, the Heritage offers two styles of quality accommodation. The hotel itself has upmarket rooms of varying sizes, and the adjacent Old Government Building has been restored and turned into stylish self-contained suites.

The George Hotel (☎ *03-379 4560,* w *www.thegeorge.co.nz, 50 Park Terrace)* Rooms from $330. Parkside George is a small, stylish boutique hotel in the luxury class. Service and facilities match the price, and there is an award-winning first-class restaurant here, *Pescatore*.

Other top-bracket Christchurch hotels include the *Chateau on the Park* (*Greater Christchurch map;* ☎ *0800 808 999, 03-348 8999,* e *res@chateau-park.co.nz, 189 Deans Ave)*, well sited at the edge of Hagley Park, *Rydges Hotel* (☎ *03-379 4700,* e *reservations_christchurch@rydges.com, cnr Worcester St & Oxford Terrace)*, in the heart of the Oxford St action, and the *Hotel Grand Chancellor* (☎ *03-379 2999,* e *res@grandc.co.nz, 161 Cashel St)*. Facilities at all are first rate; room prices start at around $200.

PLACES TO EAT
Restaurants

Oxford Terrace The largest concentration of bars, cafes and restaurants is found at 'the Strip', the eastern side of Oxford Terrace between Hereford and Cashel Sts. All of the places here have good vantage points, outdoor dining in fine weather and international dishes. The intense competition means that standards are normally quite high and prices do not differ dramatically: mains at each are in the $15 to $28 range, and all menus feature standards like gourmet pizza, pasta and vegetarian meals, and heartier dishes such as local lamb and fish. Almost all turn into popular bars as the night wears on.

Viaduct (☎ 03-377 9968) at No 136 is the perfect example of what the Strip offers – it has a good wine and beer selection, plus pizza from the wood-fired oven (with toppings like Moroccan lamb with fetta and tomato) and dishes such as Canterbury lamb stack, with roasted vegies and garlic mashed potatoes topped with goats cheese.

The *Tap Room* (☎ 03-365 0547) at No 124 is the new kid on the strip. It's a craft brewery with Monteiths' full range of beer on tap, plus seriously stylish decor and a full menu for lunch and dinner.

Sala Sala (☎ 03-366 6755) at No 184, near the Gloucester St corner, is a classy Japanese restaurant, and *Vesuvio* (☎ 03-365 4183), next door at No 182, offers an intriguing mixture – there's live jazz during the week and typical cafe fare is on offer, plus there's an adjoining room where Japanese teppenyaki is served until late every evening.

Barcelona (☎ 03-377 2100), on the corner of Oxford Terrace and Worcester St, is a bistro-bar with a cosy European feel and good Pacific Rim cuisine – eg, market-fresh fish with warm potato and roast fennel salad, tapenade and chilli and lime vinaigrette.

Popular *Sticky Fingers* (☎ 03-366 6451), in the Clarendon Towers, is a happy blend of NZ and Italian influences, with designer pizza and tasty pasta dishes on offer. Santa Fe-styled *Coyote* (☎ 03-366 6055) at No 126 has good southwestern and Tex-Mex selections, and things really get going here later on.

Asian There are number of cheap and cheerful Asian eateries around town, including the following good choices.

Mythai (☎ 03-365 1295, 84 Hereford St) Mains average $15. An old favourite, Mythai serves authentic Thai cuisine, with a good selection of seafood, noodle and rice dishes to choose from.

Ebisu (☎ 03-374 9375, 96 Hereford St) Dishes to $10. This interesting little place has the feel of a casual Japanese pub, with long bars and tables and murals on the walls. It serves up sashimi and other traditional fare, plus a range of grilled dishes ideal for sharing among a group.

Two Fat Indians (☎ 03-371 7273, 112 Manchester St) Mains average $16. Practising 'the art of curry and a pint', this modern place offers all the standards such as chicken and lamb vindaloo, rogan josh and chicken korma, plus tandoori dishes and a range of tastes to please vegetarians.

Mum's 24 (☎ 03-365 2211, cnr Colombo & Gloucester Sts) Mains $8-16. A bustling place offering cheap, simple Korean and Japanese food, Mum's serves up the good vegetarian options, sushi, noodle dishes and tasty Korean barbecued lamb or chicken.

Topkapi (☎ 03-379 4447, 185 Manchester St) Mains $9-17. Enjoy the rich decor, low tables and cushions at this atmospheric Turkish eatery, where you can sample a wonderful array of dips and starters plus a range of kebabs, including good choices for vegetarians. Finish off with some baklava or halva.

European If you're staying in one of Bealey Avenue's many motels, there's no need to travel far for good food.

Saggio di Vino (☎ 03-379 4006, 185 Victoria St, cnr Bealey Ave) Mains $25-30. This restaurant has won numerous awards for its outstanding wine selection, and the Italian-inspired food on offer is also excellent and prepared with care, but doesn't come cheap.

Santorini (☎ 03-379 6975, cnr Gloucester St & Cambridge Terrace) Mains $22. This lively eatery offers classic Greek cuisine like calamari, dolmades, spanakopita, moussaka, souvlaki and fresh fish, all downed to the strains of live bouzouki music (and you can work it off with some dancing afterwards).

Le Bon Bolli (☎ 03-374 9444, cnr Worcester & Montreal Sts) Lunch to $18, dinner mains to $30. This charming French-style brasserie is a lovely place to enjoy a coffee or light meal. Downstairs there's a small wood-panelled bar, and upstairs is a fine-dining restaurant.

Pacific Rim Apart from the fine restaurants along the Strip serving a blend of cuisines, there are many good choices scattered around town.

Blue Jean Cuisine (☎ *03-365 4130, 205 Manchester St*) Meals $15-24. Despite the slightly cheesy name, Blue Jean is a popular bar-restaurant in a sand-blasted warehouse. There are casual light meals such as burgers and pizzas for around $16, and the more substantial dishes costs $24.

Untouched World (☎ *03-357 9499, 155 Roydvale Ave,* W *www.untouchedworld .com*) Mains lunch/dinner $12-16/20-25. If you find yourself out by the airport, make a beeline for this classy 'concept store', where you can dine on fresh, well-prepared fare (organic where possible) in the sunny courtyard, and also admire or purchase some wonderful NZ-made clothing.

Tex-Mex & Cajun The original chapter of what is now a popular chain throughout NZ, the popular *Lone Star* (☎ *03-365 7086, 26 Manchester St*) serves up whopping great portions of Tex-Mex and Cajun fare. The menu makes for an entertaining read, with cleverly named items such as the Chook Berry Salad, Salmon Davis Junior and Shanks for the Memory. Mains are from $18 to $25.

Zydeco (☎ *03-365 4556, 113 Manchester St*) Mains $20-25. An unexpected find in this part of the world is this small, casual place serving up Cajun and Creole cuisine, backed by fun music and decor (check out the alligator on the wall).

Vegetarian Every town should have a place like *Dux de Lux* (☎ *03-366 6919, cnr Hereford & Montreal Sts)*. Behind the Arts Centre, it's open daily from 11am until late and specialises in seafood and vegetarian treats, including good pizzas you can wash down with one of their house brews. There's an outdoor courtyard (the perfect spot to spend a sunny afternoon), bars and a cocktail lounge upstairs, plus live music several nights a week. Mains are $15 to $22.

Main Street Cafe & Bar (☎ *03-365 0421, 840 Colombo St*) Lunch mains $5-10, dinner mains to $18. This cafe serves huge helpings of exceptionally good vegan and vegetarian food. It's a relaxed and popular place with an open-air courtyard at the

back. There are imaginative main courses, the salads are good and wholesome and the desserts mouthwatering.

Cafes

The Arts Centre has some popular cafes with outdoor areas that fill up when the sun is shining, including *Le Cafe* and the *Boulevard Bakehouse*. Many of the chic cafes are on Oxford Terrace (see Restaurants). *Caffe Roma* (☎ *03-379 3879, 176 Oxford Terrace)* is a class act, with wood-panelling, open fireplaces and great breakfast and lunch menus. Breakfast is served from 7am to 3.30pm and you can choose between muesli, eggs benedict, pancakes, bagels or brioche.

Serious coffee-drinkers will be impressed by *Cafe d'Fafo* (☎ *03-366 6083, 137 Hereford St)* and its commitment to a good brew. The coffee goes well with their extensive breakfast menu.

Java Coffee House (☎ *03-366 0195, cnr High & Lichfield Sts)* is a slightly grungy place that has good all-day breakfasts for $10, filled bagels for $4 and a very chilled-out atmosphere.

If you fancy getting out of town, down by the beach in Sumner are a couple of popular cafes. *On The Beach* (☎ *03-236 7090, 25 The Esplanade)* is, literally, on the beach, and across the road is *Rock Cafe Bar* (☎ *03-326 5358, 22 The Esplanade)*. Both are good spots for a casual meal.

Cheap Eats & Takeaways

A good variety of *food stalls* is set up daily in Cathedral Square. On Saturday and Sunday head to the Arts Centre for a general browse and a feed from one of the many food vans selling an array of cuisines from Lebanese to Thai. For delicious some homemade ice cream check out the *mobile van* that's usually parked on Armagh St near Victoria Square.

In two central locations (on the corner of New Regent and Armagh Sts, and corner of Worcester St and Oxford Terrace), *The Daily Grind* is a cool cafe churning out great coffee, fresh juices and excellent filled bagels, paninis and sandwiches to the hungry masses. Sandwiches are under $6.

There are several big fast-food outlets near the square, plus good choices like *Dimitris (709 Colombo St)* for cheap and tasty souvlaki and *New Zealand Natural (cnr Colombo & High Sts)* for great ice cream and frozen yogurt.

Hare Krishna Food for Life (602 Colombo St) is a no-frills place serving up cheap vegetarian lunches ($5 all-you-can-eat), and opposite is *Lotus Heart (595 Colombo St)*, with more vegetarian and vegan fare, including bowls of rice and curry, dahl or vegetables for $5.

City Seafood Market (277 Manchester St), next door to the YHA, sells incredibly cheap fish and chips ($3) and a variety of fresh seafood.

For fans of Japanese food, *Matsu Sushi (105 Armagh St)* has a sushi lunch box for $5, plus noodle soups and other dishes under $10. *Penang Noodle House (172 Manchester St)* is not much to look at but offers good, filling Malaysian meals.

The Loaded Hog (see Bars) knocks out excellent-value $5 cooked breakfasts on Saturday and Sunday. *Chats Bar* at the Occidental has a $6 roast and $4 barbecue, and *Bailie's Bar* at Warners on the Square also offers cheap meals that are aimed at the backpacker market.

Self-caterers should head to the large *Pak'n Save supermarket* at 297 Moorhouse Ave or to the *New World supermarket* on Colombo St, behind Air New Zealand.

ENTERTAINMENT
Pubs
The **Christchurch Pub Crawl** (☎ 021-324 537) is a tour with a difference. It operates from December to April a few times a week, leaving from Cathedral Square at around 6pm and visiting five pubs, all diverse in character. It's designed to be a fun, social time, not a hugely boozy affair. For your $30 you get transport, five free beers and a T-shirt. Bookings are essential.

Holy Grail (☎ 03-366 0140, 94 Worcester St) This is a huge – and hugely popular – sports bar that's more like an entertainment complex, with big screens and betting agents, four bars, a restaurant, pizza kitchen,

amusement arcade and pool tables. It packs in the crowds on Saturday and Sunday.

Backpackers like *Chats Bar* in the Occidental – it's a good meeting place and the beer and food are cheap. The outdoor section of the *bar* at the Stonehurst is also a popular backpacker haunt. *Bailie's (Cathedral Square)*, part of the Warners complex, is another old favourite. There's a good beer garden out the back, and cheap meals. See Places to Stay for more on these places.

No city worth its salt would be without an Irish bar nowadays. *The Bog* (☎ 03-379 7141 82 Cashel St) is among the best in town, and *Sullivans* (☎ 03-379 7790, 150 Manchester St) is also popular, particularly among the locals, and often features live music performances.

The intersection of Manchester and Cashel Sts is a good spot for drinking, with *The Loaded Hog* (☎ 03-366 6674) and the *Grumpy Mole Saloon* (☎ 03-371 9301) pulling in the crowds. The Loaded Hog is a big, airy venue with naturally brewed beers and piglet, piggyback and whole-hog-sized meals. The slightly tacky but fun Grumpy Mole is done up like a wild-west saloon, inside and out.

A night at the *Jolly Poacher* (☎ 03-379 5635, cnr Kilmore & Victoria Sts) can go on and on – it's open 24 hours and is popular with locals in the hospitality industry for an after-work drink. *The Vic and Whale* (☎ 03-366 6355, 772 Colombo St) is a large pub and restaurant opposite Victoria Square featuring big-screen TVs, pool tables and occasional bands and DJs.

One of Christchurch's best places for a beer or three is *Dux de Lux* near the Arts Centre. See Places to Eat – Vegetarian for information.

Bars & Clubs
Christchurch has a lot of cafe-bars for a night on the town; nightlife is very active on weekends. The prime area for after-dark action is Oxford Terrace, where almost all the restaurants transform into bars – many with DJs and dance floors – so there's a good selection for bar-hopping. Places like *All Bar One* and *Coyote* draw the younger

set; *Vesuvio* and *The Tap Room* will appeal to a more mature crowd. Among them is the intimate, unsigned *di lusso* (☎ *03-379 2133, 132 Oxford Terrace*), a mellow bar and lounge tucked in beside Viaduct.

For bars offering live music, head to *Sammy's Jazz Review* (☎ *03-377 8618, 14 Bedford Row*), with regular bands playing smooth tunes. The outdoor sheltered courtyard is a pleasant place for a drink on a summer evening. *Southern Blues Bar* (☎ *03-365 1654, 198 Madras St*) is the best place for aficionados of good blues music (live nightly), and it pulls a mixed crowd of workers and the city's elite.

Those in search of nightclubs should pick a copy of the weekly flyer *The Package*, which outlines the week's events and is available at various points around town. Then head down to Lichfield St, where Christchurch's bar-club scene is centred. Here you'll find *eye spy* (☎ *03-379 6634*) at No 56, *Hybrid*, upstairs at No 76 and *Church*, taking partying quite seriously and promoting 'dance religion'. *Ministry* (☎ *03-3792910*), with a popular gay following, is at No 88. *Da Box* (☎ *03-379 7977*) is a cool spot at No 112, while *Base* (☎ *03-377 7149*) is probably the city's dance scene leader with regular drum and bass, house and trance nights. It's located nearby at 674 Colombo St (upstairs).

CINEMAS

Show times for movies are listed in the local newspapers. There's a large *Hoyts* (☎ *03-366 6367*) cinema complex showing new commercial releases in the old train station on Moorhouse Ave. The *Regent on Worcester* (☎ *03-366 0140, 94 Worcester St*) is a central cinema showing Hollywood and independent productions. The *Arts Centre Cinemas* (☎ *03-366 0167*) comprises two cinemas (the Academy and Cloisters) within the Arts Centre and, appropriately enough, they show art-house films.

Performing Arts

Christchurch is the hub of the South Island's performing arts scene, with excellent theatres and the vibrant Arts Centre.

The focus is the *Town Hall* (☎ *03-366 8899, 86 Kilmore St*) by the riverside, where you can hear a chamber or symphony orchestra perform in the auditorium. The *James Hay Theatre* in the town hall and the *Theatre Royal* (☎ *03-377 0100, 145 Gloucester St*) are centres of live theatre. The *Court Theatre* (☎ *03-366 6992*, ⓦ *www.courttheatre.org.nz*), in the Arts Centre, is home to Christchurch's only professional theatre company. There are performances here, year round, of everything from from Samuel Beckett to *My Fair Lady*.

There are often free *lunch time concerts* in Cathedral Square, especially on Fridays. If you're in town in mid- to late January, check out the *World Buskers Festival* (☎ *03-377 2365*, ⓦ *www.worldbuskersfestival.com*), an annual event featuring street performers entertaining folks in various parts of the city, including Cathedral Square, the Arts Centre and Dux de Lux.

GETTING THERE & AWAY
Air

Christchurch is the main international gateway to the South Island. Christchurch airport (☎ 03-358 5029, ⓦ www.christchurch-airport.co.nz) has excellent facilities including visitors centres (☎ 03-353 7754) in both the domestic and international terminals (the domestic one is open 7.30am to 8.30pm, the international one is open for all international flight arrivals). There's also a bureau de change, ATMs, baggage storage, car-rental desks, cafes and shops.

There is a departure tax of $25 charged for passengers on international flights.

Air New Zealand (☎ 0800 737 000, ⓦ www.airnz.co.nz) offers direct domestic flights to many places in NZ, with connections to other centres. There are direct flights to and from Auckland, Blenheim, Dunedin, Hamilton, Hokitika, Invercargill, Nelson, Queenstown and Wellington, with connections to most other centres. The airline has a large travel centre (☎ 03-363 0600) at 549 Colombo St.

Qantas (☎ 0800 808 767, ⓦ www.qantas.co.nz) has half a dozen daily connections with Auckland and Wellington, and daily connections to Queenstown and Rotorua. Its Christchurch office is at 119 Armagh St.

Origin Pacific (☎ 0800 302 302, W www.originpacific.co.nz) has daily direct flights to Nelson, where you can connect to Auckland and Wellington. Freedom Air (☎ 0800 600 500, W www.freedomair.co.nz) has budget-priced connections to Auckland and Wellington.

For details of international airlines with offices in Christchurch see the Getting There & Away chapter.

Bus

InterCity (☎ 03-379 9020) buses depart from 123 Worcester St, between the cathedral and Manchester St. To the north, buses go to Kaikoura (3hrs), Blenheim (5hrs) and Picton (5½hrs), with connections to Nelson. Daily buses go direct to Queenstown (7½hrs) or to Queenstown (10hrs) via Mt Cook (5½hrs), with connections to Wanaka. To the south, daily buses run along the coast via the towns of the SH1 to Dunedin (6hrs), with connections to Invercargill, Te Anau and Queenstown.

The West Coast is sadly neglected by the major bus companies, but Coast to Coast Shuttle (☎ 0800 800 847) and Alpine Coaches (☎ 0800 274 888) have daily services to Greymouth or Hokitika (both $35) via Arthur's Pass.

Myriad shuttle buses run to most destinations including Picton, Queenstown, Wanaka, Dunedin, Akaroa, Hanmer Springs and points in between. Most can be booked at the visitors centre. See under those towns for details.

See the Getting Around chapter for details on the backpacker buses.

Train

The small, modern train station (☎ 0800 801 070) is on Clarence St in Addington, 2km southwest of the city centre, and there's a free morning bus service that picks up from many central accommodation lodges; ask at the visitors centre.

Trains run daily each way between Christchurch and Picton via Kaikoura and Blenheim. The *TranzCoastal* departs from Christchurch at 7.30am and arrives at Picton at 12.50pm, allowing plenty of time to connect with the 1.30am *Interislander* ferry to Wellington.

The *TranzAlpine* runs daily between Christchurch and Greymouth via Arthur's Pass (see the boxed text 'The *TranzAlpine*' in The West Coast chapter). The daily *Southerner* service between Christchurch and Invercargill via Dunedin ran its last journey in early 2002.

Hitching

Christchurch to Dunedin can be a long day, and tends to get harder further south until you approach Dunedin. Catch a Templeton bus (No 5) to get out of the city. Christchurch to Picton can be done in a day, although there can be long waits. Hitching north, bus R will get you to Redwood on SH74, a couple of kilometres before it joins SH1.

To hitch west take bus No 84 to Yaldhurst Rd, the start of SH73 – then keep your fingers crossed; it can be a long, hard haul, as much as two days. Pick up the train along the way if you become despondent.

GETTING AROUND

To/From the Airport The airport is 12km northwest of the city. Door-to-door airport shuttle bus companies such as Super Shuttle (☎ 0800 748 885, 03-357 9950) operate 24 hours and charge from $10 per person.

The public bus to the airport ($4, 25mins) leaves from Cathedral Square, opposite the visitors centre. On Monday to Friday, buses leave every half-hour from 6.45am to 5.45pm, then every hour until 8.45pm. They run at least every hour from 7.30am to 8.30pm Saturday, to 6.30pm Sunday. The bus operates in the opposite direction (from the airport to the city centre) at similar intervals. Phone ☎ 0800 733 287 for information.

A taxi to or from the airport will cost about $25.

Bus

Christchurch's bus service is good, cheap and efficient. Most city buses run from the well-organised Bus Exchange, with its pedestrian entrance on Colombo St opposite

Ballantynes department store. The only bus that doesn't operate from here is the airport bus (see previous paragraph). For bus information phone Bus Info (☎ 03-366 8855) between 6.30am and 10.30pm Monday to Saturday and 9am to 9pm Sunday, or stop in at the information desk in the Bus Exchange. Schedules are also available from the visitors centre. Alternatively, for a route map and timetables see W www.ecan.govt .nz, then go to the Buses and Transport page. Fares range from $1 to $2.70.

Information on the following three services can be obtained from Red Bus on ☎ 0800 733 287, W www.redbus.co.nz.

The Shuttle is a free service around the central city (as far north as Kilmore St and as far south as Moorhouse Ave) with about 20 pick-up points; during the day (8am to 7pm Monday to Thursday, until 9.30pm Friday and Saturday and 6pm Sunday) it runs every 10 minutes. The night route is every 15 minutes (until midnight Friday and Saturday) and takes in the casino.

The After Midnight Express Service operates on four suburban routes every hour between midnight and 4am on Saturday and Sunday mornings ($4).

The 'Best Attractions Direct Double Decker' links major attractions such as the International Antarctic Centre, the gondola and Willowbank Wildlife Reserve. A pass costs $10/8 adult/child and lasts two days. The bus departs from Cathedral Square.

Taxi
Christchurch has plenty of taxis. Catch them at ranks (there's one on the northwest side of Cathedral Square) or phone:

Blue Star (☎ 03-379 9799)
First Direct (☎ 03-377 5555)
Gold Band (☎ 03-379 5795)

Car & Motorcycle
The major rental companies all have offices in Christchurch, as do numerous smaller local companies. The *Yellow Pages* lists over 50 operators. Competition keeps the prices down and, though not as good as Auckland, Christchurch is the best place in the South Island to rent a car. Operators with national networks often want cars to be returned from Christchurch to Auckland because most renters travel in the opposite direction. Special rates may apply. Christchurch is also a good place to rent a motor home. For reliable national rental companies see the Getting Around chapter. Local rental companies include:

Ace Rentals (☎ 03-366 3222, @ acerentals@xtra.co.nz) 237 Lichfield St
New Zealand Motorcycle Rentals (☎ 03-377 0663, W www.nzbike.com) 166 Gloucester St. As well as renting bikes this company offers guided tours.
Pegasus Rental Cars (☎ 03-365 1100, @ info@rentalcars.co.nz) 127 Peterborough St
Renny Rentals (☎ 03-366 1790, @ renny@caverock.net.nz) 341 Madras St

If you want to buy or sell a car, the Canterbury Car Fair (☎ 03-338 5525) is held at Addington Raceway (Wrights Rd entrance) on Sunday from 9am to noon (sellers fee is $20). Turners Auctions (☎ 03-366 1807, W www.turners.co.nz), 32 Moorhouse Ave, buys and sells used cars by auction.

Bicycle
City Cycle Hire (☎ 0800 343 848, W www .cyclehire-tours.co.nz) operating out of NZ Independent Travel in Chancery Lane, off Cathedral Square, offers bike rental. Staff deliver the cycle to your accommodation and collect it at the end of the rental. Rental prices are $20/30 half/full day; mountain bikes are $30/45. You can also rent touring bikes and equipment.

Wheels n' Deals (☎ 03-377 6655), 255 Manchester St by the YHA, has mountain bikes for rent for $25 a day. It also buys and sells second-hand bikes.

Around Christchurch

LYTTELTON
pop 3100
Located southeast of Christchurch, you'll find the prominent Port Hills and, behind them, Lyttelton Harbour, Christchurch's

port. Christchurch's first European settlers landed at Lyttelton in 1850 and then made the historic trek over the hills to their promised land.

Only 12km from Christchurch, Lyttelton is an attractive small port town, with historic buildings and cafe-bars popular with Christchurch day-trippers on Saturday and Sunday. It makes a good day trip, especially if you have a car and go via the scenic **Port Hills**. Drive along the narrow Summit Rd for breathtaking views of the harbour and hillsides and vistas of Christchurch and the Southern Alps. The route is outlined in the free *Port Hills Drive* pamphlet. Alternatively, Lyttelton can be reached more quickly from Christchurch by a road tunnel, an impressive piece of engineering with gleaming tiles reminiscent of a huge, elongated public toilet.

The Lyttelton visitors centre (☎ 03-328 9093, e lyttinfo@ihug.co.nz) is at 20 Oxford St and is open 9am to 5pm daily. Pick up a copy of its self-guided historic walk pamphlet ($1).

The **Lyttelton Museum** *(☎ 03-328 8972, Gladstone Quay; admission by donation; open 2pm-4pm Tues, Thur, Sat & Sun)* has colonial displays, a maritime gallery and an Antarctic gallery. The **Timeball Station** *(☎ 03-328 7311, Reserve Terrace; adult/ child $2.50/free; open 10am-5pm daily in summer, open Wed-Sun in winter)* is one of the few remaining such places in the world. Built in 1876, it once fulfilled an important maritime duty. Every day, for 58 years, the huge timeball was hoisted on a mast and then dropped at exactly 1pm, Greenwich Mean Time, allowing ships in the harbour to set their clocks and thereby accurately calculate longitude.

Black Cat *(☎ 0800 436 574, 17 Norwich Quay)* operates 'Christchurch Wildlife Cruises', two-hour cruises on Lyttelton harbour with commentary and dolphin-spotting ($39/15 adult/child). There are one or two cruises daily, departing from B Jetty.

Paragliding operators set sail from the Gondola/Summit Rd, which is directly above Lyttelton. Ask at the visitors centre for details on operators.

Places to Stay & Eat

Accommodation in town is somewhat limited, but most of the pubs offer budget accommodation and there are also a few B&Bs and cottages. The visitors centre can help with bookings.

Tunnel Vision Backpackers *(☎ 03-328 7576, e stay@tunnelvision.co.nz, 44 London St)* Dorm beds $16-18, twins/doubles $40/44. Homely Tunnel Vision is only half an hour by bus from Christchurch. It's ideal for those who want to stay somewhere out of the city (but it is closed in winter). This attractive, refurbished old building is right in the centre of Lyttelton, close to the harbour, and has some inviting communal areas, including a courtyard and deck.

The Royal Hotel *(☎ 03-328 7114, cnr Norwich & Canterbury Sts)* has comfy, old-fashioned rooms (singles/doubles $40/70) above the pub. Local B&Bs include **Randolph House** *(☎ 03-328 8877, 49 Sumner Rd)*, with rooms for $100 to $120. **Dockside Accommodation** *(☎ 03-328 7344, 22 Sumner Rd)* has a self-contained apartment available for $75.

Lyttelton has plenty of dining choices, most of them on London St; **Volcano Cafe** *(☎ 03-328 7077, 42 London St)* is the pick. This eye-catching yellow cafe has wonderful decor and a great menu with many items boasting a distinct Mexican influence (mains $15 to $25). Next door, the equally eye-catching **Lava Bar** erupts every night.

Other very good cafe-bars on this strip are **Deluxe Cafe & Bar** *(☎ 03-328 8748, 18 London St)* and **Satchmo** *(☎ 03-328 8348, 8 London St)*. Both offer a fine range of meals and snacks in appealing surrounds.

There are also a good number of pubs and bars; there's a cosy **Irish pub** *(☎ 03-328 8085, 17a London St)* with Guinness, meals and a great deck out the back overlooking the harbour.

A night-time venue that offers a drink with a view is the very cool and quirky **Wunderbar** *(☎ 03-328 8818)*, which is rather hidden away and functions with a convoluted stairway entry, through a doorway on London St (it's signposted next to the supermarket).

GREATER CHRISTCHURCH

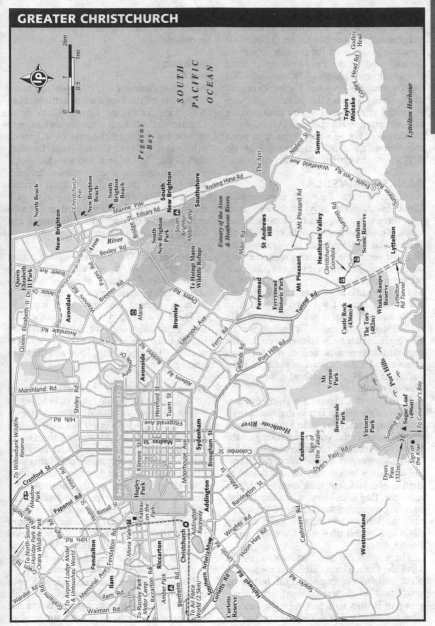

Getting There & Away

Bus No 28 runs regularly from Christchurch to Lyttelton via the road tunnel (12km). Alternatively, drive via the bayside suburb of Sumner and Evans Pass (19km) or head straight down Colombo St from Cathedral Square and go up over Dyers Pass and along scenic Summit Rd (22km).

From Lyttelton by car you can continue around Lyttelton Harbour and eventually on to Akaroa. This is a very scenic, in parts treacherous, and much longer route than via SH75 between Christchurch and Akaroa.

BANKS PENINSULA

A change from the flat area around Christchurch itself, hilly Banks Peninsula was formed by two giant volcanic eruptions. Small harbours such as Le Bons, Pigeon and Little Akaloa Bays radiate out from the peninsula's centre, giving it a cogwheel shape. The historic town of Akaroa is the main highlight.

The peninsula has a chequered history of settlement. James Cook first sighted it in 1770 and thought it was an island. He named it after naturalist Sir Joseph Banks. The Ngai Tahu tribe, who then occupied the peninsula, were attacked at the fortified Onawe *pa* by the Ngati Toa chief Te Rauparaha in 1831 and suffered a severe decline in numbers.

In 1838 Jean Langlois, a whaling captain, negotiated the sale of Banks Peninsula from local Maori and returned to France to form a trading company. With the backing of the French government, 63 settlers emigrated in 1840 under escort of the warship *L'Aube,* but only days before they arrived panicked British officials sent their own warship to raise the flag at Akaroa, claiming British sovereignty under the Treaty of Waitangi. Had the settlers arrived two years earlier, the South Island may well have become a French colony.

The French did settle at Akaroa, but in 1849 the French land claim was sold to the New Zealand Company and the following year the French were joined by a large group of British settlers. Originally heavily forested, the land was cleared for timber.

Dairy farming, later supplanted by sheep farming, became the main industry of the peninsula.

Akaroa
pop 650

Akaroa, meaning 'Long Harbour' in Maori, is the site of the first French settlement in NZ. This charming town, 82km from Christchurch, lies on a scenic harbour and strives to re-create the feel of a French provincial village. Streets (rues Lavaud, Balguerie, Jolie) and houses (Langlois-Eteveneaux) have French names, and descendants of the original French settlers reside in the town. It's a delight just to walk the streets, and to visit the gardens. Akaroa is a popular day trip from Christchurch and is also great for a longer stay.

Information The Akaroa visitors centre (☎ 03-304 8600, Ⓦ www.akaroa.com), in the post-office building, corner of rue Lavaud and Balguerie, is open 9.30am to 5pm daily in summer, 10am to 4pm in winter.

There is a Bank of NZ opposite the visitors centre; there should be an ATM in town by the time you read this. There's Internet access at Turenne Coffee Shop and the town library.

Things to See & Do The **Akaroa Museum** (☎ 03-304 7614, 71 rue Lavaud; adult/child $3.50/1; open 10.30am-4.30pm daily in summer, to 4pm in winter) has a 20-minute audiovisual on the history of the Banks Peninsula, and assorted colonial memorabilia. The old courthouse and Langlois-Eteveneaux Cottage, one of the oldest houses in NZ and partly fabricated in France, are part of the museum complex, as is the tiny Customs House by Daly's Wharf. At Okains Bay, there's a small **museum** (☎ 03-304 8611; adult/child $5/1; open 10am-5pm daily) displaying Maori and colonial history and featuring a sacred 15th-century god stick and a war canoe.

For an excellent **walking tour**, pick up a copy of the *Akaroa Historic Village Walk* booklet ($3.50); the tour starts at Waeckerle Cottage at the north end of town and finishes at the lighthouse, taking in all the wonderful old wooden buildings and churches that give the town so much of its character.

Advertised as 'four nights, four days, four beaches, four bays', the **Banks Peninsula Track** (☎ *03-304 7612,* **W** *www.banks track.co.nz)* is a 35km, four-day walk on a private track across private farmland and then around the dramatic coastline of Banks Peninsula. It costs $150, including transport from Akaroa and hut accommodation. A two-day option covers the same ground at a less leisurely pace and costs $100. Book in advance.

Akaroa Harbour Cruises (☎ *0800 436 574, 03-304 7641,* **W** *www.blackcat.co.nz)* operates two-hour cruises on the *Canterbury Cat,* departing from the Main Wharf at 1.30pm daily (also at 11am from November to March). You may well see Hectors dolphins and blue penguins on the trip. Tickets are $33/15 for adults/children; purchase them from the office on the wharf. The same company also operates **Dolphins Up Close**, dolphin-swimming tours departing four times daily from October to April. The trips cost $80/50 adult/child to swim, $33/20 to view only. Gear such as wetsuit and flippers

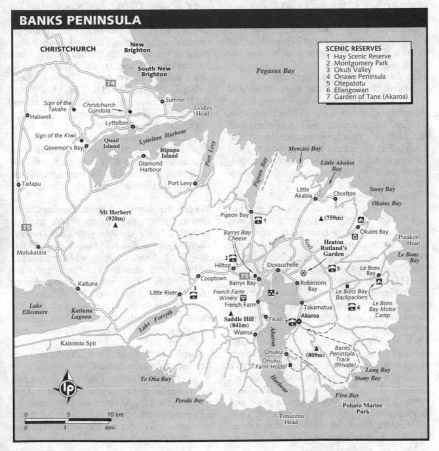

BANKS PENINSULA

SCENIC RESERVES
1 Hay Scenic Reserve
2 Montgomery Park
3 Okuti Valley
4 Onawe Peninsula
5 Otepatotu
6 Ellangowan
7 Garden of Tane (Akaroa)

is provided, and if you don't see dolphins you'll get a second trip free. **Dolphin Experience** (☎ 03-304 7726) also has popular dolphin-swimming tours, costing $75/50 adult/child; watching only is $30.

Bayline Services (☎ 03-304 7207, 108 rue Jolie) operates the Eastern Bays Scenic Mail Run, a 110km rural delivery service, and visitors can come along for the ride. You visit remote parts of the peninsula, isolated communities and seven bays. It departs from the visitors centre at 8.15am and returns at 1pm Monday to Saturday ($20); bookings are essential. It also operates an afternoon tour of the inner bays ($20).

Places to Stay – Akaroa Most of the places to stay on the Banks Peninsula are in or near Akaroa, but other possibilities are scattered around the various bays. See Places to Stay – Banks Peninsula.

Akaroa Top 10 Holiday Park (☎ 03-304 7471, e akaroa.holidaypark@xtra.co.nz, Morgans Rd) Unpowered/powered sites $18/20 for 2, cabins $44-55, self-contained units $60-65. This park, signposted off Old Coach Rd, has scenic harbour views, good facilities and a reasonably central location (there is a walking track from the park down to Woodills Rd).

Chez la Mer (☎ 03-304 7024, e chez_la _mer@clear.net.nz, 50 rue Lavaud) and *Bon Accord* (☎ 03-304 7782, e bon-accord @xtra.co.nz, 57 Rue Lavaud) are two very good backpackers, both in small historic homes set in pretty gardens in the heart of town. Prices are the same at both: dorm beds are $18, doubles and twins are $44.

Mt Vernon Lodge (☎ 03-304 7180, rue Balguerie) Camping $12.50 per person, dorm beds $15-18, en suite doubles $45-55, self-contained chalets $60. Friendly, laidback Mt Vernon Lodge, about 2km from town (free pick-up offered), is a combination hostel and guest lodge set in extensive grounds with a great assortment of farmyard animals. There's horse-trekking available (from $25 for one hour), plus a pool and large common room with an open fire.

Madeira Hotel (☎ 03-304 7009, 48 rue Lavaud) Singles/doubles with shared bath

$25/50. The Madeira has comfortable, good-value rooms above the hotel, but noise from the pub below may pose a problem on summer weekends when bands are playing.

La Rive Motel (☎ 03-304 7651, e la rive@paradise.net.nz, 1 rue Lavaud) Motel units $65-85 (Apr-Nov), $80-100 (Dec-Mar). The first motel you'll encounter as you enter Akaroa, La Rive offers well-equipped, older-style units that are clean and comfortable.

Loch Hill Country Cottages (☎ 0800 456 244, 03-304 7195, e lochhill@xtra.co.nz) Cottages $90-140 for 2 people, $18 each extra person. On the highway about 1km north of Akaroa, the eight self-contained, country-style cottages of Loch Hill are set in beautiful gardens. They're built of either stone or wood and all feature patios; some have extras like log fires and spa baths.

La Belle Villa (☎ 03-304 7084, 113 rue Jolie) Doubles $90-110. This is a pretty B&B in a historic home with private swimming pool and lovely gardens.

Oinako Lodge (☎ 03-304 8787, e oinako@oinako.co.nz, 99 Beach Rd) Doubles $165-220. This is a retreat in a grand old building near the beach, offering individually themed rooms (most with spas) and gourmet breakfasts.

Places to Stay – Banks Peninsula At **Duvauchelle**, about 10km before Akaroa, there's a basic camping ground *Duvauchelle Reserve Board Motor Camp* (☎ 03-304 5777, Seafield Rd), with unpowered and powered sites for $16, and cabins for $30 to $40. The historic *Duvauchelle Hotel* (☎ 03-304 5803, e duvauchelle .hotel@xtra.co.nz) offers good all-day bar meals plus has basic backpacker accommodation from $15 to $20, and motel units starting at $65.

Onuku is about 5km south of Akaroa and has *Onuku Farm Hostel* (☎ 03-304 7612, e onukufarm@jolyworld.com), a wonderful farmstay-cum-backpackers on a 340-hectare sheep farm. There are camp sites for $10 per person, rustic huts in the spacious grounds for $13 per person and backpacker beds in the farmhouse for $18. The owners

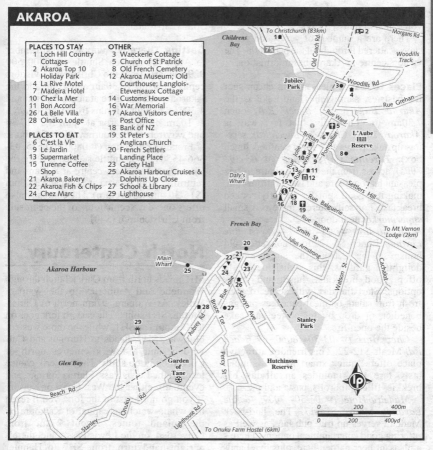

AKAROA

PLACES TO STAY
1 Loch Hill Country Cottages
2 Akaroa Top 10 Holiday Park
4 La Rive Motel
7 Madeira Hotel
10 Chez la Mer
11 Bon Accord
26 La Belle Villa
28 Oinako Lodge

PLACES TO EAT
6 C'est la Vie
9 Le Jardin
13 Supermarket
15 Turenne Coffee Shop
21 Akaroa Bakery
22 Akaroa Fish & Chips
24 Chez Marc

OTHER
3 Waeckerle Cottage
5 Church of St Patrick
8 Old French Cemetery
12 Akaroa Museum; Old Courthouse; Langlois-Eteveneaux Cottage
14 Customs House
16 War Memorial
17 Akaroa Visitors Centre; Post Office
18 Bank of NZ
19 St Peter's Anglican Church
20 French Settlers Landing Place
23 Gaiety Hall
25 Akaroa Harbour Cruises & Dolphins Up Close
27 School & Library
29 Lighthouse

also offer dolphin swimming trips ($60) and kayaking ($20) to guests, and free use of mountain bikes and fishing lines. They will pick up from Akaroa.

Le Bons Bay, 22km from Akaroa, has a camping ground, plus one of NZ's best backpackers. *Le Bons Bay Backpackers (☎ 03-304 8582; open Oct-May)* is in a restored farmhouse set in sprawling gardens with views down the valley. The friendly owner cooks up a gourmet feast every evening for guests to share (meals are remarkably good value at $10), and offers boat trips to see the wildlife ($20). Dorm beds are $18, doubles

$40 to $44; prices include breakfast. It's found about 6km before Le Bons Bay itself; the owners will pick you up from Akaroa. Book ahead as places are limited and word-of-mouth means beds are in demand. *Le Bons Bay Motor Camp (☎ 03-304 8533, e lebonsholiday@xtra.co.nz)* is a secluded, peaceful ground with unpowered & powered sites for $20 and cabins for $45.

At **Okains Bay** there's a large beachside *camping ground (☎ 03-304 8789)* with unpowered sites ($5.50 per person), kitchen and shower facilities (coin-operated). In-quire and pay at the general store a few kilometres back from the beachfront, where you can also rent sea kayaks.

There are a number of very good farmstays scattered throughout the peninsula. The visitors centre in Akaroa has information.

Places to Eat A pleasant and cheap spot for pastries, sandwiches and cake is the *Akaroa Bakery (51 Beach Rd)*, open 7.30am to 4pm daily. Not far away is *Akaroa Fish & Chips (59 Beach Rd)*, serving up takeaways ($7 for a seafood lunch box). *Turenne Coffee Shop (☎ 03-304 7005)*, across from the visitors centre, offers pleasant tearoom fare and is open from 7am, making it a good spot for an early cooked breakfast. For self-caterers there is a small *supermarket* next door.

Le Jardin (☎ 03-304 7447, 43 Rue Lavaud) Lunch $5-12. In a converted old house set back from the street among delightful gardens, this stylish new cafe offers good breakfast, lunch and snack options. Start the day with some of their fresh fruit salad, oatmeal pancakes or eggs benedict, or drop by for coffee and cake beside the open fire.

Chez Marc (☎ 03-304 8060, 69 Beach Rd) Meals $12-22. This friendly, attractive place offers 'quick smart food' – simple, tasty fare that includes an all-day big brekkie, filled pita rolls, pasta and pizza.

Madeira Hotel (☎ 03-304 7009, 48 Rue Lavaud) Mains $14-17. The laid-back Madeira serves up true pub fare, as well as offering good entertainment options. There's a pleasant beer garden here, plus live bands often perform on summer weekends.

C'est la Vie (☎ 03-304 7314, 33 Rue Lavaud) Mains $25-30. Francophiles should head to upmarket C'est la Vie for well-prepared French cuisine. Start with an entree of escargot, and move on to a main of duck a l'orange or pork fillet chasseur.

Head to the western side of Akaroa Harbour to sample good local produce: *Barrys Bay Cheese (☎ 03-304 5809)* for traditionally made cheeses; and *French Farm Winery (☎ 03-304 5785, W www.french farm.co.nz)* for a local drop. French Farm also has an alfresco pizzeria in summer,

plus an a-la-carte restaurant open 10am to 5pm year-round.

Getting There & Away From November to April the Akaroa Shuttle (☎ 0800 500 929) departs from the Christchurch visitors centre at 9am, 10.30am and 2pm, and the Akaroa visitors centre at noon, 3.35pm and 4.30pm. In winter it runs from Christchurch at 10am, from Akaroa at 4pm. It's $17/30 one way/return; the journey takes 1½ hours.

French Connection (☎ 0800 800 575, 03-366 4556) has a shuttle service leaving the Christchurch visitors centre at 8.30am and returning from Akaroa at 11am and 3.30pm ($15/30 one way/return). The company also offers one-day scenic tours of the peninsula from Christchurch ($40).

North Canterbury

SH1 heads north from Christchurch through Woodend and Amberley to the Waipara Valley. At Waipara, 57km north of Christchurch, SH1 splits. The eastern fork goes on to Kaikoura as SH1, while the more western highway, SH7, heads to Hurunui and Culverden, and a few kilometres north of Culverden it too splits. The westerly choice leads to the Lewis Pass, Maruia Springs, and eventually either the West Coast or Nelson. If you go northeast of the fork, you'll reach the whale-watching capital of Kaikoura by the inland routes. About 27km from Culverden, on the Lewis Pass route, there's a right-hand turn from SH7 to Hanmer Springs, a well-known thermal area and resort. The *Alpine Pacific Triangle Touring Guide*, free at visitors centres, outlines things to see and do in this region.

The scenic Waipara Valley has over a dozen **wineries**, all outlined in the free *Waipara Valley Vineyards* brochure. Sample a Mountford pinot noir or prize-winning Canterbury House sauvignon blanc, and stop for lunch in the lovely restaurants at Pegasus Bay or Waipara Springs. Waipara Springs, Pegasus Bay and Canterbury House are open daily for wine tasting and sales; Torlesse and Fiddler's Green on Saturday and Sunday. Most other wineries are open by appointment only. See also Organised Tours under Christchurch for details on companies offering tours of the area.

Waipara Sleepers (☎ 03-314 6003, ⓦ www.inet.net.nz/~waipara.sleepers, 12 Glenmark Drive) Dorm beds $17, doubles & twins $37-52, unpowered/powered sites $10/12 plus $5 per person. From SH1, turn onto SH7 at Waipara then take the first right (north) to get to this unique and novel accommodation, conveniently close to the local pub and general store plus walking and swimming opportunities. The excellent 'complex' features historic railway wagons set in pleasant gardens, plus old railway huts. There are four-berth share carriages in addition to doubles and twins, plus a few camp sites.

HANMER SPRINGS
pop 750

Hanmer Springs, the main thermal resort on the South Island, is about 10km off SH7, the highway to the West Coast. Apart from its hot pools, it's popular for outdoor activities including forest walks, horse treks, fishing, jetboating, rafting, bungy jumping from the Waiau ferry bridge and skiing in winter. Visitors swell the population year-round, with Hanmer being a favourite weekend spot for Christchurch folk.

Information

The helpful Hurunui visitors centre (☎ 0800 442 663, 03-315 7128, ⓔ info@hurunui .com, ⓦ www.hurunui.com) is in front of the thermal reserve. It's open 10am to 5pm daily, and staff here book accommodation, transport and local activities. Next door is a Bank of NZ ATM, open 9am to 9pm daily.

Thermal Reserve

Hanmer Springs has been attracting visitors to its thermal waters for about 130 years. Local legend has it that the thermal springs are a piece of the fires of Tamatea that dropped from the sky after an eruption of Mt Ngauruhoe on the North Island. Centuries later it has metamorphosed into the excellent **Hanmer Springs Thermal Reserve**

(☎ 03-315 7511, ⓦ www.hotfun.co.nz; adult/child $8/4; open 10am-9pm daily).

The hot spring water mixes with fresh water to produce pools of varying temperatures. In addition to the mineral pools, there are landscaped rock pools, sulphur pools, a freshwater 25m lap pool, private sauna and steam suites, a family activity area (including waterslides), massage facilities and a restaurant. Per half-hour, private suites are $15 per person.

Activities

Hanmer Springs Adventure Centre (☎ 03-315 7223, 20 Conical Hill Rd) is a good place for information on activities in the area as well as equipment rental – bikes are $15/25/30 per hour/half day/full day, plus there's scooters, roller blades, fishing gear and ski and snowboard gear. It's open 9am to 5pm daily.

There are two main skiing areas near Hanmer Springs. **Hanmer Springs Field** is the closest, 17km (unsealed) from Hanmer, and **Mt Lyford** is some 60km away. They are not as expensive as the larger resorts (see Skiing & Snowboarding in the Activities chapter). The Adventure Centre operates shuttle buses to the mountains.

The *Hanmer Forest Recreation* pamphlet outlines a number of pleasant short **walks** near town, mostly through picturesque forest. The easy Woodland Walk starts from Jollies Pass Rd, 1km from town, and goes through Douglas fir, poplar and redwood stands. It joins the Majuba Walk, which leads to Conical Hill Lookout and then back to Conical Hill Rd – about 1½ hours all up. The visitors centre has details of longer tramps in the area, including Lake Sumner Forest Park.

Thrillseekers Canyon (☎ 03-315 7046, ⓦ www.thrillseeker.co.nz) is the adrenaline centre of Hanmer Springs. Christchurch's closest bungee jumping spot, it's about 9km out of town and costs $99 to hurl yourself from the 35m-high Waiau ferry bridge. Jetboating (from $59/30 for adults/children) and white-water rafting ($75/40) on grade II to III water are also offered at the Thrillseekers Canyon centre, next to the

CANTERBURY

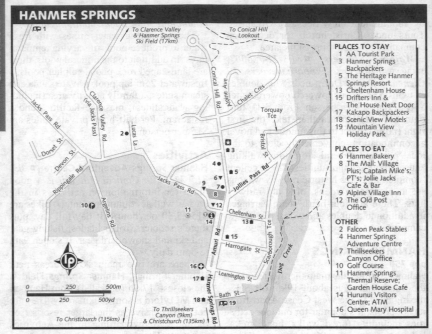

HANMER SPRINGS

To Clarence Valley & Hanmer Springs Ski Field (17km)

To Conical Hill Lookout

Jacks Pass Rd

Clarence Valley Rd (via Jacks Pass)

Lucas La

Conical Hill Rd

Alpine Ave

Chalet Cres

Torquay Tce

Dorset St

Devon St

Rippingale Rd

Jacks Pass Rd

Jollies Pass Rd

Bristol St

Argelins Rd

Amuri Rd

Cheltenham St

Scarborough Tce

Dog Creek

Harrogate St

Leamington St

Hanmer Springs Rd

Bath St

To Thrillseekers Canyon (9km) & Christchurch (135km)

To Christchurch (135km)

0   250   500m
0   250   500yd

PLACES TO STAY
1 AA Tourist Park
3 Hanmer Springs Backpackers
5 The Heritage Hanmer Springs Resort
13 Cheltenham House
15 Drifters Inn & The House Next Door
17 Kakapo Backpackers
18 Scenic View Motels
19 Mountain View Holiday Park

PLACES TO EAT
6 Hanmer Bakery
8 The Mall: Village Plus; Captain Mike's; PT's; Jollie Jacks Cafe & Bar
9 Alpine Village Inn
12 The Old Post Office

OTHER
2 Falcon Peak Stables
4 Hanmer Springs Adventure Centre
7 Thrillseekers Canyon Office
10 Golf Course
11 Hanmer Springs Thermal Reserve; Garden House Cafe
14 Hurunui Visitors Centre; ATM
16 Queen Mary Hospital

bridge where the Hanmer Springs turn-off meets SH7. There's also an office (☎ 03-315 7346) in town at the Mall for information and bookings.

Falcon Peak Stables (☎ *03-315 7444, Jacks Pass Rd; 1-hr/day treks from $35/150*) takes horse treks around Hanmer. **Alpine Horse Safaris** (☎ *03-314 4293,* Ⓦ *www .alpinehorse.co.nz*), based out of Hurunui some 60km south of Hanmer Springs, has two-hour, half-day and full-day rides, plus safaris for serious horsefolk (lasting two to 11 days).

A fun way to see the surrounding countryside is on a four-wheel motorbike safari. After some introductory instruction, you tackle the trails on farm quad-bikes up into the hills or along the river for magnificent views. **Backtrax** (☎ *03-315 7684*) does 2½ hour trips for $98 (minimum age 16). This region is also popular for mountain biking. The Adventure Centre rents bikes and can give you trail maps and advice. **Dust 'n' Dirt**

(☎ *03-315 7233*) organises four-hour bike safaris for $65.

At 500,000 acres, the vast **Molesworth Station**, north of Hanmer Springs, is the largest farm in NZ, with the country's largest cattle herd (10,000). If you're here in January or early February, inquire at the visitors centre about independent visits to Molesworth: for about six weeks most years, the farm is open to the public ($10 per car), and there are basic camping facilities, as well as cottage accommodation. Alternatively, **Trailways Safaris** (☎ *03-315 7401*) offers 4WD tours of the station from October to May (half-day/full-day tours $75/125; daytour includes picnic lunch).

Places to Stay

Mountain View Holiday Park (☎ *03-315 7113,* Ⓔ *mtview.hanmer@clear.net.nz, Bath St*) Unpowered/powered site $18/20 for 2, cabins $35-45, self-contained units $60-68. This is the most central camping ground, located on the southern edge of town and only a few minutes' walk to the thermal reserve. It's a busy ground with good amenities.

AA Tourist Park (☎ 03-315 7112, ℮ aa touristpark@xtra.co.nz, Jacks Pass Rd) Unpowered/powered sites $16/18 for 2, cabins $40, tourist flats $58. This large, well-run park is set in a peaceful location 3km from the town centre. It's well equipped and has good cabins and flats, plus AA members get a 10% discount on prices.

Hanmer Springs Backpackers (☎ 03-315 7196, ℮ hanmerbackpackers@hotmail .com, 41 Conical Hill Rd) Dorm beds $17-20, doubles $42. Long the only backpackers in town but about to face some stiff competition, this place is a small, friendly wooden chalet (a winter ski lodge) planning renovations to overcome the slightly cramped layout. It offers free pick-ups from the SH7 junction if required.

Kakapo Backpackers (☎ 03-3315 7472, ℮ stay-kakapo@xtra.co.nz, 14 Amuri Rd) Dorm beds $17, doubles & twins $40-42, en suite doubles $50. YHA-affiliated Kakapo was previously only a small cottage with limited capacity, but early 2002 saw the completion of a large new accommodation block with excellent modern facilities and plenty of common areas.

Scenic View Motels (☎ 03-315 7419, ℮ scenic.views@xtra.co.nz, 10 Amuri Ave) Units $89-139. Scenic View is an attractive stone complex with modern, colourful studios and two-bedroom apartments plus good mountain views.

Drifters Inn (☎ 03-315 7554, 0800 374 383, W www.driftersinn.co.nz, 2 Harrogate St) Rooms $87-115. Facilities at this excellent inn include a large, modern kitchen, dining and lounge area for guest use. Prices include buffet-style continental breakfast. Next door to Drifters is the aptly named **House Next Door**, with more usual budget accommodation in a lovely old house (singles, doubles and twins with shared facilities range from $40 to $50).

Cheltenham House (☎ 03-315 7545, W www.cheltenham.co.nz, 13 Cheltenham St) Singles/doubles $110/150. This B&B is superb with beautiful rooms, and two garden cottages. All rooms have bathrooms and a delightful sitting area for enjoying the substantial breakfast. The house also has a living area (with a billiards table) where free pre-dinner drinks are served.

The Heritage Hanmer Springs Resort (☎ 03-315 7021, 0800 368 888, W www .heritagehotels.co.nz, 1 Conical Hill Rd) Rooms and suites $145-275. This is a grand old resort hotel that has been extensively renovated and now offers a range of accommodation options from executive suites to garden villas and deluxe rooms. The three-bedroom self-contained villas are an excellent deal, costing $245 and sleeping up to six. Facilities at the hotel include extensive gardens, a pool, tennis court, day spa, bar and restaurant.

Places to Eat

Given that Hanmer Springs is such a popular and busy weekend resort, dining opportunities haven't kept pace with the accommodation developments. There seems to be a shortage of good cafes and interesting eateries in the area.

For excellent baked goods and cheap sandwiches, head to the **Hanmer Bakery** on Conical Hill Rd, open from 6am. The Mall has a selection of cafeteria-style places and fast-food establishments including **Village Plus** for cooked breakfasts, **Captain Mike's** for fish and chips and **PT's** for gourmet pizzas.

Jollie Jacks Cafe & Bar (☎ 03-315 7388, The Mall) Mains $14-22. Jollie Jacks is a somewhat upmarket place in a sea of takeaway stores. It's usually open late when all else is shut, and offers a good variety of meals such as spicy Asian beef salad, Thai chicken curry, bangers and mash, and fish of the day.

Alpine Village Inn (☎ 03-315 7005, Jacks Pass Rd) Meals $12-20. Alpine Village Inn, behind the Mall, is the local boozer and has reasonably priced bistro meals plus bar snacks such as nachos and burgers for under $10.

Garden House Cafe (☎ 03-315 7214) Dinner mains $16-22. This cafe in the

CANTERBURY

thermal reserve is a good spot to dry out your wrinkly skin and fill your stomach, despite the irritating elevator music. It serves up snacks, lunch and dinner, including pricey pizzas ($20), pasta dishes and the usual meat dishes.

The Old Post Office (☎ 03-315 7461, 2 Jacks Pass Rd) Mains average $29. Open daily for dinner. To blow your budget, head to the Old Post Office, one of the best restaurants in town. It's noted for its quality beef and lamb dishes.

The Heritage Restaurant (1 Conical Hill Rd) Lunch $8-17, dinner mains $24-28. This restaurant in the upmarket hotel complex is open for breakfast, lunch and dinner. It serves well-prepared food and has a good wine list featuring many Waipara drops.

Getting There & Away

The Hanmer Connection (☎ 0800 377 378, 03-315 7575) runs daily between Hanmer Springs and Christchurch ($22, 2hrs), and also operates three days a week (Tuesday, Thursday and Saturday) between Hanmer Springs and Kaikoura ($25, 2hrs).

Lazerline (☎ 03-315 7128) picks up and drops off in Hanmer Springs on request on its daily service between Nelson and Christchurch. East-West Coach Service (☎ 0800 142 622) has buses between Christchurch and Westport that will collect or set down passengers at the Hanmer Springs turn-off, but the junction is 10km from town.

Ski shuttles run to the ski areas in winter; contact the Adventure Centre for times and information.

THE LEWIS PASS HIGHWAY

SH7 continues west from the Hanmer Springs turn-off to Lewis Pass, Maruia Springs and Springs Junction. This is a beautiful route but, lying at the northern end of the Southern Alps, the 907-metre **Lewis Pass** is not as steep or the forest as dense as the routes through the Arthur's and Haast Passes. The forest near Lewis Pass is mainly red and silver beech, though the kowhai trees that grow along the river terraces are spectacular in spring.

The Lewis Pass area has some interesting walks – pick up the DOC-produced pamphlets *Lewis Pass Region* and *Lake Sumner Conservation Park*. Most tracks pass through beech forest. Snow-capped mountains form the backdrop and there are lakes, alpine tarns and mountain rivers. The most popular tramps are those around Lake Sumner in the Lake Sumner Forest Park and the St James Walkway in the Lewis Pass National Reserve. Subalpine conditions apply – sign the intentions book at the start of the St James Walkway and at Windy Point for the Lake Sumner area before heading off.

Maruia Springs is a small, self-contained thermal resort on the banks of the Maruia River, 69km from the Hanmer turn-off and 15km east of Springs Junction.

Maruia Springs Thermal Resort (☎ 03-523 8840, W www.maruia.co.nz) Camp sites $10 per person, dorm beds $26.50, motel units $95-145. The complex is located right beside the highway and includes a range of accommodation and the licensed *Hot Rocks Cafe & Bar*, which serves pricey food during the day. Rates for the units are at a premium on Saturday nights ($125 to $145 including breakfast). The main reason to visit, of course, is to bathe in the thermal pools. Here, thermal water is pumped into a sex-segregated traditional Japanese bathhouse and outdoor rock pools that are great to relax in no matter what the weather – magic in winter as the snowflakes drift down. The baths and pools are open 8am to 9pm every day ($7/4 adults/children) and there are private spa houses available from 10.30am to 5pm ($20 per hour for two adults).

From the resort, the highway continues to **Springs Junction**, where it splits: the Shenandoah Hwy (SH65) heads north to SH6 and on to Nelson; the Lewis Pass Hwy (SH7) continues west to Reefton then down to Greymouth and the West Coast. Springs Junction has a service station, a cafe and accommodation.

Alpine Inn (☎ 03-523 8813) Dorm beds $18, singles/doubles $30/60, motel units $60/74. Right on the highway junction, this large chalet offers budget accommodation with shared facilities including a lounge and kitchen. Ask at the cafe across the road.

There are DOC *camping grounds* along SH7, including Marble Hill, 6.5km east of Springs Junction (start of the Lake Daniells walk); and Deer Valley at Lewis Pass, 10km east of Maruia Springs.

At Maruia (not to be confused with Maruia Springs), about 20km north of Springs Junction on SH65, *Reids Store Backpackers* (☎ 03-523 8869) has bunk beds for $15 or B&B rooms at $35 per person.

Central Canterbury

Heading west from Christchurch on SH73 it's about a two-hour trip to Arthur's Pass National Park. The crossing from Christchurch to Greymouth, over Arthur's Pass, is a scenic route covered by both bus services and the *TranzAlpine Express* train (see the boxed text 'The *TranzAlpine*' in The West Coast chapter).

From nowhere else in NZ do you get a better picture of the climb from the sea to the mountains. From Christchurch, almost at sea level, the road cuts through the flat Canterbury Plains, through rural towns such as Kirwee, Darfield, Sheffield and Springfield. It then winds up into the skiing areas of Porter Heights and Craigieburn before following the Waimakariri and Bealey Rivers to Arthur's Pass, passing picturesque lakes along the way, including Pearson and Grasmere.

To the southwest of Christchurch and reached by SH73 and SH77 is the Mt Hutt ski resort and Methven.

CRAIGIEBURN FOREST PARK

This forest park is 110km northwest of Christchurch and 42km south of Arthur's Pass, on SH73. A good system of walking tracks crosses the park, and longer tramps are possible in the valleys west of the Craigieburn Range. The nearby country is suitable for skiing and rock climbing (particularly at Castle Hill). The predominant vegetation types are beech, tussock, totara, and turpentine scrub. If you're lucky you

may see patches of South Island edelweiss (*Leucogenes grandiceps*). Get a copy of the DOC pamphlet *Craigieburn Forest Park Day Walks* for more information.

Craigieburn is one of the best skiing areas in the country, as it has a rise of 503m. It's set in wild country and suits the advanced skier (see Skiing & Snowboarding in the Activities chapter).

Smylie's YHA & Ski Lodge Accommodation (☎ 03-318 4740, W www.smylies.co.nz) Dorm beds $20, doubles & twins $44, motel units $65. This cosy place on the main road in Springfield has a strong Japanese influence (it's run most of the year by a Kiwi-Japanese couple), featuring a Japanese bath and futons in some rooms. The friendly owners offer ski rental (from $20 per day) and transport to all the nearby fields ($20 return), plus they will pick up from Christchurch ($20). In winter (July to September) there's a dinner, bed and breakfast option for $45 per person, with Japanese and European cuisine on the menu. There's the chance for jetboating and horse riding in and around Springfield.

Flock Hill Lodge (☎ 03-318 8196, W www.flockhill.co.nz) is a high-country sheep station 44km east of Arthur's Pass on SH73, adjacent to Lake Pearson and the Craigieburn Forest Park. There are a few good accommodation options here: backpacker beds in old shearers' quarters are $18; large cottages with kitchenette sleep up to 10 (at a push) and cost $100 for two, plus $20 for each additional person; two-bedroom motel-style units with full kitchen sleep up to seven and cost $110 for two, plus $20 for each additional person. There's a kitchen in the backpackers' lodge, plus a licensed restaurant on the property. Activities include swimming, fishing, skiing, 4WD tours, walking and mountain biking; you can rent mountain bikes and basic fishing gear from the lodge, and the helpful owners can arrange rental of ski gear.

Bealey Hotel (☎ 03-318 9277, e bealey hotel@xtra.co.nz) Dorm beds $20, motel units $85. This hotel 12km east of Arthur's Pass at Bealey, is a tiny settlement famous for a hoax which led people across the nation to believe that a live moa had been sighted in the area. There are self-contained motel units and the budget Moa Lodge with 10 double rooms, plus a restaurant and bar on site.

Wilderness Lodge (☎ *03-318 9246,* **W** *www.wildernesslodge.co.nz*) Twin & double rooms $260 per person Oct-Apr, $190 per person May-Sept. This is a superb, 20-room luxury lodge on a sheep station 16km east of Arthur's Pass on SH73. Daily guided walks are included in the price, as are breakfast and a gourmet three-course dinner.

ARTHUR'S PASS

The small settlement of Arthur's Pass is 4km from the pass of the same name. The 924m pass was on the route used by the Maori to reach Westland, but its European discovery was made by Arthur Dobson in 1864, when the Westland gold rush created enormous pressure to find a crossing over the Southern Alps from Christchurch. A coach road was completed within a year of Dobson's discovery. Later on, the coal and timber trade demanded a railway, which was completed in 1923.

The town is a fine base for walks, climbs, views and winter-time skiing (at Temple Basin) in Arthur's Pass National Park, and makes a good day trip from Greymouth or Christchurch.

Information

The Arthur's Pass visitors centre (☎ 03-318 9211) in the town is open 9am to 4pm daily (8am to 5pm in summer). It has information on all the park walks, topographical maps and route guides for longer tramps with huts. Trampers can hire detailed topo maps for $1 per day (with a $20 refundable deposit). Staff also offer invaluable advice on the park's often savagely changeable weather conditions – check here before you go on any walk, and fill out an intentions card. Be sure to sign out again when you return, otherwise they'll send a search party to find you!

The visitors centre is primarily a DOC centre (ie, it doesn't make onward bookings or reservations but can help with local accommodation and transport information).

It has excellent displays, and in January there's a summer programme of guided walks and evening talks, discussions, films and slide shows.

There's an excellent website at **W** www .softrock.co.nz/apis.

About 150m from the visitors centre is the local *chapel* – make time for a visit and enjoy a lovely surprise inside.

Irie Tours (☎ *03-318 7669*) offers activities in the area including canyoning, rock climbing, abseiling and guided walks.

Arthur's Pass National Park

Day walks in the park offer 360° views of the snow-capped peaks. Many of these peaks are over 2000m, the highest being Mt Murchison (2400m). The park has huts on the tramping tracks and several areas suitable for camping. The day walks leaflet from the visitors centre lists half-day walks of one to four hours and day walks of five to eight hours. The three- to four-hour return walk to Temple Basin provides superb views of the surrounding peaks. For skiing at Temple Basin, see Skiing & Snowboarding in the Activities chapter.

Longer tramps with superb alpine scenery include the two-day **Goat Pass Track** and the difficult **Harman Pass** and **Harpers Pass Tracks**. Tracks require previous tramping experience: flooding can make the rivers dangerous to cross and the weather can be extreme; seek advice from DOC first.

Places to Stay & Eat

You can camp at the basic *public shelter* for $4 per person per night. It has stream water, a sink, tables and toilets. Camping is also available in the grounds of the *Arthur's Pass Alpine YHA* ($10 per person) and *Mountain House Backpackers* ($12 per person). Camping is free at *Klondyke Corner*, 8km east of Arthur's Pass, and *Kelleys Creek Shelter*, 17km west. Both have water, toilets and shelter.

From November to March, there is a high demand for all the available accommodation; it's advisable to book ahead.

Arthur's Pass Alpine YHA (☎ *03-318 9230*, **e** *yhaapass@yha.org.nz*) Dorm beds

RICHARD I'ANSON

Downtown Christchurch

RODNEY ZANDBERGS

Cathedral Square sculpture

DAVID WALL

Christ's College

DAVID WALL

International Antarctic Centre

FERGUS BLAKISTON

Whale mural in Kaikoura

Craigieburn ski-fields ticket office

Kaikoura pub, Canterbury

Akaroa Harbour, Canterbury

Cattle musterers with their working dogs, Dry Creek Station

$17, doubles & twins $40. The YHA is a small, laid-back and rustic hostel offering good walking information and free gear storage.

Mountain House Backpackers (☎ 03-318 9258, ☒ www.trampers.co.nz) Dorm beds $18-20. The lodge, across the road from the YHA, is an excellent choice, with a cosy feel and good facilities. The owners also have *Mountain House Cottages*, up behind the town. You can rent the comfy self-contained cottages as a whole (excellent value at $135, sleeping up to 10), or they can be used as share accommodation (singles $32, doubles & twins $49).

Alpine Motel (☎ 03-318 9233, ☒ alpine .motels@xtra.co.nz) Units $70-85. Tucked away in the southern part of town is this small complex of comfortable motel units.

The Chalet Accommodation (☎ 0800 506 550, 03-318 9236, ☒ www.arthurspass .co.nz) B&B doubles without/with en suite $110/120. This is the largest accommodation option in town with pleasant centrally-heated rooms with a TV. Downstairs the *Chalet Restaurant* is the best option for dinner, with the option of an à la carte restaurant or a cheaper bistro-bar. Meals range in price from about $13 to $28 and include pizza and pasta dishes at the cheaper end of the scale, and the likes of steak, venison and salmon at the upper end.

There are limited dining choices in Arthur's Pass. The *Arthur's Pass Store & Tearooms* (☎ 03-318 9235) offers simple fare like sandwiches and pies, and *Oscar's Haus* (☎ 03-318 9234) is a licensed cafe serving good-value meals (open until late in summer).

The Arthur's Pass Store has limited grocery supplies so it's worth stocking up in Christchurch or Greymouth beforehand.

Getting There & Around

Arthur's Pass is on the main run for buses between Christchurch ($25) and Greymouth ($20). Coast to Coast (☎ 0800 800 847), Atomic (☎ 03-322 8883) and Alpine Coaches (☎ 0800 274 888) stop here.

The *TranzAlpine* train (☎ 0800 802 802) runs between Christchurch and Greymouth

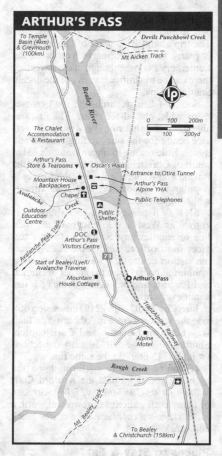

via Arthur's Pass. It leaves Arthur's Pass for Greymouth at 11.27am, for Christchurch at 4.30pm. Bus and train tickets are sold at the Arthur's Pass Store.

The road over the pass was once winding and very steep – the most tortuous of all the passes – but a new, spectacular **viaduct**, an engineering marvel in its own right, has removed many of the treacherous hairpin bends. It's slowly being extended to eliminate areas prone to rockfall.

Mountain House Taxi (☎ 03-318 9258) offers a transport service to the walking tracks and to Temple Basin ski field.

ASHBURTON
pop 15,800

The trip along SH1, south of Christchurch, is pretty flat and boring as you cross the Canterbury Plains, although in clear weather there can be magnificent views of the distant Southern Alps.

South of Christchurch, the road crosses many wide, glacial-fed rivers. The first sizable town is Ashburton, very much the service centre for the surrounding district, and there's little reason to linger long. It's 85km south of Christchurch and lies between the Rakaia and Rangitata Rivers (the former is popular for jetboating, the latter attracts white-water rafters).

SH1 as it passes through Ashburton is known as West St. Go east over the train line to parallel East St for the town's services (post office, banks etc). The Ashburton visitors centre (☎ 03-308 1064, W www .ashburton.co.nz) is on the corner of Burnett and East Sts and handles bookings for just about everything.

InterCity (☎ 03-308 8219) buses stop outside the visitors centre in Ashburton on their way between Dunedin and Christchurch. Shuttles such as South Island Connections (☎ 0508 742 669) do the same run.

If you're just driving through on the highway you'll go past the **Ashford Craft Village** (☎ 03-308 9085, 427 West St), one of many craft galleries in town and worth a look. There's a *cafe* here for a coffee break and snack.

Places to Stay & Eat

East St, in the northern part of town, is home to a string of mid-range motels and a good camping ground. ***Coronation Holiday Park*** (☎ 03-308 6603, 780 East St) has unpowered & powered sites for $20, backpackers beds for $18, cabins and tourist flats for $48 to $62 and motel units from $62 to $80. Next door, ***Academy Lodge Motel*** (☎ 03-308 5503, 782 East St) has clean and comfortable units from $75.

There are some good dining options, with the pick of them being *Jesters* (☎ 03-308 9983, 9 Mona Square) in an odd neighbourhood in the south of town, but worth seeking

out for its decor and well-priced, imaginative fare (eg, Moroccan seared tuna, pumpkin and pine nut lasagne, herb-crusted lamb, ostrich fillet). Dinner mains are $16 to $22; Monday to Friday lunches range from $7 to $13. *Cactus Jack's* (☎ 03-308 0495, 209 Wills St) is a friendly restaurant-bar offering more casual fare, including steaks, fajitas, burgers and pasta (mains $17 to $28).

METHVEN
pop 1070

Inland from Ashburton on SH77 is Methven, a good centre for the Canterbury Plains or the mountains. Methven is relatively quiet for most of the year, coming alive in winter when it fills up with skiers using it as a base for Mt Hutt and other ski areas. There are numerous year-round activities here too, including excellent hot-air ballooning, fishing and golf.

Information

The Methven visitors centre (☎ 0800 764 444, 03-302 8955, e methven@clear.net .nz) is on Main St and is open 7.30am to 8pm daily in winter, and 9am to 5pm Monday to Friday and 10am to 4.30pm Saturday and Sunday outside of the ski months. Helpful staff here make bookings for accommodation, skiing packages, transport and activities. See also the website W www .nz-holiday.co.nz/methven.

There's a Bank of New Zealand next to the visitors centre and The E-mail Centre (☎ 03-302 8700) is nearby, beside Big Al's Ski & Sport on Forest Drive.

Activities

It's **skiing** that has really set Methven on an upward growth curve. Nearby Mt Hutt offers five months of skiing (June to October), perhaps the longest ski season of any resort in NZ. See Skiing & Snowboarding in the Activities chapter for more details.

In Methven, **Big Al's Ski & Sport** (☎ 03-302 8003, W www.bigals.co.nz), located on the corner of Main St and Forest Drive, is the place to go for ski rental and advice. It also has golf clubs, mountain bikes and fishing gear for rent.

Methven Heliski (*☎ 03-302 8108,* **W** *www .heliskiing.co.nz; day trips $695*) operates from July to September and offers day trips that include five powder runs, guide service, safety equipment and lunch.

Black Diamond Safaris (*☎ 03-302 9696,* **W** *www.blackdiamondsafaris.co.nz*) offers winter trips to the uncrowded club ski fields in the area. Prices start at $40 for 4WD transport only; $95 gets you transport, a lift pass and lunch.

Mt Hutt Bungy (*☎ 03-302 9969; bungy $99*) offers unique bungy jumping on the mountain. It markets itself as 'NZ's highest bungy' – somewhat misleading as the jump is indeed at the highest altitude, but the bungy height doesn't top Nevis in Queenstown. In previous years it has operated only in winter but there's a possibility of an extended season; check first with the visitors centre.

The **Mt Hutt Forest**, an area of predominantly mountain beech, is 14km west of Methven. It's adjoined by the **Awa Awa Rata Reserve** and the **Pudding Hill Scenic Reserve**. There are two access roads available: Pudding Hill Rd leads to foot access for Pudding Hill Stream, and McLennan's Bush Rd leads to Pudding Hill Scenic Reserve and Awa Awa Rata Reserve. There are many **walking trails**: the Pudding Hill Stream Route, which requires many stream crossings, takes 2½ hours, and the Awa Awa Rata Reserve Loop Track takes 1½ hours.

The impressive **Rakaia River Gorge** is another nearby natural attraction, and there's a good, easy walk through farmland beside the river (three to four hours return). The walk begins at the car park just south of the bridge on Highway 77. **Rakaia Gorge Alpine Jet** (*☎ 03-318 6574*) and **Rakaia Gorge Scenic Jet** (*☎ 03-318 6515*) zip up to the Rakaia Gorge on jetboats for around $65 for 45 minutes.

Tandem Skydive (*☎ 025 321 135; 10,000ft dive $245*) offers jumps at Pudding Hill,

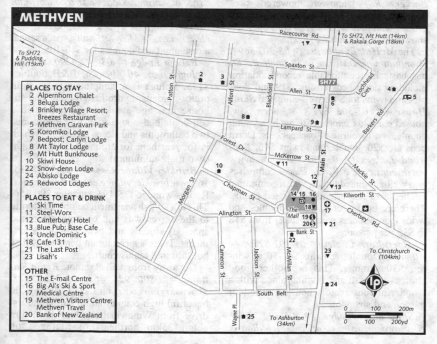

METHVEN

To SH72
& Pudding
Hill (15km)

Racecourse Rd

To SH72, Mt Hutt (14km)
& Rakaia Gorge (18km)

Spaxton St

SH77

Allen St

Lampard St

McKerrow St

Forest Dr

Chapman St

Alington St

The Mall

Bank St

South Belt

Patton St

Alford St

Blackford St

Morgan St

Cameron St

Jackson St

McMillan St

Wayne Pl

Lochhead Cres

Barkers Rd

Mackie St

Kilworth St

Chertsey Rd

To Christchurch
(104km)

To Ashburton
(34km)

PLACES TO STAY
2 Alpernhorn Chalet
3 Beluga Lodge
4 Brinkley Village Resort;
   Breezes Restaurant
5 Methven Caravan Park
6 Koromiko Lodge
7 Bedpost; Carlyn Lodge
8 Mt Taylor Lodge
9 Mt Hutt Bunkhouse
10 Skiwi House
22 Snow-denn Lodge
24 Abisko Lodge
25 Redwood Lodges

PLACES TO EAT & DRINK
1 Ski Time
11 Steel-Worx
12 Canterbury Hotel
13 Blue Pub; Base Cafe
14 Uncle Dominic's
18 Cafe 131
21 The Last Post
23 Lisah's

OTHER
15 The E-mail Centre
16 Big Al's Ski & Sport
17 Medical Centre
19 Methven Visitors Centre;
   Methven Travel
20 Bank of New Zealand

0   100   200m
0   100   200yd

15km from Methven. More sedate is a balloon flight organised through **Aoraki Hot Air Balloon Safaris** (☎ *03-302 8172*, ⓦ *www .nzballooning.com; flights $275*); the flights include a champagne breakfast and you'll enjoy spectacular views of the mountains and the plains.

Terrace Downs (☎ *0800 465 373*, ⓦ *www .terracedowns.co.nz*) is a 'high-country resort' with a world-class 18-hole golf course (green fees $80) about 25km out of town near Windwhistle on SH72.

Places to Stay

In winter Methven has some 2500 beds to cater for skiers on Mt Hutt, and many places have drying rooms and ski storage. Some places are closed in summer – the following are open year-round unless otherwise indicated, and usually offer discounted prices outside of the ski season. The visitors centre lists many more places.

Methven Caravan Park (☎ *03-302 8005, Barkers Rd*) Unpowered/powered sites $18/19, cabins $30. Methven is a basic ground with tired facilities and coin-operated showers, but it's central to town.

The *Mt Hutt Bunkhouse* (☎ *03-302 8894,* ⓔ *mthuttbunks@xtra.co.nz, 8 Lampard St*) has basic but comfortable accommodation including dorm beds costing $19 and doubles and twins for $46. Well-equipped *Skiwi House* (☎ *03-302 8772*, ⓦ *www.skiwi house.co.nz, 30 Chapman St*), run by a young couple, is a favourite of backpackers. Dorm beds are $20, doubles and twins $46. *Redwood Lodges* (☎ *03-302 8964*, ⓦ *www .methvennz.com, 5 Wayne Place*) comprises two well-appointed lodges with a communal kitchen area and brightly decorated rooms. There are bunk rooms, quads, doubles and twins (some rooms with en suite) from $18 to $35 per person.

Alpernhorn Chalet (☎ *03-302 8779, 44 Allen St*) Doubles & twins $44-50 in winter, $30 summer. This is another good choice – a small and inviting place with a wonderful conservatory housing an indoor garden and spa pool.

Snow-denn Lodge (☎ *03-302 8999,* ⓔ *snowdenn@xtra.co.nz, cnr McMillan &*

Bank Sts) Dorm beds $30/25 winter/summer, doubles & twins without/with en suite $80/100 winter, $60/70 in summer. This central lodge is modern and spacious and features wonderful kitchen-dining-living areas. It's YHA affiliated: YHA members get a discount.

Bedpost (☎ *03-302 8508*, ⓔ *beds@xtra .co.nz, 177 Main St*) Motel units $65/85 winter/summer. The Bedpost has spacious, well-appointed motel units with full kitchen and private laundry. Larger units can sleep up to eight ($16 per additional person) and are a good deal for families or groups. Next door is *Carlyn Lodge*, a backpackers lodge with dorms, doubles and twins priced from $16 to $20 per person.

Small, friendly and comfortable hotel-style lodges include *Mt Taylor Lodge* (☎ *03-302 9699*, ⓦ *www.mounttaylorlodge.co.nz, 32 Lampard St*), a stylish new place with a lovely lounge and doubles for $130/100 winter/summer; *Koromiko Lodge* (☎ *03-302 8165*, ⓔ *koromiko.lodge@xtra.co.nz, Main St*), with good B&B doubles for $95/75; and *Abisko Lodge* (☎ *03-302 8875*, ⓔ *abisko@ clear.net.nz, 74 Main St*), with a spa, a sauna, a restaurant and doubles for $80-105.

Beluga Lodge (☎ *03-302 8290*, ⓦ *www .beluga.co.nz, 40 Allen St*) B&B doubles $175. Beluga is a sumptuous lodge with pretty gardens, hydrotherapy pool and in-house massage available. There's also a self-contained house with four bedrooms, two bathrooms and sleeps up to nine, which is for rent here for around $350 per night (two night minimum).

Brinkley Village Resort (☎ *03-302 8885*, ⓦ *www.brinkleyvillage.co.nz, Barkers Rd*) Rooms winter $125-195, summer $90-150. This is a stylish apartment complex catering to the ski crowds and offering clean and spacious studios and two-bedroom apartments. There's a restaurant here, as well as hot tubs and tennis court.

Get away from it all at remote *Ryton Station* (☎ *0800 926 868, 03-318 5818*, ⓦ *www.ryton.co.nz*) on Lake Coleridge, in beautiful high country about half an hour's drive from Windwhistle (which is in turn about 25km northeast of Methven on

SH72). A variety of accommodation options are offered, including lakeside wilderness camping for $5 per site; dinner, bed and breakfast packages in chalets by the homestead for $100 per person; and a lodge with shared facilities including guest kitchen for $20 per person (linen additional). There are great activities on or near the station including fishing, walking, horse riding, mountain biking and golf.

Places to Eat

The main shopping centre has a selection of food providers, including *Uncle Dominic's* (☎ *03-302 8237)* for good takeaway meals of pizza, kebabs and souvlaki, and the cosy and inviting *Cafe 131* (☎ *03-302 9131)*, serving great breakfasts, lunch and afternoon teas.

Methven has two pubs: the *Canterbury Hotel* (☎ *03-302 8045, cnr Main St & Forest Drive)*, known as the Brown Pub, and the famous *Blue Pub* (☎ *03-302 8046)* opposite. The former is more the locals' pub, the latter is where the skiers congregate (there's often footage of the day's action on the mountain shown in the bar here). Both places serve solid, no-frills pub meals (the Brown Pub features an excellent $11 roast, costing only $7.50 at lunch time). The *Base Cafe* (☎ *03-302 9049)* at the Blue Pub offers more stylish fare.

The following restaurants do a roaring trade nightly in winter but are often open only three to five nights a week in summer – it's worth calling in advance to check they're open before you set out.

Lisah's (☎ *03-302 8070, Main St)* Mains under $20. Popular, BYO Lisah's has good-value dishes in a relaxed setting. Try the penne with avocado, pumpkin and pine nuts or the heartier steak and lamb dishes.

Ski Time (☎ *03-302 8398, Racecourse Rd)* Mains $15-25. This lovely lodge is north of town and has great food served in a dining room featuring a large open fire. Choices include good-value pizza and salad, plus fancier dishes like grilled salmon on a risotto of lemon, zucchini and peas.

Breezes (☎ *03-302 8885)* at Brinkley Village is a classy restaurant covering all bases well – vegetable, fish, chicken, lamb, steak and even ostrich dishes are in the $16 to $24 price range.

Many more restaurants and bars open in winter. *Ski Time* (see above), *Steel-worx* (☎ *03-302 9900, 36 Forest Drive)* and *The Last Post* (☎ *03-302 8259, Main St)* are extremely popular, but the last two are most likely closed in summer.

Getting There & Around

Methven Travel (☎ *0800 684 888, 03-302 8106)*, based at the visitors centre, picks up from Christchurch city and airport and will drop you off at your accommodation for about $25; other companies also offer this service during the ski season.

InterCity (☎ *03-379 9020)* has daily buses between Methven and Christchurch for $20.

Many shuttles operate to Mt Hutt ski field in winter for around $20; inquiries and pick-ups are from the visitors centre.

MT SOMERS

Mt Somers is a small settlement about 1km off Highway 72, the main road between Geraldine and Mt Hutt. The 17km, 10-hour **Mt Somers Subalpine Walkway** traverses the northern face of Mt Somers, linking the popular picnic spots of Sharplin Falls and Woolshed Creek. The highlights include volcanic formations, Maori rock drawings, deep river canyons and a variety of plant life. There are two huts, the Pinnacles and Mt Somers, on the walk. Be warned that this route is subject to sudden changes in weather and all tramping precautions should be taken. Hut tickets and information are available at the well-stocked general store (☎ *03-303 9831)* on Pattons Rd in Mt Somers township.

Also in the township is the small and well-kept *Mt Somers Holiday Park* (☎ *03-303 9719)*, with unpowered/powered sites for $16/18, standard cabins for $32 and en suite cabins for $48 (all prices for two people).

On SH72 at the turn-off to Mt Somers is Swiss-run *Stronechrubie* (☎ *03-303 9814,* Ⓦ *www.stronechrubie.co.nz)*, with pleasant accommodation set in lovely gardens and an intimate, award-winning restaurant. One reader was clearly impressed, writing that 'this is the kind of restaurant that you drive 100km to dine in rather than choose a sub-standard place!' It serves superb meals (mains $25 to $30) and is open for dinner Wednesday to Sunday; bookings are essential. Individual studio chalets here cost $80, spacious two-bedroom chalets are $120 for four people. There's also an excellent offer of $180 for dinner, bed and continental breakfast for two.

South Canterbury

TEMUKA
pop 3950

In 1853 William Hornbrook settled on his run Arowhenua, on the south bank of the Temuka River. His wife settled there a year later. Arowhenua had long been a pa site of the Ngai Tahu people. Their earth ovens, *te umu kaha* (the fierce ovens), gave Te-umu-kaha, later Temuka, its name.

The site of pioneer aviator Richard Pearse's first attempted flight and a replica of his plane are out on Main Waitohi Rd, 13.5km from Temuka towards Hanging Rock Bridge (see the boxed text 'Flights of Fancy' in this chapter).

Five kilometres south of Waitohi and towards Fairlie, **Pleasant Point** has an interesting **railway museum** (☎ *03-614 8323; adult/child $5/2.50*) at the old train station and a collection of steam locomotives and carriages that run along 3km of track on most Sundays and holidays.

Temukas visitors centre (☎ 03-615 9537) is inside the library at 72 King St.

Temuka Holiday Park *(☎ 03-615 7241,* e *temukaholiday@xtra.co.nz, 1 Fergusson Drive)*, off Domain Rd, is a large, well-maintained park set among sporting grounds with unpowered/powered sites for $18/19 and cabins for $30 to $40. There are also a handful of motels in town, including ***Benny's Getaway Motel*** *(☎ 03-615 8004, 54 King St)* with comfortable one-bedroom units for $69. Along King St are pubs offering cheap meals and accommodation, plus cafes and a number of takeaways.

About 7km north of Temuka on the highway at Winchester is the elegant ***Kavanagh House*** *(☎ 03-615 6150,* W *www.kavanagh house.co.nz)*, with a restaurant featuring cafe fare during the day and a-la-carte dining of an evening, plus two luxurious B&B rooms costing $247.

TIMARU
pop 27,350

Timaru is a thriving port city and also a convenient stopping point halfway between Christchurch and Dunedin.

Timaru comes from the Maori name Te Maru, meaning 'The Place of Shelter', but no permanent settlement existed when the first Europeans, the Weller brothers of Sydney, set up a whaling station in 1839. The *Caroline,* a sailing ship that picked up whale oil, gave the picturesque bay its name.

The town really began to boom when a landing service was established at the foot of Strathallan St. It was moved in 1868 to George St and is now a restaurant. After about 30 vessels were wrecked attempting to berth near Timaru between the mid-1860s and 1880s, an artificial harbour was built. The result is today's excellent port and Caroline Bay's beach, a result of the construction of breakwaters. The port is an important shipping point for the surrounding agricultural region.

Orientation & Information

SH1 is a road of many names as it passes through Timaru – the Hilton Highway north of town, Evans St as it enters town and then Theodosia St and Craigie Ave as it bypasses the central business district, located around Stafford St. Continuing south, the highway becomes King St and then SH1 again as it emerges from town.

The Timaru visitors centre (☎ 03-688 6163, W www.timaru.com and W www .southisland.org.nz for the region), is at 14 George St, diagonally across from the train station. It has enthusiastic staff and is open 8.30am to 5pm Monday to Friday and 10am to 3pm Saturday and Sunday. Pick up a street map and information on walks in and around the town.

Flights of Fancy

Oh, what a cute puppy!

Richard Pearse (1877–1953), a farmer and inventor, was born at Waitohi, northwest of Timaru. Once known to locals as 'Mad Pearse' and 'Bamboo Dick' (because he employed bamboo in his inventions), he may well have been the first human to fly in a heavier-than-air machine.

Pearse was a shy loner happy to tinker away in his shed building aircraft with homemade tools. His first plane, 8m wide, was constructed of scrap metal and bamboo braced by wire and powered by a simple two-cylinder engine which he designed himself; underneath were bicycle wheels.

It's reputed that he first flew about 1km in 1902 or 1903 before ignominiously crash-landing in gorse near the Ophir River. The flight was supposedly witnessed by several people, but no exact date has been ascertained. Many believe his attempts were before the Wright brothers flew at Kittyhawk, North Carolina, on 17 December 1903.

Pearse disappeared into obscurity and he died a recluse in a psychiatric hospital in Christchurch. Interest in his inventions escalated after his death and he is remembered in Auckland's Museum of Transport & Technology and in the Timaru Museum (where there is a reconstruction of his first aircraft). There's also a memorial at the point where his first flight commenced. If only they had filmed the event – Pearse's achievement will probably never be proven.

For pricey Internet access, go to either Bay City Internet (☎ 03-688 6554), 47a Stafford St, or the cybercafe in the cinema (☎ 03-684 6987) at 25 Canon St.

Things to See & Do

One of the few safe, sheltered beaches on the east coast is **Caroline Bay**, and its Christmas carnival, beginning on 26 December and running for about 10 days, is a lot of fun and attracts quite a crowd. The park along the beach has a walk-through aviary, a maze, a pleasant walkway and other attractions, including a landscaped piazza. A good walk heads north from town along Caroline Bay, past the Benvenue Cliffs and on to the Dashing Rocks and rock pools at the northern end of the bay. Caroline Bay is sheltered and calm but there's good **surfing** not far south

of the town centre (east of the hospital at Patiti Point), where you might also see sea lions. An easy 45-minute walk around the bay is outlined in a map available from the visitors centre. Also of note are the town's **Botanic Gardens** *(open 8am-dusk daily)*, entered from Queen St.

The **South Canterbury Museum** *(☎ 03-684 2212, Perth St; admission free; open 10am-4.30pm Tues-Fri, 1.30pm-4.30pm Sat & Sun)* is the main regional museum, with exhibits on the whalers and early settlers. One fascinating exhibit is a replica of the aeroplane designed and flown by Richard Pearse (see the boxed text 'Flights of Fancy').

Over 900 works of art, plus changing exhibits, feature at the **Aigantighe Art Gallery** *(☎ 03-688 4424, 49 Wai-iti Rd; admission*

CANTERBURY

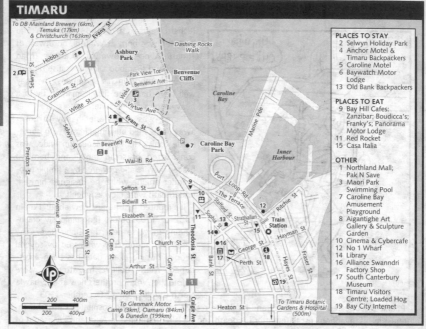

TIMARU

To DB Mainland Brewery (6km),
Temuka (17km)
& Christchurch (163km)

Evans St

Dashing Rocks
Walk

Hobbs St

Ashbury
Park

Park View Tce

Benvenue Ave

Benvenue
Cliffs

Te Weka St

Grasmere St

Selwyn St

White St

Virtue Ave

Caroline
Bay

Evans St

Beverley Rd

Caroline Bay
Park

Inner
Harbour

Wai-iti Rd

Preston St

Avenue Rd

Wilson St

Le Cren St

Sefton St

Bidwill St

Elizabeth St

Port Loop Rd

The Terrace

Stafford St

Marine Pde

Ritchie St

Strathallan St

Sophia St

Theodosia St

Bank St

Grey Rd

Church St

George St

Perth St

Caroige Ave

Arthur St

North St

Train
Station

Hayman Rd

Hayes St

Fraser St

Heaton St

To Glenmark Motor
Camp (3km), Oamaru (84km)
& Dunedin (199km)

To Timaru Botanic
Gardens & Hospital
(500m)

0   200   400m
0   200   400yd

PLACES TO STAY
2 Selwyn Holiday Park
4 Anchor Motel &
   Timaru Backpackers
5 Caroline Motel
6 Baywatch Motor
   Lodge
13 Old Bank Backpackers

PLACES TO EAT
9 Bay Hill Cafes:
   Zanzibar; Boudicca's;
   Franky's; Panorama
   Motor Lodge
11 Red Rocket
15 Casa Italia

OTHER
1 Northland Mall;
   Pak N Save
3 Maori Park
   Swimming Pool
7 Caroline Bay
   Amusement
   Playground
8 Aigantighe Art
   Gallery & Sculpture
   Garden
10 Cinema & Cybercafe
12 No 1 Wharf
14 Library
16 Alliance Swanndri
   Factory Shop
17 South Canterbury
   Museum
18 Timaru Visitors
   Centre; Loaded Hog
19 Bay City Internet

---

free; open 10am-4pm Tues-Fri & noon-4pm Sat & Sun). There's a also lovely sculpture garden here.

The **DB Mainland Brewery** (☎ *03-688 2059, Sheffield St)*, 6km north of town, has free tours at 10.30am Monday to Friday (bookings necessary). Enclosed footwear (ie, no sandals) must be worn.

Fans of the 'Swannie', the check woollen shirt famed throughout NZ, should flock to the **Alliance Swanndri Factory Shop** (☎ *03-684 9037, 24 Church St; open 10am-4pm Mon-Fri, 10am-3pm Sat).* Other woollen clothing, duvets and oilskins (all high-quality seconds) are also sold and the items are cheaper here than anywhere else.

Timaru Marine Cruises (☎ *03-688 6881)* operates cruises out of the port from October to April and a variety of marine wildlife is usually seen, including Hectors dolphins. Cruises last about 1½ hours and cost $40; they depart from the Number 1 Wharf at the corner of Port Loop Rd and Ritchie St.

Places to Stay

Selwyn Holiday Park (☎ *03-684 7690, ℮ topten@timaruholidaypark.co.nz, Selwyn St)* Unpowered/powered sites $20/21 for 2, cabins $34-58, motel units $70. Two kilometres north of the town centre, this large, well-equipped park has good facilities and a variety of accommodation options.

Glenmark Motor Camp (☎ *03-684 3682, Beaconsfield Rd)* Unpowered/powered sites $16/18 for 2 people, cabins $28-45. Peaceful Glenmark is 3km south of Timaru town centre and is a well-maintained ground with a swimming pool.

Anchor Motel & Timaru Backpackers (☎ *03-684 5067, 44 Evans St)* Dorm beds $17, twins & doubles $40, motel units $60. The YHA-affiliated backpackers here is a very small, cosy and well-equipped place and the management goes out of its way to look after you (they will pick you up from the station). The older-style motel units are comfortable and well appointed.

Old Bank Backpackers (☎ 03-684 4392, 232 Stafford St) Dorm beds $14-16, doubles $40, some with en suite. Located above the Old Bank cafe and bar in the centre of town, this small backpackers offers basic rooms and minimal kitchen facilities.

Timaru has numerous motels, especially along Evans St (SH1) at the northern end of town. *Caroline Motel (☎ 03-684 4155, 46-48 Evans St)* has good, clean units from $75, *Baywatch Motor Lodge (☎ 03-688 1886, 7 Evans St)* is more upmarket and has units – some with sea views – from $98. *Panorama Motor Lodge (☎ 03-688 0097, 52 Bay Hill)* has a good location behind the cafes of Bay Hill and offers comfortable modern units from $85.

The visitors centre has details of B&Bs and farmstays in the area.

Places to Eat

Loaded Hog (☎ 03-684 9999, 2 George St) Lunch $5-17, dinner mains under $20. Located in the former Landing Service building adjacent to the visitors centre, this casual restaurant and bar serves large portions of good food and excellent boutique brews. The $5 lunch deal is exceptional value, with dishes on offer including nachos, stuffed spuds, paninis and quiche and salad.

Red Rocket (☎ 03-688 8313, 4 Elizabeth St) Pizzas $12-21. In a converted old church you'll find this funky pizzeria and bar. There are traditional and gourmet pizzas available, with toppings including satay chicken and a good vegie option. There are simple pasta dishes available, and the coffee is excellent.

Casa Italia (☎ 03-684 5528, 2 Strathallan St) Mains $18-30. Located in a beautiful historic building, the highly acclaimed Casa Italia has an excellent wine list and serves authentic Italian food in elegant dining rooms. Pizza, pasta and risotto mains are around $18; more expensive dishes like venison and fish are in the $23 to $30 price range.

The Bay Hill area is home to three good places that overlook the bay. *Zanzibar (☎ 03-688 4367)* is a bright and airy watering hole, *Boudicca's (☎ 03-688 8550)* is a cosy cafe and wine bar with a good kebab selection, and *Franky's (☎ 03-688 0568)* is a colourful cafe. All three are popular and feature all-day menus plus dinner selections. Check out the atmosphere of each and the menus in the windows before making a decision. This area is also a good spot for evening drinks.

Getting There & Away

The visitors centre is the best place for transport inquiries and bookings. InterCity buses stop at the train station on the Christchurch to Dunedin and Invercargill routes. Numerous shuttle buses between Christchurch and Dunedin, such as Catch-a-Bus (☎ 03-453 1480) and Atomic (☎ 03-322 8883), also pass through Timaru. The average fare to Christchurch or Dunedin is $20. There's also the Cook Connection (☎ 025 583 211), with useful services three times weekly from October to April between Timaru and Mt Cook ($45, discounts for backpackers) via Fairlie, Lake Tekapo and Twizel. On alternate days it connects Mt Cook and Oamaru.

TO THE MACKENZIE COUNTRY

Those heading to Queenstown and the southern lakes from Christchurch will probably turn off SH1 onto SH79. This scenic route passes through the small towns of Geraldine and Fairlie before joining with SH8, which heads over Burkes Pass to Lake Tekapo.

Geraldine

pop 2325

Geraldine is a picturesque town with a country village atmosphere. It's noted for its pretty private gardens and active craft scene. There's a helpful visitors centre (☎ 03-693 1006, ⓔ information@geraldine.co.nz) on Talbot St, open 8am to 5.30am Monday to Friday and 10am to 4pm Saturday and Sunday.

The **Vintage Car Club & Machinery Museum** *(☎ 03-693 8756, 178 Talbot St; adult/child $5/free; open 10am-4pm daily from late Oct-early June, Sat & Sun in winter)* has over 30 vintage and veteran cars from 1907 onward. A huge shed at the back houses tractors dating from 1912.

CANTERBURY

Three Great Champions

The Timaru region has produced three great sporting champions – two human, the third a horse.

In the centre of Timaru, next to the ANZ Bank, is a statue of Robert Fitzsimmons, three-time world boxing champion with a record barely matched today. Fitzsimmons was born in 1862 and developed his impressive physique at his father's blacksmith's forge. He defeated Jack Dempsey (the Irish Jack Dempsey, not the illustrious 1920s American boxer of the same name) in 1891 to take the world middleweight crown and then Jim Corbett in 1897 in 14 rounds to win the heavyweight crown (held until 1899). Four years later, he took the world light-heavyweight championship. He died in 1917, three years after the last of his 350 or so professional bouts.

Dr John Edward (Jack) Lovelock, born in 1910, was the world record holder for the one mile. In 1936, in front of a crowd of 120,000 at the Berlin Olympics, he broke the record for the 1500m and took the gold medal. Hitler presented him with an oak tree, which is still growing in the grounds of Timaru Boys' High School on North St.

The racecourse at Washdyke is named after NZ's most famous galloper, Phar Lap, who was born at nearby Seadown. In the late 1920s and early 1930s Phar Lap swept all challengers before him. After winning Australia's top horse race, the Melbourne Cup, in 1930, he was taken to the USA, where he continued his winning streak. There he died, apparently poisoned, soon after winning the richest race in the world, the Agua Caliente Handicap in Mexico. Despite racing in the Depression years, Phar Lap was for many years the greatest stakes winner in the world. Today, Phar Lap's stuffed skin is held by the Melbourne Museum in Australia, his skeleton is in Te Papa in Wellington, and his heart is preserved at the National Museum of Australia in Canberra.

Buses between Christchurch and Queenstown usually stop in Geraldine, and the **Berry Barn Complex** on the corner of Cox and Talbot Sts caters well to passers-by with a bakery, cafes, souvenir shop and cheese shop (head here for wonderful ice cream). Also of interest is the **Barker's store**, selling excellent fruit products such as juices, sauces and jams.

Places to Stay & Eat There are basic DOC camping grounds in this region, at *Orari Gorge (Yates Rd)*, 12km northwest of Geraldine, and *Waihi Gorge (Waihi Gorge Rd)*, 14km northwest of Geraldine, with good swimming spots and picnic areas.

Geraldine Motor Camp (☎ 03-693 8147, e geraldine.motor.camp@xtra.co.nz, Hislop St) Unpowered/powered $18/20 for 2, cabins $30, new self-contained units $55. This small, well-maintained ground is set in lovely parkland (lots of trees) very central to town.

Olde Presbytery Backpackers (☎ 03-693 9644, e pkoelet@hotmail.com, 13 Jollie St) Dorm beds $18, singles $24, doubles & twins $44. This is a lovely, small, homestay backpackers with very friendly owners. The setting is great too – a large garden with a creek running through it. Prices also include bed linen.

Crown Hotel (☎ 03-693 8458, e geraldine-crown@xtra.co.nz, 31 Talbot St) Singles $60, doubles & twins $70-80. Above the large, renovated pub you'll find clean, comfortable, en suite rooms and a big guest balcony. Cheaper single rooms ($40) have TV, tea and coffee facilities and washbasins, but shared bathroom.

Geraldine Motels (☎ 0800 400 404, 03-693 8501, 97 Talbot St) Units $55-68. One of only a few motels in town, this central place has cheaper, older-style units plus three brand new and very comfortable studios.

The *Berry Barn Bakery* has good, cheap fare and is ideal for a quick pit-stop. *Plums Cafe (☎ 03-693 9770, 44 Talbot St)* is the perfect spot for a well-prepared lunch to linger over. *Geraldine Fish Supply (☎ 03-693 8441, 8 Wilson St)* does good fish and chips and other takeaway food. Of an evening, the *Totara Restaurant (☎ 03-693*

8458, 31 Talbot St), inside the Crown Hotel, has a range of meals, including pizza, pasta and assorted meat dishes, priced from $16 to $25. Just down the road is the *Village Inn* (☎ *03-693 8458, 41 Talbot St)*, a casual eatery with a pleasant outdoor area and meals in the $9 to $20 price range.

Peel Forest

The Peel Forest, 19km north of Geraldine and signposted off SH72, is one of NZ's most important areas of indigenous podocarp (conifer) forest. Mt Peel station is nearby and the road from it leads to Mesopotamia, the run of the English writer Samuel Butler (author of the satire *Erewhon*) in the 1860s.

Get information, including the *Peel Forest Park: Track Information* brochure ($1), at the *Peel Forest Store* (☎ *03-696 3567,* e *peelforest@xtra.co.nz)*, open seven days. The store has petrol, groceries, takeaway food and tearooms and also manages the excellent *DOC camping ground* on the banks of the Rangitata River, about 3km beyond the store. Camping prices are adult/child $6.50/3 plus an extra $2.50 for power, while accommodation in basic cabins costs $15/6. Facilities include kitchen, showers, card phone and laundry.

The magnificent native podocarp forest consists of totara, kahikatea and matai. One fine example of totara on the **Big Tree Walk** is 9m in circumference and over 1000 years old. Bird life attracted to this forest includes the rifleman, NZ pigeon *(kereru)*, bellbird, fantail and grey warbler. There are also picturesque waterfalls in the park – Emily Falls (1½ hours return walk), Rata Falls (two hours) and Acland Falls (one hour).

Mt Peel-based **Rangitata Rafts** (☎ *0800 251 251,* w *www.rafts.co.nz)* operates whitewater rafting on the Rangitata River. Rangitata Gorge is one of the best white-water rafting areas because of the exhilarating grade V rapids at all water levels. The company's base is at Mt Peel, about 11km past the camping ground, and there's budget accommodation here (you can get a basic bunk bed for $12, doubles for $34). The rafting trip is $130 per person, including lunch beforehand and a post-trip barbecue and hot shower; the time actually spent on the river is about three hours. Also included is return transport from Christchurch if required.

Fairlie
pop 845

Fairlie is often described as 'the gateway to the Mackenzie' because, just west of here, the landscape changes dramatically as the road mounts Burkes Pass to the open spaces of the Mackenzie Country. A few minutes' drive west of Fairlie is the historic limestone **woolshed** *(admission $5)* of the Three Springs Sheep Station, with good displays and a small cafe.

Nearby skiing is at **Fox Peak** in the Two Thumb Range, 37km northwest of Fairlie, a club ski area. **Mt Dobson**, 26km northwest of Fairlie, is in a basin 3km wide (for information see Skiing & Snowboarding in the Activities chapter). The Ski Shack (☎ 03-685 8088) on Main Rd is the place for gear rental and information.

The Resource Centre (☎ 03-685 8496, w www.fairlie.co.nz), at 64 Main St, acts as a visitors centre but is open Monday to Friday only. If closed, its windows usually display town information, or you can head to the eateries listed here to pick up brochures. Buses and shuttles pass through town on the Christchurch-Queenstown route.

Places to Stay & Eat A 'bed for every budget' is offered at the shady and well-kept *Fairlie Top 10 Holiday Park* (☎ *03-685 8375, 10 Allandale Rd)*, with unpowered and powered sites $20 for two, cabins from $32 to $42 and spacious and modern self-contained units for $60.

Fairlie Flash (☎ *03-685 8116, 7 School Rd)* has basic budget accommodation open in winter only and caters primarily to skiers. Just up the road, *Fairlie Lodge* (☎ *03-685 8452, 16 School Rd)* has good-value motel units for only $50. *Rimuwhare Country Retreat* (☎ *03-685 8058, 53 Mt Cook Rd)* has a licensed restaurant and motel units set in pretty gardens for $65.

The *Sunflower Centre* (☎ *03-685 8258, 31 Main St)* serves cheap and wholesome vegetarian food. The acclaimed *Old Library Cafe Bar* (☎ 03-685 8999, 6 Allandale Rd) is easily the pick of the town's eateries and is a great spot for coffee, snacks and well-prepared main meals.

THE MACKENZIE COUNTRY

The high country from which the Mt Cook park rises is known as the Mackenzie Country after the legendary James 'Jock' McKenzie (nobody's sure why the region and the chap himself have different spelling), who is said to have run his stolen flocks in this uninhabited region around 1843. When he was finally caught, other settlers realised the potential of the land and followed in his footsteps. The first people to traverse the Mackenzie were the Maori, who used to trek from Banks Peninsula to Otago hundreds of years ago.

Lake Tekapo
pop 295

The small settlement at the southern end of Lake Tekapo has sweeping views across the turquoise lake with the hills and snow-capped mountains as a backdrop. The turquoise colour of the lake is created by 'rock flour', finely ground particles of rock held in suspension in the glacial melt water. Tekapo derives its name from *taka* (sleeping mat) and *po* (night).

Lake Tekapo is a popular first stop on a tour of the Southern Alps. The buses heading to or from Mt Cook or Queenstown stop at the cluster of tourist shops by the main road and create chaos when they arrive.

Kiwi Treasure (☎ 03-680 6686), next to the petrol station in the string of stores and cafes on SH8, acts as a visitors centre and booking office.

The picturesque little **Church of the Good Shepherd** beside the lake was built of stone and oak in 1935. Further along is a statue of a collie dog, a touching tribute to the sheepdogs which helped develop the Mackenzie Country. It's not, as a lot of people believe, Jock McKenzie's dog Friday. It's a good idea to visit after the last bus leaves, otherwise the place is swarming with people.

Activities Popular activities around Lake Tekapo include walking, fishing, boating, skiing, cycling and horse trekking. The Godley Resort Hotel (see Places to Stay) rents out bikes, fishing rods, golf clubs and kayaks. **Lake Tekapo Adventures & Cruises** (☎ 0800 528 624) organises activities ranging from 4WD safaris to fishing and lake cruises (cruises from $30). **Mackenzie Alpine Trekking Company** (☎ 0800 628 269, 03-680 6760) offers horse riding starting at $40 for one hour.

In winter, Lake Tekapo is a base for downhill skiing at Mt Dobson or Round Hill, or cross-country skiing on Two Thumb Range. There's ski area transport and ski hire in season. Lake Tekapo also has an open-air ice-skating rink, open from June to September.

The region has a number of good **walks**. Most popular is the three-hour walk to the summit of Mt John from just beyond the camping ground (there are two options – direct or via the lake shore). From there you can continue on to Alexandrina and McGregor Lakes, an all-day walk. Other walks are detailed in the *Lake Tekapo Walkway* brochure ($1).

Alpine Recreation (☎ 03-680 6736, W www.alpinerecreation.co.nz) organises mountaineering and climbing courses and guided treks in the Mt Cook National Park. The challenging three-day Ball Pass Trek is $650 per person.

Air Safaris (☎ 0800 806 880, W www.air safaris.co.nz) operates aerial sightseeing flights from Lake Tekapo over Mt Cook and its glaciers priced at $230/150 adult/child for 50 minutes. The flights don't land on the glacier, but Air Safaris' spectacular 'Grand Traverse' takes you up the Tasman Glacier, over the upper part of the Fox and Franz Josef Glaciers, and by Mts Cook, Tasman and Elie de Beaumont. Air Safaris operates a similar flight from Glentanner, near Mt Cook, for the same price. These flights offer the most comprehensive aerial coverage of the national park, including the Godley River.

Tekapo Helicopters (☎ 0800 359 835) provides scenic helicopter flights from $175

LAKE TEKAPO

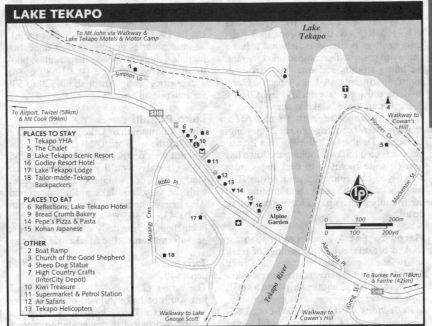

Lake Tekapo

To Mt John via Walkway & Lake Tekapo Motels & Motor Camp

To Airport, Twizel (58km) & Mt Cook (99km)

SH8

Simpson La

Pioneer Dr

Walkway to Cowan's Hill

Mackenzie St

Roto Pl

Aorangi Cres

Alpine Garden

Tekapo River

Alexandra Pl

Greig St

SH8

To Burkes Pass (18km) & Fairlie (42km)

Walkway to Lake George Scott

Walkway to Cowan's Hill

0   100   200m
0   100   200yd

PLACES TO STAY
1 Tekapo YHA
5 The Chalet
8 Lake Tekapo Scenic Resort
16 Godley Resort Hotel
17 Lake Tekapo Lodge
18 Tailor-made-Tekapo Backpackers

PLACES TO EAT
6 Reflections; Lake Tekapo Hotel
9 Bread Crumb Bakery
14 Pepe's Pizza & Pasta
15 Kohan Japanese

OTHER
2 Boat Ramp
3 Church of the Good Shepherd
4 Sheep Dog Statue
7 High Country Crafts (InterCity Depot)
10 Kiwi Treasure
11 Supermarket & Petrol Station
12 Air Safaris
13 Tekapo Helicopters

for 25 minutes (including a snow landing). The 45-minute option costs $310 and includes an icefield landing and viewings of Mt Cook and the glaciers.

Places to Stay In an exceptionally pretty setting by the lake, *Lake Tekapo Motels & Motor Camp* (☎ 0800 853 853, 03-680 6825) is a well-maintained spacious, camping ground with good facilities and an array of quality accommodation options. Unpowered & powered sites cost $20 for two people, cabins $33, tourist flats $60 and motel units from $85.

Tekapo YHA (☎ 03-680 6857, e yha tekapo@yha.org.nz) Camp sites $10 per person, dorm beds $16-17, twins & doubles $42. Tekapo YHA is a well-equipped, friendly little place. Its living room has open fireplaces and awesome views across the lake to the mountains beyond. There are limited camp sites here, and bicycles can be hired for $15 per day.

Tailor-made-Tekapo Backpackers (☎ 03-680 6700, e tailor-made-backpackers@xtra .co.nz, 9 Aorangi Crescent) Dorm beds $18, doubles & twins $40, en suite doubles $48. Spread out in a few buildings set in pretty gardens well away from the lake, this well-run backpackers has good, clean rooms – lots of twins and doubles and no bunks.

Godley Resort Hotel (☎ 03-680 6848, w www.thegodley.com) Rooms $70-145. Godley Resort is the largest hotel in town, favoured by tour groups. It has a range of options, from older-style budget rooms to smarter refurbished rooms with lake views. Facilities are good and include a pool, restaurant and sports gear for hire. There are B&B and DB&B options available.

Lake Tekapo Scenic Resort (☎ 03-680 6808, w www.laketekapo.com) Units $130-200. This resort is a centrally located, new complex of attractive, modern studio and family units. You'll find it down the small road beside the bakery.

The Chalet (☎ *03-680 6774*, e *speck@ clear.net.nz, 14 Pioneer Drive)* Apartments $110-165. Right on the lakefront, the Chalet calls itself a 'boutique motel' and it has a variety of great self-contained units for rent, including studios and one- and two-bedroom apartments. All are spacious and modern and have wonderful bright decor. Some feature superb lake views.

Lake Tekapo Lodge (☎ *03-680 6566*, w *www.laketekapolodge.co.nz, 24 Aorangi Crescent)* Doubles $200-295. This luxurious B&B on a hill overlooking the town has four en suite rooms with deck areas from which you can enjoy the great vistas. The decor is lovely, the guest areas inviting, and the friendly owners pay a lot of attention to detail.

Places to Eat A good cheap option for cooked breakfasts and all manner of fresh sandwiches, pies and pastries is *Bread Crumb Bakery*. There are also a few takeaways scattered along the strip, and a small *supermarket*.

Reflections (☎ *03-680 6808)* Lunch $5-12, dinner $14-24. Enjoy the good views here at the bistro section of the Lake Tekapo Hotel. Reflections offers good-value lunches and a range of dinner options, from light meals such as pasta to more hearty fare like fish, venison and lamb shanks.

Pepe's Pizza & Pasta (☎ *03-680 6677)* Pasta $13, pizzas $15.50. A brand new addition to the dining scene, popular Pepe's is a cosy place with a stylish bar and booths. There's a small but good menu featuring simple pasta favourites and pizza with gourmet toppings such as venison and roast tomato or chicken, cranberry and brie.

Kohan Japanese (☎ *03-680 6688)* Dishes $18-24. Down a path beside the Godley is this large Japanese restaurant built to cater to the passing tour-bus trade. It offers a full range of sushi treats plus dishes such as teriyaki chicken and tempura seafood, but has truly clinical decor.

Getting There & Away InterCity southbound services to Queenstown, Wanaka and Mt Cook come through daily, as do the northbound services to Christchurch. The InterCity booking office is at High Country Crafts (☎ 03-680 6895). Southern Link, Atomic Shuttles and the Cook Connection include Lake Tekapo on their routes; book these at Kiwi Treasure (☎ 03-680 6686). Ticket prices range from about $20 to $30 for most destinations.

Lake Pukaki

About 45km south of Lake Tekapo and 2km north of the turn-off to Mt Cook is a great **lookout** area on the shores of Lake Pukaki. On a clear day you'll get a picture-perfect view of Mt Cook and its surrounding peaks, with the very blue lake in the foreground. Also here is the Lake Pukaki visitors centre (☎ 03-435 3280, w www.mtcook.org.nz), open 10am to 5pm daily and a good place to get information on the Mackenzie Country.

Twizel
pop 1140

The rather characterless town of Twizel, just south of Lake Pukaki, only came into existence in 1968, built to service the nearby hydroelectric power station project. The town's survival beyond the completion of that project may have a bit to do with its proximity to Mt Cook (about a 45-minute drive) and its status as a good base for exploring the area. The helpful visitors centre (☎ 03-435 3124, w www.twizel.com) is in Market Place and is open 9am to 7pm daily from October to April, 9am to 5pm Monday to Saturday from May to September. Enter the town through the northern entrance off SH8 and you'll find it without problems.

Activities Twizel does have a few good diversions, including nearby **Lake Ruataniwha**, popular for rowing, boating and windsurfing. Fishing in the rivers, canals and lakes of the area is also big business; the visitors centre can help make arrangements.

Helibikes (☎ *0800 435 424*, w *www.heli biking.com)* will take you by helicopter up a mountain, which you then head down on two wheels. There are tracks to suit all levels of experience and very reasonably priced, starting from $80. The company also offers regular mountain biking trips (no helicopters involved) and heli-hiking.

The **black stilt** is the rarest wader species in the world (see the colour special section 'Fauna & Flora') and there's a DOC-run black stilt captive breeding centre near Twizel. Informative **tours** *(adult/child $12.50/5)* leave the visitors centre a few times daily – check for times. Bookings are essential.

Glacier Southern Lakes Helicopters *(☎ 0800 872 872, W www.heli-flights.co.nz)* has a range of chopper flights over the Mt Cook region from a helipad by Mackenzie Country Inn. Flights cost from $195 (25 minutes) to $495 (70 minutes), and all include either a snow or glacier landing.

Places to Stay There are a few good camping grounds in the area. Spacious *Lake Ruataniwha Holiday Park (☎ 03-435 0613, e holidaypark2000@xtra.co.nz)*, 4km south of town right beside the lake, has powered and unpowered sites for $20 and cabins from $31 to $43. It offers bikes and canoes for rent. More central is *Parklands Alpine Tourist Park (☎ 03-435 0507, e parklands1@xtra.co.nz, 122 Mackenzie Drive)*, in very pretty grounds and offering a range of excellent accommodation in a colourfully refurbished maternity hospital. Unpowered/powered sites cost $18/20 for two people, dorm beds cost $15, rooms without/with en suite cost $45/60, and self-contained cottages are $85.

High Country Holiday Lodge (☎ 03-435 0671, e erin.hchl@xtra.co.nz, 23 Mackenzie Drive) Backpackers beds $18, singles/doubles & twins with share facilities $33/48, en suite rooms $60, motel units from $75. High Country has all sorts of accommodation in cabins originally built for the hydro-scheme workers, starting with dorm beds (only two beds to a room) and working up the scale. The lodge also has a Korean restaurant.

Mackenzie Country Inn (☎ 03-435 0869, e bookings@mackenzie.co.nz, cnr Wairepo & Ostler Rds) Doubles $145-165. This prominent hotel is quite a flash place and offers two types of room – the cheaper

standard room and the newer 'deluxe'. It has an upmarket restaurant plus offers rental of bikes and golf clubs.

Mountain Chalet Motels (☎ 03-435 0785, e mt.chalets@xtra.co.nz, Wairepo Rd) Dorm beds $18, motel units $90-110. Offering comfortable, well-equipped, A-frame chalet units and a lodge with budget accommodation, this is a good choice.

Glenbrook Station (☎ 03-438 9407, e j.kelland@xtra.co.nz) Dorm beds $15, self-contained cottages $85, DB&B in homestead $125 per person. Glenbrook is a high-country sheep station offering a range of accommodation and outdoor activity options. It's 8km south of Twizel and 22km north of Omarama.

Places to Eat Market Place in the centre of town has a few choices. *Black Stilt Coffee Shop* offers the usual lunch-time fare, and *Alpine Takeaway* has good fish and chips. One of the more interesting stores here is *Aoraki Smokehouse Salmon (☎ 03-435 3144)*, where you can buy super fresh local salmon in a variety of forms – smoked salmon, salmon fillets, sushi and sashimi, pate etc. Head to the nearby supermarket and buy a few supplies for a great picnic.

Hunter's Bar & Cafe (☎ 03-435 0303) is an attractive place and the pick of the town's eateries, with lunches priced from $6 to $12 and dinner mains hovering around $20. Choose from an appealing selection that might include local salmon, rib-eye steak or Cajun chicken.

Getting There & Away InterCity buses serving Mt Cook stop at Twizel, and Christchurch-Queenstown shuttles, such as Atomic and Southern Link, also stop here. From mid-October to late April, The Cook Connection (☎ 025 583 211) services to Timaru and Oamaru call in at Twizel.

High Country Shuttles (☎ 0800 435 050) has services between Twizel and Mt Cook three times daily ($15/25 one way/return). It usually connects with the larger bus services outlined above.

Lake Ohau & Ohau Forests

Six forests in the Lake Ohau area (Dobson, Hopkins, Huxley, Temple, Ohau and Ahuriri) are administered by DOC. The walks in this vast 'outdoor recreation playground' are numerous and are outlined in the DOC pamphlet *Ohau Conservation Area* ($1). Huts are scattered throughout the region for the more adventurous trampers, and there are a few camping areas. There's a *DOC camping ground* in Temple Forest on Lake Ohau Rd, 50km southwest of Twizel. There is also a good ski field in the area.

Lake Ohau Lodge (☎ 03-438 9885, W *www.ohau.co.nz*) is a large, well-equipped place on the western shore of Lake Ohau. Its facilities including a restaurant, bar, games room and spa pools. It has a good range of accommodation available, including dorm beds ($18), budget doubles ($55), standard rooms ($92) and luxury rooms ($115). DB&B packages are available and are a good option given you're half an hour's drive from the nearest town.

MT COOK NATIONAL PARK

Mt Cook National Park, along with Fiordland, Aspiring and Westland National Parks, has been incorporated into a World Heritage area extending from the Cook River in Westland down to the base of Fiordland. The Mt Cook National Park is 700 sq km in area and one of the most spectacular in a country famous for its parks. Encompassed by the main divide, the Two Thumb, Liebig and Ben Ohau Ranges, more than one-third of the park is in permanent snow and glacial ice.

Of the 27 NZ mountains over 3050m, 22 are in this park, including the mighty Mt Cook – at 3755m this is the highest peak in Australasia. Known to the Maori as Aoraki, after a deity from Maori mythology, the tent-shaped Mt Cook was named after James Cook by Captain Stokes of the survey ship HMS *Acheron*.

The Mt Cook region has always been the focus of climbing in NZ. On 2 March 1882, William Spotswood Green and two Swiss alpinists, after a 62-hour epic, failed to reach the summit of Cook. Two years later three local climbers, Tom Fyfe, George Graham and Jack Clarke, spurred into action by the news that two well-known European alpinists, Edward Fitzgerald and Matthias Zurbriggen, were coming to attempt Cook, set off to climb it before the visitors. On Christmas Day 1884 they ascended the Hooker Glacier and north ridge, a brilliant climb in those days, and stood on the summit.

In 1913 Freda du Faur, an Australian, was the first woman to reach the summit. In 1948 Edmund Hillary's party climbed the south ridge. (Hillary went on to become, with Tenzing Norgay, the first to reach the summit of Mt Everest in the Himalaya.) Since then most of the daunting face routes have been climbed. The Mt Cook region has many great peaks including Sefton, the beguiling Tasman, Silberhorn, Elie de Beaumont, Malte Brun, Aiguilles Rouges, Nazomi, La Perouse, Hicks, De la Beche, Douglas and the Minarets. Many of the peaks can be ascended from Westland National Park, and there's a system of climbers' huts on both sides of the divide.

In the early hours of 14 December 1991, a substantial piece of the east face of Mt Cook (around 14 million cubic metres) fell away in a massive landslide. Debris spewed out over the surrounding glaciers for 7.3km, following a path down the Grand Plateau and Hochstetter Icefall and reaching as far as the Tasman Glacier.

The national park is on most itineraries of the South Island and Mt Cook is certainly an impressive sight – if you can get clear views. Most visitors to the park come on tour buses, stop quickly at the Hermitage hotel for photos, and are then off again, but the park has a few accommodation options. The park has some excellent short walks but is not a major tramping destination.

Information

The DOC visitors centre (☎ 03-435 1186, e mtcookvc@doc.govt.nz), open 8.30am to 5pm daily (to about 6.30pm in summer), will advise you on weather conditions, guided tours and tramping routes. It screens a 20-minute audiovisual on the history, mountaineering and human occupation of

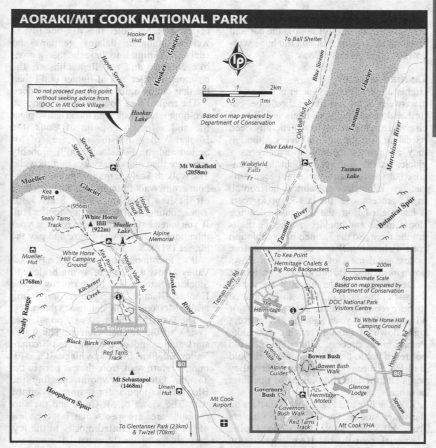

AORAKI/MT COOK NATIONAL PARK

Do not proceed past this point without seeking advice from DOC in Mt Cook Village

Based on map prepared by Department of Conservation

Hooker Hut

Hooker Glacier

To Ball Shelter

Blue Stream

Tasman Glacier

Heron Stream

Hooker Lake

Stocking Stream

Mueller Glacier

Kea Point

+(956m)

Sealy Tarns Track

White Horse Hill (922m)

Mueller Lake

Alpine Memorial

Mueller Hut

(1768m)

White Horse Hill Camping Ground

Kea Point Track

Hooker Valley Rd

Kitchener Creek

Sealy Range

Black Birch Stream

Red Tarns Track

Mt Sebastopol (1468m)

Unwin Hut

Hoophorn Spur

Mt Cook Airport

To Glentanner Park (23km) & Twizel (70km)

Mt Wakefield (2058m)

Wakefield Falls

Blue Lakes

Hooker Valley Track

Hooker River

Tasman River

Tasman Lake

Murchison River

Botanical Spur

Old Ball Hut Rd

See Enlargement

80

To Kea Point

Hermitage Chalets & Big Rock Backpackers

The Hermitage

DOC National Park Visitors Centre

To White Horse Hill Camping Ground

Glencoe Walk

Alpine Guides

Governors Bush

Governors Bush Walk

Bowen Bush

Bowen Bush Walk

Hermitage Motels

Red Tarns Track

Mt Cook YHA

Glencoe Lodge

Glencoe

Hooker Valley Rd

80

Approximate Scale
Based on map prepared by Department of Conservation

---

the Mt Cook region on the hour from 9am to 4pm ($3).

Post is handled by the souvenir store in The Hermitage, and there are a few grocery supplies sold at the coffee shop here, and at the YHA. You're well advised to stock up on both groceries and petrol before turning off SH8 to Mt Cook. Bear in mind also that Mt Cook has no banking facilities.

The Alpine Guides Mountain Shop (☎ 03-435 1834) sells equipment for skiing and mountaineering, and rents out equipment, including ice axes, crampons, day-packs and sleeping bags.

Go to ⓦ www.mountcook.org.nz and ⓦ www.mount-cook.com for details.

The Hermitage

This is the most famous hotel in NZ, principally for its location and the fantastic views of Mt Cook. Originally constructed in 1884, when the trip up from Christchurch took several days, the first hotel was destroyed in a flash flood in 1913. You can see the foundations about 1km from the current Hermitage. Rebuilt, it survived until 1957, when it was totally burnt out; the present Hermitage was built on the same site.

Even if you are unable to stay at the Hermitage, you can still sample the bar and restaurants here and look out the huge windows straight up at Mt Cook.

Tasman Glacier

Higher up, the Tasman Glacier is a spectacular sweep of ice just like it should be, but further down it's ugly. Glaciers in NZ (and elsewhere in the world) have generally been retreating over the past 100 years, although they are advancing now. Normally as a glacier retreats it melts back up the mountain, but the Tasman is unusual because its last few kilometres are almost horizontal. In the process, over the last 75-or-so years it has melted from the top down, leaving stones, rocks and boulders as the ice melts around them. So the Tasman in its 'ablation zone' (where it melts) is covered in a more or less solid mass of debris, which slows down its melting rate and makes it unsightly.

Despite this considerable melt, the ice by the site of the old Ball Hut is still estimated to be over 600m thick. In its last major advance, 17,000 years ago, the glacier crept right down to Pukaki, carving out Lake Pukaki in the process. A later advance did not reach out to the valley sides, so the old Ball Hut Rd runs between the outer valley walls and the lateral moraines of this later advance.

Like the Fox and Franz Josef Glaciers on the other side of the divide, the glaciers from Mt Cook move fast. The Alpine Memorial, near the old Hermitage site on the Hooker Valley Walk, illustrates the glaciers' speed. The memorial commemorates Mt Cook's first climbing disaster, when three climbers were killed by an avalanche in 1914. Only one of the bodies was recovered at the time but 12 years later a second one melted out of the bottom of the Hochstetter Icefall, 2000m below where the party was buried.

Walking

Various easy walks from the Hermitage area are outlined in *Walks in Aoraki/Mt Cook National Park* ($1) from the visitors centre. Be prepared for sudden climate changes.

In summer look for the large mountain buttercup, often called the Mt Cook lily, as well as mountain daisies, gentians and edelweiss. Animals include the thar, a goat-like creature and excellent climber; the chamois, smaller and of lighter build than the thar but an agile climber; and red deer.

The trail to **Kea Point** is an easy one- to two-hour return walk with much native plant life and a final viewpoint of Cook, the Hooker Valley and the ice faces of Mt Sefton and the Footstool. You'll probably see more than one cheeky kea on this walk. The walk to **Sealy Tarns** is a three- to four-hour return walk from the village, branching off the Kea Point Track. The Sealy Tarns Track continues up the ridge to Mueller Hut. If you intend staying up here register your intentions at the visitors centre and pay the hut fee ($18).

It's a four-hour return walk up the **Hooker Valley** across a couple of swing bridges to Stocking Stream and the terminus of the Hooker Glacier. After the second swing bridge Mt Cook totally dominates the valley.

The **Tasman Valley** walks are popular for a view of the Tasman Glacier. The walks start at the end of the unsealed Tasman Valley Rd, 8km from the village. It's a 40-minute return walk from the car park to the Tasman Glacier viewpoint, passing the Blue Lakes (popular for swimming) on the way. The views of Mt Cook and the surrounding area are spectacular, but the view of the glacier is limited mostly to the icy, grey sludge of the Terminal Lake and the Tasman River. To get close to the snub of the glacier, take the **Ball Shelter** route (three to four hours one way) from the car park. If you intend staying up here register your intentions at the visitors centre and pay the hut fee ($10).

Longer Walks Longer walks are only recommended for those with mountaineering experience. Advice must be sought from DOC and intentions registered. Conditions at higher altitudes are severe, the tracks dangerous and many people have died. The majority of walkers shouldn't even consider tackling them (see Mountaineering).

Guided Walks For $90, which includes lunch, **Alpine Guides Trekking** (☎ 03-435 1899, ⓔ *trekking.hermitage@xtra.co.nz*) offers a full-day, 8km walk from the Hermitage through the Hooker Valley to the terminal lake of the Hooker Glacier; half-day walks are also available.

Alpine Recreation, based in Lake Tekapo, offers high-altitude guided treks in the area. See Lake Tekapo earlier in this chapter.

Mountaineering

There's unlimited scope here for climbing for the experienced, but beware: there have been some 200 people killed in climbing accidents in the park.

The highly changeable weather is an important factor around here – Mt Cook is only 44km from the coast, catching the weather conditions blowing in over the Tasman Sea. The weather can change abruptly and you can suddenly find yourself in a storm. Unless you're experienced in such conditions, don't attempt to climb anywhere without a guide.

It's important to check with the park rangers before attempting any climb, and to heed their advice! Fill in a climber's intentions card before starting out on any climb, so they can check on you if you're overdue coming out. Be sure to sign out again when you return.

Alpine Guides (☎ 03-435 1834, ⓦ *www.alpineguides.co.nz*) has guided climbs in summer, ranging from introductory courses through to ascents of Mt Cook, but they're not cheap. **Alpine Recreation** in Lake Tekapo also offers mountaineering courses (see Lake Tekapo for contact details).

Heli-skiing & Heli-hiking

In the winter months, **Alpine Guides** (☎ 03-435 1834, ⓦ *www.heliskiing.co.nz*) offers ski-touring trips and ski-mountaineering courses, but the specialty is glacier heli-skiing. Day trips on Tasman Glacier are $650 ´ (three skiplane flights) and the 'Wilderness Heli-Skiing' trip takes in the Liebig or Malte Brun Ranges on four runs with a minimum of 3000 vertical metres of skiing for $710.

Summer trips with **Cloud 9 Helihiking** (☎ 03-435 1077, ⓦ *www.glacierexplorers .com*) take you to the 'Dark Side': you're flown to Mt Dark (approximately 2000m) and walk back down. The guided trip takes four to five hours in total and costs $148. If you prefer, you can fly up and back for $241, with time at the top for a walk around and play in the snow.

Aerial Sightseeing

The skies above Mt Cook are alive with the sound of aircraft. This is the antipodean equivalent of the Grand Canyon in the USA. The views are superb and glacier landings are a great experience – a must on any NZ adventure.

Mount Cook Ski Planes (☎ 0800 800 702, ⓦ *www.skiplanes.co.nz*) is not the cheapest option but it offers a good range of flights. The 40-minute 'Glacier Highlights' flight is $250 and a 55-minute 'Grand Circle' flight is $330; both have glacier landings. Flights without landing are much cheaper (eg, the 25-minute 'Mini Tasman' tour for $170).

From Glentanner Park, **Helicopter Line** (☎ 0800 650 651, ⓦ *www.helicopter.co.nz*) has a 20-minute 'Alpine Vista' flight for $165; an exhilarating 30-minute flight over the Ben Ohau Range $250; and a 45-minute 'Mountain High' flight over the Tasman Glacier and by Mt Cook for $350. All flights feature snow landings.

See also Lake Tekapo for details on **Air Safaris**, operating from Lake Tekapo and Glentanner Park, and Twizel for details on **Glacier Southern Lakes Helicopters**.

Other Activities

The visitors centre, the Hermitage, the YHA and Glentanner Park will be able to give information and make bookings for most activities and tours available in the area. Most are very weather-dependent.

Highly rated **Glacier Explorers** (☎ 03-435 1077, ⓦ *www.glacierexplorers.com*) has trips (adult/child $75/35) on the terminal lake of the Tasman Glacier. It involves a half-hour walk to the shore of Lake Tasman, where you board a small motorised inflatable and get up close and personal with the ice for an hour. There's good commentary and a great backdrop.

Glacier Sea-kayaking (☎ *025 229 5102)* offers three-hour trips enabling you to sea kayak into pristine glacial bays surrounded by glacial ice ($60).

There are other good ways to see the area: **Glentanner Horse Trekking** (☎ *03-435 1855)* offers guided treks in the high country over summer from $30 for a half-hour, $60 for two hours. **Alan's 4WD Tours** (☎ *03-435 0441)* has 2½-hour trips for $75/35 adult/child. Alan gives a good commentary and points out interesting alpine flora as the vehicle climbs up to Husky Flat above the glacier.

Places to Stay

The *White Horse Hill Camping Ground* is at the old Hermitage site, the starting point for the Hooker Valley Track, 1.8km from Mt Cook Village. There's running water and toilets but no electricity, showers or cooking facilities. It's run by DOC and costs $5/3 for adults/children; contact the visitors centre. There is also a handy *public shelter* in the village, with running water, toilets and coin-operated showers.

Glentanner Park (☎ *0800 453 682, 03-435 1855,* W *www.glentanner.co.nz)* Unpowered/powered sites $18/20 for 2, dorm beds $15, basic cabins $40-50, fully-equipped cabins $70. With great views of Mt Cook, this is the nearest motor camp to the park; it's 23km south on the shores of Lake Pukaki. It has good facilities, including a restaurant, and there's also a booking service in the complex for Air Safaris, Helicopter Line and Glentanner Horse Trekking.

About 3.5km before the village is the NZ Alpine Club's *Unwin Hut* (☎ *03-435 1102)*. Members get preference but beds are usually available ($20 per person) for intrepid travellers who wish to meet spider-person ascensionists. It's basic bunk accommodation but there's a big common room with a fireplace, kitchen and excellent views up the Tasman Glacier to the Minarets and Elie de Beaumont.

Mt Cook YHA (☎ *03-435 1820,* e *yha mtck@yha.org.nz, cnr Bowen & Kitchener*

Drives) Dorm beds $22, twins/doubles $58/62. This excellent hostel is well equipped with a free sauna, drying room, shop and a good video collection, plus cosy log fires. It's very popular and can get crowded in the high season (December to April), so it's worth booking a few days in advance.

Otherwise *The Hermitage* (☎ *0800 686 800, 03-435 1809,* W *www.mt-cook.com)* pretty much has a monopoly on lodging and dining in the village. *Big Rock* offers dorm beds in well-equipped chalets for $22. *Hermitage Chalets* costs $130 for four people, although they can sleep up to six ($30 for additional people). Each chalet has a double and four single beds; TVs, phones, bathrooms, well-equipped kitchens and a dining table add to the convenience.

Hermitage Motels has self-contained studios for $140 and larger units that can sleep four for $175. The *Glencoe Lodge* has good hotel rooms for $216, and the *Hermitage Hotel* itself has rooms ranging from $340 to $475. The newly completed deluxe suites at the top of the price range are quite luxurious and have good extras such a pair of binoculars to enjoy the amazing views.

Places to Eat

The Hermitage base line is the *coffee shop*, open from 7.30am daily and serving cafeteria-style meals, pies, sandwiches and coffee. The *Alpine Room* has extensive buffets ($35 at lunch time, $45 for dinner), and the *Panorama Room* is definitely an à la carte, fine-dining option. It's not cheap, however, with well-prepared mains of fish, beef, lamb and chicken hovering around $35. The view from here is up there with the world's best – you see Sefton to your left, Cook in the centre and the Ben Ohau Ranges, dark brown and forbidding, to your right. Also here is the *Snowline Bar*, with comfy lounges and the chance for pre- or post-dinner drinks. The small *Chamois Bar* is upstairs in the Glencoe Wing and offers the chance for a more relaxed eating and drinking experience, every night from 5pm. A bar menu is available from 5.30pm to 9.30pm and features a roast of the day as well as good beer-drinking food such as nachos, burgers, steak sandwiches and chicken wings. Prices are very reasonable, in the $8 to $16 range. There's a pool table here, and the bar is a popular hang-out for local workers.

There is also an all-day restaurant at *Glentanner Park*, serving meals in the $11 to $16 range. A barbecue and salad buffet here is good value at $16.

Getting There & Away

There is no longer an air link between Mt Cook and either Christchurch or Queenstown. The village's small, modern airport serves only aerial sightseeing companies, some of which may be able to combine transport to, say, the West Coast (ie, Franz Josef) with a scenic flight, but the flights are heavily weather-dependent.

There are daily InterCity buses on the Christchurch-Queenstown or Wanaka route that go to Mt Cook, where they stop for one hour. InterCity buses stop at the YHA and at the Hermitage, both of which handle bookings. High Country Shuttles (☎ 0800 435 050) have three services a day to Twizel, and you can usually connect with Atomic or Southern Link Shuttles to take you on to Queenstown, Wanaka or Christchurch. From October to April there are connections with Timaru and Oamaru courtesy of The Cook Connection (☎ 025 583 211).

There are a number of day trips to Mt Cook from Queenstown or Christchurch. InterCity (☎ 03-379 9020) offers the 'Mt Cook Wanderer', costing $124 from Christchurch, $109 from Queenstown.

Otago

OTAGO

☎ 03 • pop 187,200

Fantastic Queenstown and Wanaka with their adrenaline-inducing activities, the Otago Peninsula (NZ's first real foray into ecotourism) and Dunedin, the capital of the region, make Otago a must for any traveller. Otago's history featured a major gold rush and many aspects of the region's geography hark back to an era of prosperity, when rivers and creeks swarmed with prospectors.

Otago occupies a central position on the South Island. The main entry route is SH1 from Christchurch along the east coast. From Southland you can approach Otago via the Southern Scenic Route through the Catlins, or via SH1 from Invercargill. The most scenic way, however, is via the West Coast (SH6) and across Haast Pass.

Dunedin & the Otago Peninsula

Otago Harbour's long fiord-like inlet is the hub for many ecotourism activities, especially on the Otago Peninsula. This fauna-rich peninsula is close to Dunedin, a quaint city with many historic buildings and a convenient base for trips further afield to Central Otago and the Catlins.

DUNEDIN
pop 110,800

Dunedin is the second city of the South Island and home of NZ's first university. During the gold-rush days it was the largest city in the country. Founded by Scottish settlers (Dunedin is Celtic for Edinburgh), Dunedin has a statue of Robert Burns guarding its city centre, produces whisky at a local distillery and still has haggis ceremonies.

Dunedin's ostentatious wealth in the latter half of the 19th century produced a grand Victorian city in the South Pacific. Though central Dunedin now has modern intrusions, much of the Victorian architecture survives:

Highlights

- Enjoying the smorgasbord of activities on water, land and air at Queenstown and Wanaka
- Tackling the Routeburn and Rees-Dart tracks amid spectacular mountain scenery
- Skiing on any of the ranges near Queenstown (the Remarkables and Coronet Peak) and Wanaka (Treble Cone and Cardrona)
- Marvelling at the historic towns of the Manuherikia Valley and the Maniototo plain and the goldfields of Central Otago
- Enjoying architecturally rich Dunedin and some of the best nightlife on the South Island
- Seeing albatross, rare penguins and sea lions on the Otago Peninsula

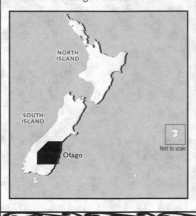

NORTH ISLAND

SOUTH ISLAND

Otago

Not to scale

solid public buildings dot the city and wooden villas are scattered across the hilly suburbs. Preservation was as much a matter of fate as of planning. After its heady start, Dunedin declined economically and much of its population drifted away. Though Dunedin's boom years are gone, it is cultured, graceful and lively for its size. The

20,000 tertiary students drive the local arts, entertainment, cafe and pub scenes.

History
The early Maori history of the Dunedin area was particularly bloody, with a three-way feud between Otago Peninsula tribes. *Utu* (revenge) followed attack as the Ngati Kahu and Ngatimamoe tribes' feud escalated in the early 19th century. Then sealing and whaling along the coast brought ravaging diseases and by 1848 the once considerable population of Otakau Pa was just over 100.

The first permanent European settlers arrived at Port Chalmers in March 1848, about six years after the plan for a Presbyterian settlement on the east coast of the South Island was initially mooted. Soon after that, gold was discovered in Otago and the province quickly became the richest and most influential one in the colony. Famous business houses were established and the province was the powerhouse of the country's economy.

Orientation & Information
Dunedin's main street changes from Princes St in the south to George St in the north as it crosses the Octagon that marks the city centre. The Dunedin visitors centre (☎ 03-474 3300, ✉ visitor.centre@dcc.govt.nz, 🅆 www.cityofdunedin.com) is at 48 The Octagon, in the magnificently restored municipal chambers. It's open 8.30am to 6pm Monday to Friday and 8.45am to 6pm Saturday and Sunday from December to March, 8.30am to 5.30pm daily from April to November.

The Department of Conservation (DOC; ☎ 03-477 0677) office at 77 Lower Stuart St has pamphlets and good information on walking tracks (open Monday to Friday only). The Automobile Association (AA; ☎ 03-477 5945) is at 450 Moray Place just east of Princes St.

A collection of banks is on George St just north of Moray Place. The central post office is at 243 Princes St; it handles poste restante. There's an inner-city post office at 233 Moray Place. Arc Cafe-Bar (☎ 03-474 1135), 135 High St, is a very popular place,

not least for its free Internet access. Many of the backpackers hostels offer access, as does the cybercafe above Governors Cafe (see Places to Eat, later in this chapter) – it has fast access for $3 an hour. Even McDonald's has got in on the act – their branch on George St has a cybercafe.

Any town full of students will do well in the bookshops department. Dunedin's finest is the University Book Shop (☎ 03-477 6976) at 378 Great King St.

Olveston
Designed by a London architect and built between 1904 and 1906, this grand house (☎ 03-477 3320, 42 Royal Terrace; tours adult/child $12/4) is preserved as it was when lived in by the Theomin family in the early 1900s. Though the building is not as extravagantly impressive as Larnach Castle (see Otago Peninsula later in this chapter), the lavish furnishings and art collections are stunning. One-hour guided tours at 9.30am, 10.45am, noon, 1.30pm, 2.45pm and 4pm offer a glimpse of the lifestyle of this fabulously wealthy family. Phone to reserve a place.

Cadbury World
By the time you read this, there should be a big new attraction for visitors to Dunedin, and a joy for those with a sweet tooth. At the time of research **Cadbury World**, a chocolate-themed tourist attraction, was being developed at the Cadbury factory in the heart of town at 280 Cumberland St. The factory opened in the early 1930s and now produces some 85% of chocolate manufactured in NZ. Check with the visitors centre for information on how to visit Cadbury World (hours, admission prices, etc), or see 🅆 www.cadbury.co.nz for updates.

Speight's Brewery
There are tours of **Speight's Brewery** (☎ 03-477 7697, 200 Rattray St) at 10am, 11.45am and 2pm daily, and evening tours Monday to Thursday at 7pm. Tours cost adult/child $12/4; bookings are essential. Tours start from the brewery's visitor centre, and at the end of the one-hour tour you get to taste a

OTAGO

few beers. There's a very good restaurant and bar here too: *The Ale House* (☎ *03-471 9050)* is open for lunch and dinner and has great tap beers, as you'd expect.

Museums

The **Otago Museum** (☎ *03-474 7474,* W *www.otagomuseum.govt.nz, 419 Great King St; admission free; open 10am-5pm daily)* has a large and varied collection of exhibits, including Maori and South Pacific cultural artefacts, a marine and maritime hall and a good Asian art collection. The natural history displays of penguins, moa

and extinct birds are particularly good and there is also a hands-on Discovery World science centre for children.

The **Otago Settlers Museum** (☎ *03-477 5052, 55 Queens Gardens; adult/child $4/free; open 10am-5pm daily),* near the train station, has a photographic collection of the region's early settlers, as well as exhibits on the loss of Maori land and the role of Chinese miners. The transport section has a variety of old vehicles.

The **New Zealand Sports Hall of Fame** (☎ *03-477 7775, Anzac Ave; adult/child $5/2; open 10am-6pm daily in summer,*

10am-4pm in winter) is inside the train station and is a must-see for keen sports fans.

The **Dunedin Public Art Gallery** *(☎ 03-474 3240, 30 The Octagon; admission free; open 10am-5pm daily)* is the oldest art gallery in NZ. Its international collection is small but contains some work by famous artists (Gainsborough, Reynolds, Constable, Turner, Dürer and Monet) even if some of the paintings are minor works. Excellent visiting exhibitions are staged.

Taieri Gorge Railway

Some visitors rate this as one of the great train journeys, similar to the Silverton to Durango line in Colorado. From October to March, four-hour excursions depart from Dunedin train station daily at 2.30pm and, from April to September, at 12.30pm. There is a 58km trip to Pukerangi ($57 return). In summer some trains continue 19km further to Middlemarch ($65). Get tickets and information from **Dunedin train station** *(☎ 03-477 4449,* **W** *www.taieri.co.nz)*.

Most people take the train as a day trip, but you can travel one way and continue by bus on to Alexandra ($95 for train and bus) or Queenstown ($110). Another option is to take your bike on the train and cycle the Otago Central Rail Trail from Middlemarch to Clyde, an excellent trip along the rail-line extension, which has been converted into a mountain-bike and walking track (see the boxed text 'Otago Central Rail Trail' in Central Otago for more details).

Other Attractions

The **University of Otago** *(☎ 03-479 1100,* **W** *www.otago.ac.nz)*, was founded with 81 students in 1869, 25 years after the settlement of Otago. It has an interesting variety of old and new styles of architecture.

Dunedin parks include the extensive **Botanic Gardens** at the northern end of the city on the lower slopes of Signal Hill. There is a good cafe, a hothouse and an aviary with kea and other native birds; the gardens are open dawn to dusk daily.

A short but definitely strenuous walk is up **Baldwin St**, listed in the *Guinness Book of Records* as the steepest street in the world

with a gradient of 1 in 1.266. From the city centre, head north up Great King St for 2km to where the road branches left to Timaru then veer right along North Rd for another kilometre. The Gut Buster race, held every year during the Dunedin Festival around February, sees the winners run up and back in around two minutes.

Swimming & Walking

The heated **outdoor saltwater pool** *(☎ 03-455 6352; open Oct-Apr)* on the headland at the end of St Clair Beach is open in summer. St Clair and St Kilda are popular beaches for walking and swimming (and St Clair for surfing also) and both are accessible by public transport from the Octagon. Otherwise **Moana Pool** *(☎ 03-471 9780, 60 Littlebourne Rd)* is the place for swimming.

There is a short walkway to **Tunnel Beach**, southwest of the city centre. Catch a Corstorphine bus from the Octagon to Stenhope Crescent and walk 1.4km along Blackhead Rd to Tunnel Beach Rd. It's then 400m to the start of the walkway. This leads down through farmland for 20 minutes to the hand-hewn stone tunnel built by John Cargill so that his family could enjoy picnics on the small, secluded beach just over the headland. The sandstone cliffs are impressive and contain fossils if you look closely. The walkway is closed from August to October for the lambing season.

Catch a Normanby bus, northeast of town from the Octagon, to the start of Norwood St, then walk two hours uphill (90 minutes down) to the **Mt Cargill-Bethunes Gully Walkway**. The highlight is the view from Mt Cargill (also accessible by car). In Maori legend the three peaks of Cargill represent the petrified head and feet of a princess of an early Otakau tribe. Captain William Cargill was a leader of the early Otago colonists. From Mt Cargill, a trail continues down to the 10-million-year-old Organ Pipes, formed by cooling lava flows that left behind giant granite crystals. From here it is half an hour to the Mt Cargill Rd on the other side of the mountain.

Northwest of Dunedin, the 5km-long **Pineapple-Flagstaff Walk** has great views

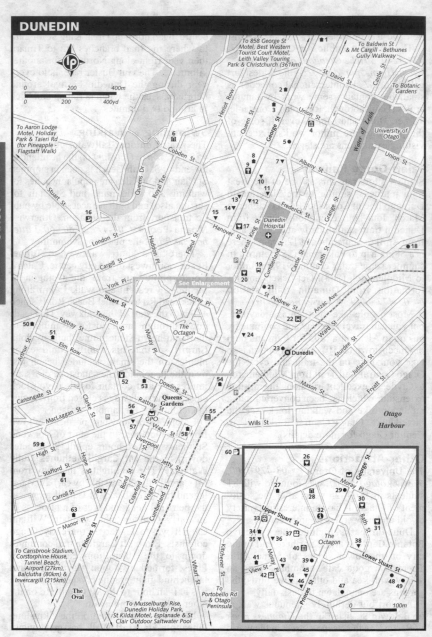

DUNEDIN

OTAGO

To 858 George St
Motel, Best Western
Tourist Court Motel,
Leith Valley Touring
Park & Christchurch (361km)

To Baldwin St
& Mt Cargill - Bethunes
Gully Walkway

To Botanic
Gardens

To Aaron Lodge
Motel, Holiday
Park & Taieri Rd
(for Pineapple -
Flagstaff Walk)

University of
Otago

Water of Leith

Dunedin
Hospital

See Enlargement

The
Octagon

Dunedin

Queens
Gardens

GPO

Otago
Harbour

The
Octagon

To Carisbrook Stadium,
Corstorphine House,
Tunnel Beach,
Airport (27km),
Balclutha (80km) &
Invercargill (215km)

The
Oval

To Musselburgh Rise,
Dunedin Holiday Park,
St Kilda Motel, Esplanade & St
Clair Outdoor Saltwater Pool

To Portobello Rd
& Otago
Peninsula

DUNEDIN

PLACES TO STAY					
1	Albatross Inn	12	Thai Over	16	Moana Pool
2	Sahara Guesthouse & Motel	13	London Lounge; Albert Arms Tavern	18	Hocken Library
3	Aunty's Backpackers	14	The Reef; Modaks	19	Suburban Bus Stop
8	Alexis Motor Lodge	15	New Satay Noodle House	21	Big Fresh Supermarket
27	Quality Hotel Dunedin	17	Abalone	22	InterCity Depot
34	97 Motel Moray Place	20	The Outback	23	New Zealand Sports Hall of Fame
41	Next Stop Dunedin Backpackers	24	Cadbury Factory	25	Countdown Supermarket
50	Elm Lodge Too	26	The Poolhouse	28	Town Hall; Metro Cinema
51	Elm Lodge Backpackers	30	Bath St	29	Library
53	Adventurer Backpackers Lodge	31	The Woolshed	32	Dunedin Visitors Centre
54	Leviathan Hotel	35	Tangenté	33	Fortune Theatre
56	Southern Cross Hotel; Casino	36	French Cafe	37	Hoyts Cinema
58	Downtown Dunedin Backpackers	38	Percolater	39	Air New Zealand
59	Chalet Backpackers	43	Mazagran	40	Dunedin Public Art Gallery; Cafe Nova
61	Stafford Gables YHA	44	Bennu	42	Rialto Cinema
63	Manor House Backpackers	45	Jizo Cafe	47	Automobile Association (AA)
		46	Etrusco at the Savoy	48	DOC; Potpourri
PLACES TO EAT & DRINK		57	Arc Cafe-Bar	49	Cycle Surgery
7	Captain Cook	62	Bell Pepper Blues	52	Speight's Brewery & The Ale House
10	Governors Café; Il Panificio; Curry Box; Azi Jaan	OTHER		55	Otago Settlers Museum
11	Fuel Café	4	Otago Museum	60	MV Monarch Harbour Cruises
		5	University Book Shop		
		6	Olveston		
		9	Knox Church		

OTAGO

of the harbour, coastline and inland ranges; look for the signpost at Flagstaff-Whare Flat Rd, off Taieri Rd.

Other Activities

Carisbrook Stadium, in the south of town, hosts regular sporting events, but rugby is what it's famous for – it's often called the 'home of NZ rugby' (and that's much softer than its other moniker, the 'House of Pain'). Attending a rugby game is a great way to experience Kiwis' passion for this sport; the season at Carisbrook usually runs from March to late October. Terrace tickets to the low-key games are usually available at the ground, but a better way for the uninitiated to go is with Bottom Bus (☎ 03-434 7370, Ⓦ www.bottombus.co.nz), on a **rugby trip** from Queenstown and Dunedin. The excursion involves getting you in the mood at one of the local student pubs, with drinks, face painting, competitions and the like, followed by attendance at Carisbrook, and after the game it's back to the pub for the post-game dissection over a meal. The price from Queenstown is $165 for the two-day trip (including accommodation); to join in Dunedin is $89.

In June 2002 the people behind Bottom Bus will stage the first **Backpacker Festival**, a four-day party for travellers highlighting rugby, student life and other features and attractions in and around Dunedin. There are plans to make this an annual event, so check the website (Ⓦ www.nzbf.com) or contact Bottom Bus for details.

Mainland Air (☎ 03-486 2200, Ⓦ www.mainlandair.com) and **Alpine Air** (☎ 03-486 2283, Ⓦ www.alpineair.co.nz) are both based at Dunedin airport and offer aerial sightseeing.

The **Otago Tramping & Mountaineering Club** (Ⓦ www.otmc.co.nz) organises 1-day and weekend tramping trips and meets every Thursday evening at 3 Young St, St Kilda; nonmembers are most welcome.

There are plenty of horse-trekking operators working in this area, including **Trojan**

Horseriding (☎ 03-465 7013) and Hare Hill (☎ 0800 437 837). Both are based north of Dunedin and offer beach rides and longer treks ($50/100 for a half/full day).

See the Otago Peninsula section later in this chapter for activities such as wildlife-spotting and sea-kayaking.

Organised Tours

Numerous tours depart Dunedin for the Otago Peninsula – see that section later in this chapter.

Behind the Tartan (☎ 03-474 3300) operates 90-minute walking tours of the city for $20/10, with an emphasis on Dunedin's history and Scottish heritage. The tours depart from the visitors centre at 10am daily.

Newton Tours (☎ 03-477 5577) has 1½-hour double-decker tours of the city at 10am, 12.45pm and 3.30pm from the visitors centre, taking in historic buildings, the university, Baldwin St and the Botanic Gardens for adult/child $20/10. The company also runs tours to the Otago Peninsula.

Monarch Wildlife Cruises (☎ 0800 666 272, 03-477 4276, W www.wildlife.co.nz) has daily cruises from one to five hours long on the MV *Monarch* from the wharf at the corner of Wharf and Fyatt Sts (a pick-up service from town is available). The half-day Otago Harbour cruise passes fur seal, shag and gull colonies and the albatross colony at Taiaroa Head and costs adult/child $58/29; for an additional cost you can also visit the penguin reserve and/or albatross observatory on this trip. You can also join the cruise at Wellers Rock on the peninsula for adult/child $27/13 and only do this shorter leg.

Places to Stay

Camping & Cabins Dunedin has three very good camping grounds, each only a few kilometres out of town. All prices given here are for two people.

Dunedin Holiday Park (☎ 0800 945 455, 03-455 4690, e office@dunedinholiday park.co.nz, 41 Victoria Rd) Powered/unpowered sites $20/18, dorm beds $18, cabins $28-50, motel units $61. This large, friendly and well-run place is near St Kilda

beach and is well positioned for forays into town or to the peninsula. There's a range of high-quality cabins and a bonus is the easy bus access – the St Kilda bus from the Octagon stops at the gate.

Aaron Lodge Motel & Holiday Park (☎ 03-476 4725, e stay@aaronlodge.co.nz, 162 Kaikorai Valley Rd) Powered/unpowered $24/22, cabins $35-38, studio flats & motels $56-71. This is a well-tended place, 2.5km northwest of the city, with good bus access (take a Bradford or Brockville bus from the Octagon). It has great gardens climbing the hill behind the main reception area, and where secluded camp sites are tucked away. Facilities are excellent, with a new heated pool, playroom and TV room.

Leith Valley Touring Park (☎ 03-467 9936, 103 Malvern St) Powered/unpowered sites $20, tourist flats $60. This small, sheltered park is by the Water of Leith, a couple of kilometres northwest of the town's centre. Take Duke St, at the top end of George St.

Hostels Many of Dunedin's backpackers are housed in wonderful old buildings. Most are rather small and relaxed places offering generally good facilities.

Stafford Gables YHA (☎ 03-474 1919, e yhadndn@yha.org.nz, 71 Stafford St) Dorm beds $16, singles $28, twins & doubles $40. Stafford Gables is only a five-minute walk from the post office. It's an elegant and sprawling old building, once used as a private hotel.

Elm Lodge Backpackers (☎ 0800 356 563, 03-474 1872, W www.elmwildlife tours.co.nz, 74 Elm Row) Dorm beds $17-18, twins & doubles $40. Friendly Elm Lodge is 10 minutes uphill (five back down) from the Octagon, and it picks up and drops off visitors. It's a fine old home with a cosy atmosphere and fantastic harbour views. It also offers brilliant wildlife tours of the Otago Peninsula. Its overflow building nearby, **Elm Lodge Too** (Arthur St), is another fine old house with the same rates.

Chalet Backpackers (☎ 0800 242 538, 03-479 2075, 296 High St) Dorm beds $18, singles $32, twins & doubles $44. This central, spacious place is a former hospital with loads of character (and rumours of a resident ghost). You will be able to pick up plenty of information here and find comfortable spots in the building's nooks and crannies to get away from it all.

Adventurer Backpackers Lodge (☎ *0800 422 257, 03-477 7367, 37 Dowling St)* Dorm beds $16-17, twins $36, doubles $38. The Adventurer is close to the action and offers high standards. This great old building has been extensively renovated and the large, open-plan common area is very inviting.

Manor House Backpackers (☎ *0800 477 0484, 03-477 0484, W www.manorhouse backpackers.co.nz, 28 Manor Place*).

Dorm beds $18, twins & doubles $42. Relaxed Manor House offers comfortable accommodation in a couple of Dunedin's old stately homes in the south of town, opposite parkland. It also operates wildlife tours to the Otago Peninsula.

Aunty's Backpackers (☎ *0800 428 689, 03-474 0708, e auntys@xtra.co.nz, 3 Union St)* Dorm beds $19, twins & doubles $44. Aunty's is a small, pleasant place in an old colonial house to the north of the centre. The staff are helpful and the kitchen is a convivial meeting place.

Next Stop Dunedin Backpackers (☎ *0800 463 987, 03-477 0447, e next stop2@hotmail.co.nz, 2 View St)* Dorm beds $15-17, twins & doubles $38. This well-located place, a converted church hall, is just a short walk from the Octagon up a steep street. Most rooms front the cavernous common room.

B&Bs & Guesthouses Close to the city centre, the *Sahara Guesthouse & Motel* (☎ *03-477 6662, 619 George St)* is a grand old house with slightly worn guestrooms (with a mix of shared and private facilities) plus older-style motel units out the back. You will find B&B singles/doubles from $55/80 and motel rooms from $80 to $90.

Albatross Inn (☎ *0800 441 441, 03-477 2727, W www.albatross.inn.co.nz, 770 George St)* B&B doubles $85-125. This charming place is superbly renovated with inviting, comfortable rooms. Breakfast is served in the stylish dining room.

Corstorphine House (☎ *03-487 1000, W www.corstorphine.co.nz, Milburn St)* B&B $275-385. For a taste of real luxury, this elegant mansion set in spacious grounds south of town has eight individually themed rooms with beautiful decor and wonderful attention to detail.

Motels Dunedin's most convenient motel row is along George St.

Best Western Tourist Court Motel (☎ *0800 244 664, 03-477 4270, e tourist court.dunedin@xtra.co.nz, 842 George St)* Units $60-99. This is a good, affordable option with clean and comfortable units.

858 George St Motel (☎ *03-474 0047, 858 George St, e reservations@858george streetmotel.co.nz)* Units $95-180. This place offers luxurious accommodation in new townhouse apartments, architecturally designed and stylishly decorated.

Alexis Motor Lodge (☎ *03-471 7268, e stay@alexis.co.nz, 475 George St)* Units $95-160. This is another new place offering quality accommodation in studio, one- and two-bedroom motel units, handily located opposite a strip of good-value eateries.

97 Motel Moray Place (☎ *0800 909 797, 03-477 2050, e info@97motel.co.nz, 97 Moray Place)* Units $95-150. This motel is very central (right behind the Octagon) and has been recently upgraded, offering good, comfortable units.

Staying out of town is an option; while opportunities on the peninsula itself are somewhat limited (see the Otago Peninsula section later in this chapter), there are a few choices in the suburbs, including *St Kilda Motel* (☎ *03-455 1151, 105 Queens Drive)*, opposite the beach and with units from $65. There are also a couple of moderately priced, older-style motels along Musselburgh Rise, on the Otago Peninsula side of town, including *Arcadian Motel* (☎ *03-455 0992, 85 Musselburgh Rise)* and *Chequers Motel* (☎ *0800 455 0778, 03-455 0778, 119 Musselburgh Rise)*. Units at both start from around $65.

Hotels The solid, reliable and central *Leviathan Hotel* (☎ *0800 773 773, 03-477*

OTAGO

3160, e leviathan@xtra.co.nz, 27 Queens Gardens) is a Dunedin landmark. It has a variety of well-appointed rooms to suit most people, with budget doubles and twins for $75, standard rooms for $90, units for $100 and suites for $125. It also has a nearby *backpackers lodge (42 Queens Gardens)*, with dorm beds for $20, and en suite singles/doubles for $45/55.

There are very few of the big hotel chains in Dunedin. *Quality Hotel Dunedin (☎ 03-477 6784, 0508 255 255, e quality.dune din@cdlhms.co.nz, 10 Smith St)* is central to the Octagon, and the top choice in town is the *Southern Cross Hotel (☎ 0800 696 963, 03-477 0752, e reservations@scenic-cir cle.co.nz, 118 High St)*, a large, well-appointed complex adjacent to Dunedin's casino (a great old building, pity about the garish pink neon). Prices at both start around the $150 to $200 mark, but it's worth inquiring about any special deals.

Places to Eat

Restaurants With a grand interior that makes it look much more expensive than it is, *Etrusco at the Savoy (☎ 03-477 3737, 8a Moray Place)* is a stylish and very popular restaurant serving authentic, affordable Italian food. Medium pastas cost $10 to $15, medium pizzas are $13 to $16.

Bell Pepper Blues (☎ 03-474 0973, 474 Princes St) Mains $25-30. This stylish restaurant is widely regarded as Dunedin's finest. It's south of the centre and worth the trip for its award-winning fare, with such delights as roasted, lemon-peppered blue cod and char-grilled cervena venison. Booking is recommended.

Bennu (☎ 03-474 5055, 12 Moray Place) Meals $10-25. A big, bustling spot, Bennu has a good menu of mainly Mexican and Italian dishes, with pizza, pasta, calzone and quesadillas proving popular. It's also a fine place for drinks around the circular bar.

Thai Over (☎ 03-477 7815, 388 George St) Meals $12-16. There's a chain of good Thai eateries popping up around town, and this central branch is a bright and relaxed place serving up good-value spicy soups and curries, plus rice and noodle dishes.

Esplanade (☎ 03-456 2544) Mains $13-26. In the old Hydro Hotel, overlooking the beach at St Clair, this inviting place is a popular spot for locals on weekends, when brunch is served from 11am. It's a good spot for lunch or dinner, with an assortment of tasty light meals and heartier fare.

French Cafe (☎ 03-477 1100, 118 Moray Place) Mains $20-25. This small, central and popular new place prepares great French provincial cuisine at very reasonable prices and has an extensive wine list. It's worth booking as seating is limited; there's also an outside deck for warmer days.

The Reef (☎ 03-471 7185, 329 George St) Mains $16-25. Serving up an assortment of fresh fish and good seafood, this colourful restaurant and bar is a good choice for a relaxed meal. There are also good menu selections for nonseafood-eaters.

Cafes Cafe society is well catered for here, particularly in and around the Octagon.

Mazagran (☎ 03-477 9959, 36 Moray Place) For an early morning caffeine fix, call in to this wee espresso bar for good, strong freshly ground coffee.

Tangenté (☎ 03-477 0232, 111 Moray Place) Breakfast & lunch to $10, meals $12-16. A great bakery-cafe (with delicious organic bread), this bright and cheery place is open from 8am daily, and also late on Friday and Saturday nights (BYO).

Every town should have a place like the wonderful *Arc Cafe-Bar (☎ 03-474 1135, 135 High St)*. It's open from noon until late daily except Sunday and has free Internet access, good vegetarian food and coffee, and there's regular live music and DJs. It's popular with locals and travellers. Check out W coffee.co.nz for more details.

Fuel Cafe (☎ 03-477 2575, 21 Frederick St) Meals average $10. In the university heartland and appropriately serving breakfast until 2pm, hip, funky Fuel is an excellent place for food during the day and evening drinks in the lounge bar out the back. Fuel is also home to Fusion, a club that regularly plays host to DJs, bands, comedy and other performances, and hosts a fortnightly gay club night called Powder.

Cafe Nova (☎ 03-479 0808, 29 The Octagon) Light meals & mains $13-25. Next to the Dunedin Public Art Gallery, this stylish spot has great cafe fare, including all-day breakfast, light meals, good coffee and decadent cakes. The weekend brunch menu is excellent.

Percolater (☎ 03-477 5462, 142 Lower Stuart St) As the name suggests, this busy place specialises in good coffee, which goes well with its reasonably priced meals and snacks.

Modaks (☎ 03-477 6563, 339 George St) Meals and snacks under $10. This is a cool and laid-back cafe in the main shopping strip, with coffee, cakes, smoothies, burgers and so on to quell the hunger pangs.

Cheap Eats & Takeaways The student pubs are great places for cheap meals. Upstairs in the Albert Arms Tavern, the *London Lounge* (George St) has hearty if unadventurous pub meals for around $10 to $12, including a $10 roast ($6 at lunch time). Serves are big enough to satisfy student appetites. The bar's cheap toasted sandwiches (around $5) are huge.

Jizo Cafe (56 Princes St) serves excellent-value Japanese dishes such as udon (noodles), miso and sushi sets. You can get eight pieces of sushi for $7.50; heartier meat and rice dishes average $11.

New Satay Noodle House (16 Hanover St) is a no-frills place that offers eat-in or takeaway service. Specialties here include huge bowls of soup, and rice and noodle dishes at rock-bottom, student-friendly prices. Dishes cost from $4 to $7.50 each.

Opposite Knox Church on George St there is an excellent strip of budget eateries. *Governors Cafe* (438 George St), open 8am until late, is something of an institution for student meals (big breakfasts, baked spuds, pies etc) and low prices. It's decorated with student notices and ads, and upstairs is a cheap Internet cafe. *Il Panificio* (430 George St) is an upmarket bakery selling delicious breads, panini and pizza slices, *Curry Box* (442 George St) has Indian dishes, and *Azi Jaan* (424 George St) sells Turkish kebabs and burgers.

Potpourri (97 Lower Stuart St) near the DOC office is a wholefood place with salads, quiche and other light meals. A simple three-course dinner here (eg, soup, burrito or baked spud with salad, and cake) will set you back all of $14.

Cumberland St is home to large supermarkets, including *Countdown* at No 309.

Entertainment

The *Otago Daily Times* newspaper lists what's on around the city, but the best publication is the free *f*INK*, available around town or online at **W** www.fink.net.nz.

Pubs, Bars & Clubs Dunedin is a drinker's town and a good place for a pub crawl. Many of the pubs and bars cater to students and are packed during term but die down in the university holidays.

Captain Cook (☎ 03-474 1935, cnr Albany & Great King Sts) or simply the 'Cook', located near the university, is *the* student pub, often so hopelessly crowded you can hardly get in the door. There's a dance floor upstairs, big-screen TVs and an outdoor beer garden, so everyone is catered for. The *Albert Arms* (☎ 03-477 2952, 387 George St) is a less crowded student pub that comes into its own on Monday and Tuesday nights when bands play.

The Woolshed (☎ 03-477 3246, 318 Moray Place) is a smaller place with good atmosphere, and *The Outback* (☎ 03-477 4414, 101 Great King St) is a casual bar.

Some of the liveliest drinking holes are the many cafe-restaurants. See Cafes earlier for details on Fuel and Arc, two excellent cafes with nightly entertainment.

Abalone (☎ 03-477 6877, cnr George & Hanover Sts) has an upmarket bar that's home to the sleek young things sipping pretty cocktails and listening to smooth tunes, especially on Saturday and Sunday evenings. *Bennu* (☎ 03-474 5055, 12 Moray Place) also has a very popular bar.

You could easily pass a few hours at *The Poolhouse* (☎ 03-477 6121, 12 Filleul St), playing pool and downing drinks from the bar. As for clubs – head to *Bath Street* (☎ 03-477 6750, 1 Bath St), the city's most popular dance venue, with DJs playing mainly house and hip-hop.

Theatre & Cinemas Dunedin is home to the very good *Fortune Theatre* company (☎ *03-477 8323,* Ⓦ *www.fortunetheatre.co .nz)*, which is housed in a refurbished 1870s church near the Octagon.

There are a number of good cinemas in the city centre. For commercial releases, *Hoyts* (☎ *03-477 7018)* is on the Octagon, *Rialto* (☎ *03-474 2200, 11 Moray Place)* shows a combination of popular and independent films and *Metro* cinema (☎ *03-474 3350)* is in the Town Hall on Moray Place, behind the visitors centre, and shows art-house titles.

Getting There & Away

Air Air New Zealand (☎ 03-477 6594) has an office on the corner of Princes St and the Octagon. It has daily direct flights to/from Auckland, Christchurch and Wellington, with connections to other centres.

Freedom Air (☎ 0800 600 500, Ⓦ www .freedomair.co.nz) has direct, budget-priced connections between Dunedin and the east coast of Australia. See the Getting There & Away chapter for details.

Bus InterCity (☎ 03-474 9600), 205 St Andrews St, has direct bus services to Christchurch, Queenstown and Te Anau.

Several door-to-door shuttles service Dunedin; the train station is the arrival and departure point for them. You can make inquiries and bookings for all services at the travel desk here (☎ 03-477 4999), or at the visitors centre. Atomic Shuttles runs to and from Christchurch ($30), Invercargill ($25) and Queenstown or Wanaka ($30). Knightrider operates a night-time service on the Christchurch-Dunedin-Invercargill route. Catch-a-Bus operates daily between Te Anau and Dunedin, and also has services to Christchurch and Queenstown.

From Dunedin, Bottom Bus (☎ 03-434 7370, Ⓦ www.bottombus.co.nz) and Catlins Coaster (☎ 03-474 3300, Ⓦ www.catlins coaster.co.nz) both do the scenic route through the Catlins (see The Catlins in the Southland chapter).

Train Dunedin's magnificent train station is on Anzac Ave. The *Southerner* train between Christchurch and Invercargill used to pass through daily but ran its final journey in early 2002. The station now only serves the Taieri Gorge Railway, and is home to the NZ Sports Hall of Fame (see earlier in this chapter).

Getting Around

Dunedin Airport (☎ 03-486 2879, Ⓦ www .dnairport.co.nz) is located 27km southwest of town. Dunedin Airport Shuttles (☎ 03-477 7777) and City Airport Shuttles (☎ 03-477 1771) offer door-to-door airport services for about $15 per person. A taxi to the city is a costly $50 to $60.

City buses leave from stops on the Octagon and buses to districts around Dunedin leave from Cumberland St. Buses run regularly during the week, but routes combine on Saturday and Sunday to form limited services or they simply stop running. The visitors centre has timetables and the average trip costs under $2. See Ⓦ www.orc .govt.nz/busTT for information.

Bike rental is available from Cycle Surgery (☎ 03-477 7473) at 67 Lower Stuart St for $25 per day. The store is a good source of information on mountain biking in the area, including the Otago Central Rail Trail.

OTAGO PENINSULA

It's possible to spend a pleasant day, or even longer, tripping around the Otago Peninsula, the most accessible wildlife area on the South Island. There are numerous stops to be made for wildlife attractions, historical sites, walkways and natural formations. The *Otago Peninsula* brochure and map is available at the Dunedin visitors centre and lists the many sights and activities. The website Ⓦ www.otago-penin sula.co.nz is very helpful.

Wildlife

For many people the peninsula's wealth of interesting fauna is the main reason for visiting. As well as albatross and yellow-eyed penguin, blue penguins *(koroa),* fur seals and sea lions can be seen here.

Jet boat model in Queenstown

Kawarau River, Queenstown

Rock-climbing at Hospital Flat

High-flying action at Cardrona Alpine resort

The view over Lake Wakatipu and Queenstown from the top of The Remarkables

RICHARD I'ANSON

Craft market near Queenstown

DAVID WALL

Rugby fans at Carisbrook Stadium, Dunedin

NEIL IRVINE

Baldwin Street, the world's steepest, in Dunedin

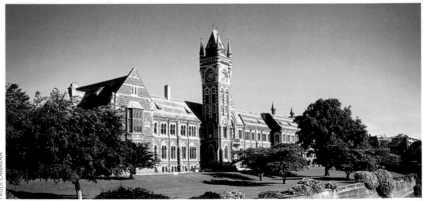
TRUDI CANAVAN

University of Otago, Dunedin

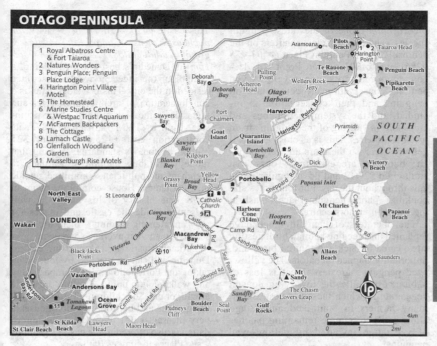

OTAGO PENINSULA

1. Royal Albatross Centre & Fort Taiaroa
2. Natures Wonders
3. Penguin Place; Penguin Place Lodge
4. Harington Point Village Motel
5. The Homestead
6. Marine Studies Centre & Westpac Trust Aquarium
7. McFarmers Backpackers
8. The Cottage
9. Larnach Castle
10. Glenfalloch Woodland Garden
11. Musselburgh Rise Motels

OTAGO

Albatross Taiaroa Head, at the end of the peninsula, has the only northern royal albatross colony in the world close to human habitation. The birds arrive at the nesting site in September, court and mate in October, lay eggs in November, then incubate the eggs until January, when the chicks hatch. Between March and September parents leave their chicks while collecting food, returning only for feeding. By September the fledged chicks leave.

The **Royal Albatross Centre** (☎ 03-478 0499, ⓔ reservations@albatrosses.com, ⓦ www.albatrosses.com; open 9am-7pm daily, shorter hours in winter) at Taiaroa has excellent displays on the albatross and other wildlife, with regular screenings of videos. The only public access to the colony is from the centre, with tours offered half-hourly (bookings essential). The one-hour tour (adult/child $24/12) includes an entertaining 30-minute introduction at the centre then heads up the hill to the glassed-in viewing

area overlooking the albatross nesting sites for 30 minutes of viewing. In calm weather it's unlikely you'll see an albatross flying, but chances are better later in the day when the wind picks up. Ask if the birds are around before you pay. The centre is open year-round but the main viewing area is closed to the public during the breeding season (mid-September to late November). At this time of year you can still enjoy the introductory talks and videos giving insight into the birds (adult/child $8/4).

Taiaroa Head is also home to the tunnels of historic **Fort Taiaroa**, built in 1886 and featuring a 150mm Armstrong Disappearing Gun. The gun was installed during the late 19th century to counter the improbable threat of attack from Tsarist Russia; it was so named because it could be withdrawn into its bunker after firing. Tours go from the albatross centre to the fort for adult/child $12/6; the 1½-hour combined albatross and fort tour costs adult/child $30/15.

Penguins The yellow-eyed penguin (in Maori, *hoiho*), one of the rarest penguin species, can be seen at close quarters on the peninsula. From **Penguin Place** (☎ 03-478 0286), just off Harington Point Rd, 1½-hour tours run to its unique yellow-eyed penguin conservation project. A talk on penguins and their conservation is included, and the system of trenches and hides allows viewing of the penguins from just a few metres. This is as close as you'll get anywhere, so the tours are very popular; bookings are essential. Tours cost adult/child $27/12 and go at regular intervals throughout the day. For tour times and bookings, phone Penguin Place or ask at the Dunedin visitors centre.

The operators of Penguin Place have replanted the breeding habitat, built nesting sites, cared for sick and injured birds and, importantly, trapped predators. The yellow-eyed penguin's greatest threat is loss of habitat, especially the low-lying coastal vegetation in which the birds nest. Sadly, many farmers in Southland and Otago allow cattle to trample remaining patches of vegetation favoured by yellow-eyed penguins.

A number of tour operators (see Transport & Tours later in this chapter) go to other yellow-eyed penguin beaches through private 'conservation reserves', ie, land owned by farmers who charge for the privilege. Yellow-eyed penguins also nest at other public beaches but numbers are small and sightings less certain. Sandfly Bay has a small colony which can be viewed from a DOC hide at the far end of the beach. Follow all signs, don't approach the penguins and view only from the hide.

Sea Lions The New Zealand (more commonly Hooker's) sea lions can usually only be seen on a tour (see Transport & Tours later in this chapter) to a 'secret' beach where the first pup was born on the NZ mainland after a breeding absence of 700 years. They are also often present at Allans Beach and Victory Beach. The sea lions, visitors from Campbell Island and the Auckland Islands, are predominantly bachelor males.

Larnach Castle

This castle (☎ 03-476 1616; **W** *www.larnachcastle.co.nz, Camp Rd; castle & grounds adult/child $12/4.50; open 9am-5pm*) is Dunedin's best-known building, a symbol of the indecent wealth that once resided in the city. This private 'castle' is a conglomeration of architectural styles and fantasies on the highest point of the peninsula. Built by JWM Larnach in 1871, its construction cost £125,000, about $25 million by today's standards. Proving that money can't buy happiness, Larnach, a merchant and politician, committed suicide in a Parliament House committee room in 1898. The history of his family is well presented inside the castle and makes for very entertaining reading – there are more scandals than your average soap opera!

Larnach Castle is 15km from central Dunedin and can be reached by tour or by taking the Portobello bus to Company Bay and walking 4km uphill. Explore the castle at will, or pay $6 (children $2) to visit only the gardens and ballroom (which houses a very pleasant cafe). Wonderful accommodation is also offered in the castle's grounds – see Places to Stay & Eat later.

Other Attractions

The **Glenfalloch Woodland Garden** (*430 Portobello Rd; open 9.30am-dusk daily*), 9km from Dunedin, is noted for its rhododendrons and azaleas and for the domestic birds freely wandering in the grounds. There's a tearoom and a restaurant popular with wedding parties. The Portobello bus stops out the front.

The University of Otago's **Marine Studies Centre & Westpac Trust Aquarium** (☎ 03-479 5826, Hatchery Rd; adult/child $7/3; open noon-4.30pm daily) is at the end of a small peninsula near Portobello (take the road beside the Portobello general store – it's about 2km of unsealed road). The aquarium has fish and invertebrates from a variety of local marine habitats, and touch-tanks with animals and plants found in shallow waters and rock pools.

Natures Wonders (☎ 0800 246 446) does trips in an eight-wheeled amphibious vehicle through property at Taiaroa Head, not far from the albatross centre. One-hour tours taking in great coastal scenery and wildlife cost about $30; bookings are advised.

Transport & Tours
There are half a dozen buse services daily between Dunedin and Portobello ($3.70 one way); two of these services continue on to Harington Point. Saturday and Sunday services are more limited. Once you get to the peninsula, however, you'll find that it's tough to get between attractions without your own transport.

There is also a wide variety of tours offered around the peninsula (most depart from Dunedin) and you'll invariably be led by a knowledgeable local guide, but, again, you have greater flexibility with your own transport.

Elm Wildlife Tours (☎ 0800 356 563, 03-474 1872, W www.elmwildlifetours.co.nz) has bird- and wildlife-spotting tours out of Dunedin. Tours take about six hours and are $55 per person; pick-up and drop-off is included. There is also the opportunity for add-on tours, such as a boat cruise or sea kayaking, at additional cost.

Back to Nature Tours (☎ 03-477 0484, W www.backtonaturetours.co.nz) is based out of Manor House Backpackers in Dunedin and does the same type of trip as Elm Wildlife for $50, departing Dunedin in the afternoon. **Bottom Bus** (☎ 03-474 7370) also offers day trips to the peninsula.

Newton Tours (☎ 03-477 5577) has tours from Dunedin to Larnach Castle along Highcliff Rd (adult/child $30/15, including castle entry). There are also wildlife tours to Taiaroa ($35/18), and options to view the albatross or penguins or take a *Monarch* cruise (all at additional cost). The company does frequent tours daily, which means you can get off and catch the next bus, thereby combining a few peninsula attractions in a half- or full-day excursion.

Otago Explorer (☎ 0800 322 240, 03-474 3300) operates tours to the peninsula and is the only operator to give guided tours inside Larnach Castle, with the guide giving a good spin on the Larnach family history.

For small group ecotours, **Otago Nature Guides** (☎ 03-454 5169, W www.nznature guides.com) is recommended. It has sunrise walks ($48) to see the yellow-eyed penguins, plus it can devise half- or full-day itineraries in the region. The owners also offer B&B accommodation.

Activities
Castle Discovery Horse Treks (☎ 0800 467 738, 03-478 0796) is based in Broad Bay and operates treks from the harbour to the hilltops around Larnach Castle. Treks cost $45 (including admission to the castle); bookings are essential.

E-Tours (☎ 03-476 1960, W www.inmark .co.nz/e-tours) operates full-day cycling tours on the peninsula. The price ($89) includes pick-up from Dunedin and a minibus ride out to the peninsula heights, then cycling along rural tracks and beach, plus admission to either the albatross or penguin centres, or a cruise.

Wild Earth Adventures (☎ 0800 699 453, 03-473 6535, W www.nzwildearth.com) has sea-kayaking trips in the area (including a sunset trip) priced from $69, including pick-up in Dunedin.

Walking
The peninsula has a number of scenic farmland and beach walks, though you really need your own transport to get to the trails. It's a half-hour walk from the car park at the end of Seal Point Rd down huge sand dunes to the beautiful beach at **Sandfly Bay**.

From the end of Sandymount Rd it's a 40-minute round-trip walk to the impressive cliff scenery of The Chasm and Lovers Leap. A one-hour side trail leads to Sandfly Bay.

Other walks include those to the Pyramids (distinct, pointed rock stacks) and Mt Charles (through private land). Get a copy of the *Otago Peninsula Tracks* pamphlet from the Dunedin visitors centre.

Places to Stay & Eat
Portobello Village Tourist Park (☎ 03-478 0359, e portobellotp@xtra.co.nz, 27 Hereweka St) Powered/unpowered sites $22/20 for 2 people, bunkrooms $30, tourist flats

$65. This lovely small park is in Portobello township and offers good facilities and excellent flats with kitchen, en suite, linen and TV. The bunkrooms are more basic.

McFarmers Backpackers (☎ *03-478 0389, 774 Portobello Rd*) Dorm beds $17, doubles & twins $40. McFarmers is a small, cosy and friendly place, only 1km from Portobello village on the Dunedin side; the local bus usually stops out the front. The place – and the owner – both have great character and you can either spend time just enjoying the fine views, or you can rent bikes, canoes or a rowing boat from here and set out to explore the area. It's worth booking ahead as places are limited.

The old pub in Portobello, the *Portobello Hotel* (☎ *03-478 0759*), has a couple of good, reasonably priced rooms that have private facilities. The cost is $35 per person, and that also includes breakfast.

Larnach Castle (☎ *03-476 1616*, w *www .larnachcastle.co.nz, Camp Rd*) Stable rooms with shared facilities $55, lodge rooms from $160. Larnach, in the grounds of the famous castle, has double rooms in the historic stable building and plush hotel-style rooms in the new lodge, with individual decor and great themed rooms. Guests staying at the castle have the option of enjoying an excellent three-course meal in the castle's dining rooms ($45). Accommodation prices include free or discounted entry to the castle and grounds.

Penguin Place Lodge (☎ *03-478 0286*, e *penguin.place@clear.net.nz, Harington Point Rd*) is alongside the tour office for Penguin Place. Simple accommodation is offered in single, double and twin rooms (shared facilities) for $15 per person, with an additional $5 for linen hire. There are kitchen facilities and a TV room, as well.

Harington Point Village Motel (☎ *03-478 0287*) on the main road, not far from the albatross centre, has spacious, self-contained units priced from $85 to $95 for two (additional people are $15 each; the units can sleep four comfortably). The owners of Harington Point are more than happy to share their extensive knowledge of the area and its wildlife.

There is also a number of cottages, homestay and B&Bs on the peninsula; the Dunedin visitors centre should be able to help you out.

The Cottage (☎ *03-478 0073*, e *the cottage@xtra.co.nz, 748 Portobello Rd*) is a charming, old-world place in a private setting at Broad Bay ($85); a breakfast hamper can be provided for an extra $25. *The Homestead* (☎ *03-478 0384*, e *thehome stead@clear.net.nz, 238 Harington Point Rd*) has excellent self-contained units a few kilometres past Portobello village. Prices are from $98 to $110 for two people; $20 per additional adult.

There are not a lot of dining options on the peninsula. Most of the bigger attractions have a cafeteria for light lunches or snacks. Portobello has a general store and adjacent takeaway shop with limited hours, plus a small cafe, and Macandrew Bay has a store and rarely-open fish-and-chip shop. The bright and breezy *Loaves & Fishes* (☎ *03-476 1357*) is also at Macandrew Bay, with a small but appealing menu and lunch dishes from $9 to $12, and dinner mains in the $14 to $22 range. It's closed Monday and Tuesday.

The best place on the peninsula for dining is the pretty *1908 Restaurant & Cafe* (☎ *03-478 0801*) in Portobello. The changing blackboard menu has a wide variety of gourmet delights, including seafood, and dinner mains are up around $30 (lunch is a more casual affair in terms of both food and price). 1908 is open for lunch and dinner daily from November to March (dinner bookings advised), with restricted hours outside these months.

Central Otago

Most Central Otago towns owe their origin to 40 years of gold mining during the 19th century. The goldfields area extends from Wanaka down to Queenstown and Glenorchy, east through Alexandra to the coast at Palmerston, and southeast from Alexandra to Milton. Interpretative pamphlets such as *Otago Goldfields: Heritage Trail* show towns and gold-mining areas. Stone buildings, gold-mining equipment and miles of tailings (waste left over from mining) are found throughout the area, while Queenstown, an important town during Otago's golden days, maintains its glory in the modern gold rush – tourism.

Most of Central Otago lies on a rugged and dry plateau, sheltered by the Southern Alps. In summer, days are warm to hot and rainfall is very low. In winter, temperatures can drop to well below freezing.

For good information on the region see W www.tco.org.nz.

CROMWELL
pop 2610

This modern but rather characterless little town is on the main route between Wanaka and Queenstown. Cromwell is the heart of stone fruit country – as testified by the giant Carmen Miranda hat-piece display in front of the town. Roadside stalls sell all manner of fruit.

The Cromwell & Districts visitors centre (☎ 03-445 0212, e cromwellvin@xtra.co .nz, W www.cromwell.org.nz) is in the Cromwell Mall and is open 10am to 4pm daily. It handles bookings and has displays on the hydroelectric projects in the Clutha Valley. The information centre also houses the town **museum** which features local mining artefacts.

On Melmore Terrace, **Old Cromwell** is a row of historic buildings overlooking Dunstan Dam (they were painstakingly removed and restored from the original Cromwell, now flooded by the waters of the dam). It's a disappointingly lifeless area, home to a few craft shops.

Gold-mining sites around Cromwell include Bannockburn, crumbling Bendigo and the Kawarau. Across a footbridge spanning the spectacular Kawarau Gorge, the **Goldfields Mining Centre** (☎ 03-445 1038, W www.goldfieldsmining.co.nz), about 7km towards Queenstown, is a rather commercial operation offering tours of the tailings and old mine machinery for a pricey $14, including the chance to pan for gold, or buy gold jewellery in their store. There's also

jetboating here with **Goldfields Jet** (☎ 03-445 3080), costing $69 for a 40-minute ride.

Further along the road to Queenstown are some excellent wineries, plus there's **bungy jumping** at the old Kawarau suspension bridge, built in 1880 for access to the Wakatipu goldfields. See Queenstown later in this chapter for information on the bungy jump.

Places to Stay & Eat

Cromwell Top 10 Holiday Park (☎ 03-445 0164, W www.cromwellholidaypark.co.nz, 1 Alpha . St) Powered/unpowered sites $20/18 for 2 people, cabins $30-55, units & motels $65-75. This huge park, 2km from the town centre, is a friendly place with excellent modern facilities. The new units are a particularly good deal.

The Chalets (☎ 0800 830 231, 03-445 1260, W www.thechalets.co.nz, 102 Barry Ave) Powered/unpowered sites $18/16 for 2 people, bunk room $15, singles $25, doubles & twins $36. The Chalets are large lodges owned by the local polytechnic and were once the quarters for dam workers. Each chalet has its own lounge and kitchen and a number of well-equipped rooms.

There are a handful of hotels and motels, including the large **Golden Gate Lodge** (☎ 0800 104 451, 03-445 1777, W www .goldengate.co.nz, Barry Ave), with hotel-style doubles from $90 to $130, plus a restaurant and public bars. The front of the mall has a good bakery, next to the **Ploughmans** (☎ 03-445 0725) cafe-bar, and there are a few takeaways at either end of the mall. For better dining options head south-east out of town to Clyde or to the **cafe** (☎ 03-445 3211) at Bannockburn Heights winery.

ALEXANDRA
pop 4620

East of Cromwell is Alexandra, the hub of Central Otago. The lure of gold brought thousands to the Dunstan goldfields but the town owes its permanence to the post-rush dredging boom of the 1890s. The orchardists followed and Alexandra owes its current prosperity to them. This pretty town is an oasis of trees among barren, rocky hills.

OTAGO

OTAGO

The helpful Central Otago visitors centre (☎ 03-448 9515, @ info@alexandra.co.nz, W www.alexandra.co.nz), 22 Centennial Ave, provides maps and plenty of local information, such as its excellent series of pamphlets outlining walks in the region. It's open 9am to 5pm Monday to Friday, 10am to 3pm Saturday and Sunday. At the time of research there were plans to relocate the centre in early 2003 to a new building across the road in Pioneer Park, which would also house the local museum.

The huge clock on the hill above town, Alexandra's answer to the Hollywood Hills sign, can be reached by a walking track or by a drive to a nearby viewpoint. The DOC office (☎ 03-440 2040) is on the outskirts of town at 43 Dunstan Rd.

The **Alexandra Historical Museum** (☎ *03-448 7077, Dunorling St; free admission; open 10am-4.30pm Mon-Fri, 10am-noon Sat*) is in temporary lodgings after it was washed out of its original premises by huge floods in 1999; visit for a look at some of the photos and articles of the devastation wreaked throughout the Central Otago region by burst riverbanks. It's usually home to a comprehensive collection of mining and pioneering relics.

Activities

Alexandra is **mountain bike** heaven with many old gold trails through the Old Man, Dunstan, Raggedy and Knobby Ranges. A highlight for keen bikers is the Dunstan Trail. The *Mountain Biking* pamphlets from the visitors centre detail exhilarating rides but check out the latest track conditions. The Otago Central Rail Trail passes through Alexandra. Alexandra Cycle World (☎ 03-448 8048), 21 Shannon St, is one of a few places in town that rents out bikes.

Dunstan Trail Rides (☎ *03-449 2445)* and **Safari Excursions** (☎ *0800 208 930, 03-448 7474)* offer horse treks and 4WD safaris respectively, through the amazing local landscapes.

Places to Stay & Eat

There are two fairly uninspiring camping grounds on the northern outskirts of town.

Both have shady settings but tired facilities. *Alexandra Holiday Park* (☎ *03-448 8297, Manuherikia Rd)* has camp sites for $19 and basic cabins from $28 to $34. *Pine Lodge Holiday Camp* (☎ *03-448 8861, 31 Ngapara St)* has powered/unpowered sites for $19.50/19, basic cabins from $32 to $36 and motel rooms for $62.

The backpackers in Alexandra was washed out in the 1999 floods and subsequently closed. At the time of research there was no backpackers in town, but it shouldn't be long before someone spies the business opportunity and opens one. Check with the visitors centre.

There is a good selection of motels along Centennial Ave, including friendly *Kiwi Motel* (☎ *03-448 8258, 115 Centennial Ave)*, with spacious, well-maintained units. Prices are from $65 to $75, making it the cheapest motel option in town. *Alexandra Motor Lodge* (☎ *0800 929 555, 03-448 7580, 85 Centennial Ave)* also has good units, starting from $85.

Thirteen kilometres south of town towards Roxburgh is *Fruitlands* (☎ *03-449 2192, W www.fruitlandscountrylodge.co.nz)*, a gallery and cafe with three lovely modern units in a restored historic stone building set in pretty grounds; accommodation is $95. The cafe here is also a good spot for lunch or a snack.

Back in town, Centennial Ave has a good *bakery* at No 82, and *La Strada Caffe* (☎ *03-448 9021)* at No 72, is an excellent spot for breakfast or lunch, serving cooked brekkies, sandwiches, muffins and fresh juices. Over the road at No 73, *Nuno's* (☎ *03-448 5444)* is a great place run by a Portuguese-Kiwi couple. The restaurant offers tempting dishes for around $20, with an emphasis on seafood (including an authentic Portuguese fish stew). Adjacent to the restaurant is a takeaway offering good fish and chips and burgers.

Getting There & Away

InterCity, Atomic and Catch-a-Bus pass through Alexandra with connections to Wanaka, Queenstown and Dunedin. Make inquiries and bookings at the visitors centre.

Otago Central Rail Trail

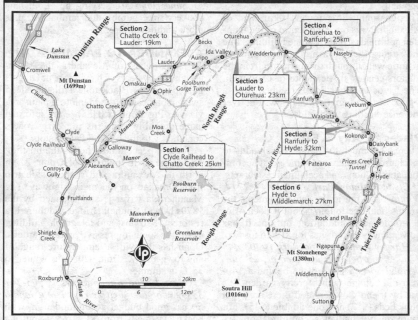

The Central Otago rail branch line was originally built to provide a reliable transport service from the goldfield towns to Dunedin, the commerce and banking centre of the region. Construction on the line began near Dunedin in 1879 and it was 28 years before the line was opened as far as Clyde in 1907.

Throughout the 20th century, as cars became more prevalent and roads in the area improved, use of the railway waned and in 1990 the 150km stretch of rail between Middlemarch and Clyde was closed permanently. DOC acquired the line and set about ripping up the tracks and resurfacing the trail, including the old rail bridges, viaducts and tunnels; the old railway line is now a year-round recreational facility, designed especially for walkers, mountain-bikers and horse-riders. It was used by some 10,000 people in the summer of 2000–01, and not surprisingly many new business have sprung up to service those using the trail.

The trail can be biked or walked in either direction, although a popular option for travellers is to take the scenic Taieri Gorge Railway from Dunedin and cycle from Pukerangi to Middlemarch (19km by road), to begin the trail the following day. The trail takes three to five days to complete in its entirety (alternatively, many people choose to do a section of the trail as a day-trip). The trail caters for all fitness levels as there are no steep hills; it offers users a chance to experience wonderful scenery and a real sense of remoteness. The towns passed though include reasonably sized settlements like Ranfurly, Omakau and Alexandra, and tiny villages such as Waipiata, Wedderburn, Oturehua and Lauder; even the small places now have a place where you can grab a bite and doss down for the night. Mountain bikes can be rented for the journey from Alexandra or Dunedin. Any of the major visitors centres in the area (Alexandra, Cromwell, Dunedin) should be able to help you with information on the trail, and everything you need to know can be found online at Ⓦ www.otagocentralrailtrail.co.nz.

OTAGO

CLYDE

pop 850

This charming little town, 10km west of Alexandra, was once the centre of the Dunstan goldfields. Historic stone buildings line the streets. Pick up a brochure detailing a historic walk through the township from the visitors centres at Alexandra or Cromwell. The Clyde **Lookout Point**, reached from a signposted road, gives great views out over the once-bustling goldfields.

Places to Stay & Eat

There's not much to Clyde, (which adds to its charm), but there are some great accommodation options and acclaimed restaurants.

Clyde Holiday Park (☎ 03-449 2714, *Whitby St)* is not in the same league as the town's boutique lodgings, but it does offer a simple accommodation option. It has powered/unpowered sites for $18/16 for two.

Hartley Arms Backpackers (☎ 03-449 2700, e hartleyarms@xtra.co.nz, 25 Sunderland St)* is a small place behind a 140-year-old cottage with a pretty garden. It's run by friendly owners and there are eight bunk beds ($17) and one double ($45). For more quality budget accommodation, try the local pub: the *Dunstan Hotel* (☎ 03-449 2869, 35 Sunderland St)* has comfortable, well-maintained rooms with shared facilities for $28/50.

Dunstan House (☎ 03-449 2295, W www .dunstanhouse.co.nz, 29 Sunderland St)* is a delightful place, its pretty rooms created with a wonderful attention to detail. Singles/doubles or twins with shared facilities are $65/85, en suite doubles cost $130; prices include breakfast. There's an inviting lounge with an open fire, and a good restaurant.

Olivers (☎ 03-449 2860, W www.olivers .co.nz, 34 Sunderland St)* is a fine-dining award-winning, restaurant that also offers elegant boutique accommodation. Rooms and unique suites range in price from $108 to $200 and are all part of a rambling old stone complex that has had its house, stable, dairy and servants quarters restored.

Other great dining options include the casual *Post Office Cafe & Bar* (☎ 03-449 2488, 2 Blythe St)* and the bright and funky

Blues Bank Cafe & Bar (☎ 03-449 2147, 31 Sunderland St)*, serving up 'Louisiana cookery' like gumbo and jambalaya, plus more traditional fare.

ALEXANDRA TO PALMERSTON

To the northeast of Alexandra, the Manuherikia Valley bears rich evidence of Otago's golden age. At Blackstone Hill the SH85 swings southeast to the Maniototo plain and, via the 'Pig Root', (SH85) – the informal name probably concerns the early road's condition – to the sea and Palmerston.

Today's peacefulness belies the bustling past of the small township of **Ophir**, 27km north of Alexandra and a short side trip from **Omakau** on the main highway. The Manuherikia River is still spanned by the 1870s Dan O'Connell Bridge and there is a restored 1886 post and telegraph building, as well as some impressive private gardens. Ophir has the widest temperature range of any town in NZ: from -20°C in winter to 35°C in summer.

Ophir Lodge Backpackers (☎ 03-447 3339, e blgaler@xtra.co.nz, 1 Macdonald St)* has good budget accommodation, with backpacker beds from $13 to $15, but it's closed from May to August. The friendly, helpful *Omakau Commercial Hotel* (☎ 03-447 3715, Main Rd)* has camp sites, backpacker beds and excellent rooms ($30/55 en suite singles/doubles, $28/48 with shared facilities), as well as tasty meals.

The road forks at Becks, where there is a great old pub. The left fork leads to **St Bathans**, once a thriving gold-mining town with a population of 2000 – today you could count the inhabitants on one hand. This is a real city escape and has original buildings like the 'haunted' *Vulcan Hotel* (☎ 03-447 3629)*, with doubles for $70 (shared facilities). This is a quaint living museum and the only survivor of the town's 14 hotels; meals are available. The **Blue Lake**, formed entirely by sluicing activity, is a popular nearby picnic spot; **horse treks** are available in the area (☎ 03-447 3512).

Back on SH85, eastbound past Blackstone Hill, **Naseby** was once the largest gold-mining town on the Maniototo. There's a museum and the surrounding area is great for walking and mountain biking. From May to September the **Maniototo Ice Rink** (☎ 03-444 9270, Channel Rd) is used for skating, curling and ice hockey.

Larchview Holiday Park (☎ 03-444 9904) is a large ground with camp sites, cabins and chalets set among native trees. There are two pubs in Naseby, both offering food and accommodation. The **Royal Hotel** (☎ 0800 262 732, 03-444 9990, **W** www .naseby.co.nz, 1 Earne St) has cheap, simple rooms ($25/40 singles/doubles with shared facilities) and the owner, Kila, is an excellent source of cycling information. He offers bike rentals and repairs and tours in the area by arrangement.

Danseys Pass, 39km north of Naseby, is another goldfields town and the home of **Danseys Pass Coach Inn** (☎ 03-444 9048, **W** www.danseyspass.co.nz), a wonderful stone inn from the 1860s and strategically located between the Maniototo and the Waitaki Valley. It has been extensively and elegantly refurbished; en suite doubles from $108 to $125. Great meals are available.

Back on the main road, you'll pass through Ranfurly and Kyeburn, 15km farther on. From Kyeburn it's 62km to Palmerston on SH85, or there's a junction with SH87, which leads south directly to Dunedin. Fifty kilometres south on this route is the tiny township of **Middlemarch**, with little going for it except an impressive backdrop (the Rock and Pillar Range) and its status as the start or end point of the Otago Central Rail Trail. **Blind Billy's Holiday Camp** (☎ 03-464 3355, **e** blind billy@xtra.co.nz) is the place to head to for cheap accommodation (camp sites, backpackers, cabins) as well as bike rental and excellent advice on the trail.

Ranfurly
pop 840

This small town is the hub of the vast inland Maniototo plain. Nearby Naseby with its goldfields and the more luckless Hamiltons goldfields near Waipiata were the original reasons for European settlement. When the railway line was closed in 1990, it came as another nail in the town's coffin, but the new rail trail brings promise of tourism, as does the town's commendable efforts to showcase its rural Art Deco architecture as an attraction ('Art Deco in a paddock', one local wittily termed it). Like Napier on the North Island, Ranfurly suffered a series of fires in the 1930s, and the town was rebuilt in the style of the time. Many of the buildings have recently been restored, and there's a great **Art Deco museum** and a few fine curio shops.

The old train station on Charlemont St is home to the helpful Maniototo visitors centre (☎ 03-444 9970, **W** www.maniototo.com) and displays on the history of the old train line. It's open 10am to 4.30pm Monday to Friday, and often on Saturday and Sunday in summer.

Catch-a-Bus (☎ 03-479 9960 in Dunedin) has a daily shuttle service between Wanaka and Dunedin that goes via Ranfurly.

Places to Stay & Eat There are a few accommodation options, including **Ranfurly Camping Ground** (☎ 03-444 9144, 8 Reade St), with sites, cabins and flats, and **Ranfurly Motels** (☎ 03-444 9383, 1 Davis Ave), with units priced from $70.

The main focus of town life is the large **Ranfurly Lion Hotel** (☎ 03-444 9140, **e** ranfurly.hotel@xtra.co.nz, 10 Charlemont St), a classic country pub with comfortable singles/doubles for $40/60 or with en suite for $45/75. It also runs the basic **backpackers** opposite, a blockhouse building charging $10 per person ($15 with linen). The pub's restaurant is the best in town.

Peter's Farm Hostel (☎ 03-444 9083) is a relaxed place in an old farmhouse, signposted 3km from Waipiata, which is 12km south-east of Ranfurly, off the highway. Apart from the peace and quiet, the main attractions are kayaking, gold-panning, fishing, cycling (free equipment supplied) and a nearby walking loop. Friendly, laid-back Peter will pick up from Ranfurly or Waipiata (there's a tavern in Waipiata for drinks and meals, but nothing else). Dorm beds are $16, doubles & twins $36 to $40. Camp on the grounds is $10 per person. The hostel is usually closed May to August.

OTAGO

OTAGO

Macraes Flat

Not all of the gold has disappeared, and the small town of Macraes Flat is the gateway to the huge Macraes Gold Mine. From Ranfurly it is 63km south-east along SH85 to Dunback and then 17km west to Macraes Flat. An alternative route is to go south from Kyeburn to Hyde (21km), then another 20km east. The open-cut mine is the largest in NZ, and tours ($10) depart at 1.30pm on Saturday and Sunday (except in summer); they can be arranged through Stanley's Hotel (☎ 03-465 2400) in Macraes Flat.

ALEXANDRA TO DUNEDIN

Southeast from Alexandra via SH8 to Dunedin there's more evidence of the 19th century's gold-seekers, and the spectacular scenery continues as you pass through small town after small town.

The first town of any size is **Roxburgh**, in an area known for fruit growing. There's a camping ground, a couple of well-priced motels and a reasonable backpackers. *Villa Rose Backpackers (☎ 03-446 8761, e re markableorchards@xtra.co.nz 79 Scotland St)* is a tidy converted house with all facilities; if the place is not completely full of itinerant fruit pickers, there are dorm beds for $14 and twins and doubles for $32.

About 9km south of Roxburgh, *The Seed Farm (☎ 03-446 6824)* has lovely studio units in converted stables, set in pretty gardens, for $100. There is also a restaurant here open daily in summer for lunch and devonshire teas.

Between Roxburgh and Milton, near Lawrence, is **Gabriels Gully**, the site of a frenzied stampede for gold by 10,000 miners in July 1861, after Gabriel Read discovered gold in the Tuapeka River. There are interesting walks in the area.

In quaint **Lawrence** you'll find the well-run *Oban House Backpackers (☎ 03-485 9600, e obanhouse@xtra.co.nz, 1 Oban St)*, with dorm beds for $15 and twins and doubles for $34. There's also a stylish cafe here, *Jazzed on Java (☎ 03-485 9234, 26 Ross St)*, which makes a great pit stop.

At Lawrence the road splits into two, one leg going to the coast and SH1 at Milton,

the other going via Lake Mahinerangi and the Waipori goldfield (and Waipori Falls) with more relics of the gold rushes. Dunedin is 57km north of Milton and about half that distance from where the Waipori Falls road meets SH1.

THE CLUTHA DISTRICT

The mighty Clutha River, flowing through the Clutha district's collection of small communities, is not NZ's longest river (the Waikato is 16km longer) but it carries the most water. The Clutha drains a huge area including Lakes Hawea, Wanaka and Wakitipu. In a number of places the river has been dammed to feed hydroelectric power stations. The Clyde Dam holds back the waters of Lake Dunstan; in the 1980s it generated great controversy at the drowning of such natural beauty. The towns of Clinton, Lawrence, Milton, Waihola, Owaka, Tapanui and Balclutha are all part of the region. Owaka is covered under The Catlins in the Southland chapter.

Balclutha
pop 4130

The largest town in South Otago, Balclutha is dominated by an impressive arched concrete bridge across the Clutha River. There's not much to the town and little reason to linger, although it may be a convenient point from which to take a guided tour of the Catlins (see The Catlins in the Southland chapter for details), or a place to stock up on groceries and petrol before heading south on the Southern Scenic Route (SH92).

The Clutha visitors centre (☎ 03-418 0388, e clutha.vin@cluthadc.govt.nz) is at 4 Clyde St and is staffed by a helpful bunch. There's a small heritage **museum** nearby on Renfrew St.

Naish Park Motor Camp (☎ 03-418 0088, 56 Charlotte St) is a small, friendly ground with sites for $18 and cabins from $27 to $40. *Rosebank Lodge (☎ 03-418 1490, 265 Clyde St)* is probably the flashest place in town, with rooms from $85. There is a good dining option here, *265 Restaurant*. Otherwise, uninspiring takeaways line the main street.

Garvan Homestead (☎ *03-417 8407,* W *www.garvan-homestead.co.nz)* is 13km north of Balclutha on SH1 and is a charming 1915 Tudor-style homestead set in magnificent gardens. It offers old-world B&B rooms for $95 to $120, and there's a good restaurant here, serving lunch and afternoon tea plus offering a-la-carte dining (reservations recommended).

North Otago

The Waitaki River, located south of Waimate, marks out North Otago. Continuing south from the Waitaki River is Oamaru, the largest town in North Otago. Follow either SH82 from Waimate or SH83 from Pukeuri Junction (8km north of Oamaru) to reach Kurow and the Waitaki Valley. From here SH83 continues to Omarama via the hydroelectric lakes of Waitaki, Aviemore and Benmore.

A good source of information on the area is W www.tourismwaitaki.co.nz.

OAMARU
pop 12,000

Pretty Oamaru was first settled by the Europeans in 1853. It was the seventh-largest town in NZ by the 1870s and early 1880s. Refrigerated meat shipping made it prosperous, and the local limestone was the favoured material for the many imposing buildings that still grace the town. The writer Janet Frame used Oamaru as the setting for some of her novels (see the boxed text 'Oamaru Framed'), and today the town is home to a number of 'artists, craftspeople and eccentrics' (in the words of one rather eccentric local!).

The town comes alive during the Heritage Celebrations in late November with penny-farthing races and other events. Oamaru also has fine public gardens and colonies of blue penguins and the rare yellow-eyed penguin.

The helpful and efficient Oamaru visitors centre (☎ 03-434 1656, e info@tourism waitaki.co.nz) is at 1 Thames St. It's open 9am to 6pm Monday to Friday and 10am to 5pm Saturday and Sunday.

Harbour-Tyne Historic Precinct

Oamaru boasts the best-preserved collection of historic commercial buildings in NZ, particularly in the harbour area and around Tyne St, which has dozens of classified buildings. The town's architecture is a mosaic of styles from Gothic revival to neoclassical Italianate and Greek. The local limestone was soft enough to saw, but it hardened when exposed to the air, so was a convenient and enduring building material. The free *Historic Oamaru* pamphlet describes this precinct.

Several small businesses have set up here, including a bookbinder, bookshop, antique shops, cafes and the *Criterion Hotel,* open daily for an old-fashioned ale. **The Woolstore** (☎ *03-434 8336)* has a good cafe, souvenirs and a car museum (entry $4). A good market is held here on Sunday.

One-hour **walking tours** ($7.50) focus on the history of the town and leave from the visitors centre on demand.

Other Attractions

The **North Otago Museum** (☎ *03-434 1652, 60 Thames St; admission free; open 1pm-4.30pm Mon-Fri, 10am-1pm Sat)* has historic and general exhibits.

The **Forrester Art Gallery** (☎ *03-434 1653, 9 Thames St; admission free; open 10.30am-4.30pm Mon-Fri, 10.30am-1pm Sat, 1pm-4.30pm Sun)* houses a good collection of local art and visiting exhibitions in an impressive historic building, a former bank built in 1883.

The town's **public gardens** date back to 1876 and are a delightful place to stroll. The main entrance gates are on Severn St where it crosses the railway line. Look out for the red Japanese bridge crossing Oamaru Creek, and the lovely *Wonderland* statue.

Penguins

Conveniently, you can walk to the yellow-eyed penguin and blue penguin colonies from the centre of town. There's lots of good information at W www.penguin.net.nz.

Blue penguins are numerous and nest right in the town around the Oamaru Harbour. Once considered a pest (they nested under buildings and on council reserves),

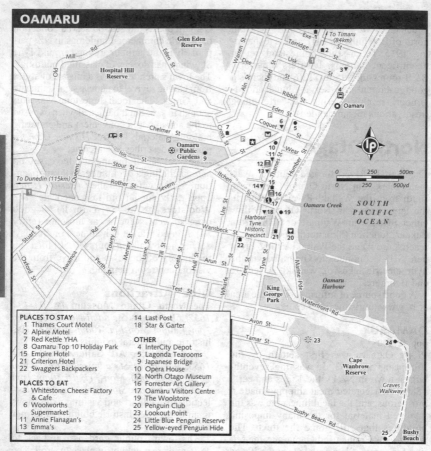

OAMARU

they are now the mascot for Oamaru and are the town's biggest tourist attraction. At the end of Waterfront Rd a nesting site has been fenced to keep out predators, and nesting boxes and a small grandstand have been built. This is a country-town version of the Phillip Island complex in Australia, the most famous site for viewing blue (or fairy) penguins. The penguins waddle ashore just after dusk year-round, although numbers are higher in summer. Viewing costs $8 per adult; children are free. The small visitors centre (☎ 03-443 1195) here has good information and souvenirs; a new, larger centre is

being built, and there are plans for new viewing grandstands to seat up to 350.

The loss of coastal forest for breeding has made **yellow-eyed penguins** among the world's rarest penguins. The Bushy Beach nesting site has good natural vegetation and a hide allows undisturbed observation of these beautiful birds. The yellow-eyeds are best seen a couple of hours before sunset, when they come ashore to feed their chicks, but they are shy and easily upset, so avoid loud noises and stick to the trail and hide. It is well worth taking a tour ($7), operated under a DOC concession, that allows closer viewing. Tours leave from the car park on Bushy Beach Rd in the early evening (the visitors centre has times).

Places to Stay

Oamaru Top 10 Holiday Park (☎ 0800 280 202, 03-434 7666, Chelmer St) Powered/ unpowered sites $20/18, cabins $32-44, self-contained units $52-62. This is a well-maintained park adjacent to the large public gardens, and has a good selection of sites, cabins and units.

Red Kettle YHA (☎ 03-434 5008, ⓔ yha oamaru@yha.org.nz, cnr Reed & Cross Sts) is a well-maintained place, small and cosy with a friendly atmosphere. It's a couple of blocks west of Thames St, near the town gardens, and is closed from June to September. Dorm beds are $16, twins and doubles $36. Another backpackers that has a similarly homey feel is *Swaggers Backpackers* (☎ 03-434 9999, ⓔ swaggers@es.co.nz, 25 Wansbeck St), close to the historic precinct and the penguin area. Dorm beds here are $17, doubles and twins $36.

Empire Hotel (☎ 03-434 3446, ⓔ empire hotel@hotmail.com, 13 Thames St) Dorm beds $17, doubles & twins $42. This brand new backpackers is run by a friendly Japanese-Kiwi couple, and you can take a shot at riding the owner's penny farthings. The hotel offers clean and comfortable new rooms and good facilities. There are plans for a cafe downstairs serving casual Japanese and English fare.

Most motels are at the top of Thames St and include the *Alpine Motel* (☎ 0800 272 710, 03-434 5038, 285 Thames St), with good units from $65, and *Thames Court Motel* (☎ 0800 223 644, 03-434 6963, 252 Thames St), with units from $70.

Criterion Hotel (☎ 03-434 6247, 3 Tyne St) Singles/doubles $60/75. Here you can stay in the heart of the historic area in pretty rooms above this excellent bar. The price includes cooked breakfast; bathroom facilities are shared.

The Waitaki Accommodation Guide is compiled by the visitors centre and lists many of the B&Bs, homestays and farmstays found in the area.

Oamaru Framed

The renowned novelist Janet Frame was born in Dunedin in 1924 but spent most of her early school years in Oamaru. Her Oamaru home, 56 Eden St, is mentioned in her autobiographies. She uses the name 'Waimaru' as a pseudonym for the town and it appears in some of her novels.

Frame first gained an international reputation in 1957 with *Owls Do Cry*. Many of the places alluded to in this novel can still be seen in town – the clock tower, the Opera House ('Miami' in the book), the Majestic (the 'Regent'), the local dump (now the site of the Red Kettle YHA) and the Duck Pond.

All of these places can be seen on the Janet Frame Trail (about a 1½-hour walk) outlined in the free *Heritage Trails of North Otago* booklet. Other sites relate to *Faces in the Water* (1961), *Scented Gardens for the Blind* (1963), *A State of Siege* (1967), *Intensive Care* (1970) and *The Edge of the Alphabet* (1962).

It was Jane Campion's film version of *An Angel at my Table*, based on the second volume of Janet Frame's autobiographical trilogy, that spurred current interest in her works. Frame had a somewhat tortured life as a young woman, and became rather reclusive. She still lives in NZ.

Places to Eat

Most eateries are concentrated along Thames St. Stylish *Emma's* (☎ 03-434 1165, 30 Thames St) is home to Oamaru's cafe society; it's the best place in town for coffee and cafe fare along the lines of quiche, soup, sandwiches and cakes.

At the *Whitestone Cheese Factory & Cafe* (☎ 03-434 8098, 3 Torridge St), you can sample the award-winning local organic cheese, amongst other fine fare. The cafe here has lunches to $10 and cheese platters for $10/15 for one/two people.

Last Post (☎ 03-434 8080, 12 Thames St) Dinner $12-25. Last Post, the town's first post office, has been revived as a fully licensed restaurant. There's a good, simple selection of bar food to $14 (enchilada, burger, baked spud) plus a fine-dining section with meals such as baked fish and fillet steak. There's the bonus of a year-round undercover courtyard garden.

Annie Flanagan's (☎ 03-434 8828, 84 Thames St) Lunch to $10, dinner $10-20. Annie Flanagan's is a fun and popular Irish bar with generous meals and a good selection of ales. There are meals in all price ranges – lunch includes great $6 specials and a $7 roast; dinner time sees snacks, light meals and more upmarket dishes like venison or steak on offer.

Star & Garter (☎ 03-434 5246, 9 Itchen St) Lunch to $10, dinner mains $11.50-22. This restaurant is a good choice, with pretty decor, an extensive menu and well-prepared food. You can't go wrong with the $11.50 roast of the day.

There's also a large, central *Woolworths Supermarket* on Thames St.

Entertainment

Criterion Hotel (☎ 03-434 6247, 3 Tyne St) This hotel is the town's best watering hole, with an open fire, cosy feel, cheap pub fare (real English pub food like pork pies, bangers and mash or ploughman's lunch) and Emerson's and Wanaka Beerworks' fine brews on tap. From here, ask for directions to the *Penguin Club*, a hot little club run by local musos that occasionally gets some top-name bands. It's down an alley off the street behind the Criterion – look out for the very small sign. Even if there's no out-of-towners headlining, the locals like to get up and have a jam. It's usually open only later in the week.

There's a cinema inside the *Opera House (☎ 03-434 1070)*, 94 Thames St.

Getting There & Around

InterCity buses between Christchurch and Dunedin stop in Oamaru, as do a number of shuttles. Atomic Shuttles (☎ 03-322 8883), Catch-a-Bus (☎ 03-489 4641) and South Island Connections (☎ 0800 742 669, 03-366 6633) charge $15 to $20 to Dunedin. To Christchurch, it's $25 to $40. Buses arrive at and depart from Lagonda Tearooms, on the corner of Eden and Thames Sts. It's best to make bookings for bus tickets with the visitors centre.

There's also The Cook Connection (☎ 025 583 211), with useful services three times weekly from October to April between Oamaru and Mt Cook ($45, discounts for backpackers) via Kurow, Omarama and Twizel. On alternate days it connects Mt Cook and Timaru.

WAITAKI VALLEY

The Waitaki Valley has some interesting towns between the turn-offs on SH1 and Omarama, including Duntroon, Kurow and Otematata. **Duntroon** has an authentic blacksmith shop, trout- and salmon-fishing nearby and jetboating on the Waitaki.

There are Maori rock drawings at **Takiroa**, about 2km west of Duntroon. The limestone cliff drawings were done with red ochre and charcoal and may date back to the moa-hunting period (AD 1000 to 1500). The Oamaru visitors centre can give directions to the site.

Kurow is at the junction of the Waitaki and Hakataramea Rivers. Since 1928, when the Waitaki power station was built, Kurow has been a service centre for the area's hydroelectric schemes such as Benmore power station and Aviemore.

Tokarahi Homestead (☎ 03-431 2500, W www.homestead.co.nz) is an elegant limestone lodge offering plush B&B rooms from $170 to $250 (dinner by arrangement). The homestead is in Tokarahi, 11km from Duntroon on the road to Danseys Pass.

Glenmac Farmstay (☎ 03-436 0200, W www.farmstaynewzealand.co.nz) has backpackers accommodation, a camping area and B&B on a sheep and cattle station about 13km from Kurow. Camping is $15 to $16 for two, dorm beds cost $15, and B&B in the homestead is available from $35 per person. Biking, fishing, horse riding and 4WD trips can all be arranged.

Otematata Country Inn (☎ 03-438 7797, 11 Rata Drive) is a YHA associate in Otematata and offers backpackers beds for $19 and budget singles/doubles (shared facilities) for $25/35, plus self-contained units from $65. There's a restaurant and bar here.

Omarama
pop 355

Omarama is located at the head of the Waitaki Valley, 119km northwest of Oamaru, at the junction of SH8 and SH83. Not far from Omarama are the **Clay Cliffs**, formed by the active Osler fault line that continually exposes clay and gravel cliffs. These clay pinnacles are on private land 15km from Omarama – about 5km north of town then 10km down a dirt road off the highway. The $5 admission is pretty steep; make sure you leave all gates as you found them.

Omarama has a worldwide reputation for gliding due to the area's northwest thermals – the world championships were held here in the summer of 1994–95. **Alpine Soaring** (☎ 03-438 9600, **W** www.soaring.co.nz) has flights costing $135 for 20 minutes.

The Omarama visitors centre is inside the Caltex service station (☎ 03-438 9544), on SH83.

Places to Stay and Eat
The **Omarama Top 10 Holiday Park** (☎ 0800 662 726, 03-438 9875, **e** omarama .holiday@xtra.co.nz) is a pretty green spot in the southern part of town with powered and unpowered sites for $20, cabins for $36 to $48, tourist flats for $65 and motel units for $75.

The **Omarama Hotel** (☎ 03-438 9713) has comfortable older-style rooms with shared facilities for $35 per person; prices include breakfast.

There are also several motels in town.

Out of Omarama on SH8 in either direction are a number of good farmstays offering budget accommodation (and usually an area for camping); beds start at about $15 at each, and all stations are closed in winter. **Dunstan Downs** (☎ 03-438 9862, **e** tim .innes@xtra.co.nz) is 17km south-west of Omarama towards Queenstown, **Killermont Station** (☎ 03-438 9864) is 15km south of Omarama and **Buscot Station** (☎ 03-438 9646, **e** buscotstn@xtra.co.nz) is 8km north of Omarama.

The best place for food is **Clay Cliffs Estate** (☎ 03-438 9654), off the highway in the southern part of town. It's a small vineyard with good lunches, devonshire teas and dinners served in a pretty restaurant or outside by a pond.

OAMARU TO DUNEDIN
The coast road south from Oamaru provides a peaceful break from SH1 with fine coastal views, good beaches and resident dolphins. Take Wharfe St out of Oamaru (following the signs for Kakanui). It joins the highway again about halfway to Moeraki at Waianakarua.

The Hall – Coastal Backpackers (☎ 03-439 5411, **e** seaside@coastalbackpackers .co.nz) on a farm at All Day Bay provides a very good standard of accommodation (dorm beds are $18, twins and doubles $40). It's 16km south of Oamaru on the coastal road, 20km north of Moeraki (from SH1 take the signposted turn-off from Maheno), and offers a wonderful chance to relax and do little, or you can take advantage of the nearby lagoon with prolific bird life, beach walks, and the area's yellow-eyed penguins, dolphins and fur seals. Mountain bikes are available.

SH1 from Oamaru to Dunedin is a pleasant stretch of highway passing through a number of small but unremarkable towns, many of them coastal. From Palmerston the 'Pig Root' to Central Otago leaves SH1. Gold miners used to prefer this route into the Maniototo, as it was far more sheltered than the Old Dunstan Trail. The much improved road makes for a great scenic trip into Central Otago.

The big attraction along the Oamaru-Dunedin stretch are the extraordinary spherical boulders, like giant marbles, at **Moeraki**, 30km south of Oamaru, and again further south at Katiki and Shag Point. There's a $2 charge to walk down to the boulders from the car park. Scientists believe the boulders were not washed up onto the beach, but eroded from the mudstone cliffs behind. Subsequent erosion has exposed an internal network of veins, which make them look very much like turtle shell.

The tiny fishing village of Moeraki is 3km south of the boulders site, off SH1 on a sheltered bay. There are camp sites and

Top Otago Tipples

For quite some time Central Otago has had an international reputation for its wonderful scenery and high-adrenaline activities, but there's a new attraction to add to the list – the local wine, including medal-winning Pinot Noir. If you do any driving in the region you'll notice the proliferation of grapes, and after tasting a fine local drop in one of the many great restaurants and bars in the area you may well conclude that wine is the region's 'new gold'.

Central Otago is NZ's newest and fastest-growing wine region, but the area is not new to grape-growing – a Frenchman named John Feraud came to area in 1862, drawn by the Dunstan gold rush. He set about growing his own grapes and produced a variety of wines, but after his departure from the area commercial wine making ceased. It wasn't revived until the 1980s, when experimental grapes were planted around Queenstown, Wanaka and Alexandra. The first modern commercial wines were produced in 1987 and it is estimated that there are now some 70 vineyards in Central Otago, with at least 10 open to the public.

To explore these wineries and learn more of the area's viticulture, pick up the excellent *Central Otago Wine Map* from any of the region's visitors centres, or check W www.otagowine.com – a wine trail is outlined here. There are numerous tours of wineries offered out of the major tourist towns like Queenstown and Wanaka.

For travellers doing some independent exploration, you don't have to venture too far out of Queenstown. On SH6, near the historic Kawarau Suspension Bridge and bungy jump, there are three excellent wineries open to the public for tastings from 10am to 5pm daily. **Peregrine** (☎ 03-442 4000, W www.peregrinewines.co.nz) is about 5km east of the bridge and produces excellent Sauvignon Blanc, Pinot Noir and Pinot Gris. **Chard Farm** (☎ 03-442 6110, W www.chardfarm.co.nz) is accessed by a truly hair-raising road off the highway, almost opposite the bridge, and if you're lucky enough to have 80-year-old Keith in charge of your tastings, you're in for a treat – his descriptions of each wine are amazing! Finally, **Gibbston Valley** (☎ 03-442 6910, W www.gvwines.co.nz), 700m from the Kawarau Bridge, is the region's largest wine producer, and its Pinot Noir is a multi-award-winner. You can do a tour of the impressive wine cave here ($9.50, including tastings), plus there's a cheese factory and a great restaurant with outdoor courtyard.

cabins at the *motor camp* (☎ 03-439 4759), a few *motel units* (☎ 03-439 4862) for $70 a double, and even a small *backpackers* (☎ 03-439 4762). Meals are available from the tourist complex near the boulders, and from the new tavern in the village. From the back of the town a gravel road leads to the lighthouse for great views of the coast, and trails lead down the cliffs to a seal colony and a yellow-eyed penguin hide.

Queenstown Region

Queenstown is the self-styled 'adventure capital of the world' but when the party ends the Wakatipu region, with its stunning lake and surrounding mountain scenery, materialises as the real attraction. The aptly name Remarkables and the Eyre Mountains form a breathtaking backdrop. Words hardly do the Remarkables justice – they're pure magic capped with snow, at sunrise or in the afterglow of dusk.

QUEENSTOWN
pop 7500

Queenstown, on the shores of Lake Wakatipu, is nestled in what is surely one of the most scenic spots in the world. It's *the* resort town of the South Island and every organised tour stops here. There's plenty of hustling for the tourist dollar, and the town can boast a fabulous range of facilities, adventure activities, restaurants, cafes and buzzing nightlife.

There's great skiing in winter and plenty of substitute adrenaline activities in summer. Most activities are centred around the lake and many rivers nearby, especially the Dart, Shotover and Kawarau. Whitewater rafting, sledging and jetboating are all great ways to get wet. Bungy jumping, tandem parachuting and parapenting are similarly exciting ways to fly. But Queenstown is also a superbly equipped resort for more urbane pursuits. Those wishing to move at a much more leisurely pace can take a cruise on the *Earnslaw,* stroll through historical Arrowtown in autumn, play a round of golf at Millbrook or shop at Queenstown's many (expensive) boutiques.

History

When the first Pakeha arrived in the mid-1850s the region was deserted, although there is evidence of Maori settlement here. Sheep farmers came first, but in 1862 two shearers discovered gold on the banks of the Shotover River, precipitating a rush of prospectors to the area. A year later Queenstown was a mining town with streets and permanent buildings. Then the gold petered out and by 1900 the population had dropped from several thousand to a mere 190.

The lake was the principal means of transport and at the height of the mining boom there were four paddle-steamers and 30 other craft plying the waters. The Queestown-Glenorchy Road along the lake was only completed in 1962.

Orientation & Information

Queenstown is a compact town sloping up the steep hills from the lakeside. The main streets are the pedestrian-only Mall and Shotover St, with its activity booking offices.

The Queenstown visitors centre (☎ 0800 668 888, 03-442 4100, e qvc@xtra.co.nz, w www.queenstown-vacation.com), is in the Clocktower Centre on the corner of Shotover and Camp Sts. It's open from 7am to 7pm in summer (until 6pm in winter). This very busy office is the biggest booking agent in town. Destination Queenstown (☎ 03-442 7440, e queenstown@xtra.co .nz, w www.queenstown-nz.co.nz) also has copious information and their website is a great source of inspiration.

The DOC office (☎ 03-442 7935) at 37 Shotover St is the place for information on the many natural attractions of the area. It's open 9am to 6pm daily. Next door, the Information & Track Centre (☎ 03-442 9708, w www.infotrack.co.nz) handles most of the transport to the trail heads for the Routeburn, Greenstone-Caples, Kepler, Milford and Rees-Dart Tracks.

On Camp St, Kiwi Discovery (☎ 0800 505 504, 03-442 7340, w www.kiwidiscovery .com) also has track transport in summer, and ski transport and hire in winter.

On Shotover St, booking offices for activities include The Station (☎ 0800 367 874, 03-442 5252, w www.thestation.co.nz), which houses AJ Hackett Bungy and various other operators. Pipeline Bungy (☎ 03-442 5455) is next door at 27 Shotover St.

Fiordland Travel (☎ 0800 656 503, 03-442 7500, e info@fiordlandtravel.co.nz, w www.fiordlandtravel.co.nz) is in the Steamer Wharf on the waterfront (it also has offices at Te Anau and Manapouri). It books a huge range of lake trips and tours to Fiordland.

The post office on Camp St (with poste restante facilities) is open 8.30am to 8pm Monday to Friday, 9am to 8pm Saturday and 10am to 6pm Sunday. Most backpackers hostels have email facilities, and Budget Communications (☎ 03-441 1562), above McDonald's on Camp St, has numerous Internet terminals ($4 to $5 per hour) and is open 9am to 11pm daily. It's just one of many cybercafes dotted around the town centre – more are on Shotover St. The handy Internet Laundry at 1 Shotover St (on the corner of Gorge Rd) allows you to check your email while doing your laundry.

Queenstown has branches of all the major banks and plenty of moneychangers are open for longer hours.

Things to See & Do

Start at the top, by catching the **Skyline Gondola** *(☎ 03-441 0101, **w** www.sky line.co.nz, Brecon St)* to the summit of the hill overlooking the town for incredible

OTAGO

QUEENSTOWN

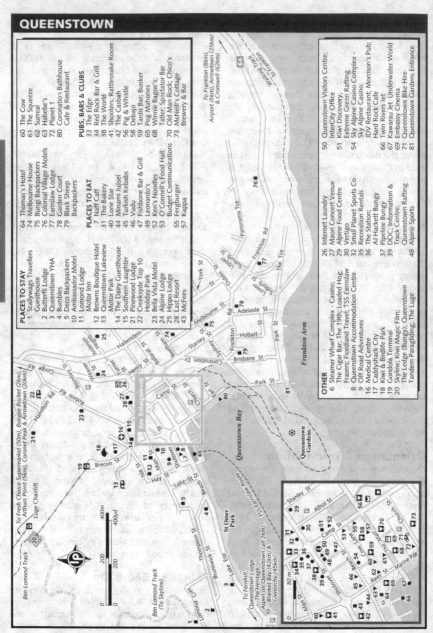

PLACES TO STAY
1 Scallywags Travellers Guesthouse
2 Butterfli Lodge
3 Queenstown YHA
4 Bumbles
5 Deco Backpackers
10 Ambassador Motel
11 Lomond Lodge Motor Inn
12 Browns Boutique Hotel
13 Queenstown Lakeview Motor Park
14 The Dairy Guesthouse
15 Southern Laughter
21 Pinewood Lodge
22 Creeksyde Top 10 Holiday Park
23 Bella Vista Motel
24 Alpine Lodge
25 Hippo Lodge
28 Last Resort
43 McFees

PLACES TO EAT
7 Naff Caff
31 The Bakery
40 Lone Star
44 Minami Jujsei
45 Turkish Kebabs
46 Vudu
47 Fishbone Bar & Grill
49 Leonardo's
52 Ken's Noodles
53 O'Connell's Food Hall; Budget Communications
55 Fergburger
57 Kappa

64 Thomas's Hotel
74 Melbourne House
75 Bungi Backpackers
76 Colonial Village Motels
77 Earnslaw Lodge
78 Garden Court
79 Black Sheep Backpackers

60 The Cow
61 The Squeeze
62 Surreal
63 Habebe's
72 Planet 1
80 Coronation Bathhouse Cafe & Restaurant

PUBS, BARS & CLUBS
33 The Edge
34 Red Rock Bar & Grill
38 The World
41 Shooters; Rattlesnake Room
42 The Casbah
56 Pig & Whistle
58 Debajo
59 Tardis Bar; Bunker
65 Pog Mahones
66 Winnie Bagoe's; Tatler; Sp>ctator Bar
68 Old Man Rock; Chico's
70 McNeill's Cottage Brewery & Bar
73

OTHER
6 Steamer Wharf Complex - Casino; The Cigar Bar; The 19th; Loaded Hog; Frasers; Fiordland Travel; TSS Earnslaw
8 Queenstown Accommodation Centre
9 Off Road Adventures
16 Medical Centre
17 Caddyshack City
18 Kiwi & Birdlife Park
19 Gondola Terminal
20 Skyline; Kiwi Magic Film; The Ledge (Bungy); Queenstown Tandem Paragliding; The Luge

26 Internet Laundry
27 Maori Concert Venue
29 Alpine Food Centre
30 Vertigo
32 Small Planet Sports Co
35 Recreation Rentals
36 The Station;
37 AJ Hackett Bungy
39 Pipeline Bungy DOC; Information & Track Centre; Queenstown Rafting
48 Alpine Sports

50 Queenstown Visitors Centre; InterCity Office
51 Kiwi Discovery; Extreme Green Rafting
54 Sky Alpine Casino Complex - Sky Alpine Casino; JDV Restaurant; Morrison's Pub; Hard Rock Cafe
66 Twin Rivers Jet
67 Kawarau Jet Underwater World
69 Embassy Cinema
71 Queenstown Bike Hire
81 Queenstown Gardens Entrance

views. The hefty return price is adult/child $14/5; the gondola operates from 9am to about 9.30pm. If the view isn't enough then check out **Kiwi Magic** *(adult/child $8/4)*, a hi-tech film that screens on the hour from 10am. It's a chance to get rid of more change from your pocket. There is also a restaurant and coffee shop.

The Luge is housed at the top of the gondola. You can zoom down in a three-wheel cart along two 800m tracks (scenic and advanced) – it's lots of fun for all ages ($4.50/16 for one ride/five rides for both adults and children, $26/19 adult/child for gondola and five luge rides).

The more energetic can walk up the vehicle track to Skyline from Lomond Crescent, but the ride is worth experiencing.

Right next to the gondola terminal is the **Kiwi & Birdlife Park** (☎ 03-442 8059, **W** *www.kiwibird.co.nz, Brecon St; adult/child $10.50/4; open 9am-5pm daily)*. It has the NZ standard – two nocturnal kiwi houses – and a small but growing programme for raising endangered species. Kea and the rare black stilt are on display in this attractive, landscaped park in the pine forest.

Nearby is **Caddyshack City** (☎ 03-442 6642, 25 Brecon St), which offers a novel indoor minigolf course that costs a steep adult/child $18/10 for a round.

On the pier at the end of the Mall, near the centre of Queenstown, is **Underwater World** (☎ 03-442 8437, adult/child $5/3), a submerged observation gallery where you can see eels and trout in the clear waters of the lake. The agile little scaup or 'diving' ducks also make periodic appearances outside the windows.

Queenstown even has a tourist-oriented **Maori concert** and *hangi*-style feast (☎ 03-442 8878, 1 Memorial St), something of a rarity in the South Island but here to cater to the throngs of tourists. Bookings are essential; the cost is $20 for the concert only, $45 for the concert and buffet meal.

Bungy Jumping
The activity that probably sparks the most interest here is bungy jumping and there's no shortage of options. **AJ Hackett Bungy**

(☎ 0800 286 495, **W** *www.ajhackett.com)* is based in The Station (see Information earlier). Hackett, world famous for his jump off the Eiffel Tower in 1986, began operating in Queenstown in November 1988.

Most jumpers are attracted to the historic **Kawarau Suspension Bridge**, 23km from Queenstown on SH6. It's 43m from the bungy-jump platform down to the river. Observation platforms accommodate spectators, and at the time of research an innovative 'underground building' was

---

Nervous on the Nevis

No safety-standard reassurances can remove trepidation prior to leaping from the gondola jump pod of the 134m (440ft) Nevis Highwire bungy. The world's first gondola jump is an engineering marvel with 30 international patents on its many innovations. It spans a remote gorge on the Nevis River and the gondola is suspended by 380m-long cables.

Although all care is taken, several aspects of the construction have been deliberately designed to maximise exposure and titillate the 'fear factor'. This increases when, bedecked in a safety harness, you take the airy cable car out to the pod, and literally thunders when you peer through the glass-bottomed floor to watch the reactions of the first jumpers.

Your turn comes. You are briefed sitting in a chair, and adjustments are made to the bungy cords based on your weight. The chair is turned and you shuffle towards the abyss.

Countdown, then six-plus seconds of free-fall with the riverbed far beneath hurtling towards you – what an incredible ground-rush! Relief as the bungy extends and you are catapulted to the top of the first bounce. At the top of the second bounce you release a rip cord and swing over into a sitting position. Now you can enjoy the bouncing and admire the view. A short bump, the clever recovery system swings into action, and you are winched back to the safety of the pod.

A relieved jumper quipped: 'This is great, you don't have to walk up from the river.'

AROUND QUEENSTOWN

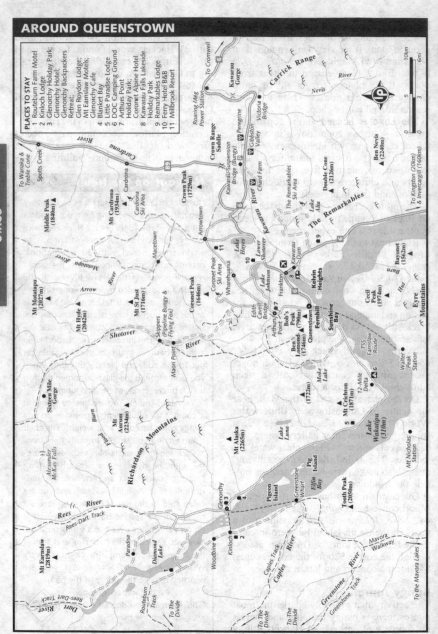

PLACES TO STAY
1 Routeburn Farm Motel
2 Kinloch Lodge
3 Glenorchy Holiday Park;
   Glenorchy Hotel;
   Glenorchy Backpackers
   Retreat;
   Glen Roydon Lodge;
   Mt Earnslaw Motels;
   Glenorchy Cafe
4 Blanket Bay
5 Little Paradise Lodge
6 DOC Camping Ground
7 Arthurs Point
   Holiday Park;
   Coronet Alpine Hotel
8 Kawarau Falls Lakeside
   Holiday Park
9 Remarkables Lodge
10 Ferry Hotel B&B
11 Millbrook Resort

OTAGO

planned for the site, to house a theatre, interactive displays, a bungy museum and cafe. A jump at the Kawarau, the world's first commercial site, costs $125 (a T-shirt is included, but photos and/or video are extra).

The closest jump to town is Hackett's **Ledge** (47m), at the top of the gondola and 400m above Queenstown. This urban option is $120, and you can even jump at night.

Not high enough? Then the **Pipeline**, the second-highest of the adrenaline 'highs', is 102m. **Pipeline Bungy** (☎ *03-442 5455,* W *www.bungy.co.nz*) built the single-span suspension bridge across Skippers Canyon on the site of an 1864 gold-sluicing water pipeline. The pipeline has been reinstated and now incorporates a walkway. From the Pipeline office on Shotover St, the cost is $150 including transport to Skippers (videos and photographs extra).

And for the highest, the engineering masterpiece that is the **Nevis Highwire** (see the boxed text 'Nervous on Nevis'), the cost is $159, which includes transport to this remote and scenic spot.

Hackett and Pipeline offer combination packages that include jetboating, helicopter flights, rafting, jumping and psychological counselling. Let's face it, after the jump the other options are chicken feed but, if you must do it all in one day, both Hackett and Pipeline charge about $370. Or if you're a true masochist, you can jump the three Hackett bungies (Kawarau, the Ledge and Nevis – the so-called 'Thrillogy') for $229.

Other Options The **Skippers Flying Fox** is milder than bungy but still a wild ride. It stretches 250m from one side of Skippers Canyon to the other. You are clipped into a cable and glide across, in a horizontal position so you can admire the view far below. The ride costs $75, including your transport to the canyon. Book with Pipeline Bungy.

At AJ Hackett's Ledge bungy site is the **Ledge Sky Swing**, where you are strapped into a harness and go into free-fall, then soar through the air on a huge arc. The swing costs $85 including the gondola trip.

A new option is the **Bungee Rocket** (☎ *03-442 9894*), off Gorge Rd on the way

out of town. There's no knee-knocking as you step up to take the plunge. This is, as one local said, 'for couch potatoes yearning for an adrenaline rush'. You're strapped into a seat in a cage-like device that's flung into the air at high speed then bounces around on the end of bungy cords ($65).

Jetboating

Hurtling up and down the rivers around Queenstown in jetboats is a very popular activity. The Shotover and Kawarau are the preferred rivers, with the Dart River less travelled, lengthy and more scenic (see Glenorchy later in this chapter).

Trips either depart straight from Queenstown or go by minibus to the river to board the jetboat. The best-known trip is with **Shotover Jet** (☎ *0800 746 868,* W *www.shotoverjet.co.nz*), which gives 30 minutes in the canyons with 360° spins for adult/child $79/39; prices include transport to their base out at Arthurs Point. This is the ride for the thrillseekers.

Twin River Jet (☎ *03-442 3257,* W *www.twinriversjet.co.nz*) and **Kawarau Jet** (☎ *03-442 6142,* W *www.kjet.co.nz*) both depart from the town pier for the Kawarau and Lower Shotover Rivers. Both offer one-hour trips on the water, with Twin Rivers being marginally cheaper at $65/35 (Kawarau is $69/39; their price includes free entry to Underwater World).

Pipeline operates the **Skippers Canyon Jet** in a remote canyon outside Queenstown, accessible only by 4WD (see under Organised Tours later). A four-hour scenic trip, which includes about 40 minutes on the Shotover River, costs $99.

Goldfields Jet (☎ *03-445 1038*) operates from the Goldfields mining centre based in the historic section of the Kawarau River outside of Cromwell (adult/child $69/39).

White-water Rafting

The rivers are equally good for rafting and again the Shotover and Kawarau Rivers are the main locations. Rivers are graded, for rafting purposes, from I (easy) to VI (unraftable). The Shotover canyon varies from III to V+, depending on the time of year and

OTAGO

includes shooting the Oxenbridge Tunnel. The Kawarau River is a grade IV and is ideal for first-time rafters. On some of the rougher stretches there's usually a minimum age of 12 or 13 years. The rafting companies supply all the equipment – it's like *Apocalypse Now* as you're lined up and given your uniform rafting gear; groups are marshalled into minibuses as others disembark from jetboats and helicopters buzz overhead.

Trips typically take four to five hours, but half of this time is getting there and back by minibus. Prices range from $109 to $129 depending on the trip and operator.

Rafting companies include **Queenstown Rafting** (☎ *03-442 9792, 0800 723 8464,* W *www.rafting.co.nz*), with its office at 35 Shotover St; **Extreme Green Rafting** (☎ *03-442 8517,* W *www.nzraft.com*) at 39 Camp St; and **Challenge Rafting** (☎ *03-442 7318,* W *www.raft.co.nz*). Extreme Green is marginally cheaper than the others and offers a barbecue snack after its trips.

River Surfing & White-water Sledging

Some of the most exciting things you can do in the water near Queenstown are river surfing and white-water sledging. **Serious Fun** (☎ *03-442 5262*) takes exhilarating trips ($119) through different sections of the Kawarau River, surfing river waves, running rapids and riding whirlpools using modified boogie boards. **Mad Dog River Boarding** (☎ *03-442 7797*) does similar trips for the same price.

Frogz Have More Fun (☎ *0800 338 738*) has trips where you get to steer highly manoeuvrable and buoyant sleds through rapids; it's a great adrenaline buzz. Trips are from $89 to $109; the cheaper trips are on gentler rivers like the Clutha and Hawea; the more expensive is on the challenging Kawarau. The company is run by a Frenchman, hence the name.

Canyoning

XII-Mile Delta Canyoning (☎ *0800 222 696,* W *www.xiimile.co.nz*) has half-day trips in the 12-Mile Delta Canyons which expose you to all the fun ingredients which go with canyoning – waterslides, rock jumps, swimming through narrow channels, abseiling and a few surprises. Trips are three hours and cost $105.

Paragliding & Parachuting

If you're up to it, why not try a tandem aerial parapente jump from Bob's Peak. **Queenstown Tandem Paragliding** (☎ *0800 759 688, 03-441 8581,* W *www.queenstowntandem-paragliding.co.nz*) is a cooperative of instructors who fly from the top of the gondola, with flights costing $160. **Flight Park Tandems** (☎ *0800 467 325,* W *www.tandemparagliding.com*) offers flights from Coronet Peak ski field for $160.

For those who prefer a delta wing there's **Skytrek Hang Gliding** (☎ *03-442 6311*) and **Antigravity** (☎ *0800 426 445,* W *www.antigravity.co.nz*), both offering flights for around $160.

The Ultimate Jump (☎ *021-325 961,* W *www.skydivetandem.co.nz*) lets you tandem freefall to terminal velocity (up to 200km/h) before your parachute opens and you are nursed safely to ground ($245).

Fly by Wire (☎ *0800 359 299, 03-442 2116,* W *www.flybywire.co.nz*) is a unique experience that allows you to control a high-speed tethered plane to speeds of up to 170km/h for a six-minute flight ($145).

Paraflying on the lake is another way to enjoy all the sights from the air. Contact **Paraflights NZ** (☎ *03-442 8507,* W *www.parasail.co.nz*); an eight-minute solo flight behind its boat is $75.

Skiing

In winter the Remarkables and Coronet Peak ski fields operate near Queenstown. See Skiing in the Activities chapter for more details.

Those who prefer motorised mobility to skis can churn up the white stuff along the Old Woman Range at 1700m, in the Garvie Mountains, with **Nevis Snowmobile Adventure** (☎ *03-442 4250, 0800 442 4250,* W *www.snowmobilenz.com*) for $359 (three hours, including a scenic helicopter flight over the Remarkables to the base).

Activities Au-go-go

There really is a dazzling array of activities in Queenstown, suitable for the old and young, the timid and the true adrenaline junkie. Learning about all the options, sifting through the information and choosing your fun can be a daunting task, but there are some things you can do to make life easier. If possible, in your trip pre-planning stages, get online and check the websites mentioned in this section to see exactly what's offered by tour operators. An excellent overview is offered by ITAG, the Independent Traveller's Adventure Guide (W www.itag.co.nz), which publishes a free guide that you can pick up once you get to Queenstown. Another good website is at W www.queenstown adventure.com.

Unless you have weeks and weeks up your sleeve, you probably won't be able to squeeze in all the activities you might like, not to mention the cash! It's a good idea to work out a rough budget and make a list of your top priorities. You may choose to stay in budget accommodation while in Queenstown in order to free up more money to go all-out on the activities.

Once in Queenstown you can either book directly with the activity company, at your place of accommodation (most backpackers, hotels and motels have a booking service) or at one of the many booking agencies in town, found mainly on Camp and Shotover Sts. Choose the most convenient, as prices will not vary from place to place. Bear in mind that there are countless combinations on offer from the large operators, eg, the $175 'K2' package gets you rafting with Queenstown Rafting and a jetboat ride with Kawarau Jet; the 'Nevis Triple Challenge' package costs $398 and involves rafting with Queenstown Rafting, a helicopter flight, jetboating with Shotover Jet and a bungy jump from the Nevis Highwire.

One thing to bear in mind in Queenstown – and throughout NZ – is that participation in all these adventure activities involves a degree of risk (they wouldn't be half as much fun if the adrenaline wasn't pumping!). Most adventure operators will do everything in their power to ensure that participants are safe and have a great time, but accidents do happen and Lonely Planet receives many letters from travellers with sad tales of broken bones and the like – and nothing wrecks a holiday more than an injury! If you plan to dive head-first into the activities in Queenstown, be aware that chances of harm are low, but they do exist. It's worth getting decent travel insurance to cover any mishap should it happen.

Heli-skiing is also popular and a full day with three runs costs around $600. **Heli Ski Queenstown** (☎ *03-442 7733)* and **Harris Mountains Heli-Ski** (☎ *03-442 6722*, W *www.heliski.co.nz)* are local operators.

Mountain Biking

The Queenstown region has opportunities for some great mountain biking. **Adventure Biking** (☎ *03-442 9708)* has 1½ trips from Moke Lake that take in river crossings and both uphill and downhill ($59).

If you're not that fit, avoid the strenuous uphill pedalling; instead choose an operator who takes you and your bike to a suitable high point. **Gravity Action** (☎ *03-442 8178)* has a trip into Skippers Canyon ($69, 4hrs),

and **Vertigo** (☎ *03-477 5411, 14 Shotover St)* has guided downhill trips from $75. Both Gravity Action and Vertigo have heli-biking options.

Motorcycling

The region around Queenstown is perfect for off-road bikes or four-wheelers on wild country tracks. The rides combine thrills with a chance to see inaccessible historical areas amid the canyons and hills of Central Otago. **Off Road Adventures** (☎ *03-442 7858*, W *www.offroad.co.nz, 61 Shotover St)* offers guided biking (motorbikes or quads) over a variety of back-country terrain. Two-hour quad-bike trips cost $119, three-hour two-wheeler trips are $199.

Walking

Many of Queenstown's activities are decidedly expensive but walks cost nothing. Stroll along the waterfront through town and keep going to the peaceful park on the peninsula. The lakeside walkway from Queenstown's Peninsula St takes just over an hour each way through beautiful parkland.

One of the shortest climbs around Queenstown is up Queenstown Hill (900m), overlooking town. It's a comfortable two to three hours up and back with good views; access is from York and Kent Sts. For a more spectacular view, climb Ben Lomond (1746m) – a difficult walk requiring a good level of fitness as it takes six hours return. As several people have underestimated this walk, we suggest you seek directions and advice locally.

There are many other walks in the area, especially from Arthurs Point and Arrowtown, areas rich in history – consult the DOC office for information. For longer walks you can hire camping equipment at **Alpine Sports** (☎ 03-442 7099, 28 Shotover St); packs, sleeping bags and boots are $5 per day. **Kiwi Discovery** (☎ 03-442 7340, 37 Camp St) and **Information & Track Centre** (☎ 03-442 9708, 37 Shotover St) also rent all the equipment you'll need. **Small Planet Sports Co** (☎ 03-442 6393, 17 Shotover St) sells new and used outdoor equipment for tramping, skiing and biking.

Guided Nature Walks (☎ 03-442 7126, W www.nzwalks.com) conducts excellent half-day walks in the area ($75) and full-day Routeburn walks ($185, including transport and picnic lunch). **Encounter Guided Day Walks** (☎ 03-442 8200, W www.ultimate hikes.co.nz) also offers a day on the Routeburn Track for $115.

Aerial Sightseeing

No possibility is ignored in Queenstown – if you can't boat up it, down it or across it or walk around it, then you can fly over it. Options range from short helicopter flights over the Remarkables (from $120) to plane flights over Milford Sound (from $200). More expensive flights to Milford include a cruise on the sound (from $250). **Over the**

Top Helicopters (☎ 03-442 2233, W www .flynz.co.nz), **Queenstown Air** (☎ 03-442 2244, Wwww.queenstownair.co.nz), **Air Fiordland** (☎ 03-442 3404, W www.air fiordland.co.nz) and **Milford Sound Scenic Flights** (☎ 03-442 3065, W www.milford flights.co.nz) are all local operators.

More exciting are aerobatic flights in a Pitts Special biplane ($215) with **Actionflite** (☎ 0800 360 264, W www.actionflite .co.nz), or a one-hour flight in a hot-air balloon with **Sunrise Balloons** (☎ 0800 468 247, 03-441 8248, W www.ballooningnz .com) costing $295.

Other Activities

Still not enough activities in Queenstown? Well there's excellent golf, fishing, horse riding, rock-climbing, mountain-climbing, diving and more, or you can just collapse in a heap. See the visitors centre or any of the major booking agencies to find out more.

Organised Tours

There are bus tours for a pleasant trip to nearby Arrowtown (see Arrowtown later).

Skippers Canyon Very popular Skippers Canyon trips take the winding 4WD-only road from Arthurs Point towards Coronet Peak and then above the Shotover River passing many sights from the gold-mining days. The scenery is spectacular, the road is hair-raising, and there's plenty of historical interest. **Outback Tours** (☎ 03-442 7386, W www.outback.net.nz) offers four-hour 4WD 'Nomad Safaris' for adult/child $75/50, including a stop to pan for gold.

Skippers Grand Canyon is run by Pipeline, who operate a bungy jump here as well as a flying fox across the canyon and jetboating on the river below. Pipeline offers trips to Skippers in conjunction with all the activities, as well as purely sightseeing trips. A four-hour trip is $59; with jetboating the cost is $105.

Lake Cruises The stately steel-hulled TSS (Twin Screw Steamer) *Earnslaw* is the most famous of the lake's many cruise boats. Licensed to carry 810 passengers, it churns across the lake at 13 knots, burns a tonne of coal an hour and was once the major means of transport on the lake. The development of modern roads ended its career with NZ Railways. Since 1969 it has been used for lake cruises and now works harder than ever. Inquiries and bookings should be made at Fiordland Travel (☎ 03-442 7500) at Steamers Wharf.

Earnslaw Cruise Scenic Lake Wakatipu cruise; daily year-round at noon, 2pm and 4pm, with additional cruises from October to mid-April (adult/child $34/15, 1½hrs).
Evening Dining Cruise A four-hour cruise with a carvery buffet at Walter Peak. Leaves at 6pm August to May (adult/child $88/44).
Walter Peak Station Excursion Cruise to Walter Peak Station for a farmyard tour. Tours leave year-round at noon and 2pm, with additional tours in summer. Tours are 3½ hours, and you see sheepdogs and sheep shearing at the station ($52/15). for an additional cost, there is also the option of horse-trekking or wagon rides on these cruises.

Milford Sound Day trips via Te Anau to Milford Sound take 12 to 13 hours and cost around adult/child $170/90, including a two-hour cruise on the Sound. Bus-cruise-flight options are also available. The main operators are **Fiordland Travel** (☎ 0800 656 503, 03-442 7500), **Great Sights** (☎ 0800 744 487) and **InterCity** (☎ 03-442 8238). Milford Sound is a long way from Queenstown and Te Anau is a better departure point. The same is true for trips to Doubtful Sound, which cost $245/122.50 from Queenstown.

Kiwi Discovery (☎ 03-442 7340, 37 Camp St) has a Milford Sound day excursion for $139, including a cruise on the small *Friendship*. **The BBQ Bus** (☎ 03-442 1045, W www.milford.net.nz) has tours for $159, including a barbecue lunch.

From October to March, Fiordland Travel has two-day trips that allow you to overnight on either Milford or Doubtful Sound (for details see the Southland chapter).

Winery Tours There's an ever-growing number of operators offering guided tours to the great wineries of the region, and it's a good way to be able to enjoy a drink or three without having to drive yourself. **Queenstown Wine Trail** (☎ 03-442 3799, W www.queenstownwinetrail.co.nz) offers a good, casual and informative five-hour trip for $69; for $135 you can do the trip and return to Queenstown by jetboat. **It's Wine Time** (☎ 0508 946 384) offers a short, three-hour afternoon tour for $59, or a full-day trip for $162, including lunch.

Kingston Flyer About 45km south of Queenstown, at Kingston on the southern tip of Lake Wakatipu, is the **Kingston Flyer** (☎ 0800 435 937, 03-248 8848, W www .kingstonflyer.co.nz), a heritage steam train that operates from October to April. It runs morning and afternoon on a 14km stretch of track between Kingston and Fairlight. The cost is adult/child $20/7 return; a connection service (☎ 03-442 6666) operates out of Queenstown to meet the morning train ($50 including train ride).

Rugby Trips The Bottom Bus (☎ 03-474 7370, W www.bottombus.co.nz) operates backpacker-focused, two-day trips to Dunedin to see a rugby game at Carisbrook, the 'House of Pain'. For details see Other Activities under Dunedin at the start of this chapter.

Places to Stay

Despite Queenstown's 15,000 beds, finding a room at peak periods can be difficult. Prices go sky-high during the summer and ski-season peaks. Prices given are for the high season; try to negotiate for a better deal in the shoulder seasons.

Camping & Cabins Prices given here are for two people.

Queenstown Lakeview Motor Park (☎ 0800 482 735, 03-442 7252, W www.mo torpark.co.nz, 53 Man St) Powered/unpowered sites $22, basic cabins $40, flats, units, motels $60-95. This recently revamped ground is very well equipped with a good kitchen, coin-operated laundry, TV room etc, but the rather big downside is a lack of shade or privacy in the camping areas, plus coin-operated showers. Still, it's in the heart of town, and the facilities are all brand new, so you might be able to overlook these things. The new accommodation options are very slick and represent good value.

Creeksyde Top 10 Holiday Park (☎ 0800 786 222, 03-442 9447, **W** www.camp.co.nz, 54 Robins Rd) Powered/unpowered sites $26, cabins $42-62, tourist flats & motel units $70-98. Creeksyde is a modern, neat and green little ground catering primarily to campervans, but also home to a number of good cabin and flat options. It's also quite central – about a 10-minute walk from the heart of town.

Kawarau Falls Lakeside Holiday Park (☎ 0800 226 774, 03-442 3510, **e** relax@ campsite.co.nz) Powered/unpowered sites $24/22, cabins $45, tourist & en suite cabins $60-85. Peaceful, well-maintained Kawarau Falls is on SH6 at Frankton (past the airport) in a beautiful setting by the lake.

Arthurs Point Holiday Park (☎ 0800 462 267, 03-442 9311, **e** top10.queen stown@xtra.co.nz) Powered/unpowered sites $22/20, backpackers beds $15, basic cabins $38, self-contained units $67-90. In a scenic setting surrounded by great mountain views, this park is about 5km from town towards Arrowtown.

Fifteen kilometres from Queenstown on the road to Glenorchy. There is a *DOC camping ground* at 12-Mile Creek Reserve. Charges are adult/child $4/2.

Hostels The large, ever-busy place *Queenstown YHA* (☎ 03-442 8413, **e** yhaqutn@ yha.org.nz, 88 Lake Esplanade) is right by the lake and offers all the expected high-quality facilities, having been renovated recently. There are friendly staff and good communal areas. Dorm beds are $20, twins and doubles range from $44 to $52.

Butterfli Lodge (☎ 03-442 6367, **W** www .butterfli.co.nz, 62 Thompson St) Dorm beds $18, doubles & twins $55. This is a classy new backpackers, a small place where you'll easily feel at home. Decor and facilities are first rate, and there's a lovely outdoor area where you can enjoy the views.

Pinewood Lodge (☎ 0800 746 3966, 03-442 8273, **W** www.pinewood.co.nz, 48

Hamilton Rd) Dorm beds $18, twins/ doubles from $45. Pinewood Lodge is a little way out of the centre but is an excellent option, with a variety of old and new lodges in spacious grounds. Each lodge has its own lounge and accommodation for families and groups as well as backpacker lodgings. There are well-equipped kitchens, a spa and a great TV room in what looks to be a barn.

Bumbles (☎ 0800 428 6253, 03-442 6298, 2 Brunswick St) Dorm beds $18, twin bunkrooms $40, twins & doubles $45. Bumbles is friendly place along Lake Esplanade. It has good communal areas with views across the lake; most dorms have their own bathroom and fridge.

Thomas's Hotel (☎ 03-442 7180, **W** www .thomashotel.co.nz, 50 Beach St) Dorm beds $19-20, budget twins & doubles $69, hotel doubles & twins $79-109. Thomas's is popular for its great lakeside location as well as its backpacker rooms. All are heated and have their own bathrooms, TV and fridges – as well as the regular, well-equipped hotel rooms, and 'deluxe' rooms with lake views.

Black Sheep Backpackers (☎ 03-442 7289, **W** www.blacksheepbackpackers.co .nz, 13 Frankton Rd) Dorm beds $19, doubles & twins $50. Just a short walk to town, this former motel has two spa pools, a deck, a bar and Internet. Its standards are high and reception is open 24 hours.

Alpine Lodge (☎ 03-442 7220, **e** alpine lodge@xtra.co.nz, 13 Gorge Rd) Dorm beds $19, twins & doubles $48. Alpine Lodge is small and cosy with a friendly ski-lodge feel, including an open fire in the lounge area.

Deco Backpackers (☎ 03-442 7384, 52 Man St) Dorm beds $18, twins & doubles $44. Deco, a short walk from town, is in a restored Art Deco building. It's a small and friendly place and offers two kitchens, good outdoor areas and freshly brewed coffee every morning.

Bungi Backpackers (☎ 0800 728 286, 03-442 8725, 15 Sydney St) Dorm beds $16, doubles & twins $40. Brightly painted Bungi is one of the cheaper options and is an older-style and slightly ramshackle place. Rooms are small but there's a large yard with good barbecue area and volleyball court, plus spa.

Southern Laughter (☎ *0800 5284 4837, 03-441 8828, 4 Isle St*) Dorm beds $18-22, twins & doubles $45-55. This is a well-positioned place with excellent facilities: some dorms have an en suite, some have their own small kitchen. The decor is bright and cheery and the atmosphere is lively.

Scallywags Travellers Guesthouse (☎ *03-442 7083, 27 Lomond Crescent*) Dorm beds $20, doubles & twins $55. Scallywags is a small, well-run backpackers high up over the town (reached by a short cut up through the motor park), hence with great views. There's also a lovely indoor-outdoor area and barbecue.

Hippo Lodge (☎ *03-442 5785,* W *www .hippolodge.co.nz, 4 Anderson Heights*) Dorm beds $22, doubles/twins $54, limited camping space $12 per person. This is a delightful little place with some of the best views in town. To walk here, head up Shotover St, then take Turner St and the stairs to Hallenstein St; Anderson Heights is just to the left. The walk up with a backpack may be exhausting, but it's worth the climb. The friendly owners have another quality accommodation option that may appeal if you have your own transport. ***Hippo Hideaway*** is about 5km out of town in Arthurs Point.

Last Resort (☎ *03-442 4320, Man St*) Dorm beds $20. The Last Resort, at the east end of Man St, is approached from a small bridge over a stream. All rooms are shared – there are three four-bed dorms and one six-bed dorm – and the cost includes linen and towels. It's friendly, small, centrally located and popular.

McFees (☎ *03-442 7400, 48A Shotover St*) Dorm beds $20, doubles & twins $65-75. McFees is a good budget hotel in the centre of town, offering shared rooms with a limit of four per room. All rooms have en suite, phone and TV. There's a lovely large kitchen area with great views.

B&Bs & Guesthouses There are wonderful guesthouses located in and around Queenstown, some offering true luxury.

Melbourne House (☎ *03-442 8431,* e *stay@mmlodge.co.nz, 35 Melbourne St*) Singles/doubles with shared facilities $55/85. This small, older-style guesthouse is friendly and well organised. B&B rooms share bathroom facilities. There is also a motor lodge here, with comfortable units from $95.

Little Paradise Lodge (☎ *03-442 6196,* W *www.littleparadise.com, Glenorchy-Queenstown Rd*) Beds in shared room $35-45, double rooms $100-120. This unique place, halfway between Queenstown and Glenorchy, has magnificent views. It has delightful gardens and wildlife and offers kayaks and fishing gear for use. There are four rooms in the farmhouse (some with share facilities, all with use of the kitchen), and the decor is wonderfully bizarre.

Ferry Hotel B&B (☎ *03-442 2194,* W *www.ferry.co.nz, Spence Rd*) Rooms from $155-185. About 11km out of town (signposted off SH6 at the Lower Shotover Rd), this charming building dates from the 1870s and is chock-full of history. The gardens are delightful, the owners welcoming and the rooms top-notch.

The Dairy Guesthouse (☎ *03-442 5164,* W *www.thedairy.co.nz, 10 Isle St*) Rooms $260-295. In a great central location, part of this classy guesthouse was a general store in the 1920s (and it's now where the great breakfasts are served). The Dairy is now an upmarket establishment offering stylish and inviting boutique-style accommodation.

Remarkables Lodge (☎ *03-442 2720,* W *www.remarkables.co.nz*) Lodge rooms $580, cottage $660 (GST extra). This gorgeous, exclusive lodge, in a fantastic location, has the Remarkables at its back door; and is only a few kilometres south of the ski field entrance on SH6. A multi-award winner, facilities are superb and include a pool, hot tub, log fire, bar and restaurant. For your money you will be totally spoilt, with prices including airport transfers, breakfast, pre-dinner drinks and a three-course dinner.

Motels Queenstown motels are generally expensive but prices fluctuate with the seasons; the best place to look for them is along Frankton Rd, or Gorge Rd on the other side of town.

Colonial Village Motels (☎ *03-442 7629,* e *colonial@queenstown.co.nz, 136 Frankton Rd)* has budget units for $68, and more polished options from $78 to $110. **Earnslaw Lodge** (☎ *03-442 8728,* e *earnslawlodge@xtra.co.nz,, 77 Frankton Rd)* is an older-style place with a range of studios and apartments priced from $89. **Garden Court** (☎ *0800 427 336, 03-442 9713,* e *stay@gardencourt.co.nz, 41 Frankton Rd)* has lovely modern studios and spacious apartments priced from $125.

Lomond Lodge Motor Inn (☎ *03-442 8235,* e *info@lomondlodge.com, 33 Man St)* is a very central, affordable option, with comfortable older-style units from around $89. **Ambassador Motel** (☎ *03-442 8593,* e *amb@clear.net.nz, 2 Man St)* nearby isn't much to look at but offers reasonable units for about $80.

➤ **Bella Vista** (☎ *0800 610 171, 03-442 4468,* e *bellavista.queenstown@xtra.co .nz, 36 Robins St)* Units $89-110. This is the newest motel in Queenstown (one of very few to have been built here in the last 10 or so years – most development nowadays is modern apartment-style complexes). Bella Vista offers clean and comfortable if slightly bland units in a good location, not far from the centre of town.

Hotels See also the listings under Hostels, earlier, for details of budget hotels like Thomas's and McFees.

Queenstown Lodge (☎ *0800 756 343, 03-442 7107,* W *www.qlodge.co.nz, Sainsbury Rd)* Bed in 4-bed room $30, doubles & twins $85-95. This lodge is in Fernhill, 2km west of the centre, and has a magnificent view of the lake. This huge place is like a cross between a ski lodge and an upmarket student-college house, with dozens of rooms on different levels down the hillside. It caters mostly to cheap tour groups but has plenty of rooms for independent travellers. The lodge has a large communal kitchen and licensed restaurant, bar and deck, plus spa and sauna. Self-contained apartments are also available from $150.

Coronet Alpine Hotel (☎ *03-442 7850, Malaghans Rd)* Rooms around $140. Out of town at Arthurs Point, this large hotel in spacious grounds is the closest hotel to Coronet Peak and offers great facilities for skiers, plus summer extras like a swimming pool. Rooms are pleasant and comfortable.

Browns Boutique Hotel (☎ *03-441 2050,* W *www.brownshotel.co.nz, 26 Isle St)* Rooms $190-220. This small, intimate hotel is modelled on the pensions of Europe and offers spacious, tastefully decorated rooms with good facilities. There's a very pleasant guest lounge and courtyard area.

There are dozens of large hotels and all the major chains are well represented. Prime hunting grounds are along the waterfront and at Fernhill, a few kilometres west of the town. In most of the larger hotel complexes you'll find all the facilities travellers would expect, and some more, eg, bars, restaurants, possibly a pool and spa. You'll pay extra for rooms with guaranteed lake views. Rack rates are generally high, but there are often good deals to be had – its pays to ask.

Aspen on Queenstown (☎ *0800 427 7688, 03-442 7677,* e *aspen@xtra.co.nz, 139 Fernhill Rd)* Doubles $135-160, 1-/2-bedroom apartments $225/295. Aspen on Queenstown has a good range of quality accommodation, with comfortable hotel-style rooms and serviced apartments that are spacious. The complex has spectacular views and excellent facilities, including pool and restaurant.

The Heritage (☎ *0800 368 888, 03-442 4988, 91 Fernhill Rd)* Rack rate $290-510, depending on size, view, season. Good specials can reduce the price considerably. This is one of the best choices if you're after a first-rate hotel. It's a large complex with classy decor (the reception building is beautiful) and professional staff, and excellent rooms and suites are offered.

Holiday Homes & Apartments The visitors centre can help with finding accommodation. Another good option, especially for families and groups, is **Queenstown Accommodation Centre** (☎ *03-442 7518,* e *holiday@qac.co.nz,* W *www.qac.co.nz,*

30 Shotover St), which has a range of great holiday homes and apartments (sleeping four to twelve) on its books; you need to be staying a minimum of three days. Prices range from $100 to $650 a night.

Places to Eat

Queenstown has a thriving restaurant scene, with the South Island's best dining outside Christchurch and Dunedin.

Restaurants Something of a Queenstown institution and very busy, *The Cow (☎ 03-442 8588, Cow Lane)* is a cosy place with an open fire and the pasta and pizza are good – that's if you get time seated to digest them; the popularity of the place means turnover of tables is expected to be very fast, which is unsettling to diners wanting to linger a little! Meals are around $16. Other popular places for tasty pizza are *McNeill's Cottage Brewery* and *Winnie Bagoes* (see Entertainment later).

Surreal (☎ 03-441 8492, 7 Rees St) Mains $17-21. This is a fine spot to sample meals of Asian-inspired flavours (served on either rice or noodles), to a backing of smooth tunes. Surreal transforms from a restaurant into a popular bar, later in the evening. Other popular eateries with stylish decor and extensive menus featuring well-prepared Pacific-Rim dishes include *JDV (☎ 03-441 2747)*, part of the Alpine Casino Complex; *The 19th (☎ 03-442 4006)*, at Steamers Wharf; and *Tatler (☎ 03-442 8372)*, in the Mall.

Coronation Bathhouse Cafe & Restaurant (☎ 03-442 5625, Marine Parade) Dinner mains $25-30, lunch around $15. Treat yourself to brunch, lunch or dinner at this delightful place in a restored historic bathhouse from 1911. The setting is superb – on the lake and right next to gardens and a children's playground.

Lone Star (☎ 03-442 9995, 14 Brecon St) Mains $18-25. Lone Star is found in most of the larger South Islands towns, and Queenstown is no exception. With a 'deep south' bent, it serves up huge portions of cleverly named Tex-Mex and Cajun fare in a fun, laid-back atmosphere.

Fishbone Bar & Grill (☎ 03-442 6768, 7 Beach St) Mains $15-27. Another good casual eatery is this colourful place, specialising in all things fishy. There's reef & beef, seafood pasta and plenty of fresh fish – fried, baked, smoked and char-grilled.

Minami Jujisei (☎ 03-442 9854, 45 Beach St) Mains $20-28. The name is a bit of a mouthful (it means 'Southern Cross'), but you'll have no trouble wrapping your tongue around the superb food here. This fine place is often voted NZ's best Japanese restaurant.

Gantley's (☎ 03-442 8999, Malaghans Rd) Mains $24-38. Gantley's, situated in a historic 1863 stone building at Arthurs Point, is a great place for fine dining by candlelight. It's one of Queenstown's finest – and priciest – restaurants, with well-prepared dishes including crispy braised duckling, fillet of beef or fish of the day. Reservations are essential; there's a courtesy bus into town if you wish to sample from their award-winning wine list.

Cafes & Cheap Eats Queenstown's best cafe is the funky *Vudu (☎ 03-442 5357, 23 Beach St)*, open daily from 8am to late and serving breakfast to 3pm. It has an eclectic menu of classic cafe fare and great coffee, plus a tiny side courtyard for outdoor eating.

Other excellent cafe choices are *Naff Caff (☎ 03-442 8211, 62 Shotover St)* and bustling *Leonardo's (☎ 03-442 8542, 22 Shotover St)*. Both offer breakfast, lunch and snacks, and the perfect espresso.

When it comes to fast food, all the usual suspects are easy to find along Camp St, but there are other excellent options, where you'll get a good feed for $10 or under. *The World* and *Pig & Whistle* (see Entertainment) are good choices.

Inside the shopping centre is *O'Connell's Food Hall (Camp St)*, with a great collection of cheap stalls, including Thai and Japanese. *Ken's Noodles*, opposite on Camp St, is a local favourite for udon (noodles) and sushi at reasonable prices. *Kappa (36 The Mall, upstairs)* is another safe bet for good-value Japanese cuisine. *Planet 1 (cnr Church St & Marine Parade)* is a great

OTAGO

kiosk on the waterfront offering a small but interesting range of Japanese dishes including good-value sushi and curry.

The Bakery (11 Shotover St), just beyond Camp St, serves up pies, sandwiches and pizzas and is open 24 hours. Tucked away in Cow Lane, right behind the wine shop, is *Fergburger*, which serves up traditional and gourmet burgers. *The Squeeze* on the Mall has steak sandwiches, panini, hot dogs and pasta to go for under $8.

Habebes (cnr Rees & Beach Sts) is a tiny place inside the Wakatipu Arcade serving Middle Eastern and vegetarian dishes, including huge pita wraps (lamb, chicken or vegie). *Turkish Kebabs (31 Beach St)* is a central place serving, well, Turkish kebabs.

For self-catering, the central *Alpine Food Centre* is at the top of Shotover St and is open until 9pm daily. The larger *Fresh Choice* supermarket is located out of town on Gorge Rd.

Entertainment

There is nothing small-town about the excellent nightlife in Queenstown – it's action-packed every night of the week. And with the compact size of Queenstown's 'downtown' area, everything is almost next door to each other. To find out what's on where, check out *The Source*, a free weekly flyer that's widely available around town.

McNeill's Cottage Brewery & Bar (☎ 03-442 9688, 14 Church St), around the corner from the Mall, is a great place to head to for reasonably priced pub fare (great pizzas) and its own excellent beers, brewed on the premises. *Winnie Bagoes (☎ 03-442 8635)* upstairs on the Mall is another very popular place (also serving gourmet pizzas late into the night). The added attraction here is a retractable roof for sunny days.

A few doors down is *Tatler*, an upmarket restaurant, with the upstairs *Spectator Bar* and balcony overlooking the Mall. Nearby is *Old Man Rock* (downstairs), a cosy cafe-bar, and the very popular *Chico's (☎ 03-442 8349)*, upstairs, a restaurant that transforms into a disco later in the night, playing old hits and attracting a wide mix.

Pog Mahones (☎ 03-442 5382, 14 Rees St) is *the* Irish pub in town; it's a popular place for a drop of Guinness and occasional live music, and it can get pretty crowded. Other pubs include *Morrison's (☎ 03-441 3191)*, in the new casino complex on Beach St and with regular live music, and the English-style *Pig & Whistle (☎ 03-442 9055, 19 Camp St)*, with an older crowd and cheap pub fare.

Red Rock Bar & Grill (☎ 03-442 6850, 48 Camp St) is hugely popular in the ski season, but even in summer the crowds are here enjoying a drink at the outdoor tables. Opposite is the slightly cheesy nightclub, *The Edge*; the *Casbah (☎ 03-442 7833, 54 Shotover St)* has a similar feel and is often packed with bus-going backpackers (and the word is that the only locals who go here are the ones looking to pick up inebriated travellers!).

A step up from the Casbah, *The World (☎ 03-442 6757, 27 Shotover St)* is usually wall-to-wall with party-goers and is one of Queenstown's most popular late-night backpacker venues – it's also a good stop for a cheap and filling feed.

Shooters (☎ 03-442 4144, 10 Brecon St) is Queenstown's big sports bar, and next door is *Rattlesnake Room*, a bar usually playing dance music. *Surreal (☎ 03-441 8492, 7 Rees St)* has a similar theme, attracting many of NZ's big-name DJs, and doubles as a slick restaurant until 10pm.

Steamers Wharf is an excellent spot for restaurants and nightlife, with the *Loaded Hog (☎ 03-441 2969)* featuring a pub-style atmosphere, and bars including *Frasers (☎ 03-442 5111)* and the rather swish *Cigar Bar (☎ 03-442 0534)*, often with live jazz performances on Fridays.

Most bars in town close around 2am or 3am, but night owls can continue at a few exclusive venues tucked away down Cow Lane, off Camp St. Funky, Spanish-themed *Debajo (☎ 03-442 6099)* and the hip *Tardis Bar (☎ 03-441 8397)* both play dance music; close to Tardis is the chic, unsigned *Bunker (☎ 03-441 8030)*. Squeeze through the crowd at the bar, or head for the couches near the open fire.

Queenstown now has two casinos in which you can lose your money. ***The Wharf Casino*** *(☎ 03-441 1495)*, in the Steamer Wharf building and the new ***Sky Alpine Casino*** *(☎ 03-441 0400)*, on Beach St, both attempt to bring a touch of Monaco to the town that has just about everything. The latter is home to the ***Hard Rock Cafe*** *(☎ 03-441 3113)*, the first of the chain in NZ.

And for those after something quieter, the ***Embassy Cinema*** *(☎ 03-442 9994, 11 The Mall)* shows new-release movies for $11.

Getting There & Away

Air Air New Zealand (☎ 03-441 1900, W www.airnewzealand.co.nz) operates daily direct flights between Queenstown and Auckland, Christchurch, Rotorua and Wellington, with connections to other major centres. Qantas (☎ 0800 808 767, W www .qantas.co.nz) has direct daily connections to/from Christchurch, with connections to Auckland and Rotorua.

Bus The InterCity booking office (☎ 03-442 2800), in the visitors centre on the corner of Shotover and Camp Sts, has several daily services to and from Queenstown: there are routes to Christchurch, Te Anau and Milford Sound, Dunedin and Invercargill, and also a daily West Coast service to the glaciers via Wanaka and Haast Pass.

'Alternative' bus tours such as the West Coast Express, Kiwi Experience, Magic Bus or the Flying Kiwi also go up the West Coast to Nelson. See Backpackers Buses in the Getting Around chapter for details.

The Bottom Bus does a loop service around the 'deep south' of the South Island (see Tours & Transport under The Catlins in the Southland chapter for details). Book tickets at the Information & Track Centre (☎ 03-442 9708).

Myriad shuttle buses operate from out of Queenstown. The visitors centre books most of them; to Wanaka the price ranges from $15 to $25, to Dunedin the price is $30, to Te Anau it's $25 to $35, to Christchurch $45 to $50. Wanaka Connexions offers some five services to Wanaka daily ($25); Atomic Shuttles goes to Christchurch, Dunedin and Invercargill; Southern Link has services to Dunedin, Christ-church and Wanaka; Catch-a-Bus goes to Dunedin and Topline Tours goes to Te Anau.

Trampers Transport Information & Track Centre and Kiwi Discovery can help make arrangements to get you to the tracks. Backpacker Express (☎ 03-442 9939, W www .glenorchyinfocentre.co.nz) runs to and from the Routeburn, Greenstone, Caples and Rees-Dart Tracks, all via Glenorchy. The morning bus picks up at various accommodation points around Queenstown. Prices are $15 between Queenstown and Glenorchy, and between Glenorchy and any of the tracks is $15.

Bus services between Queenstown and Milford Sound via Te Anau can be used for track transport. See the Te Anau in the Southland chapter for information on Tracknet, a Te Anau-based company that operates services for trampers.

Getting Around

To/From the Airport The airport is at Frankton, 8km from town. Super Shuttle (☎ 03-442 3639, e supershuttle@queens town.co.nz) picks up and drops off in Queenstown for $8 per person. Taxis cost about $18 – phone Alpine Taxis (☎ 03-442 6666) or Queenstown Taxis (☎ 03-442 7788).

Bus The Shopper Bus (☎ 03-442 6647) has buses that leave from outside McDonald's on Camp St. It has services to Fernhill and Frankton accommodation ($2), and there is a regular service to the airport ($3.50). In December and January there is a 'Niteclub Express' bus running in the wee hours of Friday, Saturday and Sunday mornings.

Kiwi Discovery operates ski-season shuttles to Coronet Peak and the Remarkables (about $25) and Cardrona and Treble Cone ($30).

Bicycle & Moped Queenstown Bike Hire (☎ 03-442 6039) is down on the lakefront on the corner of Marine Parade and Church St and has a wide variety of bikes from $20 a day, and good suggestions on where to

OTAGO

cycle. Rental kayaks are also available ($18 for two hours).

Recreation Rentals (☎ 03-442 5311), behind The Station on Camp St, has bikes and mopeds for rent (mountain bikes are $15 for a half day, moped rates are $35/80 for one/four hours). Vertigo (☎ 0800 837 8446) at 14 Shotover St, opposite Small Planet, has mountain bikes from $35 a day.

ARROWTOWN
pop 1700

Between Cromwell and Queenstown is the loop road turn-off to Arrowtown. The faithfully restored early gold-mining settlement has a beautiful avenue of deciduous trees, especially pretty in autumn (you'll see postcards featuring this scene around town). Lined with wooden buildings (over 60 of them from the 19th century), the main street looks a lot like a movie set for a Western, except for all the tourist shops.

The visitors centre (☎ 03-442 1824, W www.arrowtown.org.nz) is open 9am to 5pm daily and is inside the **Lake District Museum** (*adult/child $4/50c, Buckingham St*), which has good displays on gold mining and local history. Purchase copies of

Historic Arrowtown and *Arrowtown Walks* from the museum. The latter has plenty of information about getting to Macetown and historic notes about the area.

The best example of a gold-era **Chinese settlement** in NZ is near Bush Creek, at the top end of Buckingham St. A few huts have been restored as a reminder of the role played by Chinese 'diggers' during and after the gold rush, and there are good interpretive signs explaining the lives of residents. The Chinese were subjected to prejudice, especially during the 1880s economic depression. They often did not seek new claims but worked through the tailings looking for the fine gold undetected by earlier miners.

The **golf course** (*☎ 03-442 1719*) here is picturesque and challenging, with narrow defiles and rock obstacles adding to the fun. Green fees are $30; hiring clubs costs $15.

Macetown

Just north of Arrowtown is Macetown, a ghost town reached only via a long, unimproved and flood-prone road – the original miners' wagon track – which crosses the Arrow River over 25 times! Trips are made from Queenstown by 4WD vehicle, and

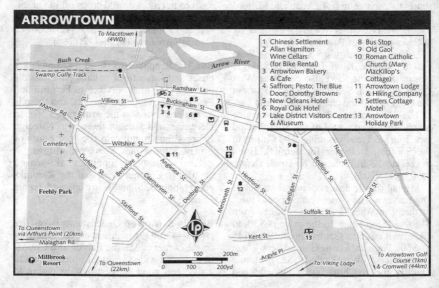

ARROWTOWN

1 Chinese Settlement	8 Bus Stop
2 Allan Hamilton	9 Old Gaol
Wine Cellars	10 Roman Catholic
(for Bike Rental)	Church (Mary
3 Arrowtown Bakery	MacKillop's
& Cafe	Cottage)
4 Saffron; Pesto; The Blue	11 Arrowtown Lodge
Door; Dorothy Browns	& Hiking Company
5 New Orleans Hotel	12 Settlers Cottage
6 Royal Oak Hotel	Motel
7 Lake District Visitors Centre	13 Arrowtown
& Museum	Holiday Park

gold panning time is included. The main operator is **Outback Tours** (☎ *03-442 7386*, W *www.outback.net.nz)*, which offers 4½-hour 'Nomad Safaris' to Macetown for $75/50 adult/child. They have a pick-up service for passengers in Arrowtown.

This area is also good for mountain biking; Allan Hamilton Wine Cellars (☎ *03-442 1026)* on Ramshaw Lane St rents out mountain bikes for $25/40 half/full day, and also gold pans if you feel like trying your luck.

Places to Stay

Arrowtown Holiday Park (☎ *03-442 1876,* e *gibb@southnet.co.nz, Suffolk St)* Powered/unpowered sites $20/19 for 2 people, cabins $35. This large ground is the only choice in town for campers. Facilities at Arrowtown are slightly tired but the mountain views are magnificent.

There are no backpackers, but both the pubs on the main street have good cheap accommodation. The *New Orleans Hotel* (☎ *03-442 1745, 27 Buckingham St)* has simple dorm bunks for $12, plus comfortable singles/doubles with en suite for $40/60. The *Royal Oak Hotel* (☎ *03-442 1700, 42 Buckingham St)* has dorm beds for $15 and singles/doubles (shared facilities) for $25/50.

There are a handful of motels in town. The friendly *Viking Lodge* (☎ *0800 181 900, 03-442 1765,* e *viking@inq.co.nz, 21 Inverness Crescent)* has A-frame chalets, each with its own washing machine and video player, from $80.

Settlers Cottage Motel (☎ *0800 803 801, 03-442 1734,* e *settlersmotel@clear.net.nz, 22 Hertford St)* has spacious, comfortable units set in pretty gardens from $92 for a studio to $110 for a two-bedroom unit.

There are several good B&Bs in the vicinity of Arrowtown; contact the visitors centre for details. One excellent option is *Arrowtown Lodge & Hiking Company* (☎ *0800 258 802, 03-442 1101,* W *www.arrowtownlodge.co.nz, 7 Anglesea St)*, which has four cottage-style suites; B&B singles/doubles start at $70/120. The owners also conduct guided alpine tramps, historic hikes

and scenic bushwalks for $80 per day, which includes transport and lunch.

Millbrook (☎ *0800 800 604, 03-441 7000,* W *www.millbrook.co.nz, Malaghan Rd)* Rates $290-430 Apr-Sept, $320-495 Oct-Mar. Magnificent Millbrook is one of the region's top resorts and is not far out of Arrowtown towards Queenstown. It has beautiful scenery and luxurious accommodation (rooms, suites, villas and cottages of varying sizes). Its grounds are home to restored historic buildings, a health spa, sports facilities and good restaurants – the golf course here is superb.

Places to Eat

There are plenty of options, along pretty Buckingham St, catering to most budgets. The *Arrowtown Bakery* has excellent pies and rolls; the adjacent *cafe* serves up hearty cooked breakfasts. There are a few good takeaways offering burgers and fish and chips, and the *New Orleans* and *Royal Oak Hotels* have bistros with quality pub fare.

Arrowtown has developed a reputation as a foodies' retreat, and it's not hard to see why. Elegant *Saffron* (☎ *03-442 0131, 18 Buckingham St)* is acclaimed as one of the country's finest restaurants (mains around $30; book ahead). The owners have opened a more casual eatery behind it: stylish *Pesto* (☎ *03-442 0885)* serves up a great selection of affordable pizzas, pasta and salads, with mains costing from $13 to $19. To round off this 'mini-empire', a small, intimate bar has recently been opened next door to the restaurants, called *The Blue Door*.

And to add to the outpouring of good taste, down the alley beside the restaurants is *Dorothy Browns* (☎ *03-442 1968)*, a classy cinema and bar.

Getting There & Away

From Queenstown, the Double Decker Bus (☎ *03-442 6067)* does a three-hour round-trip to Arrowtown at 10am and 2pm daily for $27, which you can ride as one-way transport ($15) or as a sightseeing trip. Arrow Express (☎ *03-442 1535)* has three scheduled services daily that can be picked up outside the museum in Arrowtown, and outside McDonald's on Camp St in Queenstown ($10/18 one way/return, 25mins).

For prebooked passengers, InterCity buses to Dunedin and Christchurch can also stop at Arrowtown.

GLENORCHY
pop 215

At the head of Lake Wakatipu, the tiny picturesque, hamlet of Glenorchy is 47km (a scenic 40-minute drive) from Queenstown and offers a tranquil escape. Many people pass through briefly in their rush to knock off the Routeburn Track, and thus bypass perhaps one of the greatest tramping opportunities – the Rees and Dart River valleys.

Those with a car can explore the superb valleys north of Glenorchy. For those who have always been searching for **Paradise**, it lies some 15km northwest of Glenorchy at the start of the Rees-Dart Track. Paradise is just a paddock but the gravel road there runs through beautiful farmland surrounded by majestic mountains (there are a couple of small creek crossings). Alternatively, you can explore the Rees Valley or take the road to Routeburn, which goes via the Dart River Bridge. Near the start of the Routeburn Track in Mt Aspiring National Park there is a day hut and a couple of short walks – the Double Barrel and the Lake Sylvan walks – if you are not tackling the Routeburn.

The town has a **golf course** and pleasant **walks** around the lake. There's a helpful DOC visitors centre (☎ 03-442 9937, e glenorchyvc@doc.govt.nz) here, with the latest track conditions, hut tickets and general information. It's open 8.30am to 4.30pm daily in summer, with reduced hours in winter. Get camping gear and supplies in Queenstown or Te Anau.

A good source of information is W www.glenorchy.com.

Jetboating & Kayaking

The Dart River jetboat trip offers a scenic trip into the heart of the Dart River wilderness, one of NZ's most beautiful places. Savour the grandeur of the slopes of Mt Earnslaw and the bush-clad mountain walls on both sides of the river. The breathtaking scenery lasts for two hours then there's a stop to take a guided walk through beech forest, and a 4WD journey on the back road to Paradise.

Dart River Safaris (☎ 0800 327 8538, 03-442 9992, W www.dartriver.co.nz) has a shuttle service departing Queenstown at 8am and noon year-round; from Queenstown the trip is six hours in total and costs adult/child $159/80. If you make your own way to Glenorchy the 'wilderness safari' is about three hours and costs $145/72.50. Reservations are essential.

Also offered by the company is 'The Heritage Trail', a fully catered luxury option with limited numbers that involves jetboating for 1½ hours, walking for 1½ hours and a one-hour 4WD journey, plus a gourmet picnic in the wilderness. The shuttle service for this trip leaves Queenstown at 9.30am year-round; the seven-hour trip costs $299/225 whether you join from Queenstown or Glenorchy.

And finally, a great option is to take a 75-minute jetboat ride up the Dart and then descend the river in an inflatable three-seater canoe (a 'funyak'; see W www.funyaks.co.nz); the canoe section is 2¼ hours and no experience is necessary. The journey from Queenstown is a total of eight to nine hours and the return cost is $209/157; from Glenorchy the duration is five hours and the cost is $195/147.

Dart Wilderness Adventures (☎ 03-442 9939, W www.glenorchyinfocentre.co.nz) also operates jetboating trips on the Dart River out of Glenorchy, and offers pick-up and drop-off from Queenstown. It has 70km of jetboating; from Queenstown the total duration is six hours and the cost is $145/72.50 adult/child; if you join the trip in Glenorchy the cost is $135/67.50.

Other Activities

There are two companies in Glenorchy offering you the chance to explore this stunning area on horseback and they cater to all levels of riding experience. **Dart Stables** (☎ 0800 474 3464, 03-442 5688, W www.glenorchy.co.nz) has a number of options, including a two-hour ride for $65, a full day for $130 or an overnight trek from $250, including meals and accommodation. **High Country Horses** (☎ *03-442 9915,* **W** *www.high-country-horses.co.nz)* also offers a great range, including twilight treks from $50. Both companies will arrange transfers from Queenstown, if one is required, for an additional fee.

Glenorchy Air (☎ *03-442 2207,* **W** *www .glenorchy.net.nz)* has a 20-minute local aerial sightseeing trip around Mt Earnslaw and the Routeburn for $120. Mt Aspiring and the Olivine Ice Plateau are included in 45 minutes for $210. A flight over Milford Sound is $195; a Milford cruise option costs from $260. The flights are available from Glenorchy or Queenstown.

Glenorchy Cruising (☎ *03-442 9951.* **e** *wakatipu@xtra.co.nz)* organises fishing trips ($105 per person for two hours, gear included) and eco-cruises, and also operates a water-taxi service.

Places to Stay & Eat

Glenorchy Holiday Park (☎ *03-442 9939,* **W** *www.glenorchyinfocentre.co.nz, 2 Oban St)* Powered/unpowered sites $18/16 for 2 people, dorm bunks $13, cabins $30. This spacious park is well set up for trampers and offers rustic accommodation. You can buy limited supplies from the store here; the Backpacker Express for transport to the tracks also operates out of here.

Glenorchy Hotel (☎ *0800 453 667, 03-442 9902,* **e** *ehotel@glenorchy.org.nz)* has very comfortable rooms behind the pub. Doubles with shared facilities are $59, with en suite $79. The owners also have the *Glenorchy Backpackers Retreat*, a simple lodge with good facilities out the back of the hotel; dorm beds are $16. The pub offers good food and great views from its lovely outdoor deck.

Directly across the lake from Glenorchy is the excellent *Kinloch Lodge* (☎ *03-442 4900,* **W** *www.kinlochlodge.co.nz)*, a great place to unwind. In a peaceful lakeside setting, the quality accommodation ranges from bunk rooms ($18 to $22 per person), simple doubles and twins from $55, and

more upmarket rooms costing from $88 per person, including breakfast and dinner (there are no en suite rooms). There are self-catering facilities, or meals can be enjoyed at the restaurant here. The lodge is a 26km drive from Glenorchy around the head of the lake, or you can take a three-minute boat transfer across the lake for a small charge (organise with the owners when booking).

The *Glen Roydon Lodge* (☎ *03-442 9968,* **W** *www.glenroydon.com)*, near the Glenorchy Hotel, has well-appointed hotel-style rooms from $90, plus a restaurant, cafe and bar. The friendly owner is a great source of information on the area.

Mt Earnslaw Motels (☎ *03-422 6993,* **W** *www.earnslaw.bizland.com)* is a new place with modern units (from $85 to $95). The owner has a rather novel store in town selling products made from possum fur!

Routeburn Farm is on the road to the Routeburn Track, 6km before the start of the walk and 21km from Glenorchy. The owners have the spacious *Routeburn Farm Motel* (☎ *03-442 9901,* **e** *elfinbay@queens town.co.nz)*, a three-bedroom self-contained cottage set in farmland, with good walking opportunities all around. The cottage costs $85 for two, $10 each additional person.

Blanket Bay (☎ *03-442 9442,* **W** *www .blanketbay.com)* Doubles $1090-1690, chalets $1690-2390. Out of the range of many, but hey, it's nice to dream! Blanket Bay is a truly exclusive world-class resort on the shores of Lake Wakatipu near Glenorchy. It's a breathtaking place both inside and out, to match the stunning setting. The lodge is constructed of native timber and local schist stone, and has some brilliant facilities, including a luxurious lounge with open fire, dining room, bar and outdoor heated pool.

Back in the real world, both the pub and the Glen Roydon Lodge have food on offer, but the best place in town for a meal is the *Glenorchy Cafe* (☎ *03-442 9958)*, a great place with loads of character, interesting decor and old vinyl records on the turntable. It offers tasty home-cooked food, with lunch such as soup, panini and pies to $10 and dinner from $15 to $28 (dinner served

November to April). There's a good outdoor area, and on Thursdays in summer there's a popular jam session and barbecue.

Stock up on groceries in Queenstown.

Getting There & Away
Wonderfully scenic Glenorchy-Queenstown Rd is now sealed all the way, but its constant hills are a killer for cyclists. In summer there are daily trampers' buses connecting the two areas, such as Backpacker Express, based at the Glenorchy Holiday Park. Backpacker Express operates transport to the start of the Routeburn and other tramps in the area, plus a boat service to Kinloch and the Greenstone and Caples Valleys.

LAKE WAKATIPU REGION TRAMPS
The mountainous region at the northern head of Lake Wakatipu combines some of the greatest scenery in NZ with some of the best tramping tracks: the famous Routeburn and lesser-known Greenstone, Caples and Rees-Dart Tracks are all here. Glenorchy is a convenient base for all these tramps.

Track Information
For accommodation details, transport to and from all trail heads and the location of DOC information offices and ranger stations, see the Queenstown and Glenorchy sections earlier in this chapter and Te Anau in the Southland chapter.

Staff at the DOC offices can give you advice on the best maps to use, outline track conditions and sell hut and Great Walks Passes. For more detailed information on these tracks see Lonely Planet's *Tramping in New Zealand*.

The Routeburn Track
The three- to four-day Routeburn Track is one of the best rainforest/subalpine tracks in the country because of the great variety of countryside and scenery. Unfortunately, it has become the surrogate for those who have missed out on the Milford Track and pressures on the track have necessitated the introduction of a booking system, as there is for Milford.

Advance bookings are required throughout the main season (November to April), either through DOC in Te Anau, Queenstown or Glenorchy, or by email at e greatwalksbooking@doc.govt.nz. The Great Walks Pass (adult/child $35/17.50 per night) allows you to stay at Routeburn Flats, Routeburn Falls, Lake Mackenzie and Lake Howden huts. A camping pass (Routeburn Flats and Lake Mackenzie only) is $15/7.50 per adult/child per night.

Off season, from late April to late October, the Routeburn Flats and Routeburn Falls huts are $10, and Lake Mackenzie and Howden Huts are $5. Note that the Routeburn Track is often closed by snow in the winter and stretches of the track are very exposed and dangerous in bad weather, so check with DOC.

Routeburn Walk Ltd (☎ 03-442 8200, W *www.routeburn.co.nz*) has a three-day guided walk on the Routeburn ($950/1050 low/high season), a three-day walk on the Greenstone ($950/1050), and a six-day 'Grand Traverse' ($1325/1425), which combines the two. Prices include return transport, accommodation and all meals. See Walking in the Queenstown section of this chapter for details of guided one-day walks on the Routeburn.

There are car parks at the Divide and the Glenorchy end of the Routeburn but they are not attended so don't leave valuables in your car. Glenorchy Holiday Park stores gear for free if you use its transport (otherwise there's a small daily charge).

Walking the Track The track can be started from either end. Many people travelling from the Queenstown end try to reach the Divide in time to catch the bus to Milford, and connect with a cruise on the sound. Highlights of the track are the view from the Harris Saddle and from the top of nearby Conical Hill. You can see the waves breaking on the West Coast beach at Martins Bay. The view is almost as good as the view from Key Summit, which offers a panorama not only of the Hollyford Valley but also of the Eglinton and Greenstone River valleys.

Estimated walking times are:

route	time
Routeburn Shelter to Flats Hut	3 hrs
Flats Hut to Falls Hut	1 to 1½ hrs
Falls Hut to Mackenzie Hut	4½ to 6 hrs
Mackenzie Hut to Howden Hut	3 to 4 hrs
Howden Hut to the Divide	1 to 1½ hrs

Greenstone & Caples Tracks

The Routeburn can be combined with the Caples and Greenstone Tracks for a round trip back to the Glenorchy area. Access at the Caples and Greenstone end is at Greenstone Wharf; the road from Kinloch to Greenstone Wharf is unsealed and rough; Backpacker Express usually runs a boat across the lake from Glenorchy. These two tracks form a loop; the huts are Mid Caples, Upper Caples, McKellar, Mid Greenstone (all $10 per person per night) and Sly Burn ($5). Estimated walking times are:

route	time
Greenstone Wharf to Mid Caples Hut	3 hrs
Mid Caples Hut to Upper Caples Hut	2 to 3 hrs
Upper Caples Hut to McKellar Hut	6 to 8 hrs
McKellar Hut to Mid Greenstone	4 to 6 hrs
Mid Greenstone to Sly Burn	1 to 1½ hrs
Sly Burn to road end	3 to 5 hrs

From McKellar Hut you can walk two to 2½ hours to Howden Hut on to the Routeburn Track as described earlier (you will need a booking for this hut from November to April). Other options from McKellar Hut include turning off for the Divide before reaching Howden Hut.

Rees-Dart Track

This difficult four- to five-day circular route goes from the head of Lake Wakatipu by way of the Dart River, Rees Saddle and Rees River valley, with the possibility of a side trip to the Dart Glacier, if you're suitably equipped. Access by vehicle is possible as far as Muddy Creek on the Rees side, from where it's two hours to 25-Mile Hut.

You can park at Muddy Creek; transport is also available to and from the tracks. Most people go up the Rees first and then back down the Dart. The three DOC huts, Shelter Rock, Dart and Daleys Flat, cost $10 per person a night.

Estimated walking times are:

route	time
Muddy Creek to Shelter Rock Hut	6 hrs
Shelter Rock Hut to Dart Hut	5 to 7 hrs
Dart Hut to Daleys Flat Hut	6 to 8 hrs
Daleys Flat Hut to Paradise	6 to 7½ hrs

Wanaka Region

Entering Otago via the Haast Pass, you first come to the tiny hamlet of Makarora. The first sizable towns, however, are Hawea and Wanaka, reached by passing between Lakes Wanaka and Hawea at the Neck. The central feature of this region is Mt Aspiring, surrounded by the national park of the same name.

MAKARORA
pop 40

When you reach Makarora you've left the West Coast and entered Otago, but it still has a West Coast frontier feel. It's the southern gateway to the Haast Pass and it can accommodate about 140 people, mostly trampers and adventure-seekers. There isn't much else to this township – which is part of its charm.

OTAGO

The DOC visitors centre (☎ 03-443 8365) on the highway has information on the Haast region and should be consulted before undertaking any tramps; the office is manned from 8am to 4.45pm daily from November to April; Monday to Friday only from May to October. See also W www .makarora.co.nz for information.

'Siberia Experience'

Makarora is the base for one of NZ's great outdoor adventures: the Siberia Experience. This is one of those Kiwi extravaganzas that combine sundry thrill-seeking activities – in this case a scenic small-plane flight (25 minutes), a three-hour bushwalk through a remote mountain valley and a jetboat trip (30 minutes) down a river valley. Make sure you follow the markers as you descend from Siberia; people have become lost and have had to spend the night in the open. (Just a quick note to explain the name: an early traveller through the region named one of the world's most beautiful valleys Siberia and, equally bizarrely, called the nearby Matterhornesque peaks Dreadful and Awful.) You might consider spreading the whole experience out over two days and overnighting in Siberia – the 20-bed DOC hut in Siberia Valley costs $10 per night.

Southern Alps Air (☎ 0800 345 666, 03-443 8666, e rpcooper@xtra.co.nz) offers the 'experience' from mid-October to mid-April ($185, minimum numbers required). It also has 40-minute scenic flights over Mt Aspiring ($150 per person), 75-minute trips to Mt Cook and the glaciers ($240) and landings at Milford Sound ($250).

Jetboating

A 50km, one-hour jetboating trip into Mt Aspiring National Park on the Makarora and Wilkin Rivers costs adult/child $55/27 (minimum numbers required) with **Wilkin River Jets** (☎ 03-443 8351), much cheaper than Queenstown trips.

For trampers, boats go to Kerin Forks at the top of the Wilkin River and a service goes across the Young River mouth when the Makarora floods. Inquire at the jetboat company or with DOC.

Walking

Of the area's many walks, shorter ones include the Old Bridal Track (1½ hours one way), which heads from the top of the Haast Pass to Davis Flat; a 15-minute nature walk around Makarora; and the Blue Pools River Walk (30 minutes return), where you can see huge rainbow trout.

Longer tramps go through magnificent countryside, but are not to be undertaken lightly. Alpine conditions, flooding and the possibility of avalanches mean that you must be well prepared and consult with DOC before heading off. The *Tramping Guide to the Makarora Region* ($3.50) published by DOC is a good investment.

The three-day **Gillespie Pass** tramp goes via the Young, Siberia and Wilkin Rivers but this is a high pass with avalanche danger. With a jetboat ride down the Wilkin to complete it, this surely could rate alongside the Milford Track as one of the great tramps. The **Wilkin Valley Track** heads off from Kerin Forks Hut, reached by jetboat, or you can fly in to Top Forks. From Kerin Forks the track leads to Top Forks Hut, then the north branch of the Wilkin. Here are the picturesque Lakes Diana, Lucidus and Castalia (one hour, 1½ hours and 3–4 hours respectively from Top Forks Hut).

Places to Stay & Eat

Makarora Tourist Centre (☎ 03-443 8372, e touristcentre@makarora.co.nz) Powered/unpowered sites $17/16 for 2 people, dorm beds $18, cabins $50 (linen additional), self-contained motel units $80. This large complex is behind the tearooms and store. It offers good accommodation in a peaceful bush setting, with motel rooms, A-frame cabins, camp sites and dorm beds in a backpackers lodge. The self-contained 15-bed homestead is perfect for groups and has awesome views (price based on numbers).

Larrivee Homestead (☎ 03-443 9177, e andiepaul@xtra.co.nz) B&B singles/doubles $80/110; self-contained cottage $100 for 2 people plus $20 each extra adult. Larrivee is not far from the Makarora Tourist Centre – take the road closest to the DOC visitors centre and follow it until you reach the octagonal masterpiece at the end of the drive; the house and cottage are made of local stone and hand-split cedar. On offer here is a friendly homestay B&B, plus a very comfortable, self-contained cottage that sleeps four. There are free bikes and kayaks for guest use; dinners are prepared by arrangement for $35 per person.

The nearest **DOC camping grounds** are on SH6 at Cameron Flat, about 14km north of Makarora, and at Boundary Creek Reserve, about 18km south of Makarora on the shores of Lake Wanaka.

The **tea rooms** at the tourist centre are open 9am to 5pm daily, with longer hours in summer. You can get good light meals and snacks, and there's a grocery store for basic supplies, plus Internet access and petrol. A few kilometres south is another petrol station and tearooms, the **Country Cafe**.

Getting There & Away

West Coast Express, Magic Bus and Kiwi Experience buses stop here regularly while InterCity has one northbound bus (to the glaciers) and one southbound bus (to Hawea, Wanaka and Queenstown) per day.

If you're driving from the south, you'll first pass a tiny settlement, but you need to continue on for a few kilometres to reach the main village (if you can call it that!).

HAWEA

Lake Hawea, separated from Lake Wanaka by a narrow isthmus, is 35km long and 410m deep. The lake was raised 20m in 1958 to provide those important cusecs for power stations downriver. Trout and landlocked salmon can be caught in its waters. Local character Harry Urquhart (☎ 03-443 1535) has recommended fishing trips on the lake.

The small town of Hawea has yet more spectacular lake and mountain views, but is mostly just a collection of holiday and retiree homes. At the lakeshore, **Lake Hawea Motor Camp** (☎ 03-443 1767, e lake.hawea@xtra.co.nz) has powered/unpowered sites for $20, basic cabins for $35 and cottages with kitchen and bathroom for $65 to $75.

The **Lake Hawea Motor Inn** (☎ 0800 429 324, 03-443 1224, e lakehawea@xtra

.co.nz, 1 Capell Ave) has a backpackers lodge with dorm beds for $20, plus comfortable but pricey units for $90 to $120. There's a restaurant, bar and good beer garden here.

WANAKA
pop 3500

Long a Kiwi summer resort known for its New Year revelries and a popular ski town in winter, Wanaka has a host of activities and natural mountain and lake splendour attracting visitors year-round.

Although not in quite the same league as Queenstown, the town is nirvana for adrenaline buzz seekers, with fine living and an overdose on scenery and the outdoors. Just over 100km from Queenstown, at the southern end of Lake Wanaka, it's the gateway to Mt Aspiring National Park and the Treble Cone, Cardrona, Harris Mountains and Pisa Range ski areas. This laid-back town offers a sharp contrast to the hype of Queenstown, though many locals fear that all the development taking place here will change that.

Every second Easter (even-numbered years) Wanaka hosts the incredibly popular **Warbirds over Lake Wanaka**, a huge international air show that sees the town and surrounding area fill up with visitors (in 2000 some 110,000 people attended the three-day event) and the skies fill with aircraft. Information can be obtained from the visitors centre or on ☎ 03-356 0296 and w www.warbirdsoverwanaka.com.

Information

The Wanaka visitors centre (☎ 03-443 1233, e info@lakewanaka.co.nz, w www.lakewanaka.co.nz) is down on the waterfront. It's inside the log cabin that is also home to Lakeland Adventures (☎ 03-443 7495, w www.lakelandadventures.co.nz), which rents out kayaks and bikes and operates a few activities in the area such as jetboating and lake cruises. The visitors centre is open 8.30am to 5.30pm Monday to Friday, 9am to 5pm Saturday and Sunday.

The DOC Mt Aspiring National Park visitors centre (☎ 03-443 7660, e wanakavc@doc.govt.nz) is on Ardmore St. It's open

OTAGO

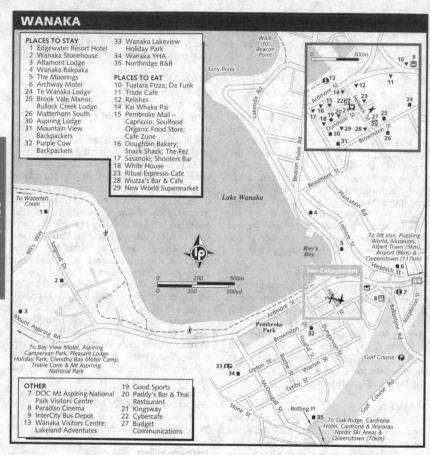

WANAKA

PLACES TO STAY
1 Edgewater Resort Hotel
2 Wanaka Stonehouse
3 Altamont Lodge
4 Wanaka Bakpaka
5 The Moorings
6 Archway Motel
24 Te Wanaka Lodge
25 Brook Vale Manor;
   Bullock Creek Lodge
26 Matterhorn South
30 Aspiring Lodge
31 Mountain View
   Backpackers
32 Purple Cow
   Backpackers

33 Wanaka Lakeview
   Holiday Park
34 Wanaka YHA
35 Northridge B&B

PLACES TO EAT
10 Tuatara Pizza; Da Funk
11 Trade Cafe
12 Relishes
14 Kai Whaka Pai
15 Pembroke Mall –
   Capriccio; Soulfood
   Organic Food Store;
   Cafe Zone
16 Doughbin Bakery;
   Snack Shack; The Fez
17 Sasanoki; Shooters Bar
18 White House
23 Ritual Espresso Cafe
28 Muzza's Bar & Cafe
29 New World Supermarket

OTHER
7 DOC Mt Aspiring National
  Park Visitors Centre
8 Paradiso Cinema
9 InterCity Bus Depot
13 Wanaka Visitors Centre;
   Lakeland Adventures

19 Good Sports
20 Paddy's Bar & Thai
   Restaurant
21 Kingsway
22 Cybercafe
27 Budget
   Communications

8am to 4.45pm daily from November to April. From May to October its hours are 8am to 4.45pm Monday to Friday, 9.30am to 3.45pm Saturday (closed Sunday). It has displays and audiovisuals, and is the place to inquire about walks and tramps.

Cybercafes include Budget Communications (☎ 03-443 4440) at 38 Helwick St, and the laid-back cafe (☎ 03-443 7429) upstairs at 3 Helwick St.

Puzzling World Maze

Three-dimensional mazes have become a NZ craze and an export activity, and this maze (☎ 03-443 7489, W www.puzzling world.com; adult/child $7/4.50; open 8am-5.30pm daily) was the original. The idea is to find your way along 1.5km of puzzling passages to the towers at each corner and then back to the exit. It's guaranteed to be more difficult than you think. The Tilted House, built on a 15° angle, is designed to confuse your sense of perspective, balance and direction. The maze complex includes a Puzzle Centre, with a variety of puzzles to test your skills, and the Hologram Hall. It's on the road to Cromwell, 2km from Wanaka.

Museums

Wanaka airport, 8km from town, is quite an aviation centre. As well as offering many aerial sightseeing activities, it has the well-presented **New Zealand Fighter Pilots Museum** (☎ 03-443 7010; adult/child $7/4; open 9am-4pm daily), which chronicles the history and exploits of NZ's fighter pilots and displays lovingly restored war planes.

Just outside the airport, the excellent **Wanaka Transport & Toy Museum** (☎ 03-443 8765; adult/child $5/2; open summer 8.30am-5pm daily) has an amazing collection of, well, stuff – everything from aircraft to motorbikes, vintage cars and the most incredible assortment of toys. It's the private collection of a man who obviously loves to collect – the treasures he has amassed and restored are quite something.

Not a museum but well worth visiting if you're out this way is **Wanaka Beer Works** (☎ 03-443 1865), next door to the Wanaka Transport & Toy Museum. You can drop by anytime to taste their fine brews, or join a daily tour ($5) of their small brewery at 2pm (bookings recommended).

Mt Aspiring National Park

In 1964, a mountainous area in northwestern Otago and southern Westland was earmarked as a national park, named after its highest peak, 3027m Mt Aspiring, the highest peak outside the Mt Cook region. The park now extends over 3500 sq km along the Southern Alps from the Haast River in the north to its border with Fiordland National Park in the south.

The park has wide valleys, secluded flats, over 100 glaciers and towering mountains. The southern end of the park around Glenorchy is the most trafficked by visitors and includes popular tramps such as the Routeburn, but there are good short walks and more demanding tramps in the Matukituki Valley close to Wanaka. Tracks are reached from Raspberry Creek at the end of Mt Aspiring Rd, 54km from Wanaka. See Getting Around later in this chapter for details of shuttle services.

The popular three-hour return **Rob Roy** walk has good views. From Raspberry Creek follow the West Matukituki Valley, from where the walk goes up the Rob Roy Stream to a point below the Rob Roy Glacier.

The **West Matukituki Valley Track** goes on to Aspiring Hut, a scenic four- to five-hour return walk over mostly grassy flats. Overnight or longer tramps continue up the valley to French Ridge Hut and Liverpool Bivvy for great views of Mt Aspiring, or over the very scenic but difficult Cascade Saddle to link up with the Rees-Dart Track north of Glenorchy.

Longer tramps are subject to snow and can be treacherous in adverse weather. Register intentions and seek advice from DOC in Wanaka before heading off.

Mountain Recreation (☎ 03-443 7330, W www.mountainrec.co.nz) offers a four-day guided West Matukituki Valley trek goes to the comfortable Shovel Flat base camp, treks up to the valley head to see glaciers and waterfalls, stops overnight in the French Ridge Hut and climbs on Mt French, with superb views of Bonar Glacier and Mt Aspiring ($895). An easier three-day option costs $595. All equipment, accommodation and food is provided.

With all the snowy peaks, the park is popular for mountaineering and alpine climbing courses. Both **Mount Aspiring Guides** (☎ 03-443 9422, W www.mtaspiringguides .co.nz), **Alpinism & Ski** (☎ 03-443 6593, W www.alpinismski.co.nz) and **Mountain Recreation** offer beginner courses, guided ascents of Mt Aspiring for the more experienced and ski-mountaineering tours.

Wanaka Rock Climbing (☎ 025 762 525, W www.rockclimb.net.nz) specialises in rock-climbing instruction and private guides in the Matukituki Valley.

Walking

The *Wanaka Walks and Trails* brochure ($1) published by DOC outlines walks around the town, including the easy 30-minute lakeside walk to Eely Point and on to Beacon Point, and the Waterfall Creek walk.

The fairly gentle climb up **Mt Iron** (549m), near the maze, takes 45 minutes to the top with views of rivers, lakes and mountains. There's a more exhausting trek up **Mt Roy** (1578m), starting 6km from Wanaka on the Mt Aspiring Rd, which takes about three hours to get to the top if you're fit. The 8km track winds at every step of the way, but the view of Mt Aspiring is a knockout. The track crosses private land and is closed from October to mid-November for the lambing season.

The **Diamond Lake Track**, a 25-minute drive from town, offers a two- or three-hour walk to the great views from the top of Rocky Hill.

Jetboating, Rafting & Kayaking
A 50-minute jetboat trip with **Lakeland Adventures** across the lake and then up the Clutha River costs adult/child $60/30.

Pioneer Rafting (☎ 03-443 1246) has easy white-water rafting trips with an eco bent for $95/145 for a half/full day.

Contact **Alpine River Guides** (☎ 03-443 9023, W www.alpinekayaks.co.nz) to find out about kayak trips on the Hawea, Clutha, Matukituki, Makarora and Kawarau Rivers for beginners and experienced paddlers. A full day (seven hours) costs $120, a half day is $90.

Canyoning & River Sledging
Those with a sense of adventure will love this unique summertime-only (November to April) activity involving climbing, swimming and waterfall-abseiling through confined, steep and wild gorges. Transport to the canyon, lunch, instruction and equipment are included for $175. The trips are operated by **Deep Canyon** (☎ 03-443 7922, W www.deepcanyon.co.nz).

Frogz Have More Fun (☎ 0800 338 737), also from Queenstown, has white-water sledging on boogie-board-style rafts. The cheaper trips ($89) are on gentler rivers like the Clutha and Hawea, the more expensive ($109) on the challenging Kawarau.

Aerial Activities
Tandem Skydive Wanaka (☎ 03-443 7207, W www.skydivenz.com) does tandem sky diving from 9000ft ($225) and from 12,000ft ($295). As well as the adrenaline buzz, views of the mountains are stunning.

Wanaka is ideally suited for paragliding and **Wanaka Paragliding School** (☎ 03-443 9193, W www.wanakaparagliding.co.nz) has introductory courses for $180 (by the end of which you will be doing 100m flights from Mt Iron).

Aerial Sightseeing
All the following companies are based at Wanaka's airport.

Aspiring Air (☎ 0800 100 943, 03-443 7943, W www.nz-flights.com) has a range of scenic flights, including a 20-minute flight over the Wanaka area for $90, a 50-minute flight over Mt Aspiring for $155, a Mt Cook and glacier flight for $280 and Milford Sound for $255. A flight plus cruise on the sound costs $295.

Wanaka Flightseeing (☎ 0800 435 444, 03-443 8787, W www.flightseeing.co.nz) offers a similarly wide range, with a Mt Aspiring flight costing $145; **Wanaka Helicopters** (☎ 03-443 1085, W www.heliflights.co.nz) has similar sightseeing routes but is considerably more expensive.

Other Activities
Lakes Wanaka and Hawea (16km away) are excellent for trout fishing and there are numerous guides who will organise trips. **Lakeland Adventures** has 2½-hour guided trips for $250, including boat hire for three people. Alternatively, on your own, you could hire a motorised runabout for $40 per hour and rod for $12 per day; a licence will cost another $13.

Alpine & Heli Mountain Biking (☎ 03-443 8943, W www.mountainbiking.co.nz) does just that – high-altitude guided mountain biking. There are half-day and full-day trips ($95/165) that take you high into the Pisa Range by 4WD and then you head downhill back to town. Heli-biking trips from around 2000m are also offered, priced from $235.

Backcountry Saddle Expeditions (☎ 03-443 8151), 26km from Wanaka on the Cardrona Rd (just south of the Cardrona Hotel), offers two-hour horse treks for $50 and overnight wilderness trips from $140. **Mt Iron Saddle Adventures** (☎ 03-443 7777) has two-hour treks from $45.

Criffel Peak Safaris (☎ 03-443 1711, W www.criffelpeaksafaris.com), out near the airport, has quad-bike trips in the Upper Clutha basin. Prices vary depending on the duration and destination; a two-hour challenging climb to the top of Criffel Bluffs is $75; a cruisy three-hour journey through a deer farm is $130.

Good skiing areas nearby include **Treble Cone**, **Cardrona**, the **Waiorau Nordic Ski Area** (for cross-country skiing) and **Harris Mountain** for heli-skiing (see Skiing & Snowboarding in the Activities chapter).

Good Sports (☎ 03-443 7966, W www.good-sports.co.nz, Dunmore St) hires out a vast array of sports equipment, including bikes, camping and hiking gear, fishing rods and water-sports gear.

Organised Tours

Lakeland Adventures on the waterfront has one-hour lake cruises for $50/25. The **Mizzy Bee** (☎ 0800 464 999, 03-443 1855) offers a guided bus trip around the sights of town and the Wanaka back country. Tours generally last for three hours and cost $59, but cheaper, shorter options are also available.

During the summer months, **Alpine Shuttles** (☎ 03-443 7966) has tours around the local area, including 'Wine Encounters of Central Otago', which visits a selection of vineyards in the area ($75/95 for a half/full day), and 'Country Gardens', which calls on some of the outstanding private gardens around Wanaka ($59).

Places to Stay

Camping & Cabins All prices given in this section are for two.

Wanaka Lakeview Holiday Park (☎ 03-443 7883, 212 Brownston St) Powered/unpowered sites $20, cabins $32, tourist flats $52-59. This sprawling park is the most central, only 1km from town. It has lake views and treed areas and good facilities.

Aspiring Campervan Park (☎ 03-445 6603, W www.campervanpark.co.nz, Studholme Rd) Sites $30. Catering exclusively to campervans, this neat little park is new, modern and very well equipped. There's free use of the spa and sauna, plus a large

lounge and kitchen and a great barbecue area. It's a couple of kilometres out of town on the road to Mt Aspiring.

Pleasant Lodge Holiday Park (☎ 03-443 7360, e plelow@xtra.co.nz, 217 Mount Aspiring Rd) Powered/unpowered sites $20, cabins $35, tourist flats $65, motels $80. This park is 3km from Wanaka, has extensive grounds, good facilities, and a pool.

Glendhu Bay Motor Camp (☎ 03-443 7243, e glendhucamp@xtra.co.nz, Mt Aspiring Rd) Powered/unpowered sites $19, cabins $27-36. The top choice for its truly lakefront location, scenic Glendhu Bay is right on Lake Wanaka 12km from town, in spacious grounds.

There is a *DOC camping ground* at Albert Town reserve, adjacent to SH6, 5km northeast of Wanaka.

Hostels There are some very good backpackers in Wanaka; most have a pleasant and inviting small-town feel.

Matterhorn South (☎ 03-443 1119, e matterhorn@xtra.co.nz, 56 Brownston St) Dorm beds $19-22, doubles & twins $42, lodge rooms $70 for 2 people. Friendly Matterhorn South is a delightful place with great accommodation options plus very pleasant deck and barbecue areas. Lodge rooms sleep four and have en suite, fridge and TV.

Wanaka YHA (☎ 03-443 7405, e yha wnka@yha.org.nz, 181 Upton St) Camp sites $10 per person, dorm beds $17, twins & doubles $38. The small, well-run YHA has a relaxed, friendly atmosphere and good accommodation in spacious grounds. Mountain bikes are available.

Wanaka Bakpaka (☎ 03-443 7837, e wanakabakpaka@xtra.co.nz, 117 Lakeside Rd) Dorm beds $18-19, twins $42, doubles $47. Wanaka Bakpaka is opposite the jetty on the northern side of Roy's Bay, with great views of the lake and mountains from its cosy lounge area. It's well set up for travel and tramping information. Mountain bikes, kayaks and canoes can be hired.

Purple Cow Backpackers (☎ 0800 772 277, 03-443 1880, W www.purplecow.co.nz, 94 Brownston St) Dorm beds $19, twins &

doubles with en suite $52. This great place has modern facilities, huge common areas and spectacular views, and the added bonus of en suites for all rooms. It's a spacious and friendly backpackers with a ski-lodge feel; bikes and kayaks can be rented.

Bullock Creek Lodge (☎ *03-443 1265,* e *bullockcreeklodge@clear.net.nz, 46 Brownston St)* Dorm beds $20, twins & doubles from $45, with en suite $60. This lodge has excellent grounds, with decks, lawns and a pleasant stream. Dorms and rooms are clean and comfortable, and the communal areas are very appealing.

Mountain View (☎ *03-443 9010,* e *mountainview@madmail.com, 71 Brownston St)* Dorm beds $18, doubles $45. This is a small and friendly new place that's well located and provides all the essentials for a good stay.

Altamont Lodge (☎ *03-443 8864,* e *altamontlodge@xtra.co.nz, 121 Mt Aspiring Rd)* Singles/doubles $30/48; linen additional $5. Altamont Lodge, on the edge of town towards Treble Cone, is not technically a backpackers but does offer excellent budget accommodation. It's very popular with skiers in winter and is well set up for winter pursuits, with a drying room and ski storage. The lodge has comfortable rooms, all with shared bathroom amenities, and facilities include a communal kitchen and spacious lounge area with open fire, plus tennis court and spa.

B&Bs & Guesthouses A dozen or so B&B-style places (with doubles averaging $100 to $120) are in and around Wanaka; contact the visitors centre for information.

Of particular note are **Northridge B&B** (☎ *03-443 8835,* e *s.atkinson@xtra.co.nz, 11 Botting Place),* on a ridge overlooking Wanaka (rooms $140), and the **Wanaka Stonehouse** (☎ *03-443 1933,* e *stonehouse@xtra.co.nz, 21 Sargood Drive),* an English-style manor with doubles from $160 to $180.

Te Wanaka Lodge (☎ *0800 926 252, 03-443 9224,* w *www.tewanaka.co.nz, 23 Brownston St)* B&B rooms $140-185. Te Wanaka is a superb, central lodge with warm and inviting decor and stylish nooks and crannies to enjoy, and a secluded garden hot tub. There's a gourmet breakfast to start the day, and a bar at which to end it. All the spacious rooms have en suites and balconies (there is also a self-contained cottage).

Oak Ridge (☎ *0800 869 262, 03-443 7707,* w *www.oakridge.co.nz, cnr Cardrona Valley & Studholme Rds)* Rooms $160-240. In a lovely setting a few minutes out of town on the way to Cardrona, Oak Ridge is a luxury lodge with stylish common areas decorated with art and antiques. There's also a highly rated restaurant here, Tea Thyme, plus facilities including a pool, spa and tennis court.

Lady Pembroke (☎ *0800 465 036, 03-443 7181,* w *www.houseboats.co.nz)* This is the perfect way to see the lake: on a self-contained houseboat with two king-size bedrooms and two bunkrooms, ideal for a party of eight. The daily rate ranges from $500 to $650 depending on time of year, with a usual minimum of two nights; linen is additional.

Motels & Hotels A small distance from the central action but with some of Wanaka's cheapest motel units, **Archway Motel** (☎ *03-443 7698, 64 Hedditch St)* offers comfortable, older-style studios from $75. For a little more ($85) you can move up a notch in quality in their chalet units.

Brook Vale Manor (☎ *0800 438 333, 03-443 8333,* e *brookvle@voyager.co.nz, 35 Brownston St)* Units $80-110. The immaculate Brook Vale is centrally located, with lovely gardens by a stream. The modern units are equipped with full kitchens, and there's a pool for guests in summer and a spa in winter.

Aspiring Lodge (☎ *0800 269 367, 03-443 7816,* e *aspiring@voyager.co.nz, cnr Dunmore & Dungarvon Sts)* Units $95-130. This friendly older-style place offering spacious, comfortable motel units.

Bay View Motel (☎ *0800 229 8439, 03-443 7766, Mt Aspiring Rd)* Units $110-145. The excellent Bay View is 3km from town on the road to Mt Aspiring and is very popular in winter; it's well set up for skiers and some larger units have fireplaces. All have full kitchens and great views over the spacious grounds to the lake and mountains.

The Moorings (☎ 0800 843 666, 03-443 8479, Ꝓ www.themoorings.co.nz, 17 Lakeside Rd) This is a fashionable lakefront complex of stylish studio units ($99 to $150) and modern, well-equipped two- or three-bedroom apartments ($150 to $300).

Edgewater Resort Hotel (☎ 0800 108 311, 03-443 8311, Ꝓ www.edgewater.co.nz, Sargood Drive) This huge resort is a flash lakefront establishment with an excellent range of activities and facilities, including restaurant and bar, outdoor dining area with great views, spa, sauna, and tennis court. Accommodation ranges from hotel-style rooms ($160) and one-bedroom suites ($250) to deluxe two-bedroom apartments that sleep four ($410).

Places to Eat

Restaurants Wanaka is well endowed with restaurants.

Relishes (☎ 03-443 9018, 99 Ardmore St) Mains $17-27. A definite favourite of the locals, this classy restaurant features imaginatively prepared meals and a great selection of wines from the area.

White House (☎ 03-443 9595, 33 Dungarvon St) Dinner mains to $25. With its whitewashed walls and blue shutters, the wonderful White House looks like it would be more at home somewhere on the Med than on a NZ lake, and the menu borrows heavily from Mediterranean and Middle Eastern cuisine, with an extensive selection for vegetarians. It's a friendly place with a changing blackboard menu; it's cosy inside with an open fire for winter, plus it has a lovely outdoor terrace.

Sasanoki (☎ 03-443 1188, 145 Ardmore St) Dinner mains $18-25. In a classy new restaurant with Japanese decor, Sasanoki serves up an intriguing mix of Japanese and Kiwi cuisine, with a little bit of everything else thrown in (they even have paella on the menu!). You can opt for traditional Japanese cuisine such as udon noodles, a sushi platter or chicken teriyaki, or go for the lamb shanks simmered in a soy-based stock.

Capriccio (☎ 03-443 8579, 123 Ardmore St) Mains $15-28. As well as good authentic Italian pastas at reasonable prices, this restaurant's menu has a heavy emphasis on seafood, with scallops, mussels and crayfish on offer. Other tempting mains include rack of lamb and Stewart Island salmon.

Tuatara Pizza Bar (☎ 03-443 8186, 76 Ardmore St) Pizzas $15-25. Tuatara is a good choice for a casual bite, with interesting pizza combos on the menu (eg, venison and cranberry, tofu with teriyaki sauce) and a relaxed feel.

Muzza's Bar & Cafe (☎ 03-443 7296, 59 Helwick St) Mains $15-24. With a name like that, this couldn't be anything but a casual, laid-back place with a friendly atmosphere. Family-friendly Muzza's has an open fire, couches and tables. The roast lamb and vegies meal ($14.95) is good value.

Cafes & Cheap Eats Good cafes are scattered throughout town. Among those worth lingering over a coffee at are the cool *Trade Cafe* (☎ 03-443 6722, 71 Ardmore St) at the front of the Wanaka Hotel and *Ritual Espresso Cafe* (☎ 03-443 6662, 18 Helwick St), with classic cafe fare like salads, panini, pasta and burgers to about $14.

Kai Whaka Pai (☎ 03-443 7795, cnr Helwick & Ardmore Sts) Lunch $5-20, dinner mains to $30. The name means 'good food here' and that's exactly what you'll find. It's a popular cafe-bakery by day and restaurant-bar by night, serving up breakfast, lunch and dinner, and with a reputation for some of the best food in the area.

Cafe Zone (☎ 03-443 9220, Pembroke Mall) Breakfasts and lunch $4-14. A favourite of the local ski crowd, funky and colourful Cafe Zone, situated behind the strip of takeaways, offers great all-day breakfasts plus perfect lunch treats, such as toasted bagels, wraps and quesadillas. It's usually open for dinner in the peak summer and winter seasons.

There are three lakefront places offering cheap food. *Doughbin Bakery* offers sandwiches and baked goods, *The Fez* next door sells cheap Turkish kebabs, and the *Snack Shack* has pizzas, hamburgers and fish and

OTAGO

chips. In winter, stop by the *Soulfood Organic Food Store* in the Pembroke Mall for cheap serves of warming soup.

For self-caterers, there's a *New World* supermarket on Dunmore St.

Entertainment The best entertainment in Wanaka is provided by the brilliant *Cinema Paradiso* (☎ 03-443 1531, **w** *www.paradiso .net.nz, 3 Ardmore St)*. This former town hall has been turned into a small cinema with loads of character: it's filled with old lounge chairs and sofas (and a Morris Minor!); many films are personally introduced, and there's an interval when you can purchase freshly baked cookies, coffee and great ice cream. Tickets are adult/child $10/6, and it's worth going even if you're not particularly interested in the movie being shown.

Shooters (☎ 03-443 4345, 145 Ardmore St) is a new and incongruous waterfront place that'd look more at home in Queenstown than Wanaka. Still, it has become a popular drinking hole, with good-value happy hours, pool tables, cheap bar snacks and a large deck overlooking the lake.

Other nightspots include *Kingsway* (☎ 03-443 7663, 21 Helwick St), a popular bar and diner with pool tables and often DJs, and *Paddy's Bar* (☎ 03-443 7645, 21 Dunmore St), with occasional live music (and if you're feeling peckish there's a Thai restaurant attached).

Just up from Tuatara Pizza, you'll find *Da Funk* (☎ 03-443 8269, 68 Ardmore St), a cool coffee house and bar that is sometimes a venue for live music.

Getting There & Away

Air Aspiring Air (☎ 0800 100 943) has up to three flights daily between Queenstown and Wanaka ($100 one way, $150 return, 20mins).

Bus The InterCity bus depot at Paper Place (☎ 03-443 7805), 84 Ardmore St, has daily Queenstown buses going to Franz Josef via Haast Pass from via Wanaka. Buses from Queenstown to Christchurch via Mt Cook stop here and a daily bus to Cromwell connects with the Queenstown to Dunedin route.

Wanaka is well serviced by door-to-door shuttles, most of which can be booked at the visitors centre. Southern Link (☎ 03-443 7414) goes to Queenstown ($15) and Christchurch ($50), Wanaka Connexions (☎ 03-443 9122) goes to Queenstown (including the airport) five times daily ($25, backpackers fare $22) and Atomic Shuttles (☎ 03-442 9708 in Queenstown) goes to Queenstown ($15), Dunedin ($30), Invercargill ($35) and Greymouth ($80).

Getting Around

Alpine Shuttles (☎ 03-443 7966), operating from Good Sports on Dunmore St, has regular transport to Raspberry Flat at the national park for $25/45 one way/return, and to the ski fields of Cardrona, Waiorau and Treble Cone (adult/child $22/15 return). Alpine Shuttles can also arrange transport to Makarora. Mount Aspiring Express (☎ 03-443 8422) has two services daily to Raspberry Creek in summer for the same price as Alpine Shuttles.

Numerous backpacker places around town rent out mountain bikes, as do Lakeland Adventures and Good Sports.

CARDRONA

Although the Crown Range Rd to Queenstown via Cardrona looks much shorter on the map than the route via Cromwell, it's a winding, climbing mountain road that has only recently been sealed. It's a drive well worth doing for the incredible scenery, but be warned that it is hair-raising! Take care, especially in poor weather.

Another good reason to take this road is to visit the historic *Cardrona Hotel* (☎ 03-443 8153), an old place (established 1863) full of character and set in pretty gardens. It fills up considerably on winter afternoons as skiers come off the nearby fields. Casual bar meals are on offer and there's an à-la-carte restaurant, plus accommodation. Budget rooms are $20 per person and there are double rooms for $85, a bit steep considering that facilities are shared. The hotel is right near the turn-off for the **Waiorau Snow Farm** (☎ 03-443 9717, **w** *www.snowfarm nz.com)*, a cross-country skiing area.

Southland

☎ 03 • pop 100,800

Southland is famous for its Milford Sound, and while many visit Milford on day trips from Queenstown, they don't usually get any further into this frontier province of rugged fiords, mountains, fine coastal scenery and abundant flora and fauna.

There are three main routes into Southland: via Queenstown to Fiordland; from Queenstown down SH6 to Invercargill; and from Dunedin to Invercargill on SH1. All three, however, miss spectacular scenery, so some interesting local routes are described in this chapter.

Southland has a predominantly Scottish heritage, and there's also a considerable Maori population, whose *marae* (traditional ancestral villages) are being re-established.

Fiordland

The spectacular Fiordland National Park, part of Te Wahipounamu World Heritage Area, includes some of New Zealand's most famous walks, including the best-known of the lot, the Milford Track. The tracks, however, barely penetrate this raw, powerful region. The immensity of it can only really be appreciated from the air or from a boat or kayak out on the sounds.

TE ANAU
pop 1785

Lake Te Anau, with three arms that penetrate into the mountainous forested shore, was gouged out by a huge glacier. It's 417m at its deepest, 53km long and 10km across at its widest point, making it NZ's second-largest lake after Taupo in the North Island. The lake takes its name from the caves discovered on its western shore, Te Ana-au, meaning 'cave with a current of swirling water'.

The township is beautifully situated on the lakeshore and is the main tourist centre of the region. It has all manner of activities to keep

Highlights

• Cruising Lakes Te Anau and Manapouri to Te Anau Glowworm Caves and Doubtful Sound

• Tramping the Milford and Kepler Tracks in stunning Fiordland National Park

• Sea kayaking on magnificent Milford Sound

• Driving the Southern Scenic Route from Manapouri to Invercargill

• Exploring the flora- and fauna-rich Catlins, with fossilised forests, native bushland, Hector's dolphins, penguins and rare birds

• Visiting the critters that inhabit the tuatara house at Southland Museum, Invercargill

NORTH ISLAND

SOUTH ISLAND

Not to scale

Southland

SOUTHLAND

you busy, although for many visitors the town is just a jumping-off point for Milford.

Information

The Department of Conservation's (DOC) Fiordland National Park visitors centre (☎ 03-249 7924, **e** fiordlandvc@doc.govt .nz) is on Lake Front Drive near the turn-off

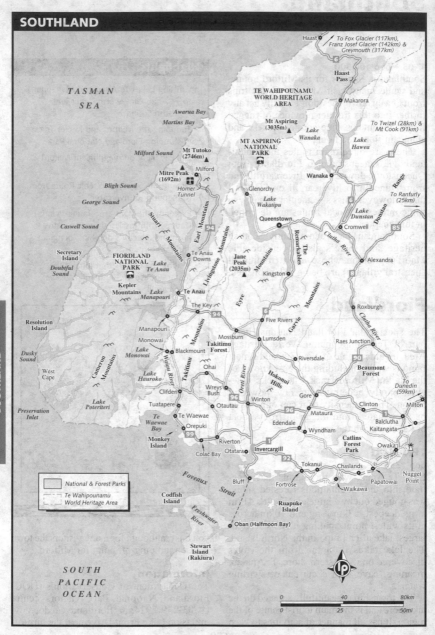

SOUTHLAND

SOUTHLAND

Haast
To Fox Glacier (117km),
Franz Josef Glacier (142km) &
Greymouth (317km)

Haast
Pass

TE WAHIPOUNAMU
WORLD HERITAGE
AREA

Makarora

*TASMAN
SEA*

Awarua Bay

Martins Bay

Mt Aspiring
(3035m)

Lake
Wanaka

To Twizel (28km) &
Mt Cook (91km)

Milford Sound

Mt Tutoko
(2746m)

MT ASPIRING
NATIONAL
PARK

Lake
Hawea

Mitre Peak
(1692m)

Milford

Bligh Sound

Homer
Tunnel

Glenorchy

Wanaka

George Sound

Lake
Wakatipu

To Ranfurly
(25km)

Caswell Sound

Queenstown

Lake
Dunstan

Cromwell

*Secretary
Island*

FIORDLAND
NATIONAL
PARK

Lake
Te Anau

Te Anau
Downs

Jane
Peak
(2035m)

The
Remarkables

Alexandra

*Doubtful
Sound*

Kepler
Mountains

Lake
Manapouri

Te Anau

Kingston

*Resolution
Island*

The Key

Five Rivers

Roxburgh

Manapouri

Mossburn

*Dusky
Sound*

Monowai

Lake
Monowai

Blackmount

Takitimu
Forest

Lumsden

Riversdale

Raes Junction

Beaumont
Forest

*West
Cape*

Lake
Hauroko

Ohai

Hokonui
Hills

To
Dunedin
(59km)

*Preservation
Inlet*

Lake
Poteriteri

Clifden

Wreys
Bush

Winton

Gore

Clinton

Milton

Tuatapere

Otautau

Mataura

Balclutha
Kaitangata

Te Waewae

Orepuki

Edendale

Wyndham

Catlins
Forest
Park

Owaka

*Te
Waewae
Bay*

Riverton

Invercargill

Monkey
Island

Colac Bay

Otatara

Nugget
Point

National & Forest Parks
Te Wahipounamu
World Heritage Area

Tokanui

Chaslands

*Foveaux
Strait*

Bluff

Fortrose

Papatowai

Waikawa

*Codfish
Island*

*Freshwater
River*

Ruapuke
Island

Oban (Halfmoon Bay)

*Stewart
Island
(Rakiura)*

*SOUTH
PACIFIC
OCEAN*

0   40   80km
0   25   50mi

to Manapouri. It's an excellent resource centre with a museum, park exhibits and information on tramping and shorter walks. It's open 8.30am to 4.30pm daily; summer hours are often extended. Independent walkers for the Milford and Routeburn Tracks can book here at the Great Walks Booking Desk (☎ 03-249 8514, e great walksbooking@doc.govt.nz).

The Te Anau visitors centre (☎ 03-249 8900, e teanau1@fiordlandtravel.co.nz) is inside the central-waterfront Fiordland Travel office. It's open 8.30am to 5.30pm daily. Fiordland Travel (☎ 0800 656 501, 03-249 7416, e info@fiordlandtravel.co.nz, w www.fiordlandtravel.co.nz) is a large company with a high profile on the South Island. It operates a variety of cruises and tours in the Fiordland area; it also has offices in Manapouri and Queenstown.

Air Fiordland's office (☎ 03-249 7505) and booking agency on the main street is another good place to find out about various activities and transport in the area; it is the town's intercity bus depot and you can also access the Internet here.

The Te Anau post office is in the centre of town (the main shopping strip is referred to

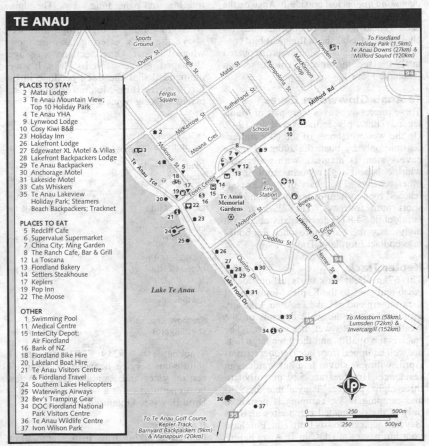

TE ANAU

PLACES TO STAY
2 Matai Lodge
3 Te Anau Mountain View; Top 10 Holiday Park
4 Te Anau YHA
9 Lynwood Lodge
10 Cosy Kiwi B&B
23 Holiday Inn
26 Lakefront Lodge
27 Edgewater XL Motel & Villas
28 Lakefront Backpackers Lodge
29 Te Anau Backpackers
30 Anchorage Motel
31 Lakeside Motel
33 Cats Whiskers
35 Te Anau Lakeview Holiday Park; Steamers Beach Backpackers; Tracknet

PLACES TO EAT
5 Redcliff Cafe
6 Supervalue Supermarket
7 China City; Ming Garden
8 The Ranch Cafe, Bar & Grill
12 La Toscana
13 Fiordland Bakery
14 Settlers Steakhouse
17 Keplers
19 Pop Inn
22 The Moose

OTHER
1 Swimming Pool
11 Medical Centre
15 InterCity Depot; Air Fiordland
16 Bank of NZ
18 Fiordland Bike Hire
20 Lakeland Boat Hire
21 Te Anau Visitors Centre & Fiordland Travel
24 Southern Lakes Helicopters
25 Waterwings Airways
32 Bev's Tramping Gear
34 DOC Fiordland National Park Visitors Centre
36 Te Anau Wildlife Centre
37 Ivon Wilson Park

Sports Ground

To Fiordland Holiday Park (1.5km), Te Anau Downs (27km) & Milford Sound (120km)

Fergus Square

School

Te Anau Memorial Gardens

Fire Station

Lake Te Anau

To Mossburn (58km), Lumsden (72km) & Invercargill (152km)

To Te Anau Golf Course, Kepler Track, Barnyard Backpackers (9km) & Manapouri (20km)

SOUTHLAND

as 'Town Centre'), and there are also banks located here.

Te Anau is the jumping-off point for the Milford Track and many other walks (the Kepler, Dusky, Routeburn and Hollyford). Bev's Tramping Gear (☎ 03-249 7389, ℮ bevs.hire@maxnet.co.nz), 16 Homer St, rents out all manner of tramping and camping equipment, including topo maps. It's open 9am to noon and 6pm to 8pm daily or by arrangement.

Te Anau Wildlife Centre

This DOC-run centre (☎ 03-249 7921; admission free) is just outside Te Anau on the road to Manapouri. The grounds and mostly natural enclosures house numerous birds, including the rare takahe, a flightless bird considered extinct until a colony was discovered in 1948 (see the special colour section 'Fauna & Flora').

Te Anau Glowworm Caves

These impressive caves were part of Maori legends but only rediscovered in 1948. On the western shores of the lake and accessible only by boat, the 200m of active cave system is magical, with waterfalls, whirlpools and a glowworm grotto in the inner reaches. The heart of the caves is reached by a system of walkways and two short punt journeys. The 2½-hour trip (adult/child $44/15) departs daily at 2pm; in high season there are more tours. For bookings contact Fiordland Travel.

Kepler Track

This 67km Great Walk starts just outside Te Anau and goes to the Kepler Mountains at the southern end of Lake Te Anau. Like any Fiordland track, the walk depends on the weather; when it's wet, it's *very* wet. The track is top quality, and the three large huts are well equipped from late October to mid-April, with gas stoves and hut wardens in residence. Hut fees are $20 per night (a three-night 'package' is available for $50) and camping is $9; camping is permitted only at the designated camp sites at Brod Bay and adjacent to Iris Burn Hut. Purchase your hut passes at DOC in Te Anau before

setting out; passes purchased at the huts will incur a surcharge.

The alpine sections of the track may be closed in winter due to weather conditions. These sections require a good level of fitness, though other sections are much easier. From mid-April to late October the huts have no heating or cooking facilities; the hut fee for these months is $10 per night, and camping is free.

The walk can be done over four days and features a variety of vegetation and terrain, including lakeside and riverside sections, then a climb out of the beech forest to the tree line and panoramic views. The alpine stretch between Luxmore and Iris Burn Huts goes along a high ridge line, well above the bush, offering fantastic views when it's clear. Other sections cross over U-shaped, glacier-carved valleys. It's recommended that the track be done in the Luxmore-Iris Burn-Moturau direction. Estimated walking times are as follows:

route	time
DOC Fiordland visitors centre to control gates	45 mins
Control gates to Brod Bay	1½ hrs
Brod Bay to Luxmore Hut	3½ to 4½ hrs
Luxmore Hut to Iris Burn Hut	5 to 6 hrs
Iris Burn Hut to Moturau Hut	5 to 6 hrs
Moturau Hut to Rainbow Reach	1½ to 2 hrs
Rainbow Reach to control gates	2½ to 3½ hrs

Tracknet (☎ 03-249 7777) operates a shuttle-bus service between Te Anau, the control gates and Rainbow Reach. A few boat operators offer a water-taxi service to Brod Bay (see Organised Tours).

Kayaking

Guided kayaking trips in this enthralling

KEPLER TRACK

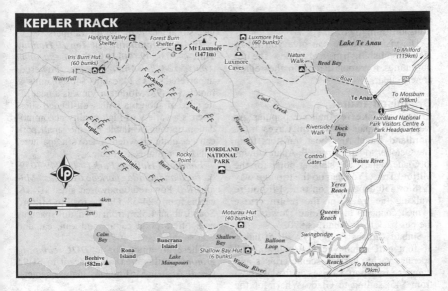

natural environment are run by **Fiordland Wilderness Experiences** (☎ *0800 200 434, 03-249 7700,* **W** *www.fiordlandseakayak.co .nz).* All trips are in the World Heritage Area and could include Lakes Te Anau and Manapouri, or Doubtful and Milford Sounds. The view of the lakes, waterfalls and fiords from this vantage point are overwhelming.

Among its many great options, the company has day paddles on Milford Sound for $90 (including transport from Te Anau) and a two-day guided trip on serene Doubtful Sound ($260). Independent kayak rental costs around $50 per day.

Aerial Sightseeing

Waterwings Airways (☎ *03-249 7405,* **e** *waterwings@teanau.co.nz)* has floatplane flights from right off Te Anau Terrace in the town centre. There's a quick zip around the local area for $55, a 20-minute flight over the Kepler Track for $110, and another over Doubtful Sound for $195 (40 minutes). There are also trips over the Milford Sound ($295, one hour) and a 'Fiordland Fantastic' trip over the remote Dusky and Doubtful Sounds ($335, 75 minutes). Waterwings also offers air transport for trampers.

Air Fiordland (☎ *03-249 7505,* **W** *www .airfiordland.co.nz)* has scenic flights on fixed-wing aircraft. A 20-minute scenic trip over Te Anau is $90, a 70-minute trip over the Milford Sound, $230, and over Doubtful Sound, $165, (40 minutes). It also offers Milford Sound flight-and-cruise packages from $270. Its head office is on Town Centre; it also has operations out of Queenstown.

Southern Lakes Helicopters (☎ *03-249 7167, 0508 249 7167,* **W** *www.southern lakeshelicopters.co.nz),* on the Lakefront Drive helipad, also has scenic flights around the area. On one combination trip you can 'heli-hike-sail' for $130 to $155 (depending on numbers). Southern Lakes takes you up to Mt Luxmore, then you walk to Brod Bay (about three hours) and take a boat back to Te Anau.

As well as scenic flights, most of these operators offer the option of one-way flights to Milford Sound.

Other Activities

High Ride Four Wheeler Adventures (☎ *0800 822 882,* **W** *www.highride.co.nz)* offers 3½-hour quad-bike trips through the back country of Te Anau, with great views over the lakes. The cost is $98, including transport from town.

The visitors centre can give you information on **fishing** trips and guides. The opportunities for trout fishing in the region are excellent.

Organised Tours

Cruises on Lake Te Anau are popular. As well as Te Anau Glowworm Caves trips, **Fiordland Travel** runs boat transfers from late October to April from Te Anau Downs to Glade Wharf, the starting point for the Milford Track. You can do the trip one way ($38 or $50 depending on times) if you're walking the track, or the return cruise (which connects at Te Anau Downs with the bus back to Te Anau) is $70.

Sinbad Cruises (*☎ 03-249 7106*) has a 36-foot gaff ketch yacht, *Manuska,* and operates yacht charters, scenic cruises and trampers' transport. Cruises on the lake cost from $45; sailing to Glade Wharf for the Milford Track is $60, to Brod Bay for the Kepler is $15.

Lakeland Boat Hire (*☎ 03-249 8364*) rents out rowing boats, pedal boats and canoes from a caravan beside the lake, opposite Pop Inn. It also operates the Kepler Water Taxi, which does regular trips to Brod Bay.

Trips'n'Tramps (*☎ 03-249 7081,* **w** *www .milfordtourswalks.co.nz*) offers guided hikes in the area, with small groups and personalised service. It operates a Milford Track day walk (10km to 12km) for $110.

Places to Stay

Camping & Cabins All prices listed here are based on two people sharing.

Te Anau Lakeview Holiday Park (*☎ 03-249 7457,* **e** *reservations@destinationnz .com, Te Annau-Manapouri Rd*) Powered/ unpowered sites $24/22, cabins $46-53, tourist flats $82, motel units $92-120. This large, well-equipped park is opposite the lake and 1km from Te Anau on the road to Manapouri. It has attractive grounds and numerous accommodation options, from a backpacker lodge (see Steamers Beach under Hostels later) to five-star motel units. Staff

can organise track transfers, and car, van and gear storage is available for trampers.

Te Anau Mountain View Top 10 Holiday Park (*☎ 03-249 7462,* **e** *fivestar@teanau .co.nz, 128 Te Anau Terrace*) Powered/ unpowered sites $24, cabins $46-50, units & motels $75-98. Mountain View is a neat little slice of suburbia with well-tended sites. There's a variety of high-quality accommodation options available but the small park can get quite crowded. There's a spa here, plus bike rental is available.

Fiordland Holiday Park (*☎ 03-249 7059,* **e** *fiordland.holiday.park@xtra.co.nz, Milford Rd*) Powered/unpowered sites $18/16, cabins from $24-58. On the road to Milford Sound, about 1.5km from town, this spacious park offers good cabins and van, car and gear storage.

There are many basic *DOC camping grounds* in this area, all adjacent to SH94 (see Te Anau to Milford later in this chapter).

Hostels Te Anau gets crowded in summer, so it's well worth booking ahead.

Te Anau Backpackers (*☎ 0800 200 074, 03-249 7713,* **e** *info@teanaubackpack ers.co.nz, 48 Lake Front Drive*) Dorm beds $19, twins & doubles $46. This is a large, friendly place, set among the town's prime real estate with great lake views. Extras include spa, bike hire, and car and gear storage for trampers. The staff will help arrange transport to the tracks and various activities in the area. Next door is the smaller *Lakefront Backpackers Lodge* (*☎ 03-249 7974, 50 Lake Front Drive*), a 'sister operation' of the larger hostel and usually only open in summer, with much the same prices as its neighbour.

Te Anau YHA (*☎ 03-249 7847,* **e** *yha tanau@yha.org.nz, Mokonui St*) Dorm beds $19, twins & doubles $46. This bright, clean and modern hostel has excellent facilities and a pleasantly laid-back feel. It's well set up for trampers and will store gear.

Steamers Beach Backpackers (*☎ 03-249 7737,* **e** *steamers@destinationnz.com*) Dorm beds $18-19, twins/doubles $46/48. At Lakeview Holiday Park on the road to Manapouri, Steamers Beach offers comfortable rooms and luxurious communal areas, with a great new kitchen, dining room and lounge. Extras include car and gear storage plus track transport.

Barnyard Backpackers (☎ 03-249 8006, e rainbowdowns@xtra.co.nz, 80 Mt York Rd) Dorm beds $18-19, twins & doubles $46. Barnyard is an excellent place on a deer farm 9km from Te Anau on the way to Manapouri, with stunning views. There are rooms in the homestead, which has a cosy lounge area and open fire, plus separate log cabins with bathroom. Horses roam the property and horse-trekking is available (from $25 for an hour).

B&Bs & Guesthouses There are a handful of well-kept B&B places. The visitors centre can help find and book one to suit your needs.

Matai Lodge (☎ 03-249 7360, 0800 249 7360, e matailodge@wxe.net.nz, 42 Mokonui St) B&B singles/doubles & twins $55/76. Cosy Matai Lodge is in a central location and offers comfortable, older-style rooms with shared facilities.

Cats Whiskers (☎ 03-249 8112, e i.t .maher@paradise.net.nz, 2 Lake Front Drive) B&B rooms $120-135. Opposite the DOC visitors centre, this small guesthouse is set in pretty gardens and offers pleasant, spacious rooms.

Cosy Kiwi B&B (☎ 03-249 7475, e cosykiwi@teanau.co.nz, 186 Milford Rd) Singles/doubles from $60/85. The Cosy Kiwi is run by a friendly, helpful Kiwi-Austrian couple who provide a gourmet breakfast buffet for guests. The comfortable, modern rooms have good amenities and there's an inviting guest lounge.

Motels & Hotels There are numerous motels along Lake Front Drive. You can negotiate prices in winter (and often in the shoulder seasons) to get a good deal.

Lynwood Lodge (☎ 03-249 8538, e lyn woodlodge@xtra.co.nz, cnr Luxmore Drive & Milford Rd) Rooms $90-95. Closed in winter. At the top of town, the sprawling Lynwood Lodge offers simple but comfortable hotel-style rooms.

Edgewater XL Motel & Villas (☎ 03-249 7258, 52 Lake Front Drive) Rooms $85-115 for 2 people, additional people $15. This place is slightly dated but its rooms are comfortable and well priced. Larger, fully self-contained units and villas can sleep up to five. Guests also have free use of canoes.

Other motels include **Lakeside Motel** (☎ 0800 452 537, 03-249 7435, e lakeside .teanau@xtra.co.nz, 36 Lake Front Drive), with units from $85, and **Anchorage Motel** (☎ 03-249 7256, e anchorage.te-anau@ xtra.co.nz, 47 Quintin Drive), with units from $75.

Holiday Inn (☎ 0800 223 687, 03-249 9700, e holidayinn.teanau@xtra.co.nz, Lake Front Drive) Rooms & suites $125-270. The lakefront Holiday Inn is a large complex with a good range of rooms and suites spread throughout its grounds. Features here include a restaurant, pool, and spa.

Lakefront Lodge (☎ 0800 525 337, 03-249 7728, e anne@lakefront.co.nz, 58 Lake Front Drive) Units $120-150. This is a well-maintained lodge that offers immaculate and quite luxurious units with all the creature comforts in a great lakeside setting.

Places to Eat

The **Pop Inn** near the lakefront has light snacks and sandwiches, and is often crammed with bus travellers. **Fiordland Bakery** on the main strip is the place for pies, sandwiches and cakes and cheap cooked breakfasts daily from 7am.

For some excellent cafe fare, head to the delightful **Redcliff Cafe** (☎ 03-249 7431, 12 Mokonui St), a restaurant-bar in a restored cottage with cosy indoor and outdoor dining areas. Light meals such as soup or salad are priced from $8 to $15; fine dinners are also served.

Keplers (☎ 03-249 7909) Mains $17-29. Te Anau has a decent restaurant scene for its size, and popular Keplers is among the better choices. The menu features lots of seafood, plus local lamb and venison dishes. If you can afford to splurge, Fiordland crayfish is around $60.

La Toscana (☎ 03-249 7756) Pasta mains $15, pizzas $20. La Toscana, in the town centre, is modelled on a traditional pizzeria and spaghetteria and is the perfect choice for cheap and cheerful dining. It serves authentic Italian dishes and tasty desserts.

If all the walking has given you a healthy appetite, head to *Settlers Steakhouse* (☎ *03-249 8454)*, the local hunting ground for carnivores. There are also two reasonable *Chinese restaurants* at the top of the strip.

The Ranch Cafe, Bar & Grill (☎ *03-249 8801)*, on the main road, and *The Moose* (☎ *03-249 7100)*, on the lakefront, are the main entertainment venues in town. The bar upstairs at The Ranch attracts a younger crowd, primarily drawn to its cheap happy-hour drinks. Both places serve food and have occasional live music.

Get supplies at the well-stocked *Supervalue Supermarket* in the town centre.

Getting There & Away
InterCity (☎ 03-249 7559) has daily bus services between Queenstown and Milford via Te Anau. Daily services also go to Invercargill and to Dunedin, continuing on to Christchurch.

Topline Tours (☎ 0508 832 628) operates a daily shuttle service between Te Anau and Queenstown, departing Te Anau at 10am and Queenstown at 2pm ($35). Tracknet (03-249 7777) also operates on this route, and offers regular service between Te Anau and Milford Sound.

Spitfire Shuttle (☎ 03-249 7505) departs Te Anau daily for Invercargill (via Manapouri) at 8.30am, returning at 1pm ($40). Catch-a-Bus (☎ 03-249 8900) operates between Te Anau and Dunedin, leaving Dunedin around 9am and Te Anau at 1pm.

Fiordland Travel has buses to Queenstown and Milford.

Drivers should fill up with petrol in Te Anau before setting off for Milford Sound. Chains should be carried in winter – they can be rented from many of the service stations.

Trampers' Transport Tracknet (☎ 03-249 7777), operating out of Lake View Motor Park, has daily shuttle buses from October to May for the Kepler, Routeburn and Hollyford Tracks and to Milford (call to inquire

about winter services). The Kepler shuttle runs to the control gates and the swing bridge. The shuttle to Milford passes the Divide at the start/end of the Routeburn and Greenstone Tracks.

Kiwi Discovery (☎ 03-249 7505) from Queenstown also provides trampers' transport, passing through Te Anau mid-morning on the way to Milford.

Getting Around
You can hire bicycles for $20 to $25 per day from Fiordland Bike Hire (☎ 03-249 7211) at 7 Mokonui St and from some of the camping grounds and backpackers.

TE ANAU TO MILFORD
It's 119km from Te Anau to Milford on one of the most scenic roads you could hope for. The first part is through relatively undulating farmland that sits atop the lateral moraine of the glacier that once gouged out Lake Te Anau. At 16km the road enters a patch of mountain beech forest, passes **Te Anau Downs** at 29km and heads towards the entrance of Fiordland National Park and the Eglinton Valley. Again, you pass patches of beech – red, silver and mountain – as well as alluvial flats and meadows.

At **Mirror Lakes**, 58km from Te Anau, there's a five-minute walk to the reflective lakes (you need good weather to enjoy them). **Knobs Flat**, 5km on, has an unmanned

---

Frustrating Fiordland Features

Once you leave Te Anau, you hit two of the menaces of Fiordland: rain and sandflies. Rain in this area is very heavy – Milford gets over 6m annually! Sandflies, for those who haven't met them, are nasty little biting insects. They're smaller than mosquitoes, with a similar bite, and you'll see clouds of them in Milford. Don't be put off sightseeing by rain; the masses of water hurtling down the sheer walls of Milford Sound are an incredible sight and the rain tends to keep the sandflies away.

For walking and tramping it's a different story, as the rain means flooded rivers and poor visibility.

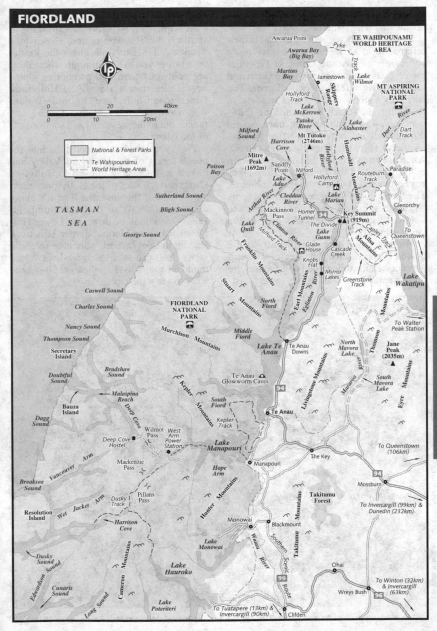

FIORDLAND

National & Forest Parks

Te Wahipounamu
World Heritage Areas

TE WAHIPOUNAMU
WORLD HERITAGE
AREA

MT ASPIRING
NATIONAL
PARK

Awarua Point

Awarua Bay
(Big Bay)

Martins
Bay

Jamestown

Pyke

Track

Lake
Wilmot

Hollyford
Track

Skippers
Range

Lake
McKerrow

Milford
Sound

Tutoko
River

Harrison
Cove

Mt Tutoko
(2746m)

Lake
Alabaster

Dart
River

Dart
Track

Mitre
Peak
(1692m)

Sandfly
Point

Poison
Bay

Lake
Ada

Milford

Hollyford
Camp

Hollyford
River

Humboldt

Mountains

Routeburn
Track

Paradise

TASMAN
SEA

Sutherland Sound

Bligh Sound

Arthur River

Cleddau
River

Mackinnon
Pass

Homer
Tunnel

Lake
Marian

Glenorchy

George Sound

Lake
Quill

Clinton River

The Divide

Key Summit
(919m)

Caples Track

To
Queenstown

Milford Track

Lake
Gunn

Ailsa
Mountains

Franklin Mountains

Glade
House

Cascade
Creek

Caswell Sound

Charles Sound

Stuart

Mountains

North
Fiord

Knobs
Flat

Mirror
Lakes

Eglinton

River

Earl Mountains

Greenstone
Track

Lake
Wakatipu

Nancy Sound

FIORDLAND
NATIONAL
PARK

Murchison

Mountains

Middle
Fiord

Lake Te
Anau

Te Anau
Downs

North
Mavora
Lake

Livingstone Mountains

Thomson

Mountains

Jane
Peak
(2035m)

To Walter
Peak Station

Thompson Sound

Secretary
Island

Doubtful
Sound

Bradshaw
Sound

Kepler

Mountains

Te Anau
Glowworm Caves

South
Fiord

Te Anau

Mararoa River

South
Mavora
Lake

Eyre
Mountains

Malaspina
Reach

Bauza
Island

Deep Cove

Arm

Kepler
Track

Dagg
Sound

Wilmot
Pass

West
Arm
Power
Station

Deep Cove
Hostel

Lake
Manapouri

To Queenstown
(106km)

Breaksea
Sound

Mackenzie
Pass

Hope
Arm

Manapouri

The Key

Mossburn

Resolution
Island

Vancouver Arm

Wet Jacket Arm

Dusky
Track

Pillans
Pass

Hunter

Mountains

Takitimu
Forest

To Invercargill (99km) &
Dunedin (232km)

Harrison
Cove

Monowai

Blackmount

Takitimu

Mountains

Dusky
Sound

Edwardson Sound

Cameron

Mountains

Lake
Monowai

Waiau

River

Southern

Scenic

Route

Ohai

To Winton (32km) &
Invercargill (63km)

Cunaris
Sound

Long Sound

Lake
Hauroko

Lake
Poteriteri

To Tuatapere (13km) &
Invercargill (90km)

Wreys Bush

Clifden

SOUTHLAND

visitors centre with exhibits, toilets, a telephone, dumping station and water.

At the 77km mark is the area that is now
referred to as O Tapara, but known more
commonly as **Cascade Creek**. O Tapara is
the original name of nearby Lake Gunn and
refers to a Ngai Tahu ancestor, Tapara. The
lake was a stopover for parties heading to
Anita Bay in search of greenstone *(pounamu)*. A 45-minute walking track passes
through tall red beech forest that shelters
a variety of bird life. Paradise ducks and NZ
scaup are often seen on the lake. Lake Gunn
is the largest of the Eglinton Valley lakes
but Fergus and Lochie are higher in altitude.
The forest floor is an array of mosses, ferns
and lichens. In Cascade Creek you may see
long-tail bats, which are NZ's only native
land mammals.

The vegetation alters significantly as the
Divide is approached. The size of the bush
is reduced and ribbonwood and fuchsia are
prominent. The Divide is the lowest east-

west pass in the Southern Alps, and there's
a shelter here for walkers either finishing or
starting the Routeburn and Greenstone
Tracks. A 1½-hour walk along the Routeburn brings you to **Key Summit**, where there
are numerous tarns and patches of alpine
bog. Three river systems (the Hollyford,
Greenstone/Clutha and Eglinton/Waiau)
start from the sides of this feature and
radiate out to the west, east and south coasts
of the island.

From the Divide, the road falls into the
beech forest of the **Hollyford Valley** and
there's an interesting turn-off to Hollyford
Camp and the start of the Hollyford Track.
At the end of the unsealed road it's about
a 10-minute walk to the high **Humboldt
Falls**. One kilometre down the Lower Hollyford Rd from Marian Corner is a track
leading to **Lake Marian**, which has splendid
views. You can take the three-hour return
tramp or, alternatively, a pleasant 20-minute
walk to view the rapids.

SOUTHLAND

ALEXANDER TURNBULL LIBRARY, WELLINGTON NZ

Men working with picks and shovels inside the Homer Tunnel (William Hall Raine, circa 1935-53)

Back at the corner, the road to Milford rises up to the east portal of the **Homer Tunnel**, 101km from Te Anau. The tunnel is named after Harry Homer, who discovered the Homer Saddle in 1889. Work on the tunnel didn't begin until 1935, providing relief for unemployed people during the Depression. It wasn't finished until 1953. Rough-hewn, the tunnel has a steep east to west gradient, but emerges after 1207m into the spectacular **Cleddau Canyon** on its Milford side. At the portals are short nature walks, with descriptions of alpine species found here. Cheeky kea greet buses. The road may be closed in winter by high snowfalls and avalanches.

About 10km before reaching Milford is the **Chasm Walk** (20 minutes return). The Cleddau River plunges through eroded boulders in a narrow chasm, the Upper Fall, which is 22m deep. About 16m lower it cascades under a natural rock bridge to another waterfall. There are views of **Mt Tutoko** (2746m), Fiordland's highest peak, glimpsed above the beech forest just before you arrive in Milford. A track leads off from the western side of the bridge over Tutoko River. After a two-hour walk through bush, the scenery here is overpowering. Don't venture any further unless you are a competent tramper and well equipped. There's no development in this region – nature, swarms of gigantic sandflies and abundant rainfall seem to retort 'Just you try'.

Hollyford Track

This is a well-known track along the broad Hollyford Valley through rainforest to the Tasman Sea at Martins Bay. Because of its length (four days one way), it should not be undertaken lightly. Check with DOC in Te Anau for detailed information and the latest track and weather conditions.

Hollyford Valley Walk (☎ 0800 832 226, 03-442 3760, W www.hollyfordtrack.co.nz) offers guided walks on this track that include a flight to Milford Sound and a jetboat trip on Lake McKerrow. It avoids the hardest and most tedious part of the walk, Demon Trail. The three-day trip is $1550, the four-day trip from $1670.

Tracknet (☎ 03-249 7777) has a regular shuttle from Te Anau to the start of the trail. The cost of chartering an **Air Fiordland** (☎ 03-249 7505) plane between Milford and Martins Bay is $375; between Te Anau and Martins Bay is $750 (the charge is per load – four people can be transported).

There are six DOC huts (Hidden Falls, Alabaster, McKerrow Island, Demon Trail, Hokuri and Martins Bay Hut), each costing $5 per night.

Estimated walking times are:

route	time
Lower Hollyford Rd car park to Hidden Falls	2 to 3 hrs
Hidden Falls to Lake Alabaster	3 to 4 hrs
Lake Alabaster to Lake McKerrow	3 hrs
Lake McKerrow to Trail	1½ hrs
Demon Trail to Hokuri	5 to 6 hrs
Hokuri to Martins Bay	4 to 5 hrs

Places to Stay & Eat

Along SH94 are many basic *DOC camping grounds*. They operate on an honesty system, and fees per night are adult/child $5/2.50. Their distances from Te Anau are:

location	km
Ten Mile Bush	17
Henry Creek	25
Walker Creek	49
Totara	53
McKay Creek	53
East Branch Eglinton	56
Deer Flat	62
Kiosk Creek	65
Smithy Creek	67
Upper Eglinton	71
Lake Gunn	81

There are three good options at Te Anau Downs, 27km from Te Anau on the road to Milford, near where boats depart for Glade

SOUTHLAND

Wharf and the Milford Track. Inquiries for the three can be directed to e grumpys@ xtra.co.nz, but specify which one you're interested in. There's a restaurant and bar here and some supplies are sold. Staff can help with local travel arrangements.

Grumpy's Backpackers (☎ 0800 478 6797, 03-249 8133) has dorm beds for $18 to 20, and doubles and twins from $48 to $53 ($53 gets you a magnificent view). All rooms have en suite, and don't be fooled by the name of the establishment – Dave, the owner, is a top bloke! There's a good kitchen and lounge area.

Also here is *Te Anau Downs B&B Hotel (☎ 0800 500 706, 03-249 7510, e grump ys@xtra.co.nz)*, with comfortable hotel-style rooms priced from $85 to $95; the tariff includes continental breakfast. Finally, *Te Anau Downs Motor Inn (☎ 0800 500 805, 03-249 7811)* has modern, self-contained motel units priced from $95 to $109 for two; larger units sleep up to six.

Formerly known as Gunn's Camp and still often referred to as such, *Hollyford Camp (no phone)* in the scenic Hollyford Valley (8km off the main road) offers very rustic cabins and camp sites. Cabins cost $17/34 for a single/double; camping ($4 per person) is possible but there are no kitchen facilities for campers. The camp also has a shop with basic trampers' supplies (sorted into 'pack-friendly' bags), plus an interesting little **museum**. Entry is free if you stay at the camp, $1 otherwise.

Possibly the most remote homestay in NZ is *Charlie's Place (☎ 07-332 2093 after hours, e john-p@wave.co.nz)* at James-town on the shores of Lake McKerrow in the Hollyford Valley. This small and wonderfully remote wilderness lodge has B&B for $55 and DB&B for $105. The contact details listed here are for Charlie's brother. Check out w www.purewilderness.co.nz for information on the area, the facilities and, importantly, how to get here.

MILFORD SOUND
pop 170
One of NZ's most famous tourist destinations, Milford Sound is the most visited of all the fiords, and the most instantly breath-taking. The 22km-long fiord is dominated by beautiful, 1695m-high Mitre Peak. The calm water mirrors the sheer peaks that rise all around. Busy through much of the day, in the morning and late afternoon Milford is serene, but don't expect blue skies. Milford is synonymous with rain: 5.5m of it a year is only average. Consider yourself lucky if you strike a fine day, otherwise take in the spectacular waterfalls.

Although remote, Milford Sound has thousands of visitors each year. Some come via the Milford Track, which ends at the sound, but most come by the buses that pull into the cruise wharf. The visitors centre here resembles a busy international air terminal when all the buses arrive.

Milford Track
Described by some as the finest walk in the world, this four-day, 53.5km walk is along a very scenic track. It's the country's best-known walk and many visitors make a special effort to do it although, sadly, they often leave NZ without realising that many other great tracks exist.

The number of walkers is limited each year; accommodation is only in huts, camping is not allowed and you have to follow a set itinerary. Some walkers resent these restrictions, but the benefits outweigh the inconvenience: keeping numbers down protects the environment and, though it's a hassle to book, you're guaranteed the track won't be overcrowded.

In the off-season it's still possible to walk the track, but there's limited trail transport, the huts aren't staffed and some of the bridges are removed. In the height of winter, snow and avalanches make it unwise.

Expect lots of rain. And when it does, the effect is an experience not to be missed. Water cascades *everywhere* and small streams become raging torrents within minutes. Remember to bring a raincoat and pack belongings in an extra plastic bag.

Bookings You can walk the track as an independent tramper or part of a guided tour. For independent bookings contact the Great

MILFORD TRACK

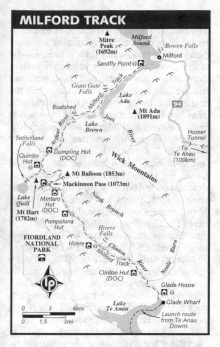

Walks Booking Desk at DOC Fiordland National Park visitors centre (see Information under Te Anau earlier in this chapter). The track can only be done in one direction – from Lake Te Anau to Milford; your DOC permit allows you to enter the track on a particular day and no other. The track must be booked from late October to late April; bookings can be heavy and it pays to book as far ahead as possible (bookings commence on 1 July for the following season).

A track permit costs $105, which includes three nights in the huts. The booking desk can also book transport: bus from Te Anau to Te Anau Downs ($12), ferry to Glade House ($38 to $50), launch from Sandfly Point (the track's end) to the Milford Sound cruise terminal ($19.80) and bus back to Te Anau ($37). All up the cost is from $212 per person.

Milford Track Guided Walk (☎ 03-441 1138, **W** www.milfordtrack.co.nz) has guided walks on the track for $1490 in low

season (late October to late November and mid-March to late April) and $1690 in high season (early December to mid-March). These organised parties stay at a different chain of huts from the independent walkers; the guided walk is all-inclusive for five days and four nights, but walkers still only get three days on the trail. The final night is spent at Mitre Peak Lodge at Milford Sound.

Walking the Track The trail starts at Glade House, at the northern end of Lake Te Anau, accessed by boat from Te Anau Downs or Te Anau. The track follows the fairly flat Clinton River valley up to Mintaro Hut, passing through rainforest. From Mintaro it passes over the scenic Mackinnon Pass, down to Quintin Hut and through the rainforest in the Arthur River valley to Milford Sound. You can leave your pack at Quintin Hut while you make the return walk to Sutherland Falls, NZ's highest. If the pass appears clear when you arrive at Mintaro Hut, make the effort to climb it – after a hot drink – as it may not be clear the next day. The highlights of Milford are the beautiful views from the **Mackinnon Pass**, the 630m **Sutherland Falls**, the rainforest and the crystal-clear streams. An intricate and very unnatural staircase has been built down beside the rapids on the descent from Mackinnon Pass. Estimated walking times are:

route	time
Glade House to Clinton Hut	1 to 1½ hrs
Clinton Hut to Mintaro Hut	5½ hrs
Mintaro Hut to Dumpling Hut	6 hrs
Side trip to Sutherland Falls	1½ hrs return
Dumpling Hut to Sandfly Point	5½ to 6 hrs

Guided walkers stop at their own huts – Glade House, Pompolona and Quintin.

SOUTHLAND

Transport to Glade Wharf Tracknet (☎ 03-249 7777) operates bus services from Te Anau to Te Anau Downs ($12), and Fiordland Travel (☎ 03-249 7416) has two boat services daily from Te Anau Downs to Glade Wharf (one service leaves at 10.30am and costs $38, a second service at 2pm has limited seats and costs $50). Alternatively, Sinbad Cruises (☎ 03-249 7106) sails from Te Anau to Glade Wharf for $60.

Transport from Sandfly Point Ferries leave Sandfly Point at 2.30pm and 3.15pm for the Milford Sound cruise wharf. Or you could kayak: Rosco's has guided kayaking from Sandfly Point to Milford for $20 (or $49 including transport back to Te Anau). Fiordland Wilderness Experiences (☎ 03-249 7700) offers the same service for much the same price (see under Te Anau earlier in this chapter). Many operators offer complete packages covering both ends of the walk for around $110.

Sea Kayaking
Probably one of the most spectacular ways you can see Milford Sound is sitting at water level in a sea kayak. In that plastic shell, you fully realise your relative insignificance to the Sound's huge natural amphitheatre. Whatever the weather, looking up to the towering bulk of the mountains is nothing short of awesome.

Rosco's Milford Sound Sea Kayaks (☎ 0800 476 726, 03-249 7695) has trips that take in Stirling Falls, Harrison Cove beneath the bulk of the Pembroke Glacier, Bowen Falls and flora and fauna from an almost 'reach-out-and-touch-it' vantage point. The cost of the trip is $99 including return transport to Te Anau, $79 if you meet him in Milford. Trips are good value and well within the bounds of someone with average fitness. There's also an afternoon trip at 4pm that includes a short paddle to Sandfly Point and a walk on the Milford Track ($49).

See Kayaking in the Te Anau section earlier in this chapter the contact details for **Fiordland Wilderness Experiences**, which offers similar guided trips on the sound.

Underwater Exploration
The marine life of the sound is as unique as its land vegetation. Heavy rainfall creates a permanent freshwater layer (stained by tannins washed out of the vegetation) above the warmer sea water, and this filters out much of the light and restricts almost all the marine life to the top 40m of water depth. This band of water is clear and calm and is home to diverse sponges, corals and fish.

There is an **underwater observatory** (☎ 0800 326 969, 03-249 9442, W www .milforddeep.co.nz) moored at Harrison Cove on the sound, and here you can descend over 10m to a viewing chamber to see the reef system and have it explained. Many cruises on the sound include a stop here (usually at an additional cost), or you can take a shuttle operated by the observatory from the Milford cruise wharf ($40).

Tawaki Dive (☎ 03-249 9006, W www .tawakidive.co.nz) operates diving trips in the sound. Day trips from Te Anau, which include two dives and full gear/own gear, cost $225/180. The cost is $40 less if you take your own transport to Milford.

A unique experience for those wanting to check out the underwater life is offered by **Submarine Adventures** (☎ 0800 478 262, 03-474 1782, W www.submarines.co.nz). Passengers can board a small submersible (maximum four passengers plus pilot) for a 50-minute underwater journey. Prices aren't cheap: $395 or $495 per person (the lower rate is for early-morning and late-afternoon dives).

Milford Sound Cruises
Cruises on Milford Sound are hugely popular, so it's a good idea to book a few days ahead. On all trips you can expect to see Bowen Falls, Mitre Peak, Anita Bay, the Elephant and Stirling Falls.

All cruises leave from the huge wharf visitors centre, a five-minute walk from the cafe and car park on an elevated walkway through a patch of Fiordland bush.

Fiordland Travel (☎ 0800 656 501, 03-249 7419, W www.fiordlandtravel.co.nz) has 1½-hour scenic cruises for adult/child $45/15 and 2½-hour nature cruises that have a nature guide on board for commentary and to answer questions ($60/15). From October to April a good choice is the MV *Friendship*, with cruises at 10.30am and/or 12.45pm ($55/15). The small *Friendship* has a capacity of only 45, so offers a more personal trip. Buffet lunches are available on the larger boats ($24), or you can pre-order a picnic lunch ($12). Most trips offer the option of stopping in at the underwater observatory for an additional $20/13.

Mitre Peak Cruises (☎ *03-249 8110,* W *www.mitrepeak.com)* has small boats (capacity 60). Cruises cost $47/20 per adult/child for 1¾-hour cruises, or $56/20 for longer cruises (two hours and 10 minutes) that venture out to the Tasman Sea. The summer cruise at 4.50pm is an excellent choice as many of the larger boats are heading back at this time. It's an additional $20/10 to visit the underwater observatory.

Red Boat Cruises (☎ *0800 657 444, 03-441 1137,* W *www.redboats.co.nz)* organises 1¾-hour cruises for $45/12, and 2¼-hour trips that take in the observatory and cost $62/20. A buffet lunch on the 1.30pm cruise costs $26, a snack pack is available on all cruises and costs $13.

Between them, these operators have well over a dozen cruises a day in summer between 9am and 3pm; it's a good idea to go on the first or last cruise of the day (or an overnight cruise) to avoid the noon-time crowds.

Overnight Cruises Fiordland Travel has overnight cruises on a choice of two boats; these allow you to appreciate the fiord when all other traffic has ceased. Kayaking, shore visits and swimming are offered as the boats sail the full length of the sound, and you'll probably see wildlife such as dolphins, seals and penguins.

The budget-oriented *Milford Wanderer*, modelled on an old trading scow, carries 60 passengers overnight from October to April. The trip leaves around 4.30pm or 5pm, returning the next morning at 9.15am. Staying overnight in tiny four-bunk cabins (shared bathrooms) costs $265 per person with connections from Queenstown, $225

from Te Anau or $155 from Milford; linen and meals are provided. The *Wanderer* is a YHA associate, so YHA discounts apply.

The *Milford Mariner* also sleeps 60 but offers more upmarket accommodation in en suite twin-share cabins. This trip operates from September to May, departs Milford at 4.30pm and returns the following day at 9.30am. The cost is $360 per person from Queenstown, $320 from Te Anau and $250 from Milford (prices based on a twin-share basis).

Places to Stay & Eat

Independent walkers seeking a bit of luxury after completing the Milford Track will be disappointed. The *Mitre Peak Lodge* caters only to those who do the guided walk.

Milford Sound Lodge (☎ *03-249 8071,* e *milford.sound.lodge@xtra.co.nz)* Powered/unpowered sites $12/10 per person, dorm beds $21, twins & doubles $52. This backpackers is the only accommodation in Milford. Under new management, there are huge renovations going on, and these are producing good results. It's worth noting that the generator is turned off at around 11pm, so it's lights off for everyone until about 6.30am; bring your torch. There's a lounge and dining area where cheap and tasty meals are served, a kitchen for guest use and a small shop selling supplies. The lodge is a couple of kilometres from the ferry wharf, off the main road.

Mitre Peak Cafe (☎ *03-249 7931)* is by the car park near the sound and offers coffee, snacks, sandwiches and reasonably priced meals. It's open 9am to 4.30pm or 5pm daily and sells souvenirs and camera film. It also has a booking desk for cruises, kayaking trips and scenic flights. The *Milford Tavern* (☎ *03-249 7427)* next door is the local pub. It has limited snacks, beer and a smattering of local workers, but not much else. It's open from about 4.30pm, although in peak season it may open at 11am.

Getting There & Away

You can reach Milford Sound by four methods: hike, fly, bus or drive. The most spectacular is by flying from Queenstown or Te Anau (see Queenstown in the Otago chapter and Te Anau earlier in this chapter). A good combination trip is to go to Milford by bus and return by air, or vice versa. Numerous scenic flights are also offered in Milford: Milford Sound Flightseeing (☎ 03-249 7778) has a 10-minute fight to the mouth of the sound for $55, plus lengthier options; book at the visitors centre or at the booking desk inside the cafe.

The 120km road trip passing through the Homer Tunnel is also spectacular. InterCity runs daily bus services from Queenstown and Te Anau, but most passengers come on day trips which include a cruise. Trampers' buses also operate from Te Anau and Queenstown and will pick up at the Milford Sound Lodge. All these buses pass the Divide and the start/end of the Routeburn and Greenstone Tracks.

Many visitors make the return trip from Queenstown in one long 12-hour day. Te Anau is a better starting point as it's only five hours return by bus. Fiordland Travel's coach-cruise-coach excursion, leaving Te Anau at 8am and returning at 4.30pm, costs $100 (children $50). InterCity has basically the same excursion for much the same price, except the cruise is with Red Boat. There are a number of other operators, including two companies that usually guide small groups. Trips'n'Tramps (☎ 03-249 7081) has a coach-and-cruise option out of Te Anau for $115, the BBQ Bus (☎ 03-442 1045) offers small, personal trips from Queenstown, picking up also in Te Anau, and the price ($139 from Te Anau, $159 from Queenstown) includes a barbecue lunch.

By car, the drive from Te Anau should take about 2½ hours, not allowing for stops. Fill up with petrol in Te Anau.

MANAPOURI
pop 210
Just 19km south of Te Anau, on the shores of the lake of the same name, Manapouri is a popular centre for trips, cruises and walking expeditions into the Fiordland area. The lake, the second-deepest in NZ after Hauroko, is in a spectacular setting, surrounded by mountains covered by native bush in their lower reaches. Close to town its shoreline forms the picturesque and popular Frasers Beach. The town survives on a combination of hydroelectricity generation and tourism, an uneasy mix at the best of times.

Information
The main information centre is Fiordland Travel (☎ 0800 656 502, 03-249 6602, e info@fiordlandtravel.co.nz, w www.fiordlandtravel.co.nz). The Pearl Harbour office organises most West Arm Power Station and Doubtful Sound trips, so it's very busy just prior to departures.

Doubtful Sound
Milford Sound, dominated by Mitre Peak, may be more immediately spectacular, but Doubtful Sound is larger, gets much less tourist traffic and is also a magnificent wilderness area of rugged peaks, dense forest and thundering waterfalls after rain.

Until relatively recently, only the most intrepid tramper or sailor entered the inner reaches of Doubtful Sound. Even Captain Cook, who named it, did not enter. Observing it from off the coast in 1770, he was 'doubtful' whether the winds in the sound would be sufficient to blow the ship back out to sea, and sailed on. In 1793 the Spanish entered the sound; Malsapina Reach was named after one of the leaders of this expedition, Bauza Island after another.

Doubtful Sound became accessible when the road over the Wilmot Pass opened in 1959 to facilitate construction of the West Arm Power Station, built to provide electricity for the aluminium smelter near Bluff. A tunnel was dug through the mountain from Lake Manapouri to Doubtful Sound, and the massive flow of water into the sounds drives the power station turbines. The project sparked intense environmental battles; in the 1970s plans to considerably raise the level of Lake Manapouri were defeated by the Save Manapouri Petition – the longest petition in NZ history. It's hard to imagine anyone would want to destroy what's described as 'New Zealand's loveliest lake'.

Today, Doubtful Sound is exquisitely peaceful. Bottlenose and dusky dolphins and fur seals can be seen in its waters, and Fiordland crested penguins nest in October and November. Below the surface, black coral and other deep-sea life exist at unusually shallow levels because sunlight is filtered out by a permanent layer of fresh water on top of the sea water. As well as the water pumped down from Lake Manapouri, Doubtful Sound receives some 6m of rain annually.

Activities

Adventure Kayak & Cruise (☎ *0800 324 966, 03-249 6626*, W *www.fiordlandadven ture.co.nz*), next to the garage in Manapouri, rents kayaks and gear at $40 per day for paddling on Lake Manapouri and also has day trips to Doubtful Sound that combine a cruise and kayaking ($165). Dinghies can be hired for $5 per person per day.

With a dinghy or kayak you can cross the Waiau River for the best **walks** close to town – the three-hour Circle Track or out to Hope Arm. Although Te Anau is the usual access point for the Kepler Track, the trail touches the top end of Lake Manapouri. Part of the Kepler can also be done as a day walk from Manapouri – access is via the swing bridge at Rainbow Reach about 10km north of town.

Manapouri is also a staging point for the remote, five-day **Dusky Track**, a real walk into the wilderness of Dusky Sound. This challenging walk is only for experienced trampers prepared for plenty of rain. See DOC and Lonely Planet's *Tramping in New Zealand* for more details.

For fishing tours contact **4 in Fiordland** (☎ *03-249 8070*). The company also offers mountain biking, kayaking and boat hire.

Organised Tours

Fiordland Travel has a half-hour cruise across Lake Manapouri; the next leg is by bus to Doubtful Sound with a side trip venturing 2km underground by road to the West Arm Power Station. After a tour of the power station, the bus travels over Wilmot Pass to the sea, where you then explore the sound on a three-hour cruise. The eight-hour trip costs $185/45 per adult/child

from Manapouri, $198/51.50 from Te Anau and $245/122.50 if you require transport from Queenstown. You can pre-order a picnic lunch ($18) or take your own.

From October to April, Fiordland Travel also offers an **overnight cruise** on Doubtful Sound, a wonderful way to experience this 'sound of silence'. The *Fiordland Navigator* sleeps 70 and offers two types of accommodation options: twin-share private cabins with en suite ($340 per person from Manapouri, $353 from Te Anau, $390 from Queenstown; prices based on twin-share occupancy), or else quad-share bunk-style accommodation ($245 per person from Manapouri, $258 from Te Anau, $295 from Queenstown); YHA discounts apply. Prices include meals and kayaking; the trip leaves Manapouri at 12.30pm and returns at 12.15pm the following day.

Fiordland Ecology Holidays (☎ *03-249 6600*, W *www.fiordland.gen.nz, 1 Home St)* offers a unique experience to a small number of clients. Its tours are run by people who are very familiar with the flora and fauna of the area, and who sail their superbly equipped yacht into various remote parts of the World Heritage Area. They take a maximum of 12 passengers, and four-day, three-night trips on Doubtful Sound cost around $890; other interesting trips go to Dusky Sound, Preservation Inlet and Stewart Island (and even NZ's Subantarctic Islands – see the Outer Islands chapter for details).

Fiordland Explorer Charters (☎ *0800 434 673, 03-249 6644)* also has daily wilderness trips to Doubtful Sound. It takes small groups out (maximum 10) on a 7½-hour trip ($150), and will pick up from Te Anau. It also rents out kayaks ($20 for half a day) and mountain bikes ($10) for exploring the Manapouri area.

Places to Stay & Eat

Manapouri Glade Motel & Motor Park (☎ *03-249 6623, Murrell Ave)* Powered/unpowered sites $17 for 2 people, cabins $30, motel units $70. This small, pretty, well-maintained park is in a peaceful location next to the lake. It's closed in winter.

Manapouri Lake View Motels & Motor Park (☎ *03-249 6624)* Powered/unpowered sites $20/19 for 2 people, backpackers dorm beds $16, cabins from $33, motel units $60-95. Set in sprawling grounds, this friendly place has good amenities and loads of character, including some quaint and quirky cabins. Not far away is the *Manapouri Lakeview Motor Inn* (☎ *03-249 6652,* e *manapouri@clear.net.nz, 68 Cathedral Drive)*, with backpackers dorm beds for $18 and units from $60.

Freestone Backpackers (☎ *03-249 6893)* is a secluded place set back from the road 3km east of Manapouri on the Manapouri-Hillside Rd. There are dorm beds inside the house for $17 and doubles for $45, plus rustic huts with pot belly stoves, gas cookers and verandas for $60. It's closed June to September.

Deep Cove Hostel (☎ *03-249 6602, 03-216 1340)* is on Doubtful Sound and is well set up for sea and walking activities. It normally only takes school groups; in summer independent travellers may be able to stay. Arrangements must be made in advance.

There are two lovely B&Bs in town. *The Cottage* (☎ *03-249 6838, Waiau St)* is a small place near the river set in a pretty, flower-filled garden. It has two comfy rooms costing $75 to $90. The more up-market *Murrell's Grand View House* (☎ *03-249 6642,* e *murrell@xtra.co.nz, 7 Murrell Ave)* was built in 1889 and features wide verandas, spacious grounds and great views over the lake. It serves up hearty breakfasts and has three comfortable rooms costing $230 to $250.

Cathedral Cafe (☎ *03-249 6619)*, attached to the general store/post office, has home-cooked meals and snacks. The only other option is the *Beehive* cafe at the Lake View Motor Inn, which is open all day. It's wise to stock up on groceries in Te Anau.

Getting There & Away

Public transport options are limited. Spitfire Shuttle (☎ 03-249 7505) runs a daily service between Invercargill and Te Anau and stops in at Manapouri on each journey. To Invercargill costs $35, to Te Anau it's $15.

Otherwise you could ask at Fiordland Travel if there are spare seats on its coaches to Te Anau.

SOUTHERN SCENIC ROUTE

The Southern Scenic Route starts in Te Anau and goes via Manapouri, Blackmount and Clifden to Tuatapere. At Tuatapere, SH99 goes to Invercargill via Colac Bay and Riverton. From Invercargill to Dunedin you can take the scenic east-coast route through the Catlins. Public transport is limited but the Bottom Bus provides a good backpacker shuttle.

The town of **Clifden** has a cave system nearby and the Clifden Suspension Bridge, built in 1899. The mystical Clifden (Waiau) Caves can be explored but you should heed all warnings. You'll need torches; ladders are provided in steep sections. The caves are signposted on the Otautau Rd, 2km from the Clifden Rd corner. See the visitors centre in Tuatapere for information beforehand.

Just south of the suspension bridge is a turn-off to a walking track through a reserve of 1000-year-old totara trees (23km off the main road). From Clifden you can also drive 30km (of mostly unsealed road) to **Lake Hauroko**, the deepest in NZ. Hauroko lies in a beautiful bush setting, with precipitous slopes on its sides. In 1967 an interesting example of a Maori cave burial was discovered on Mary Island, on the lake. In this *tapu* place a woman of high rank was buried, sitting upright, in about 1660.

The challenging, 84km **Dusky Track** starts at Hauroko Burn and leads to Lake Manapouri, with a two-day detour to Supper Cove on Dusky Sound. This is a rugged but rewarding tramp for the well-prepared. Consult the DOC and Lonely Planet's *Tramping in New Zealand*. **Lake Hauroko Tours** (☎ 03-226 6681) has day-trips to the lake and organises four- or eight-day tramps from Hauroko to Lake Manapouri, and provides trampers' transport in the area.

Tuatapere
pop 740

Once a timber milling town, Tuatapere is now a sleepy farming centre situated on the banks of the Waiau River, famous as the 'sausage capital' of NZ. The woodchoppers were so effective, only the small remnant of native forest in the town's domain remains; once most of the area looked like this. The town can be used as a base for trips to Lake Hauroko or Te Waewae Bay.

The Tuatapere visitors centre (☎ 03-226 6399, e reinfo@es.co.nz) on the main road has information on many activities, and will provide a map to the Clifden Caves or hut passes for walks. Jetboats operate on the Wairaurahiri River, and helicopter tours and trampers' transport can be arranged through the centre. The Spitfire Shuttle that operates daily between Te Anau and Invercargill stops here.

Hump Ridge Track The biggest thing to hit Tuatapere in years is the Hump Ridge Track, which opened in late 2001. NZ's newest walking track is a 53km circuit that begins and ends at Bluecliffs Beach on Te Waewae Bay, 20km from Tuatapere. This excellent walk takes three days to complete and the track passes through coastline, forests of podocarp and beech, subalpine settings and sandstone outcrops. Estimated walking times are as follows:

route	time
Bluecliffs Bay Car Park to Okaka Hut	8 to 9 hrs
Okaka Hut to Port Craig Village	7 hrs
Port Craig Village to Bluecliffs Bay	6 to 7 hrs

It's essential to book for this track, which is administered by a local trust rather than DOC. Contact the Tuatapere Hump Ridge Track Trust (☎ 03-226 6739, 0800 486 774, e info@humpridgetrack.co.nz); the cost is $80. Good information is online at w www .humpridgetrack.co.nz.

Places to Stay & Eat There are a couple of cheap and very basic camping grounds, including the riverside *Tuatapere Motor Camp* (☎ 03-226 6502), and *Mickaela*

Camping Ground (☎ 03-226 6626, Peace St), which is just a suburban block. *Hump Track Backpackers* (☎ 03-226 6418, 6 Clifden St) has budget beds in bunkhouses and cabins from $10 to $20; don't expect luxury at the price, but the rooms are functional. You can also camp in the grounds here. The owner is a good source of information on the tramping and activity options in the area, and hires out bikes and kayaks.

The friendly *Waiau Hotel* (☎ 03-226 6409, 47 Main St) has comfortable rooms set in gardens behind the pub priced from $55 (shared facilities) or $65 (with en suite). This is also the best place in town for meals, with solid country fare and the 'famous' local sausages.

The visitors centre has lists of B&Bs and farmstays, and along Main St there are a couple of *takeaways*. The anticipated influx of visitors for the new walking track may possibly bring about welcome development.

Tuatapere to Riverton

About 10km south of Tuatapere the scenic route reaches the cliffs above **Te Waewae Bay**, where Hector's dolphins and southern right whales are sometimes seen. At the eastern end of the bay is tiny Monkey Island, or Te Poka a Takatimu (Anchor Stone of the *Taka-timu* Canoe). Nearby is **Orepuki**, where strong southerlies have had a dramatic effect on the growth of macrocarpas, trees so windblown that they grow in a direction away from the shore.

Seven kilometres past Orepuki on SH99 is *Hillcrest* (☎ 03-234 5129, e *hillcrest backpackers@xtra.co.nz*), a sheep farm with popular backpacker accommodation and interesting walks. Accommodation is mostly in doubles and twins and costs $16 per person. Camp sites are also available for $8 per person. Hillcrest is closed May to October.

It's worth taking a detour off the main road to check out **Cosy Nook**, a picturesque wee settlement of baches. The next point of interest is **Colac Bay**, an old Maori settlement and now a popular holiday and surfing spot for Southlanders.

Colac Bay Tavern & Camping Ground (☎ 03-234 8399, e *dustez@xtra.co.nz*) has

SOUTHLAND

food, drink and accommodation. Camping is available for $8/9 per person for powered/unpowered sites, and there are basic cabins for $17 per person. There's a communal kitchen and barbecue.

Riverton
pop 1850

Riverton, 38km west of Invercargill, is considered to be one of the oldest European settlements in NZ, dating from the sealing and whaling days. This pretty town has good beaches and proclaims itself the 'Riviera of the South' – quite a stretch, but it is a pleasant, relaxed place. The Riverton Rocks area is a popular (if cold) local beach and Taramea Bay is a safe place to swim.

The town's visitors centre (☎ 03-234 9991) is located inside the **Early Settlers Museum** at 172 Palmerston St and is usually open 10.30am to 4pm daily from November to April (2pm to 4pm daily outside these months). It takes bookings for the Bottom Bus, which overnights in Riverton.

Places to Stay & Eat Basic but functional *Riverton Caravan Park* (☎ 03-234 8526, Hamlet St) is about 4km from the visitors centre by Riverton Rocks beach and has powered/unpowered sites for $16/15 for two, plus a smattering of cheap cabin beds.

Globe Backpackers & Bar (☎ 0800 843 456, 03-234 8527, e globebackers@xtra.co .nz, 144 Palmerston St) Dorm beds $17, twins & doubles $40. This lively old pub in the town centre is a friendly, well-run place. Accommodation is plentiful and comfortable, the guest kitchen is great, and there's good, cheap food available in the bar.

Riverton Rock (☎ 03-234 8886, e guest houseriverston@xtra.co.nz, 136 Palmerston St) Doubles without/with bath $50/88. Riverton Rock is a beautifully renovated guesthouse with plenty of character and warm and inviting rooms.

Takeaways line the main street, but the town has two excellent dining choices. *Country Nostalgia* (☎ 03-234 9154, 108 Palmerston St) is on the main road and has funky decor and creative, well-prepared food; casual *Beach House Cafe* (☎ 03-234

8274, 126 Rocks Highway), on the other side of town, has great sea views and a wide range of appetising meals.

Central Southland

From Invercargill to Gore, SH1 effectively divides the province of Southland into two. To the west of the highway is Fiordland and to the southeast is the Catlins. The majority of Southland's population is concentrated in the centre of the province along SH1, and in the city of Invercargill.

INVERCARGILL
pop 49,300

Invercargill is the southernmost city in NZ, the main city of Southland and very much a farm-service community. It's missed out on a lot of the tourism wealth you'll find in many South Island towns, however an increasing number of travellers are stopping over on the way to the tramping tracks of Stewart Island, the nearby Catlins and the wild areas of southern Fiordland.

Many locals have been offended by our previous descriptions of Invercargill (including the now infamous 'checked shirt and bad haircuts' line) and wrote to us to defend their city. Invercargill has its good points, but there's not a great deal here to sell to most travellers. Urban regeneration is under way and there's a growing number of students (thanks largely to the local polytechnic's clever initiative to lure them with fee-free tuition), hence more cafes and bars are starting to appear, but Invercargill is still primarily a town most travellers will pass through quite quickly.

Information

Invercargill is a remarkably ordered city based on a grid pattern crisscrossing a flat plain. In the museum building, near the main entrance to Queens Park on Gala St, is the Invercargill visitors centre (☎ 03-214 6243, e tourismandtravel.invercargill@thenet.net .nz, w www.invercargill.org.nz). It's open 9am to 5pm Monday to Friday, 10am to 5pm Saturday and Sunday.

INVERCARGILL

PLACES TO STAY
1 Queens Park Motel
2 Homestead Villa Motels
4 Invercargill Caravan Park
   & Camping Ground
5 Southern Comfort
8 Ascot Park Hotel
9 Coachman's Inn
25 Tuatara Lodge
26 Gerrard's Hotel
34 Birchwood Manor

PLACES TO EAT
12 Lone Star Cafe
13 Global Byte Cafe
14 Louie's
15 The Cod Pot
17 Tillerman's Cafe & Bar
18 In a Pickle
21 Robert Harris Cafe
23 The Fat Indian
27 The Crescent
28 Thai Dee; Movieland 5
29 Frog 'n' Firkin
30 Kyoto
31 Zookeepers

OTHER
3 Queens Park Golf Course
   Clubhouse
6 Invercargill Visitors Centre;
   Southland Museum; Tuatara House
7 Queens Park Main Entrance
10 Water Tower
11 Automobile Association (AA)
16 Embassy
19 DOC
20 Air New Zealand
22 Library
24 Saints & Sinners
32 Wensley's Cycles
33 Pak n Save Supermarket
35 Southland Aquatic Centre
36 Homestead Rugby Park

The main post office can be found at 50 Don St. Internet access is available at the library (☎ 03-218 7025), 50 Dee St; inside the visitors centre; and at Global Byte Cafe (☎ 03-214 4724), 150 Dee St.

The Automobile Association (AA; ☎ 03-218 9033) is at 47 Gala St. The DOC office (☎ 03-214 4589) is on the 7th floor of the State Insurance building on Don St.

Southland Museum & Tuatara House

Located by the main entrance to Queens Park, Southland Museum (☎ *03-218 9753,*

Ⓦ *www.southlandmuseum.com; admission by donation; open 9am-5pm Mon-Fri, 10am-5pm Sat & Sun*) features natural history and technology displays, Maori galleries, and art galleries featuring touring exhibitions. Pride of place, however, goes to the exhibitions about NZ's subantarctic islands, and the **Roaring Forties Experience** *(adult/child $2/50c)* which takes you on a 25-minute audiovisual journey to the islands between NZ and the Antarctic. Andris Apse's photography captures the remote and surreal atmosphere of the last stands of the great untouched.

Invercargill's most famous attraction is the tuatara house inside the museum. The ancient and rare NZ reptiles on show include Henry, who is over 100 years old and going strong (a tuatara can live to 150 in captivity). Don't expect to see him doing much!

Other Attractions

From the museum, wander around delightful **Queens Park**. Among the park's attractions are various animals, an aviary, duck ponds, rose gardens and a tea kiosk. The 18-hole Queens Park **Golf Course** (☎ *03-218 8371, clubhouse on Kelvin St)* is good value at around $25 for club hire and green fees.

Anderson Park Gardens and Art Gallery *(☎ 03-215 7432, McIvor Rd; entry to some exhibitions $2; open 10.30am-5pm daily)* displays NZ art collections in a Georgian-style mansion set among lovely gardens. It's 7km north of the city centre, off the main road to Queenstown.

The curious **water tower** *(Leet St; $1; open 1.30pm-4.30pm Sun only)* was built in 1889. You can climb to the top for a bird's-eye view of the town and surrounding area.

Invercargill's long, sweeping beach is **Oreti**, 10km west of the city. The water is milder than expected because of warm currents, and you can drive on the hard sands (but take care). If you're not up to braving the sea, the **Southland Aquatic Centre** *(☎ 03-317 3838, Elles Rd; admission $3.50)*, also known as 'Splash Palace', is a huge swimming pool complex with slides and a wave machine.

Activities

For local sites of interest, pick up a walking-tour leaflet of Invercargill's historical places from the museum. **Thomson's Bush** *(Queens Drive)*, is the last remnant of Taurakitewaru Wood, the forest that once covered Invercargill. It's about 3.5km north of the main post office. The best of the area's short walks are at the **Sandy Point Domain**, on the way to Oreti Beach, with a mixture of totara scrub forest, fern gullies, coastal views and bird life.

There are several other walks, plus activities such as golf, horse riding and scenic flights; inquire at the visitors centre.

Places to Stay

Camping & Cabins All prices given are for two people.

Lorneville Holiday Park (☎ *03-235 8031,* e *lornepark@xtra.co.nz)* Powered/unpowered sites $19, cabins $36-40, tourist flats $58-65, B&B in homestead $90. Excellent Lorneville is a large, well-maintained camping ground on a friendly farmlet, offering numerous accommodation choices. From town, head north along SH6 for 8km, then turn right onto SH98 and travel a further 3.5km.

Gum Tree Farm Motor Park (☎ *03-215 9032,* e *gumtreefarmmp@xtra.co.nz, 77 McIvor Rd)* Powered/unpowered sites $18/16. This new camping ground, close to Anderson Park Gardens and Art Gallery, is small and sweet with good facilities. The turn-off to McIvor Rd is about 7km north of the city centre.

Invercargill Caravan Park & Camping Ground (☎ *03-218 8787, 20 Victoria Ave)* Powered/unpowered sites $17/15, cabins $28-36. The most central camping area is an OK place to spend a night or two, but the parks to the north of town are better. The owners offer car and van storage for people heading to Stewart Island ($3 per day).

Hostels Invercargill is home to a couple of excellent backpackers.

Tuatara Lodge (☎ *0800 488 282, 03-214 0954,* e *tuataralodge@xtra.co.nz, 30 Dee St)* Dorm beds $19, doubles $45, en suite doubles $70. This is an excellent new backpackers and YHA affiliate (the world's southernmost YHA), centrally located and featuring friendly, helpful staff, sparkling modern facilities, clean, spacious rooms and good security.

Southern Comfort (☎ *03-218 3838, 30 Thomson St)* Dorm beds $18, twins & doubles $42. Consistently rated one of the best backpackers in the country, classy Southern Comfort is housed in a late-19th-century Art Nouveau villa, with tasteful decor and beautifully manicured gardens. The common areas are wonderfully inviting and dorms here are pleasant and clean, plus there are free bikes for guest use.

SOUTHLAND

Hotels & Motels Invercargill has over 30 motels; North Rd and Tay St are the best hunting grounds.

Gerrard's Hotel (☎ 03-218 3406, ✉ in fo@gerrards.co.nz, 3 Leven St) Rooms with own facilities $70-90. Central Gerrard's, opposite the train station, is an ornate 1896 building with character and charm. Each of the rooms in this small, boutique-style hotel is decorated differently; the newer doubles are particularly pleasant.

Ascot Park Hotel (☎ 03-217 6195, ✉ ascot@ilt.co.nz, cnr Tay St & Racecourse Rd) Motel units $92, hotel rooms from $150. About 3km from the city centre, Ascot Park is a large, upmarket complex with an indoor pool, spa and sauna, restaurant, motel units and deluxe hotel rooms.

Queens Park Motel (☎ 0800 800 504, 03-214 4504, ✉ queens.park.motels@xtra .co.nz, 85 Alice St) Units $80-95. With the bonus of the property's rear gate opening onto lovely Queens Park, this friendly, well-maintained motel is in a quiet, residential area and is an excellent choice.

Coachman's Inn (☎ 03-217 6046, 0508 426 224, ✉ twilkes@southnet.co.nz, 705 Tay St) offers a variety of good-value options, including nicely updated studio motel units for $65, plus budget cabin accommodation (from $25) and even a small strip for camping (sites $15 for two).

Among the newer motels, central **Birchwood Manor** (☎ 03-218 8881, ✉ birch@ birchwood.co.nz, 189 Tay St) has modern, well-equipped units from $86, and **Homestead Villa Motels** (☎ 03-214 0408, ✉ vil la@southnet.co.nz, cnr Avenal & Dee Sts) offers much the same, with prices starting from $90.

Places to Eat

Restaurants & Cafes Invercargill has some good eating options, and a few new players on the scene offer Asian cuisine.

Zookeepers (☎ 03-218 3373, 50 Tay St) Meals $6-20. You're welcomed into this cool cafe-bar by a giant elephant on the roof, and the animal theme runs through the decor. It's a popular place and serves a range of meals, from lighter fare like soup, dips and pasta to meals such as crumbed blue cod and rib-eye steak.

Tillerman's Cafe & Bar (☎ 03-218 9240, 16 Don St) Mains to $20. Tillerman's is another good local gathering spot. It has a wide menu that features the well-prepared standards (beef, blue cod, lamb), plus Asian and vegetarian dishes. Upstairs is Tillerman's music lounge, popular for DJs and occasional live music.

Lone Star Cafe (☎ 03-214 6225, cnr Dee & Leet Sts) Light meals to $15, mains $20-25. Rowdy, ever-popular Lone Star has two parts: a back bar and a dining area. The restaurant serves huge nachos, steaks, pork ribs and other Tex-Mex-inspired food; the bar is a fine place for a sociable drink.

Louie's (☎ 03-214 2913, 142 Dee St) Mains to $25. Louie's is a lively and fashionable cafe-tapas bar with a great selection of food tastes, including Asian, Mediterranean and Pacific Rim flavours. The bar area is popular on weekends with Invercargill's hip crowd.

The Fat Indian (☎ 03-218 9933, Piccadilly Lane, 38 Dee St) Mains around $15. In a laneway off Dee St, next to the library, is this welcoming new curry house, with classic dishes like beef vindaloo, lamb korma and assorted tandoori treats.

Thai Dee (☎ 03-214 5112, 9 Dee St) Mains around $15. Centrally located and offering a variety of Thai noodle, rice and curry dishes as well as spicy soups, this place is perfect for a pre- or post-movie meal (the cinema is next door).

The Crescent (☎ 03-214 6189, 11 The Crescent) Dinner mains $19-26. The newest addition to Invercargill's dining scene is this upmarket restaurant and wine bar, housed in a renovated 1900s building. It deserves to do well, with a creative menu featuring the likes of fresh fish on a clam, crawfish and snowpea risotto.

Cafes & Cheap Eats Along Dee St and around the town centre there's the usual collection of fast-food and sandwich places. There's also a steadily growing set of cafes for light meals or a coffee stop. **Robert Harris Cafe** (☎ 03-214 1914, 73 Dee St) is

SOUTHLAND

an agreeable breakfast spot, and *In a Pickle* (☎ 03-218 7340, 16 Don St) is one of the best lunch places in town, with a range of food that includes quiches, panini and bagels. *Global Byte Cafe* (☎ 03-214 4724, 150 Dee St) offers Internet access plus snacks such as pastries and sandwiches as well as coffee and cake.

Kyoto (☎ 03-218 1292, 31 Esk St) is a low-key Japanese cafe serving excellent cheap dishes, including sushi and noodles. *The Cod Pot* (☎ 03-218 2354, 136 Dee St) turns out consistently good fish and chips, and offers delicious Bluff oysters in season.

For self-caterers, there's a large *Pak'n Save* supermarket at 95 Tay St.

Entertainment

Lively places with the best atmosphere include *Zookeepers*, which has laid-back staff and some of Invercargill's brighter party animals, *Louie's*, where the smart young things go, and *Tillerman's Cafe & Bar*, with a bar and separate music lounge. The casual *Lone Star Cafe* is often crowded, and the *Frog 'n' Firkin* (☎ 03-214 4001, 31 Dee St) is a good pub for a beer and bar snack. See Places to Eat for more details.

The big nightclub in town is *Saints and Sinners (34 Dee St)*. The *Embassy (122 Dee St)* is a live music venue that can hold 500 people. Even when it's not hosting bands, the foyer bar here is a popular weekend drinking spot.

Movieland 5 (☎ 03-214 1110, 29 Dee St), near Thai Dee, shows latest-release movies for $10.

Getting There & Away

Air Air New Zealand (☎ 03-215 0000), at 46 Esk St, has direct flights daily to Christchurch and Wellington, with connections to other major centres.

Stewart Island Flights (☎ 03-218 9129, ℯ sif@xtra.co.nz, ☒ www.stewartisland flights.com) flies between Invercargill and Stewart Island three times daily (see Stewart Island in the Outer Islands chapter).

Bus InterCity (☎ 03-214 0598) buses are based at the train station on Leven St. Buses run daily from Invercargill to Te Anau and to Dunedin and Christchurch. Hazlett Tours (☎ 03-216 0717) does the leg to Queenstown for InterCity daily.

Spitfire Shuttle (☎ 03-214 1851) operates daily between Invercargill and Te Anau. Catch-A-Bus (☎ 03-214 5652) and Atomic Shuttles (☎ 03-214 6243) runs buses between Invercargill and Dunedin, and Knightrider (☎ 03-342 8055) operates a night-time service on the Christchurch-Dunedin-Invercargill route.

Campbelltown Passenger Services (☎ 03-212 7404) has a door-to-door service between Invercargill and Bluff ($10); services connect with the Stewart Island ferry.

Catlins Coaster and Bottom Bus services pass through Invercargill (see The Catlins later in this chapter).

The *Southerner* train between Invercargill and Christchurch via Dunedin ran its final journey in early 2002.

Getting Around

The airport (☎ 03-218 9129) is 2.5km from the centre. It's about $10 by taxi or $6 with Spitfire Shuttle (☎ 03-214 1851), which will pick you up from your hotel. There are two taxi companies: Taxi Co (☎ 03-214 4478) and Blue Star (☎ 03-218 6079).

The Southland Express Freebie is a useful bus service around the town centre (Dee, Tay, Esk, Kelvin and Gala Sts) every 15 minutes between 10am and 4.30pm Monday to Friday; travel is free. Otherwise city buses (☎ 03-218 7108) run to the suburbs on Monday to Friday from around 7am to 6pm (free between 9am and 2.30pm; otherwise $1.20).

Wensley's Cycles (☎ 03-218 6206), on the corner of Tay and Nith Sts, hires out bikes for $20 a day.

BLUFF
pop 2100

Invercargill's port, and the departure point for the Stewart Island catamaran, the sprawling and not terribly appealing Bluff is 27km to the south. Popular folklore has it that Bluff is the Land's End of NZ, though it's not the South Island's southernmost point (this claim to fame rests with Slope

Point in the Catlins). 'From Cape Reinga to Bluff' is an oft-quoted phrase signifying the entire length of NZ. The country's main highway, SH1, runs between the two and terminates at the **Stirling Point signpost** in the south, which indicates distances to the South Pole and elsewhere in the world.

Foveaux Walk is a good 6.6km coastal walkway from the signpost to Ocean Beach (2½ hours). Alternatively, take the trail for about 1km and then return by the 1.5km Glory Track. You can drive or walk the 3km to the observation point at the top of 265m **Bluff Hill** for unobstructed views of the flat surrounding area and across to Stewart Island. It's accessed off Lee St.

The **Bluff Maritime Museum** (☎ 03-212 7534; admission $2, open 10am-4.30pm Mon-Fri, 1pm-5pm Sat & Sun) is on Fore-shore Rd. The **Paua Shell House** (258 Marine Parade; admission by donation; open 9am-5pm daily) has an amazing array of kitsch statuary (check out the fountain) and shells from all over the world, including some 1100 paua shells decorating its walls.

Across the harbour from Bluff is the huge **Tiwai Point aluminium smelter**, a major source of employment for Invercargill's citizens. Aluminium is an important NZ export. Free tours at 10am Monday to Friday can be arranged by phoning ☎ 03-218 5494 well in advance.

Foveaux Souvenirs & Antiques (☎ 03-212 8305), 74 Gore St, acts as the local visitors centre. The **Bluff Oyster & Southland Seafood Festival** is held annually in early May, celebrating Bluff's famous delicacy. The oysters are in season from late March to late August. See W www.bluff.co.nz for information.

Places to Stay & Eat

Bluff Motor Camp (☎ 03-212 8704, Argyle Park, Gregory St) Powered/unpowered sites $6/5 per person, cabins $8 per person. This small camping ground operates on an honesty policy as it's usually unstaffed. Facilities are very basic.

For backpacker accommodation you're better off staying in Invercargill. About the only choice in Bluff is the scruffy *Property*

Arcade Backpackers (☎ 025 207 7301, 120 Gore St), opposite the ferry wharf. Dorm beds are $12, doubles and twins $28. Otherwise **Bayview Hotel** (☎ 03-212 8615, 48 Gore St) has basic but comfortable rooms above the bar for $25 per person with shared facilities, $30 per person with en suite; breakfast is included in the price.

Land's End NZ (☎ 03-212 7575, e landsend@southnet.co.nz) Singles/doubles $85/115. This B&B at the end of SH1, opposite the signpost, has pleasant, comfortable rooms (most with sea views). The friendly owners give useful information on touring the South Island.

The main street of Bluff is lined with a pretty uninspiring collection of pubs and takeaways. Best to head to Stirling Point, where the *cafe* adjoining Land's End NZ has an excellent selection of meals and wine, specialising in local seafood (try the unique kumara and blue cod soup). Next door is *The Drunken Sailor* (☎ 03-212 8855), a cafe-bar with a menu that also features local produce.

Getting There & Away

Campbelltown Passenger Services (☎ 03-212 7404) has a door-to-door service between Invercargill and Bluff ($10); services connect with the Stewart Island ferry. See Stewart Island in the Outer Islands chapter for ferry details.

Campbelltown also offers secure vehicle storage down by the wharf for those heading to Stewart Island, at a cost of $5 per day. The office is inside the ferry terminal.

INVERCARGILL TO DUNEDIN

From Invercargill to Dunedin, SH1 via Gore and Balclutha is the quick, direct route. Much more scenic is the continuation of the Southern Scenic Route, SH92, via the coastal road through the Catlins.

SH1 passes through Mataura, site of a huge freezing works; Gore, home of the Big Brown Trout and country music; and Balclutha (see the Otago chapter). Visitors, particularly US ones, may get a kick out of the 'Presidential Highway', a 44km stretch of SH1 linking the towns of Clinton and Gore.

SOUTHLAND

Gore

pop 8500

This farming service town, Southland's second largest, spans the Mataura River and has the Hokonui Hills as a great backdrop. In early June, Gore hosts the NZ Gold Guitars, an annual country and western festival, during which the town is booked out.

The helpful Gore visitors centre (☎ 03-208 9908, ⓔ goreinfo@esi.co.nz, ⓦ www .mataura.co.nz) is on Norfolk St, in the **Hokonui Heritage Centre**, a complex that includes the historical museum (free entry) and the Hokonui Moonshine Museum ($5), which explores 51 years of Prohibition in this area. Opposite is the recently expanded **Eastern Southland Gallery**.

Croydon Aircraft Company (☎ 03-208 9755) at Mandeville, 16km towards Queenstown, restores vintage aircraft and offers Tiger Moth flights. There's also a good restaurant here.

With luck, you may catch a trout the size of the 'big one' in one of the many (40 or so) excellent nearby streams. For information contact the visitors centre, which can put you in touch with one of the area's many fishing guides.

Places to Stay & Eat This small, well-maintained *Gore Motor Camp* (☎ 03-208 4919, ⓔ gorecamp@xtra.co.nz, 35 Broughton St) is at the southern end of town. It has powered and unpowered sites $20 for two people and cabins for $24.

Old Fire Station Backpackers (☎ 03-208 1925, ⓔ oldfirestation@ispnz.co.nz, 19 Hokonui Drive) Dorm beds $18, twins/doubles $40/45. This small, friendly backpackers, opposite the visitors centre, has been stylishly renovated and now has bright and comfortable rooms and some excellent facilities, including an attractive courtyard and barbecue area.

There are a few motels in town, including the older-style *Charlton Motel* (☎ 03-208 9733, 9 Charlton Rd), which has units from $60, and the newer, more expensive *Riverlea Motel* (☎ 03-208 3130, 46 Hokonui Drive), with modern, spacious units starting from $80.

Main St has a number of places to keep the wolf from the door. *Howl at the Moon* (☎ 03-208 4145, 2 Main St) is popular for eating or drinking, and the nearby *Green Room Cafe* (☎ 03-208 1005, 59 Irk St), by the town's small cinema, is a cool place for a coffee stop.

The Catlins

If you're travelling between Invercargill and Dunedin with your own transport, consider taking the longer coastal route, allowing a couple of days for stopovers. The distance is similar to the inland route but you travel much slower as some 22km is unsealed (although there is talk of the road being tar-sealed sometime in the not-too-distant future). The route goes through the region known as the Catlins, which stretches from Waipapa Point in Southland to Nugget Point in South Otago. It includes a number of forests, bays and scenic reserves and is a totally absorbing area.

History

The area was once inhabited by moa hunters and evidence of their camp sites and middens has been found at Papatowai. Between AD 1600 and 1800 the Maori population thinned out because of the decline of the moa, the lack of kumara cultivation and fear of the *maeroero* – the wild, yeti-like creature of the Tautuku bush, reputed to have snatched children and young women.

Later, whalers occupied sites along the shoreline, such as at Waikawa Harbour, Tautuku Peninsula and Port Molyneaux. Then timber millers, serving the Dunedin market, moved into the dense stands of beech forest in the 1860s. At the height of logging there were about 30 mills in the area. As in many other parts of NZ, the pastoralists constituted the final wave of settlement.

Flora & Fauna

There are still reserves of podocarp forests in the Catlins, containing trees such as kahikatea, totara, rimu and miro. Behind the sand dunes of Tahakopa and Tautuku Bays

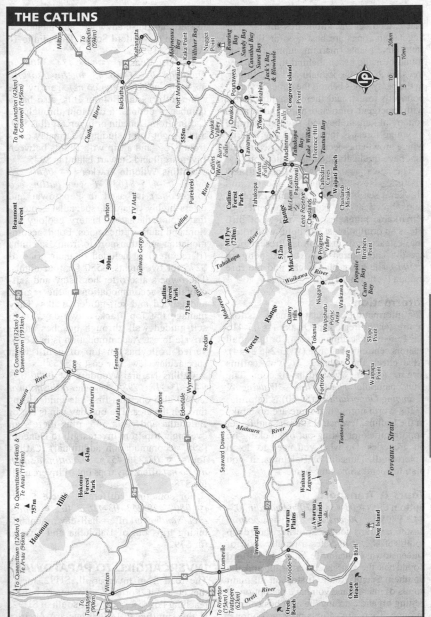

THE CATLINS

SOUTHLAND

there are excellent examples of native forest that extend several kilometres inland. The vegetation zones are best seen at Tautuku: sand-dune plants (marram, lupin, flax) are found near the beach; behind these are low trees, such as rata, kamahi and five-finger; in the peaty sands behind the dunes is young podocarp forest; and there's mature forest with emergent rimu and miro and a main canopy of kamahi beyond. A good example of young forest is found near Lake Wilkie, where growth has occurred on the sediments that have gradually filled in the lagoon.

The fauna, as much as the flora, attracts visitors. New Zealand fur seals and Hooker's sea lions are abundant. Elephant seals breed at the Nuggets, a series of remarkable pinnacles. The variety of bird life is an ornithologist's delight, with many sea, estuary and forest birds. Present here are the endangered yellow-eyed penguin *(hoiho)*, the kaka, blue ducks and the rare mohua (yellowhead).

Information

For information contact the main visitors centre for the region in Owaka (☎ 03-415 8371, ⓔ info@catlins-nz.com), or the small visitors centre in Waikawa (☎ 03-246 8444). Also check the websites Ⓦ www.catlins .org.nz and Ⓦ www.catlins-nz.com. The DOC pamphlet *The Catlins – Walking & Tramping Opportunities* ($3.50) is helpful.

It's worth noting that there are no banks in the Catlins, few petrol stations and fewer opportunities for eating out or stocking up on groceries. Do what you need to do in Invercargill, Dunedin or Balclutha, if you plan to spend some time here.

Tours & Transport

Bottom Bus *(☎ 03-434 7370 in Dunedin, 03-442 9708 in Queenstown,* Ⓦ *www.bottom bus.co.nz)* runs tours exploring the 'deep south' of NZ. It operates a regular loop of Queenstown, Dunedin, Te Anau and Milford Sound via the Catlins, Invercargill and the Southern Scenic Route. It stops at all main points of interest and you have the option of getting off and catching the next bus coming through. There are various package options;

the Southlander pass costs $275, allows you to start and finish anywhere and includes a cruise on the Milford Sound. Dunedin to Te Anau is $119.

Catlins Coaster *(☎ 03-474 3300 in Dunedin, 03-214 6243 in Invercargill,* Ⓦ *www.catlinscoaster.co.nz)*, run by the same folks as the Bottom Bus, also has a number of options: a day tour through the Catlins from Dunedin or Invercargill is $99, a two-night trip including a farmstay costs from $165, and a trip with flights between Invercargill and Stewart Island is $245.

Catlins Wildlife Trackers *(☎ 0800 228 5467, 03-415 8163,* Ⓦ *www.catlins-eco tours.co.nz)* is based in Papatowai and offers highly regarded, specialist ecotours that explore the natural history, geology and flora and fauna of the region. Food, accommodation and transport to/from Balclutha (if required) is included in their price of $275 for two nights, $550 for four nights. The owners also offer homestay and self-contained accommodation in the region, and guided and self-guided walks. They manage the **Top Track**, a two-day, 26km self-guided walk through beaches and a private forest. Accommodation is in a converted trolleybus on top of a hill with spectacular views; the cost is $25.

Catlins Natural Wonders *(☎ 0800 353 941, 03-418 1798,* Ⓦ *www.catlinsnatural .co.nz)* also operates first-rate guided trips through the area. The one-day trip is out of Balclutha and costs $85, plus there's an overnight trip from Invercargill to Dunedin ($95, accommodation additional). **Catlins Tours** *(☎ 03-230 4576,* ⓔ *catlins@south net.co.nz)* offers day trips out of Invercargill for $78.

For something different, **Cycle South** *(☎ 0800 429 253, 03-418 2202,* ⓔ *toni@ cycle south.com)* offers half-day mountain-biking trips out of Balclutha and Owaka for $79.

INVERCARGILL TO PAPATOWAI

The road from Invercargill, SH92, meets the coast at Fortrose. However, before reaching Fortrose, and to the south of SH92, is the significant 14,000-hectare **Awarua**

Wetlands, which supports various wading bird species and many vegetation types.

At Fortrose, take a turn-off to the south to Waipapa Point. The lighthouse here was erected in 1884, after the second-worst maritime disaster in NZ's history. In 1881 the SS *Tararua* struck the Otara Reef, 1km offshore. Of the 151 passengers and crew only 20 survived; 65 victims are buried in the nearby graveyard.

The next detour is to Slope Point, the most southerly point on the South Island. A small beacon lies across private land, a 20-minute walk from the road (the track is closed in September and October due to lambing).

Curio Bay is the next place of interest. At low tide, you can see one of the most extensive fossil forests (160 million years old) in the world. The petrified stumps and fallen log fossils are proof of NZ's location in the ancient supercontinent Gondwanaland, and the plant species identified here are similar to those of South America.

Just around the corner in Porpoise Bay you may see Hector's dolphins surfing in the waves breaking on the beach, and you can swim with them. Be careful not to touch or otherwise harass the dolphins, which come close into shore over summer to rear their young. Yellow-eyed penguins, fur seals and sea lions also inhabit the area.

At Waikawa, a bit further on, Dolphin Magic (☎ 0800 377 581, 03-246 8444, e dolphinmagic@xtra.co.nz) does boat trips (1½ hours, three daily from October to April) to see the dolphins. Some trips go to the Brothers Point, where there are fur seals and many species of sea bird. The dolphin cruise is $50, a twilight cruise $75. The company is based in the old church here, and acts as an information centre and store.

The Cathedral Caves on Waipati Beach, so-named for their resemblance to an English cathedral, are only accessible at low tide (tide tables are posted at the turn-off from SH92, or can be obtained from the Owaka and Waikawa visitors centres). From the road it's 2km to the car park, then a 15-minute walk to the beach and a further 25 minutes to the caves. The cost to visit is $5 per car load; cyclists and trampers pay $2.

The turn-off to pretty McLean Falls is just before the parking area for Cathedral Cave. The falls are 3.5km up a dirt road, then it's a 40-minute return walk. Next along is Lenz Reserve, with a bird lodge and the remains of the old Tautuku sawmill just a short walk from the road.

At Tautuku Bay there's a 15-minute walk to the beach, a stunning sweep of sand punctuated by drifts of seaweed, and a walk to Lake Wilkie, where there are unique forms of plant life. Just past Tautuku is a great lookout point at Florence Hill.

Papatowai, at the mouth of the Tahakopa River, is the next tiny town reached along this route. This is the base for Catlins Wildlife Trackers (see Tours & Transport at the start of this section) and for some amazing forays into the nearby forests.

Places to Stay & Eat

From Tokanui, the turn-off to the coast leads 13km to Slope Point, where there are two choices for budget accommodation. Welcoming *Slope Point Backpackers* (☎ 03-246 8420, e hollybrook@xtra.co.nz) (formerly Pope's Place) has camp sites for $8 per person, dorm beds for $15 and doubles and twins for $35. You can have a 'hands-on' tour of the farm and help feed the animals.

Right next door, *Nadir Outpost* (☎ 03-246 8544, e nadir.outpost@ihug.co.nz) is home to the novel Little Shoppe, which is indeed tiny and sells a decent range of supplies. The friendly owners also provide good information for touring in NZ, and offer camp sites for $8 per person, dorm beds from $16, and B&B inside the family home for $35 per person. The entry point for the walk to Slope Point is a further 3.5km from these two places.

Curio Bay Camping Ground (☎ 03-246 8897), right on the beach, has pleasant, sheltered powered/unpowered sites for $15/10 per double. Nearby, tiny *Curio Bay Backpackers* (☎ 03-246 8797, e strats nz@yahoo.com) has beds for $18 per person. It's an inviting and casual place with a deck area overlooking the beach.

Waikawa Holiday Lodge (☎ 03-246 8552, e greg.stephens@xtra.co.nz) Dorm beds

$20, twins & doubles $44. Halfway along the route at Waikawa, opposite the dolphin centre, is this comfortable, self-contained house with spotless rooms and a lovely open fire.

Catlins Farmstay (☎ *03-246 8843,* e *catlinsfarmstay@xtra.co.nz, Progress Valley Rd)* B&B doubles $90-110. On a 1000-acre farm not far from Waikawa is this excellent option, with B&B offered in a comfortable house set in a flower-filled garden; dinners cost $30. The owners can also arrange accommodation for you in self-contained cottages in Waikawa for $70.

In Papatowai you'll find *Papatowai Scenic Highway Motels & Store* (☎ *03-415 8147)*. The handy, well-stocked store has some takeaway food plus petrol and grocery supplies, and there's a public phone here. Behind it are well-appointed motel units ($70), but the name of the establishment is misleading – views are of the general store!

Also behind the store is the simple *Papatowai Motor Camp* (☎ *03-415 8500,* e *pest@es.co.nz)*, with powered/unpowered sites for $14/12 per double, backpackers beds for $12 and cabins for $30.

Still in Papatowai, your best option may be *Southern Secret Motels* (☎ *03-415 8600,* e *catlinsbb@xtra.co.nz)*, with new and stylish studio motel units for $80.

Hilltop (☎ *03-415 8028,* e *hilltop@ihug.co.nz, Tahakopa Rd)* Dorm beds $20, twins & doubles $50, en suite doubles $55. This exceptional backpackers is reached on the road just before the bridge near Papatowai and offers fantastic views and great sunsets. A little over 1km from the main road and then another 500m up a steep hill, you'll find two beautifully furnished farmhouses offering accommodation in three-bed dorms and doubles. There's also free use of bikes, canoes, boogie boards and wetsuits.

PAPATOWAI TO BALCLUTHA

Between Papatowai and the regional centre of Owaka are many interesting places to visit. First, follow SH92 north to **Matai Falls** on the Maclennan River, then head southeast on the signposted road to the more scenic **Purakaunui Falls**. It's only a short walk through bush to these tiered falls, best viewed from a platform at their base.

About five minutes beyond Purakaunui Falls is *The Falls Backpackers* (☎ *03-415 8724,* e *sparx@es.co.nz)*, offering quality accommodation in an old and lovely relocated farmhouse. Beds in shared rooms are $20, twins are $40 and doubles $45. Down on the water, there's a *DOC camping ground* at Purakaunui Bay.

In the **Catlins Forest Park** you can do the river walk, a good day trip out of Owaka. There's a five-hour track to Tawanui from the Wisp camping area – observant walkers may see the rare mohua (yellowhead) here. There's a *DOC camping ground* at Tawanui.

Out near the mouth of the Catlins River, on the southern side, is **Jack's Blowhole**, a 55m-deep hole in the middle of paddocks. It's 200m from the sea but connected by a subterranean cavern. Access is closed in September and October due to lambing.

On the northern side, southeast of Owaka, is the **Pounawea Nature Walk**, a 45-minute loop through kahikatea, ferns, kamahi, rimu, totara and southern rata. There's a salt marsh near the Catlins River estuary.

Owaka
pop 395

Owaka is the main town of the Catlins area. The main Catlins visitors centre (☎ 03-415 8371, e info@catlins-nz.com) and the DOC field office (☎ 03-415 8341) are both at 20 Ryley St. The visitors centre has quite extensive information on the region and accommodation listings, including details of the many farmstays in the area.

Valley View Horse Treks (☎ *03-415 8464)* operates in hill country 24km from Owaka. Over the summer months (November to April) the two-hour rides traverse tussock country, among sheep and cattle, to a lofty viewpoint. It costs $60 per person, including refreshments. Bookings are essential.

Places to Stay & Eat There's a reasonable selection of accommodation options in Owaka, plus a pub, takeaway outlets, a cybercafe, a petrol station, a supermarket and the best dining option in the region.

SOUTHLAND

Keswick Park Camping Ground (☎ 03-419 1110, ⓔ pounawea@ihug.co.nz, Pounawea Rd) Powered/unpowered sites $16/12 for 2 people, dorm beds $12, self-contained tourist flats $49. Keswick Park is on the waterfront a few kilometres out of town – take Royal Terrace. It's quite basic but is in a lovely setting.

There are two excellent backpackers in or near Owaka. *Blowhole Backpackers* (☎ 03-415 8830, 24 Main Rd) is in a brightly decorated old house with a sunny veranda in summer and a cosy fire in winter. Dorm beds are $17, doubles are $45. Friendly and inviting *Surat Bay Lodge* (☎ 03-415 8099, ⓔ suratbay@actrix.gen.nz, Surat Bay Rd) is in a great spot in Newhaven, 5km east of Owaka overlooking the Catlins estuary. It's an ideal place to unwind, with bikes and canoes for hire. Only metres from the lodge is a beach where sea lions hang out. Dorm beds are $18, twins/doubles are $40/45.

Of the many B&Bs in the area, fine choices are the central *Catlins Retreat B&B* (☎ 03-415 8830, ⓔ catlinsbb@xtra.co.nz, 27 Main Rd), with pretty singles/doubles behind a picket fence for $45/75. *Kepplestone* (☎ 03-415 8134, ⓔ kepplestone@xtra.co.nz) is on lovely Surat Bay, 5km from town, and has singles/doubles for $60/95.

Owaka Lodge Motel (☎ 03-415 8728, ⓔ owakalodgemotel@xtra.co.nz, 12 Ryley St) and *Catlins Area Motel* (☎ 03-415 8821, ⓔ catlinsareamotel@hotmail.com, cnr Clark & Ryley Sts) both have clean and comfortable units priced from $70.

The *Lumberjack Bar & Cafe* (☎ 03-415 8747, 3 Saunders St) is an inviting spot to enjoy the great lunch and dinner menu, plus there's an open fire, lounge area and an amazing timber bar.

Owaka to Balclutha

East of Owaka, **Cannibal Bay** is home to a Hooker's sea lion breeding ground. The bay gets its name from the surveyor Hector, who discovered human bones in a midden here and assumed it was part of a feast. Te Rauparaha is also known to have exacted revenge here. There's a good 30-minute walk between here and Surat Bay.

Further around the coast, on a not-to-be-missed side track from the Kaka Point road, is **Nugget Point**. The islands sitting out from the lighthouse promontory (a 15-minute walk from the car park) seem to lead off to the very edge of the world. Fur seals bask below on the rocks, as do Hooker's sea lions and elephant seals on occasions; it's the only place on the NZ mainland where these species coexist. There's a wealth of bird life: yellow-eyed and blue penguins, gannets, shags and sooty shearwaters breed here and many other pelagic species pass by. The stone lighthouse was built in 1869. On your way to the lighthouse area you'll pass **Roaring Bay**, with a well-placed hide from where you may be able to observe yellow-eyed penguins coming ashore (normally about two hours before sunset).

Nugget Lodge Motels (☎ 03-412 8783, ⓔ lighthouse@nuggetlodge.co.nz), only 2km from the lighthouse, has two comfortable, fully self-contained units perched on the water's edge. The cost is $95, with evening meals (by arrangement) costing $35.

From Nugget Point the road loops back around through Kaka Point and Port Molyneaux to SH92 and Balclutha (see the Otago chapter). **Kaka Point** is a pleasant little town on a good beach. Above the town is the small *Kaka Point Camping Ground* (☎ 03-412 8814, 39 Tarata St), with powered/unpowered sites for $15 for two, and basic cabins from $25. *Fernlea Backpackers* (☎ 03-412 8834) is in a small, cosy cottage, near the beach and up the steps from Moana St. Beds are $15.

Nugget View & Kaka Point Motels (☎ 0800 525 278, 03-412 8602, ⓔ nugview@catlins.co.nz, 11 Rata St) Units $65-150. The friendly owners of these motels have a great range of comfortable and spacious self-contained units, from budget ($65) to mid-range ($99) and luxury ($150, with great sea views, spas and all the trimmings). **Nugget Point Ecotours** operates from here (one-hour tours from $30), and the owners can also arrange fishing trips ($85).

On the Esplanade in Kaka Point is a store with takeaways, and an attractive cafe-bar, *The Point* (☎ 03-419 8800).

Outer Islands

New Zealand is often mistakenly believed to consist of just the two islands, North and South. In fact there are a number of island groups off its shores and these are home to fascinating cultures, unique flora and fauna, magnificent scenery and solitude.

Stewart Island

☎ 03 • pop 420

Called Rakiura by the Maori, NZ's third-largest island is an increasingly popular destination for getting away from it all. Rakiura means 'Glowing Skies' in Maori, perhaps referring to the *aurora australis* that's often seen in this southern sky, or the spectacular blood-red sunrises and sunsets. In 2002 Stewart Island became NZ's newest and most southerly national park. It's often thought of as being isolated and battered by harsh southern winds – actually it's not so inhospitable, but it certainly is unspoilt.

The minuscule population of hardy, independent islanders is congregated in the only town of any size, Oban, on Halfmoon Bay. Half an hour's walk away is a sanctuary of forest, beaches and hills. The weather is incredibly changeable – brilliant sunshine one minute, pouring rain the next. It can get very muddy underfoot and you will need boots and waterproof clothing, but the temperature is milder than you would expect (the winter average is around 10°, summer is 16.5°). There are also some lovely bathing beaches here, including some that are easily accessible off Kamahi Rd in Oban. The water looks clear and inviting but the water temperature is invariably chilly.

History

There is evidence that parts of Rakiura were occupied by moa hunters as early as the 13th century AD. According to myth, NZ was hauled up from the ocean by Maui (see the 'Maori Culture & Arts' special section), who said 'Let us go out of sight of land, far

Highlights

- Enjoying the isolation and peace of sleepy Halfmoon Bay on Stewart Island
- Walking on any of Stewart Island's tracks – truly a remote walking experience
- Seeing the rich birdlife of Stewart and Ulva Islands, including kiwis
- Exploring Chatham Island, its isolated lagoons, ramshackle fishing settlements and wild landscapes
- Tracing Moriori culture on Chatham Island, especially the tree carvings at Te Hapupu

out in the open sea, and when we have quite lost sight of land, then let the anchor be dropped'. The North Island was the fish that Maui caught; the South Island his canoe and Rakiura was the anchor – 'Te Punga o te Waka o Maui'.

The first European visitor was Captain Cook, who sailed around the eastern, southern and western coasts in 1770 but could not make up his mind whether it was an island or a peninsula. Deciding it was part of the South Island mainland he called it Cape South. In 1809 the sealing vessel

OUTER ISLANDS

Pegasus, under the command of Captain Chase, circumnavigated Stewart Island and proved it to be an island. It was named after William Stewart, first officer of the *Pegasus,* who charted the southern coast of the island in detail.

In June 1864 Stewart and the adjacent islands were bought from the Maori for £6000. Early industries consisted of sealing, timber milling, fish curing and shipbuilding. The discovery of gold and tin towards the end of the 19th century also led to an increase in settlement but the rush didn't last long and today the island's economy is only based on fishing – crayfish (lobster), paua (abalone), salmon, mussels and cod – and tourism.

Flora & Fauna

Unlike the North and South Islands, there is no beech forest on Stewart Island. The predominant lowland vegetation is hardwood but there are also lots of tree ferns, a variety of ground ferns and several different kinds of orchid. Along the coast the vegetation consists of mutton bird scrub, grass tree, tree daisies, supplejack and leatherwood. But there are warnings not to go tramping off the beaten track, as the bush is impenetrable in most places.

Stewart Island is an ornithologist's delight. Apart from the many sea birds that breed here, bush birds such as tui, parakeets, kaka, bellbirds, fernbirds, robins, dotterels and kiwis abound. The weka can sometimes be spotted here, as well as the Fiordland crested, yellow-eyed and blue penguins.

Two species of deer, the red and the Virginia (whitetail), were introduced to the island early in the 20th century. Also introduced were brush-tailed possums, which are numerous in the northern half of the island and highly destructive to the native bush. Stewart Island has lots of NZ fur seals too.

Around the shores are clusters of bull kelp, common kelp, fine red weeds, delicate green thallus and bladders of all shapes and sizes.

Orientation

Stewart Island is roughly 65km long and 40km across at its widest point. It has less

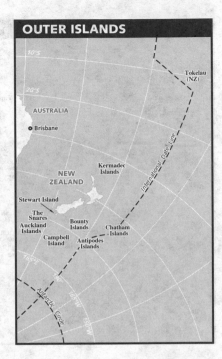

OUTER ISLANDS

than 20km of roads and a rocky coastline incised by numerous inlets, the largest of which is Paterson. The highest point on the island is Mt Anglem (980m). The principal settlement is Oban on the shores of Halfmoon Bay. It is named after a place in Scotland and the name means 'many coves' in Gaelic. Roads extend a few kilometres out from Oban. There are some 360 homes on the island – many of them holiday homes.

Information

The friendly and helpful DOC visitors centre (☎ 03-219 0002, ⓔ stewartisland fc@doc.govt.nz) is a few minutes' walk from the wharf on Main Rd. In addition to excellent practical information it has some good displays on flora, fauna, walks and so on. The centre is open 8am to 7pm Monday to Friday and 9am to 7pm Saturday and Sunday in summer, and 8am to 5pm Monday to Friday and 10am to noon Saturday and Sunday in winter.

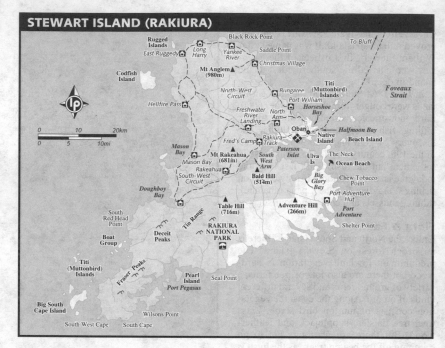

STEWART ISLAND (RAKIURA)

The visitors centre (☎ 03-219 0009) has good track information; it also sells hut passes. Several handy pamphlets on tramps on the island, including *Day Walks, Rakiura Track* and *North West Circuit & Southern Circuit Tracks* ($1 each), can be purchased there. There are lockers here for gear-storage while you're tramping.

For good online information, see Ⓦ www .stewartisland.co.nz.

There are no banks on Stewart Island. Credit card payment is accepted for many services, but it's wise to bring a supply of cash to last the duration of your stay.

The post office is at Stewart Island Flights (☎ 03-218 9129), about five minutes' walk from the wharf. Stewart Island is a local (not long-distance) phone call from Invercargill. There are card phones outside the Lighthouse Wine Bar and at the Shearwater Inn, and coin phones in the South Sea Hotel foyer and the foyer of the visitors centre. You can access the Internet at a coin-operated computer inside the South Sea Hotel, or at Justcafe on Main Rd.

The Stewart Island Adventure Centre (☎ 03-219 1134), at the end of the wharf, is a booking agency for activities on the island, and handles ferry bookings and water taxis. Oban Tours & Taxis (☎ 03-219 1456, ⓔ obantours@clear.net.nz) also does bookings for activities as well as operating sightseeing tours and renting scooters, cars, fishing rods, dive gear, and even golf clubs.

On Main Rd, Halfmoon Bay's general store, Ship to Shore (☎ 03-219 1069), has a wide variety of supplies such as fresh fruit and vegetables, dried foods and gas canisters (open seven days).

Things to See & Do

The **Rakiura Museum** (*Ayr St; adult/child $2/50c; open 10am-noon Mon-Sat, noon-2pm Sun*) is worth a visit if you're interested in the history of the island as it features whaling, sealing, tin mining, timber milling and fishing. Particularly interesting is the section dealing with Maori heritage. It is believed that Maori have lived on Rakiura for 800 years or more. The *titi* (mutton birds) on the islands adjacent to Rakiura were an important seasonal food source for the southern Maori (and their annual harvest continues). Today's southern Maori population is predominantly Ngai Tahu, with earlier lineages to Kati Mamoe and Waitaho.

In a bush setting off Golden Bay Rd is a pretty craft shop and gallery, **The Fernery** (☎ 03-219 1453).

At Harrold Bay, about 3km southeast of town, is an **old stone house** built by Lewis Acker around 1835. It's one of the oldest stone buildings in NZ.

The island's new **Community Centre** (☎ 03-219 1477, *Ayr St*) houses the library (seldom open) and gym facilities, which are open to visitors ($5).

Construction of a waterfront **aquarium** and cafe complex had begun at the time of research.

Ulva Island

Ever dreamed of paradise? It may well be Ulva Island in Paterson Inlet. It's only 250 hectares, but a lot is packed into it. An early naturalist, Charles Traill, was honorary postmaster here. He would hoist a flag to signal to other islands, including Stewart, that the mail had arrived and hopefuls would come from everywhere. His postal service fell out of favour, however, and was replaced by one at Oban. A year later, in 1922, the island was declared a bird sanctuary.

Ulva is a joy for bird-watchers. As soon as you get off the launch the air is alive with the song of tui and bellbirds. You'll see kaka, weka, kakariki and NZ pigeon (*kereru*). This has a lot to do with the absence of predators here.

Good walking tracks have been developed in the island's northwest. The forest has a mossy floor and many tracks intersect the stands of rimu, miro, totara and rata – all of which, when added to the delight of the birdsong, create a setting you won't forget. The birds come so close that you don't need a telephoto lens.

You can get to Ulva by water taxi; expect to pay about $20 return (see Getting Around later in this chapter). Pick up a booklet on the island from the DOC visitors centre in Oban before you go, which outlines excellent self-guided walks.

Walking

There are numerous walks on Stewart Island: it's a tramper's heaven. Although some take only a couple of hours, a day trip to the island is hardly worthwhile. You should plan on spending at least a few days here so you can enjoy the beaches and rare bird and plant life.

There's a good network of tracks and huts in the northern part of the island, but the southern part is undeveloped and can be very desolate and isolated. You are advised not to go off on your own, particularly from the established walks, unless you have discussed your itinerary with someone else beforehand. For the more distant walks, pay your hut fees and get pamphlets at the visitors centre. These pamphlets have detailed information on the walks, their duration, when to go and hut facilities.

Each hut has foam rubber mattresses, wood stoves, running water and toilet facilities, but you need to take food, sleeping bags, ground sheets, eating and cooking utensils, first-aid equipment with you. If you have them, a tent and portable gas stove are very useful as the huts can fill up over summer holidays and at Easter.

The **Rakiura Track**, starting from Oban, is one of NZ's Great Walks (see Tramping in the Activities chapter) and makes an interesting three-day circular tramp. The track is well defined (it has been extensively boardwalked) and it's an easy walk, the major drawback being that it gets very crowded in summer. Huts at Port William and North Arm have space for 30 trampers. If you prebook, the cost of a bed is $10 and camping is $6 (costs are $15 and $8 if you just turn up). There's a maximum stay of two nights in a hut.

The northern portion of the island has the **North-West Circuit Track** but it's long – 125km – and takes some 10 to 12 days to complete. Fees for most of the North-West Circuit huts are $5 per bed. The tracks further away from Halfmoon Bay can be very muddy and quite steep in places, so this walk is for well-equipped and experienced trampers. These longer walks are detailed in Lonely Planet's *Tramping in New Zealand*.

There are shorter walks around Halfmoon Bay. Take the 15-minute walk to **Observation Rock**, which has good views over Paterson Inlet. With three hours to spare, you can continue past the old stone house at Harrold Bay to **Ackers Point Lighthouse**, where there are good views of Foveaux Strait. Blue penguins and a colony of shearwaters (mutton birds) can be seen near the rocks here. There are many other walks outlined in DOC's *Day Walks* brochure.

Ruggedy Range Wilderness Experience (☎ 03-219 1066, **W** *www.ruggedyrange .com*) is an excellent ecotourism operator offering nature tours and guided walks and tramps on the island. Destinations and prices vary from $60 for a half-day trip to Ulva Island to $750 for a three-day tramp taking in Freshwater Valley and Mason Bay (food and equipment supplied).

Organised Tours

A good way to see what's on offer is to take a minibus tour around Halfmoon Bay, Horseshoe Bay and various other places. Costing around $20, they are zippy little 1½-hour trips – because there really isn't very far you can drive on Stewart Island! Check with **Oban Tours & Taxis** (☎ 03-219 1456, **e** *obantours@clear.net.nz*) for details.

With a lack of roads, a boat trip is another good option to get a feel for the island. There are a large number of companies offering cruises and specialist trips (eg, fishing, diving, marine farms, wildlife viewing). The visitors centre has details of all the options; the going rate is $50 per person for general half-day trips.

Bravo Adventure Cruises (☎ 03-219 1144, **e** *philldismith@xtra.co.nz*) has daily trips to Ulva Island and salmon farms, plus offers charters for fishing or bird-watching parties (see the Kiwi Spotting section a little later in this chapter).

Thorfinn Charters (☎ 03-219 1210, **e** *thorfinn@southnet.co.nz*) has an 11m launch available for half-day and full-day cruises; nature tours are its speciality and it also runs fishing trips.

Talisker Charters (☎ 03-219 115, **e** *ta it@taliskercharter.co.nz*) has the *Talisker*, a 17m steel sailing ketch available for cruises from half a day ($50) to several days (live aboard for $110 per person per night), with possible itineraries including the Fiordland coast.

Seabuzzz (☎ 03-219 1282, **e** *seabuzzz@ southnet.co.nz*), runs one-hour glass-bottom boat trips for underwater viewing ($25) and a water taxi service.

Kayaks can be rented for about $45 a day for independent exploring of Paterson Inlet, and guided kayaking is also offered; see the visitors centre for information. The inlet consists of 100 sq km of bush-clad sheltered waterways, with 20 islands, DOC huts and two navigable rivers. A popular trip is a paddle to Freshwater River Landing (7km upriver from the inlet) followed by a three- to four-hour walk to Mason Bay to see kiwis in the wild.

Kiwi Spotting This is one of the best eco-activities of NZ. The search for *Apteryx australis lawryi* would be a difficult one if you didn't know where to look. The Stewart Island kiwi is a distinct subspecies of the brown kiwi, and has a larger beak and legs than its northern cousins. These kiwi are common over much of Stewart Island, particularly around beaches, where they forage for sandhoppers under the washed-up kelp. Unusually, *A. australis lawryi* is active during the day as well as night – the birds are forced to forage for longer to attain breeding condition. Many trampers on the North-West Circuit spot them, especially at Mason Bay.

Bravo Adventure Cruises (☎ 03-219 1144, **e** *philldismith@xtra.co.nz*) runs popular kiwi-spotting tours to view these flightless marvels. Numbers are limited for protection of the kiwi – only 15 people can travel on the MV *Volantis*. Demand well outstrips supply and trips don't go every

OUTER ISLANDS

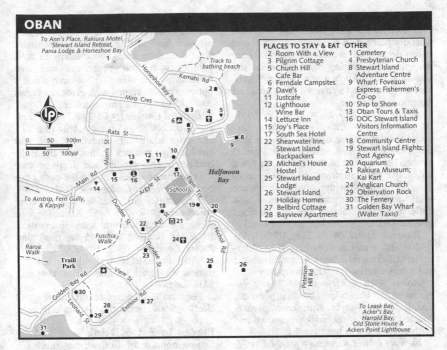

OBAN

To Ann's Place, Rakiura Motel, Stewart Island Retreat, Pania Lodge & Horseshoe Bay

Track to bathing beach

Horseshoe Bay Rd
Kamahi Rd
Miro Cres
Rata St
Morris St
Main Rd

To Airstrip, Fern Gully, & Kaipipi

Argyle St
Elgin Tce
School
Dundee St
Ayr St
Fuschia Walk
Raroa Walk
Traill Park
Golden Bay Rd
View St
Leonard St
Exelsior Rd

Halfmoon Bay

Nichol Rd
Peterson Hill Rd

To Leask Bay, Acker's Bay, Harrold Bay, Old Stone House & Ackers Point Lighthouse

PLACES TO STAY & EAT	OTHER
2 Room With a View	1 Cemetery
3 Pilgrim Cottage	4 Presbyterian Church
5 Church Hill	8 Stewart Island
Cafe Bar	Adventure Centre
6 Ferndale Campsites	9 Wharf; Foveaux
7 Dave's	Express; Fishermen's
11 Justcafe	Co-op
12 Lighthouse	10 Ship to Shore
Wine Bar	13 Oban Tours & Taxis
14 Lettuce Inn	16 DOC Stewart Island
15 Joy's Place	Visitors Information
17 South Sea Hotel	Centre
22 Shearwater Inn;	18 Community Centre
Stewart Island	19 Stewart Island Flights;
Backpackers	Post Agency
23 Michael's House	20 Aquarium
Hostel	21 Rakiura Museum;
25 Stewart Island	Kai Kart
Lodge	24 Anglican Church
26 Stewart Island	29 Observation Rock
Holiday Homes	30 The Fernery
27 Bellbird Cottage	31 Golden Bay Wharf
28 Bayview Apartment	(Water Taxis)

day, so make sure you book *well* ahead to avoid disappointment. The tours cost $60, and a good level of fitness is required.

Places to Stay

The visitors centre has information on all accommodation options. Many B&Bs and holiday homes offer courtesy transfers on arrival.

Ferndale Campsites (☎ 03-219 1176) Camping $8 per person. Ferndale has an ablution block with coin-operated showers ($2), a washing machine, cooking shelter and picnic tables. There are tents and cookers for hire also. Shower and laundry facilities are open to the general public.

Several *homes* in and around Oban offer backpacker-style accommodation at low rates (usually no advance booking is possible). The visitors centre can show you photographs of all these places and direct you to them; for most you'll need your own sleeping bag and food.

Rumours have circulated on the NZ backpacker circuit about the safety of female travellers in one or two of Oban's hostels, which are not listed here. Your best bet is to check with the visitors centre first, and if you don't feel comfortable in the place you're staying, move on.

Probably the best of the backpackers, *Ann's Place* (☎ 03-219 1065), north of the township, offers tramping-style accommodation in a family house. It's good value at $12 and it's a friendly place to stay.

Joy's Place (☎ 03-219 1376, Main Rd) has bunkroom beds for $15; there is definitely no drinking or smoking here.

There are a few converted bachelor pads on the island: *Michael's House Hostel* (☎ 03-219 1425) and *Dave's* (☎ 03-219 1427) both will offer basic accommodation for $20.

Shearwater Inn/Stewart Island Backpackers (☎ 03-219 1114, ⓔ *shearwater .inn@stewart-island.co.nz, Ayr St*) Dorm beds $18, singles $24, doubles & twins $40, singles/doubles with linen $36/60. This friendly place is in the centre of town and offers decent budget accommodation. There are plans to develop camp sites on the grounds. It has kitchen and laundry facilities for guests, and a covered BBQ area and large common room.

South Sea Hotel (☎ *03-219 1059,* W *www.stewart-island.co.nz, Elgin Terrace)* Singles $40-60, doubles & twins $80, sea view rooms $90, self-contained motel units $120. Central to the 'action' of town (ie, above the waterfront pub), these comfortable rooms, all with shared facilities, are well located, but in peak season may be a little noisy. The motel units are spacious and modern and located behind the hotel.

Rakiura Motel (☎ *03-219 1096)* Units $120. This small motel offers five older-style self-contained units 1.5km from the township, overlooking Halfmoon Bay.

Room With A View (☎ *03-214 9040, Kamahi Rd)* Unit $75. This is a pleasant, spacious motel-style unit, conveniently located a few minutes' walk from town and with easy access to beach paths.

Stewart Island Retreat (☎ *03-219 1071,* e *retreat@southnet.co.nz)* Singles/doubles $80/160. The Retreat on tranquil Horseshoe Bay has a mission to 'enhance your health and wellbeing in an eco-friendly environment'. It offers B&B plus other meals by arrangement, with the emphasis on organic cuisine and vegetarian and seafood menus.

Stewart Island Lodge (☎ *03-219 1085,* W *www.stewartislandlodge.co.nz, Nichol Rd)* Singles $262, doubles & twins $216 per person. This plush lodge offers upmarket accommodation on Halfmoon Bay. Its five suites have private facilities and enjoy good views. Prices include breakfast and three-course gourmet dinner (local seafood is featured).

Another accommodation option is to hire one of the many self-contained flats or holiday homes, which often represent good value, especially if there's a few of you sharing.

Stewart Island Holiday Homes (☎ *03-217 6585, 219 1057)* Houses $100 for 2 people plus $25 per extra adult. There are two fully-equipped houses on offer in a pleasant bush setting, about a five-minute walk from town. Each house sleeps up to 10 people, with four bedrooms and two bathrooms. The owners also have a B&B option: en suite rooms with great sea views cost $120/140 for a single/double.

Bellbird Cottage (☎ *03-219 1416, Excelsior Rd)* Cottage $95 for 2 people plus $15 per extra adult. Surrounded by bush and birdlife, five minutes from town, the Bellbird has three bedrooms and sleeps seven.

Other possibilities include the cosy one-bedroom **Pilgrim Cottage** (☎ *03-219 1144, Horseshoe Bay Rd)* at $85 for two; **Bayview Apartment** (☎ *03-219 1465, Excelsior Rd),* in an elevated position near Observation Rock and sleeping six ($95 for two); and **Pania Lodge** (☎ *03-215 7733,* e *halstead@xtra.co.nz)* at Butterfield Beach, a 25-minute walk from Halfmoon Bay, charging $110 for two.

For details of other rental houses and B&B options contact the visitors centre.

Places to Eat & Drink

Dining options are limited, but there are some surprisingly good choices.

South Sea Hotel (☎ *03-219 1059)* With an aim to please everyone, the restaurant inside the waterfront hotel serves up breakfast, lunch and dinner, plus there's a more casual bar menu featuring burgers, potato wedges etc. The dinner menu (mains $19 to $30) features local seafood such as steamed mussels, fresh oysters, seafood chowder and pan-fried or battered blue cod. If you're feeling brave, you can also try the local delicacy: roasted mutton bird.

Church Hill Cafe Bar (☎ *03-219 1323, Kamahi Rd)* Dinner mains $20-27. With attractive decor and a menu that wouldn't be out of place in a mainland city (except perhaps for the mutton bird dish), this cafe is a good place for coffee or something more substantial as you enjoy the fine views over Halfmoon Bay.

Lighthouse Wine Bar (☎ *03-219 1208, Main Rd)* Pizzas to $20. This atmospheric place serves up excellent antipasto platters and gourmet woodfired pizzas such as the Popeye, with spinach, garlic and feta cheese. It's a good choice just for a drink too, with an extensive selection of quality NZ wines and beers.

Justcafe (☎ *03-219 1422, Main Rd)* Sandwiches around $5. Enjoy some of Justcafe's coffee, sandwiches, muffins, soup or other lunch fare as you access the Internet or browse through their magazines.

Kai Kart (☎ *03-219 1225, Ayr St)* Takeaways average $7. Out the front of the museum is this convenient van selling all manner of takeaway food, including fish and chips, paua patties, hamburgers, hot dogs and souvlaki.

Crystals & Coffee (☎ *03-219 1269)* Over on Horseshoe Bay, Stewart Island Retreat offers this place for trampers to take a rest and enjoy cake and coffee.

Self-caterers can also get groceries from *Ship to Shore* general store or *Lettuce Inn* (☎ *03-219 1243, 31 Main Rd)*. Often the *Fishermen's Co-op* on the Halfmoon Bay wharf and *Southern Seafoods* at Horseshoe Bay have fresh fish and crayfish for sale, or you can catch your own fish, of course.

One of the very few places for nightlife is the pub, the South Sea Hotel – observe the evening life-cycle of the endangered, white-gumbooted Stewart Islander. Alternatively, head for a drink at the Lighthouse Wine Bar.

Getting There & Away

For a quick look at Stewart Island, inquire at the Invercargill visitors centre about packages, which can be good value and often include air fares, accommodation and tours.

Air Stewart Island Flights (☎ 03-218 9129, ⓔ sif@xtra.co.nz, Ⓦ www.stewartisland flights.com) flies between Invercargill and Stewart Island for $80/145 one way/return (children $45/75). There are often discount standby fares but phone ahead.

Flights depart three times daily, all year round, and it only takes 20 minutes to fly over the narrow strait. On Stewart Island, the bus from the Ryans Creek airstrip to Oban is included in the air fare.

Boat Stewart Island Marine's (☎ 03-212 7660, ⓔ foveauxexpress@southnet.co.nz) passenger-only *Foveaux Express* runs between Bluff and Stewart Island for $45/84 one way/return (children half-price). There are departures twice daily year-round. See Ⓦ www.stewartisland.co.nz for the most up-to-date schedule. Definitely book a few days ahead in summer.

The crossing takes one hour across Foveaux Strait, noted for its often stormy weather, so the journey can be pretty rough going.

Campbelltown Passenger (☎ 03-212 7404) has a shuttle service connecting with the ferry and picks up from anywhere in Invercargill ($10).

Getting Around

Oban Tours & Taxis (☎ 03-219 1456, ⓔ obantours@clear.net.nz) arranges bus tours, water taxis, rental cars, motor scooters, boat charters and excursions. Car rental costs $50/70 half/full day, petrol and mileage included. Motor scooters start at $20 for one hour, $35 for three hours and $50 for 24 hours.

Innes Backpackers (☎ 03-219 1080) has mountain bikes for hire for $10 per day.

A number of charter boats do pick-ups and drop-offs to remote parts of the island, which may be useful for trampers. Stewart Island Water Taxi (☎ 03-219 1394) and Seaview Water Taxi (☎ 03-219 1014) both offer such a service, and also go regularly to Ulva Island ($25 return for one person; $20 for two or more). They operate from Golden Bay Wharf, about a 10-minute walk from the township.

Chatham Islands

☎ 03 • pop 770

The Chathams are an isolated, mysterious and wild group of islands, very much off the beaten track. Named Rekohu (Misty Sun) by the Morori, they are way out in the Pacific, about 850km due east of Christchurch. The islands are the first human habitation over the international dateline, and marketed

OUTER ISLANDS

CHATHAM ISLANDS

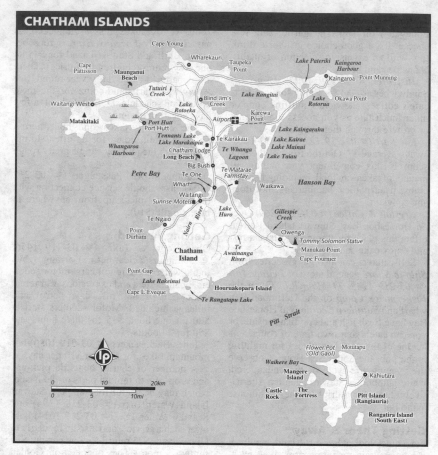

themselves as the first to see the dawn of the new millennium. There are 10 islands in the group but apart from the 35 or so people on Pitt Island, only Chatham Island, with 735 people, is significantly populated.

The islands offer a world of contrast: rugged coastlines and towering cliffs; volcanic peaks; lagoons and peat bogs; sweeping beaches devoid of human habitation; isolated farms; wind-stunted vegetation and dense patches of forest. Apart from farming and tourism (particularly ecotourism), the other main industry is crayfish processing, and there are plants at Waitangi, Kaingaroa,

Owenga and Port Hutt. These four towns look like neglected junk heaps choking in the flotsam and jetsam of their raison d'être. They may not be flash, but they do have a dilapidated charm.

History

The Chatham Islands were formed eons ago by volcanic upthrust. The main island is known as the home of the Moriori tribe, who settled these islands from the South Island about 1000 years ago. In isolation from the mainland Maori, the Moriori maintained a more ancient Polynesian culture.

OUTER ISLANDS

The Last of the Moriori

One of the most fascinating aspects of the Chathams is the cultural legacy of the Moriori. There are still Moriori descendants on the islands and there are a few remnants of their once flourishing culture.

There has been much speculation as to where the Moriori came from (for an old-fashioned theory, see History in the Facts about New Zealand chapter). It is now scientifically accepted that the Moriori were Maori who sailed to the Chathams from NZ. The date of their arrival is in dispute, but it was some time between AD 900 and AD 1500.

Once in the Chathams, the Moriori began to develop a separate identity from the mainland Maori. They did not have rigid social divisions, they forbade tribal warfare and settled disputes on a one-to-one basis with hand-to-hand combat, and their language developed subtle differences. They carved their symbols into trees (dendroglyphs) and into the rocks (petroglyphs) fringing Te Whanga Lagoon. When the HMS *Chatham* visited in 1791 there were believed to be about 2000 Moriori on the islands.

From about 1835, groups of mainland Maori began to arrive in the Chathams and soon there were about 900 new residents made up of the Ngati Tama and Ngati Mutunga of the Taranaki Ati-awa. They began to occupy the land in a process known as *takahi,* killing about 300 Moriori who resisted and enslaving others. By 1841 there were believed to be only 160 Moriori and over 400 Maori and it was not until two years later that the Ngati Tama and Te Ati-awa released the last of the Moriori slaves. In 1870 the Native Land Court Hearings recognised that the two mainland tribes had sovereignty over 97% of the Chathams by right of conquest; small reserves were created for the surviving 90 Moriori. The Moriori intermarried in time and slowly their unique culture and identity faded. Their language died with the last great Moriori scholar, Hirawanu Tapu, in 1900. There were only 12 full-blooded Moriori left at this stage.

Today, Moriori, Pakeha and descendants of the mainland Maori live side by side as Chatham Islanders. The last full-blooded Moriori was Tommy Solomon, who died in 1933. His passing was seen at the time as the extinction of a particular race, but it was far from that. His three sons and two daughters are identified as Moriori and there were many other families on the island who claimed Moriori ancestry. There are now believed to be over 300 Moriori descendants and there has been a revival of Moriori consciousness, particularly strong after the building of the Solomon monument at Manukau Point near Owenga in the southeast of the island.

In August 2001 the Waitangi Tribunal, charged with investigating Maori land claims, decided that the ancestral rights to the Chatham Islands belong to the Moriori. The Tribunal found that Moriori should receive compensation for the lasting impact of the Crown's failure to intervene after the 1835 mainland Maori invasion, and called the 1870 decision to award Maori sovereignty over the Chathams by right of conquest 'patently wrong'. Moriori descendants should finally get some compensation for their ancestors' sufferings.

However, with the arrival of Europeans things rapidly began to go wrong: the Moriori population crashed from around 2000 at the time of the first European arrival in 1791 to only about 100 in the 1860s. By the beginning of the 20th century there were just 12 full-blooded Moriori left (see the boxed text 'The Last of the Moriori').

Fauna

There are 18 species of bird unique to the islands and, because of their isolation, there is a large degree of endemism, as with the local tomtit, pigeon and robin. Entry to the sanctuaries, such as those at Pitt and Rangatira (South East) Islands, is prohibited, but many species can still be seen. The staff at DOC will outline the best viewing spots for bird-watchers. Rare and unusual birds include the endangered black robin, which at one stage was perilously close to extinction in its last refuge, Mangere Island near Pitt Island (read more about the black robin story in the 'Watching Wildlife' colour section). The very rare Chatham Island taiko *(Pterodroma magentae)* was recently rediscovered nesting in the Tuku River region of the south coast of Chatham.

Black swans, pukeko, weka and many species of ducks are common.

There's a fur seal colony near Kaingaroa in the northeast of Chatham Island. The only access to the seals is across private land and permission must first be obtained from the landowner.

Information

Information on the islands is available from the Trust Board (☎ 03-305 0066, ⓔ info@ chathams.govt.nz), PO Box 65, Waitangi; Air Chathams (☎ 03-305 0209, ⓔ air chats@xtra.co.nz); or the local council (☎ 03-305 0033), PO Box 24, Waitangi. Once on Chatham Island, the best option is to ask around for information and talk to the locals, particularly your accommodation hosts. The signposted DOC office (☎ 03-305 0098) is in Te One; call before you go as it may be unattended.

The websites ⓦ www.chathams.com and ⓦ www.chathams.govt.nz are good sources of information, although they don't seem to be updated regularly. *A Land Apart,* by Michael King & Robin Morrison, provides a wealth of information about the islands.

Waitangi is the only sizable town on the islands. There are a couple of shops, a hotel, small hospital, museum and golf course. There is an ANZ bank here (which also acts as a post office) but no ATM – bring sufficient cash with you.

The monthly *Chatham Islander* carries the local news. The islands also have their own radio station, Radio Weka (92.1 FM), and a TV station run in conjunction with TVNZ. There is an STD and fax link with the mainland, and a card phone in Waitangi.

The Chatham Islands are very exposed but they have a temperate climate. Average daily temperatures vary from 12°C to 18°C in February and 6°C to 10°C in July. The best time to visit is in December and January; often the temperatures then reach 23°C to 24°C. Chatham Islands time is 45 minutes ahead of mainland NZ time.

Things to See & Do

The islands have plenty of fine beaches popular for **fishing** and particularly for catching crayfish. Crayfish are a major industry in the Chatham Islands, and they're exported to North America and Japan. There are daily quotas as to how many crays or paua each person can catch; check with DOC office in Te One.

Scuba divers can explore the **shipwrecks** around the islands while trampers will also find interesting country to explore, and there are **walking tracks** in the reserves established by DOC. There's a small **museum** (☎ 03-305 0054; open 8.30am- 4.30pm Mon-Fri) with Moriori artefacts in the council offices in Waitangi.

The mysterious 200-year-old Moriori **tree carvings** (dendroglyphs) can be found in a grove adjacent to the old Te Hapupu aerodrome, in a signposted and fenced-off area open to the public. **Rock engravings** (petroglyphs) are found on the shores of Te Whanga Lagoon, not far from the airstrip. **Fossilised sharks' teeth** can be found at Blind Jim's Creek, also on the shores of Te Whanga Lagoon. These teeth are about 40 million years old and a local heritage – please leave them where you see them. Their appearance here, pushed up by the waves of the lagoon, has not yet been fully explained.

There is a **statue** of the 'last Moriori', Tommy Solomon, at Manukau Point near Owenga (see the boxed text 'The Last of the Moriori' earlier in this chapter). Tommy's eyes seem to follow you as you scramble around the rocks below.

Places to Stay & Eat

Hotel Chathams (☎ 0800 566 000, 03-305 0048, ⓔ vcroon@voyager.co.nz, Waitangi) Singles with shared facilities $75, singles/ doubles with en suite $100/110. This newly renovated hotel in Waitangi is the focal point of town. It has good rooms, most with balconies and sea views. It also has a small souvenir shop (where you can get the highly prized Chathams T-shirt), plus rents out cars and organises tours of the island's attractions. Good meals are served here – the restaurant specialises in local seafood.

Travellers Rest Guesthouse (☎ 0800 566 000, 03-305 0048, ⓔ travellersrest@xtra .co.nz, Waitangi) Singles/doubles $110/120.

This guesthouse is run by the owners of Hotel Chathams. It offers more luxurious rooms, all with TV, phone and en suite.

Sunrise Motels (☎ 03-305 0215, W sunrisemotels.hypermart.net, Tuku Rd 500m south of Waitangi) Singles/doubles with shared facilities $50/70, self-contained units $75. Sunrise Motels is a five-bedroom house with share facilities, plus two self-contained units. The owners also run **Roo's Roost Backpackers** in central Waitangi near the community hall ($25 per person; linen extra). The units have their own kitchen facilities, other accommodation has access to equipped kitchens.

Chatham Lodge (☎ 03-305 0196, W www.chathamlodge.net.nz, north of the Kaingaroa and Airport Rds junction) Singles/doubles $102/112. Chatham Lodge has quiet, comfortable rooms and hires out vehicles. Activities offered include fishing, boating and tramping in nearby Henga Scenic Reserve. Meals cost $15 for cooked breakfast, $15 for lunch (packed or served), and $30 for dinner. The lodge also organises package tours from Wellington, which include air fares, airport transfers, all meals, accommodation and daily tours.

Te Matarae Farmstay (☎ 03-305 0144) B&B en suite singles/doubles $73/85. The Smith family farmstay near the shores of Te Whanga Lagoon, 11km from Waitangi, is surrounded by natural bush and offers a good opportunity for kayaking. The friendly owners offer free airport transfers, rental of a 4WD vehicle, and meals are available (cut lunch $10, dinner $25).

Campers and backpackers should head to Owenga, where there is a small **camping area** (☎ 03-305 0271) on a family property. You can pitch a tent (payment by *koha* or donation) or sleep in the sleepout ($20 per person) and use the cooking and bathroom facilities of the house. The friendly, laid-back owners usually invite guests in to share the family dinner and will help arrange access to the properties of the area, so this is a great homestay-type arrangement.

Hotel Chathams is the best place to go for meals, and most accommodation hosts offer meals. Other central options include the **Waitangi Cafe** (☎ 03-305 0505) on Tuku Rd, with standard takeaway and tearoom fare, and **Petre Bat Take-Aways** (☎ 03-305 0132). The fast-food option for those visiting Kaingaroa is **Kaingaroa Kai Kart** (☎ 03-305 0327). For self-caterers, the **Waitangi General Store** (☎ 03-305 0041) is the island's main store and stocks a decent range of food and assorted household goods. You can buy crayfish and blue cod at the packaging factory in Waitangi. Flounder and whitebait can be caught in the lagoon, and paua and kina gathered just offshore.

Entertainment – bring your own or head to Waitangi's local, **Hotel Chathams**.

Getting There & Away

Your only option is by air with Air Chathams (☎ 03-305 0209, e airchats@xtra.co.nz), which can also be booked through Air New Zealand. Air Chathams flies to/from Wellington on Monday, Wednesday, Friday and Saturday, and Christchurch on Wednesday and Saturday. Return fares from either destination start from $576. The flight takes two hours and since seats are limited it's wise to book well ahead.

Getting Around

Beyond Waitangi most roads are unsealed and there is no public transport. Accommodation owners will pick you up from Karewa airport (usually for a fee of $10 to $20) if they know of your arrival – some visitors have been left stranded at the airport, which is 21km north of Waitangi.

Chatham Motors (☎ 03-305 0093, e chathammotors@yahoo.com) hires out 4WD vehicles starting at around $82 per day, and 4WD motorbikes for $52; cars cost from $62 to $82 (delivery to the airport is extra). All prices include insurance but not kilometres, fuel or GST.

Chatham Lodge, Te Matarae and Hotel Chathams hire out vehicles – expect to pay around $80 for a car, around $100 for a 4WD. It's also quite easy to hitch around the island.

Air Chathams operates a light aircraft for aerial sightseeing and trips to Pitt Island. It may be possible to hitch a ride with fishing vessels across to Pitt Island (19km from main Chatham Island), but the seas there are very rough.

Tours are available from Hotel Chathams and Chatham Lodge; prices are advised on application. It is relatively easy to hire a vehicle and see most of the island's sights by yourself. Walking is a popular form of transport but check with the DOC about access across private land.

Other Islands

New Zealand administers a number of the outlying islands. The Subantarctic Islands, are to the south, towards Antarctica, and to the north, in the Pacific Ocean, are the Kermadecs.

SUBANTARCTIC ISLANDS

The Snares, Auckland, Bounty and Antipodes Islands and Campbell Island are established nature reserves run by DOC in Invercargill. Entry is restricted and by permit only. To get some idea of this wild environment, visit the Southland Museum & Art Gallery in Invercargill and watch the *Roaring Forties Experience* audiovisual.

The islands have a colourful human history of sealing, shipwrecks and forlorn attempts at farming. Now the islands are important as a reserve for remaining areas of vegetation unmodified by humans and as breeding grounds for sea birds, penguins and mammals such as the elephant seal.

The Subantarctic Islands' remarkable wealth of birdlife saw their gazettal by Unesco as a World Heritage Site in 1998. This recognises their outstanding value not only to NZ but to the whole world.

Few are fortunate enough to visit these remote islands but increasing ecotourism possibilities, well managed and guided, are possible by boat. They are strictly controlled by DOC and are not cheap.

Fiordland Ecology Holidays (☎ 03-249 6600, W *www.fiordland.gen.nz, PO Box 40, Manapouri)* is based in Manapouri in Southland and takes a number of scientific trips to the Subantarctic Islands every year,

selling leftover berths to help fund the trips. Costs are around $275 per day plus various government fees (landing permits and the like). These trips are very popular and spaces are limited so there is a waiting list of interested persons; a good level of fitness is required.

Heritage Expeditions (NZ) (☎ 03-338 9944, W *www.heritage-expeditions.com, PO Box 6282, Christchurch)* has a range of expensive upmarket tours taking in New Zealand as well as the Australian subantarctic islands, and Antarctica.

Snares Islands

The Snares Islands are most famous for the incredible number of sooty shearwaters (mutton birds) that breed there. It has been estimated that on any one evening during the season (from November to April) there will be five million in the air before they crash-land to return to their burrows.

Other birds found here are the endemic Snares crested penguin, cape pigeon and Bullers mollymawks.

Auckland Islands

These are probably the most accessible of NZ's Subantarctic Islands.

Many species of birds make Enderby Island their home (either temporary or permanent), including endemic shags, the flightless teal and the royal albatross. Skuas (gull-like birds) are ever present in the skies above the sea lion colony.

Discovered in 1806, the Auckland Islands were an infamous shipwreck risk in the 19th century. Settlement was once attempted in Erebus Cove, and it was not until 1992 that the last of the introduced cattle were destroyed.

On Disappointment Island there are some 60,000 white-capped mollymawks.

Campbell Island

Campbell Island is the true domain of the pelagic bird species. It is estimated that there are over 7500 pairs of southern royal albatross based here, not to mention the colonies of greyheaded and blackbrowed mollymawks.

OUTER ISLANDS

The Campbell Island teal is one of NZ's rarest birds (perhaps 50 to 100 remain).

Antipodes Islands

These islands get their name from the fact that, at latitude 180°, they are opposite latitude 0° at Greenwich, England. The real treat on these islands is the endemic Antipodes Island parakeet, which is found with, but does not breed with, the red-crowned parakeet (similar to the NZ species of parakeet). Wandering albatross nest in the short grass at the top of the islands.

Bounty Islands

Landing is not permitted on any of the 13 Bounty Islands – there is a good chance that you would step on the wildlife anyway, as the 135 hectares of land that makes up these granite islands is covered with mammals and birds. There are literally thousands of erect crested penguins, fulmar prions and salvins mollymawks clustered in crevices near the lower slopes and on all other available pieces of real estate.

THE KERMADECS

These islands, 1000km northeast of NZ, were annexed to NZ in 1887, and consist of Raoul, McCauley and Curtis Islands, L'Esperance Rock and several other rocky outcrops. Their Polynesian name is Rangitahua. Only Raoul has water and has been settled periodically, most notably in the early 19th century when whaling was conducted here. There are a number of protected archaeological and historical sites. Most of the islands have boulder-strewn beaches and steep, rocky cliffs.

The islands cannot be reached without difficulty and permits are not readily granted because of the frequency of earthquakes and volcanic eruptions, common in this region of the Pacific 'ring of fire'.

The Kermadec Islands constitute NZ's largest marine reserve, created in 1990, and it's interesting as it is a transitional zone between temperate and tropical waters. Diving is popular in the reserve, which has corals but not reefs, and an elusive goal is the rare spotted black groper.

TOKELAU
☎ 690 • pop 1500

These three atolls (Atafu, Nukunonu and Fakaofo), with their tiny populations and covering only 10 sq km, lie about halfway between NZ and Hawaii. They have been administered by NZ since 1925; more recently, Samoa has also aided in their administration and Tokelau is now moving towards self-determination and a degree of independence from Wellington.

The small atolls of Tokelau cannot support a large population and there has been a steady stream of Tokelauans leaving for overseas (Samoa or NZ) for many years – there are now many more Tokelauans living in NZ than on the atolls themselves. In NZ, Tokelauans maintain their culture and their language through social and church groups.

Tokelau, with other low-lying Pacific nations such as Tuvalu, Kiribati and the Marshall Islands, is at extreme risk from the effects of global warming, with rising sea levels, increased severity of storms and the death of coral reefs all predicted. United Nations study teams do not expect Tokelau to be inhabitable beyond the 21st century.

If you want to visit Tokelau you're probably out of luck because there's only one cargo and passenger ship a month (from Samoa) and it's usually fully booked with islanders returning home from Samoa or NZ. There is no tourism to speak of and almost no established facilities for tourists, although there are a couple of places to stay.

Visitor permits are issued by the Tokelau Apia Liaison Office in Samoa (NZ$20 for a one-month stay); consent to visit must be given by the village elders, accommodation must be arranged prior to departure and a return ticket to Samoa must be booked. If you're determined to visit, make inquiries at the Tokelau Apia Liaison Office in Samoa (☎ 685-20822, fax 685-21761), PO Box 865, Apia.

Read about Tokelau online at W www.tokelau.org.nz and W www.xl.net.nz, and for more information see Lonely Planet's *South Pacific* guide, which has a chapter on Tokelau.

OUTER ISLANDS

Language

New Zealand has two official languages: English and Maori. English is the language you'll usually hear spoken, but Maori, long on the decline, is making a comeback. You can use English to speak to anyone in NZ – all Maori people speak English. There are some occasions, though, when knowing a little Maori would be useful, such as visiting a *marae*, where often only Maori is spoken. Maori is also useful to know since many places in NZ have Maori names.

KIWI ENGLISH

Like the people of other countries in the world who speak English, New Zealanders have a unique way of speaking the language. The flattening (some would call it slaughtering) of vowels is the most distinctive feature of Kiwi pronunciation. The NZ treatment of 'fish and chips' – 'fush and chups' – is an endless source of delight for Australians. In the North Island sentences often have 'eh!' attached to the end. In the far south a rolled 'r' is practised widely, a holdover from that region's Scottish heritage – it's especially noticeable in Southland. See the glossary at the back of this book for an explanation of Kiwi English words and phrases.

A *Personal Kiwi-Yankee Dictionary* by Louis S. Leland Jr is a fine and often hilarious book of translations and explanations of quirks between the Kiwi and American ways of speaking English. Yanks will love it.

MAORI

The Maori have a vividly chronicled history, recorded in songs and chants which dramatically recall the migration to NZ from Polynesian Hawaiki and other important events. Early missionaries first recorded the language in a written form by using only 15 letters of the English alphabet.

Maori is closely related to other Polynesian languages (including Hawaiian, Tahitian and Cook Islands Maori). In fact, NZ Maori and Hawaiian have the same lexical similarity as Spanish and French, although over 7000km separates Honolulu and Auckland.

The Maori language was never dead – it was always used in Maori ceremonies – but over time familiarity with it was definitely on the decline. Recent years have seen a revival of interest in it, however, and this forms an integral part of the renaissance of *Maoritanga* (Maori culture). Many Maori people who had heard the language spoken on the *marae* for years but had not used it in their day-to-day lives are now studying it and speaking it fluently. Maori is now taught in schools throughout NZ, some TV programs and news reports are broadcast in it and many English place names are being renamed in Maori. Even government departments have been rechristened with Maori names: for example the Inland Revenue Department is also known as Te Tari Taake (the last word is actually *take*, meaning 'levy', but the department has chosen to stress the long 'a' by spelling it 'aa').

In many places, Maori people have come together to provide instruction in their language and culture to young children; the idea is for them to grow up speaking both Maori and English, and to develop a familiarity with Maori tradition. It's a matter of some pride to have fluency in the language. On some *marae* only Maori can be spoken, encouraging everyone to speak it and emphasising the distinct Maori character of the *marae*.

Pronunciation

Maori is a fluid, poetic language and surprisingly easy to pronounce once you remember to split each word (and some can be amazingly long) into separate syllables.

Most consonants in Maori – h, k, m, n, p, t and w – are pronounced much the same as in English. The Maori r is a flapped sound (not rolled) with the tongue near the front of the mouth. It is closer to the English 'l' in pronunciation.

Two combinations of consonants require special attention: **ng**, pronounced as in the English words singing or running, can be used at the beginning of words as well as at the end. To practise, just say 'ing' over and over, isolate the 'ng' part of it and then practise using it to begin a word rather than end one. The **wh** also has a unique pronunciation in Maori – generally as a soft English 'f'. This pronunciation is used in many place names in NZ, eg, Whakatane, Whangaroa and Whakapapa (all pronounced as if they begin with a soft 'f'). There is some regional variation, however: in the region around the Whanganui River, for example, the **wh** is pronounced as in the English words 'when' and 'why'.

When learning to speak Maori the correct pronunciation of the vowels is all-important. The examples below are only a rough guideline – to really get it right you'll have to listen carefully to someone who knows how to pronounce the language correctly. Each vowel has both a long and a short sound with long vowels often denoted in text by a macron (a line over the letter) or a double vowel. We have not indicated long/short vowel forms in this book.

Vowels

a	as in 'large'
e	as in 'get'
i	as in 'marine'
o	as in 'pork'
u	as the 'oo' in 'moon'

Diphthongs

ae, ai	as the 'y' in 'sky'
ao, au	as the 'ow' in 'how'
ea	as in 'bear'
ei	as in 'vein'
eo	as 'eh-oh'
eu	as 'eh-oo'
ia	as in the name 'Ian'
ie	as the 'ye' in 'yet'
io	as the 'ye o' in 'ye old'
iu	as the 'ue' in 'cue'
oa	as in 'roar'
oe	as in 'toe'
oi	as in 'toil'
ou	as the 'ow' in 'sow'
ua	as the 'ewe' in 'fewer'

Each syllable ends in a vowel and there is never more than one vowel in a syllable. There are no silent letters.

There are many Maori phrasebooks, grammar books and Maori-English dictionaries if you want to take a closer look at the language. Learning a few basic greetings is an excellent thing to do, especially if you plan to go onto a marae, where you'll be greeted in Maori.

The *Collins Maori Phrase Book* by Patricia Tauroa is an excellent book for starting to speak the language, with sections on every-day conversation and also on how the language is used in a cultural context (such as on a marae). Lonely Planet's *South Pacific phrasebook* has a useful section on the Maori language as well as several Pacific languages (Tongan, Samoan, Cook Island Maori) that you may have heard spoken around Wellington or South Auckland.

Other English-Maori dictionaries include the *English-Maori Maori-English Dictionary* by Bruce Biggs, and the *Reed Dictionary of Modern Maori* by PM Ryan, one of the most authoritative.

Greetings & Small Talk

Maori greetings are finding increased popularity; don't be surprised if you're greeted on the phone or on the street with *Kia ora*. Try these ones:

Haere mai!	Welcome!
Haere ra.	Goodbye. (one staying to one going)
E noho ra.	Goodbye. (to one staying)
Kia ora.	Hello/Good luck/Good health.
Tena koe.	Hello. (to one person)
Tena korua.	Hello. (to two people)
Tena koutou.	Hello. (to three or more people)

Kei te pehea koe?
  How are you? (to one person)
Kei te pehea korua?
  How are you? (to two people)
Kei te pehea koutou?
  How are you? (to three or more)
Kei te pai.
  Very well, thanks/That's fine.

Maori Geographical Terms

The following words form part of many place names in NZ:

a – of
ana – cave
ara – way, path, road
awa – river or valley
heke – descend
hiku – end, tail
hine – girl, daughter
ika – fish
iti – small
kahurangi – treasured possession; special greenstone
kai – food
kainga – village
kaka – parrot
kare – rippling
kati – shut or close
koura – crayfish
makariri – cold
manga – stream or tributary
manu – bird
maunga – mountain
moana – sea or lake
moko – tattoo
motu – island

mutu – finished, ended, over
nga – the (plural)
noa – ordinary, not *tapu*
nui – big, great
nuku – distance
o – of, place of ...
one – beach, sand or mud
pa – fortified village
papa – flat land, broad slab
pipi – shellfish
pohatu – stone
poto – short
pouri – sad, dark, gloomy
puke – hill
puna – spring, hole, fountain
rangi – sky, heavens
raro – north
rei – cherished possesion
roa – long
roto – lake
rua – hole in the ground, two
runga – above
tahuna – beach, sandbank
tane – man

tangata – people
tata – close to; dash against;
twin islands
tawaha – entrance, opening
tawahi – the other side (of a
river or lake)
te – the (singular)
tonga – south
ure – male genitals
uru – west
wahine – woman
wai – water
waingaro – lost; waters that
disappear in certain seasons
waha – broken
waka – canoe
wera – burnt or warm; floating
wero – challenge
whaka... – to act as...
whanau – extended family
whanga – harbour, bay or inlet
whare – house
whenua – land or country
whiti – east

Knowledge of just a few such words can help you make sense of many Maori place names. For example: Waikaremoana is the Sea *(moana)* of Rippling *(kare)* Waters *(wai)*; Rotorua means the Second *(rua)* Lake *(roto)*; and Taumatawhakatangihangakoauauotamateaturipukakapikimaunga-horonukupokaiwhenuakitanatahu means ... well ... perhaps you'd better read 'The Longest Place Name in the World' in the East Coast chapter for that translation. Some easier place names composed of words in this list are:

Aramoana – Sea *(moana)* Path *(ara)*
Awaroa – Long *(roa)* River *(awa)*
Kaitangata – Eat *(kai)* People *(tangata)*
Maunganui – Great *(nui)* Mountain *(maunga)*
Opouri – Place of *(o)* Sadness *(pouri)*
Te Araroa – The *(te)* Long *(roa)* Path *(ara)*

Te Puke – The *(te)* Hill *(puke)*
Urewera – Burnt *(wera)* Penis *(ure)*
Waimakariri – Cold *(makariri)* Water *(wai)*
Wainui – Great *(nui)* Waters *(wai)*
Whakatane – To Act *(whaka)* As A Man *(tane)*
Whangarei – Cherished *(rei)* Harbour *(whanga)*

(Note that the adjective comes after the noun in Maori constructions. Thus 'cold water' is *wai makariri* not *makariri wai*.)

Glossary

This glossary is a list of 'Kiwi English' and Maori terms you will come across often in New Zealand.

Also see the boxed text 'Maori Geographical Terms' in the Language chapter for some Maori words that pop up again and again in NZ place names.

AA – New Zealand Automobile Association; the organisation which provides road information and roadside assistance

afghan – popular homemade chocolate biscuit

All Blacks – NZ's revered national rugby union team (the name comes from 'All Backs', which the press called the NZ rugby team on an early visit to England)

Aoraki – Maori name for Mt Cook, meaning 'Cloud Piercer'. Aoraki is the South Island pronunciation; otherwise it would be Aorangi.

Aotearoa – Maori name for NZ; most often translated as 'Land of the Long White Cloud'

atua – spirits or gods

bach – a holiday home, usually a wooden cottage (pronounced 'batch'); see also *crib*

Barrier, the – local name for Great Barrier Island in the Hauraki Gulf

baths – swimming pool, often referred to as municipal baths

Beehive – Parliament House in Wellington, so-called because of its distinctive shape

Black Power – a large, well-organised and mainly Maori bikie-style gang

black-water rafting – rafting or tubing underground in a cave or *tomo*

boozer – a public bar

box of birds – an expression meaning 'on top of the world', usually in response to 'How are you?'

bro' – literally 'brother'; usually meaning mate, as in 'just off to see the bros'

bush – heavily forested areas

Buzzy Bee – a child's toy as essential to NZ child development as dinosaur models; a wooden bee dragged along by a string to produce a whirring noise

BYO – bring your own (usually applies to alcohol at a restaurant or cafe)

Captain Cooker – a large feral pig, introduced by Captain Cook and now roaming wild over most of NZ's rugged bush land (see also *kune kune*)

CHE – not the revolutionary but Crown Health Enterprise (regional, privatised health authorities)

chillie bin – cooler; esky; large insulated box for keeping food and drink cold

choice – fantastic; great

ciggies – cigarettes

crib – the name for a *bach* in Otago and Southland

cuzzie or cuz' – cousin; relative or just mate; see *bro'*

dairy – a small corner store which sells just about everything, especially milk, bread, the newspaper and ice cream

Dalmatian – a term applied to the predominantly Yugoslav gum diggers who fossicked for kauri gum (used as furniture polish) in the gum fields of Northland

DOC – Department of Conservation (or *Te Papa Atawhai*); the government department which administers national parks and thus all tracks and huts

domain – open grassed area in a town or city, often the focus of civic amenities such as gardens, picnic areas and bowling clubs

DOSLI – the former name of Land Information NZ

doss house – temporary accommodation

DPB – a government handout, increasingly used in the vernacular as more families struggle in the free market economy

dropkick – a certain method of kicking a rugby ball; a personal insult

EFTPOS – electronic funds transfer at point of sale. A facility to pay over the counter using your ATM card.

farmstay – accommodation on a typical Kiwi farm where you are encouraged to join with in the day-to-day activities

fiscal envelope – money set aside by the NZ government to make financial reparation for injustices to Maori people since the Treaty of Waitangi

football – rugby, either union or league

freezing works – slaughterhouse or abattoir for sheep and/or cattle

Gilbert – the most popular brand of rugby football

Godzone – New Zealand (from Richard Seddon who referred to NZ as 'God's own country')

good as gold, good as – very good

greenstone – jade, *pounamu*

haka – any dance but usually refers to the traditional challenge; war dance

hakari – feast

handle – a beer glass with a handle

hangi – oven made by digging a hole and steaming food in baskets over embers in the hole; a feast of traditional Maori food

hapu – sub-tribe or smaller tribal grouping

hard case – an unusual or strong-willed character

Hawaiki – the Polynesian homeland from where the Maori tribes migrated by canoe (probably Ra'iatea in the Society Islands). Also a name for the Afterworld.

hei tiki – carved, stylised human figure worn around the neck, often a carved representation of an ancestor; also called a *tiki*

hoa – friend; usually pronounced 'e hoa'

hokey pokey – a delicious variety of ice cream with butterscotch chips

hoki – a fish common in fish and chip shops

homestay – accommodation in a family house where you are treated (temporarily, thank God) as one of the family

hongi – Maori greeting; the pressing of noses and sharing of life breath

hui – gathering; meeting

huntaway – a loud-barking sheep dog, usually a sturdy black-and-brown hound

Ika a Maui, Te – (The Fish of Maui) the North Island

Instant Kiwi – state-run lottery

Interislander – any of the big old ferries which make the crossing across Cook Strait between Wellington (North Island) and Picton (South Island)

'Is it what!' – strong affirmation or agreement; 'Yes isn't it!'

iwi – a large tribal grouping with common lineage back to the original migration from Hawaiki; people; tribe

jandals – sandals; flip-flops; thongs; usually rubber footwear

jersey – a jumper, usually woollen (also the shirt worn by rugby players, eg grab him by the jersey)

judder bars – bumps in the road to make you drive slowly; speed humps

K Rd – Karangahape Rd in Auckland

kai – food; almost any word with kai in it has some food connection

kainga – village; pre-European unfortified Maori village

ka pai – good; excellent

karakia – prayer

kaumatua – highly respected members of a tribe; the people you would ask for permission to enter a *marae*.

kina – sea urchins; a Maori delicacy

kiwi – the flightless, nocturnal brown bird with a long beak which is the national symbol; the New Zealand dollar; a New Zealander; a member of the national rugby league team; an adjective to mean anything of or relating to NZ

kiwi bear – the introduced Australian brush-tailed possum

kiwi fruit – a small, succulent fruit with fuzzy brown skin and juicy green flesh; a Chinese gooseberry

koe – you (singular)

koha – a donation

kohanga reo – schools where Maori language and culture are at the forefront of the education process; also called 'language nest' schools

korua – you (two people)

koutou – you (more than two people)

kumara – Polynesian sweet potato; a Maori staple food

kunekune – another type of wild pig introduced by Chinese gold diggers in the 19th century (see *Captain Cooker*)
Kupe – an early Polynesian navigator, from *Hawaiki*, credited with the discovery of the islands that are now NZ

league – rugby league football
lounge bar – a more upmarket bar than a public bar; called a 'ladies bar' in some countries

mana – the spiritual quality of a person or object; authority of a chief or priest
manaia – a traditional carving design; literally means 'bird-headed man'
manuhiri – visitor; guest
Maori – the indigenous people of New Zealand
Maoritanga – Maori culture
marae – literally refers to the sacred ground in front of the Maori meeting house; now more commonly used to refer to the entire complex of buildings
Maui – an important figure in Maori (Polynesian) mythology
mere – flat, *greenstone* war club
metal/metalled road – gravel road (unsealed)
MMP – Mixed Member Proportional; a cumbersome electoral system used in NZ and Germany; a limited form of proportional voting
moko – tattoo; usually refers to facial tattoos
Mongrel Mob – a large, well-organised and mainly Maori bikie-style gang
Moriori – an isolated Polynesian group; inhabitants of the Chatham Islands
motor camp – well-equipped camping grounds with tent sites, caravan and campervan sites, on-site caravans, cabins and tourist flats
motorway – freeway or expressway

naiad – a rigid hull inflatable boat (used for dolphin swimming, whale-watching etc)
ngati – literally 'the people of' or 'the descendants of'; tribe; (in the South Island, it's pronounced 'kai')
nga – the (plural); see *te*
nifty-fifty – 50cc motorcycle

NZ – the universal appellation for New Zealand; pronounced 'enzed'

pa – fortified Maori village, usually on a hill top
Pacific Rim – a term used to describe modern NZ cuisine; cuisine with an innovative use of local produce, especially seafood, with imported styles
Pakeha – Maori for a white or European person; once derogatory, and still considered so by some, this term is now widely used for white New Zealanders
pakihi – unproductive and often swampy land on South Island's west coast; pronounced 'par-kee'
papa – large blue-grey mudstones; the word comes from the Maori for the Earth Mother
Papa, Te – literally 'our place', a term of endearment for the new national museum in Wellington
parapenting – paragliding
paua – abalone; tough shellfish pounded, minced, then made into patties (fritters), which are available in almost every NZ fish and chip shop
peneplain – area worn almost flat by erosion
PC – 'politically correct' (definition varies according to who you talk to)
pig islander – derogatory term used by a person from one island for someone from the other island
pillocking – 'surfing' across mud flats on a rubbish-bin lid
Plunket – an adjective to describe the Plunket Society's services to promote the health of babies eg Plunket rooms (baby clinics), Plunket nurses (baby nurses)
polly – politician
ponga – the silver tree fern; called a bungy (pronounced 'bungee', with a soft 'g', in parts of the South Island)
pounamu – the Maori name for *greenstone*
powhiri – a traditional Maori welcome onto the *marae*

quad bikes – four-wheel farm bikes

Rakiura – literally 'Land of Glowing Skies'; Maori name for Stewart Island, which is important in Maori mythology as the anchor of Maui's canoe

rap jump – face-down abseil

Ratana – a Protestant Maori church; adherents of the Ratana faith

raupo – bullrush

Rheiny – affectionate term for Rheineck beer

rigger – a refillable half-gallon plastic bottle for holding draught beer

Ringatu – an East Coast Maori church formed by Te Kooti

riptide – a dangerously strong current running away from the shore at a beach

Roaring Forties – the ocean between 40° and 50° south, known for very strong winds

scrap – a fight, not uncommon at the pub

section – a small block of land

silver fern – the symbol worn by the All Blacks and other national sportsfolk on their jerseys, representative of the underside of a *ponga* leaf. The national netball team are the Silver Ferns.

Steinie – affectionate term for Steinlager beer

Syndicate, the – the NZ defenders of the America's Cup in 2000

Tamaki Makaurau – Maori name for Auckland

tane – man

tangata – people

tangata whenua – people of the land; local people

taniwha – fear-inspiring water spirit

taonga – something of great value; a treasure

tapu – sacred; forbidden; taboo

tarseal – sealed road; bitumen

te – the (singular); see *nga*

Te Kooti – a prominent East Coast Maori prophet and rebellion leader

Te Papa Atawhai – Maori name for *DOC*

tiki – short for *hei tiki*

toi toi – a tall native grass

tohunga – priest; wizard; general expert

tomo – hole; entrance to a cave

tramp – bushwalk; trek; hike; a more serious undertaking than an ordinary walk, requiring some experience and equipment

tua tua – a type of shellfish

tuatara – a prehistoric reptile dating back to the age of the dinosaurs (perhaps 260 million years)

tukutuku – Maori wall panellings in *marae* and churches

tuna – eel

varsity – university

VIN – Visitor Information Network; the umbrella organisation of the visitor information centres and offices

wahine – woman

wai – water

waiata – song

Waikikamukau – mythical NZ town; somewhere in the *wopwops*

Wai Pounamu, Te – (The Water of Greenstone) Maori for the South Island

Waitangi – short way of referring to the Treaty of Waitangi

waka – canoe

Watties – the NZ food and canning giant; New Zealand's answer to Heinz, until Heinz took over the company

whakapapa – genealogy

whare – house

whare runanga – meeting house

whare taonga – a treasure house; a museum

whare whakairo – carved house

whenua – land

whitebait – a small elongated translucent fish which is scooped up in nets and eaten whole (head, eyes and all!) or made into patties

wopwops – remote ('out in the wopwops' is out in the middle of nowhere)

Thanks

THANKS

Many thanks to the huge number of travellers who used the last edition and wrote to us with helpful hints, useful advice and interesting anecdotes. Almost a thousand people have written to us since the last edition – a sign of how popular the book is (we hope!). The following people wrote, emailed or faxed in information:

David Absdum, Liam Adam, Michael Adler, Helen Ahern, Maurice Alberts, Friederike Albrecht, David Alford, Deal Allison, Clive Alsop, Girry Amaya, Ruth Amos, Frede Andersen, Ulla Andersen, Ryan Anderson, Wayne & Jean Andreen, Jami Andrews, Raymond Ang, Mary Beth Armstrong, Charles G Aschmann, Eskerriz Asco, Harriet Ashman, Keith Atkin, Lyndsay Atkinson, Ana Bailey, Peter Bailey, JH Baird, Luc Bajot, Glenn Baker, Richard Bakker, Tracy Baksa, Carmel Ballinger, Margaret Barbour, Annabelle Barlow, Peter Barnao, Ashleigh Barrett, Rebecca Barroso, Marianne Barsoe, Jennie Bary, Lucy Bebbington, Ellen Beck, Simon Beck, Gerrit Beckmann, Vivienne Beddoe, Archie Bell, Judy Bell, Tony Benfield, Sarah Bennet, Gordon & Christina Bennett, Rolf Benzinger, Jan Beranek, Ray Bergfeld, Mort & Judy Berman, Dick Bernstein, Andreas Bertram, Kristin Bervig Valentine, Petra Bettess, Karen Bevan-Magg, Marian Beymon, Don Bialos, Scott Bickerton, Susan Bidwell, Andreas Biebersdorf, Lothar Biermann, Alan Bill, Martina Binder, Ivan & Christina Blackwell, Ramie Blatt, RF Blesing, Dani Bless, Laurie Blue, Evi Blueth, Kelly Blumer, Bev Blythe, Nina Boldt, Mr & Mrs R Bonner, Richard Boon, Jurgen Bootsveld, Agnes Boskovitz, Angela Bowen, Heather Bowles, Ann-Maree Bowman, BJ Boxall, Leo Brace, Ann Brame, David Brame, Andrew Brannigan, Michael Brasier, Katie Bratby, Shirley Breeuwer, Andy Brice, David Brick, Colleen Bright, Emmanuele Brissat, Ben Brock, Fay Brooks, David Brown, Peter Brown, Robert Brown, Sue & Paul Brown, Maike Brunink, Alexander Brunner, Richard Brunt, Lydia Buchholz, Simon Buckingham, Margriet Buis, Lou Buller, Lee Bumsted, Piers Burgess, Adam Burk, Leslie Burnett, Nicole Burns, Penny Burton, David Butler, Judy Butler, Les Butter, Christine Cachemaille, Alastair Cadzow, Gary Calderbank, Jan Calkins, Laura Cameron, Monika Carlen, Haydn Carmichael, Steven Carrick, Ben Carroll, Blair Carruthers, Maggi Carstairs, Denise Caruth, Jackie Carver, Janet Castle, Harvey Chamberlain, Irene Chan, Russell Chan, Kath Chandler, Tom Channell, Marie Chrysander, Louisa Clarke, Hannah Clements, Christina & Douglas Cleworth, Kate Clode, Nicki Close, Ian Coates, Nicci Coffey, Simon Coffey, Tom Cohen, Tina Coleman, Salvatore Consalvi, Sharon Cooper, Barbara Corbett, Rod Corbett, Derek Cordell, Charlotte Cotrell, Barbara Couden Ochs, Christena Coutsoubos, Katherine Cowan, Roger C Cowell, Ken Crago, Stewart J Crichton, John & Judy Critchfield, R&M Crook, Emma Crookes, RM Cross, Gale Crouch, Michael Crouser, MJ Crozier, Fiona S Cumming, Christopher Currie, Fran Curtis, Dave Cutchin, Toby Cygman, Paul Dale, Jacquie Daly, Jerome J Dambro, Neca Dantas, Lois-Ellin Datta, Eluned Davies, Don Davison, Anna Day, Marcel de Jong, Jan Robert de Rijk, Marleen de Waardt, John Deason, Deborah Dereham, Michael Derieg, Sander Derikx, Julie Desjardins, Friederike Dewitz, Glen Ditchfield, Elizabeth Docking, Jill Don, Mike Dooley, Gulielma Dowrick, Geraldine & David Drabble, Peter Drake, Kate Drakes, Lucy Drane, Inger Drengsgaard, Mette Droegemuller, George Duff, Nadia Duguay, Mr & Mrs Duncan, Anthony Dunk, Nelly Dupuis, Yuvald Dvir, Stuart Dyer, Phillip East, Caroline Eastmond, Alan Eberst, Ron Ebert, Mark Ebrey, Frances Edwards, Sabine Ehlers, Sjoerd Eickmans, Thalia Eley, Jill Elias, Rachel Elliott, Hugh Elsol, Stephen Emanuel, Ryan M Emond, Iliya Englin, Norman Erlichman, Ralph & Kay Erwin, Jenny Esots, Dominique Estiral, Ngaire Evans, Sue Evans, Grant Everett, Claire Eveson, Pauline Evill, Jane & Rory Ewins, Beryl Exley, Brian Fagan, Caryll Fagan, Fay Farrant, Megan Felton, Doug Fenna, Nicky Fenton, Roualeyn Fenton-May, Diane Ferguson, Michele Fernandez-Warren, Rachael Fewster, Geert Fijnaut, Col Finnie, Linda Fitch, Kevin Flaherty, Kate Flanagan, Hugh & Julia Fleming, Faith Flower, Mark Foley, Nancy Ford, Fiona Foster, Jo Fox, J Fraenkel, Elizabeth France, Till Francke, Helene Frankel, Lennie Fredskov, Barry Freed, Abby Freeman, Sander Freenstra, Harriet Friedlander, Carola Friesen, Cecilia Fyfe, Kathleen Gallichan, Clea & Hilary Gardiner, Jeanette & Teri Garnier, Lubbe Garrell, Steve Gaudun, WM Gemmill, David Gentry, Paul Geyer, Nick Geyman, Doris Gfeller, Barbara Giese, Clare Gifford, Adam Gillett, Dr GT Gillett, Cameron Glass, Ken Glassey, Catherine Godfrey, Judith Goldsman, Jennifer M Goodhand, Ilana Gordon, Glenn Gorman, John Gould,

Lise Goyette, Erik Graafland, Brian Graham, Alision Gray, Jane Gray, Jason Gray, Peter Gray, MA Greenhalgh, Paul Greest, Katinka Gregoire, Penny Grieve, Fiona Griffith, Jean Grudgings, J Grutemann, P&M Gutmann, Wouter Haar, Niels Haarsma, Anne Hague, Susan Haines, Ben Hales, Katrina Hall, Tim Hallam, Birgit Hamel, Thera Hamel, Steve Hamnett, Gina Han, Jo Hancock, Armin Hanik, Yvonne Hanks, Linda Hansen, Darcey Harding, Stephen Hardwick, Claire Harman, Kim Harman, Tom Harriman, Paul Harris, Leanne Harrison, Mark Harrison, George Hart, Stewart Harvey, Hadas Haspel, Tony Hastie, Thain Hatherly, Fiona Hawke, Helen Hayes, Karan Hayman, Darren Hazell, Bruce Healy, Shane Heaps, Carol & Dennis Hegarty, Jim Heiser, Jennifer Heitin, Helena Hellidelli, Shaula Hemmer, Jay Hemstapat, Ruth Henderson, Rachel Henwood, Dennis Hesseling, Samatha Hewton, Alyson Higgs, BJ Hill, Carol-Lynn Hill, Julie Hilton, Ben & Alex Hitchens, Guy Hoare, Anne Hodge, Sarah Hodgetts, Rene & Jette Hoeg, Ina Hoffman, Jane Hole, Lori Holland, Simon Holliday, Rob & Julie Hollifield, John Holton, Mark & Michelle Homberg, Anne Homes, Monique Hoolt, Robin Hopf, Kevin & Dawn Hopkins, Jules Hospers, Leonie Houlahan, Denis Howe, Richard Howitt, Diane & Geoff Howlett, Tania Huckle, Luke Huges, Chad Huggett, Keri Hulme, Kristina Humohris, Ron Hunt, Susan Hunting, Hester Hunziker, Lynn Hurton, Jacqueline Hutchinson, Chua Hwee Koon, Jaki Ilbery, Jeff Ingliss, Linus Ingulfson, Maike Intemann, Sandra Irvine, Susan Irwin, Bryan & Phyllida Isles, Francis B Jackson, Paul Jacobs, John Jacobsen, Christiane Jagailloux, Loretta Jakubiec, John & Di James, Simon James, Dagmar Janousek, Vibeke Jansteen, Ewa Jaremkiewicz, Derek Jeary, Derek Jennings, Lene Jensen, Gitta & Peter Jenson, June & Graeme Jessop, Sven Jisander, David Johnson, S Jollivant, Matt Jones, Susan Jones, Warren Jowett, George Juchnowicz, Zain Kapasi, Wendy Keane, Calire Keith, Shawn Kelley, Jo & Chommy Kelly, Morgan Kelly, Brett Kelsall, Kristel & Filip Kennis-Verbeek, Elaine Kerr, the Kerr family, Eileen King, Jan King, Murdoch King, Robert King, Merav Kirat, David Kirklam, Dorothy Klease, Michelle Knight, Joy Kobayashi, Deborah Koch, Magnus Koldau, Silke Korbl, Vera Kotz, Kordula & Uwe Kroll, Meike Krug, Sandra Kruizenga, Sacha Kuijs, Tina Kunkel, Marieke Kupers, Johanna Kurvits, Tess Laidlaw, Philip & Linley Lake, Lisa Lamb, Robert Lamb, Terry Lambeth, Nina Laney, Gavin Lang, Arnoud Langelaar, Pamela Lannon, Jon Lasenby, Adam Latham, Alexander L Laur, John Lawlor, Louise Lawrence, Jacques Yves Le Marec, Adam Leader, Grace Lee, Michelle Lee, Jane Lees, Sue Leggate, Dorit Lehmann, Pete Lens, Joyce Lepperd, Jan John Leslie,

Noa Lev, Milton Lever, Keith Levi, Don Levy, Stu Leyland, Anthony Liechti, Peter Lightburn, Sally Lilley, Gim Lim, Michelle Linder, Douwe Linders, Linda Lines, Romeo Lipizzi, Alan Lloyd, Jill Lloyd, Ken Lodge, Anne Loeser, Magnus Lofgvist, Sara Lolly, John & Judy Long, Therese Longhurst, Robert Longley, Tommy & Katie Lorden, Jemima Lovell, Megan Lowden, Les Lowe, Katia Ludwig, Kirsten Lueders, Carl Lundqvist, Ann Lunn, Els Luyten, C Maclillrick, Lauren Mackenzie, AP Mackie, Maree Madden, D Maher, Tony Mahers, J Maidment, Norm & Mary Mainland, Hitesh Makwana, Mary Male, Rachel Malkin, Norman & Vera Mangold, Andreas Manthey, Marie-France Marais, Luke & Marigold Marsden-Smedley, Michael Marsh, Stuart Marsh, Marilyn Marsh-Booth, Cliff Martin, Elizabeth Martin, Herve Martin, James Martin, Ruth Martins, Carol Mason, Peter Mason, M Mata, Ann Kathrin Mathe, Vic Mau, Sarah McAllister, Glenys McCallum, Lucy Mccann, Kelly McCarthy, Darren McClelland, Andrew McClintock, June & Ian McCormack, Donald McDonald, Mike McGrath, Kathryn McHenry, Sarah & Sean McHugh, Nick McIntosh, Howard McKay, Lauren McKenzie, Tony McKevitt, P McKinna, Aaron McLean, Angus Mclean, Tammy McMinn, D McNicole, Michael McRitchie, Sonja McShane, Carlien Melrose, Carey Meyers, Johanna Micklam, Megan Middleton, Jennifer Milano, Enid Miller, Norm Miller, Sarah Milne, Sherwick Min, Angie Mishkin, Annick & Keith Mitchell, Dee Mitchell, Joan Mitchell, Paul Mitchell, Stuart Mitchell, Sue Mobley, Masniza Mokhtar, Catherine Mollan, Stuart & Vine Molony, Marion Monks, Angie Moody, Jim & Jill Moore, Chris Moores, Ann Moorhouse, S Morgan, Shaun Morgan, Caroline Morris, Miranda Morris, John Morrow, Professor Alan Mortimer, Geoff & Beryl Mortlock, Hugh Morton, Lizzy Moxey, Andrea Mullin, Carole Murdoch, Alan Murgatroyd, Ruth Murphy, Janine Murray, Ishay Nadler, Victoria Nason, Kathy Nelson, Sheri Nelson, Nathalie & Nick Nerd, David & Sarah Newsham, John Nicholls, Ysolde Nichols, Casper Nielsen, Marjan Nieuwland, Yoav Nimron, Geoff Ninnes, Mette Nissen, Justin Nobbs, Ina Noll, Ton Noorduyn, Jette Nornberg Pedersen, BJ Null, Shauna Nyborg, Justin Oates, Nina O'Connell, Hiromi Ogata, Ellie Ogilvie, Aillil O'Reilly, Charlie Oscroft, Robert Osserman, Mary Owen, Mika Oyry, Elisa & Debora Paglerani, Colin Pander, Chris Pappas, Edson Parra, Alpesh Patel, G Patena, Rachel Paton, Wendy Paton, Janice Patterson, Christiane Paul, Margaret Payze, Jemma Pearce, E Pell, Santos Penha, Mark Penny, Christina Pensze, Anita Penttila, Gualberto Perez, Lynnette Perry, Patrik Persson, Chris Peterson, Ulla Peterson, Caroline Pheeny, Ray Phelan, Helen Phillips, Lyn

Pierpoint, Roger Pierpoint, Jaap Pijbes, Sara Pines, Margot & Spencer Platt, Lynne & Gordon Plenderleith, Herbert Plenker, Ruth Pojer, Helen Porter, Ben Post, Pam Potas, Joe Potter, Bill Preis, Dina Priess, Jerome Prince-Foster, Annette Pullin, Hilton Purvis, Alexis Pym, Rozy R, Mary Rabling, Malcolm Raiser, Keith Rakow, Maria Ralph, Eliot Randle, Margaret Rankin, Vladimir Rashev, Tilak Ratnanather, Judith Rattenbury, Michael Rausch, Lou Rauschenberger, Sophia Read, Pete Reames, Diane-Elizabeth Reaxure, Janice Redpath, Ken Reed, Shannon Reed, Sofia Rehn, Bernhard Reinmann, John Rennie, Wendy Reyno, Tom Reynolds, Emma Richards, John Richards, Ruth & Bruce Richards, William & Thomas Richards, Rhonda Richardson, Alison Rickerby, Don Rietbroek, Rose M Rijcken, Lori Riviere, Larry Robbins, Lousie Roberts, Max Roberts, John Robertson, Catherine Robinson, Susan Robinson, Declan Roche, Victor Rochow, Yvette Rogier, Jan Rolf-Larsen, Myra Ron, Svenja Roolfs, Michael & Melissa Rooney, Diane & Steven Rose, Frank E Rose, David Rosenthal, Daniel Ross, Johanna Roughley, Stephanie Rowatt, Sarah Rowlands, Murray & Adrianne Roy, Ido Rozental, Caolyn Ruben, Meike Rumpold, Anna Jen Rusden, Peter Rutter, Katrin Salzman, Ronald W Sandefer, Donald Sarten, Val Sarver, Scott Sather, Michiel Satink, Yoshiki Sato, Jan Sauerwald, Yvonne Schefer, Martin Schievink, Nadia Schmid, Thomas Schmidt, Alaric Schraven, Stefan Schulz, Nik Schumacher, Seth Schweitzer, Judith Sear, Helene Seddon-Glass, Merrore Selenstoch, E Sesso, Karina Severin, Kurt Shafer, Fraser Shearer, Noralene Sheehan, Anne Shepherd, Jan & Tony Sheppard, Lyndon Shirley, Richard Shive, Bronwyn & Deane Shute, Jennifer Shutt, Lynette Sieners, Christina Silkstone, Mic & Gloria Simpson, Gordon & Jane Sims, Deborah Sinclair, Roy Sinclair, Loren Sirl, Judi Skinner, Jo Sladen, Brett Slatter, Derek Smith, Elizabeth Smith, Kathleen Smith, Lisa Smith, Martin Smith, Michael Smith, Robert & Peggy Smith, Sandra Smith, Suzy Smith, Victoria Smith, Virginia Smith, Wes Smith, Daphne Snartt, Peter Snartt, Zoe Snellgrove, Rebecca Snowey, PM Soper, Andy Sparrow, Carol Spence, Gerry & Audrey Spencer, Kieran Spillane, Edith & Henk Spreeuw, Florence & Paul Spurling, Gordon Stanger, Dr Mary Stannard, Margaret Stare, Helen Stasa, Eva Stassig, L William Staudenmaier, John Steven, Martine Stevens, Zena Stevens, Joyce L Stevenson, Lyn Stoker, Adrian Stokes, Derek Stone, P Stone, Richard Stott, Caroline Stout, Janet Stucken, Omar Studer, Karen Sugars, John & Lynn Sullivan, David Summergreene, Conal Summers, Val Sutcliffe, Jarden Svensson, David Swanson, Kelly Swanson, John Sweet, Hugh Symons, J Symons, Miho Tabuchi, Patrick Tai, Murray Takle, Jocelyn Tay, Duncan Taylor, Linda Taylor, Liz Taylor, Mark & Lynne Taylor, Ruth Taylor, Ray Te Paiho, Scott Teagle, Sonya Teale, Giri Tenneti, Anne-Marie ter Beek, Carolijn Theunissen, Bruce Thomas, Jared Thomas, Birgid & Keith Thompson, Pam Tindall, Rossindra Tiruchelvam, Margaret Titterington, Kevin Townroe, Samantha Trott, Leigh Trutwein, John Turner, Joerg Tuske, Browyn Tweedie, Sarah Urlich, Joost Vallinga, Caroline & Herman van den Wall Bake, Thomas van der Ljke, Sander van der Meijs, Sune van Deurs Jonsson, Joyce Van Gelder, Caroline Van Halteren, Kris van Kooten, Peter Paul van Reenen, Judy van Veen, Isabel van Weel, Marguerite Vanderkolk, Paul D Varady, Paul & Tracey Veitch, Richard Venmore, Caroline Verbist, Claske Vingerling, Wanda Vivequin, Arlinde Vletter, Cees Vletter, Hinrich Voges, Ludwig Vogler, Daniela von Babo, Lawrence Wainwright, Jim & Jill Waits, Gil Walker, Giovanna Walker, Max Walker, Sally Wallen, Michael Wallis, Chris Walsh, James Walters, Erika Walther, Dana Wang, Rachel Warach, Sharon Ward, Megan Wather, Natalie Watson, Natasha Watson, RL Watson, Glenn Weaver, Chris & Wendy Webb, Joyce Webster, Simon Webster, Bruno Weder, Miri Weinberger, Sandra Wessels, Irene Westendorp, Christine Wheatley, Donna Wheatley, Robert Wheatley, Kate Whetham, Nicole White, Anne Whitehall, Andrea Wild, Hans Willems, Lummie Williams, Sharon Williams, Jeremy Wills, Mary Wills, Grant Wilson, Michael Wilson, Bentzi Winter, Sandra Wolf, Stefan Wolf, Antony Wolowiec, Hjalmar Wolvekamp, Arnd Wolvetang, Guy Wong, Bridget & Phil Wood, Julie & Mark Wood, M Wood, Neil & Helen Wood-Mitchell, Barbara & Gerry Woolf, Angie Wright, Alec Yarrow, Steve Yeoman, Aya Yzhaki, Georges Zucker

LONELY PLANET

ON THE ROAD

Travel Guides explore cities, regions and countries, and supply information on transport, restaurants and accommodation, covering all budgets. They come with reliable, easy-to-use maps, practical advice, cultural and historical facts and a rundown on attractions both on and off the beaten track. There are over 200 titles in this classic series, covering nearly every country in the world.

 Lonely Planet Upgrades extend the shelf life of existing travel guides by detailing any changes that may affect travel in a region since a book has been published. Upgrades can be downloaded for free from **www.lonelyplanet.com/upgrades**

For travellers with more time than money, **Shoestring** guides offer dependable, first-hand information with hundreds of detailed maps, plus insider tips for stretching money as far as possible. Covering entire continents in most cases, the six-volume shoestring guides are known around the world as 'backpackers bibles'.

For the discerning short-term visitor, **Condensed** guides highlight the best a destination has to offer in a full-colour, pocket-sized format designed for quick access. They include everything from top sights and walking tours to opinionated reviews of where to eat, stay, shop and have fun.

CitySync lets travellers use their Palm™ or Visor™ hand-held computers to guide them through a city with handy tips on transport, history, cultural life, major sights, and shopping and entertainment options. It can also quickly search and sort hundreds of reviews of hotels, restaurants and attractions, and pinpoint their location on scrollable street maps. CitySync can be downloaded from **www.citysync.com**

MAPS & ATLASES

Lonely Planet's **City Maps** feature downtown and metropolitan maps, as well as transit routes and walking tours. The maps come complete with an index of streets, a listing of sights and a plastic coat for extra durability.

Road Atlases are an essential navigation tool for serious travellers. Cross-referenced with the guidebooks, they also feature distance and climate charts and a complete site index.

LONELY PLANET

ESSENTIALS

Read This First books help new travellers to hit the road with confidence. These invaluable predeparture guides give step-by-step advice on preparing for a trip, budgeting, arranging a visa, planning an itinerary and staying safe while still getting off the beaten track.

Healthy Travel pocket guides offer a regional rundown on disease hot spots and practical advice on predeparture health measures, staying well on the road and what to do in emergencies. The guides come with a user-friendly design and helpful diagrams and tables.

Lonely Planet's **Phrasebooks** cover the essential words and phrases travellers need when they're strangers in a strange land. They come in a pocket-sized format with colour tabs for quick reference, extensive vocabulary lists, easy-to-follow pronunciation keys and two-way dictionaries.

Miffed by blurry photos of the Taj Mahal? Tired of the classic 'top of the head cut off' shot? **Travel Photography: A Guide to Taking Better Pictures** will help you turn ordinary holiday snaps into striking images and give you the know-how to capture every scene, from frenetic festivals to peaceful beach sunrises.

Lonely Planet's **Travel Journal** is a lightweight but sturdy travel diary for jotting down all those on-the-road observations and significant travel moments. It comes with a handy time-zone wheel, a world map and useful travel information.

Lonely Planet's eKno is an all-in-one communication service developed especially for travellers. It offers low-cost international calls and free email and voicemail so that you can keep in touch while on the road. Check it out on **www.ekno.lonelyplanet.com**

FOOD & RESTAURANT GUIDES

Lonely Planet's **Out to Eat** guides recommend the brightest and best places to eat and drink in top international cities. These gourmet companions are arranged by neighbourhood, packed with dependable maps, garnished with scene-setting photos and served with quirky features.

For people who live to eat, drink and travel, **World Food** guides explore the culinary culture of each country. Entertaining and adventurous, each guide is packed with detail on staples and specialities, regional cuisine and local markets, as well as sumptuous recipes, comprehensive culinary dictionaries and lavish photos good enough to eat.

OUTDOOR GUIDES

For those who believe the best way to see the world is on foot, Lonely Planet's **Walking Guides** detail everything from family strolls to difficult treks, with 'when to go and how to do it' advice supplemented by reliable maps and essential travel information.

Cycling Guides map a destination's best bike tours, long and short, in day-by-day detail. They contain all the information a cyclist needs, including advice on bike maintenance, places to eat and stay, innovative maps with detailed cues to the rides, and elevation charts.

The **Watching Wildlife** series is perfect for travellers who want authoritative information but don't want to tote a heavy field guide. Packed with advice on where, when and how to view a region's wildlife, each title features photos of over 300 species and contains engaging comments on the local flora and fauna.

With underwater colour photos throughout, **Pisces Books** explore the world's best diving and snorkelling areas. Each book contains listings of diving services and dive resorts, detailed information on depth, visibility and difficulty of dives, and a roundup of the marine life you're likely to see through your mask.

OFF THE ROAD

Journeys, the travel literature series written by renowned travel authors, capture the spirit of a place or illuminate a culture with a journalist's attention to detail and a novelist's flair for words. These are tales to soak up while you're actually on the road or dip into as an at-home armchair indulgence.

The range of lavishly illustrated **Pictorial** books is just the ticket for both travellers and dreamers. Off-beat tales and vivid photographs bring the adventure of travel to your doorstep long before the journey begins and long after it is over.

Lonely Planet **Videos** encourage the same independent, tough-minded approach as the guidebooks. Currently airing throughout the world, this award-winning series features innovative footage and an original soundtrack.

Yes, we know, work is tough, so do a little bit of deskside dreaming with the spiral-bound Lonely Planet **Diary** or a Lonely Planet **Wall Calendar**, filled with great photos from around the world.

TRAVELLERS NETWORK

Lonely Planet Online. Lonely Planet's award-winning Web site has insider information on hundreds of destinations, from Amsterdam to Zimbabwe, complete with interactive maps and relevant links. The site also offers the latest travel news, recent reports from travellers on the road, guidebook upgrades, a travel links site, an online book-buying option and a lively travellers bulletin board. It can be viewed at **www.lonelyplanet.com** or AOL keyword: lp.

Planet Talk is a quarterly print newsletter, full of gossip, advice, anecdotes and author articles. It provides an antidote to the being-at-home blues and lets you plan and dream for the next trip. Contact the nearest Lonely Planet office for your free copy.

Comet, the free Lonely Planet newsletter, comes via email once a month. It's loaded with travel news, advice, dispatches from authors, travel competitions and letters from readers. To subscribe, click on the Comet subscription link on the front page of the Web site.

Lonely Planet Guides by Region

Lonely Planet is known worldwide for publishing practical, reliable and no-nonsense travel information in our guides and on our Web site. The Lonely Planet list covers just about every accessible part of the world. Currently there are 16 series: Travel guides, Shoestring guides, Condensed guides, Phrasebooks, Read This First, Healthy Travel, Walking guides, Cycling guides, Watching Wildlife guides, Pisces Diving & Snorkeling guides, City Maps, Road Atlases, Out to Eat, World Food, Journeys travel literature and Pictorials.

AFRICA Africa on a shoestring • Botswana • Cairo • Cairo City Map • Cape Town • Cape Town City Map • East Africa • Egypt • Egyptian Arabic phrasebook • Ethiopia, Eritrea & Djibouti • Ethiopian Amharic phrasebook • The Gambia & Senegal • Healthy Travel Africa • Kenya • Malawi • Morocco • Moroccan Arabic phrasebook • Mozambique • Namibia • Read This First: Africa • South Africa, Lesotho & Swaziland • Southern Africa • Southern Africa Road Atlas • Swahili phrasebook • Tanzania, Zanzibar & Pemba • Trekking in East Africa • Tunisia • Watching Wildlife East Africa • Watching Wildlife Southern Africa • West Africa • World Food Morocco • Zambia • Zimbabwe, Botswana & Namibia
Travel Literature: Mali Blues: Traveling to an African Beat • The Rainbird: A Central African Journey • Songs to an African Sunset: A Zimbabwean Story

AUSTRALIA & THE PACIFIC Aboriginal Australia & the Torres Strait Islands •Auckland • Australia • Australian phrasebook • Australia Road Atlas • Cycling Australia • Cycling New Zealand • Fiji • Fijian phrasebook • Healthy Travel Australia, NZ & the Pacific • Islands of Australia's Great Barrier Reef • Melbourne • Melbourne City Map • Micronesia • New Caledonia • New South Wales • New Zealand • Northern Territory • Outback Australia • Out to Eat – Melbourne • Out to Eat – Sydney • Papua New Guinea • Pidgin phrasebook • Queensland • Rarotonga & the Cook Islands • Samoa • Solomon Islands • South Australia • South Pacific • South Pacific phrasebook • Sydney • Sydney City Map • Sydney Condensed • Tahiti & French Polynesia • Tasmania • Tonga • Tramping in New Zealand • Vanuatu • Victoria • Walking in Australia • Watching Wildlife Australia • Western Australia
Travel Literature: Islands in the Clouds: Travels in the Highlands of New Guinea • Kiwi Tracks: A New Zealand Journey • Sean & David's Long Drive

CENTRAL AMERICA & THE CARIBBEAN Bahamas, Turks & Caicos • Baja California • Belize, Guatemala & Yucatán • Bermuda • Central America on a shoestring • Costa Rica • Costa Rica Spanish phrasebook • Cuba • Cycling Cuba • Dominican Republic & Haiti • Eastern Caribbean • Guatemala • Havana • Healthy Travel Central & South America • Jamaica • Mexico • Mexico City • Panama • Puerto Rico • Read This First: Central & South America • Virgin Islands • World Food Caribbean • World Food Mexico • Yucatán
Travel Literature: Green Dreams: Travels in Central America

EUROPE Amsterdam • Amsterdam City Map • Amsterdam Condensed • Andalucía • Athens • Austria • Baltic States phrasebook • Barcelona • Barcelona City Map • Belgium & Luxembourg • Berlin • Berlin City Map • Britain • British phrasebook • Brussels, Bruges & Antwerp • Brussels City Map • Budapest • Budapest City Map • Canary Islands • Catalunya & the Costa Brava • Central Europe • Central Europe phrasebook • Copenhagen • Corfu & the Ionians • Corsica • Crete • Crete Condensed • Croatia • Cycling Britain • Cycling France • Cyprus • Czech & Slovak Republics • Czech phrasebook • Denmark • Dublin • Dublin City Map • Dublin Condensed • Eastern Europe • Eastern Europe phrasebook • Edinburgh • Edinburgh City Map • England • Estonia, Latvia & Lithuania • Europe on a shoestring • Europe phrasebook • Finland • Florence • Florence City Map • France • Frankfurt City Map • Frankfurt Condensed • French phrasebook • Georgia, Armenia & Azerbaijan • Germany • German phrasebook • Greece • Greek Islands • Greek phrasebook • Hungary • Iceland, Greenland & the Faroe Islands • Ireland • Italian phrasebook • Italy • Kraków • Lisbon • The Loire • London • London City Map • London Condensed • Madrid • Madrid City Map • Malta • Mediterranean Europe • Milan, Turin & Genoa • Moscow • Munich • Netherlands • Normandy • Norway • Out to Eat – London • Out to Eat – Paris • Paris • Paris City Map • Paris Condensed • Poland • Polish phrasebook • Portugal • Portuguese phrasebook • Prague • Prague City Map • Provence & the Côte d'Azur • Read This First: Europe • Rhodes & the Dodecanese • Romania & Moldova • Rome • Rome City Map • Rome Condensed • Russia, Ukraine & Belarus • Russian phrasebook • Scandinavian & Baltic Europe • Scandinavian phrasebook • Scotland • Sicily • Slovenia • South-West France • Spain • Spanish phrasebook • Stockholm • St Petersburg • St Petersburg City Map • Sweden • Switzerland • Tuscany • Ukrainian phrasebook • Venice • Vienna • Wales • Walking in Britain • Walking in France • Walking in Ireland • Walking in Italy • Walking in Scotland • Walking in Spain • Walking in Switzerland • Western Europe • World Food France • World Food Greece • World Food Ireland • World Food Italy • World Food Spain **Travel Literature:** After Yugoslavia • Love and War in the Apennines • The Olive Grove: Travels in Greece • On the Shores of the Mediterranean • Round Ireland in Low Gear • A Small Place in Italy

Lonely Planet Mail Order

onely Planet products are distributed worldwide. They are also available by mail order from Lonely Planet, so if you have difficulty finding a title please write to us. North and South American residents should write to 150 Linden St, Oakland, CA 94607, USA; European and African residents should write to 10a Spring Place, London NW5 3BH, UK; and residents of other countries to Locked Bag 1, Footscray, Victoria 3011, Australia.

INDIAN SUBCONTINENT & THE INDIAN OCEAN Bangladesh • Bengali phrasebook • Bhutan • Delhi • Goa • Healthy Travel Asia & India • Hindi & Urdu phrasebook • India • India & Bangladesh City Map • Indian Himalaya • Karakoram Highway • Kathmandu City Map • Kerala • Madagascar • Maldives • Mauritius, Réunion & Seychelles • Mumbai (Bombay) • Nepal • Nepali phrasebook • North India • Pakistan • Rajasthan • Read This First: Asia & India • South India • Sri Lanka • Sri Lanka phrasebook • Tibet • Tibetan phrasebook • Trekking in the Indian Himalaya • Trekking in the Karakoram & Hindukush • Trekking in the Nepal Himalaya • World Food India **Travel Literature:** The Age of Kali: Indian Travels and Encounters • Hello Goodnight: A Life of Goa • In Rajasthan • Maverick in Madagascar • A Season in Heaven: True Tales from the Road to Kathmandu • Shopping for Buddhas • A Short Walk in the Hindu Kush • Slowly Down the Ganges

MIDDLE EAST & CENTRAL ASIA Bahrain, Kuwait & Qatar • Central Asia • Central Asia phrasebook • Dubai • Farsi (Persian) phrasebook • Hebrew phrasebook • Iran • Israel & the Palestinian Territories • Istanbul • Istanbul City Map • Istanbul to Cairo • Istanbul to Kathmandu • Jerusalem • Jerusalem City Map • Jordan • Lebanon • Middle East • Oman & the United Arab Emirates • Syria • Turkey • Turkish phrasebook • World Food Turkey • Yemen **Travel Literature:** Black on Black: Iran Revisited • Breaking Ranks: Turbulent Travels in the Promised Land • The Gates of Damascus • Kingdom of the Film Stars: Journey into Jordan

NORTH AMERICA Alaska • Boston • Boston City Map • Boston Condensed • British Columbia • California & Nevada • California Condensed • Canada • Chicago • Chicago City Map • Chicago Condensed • Florida • Georgia & the Carolinas • Great Lakes • Hawaii • Hiking in Alaska • Hiking in the USA • Honolulu & Oahu City Map • Las Vegas • Los Angeles • Los Angeles City Map • Louisiana & the Deep South • Miami • Miami City Map • Montreal • New England • New Orleans • New Orleans City Map • New York City • New York City City Map • New York City Condensed • New York, New Jersey & Pennsylvania • Oahu • Out to Eat – San Francisco • Pacific Northwest • Rocky Mountains • San Diego & Tijuana • San Francisco • San Francisco City Map • Seattle • Seattle City Map • Southwest • Texas • Toronto • USA • USA phrasebook • Vancouver • Vancouver City Map • Virginia & the Capital Region • Washington, DC • Washington, DC City Map • World Food New Orleans **Travel Literature**: Caught Inside: A Surfer's Year on the California Coast • Drive Thru America

NORTH-EAST ASIA Beijing • Beijing City Map • Cantonese phrasebook • China • Hiking in Japan • Hong Kong & Macau • Hong Kong City Map • Hong Kong Condensed • Japan • Japanese phrasebook • Korea • Korean phrasebook • Kyoto • Mandarin phrasebook • Mongolia • Mongolian phrasebook • Seoul • Shanghai • South-West China • Taiwan • Tokyo • Tokyo Condensed • World Food Hong Kong • World Food Japan **Travel Literature:** In Xanadu: A Quest • Lost Japan

SOUTH AMERICA Argentina, Uruguay & Paraguay • Bolivia • Brazil • Brazilian phrasebook • Buenos Aires • Buenos Aires City Map • Chile & Easter Island • Colombia • Ecuador & the Galapagos Islands • Healthy Travel Central & South America • Latin American Spanish phrasebook • Peru • Quechua phrasebook • Read This First: Central & South America • Rio de Janeiro • Rio de Janeiro City Map • Santiago de Chile • South America on a shoestring • Trekking in the Patagonian Andes • Venezuela **Travel Literature**: Full Circle: A South American Journey

SOUTH-EAST ASIA Bali & Lombok • Bangkok • Bangkok City Map • Burmese phrasebook • Cambodia • Cycling Vietnam, Laos & Cambodia • East Timor phrasebook • Hanoi • Healthy Travel Asia & India • Hill Tribes phrasebook • Ho Chi Minh City (Saigon) • Indonesia • Indonesian phrasebook • Indonesia's Eastern Islands • Java • Lao phrasebook • Laos • Malay phrasebook • Malaysia, Singapore & Brunei • Myanmar (Burma) • Philippines • Pilipino (Tagalog) phrasebook • Read This First: Asia & India • Singapore • Singapore City Map • South-East Asia on a shoestring • South-East Asia phrasebook • Thailand • Thailand's Islands & Beaches • Thailand, Vietnam, Laos & Cambodia Road Atlas • Thai phrasebook • Vietnam • Vietnamese phrasebook • World Food Indonesia • World Food Thailand • World Food Vietnam

ALSO AVAILABLE: Antarctica • The Arctic • The Blue Man: Tales of Travel, Love and Coffee • Brief Encounters: Stories of Love, Sex & Travel • Buddhist Stupas in Asia: The Shape of Perfection • Chasing Rickshaws • The Last Grain Race • Lonely Planet ... On the Edge: Adventurous Escapades from Around the World • Lonely Planet Unpacked • Lonely Planet Unpacked Again • Not the Only Planet: Science Fiction Travel Stories • Ports of Call: A Journey by Sea • Sacred India • Travel Photography: A Guide to Taking Better Pictures • Travel with Children • Tuvalu: Portrait of an Island Nation

LONELY PLANET

You already know that Lonely Planet produces more than this one guidebook, but you might not be aware of the other products we have on this region. Here is a selection of titles that you may want to check out as well:

Auckland
ISBN 1 86450 092 1
US$14.95 • UK£8.99

South Pacific
ISBN 0 86442 717 4
US$24.95 • UK£15.99

Antarctica
ISBN 0 86442 772 7
US$19.99 • UK£12.99

Kiwi Tracks
ISBN 0 86442 787 5
US$12.95 • UK£6.99

Cycling New Zealand
ISBN 1 86450 031 X
US$12.95 • UK£6.99

Tramping in New Zealand
ISBN 1 74059 234 4
US$19.99 • UK£12.99

**Diving & Snorkeling
New Zealand**
ISBN 1 74059 267 0
US$16.99 • UK£12.99

**Healthy Travel
Australia, NZ & The Pacific**
ISBN 1 86450 052 2
US$5.95 • UK£3.99

South Pacific phrasebook
ISBN 0 86442 595 3
US$6.95 • UK£4.99

Travel Photography
ISBN 1 86450 207 X
US$16.99 • UK£9.99

Travel with Children
ISBN 0 86442 729 8
US$14.99 • UK£8.99

Lonely Planet...On the Edge
ISBN 1 86450 222 3
US$12.99 • UK£6.99

Available wherever books are sold

Index

Text

Bold indicates maps.

Bold indicates maps.

Bold indicates maps.

Bold indicates maps.

Bold indicates maps.

Bold indicates maps.

Boxed Text

Bold indicates maps.

MAP LEGEND

CITY ROUTES

Motorway	Motorway
Highway	Primary Road
Road	Secondary Road
Street	Street
Lane	Lane
	On/Off Ramp

⊐⊐⊐⊐	Unsealed Road
→	One Way Street
	Pedestrian Mall
⊓⊓⊓⊓	Stepped Street
)==	Tunnel
	Footbridge

REGIONAL ROUTES

	Motorway, Freeway
	Primary Road
	Secondary Road
	Minor Road

BOUNDARIES

	International
	State
— — —	Disputed
	Cliff

HYDROGRAPHY

	River, Creek
	Lake

◉	Spring
⌐⌐	Waterfalls

TRANSPORT ROUTES & STATIONS

◎	Train
	Train - disused
	Bus Route
⇥⇥⊟	Cable Car, Chairlift

⌐	Ferry
⋏	Walking Trail
	Pier or Jetty
	Path

AREA FEATURES

	Building
⊛	Park, Gardens

	Market
	Forest

	Beach
+ + +	Cemetery

	Glacier
	Plaza

POPULATION SYMBOLS

✪ CAPITAL	National Capital
◉ AUCKLAND	City

● Timaru	Town
◉ Mokau	Village

	Urban Area

MAP SYMBOLS

▪	Place to Stay
▼	Place to Eat
●	Point of Interest

✈	International Airport	⌂	Cave	☼	Lookout	⊠	Shopping Centre
⊟	Domestic Airport	✚ ✝	Church	⌂	Marae	⚜	Ski Field/Club
⑨	Bank	⬎	Dive Site	⚑	Monument	⌂	Stately Home
⬲	Bicycle Rental	✛	Hospital	⊞	Museum/Art Gallery	☎	Telephone
⬈	Bird Sanctuary	⬡ ⬡	Hut/Shelter	⬒	National Park	⊙	Toilet
⬚ ⬚	Brewery/Pub or Bar	⬒	Internet Cafe	✚	Police Station	❶	Tourist Information
⊟ ⊟	Bus Terminal/Stop	♣	Kauri Tree/Forest	✉	Post Office	⚲	Winery
⊞ ⬚	Caravan/Camping	⚲	Lighthouse	⊞	Ruins	♠	Zoo/Wildlife Park

Note: not all symbols displayed above appear in this book

LONELY PLANET OFFICES

Australia
Locked Bag 1, Footscray, Victoria 3011
☎ 03 8379 8000 fax 03 8379 8111
email: talk2us@lonelyplanet.com.au

USA
150 Linden St, Oakland, CA 94607
☎ 510 893 8555 TOLL FREE: 800 275 8555
fax 510 893 8572
email: info@lonelyplanet.com

UK
10a Spring Place, London NW5 3BH
☎ 020 7428 4800 fax 020 7428 4828
email: go@lonelyplanet.co.uk

France
1 rue du Dahomey, 75011 Paris
☎ 01 55 25 33 00 fax 01 55 25 33 01
email: bip@lonelyplanet.fr
www.lonelyplanet.fr

World Wide Web: www.lonelyplanet.com *or* AOL keyword: lp
Lonely Planet Images: www.lonelyplanetimages.com